ENCYCLOPEDIA OF
ARCHITECTURE
DESIGN, ENGINEERING & CONSTRUCTION

EDITORIAL BOARD

ENCYCLOPEDIA OF
ARCHITECTURE
DESIGN, ENGINEERING & CONSTRUCTION

JOSEPH A. WILKES, FAIA
Editor-in-Chief

ROBERT T. PACKARD, AIA
Associate Editor

VOLUME 5
Tabler, William B.
to
Zoos

Supplement

Index for Volumes 1–5

A WILEY-INTERSCIENCE PUBLICATION

JOHN WILEY & SONS

New York • Chichester • Brisbane • Toronto • Singapore

For her help in so many ways,
this encyclopedia is dedicated to
my wife Margaret.

Library of Congress Cataloging in Publication Data:

Encyclopedia of architecture.

   "A Wiley-Interscience publication."
   Includes bibliographies.
   Contents: v. 4. Pope, John Russell to Systems Integration
   1. Architecture—Dictionaries.   I. Wilkes, Joseph A.
II. Packard, Robert T.

NA31.E59   1988   720′.3   87–25222
ISBN 0–471–63243–0 (v. 5)
ISBN 0–471–63351–8 (set)

Printed in the United States of America

10 9 8 7 6 5 4 3 2 1

EDITORIAL STAFF

Editor-in-chief: Joseph A. Wilkes, FAIA
Associate Editor: Robert T. Packard, AIA
Managing Editor: Stephen A. Kliment, FAIA
Editorial Supervisor: Samuel Christian

Production Manager: Jenet McIver
Production Supervisor: Jean Spranger
Production Assistant: John T. Steen
Designer: Jean Morley

CONTRIBUTORS

Kathryn H. Anthony, PhD, *University of Illinois at Urbana-Champaign, Champaign, Ill.,* Wurster, William

Steven Bedford, *Middlebury, Conn.,* Weidlinger, Paul

John C. Birchfield, *Birchfield Foodsystems, Inc., Annapolis, Md.,* Restaurant and Service Kitchens (supplement)

Jean-Paul Bourdier, *Berkeley, Calif.,* West African Vernacular Architecture

Gunnar Brinck, *Western Wood Products Association, Portland, Oreg.,* Wood in Construction

Denise Scott Brown, *Venturi, Rauch & Scott Brown, Philadelphia, Pa.,* Venturi, Rauch and Scott Brown

Dennis B. Brown, AIA, *Washington, D.C.,* Working Drawings

Charles Brownell, *University of Virginia, Charlottesville, Va.,* Thornton, William

Beth Buffington, *Washington, D.C.,* Vertical Transportation

John W. Chapman, *KCCT Architects, Washington, D.C.,* Transit Systems

Meredith L. Clausen, *Seattle, Wash.,* Thiry, Paul

Seymour K. Coburn, *Corrosion Consultants, Inc., Pittsburgh, Pa.,* Steel, Weathering (supplement)

Anthony Consoli, *Hyattsville, Md.,* Tilt-up Construction

Eason Cross, FAIA, *Cross Associates, Alexandria, Va.,* Urban Design—Architecture at Urban Scale

Manuel Cuadra, *Technische Hochschule Darmstadt, Darmstadt, FRG,* Ungers, Oswald M.

Gordon Culp, *HDR Engineering, Inc., Bellevue, Wash.,* Wastewater Management; Water Treatment

Karen J. Dominguez, *Whitewater, Wis.,* Time-Adaptive Housing

James H. Fitzwater, AIA, *Fitzwater & Fitzwater, Houston, Tex.,* Termites—Control by Soil Poisoning; Wood Treatment

David P. Fogle, AICP, *Rehoboth, Del.,* Restoration, Historic (supplement)

Alan J. Friedman, PhD, *New York Hall of Science, Corona, N.Y.,* Science and Technology Facilities (supplement)

Peter Frink, *Assembly Places International, Philadelphia, Pa.,* Theaters and Opera Houses

Gary C. Greenan, AICP, *University of Miami, Coral Gables, Fla.,* Site Development (supplement)

Sarah Harkness, FAIA *The Architects Collaborative, Cambridge, Mass.,* The Architects Collaborative

Lynne Iadarola, *Chevy Chase, Md.,* Zoos

Edwin J. Jakacki, *U.S. Gypsum Corp., Libertyville, Ill.,* Wallboard and Plaster Systems

Robert J. Karn, *KCCT Architects, Washington, D.C.,* Transit Systems

Thomas C. Klingler, *Dow Chemical USA, Midland, Mich.,* Styrene Resins (supplement)

Jerome Klosowski, *Dow Corning Corporation, Midland, Mich.,* Silicones (supplement)

Robert Linck, *Philadelphia, Pa.,* Sheet Metal (supplement)

Clark Lundell, AIA, *Auburn University, Auburn, Ala.,* Tange, Kenzo; Yamasaki, Minoru

Harry F. Mallgrave, *Afton, Minn.,* Theory of Architecture

Sara P. O'Neil-Manion, AIA, *O'Neil and Manion, Architects, Bethesda, Md.,* Interior Partitions and Partition Coverings (supplement)

Jack Merry, *American Plywood Association, Tacoma, Wash.,* Wood, Structural Panel Composites

Trinh T. Minh-ha, *Berkeley, Calif.,* West African Vernacular Architecture

Arthur H. Mittelstaedt, Jr., Ed.D., *Ward Associates, Bohemia, N.Y.,* Recreational Facilities (supplement)

Marilyn de Moire, *American Plywood Association, Tacoma, Wash.,* Wood, Structural Panel Composites

Edward J. Nichols, *Alexandria, Va.,* Value Engineering

Robert T. Packard, AIA, *Reston, Va.,* Adam, Robert and James (supplement); Metric System (supplement); Moisture Protection (supplement); Quantity Surveying (supplement); Regulations—Zoning and Building Codes (supplement); Telford, Thomas; Terrazzo; Union Internationale des Architectes (UIA); Van de Velde, Henry Clement; Van Eyck, Aldo; Viollet-le-duc, Eugene-Emmanuel; Visionary Architecture; Wachsmann, Konrad; Wagner, Otto Koloman

Wayne E. Peterson, Jr., *Dow Chemical Company, Midland, Michigan,* Styrene Resins (supplement)

Laurie Putscher, *Annapolis, Md.,* Rugs and Carpets (supplement)

Barry Riccio, *University of Illinois, Urbana, Ill.,* Wright, Frank Lloyd

Irving Rosner, *Rosner Television Systems, Inc., New York, N.Y.,* Television and Radio Studios

J. Walter Roth, AIA, *Alexandria, Va.,* Tennessee Valley Authority (TVA) Architecture; United States Capitol; White House

Thomas L. Schumacher, *FAAR, Washington, D.C.,* Terragni, Giuseppe

Alan Schwartzman, FAIA *Davis, Brody & Associates, New York, N.Y.,* Science and Technology Centers (supplement)

Anatole Senkevitch, *University of Michigan, Ann Arbor, Mich.,* Soviet Union Architecture (supplement)

John Ormsbee Simonds, *FASLA, The Loft,* Pittsburgh, Pa., Urban Design—Creation of Livable Cities

Norma Sklarek, FAIA, *The Jerde Partnership, Los Angeles, Calif.,* Women in Architecture

Nancy Somerville, *The American Institute of Architects, Washington, D.C.,* Registration of Professionals in Construction (supplement)

Frank Spink, *Urban Land Institute, Washington, D.C.,* Urban Land Institute

David Stahl, *Urban Land Institute, Washington, D.C.,* Urban Land Institute

Richard F. Stone, *U.S. Gypsum Corp., Libertyville, Ill.,* Wallboard and Plaster Systems

Rober C. Stroh, *NAHB Research Center, Upper Marlborough, Md.,* Framing, Wood (supplement)

William B. Tabler, Sr., FAIA, *New York, N.Y.,* Tabler, William B.

John Templer, *Georgia Institute of Technology, Atlanta, Ga.,* Sight-Impaired Design for; Stair Design (supplement)

Guiliana Tesoro, *Dobbs Ferry, N.Y.,* Textiles

Jane Thompson, *Benjamin Thompson & Associates, Cambridge, Mass.,* Thompson, Benjamin

Thomas Vonier, AIA, *Thomas Vonier Associates, Inc., Washington, D.C.,* Windows

Don Wallace, *Western Wood Products Association, Portland, Oreg.,* Wood in Construction

Ralph Warburton, FAIA, *University of Miami, Coral Gables, Fla.,* Wren, Sir Christopher

Catherine Weese, *Harry Weese & Associates, Chicago, Ill.,* Weese, Harry

Joseph A. Wilkes, FAIA, *Annapolis, Md.,* Concrete—Admixtures, Curing, and Testing; Flooring, Wood (supplement)

James Ziska, *Dow Chemical Company, Midland, Mich.,* Styrene Resins (supplement)

Karl Zupic, *Dow Chemical Company, Midland, Mich.,* Styrene Resins (supplement)

ENCYCLOPEDIA REVIEWERS

To ensure that articles were complete in coverage, accurate in detail, and timely, copies of the authors' drafts were submitted for review to known experts in the many fields covered by the Encyclopedia. Some reviewers were suggested by the authors themselves; mostly they represented a pool of volunteers recruited for this task.

The suggestions and comments were submitted to the authors for use in preparing final drafts. In most cases reviewers remained anonymous to the authors.

The review process required time, expertise, and a great deal of effort on the part of the reviewers, and the editors and publisher deeply appreciate their help and support.

CONTENTS

CONVERSION FACTORS, ABBREVIATIONS, AND UNIT SYMBOLS

Selected SI Units (Adopted 1960)

Quantity	Unit	Symbol	Acceptable equivalent
BASE UNITS			
length	meter[†]	m	
mass[‡]	kilogram	kg	
time	second	s	
electric current	ampere	A	
thermodynamic temperature[§]	kelvin	K	
DERIVED UNITS AND OTHER ACCEPTABLE UNITS			
* absorbed dose	gray	Gy	J/kg
acceleration	meter per second squared	m/s^2	
* activity (of ionizing radiation source)	becquerel	Bq	1/s
area	square kilometer	km^2	
	square hectometer	hm^2	ha (hectare)
	square meter	m^2	
density, mass density	kilogram per cubic meter	kg/m^3	g/L; mg/cm^3
* electric potential, potential difference, electromotive force	volt	V	W/A
* electric resistance	ohm	Ω	V/A
* energy, work, quantity of heat	megajoule	MJ	
	kilojoule	kJ	
	joule	J	N·m
	electron volt[x]	eV[x]	
	kilowatt hour[x]	kW·h[x]	
* force	kilonewton	kN	
	newton	N	kg·m/s^2
* frequency	megahertz	MHz	
	hertz	Hz	1/s
heat capacity, entropy	joule per kelvin	J/K	
heat capacity (specific), specific entropy	joule per kilogram kelvin	J/(kg·K)	
heat transfer coefficient	watt per square meter kelvin	W/(m^2·K)	
linear density	kilogram per meter	kg/m	
magnetic field strength	ampere per meter	A/m	
moment of force, torque	newton meter	N·m	
momentum	kilogram meter per second	kg·m/s	
* power, heat flow rate, radiant flux	kilowatt	kW	
	watt	W	J/s
power density, heat flux density, irradiance	watt per square meter	W/m^2	
* pressure, stress	megapascal	MPa	
	kilopascal	kPa	
	pascal	Pa	
sound level	decibel	dB	
specific energy	joule per kilogram	J/kg	
specific volume	cubic meter per kilogram	m^3/kg	

Quantity	Unit	Symbol	Acceptable equivalent
surface tension	newton per meter	N/m	
thermal conductivity	watt per meter kelvin	W/(m·K)	
velocity	meter per second	m/s	
	kilometer per hour	km/h	
viscosity, dynamic	pascal second	Pa·s	
	millipascal second	mPa·s	
volume	cubic meter	m^3	
	cubic decimeter	dm^3	L (liter)
	cubic centimeter	cm^3	mL

* The asterisk denotes those units having special names and symbols.

† The spellings "metre" and "litre" are preferred by ASTM; however "er-" is used in the Encyclopedia.

‡ "Weight" is the commonly used term for "mass."

§ Wide use is made of "Celsius temperature" (t) defined by

$$t = T - T_0$$

where t is the thermodynamic temperature, expressed in kelvins, and $T_0 = 273.15$ by definition. A temperature interval may be expressed in degrees Celsius as well as in kelvins.

x This non-SI unit is recognized by the CIPM as having to be retained because of practical importance or use in specialized fields.

In addition, there are 16 prefixes used to indicate order of magnitude, as follows:

Multiplication factor	Prefix	Symbol
10^{18}	exa	E
10^{15}	peta	P
10^{12}	tera	T
10^9	giga	G
10^6	mega	M
10^3	kilo	k
10^2	hecto	h[a]
10	deka	da[a]
10^{-1}	deci	d[a]
10^{-2}	centi	c[a]
10^{-3}	milli	m
10^{-6}	micro	μ
10^{-9}	nano	n
10^{-12}	pico	p
10^{-15}	femto	f
10^{-18}	atto	a

[a] Although hecto, deka, deci, and centi are SI prefixes, their use should be avoided except for SI unit-multiples for area and volume and nontechnical use of centimeter, as for body and clothing measurement.

Conversion Factors to SI Units

To convert from	To	Multiply by
acre	square meter (m^2)	4.047×10^3
angstrom	meter (m)	1.0×10^{-10}†
atmosphere	pascal (Pa)	1.013×10^5
bar	pascal (Pa)	1.0×10^5†
barn	square meter (m^2)	1.0×10^{-28}†
barrel (42 U.S. liquid gallons)	cubic meter (m^3)	0.1590
Btu (thermochemical)	joule (J)	1.054×10^3
bushel	cubic meter (m^3)	3.524×10^{-2}
calorie (thermochemical)	joule (J)	4.184†
centipoise	pascal second (Pa·s)	1.0×10^{-3}†
cfm (cubic foot per minute)	cubic meter per second (m^3/s)	4.72×10^{-4}
cubic inch	cubic meter (m^3)	1.639×10^{-5}
cubic foot	cubic meter (m^3)	2.832×10^{-2}
cubic yard	cubic meter (m^3)	0.7646

To convert from	To	Multiply by
dram (apothecaries')	kilogram (kg)	3.888×10^{-3}
dram (avoirdupois)	kilogram (kg)	1.772×10^{-3}
dram (U.S. fluid)	cubic meter (m³)	3.697×10^{-6}
dyne	newton (N)	$1.0 \times 10^{-5\dagger}$
dyne/cm	newton per meter (N/m)	$1.0 \times 10^{-3\dagger}$
fluid ounce (U.S.)	cubic meter (m³)	2.957×10^{-5}
foot	meter (m)	$0.3048^\dagger$
gallon (U.S. dry)	cubic meter (m³)	4.405×10^{-3}
gallon (U.S. liquid)	cubic meter (m³)	3.785×10^{-3}
gallon per minute (gpm)	cubic meter per second (m³/s)	6.308×10^{-5}
	cubic meter per hour (m³/h)	0.2271
grain	kilogram (kg)	6.480×10^{-5}
horsepower (550 ft·lbf/s)	watt (W)	7.457×10^{2}
inch	meter (m)	$2.54 \times 10^{-2\dagger}$
inch of mercury (32°F)	pascal (Pa)	3.386×10^{3}
inch of water (39.2°F)	pascal (Pa)	2.491×10^{2}
kilogram-force	newton (N)	9.807
kilowatt hour	megajoule (MJ)	$3.6^\dagger$
liter (for fluids only)	cubic meter (m³)	$1.0 \times 10^{-3\dagger}$
micron	meter (m)	$1.0 \times 10^{-6\dagger}$
mil	meter (m)	$2.54 \times 10^{-5\dagger}$
mile (statute)	meter (m)	1.609×10^{3}
mile per hour	meter per second (m/s)	0.4470
millimeter of mercury (0°C)	pascal (Pa)	$1.333 \times 10^{2\dagger}$
ounce (avoirdupois)	kilogram (kg)	2.835×10^{-2}
ounce (troy)	kilogram (kg)	3.110×10^{-2}
ounce (U.S. fluid)	cubic meter (m³)	2.957×10^{-5}
ounce-force	newton (N)	0.2780
peck (U.S.)	cubic meter (m³)	8.810×10^{-3}
pennyweight	kilogram (kg)	1.555×10^{-3}
pint (U.S. dry)	cubic meter (m³)	5.506×10^{-4}
pint (U.S. liquid)	cubic meter (m³)	4.732×10^{-4}
poise (absolute viscosity)	pascal second (Pa·s)	$0.10^\dagger$
pound (avoirdupois)	kilogram (kg)	0.4536
pound (troy)	kilogram (kg)	0.3732
pound-force	newton (N)	4.448
pound-force per square inch (psi)	pascal (Pa)	6.895×10^{3}
quart (U.S. dry)	cubic meter (m³)	1.101×10^{-3}
quart (U.S. liquid)	cubic meter (m³)	9.464×10^{-4}
quintal	kilogram (kg)	$1.0 \times 10^{2\dagger}$
rad	gray (Gy)	$1.0 \times 10^{-2\dagger}$
square inch	square meter (m²)	6.452×10^{-4}
square foot	square meter (m²)	9.290×10^{-2}
square mile	square meter (m²)	2.590×10^{6}
square yard	square meter (m²)	0.8361
ton (long, 2240 pounds)	kilogram (kg)	1.016×10^{3}
ton (metric)	kilogram (kg)	$1.0 \times 10^{3\dagger}$
ton (short, 2000 pounds)	kilogram (kg)	9.072×10^{2}
torr	pascal (Pa)	1.333×10^{2}
yard	meter (m)	$0.9144^\dagger$

† Exact.

Acronyms and Abbreviations

AA	Archigram Architects	AASHTO	American Association of State Highway and Transportation Officials
AAA	American Arbitration Association		
AACA	Architects Accreditation Council of Australia	AAT	Art and Architecture Thesaurus
AAL	Association of Architectural Librarians	ABA	Architectural Barriers Act
AAMA	American Architectural Manufacturers Association	ABC	Alternate birthing center; Associate Builders and Contractors
AASHO	American Association of State Highway Officials	ABNT	Associacao Brasileira de Normas Tecnicas

ABPMA	Acoustical and Board Products Manufacturers Association
ABS	Acrylonitrile–butadiene–styrene
AC	Alternating current
ACA	American Correction Association; Ammoniacal copper arsenate
ACEC	American Consulting Engineers Council
ACI	American Concrete Institute
ACS	Acrylonitrile–chlorinated polyethylene–styrene
ACSA	Association of Collegiate Schools of Architecture
ADC	Air Diffusion Council
ADL	Activities of daily living
ADPI	Air Distribution Performance Index
ADR	Alternative dispute resolution
AEC	Atomic Energy Commission
AEG	Allgemeine Elektricitats-Geselschaft
AEIC	Association of Edison Illuminating Companies
AEPIC	Architecture and Engineering Performance Information Center
AFD	Air filtration devices
AFL/CIO	American Federation of Labor and Congress of Industrial Organizations
AFNOR	Association Francaise de Normalisation
AFUE	Annual fuel utilization efficiency
AGA	American Gas Association
AGC	Associated General Contractors of America
AGIC	Architectural Group for Industry and Commerce
AGTS	Automated guideway transit systems
AHA	American Hardboard Association
AHAM	Association of Home Appliance Manufacturers
AHU	Air handler unit
AI	Articulation Index; Artificial Intelligence
AIA	American Institute of Architects
AIA/F	American Institute of Architects Foundation
AIAS	American Institute of Architecture Students
AIA/SC	American Institute of Architects Service Corporation
AICP	American Institute of Certified Planners
AID	Agency for International Development
AIKD	American Institute of Kitchen Dealers
AIREA	American Institute of Real Estate Appraisers
AISC	American Institute of Steel Construction
AISI	American Iron and Steel Institute
AITC	American Institute of Timber Construction
ALS	American Lumber Standards
AMA	Acoustical Materials Association
AMCA	Air Moving and Conditioning Association
ANSI	American National Standards Institute

APA	American Planning Association; American Plywood Association
APR	Air purifying respirators; Architectural program report
APS	Arrival point of sight
ARCC	Architectural Research Centers Consortium
ARCUK	Architects Registration Council of the United Kingdom
ARE	Architect Registration Examination
ARI	Air-Conditioning and Refrigeration Institute
ARLIS/N	Art Libraries Society of North America
ARMA	Asphalt Roofing Manufacturers Association
ARP	Air raid precaution
ASA	Acoustical Society of America; American Subcontractors Association
ASCE	American Society of Civil Engineers
ASET	Available safe egress time
ASHRAE	American Society of Heating, Refrigerating, and Air Conditioning Engineers
ASHVE	American Society of Heating and Ventilating Engineers
ASID	American Society of Interior Designers
ASLA	American Society of Landscape Architects
ASM	American Society for Metals
ASME	American Society of Mechanical Engineers
ASTM	American Society for Testing and Materials
ATA	Air Transportation Association of America
AtBat	l'Atelier des Batisseurs
ATBCB	Architectural and Transportation Barriers Compliance Board
ATC	Air Transport Command
ATM	Automatic teller machine
ATMA	American Textile Machinery Association
A/V	Audio/video
AWG	American wire gauge
AWI	Architectural Woodwork Institute
AWPA	American Wood Preservers Association
AWPB	American Wood Preservers Bureau
AWT	Advanced wastewater treatment
BBC	British Broadcasting Company
BBN	Bolt Beranek and Newman
BBP	Butylbenzyl phthalate
BCMC	Board for the Coordination of the Model Codes
BDA	Bund Deutscher Architekten
BEEP	Black Executive Exchange Program
BEL	*Bauentwerfslehre*
BEPS	Building Energy Performance Standard
BFE	Base flood elevation
BFSM	Building Fire Simulation Model
BH	Boxed heart
BIA	Brick Institute of America

BJS	Bureau of Justice Statistics	CON	Certificate of need
BOCA	Building Officials and Code Administrators International	CP	Cellulose propionate
		CPD	Continuing professional development
BOD	Biological oxygen demand	CPE	Chlorinated polyethylene
BOMA	Building Owners and Managers Association International	CPM	Critical path method
		cps	cycles per second
BOSTI	Buffalo Organization for Social and Technological Innovation	CPSC	Consumer Product Safety Commission
		CPU	Central processing unit; Computer processing unit
BPST	British portable skid tester		
BRA	Boston Redevelopment Authority	CPVC	Chlorinated poly(vinyl chloride); Critical pigment volume concentration
BRAB	Building Research Advisory Board		
BRB	Building Research Board		
BRI	Building related illness	CR	Cavity ratio; Condensation resistance
BS	Building standards		
BSR	Board of Standards Review	CRI	Color Rendering Index
BSSC	Building Seismic Safety Council	CRREL	Cold Regions Research and Engineering Laboratory
Btu	British thermal unit		
BUR	Built-up roofing	CRS	Caudill Rowlett Scott
BV	Bolt value	CRSI	Concrete Reinforcing Steel Institute
		CRSS	Caudill Rowlett Scott Sirrine
CA	Cellulose acetate	CRT	Cathode ray tube; Computer relay terminal
CAA	Clean Air Act		
CABO	Council of American Building Officials	CSI	Construction Specifications Institute
CACE	Council of Architectural Component Executives		
		CSPE	Chlorosulfonated polyethylene
CAD	Computer-aided Design	CSRF	Construction Science Research Foundation
CADD	Computer-aided Design and Drafting		
CAGI	Compressed Air and Gas Institute	CU	Coefficient of utilization
CAJ	Committee on Architecture for Justice	CUA	The Catholic University of America
CARF	Committee on Accreditation of Rehabilitation Facilities	CVS	Certified value specialist
CB	Cellulose butyrate	DAL	Federation of Danish Architects
CBD	Central business district	dB	decibel
CBR	California bearing ratio	DC	Direct current
CCA	Chromated copper arsenate	DEW	Distant Early Warning
CCC	Civilian Conservation Corps	DHHS	Department of Health and Human Services
CCR	Ceiling cavity ratio		
CCTV	Closed-circuit television	DOD	Department of Defense
cd	candela	DOE	Department of Energy
CDA	Copper Development Association	DOL	Department of Labor
CDC	Community design center	DOP	Dioctyl phthalate
CEC	Canadian Electrical Code; Consulting Engineers Council	DOT	Department of Transportation
		DP	Data processing; Degree of polymerization
cfm	cubic feet per minute		
CFR	Airport Crash, Fire and Rescue Service; Code of Federal Regulations	DPIC	Design Professionals Insurance Company
		DPLG	Diplome par le gouvernmente
CIAM	Les Congres Internationaux d'Architecture Moderne	DPU	Data processing unit
		DWV	Drain–waste–vent
CIB	International Council for Building Research, Studies, and Documentation	DX	Direct-expansion
		EDRA	Environmental Design Research Association
CIMA	Construction Industry Manufacturers Association		
		EENT	Eye, ear, nose, and throat
CKD	Certified kitchen designer	EER	Energy efficiency ratio
CLARB	National Council of Landscape Architectural Registration Boards	EERI	Earthquake Engineering Research Institute
CLEP	College-level Examination Program	EESA	Education Evaluation Services for Architects
CLTD	Cooling load temperature difference		
CM	Construction management; Construction manager	EIP	Ethylene interpolymers
		EJCDC	Engineers Joint Contract Documents Committee
CMAA	Construction Management Association of America		
		ELR	Equivalent length of run
CMU	Concrete masonry unit(s)	EMT	Electrical metallic tubing
CN	Cellulose nitrate	ENT	Ear, nose, and throat
COD	Chemical oxygen demand	EP	Epoxies
COF	Coefficient of friction	EPA	Environmental Protection Agency

EPCOT	Experimental Prototype Community of Tomorrow
EPDM	Ethylene propylene diene monomer
EPI	Emulsion polymer/isocyanate
EPS	Expandable polystyrene
ERM	Escape and rescue model
ESD	Electrostatic discharge
ESI	Equivalent sphere illumination
ESP	Education Services for the Professions
ET	Evapotranspiration
ETP	Electrolytic tough pitch
ETS	Environmental tobacco smoke
E&B	*Environment and Behavior* (journal)
f	Fiber(s)
FAA	Federal Aviation Administration
FAIA	Fellow of the American Institute of Architects
FAR	Floor area ratio
FBI	Federal Bureau of Investigation
FBO	Foreign Building Operations
fc	footcandle(s)
FCARM	Federation of Colleges of Architects of the Mexican Republic
FCR	Floor cavity ratio
FEMA	Federal Emergency Management Agency
FG	Flat grain
FHA	Federal Housing Administration
FHWA	Federal Highway Administration
FIDCR	Federal Interagency Day Care Requirements
FIDIC	Federation Internationale des Ingenieurs-conseils (Federation of Consulting Engineers)
FIDS	Flight Information Display Systems
FIRM	Flood insurance rate map
FM	Fineness modulus
FmHA	Farmers Home Administration
FMRL	Factory Mutual Research Laboratories
FOHC	Free-of-heart center
fpm	feet per minute
fps	feet per second
FR	Flame retardant
FRP	Fiber glass-reinforced plastic
FRT	Fire retardant treated
FS	Factor of safety
FSES	Fire Safety Evaluation System
ft	foot (feet)
FU	Fixture units
GA	Gypsum Association
GAO	General Accounting Office
GATT	General Agreement on Tariffs and Trade
GDP	Gross domestic product
GFCI	Ground fault circuit interrupter
Glulam	Glued laminated wood
GMAW	Gas metal arc welding
GMP	Guaranteed maximum price
gpm	gallons per minute
GRP	Glass reinforced plastic
GSA	General Services Administration

GSIS	Government Service Insurance System
GTAW	Gas tungsten arc welding
h	hour(s)
HABS	Historic American Buildings Survey
HDO	High density overlay
HDPE	High density polyethylene
HEGIS	Higher Education General Information Survey
HEPA	High-efficiency particulate absolute
HGSD	Harvard Graduate School of Design
HHS	Department of Health & Human Services
HID	High-intensity discharge
HOK	Hellmuth Obata and Kassabaum
HPL	High-pressure laminate
HPS	High-pressure sodium
HUD	Department of Housing & Urban Development
HVAC	Heating, ventilating, and air conditioning
Hz	Hertz
I	Candlepower
IACC	International Association of Conference Centers
IALD	International Association of Lighting Designers
IAPS	International Association for the Study of People and their Physical Surroundings
IATA	International Air Transport Association
IBD	Institute of Business Designers
ICAO	International Civil Aviation Organization
ICBO	International Conference of Building Officials
ICEA	Insulated Cable Engineers Association
ICOR	Interprofessional Council on Registration
IDP	Intern–Architect Development Program
IDSA	Industrial Designers Society of America
IEC	International Electrotechnical Commission
IEEE	Institute of Electrical and Electronics Engineers
IES	Illuminating Engineering Society of North America
IF	Industrialization Forum
IG	International Group
IIC	Impact insulation class
IIT	Illinois Institute of Technology
ILS	Instrument landing system
in.	inch(es)
INCRA	International Copper Research Association
IP	Image processing
ir	infrared
IRA	Initial rate of water absorption
ISO	International Organization for Standardization

IUA	Institute Universitario di Architettura; International Union of Architects	mpy	mils per year
		msec	millisecond(s)
		MSHA	Mine Safety and Health Administration
JAE	*Journal of Architectural Education*	MSR	Machine stress-rated
JAPR	*Journal of Architectural and Planning Research*	MV	Mercury vapor
		μm	micrometer
JCAH	Joint Commission on Accreditation of Hospitals		
		NAAB	National Architectural Accrediting Board
JEP	*Journal of Environmental Psychology*	NACA	National Advisory Council on Aging
JIS	Japanese industry standards	NAEC	National Association of Elevator Contractors
JIT	Just in time		
JSAH	*Journal of the Society of Architectural Historians*	NAHB	National Association of Home Builders of the United States
		NAPF	National Association of Plastic Fabricators
KCPI	Knife cuts per inch		
KD	Kiln-dried	NASA	National Aeronautics and Space Administration
kg	kilogram		
kip	1000 pounds	NASFCA	National Automatic Sprinkler and Fire Control Association
km	kilometer		
kPa	kilopascal	NAVFAC	Naval Facilities Engineering Command
ksi	kips per square inch		
kW	kilowatt(s)	NBC	National Building Code
		NBCC	National Building Code of Canada
L	liter	NBFU	National Board of Fire Underwriters
lb	pound	NBM	National Building Museum
LCC	London County Council		National Institute of Science and
LDPE	Low density polyethylene	NBS	Technology (Formerly National
LDR	Luminaire dirt replacement; Labor/delivery/recovery		Bureau of Standards)
		NC	Network communications; Noise criteria
LDRP	Labor/delivery/recovery/postpartum		
LFT	Laminated floor tile	NCA	National Constructors Association
LLDPE	Linear low density polyethylene	NCAR	National Council of Architectural Registration
LLF	Light loss factor		
LOF	Large ordering framework	NCARB	National Council of Architectural Registration Boards
LPS	Low-pressure sodium		
LRI	Lighting Research Institute	NCEE	National Council of Engineering Examiners
LSC	Life Safety Code		
		NCIDQ	National Council of Interior Design Qualification
m	meter		
MAAT	Mean average air temperature	NCMA	National Concrete Masonry Association
MAI	Member of the Appraisers Institute		
MARTA	Metropolitan Atlanta Rapid Transit Authority	NCS	Natural color system
		NCSBCS	National Conference of States on Building Codes and Standards
MBMA	Metal Building Manufacturers Association		
		NDS	National design specifications
MC	Moisture content	NEA	National Endowment for the Arts
MDF	Medium density fiberboard	NEC	National Electrical Code
MDI	Methylene diisocyanate	NECA	National Electrical Contractors Association
MDO	Medium density overlay		
MDP	Main distribution panelboard	NEH	National Endowment for the Humanities
MDPE	Medium density polyethylene		
MERA	Man and Environment Research Association	NEISS	National Electronic Injury Surveillance System
		NEMA	National Electrical Manufacturers Association
MG	Motor generator		
MGRAD	Minimum Guidelines and Requirements for Accessible Design	NFIP	National Flood Insurance Program
		NFPA	National Fire Protection Association; National Forest Products Association
MH	Metal halide		
MIA	Marble Institute of America		
min	minute(s)		
MIT	Massachusetts Institute of Technology	NGR	National grading rule
MLS	Master of Library Science	NIBS	National Institute of Building
mm	millimeter	NIC	Noise insulation class
MOE	Modulus of elasticity	NIOSH	National Institute for Occupational Safety and Health
MOR	Modulus of rupture		
MPa	Megapascal		
MPS	Minimum property standards		

NKCA	National Kitchen Cabinet Association		psf	pounds per square foot
nm	nanometers		PSFS	Philadelphia Savings Fund Society
NMS	Nonmetallic sheathed		psi	pounds per square inch
NMTB	National Machine Tool Builders Association		PTFE	Polytetrafluoroethylene
			PTO	Power take-off
NPS	National Park Service		PTV	Passenger transfer vehicle
NR	Noise reduction		PUD	Planned unit development
NRC	Noise reduction coefficient		PVA	Paralyzed Veterans of America; Poly(vinyl acrylic)
NRCA	National Roofing Contractors Association		PVAC	Polyvinyl acetate
NSF	National Science Foundation; National Sanitation Foundation		PVAL	Polyvinyl alcohol
			PVB	Polyvinyl butyral
NSPE	National Society of Professional Engineers		PVC	Poly(vinyl chloride); Pigment volume concentration
NSSEA	National School Supply and Equipment Association		PVDC	Polyvinylidene chloride
			PVDF	Polyvinylidene fluoride
			PVF	Polyvinyl fluoride; Polyvinyl formal
oc	on center		PW	Present worth
OEM	Original equipment manufacturer		PWA	Present worth of annuity
OPLR	Office for Professional Liability Research		PWF	Permanent wood foundation
ORBIT-2	Organizations, Buildings and Information Technology (study)		RAIC	Royal Architectural Institute of Canada
OSA	Olefin–styrene–acrylonitrile		RBM	Reinforced brick masonry
OSB	Oriented strand board		RCR	Room cavity ratio
OSHA	Occupational Safety and Health Administration		REA	Rural Electrification Administration
			REI	Relative exposure index
			REIT	Real estate investment trust
PA	Polyamide		RF	Resorcinol–formaldehyde
P/A	*Progressive Architecture* (journal)		RFC	Reconstruction Finance Corporation
PACO	Probing Alternate Career Opportunities		RFP	Request for proposal
			rh	Relative humidity
PADC	Pennsylvania Avenue Development Corporation		RIBA	Royal Institute of British Architects
			RIM	Reaction injection molding
PAPER	People and the Physical Environment Research		RL, R/L	Random length
			ROI	Return on investment
PAT	Proficiency analytical testing		rpm	revolutions per minute
PB	Polybutylene		R/UDAT	Regional/Urban Design Assistance Team(s)
PBS	Public Building Service			
PBT	Polybutylene terephthalate			
PC	Personal computer; Polycarbonate; Polymer concrete		SAC	Sound absorption coefficient
PCA	Portland Cement Association		SAE	Society of Automotive Engineers, Inc.
PCB	Pentachlorobiphenyl		SAN	Styrene–acrylonitrile
PCC	Polymer cement concrete		SAR	Stichting Architekten Research
PCD	Planned community development		SAVE	Society of American Value Engineers
PCEH	President's Committee for the Employment of Handicapped		SBCC	Standard Building Construction Code
PCI	Prestressed Concrete Institute		SBCCI	Southern Building Code Congress International, Inc.
PE	Polyethylene		SBR	Styrene butadiene rubber
PEPP	Professional Engineers in Private Practice		SBS	Sick building syndrome
			SCFF	Silicone-coated fiber glass fabrics
PERT	Program evaluation and review technique		SCS	Soil Conservation Service
PET	Polyethylene terephthalate		SCSD	School Construction System Development
PIB	Polyisobutylene			
PIC	Polymer-impregnated concrete		SE	Service entrance
PMMA	Polymethyl methacrylate		sec	second(s)
PMR	Protected membrane roof		SERI	Solar Energy Research Institute
PMS	Pavement management system		SG	Slash grain
POE	Post-occupancy evaluation		SHHA	Self-help Housing Agency
PP	Period payment; Polypropylene		SIC	Standard Industrial Classification
ppm	parts per million		SIR	Society of Industrial Realtors
PRF	Phenol–resorcinol–formaldehyde		SJI	Steel Joist Institute
PS	Polystyrene		SLA	Special Libraries Association
PSAE	Production Systems for Architects and Engineers		SMACNA	Sheet Metal and Air Conditioning Contractors National Association
			SMH	Super metal halide

SMPS	Society for Marketing Professional Services	UFI	Urea–formaldehyde foam insulation
SMU	Southern Methodist University	UHMWPE	Ultra-high molecular weight polyethylene
SOCOTEC	Societe de Controle Technique	UIA	Union Internationale des Architects
SOM	Skidmore Owings and Merrill	UIDC	Urban Investment Development Company
SPD	Supply, processing, and distribution		
SPI	Society of the Plastics Industry	UL	Underwriters Laboratories
SPP	Speech privacy potential	ULI	Urban Land Institute
SPRI	Single Ply Roofing Institute	UNESCO	United Nations Educational, Scientific, and Cultural Organization
SSPB	South Side Planning Board (Chicago)		
ST	Structural tubing		
STC	Sound transmission class	UNS	Unified numbering systems
STD	Standard	UPS	Uninterruptible power supply
STL	Sound transmission loss	USCOLD	United States Committee on Large Dams
TAC	The Architects Collaborative	USDA	United States Department of Agriculture
TAS	Technical Assistance Series		
TCFF	Teflon-coated fiber glass fabrics	USIA	United States Information Agency
TDD	Telecommunication devices for deaf persons	USPS	United States Postal Service
		uv	ultraviolet
TDI	Toluene diisocyanate		
TEM	Transmission electron microscopy	VA	Veterans Administration
TH	Technische Hochschule	VAT	Vinyl asbestos tile
THB	Technische Hochschule Braunschweig	VCP	Visual Comfort Probability Factor
TIMA	Thermal Insulation Manufacturers Association	VCT	Vinyl composition tile
		VDT	Video display terminal
TL	Transmission loss	VG	Vertical grain
T-PV	Temperature–pressure relief valve	VISTA	Volunteers in Service to America
TV	Television	VLH	Very low heat
TVA	Tennessee Valley Authority	VMA	Voids in the mineral aggregate
TWA	Time-weighted average	VOC	Volatile organic compound
T & G	Tongue and groove	VU	Value unit(s)
T & P	Temperature and pressure		
UBC	Uniform Building Code	WAA	War Assets Administration; Western Association of Architects
UCC	Uniform Commercial Code		
UCI	Uniform Construction Index	WHO	World Health Organization
UDDC	Urban Design and Development Corporation	WMMA	Woodworking Machinery Manufacturers Association
UF	Urea–formaldehyde	WP	Word processing; Word processor
UFAS	Uniform Federal Accessibility Standards	WPA	Work Progress Administration; Work Projects Administration

T

TABLER, WILLIAM B.

Over the past 40 years, William B. Tabler Architects, of New York City, has designed and drawn the plans for more than 350 hotels in some 20 countries, more hotels, by far, than any other firm or individual.

"Cherubic William Benjamin Tabler, Sr.,"—founder and still head of the company in 1989—*Time* magazine has said, "has become the world's busiest designer of big hotels . . . The world's major innkeepers knock on Tabler's door because he has developed a . . . precision for slashing frills and space out of his buildings to make them cheaper to construct and operate. . . . Few Tabler hotels win design prizes; but the architect is proud that no hotel of his design has lost money" (1).

The Tabler-designed hotels range from the 2500-room New York Hilton, to the 150-room Jordan Inter-Continental at Amman and the 198-room Nairobi Serena in Kenya. Tabler has created more than 20 Hiltons. Aside from the one in New York City, some of the largest are in Washington, D.C., Pittsburgh, Dallas, San Francisco, St. Paul, Baltimore, and Indianapolis.

He has done a number of Sheraton hotels, including the Universal Hotel of the Stars at Universal City, California; hotels for Stouffer, including the Riverfront Inn on the Mississippi River, in St. Louis; a number of Registry Hotels, among them the recently completed luxury Dallas Registry; three hotels in Ireland, two in Turkey, hotels in Saudi Arabia, Egypt, Kenya, Zambia, Jordan, Pakistan, a dozen or more in Canada, others in Bermuda, South Korea, and Sri Lanka, as well as hotels in Central and South America, Nassau, and Montego Bay, Jamaica. Mr. Tabler was consulting architect to such hotels as the London Hilton, the New Otani in Tokyo, the Manila Hotel, and the Manila Mandarin in the Philippines, the Dorchester, London, and scores of others.

Tabler took degrees in engineering at Harvard College, then Bachelor's and Master's degrees in architecture at the Harvard Graduate School of Design. He finished nine years of college and graduate work in seven years and led his class. Tabler graduated in 1939 and, despite the Depression, managed to find employment with Holabird & Root of Chicago, which was designing the new Statler Hotel in Washington, D.C. Tabler was put in charge of drawing the plans and later on-site supervision of construction as job captain. This headed him in the direction that Tabler's career has followed ever since.

The Washington Statler, which opened in 1943, was the first hotel of consequence built in the United States during the 12 years since the new Waldorf Astoria was completed in New York City in 1931. The Depression had driven 80% of U.S. hotels into bankruptcy, including three of the four large chains. This caused many hotel owners and especially financial institutions to doubt that it was possible any longer to build a fine hotel that would be financially profitable—even by the Statler Company, ad-

mittedly the most scientific designers and operators of hotels, the only chain that did not bankrupt in the Depression.

The main reason for so many hotel failures was that most large hotels had been so poorly arranged that they required twice as many employees as they should have. Thus, the architects built into the new Washington hotel all of the know-how for economical operation that the Statler people had learned over the company's 40 years of existence, plus new mechanical and electrical labor-saving and guest-pleasing innovations that had developed over the 12-year dearth of hotel building. These ranged from central air-conditioning to new types of dishwashers. As a result, during the dramatic revival in hotel occupancy brought on by World War II, the 800-room Washington Statler became probably the most profitable hotel for its size in the world.

As soon as the Washington Statler opened, Tabler joined the Seabees and spent the rest of the war designing airfields, hospitals, docks, and other military and naval installations in the islands of the Central and South Pacific. His Washington experience had made Tabler fascinated with hotels, and as soon as the war was over, he opened his own architectural office in New York City specializing in hotel design, with the Statler Company as his principal client.

Determined to build maximum efficiency into his hotels, Tabler laboriously measured every room in every service and mechanical department of every Statler Hotel. He interviewed the managements of each department and the employees to learn how many employees were required for efficiently operating each department and the general level of efficiency, depending on the area of its floor space, the number of employees required, its location in the hotel with regard to areas to be served, and the type and equipment used.

These data allowed Tabler to prepare the first set of standards ever written on how to build a hotel with regard to the size and location of each department to provide maximum service at minimum cost. His company has continued to refine this information over the years on the basis of experience.

A number of hotel companies, including such large ones as Sheraton, Inter-Continental, Westin Hotels, Hilton, and, in fact, all major hotel operators have adopted Tabler's standards into their own guidelines; thus Tabler's influence is evident in the hundreds of hotels around the world designed by other architects, as well as by Tabler's own firm. His commercial–convention type of hotel is planned to require about half as many employees as that hotel has guest rooms. The same type of hotel, built prior to the 1930s depression, requires three or four times that many employees.

Tabler and his architects have also developed rules of thumb, based on long experience, that indicate the percentage of entire cost of building, equipping, and furnishing a hotel that each department, operation, or area should bear, depending on the hotel's location—central city, suburban, or third world. This information ranges from the proportion of the cost of the entire project that table service, for example, should bear, on up to guest rooms, heating, kitchen and mechanical equipment, land, and various types of parking facility. Tabler even tells the prospective hotel builders the average room rent to charge per day in order to amortize the mortgage and break even in operations at 60–65% occupancy.

Tabler was first to put music in hotel elevators—not especially to please passengers, but mainly to entertain elevator operators and keep them from quitting their jobs because of boredom. Later, he promoted self-service elevators, and dial telephones in guest rooms despite the objection by many hotel managements that each of these innovations cheapened service. It turned out that guests liked the independence that self-service elevators and telephones offered.

Some Tabler innovations have extended beyond hotels into general use. Among these are the new-style escalators with sides of tempered glass, increasingly popular in department stores, office and public buildings, as well as hotels. The idea originated when Tabler wanted to install an escalator to carry guests from the lobby to the mezzanine and ballroom in the New York Hilton, which his firm was designing. The late Wallace K. Harrison, architect for Rockefeller Center, however, insisted on a "monumental staircase" instead. To Harrison, regular escalators were like a back stairs. Tabler then suggested making the sides of the escalator of tempered, transparent glass. Harrison agreed that such an escalator would be sufficiently "monumental" and Tabler took his idea to the manufacturers of escalators. The Otis and Westinghouse Elevator companies removed the machinery that moved the stair steps from the sides of the escalator to the bottom, so that transparent glass could be used. The glass-sided escalator has enjoyed increasing popularity ever since.

Most notable of Tabler's innovations that have extended beyond hotels is the nonslip bathtub, now standard equipment in most recently built homes, as well as in hotels. A main cause of injuries to hotel guests, as well as people in their homes, had long been slipping and falling on the high gloss porcelain finish of bathtubs. The so-called matte finish was rough and nonslippery but extremely difficult to clean. Tabler kept looking for a solution and finally found it in his suite in the Inter-Continental Hotel in Geneva, Switzerland, in 1964. Workmen had sanded the bottom of his bathtub, trying to remedy some areas of chipped enamel. In those spots the bottom of the tub was a sort of semigloss that held Tabler's feet like adhesive when he stood there. He tried soiling the areas and found they were easy to clean.

The architect now collected different types of tile used for other purposes until he found a finish almost like the bottom of the bathtub in Geneva. Tabler gave samples to representatives of the Crane Company, American Standard, and Kohler. Pretty soon all three plumbing manufacturers were coming out with nonslip bathtubs. Nonslip bathtubs are now safety features in probably hundreds of thousands of U.S. homes.

In the area of professional ethics, Tabler has written that "an architect, being a professional, designs not just according to the requirements of the owner. Being a professional, the architect must also design to the requirements of the people who are going to be hotel guests; and he must design to the generalized needs of society. Any truly conscientious architect should refuse to design a building that abuses this public trust" (2). Such an attitude has prompted one source to describe Tabler as "a philosopher and the [hotel] industry's conscience-keeper" (3).

BIBLIOGRAPHY

1. *Time*, 78 (Aug. 6, 1965).
2. W. Tabler, "American Hotel Design Today," *Statler Lectures*, University of Massachusetts and The Statler Foundation, Amherst, Mass., 1971, p. 2.
3. R. Skyme, ed., *Hotel Specification International*, Pennington Press Ltd., Kent, UK, p. 84.

See also HOTELS

WILLIAM B. TABLER, SR.,
FAIA
New York, New York

TAKAMATUS, SHIN.   See ORIENTAL ARCHITECTURE

TANGE, KENZO

Kenzo Tange (b. 1913) is a world-renowned Japanese architect of the second half of the twentieth century who has fused the architectural traditions of his native Japan with the contemporary philosophy and traditions of the western world. Tange, as well as most architects of his generation, was greatly influenced by the principles of the Congres Internationaux d'Architecture Moderne (CIAM) (1928) and the individuals identified with that organization including Le Corbusier, Walter Gropius, and Siegfried Giedion.

Tange believed that the Japanese people were searching for a freedom of expression that would symbolize a new postwar Japanese society free from the technocratic regimes of the past. His work marked a revived awareness of Japanese architectural traditions expressed through a contemporary interpretation of architectural form. Tange has become an architect of the world largely because his work is so intensely Japanese. He demonstrated that a unique regionalism could be developed, and recognized, within the circumstance of the international style.

Kenzo Tange was born on September 4, 1913 in the port city of Imabari, Ehime Prefecture. Imabari is on the Takanawa peninsula, which is located on the island of Shikoku, the smallest (50 mi wide by 150 mi long) of the four major islands of Japan. Shikoku is nationally recognized as the land of 88 holy temples and shrines that honor the scholar–priest Kukai. Imabari is the ancient site of early Yayoi (100 B.C.) settlements.

Tange attended high school in Hiroshima on the main island of Honsho some 40 miles across the inland sea from his home in Imabari. All of his formal professional education was acquired in Imperial Japan before the end of World War II. In 1935, at the age of 22, he entered the Tokyo Imperial University and took architectural courses in the Department of Engineering, graduating in 1938.

In 1938 Tange sought employment in the office of Kunio Maekawa. Bauhaus principles had a strong influence on Japanese architects in the 1930s and Maekawa was clearly one of the most influential Japanese architects of his generation. In design competitions calling for a traditional Japanese approach, Maekawa's unsuccessful submissions were clearly developed in the international style. In perfecting his design philosophy Maekawa drew on his five-year work experience with Antonin Raymond in Japan and his experience in Paris with the office of Le Corbusier working on the Villa Savoye and the Swiss Pavilion. In Tange's four years of employment with Maekawa, he assimilated these experiences from his mentor. While in Maekawa's office, Tange joined the Japanese Werkbund and was responsible for the planning of the Kishi Memorial Gymnasium. A generation later the office of Kenzo Tange and URTEC was to provide the same type of vital work environment for such notable young Japanese architects as Kisho Kurokawa, Fumihiko Maki (two of the five metabolist group), Arata Isozaki, and Sachio Otani.

Tange returned to Tokyo University in 1942 for graduate study. It was during this period that he developed his lifelong interest in urban design. Under the influence of a classmate, Ryuichi Hamaguchi, Tange was attracted to western Renaissance architecture, especially the works of Michelangelo. He developed a strong sense of the greatness of Rome and Greece. While in graduate school, Tange identified the concept of "communication space," which was to be an important part of his future work. This concept, derived from his study of the Greek agora and European plazas as public meeting places, was a revolutionary one within the Japanese culture where there is no tradition of public space.

In 1942, Tange was awarded first prize for his design for a Far East memorial building, which was sponsored by the Japanese Architectural Institute. In 1943, he won a prize for his plan for a Japanese–Thai cultural center in Bangkok. Tange completed his graduate study in 1945 at the age of 32. In 1946 Tange accepted a professorship at Tokyo University.

Tange's private practice began in 1949 with his successful submission to the open competition for the Hiroshima Peace Center located in the city of his high school experience. This project ultimately became his first executed permanent building (1950). Previously, Tange had designed a pavilion of local products for the Kobe Industry and Trade Fair, but it was torn down at the end of the exposition. The Hiroshima Peace Center was one of the first postwar buildings in Japan to develop fully the characteristics of the international style, with an exposed concrete structure, and architectural elements that were in-

dividually articulated. The influence of Le Corbusier was clearly evident.

In 1951, Tange and Maekawa attended the eighth CIAM (Congres Internationaux d'Architecture Moderne) conference. "The Heart of the City" was the theme of the conference, and Tange was requested to present his award-winning design for the Hiroshima plan reconstruction. After meeting with Le Corbusier and visiting the construction site of Unite d'Habitation in Marseilles, Tange was convinced of the viability of his plan for Hiroshima.

Because of the reorganization of local governments after World War II, a large number of commissions for municipal and prefectual headquarters became available. Tange's success with the Hiroshima Peace Center provided him with a number of these commissions, and allowed him to develop further his use of the exposed concrete structural frame, which culminated in the construction of the Kurashiki City Hall, Okayama Prefecture (1958–1960) (Fig. 1).

By 1957, Tange and his associates had adopted the firm name Kenzo Tange and URTEC (derived from the term urbanist architect). It is most probable that this team approach was developed on the model of Walter Gropius and TAC (The Architects Collaborative).

The international design community was focused on Japan and the Tokyo World Design Conference scheduled for 1960. As the program chairman for the conference, Tange was inspired to work on a proposal for a large-scale urban design scheme. During his visiting professorship at the Massachusetts Institute of Technology in 1959, Tange worked for four months with a fifth-year design studio on an urban design scheme that would accommodate housing for 25,000 people over the Boston Bay. This experience helped to develop and clarify Tange's ideas on a plan for Tokyo.

A Plan for Tokyo, 1960: Toward a Structural Reorganization was published and presented by Tange at the Tokyo World Design Conference. The plan proposed a linear organized matrix for Tokyo Bay, which was to be an extension of the uncontrolled expansion of the city proper. This urban matrix was an adaptation of Tange's architectural notions of structural order, expression, and urban "communication space." This approach to large-scale urban de-

Figure 1. Kurashiki City Hall, Kurashiki, Japan, 1958. Courtesy of Clark Lundell.

sign was later applied to the award-winning proposal Tange submitted for the reconstruction of the city of Skopje in Yugoslavia (1965).

The Tokyo plan led Tange to begin an architectural exploration of the plastic nature of suspended structural form in his design for Saint Mary's Cathedral, Tokyo (1961–1964). This exploration demonstrated a significant break with his Corbusian past, and culminated in his design for the Olympic Sports Hall, Tokyo (1964). In 1966, the first megastructural complex combining Tange's notions of structural expression and the metabolists' notions of growth systems was constructed. Tange's design for the Yamanashi Press and Broadcasting Center, built in Kofu, Japan, allowed Tange to give metabolic life to Arata Isozaki's (URTEC) seminal studies for City in the Air (1962).

Tange continued to develop the ideas brought together in the Yamanashi Press and Broadcasting Center. The Kuwait Embassy and Chancery Building in Tokyo (1970) and the University of Oran proposal in Algeria (1972) each demonstrate further development of a metabolic architecture that suggests incompleteness, flexibility, and the potential for change and growth.

The international oil crisis and popular skepticism, in the mid-1970s, of large-scale urban projects based on megastructures reduced the number of projects of this type in Japan. Most of Tange's practice shifted to the developing, oil-rich Arab countries where he continued to apply his structuralist–metabolistic ideas to projects such as the Moroccan Capital and International Congress Hall (1978).

Tange's smaller, individual projects reflect his return to the aesthetics of the late modern movement, as can be seen in the Minneapolis Society of Fine Arts Building, Minnesota (1974), the Hanae Moi Building in Tokyo (1978), and the Akasaka Prince Hotel, Tokyo (1982). Tange's interest in old Japanese traditions, in which many of his aesthetic principles have their roots, has been demonstrated by his collaboration with Naburo Kawazoe on the following publications: *Katsura: Tradition and Creation in Japanese Architecture* (1960), foreword by Walter Gropius, and *Ise: Prototype of Japanese Architecture* (1965).

In a discussion of postmodernism in 1983, Tange suggested that if young architects are not allowed to lapse into flights of fancy without being labeled for their divergence, then architecture as expression cannot progress. If the expression of reality is considered modernism, then the architectural expression of a shift from an agrarian to an industrial to an information-based society must also be a type of modernism.

BIBLIOGRAPHY

General References

R. Boyd, *Kenzo Tange,* Braziller, New York, 1962.

B. Bognar, *Contemporary Japanese Architecture,* Van Nostrand Reinhold Co., Inc., New York, 1985.

M. F. Ross, *Beyond Metabolism,* Architectural Record Books, Mc-Graw-Hill Inc., New York, 1978.

K. Tange and N. Kawazoe, *Katsura: Tradition and Creation in Japanese Architecture,* Yale University Press, New Haven, 1960.

K. Tange and N. Kawazoe, *Ise: Prototype of Japanese Architecture,* M.I.T. Press, Cambridge Mass, 1965.

CLARK LUNDELL, AIA
Auburn University
Auburn, Alabama

TAPES, GLAZING.   See SEALANTS

TELEVISION AND RADIO STUDIOS

Television and radio studios are the architectural designations for all facilities related to program production in the television and radio industries. The television medium is concerned with communication by picture and sound transmission by means of radio and cable. Radio is communication over a distance by converting sounds or signals into electromagnetic waves and transmitting these directly through space without connecting wires (1). Radio programming is produced for sound broadcasting. Television programming is intended for broadcasting, cable transmission, and recording.

Both radio and television were initiated in laboratory environments and later evolved into their industrial settings. Radio is the older medium. Sound broadcasts were initiated in 1907 on an experimental basis. By 1910, several radio stations were broadcasting experimentally. In 1920, just one station was licensed to render a regular broadcast service. In 1922, more than 500 broadcasting stations went on the air (2). The production and transmission facilities of these earlier stations were usually located together at a desirable transmission site. The production facilities and the radio transmitter were housed in a common space, frequently a shack on the roof of a tall building, adjacent to the radio antenna and support tower. Television broadcasting originated in the mid-1920s on an experimental basis. Radio transmissions of moving "shadow graphs" were demonstrated in 1925. The first pictures with tones of gray were broadcast in 1926. By the late 1920s, several experimental television broadcast licenses for regularly scheduled transmissions had been issued. Television broadcasting continued on an experimental basis until after World War II (the mid-1940s), when several commercial licenses were issued (3). As with radio, the earlier stations located their production and transmission facilities together.

RADIO STUDIOS

The radio industry currently transmits programs on two broadcast bands. The lower-frequency band is used for amplitude modulated (AM) broadcasts, and the higher-frequency band is used for frequency modulated (FM) broadcasts. The AM technology is the older of the two and initiated the industry. FM broadcasting, introduced commercially in 1940 (4), provides higher-fidelity sound reproduction, as well as a more noise-free transmission. Both AM and FM radio stations require program-originating studio facilities and a transmitting plant containing the transmitter and antenna system. Studio and transmitter facilities may be at a common location or in different buildings separated by some distance and interconnected by telephone lines or highly directional microwave radio (Fig. 1). The transmitter and antenna tower, however, must be at the same location in close proximity to each other. The location of both studio and antenna sites is subject to approval by the Federal Communications Commission (FCC). Consideration is given to existing stations in the area and potential signal interference.

SITE CONSIDERATIONS

It is more economical to combine studio and transmitter equipment in one building. This minimizes the investment for both land and equipment, lower costs for heating

and air conditioning, and may reduce the operating staff. The combined site must meet the requirements for a good antenna location, providing adequate room for a tower and achieving the desired signal coverage. The studio preference is for convenient access to station personnel, guests, and clients. Separate sites are sometimes advisable to accommodate conflicting requirements. A high altitude and good grounding are desirable for antenna location, whereas a good studio site is one located close to a city and easily accessible. Zoning regulations may prohibit erecting towers on otherwise ideal combined site locations. Radio studios are frequently located near centers of business activity, on view to the community, with the station transmitting plant on a more remote tall building or mountain peak.

The environmental impact of the station antennas' electromagnetic radiation should be assessed when evaluating sites.

Acoustic requirements need to be taken into account when sites are being selected for radio studios. Noise and

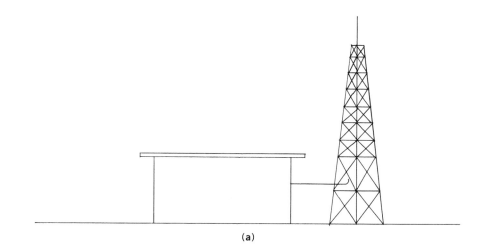

(a)

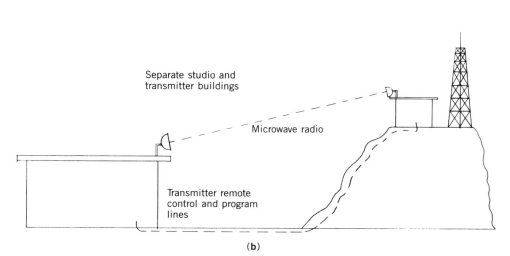

Separate studio and transmitter buildings

Microwave radio

Transmitter remote control and program lines

(b)

Figure 1. (a) Common studio and transmitter building. (b) Remote-controlled transmitter.

vibration from nearby airports, overhead flight paths, street and highway motor traffic, underground and surface rail traffic, local industry, and building mechanical systems must be evaluated. The studio construction should provide adequate protection against these noises either by provision of effective external sound insulation or by the use of other structures, such as screens. Studios should be acoustically separated, as far as possible, from buildings, plants, shops, or malls capable of generating noise or vibration (5).

PLANT LAYOUT

The appropriate configuration for a radio studio is determined by its program requirements. Program elements have varied little since the early days of radio. News, music, drama, interviews, discussions, and light entertainment, both live and recorded, have been the mainstays of radio programming. A variety of formats, such as those with disk jockeys, choral groups, telephone call-in discussions, and studio audiences, have been used successfully. The presentation of these materials changes continuously, as does the technology. Current radio operations, both AM and FM, broadcast more recorded than live material. Whereas the phonograph record was once the only source of recorded programs, today there are, additionally, reel, cassette, and cartridge tapes and compact disks, all in a variety of analogue and digital recordings.

STUDIO AND CONTROL ROOM

In the past, many radio studios were built to accommodate large studio audiences. That requirement no longer exists, studio audiences not being a popular current format. Similarly, most radio studios need not accommodate large orchestral or choral groups. These performances are generally prerecorded, or if live, are broadcast from a concert hall as a remote feed to the radio studio. Generally, the material used for AM and FM radio broadcasting is in the form of live speech for news and commentary or prerecordings. However, a number of broadcasts exist for which the preferred origin is a broadcast studio. A control room, which functions to control, mix, and monitor the program sound sources, is always associated with the studio. The distinction between the control room and the studio is no longer as clear as it once was. It is now common practice to design and utilize the control room as a studio and to exercise some form of program control from the studio. The performer and the control operator are frequently one and the same.

STUDIO-RELATED SPACES

Announce booths, once a standard accessory to the broadcast studio, are no longer so considered. Announcements are generally made from the studio or control room. Announce booths are still used for special applications and, although not mandatory, may be useful.

Sound locks are necessary in circumstances where there is the possibility of a door being open between an active recording microphone and a loudspeaker playing back the same recording. This feedback situation can initiate a sound oscillation that howls. The sound lock is simply an entry arrangement that ensures a closed door between the recording microphone and a monitoring loudspeaker.

The prominent role of news in radio may require the location of a news facility adjacent to the studio. The facility can be as simple as a news wire service or as complex as a news room with elaborate communications capabilities. In either case, the noise of the news operation cannot be allowed to intrude into the program microphones, except by intent.

Since the advent of audio tape recording in the late 1940s, tape editing facilities have become a necessary adjunct to the radio studio. These facilities can be accommodated in spaces as small as a workbench, but in large operations may require small sound-isolated rooms.

Recorded programs are usually stored on a daily basis in the control room. A radio station's collection of recorded programs is one of its valuable assets. The provision of long-term storage and retrieval facilities is served by a library. At small stations, the library need not be more than adequate space and shelving in an unoccupied space. Larger stations may require separate climate-controlled library rooms to safely store their recorded materials. The library need not be adjacent to studio spaces, but should have easy access.

Studios that are often used for live musical performances make good use of a multipurpose space. It can serve as a rehearsal room, listening room, or quality-monitoring room. The room acoustics should be similar to those of a music studio. The location of the space in relation to the studio is not critical.

Radio studios that frequently program live performers and guests should consider the provision of a comfortable, quiet, and attractive waiting room or "green room." The space serves to provide calm and seclusion in the hectic radio environment. It is best located within easy access of the studio area.

An on-air or master control room is used to route incoming and outgoing signals for the radio station. At a small station, this function may be performed by a studio control room that is equipped to serve the dual purpose. Larger stations have a dedicated control room, not associated with program origination, assigned that role.

STUDIO PLANT SIZE

The size of the radio studio plant is a function of the size of the market that the station serves. Large stations are usually located in highly populated market areas. Size is also dependent on whether the station is a dual AM–FM operation with independent programming and on the program formats it favors. The station's program format can change relatively frequently. Ideally, the plant should be designed to cope with a variety of formats. A combined AM–FM plant with separate AM and FM programming

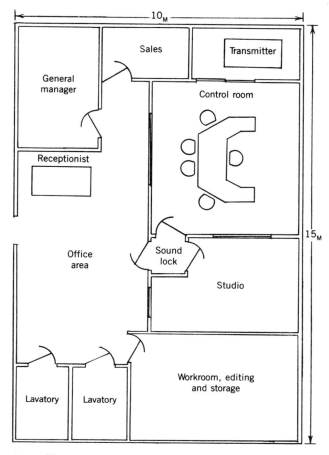

Figure 2. A 10 × 15-m radio station floor plan.

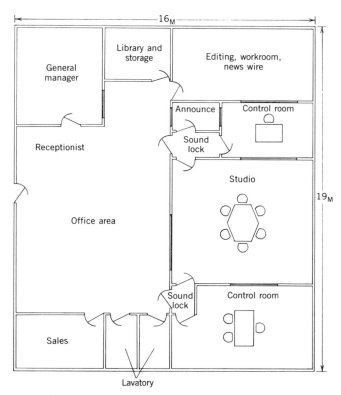

Figure 3. A 16 × 19-m radio station floor plan.

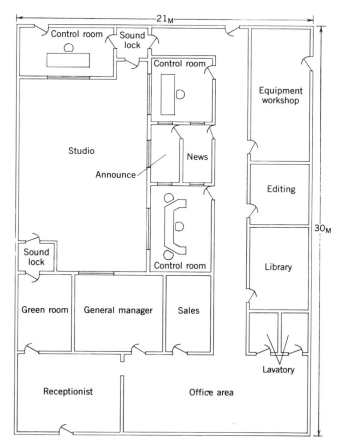

Figure 4. A 21 × 30-m radio station floor plan.

will always have greater studio space requirements than an individual AM or FM station in the same market with a similar program format.

Figures 2 through 5 present a set of floor plans suitable for four different-sized stations.

PROGRAM PRODUCTION AREA CONSTRUCTION CONSIDERATIONS

Construction practices must take into account local conditions and code requirements. Electrical and fire codes are especially significant because of the nature of the equipment contained in the radio studio. Access for the handicapped is another requirement that must be accommodated in a new facility. Suitable incoming electrical power and telephone services should be available to meet the needs of the operation.

NOISE AND ACOUSTICS

Program sound is the output product of a radio studio. The quality of the sound is of prime importance to studio operation. The sound environment of a radio studio is therefore of utmost concern in construction design. The site and its layout should be selected to minimize the effect of traf-

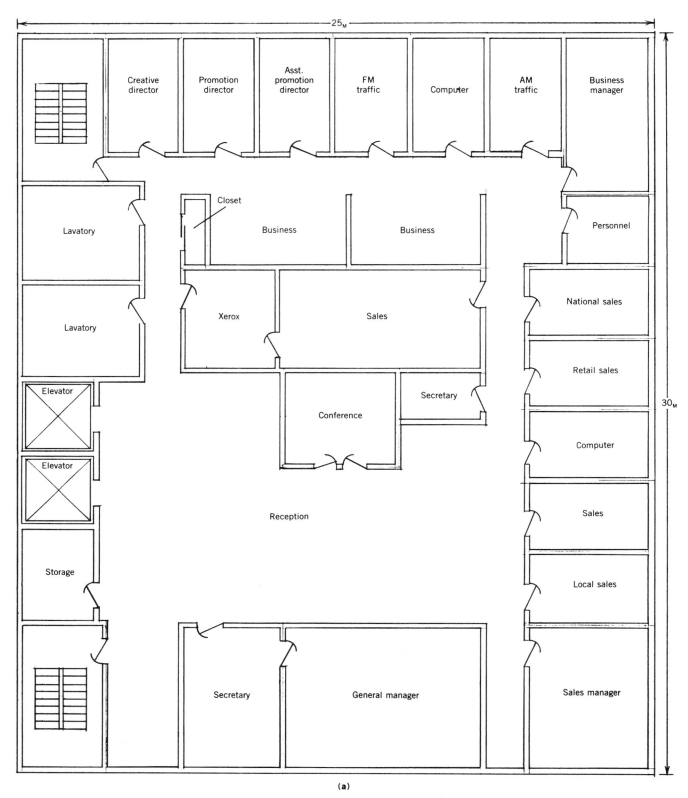

Figure 5. Large AM–FM radio station floor plan. (a) First floor. (b) Second floor. (c) Third floor.

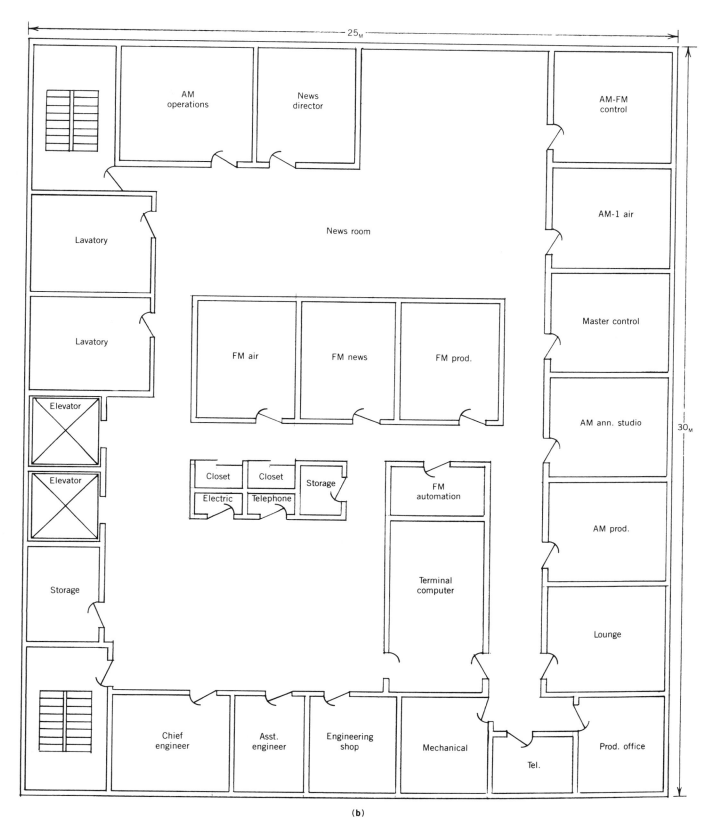

Figure 5. (*Continued*)

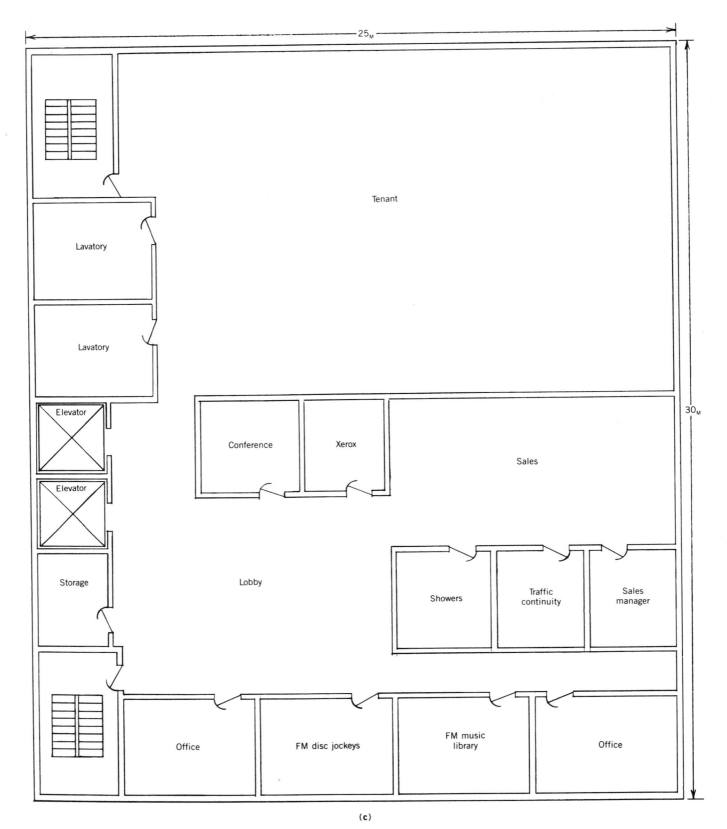

(c)

Figure 5. (*Continued*)

fic and aircraft noise and other noise-producing areas on the studio. Sound leakage into and out of the studio should also be avoided.

In the design of a multistudio plant, studios should be separated as far as possible from each other by less sensitive areas or corridors. If the design precludes that, provision should be made for relatively massive walls to provide sound-level reduction. Sound-reducing doors and windows should be utilized for all of the necessary wall openings. It may also be necessary to consider additional space for the studio to allow for floating its floor against structure-borne noise and vibrations. Additionally, the floating floor studio should be separated from its neighboring spaces by a structural wall joining the main solid shell of the building and an independent inner wall integral with the floated floor. Space will also be required for a false ceiling isolated from the building shell and having room for sound absorbers and services. Details of sound-isolating construction, such as gasketing for sound-control doors, are described elsewhere in this Encyclopedia.

The ventilation system serving all technical areas must be quiet, necessitating large section ducts and attenuators. Ideally, the refrigeration equipment, the heating system boilers, and other potentially noisy building operations should be spatially separated from the studio area.

The limits for noise that can be tolerated in a radio studio can be determined by reference to the noise criteria curves shown in Figure 6. These curves show a series of noise levels, each with a noise criteria level (NC) related to it. The curves take into account the frequency response of the ear to noise in the audible octave bands from 40 to 1120 Hz. The ear's sensitivity to noise increases with frequency. The acceptable level for a radio studio is the NC20 curve, which is barely audible.

SPEECH STUDIOS

Most current program origination and control operations are being carried out in small rooms. Economics dictates that these rooms not be large, but if they are made too small, speech quality will be impaired by poor room acoustics. It is possible, with proper design, to keep studio dimensions small without undue performance degradation. The volume dimensions of the room are critical. The volume should not be less than about 60 m³, nor does it need to be above 80 m³ for acceptable quality, although the European Organisation Internationale de Radiodiffusion et Television (OIRT) recommends 120 m³. Good sound diffusion is a requirement for any acoustically sensitive area. It can be achieved in the speech studio by the proper arrangement of sound absorbers on the room surfaces. Sound impairment caused by the repeated reflection of sound from two facing surfaces, or flutter echo, can be eliminated by adding a few patches of sound-absorbing material to the offending walls. Some acousticians recommend slanting the studio walls to avoid parallel surfaces. This does effectively reduce flutter echo, but does not remove colorations. The subjective significance of the slanted wall is difficult to assess, and the nonrectangular construction is expensive and difficult to deal with.

The recommended reverberation time for a speech studio is 0.3–0.4 s, depending on its volume. The lower figure is for very small studios, and the higher figure for a large speech studio of about 150 m³ (5).

MUSIC STUDIOS

Few radio studios are being used to broadcast live musical performances. Recorded music performances are the more popular current format. The requirements for broadcasting live music vary with the type of music. Classical orchestral music, chamber music, and popular music all have differing acoustical needs. Popular music covers such a wide variety of types that it is impossible to generalize its exact radio studio requirements. Popular music includes performances associated with electroacoustic devices, vocalists, large and small groups, and heavy rhythm as well as with older, more traditional music forms. All new music studios have to be suitable for stereophonic broadcast.

The orchestral studio should be comparable in size to a medium-sized concert hall. A volume of 10,000 m³ is sufficient, unless a large studio audience is to be accommodated without detriment to the acoustics. The reverberation time should be about the same as that of a concert hall of similar size, being longer for a large studio than for a smaller one. The recommended reverberation time for radio music studios ranges from 0.8 s for a 1,000-m³ studio volume to 2.0 s for a 10,000-m³ studio volume (5). Similarly, the shape of the studio can be guided by good concert hall practice. The height of the studio should be greater

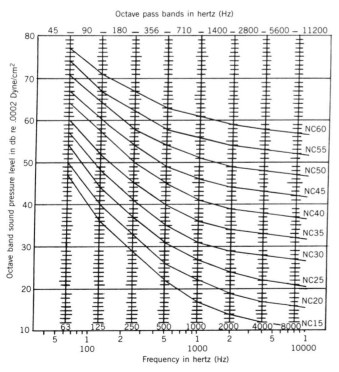

Figure 6. Announce booth acoustics frequency level band in hertz (Hz).

than half the width, and the length should be greater than the width. It is desirable to be able to seat the orchestra within half of the studio to permit the pickup to have the right perspective and balance.

Studios designed for chamber music performances, solos, or small vocal groups have the same general requirements as the orchestral studios. The volume, however, should be much smaller to preserve the intimacy appropriate to the setting of the music as well as for the smaller distances required for microphone coverage. The liveness of the sound should be similar to that of an orchestral studio, and the reverberation time should be lower, in approximately the same ratio as the linear dimensions.

Popular music performances cover such a wide variety that it is impossible to generalize the exact requirements for a studio. Fashions in desired performance have changed cyclically in the past, with alternating requests for live and dead sounds. Artificial reverberation is easily and effectively implemented with current digital electronic equipment. There is less need for highly reverberant studios. Some current designs for popular music performances feature a live end, or reverberant portion, and a dead end, or nonreverberant portion.

ANNOUNCE BOOTHS

Announce booth acoustics must provide the same sound quality as other areas. A reverberation time of less than 0.25 s is a good compromise. It should be independent of frequency over the range of 200–8000 Hz, with decreasing reverberation below 200 Hz. The ambient noise level should not exceed NC20 (Fig. 6).

COMBINATION STUDIO AND CONTROL

A popular current radio format utilizes the combination of performance and control functions by one person. This style requires that an area operate as both control room and studio. The spaces that have been developed to fulfill the requirement are small, on the order of 200–400 m³ in volume. Low reverberation times are desirable for these combination rooms because of the inherent activity-generated noise that accompanies such operations. Interviews are often conducted in this environment, and although a low reverberation time is preferred, the space should not be acoustically dead.

PREFABRICATED CONTROL ROOMS AND STUDIOS

Several manufacturers currently offer prefabricated, acoustically designed rooms intended for on-site installation and use as radio control rooms and studios. The rooms are usually small and can be used in existing spaces. They can be designed to a variety of requirements, but are more limited in performance than structural space. Special situations arise that make consideration of such a facility worthwhile.

LIGHTING

The lighting requirements for radio studios are not difficult. Two types of lighting should be considered: general and work space illumination. General illumination should be diffused, uniformly distributed illumination, similar to office lighting (6). Work lighting should be directional illumination of about 320 lx, provided for operators' consoles, audio consoles, and technical equipment. Emergency lighting should be provided for operation from emergency power in the event of failure of the regular lighting circuits.

ELECTROMAGNETIC FIELDS

Intense electromagnetic fields can interfere with the operation of a radio studio. Strong magnetic and electric fields affect the performance of microphones, amplifiers, and recording devices. Shielding from magnetic fields is accomplished by enclosing the space affected with a magnetically permeable material, such as iron-based mu-metal. Shielding from high-frequency electric fields is achieved by enclosure of the space with electrically conductive material, such as copper screen or solid aluminum. The high cost of materials and construction for effectively shielding large studio spaces makes the concept of shielding the studio impractical. It is more desirable to remove or shield the source of interference or the specific items of equipment affected by the interference.

Physical avoidance is most effective. Magnetic fields exceeding 0.5 gauss should be avoided because of the difficulty of providing effective shielding from strong magnetic fields. Conductive metallic enclosures on studio equipment provide shielding from most electric field interference when properly grounded.

AIR CONDITIONING

Air conditioning in radio studios is required to remove heat dissipated by equipment, to supply heat when required, and to regulate the moisture content. An appropriate environment must be maintained for proper equipment operation and personnel comfort. The operating area temperatures should be maintained at approximately 22°C. In nonoperating areas, the temperature can be slightly higher, at 26°C. The relative humidity should not exceed 60% in any operating area, nor should it be less than 40% in any magnetic tape handling area. Air velocities should be kept low for both noise reduction and personnel comfort. The velocity at air supply vents should be less than 100 m/min and less than 10 m/min at personnel positions.

The nature of radio operations requires that their air-conditioning systems be independent and available at all hours during all seasons. Radio operating area air requirements do not always coincide with normal office needs. An economy can be effected during the heating season by recirculating the excess heat generated by the electronic equipment, particularly the transmitter, to heat the plant.

PRIMARY POWER

The primary power for the technical facilities should be provided on a distribution panel that is independent of the rest of the plant power distribution. It is desirable to provide regulation and line conditioning for the technical facility's primary power. An emergency power source should be considered. Uninterruptible emergency power can be provided by battery-driven alternators. The running time of these emergency generators is limited by the battery discharge time. Large loads cannot be sustained for long periods. Diesel-driven generators are an effective alternative emergency power source because of the relative safety of diesel fuel storage and their long running-time capability.

The primary power distribution panel should include a ground terminal that is independent of the electrical neutral. Although the electrical neutral is grounded for safety, it usually has a small voltage difference with respect to an independent ground because of the unbalanced phase currents that flow through the neutral.

The load requirements for primary power are dependent on the facilities encompassed. Transmitters require power ranging from a few kilowatts to several megawatts. Typical studio components require less than 10 kW of primary power supply.

FIRE PROTECTION

Until recently, the preferred fire deterrents in areas containing radio electronic equipment were chemical. Manually operated carbon dioxide fire extinguishers or automatic halon systems were deemed to cause less equipment damage than water. These deterrents, however, have drawbacks. Manually operated extinguishers require that personnel assume some risk in handling the equipment during a fire and are effective only on small fires. The halon systems are expensive, operate only once on the fire, and pose some inhalation risk. Water is currently the best choice of deterrent for equipment fires and is preferred by fire insurance companies. Although there is the potential for electrical shock, the equipment generally shuts itself down when this possibility occurs. A time-delayed automatic sprinkler system provides the best deterrent to significant harm to the personnel and plant in the event of a fire and minimizes the risk of false alarms. Water damage to electronic equipment can be dealt with more readily than fire or chemical damage.

TELEVISION STUDIOS

The television industry (broadcast, cable, and recording) can be categorized to a greater extent than radio into network and local operations. Although radio networks do exist, the preponderance of radio operations are local in reach. The large network plants include specialized facilities dedicated to network operations such as network transmission. Network transmission facilities do not originate programs and are not considered in detail because of their uniqueness as compared to program source facilities.

Cable television differs from broadcast television in the technology utilized to transmit programs to its audience. Broadcast television uses radio transmission to reach its audience, whereas cable television is wired into its subscribers' homes. Both require program-originating facilities and a transmission facility. The cable transmission facility, referred to as the "head end" of its distribution system, is the cable television equivalent of the transmitter and antenna facilities of radio and broadcast television. As with radio, studio and transmission facilities may be at a common location or separated and interconnected by cable or directional microwave radio. Considerations for the location of broadcast television studio and antenna sites are similar to those for radio, requiring FCC approval and proof of noninterference with existing stations. Cable television studio and head end locations do not require FCC approval if no interconnecting microwave is used.

Television recording studios differ from those of both broadcast and cable when they have no transmission facilities. The programs that are produced at these studios end up on a recording medium such as videotape and are physically transported to their next destination. Some recording studios now utilize satellites for distributing signals to their destination and for incoming signals from external sources. These studios utilize a master or transmission control and are similar in operating and design requirements to a local television broadcast station, including FCC approval for transmitting antenna locations.

SITE CONSIDERATIONS

Site considerations for broadcast television are similar to those given for radio. Cable television head end sites do not have the same preferences for altitude or grounding unless they utilize microwave interconnections that require height. They are generally best located centrally or as close to their market area as possible. The site ambient noise requirements for television studios are the same as those for radio studios since live sound is an integral part of both radio and television programming.

PLANT LAYOUT

The television networks, because of the large market that they serve, originate more programs from their own plants than either broadcast stations or cable systems. The latter transmit mostly prerecorded programs, network programs, and live news or events of local interest. Network-originated programming, in addition to live news and events of national interest, includes dramas, soap operas, situation comedies, and other entertainment performed in the presence of live audiences. Network plants are designed to accommodate a more diverse range of programs and incorporate greater capabilities than nonnetwork plants. The support facilities for television are greater in scope and more complex than those required for radio. The visual aspect of the medium requires additional technological and theatrical facilities. The visual staging required for television necessitates the use of stage design, scenery, specialized lighting, makeup, wardrobe, props, dressing rooms, graphics, and larger organizations and spaces to contain them. The electronics equipment is similarly more complex and needs larger spaces. Figures 7 and 8 illustrate variations in layout for medium-sized network and station facilities.

STUDIO AND CONTROL ROOM

A wide variety of program formats are originated in television studios. The smallest studios are required for news or talk shows involving one or two performers. Unlike in radio, even these small shows do not usually combine the control room and the studio on a common stage. The lighting requirements for a television studio are different from those for a television control room. The control room requires a low level of ambient lighting, with no lights reflecting from the faces of the television monitors and moderate work light levels directed at work spaces. The television studio requires a flexible arrangement suitable to staging a variety of events with appropriate lighting for television cameras. Although the control room can be

brought out to the news room area, it is more common to utilize a control room stage set and a separate control room for news programs whose performers are to appear in a control room setting. The larger studios, those used for large musical performances, audience participation programs, and dramatic programs, all utilize separate control rooms.

Earlier control rooms were designed with viewing windows to permit the director to view the studio. It was soon discovered that not only was the window generally blocked from view by a curtain or large scenery flat, but that it was also more desirable for the director to concentrate on the television images on monitor screens. Control room windows are now used only in special-purpose facilities, for the control room design is more functional without them. When they are used, consideration must be given to their sight lines as well as to those of the production monitors. The windows should be angled in order to avoid annoying reflections toward control room operating personnel. They should provide the required sound isolation and have provisions for minimizing glare from studio lighting. This last requirement can be accomplished by

FACILITIES LEGEND			
Space	Area sq. meters	Space	Area sq. meters
Rehearsal halls	716	Offices	358
Video control	81	Video equip. center	76
Green rooms	112	Maintenance storage	54
Wardrobe rooms	102	Eng. maintenance	60
Lighting	47	Elec. & telco	22
Announce	10	Dimmer rooms	124
Audio	39	Storage	54
Control	251	Video screening rooms	124
Star dressing rooms	372	Studios	1860
Dressing rooms	332	Master control	200
Make-up room w/7 make-up tables	95	Total	5158
Video tape & telecine	69		

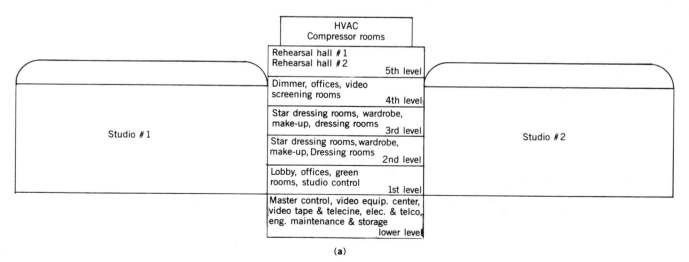

(a)

Figure 7. (a) Television production facility. (b) Lower level. (c) First level. (d) Second and third levels. (e) Fourth and fifth levels.

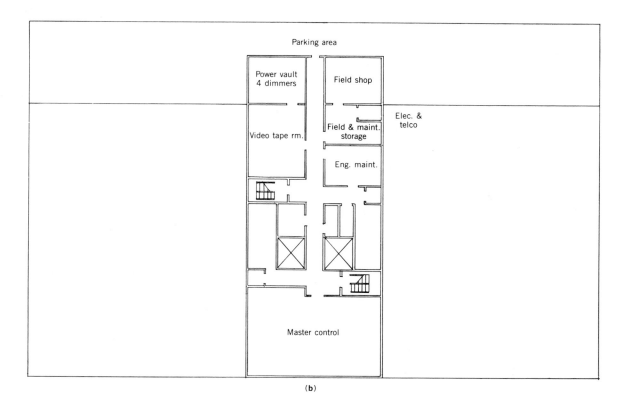

(b)

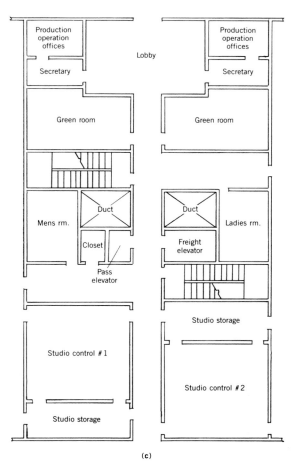

(c)

Figure 7. (*Continued*)

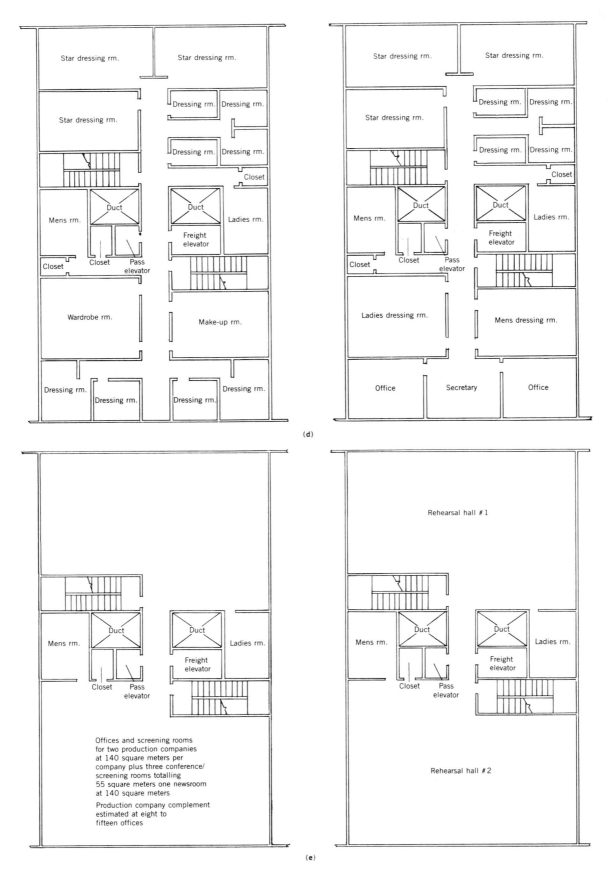

Figure 7. (*Continued*)

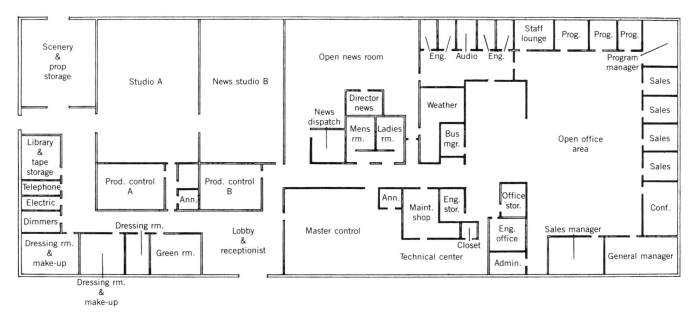

Figure 8. Television station.

the use of neutral density glass or window shades having photometric light transmission of approximately 15%.

It is desirable to allow the program personnel easy access to the studio from the control room. Control rooms are therefore preferably located on the same floor level and adjacent to their related studios.

The functional layout of television studio control rooms is based on arranging the operating functions in a group around the program director, the key person. Although layouts vary with the operating style of the facility, the control room occupants are more consistent. There are always a video switcher and an audio control operator in the control room. Frequently, there is space for an assistant director, a lighting director, a video operator, a character generator operator, and a producer in the grouping around the director and the monitors. The spaces may be part of the same control room or contiguous to it with window separation. An announce booth and announcer may be associated with the control room. Visual signaling between the director, video switcher operator, audio control operator, and announcer should be possible.

STUDIO-RELATED SPACES

The support spaces required for television studios are larger than the studio spaces, the ratio depending on the program formats for which the studio is intended. All studios require control room, tape recording, editing, viewing and screening, graphics, library, scenery, prop, and some form of performance personnel support spaces. News and information programs have the least demanding support requirements; dramatic and musical variety programs have more elaborate needs.

In considering scenery spaces, the need for on-site scenery construction should be considered. If scenery construction is necessary, space must be allocated for carpentry and scenery shops and their associated storage requirements. Minimally, scenery and prop storage spaces should be provided for any television studio. These spaces should have access to truck loading areas and require modest environmental control. They can have open walls and ceilings with simple paint finishes and sealed floors.

Performance personnel support spaces include star dressing rooms, cast dressing rooms, wardrobe, makeup, and offstage holding areas called green rooms. News and information programs have modest requirements for these spaces. Drama programs and musical variety shows employing large production companies need larger spaces.

A rehearsal hall is a necessary adjunct to any television studio that is used for drama programs. The space needed for that use is fairly large and should be considered multipurpose, to be utilized as a meeting or conference room when available.

News plays a significant role in television programming. A newsroom is part of many television plants, with capabilities ranging from local to national and international news gathering. The traditional television news room is an open area with enough desk space to house the news staff. A large communications and dispatch desk is also accommodated in the news room area. Some closed office space for the news executive personnel is needed, but in general, open communication is desirable. Local weather forecasting is an important feature of many local news programs. Weather forecasting facilities space is a useful adjunct to the television news room.

Announce booths, as in radio, are useful for narration, but not necessary for every television studio. They are best located in the studio control room, with a line of sight to the director and audio operator.

Sound locks should be utilized at studio entrances where the possibility of program sound feeding back into the studio exists.

Graphics are a significant source of program material.

Graphics production for television has become increasingly electronic and integrated into programs. The graphics spaces should be accessible to the control room space, but need not be adjacent to it or large in relative size.

Editing, or postproduction, is an important function in television programming. Most television programs are not played on the air live, as they occur. Editing suites must be provided for use by production personnel, news gatherers, and technical personnel. Production personnel usually require limited editing capability and can operate in small, limited-use, or off-line suites. The news operation requires off-line editing support, as well as larger, more complex, on-line suites for its program production. The larger, on-line suites are required for final program assembly by technically competent operators in association with programming decision makers. Appropriate design and adequate provision of postproduction capability are essential to any self-contained television operation.

In order to display the end product of a television production to its best advantage, provision should be made for viewing rooms designed for that purpose. In a large plant, enough use can be made of these rooms to permit them to be designed for that purpose only. In smaller plants, the viewing room can easily be designed to double as a conference room.

Library storage of recorded material is required at every television facility. At larger plants, the storage may be divided into archival and frequent-use areas. In smaller plants, long- and short-term library storage may be shared with incoming film and tape storage because the desired environmental conditions are identical.

The size and complexity of videotape and film projection equipment, coupled with the noise generated by the machinery, require that spaces apart from the studio and control room be allocated to them. At large plants, this equipment may be controlled or have control assigned to a studio control room by an intermediate control room, which may be designated as program control. The grouping of film projection equipment in an area called the telecine, and of videotape record/playback equipment in a common videotape area, is done at large plants. Smaller facilities may combine the telecine and videotape functions in a single area without an intermediate program control.

Control of incoming and outgoing signals for a television plant is through a master or transmission control room. The main function of this control room is to route incoming signals through the plant and assign the plant outputs to their proper destinations. An announce booth may be associated with this control room to permit special announcements to be added to the signals. At the larger plants, no programs are originated from this control room. Smaller plants may utilize their master control room to originate simple news or information programs.

STUDIO PLANT SIZE

Television plant size is related to the size of the market served and to the desired program format. Small plants are usually found in small market areas, and large plants in large market areas. The economics of the potential market limits the capital investment in plant facilities. Small plants are frequently found in large markets if their formats are such that little space must be allocated to live programming, or if their potential market share is small. A small plant usually has only one studio capable of program production. Most television stations have at least two studios available for program production, permitting more locally produced material.

Studio size is determined by the type of production it is to serve. Small studios of about 125 m² are best suited to news and information programs. A good-sized multipurpose studio capable of some dramatic and musical production would be about 600 m². Larger studios of approximately 1200 m² are less limited in application and may be used to produce dramas requiring large fixed sets (such as for soap operas), live audience participation programs, or large variety shows. The height requirement for these studios varies with the size. In the smallest studios, the minimum desirable height to the bottom of the overhead stage lighting fixtures is 4 m. In the larger studios, minimum heights of 7 or 8 m are desirable in order to permit the use of high backdrops. Higher studio heights permit wider camera angles with more panoramic perspectives.

PROGRAM PRODUCTION AREA CONSTRUCTION CONSIDERATIONS

As with any new construction, local conditions and code requirements as well as federal regulations concerning access for the handicapped must be considered. Electrical power and telephone service demands for a television plant are high. Their adequate availability should be arranged. Air-conditioning needs are also unusual and should be recognized in early planning. The need for studio space to be clear of support columns is another unusual design requirement. A large open studio space may require special support for its overhead structure, which may contain a heavy lighting grid and large air ducts.

NOISE AND ACOUSTICS

The same general constraints that are placed on noise in the radio studio plant apply to the television studio. The acoustic requirements, however, differ. Television studios must be considerably less reverberant than radio studios of comparable size. The dominant reason for the lower reverberation is the background noise created in television production by the movement of cameras, personnel, and scenery. These noises would be exaggerated by a reverberant studio. Another reason is that on many television programs the microphones are placed farther away from the performers, out of the picture. The studio, in those cases, requires low reverberation in order to provide the appropriate ratio of direct to reverberant sound to accompany the picture. A reverberant studio would not permit the illusion of intimacy necessary to many television programs. The recommended reverberation time for television studios as related to volume ranges from a minimum of 0.25 s for a 100-m³ studio volume to 0.5 s for a

10,000-m^3 studio volume. It is difficult to make very large studios with acceptable acoustics because their reverberation times tend to be longer than desirable (5).

The limits for noise that can be tolerated in a television studio are determined by the noise criteria curves shown in Fig. 6. The acceptable level for a television studio is greater than that for a radio or recording studio because the necessary movement of equipment and personnel generates an ambient noise that must be allowed. The NC25 level, a relatively quiet noise level, is a good design criterion for television studios.

Conference rooms equipped with viewing facilities and screening or viewing rooms should have acoustics similar to those in a living room. These rooms are used to judge program sound critically under typical audience conditions. The reverberation time and noise level should be the same as in a quiet home.

Many of the conditions concerning radio studio construction, except for the noise criteria, are applicable to television studio design as well. Television announce booths follow criteria similar to those for radio announce booths described above.

LIGHTING

The lighting requirements for the television stage more closely resemble those for theatrical stage lighting than other technical areas of the television studio plant. They are therefore considered separately.

TELEVISION STUDIO STAGE

The television studio stage lighting system may be subdivided into three areas of concern: the overhead suspension for stage lighting, set enclosure or cyclorama lighting, and lighting equipment.

The overhead suspension system is the ceiling-mounted support for the stage lighting outlets and fixtures. The grid configuration of the structure allows lights to be hung throughout a matrix network, at roughly 1.5 × 1.5-m spacings. The simplest of these structures is a fixed pipe grid that is mounted to the ceiling at approximately 1.5-m intervals. The fixed grid is best utilized in small studios where stage settings are space limited. A fixed grid height of 5 m permits lighting fixtures to be suspended 4 m above the floor and also allows ladder access. A more complex form of the fixed grid is the catwalk. The catwalk permits overhead access to lighting fixtures that are mounted to it without interfering with activities on stage. Catwalks can be mounted higher than pipe grids, and when used do not require final focusing of the fixtures to take place from the floor either by ladder or pole. Catwalks can be used in combination with other forms of suspension that are movable. A movable suspension system has the advantage that it can be located higher than a fixed grid when desired. The simplest of the movable suspension systems is the counterweighted batten. Battens consist of lengths of pipe that run across the width of the studio. These pipes, or battens, move up and down on steel cables, over pulleys, counterbalanced by adjustable weights. The disadvantages of the counterweighted adjustable batten are the need to rebalance the weights when different fixtures are used, the added stress to the roof support system from the counterweights, and the floor space taken up by the counterweights.

The disadvantages of the counterweighted battens can be overcome by the use of electric-motor-driven winches to raise and lower the battens. The electric motor drive permits precise remote location of the battens manually or by computer. Loads on the battens within the capacity of the motors can be changed without readjustment. A variation on the electric-motor-driven batten is the electric-motor-driven modular grid. The modular grid is composed of several short battens joined together in a single module that can be raised and lowered by a single motor-driven winch. It has all of the advantages of the motor-driven batten with the additional feature of requiring only one motor and winch for a number of pipes.

Motor-driven suspension systems are frequently combined with catwalk grids that provide easy access to the fixtures. The overhead suspension system can be quite complex. It occupies the same space as overhead air-conditioning ducts and electrical cables and adds weight to the ceiling support. Design coordination is required.

The suspension system must provide mounting positions for the fixtures used to light the cyclorama in the studio. The cyclorama can be of hard or soft construction. A hard cyclorama is a smooth, plastered surface parallel to the studio wall that blends flush to the floor. It is limited in use to small areas in a television studio because of the acoustical problems it can create. A soft cyclorama is constructed of a seamless drapery material that is hung on rollers, which move along a track and allow it to be positioned anywhere around the perimeter of the studio. In large studios, two parallel tracks are sometimes utilized to permit greater background flexibility. Both hard and soft cycloramas may utilize lights at floor level to create special lighting effects. These cyclorama floor lights can be hidden from view if cyclorama pits are provided at the base of the cyclorama. These pits are dug into the studio floor and, in some cases, may extend around the studio perimeter. The light fixtures are mounted in the pits below floor level.

Lighting equipment can be classified into three categories: control, distribution, and fixtures. The control equipment consists of the operator's control console and the dimmers. Although it is possible to light a television stage without dimming capability, the technique is cumbersome and artistically limited. Dimming capability should be provided for every television studio. Dimmers are available in modules that can be rack mounted. They dissipate a good deal of heat, and may generate noise and electrical interference. They are best located away from the studio, in an area where these emissions do not cause any problems. They should not be too distant from the studio distribution that they serve in order to minimize the lengths of electrical cable required. In some designs, the dimmers are routed to the lighting outlets by a patchbay. This technique allows the outlets to be assigned to each dimmer as needed for a specific scene. The number of required dimmers can be kept down, and capital costs minimized. A more current and preferable design permanently assigns a dimmer to each lighting outlet. This technique minimizes the time and labor involved in resetting the dimmers for differing scenes and provides for greater artistic capability. In view of the trend toward decreasing component costs and increasing labor costs, the dimmer-per-outlet design is increasingly economical. The decreasing cost of microprocessor components has made computerized control of dimmers economical. Sophisticated lighting control consoles using microprocessor components are available at moderate cost. These consoles are relatively small and are best located in the studio control room, permitting close coordination between the lighting director and the rest of the production team. Some of the larger studio systems use two microprocessor control consoles. One is located in the control room for the lighting director to use to set up the lighting design for the program on a computer. The second one is larger and located away from the control room, closer to the dimmers, for operation by an electrician. It has manual control as well as control of the computer set up by the lighting director. The lighting director can work from either location.

The distribution equipment consists of connector strips and floor and wall outlets located throughout the studio. The connector strips are mounted on the suspension system. Wall outlets are mounted in conveniently located wall boxes, and floor outlets may be provided in cyclorama pits.

The fixtures consist of theatrical lighting fixtures, including scoops for base and fill lights, Fresnels for key and back lights, and cyclorama lights and lekolights for pattern projection. They are mounted on the pipes in the suspension grid or on stands on the floor or are set in the cyclorama pit.

The electrical load requirement for a television stage lighting system is determined by the light levels required for color television cameras in the stage production area. For the illumination required by most television production, 450 W of electrical power per square meter of usable stage area is adequate.

OTHER TECHNICAL AREAS

The other technical areas consist of two groups, one having operating requirements and the other not. The operating areas require two types of lighting: one for operational periods and one for general illumination. The nonoperational areas require only general illumination suited to their use. In all technical areas, light from outdoor sources is undesirable.

The task lights for operational areas such as those for studio control, transmission control, videotape, and telecine require localized lighting of 30–40 lx on the director's, editing, video switching and audio console, and other operating positions. Lighting fixtures should be designed and located to prevent stray light from striking monitor faces or control room windows. Conveniently located dimmer control of functionally grouped or individual light sources is needed. The general illumination for these areas should be well diffused and uniformly distributed at about 100 lx. Sources should be located so that reflections from windows, monitors, and clocks are avoided. Separate control of task lights and general illumination is required. To permit critical color viewing, a color temperature of 6500 K is desirable in all technical operating areas. Emergency lighting, powered by fully charged batteries, should be provided in all technical areas. Technical operating areas containing equipment racks should be provided with retractable reel lights to be used by maintenance personnel as trouble lights.

Critical viewing can take place in television viewing, film screening, and multipurpose conference rooms. Care must be given to the design of the lighting system in these rooms, just as in operating areas. Two types of illumination are required: one for viewing times and one for general illumination. During viewing times, light from outdoor sources is undesirable and should be blocked. At such times, a diffused, uniformly distributed illumination of 110 lx in the seating area is suitable for conference and viewing rooms. Film screening rooms should have no illumination during screening. General illumination during other periods should be suitable to the intended use, as a conference or presentation room. Rooms used for applying makeup for color television should be lit so that correct judgment of color balance can be made. To that purpose, incandescent lighting operated at a color temperature of 3200 K is used for both general and task illumination. A general illumination of 540 lx, evenly distributed, is suitable. Both daylight and fluorescent light should be excluded.

ELECTROMAGNETIC FIELDS

As with the considerations described for radio studios, intense electromagnetic fields can seriously interfere with television cameras, tape recorders, and microphones. Although the equipment is usually well shielded against this type of interference, the same precautions advised for radio studios are applicable to television studios. Physical separation from interference sources is the most effective preventive. Magnetic fields exceeding 0.5 gauss are to be avoided because of the difficulty in providing shielding from strong magnetic fields.

AIR CONDITIONING

The air-conditioning requirements cited for radio studios are also applicable to television studios. The relative humidity requirements for film storage or handling areas are identical to those noted for magnetic tape.

Achieving the desired ambient conditions is difficult in a television studio stage because of the large amount of heat generated by theatrical lights, the large space involved, and the need to avoid visible air movement on sets and cycloramas and annoying drafts on performers. The low noise and air velocity requirements necessitate the use of large ducts and vents. A commonly used technique makes use of several large air outlets located throughout the staging area at the level of the stage lighting fixtures.

The accompanying large exhaust vents are located in the studio walls.

PRIMARY POWER

Radio studio needs for primary power are applicable to television studios. The requirements for emergency power for television facilities are more complex than those for radio because of the much larger television equipment load. Generally, only selected parts of the television plant are provided emergency power. A special emergency power load distribution is set up to keep the minimal essential facilities operational in the event of primary power loss.

FIRE PROTECTION

The fire protection requirements for television studios are similar to those for radio studios, described earlier.

STUDIO FLOORS

Television studio floors require special consideration. A rough or uneven floor interferes with camera shots taken while the camera is in motion, rolling on the floor. The resultant pictures are jerky. It is also difficult to move any camera equipment across such a floor, an operation that is essential to television operation.

Smooth concrete floors are best for a television studio. The required degree of smoothness is achieved with a suitable floor covering, such as rubber, linoleum or poured resin compound. Concrete floors can accommodate the heavy television studio equipment loads without deforming or being noisy. Wooden floor structures are preferred for dance programs and can be used if solidly constructed, evenly surfaced, and free from squeaks.

Television studio floor coverings have special requirements. They must minimize noise created by movement on them, have the ability to recover from surface deformation, be resistant to abrasion and accidental burns, be a neutral color with a diffuse reflectance on the order of 15–20%, be free of any pattern, and be free of cold flow. The covering must also be capable of being painted with water paints, washed, and repainted frequently with minimum deterioration. Highly polished, waxed finishes are to be avoided. A dull finished surface is preferred. Acceptable coverings include sheet rubber and linoleum, rubber and asphalt tile, plastic and hard resin materials, cork, and hardwood. Any steel in the studio walls, ceiling, or floor should be in contact with the metal frame of the building in order for it to be grounded. Grounding of the steel is necessary in order to minimize electromagnetic interference.

The finished studio floor should be as smooth and level as possible. Abrupt level changes of more than 0.8 mm are to be avoided. Gradual level changes should not exceed 3.2 mm in a 1-m length.

RAISED ACCESS FLOORS

Television plants have a large number of electrical and electronic interconnections running through the technical areas. Raised access floors provide a convenient path between various pieces of equipment and also conceal the interconnecting wires, cables, and conduits. These floors cannot be used in the studio areas because of the studio floor requirements cited. Their use in all other technical equipment and control areas is advantageous from both design and cost viewpoints. Current code requirements necessitate the provision of ramps for the handicapped in areas utilizing raised floors.

BIBLIOGRAPHY

1. *Webster's New World Dictionary*, 2nd college ed., William Collins + World Publishing Co., Inc., Cleveland, OH, and New York, 1974.
2. E. Barnouw, *A Tower in Babel—A History of Broadcasting in the United States to 1933*, Vol. I, Oxford University Press, New York, 1966.
3. R. S. O'Brien and R. B. Monroe, "101 Years of Television," *Journal of the SMPTE* **85,** 457 (July 1976).
4. E. Barnouw, *The Golden Web—A History of Broadcasting in the United States 1933 to 1953*, Vol. II, Oxford University Press, New York, 1968.
5. C. Gilford, *Acoustics for Radio and Television Studios*, IEE Monogr. Ser. 11, Peter Peregrinus Ltd., London, 1972, p. 188.
6. *IES Lighting Handbook,* 5th ed., Illuminating Engineering Society, New York, 1972, sects. 10, 11.

General References

Engineering Handbook, 7th ed., National Association of Broadcasters, Washington, D.C., 1985, sects. 5.1, 5.2.

IRVING ROSNER
Rosner Television Systems Inc.
New York, New York

See also ACOUSTICAL DESIGN—PLACES OF ASSEMBLY; ACOUSTICAL INSULATION AND MATERIALS; ACOUSTICS—GENERAL PRINCIPLES; NOISE CONTROL IN BUILDINGS; THEATERS AND OPERA HOUSES

TELFORD, THOMAS

British engineer Thomas Telford (1757–1832) represents a generation of engineers who applied the new materials produced by the Industrial Revolution to their work. Telford was a pioneer in the application of cast iron to bridge construction. His interests were wide ranging, and among his achievements, he is credited with the founding of the world's first engineering society, the Institution of Civil Engineers, which he served as its first president. Active before the age of the railroad, Telford worked on roads and canals.

Telford was born in Glendinning, United Kingdom, in 1757. The son of a shepherd, his early education was obtained at a parish school. Because he was poor, he was apprenticed to a stone mason. For over 20 years, in his evenings he read books in many fields, including stone carving, drawing, architecture, and science. In 1780, he started working in Edinburgh and, in 1782, went to London, where for two years he worked as a mason on Sir William Chamber's Somerset House. By age 30, he was at Shrewsbury under the patronage of the wealthy William Pulteney. He designed and built a number of stone toll-houses and churches, and his first bridge, over the Severn River, dates from 1790–1792. He was responsible for the maintenance and repair of local bridges. The flood of the Severn River in February 1795 destroyed many bridges, and Telford was asked to design new ones as well as being appointed the engineer of the Shrewsbury Canal. This was the beginning of his productive career.

The Industrial Revolution was possible because of developments in the refining of iron. The substitution of coke for charcoal started in 1709. Crucible steel was first made in 1740, and wrought iron in 1784. The foundries developed near the coal mines. In the United Kingdom, this area was the Midlands.

Dependent on local iron foundries, the early engineers were able to have sections cast to their designs. Early uses were for steam engines and in industrial buildings, which began to be built using cast-iron columns and brick arches spanning between beams as a standard mill type. Wrought iron came into general use, using rolled sections, in about 1845. It was not until about 1855 that Sir Henry Bessemer invented a way to make steel in large amounts.

None of the early engineers had guidebooks or formulas to help them in their designs. Telford, the most brilliant of the early British civil engineers, developed good judgment on the basis of experience he and others had in construction. Although many buildings had iron columns, it was in bridge design that the greatest advances occurred, and Telford led the field. Telford was untrained in mathematical calculation and had little regard for abstract scientific work, but depended on frequent tests and observation of the behavior of existing structures. Many of his bridge designs were reviewed by other engineers and scientists, and he had reason to modify some of his designs in response to their recommendations. As a stone mason, he also had high regard for good foundations.

Telford was not the only designer using cast iron for bridges. However, his are more aesthetically appealing and, from an engineering analysis, more efficient in their use of materials. He was among the first to feel that beauty was based on technical and economic efficiency, rather than on historic styles. Telford was sensitive to the landscape in the placement and detailing of his bridges. He emphasized the contrast between engineering and architecture in his writings.

The earliest of the iron bridges that has endured is the Iron Bridge over the Severn River at Coalbrookdale, dating from 1777–1779. Designed by architect Thomas Farnolls Pritchard (?–1777) and Abraham Darby III, the iron parts were cast at Darby's Coalbrookdale Foundry.

Telford observed that the Iron Bridge at Coalbrookdale had survived the 1795 flood. Although expert in stone construction, he was convinced that cast iron was a suitable material for bridges. His designs for the 130-ft single-arch iron bridge at Buildwas is dated April 1795 and was built in 1796. Throughout his career, he designed both cast-iron and stone bridges, but it was in his canal work that he developed the use of cast iron. For the Ellesmere Canal (1795–1805), he designed two large aqueducts to carry the canal over the River Dee at Llangollen and at Pont Cysyllte.

When it came to the Dee Valley at Pont Cysyllte, normal canal builders were at a loss. The valley was 2500 ft wide, and even with fill, the remaining span of 1000 ft needed a new solution. Piers of over 120 ft in height were needed, and Telford designed a cast-iron trough to hold the water, supported on cast-iron arch ribs spanning between masonry piers. The reduction in load by using iron allowed the piers to be hollow above the 70-ft height. The visual lightness of the canal aqueduct is its chief attribute.

The surviving Waterloo bridge over the Conway River at Bettwys-Coed, dated 1815, includes decorative castings celebrating the victory over Napoleon. The same year, Telford designed a still-standing 150-ft span, the Craigellachie Bridge, over the River Spey in Scotland. This was a simple iron truss arch with light iron struts and bracing above. It was restored in 1963.

His most famous bridge, with a 580-ft span, is the one he designed in 1810 to bridge the Menai Strait in Wales. Funding was not approved by Parliament until 1815, and construction of the bridge occurred from 1819 to 1826. This was the first cable suspension bridge. It was not possible to fabricate the continuous cables Telford wanted, and he used wrought-iron chain instead. The roadway is 100 ft above the water. Subject to high winds, the bridge suffered frequent damage, and modern vehicle loading exceeds Telford's estimates for horse-drawn vehicles. The bridge was largely rebuilt in 1938–1940 using high-tensile-strength steel cables, and the roadway was widened. Its appearance is similar to that of the earlier construction because of an effort to protect the famous monument of early engineering. For many years this remained the longest suspension bridge in the United Kingdom.

The masonry piers at the entrance to the bridge were simply detailed with arched openings. Elsewhere, he used Gothic crenelated detailing, as at Conway, and in 1826, the Tewkesbury bridge had Gothic detailing in the cast-iron members. Telford's work opened the way to the later railroad age, where bridge building and construction of railway stations occurred on an unprecedented scale. The parallel use of cast iron and glass in greenhouses and other buildings benefited from the early use of cast iron for bridges.

Telford proposed greater spans. One was to bridge the Thames at London in a single 600-ft span. It received detailed consideration, but Parliament failed to act, probably in recognition of the high cost of the approaches. It was fortunate that this was not built since the materials available were not suitable for modern traffic. Considering the structural failures that have occurred, Telford's work survives as an example of good engineering.

Telford's writings include an autobiography published posthumously in 1838 (1) and sections on "History" and "Practice" for the article "Bridge" (1812) in the *Edinburgh*

Encyclopaedia (2). He also collaborated with A. Nimmo, who authored the section on "Theory" for the "Bridge" article. Telford's work is discussed in detail in many histories of civil engineering.

BIBLIOGRAPHY

1. J. Rickman, ed., *Life of Thomas Telford, Civil Engineer,* James and Luke G. Hansard and Sons, London, 1838.
2. T. Telford in "Bridge," in *Edinburgh Encyclopaedia,* Vol. VI, Edinburgh, UK, 1830, pp. 479–545; *New Edinburgh Encyclopedia,* Whiting and Watson, New York, 1814, pp. 470–532.

General References

R. J. M. Sutherland, "Telford," *Architectural Review,* 338 (Dec. 1953).

H. R. Hitchcock, "Building with Iron and Glass: 1790–1855," *Architecture: Nineteenth and Twentieth Centuries,* The Pelican History of Art, Penguin Books, Harmondsworth, UK, 1977, chapt. 7.

T. Ruddock, *Arch Bridges and Their Builders: 1735–1835,* Cambridge University Press, Cambridge, UK, 1979.

D. P. Billington, *The Tower and the Bridge: The New Art of Structural Engineering,* Basic Books, Inc., New York, 1983.

See also BRIDGES; EIFFEL, GUSTAV; STRUCTURAL STEEL

ROBERT T. PACKARD, AIA
Reston, Virginia

TENNESSEE VALLEY AUTHORITY (TVA) ARCHITECTURE

A timely fusion of factors, directly or indirectly combining ideal conditions, can foster exceptional architectural achievement. That is especially true of government programs and projects, and few examples in modern times can match that marvel of the twentieth century, the Tennessee Valley Authority (TVA). Success in the accomplishment of physical developments under governmental sponsorship is typically supported by an alliterative triad of programs, principals, and professionals.

In the case of TVA, the program was exceedingly great, a stupendous opportunity for the practical application of broad-scale New Deal theories. The principal figures associated with the realization of the socioeconomic and political ideas; the concepts of physical planning, design, and construction; and the viability of the actual enterprise of operation and production were men of vision and purpose: Senator George W. Norris of Nebraska, chairman of the Senate Committee on Agriculture and Forestry, who constantly pushed for the necessary legislation; David E. Lilienthal, the TVA administrator who had the vision and faith required to make new departures; and President Franklin D. Roosevelt, the national leader who seized the opportunity to demonstrate that new approaches need not obviate old values and could, in fact, set the example for additional excursions into regional, national, and even international progress. Professional talent and enthusiasm were plentiful, much as a result of the Great Depression, which had brought development programs almost to a standstill before federal government intervention. The architectural expertise and ambition available to TVA were exemplified by Roland A. Wank, whose contribution to the reconciliation of engineering and architectural considerations, as well as to the appreciation and conservation of the environment, have been increasingly valued with the passage of time.

Long before TVA came into being in 1933, conservation of land and water resources had been championed by such national leaders as President Theodore Roosevelt and Gifford Pinchot, a founder of the Bull Moose Party. Pinchot, who headed forestry services under presidents McKinley, Roosevelt, and Taft and served as president of the National Conservation Association, subsequently served two terms as governor of Pennsylvania. Regional and national concerns over the interrelated activities of inland navigation and flood control demanded planning, if not operational, authority superseding that of individual states. The tremendous construction budgets required for effective flood control projects and their accompanying hydroelectric power production facilities also indicated the need for federal funding just as the multistate electricity distribution networks carrying power generated by regional water control projects indicated a need for federal administration.

The shallows, rapids, and pools of an extensive portion of the Tennessee River called Muscle Shoals posed a serious obstruction to steamship traffic developing on that watercourse in the early 1800s. The state of Tennessee relieved the problem by constructing a canal (1824–1836), followed by construction of a portage railroad. The federal government built two canals toward the end of the nineteenth century that provided year-round passage until the end of World War I. Responding to the wartime need for explosives production, the National Defense Act of 1916 authorized construction of dams and nitrate processing plants along Muscle Shoals. Funding for the project terminated with the war, although construction of Wilson Dam was continued until its completion in 1925. Senator Norris repeatedly sponsored legislation for public operation of the Muscle Shoals facilities to produce peacetime electric power and phosphate fertilizers, but his proposals were vetoed by presidents Coolidge and Hoover. Norris's efforts were eventually rewarded in 1933 with the creation of TVA, incorporating the Muscle Shoals project.

TVA was among the many public works agencies to appear early in the first administration of President Franklin D. Roosevelt; its purpose was to provide publicly developed electric power and to conserve natural resources throughout the Tennessee River watershed. This entailed the obvious activity of dam construction for electricity generation and flood control, but it also included the construction of navigation locks. Beyond those specialized facilities, TVA was involved, through planning, design, and construction, in community and industrial development, agricultural and forestry management, and large-scale land and water-based recreational installations. Roosevelt envisaged a broad role for TVA, including planning for conservation as well as development of natural resources along the Tennessee River and adjacent areas for purposes of enhancing the national social and economic welfare. He saw it going far beyond hydroelectric power, vitalizing all kinds of human concerns. He referred to TVA as a corporation clothed with the power of government, but possessed of the flexibility and initiative of a private enterprise.

Physical planning provided opportunities for comprehensiveness in intention and continuity in design. Concepts incorporated progressive ideas including curved roads and footpaths following topographic contours, as well as public land encircling residential areas to provide buffers against occupational, business, or manufacturing districts. TVA road systems incorporated a series of bridges whose integration of design requirements expressed an advanced architectural aesthetic similar to that of the contemporary Swiss master bridge-builder Robert Maillart. TVA planning benefited the entire region by including as basic requirements in their design agenda the conservation of natural beauty and public accessibility for recreation. For example, at the Land Between the Lakes recreation area in western Kentucky and Tennessee there is a Conservation Education Center (1966) with simple camp structures of sophisticated design where schoolchildren of the fourth to ninth grades attend week-long study sessions. Where TVA river impoundments required flooding of natural areas, extensive wildlife refuges were provided and turned over to the states as well as to federal agencies.

Early in the program, TVA's Land Planning and Housing Division produced, within one month, a master plan for Norris, Tennessee, to house the project work force during construction and to remain as a new town following completion of the dam. Planned for approximately 300 individual houses and 30 apartments, the urban planning and architectural design attempted to express traditional local characteristics on the exteriors of the dwellings while incorporating modern advances in the interior finishes and fixtures. Although the layout of the urban plan sensitively followed existing landscape features and had relatively few street intersections, some critics felt that an opportunity to continue the dynamic modern design momentum of the dam structures had been missed in the design of the town's residential buildings. The concept of a design continuum was captured in broad and romantic

landscape design features associated with the roadways, pullouts, and parking areas, as it was also consciously woven through the smallest, specially designed architectural details of the major structures: surface finishes and colors, hardware, graphics, railings, lighting fixtures, and other accessories.

Initially perceived as a program of engineering design and heavy construction, the aesthetics were entrusted to the staff engineers, who were inclined to embellish their powerhouses with exterior architectural ornamentation, more or less Georgian or Gothic in their stylistic strivings, as in the pre-TVA Wilson Dam (1918–1925) where an earlier eclectic architectural ornamentation cloaked the steel skeleton with a covering of concrete in attempts to copy the stonemasonry details of the traditional classic orders. TVA's early chief staff architect, Roland A. Wank (1898–1970) received stalwart support from Albert Kahn (1869–1942), the United States' foremost industrial architect, who encouraged the TVA architectural staff in their preference for an unembellished "clean line" approach. The dramatic masses and powerful lines of the dams and their adjunct structures held great appeal for a young generation of government architects who could apply their enthusiasm for direct, honest expression of function, structure, and materials on a truly monumental scale. Thus the grand powerhouse at Norris Dam (1933–1936) could exhibit a checkered pattern of form-board impressions on its exposed concrete surface, something that would not be tolerated in other government buildings of the time. As in other government programs where staff housing had to be provided at low cost and in remote locations, challenges to design within strict constraints of limited size, space, materials, and equipment, as well as prefabrication and portability, brought forth imaginative but disciplined solutions to complicated problems (Fig. 1). TVA's designs for diverse building types, produced over an extended period of time, maintain high architectural standards, instilling a sense of accomplishment and pride among government agencies and their architects.

The most striking examples of TVA architecture are the dramatic and, in many cases, awesome dams (Fig. 2). They range in variety of purpose from main river dams to storage dams, from producers of electric power to controllers of navigation and irrigation, to preventers of flood damage. They also vary in size: up to 8422 ft (2567 m) in

Figure 1. Prefabricated housing units at Fontana Dam, North Carolina (1942–1945) were used to house the staff of 5000 in a "construction village," and later for resort lodgings and as housing at the Oak Ridge, Tennessee Atomic Energy Center. Courtesy of Tennessee Valley Authority.

Figure 2. The highest dam east of the Rocky Mountains, Fontana Dam, North Carolina (1942–1945) incorporates a motor road and the Maine to Georgia Appalachian Trail, plus a visitors' building and scenic overlook structure at the top, as well as a powerhouse and electric generating–distributing station below. Courtesy of Tennessee Valley Authority.

length and 480 ft (146.3 m) in height. They incorporate powerhouses and control buildings, visitors buildings and observation towers, and recreational facilities (boat basins, inclined railways, viewing platforms, picnic areas, etc), traversing highways and railways. Reflecting the Great Depression era of its initial development, the dams and associated installations feature mural art in many of the visitor facilities, depicting TVA constructions and the regional environments and cultures. Rustic vacation cabins and recreation facilities at Norris Lake were designed and built in cooperation with the Civilian Conservation Corps (CCC) and the National Park Service (NPS). Many TVA visitor facilities bear a family resemblance to those in the national parks and the public recreation or camping areas under the management of the U.S. Forest Service (Department of Agriculture) or the Corps of Engineers (U.S. Army), demonstrating a high degree of design information interchange among government agencies.

Perhaps more unique to TVA, because of its particular design programs, was the emergence of striking designs for their great traveling gantry crane structures. Especially handsome even in their early versions, these large mobile pieces of specialized moving and dumping equipment were much improved on in subsequent staff designs, and came to be almost a stock feature of dramatic photographs taken with the gigantic powerhouses or dams serving as massive backdrops (Fig. 3). Reflecting the World War II period of their development, the dams were typically built in record time (ie, Douglas Dam, February 1942 to March 1943) and the structural elements of the

powerhouses of that time (ie, Fontana Dam 1942–1945) appear outsized as they utilized reinforced concrete instead of structural steel, unavailable because of wartime armament priorities.

In the interest of saving time and money, a number of

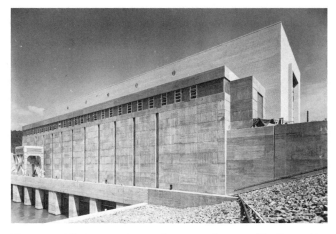

Figure 3. The concrete powerhouse at Guntersville Dam, Alabama (1935–1939) is part of a regional electric power system that serves more than 3 million customers in seven states. Note the characteristic traveling gantry crane stressing, by contrast, the static monumentality of the massive concrete structure. Courtesy of Tennessee Valley Authority.

TVA structures were designed with elements or details taken from earlier constructions in the program. Provided slavish and stultifying repetition is avoided, such an approach can yield improvements as well as savings. The adoption of standardized or site-adapted designs by government agencies is a familiar and dangerous device, liable to stifle creativity and produce unnecessarily severe impacts on the environment. With the exception of some limited use of standardized designs and prefabrication to house construction workers in temporary villages (reused as lodgings in the recreation resort areas and as housing at the Atomic Energy Commission installations in Oak Ridge, Tennessee), TVA followed the enlightened and inspiring course of designing to specific sites, determinants, and restraints. As a result, the bridges (some of them built with steel members salvaged from dam construction support systems), while displaying an overall design concept in certain associated groups, also demonstrate directness in their geometry and refinement in their details that express individuality in their melding of materials, form, and function. The more strictly architectural components of TVA's constructions—the powerhouses, steam plants, control buildings, and administrative facilities—are impressive, yet sensitively designed, demonstrating adherence to principles derived from both the Ecole des Beaux Arts and the Bauhaus.

TVA's various building types functionally respond to their specific design programs while satisfying schooled tastes by their arrangements of masses, compositions of solids, voids, textures and colors, and the proper placement of accent motifs. Thus, extensive window walls lighten masses on the exteriors while they light up the spaces of the interiors; lightweight aluminum-paneled exterior walls are solidly supported and visually anchored by masonry bases; utilitarian elements, such as conveyor structures, are boldly expressed by their housings and sensibly finished in colors compatible with their dust or soot collecting situations. The Watauga Dam visitors reception building (1944) has a simple plan of three elements. A central lobby with a sheltered, recessed entrance joins, yet separates, a viewing lounge overlooking a lake from secluded restrooms at the rear. It features dressed ashlar local stone and extensive exterior window walls, easily compared to countless successor visitor centers in parks and nature preserves throughout the United States. Coal-fired steam plants built following World War II and into the 1970s were worthy architectural successors to the earlier hydroelectric generator stations, but could not match the monumental drama contributed by the accompanying massive dams. Even later, the nuclear plants demonstrated a certain dissolution of the TVA image; looking much like anyone else's nuclear plants, and not open to the public, they had little effect on the public consciousness of the philosophical and historical TVA.

TVA's architectural distinction can be credited, in great part, to Roland Wank, who was born in Hungary and educated as an architect in Central Europe, coming under the Viennese modernist influence of Otto Wagner (1841–1918) and the secession movement. These influences directly reflected a geometric and abstract expression of structure as found in their public buildings, bridges, and dams related to Vienna's regional transportation systems. As a designer with the New York firm of Fellheimer and Wagner, Wank was closely involved with the design of their impressively modernistic and highly conspicuous Cincinnati Railroad Terminal (1929–1933), a monumental concrete structure of quadrispherical form. It helped bring him to TVA as Chief Architect during the early years of the program (1933–1944), where he played an important role in giving the monumental structures of the system drama and symbolism in their form and interpretation through expression in their materials. Wank was originally assigned to town planning for Norris, to which he was well suited because of his European background of sensitivity to urban design on a smaller, environmentally conservative scale, and for which he intended a design interaction that could relate to Norris Dam itself.

Eventually, he returned to Fellheimer and Wagner, continuing as Chief Consulting Architect for TVA while ending his career as a partner in the successor firm of Wank, Adams, Slavin and Associates. Speaking on the subject of democratic planning at the Princeton University Bicentennial Celebration (1947), Wank noted that the Great Depression and the New Deal produced some positive accomplishments whose intrinsic worth is minor compared to their promotional value; that projects fall short of their potential, as conceived by the designers; that the planning process can be discouragingly slow; and that mortals pass on, knowing that they have not achieved their full potential. He concluded that the progress of planning in a democracy, by its nature, is slow and intermittent (he termed it "leapfrogging" and "bridge building"). He also pointed out that acceptance of the rates of speed and success inherent in that process is the test of faith in democracy.

Throughout its history, TVA has faced challenges to its roles as socioeconomic and physical planner, as designer and builder, as producer of commercial commodities, and as agent of environmental impact. These challenges resulted in constant reexamination of its missions, functions, and operations, as well as the rights and interests of private enterprise and public welfare. Concern over its essential missions were faced from the time of its creation; perceived conflicts with private power production interests were contested throughout the 1930s, and attempts at privatization were fought off well into the 1950s. By the 1960s, new legislation permitted TVA to make its own decisions on time and place for construction of new facilities and to issue its own bonds for that purpose (conversely, limiting TVA's service area and preventing expansion into private domains). By the 1970s, injunctions resulting from adverse environmental impacts produced beneficial effects on threats to the survival of endangered species, the ravages of strip-mining coal, and the dangers of air pollution. The TVA nuclear power plant program of the 1960s and 1970s was slowed by energy consumption demand decreases following OPEC oil embargoes, the application of energy conservation measures, and the general adoption of a more cautious attitude toward proliferation of nuclear plants (by the late 1970s and early 1980s TVA discontinued three new construction projects). TVA has, at the same time, encouraged energy conservation by promoting alternate sources (ie, wood and solar), by providing free surveys and design assistance to customers and professionals, and by offering low cost loans for the installation of special materials and equipment.

Whatever effects these initiatives may have on the future of architecture, the fact remains that TVA has made its mark, reflecting not only the confidence of its original sponsors when they first emblazoned its earliest buildings with the motto Built for the People of the United States, but also in its inspiration for similar river valley programs throughout the world, many of them involving former TVA staff. Recent projects in various parts of the world (Australia, Egypt, India, and the USSR) may rival TVA's in the size or capacity of their significant features (ie, dam sizes and generator capacities), but in the unification of all of the various elements of its comprehensive program of rehabilitation, the uniqueness of TVA's accomplishment is unmatched.

BIBLIOGRAPHY

General References

"Tennessee Valley Authority," *Architectural Forum* **71,** 73–114 (Aug. 1939).

E. L. Armstrong, ed., *History of Public Works in the United States, 1776–1976,* American Public Works Association, Chicago, Ill., 1976.

L. Craig and the staff of the Federal Architecture Project, *The Federal Presence: Architecture, Politics and Symbols in U.S. Government Building,* Massachusetts Institute of Technology, Cambridge, Mass., 1978.

R. A. Wank, "Democratic Planning," in T. H. Creighton, ed., *Building for Modern Man,* Princeton University, Princeton, N.J., 1949, pp. 149–154.

Tennessee: A Guide to the State, Federal Writer's Project, American Guide Series, Hastings House, New York, 1939 (1949).

J. H. Kyle, *The Building of TVA—An Illustrated History,* Louisiana State University, Baton Rouge, La., 1958.

D. Lilienthal, *TVA, Democracy on the March,* Harper Brothers, New York, 1944.

M. Moffett and L. Wodehouse, *Built for the People of the United States: Fifty Years of TVA Architecture,* University of Tennessee, Chattanooga, Tenn., 1983. A catalog for an exhibition by that title at the University of Tennessee's Art and Architecture Gallery, contains an extensive bibliography, including numerous periodical articles.

L. Mumford, *The Culture of Cities,* Secker and Warburg, London, 1946. *From Sea to Shining Sea,* report prepared for the President's Council on Recreation and Natural Beauty, Vice President Hubert H. Humphrey, Chairman, U.S. Government Printing Office, Washington, D.C., 1968.

G. E. Sandstrom, *Man the Builder,* McGraw-Hill Inc., New York, 1970–1978.

See also GOVERNMENT BUILDINGS; POWER GENERATION—FOSSIL FUELS

J. WALTER ROTH, AIA
Alexandria, Virginia

TENNIS COURTS.   See RECREATIONAL FACILITIES—SUPPLEMENT

TERMITES—CONTROL BY SOIL POISONING

Even proper or excellent architectural design, detailing, and construction cannot totally prevent infestation by termites. Soil treatment chemicals that can stay active for decades are an effective defense against termite attack. Termites may live in rotting debris left at the site during construction. Dead tree limbs or neighboring buildings may harbor active nests of termites. Soil treatment provides a lasting barrier of poison that invading termites must cross. Treatment during construction allows the poison to be easily placed in all foundation areas. Even with proper soil treatment, structures that contain wood products should be checked at least every year for termites.

Termites are social insects like ants and bees. The colony is composed of several castes with specific functions. There are workers, soldiers, and both primary and secondary reproductive castes. Few eggs are laid during the first year of a colony. Three to four years will pass before winged reproductive termites are seen. Within 90 days, mature termites can do significant damage. Termites lack highly segmented bodies and can be distinguished from ants by the ants' tiny "wasplike" waists (Fig. 1). Termite wings may be twice their body length as opposed to ant wings, which are about the length of the ant's body. Loose

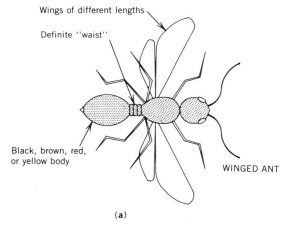

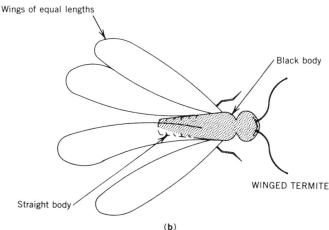

Figure 1. (**a**) Winged ant; (**b**) Winged termite.

wings left by swarming reproductives are a good indication of termite infestation. On detection, the colony should be killed and the surrounding wood removed or treated. Termites live in the soil and eat wood. They build galleries or paths in their search for food. Sometimes termites can be quite selective in the wood they eat. Wood that has been honeycombed with termite tunnels can exist far from the nest while closer pieces of wood are ignored. Subterranean termites cause 95% of the damage (genera *Reticultermes* and *Coptotermes*). Tropical or Asiatic types such as the Formosan termites can be especially aggressive and are spreading across the United States and the world. Termites infest large parts of the United States.

Luckily for homeowners, there are some very effective chemicals against termite infestation. Termite poisons are called termiticides. The Environmental Protection Agency (EPA) of the United States has studied termiticides extensively. They estimate that "0.75–1.00 billion dollars per anum appears to be the best available estimate of the magnitude of the subterranean termite problem in the U.S." (1). The EPA also found that "in summary, the benefits of the termiticides, particularly the cyclodienes, are very high" (2). The cyclodiene class of chemicals, including chlordane, is cheap and effective. These chemicals have been proven to remain active after over three decades in the soil. The EPA further remarked that "the benefits from the use of the currently registered termiticide products outweigh the potential risks" (3). The risks are more from immediate poisoning than from long-term cancers, which have been demonstrated in small mammals exposed to large doses.

CHEMICALS FOR SOIL TREATMENT

By their nature, termiticides are poisons. The EPA and other government agencies have set standards of use and maximum allowable concentrations (Table 1). Improper application may poison plants or animals, such as cats and dogs. Small children can consume soil and become poisoned. The person applying the chemical is in the most danger. Certified pesticide companies will have special suits of clothes, gloves, and special cleaning procedures. "Do-it-yourself" application should be avoided. The EPA is now requiring more extensive labeling procedures. There are three major classes of chemicals used as termiticides, the cyclodienes, chlorinated hydrocarbons, and organophosphates (5).

Table 1. Maximum Allowable Concentrations[a]

Chemical	ACGHI Level,[b] $\mu g/m^3$	OSHA Level, $\mu g/m^3$
Chlordane		500
Heptachlor	500	500
Aldrin–Dieldrin	250	250
Lindane	500	500
Pentachlorophenol	500	500
Chloropyrifos	200	

[a] Ref. 4.
[b] American Conference of Governmental Industrial Hygienists, 1982.

Table 2. Typical Mixtures[a]

Chemical	Concentration[b]
Aldrin	0.5%
Chlordane	1.0%
Dieldrin	0.5%
Heptachlor	0.5%

[a] Ref. 6.
[b] Applied in oil solution or water emulsion.

The Cyclodienes

The cyclodienes are aldrin, chlordane, dieldrin, and heptachlor (Table 2). Symptoms of acute poisoning in man are dizziness, nervousness, convulsions, and loss of coordination. Almost all termiticides used are cyclodienes. Chlordane and chlordane mixtures comprise 80% or more of the chemical termiticides used. The cyclodienes are very persistent on the environment. Chemicals tested after 34 years in the soil are still potent. Chlordane and chlordane–heptachlor mixtures are typically half to a quarter the cost of competing chemicals when compared on a dollar per year basis (7). Before 1974, aldrin had a major share of the market. Dieldrin is rarely used because of its high cost.

Chlorinated Hydrocarbons

Lindane is about half as persistent as the cyclodienes. Early signs of lindane poisoning are headache, dizziness, and vomiting. Other symptoms of poisoning are diarrhea, hypothermia, hyperirritability, uncoordination, and convulsions. Pentachlorophenol is also a chlorinated hydrocarbon. Symptoms of intoxication are accelerated respiration, vomiting, increased body temperature, tachycardia, neuromuscular weakness, and cardiac failure. It is only indirectly related to termite treatment in that it is a major chemical used in treated lumber. Properly constructed and drained wooden foundations composed of pentachlorophenol-treated wood are acceptable alternatives to concrete foundations. They have been used for many years and are accepted by many building codes. Pentachlorophenol has been restricted by the EPA and cannot be applied by the homeowner. Although not as effective as creosote, it is a persistent poison for both insects and fungi.

Organophosphates

Chloropyrifos is an organophosphate pesticide. Applicators should have their blood chlorinesterase levels measured before application and periodically afterward. Symptoms of poisoning include nervousness, giddiness, headache, blurred vision, weakness, nausea, cramps, diarrhea, and discomfort in the chest. Chloropyrifos pesticides are relatively new and are used mainly in California.

OTHER CONTROL METHODS

There are also several kinds of "nonchemical" approaches to controlling termites (8). The Integrated Pest Management (IPM) technique stresses proper construction, moisture control, environmental modification, and inspection along with some chemical treatment. IPM procedures include the use of "bait blocks" to deliver conventional termiticides, insect growth regulators, antibiotics, and others. One interesting "birth control" method uses the juvenile hormone analogue methoprene. This kills termites by disrupting their development. Methoprene is currently registered for use against mosquitoes, some flies, and fleas.

The Steinernematid Nematode ("Spear") is a microscopic organism that attacks termites. It searches for termites by sensing their body heat, carbon dioxide, and waste trails. "Spear" then enters the termite through a body opening and destroys the insect within 48 hours. The nematodes are packages in a water-soluble gel and applied with conventional pest control equipment. These biological control agents are exempt from registration by the EPA. They are controlled by other U.S. agencies.

APPLICATION TECHNIQUES

The applicator is attempting to create a barrier of treated soil adjacent to walls or piers from grade to footing. Shallow trenches may need to be dug and rods or probes thrust into the ground to aid absorption. Concrete slab-on-grade treatments should be applied to the fill just before the concrete pour or the treated fill should be protected from disturbance by vapor barriers or other means. Excessively wet fills should not be treated. To treat soils or fill below existing concrete slabs, holes should be drilled in the slab at even spacings determined by the termiticide applicator. Termiticides may be applied in oil or water solutions. Oil solutions should be avoided because oils are toxic to plants and may cause a fire hazard. They can stain building materials and destroy plastic vapor barriers (9).

Concrete Slab-on-grade

For chemicals at standard concentrations overall treatment of 1 gal/10 ft^2 (4 L/m^2) under slab and attached porches is usual. Gravel fills or absorbent materials require an extra 0.5 gal/10 ft^2 (2 L/m^2). Critical areas require 2 gallons per 5 lineal ft (5 L/m). These areas include along the inside and outside of foundation walls, interior partitions, and utility entrance places.

Crawl-space or Basement Construction

On the inside of the foundation walls, at piers, and at utility entrances, apply 2 gal/5 lineal ft (5 L/m) of chemicals at standard concentrations. Do not make an overall treatment of the soil. On the outside foundation walls apply 2 gal/5 lineal ft (5 L/m). Where foundations are deep, use probes to apply 4 gal/5 lineal ft (10 L/m).

CONSTRUCTION PRACTICES

The general principle is to keep untreated wood dry and separated from the soil by concrete, masonry, or treated-wood construction. Fungus or damp conditions may attract termites. Clean, dry foundations next to treated soils are the best defense against termites. Termite shields are not effective. "The value of shields are better demonstrated in theory than in practice" (10). The shields usually only act to make the termites more visible as they extend their tubes around the shields. In highly infested southern regions of the United States traditional residential construction uses concrete pier foundations supporting wooden beams set 20 in. (500 mm) or so above ground level. This gap allows air movement to dry the wood and gives access for periodic inspections and repair if necessary. Modern concrete slab-on-grade construction techniques can hide damage caused by trapped moisture. Slab-on-grade foundations can leave the wooden frame construction above more vulnerable to attack than traditional pier-and-beam foundations. Water accumulation should be prevented by proper flashing and positive drainage off roofs, walls, and away from foundations. A dripping faucet in the back that no one sees can keep an area permanently damp. Fungus and termites will find these damp areas attractive. Even though masonry, concrete, and steel structures are immune from termite attack, their contents are not. Books, cardboard containers, and other wood products left in storerooms and warehouses can be rapidly destroyed. Architects should not assume that they can avoid soil treatment just because building materials are "nonedible." Soil treatment should also be considered to protect a building's contents.

CONCLUSION

Soil treatment by poisoning is an effective way to help prevent termite attack. Pretreatment of soils under and around foundations is superior to treatment of existing buildings. If long-lasting pesticides of the cyclodiene family are used, periodic retreatment is not necessary. All accessible foundation areas should be checked once a year.

BIBLIOGRAPHY

1. United States Environmental Protection Agency, *Analysis of the Risks and Benefits of Seven Chemicals Used for Subterranean Termite Control,* Office of Pesticides and Toxic Substances, Office of Pesticide Programs, Washington, D.C., Nov. 1983, p. III–4.

2. Ref. 1, p. V–4.

3. Ref. 1, p. V–5.

4. Ref. 1, p. IV–8.

5. P. J. Spear, "Principles of Termite Control," in K. Krishna and F. M. Weesner, *Biology of Termites,* Academic Press, Inc., Orlando, Fla., 1969, p. 593.

6. D. H. Percival, *Council Notes, Termite Control,* Vol. 3, no. 4, University of Illinois at Urbana–Champaign, Small Homes Council—Build Research Council, Champaign, Ill. Winter 1980, p. 5.

7. Ref. 1, Table III–3, p. III–16.

8. Ref. 1, p. III–8.

9. Ref. 5, p. 599.

10. Ref. 5, p. 586.

General References

R. H. Beal, J. K. Mauldin, and S. C. Jones "Subterranean Termites, Their Prevention and Control in Buildings," *U.S. Department of Agriculture Home & Garden Bulletin* 64 (1986).

R. T. Meister, ed., *Farm Chemicals Handbook*, Meister Publishing Co., Willoughby, Ohio, 1981.

Federal Housing Administration, *Minimum Property Standards*, U.S. Department of Housing and Urban Development, Office of Housing, USGPO, Washington, D.C. 1982. See sections 602–3.2 and 606–2 in document 4900.1, "One and Two Family Dwellings."

G. M. Hunt and G. A. Garrett, *Wood Preservation*, McGraw-Hill Inc., New York, 1967.

C. G. Wright and R. B. Leidy, "Termite Control Produces Low Levels Chlordane and Heptachlor in Treated Houses," in *Pest Control Technology*, 44–45, 55 (July 1982).

JAMES H. FITZWATER, AIA
Design Automation
Houston, Texas

TERRAGNI, GIUSEPPE

In December, 1926 the first of four articles on the state of Italian architecture was published in the obscure journal *Rassegna Italiana*. The articles were the first theoretical writings of the modern movement in Italy and were signed by seven young architects from the *Politecnico:* Terragni, Luigi Figini, Gino Pollini, Sebastiano Larco, Ubaldo Castagnoli, Guido Frette, and Carlo Enrico Rava, known as the *Gruppo 7*. The articles are often referred to as the "Rationalist Manifesto," and the modern movement architects who followed in the direction set by these avant-garde pathfinders are called the "rationalists." Terragni has been often viewed as the leader of the group. But the Gruppo 7 were, above all, schooled in the classicism of the academy, and they were part of a nationalistic movement that had begun long before fascism.

As a consequence of this classical substratum their manifesto was laced with references to the stability that recent architectural events had created. After the uncertainties of futurism and the decorative excesses of the eclectic styles of the early twentieth century, Italian architecture looked like it was once again back on the road to classicism.

Terragni was born in the small town of Meda, between Milan and Como, on April 18, 1904. His father, Michele, was a building contractor who came from Seveso (also near Milan) but his itinerant construction business took them to Meda. Giuseppe, the youngest of four sons, moved to Como when he was school aged, and stayed there with his mother's relatives. In 1917, he enrolled in the Istituto Tecnico in Como and, after graduating from the physics and mathematics department of the Istituto in 1921, he enrolled in the Scuola Superiore di Architettura of the Politecnico of Milan. Terragni had painted avidly as a young man, and when he finished his architectural education he had to make the decision either to be a painter or an architect.

In 1927, Terragni opened his office in Como on Via Indipendenza 23 with Luigi Zuccoli as his assistant. Zuccoli was to remain with him until the end in 1943, completing the last major work, Casa Giuliani-Frigerio, after Terragni returned to active military duty in the army in World War II. Terragni's brother Attilio (1896–1958) worked with Giuseppe on most of the projects in and for Como, while Pietro Lingeri was Terragni's partner for most of the competition projects and for the apartment buildings erected in Milan.

In 1928, Terragni was invited along with other Italian avant-garde architects to exhibit at the Weissenhof Exhibition in Stuttgart, and in the same year MIAR (Movimento Italiano per L'Architettura Moderna—Italian Movement for Modern Architecture) was formed as a kind of Italian version of CIAM. MIAR held its first exhibition in Rome in 1928 and Terragni and the Gruppo 7 participated. He exhibited the Novocomum apartment house project, then still in construction. This building is usually considered the first executed work of Italian rationalism, and along with Lingeri's Amila Motorboat Club in Tremezzo on Lake Como, remained one of the few constructed works of Italian rationalism for almost five years after its completion.

The ambiance of Como was strongly influenced by two factors. First was the persistence of the myth of the Maestri Comacini, the legendary master masons who influenced European architecture in the Middle Ages. The second factor was the local silk industry, the most important industry of the region. These factors engendered an intense craft orientation in the architects of the region. Terragni and his associates possessed perhaps the most uncompromising will to build well of any architects in Italy during the fascist period.

The artistic activity in Como—a small, almost backwater town in the lake district—revolved around the Café Rebecchi where Terragni and his friends would congregate to talk about architecture and art. Café Rebecchi was nothing like the Parisian cafés of the period, however, but more like the working class *Enoteca* of the region, a place where friends could enjoy an *ombretto* (an afternoon drink—literally, "a shadow") among men of many walks of life. Como had a small coterie of abstract painters including Mario Radice, Manlio Rho, and Aldo Galli, with Terragni, Lingeri, Zuccoli, and Cesare Cattaneo as the participating architects.

Another factor in Terragni's personality was his Catholicism, which was very personal and individual. A devout believer, as well as a card-carrying fascist, Terragni would go to mass at the Church of the Crocifisso on the edge of the old town, in order to be alone and away from the crowded cathedral with its elaborate decorations and "distractions." It was possibly this devotion that pushed Terragni to attempt to strike a balance between the traditional and the avant-garde in architecture, the one representing faith, the other reason.

At the beginning of the 1930s came, along with the Great Depression, a number of significant events in the history of Italian architecture in the period. In 1931 was the famous Second Exhibition of Rationalist Architecture in Pietro Maria Bardi's gallery in Via Veneto in Rome, which included Bardi's acerbic "Table of Horrors." Terragni exhibited there, and the following year he was also chosen to design the decorations of the room celebrating 1922, the year of the Fascist March on Rome and the seizure of power, in the Tenth Anniversary Exhibit of the Fascist Revolution, held in the great exposition hall on Via Nazionale in Rome.

In 1932 Terragni received the most important commission of his career: the Casa del Fascio in Como. It was at this time that he also renewed his collaboration with Pietro Lingeri. It was during this period that the five Milan apartment houses, the pair's most fruitful collaborative effort, were designed.

In 1934, Terragni's project was among those premiated in the national competition for the Palazzo Littorio in Rome (the National Fascist Party headquarters). This was the so-called Solution A, produced with Lingeri and Luigi Vietti. The same team produced another scheme, Solution B, not premiated. This project, and the competition in general, often serves as an index to the confrontation between the Roman and the Milanese architects, a confrontation that became one between (mainly) Milanese rationalism and the more conservative Roman architecture, sometimes referred to as monumentalism. The debate revolved around which architecture would become the "Fascist style," and therefore which would represent the architecture of the State.

The Casa del Fascio in Como was Terragni's most famous building then, and remains so now, even though the success of the Casa del Fascio was tempered by the adverse criticism leveled at Terragni by Giuseppe Pagano, himself an important rationalist architect and the editor of *Casabella* magazine. Pagano argued that there was a narcissistic streak in Terragni's work.

The period of the mid-1930s was perhaps the most creative for Terragni in his entire career and corresponded to his all-out embrace of the forms of the international style. Indeed, this was an important period for all Italy, just when the modern movement was being suppressed and even outlawed in other European countries.

In 1938 Rino Valdameri, a Milanese lawyer and director of the Brera, commissioned Terragni and Lingeri to design a "Danteum" for Rome. This project remained unbuilt, even though it was approved by Mussolini. Also in 1938, Terragni collaborated with Alberto Sartoris on a plan for workers' housing in the Rebbio quarter of Como. Terragni's major work of this last period, 1939–1943, is the Casa Giuliani-Frigerio in Como, completed by Zuccoli from Terragni's preliminary drawings. In 1939, Terragni also received a commission to design a Casa del Fascio in Rome, in the Trastevere quarter. This commission went barely beyond the stage of preliminary sketches, however, before Terragni was called up into the Italian army.

On September 5, 1939, five days after the Nazi invasion of Poland (and, ironically, the day after receiving the news of the cancellation of the Danteum project), Terragni was called up once again to serve in Mussolini's army. He was sent first to Verona, where he continued to make sketches for the Casa Giuliani-Frigerio. In 1940, he left for the Balkans and on July 11, 1941 he was sent to Russia as a captain in the artillery. During this time he continued to

devote as much time as he could to architecture. He sketched incessantly, creating schemes for a "Total Theater," the Casa del Fascio in the Trastevere section of Rome, a stepped-section apartment house, and an urban design scheme for the "Cortesella" district of Como.

In the battle of Stalingrad, Terragni found himself ordering artillery barrages against teenage boys. He cracked. After a brief hospitalization abroad he was brought back to Italy in January 1943, where he spent some time in a hospital in Pavia. He was diagnosed as having suffered a nervous collapse. He was treated by a specialist in nervous and mental illness, and made some last sketches in Pavia. At least one of these sketches is on his doctor's stationery. Terragni was clearly in terrible shape mentally as well as physically. Through family influence he was brought back to Como. His very last project was for a cathedral to be executed in reinforced concrete in a parabolic section.

Giuseppe Terragni died on July 19, 1943, six days before the coup d'état that deposed Mussolini and led to Italy's withdrawal from World War II; he was 39. Terragni was buried in the family tomb in the cemetery near Séveso. The circumstances surrounding his death are somewhat mysterious. The official account is that he had suffered an embolism. Many believed, and some still do, that he took his own life. What is certain is that Terragni took much of the guilt and shame for fascism on himself.

International interest in the architecture of Giuseppe Terragni is a fairly recent phenomenon. Although Terragni was acknowledged during his all-too-short lifetime as one of the leading figures of the Italian modern movement and its most talented practitioner, interest in his work ebbed after World War II, not to surface again until the late 1960s. While his work was well known in Italy during the 1940s and 1950s—he was, of course included, as were many other Italians, in Zevi's monumental *Storia dell'Architettura Moderna* first published in 1953—in the English-speaking world he was little known until Panos Koulermos published a short article on the work of Terragni and Lingeri in *Architectural Design* in the early 1960s. At about that time, Peter Eisenman began his research on Terragni, later publishing articles in *Casabella, Perspecta,* and *Oppositions.*

It is interesting to note that Terragni's name does not appear in any of the influential books on modern architecture published in English between 1940 and the mid-1960s. One technical exception is Banham's inclusion of Terragni's name in his *Theory and Design in the First Machine Age* as the architect who completed the Como monument to those killed in World War I, after the designs of Antonio Sant'Elia.

For many scholars, the problem of Terragni was the problem of Italy: fascism. Italian fascism still infected the atmosphere of the postwar period. Most Italians preferred to forget the politics of the period—what Benedetto Croce described as the "unfortunate episode" of the fascist era—and foreign architects associated the architecture with the politics so closely that the only acceptable designer was Pier Luigi Nervi. In order to disinfect the atmosphere, many of the early postwar writers placed Terragni and the other rationalists outside the politics of the period, or even absolved them of culpability in the policies of fascism. The fact that Giuseppe Pagano, Raffaele Giolli, Gianluigi Banfi, and Terragni (among others) all died during the war, and some literally were martyred, helped remove them from mainstream of politics. (For Pagano and Giolli, who had turned against fascism and paid with their lives, such martydom was unambiguous.) Furthermore, the fact that these martyrs were also rationalists made it easier to associate modernism with more liberal causes, even to claim a left wing of fascism. Attempts to place figures such as Terragni outside the political sphere and above the fray continued into the 1970s.

Terragni, then, rested—if not in peace—in relative obscurity outside Italy. In the United States, he began to receive some recognition after the publication of the monograph number of *L'Architettura,* later republished as *Omaggio a Terragni,* edited by Bruno Zevi. This publication, in Italian only, became a copybook for some U.S. students of architecture, but it did not whet the appetite of U.S. historians. No books in English had yet been written on Terragni as an architect and creative genius. Here was an architect who, Zevi recently has argued, was on the same plane with Wright and Le Corbusier, being excluded from the pantheon of worthies.

Even after interest in Terragni surfaced, he was not simply accepted as an important international figure in the modern movement, but rather as a talented architect from the provinces. And while some of his projects were recognized as masterpieces, many of his works were disparaged by postwar critics and historians. Como architect Giuseppe Rocchi called him "an able eclectic, collecting a pile of disparate references," (1) and Terragni's apparent lack of interest in a Corbusian elegance of the free plan has made some architects refrain from studying him in depth, even if they admire his facades. Still others consider him nonspatial.

But if the problem of Terragni is the problem of Italy in the interwar period, then the same misconceptions about him and his country that have developed in the wake of modern movement polemics and histories need the same revisions. Significantly, many of the values and directives of the modern movement that have come under fire in the last two decades are the same values and directives that Italians also questioned during the 1920s and 1930s. A sort of revisionist history in relation to the polemics of orthodox modernism has been written for many other persons and countries. Italy has lagged behind.

BIBLIOGRAPHY

1. *L'Architettura,* 163 (1969).

General References

B. Zevi, *Giuseppe Terragni,* Zanichelli, Bologna, 1980.

E. Mantero, *Giuseppe Terragni e l città del razionalismo in Italia,* Dedalo, Rome, 1969.

B. Zevi and co-workers, *Ommaggio a Terragni,* Etas Kompas, Rome, 1968.

M. Tafuri, "Terragni: Subject and Mask," *Oppositions* **11,** (1978).

P. Eisenman, "From Object to Relationship," *Casabella* **344,** (Jan. 1970).

P. Eisenman, "From Object to Relationship II," *Perspecta* **13/14,** (1971).

D. Ghirardo, "The Vicenda of the Casa del Fascio in Como," *The Art Bulletin* (Oct. 1980).

M. Labò, *Giuseppe Terragni,* Il Balcone, Milan, 1949.

T. Schumacher, *The Danteum,* Princeton Architectural Press, Princeton, N.J., 1985.

Thomas L. Schumacher,
FAAR
University of Maryland
College Park, Maryland

TERRAZZO

DEFINITION

Terrazzo is an exceptionally durable poured floor, base, or stair system of aggregate in a matrix, manufactured on the job site from basic materials by skilled workers. Terrazzo finishes consist of a topping applied either directly to a concrete substrate or over a portland cement underbed.

HISTORY

The earliest arrangements of pebbles on floors in patterns date from the seventh or eighth century B.C. and were probably Phrygian. Black and white stones were used in the earliest work, in geometric patterns. The limited color range did not prevent fine work in northern Greece by the fourth century B.C. Advances in mosaic work came with the development of cut and shaped stones, which the workers could use to create finer work. These cut stones, marble, and glass were called tesserae and were usually small cubes. Glass was used to supply brightness and color variations, but was too easily damaged to be often used on floors. By Hellenistic times, mosaics were a fine art. Elaborate mosaic scenes were often surrounded by geometric patterns to form a border. The effect can be compared to that of a carpet laid on a floor.

Few of the early floor mosaics have survived. Those that have often were in remote areas where buildings did not receive the hard use of urban locations. Even these durable floors, using materials such as marble, other stones, or terracotta with occasional glass tesserae, tended to be repaired or replaced over time.

Wall mosaics fared better. For these areas, smoothness was not a criteria, so the tesserae could be set to catch the changing light. Entire walls, columns, and vaults were covered with mosaics in the Byzantine period. They created dramatic effects that still survive in many locations. The colored glass (smalto) was most used on the vertical and ceiling mosaics. A large group of mosaics survive in several buildings at Ravenna, Italy, dating from the fifth and sixth centuries A.D.

The early mosaics used gypsum as the cementitious material. Lime mortars, developed by the Romans, were used later.

MODERN TERRAZZO

Terrazzo used today was developed after the discovery of portland cement about 1820. With the research and experimentation in plastics after World War II, a new type of terrazzo flooring was developed in which synthetic resins serve as the binder (matrix) instead of portland cement.

In the United States, The National Terrazzo and Mosaic Association, Inc., Des Plaines, Illinois, produces standard specifications and supports an awards program for terrazzo installations.

TERRAZZO SYSTEMS

Portland Cement

Portland cement terrazzo is available in three basic systems: sand cushion, bonded terrazzo over concrete, or monolithic terrazzo.

Sand Cushion. Sand-cushion terrazzo may be used for interior floors. Separated from the concrete substrata by an isolation membrane, the 3-in. depth weighs 30 lb/ft^2. Divider strips control anticipated contraction and allow color separation (Fig. 1).

Bonded. Bonded terrazzo is used for interior and exterior surfaces, the 1¾ to 2¼ in. depth weighs 18 lb/ft^2. Divider strips spaced 6–8-ft oc should also be placed over all breaks in the substrate (Fig. 2).

Monolithic. Placed over concrete slabs, monolithic terrazzo is an economical ½-in.-thick system used for large floor areas, such as in shopping malls. It is dependent on the quality of the concrete beneath, with divider strips 10–15-ft oc, including over all joints in the slab. Angle divider strips are glued to the slab (Fig. 3).

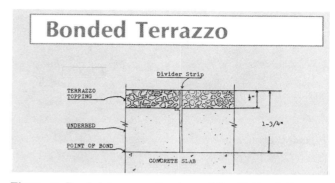

Figure 2. Bonded terrazzo. Courtesy of the National Terrazzo and Mosaic Association, Inc.

Structural. Structural terrazzo is used over a 4-in. concrete base, where the slab and terrazzo are placed by one contractor. Dividers are set into concrete slab on 8–10-ft centers and are placed on column lines. Total weight of slab and topping is approximately 60 lb/ft^2 (Fig. 4).

Thin-set Terrazzo

Thin Set. Thin-set terrazzo is available using epoxy or polyester matrix in a ¼-in. thickness, which is economical for ground-level or multistory buildings and is used for both vertical and horizontal restorations. Angle dividers are spaced 10–15-ft oc. Small stone chips are required. The total weight on the system is only 3 lb/ft^2 (Fig. 5).

Polyacrylate. Polyacrylate terrazzo is a modified cement composite using a blend of marble chips or other suitable aggregates over concrete slabs. The topping is ¼- to ⅜-in. thick.

Other Applications

Rustic. Rustic terrazzo refers to a textured surface for exterior use. This slip-resistant surfacing may be used with sand-cushion, bonded, structural, and monolithic systems. Temporary wood strips are used, then replaced by a pourable sealant inserted into the joint. Divider strips also may be used. The weight depends on the system used and thickness of the systems.

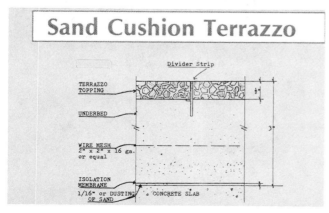

Figure 1. Sand cushion terrazzo. Courtesy of the National Terrazzo and Mosaic Association, Inc.

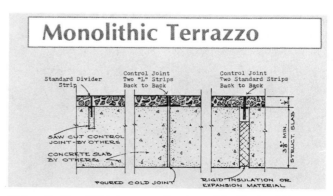

Figure 3. Monolithic terrazzo. Courtesy of the National Terrazzo and Mosaic Association, Inc.

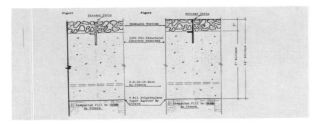

Figure 4. Structural terrazzo. Courtesy of the National Terrazzo and Mosaic Association, Inc.

Precast. Terrazzo may be used in precast items for steps, bases, planter, benches, wall panels, and other uses.

MATERIALS

Aggregates are marble chips of various sizes. For terrazzo, marble may be defined as any calcareous rocks capable of taking a polish, including onyx, travertine, and serpentine rocks. Occasionally granite chips are used. Chips are now available in a wide variety of colors (Table 1).

Customary sizes for toppings are:

1. Standard: No. 1 and No. 2, equal parts.
2. Intermediate: No. 1, 2, 3, and 4.
3. Venetian: No. 1, 2, 3, 4, and 5; and/or 6, 7, and 8.

MATRIX MATERIALS AND DIVIDER STRIPS

Matrix material may be either a portland cement–sand mixture, epoxy, or polyester resin. Divider strips are essential in all systems of terrazzo and are designed to control damage to the floor system caused by anticipated movement of the structure. Materials may be metal (zinc alloy or brass) or plastic of varying gauges. Occasionally marble may be used for divider strips.

Abrasive inserts are used at the edge of stair treads. Dividers may be used to separate colors of terrazzo, allowing decorative patterns to be built into the floor.

SURFACING

Once the terrazzo topping is placed and the matrix has set, the surface is ground using electric-powered floor grinders

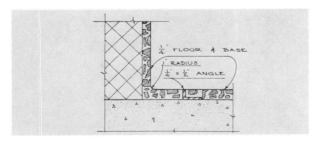

Figure 5. Thin-set terrazzo. Courtesy of the National Terrazzo and Mosaic Association, Inc.

Table 1. Marble-chip Sizes

Number	Passes Screen, in.	Retained on Screen, in.
0	1/8	1/16
1	1/4	1/8
2	3/8	1/4
3	1/2	3/8
4	5/8	1/2
5	3/4	5/8
6	7/8	3/4
7	1	7/8
8	1 1/8	1

and hand-held edging machines in a wet slurry and grouted with matching materials and polished to reveal 70% of the aggregate. Penetrating sealers and cleaning materials should be specifically formulated for use on terrazzo. Floors should never be waxed.

The use of abrasive materials can provide slip-resistant surfaces for ramps and stairways. Terrazzo floors are durable and can be repaired (Figs. 6 and 7). A notable recent installation is in the Jacob K. Javits Convention Center, New York City (I.M. Pei & Partners).

Figure 6. Minnesota World Trade Center, St. Paul, Minn. Courtesy of the National Terrazzo and Mosaic Association, Inc.

Figure 7. Northlake Mall, Atlanta, Ga. Courtesy of the National Terrazzo and Mosaic Association, Inc.

BIBLIOGRAPHY

General References

The National Terrazzo and Mosaic Association, Inc. publishes technical publications for the construction industry.
M. Gough, *The Origins of Christian Art,* Praeger Publishers, New York, 1973.
A. Grabar, *Byzantine Painting,* Skira, Inc., New York, 1953.

Material for this article was derived in large part from the publications of the National Terrazzo and Mosaic Association, Inc., with permission.

See also CERAMIC TILE; FLOORING, WOOD; RESILIENT FLOORING; RUGS AND CARPETS

ROBERT T. PACKARD, AIA
Reston, Virginia

TESTING. See DIAGNOSTICS, BUILDING; VALUE ENGINEERING

TEST METHODS—ADDITIVES, CURING AND WINTER CONCRETING. See CONCRETE—
ADMIXTURES, CURING AND TESTING

TEXTILES

The modern textile industry is a vast industrial complex in which many segments interact in the development, production, and marketing of technologically sophisticated products. The interrelationships of key sectors of the industry shown schematically in Figure 1 suggest the essential elements of textile materials, and the sequence of processing steps required for the conversion of the starting materials—fibers—to finished products for use by consumers or in other industries.

While there are common elements in textiles intended for apparel use and for other applications, this article will focus on fabrics for home furnishings and for use in building interiors. In the United States, this represents approximately half of the total volume of fiber consumed. In this segment of the industry, perhaps even more than in apparel textiles, the evolution of the synthetic fiber industry has had a dramatic impact on the development of new

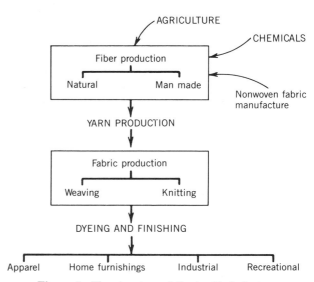

Figure 1. The structure of the textile industry.

products, and on the development of nontraditional applications of textile materials in building.

A brief description of the elements that make up a textile fabric requires definition of commonly used terms as follows. Fibers are classified as natural and man-made. Man-made fibers are subdivided into cellulosic and noncellulosic. Yarn is typically classified as continuous filament or spun staple. Staple fiber spun yarn is made by processing discontinuous fibers (one to several inches in length) that are bound together by twist; continuous filament yarn is produced by passing a fluid through a spinnerette at a controlled rate, after which the filaments are solidified and stretched. Fabric is made by weaving, knitting, or tufting of yarns. Nonwoven fabrics may be made directly from fiber without conversion to yarn.

Dyeing and Finishing (wet processing) of fabrics are processes that provide aesthetic and functional properties that have significant effects on consumer acceptance and on performance in use. Coated fabrics are those to which a polymeric substance such as plastic or rubber has been applied in a firmly adhering layer onto fabric to provide specific properties (eg, water impermeability).

Each element of the fabric structure plays a role in the properties. Thus, the properties of a textile ultimately depend on combining fiber composition, type of yarn, fabric construction, finish, and combination with other materials, as in coating or carpet backing. To a very significant degree, the requirements of a particular end use or application can be met by judicious selection of these parameters in the design of the fabric, and by the technology of manufacturing.

FIBER TO FABRIC

The world production of fibers is shown schematically in Figure 2. In the United States, mill consumption of man-made fibers has reached approximately 70% of the total (Table 1) (2,3). The volume of man-made fibers produced continues to grow, and the number of different fibers available singly and in blends for the manufacture of yarns and fabrics exhibiting specific properties increases from year to year. Generic names and part of the Federal Trade Commission Definitions for commercial man-made fibers are shown in Table 2 (2,3).

Fiber properties are only one factor to be considered in the selection and evaluation of a textile material for a given application. However, some generalizations are possible concerning the features of importance. It is evident, for example, that fibers used in window fabrics must resist sunlight and that fiber strength can have overriding importance in fabrics for industrial use. Table 3 is a brief summary of selected properties of man-made fibers (3) and Table 4 shows the same properties for the natural fibers and their place in the fiber classification scheme.

The properties of fibers depend on several factors, including the chemical structure of the polymers from which they are formed, the morphology or fiber microstructure, and, in the case of man-made fibers, on the conditions employed in manufacture. The properties shown in Table 3 are indicative of those which may be correlated with some aspects of performance in fabrics designed for specific end uses.

A discussion of manufacturing steps and variables in the conversion of fiber to yarn and yarn to fabric is beyond the scope of this review, but a few words about fabric constructions are appropriate because construction variables play a significant role in determining the suitability of a textile material for a specific end use. Fabric may be woven, knitted, or it may be a nonwoven structure. The fundamental construction parameters of woven fabrics include weight per unit area (usually expressed as ounces per square yard), count (yarns per inch in the warp, or lengthwise), filling (cross direction of the fabric), and weave. Fundamental types of weave, named in accordance with the design followed in interlacing the yarns to form the textile structure, are plain, twill, satin, pile. Schematic drawings of common weaves and of a knitted fabric structure are shown in Figure 3. In addition, there are more complex novelty weaves (eg, damask and jacquard) that provide textile pattern, or surface effects not found in the basic weaves, and are generally intended for aesthetic effects.

Fiber composition and fabric construction together determine in large measure whether a fabric is suitable for a given industrial use—where performance properties are a dominant consideration. On the other hand, dyeing and finishing of fabrics produce the aesthetic and performance features that are factors of major importance in fabrics for interior furnishings. The technology of dyeing and finishing has become more complex and sophisticated with the growth of man-made fibers and with the large number of fibers and material combinations employed in the manufacture of textiles.

For many applications, textile products must comply with performance standards promulgated by federal, state, and local regulatory agencies and must also satisfy labeling requirements. This is, of course, in addition to the need for meeting the specifications imposed by the buyer, which generally include performance properties under conditions of use.

FABRIC PROPERTIES AND USES

For each application, the critical fabric properties must be determined. There are, however, also some general properties depending on composition, design, and quality that must be considered in all situations. These include the following:

- Colorfastness (to washing, dry cleaning, sunlight).
- Wear life (under conditions of use), including tear, tensile strength, and abrasion resistance.
- Cleanability (dimensional stability in laundering or dry cleaning).
- Resistance to sunlight, rot, and fungus.
- Flammability.

In addition, the response of a fabric to humid environment, soiling (dry soiling and staining), and wrinkle resistance may be of significance. Special properties such as

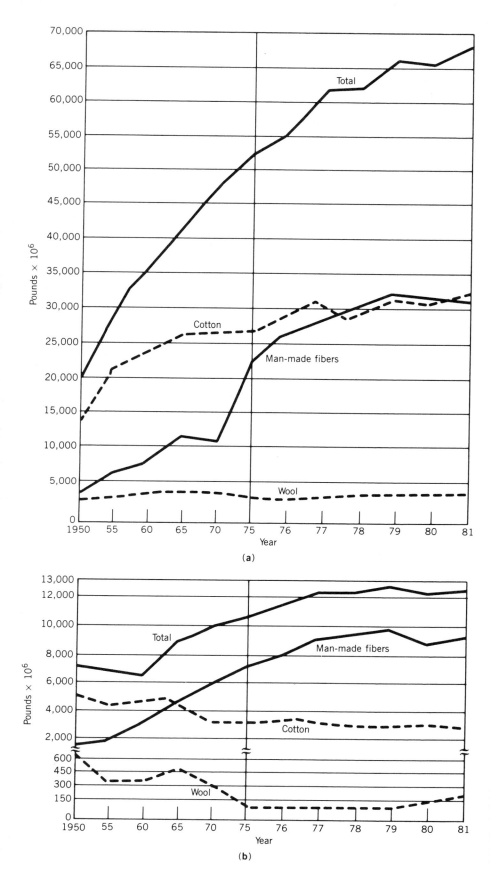

Figure 2. (a) World production of cotton, wool, and man-made fibers; (b) U.S. textile mill consumption of cotton, wool, and man-made fibers. Courtesy of the Man Made Fiber Producers Association, Inc.

Table 1. U.S. End Use Summary, 1984[a]

End Use	Total[b]	Cotton[b]	Wool[b]	Man-made[b] Fibers
Apparel	4,373	1,692	172	2,509
Home Furnishings	4,076	815	35	3,226
Industrial	3,754	389	21	3,344
Exports of				
Domestic Products	279	84	4	191
Total	*12,482*	*2,980*	*232*	*9,270*

[a] Ref. 2.
[b] In millions of pounds.

soil repellency or water repellency may also be required in some applications.

As the uses of textiles for architects and designers are explored in the discussion that follows, properties will be discussed only with reference to the elements that can guide the selection of specific materials. The uses of textiles in the built environment of interest to the readers of this article are summarized in Table 5, excluding apparel, and also those textiles (bed, table, bathroom) that are selected and controlled by consumers exclusively. Home furnishings comprise about two-thirds of nonapparel use of fibers. Fabrics for home furnishings other than floor cover-

Table 2. Commercial Man-made Fibers in the United States, 1984

Fiber	FTC Definition (in part)	Major Uses	First U.S. Commercial Production
Acetate	The fiber-forming substance is cellulose acetate; when not less than 92% of the hydroxyls are acetylated, the term triacetate may be used	Apparel	1924; Celanese Corp.
Acrylic	The fiber-forming substance is a synthetic polymer composed of at least 85% by weight of acrylonitrile units ($-CH_2-CH-$, CN)	Apparel; home furnishings	1950; DuPont
Aramid	The fiber-forming substance is a long-chain synthetic polyamide in which at least 85% of the amide linkages are attached directly to two aromatic rings	Industrial; military; ropes and cables; tires; FRP (composites)	1961; DuPont
Glass	A manufactured fiber in which the fiber-forming substance is glass	Curtains and drapes; FRP (laminates)	1936; Owens-Corning Fiberglass
Metallic	A manufactured fiber composed of metal, plastic-coated metal, metal-coated plastic, or a core completely covered by metal	Decorative filaments	1946; Dobeckmun Co. (Brunswick Corp.)
Modacrylic	The fiber-forming substance is any synthetic polymer composed of less than 85% but at least 35% by weight of acrylonitrile units ($-CH_2-CH-$, CN)	Pile fabrics; carpets and rugs; drapes; blankets	1949; Union Carbide Corp.
Nylon	The fiber-forming substance is a long-chain synthetic polyamide in which less than 85% of the amide ($-C-NH-$, O) linkages are attached directly to two aromatic rings	Apparel; furnishings; industrial	1939; DuPont
Olefin	The fiber-forming substance is any long-chain synthetic polymer composed of at least 85% by weight of ethylene, propylene, or other olefin units	Home furnishings; industrial; cordage	1961; Hercules Inc.
Polyester	The fiber-forming substance is any long-chain synthetic polymer composed of at least 85% by weight of an ester of a substituted aromatic carboxylic acid	Apparel; furnishings; industrial	1953; DuPont
Rayon	Manufactured fiber composed of regenerated cellulose	Apparel; home furnishings	1910; Avtex Fibers Inc.; American Viscose
Saran	The fiber-forming substance is any long-chain synthetic polymer composed of at least 80% by weight of vinylidene chloride units ($-CH_2-CCl_2-$)	Garden furniture; upholstery; public conveyances	1941; Firestone Plastics Co.
Spandex	The fiber-forming substance is a long chain synthetic polymer composed of at least 85% of a segmented polyurethane	Elastic fiber (apparel and undergarments)	1959; DuPont
Vinyon	The fiber-forming substance is a long-chain synthetic polymer composed of at least 85% by weight of vinyl chloride units ($-CH_2-CH\,Cl-$)	Industrial (nonwoven)	1939; FMC Corp.

Table 3. Properties of Man-made Fibers[a]

Fiber	Breaking Tenacity g/den[b]	Moisture Regain,[c] %	Effects on Heat[d]	Specific Gravity	Specific Qualities
Acetate, filament and staple	1.2–1.5	6.0	Softens at 205°C	1.32	
Acrylic, filament and staple	2.0–3.5	1.3–2.5		1.14–1.19	
Aramid					
Kevlar, filament	20–22	4.5–7.0	Dec. 482°C	1.38–1.44	High strength thermal stability
Nomex, filament and staple	4.0–5.3	6.5	Dec. 427°C		High strength thermal stability
Modacrylic, filament and staple	2.0–3.5	0.4–4.0	Shrinks at 121°C	1.30–1.37	Flame resistant
Nylon, filament and staple	3.0–9.5	4.5	Melts at 212–220°C	1.14	
Olefin (polypropylene), filament and staple	4.8–7.0		Melts at 163°C	0.91	Lightweight; strong
Polyester, filament and staple	4.0–9.5	0.4–0.8	Melts at 294–298°C	1.22–1.38	
Rayon, filament and staple	0.73–6.0	13	Dec. 177–240°C	1.50–1.53	Easy to dye; versatile
Spandex, filament	0.6–0.9	0.75–1.3	Dec. 149°C	1.20–1.21	Elastic
Saran, filament	to 1.5		Softens at 116°C; does not burn	1.70	Resistant to weather, mildew, and fire
Triacetate, filament and staple	1.2–1.4	3.2	Melts at 302°C	1.3	

[a] Ref. 3.
[b] Stress at which fiber breaks.
[c] Percent of moisture—free weight at 70°F and 65% rh.
[d] Dec. = decomposes.

ings are generally more similar to apparel fabrics and less technologically specialized than those developed for outdoor, industrial, or building applications. Aesthetic factors, economic considerations, and marketing play important roles.

INTERIOR FURNISHINGS

Textiles for Seating

These include upholstery fabrics for domestic applications (fixed upholstery or loose covers) and upholstery fabrics for contract use (4). In the first instance, the upholstered furniture must initially satisfy consumer demands as to aesthetics and comfort. Wear life and functional properties, as well as retention of appearance, are more important in upholstered furniture for contract use, where a life cycle of 5 to 10 years is frequently demanded, and such properties as flame resistance may be required to meet applicable standards. Materials used for seating upholstery (contract) are selected in this context. Fabrics commonly used for domestic applications are not suitable: stronger, heavier fabrics are generally back coated to provide dimensional stability, and treated with functional finishes to improve stain repellency, flame resistance, and other properties. A summary of preferred fibers and key properties for upholstery fabrics is shown in Table 6.

Window Textiles

Distinguishing "sheers" (sun filters) from drapery fabrics, it is important to note that the former is functional and

Table 4. Natural Fibers

	Breaking Tenacity g/den	Moisture Regain, %	Effects of Heat[a]	Specific Qualities
Cotton	3–5	6–8	Dec. 150°C	Too numerous to list
Wool	1.0–1.7	16–18	Dec. 130°C	Warmth, flexibility, and resilience
Silk	3.5–5.0	ca 11	Dec. 175°C	Strength and flexibility; luxurious appearance

Cellulosic Fibers			Mineral Fibers	Protein Fibers		
Seed fibers	Bast (stem)	Hard (leaf)	Asbestos	Silk	Hair fibers	Wool
Cotton	Linen Hemp Jute Ramie	Sisal			Alpaca Cashmere Mohair	

[a] Dec. = decomposes.

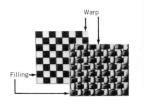

(a)

Common herringbone twill

Characteristic diagonal of the twill weave

Right-hand twills

Even $(\frac{2}{2})$

(b)

(c)

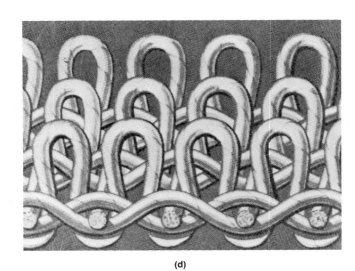

(d)

Figure 3. Fabric constructions. **(a)** Plain; **(b)** twill; **(c)** satin; **(d)** knitted. **(b)** Courtesy of National Association Wool Manufacturers.

Table 5. Uses of Textiles in Architecture

Interior furnishings	Seating fabrics (upholstered furniture); window fabrics (curtains and drapes); wall coverings, wall hangings; screens and room dividers; floor coverings
Outdoor and recreational	Awnings; outdoor carpets; sports surfaces; coated fabrics for pool covers, terrace awnings, and marquees
Buildings and industrial	Fabric structures as building materials and membrane structures; roofing

essentially "standardized," whereas the latter is an important decorative element. For the sheer nets used in close proximity to window panes, the preferred fibers are currently polyester or polyester–cellulose blends. Glass fabrics were popular for a time, but shedding of glass fibers in laundering as a result of fiber-to-fiber abrasion was a serious problem. Polyester sheers provide the desired laundering, dimensional stability, and smooth-drying properties. Blends with cellulosics may be used for special design effects by selectively removing the minor component fiber in processing (burn-out, etching). For drapery fabrics, decorative effects are dominant considerations and numerous fiber compositions and weaves have a place. Heavy fabrics are generally preferred; ease of coloration and texture are desirable. Cotton and cellulosics (acrylics, nylon, and polyesters) are widely used. The demand for flame-resistant materials has increased in recent years, and developmental fiber products are receiving attention for this reason (eg, modacrylics), even though there are no federal regulations governing drapery fabrics at this time.

Table 6. Upholstery Fabrics

Preferred Fibers and Weaves	Key Properties Required
Domestic Applications	
Fixed upholstery	
Rayon, flat weaves	Bright colors
Acrylic, velvet or pile	Colorfastness to light, gas fading, and crocking (rubbing)
Nylon, textured	Spongeability; stain resistance
Polypropylene, textured	Abrasion resistance
Wool, tweeds	
Loose Covers	
Cotton and cotton blends	Washability; dimensional stability
Stretch nylon, knitted	Abrasion resistance
Contract Use[a]	
Furniture manufacturers' specifications must be met and guarantees must be provided for long life cycle; numerous materials are used and changes are frequent	Abrasion resistance; light fastness; color fastness to light, fading, and crocking; resistance to seam slippage; flame resistance; stain repellency; spongeability

[a] Includes such uses as commercial, educational, and industrial.

Wall Coverings

Fabrics for wall coverings have enjoyed popularity in some areas. An interesting development in wall fabrics in western Europe has been that of suspending and tensioning fabric from ceiling to baseboard, after covering the wall surface with a liner or fill that helps with thermal and acoustic properties. The primary fabric can be removed easily for cleaning or replacement, and the gap between fabric and wall can be used to accommodate wiring. Wall covering fabrics as decorative elements have employed a broad range of materials, but recent awareness of flammability issues has cast some doubts on future exploitation of fabrics in this vein. Similar considerations apply in the case of wall hangings, which may range from individual handwoven tapestries to carpetlike structures of repeating pattern.

Floor Coverings (Rugs and Carpets)

The terms rugs and carpets are not interchangeable (5). A rug is a soft-surfaced floor covering, usually patterned, of a size to cover the greater part of the floor area in a room. Carpets are made of the same fibers as rugs but they generally have a plain surface, and they are cut to cover the floor from wall to wall. Carpets woven in wide widths to fit a room cross section are called broadloom. Rugs and carpets have a pile surface that can be characterized as cut pile: fiber ends stand vertically, or they are of tufted or twisted construction, with vertical loops of pile yarns as the wearing surface. This construction gives a floor covering that is heat retentive, absorbs noise, and is less tiring to walk on than are hard surfaces. For most homemakers, rugs and carpets are major textile purchases. The consumption trends of fibers for face yarns used in carpets is shown in Figure 4 (6) and actual U.S. total fiber use (1984) is summarized in Table 7.

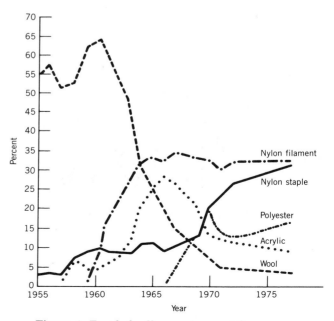

Figure 4. Trends for fiber use in carpet face yarns.

Table 7. U.S. Fiber use in Carpets and Rugs, 1984[a]

Use	Total Fiber[b]	Man-made Fibers[b]	Cotton[b]	Wool[b]
Total carpets and rugs	2287.7	2258.4	14.9	14.4
Face yarns	1976.5	1954.5	7.6	14.4
Backing	311.2	303.9	7.3	

[a] Ref. 2.
[b] In millions of pounds.

Traditional constructions of carpets and rugs, such as the one shown in Figure 5a, have little significance in the industry today. Both materials and manufacturing methods have changed dramatically with the advent of high speed tufting machinery. Tufting is done by punching extra yarns into a base fabric of desired weight and yarn content. Rows of needles, each of which carries yarn from a spool held in a creel, simultaneously punch through the horizontally held fabric to a predetermined distance. As the needles are withdrawn, hooks move forward to hold the loops, thus forming uncut pile. When cut pile is desired, knives that are attached to the hooks move in scissorlike fashion and cut the loops as the needles are drawn up. The fabric moves a predetermined distance forward each time the needles are retracted. The tufts of yarn are held in place by their own untwisting, and by the shrinkage of the ground fabric in the finishing process. In rugs, where there is much abrasion, the back is coated with latex to hold the tufts (Fig. 5b).

Tufting is extremely rapid and therefore economical. A rug can be tufted at about 645 yd^2/min. Both cut and uncut pile may be combined. Sculptured and textural effects can be obtained by controlling the depths of the individual needle punchings.

Economic benefits of high speed tufting have brought about widespread use of soft floor covering in hospitals, schools, and other public occupancies. Data available from the Department of Commerce for shipments of rugs and carpets show parallel trends for "total" and "tufted" types (Fig. 6). With increasing use and with increasing emphasis on functional properties, wear life, and economics on the part of users, the choice of fibers for face yarns has narrowed essentially as predicted by the trends shown in Figure 4.

Some features of pile fibers of major commercial utility include the following.

1. *Wool.* Good durability, springiness, colorfastness, moderately fire resistant, dry cleanable, water absorbent, subject to insect damage.

2. *Nylon.* Wear resistant, washable, resistant to waterborne stains, easily dyed in bright color, oil stains are difficult to remove, tends to static accumulation at low humidity.

3. *Modacrylic.* Approaches the wear and durability of nylon, somewhat less prone to static accumulation, flame resistant.

4. *Polyester.* Excellent durability, colorfastness, light fastness, subject to oily staining and to static accumulation.

5. *Olefins.* Stiff fibers used for athletic fields and indoor–outdoor carpeting, colorfast to sun and moisture, but subject to oil and grease stains, not resilient in recovery from load.

Rayon and cotton are not significant as pile fibers because of their poor resilience and durability as compared to other fibers.

In addition to pile fibers, floor coverings include backing fibers and fabrics as important components of the textile structure. Tufted carpets have a primary backing where polypropylene fabrics have captured about 80% of the market (replacing jute fabrics). For secondary backings, jute remains important. Backing products combining polypropylene and jute in various ways have also been developed. A small number of nonwoven backing of various types have been introduced.

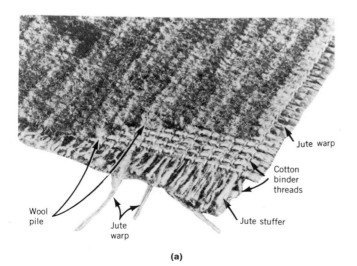

(a)

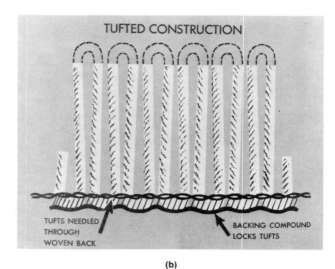

(b)

Figure 5. Carpet constructions. **(a)** Traditional woven carpet; **(b)** tufted carpet schematic.

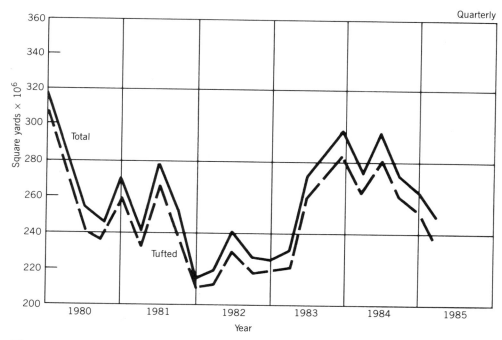

Figure 6. Rug and carpet shipments. The quantity of shipments represents rugs, carpets, and carpeting physically shipped during the period. Includes transfers to other divisions of the same company, such as sales offices. Excluded are products fabricated from carpeting or roll goods not produced in the reporting establishments. Courtesy of the U.S. Department of Commerce, Bureau of the Census.

The Issue of Flammability

Awareness of and concern with the issues of textile flammability and, more specifically, of the flame resistance of fabrics used in interior furnishings has increased dramatically after the amendment to the Flammable Fabrics Act was signed in December 1967. Fabrics used in interior furnishings became subject to regulation, and broader authority concerning promulgation of specific standards was granted to the Department of Commerce. Federal standards for surface flammability of carpets and rugs (DOC–FF–1–70 and FF–2–70), and for the flammability of mattresses (FF–4–72), became effective within a short time. Regulatory activity by state agencies was greatly accelerated. In the state of California (Bureau of Home Furnishings) stringent requirements apply to materials used in upholstered furniture, and the development of test methods that simulate fire hazard in interior furnishings has also been a factor in the response of industry to the pressure of regulation.

Currently, there is no federal standard specifically covering the flammability of fabrics for upholstered furniture, or window fabrics, but increasing awareness of the issues during the last decade has led to voluntary industry programs, and to more stringent specifications for materials used in commercial, public, or institutional occupancy buildings. The promulgation of federal standards regulating the entire item of upholstered furniture (as distinct from materials used in manufacture) has been discussed for many years. It is extremely difficult, primarily because the importance of materials' interactions and of design in flammability hazard cannot be adequately simulated in laboratory tests.

For floor coverings, the situation has been more easily evaluated and controlled. For domestic applications, compliance with the federal standard can be attained by employing wool, modacrylic fibers, or nylon in the pile. For carpets used in public or in high-rise buildings, compliance with more severe tests (eg, radiant panel tests) may be required, and additional specifications may be imposed by state or local agencies or by private organizations. In such instances, fibers treated with appropriate fire retardants, fire retardant backings, and other specialized materials in the carpets may be necessary.

Outdoor Textiles

The use of carpets for poolside, terraces, and other outdoor applications has been briefly mentioned in the context of floor coverings. The technology of fabrics for awnings is somewhat specialized because the outdoor exposure of the materials demands properties such as resistance to sunlight and water repellency, as well as strength and wear resistance related to the design of the structure.

The fabric used for awnings is canvas—or duck—a compact, firm, plain weave fabric with a weight of 8–50 oz/yd². Traditionally made from cotton or linen fibers, canvas fabrics for window awnings and similar applications are now manufactured from synthetic fibers as well. Awning stripe fabric, specifically used for awnings, beach umbrellas, etc, is generally a heavy, firm-woven cotton duck or canvas with either yarn-dyed or printed (or even painted) stripes in bright colors.

BUILDING WITH COATED FABRICS

With the exception of traditional canvas awnings for windows, fabrics considered as modern building materials are, in effect, specialty coated fabrics that combine the beneficial properties of a textile and a polymer—the textile component providing tensile strength, tearing strength, and elongation control, and the coating, protection against the environment to which the fabric is subjected.

Lightweight Structures

For many people, "building with textiles," or the use of coated fabrics in building constructions, is synonymous with air-supported structures or spectacular major projects such as the roof of the Olympic Stadium in Montreal. However, lightweight, load-bearing structures have also established themselves in areas that used to be reserved for more conventional structures and materials. The awning over a terrace and the marquee over the entrance to hotels or restaurants may be already considered as textile architecture. Textile roofings as weather protection over swimming pools or playgrounds consist of coated fabrics woven from high tenacity synthetic fiber yarns. There is thus a significant use of textiles in lightweight, plane, load-bearing structures consisting of flexible elements for everyday uses, in addition to the emerging opportunities for larger roofings where the emphasis is on tensile-stressed and pneumatic structures. The requirements of coated fabrics for these applications are diverse, less demanding than those of textiles for large roofings and membrane structures, but nevertheless more critical and specialized than in the case of simple window awnings.

Roofings and Membrane Structures

The first air-supported structures were erected in the late 1950s, but their important advantages were realized about a decade later when the economic value of erecting the structures at low cost in a short time and of dismantling them when required became an overriding factor (7,8). Furthermore, the advancing technology of materials for coated fabrics provided new opportunities (9). The history of major projects in the construction of flexible roofings from 1967 to the mid-1970s reflects technological progress, problems, and successful major undertakings, as well as the role of coated textile developments in the industrial world (10).

Tensile stressed and pneumatic structures in the United States, western Europe, and Japan have been characterized as air houses, large pneumatic structures, arched structures, and prestressed structures. Discussion of the design and engineering principles that differentiate the structures is beyond the scope of this article. However, these principles are important in the selection of the materials—including coated fabrics—used in each case.

The textiles must withstand the mechanical stresses of the structure, as well as climatic and environmental conditions; compliance with regulations is essential. In western Europe and in the United States, polyvinyl chloride (PVC) coated fabrics made from high tenacity polyester and polyamide fiber yarns have been used almost exclusively to date. From a technical point of view, yarns from polyester fibers are preferable to nylon yarns in prestressed constructions because of better dimensional stability under changing climatic conditions. The most important property of the coated fabrics is residual strength under loading for long periods of time. For example, the PVC-coated polyester fabric used for an air-supported structure in Europe (Bochum Radome) was found to have retained 90% of its original strength after eight years under actual service conditions (10).

Other properties that are important in the life of the coated fabrics depend also on the coating, and attempts have been made to replace PVC by other coating materials. A comparison of PVC-coated polyester fabric with Teflon-coated glass fabric for a "standard" air house has been made. The qualitative results shown in Table 8 provide an interesting example of the necessary trade-offs, and also an illustrative list of critical properties that must be evaluated in selecting the textile material. The structural properties of coated fabrics for membrane roof structures have been investigated and described in the literature (11).

The development of yarns from high tenacity, high modulus aromatic polyamide (aramid) fibers, and fabrics made from them, affords an opportunity to build air-supported structures of up to 350 m in diameter, while the technical limit for coated fabrics made from high tenacity polyester is a diameter of about 150 m (10).

A new opportunity for textiles in buildings is flat-roof covering with PVC-coated fabrics. In this roofing configuration, the coated fabric can replace part of the conventional bitumen roof covering. Coated fabrics offer advan-

Table 8. Qualitative Comparison of Teflon-coated Glass and PVC-coated Polyester Fabrics for an Air House

Fabric Appearance	Teflon-coated Glass[a]	PVC-coated Polyester[a]
		++
Tear strength		++
Dimensional stability	+	
Flammability	+	
Translucency		+
Seam strength	+	
Cleanability	+	
Processing		++
Flexibility		++
Chemical resistance	++	
Heat resistance	++	
Resistance to cold	+	

[a] + = somewhat better; ++ = distinctly better.

tages over nonreinforced films because of low shrinkage, higher strength, and lower elongation and may allow dispensing with the gravel layer in the traditional multilayered structure of flat roofings. While the requirements of coated fabrics for flat-roof coverings have been defined (8), the development of satisfactory materials has not been fully implemented to date.

Architectural Fabrics as Permanent Construction Materials

In 1982, silicone-coated glass fabrics were introduced commercially under the Vestar trade name. These are believed to represent the latest development in the evolution of permanent structural fabric technology, combining the strength and durability of fiberglass with the weathering properties of silicones. The materials meet the stringent requirements for classification as permanent construction materials and exhibit an excellent balance of properties including flexibility, durability, low weight, and translucency (12,13). These fabrics were used for the roofing of the gymnastics and fencing stadiums built for the 1988 Olympic Games in Seoul, Korea. The roofing of the Gymnastics Hall, with a clear span of 350 ft was not air supported, but it featured a novel cable and tension-ring support system. Both material and design thus reflect a significant advance in the technology of coated fabrics in buildings.

FUTURE TRENDS

The evolution of textiles for the home and office has been a product of the dramatic developments in the synthetic fiber industry after World War II. The new fibers and the technological progress of the textile industry have created a broad spectrum of materials that provides the consumer and the architect with a choice of style, performance, and cost. New fibers may be developed for special applications, but the principal thrust of future development in home furnishing is believed to be an increasing emphasis on functional properties and economics.

Building fabrics have come a long way during the last 15 years, and fabric structures are now considered a mature building technology. With the availability of new materials and design techniques, fabric structures are becoming attractive for permanent buildings as well as for the semipermanent structures where they are now considered with increasing frequency.

BIBLIOGRAPHY

1. *The Competitive Status of the U.S. Fibers, Textiles and Apparel Complex,* report of the Committee of the National Research Council, National Academy Press, Washington, D.C., 1983.
2. *Textile Organon* **56**(9), (Sept. 1985).
3. *Man-Made Fibers Fact Book,* Man-Made Fibers Producers Association, Inc., Washington, D.C., 1983.
4. M. O'Shea, "Interior Furnishings," *Textile Progress* **11**(1), 1–63 (1981).
5. G. H. Crawshaw, "Textile Floor Coverings," *Textile Progress* **9**(2), 1–72 (1977).
6. J. Labarthe, *Elements of Textiles,* Macmillan Publishing Co., New York, 1975.
7. P. W. Harrison, *The Design of Textiles for Industrial Applications,* The Textile Institute, Manchester, UK, 1977.
8. P. Bajaj, A. K. Sengupta, "Industrial Applications of Textiles," *Textile Progress* **14**(1), 1–30 (1985).
9. "The use of tensioned fabric structures by Federal Agencies," *Architectural Fabric Structures,* report of the Advisory Board on the Built Environment, National Academy Press, Washington, D.C., 1985.
10. H. Blumberg, "Building with Coated Fabrics. The Present Position and World-Wide Trends," in Ref. 7, pp. 137–159.
11. Y. Nakahara, *J. Text. Mach. Soc. Japan* **31**, 79 (1978).
12. *Vestar Architectural Fabric Systems,* ODC, a subsidiary of Dow Corning Corp., Norcross, Ga., 1985.
13. "ODC Fabrics to cover stadium for 1988 Olympics," *Dow Corning Materials News,* 5 (July/Aug. 1985).

GIULIANA C. TESORO
Dobbs Ferry, New York

THE ARCHITECTS COLLABORATIVE

The Architects Collaborative (TAC) has been a bellwether for many other U.S. architectural offices. Started immediately after World War II in a state of optimism to rebuild the world, it has grown from its original eight founders to be one of the largest architectural offices in the country. Many have emulated its dream of a collaborative way of working. Preserving the dream and retaining design quality at TAC through the vicissitudes of growth and outside influences over a long period of time has provided a test case that has been watched by others in the design profession.

Architects are not independent (although the myth of the genius–innovator–artist is still treasured and kept alive, both by the media and by the architects themselves). Through 40 years of practice, TAC's typical client has changed from a single owner–user to building committee to developer. The types of building needed have changed from housing to education to health facilities to tourist facilities to office buildings and mixed-use complexes. Opportunities for work in other countries have come and gone and will probably continue to do so.

When TAC was begun, elevator technology was well accepted (which made high-rise buildings possible), but air-conditioning was not universally expected (which meant that the form of medium-rise buildings was still influenced by dependence on natural ventilation). Computer technology has hastened the change from the industrial age to the information age, with the result that office buildings have replaced factories.

Through the period of TAC's existence the financial climate has gone from racing inflation to violent increases in liability costs; the social climate has changed from one in which the public ignored its surroundings to one in which intense community involvement is the norm; prevailing architectural design moved from the influence of eclecticism to functionalism to exploitation of modernism to historic preservation and postmodernism. Last, the psychological climate within the practice of architecture has gone from the exuberance that followed World War II to conservatism and business orientation.

These changes have affected architectural design and practice for all architects. Whether or not the original dreams of TAC and the influence of Walter Gropius have survived or grown can best be seen through the work of the office over the last 40 years.

BEGINNINGS

> The whole postwar-reconstruction problem—so vast and complex—hangs upon our ability to cooperate. The architect as a coordinator by vocation should lead the way—first in his own office—to develop a new "technique of collaboration" in teams. The essence of such technique will be to emphasize individual freedom of initiative instead of authoritative direction by a boss. Synchronizing all individual efforts by a continuous give and take of its members a team can raise its integrated work to higher potentials than the sum of the work of just as many individuals (1).

The Architects Collaborative began in 1945 with an idea. That idea was more concerned with a method of operation and with a set of ideals to be achieved than with formulas of design or specific solutions. Gropius summarized this in the statement above, written at about that time.

This was a time of great hope and great expectations. The development of technology was at a point where it could be turned to the advantage of all people. With the war over, this great potential could be put to peaceful use. In the United States, there had been a period of over 15 years with virtually no construction for basic human needs—housing, schools, hospitals, and commercial buildings. Certainly there was a need and the technology was available.

TAC was formed by eight partners: Walter Gropius, already a world-famous architect and chairman of the Department of Architecture at Harvard, and seven younger partners, all in their late twenties or early thirties. The younger partners were Jean B. Fletcher, Norman Fletcher, Sarah P. Harkness, John C. Harkness, Louis McMillen, Robert McMillan, and Benjamin Thompson. The collaborative process was not based on the concept of a group of specialists working together, each with a particular expertise to add to the whole. Rather, the TAC partners aspired to be generalists, interested in the whole scope of architecture, and they all had basically the same educational background.

The first bit of TAC's good fortune resulted from the competition for dormitories for Smith College, which took place just as the office was starting in the fall of 1945. About 250 architects entered the competition. The team of J. Fletcher, N. Fletcher, and Thompson won first prize, and S. Harkness and J. Harkness received second. Although the project was finally not built, the prize money ($3000 for first place and $2000 for second) was the financial base on which the office was started.

From the beginning, TAC established a procedure of regular Thursday office meetings for the partners to discuss business and design. The concept was not to establish design by committee but to have an active exchange of ideas on work at various stages of development. Final decisions, however, were and still are up to the principal in charge of the project.

HISTORY: 40 YEARS OF TAC

1945–1956

In reviewing TAC's work, it is interesting to note how early the first seeds of project types were planted and the length of time before the project type became a sizable percentage of TAC work. Sometimes the type of project had a definite life span, due to outside influences. A case in point was the design of school buildings, which came and went with the baby boom. Sometimes seeds that were planted earlier came to fruition when circumstances were appropriate. In the last few years, for example, office buildings have been a major part of TAC work; the first office building designed by TAC was built in 1958. Hospital work and buildings for health care, on the other hand, once TAC had made an entry into this highly technical type of work, became an ongoing background activity.

Housing was a major type of work in TAC's first decade, which is not surprising. Single-family houses were in short supply, and the G.I. bill enabled returning veterans to build. Gropius had already built his house in Lincoln, Massachusetts (now owned by the Society for the Preservation of New England Antiquities), but the younger partners solved their own housing needs and developed work for the new firm by planning and building Six Moon Hill, a community of 28 families in Lexington, Massachusetts. Although custom designed, Six Moon Hill houses shared common details and materials: "open plans" accentuated the concept of "space flow" and adapted to modern servantless living, large glass openings brought in the sun on south orientations, and neighborliness with privacy was achieved through site planning.

Six Moon Hill was followed by Five Fields, also in Lexington. A much larger development, Five Fields offered a variety of standard plans. Frugality of cost, functionalism for family living, and planning in relation to natural terrain and growth were guiding forces in both developments.

In 1955, the commission for design of the Hansa Apartment Block in the FRG was awarded to Gropius. Built with wall fillings of bomb rubble, the building was the first postwar project of many for Gropius in his homeland, and the first high-rise multifamily housing project for TAC.

By 1952, the baby boom had hit school age. For the next 10 years, the major work of TAC was in education—elementary, junior high, and high schools, followed by college and university work. Early beginnings in the field were the competition in 1946 for the Peter Thacher Elementary School in Attleboro, Massachusetts, won by TAC (later redesigned and built as the Peter Thacher Junior

High School) and the commission in 1949 for the Harvard Graduate Center. The Harvard Graduate Center program called for an economy of space that would be unacceptable today, but Gropius, as in his Bauhaus days, succeeded in bringing in artists and sculptors to work with the architects.

One of the most important projects in this first decade was the U.S. Embassy in Athens, Greece. With much attention to context, scale, program, and serviceability, the design was at the same time a contemporary interpretation of Greek classicism—a departure from bare-bones functionalism. Other early beginnings were projects for health care, community facilities, commercial facilities, and master planning.

1956–1966

By 1956, TAC was well established, and the following decade saw recognition and expansion. Gropius received the AIA Gold Medal in 1959, TAC received the AIA Architectural Firm Award in 1964, and *The Architects Collaborative, 1945–1965* edited by Gropius and the other TAC partners was published by Arthur Niggli, Ltd., in 1966 (2). The housing shortage was less acute, but the baby boom reached schools at all levels. Design of school buildings replaced single-family houses and became an increasingly large segment of TAC work. In 1957, the commission for the University of Baghdad (which had come through a former Iraqi student of Walter Gropius) started TAC's involvement in the Middle East.

This led, in 1960, to the opening of a TAC branch office in Rome under the direction of Louis McMillen. He was joined shortly by Robert McMillan and Richard Brooker. Louis McMillen returned to TAC Cambridge in 1962 and Robert McMillan left TAC in 1963 to start his own office. Richard Brooker took over the running of the office from 1963 until its closing in 1969. Major work in the Rome office from 1960 to 1962 was for the University of Baghdad. At its height, the combined architectural–engineering staff numbered over 200, which included more than 80 architects. Subsequent work in the Rome office included the University of Tunis, Tunisia; the School of Agriculture in Sousse, Tunisia; Kano Teacher Training College in Kano, Nigeria; and The Central Veterinary Laboratory and the Higher Teacher Training College, both in Bamako, Mali.

In 1958, the commission for the Pan American Airways Building in New York City was awarded to TAC, with Walter Gropius as principal, associated with Pietro Belluschi and Emery Roth & Sons. The building aroused controversy, but Gropius always maintained that crowding and congestion would be minimized by concentrating development immediately over the transit system. As early as 1952, TAC had consulted on design for the Michael Reese Hospital in Chicago, and in 1954 TAC's first health-related facility, the Overholt Thoracic Clinic in Boston, Massachusetts, was completed. With the commission in 1963 for work for the Children's Hospital Medical Center in Boston (a client relationship that lasted for more than 20 years), projects for health care became a major segment of TAC work.

TAC's design approach was typified in design for school buildings, where concern was with new advances in construction, materials, and program solutions. Schools were child centered, and planning followed educational theories promoted by Educational Facilities Laboratory (a Division of the Ford Foundation). As schools of 3000 students replaced schools for 600 students, the "house system" and "team teaching" replaced the old system of classrooms and corridors. Open plans replaced bearing walls, but the building form became typically more compact, multi-story, and urban. New departures in construction were the use of folded plate roofs (Hanscomb Elementary School, Lincoln, Mass., 1958–1960); use of Plexiglas skylights (the result of a 1947 research study for Rohm & Haas); developments in concrete technology, including "lift slab" (Northeast Elementary School, Waltham, Mass. 1953–1955), poured-in-place and precast concrete, and bush hammering or exposed aggregate finishes (New Trier Township High School, Illinois, 1962–1966); use of coffered concrete ceilings with integrated lighting (Academic Quadrangle, Brandeis University, Waltham, Mass., 1958–1960); use of laminated wood beams for large-span structures (Wayland High School Field House, Wayland, Mass., 1958–1960); and the first incorporation of an air-supported structure in a permanent facility (Forman School, Litchfield, Conn., 1962–1964).

A major change in office organization took place in 1964, when the partnership was changed to a corporation and a stockholder's group was created. With the exception of McMillan and Thompson, who had left the firm in 1963 and 1965, respectively, to start their own offices, the original partners became principals and new principals were added. These were Alex Cvijanovic (1964–present), William Geddes (1964–1978), Herbert Gallagher (1964–1975), Morse Payne (1964–1986), Richard Brooker (1964–present), Ernest Birdsall, comptroller (1964–1982), Peter Morton (1965–1986), and Roland Kluver (1966–present). Walter Gropius was elected the first president.

The first loss from the original group occurred with the death of Jean Fletcher in 1965. She had played a strong part in the development of Six Moon Hill and Five Fields, was instrumental in developing hospital work for the office, and had promoted the plan for incorporation.

By 1964, members of TAC were scattered in several rented spaces around Cambridge, Mass. To bring everyone together under one roof, TAC built its own office building at 46 Brattle Street, Cambridge. The building continues to serve as headquarters for the firm today.

1966–1976

The late 1960s and early 1970s were a time of social change. Environmentalism and the minority and women's movements were accompanied by antiwar demonstrations, riots, and vandalism. The baby boomers had come of age and were speaking out, but the elderly population was also increasing and disabled veterans were returning from the Vietnam War. Some of the effects on architecture were: requirements for defensive (vandal-proof) design, such as the "windowless school" (which TAC had always resisted); laws for government subsidized housing that required 10% of the units be accessible to the handicapped and elderly; and, after the 1973 oil crisis, the development and requirements for energy efficiency in buildings.

TAC work in housing was for the elderly (Baptist Home for the Aged, Columbus, Indiana, 1964–1967) and for multifamily use (Ely Park Housing, Binghamton, N.Y., 1969–1974). It also involved community planning (Redwood Shores, Redwood City, Calif., 1964–1966, Gropiusstadt, West Berlin, FRG, 1968–1970; Veterans' Housing, Oxford, N.Y., 1973–1979).

Although school construction had passed its peak, some of the most interesting schools designed by TAC were built in this period. Examples are the Bronx Intermediate School #137 (Bronx, N.Y., 1970–1976) and the Josiah Quincy Community School (Boston, Mass., 1970–1976). In both projects, design efforts were directed toward humanization and community involvement. College and university work continued, often with specialized buildings such as libraries (Bates College, Lewiston, Me., 1970–1973), buildings for the arts (Virginia Commonwealth University Performing Arts Center, Richmond, Va., 1972–1982), and athletic facilities (Ainsworth Gymnasium, Smith College, Northampton, Mass., 1973–1977). Work of the University of Baghdad went on, in spite of interruptions due to revolutions in Iraq. Work in health care continued with clients such as Harvard University Medical School, University of Minnesota, and Lahey Clinic in Burlington, Mass. Design of tourist facilities included hotels and resorts in Greece, Yugoslavia, and Iraq. Town and city planning and master planning included studies made for projects in the United States, Europe, and the Middle East. Commissions in Kuwait followed a visit by Louis McMillen with a "trade mission" of professionals and businessmen. TAC's involvement in the Middle East grew to more than half of the total office work, until it suddenly slowed down with the onset of the Iran–Iraq war in 1980.

Some of TAC's outstanding projects during this period were the Rosenthal Glass Factory (Amberg, FRG, 1967–1970), which received the Owens-Corning Fiberglas Corp. Energy Conservation Award; National Shawmut Bank (Boston, Mass., 1967–1975); the AIA Headquarters Building in Washington, D.C. (1969–1973); and the Bernardine Hotel Resort Complex (Piran, Yogoslavia, 1971–1976). TAC's own organization became more specialized with the establishment of the Landscape Department in 1965, the Interiors Department in 1968, and Graphics in 1977. Gropius stepped down from the TAC presidency after two years and was followed by J. Harkness, N. Fletcher, L. McMillen, Gallagher, and Payne, each for a two-year term, with the exception of Gallagher, who served for three years. Walter Gropius died in 1969.

1976–1986

In the period from 1976 to 1986, primarily due to outside influences, major changes took place both in practice and design. Fuel shortages that continued until 1978 stimulated "energy-conscious design," and grants from the Department of Energy (DOE) encouraged research in active and passive solar systems in buildings. Historic preserva-

tion had become a public trend, and rehabilitation tax credits (up to 20%) allowed and encouraged preservation projects for which, without these incentives, the financial risk would have been too great. Competition for architectural commissions was stimulated by the antitrust ruling of the Department of Justice, which disallowed standard fee setting as had been recommended in the American Institute of Architects' "Blue Book"; as a result, the AIA Convention in 1978 voted to allow "design-build" and advertising.

The practice of architecture was further confused by the combination of inflation and unemployment that went hand in hand in the 1970s. Architects everywhere became more concerned about office management and about architecture as a business. The AIA, along with other organizations, conducted courses on everything from management to how to conduct winning interviews; in 1984, a series of AIA conferences on "Power, Image, and Compensation" faced the issues. A greatly increased public interest in design and the built environment was expressed by community involvement in the design process; it was also accompanied in the 1980s by increases in professional liability insurance rates for architects of up to 400%. Last, in architectural design, postmodernism, perhaps originally started by Robert Venturi with his book *Complexity and Contradiction in Architecture* (3), had challenged the concepts of what had become conventional modern architecture.

TAC responded to the energy crisis by addressing the problem in large buildings. It was found that the greatest savings could be made through the use of daylighting, which reduced the need for artificial lighting and air-conditioning. But perhaps the greatest advantage of designing for daylighting was the pleasantness of the building. Outstanding examples of energy-conscious design by TAC are the CIGNA South Office Building in Bloomfield, Connecticut (1979–1984), and design for the Government Service Insurance System (GSIS) Headquarters Building in Manila, Philippines (1977–1980). At CIGNA, long office wings are separated by a skylit garden atrium; at GSIS, daylit "pods" of office space, with potential for natural ventilation, offset frequent brownouts.

During the downturn that affected most architects in the late 1970s, TAC's fortunes were saved by work in the Middle East. In 1977, a large commission was received for urban design and architectural components of the Master Plan for Jubail, a new city in Saudi Arabia on the Arabian Gulf. This high level of activity led to the opening of a TAC office in Kuwait and later in Baghdad. In the 1980s, the TAC staff reached an all-time high number of 380, with more than 100 architects working on projects for the city of Baghdad. At one time, 53 buildings were under construction for the University of Baghdad, with more in design. A large project for Baghdad was the redesign of Khulafa Street, which included design of new buildings as well as urban design of the street itself. Work continued even after the onset of the Iran–Iraq war in 1980, but was stopped in 1982 when the site for the Conference of Unaligned Nations was changed from Baghdad to Karachi, Pakistan. At this time, TAC's numbers were reduced by about 100, and except for work that continues in Kuwait, business development efforts were redirected toward work in the Far East and the United States.

In 1974, Howard Elkus participated in a trade mission to the Far East, as had L. McMillen to the Middle East. The GSIS in Manila, mentioned earlier, resulted from that trip, and work with Asian interests in the United States is ongoing.

A period of concentration in the design of office buildings was launched in 1973 when TAC won a national competition for design of the Johns-Manville Corp. World Headquarters to be built in the foothills outside Denver, Colorado. Completed in 1976, the building's gleaming aluminum skin and mirrored glass windows contrast dramatically with the rugged terrain of the Rocky Mountains.

A growing segment of TAC work is with real estate developers. A major project was Copley Place, Boston, for which TAC was master architect and planner with Urban Investment Development Co. (UIDC). Commissioned in 1978 and dedicated in 1984, it includes two hotels, retail and office space, a 9-cinema complex, housing, and parking. The development is built on air rights over the Massachusetts Turnpike, two railroads, a commuter line, and major city roadways. Extensive citizen review accompanied the planning process.

The office building of today is frequently built on speculation. Developers set the rules that will allow the most efficient and most flexible use of space. Because the eventual users are unknown, design of the building shell is separated from interior design, which comes later and may be changed with each new tenant. From the beginning, TAC's interest was in total design. Responding to the changed situation, the TAC Interior Design and Graphics departments increased their services in programming, office layout, planning for communications technology, and design of signage and graphics, both for buildings where TAC was the architect and for other existing spaces. In 1985 the office was commissioned to reprogram and redesign interiors of the AIA Headquarters Building in Washington, D.C., originally designed by TAC in 1969.

While the design of office buildings tended to be high-tech—a natural development in the modern movement—design of residential buildings or of buildings in old neighborhoods was influenced by the preservation movement. Rehabilitation of existing buildings such as the Prescott Mill in Clinton, Mass. (converted to housing, 1977–1982), or the Charlestown Navy Yard in Boston (to be converted to housing, hotel, and medical research space) reflected public recognition of the nation's heritage. In the Back Bay area of Boston, a historic area, new buildings such as Heritage on the Garden, a residential, retail, and office complex to be completed in 1988, followed height and setback rules set by the Boston Redevelopment Authority (BRA) and looked to its neighbors for design inspiration.

In 1976, TAC undertook a close examination of its management needs. After consultation with experts in management, TAC created a Policy Board, in 1977, to be responsible for long-range planning and design direction, while the president and specialized Board of Managing Directors took care of day-to-day affairs in personnel, technical services, finance, and marketing. TAC presidents in this time period were John Harkness, 1977–1984, and John Hayes, 1984–present. The Policy Board was chaired by Norman Fletcher, 1977–1984; John Harkness, 1984–1986; and Perry Neubauer, 1986–present.

By 1986, there were 18 principals, of whom 9 are members of the Policy Board on a rotating basis. Present principals are Richard Brooker, James Burlage, Sherry Caplan, Alex Cvijanovic, Royston Daley, Gregory Downes, Howard Elkus, Norman Fletcher, John Harkness, Sarah Harkness, John Hayes, Roland Kluver, Perry Neubauer, Leonard Notkin, Richard Sabin, John Sheehy, David Sheffield, and Malcolm Ticknor.

In the late 1970s and early 1980s TAC became increasingly aware of demographic differences and market forces within the United States. This led to the conclusion that to be a national firm, TAC needed to develop a West Coast presence. In 1985, TAC established an office in San Francisco under the direction of Burlage and Elkus. The West Coast staff was rewarded when they received a Progressive Architecture Citation in Urban Design for the redevelopment plan of the Near West Campus, Stanford University, in 1986. The history of TAC continues to be made with changing people and changing circumstances.

LOOKING BACK

The Architects Collaborative could be said to be the same age as the period of growth and acceptance of the modern movement in the United States. Although the principles of modern architecture had been demonstrated and promoted earlier (Gropius came to Harvard in 1937), they had not become reality until after World War II, at which time TAC was born.

The struggle for existence was acute in the early years, but virtually all the seeds for future work were laid in the first 10 years. The second 10 years saw major expansion and recognition, and a large segment of work in buildings for education. By the third decade, TAC had become one of the largest architectural offices in the country, and the earlier informalities of operation gave way to more defined structure and departmentalization, and commissions were international. The fourth decade saw greater attention being paid to systems of management within the office, a shift of emphasis from work in foreign countries to expansion of work in the United States, and a surge in design of office buildings and work with developers.

What remains of Gropius's teaching? What endures of the original TAC spirit? What about collaboration? The original search for new ideas for a new world has been replaced by a client-centered approach. Innovation occurs more often in refinement of the building skin and design for the office workplace than in invention at the large scale in building structure. If Gropius were alive, he would probably be intrigued by the new types of glass presently available and the use of CADD; he might be dismayed to see the prevalence of pitched roofs and dormer windows in TAC design, but he should be relieved to find that functionalism—in planning, structure, and all aspects of design—is still the wellspring of TAC work. Last, he would find that TAC members are convinced, through experience, of the validity of his maxim that "a team can raise its integrated work to higher potentials than the sum of the work of just as many individuals".

The following is a sampling of TAC's projects (Figs. 1–7).

Figure 1. CIGNA Corporation Office Building, Bloomfield, Connecticut, 1984. In response to energy conservation objectives, the design of CIGNA Corporation's suburban office building takes maximum advantage of daylighting technology. The headquarters facility serves 2200 employees and is organized around a 470-ft long multiuse atrium. Photograph by Steve Rosenthal.

Figure 2. The Heritage on the Garden, Boston, Massachusetts, 1988. The Heritage on the Garden is a luxury residential project overlooking the Public Garden in Boston. The winner of a city-sponsored competition, it relates to its historic urban surroundings and observes strict city guidelines. The mixed-use development also contains retail and office space. Photograph by Steve Rosenthal.

Figure 3. The American Institute of Architects Headquarters, Washington, D.C., 1973. The AIA Headquarters building was designed to be a subtle backdrop to the eighteenth-century brick Octagon House already occupying the site. The new structure is separated from the historic one by a pedestrian plaza. Photograph by Ezra Stoller/ESTO.

Figure 4. Rendering of the University of Baghdad, Baghdad, Iraq, 1957–1986. The University of Baghdad was originally commissioned in 1957 and includes academic, residential, recreational, and service areas for 18,000 students on 566 acres. The focus of the campus is a central plaza that includes student and cultural centers and faculty and administrative offices. The entrance to the University, an 80-ft arch, was Gropius's design and is meant to represent the open mind. Jacoby rendering.

Figure 5. Olin Arts Center, Bates College, Lewiston, Maine, 1986. This study and performance center for music and art contains the College art museum, a 300-seat performance hall, and a variety of studio, classroom, and faculty office spaces. The building is also a cultural resource for the surrounding communities. Photograph by Brian Vanden Brink.

Figure 6. Josiah F. Quincy School & Community Center, Boston, Massachusetts, 1976. The Quincy School, serving several inner-city neighborhoods, houses an elementary school for 820 students, recreation and public spaces, and community facilities that include a health center, "Little City Hall," offices, gymnasium, pool, theater, and library. Photograph by Steve Rosenthal.

Figure 7. Lahey Clinic Medical Center, Burlington, Massachusetts, 1980. This center brings together under one roof the diverse health care services of an internationally renowned medical institution, which formerly were delivered in ten different locations. A 200-bed acute-care hospital allows Lahey to provide inpatient care for the first time in its 50-year history. Photograph by Steve Rosenthal.

BIBLIOGRAPHY

1. W. Gropius, handwritten note.
2. *The Architects Collaborative, 1945–1965,* Arthur Niggli, Ltd., 1966.
3. R. Venturi, *Complexity and Contradiction in Architecture,* 1963.

SARAH P. HARKNESS, FAIA
The Architects Collaborative
Cambridge, Massachusetts

THEATERS AND OPERA HOUSES

A theater can be characterized as an assembly of persons to witness a commonly focused performing activity. The space may be a conventional theater, a square or street, or even an elaborately decorated performance environment, such as a carnival midway or amusement park. A necessary ingredient is communication, usually both visual and aural. The term theater comes from the Greek verb *theatai,* meaning to see, watch, look at, or behold.

The theater experience in its most basic form has always played a role in human culture. Here an historical survey of buildings built specifically to house performances is given and a discussion of design considerations is presented.

ANCIENT GREEK THEATER

The ancient Greeks disguised themselves and performed dances and rituals to the gods of nature. By the sixth century B.C. festivals in honor of Dionysus, the god of wine, took place every year in March. During these rituals, priests, accompanied by flute players and dancers, made sacrifices at an altar. In countryside villages, the rituals took place in a flat, open space. In Athens the *agora,* or open-air marketplace, was the site of these events. In the marketplace, there was reputedly a place called the *orchestra* (what we now consider a performance area) and wooden benches or scaffolding from which an audience could watch.

Temple and the Theater of Dionysus

At the time performances were being held in the marketplace, a temple and altar to Dionysus were being built on the southeast slope of the Acropolis. This is considered to be the first specifically constructed theatrical environment. At the time of Aeschylus (525–456 B.C.), a performance area was built in this precinct. The hill rising from the performance area enabled the spectators to sit and watch, at first on the ground or on small outcroppings of rock, and eventually on wooden seats built on the mountainside. Around the middle of the fourth century B.C., permanent stone seating was introduced to replace the wooden seats. The seating rows were circular, stepped tiers arranged in three galleries separated by horizontal aisles or crossovers. Each tier had a horizontal projection

of about 30 in. (76.2 cm) and a rise of about one foot (30.5 cm). The new permanent arrangement was called the *theatron* and had a capacity of 10,000–20,000. The lowest row of seats was occupied by the priests or other important persons. Behind the priests, the tribes sat in various sections of the same gallery.

The entrance for the spectators was through the open space between the *theatron* and the *scaena,* a building that served as a shelter for the performer and as a background for the performance space. There was no raised stage as yet.

Theater at Epidaurus

The Theater of Dionysus served as a model for other theaters throughout the Greek empire. One of the best-preserved structures is the Theater at Epidaurus, about 92 miles (149 km) southwest of Athens, built by Polycleitus the Younger in c 350 B.C. (Fig. 1). The Theater at Epidaurus, situated on a hillside, still retains its circular orchestra. (The majority of Greek theaters that have survived have been altered by the ancient Romans, who usually reduced the orchestra to a semicircle.) The plan of the theater consists of two galleries and has a seating capacity of some 17,000. Each row of seats has a horizontal projection of 30 in. (76.2 cm) and a constant rise of 13 in. (33 cm). The viewing distance from the farthest seat to

Figure 1. Last row from Theater at Epidaurus, Greece. Courtesy of Peter H. Frink.

the middle of the orchestra is approximately 200 ft (61 m). From the uppermost seat, a person speaking in a normal voice who is positioned at the orchestra can be heard quite distinctly.

HELLENISTIC PERIOD

Introduction of the Actor and the Development of the Scaena as a Stage

The introduction of the actor in Greek theater began during the Hellenistic period in the middle of the fourth century B.C. This made it possible to establish a dialogue between the actor and the chorus and to have, for the first time, the notion of conflict.

At the Theater of Dionysus at the Acropolis in Athens, the *scaena* was a long stone building that provided dressing spaces for the chorus. The wall of the structure coincided with a wall of the original temple to Dionysus that was later replaced with a new Doric temple farther back.

The addition of the actor into the theatrical performance required an architectural change to provide for it. To differentiate the chorus from the actor a platform, or *proscaena,* was added to the front of the higher *scaena* building.

The earliest examples looked very much like the street front of a two-story building with a one-story front porch. It is possible that the Greeks had such a building in mind when they constructed the *scaena.*

A typical scheme gradually developed for the design of the *scaena* and *proscaena.* The upper story of the *scaena* contained three to five large openings. These openings were usually filled with panels of painted scenery. The *proscaena* was composed of columns that supported the acting platform in a porchlike manner. Painted panels were often placed between the columns. The platform of the *proscaena* could be reached either from inside the *scaena* building, or often by ramps located at each end of the *proscaena* platform.

By the end of the Hellenistic period the four elements of the Greek theater had been developed: the orchestra, the *theatron,* the *scaena,* and the *proscaena.* Each of these elements was fully developed individually, but they were not completely incorporated into a fused theater design.

Development of the Odeum

Soon after the construction of the wooden seats at the Theater of Dionysus an odeum, or covered assembly hall, was built (446–442 B.C.) by Pericles. It had a sustaining wall around the seating area. The odeum, a structure about 170-ft (51.8-m) square, was used for musical competitions and provided room for chorus rehearsals. The odeum's position cut a small slice out of the seating area of the theater and was partially responsible for shifting the entire theater slightly off its natural axis. Some authorities maintain that the odeum was placed in such a position to provide a view of the performance area for those within the odeum. The odeum was burned in 86 B.C. by Sulla and little more than the outlining foundation wall remains today.

MAGNA GRAECIA

By the eighth century B.C., the large number of colonies that sprang up along the coast of southern Italy and Sicily became known as Magna Graecia. The Sicilian city of Syracuse became so powerful from shipping and commerce that it eventually became a rival of Athens.

The early Greeks brought their theater with them to the shores of Magna Graecia. There was a significant development of the popular comedy. They also brought their designs for the construction of the theaters. The earliest, best-preserved Greek theaters in Magna Graecia can be found in the Sicilian towns of Syracuse and Taormina.

The Theater of Taormina. Built high into the side of a hill overlooking the town of Tauromenion (Taormina today), with the view of the coast of Sicily almost all the way to Syracuse and snow covered Mount Etna in the background, the Theater of Taormina (Fig. 2), is a remodeled Greek theater. Very little remains from the original Greek theater built during the rule of Hieron II (275–216 B.C.). The Romans almost completely rebuilt it in brick during the time of Augustus, substantially changing its form to a Roman theater typical of the period.

The first tragedies and comedies were brought to Rome as adaptations and translations of their Greek sources in 240 B.C. They were usually performed on wooden stages.

In 154 B.C., the Roman Senate prohibited the construction of stone theaters in Rome, although seating was allowed in theaters built at least a mile from the city. By banning permanent theaters, the Senate sought to discourage people from spending too much time at theatrical presentations.

Odeum at Pompeii. After the defeat of Sulla in 80 B.C., a small covered theater, or odeum, was built to the front and east of the large theater (Fig. 3). This odeum, seating about 1500, was quite similar to the Greek bouletarians but without interior columns usually found in the Greek structures. It might be called the first, pure Roman theater.

The rectilinear enclosing walls contained the spectators, orchestra, and stage in a unified form with the extremities of the highest rows and cut off at each end. The entrances to the orchestra were vaulted, providing extra places for seating above them that, at least in later examples, was reserved for magistrates, tribunes, and the providers of the performances. Access to these spaces was by a set of narrow steps within the stage area but behind the vaulted side entrances. Four marble steps for the tribunes or other honored guests were placed below the steeply sloped *cavea* within the performance area, reducing its size.

Change in Emphasis from the Chorus to the Actor

With a decline of the chorus and the rise of the actor, an architectural change was also needed. In Pompeii in 75 B.C., the odeum was used as model to make changes in the larger and older theater. The stage was lowered to allow a better view for those sitting in the orchestra. The *paras-*

Figure 2. Theater at Taormina, Sicily, Italy. Courtesy of Peter H. Frink.

Figure 3. The Large Theater at Pompeii, Italy. Courtesy of Peter H. Frink.

caenae were then removed and vaulted, providing entrances at the ends of the stage for the actors.

Unification of the Theater Structure

It was also around this time that the *parodoi* were vaulted and the *cavea* was extended above and across the vaulted entrances. This can be seen at the theater at Fiesole, near Florence, built in 80 B.C.

Further changes were made to the large theater in Pompeii during the rule of Augustus who died in 14 A.D. A covered, vaulted corridor was built behind the second gallery, with doors leading to each of the five dividing aisles. A third gallery was built above the vaulted corridor, and the marble steps in the orchestra for the magistrates may have been added at this time. It is possible that the paradoi were uncovered until this time, and that the sweeping changes, unifying the theater into a single form, were made all at once.

It was also during this period that alterations were made to the theaters at Taormina and Syracuse. In the theater at Taormina, a corridor was constructed above and around the top of the *cavea* unifying the *cavea* structure with the tall *scaena* structure, as was done in Pompeii. In both Syracuse and Taormina, the stage and *scaena frons* were moved forward, cutting off the former access to the performance area through the *parodoi,* and thereby requiring the construction of tunnels to give access to the performance from outside the theater.

THE ANCIENT ROMANS

The first stone theater in Rome was built by Pompey in 55 B.C. It was built on level ground and was therefore one of the earliest theaters to be raised on a stone substructure of arches and vaults.

Ostia. The oldest purely Roman open-air theater in existence was built by Agrippa in Ostia. It is raised above the level ground on arches and vaults.

Odeum of Agrippa. In 15 B.C. Agrippa also built an odeum in the Agora of Athens, located approximately where the original dances to Dionysus were performed. The original auditorium could seat about 1000. It was probably built to replace the Odeum of Pericles, next to the theater of Dionysus, whose maze of interior columns interfered with visibility and general use. The Odeum of Agrippa was similar in form to the Greek bouletarian. The Romans, however, eliminated the interior supporting columns usually found in the Greek odea by tightly compressing the walls, shortening the upper tiers, reducing the size of the orchestra and stage, and strengthening the walls. These measures did not entirely succeed in Agrippa's odeum—the roof collapsed in 150 A.D. The Romans then reduced the size by half (from 1000 to 500 persons) and the span from 80 ft (24 m) to 40 ft (12 m). The building was burned by barbarians in 267 A.D. and a gymnasium was built on the same spot in 400 A.D.

Odea next to open-air theaters. The Romans as well as the Greeks often built odea near larger open-air theaters. They served not only as places for lectures and musical presentations, but could be used for rehearsals. The-

ater-odeum combinations can be found in Pompeii; Taormina; Syracuse, Italy; Lyons, France; and Corinth, Greece.

Prototype Roman Theater

By the time of Augustus, a definite form had been established. The *cavea* and the *scaena* were pushed together, reducing the Greek circular performance area to a semicircle. While access to the orchestra in the Greek theater was through open *parodoi*, it was now through vaulted passages below the *parodoi*. The seats for the tribunes and magistrates and the providers or producers of the play were in boxes above the vaulted entrances to the orchestra, while senators, members of the city council, and other distinguished guests were seated on the lowest tiers in the orchestra.

The stage of the Roman theater is low and deep compared to the Greek stage. The *scaena frons* is solid, richly decorated, and designed with three entrances in the front and one in each wall of the stage. The room behind the *scaena frons* became narrower, eventually serving only as a corridor connecting the large rooms flanking the stage.

The Greek theater played a role in Greek religion and was subsequently built in sanctuaries, always on the slope of a hill. The Roman performances catered to the taste of the public so their theaters were built on any good site. They were erected on level ground with substructures of arches and vaults, and on slopes of hills as were those of the Greeks.

The facades of the raised theaters were quite handsome and well-thought-out substructures consisting of ribs, arches, and vaults interlaced with exits, stairways, and corridors leading from the various parts of the building.

An awning protecting spectators from the rain and sun was often suspended over the *cavea* from masts cantilevered from the portico or walls surrounding the *cavea*.

A curtain was often suspended from the structures flanking the stage, dropped into a ditch behind the front of the stage at the beginning of the play, and raised at the end of the play by means of a systems of levers and pulleys. Smaller curtains were hung from the *scaena frons* and used to cover certain portions of it.

A slanted wooden roof was usually built high over the stage, the main purpose of which was to protect the curtains and the expensive statues and decorations on the *scaena frons*. It also served to visually focus the attention of the spectator to the stage.

Theaters built during the last century of the Republic became more standardized in plan and elevation. There was also a tendency to make everything more luxurious. The earlier theaters were often redecorated.

Vitruvius

In *The Ten Books on Architecture,* Vitruvius made definite rules for the shape, size, proportions, and orientation of the theater. He recommended, for example, that the theater face north or northwest partly to keep the sun out of the eyes of the spectators.

Vitruvius divided the orchestra into four equilateral triangles, the points determining the aisles, the center

Figure 4. Theater of Herodes Atticus, Athens, Greece. Courtesy of Peter H. Frink.

chord, and the edge of the stage. He also recommended that the stage be 5-ft (1.5-m) high so persons standing in the orchestra could see the stage.

Existing Examples

The Theater of Orange in France, built in 50 A.D. with seating for 7000, and the Theater of Herodes Atticus on the slope of the Acropolis in Athens (Fig. 4), built in 161 A.D. with seating for 6000, are among the better-preserved examples. Each was built against the slope of a hill, minimizing the need for supports to hold up the cavea.

Audience circulation patterns in both theaters are better developed than in the Greek theaters. Between each of the three galleries of the Theater of Orange is located an open aisle and a closed vaulted corridor with exits at each of the radiating aisles. These covered corridors lead to long, steep stairways at each end, and also provide a convenient place to run in case of rain as well as access to other rooms.

The theater of Herodes Atticus has no covered corridors. There is a single horizontal aisle dividing the cavea into two galleries leading to stairways located within the large masses flanking the stage.

The difficulty in providing access to the upper galleries in both of these examples is due to the theater's construction against a hill. It was easier to provide better means of access to the *cavea* in theaters built on flat ground. With the *cavea* raised on arches and vaults, the necessary stairs, corridors, and exits could be inserted between the supports.

Performer-Spectator Interrelationships

The visual contact between the actor and the spectator is intimate as is found in the Greek theater, for most of the seats. The *cavea* of Roman theaters, particularly the later ones, is steeper than that of Greek theaters, producing better sound and sight lines. The horizontal projection of the depth of the tiers of the Theater of Herodes Atticus is a narrow 25 in. (63.5 cm).

THE DARK AND MIDDLE AGES—MEDIEVAL THEATER

By the sixth century A.D. in Europe, with the attack of the barbaric tribes from the north and the decline of the Roman Empire, the classical theater, as performed in a permanent, single-purpose structure, almost completely disappeared.

Theatrical performance during the Dark Ages was maintained by the people through folk festivals, and by strolling players such as minstrels, vagabonds, mimes, conjurers, acrobats, jugglers, dancers, ballad singers, and animal handlers. The strolling players performed on market-day festivals or holy days, attracting crowds in the streets and the squares throughout Western Europe. The thirteenth century saw the introduction of puppet and marionette shows. With the increasing power of the church, public (versus court) theater not only found itself without patronage, but was condemned by Christian authorities.

LITURGICAL THEATER

Theater Performances in the Church

Around the ninth century the Catholic Church developed religious plays within the liturgy of the Mass. These plays were first performed on the steps of the altar. With a desire to place the story of Christ more realistically before its congregations, the church translated its religious history and dogma into a theatrical form. The plays produced by the church were known as mystery plays. The plays were originally written in Latin, but later translated into the language of the people.

Originally, everything was sung by soloists with a chorus and accompanied by the organ, but as the plays gradually grew away from the church, there was more speaking and less music.

Movement Out of the Church Structure

As the productions became more popular, they attracted larger audiences. The plays and the productions became more secular, and the productions used more special effects. As such, the church moved the productions to the steps outside the church but often performed them in a churchlike arrangement of the acting area, although the later dramas were sometimes performed in the round. Stationary settings were eventually built as well as a structure with a curtained platform.

The Center Stage. It is presumed that the center stage was the common staging technique for such events sometimes using a platform. When the back of the platform has a curtained tiring room for performers, this arrangement is sometimes called a booth stage. The Transverse stage is a special form of center stage. It is characterized by the separation of the audience into two parts that face opposite sides of a performing area. This staging arrangement fits into a narrow hall or a chapel, with royalty on one side and commoners on the other.

Transformation from the Sacred to the Secular

It is common to regard the Dark and Middle Ages (300–1500), between the decline of the Roman empire to the beginning of the Renaissance, as a discontinuous or missing period for theater architecture. This tendency is partly due to the absence of special, single-use buildings for theatrical performances. But churches, plazas, and streets became the theatrical environment of the time, and the roles of actors and spectators were interchanged at different moments.

THE RENAISSANCE THEATER

Rebirth of Interest in Ancient Greece and Rome

A new element in the Renaissance was an interest in perspective. There was also a great striving to learn how to present realistically the forms of nature as seen through the eyes of the artists. Both of these characteristics were to have a profound effect on theater structures of the period.

Fusion of Existing Theater Forms

The form of the proscenium theater structure as it is known today has its origins in the Renaissance, as a fusion of three already existing forms. The first form was the curtained hall with a simple, raised dais, as was used with the French farce, in which a raised platform was terminated by a simple back cloth painted in perspective.

The second form was suggested by Sebastiano Serlio (1475–1552). In *Architettura* (1551), he suggests a structure consisting of a raked set of tiers for spectators and a stage bound by rectangular outside enclosing walls. Part of the stage was flat and the rear raked slightly. On the stage was placed one of three sets of scenes, constructed of lath and plaster and painted in perspective, depicting a scene for a comedy, tragedy, or a satire.

The third form, influenced by Roman theaters, was the desire for a more permanent setting.

Development of the Proscenium Theater Form

Teatro Olimpico of Vicenza. The first covered theater in Europe was built in the city of Vicenza in 1580. Teatro Olimpico was begun by Andrea Palladio (1518–1580), and finished by Vincenzo Scamozzi (1552–1616) in 1583. Teatro Olimpico (Fig. 5) contains most of the elements of a typical Roman theater. It is about the same size (about 900 persons), and has a raised stage, an orchestra, and a set of raked tiers. The center of curvature is located in the center of the stage, instead of within or at the edge of the orchestra as found in the Roman theater, improving the actor-audience relationship.

The three doors in the Roman *scaena frons,* and the doors in each end of the stage found in the Roman theater prototype, have been retained in the Teatro Olimpico, although the central entrance has been given special emphasis by increasing its size, and by spanning the opening with an arch.

Perspective Vistas. The most significant new element in the Teatro Olimpico is the construction of vistas, in a forced perspective, at diverging angles behind each of the openings to the stage. They depict the street scene in Vicenza, are permanent, and are not meant to be changed.

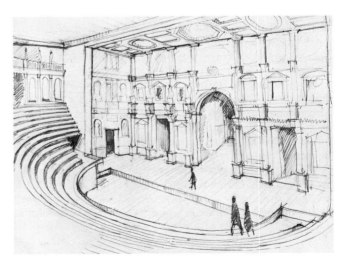

Figure 5. Teatro Olimpico, Vicenza, Italy. Courtesy of Peter H. Frink.

Circular Colonnade. A circular colonnade, solid in the middle and open in the ends, provides access to the cavea and encloses the *cavea* behind the last row of tiers in a manner similar to the enclosing colonnades or arcades about the last tier in the Roman theater.

The *cavea* is of wood. The *scaena frons* and perspective vistas are constructed of wood and brick and covered with plaster. The roof above the *cavea,* now smooth and painted, was once similar in appearance to the coffered ceiling above the stage.

Teatro Olimpico at Sabbionetta. In the small town of Sabbionetta, about 70 mi (110 km) southwest of Vicenza, Scamozzi built the Teatro Olimpico of Sabbionetta in 1588.

Fixed Vista Behind a Single Opening. In this theater Scamozzi combined the intent for the permanent setting of the Roman theater with the concept by Sebastiano Serlio in which a single scene in a forced perspective was erected behind the stage. This was done by widening the central door and eliminating (or combining) the other two doors on the Roman *scaena frons.* This resulted in a single opening behind which was built a single, permanent vista in perspective—similar to those at Vicenza—within which action could take place.

Scamozzi reshaped the Roman *cavea* into a sharp ∪ that left room on the flat ground floor for the placement of seats for spectators. The theater has a capacity of 350–400.

An open colonnade, similar to the partly open one in Vicenza, was built behind and above the *cavea* with the purpose of providing a gallery from which the stage could be seen.

Teatro Farnese at Parma. The third phase in the evolution of the Renaissance theater occurred in the city of Parma, not far from Vicenza and Sabbionetta, with the construction of the Teatro Farnese (often called the first modern theater), within the Pilotta Palace, by Giovanni Battista Aleotti (1546–1636), in 1618.

Creation of a Nonpermanent Setting. To allow for the possibility of changing scenery in a permanent structure, the acting area was pushed entirely behind the central opening. A curtain was placed behind what was to become known as the proscenium arch.

The front of the stage still retains the rectangular shape of the Roman stage and, while all but the central opening of the Roman stage front have been eliminated, there remains a subtle suggestion of the previous openings, with the general areas still flanked by engaged columns. The sides of the proscenium opening were designed in a forced perspective and the floor of the stage ramps upward to the rear.

Changeable Scenery. Instead of a permanently constructed vista or scene, the Renaissance theater designers learned the theories of perspective drawing to recreate these same visual effects by painting scenic perspective on a series of vertical, parallel flats. Since these flats were relatively light and movable, a large number of scenes could be switched by moving or sliding the flats into the wings of the stage.

U-shaped Cavea. Although the Teatro Farnese, with a capacity of about 3000 persons, is much larger than the Teatro Olimpico at Sabbionetta, both were built within similarly proportioned pre-existing enclosures, resulting in similarly shaped *caveas* in the form of a ∪ about a flat ground floor with galleries above. While the view of the stage from the *cavea* of the Teatro Farnese is not very good, the hall was also used for banquets and balls making convenient use of the flat space on the main floor. The ∪-shaped *cavea* was to become quite influential in the design of opera houses in Italy in the future.

Galleries. In the Teatro Farnese, the colonnade and galleries were above and behind the *cavea.* It was possible to provide three gallery levels, due to the size of the theater, whereas the Teatro Olimpico at Sabbionetta had only one. The splendid view of the stage from the galleries, as well as the subsequent increase in the capacity of the theater, were important advantages and influenced the design of the early opera houses in Europe. Access to the galleries is by means of stairways located between the *cavea* and the corners of the enclosing structure. The entrance to the main floor of the theater, as in Sabbionetta, is located at the central rear of the hall.

ELIZABETHAN THEATER

Form of the Early Theater

There are at least three theories on the form of the early Elizabethan theater. The first form was the hall stage, a simple curtained hall similar to that used with the French farce.

The second was characterized by a setting similar to that recommended by Sebastiano Serlio. This form was often used for court shows, particularly at universities.

The third form, and the most influential on opera houses built on the continent of Europe, was the structure used by the public theater.

The earliest Elizabethan public playhouses were little more than converted inn courtyards. Actors performed at one end of the open court while some spectators watched from the windows of surrounding structures that provided covered seats for those willing to pay more for admission. Other spectators sat on benches or stood in the courtyard surrounding the stage.

Specially Built Structures

The first specially built Elizabethan theater structures were found outside of London. The three most famous were the Swan Theater built in 1596, the Globe (the home of Shakespeare's company) built in 1600, and the Red Bull Theater, built in 1662. Although no plans of these structures exist, it is possible to obtain a fairly accurate description by combining rough sketches made at the time, written descriptions, and stage directions from the plays themselves.

The basic form of the theater consisted of an open court surrounded by a circular structure composed of perhaps three covered tiers or galleries. These were divided into individual compartments that looked out into the open court. The compartments for the spectators were connected by an aisle behind them. The shape of the play was square, as in the original inn yards; polygonal; or round, as in a bull-baiting ring.

A raised platform, placed against one of the inner walls, served as the stage. Undoubtedly the wall behind the platform was decorated, and probably was provided with one large central door and two smaller ones flanking it. Behind the stage were two levels of roofed performing areas that could be curtained off from the audience and used as entrances and exits as well as settings for small-scale interior scenes. A roof was probably placed over the raised platform and supported by carved and painted pillars.

Private Theaters

Later, private theaters were constructed along the same lines, but with roofs that covered the entire audience. Very little scenery was used because in the Elizabethan theater, the play and the acting company itself were the most important elements of the theatrical experience.

BAROQUE AND ROMANTIC THEATERS AND OPERA HOUSES

The forms of the performing arts as known today, have their roots in the Renaissance and the post-Renaissance periods. Music was a favorite feature of court entertainment, festivals, tournaments, and banquets during the fifteenth and sixteenth centuries.

Italian opera and ballet began to develop at the end of the sixteenth century. Both forms were performed indoors in palace banquet halls and formal outdoor gardens. For example, large casts enacted masques, allegorical plays for special occasions, using scenic design and mechanical effects, dance, singing, and procession. Around 1600, these productions gave impetus to the development of the proscenium stage in Italy that began to have influence in the other European countries. The rise of secular drama, with music often playing a secondary or decorative role, was also a prominent feature of the Renaissance.

While the aristocrats regarded early operas as a recreation of classical Greek theater, eighteenth-century opera could be more accurately characterized as dedicated to a secular exhibition of earthly delight. There was an emphasis on spectacle and the use of well-paid soloists. Theaters for opera were correspondingly elaborate. The productions existed principally for the wealthy classes.

The eighteenth-century opera houses were built specifically for music of contemporary composers including Glück, Hayden, and Mozart.

Development of the Opera House

The shape of the majority of opera houses built during the seventeenth, eighteenth, and nineteenth centuries is thought to have developed from the Renaissance and Elizabethan theaters.

In Italy and France at this time, there was a constant striving to achieve something new in theater design. Experimentation with theater form was divided into two schools. Some artists devoted their energies creating elaborate settings and sophisticated stage machinery; others strove to design seating arrangements that would best aid the spectators in viewing the performance.

Since buildings and scenery were often designed and built at the same time, their character was similar and usually quite extravagant. The proscenium arch can be seen as a visually transitional element, rather than a border. The development of opera, the elaborate scenic design, and the magnificent theaters was contemporaneous. Early stages were connected to the main floor with steps or ramps. The performers could descend from the stage and join the audience in dancing at the end of a performance.

Development of the Horseshoe-shaped Opera House

The first step in the transformation from Teatro Farnese of Parma to the horseshoe-shaped opera house was the elimination of the ∪-shaped wooden steps or tiers. In their place were several stories of superimposed galleries forming a cellular structure similar to the Elizabethan theater, but that extended from one side of the stage opening to the other in the ∪ shape similar to that of the Teatro Farnese.

The Molière Theater, constructed within the Palais Royal in Paris for Richelieu in 1640, combined a number of elements including the cellularlike walls of the Elizabethan theater and a hall and stage structure similar to the Teatro Farnese, but with the walls forming a trapezoidal shape. The hall was destroyed by fire in 1763.

A further improvement included the construction of galleries with parallel sides, but with the partitions between the compartments angled in an attempt to give the spectators a better view of the stage. This is illustrated by Teatro della Fortuna (1677), built in Fano by Giacomo Torelli (1608–1678).

A greater capacity was achieved by pushing the side walls out, creating a wider hall with more room on the ground floor and more room for a greater number of boxes. This is illustrated by the plan of Teatro del Falcone in Genoa, reconstructed by Carlo Fontana in 1702.

The bell-shaped plan of the interior of the Teatro Delli quattro Cavaglieri, built in Pavia in 1713 by Francesco Galli Bibiena (1659–1739) was created with a continuously curved structure of four galleries of boxes, with the partitions pointed toward the stage. The seating capacity is 1000. The main entrance to the orchestra floor is located at the rear of the well and leads to a central aisle. The galleries are supported on arches giving access to the entire perimeter of the orchestra floor. The stairs to the galleries are located in the rear corners of the building behind the boxes. The facade of the galleries has a vertical emphasis, defined by the visually dominant system of supporting columns and arches, resulting in an effect similar to that of the Teatro Farnese at Parma.

Stage House and Technology

Around 1640 a significant modification in the stage structure was introduced. Instead of the permanent or semipermanent scenery of the Renaissance theater, devices were invented for lifting (flying) the scenery into a space above the stage. Flying scenery, an extension of offstage spaces, slots in the stage floor for horizontal movement of wings, counterweighted machinery, and stage gridirons, were all major innovations.

Scenery

The scenery for the Baroque opera houses of the eighteenth century developed in England and Italy used exaggerated perspective views. The auditoriums were horseshoe-shaped with the proscenium openings often 32-ft (9.75-m) wide, and stage depths sometimes as much as 132 ft (40 m). The shape of the assembly envelope, combined with the one-point perspective, gave the best view in the auditorium to the patron seated front and center in an elevated royal box.

Teatro Argentina in Rome, designed by Girolamo Teodoli in 1731, was perhaps the first hall with a horseshoe-shaped plan, and was to become the pattern for the majority of opera houses. It was determined that the selection of a carefully proportioned horseshoe-shaped curve could enclose a large number of people close to the stage on the orchestra floor. Numerous boxes were angled toward the stage by carefully positioning the partitions between the boxes. There were a great number of variations in the proportion of the horseshoe from wide to narrow and probably equally as many schemes for constructing the ideal proportion.

Visibility was further improved by projecting the boxes slightly beyond the vertical supports. This device also tended to change the character of the facade of the galleries from a vertical emphasis (due to the dominance of the vertical members) to a horizontal emphasis.

Residenz Theater, Munich

A revolving stage was first installed at the Residenz Theater (der Hofgarten) in Munich in 1896 by Karl Lautenschläger (1843–1906). This stage was motivated by the need to shift the heavy three-dimensional settings which were replacing the wings and drops designed for movement by the chariot-and-pole system. The Residenz had been the home of Maximilian I (1597–1651) and then of King Ludwig I. The various buildings and courtyards are used for theatrical performances. Figure 6 is Im hof der Residenz where outdoor performances are held.

The Galli-Bibienas

From 1680 to 1780, the Galli-Bibienas were among the most influential theater architects and stage designers in Europe. The two sons of Ferdinando (1657–1743), Giuseppi (1696–1757) and Antonio (1700–1774), were the principal theater designers and architects. They played an important role in defining court theater design and the modern public playhouses, as well as establishing opera as a visual spectacle in Italy.

Teatro San Carlo of Naples. The earliest building of the Teatro San Carlo of Naples was built in 1737 from a design by Giovannio Antonio Medrano and Angelo Carasale.

Figure 6. Im Hof der Residenz, Munich, Germany. Courtesy of Bavaria-Verlag, Bildagentur, Munich. See also color plates.

It was rebuilt in 1810–1812 by Antonio Niccolini. The foyer was recently rebuilt, having been destroyed during World War II. It has six tiers of galleries arranged in the typical horseshoe plan. A royal box is located above the central rear entrance to the assembly hall.

Teatro della Pergola in Florence. In 1738, a new horseshoe-shaped well was built within the interior of the Teatro della Pergola in Florence after the original wooden structure was destroyed by fire. The current structure has a seating capacity of approximately 1500. The two upper rings of boxes were combined to form a larger single gallery around 1930 (Fig. 7).

The orchestra floor of most of the opera houses to follow was usually built above street level, and usually was reached by a central stairway from an entrance foyer. A central door at the rear of the auditorium, often under a royal box, led from the circulation space behind the auditorium to a central aisle. The rings were reached by stairways located in the rear corners of the circulation space behind the auditorium. In some opera houses, a class differentiation was maintained by allowing access to the upper rings or galleries by means of separate side stairs.

Teatro alla Scala of Milan. This well-known landmark that dominates the Piazza alla Scala was built in 1778 by Giuseppi Piermarini (1734–1808). With a seating capacity of approximately 3000, it is the largest opera house in Europe. The six rings of balconies, sweeping around the huge well, visually define this most impressive opera house (Fig. 8).

The most significant developments in the design of opera houses of the nineteenth century were the greater emphasis on the lobby, circulation, and public spaces; the

Figure 7. Teatro della Pergola, Florence, Italy. Courtesy of Peter H. Frink.

incorporation of larger balconies or galleries; and a monumental exterior massing and placement within the urban environment.

Theatre de l'Opera of Paris

Theatre de l'Opera of Paris (Fig. 9), built in 1876, was the largest in Second-Empire France. The entire design was conceived around the event of opera-going as a spectacular ritual. Architect J. L. Charles Garnier (1825–1898)

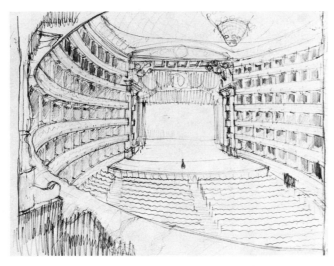

Figure 8. Teatro alla Scala, Milan, Italy. View of assembly envelope. Courtesy of Peter H. Frink.

Figure 9. Theatre de l'Opera of Paris, J. L. Garnier, Architect. Courtesy of Jacques Moatti/Explorer, Paris, France. See also color plates.

believed that the role of public architecture, especially theater buildings, was to provide an elaborate setting for the theater of life. According to Garnier, the assembling of several people became a theater event, people as actors in a human drama.

The sequence of the circulation movement into the assembly envelope becomes a series of progressive spaces—clearly expressed in exterior massing—from the ceremony of the arrival of carriages, to the auditorium itself by means of the monumental stairwell.

The public circulation and lobby space of the Theatre de l'Opera of Paris is at least nine times the area of the auditorium proper. The grand stairwell, seven or eight stories high, is larger than the well of the auditorium and is a much more impressive space. The auditorium pales in visual impact in comparison to these public areas. The monumental, gracefully curving stairway takes the theatergoer from the entrance lobby to the level of the orchestra floor. From the central stairway, the theatergoer can move to either side of the central well where the rings of the balcony are reached by means of double stairways separated by an elevator. The upper lobbies overlook the central stairwell at each level.

The Horseshoe-shaped Opera House

The horseshoe-shaped, Baroque opera house is an historical form that, although somewhat modified, continues to be replicated today. In its historic form of horizontal rings or galleries, the theater has seats at the sides with poor sight lines to the stage. The galleried opera house promotes the shared experience, reinforced by the support of the audience. The awareness of co-participants in the peripheral view of other participants creates a sense of togetherness. The horizontal rings or balconies of the historical, horseshoe-shaped opera house, however, do not always function as well as the orchestra.

If an assembly envelope is perceived by an assembly participant to be complete without the stage environment or with an act curtain in front of a stage setting, the performing activity might be defined as an event adjunctive to the assembly experience. While this experience may be effective or attractive, it may have little to do with what happens on the stage.

Bayreuth Festspielhaus

The origins of the form of the Festspielhaus go back to designs by architect Gottfried Semper (1803–1879), one of the leading architectural theorists and practitioners of his day. The Festspielhaus is principally the product of Richard Wagner and his theater consultant, Karl Brandt.

While theater plans by Semper were sent to Bayreuth by Ludwig II, king of Bavaria and Wagner's patron, for reference, Otto Brückwald (1841–1904) was selected as the architect for the Festspielhaus.

The individualized experience at the Festspielhaus was reinforced by incorporating the following physical elements, many of which have remained influential.

1. Use of continental seating (no center aisles) with public entrances from the sides of the assembly envelope.
2. Elimination of side boxes with poor sight lines.
3. Use of a generous floor slope for improved sight lines.
4. Diffusion of the prominence of the proscenium arch that became a series of eight house portals or wings.
5. Democratic seating layout.
6. Concealed orchestra pit to avoid a distractive separation between the audience and the performing area.
7. Darkening the theater for the performance.

Wagner conceived his operas as *Gesamkunstwerke*, a combination of dance, drama, and music in a large-scale production involving the participation of the audience. He was able to achieve an environment appropriate for this approach in the Festspielhaus at Bayreuth (1872–1876). The intent to promote the individualized experience was supported by a desire to dissolve the concept of the separation between the stage and the auditorium, and the desire to create a democratic arrangement of the audience with the elimination of physical separations within the audience.

New Construction Technologies

The Viennese architectural firm of Ferdinand Fellner and Hermann Helmer promoted the Italian-Baroque model.

The firm designed and realized approximately 50 theaters and opera houses throughout the world. The architects utilized the available architectural technology with changes in construction from wood to metal. For example, steel was used to construct cantilevered balconies. This period saw the common use of electric lights and hydraulic stage lifts.

TWENTIETH-CENTURY THEORIES

The end of the nineteenth and the beginning of the twentieth centuries saw the emergence of a reaction against the enlightenment of the seventeenth and eighteenth centuries characterized by concerns for reason, rationality, and the Western desire to "figure things out."

Even before the emergence of the cinema, there was an interest in evaluating the performing experience. As previously discussed, Wagner saw his creation of music-drama as more than an intellectual perception. While the Bayreuth Festspielhaus left the concept of the picture-frame stage intact, Wagner's vision was a transformation of the common experience of his time.

It is useful to look at the performing arts from the concept of phenomenology, or human experience that goes beyond the consideration of both objective reality and purely subjective response.

Sir Tyrone Guthrie (Irish; 1900–1971). It was the view of stage director Sir Tyrone Guthrie that adults do not submit to illusion in the theater. In an age when movies provided a ubiquitous illusion of reality, Guthrie contended that the live theater should stress the differences. His stated aim was "to present a ritual of sufficient interest to hold the attention of . . . an adult audience." He argued that an encirclement of the audience area in a greater degree about an open performing area placed an equal number of people closer to the performing area.

Adophe Appia (Swiss; 1862–1928). In the interest of a deeper reality, stage designer Adolphe Appia recommended that stage designers give up trying to represent the real world and instead convey mood, atmosphere, and emotion. Appia pronounced the stage picture to be a genuine work of the imagination rather than a flimsy representation of something else. He saw the play as something unique in its own being rather than the interpretation of a written script.

Gordon Craig (British; 1872–1966). Craig, who was a contemporary of Appia, held that the art of the theater was not the play or the drama, nor the acting or the scene, but the action itself. The spirit of acting, he believed, was composed of words as the body of the play; line and color as the very heart of the scene; and rhythm as the very essence of dance. Craig believed that a truly theatrical work is incomplete until it is performed.

The picture-framed proscenium, as does a frame around a representational painting, symbolizes the looking into a scene to observe a representation of something. The absence of a frame around an expressionistic painting results from the intent to promote the involvement or participation in the action of the painting itself. In the theater, this intent may involve the banishing of all forms of theatrical realism except the only one that may really matter, the emotional truth.

Antonin Artaud (French; 1895–1947). Artaud, a dramatist, wrote that the theater of illusion was characterized by a great gulf separating the world of the actor from that of the audience. The fiction, he believed, is that the play is like a slice of life that the audience, sitting passively in the dark, accidentally observes. According to this attitude, the play is controlled by the author, who creates his characters, the social message, or the poetry by himself, and who then presents them, via the actors, to the public. Actors, according to Artaud, need not be like ventriloquists' dummies.

Bertolt Brecht (German; 1898–1956). Brecht compared the actor to a witness giving an account of a street action. According to Brecht, once the pretense is given up that the stage is, or represents, a place other than a platform in front of an audience, there is no reason to preserve the proscenium.

Search for New Theater Forms and Technologies

The objection to the proscenium-framed stage continued into the twentieth century. The first steps involved the incorporation of the proscenium area as a performance area with the use of a deep extension of the stage apron.

The Hoftheater with a seating capacity of 1050, constructed at Weimar (1908) by Max Littman (1862–1931), incorporates an adjustable proscenium zone. The organizational form of its assembly envelope is characterized as a zero-degree encirclement arrangement.

Max Reinhardt (German; 1873–1943). Stage director Max Reinhardt experimented with new relationships between the performers and the spectators.

The Grosses Schauspielhaus

The Grosses Schauspielhaus was designed by the German expressionistic architect Hans Poelzig (1869–1936) for Max Reinhardt in Berlin in 1919. It was constructed within an existing structure for a circus that itself was remodeled from a still older public market. This project, with seating for approximately 3500, is an example of the concept of the creation of a "great room" as a complement to a theatrical event.

The design intent within the assembly envelope was to evoke the experience of the ancient Greek theater form where the action takes place within the audience space. To do this, an open stage was encircled on three sides by seating areas. A stage house with a proscenium arch was appended at the open end.

An optional replacement of the central platform with seating was conceived to allow the conversion of the assembly envelope into a proscenium form, thus creating perhaps the first multiple-form theater on a large scale. The scheme did not work well, however. The focus of most of the seats remained on the open stage area, regardless of

whether it was filled with seats or a performing area. The view into the proscenium frame was obstructed for a large number of seats at the sides. The enclosure of the assembly envelope with a dome (even with the added stalactite-like elements) created acoustic problems.

The importance of this building lies in its attempt to evoke the anticipation that something extraordinary awaited the audience that would cause it to lose its sense of reality.

THEATER DESIGN IN AMERICA

In the United States, the nineteenth century was characterized by the construction of theaters and opera houses, the designs of which were based loosely on nineteenth-century European theaters. There were no public subsidies for opera companies as in Europe.

Chicago Auditorium-Theater

Completed in 1889, designed by the Chicago architectural firm of Louis Sullivan and Dankmar Adler, The Chicago Auditorium-Theater was part of a mixed-use structure that included an office building and a hotel as flanking elements, combined with a 15-story office tower.

Seating a maximum of about 4000, this facility is a landmark, multiple-use theater on the basis of its well-thought-out innovations in technology. It is considered one of the most innovative American auditorium designs of the nineteenth century.

The theater envelope was designed with seating floor slope sections based on the iscidomal theories of John Scott Russell. A variable seating capacity capability was incorporated with the use of hinged ceilings that shut off flying balconies, and the use of a cutoff curtain. The innovative theater engineering made use of hydraulic water-powered stage equipment. The project included an on-site electric generating plant for lighting, forced mechanical ventilation, and an air cooling system. The design of the building required the use of structural engineering daring for its time.

Commercial Theater Boom in New York City

The beginning of the twentieth century brought a boom in the construction of playhouses in New York City with a peak between 1911 and 1928. The average seating capacity of the theaters that have remained into the middle of the twentieth century was about 1200. Since the theaters were built to make a profit, they included as many seats as possible, with only a minimum space set aside for the stage and lobby. The stages were often no deeper than about 30 ft (9.15 m), and the sidewalks were often the only place to gather at intermission.

The development of sound motion pictures provided entertainment for the masses at a fraction of the cost of a theater production, and eventually halted the construction of new playhouses around 1928. Many playhouses were converted into movie houses.

DEVELOPMENT OF MOTION PICTURES

Peep Shows

The Kinetoscope. This invention by Thomas Alva Edison (1847–1931) in 1889, consisted of 50 ft (15.25 m) of film that presented a one-minute silent film to an individual viewer. Edison originally intended to combine moving pictures with sound, but discontinued experiments with the Kinetophone following the success of Kinetoscope. The film presentations were sometimes referred to as peep shows (1894), and were available in penny arcades.

The Vitascope. Unveiled by Edison in New York in 1896, this advancement allowed for the projection of Kinetoscope images onto a wall. This technological change transformed the entertainment from a purely individualized experience to a shared experience with an audience.

Silent movies became such a popular entertainment that there was not always enough time to construct buildings exclusively for films. The early films were shown in the back of stores converted exclusively to show films. In 1905, the name nickelodeon was coined by Harry Davis and John Davis for their facility in McKeesport, Pennsylvania, as a combination of ticket price with the Greek name for a covered theater.

The Movie Palace

When attendance at movies began to decline, filmmakers needed to develop something different to maintain public interest. The store-show theaters with piano accompaniment were satisfactory for the working class, but not for the middle class. In 1914, the Strand Theater on Broadway in New York City began a new era of movie houses. While ticket prices increased from five cents to 25 cents, the price included an opportunity to hear a 30-piece orchestra and a Wurlitzer organ. This upgrade made movies more dignified. By 1915, in New York City going to a movie palace became as respectable as the legitimate stage.

In movie theaters during World War I (1914–1918), newsreels provided information, and were followed by entertainment. Hollywood movies with stars such as Charlie Chaplin, Mary Pickford, and Douglas Fairbanks, Sr., provided romance and adventure in contrast to the bad news from Europe.

The next decade, following the end of the war, was a period of unparalleled flamboyance and affluence. There was money to spend, things to buy, and time for leisure and mobility. The prosperity of the times made financing available for the development of the movie palace. Movie palaces were the most splendid structures many patrons had ever seen.

While silent films were popular, they were not trusted to stand on their own. Since they required a musical accompaniment, such as an orchestra or a theater organ, movies were considered only a part of the entertainment to be presented in the movie palace. The movie palace event often consisted of a Wurlitzer organ, an atmospheric architectural environment, an orchestra that rose out of a pit, musical numbers, dancers, vaudeville acts, captioned newsreels, musical solos, then the silent film.

Samuel Lionel Rothafel. Beginning with the transformation of a tavern owned by his father-in-law into a movie theater, Samuel Lionel "Roxy" Rothafel (1882–1936) began a career that led to his position as the maestro of the movie palace. In New York City (1914–1922), he was associated with such theaters as the Regent, Strand, Rialto, Rivoli, and Capital.

The Roxy Theater. Offered the prospect of building his own theater with William Fox, Roxy created his masterpiece—the Roxy. It opened in 1927, with a seating capacity of nearly 6000, and was designed by architect W. W. Ahlschlager with decorator Harold Rambusch. Roxy was concerned with every detail. The facility had a music library with over 50,000 scores, a hospital, five floors of dressing rooms, lodging for animals, and a radio broadcast studio.

Roxy was a master impressario. He recognized the public's hunger for spectacle and escapist shows, and provided a total environment for his audience. He put them in the mood for architectural, musical, and cinematic art. The patron public was considered a guest and was treated well.

Roxy recognized the importance of music with silent film. Music was considered more important to him than the movies themselves. A skilled and intuitive musical arranger, he scored the movie music himself.

Radio City Music Hall. A building lot in New York City, leased from Columbia University by John D. Rockefeller, Jr., was offered to the Radio Corporation of America (Fig. 10). Roxy was a natural choice to become director for planning a new theater. He resigned from his own theater to take on the challenge.

The new theater was designed by The Associated Architects, an organization that included Raymond Hood and Edward Durell Stone. The interior design by Donald Desky followed the Art Deco movement. The interior design is characterized by the elegant simplicity of a series of curved bands that reach down to become the proscenium opening. A seating capacity of about 6000 is organized on a large ground floor with three relatively short balconies. The stage was built with some of the most well-engineered theater equipment available.

The theater had an extravagant grand opening on December 27, 1932. By the end of performance at 2:30 A.M half of the audience had left. Roxy devised his show on the premise that silent movies were passé and offered classy vaudeville acts instead. The movies, sound films by that time, had since become the main focus.

Architecture of the Movie Palace

The seating capacities of movie palaces in larger cities averaged between 3500–4500, up to a limit of approximately 6000. Movie palaces in the smaller cities had seating capacities of approximately 2500. Until the arrival of sound films, theaters were built with the premise that the

Figure 10. Radio City Music Hall, New York, N.Y. (**a**) entertainment center's grand foyer. Dominated by Ezra Winter's 30 × 60 ft mural, "The Author of Life" which follows the sweeping curve of the stairway leading up to the mezzanines. (**b**) auditorium. Courtesy of George A. Le Moine and Radio City Music Hall. See also color plates.

silent film played only a part of a variety of entertainment. The theaters were built with stage houses with flying lofts, orchestra pits, and pipe organs.

The theaters commonly had very large balconies with low and deep overhangs. Larger theaters sometimes incorporated a loge—a small balcony tucked under the main balcony—that offered a special seating area and improved the sight lines from the rear seats of the main floor below.

Movie Palace Architects and Architectural Styles

Thomas W. Lamb designed more than 300 theaters during his career, beginning in about 1909. He was a Neoclassi-
cist and made extensive use of columns, domes, and arches. He later moved to the Rococo, the Italian-Baroque and Louis XVI styles, and followed with Hindu, Persian, Chinese, and Spanish influences.

John Eberson, also responsible for hundreds of theaters, created the atmospheric theater style. Beginning in 1922, in place of ornamented ceilings, he designed theaters with cloud machines and plaster sky ceilings with pin-hole stars arranged in accurate constellations. Once inside, the patrons would find themselves magically seated in a Spanish patio, an Egyptian temple, a Persian court, or an Italian garden, all with a romantic night sky above.

Construction costs were often lower for atmospheric theater because elaborate and expensive decoration was required only on the sides and around the proscenium frame.

The End of the 1920s and the Introduction of Talkies

By the end of the 1920s, the number of moviegoers began to diminish. The introduction of sound by the Vitaphone in 1926 by Warner Brothers was a business gamble by a company facing bankruptcy. Its unsuccessful debut at the Metropolitan Opera House in New York was in *Don Juan* with John Barrymore.

The Jazz Singer, the first "talkie" with Al Jolson, started a revolution in 1927 that saved the movie industry. The addition of sound transformed the film itself into a vehicle for the creation of an illusion of reality, characterized by the individualized experience. The Great Depression gave the movies an opportunity to relieve the existing worries. The experience of the cinema itself into a vehicle for the creation of a sense of illusion, reinforced with the provision of sound, did not need the support, nor could people often afford, the lavish escape of the movie palace.

POST-WORLD WAR II CULTURAL EXPLOSION

The period following World War II saw another cultural explosion similar to the one after World War I. There was a new boom in the theater construction in the United States as well as in Europe. The U.S. boom was characterized by a new increase in affluence and a more mobile population. The increase in new theater construction did not emerge from an experience in theater building design, however.

Civic and Cultural Centers

A number of larger cities planned and built multi-facility cultural complexes with three to five or more performing-arts facilities. Prominent among these were the Lincoln Center for the Performing Arts in New York City (1966), the Music Center in Los Angeles, Calif. (1971), and The Kennedy Center in Washington, D.C. (1966–1971). A number of medium-sized cities combined performing-arts facilities with sports and convention facilities.

Multiple-use Facilities in The United States

With the exception of the largest cities with major orchestras and full-time opera companies, the small-to-medium sized cities (30,000–1,500,000) could often afford to build and operate only a single theater or auditorium. To keep such a facility busy (100–250 performances per year), it became necessary for it to serve a variety of performing-arts uses, including drama, dance, opera, musical comedy, and orchestra concerts.

The facilities that worked best were often designed to incorporate an adjustable reverberation time, adjustability in the size and scale of performing area, a demountable orchestra shell, and sometimes an adjustable seating capacity.

Theaters for Colleges and Universities in the United States

Colleges and universities have served as a second major site for new performing-arts facilities. The institutions that have the strongest or most committed music and drama schools have often been able to provide single-use theaters for their arts programs. Other institutions have provided multiple-use facilities.

Motion Picture Theaters and Television

Around 1948 television began to compete with theaters and movie houses for audiences. The motion picture industry countered with technological changes that included wider and/or larger screens. Cinerama, originally a process that used three cameras and projectors and later one camera and projector; 70-mm film (Todd AO); and anamorphic lenses (Cinema-Scope) with standard 35-mm film, all were processes used to project onto wider and sometimes higher screens, and were usually combined with stereophonic sound, with the intent of giving the viewer a greater sense of involvement in the film. Motion pictures were also shown in three dimensions, requiring the wearing of special glasses with polarized lenses.

Some of the most recent large-screen ventures, commonly created for world fairs, include circular-screen theaters (using a number of projectors), and the very large-screen (up to 60 × 120 ft) Imax process and Omnimax.

A recent response to competition from the home entertainment industry is the multiple cinema (multiplex) facilities with an average of 4–12 theaters each with 150–350 seats. A greater variety of available films combined with a smaller audience for each allows for increased efficiency with the use of a common projection room, lobby and facilities, ticket booth, and refreshment stand, resulting in lower capital and overhead costs per film presentation.

The proliferation of the video cassette recorder (VCR) in homes in the 1980s, combined with video cassette rental stores, seems to have increased interest in movies, but has provided competition for viewing time. As the size of screens in theaters become smaller and that of television screens at home become larger, perhaps with high-definition television (HDTV), it is unclear as to whether or not the motion picture industry will need a new way to promote the viewing of films in theaters in the future.

EXPLORATION OF NEW AND OLD THEATER FORMS

Center Stages (Arena Theater Form) or Island Stage

While the center stage does not have a significant place in the history of drama, it was used in ancient Greece and Rome for the performance of sports and spectacles in coliseums, and continues to be used today for such events. As already mentioned, the center stage form was also used during the Middle Ages.

One practical reason for the choice of the center stage for drama, it has been contended, is that the theater may be cheaper to build, and may require the provision or construction of a lesser amount of scenery. The form has been popular with amateur and smaller theater organizations.

The credit for one of the first theater-in-the-round productions in the United States is usually given to the Teachers College of Columbia University in 1914.

In the 1920s and 1930s there was an increased interest in the center stage. The first permanent theater to be built as a center stage was the Penthouse Theater at the University of Washington in Seattle, Wash. in 1932. It was designed by Glen Hughes with a seating capacity of 172. The first professional company to use the central stage was formed in 1947 by Margo Jones in Dallas, Tex. The theater had a seating capacity of 198. The Alley Theater of Houston, Tex., with director Nina Vance, is a center-stage theater constructed within a fan factory.

Arena Stage, completed in 1961 in Washington, D.C. is one of the best-known modern examples of the center or arena stage. It seats 811, and was designed by Harry Weese for founder and director Zelda Fichandler (Fig. 11). The actors' access to the performing area that is independent of public circulation, is provided by means of vomitory passages through and under the seating area at the four corners.

Open Three-quarter-arena Form

As already mentioned, Sir Tyrone Guthrie played an influential role in the contemporary exploration of the three-quarter-arena theater form. Festival Theater at Stratford was Guthrie's opportunity to realize the theater form he had advocated. The first theater structure was covered by a tent, but was later transformed into a permanent structure. The three-quarter-arena concept that provided the first prototype for a renewed interest in this form, was worked out with stage designer Tanya Moisewitsch. It was completed in 1957. The actors' access to the performing area, independent of public circulation, is provided by means of two vomitory passages through and under the seating area.

The Tyrone Guthrie Theater (Fig. 12), at Minneapolis, seating 1437, provided a second opportunity for Guthrie and Moisewitsch to repeat and refine the lessons of the Ontario Shakespearean Theater with the help of architect Ralph Rapson. An unusual characteristic of the assembly envelope of this theater is the non-symmetry of its seating plan in which a balcony transforms itself into a steep, single floor at one side. This theater has served as a model for the three-quarter-arena form for over 25 years.

Pictorial-Open Theater Form

Some critics of theater shape and form have considered legitimate only the prototypical or historical forms (proscenium, arena, and three-quarter-arena).

There is a fourth form, however, that fits between the proscenium and the three-quarter-arena forms. Names given to this form include the pictorial-open, wide fan, hybrid, and thrust. This form has the potential of combining the best characteristics of the proscenium and three-quarter-arena forms while avoiding the limitations of both.

The pictorial-open form may allow for the creation of a degree of scenic magic associated with the creation of illusion, while keeping the audience close to the performing

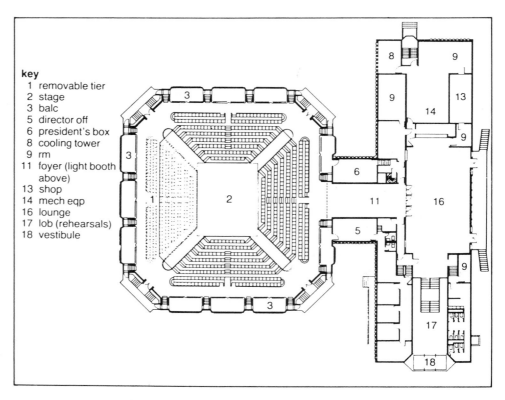

Figure 11. Arena Stage, Washington, D.C. Upper level plan, Harry Weese, Architect. Courtesy of Peter H. Frink.

key
1 removable tier
2 stage
3 balc
5 director off
6 president's box
8 cooling tower
9 rm
11 foyer (light booth above)
13 shop
14 mech eqp
16 lounge
17 lob (rehearsals)
18 vestibule

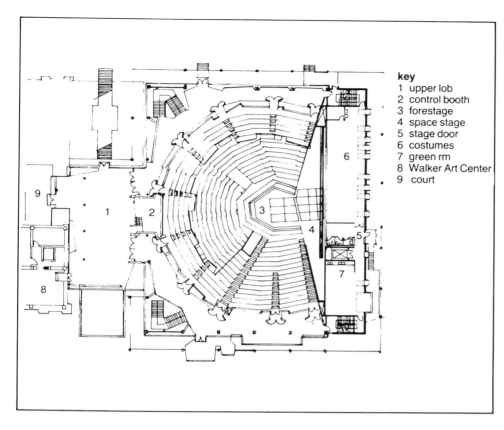

key
1 upper lob
2 control booth
3 forestage
4 space stage
5 stage door
6 costumes
7 green rm
8 Walker Art Center
9 court

Figure 12. Tyrone Guthrie Theater, Minneapolis, Minn. Plan of assembly envelope, Ralph Rapson, Architect. Reprinted by permission of Blackwell Scientific Publications Ltd., Oxford, England, *Architect's Data*, Neufert.

area. The 90–130° encirclement may lead to the dissolution of the picture frame and its two dimensionality. The seating encirclement corresponds to the binocular, peripheral field of view of an actor standing at a point of command within the performing area. This interrelationship allows a performer to see the entire audience simultaneously and, conversely, allows the entire audience to see the eyes of a performer simultaneously.

The greatest design challenge in the pictorial-open form is the transition zone between the audience and performing areas. The proscenium form consists of two rooms separated by the proscenium frame. The three-quarter-arena form consists of one room where both the audience and performing areas are located. The pictorial-open form invites the creation of a perceived sense of one room for both performers and spectators while also providing the flexibility of a second room for the containment of offstage support space.

Built-in adjustability at the boundary of the physical limits of the assembly envelope may be desired to avoid having to provide (and pay for) huge amounts of three-dimensional scenery or masking elements to fill the void space.

Norman Bel Geddes. Historical prototypes for the pictorial-open form are the theater projects (none were built) of the American designer Norman Bel Geddes (1893–1958). While his Intimate Theater projects of the 1920s suggest an effective performer-spectator interrelationship in plan, the vertical sections of his projects show problems that

would not have allowed them to work acoustically or technically.

Bel Geddes invariably used a dome as a three-dimensional enclosing element for the performing end of the assembly envelope. The exposed dome would have resulted in acoustical problems, and would have created problems for the closure of the scenic environment. It is not clear how technical support and stage lighting equipment were to be integrated.

The Olivier Theatre at the National Theatre of London (Fig. 13), completed in 1976, with a seating capacity of 1160, is a prominent example of the pictorial-open-form theater. The performing area is surrounded by a large flying loft, offstage space, and three wagon wings. The architect was Denys Lasdun.

The Olivier Theater does not have a built-in means of reducing the scale of the transition zone between the performing and seating areas. The vast, open stage requires the provision of large amounts of masking and/or scenery.

The New Alley Theater in Houston, Tex., the larger (800 seats) of two theaters in the facility, was completed in 1968. Working with theater founder and director Nina Vance, architect Ulrich Franzen provided a pictorial-open seating arrangement. The transition zone between the performing and seating areas was addressed by avoiding the provision of a large amount of flexibility by building a permanent stage setting.

Kreeger Theater was added to the Arena Theater facility in Washington, D.C. in 1968 by architect Harry Weese. The seating capacity of 500, organized on a main floor and

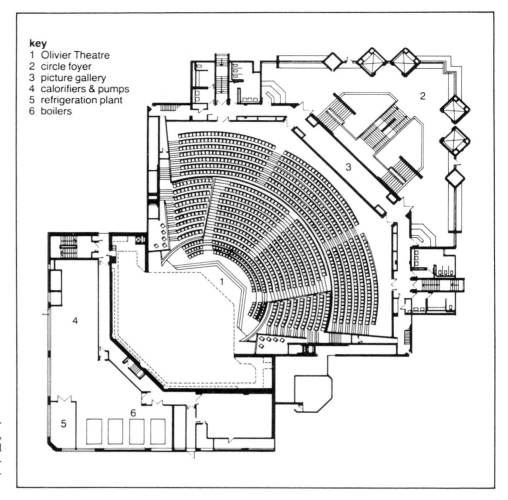

key
1 Olivier Theatre
2 circle foyer
3 picture gallery
4 calorifiers & pumps
5 refrigeration plant
6 boilers

Figure 13. Olivier Theatre, National Theatre, London, England, Denys Lasdun, Architect. Reprinted by permission of Blackwell Scientific Publications Ltd., Oxford, England, *Architect's Data,* Neufert.

a balcony, combines the pictorial-open seating organization with a stage flying loft.

Multiple-form Theater

An alternate approach for those not wanting to make a permanent commitment to a specific theater form is the mechanically adjustable, multiple-form theater. As already described, the Grosses Festspielhaus in Berlin was an attempt by Reinhardt and Poelzig to provide a multiple-form facility. The failure to make a corresponding adjustment in the orientation of the seating that related to the shift in the location of the performing area, did not provide a workable solution, however.

The Total Theater. Proposed by Walter Gropius during his Bauhaus days, this project is well known as an attempt to create a true, multiple-form theater. This project, assisted by stage director Erwin Piscator in 1926, transformed seating and performing areas of the three prototypical seating arrangements by means of a turntable.

The performer-spectator relationships of each of the three arrangements are somewhat contrived compared to prototypical fixed designs. Convenient performers' access to the performing area in the open theater arrangements seems not to have been considered.

The Loeb Drama Center. This theater, with a seating capacity of 600, is among the best-known existing examples of a multiple-form theater. It was completed in Cambridge, Mass. in 1960 by architect Hugh Stubbins and theater consultant George C. Izenour. The change-over system involves splitting and rotating seating banks, the height of which is adjusted by means of powered lifts.

The project does not provide a method of allowing actors to reach the performing area independent of the audience circulation. Access is commonly done by means of actors' vomitories in the fixed three-quarter theater.

Vivian Beaumont Theater. This multiple-form theater in Lincoln Center, New York City was built over the anxiety of its theater consultant, Jo Mielziner, who has written that he recommended the construction of a single-form theater. What was built is a very good three-quarter-arena theater backed up by a large stage house. (This is a small-scale version of the arrangement at the Grosses Schauspielhaus in Berlin, already discussed.)

As originally built, a change-over between the proscenium and three-quarter-arena forms was done by the use of seating wagons, a lift, and a turntable. This mechanism interchanged the front third of the seating area between two differently shaped seating banks, one of which incorporated a thrust stage. A problem with this arrangement is that the fixed seats at the sides maintain their focus within the auditorium, and the view into the stage house is not good.

An alternative solution might have been to establish a fixed performing area that is a compromise between the thrust and proscenium arrangements, and to reshape the seating slightly to match. The result would have been the pictorial-open theater form already discussed.

ANALYSIS AND DESIGN CONSIDERATIONS

The size and design of theater and opera-house facilities today depends on a number of factors including the cultural role in the society, the nature of the operation, the ownership, and the seating capacity of the facility.

CULTURAL ROLE—GERMANY VERSUS THE UNITED STATES

Theaters and Opera Houses in Germany

Theater-going plays an important role in German lifestyle. An evening at the theater, opera, or concert, while always regarded as a special occasion, is not a once-in-a-lifetime event, but is a normal, free-time diversion that has not seemed to have suffered from competition by television or the movies. It is not surprising, therefore, that this country has a greater number of major theaters, opera houses, and concert halls per person than any other country. Towns with as few as 30,000 inhabitants can usually boast of at least one major theater facility of some sort. The theater in Germany, as in other European countries, is supported by the state and/or city government. This fact, however, is only partially responsible for the large number of theaters. Equally important is the observation that the citizens are usually proud of their city theaters, a part of the cityscape and consider them to be as necessary as the city hall.

The nearly total destruction of German cities during the World War II either partially or completely destroyed most of the theaters. In less than a decade, however, not only did the Germans rebuild the center of every city, but rebuilt them with some of the finest theaters found today anywhere in the world.

The seating capacity of the average German theater–opera house is approximately 1000. The size of the average performing-arts facility is over 1,000,000 ft^2 (over 100,000 m^2) or close to 1000 ft^2 (100 m^2) per seat. Most of these facilities have backstage support spaces for the construction of scenery, rehearsal rooms, and large storage areas.

Theaters and Opera Houses in the United States

In comparison, the construction and operation of theaters and opera houses in the United States is diverse. There is a parallel operation between the commercial theater (perhaps best known as the Broadway theater) and nonprofit theater organizations. The capital cost for nonprofit theaters is typically financed by private philanthropy (donations, etc.) or public philanthropy (public taxes and bonds). The capital cost of theater buildings for the live performing arts cannot be financed practically by a portion of ticket sales. Developers for new theaters and opera houses are usually independent, nonprofit organizations formed for the purpose of operating a center, cities or municipal authorities, educational institutions, cultural institutions such as museums, and sometimes performing-arts groups themselves, such as professional repertory theater companies, opera companies, and orchestras.

The wide spectrum of developers leads to a divergence in facility size. The size of the total theater facility in the United States varies approximately from 20 ft^2 (1.9 m^2) per seat to about 120 ft^2 (11 m^2), with an average of approximately 63 ft^2 (5.9 m^2) per seat. The extent of backstage support for scenery construction, storage, and rehearsal area varies greatly depending on the role of the facility—from a roadhouse for outdoor shows to in-house production of theater programs.

PERFORMING AREA WITHIN THE ASSEMBLY ENVELOPE

Size of the Performing Area

The performing or acting area (distinct from the total stage area including offstage wing and upstage spaces) is the limit of the area capable of being seen by the spectators simultaneously. The appropriate size of the performing area is determined by several factors.

The number of performers on the stage at one time is one determining factor. On the one hand, a scene from a major production of *Turandot* at the Metropolitan Opera in New York, for example, is reported to have had 286 performers on the stage at one time.

On the other hand, a two-character play taking place in an intimate stage setting may not be perceived as natural if the scale of the scenic environment is the same size as a setting for 286.

Scale of Scenic Environment. Even if a stage space is intended for a single use such as drama, the possibility for flexibility in the size of the performing area is useful for a repertory that includes Shakespeare's *Richard III,* for example, and an intimate, two-character play.

Table 1 indicates the range of performing area sizes for various types of performing activities.

Table 1. Performing Area Sizes (Not Including Offstage Support Space)

	Minimum		Average		Maximum	
	ft^2	m^2	ft^2	m^2	ft^2	m^2
Lectures	150	(14)	240	(22)	500	(46)
Revue, nightclub	350	(33)	450	(42)	700	(65)
Legitimate drama	250	(23)	550	(51)	1000	(93)
Dance	800	(74)	1200	(112)	1800	(167)
Musicals	800	(74)	1200	(112)	1800	(167)
Symphonic concerts	1500	(139)	2000	(186)	2500	(232)
Opera	1000	(93)	2500	(232)	4000	(372)
Pageant	2000	(186)	3500	(325)	5000	(465)

SEATING AREA

Seating Capacity of the Auditorium

In a pure sense, the size of the audience, or seating capacity, is a consideration independent of the size of the performing area. Financial considerations may, of course, dictate against an opera setting with 286 performers in an assembly envelope with a seating capacity of 500.

Table 2 indicates the range of seating capacities for theaters in the United States.

Larger capacity halls may result from the need to keep ticket prices within a range the audience is willing to pay. A larger capacity may also result from the need to accommodate a given enrollment at an educational institution.

Need for a smaller capacity may arise from the expectation of attracting a smaller audience or preferring to present more than one performance of a given activity. Practical considerations of distance can dictate against a use of a very large theater for drama, where facial features and the unamplified voice needs to be communicated.

A user group that may attract a small audience at one performance will not want their patrons to find many empty seats, this giving the impression of a less-than-successful event.

Multiple-capacity Facilities

To keep performing-arts facilities as useful and busy as possible, localities and institutions have been provided with theater facilities that incorporate a variable seating capacity. The simplest method of achieving a multiple-capacity facility is by not using a balcony. Other methods include organizing the seating and circulation with cross aisles and controlling the house lights for rear sections. Masking walls and movable (flying and/or hinged) house ceilings that visually (and sometimes acoustically) cut off balconies from the seating below also have been used.

Size of the Seating Area

The size of the audience area portion of the assembly envelope is a function of the product of the seating capacity times the seating efficiency in area per seat. While the seating area including aisle widths of up to approximately 44 in. (112 cm) will range from 6–7.5 ft^2 (0.56–0.70 m^2) per seat, an area per seat for the audience area portion of the assembly envelope of 9–10 ft^2 (0.84–0.93 m^2) will allow for room-shaping, acoustic adjustments, and other requirements.

PERFORMER-SPECTATOR INTERRELATIONSHIPS— HORIZONTAL PLANE

Seating Row Arrangements

The multiple-aisle seating pattern, the most common in the United States—as defined by many building codes—is characterized by row lengths of 14 chairs separated by aisles at both ends, and row lengths of 7 chairs with an aisle at one end. Row spacing is typically 32–36 in. (81–91 cm). Maximum efficiency (minimum area per seat) with the multiple-aisle seating is achieved by maintaining one aisle per 14 seats. This arrangement lends itself to rectilinearly-shaped envelopes the widths of which are multiples of approximately 30 ft (9.15 m). An internal circulation with longitudinal aisles leading to public lobbies at the rear of the assembly envelope works efficiently.

The Continental seating pattern, so-called because of its common use on the European continent, is characterized by longer, continuous rows of seats extending between aisles and exits at the side walls of the assembly envelope. Building codes (and ease of patron access past seated persons) dictate row spacings of 38–42 in. (97.6–107.6 cm). Continental seating allows more design flexibility in the overall shape of seating area (fan or circular) without sacrificing efficiency, by maintaining the permissible maximum number of seats per aisle. Even though wider row-spacing may allow access passage in front of a seated spectator, longer rows do not appeal universally to theater patrons in the United States.

Continental seating may require a larger public lobby circulation system because of the need for access both at the sides of the assembly envelope in addition to an entrance lobby.

The long, anonymous rows can promote the individualized experience resulting from a loss of a sense of place, thus encouraging attention to the performance. In contrast, the multiple-aisle seating arrangement can promote the shared experience by giving the spectator more clues as to where he is located within a room where the performing activity may be perceived as an adjunct to the theater-going event.

Many building codes in the United States permit hybrid or modified continental seating patterns characterized by row lengths from 18–30 chairs with row spacings from 35–38 in.

Performer-spectator Interrelationships

An empirical approach to the design of performer-spectator interrelationships is to reproduce historical theater forms. This approach may be characterized by a choice between the proscenium, three-quarter-arena, or the arena (theater-in-the-round) theater forms.

An analytic approach is to choose a trade-off (for a given seating capacity) between the degree of encirclement (the angular relationship between the performing area and the spectators at the front sides of the performing area) and the distance between the stage and the

Table 2. Theater Facility Sizes in the United States

Capacity	Theater
35–75	Classroom
75–150	Lecture room, experimental theater
150–300	Large lecture room, small theater
300–750	Average drama theater in educational setting
750–1500	Small commercial theater, repertory theater
1500–2000	Medium–large theater, large commercial theater
2000–3000	Average civic theater, multiple-use hall
3000–6000	Very large auditorium
Over 6000	Special assembly facilities

farthest viewer. The *angle of encounter* is the measurement between a performer, standing in the middle of the performing area, and the spread or surround of the audience area. *Simultaneous facial encounter* is achieved when a performer, standing at a point of command on the stage can see the entire audience at one time. The binocular, peripheral field of view for the human is about 130°.

Flexibility in the size of performing area is easier to achieve with less encirclement. The size of the performing area is fixed with a 360° encirclement. Horizontal movement of scenery is easier to accomplish with less encirclement and is impossible with 360° encirclement.

Encirclement—Theater Forms

Encirclement, an analytical definition of historical or empirical theater forms, is a measurement of how completely the audience area surrounds or envelops the performing area.

Zero-Degree Encirclement. In zero-degree encirclement (proscenium stage, picture-frame stage, end stage), the angle of audience spread in front of a masking frame is determined by the maximum amount of the corner cutoff from a rectangularly-shaped performing area that can be tolerated by the seats at the side (Fig. 14). The audience area does not fill the angle of encounter from the point of command, resulting in the audience being farthest from the performing area. This theater form offers the largest amount of flexibility in the size of the performing area. Physical relationships provide for a large amount of scenic wall surfaces without masking sight lines. Horizontal movement of scenery can be made both perpendicularly and parallel to the centerline. There is a possibility of a short difference in arrival time between direct and reflected sounds at the spectator that may be beneficial for music performances.

90–130° Encirclement. In 90–130° encirclement (pictorial-open stage, wide fan, hybrid, thrust stage), the audience spread is defined and limited by the angle of encounter from the point of command (Fig. 15). The shape of the performing area may be trapezoidal, rhombic, or circular.

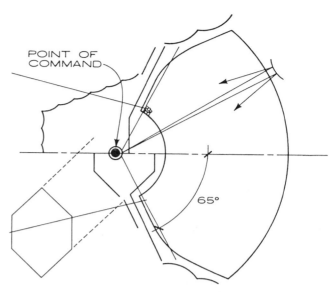

Figure 15. 90°–130° encirclement plan. Reprinted by permission of John Wiley & Sons, Inc., *Architectural Graphic Standards,* C. G. Ramsey and H. R. Sleeper, 8th ed., 1988.

The audience is closer to the performing area than in zero-degree encirclement. The picture frame may be less dominant. There is some flexibility in the size of the performing area. The provision for some amount of scenic wall surface is possible without obscuring the performing area. Horizontal movement of scenery is possible in directions at 45° along the centerline. The shape of the seating area places a maximum number of seats within the directional limits of the sound of the unaided voice, a benefit for speech performance.

180–270° Encirclement. In 180–270° encirclement (Greek theater, peninsular, three-sided, thrust stage,

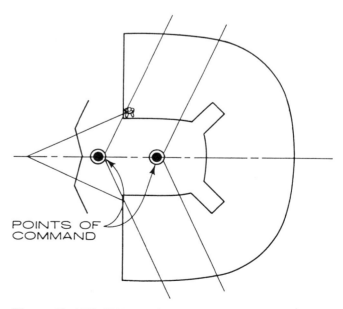

Figure 16. 180°–270° encirclement plan. Reprinted by permission of John Wiley & Sons, Inc., *Architectural Graphic Standards,* C. G. Ramsey and H. R. Sleeper, 8th ed., 1988.

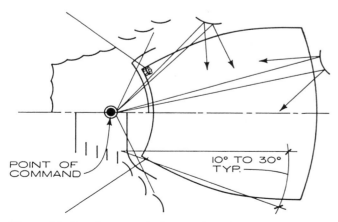

Figure 14. Zero degree encirclement plan. Reprinted by permission of John Wiley & Sons, Inc., *Architectural Graphic Standards,* C. G. Ramsey and H. R. Sleeper, 8th ed., 1988.

three-quarter arena, Elizabethan stage), the audience spread is well beyond the angle of encounter from a point of command to bring the audience closer to the performing area. Simultaneous eye contact between the performer and all spectators is not possible. There is a minimum flexibility in the size of the performing area. Only a minimum amount of scenic wall surface is possible without masking sight lines. Horizontal movement of scenery is possible along the centerline. The large encirclement by the seating area usually demands actors' vomitory entrances through or from under the audience (Fig. 16).

360° Encirclement. With the 360° encirclement (Arena stage, theater-in-the-round, island stage, center stage), the performer will always be seen from the rear by some spectators. Simultaneous eye contact between performer and all spectators is not possible. The audience is closest to the performance. There is no flexibility in the size of the performing area. There are no scenic wall surfaces possible without obscuring the view of the performing area. Horizontal movement of scenery is not readily possible. Total encirclement by seating area demands actors' vomitory entrances through or from under the audience (Fig. 17).

Multiple-form Theater

Black box, experimental, or studio theaters are intended for those not willing to commit to a permanent choice in degree of encirclement or theater form. These theaters have been designed and built to allow a transformation from one form to another. The theater architect, however, will face the balance between the three Cs: changeability, commitment, and complexity–cost.

Changeability. Theater-users often request that the assembly envelope offer a maximum degree of flexibility. The type of flexibility in mind often relates to the wish to change the type or degree of encirclement in the specta-

tor-performer interrelationships. This can be called the desire for flexibility, or changeability.

Commitment. A second concern among theater users is the desire for the theater to be a committed space. Most theater users are interested in the assembly envelope being well designed and with architectural characteristics that support the intended theater design concept, such as good conditions for seeing and hearing. Some theater-users say that they are less interested in flexibility or changeability than in the availability of a wonderful, workable, and efficient place in which to work.

While there are some requests for uncommitted spaces, this may really be a request for changeability. Assuming that a space can be designed to satisfy a particular arrangement, it is difficult to see why as much commitment as possible to that particular arrangement would not be welcome.

Complexity and Cost. Theater-users are sometimes anxious over complicated conversion equipment systems that may result in high installation and maintenance costs. The desire for great changeability, however, while having great commitment to a given arrangement, will result in the need for greater complexity and/or cost.

The choice of a simpler changing system will usually require another choice involving a trade-off between the degree of changeability and the degree of commitment to a particular arrangement.

Side Stage Adjustability

The relationship between the seating at the front and the performing area becomes the critical design consideration for theaters that incorporate the need for variability in size of the performing area.

Adjustability at the sides of the performing area in front of the structural proscenium opening offers opportunities for architectural shaping, side stage lighting, natural acoustic reflections, side entrances for actors to a thrust or apron stage, and extended (caliper) stage uses (Fig. 18).

PERFORMER-SPECTATOR INTERRELATIONSHIPS— VERTICAL PLANE

Vertical Sight Lines

Sight Line Geometry. The average height of the eyes of a seated person above the floor of a seating tier is 44 in. (1.12 m) with a 7-in. (18-cm) deviation. The head clearance is the vertical distance between the eyes and the sight line from the row behind (C_1 in Fig. 19). The distance from the eyes to the top of the head is about 5 in. (12.7 cm) (C_2 in Fig. 19). A viewing sight line for a given row is the line from the eyes of the seated person—44 in. (1.12 m) above the floor—through a point at the head clearance distance above the sight line of the row in front. The point where the sight line from the worst row intersects a plane, 2 in. (5 cm) above the stage, is called the arrival point of sight (APS) (Fig. 19).

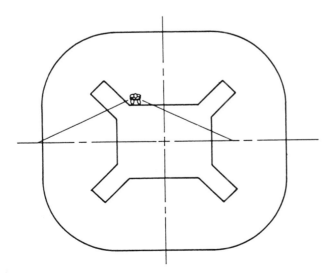

Figure 17. 360° encirclement plan. Reprinted by permission of John Wiley & Sons, Inc., *Architectural Graphic Standards*, C. G. Ramsey and H. R. Sleeper, 8th ed., 1988.

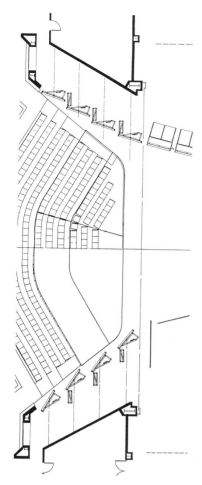

$$R = \frac{T}{D_1}\left[E_1 + (N-1)\,C\right] + C \qquad R = \frac{T}{D_B}\left[E_B + (N-1)\,C\right] + C$$

$$D_1 = \frac{T}{R-C}\left[E_1 + (N-1)\,C\right] \qquad D_B = \frac{T}{R-C}\left[E_B + (N-1)\,C\right]$$

$$E_1 = \frac{D_1}{T}(R-C) - C\,(N-1) \qquad E_B = \frac{D_B}{T}(R-C) - C\,(N-1)$$

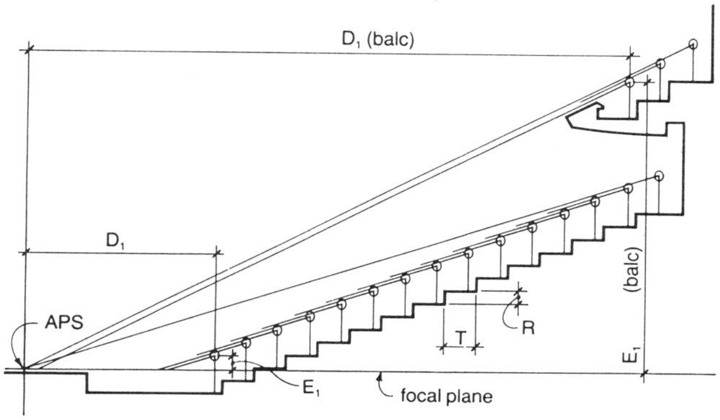

Figure 20. Constant rise floor slope. Reprinted by permission of Blackwell Scientific Publications Ltd., Oxford, England, *Architect's Data*, Neufert.

ceptable to see between the heads of the row directly in front, allowing a shallower floor slope.

Stage Height. The maximum stage height, resulting in the shallowest floor slope, is slightly below the eye height of a seated person in the front row or about 42 in. (1.07 cm), corresponding to an APS at 2 in. (5 cm) above the stage floor. If and as the stage height is reduced—improving relationship of the front rows to the stage—a correspondingly steeper floor slope is required. If the APS is at a height above the eye height of the first row, the resulting shape of the floor slope will be a reverse curve.

The closer the APS is to the first row, the steeper will be the resulting floor slope.

Constant Rise Floor Slope. The design of a seating floor slope with a constant rise per row results in the sight lines from each row being parallel. To allow those in the last row to see to a given point (APS) on the stage, it is necessary to give each subsequent row in front a better-than-required view of the stage (Fig. 20)

Iscidomal Floor Slope. The design of the floor slope generated by having all the sight lines of a given seating bank pass through a single focal point, or the APS, results in a floor that is exponential in shape. The row risers increase in height the farther the row is from the APS. The iscidomal floor slope will permit the last row of a seating bank to be at a lower elevation than with a constant rise floor slope, assuming the APS is at the same distance from the front row (Fig. 21).

Balconies

A balcony is a useful consideration in an assembly envelope with a seating capacity of greater than 500.

Advantages. Some seats can be closer to the stage as a result of the overlap. Balconies create three-dimensional

Figure 18. Side stage adjustability plan. Courtesy of Peter Frink.

Every-row vision floor slopes incorporate a head clearance of 5 in. (12.7 cm) over the row directly in front.

Every-other-row vision floor slopes incorporate a head clearance of 5 in. (12.7 cm) over the second row in front or 2.5 in. (6.35 cm) over the row directly in front. This arrangement, the most common system, assumes it is ac-

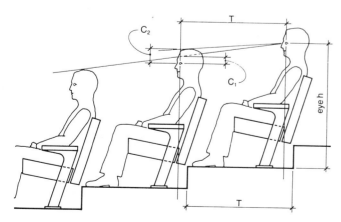

Figure 19. Typical seated spectator. Reprinted by permission of Blackwell Scientific Publications Ltd., Oxford, England, *Architect's Data*, Neufert.

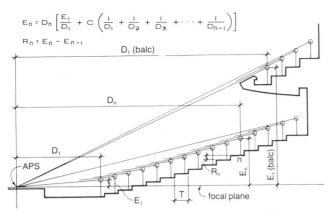

$$E_n = D_n \left[\frac{E_1}{D_1} + C \left(\frac{1}{D_1} + \frac{1}{D_2} + \frac{1}{D_3} + \cdots + \frac{1}{D_{n-1}} \right) \right]$$

$$R_n = E_n - E_{n-1}$$

Figure 21. Iscidomal floor slope. Reprinted by permission of Blackwell Scientific Publications Ltd., Oxford, England, *Architect's Data,* Neufert.

complexities within the envelope that may increase the shared experience among participants. A balcony may allow the facility to have a smaller footprint as a result of the overlap of both seats and lobby spaces, and/or control or projection rooms.

Pitfalls. Balconies with too great a depth or overhang for the height at the front can shade the natural sound to seating underneath, isolate sections of audience, and block sight and sound lines to the top of proscenium opening. Second balconies may be interpreted as second-class seating, conflicting with a democratic ideal. Second-class status can be avoided by using the same standards for row spacing, sight lines, and seating furniture used for orchestra seating.

Three short balconies with six rows may be preferable to one balcony with 18 rows. A short balcony may seem to be more intimate because there are fewer heads in between the spectator and the stage.

The maximum slope or rake is about 30°, the equivalent of three step risers per row.

Flying balconies, open to the assembly envelope behind, may allow a greater overhang without shading the reverberant energy to the seating underneath (Figs. 22–26).

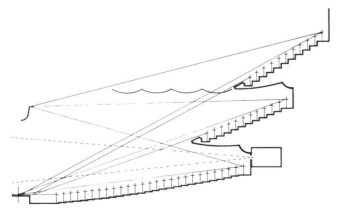

Figure 22. Longitudinal section—two attached balconies. Reprinted by permission of Blackwell Scientific Publications Ltd., Oxford, England, *Architect's Data,* Neufert.

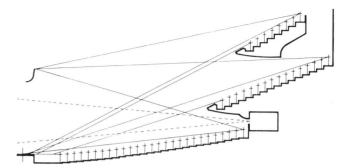

Figure 23. Longitudinal section—lower attached balcony and upper flying balcony. Reprinted by permission of Blackwell Scientific Publications Ltd., Oxford, England, *Architect's Data,* Neufert.

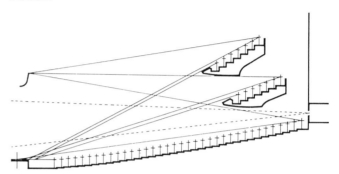

Figure 24. Longitudinal section—two flying balconies. Reprinted by permission of Blackwell Scientific Publications Ltd., Oxford, England, *Architect's Data,* Neufert.

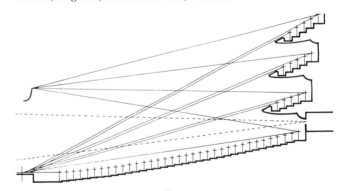

Figure 25. Longitudinal section—three attached balconies. Reprinted by permission of Blackwell Scientific Publications Ltd., Oxford, England, *Architect's Data,* Neufert.

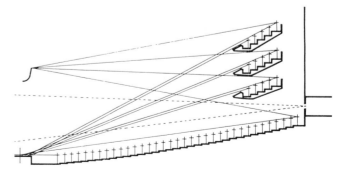

Figure 26. Longitudinal section—three flying balconies. Reprinted by permission of Blackwell Scientific Publications Ltd., Oxford, England, *Architect's Data,* Neufert.

Side Balconies. Side or wing balconies, galleries, and boxes promote the shared experience within the assembly envelope. While the amount of seating side balconies add is small and the capital cost per seat is high when compared with adding extra rows at the rear, defining the limits of the assembly envelope with people rather than architectural walls can create a more interesting sense of place. The design of side balconies with good sight lines to the stage may require design complexities in the risers and railings that is sometimes ignored for the sake of concerns other than providing clear vision to the stage. Side balconies with obstructed sight lines are not recommended.

ASSEMBLY ENVELOPE CEILING

The ceiling of the modern theater and opera house is commonly designed to satisfy a number of requirements. Shaping the ceiling to provide natural distribution of reflected sound to the seating below is normally beneficial. The ceiling also commonly provides for house lighting and access, and mechanical air supply grilles and ducts. In addition, theaters and opera houses require the integration of positions for portable stage lighting and catwalk access. The ceilings of modern, multiple-use theaters also require the integration of a sound reinforcement speakers cluster or a distributed array.

ORCHESTRA PIT

The orchestra pit has served as the normal solution for musicians accompanying a performance on stage since the seventeenth century and continues to solve that need today.

The shape and location of the orchestra pit results from such functional requirements as size related to the number of musicians and their comfort, viewing sight lines simultaneously available between the conductor and both the musicians and the stage, and acoustics as experienced in the pit, on stage, and in the auditorium (Fig. 27).

The orchestra pit can be a distracting element because it separates the performance from the audience area. The best-known solution to this problem is Wagner's sunken pit at the Bayreuth Festspielhaus where more than 40% of the area of the pit is stepped down under the apron or front edge of the stage, and 20% is covered by a curved cowling in front of the first seating row.

While the Wagner pit is normally considered appropriate only for his music, it is recommended that some portion of all orchestra pits have an alcove extending under the apron of the stage. The alcove extension helps to provide an acoustic balance between orchestra and singers. The stage overlap also reduces the visual distraction of the pit and permits the seating to be closer to the stage.

Creating sight lines from the conductor to both the musicians and the stage with a minimum of head strain requires that the pit floor be as high as possible. This relationship means that the thickness of the stage apron extension over the pit alcove needs to be as thin as is structurally possible while still providing minimally adequate headroom for standing musicians underneath.

A solution to the visual distraction problem has included the covering of the pit with a sound-transparent, netting material. The use of electronic reproduction of sound for popular musicals has sometimes resulted in a shift of the orchestra to an isolated backstage area hidden from view of the audience.

If an orchestra pit is included, the use of adjustable floor equipment to make this area as flexible as the budget allows is recommended. When not used as a pit, this area can serve as an apron stage extension (assuming the seating floor slopes have been properly designed to provide sight lines to this area), and for extra seating at the front. The best solution for creating an adjustable floor is a powered pit lift or lifts. Mounting seats in this area on traveling wagons, with storage alcoves below the seating floor, makes the change-over easier. More time-consuming substitutes include manual scaffolding or pit fillers.

The size of the orchestra pit is 10–16 ft^2 (1.0–1.5 m^2) per musician. (Pianists and tympanists require more space than clarinets.) A pit orchestra may vary in size from a few musicians to a full orchestra of 100 or more.

A variable-size orchestra pit is recommended for a multiple-use facility.

SUBJECTIVE DESIGN CONSIDERATIONS

Row-Shaping

Much of the character of the assembly envelope results from the shaping or alignment of seating rows, particularly when the encirclement is great and/or the seating is broad with respect to the performing area. Although a seated spectator can rotate his head about 45° from the centerline axis with relative comfort, most people prefer to have the seating furniture positioned so that they face the center of action in the performing area. Geometrical shaping of the seating rows is commonly done using concentric arcs, straight-line segment geometry, or some combination.

Curved Rows. There is no proper or ideal location for a center of curvature for concentric row arcs. The best choice is that which feels the best. A combination of concentric curves with a center of curvature in the middle of the performing area for the seating in the center, and straight-line tangents at the ends may give a good result.

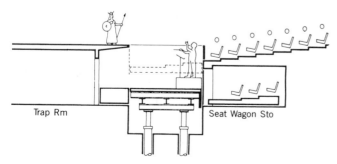

Figure 27. Section through orchestra pit with a powered lift. Reprinted by permission of Blackwell Scientific Publications Ltd., Oxford, England, *Architect's Data,* Neufert.

Straight-line Segments. A polygonal arrangement with straight-line segments is sometimes used. Some designers think that a segmented arrangement with straight-line segments is more dynamic than the more common curved-row scheme. A double herringbone pattern is a popular alternative. A break line bisecting the angle between the segments keeps the rows at the same spacing.

Experiential Considerations

The overall design of the seating arrangement within the assembly envelope may be influenced by a distinction and choice between the creation of the individualized experience and the shared experience for the assembly participant.

Massed Assembly. The individualized experience is encouraged by the creation of a ubiquitous, anonymous character to the seating organization. An intent behind creation of the lack of definition is to encourage the spectator to lose his sense of place within the assembly envelope, promoting his individualized absorption in the performing event on the stage.

Assemblyhood. The shared experience is encouraged by an arrayed or segmented organization of the seating areas to create a series of assemblyhoods. Assemblyhoods, or grouped audience areas, can be articulated by the use of low walls, aisles, small balconies, boxes, and changes in floor slope pitch. The purpose here is to give the spectator a sense of place within the assembly envelope.

SYMMETRY AND ASYMMETRY

Symmetry. Most theaters and opera houses have assembly envelopes that are symmetrical about a centerline axis. Symmetry is a safe approach toward presenting a

Figure 28. Concert Hall, Birmingham-Jefferson Civic Center, Alabama. Geddes Brecher Qualls Cunningham, Architects, 1974, 2965 seats. Courtesy of Peter H. Frink.

neutral organization of the fixed elements to the creation of the stage environment.

Asymmetry. It has been asserted that the centerline axis of the symmetrical assembly envelope creates a force that overdominates the performance. An asymmetrical arrangement may be perceived as being more dynamic than a symmetrical scheme.

Asymmetrical assembly envelopes such as the 1500-seat Tyrone Guthrie Theater of Minneapolis, Minn., the 2965-seat Concert Hall at the Birmingham-Jefferson Civic Center, Ala., (Fig. 28), and the 3000-seat Orange County Theater near Los Angeles, Calif. have been built. The assembly places by Finnish architect Alvar Aalto invariably incorporate an asymmetrical arrangement. While asymmetry may or may not be acceptable, a balanced organization is always recommended.

MULTIPLE-USE FACILITIES

Multiple-use Theaters. To keep performing-arts facilities as useful and busy as possible, municipalities and institutions often need theater facilities that can serve a variety of functions such as drama, dance, opera, musicals, concerts, lectures, and film presentations. Multiple-use capability commonly requires a stage equipped for scenic productions; an electronic sound system; a demountable orchestra shell; an adjustable reverberation control flexibility in the size of the performing area (Fig. 18). It may also require a multiple seating capacity capability.

STAGE AREAS

Size and Shape in Plan

The total stage area is the sum of the performing area plus the surrounding offstage areas. An ideal, large stage area for a proscenium arrangement consists of a duplication of the performing area, typically defined by a stage wagon, at either side of the stage (wagon wings) and upstage of the performing area. This arrangement is the cruciform layout commonly found in new European theaters and opera houses. The ceiling height of the wagon wings needed to accommodate the highest stage setting can be lower than the height of a flying loft above the performing area. The platform height of scenery wagons may be accommodated by means of slip stages, equalizer lifts, and/or stage or plateau elevators.

A less costly stage results by deleting the upstage wagon storage area and one or both full wagon wings. A minimum stage area without full wagon wings is a function of the necessary offstage space to accommodate masking and backstage circulation around the stage setting. A minimum stage width is about twice the maximum portal opening for the stage set, and at least 16 ft (4.9 m) beyond the maximum portal opening. A minimum stage depth is 5–6 ft (1.5–1.8 m) greater than the anticipated position of most upstage backdrop, with a very minimum of 30 ft (9.2 m) from the plaster line (inside face of the proscenium wall) to the rear wall for the smallest theaters (Fig. 29).

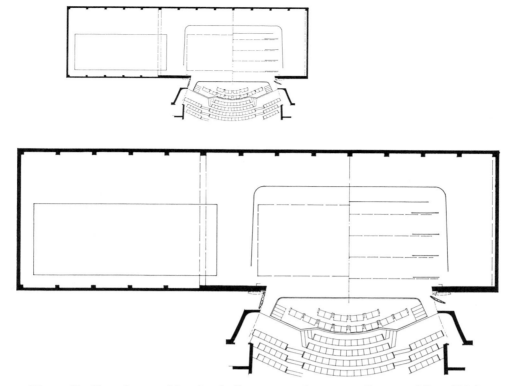

Figure 29. Plan of stage with reduced offstage spaces for wagons. Courtesy of Peter Frink.

Stage Area Ceiling Heights

The simplest and often least expensive method of installing a scenic environment is by hanging the setting, lighting, and sight line masking. The space and stage equipment above the top of the highest setting is an important consideration.

Permanent or Fixed Performing Area Enclosure. A stage area with a permanent ceiling at the height of the anticipated scenic environment limits the use of stage area for scenic productions and is typically found in lecture, recital, or concert halls. Spotline rigging through small openings or hinged panels in permanent ceilings will provide some flexibility.

Low Loft Rigging Space. A stage volume with a minimum height of at least 7–15 ft (2.1–4.5 m) above the top of the highest setting, equipped with a rigging system to hang the setting, lighting, and masking is the minimum recommendation for a theater stage.

An alternate to a low, open loft with a rigging system is a series of access catwalks, or a wire mesh walking grid.

Flyloft. A rigging loft allows for the changing and storage of hanging scenery. To provide storage height above the top of the highest setting out of sight from the seated spectator, the height of the rigging loft must be 2.5 to three times the height of the front portal or proscenium opening. Clear flyloft heights to the bottom of the rigging steel or the gridiron vary from a low range of 55–65 ft (17–20 m), an average of 75–85 ft (23–26 m), to a high of 95–100 ft (29–30 m) and above.

Flylofts commonly have a steel gridiron with walking headroom below the stage roof or ceiling that, in turn, may be structurally hung from the roof structure. A typical gridiron floor structure consists of 3-in. (7.5-cm) steel channels at about 6-in. (15-cm) centers separated by 10-in. (25-cm) open wells 10–12 ft (3–3.65 m) apart for hanging lines for scenery battens. This arrangement provides for the installation of spot-line sheaves or pulleys and a walking surface at the same time.

The loft-block sheaves for the rigging system are traditionally mounted on the gridiron wells, but may be more conveniently underhung from the bottom of loft block beams above the wells that might also be the bottom of the stage roof supporting beams.

Flyloft Without a Gridiron. If a rigging system is hung from the underside of loft-block and/or roof beams, the gridiron is sometimes deleted for cost savings in steel and stage house volume. Elimination of the gridiron, however, results in the following problems:

1. Installation of rigging for isolated spotlines is very difficult.
2. Repositioning of loft blocks is difficult.
3. Inspection and service of rigging and stage electrical equipment is very difficult.

Fire Curtain

Because of the storage of scenery, a flyloft normally requires special consideration with respect to its separation from the seating area. Many building codes require the separation of the stage and seating areas by means of an operating fire curtain. Some building codes do not consider the stage and seating as separate areas. When scenery can be stored above the performing area, however, special requirements are still necessary with respect to the performing area. Among other requirements is the provision of a deluge water curtain.

The fire curtain can provide a serious design impediment to the consideration of the assembly envelope as one room consisting of the seating area and the performing area. In Germany, many new theaters and opera houses locate a fire curtain at the audience edge of an orchestra pit to give design flexibility at the proscenium transition zone.

PUBLIC SPACES

Physical Considerations

Function. From a functional viewpoint, the purpose of foyers, lobbies, and lounges is to provide for (1) circulation between the outside doors and entrances to assembly envelope; (2) a gathering place for audiences and refreshments at intermissions; and (3) access to toilets and coatroom.

Size. A minimum area of open circulation space exclusive of furniture and counters, as defined by some building codes, is 2 ft^2 (0.19 m^2) per seat. An area of 4–6 ft^2 (0.37–0.56 m^2) per seat provides minimum comfort. An area of 10 ft^2 (1.0 m^2) per seat is generous with 15 ft^2 (1.4 m^2) per seat being luxurious. A lobby that is too vast for the size of the audience may not promote the shared experience.

To determine the quantity of public toilets needed it must be taken into account that they are commonly available to the entire audience at the same, limited times. Women's facilities need to be larger than men's.

Experiential Considerations

The design of the lobby is affected by the attitude about its role in the total performance experience. One attitude is to perceive the public lobby as an architecturally complete space independent of its relationship to the assembly envelope. Another is to see the lobby principally in its role as a circulation journey from the outside entrance to the doors of the assembly envelope.

The individualized experience of the assembly participant, on the one hand, is promoted by the physical isolation of the assembly envelope from the lobbies. Visual and acoustic isolation is accomplished at the entrance doors to the assembly envelope by means of vestibules serving as sound and light locks.

The shared experience among participants, on the other hand, may result from regarding the ritual of theater-going as *sui generis,* or the actual event itself. The theater-going experience may be perceived as a planned sequence of progressive spaces and events.

It is sometimes forgotten that contemporary theater-going is most commonly experienced under artificial illumination.

The Theater Facility in Its Environment

In a larger architectural context, a performing-arts facility often plays an important role in its setting. On the one hand, the theater structure may be considered an individualized entity. On the other, it may be considered an integral part of the cityscape inasmuch as the foyer, lobby, auditorium, and other rooms are designed to be an extension of the city.

BACKSTAGE SUPPORT SPACES

The size of the backstage support space varies greatly among facilities in the United States, depending on the role, use, and capital budget available to support the envisioned role of the facility.

Road House—No In-house Production Support

For touring shows, the minimum backstage support includes dressing rooms for actors, dancers, musicians; a green room (an offstage lounge for performers); space for stagehands; the stage entrance; and a truck dock and loading door for delivering scenery to the stage. These functions support the use of the facility as a roadhouse where all productions are brought in from outside the facility. In the United States the range in sizes for these areas usually varies from 1500 ft^2 (140 m^2) to 4000 ft^2 (370 m^2), but can be larger.

In-house Production Support

An early planning and programming determination is whether, or to what degree, the facility is envisioned as an in-house, self-producing, cultural institution. Most German theater–opera facilities, for example, are planned and built as complete, self-contained, production facilities.

A theater facility designed to be an in-house, self-producing organization will normally include such facilities as scenery and property shops, scenery and property storage, costume shops and storage, rehearsal and practice rooms, and administrative offices for support personnel. These facilities are in addition to the minimum roadhouse backstage facilities.

Production and rehearsal facilities for professional theater, opera, and dance companies in the United States vary greatly in size and scope. The larger, older, or better-established institutions are likely to have more extensive production and rehearsal facilities. Some professional companies have production and rehearsal facilities at locations separate from the theater where they normally perform.

Theaters at educational institutions in the United States, sometimes as part of a fine-arts or performing-arts facility, often serve as an integral part of theater (drama), dance, or opera program, making the institution a self-producing organization. These performing-arts programs have a great variation in their mission and the size of the support facilities. While many first-class educational and professional performing-arts institutions in the United States have large, complete, well-planned, and well-designed facilities, the better performing-arts programs do not always have the better facilities.

Civic theaters and cultural and performing-arts centers are sometimes but not always built with in-house production facilities.

Sizes and Adjacencies

Scenery Construction Shops. These spaces work best when located near and on the same level as the stage and are provided with as large a door-opening as the budget will allow. The opening needs doors with a sound rating that will allow the stage and shop to be used simultaneously. Scenery shops also need access to a truck loading dock.

Rehearsal Rooms. These rooms often begin to lose their usefulness when they are less than approximately 40 ft × 50 ft (12.2 m × 15.2 m); these specifications will just barely contain an average-sized performing area.

RENOVATED THEATERS

There has been a recent increase in the renovation of older theaters, movie theaters of the late 1920s in particular, into performing-arts facilities. Choosing to transform these buildings into facilities for the live performing arts offers advantages but may involve some limitations.

Advantages. These facilities often have an architectural character of merit that would be expensive to reproduce, and that may have historical sentiment in the community, or have landmark recognition. The facilities often occupy a prime location and are often integrated into the urban fabric. Reuse of the existing structure and character can reduce costs over a completely new structure.

Disadvantages. The potential deficiencies also need to be considered. Many of these older facilities have shallow stage depths (often only 30-ft (9.1-m) deep, or less) and limited offstage or wing space. It is not always practical to increase the size of the stage.

The older movie theaters often incorporated balconies that are too deep and low for the live, performing arts. Solutions to this problem have included rebuilding the balconies—an expensive proposition—and reducing the number of seating rows under the balcony, that may result in the loss of too many seats.

The seating row spacing of 30–32 in. (11.8–12.6 cm) is common but is often too tight for contemporary standards. While reseating with wider spacing may not be difficult on a ground floor, rebuilding a balcony may be expensive or impractical.

The seating floor slopes, particularly on the main floor, are often too shallow, or inefficiently shaped. Reconstruction with steeper and reshaped floor slopes may be practical if there is enough headroom under an existing balcony, and if access to existing lobby levels can be managed.

The older movie houses usually lacked overhead, front stage lighting positions. Catwalks have been incorporated both by means of bridges suspended and exposed below the ceiling, and above the ceiling behind opening slots or hinged ceiling panels.

The older movie houses were normally not designed to incorporate central loudspeaker clusters above the proscenium opening. Adding this necessary item can provide challenging design problems.

Reverberation time is often too short for music and too long for speech. Too long a reverberation time can be reduced by adding acoustical absorption such as curtains. Lengthening the reverberation time is normally not easy because this usually requires adding volume to the assembly envelope. Solutions to this problem have included both the creation of a reverberation orchestra shell on stage (Fig. 30) or by means of electronic sound.

FILM PROJECTION

Single-use Film Theaters

The limits of the seating plan area of a film theater are determined by the top and vertical edges of the screen. A projected image on a screen will have an apparent distortion when viewed from an angle beyond the perpendicular to a point on the screen in plan and section. The boundary of the seating area for which spectators will see the same apparent distortion is called the line of isodeformation. The shape in plan is a hyperbola for viewing a point on the screen (Fig. 31).

Seating Zone I is the area in plan where the apparent distortion of a projected image exists but will not be noticed. It is defined by the hyperbola related to a cone with its apex on a point on the screen and its sides at 30° from the perpendicular axis at that point on the screen.

Seating Zone II is the area in plan where the apparent distortion of a projected image will be noticed but tolerated. It is defined by the area outside of Zone I but within the hyperbola related to a cone with its apex on a point on the screen and its sides at 45° from the perpendicular axis at that point on the screen.

Seating Zone III is the area in plan beyond the limits of Zone II where the apparent distortion of the projected image will not be tolerated; the viewers there will refuse to use the seats.

Viewing of a Flat Screen

Since a projected image occupies a space on a screen rather than a point, the seating area, defined by the isodeformation lines for which the entire width of the projected image is considered, is represented by the area common to the hyperbolas for both upper corners of the projected image (Fig. 32).

Viewing of a Curved Screen

Seating with less apparent distortion closer to a screen with a given width can be increased by curving the screen. An appropriate screen curvature will cause an overlap of the hyperbolas drawn from the sides of the projected image in such a way that they define a greater common seating area (Fig. 33).

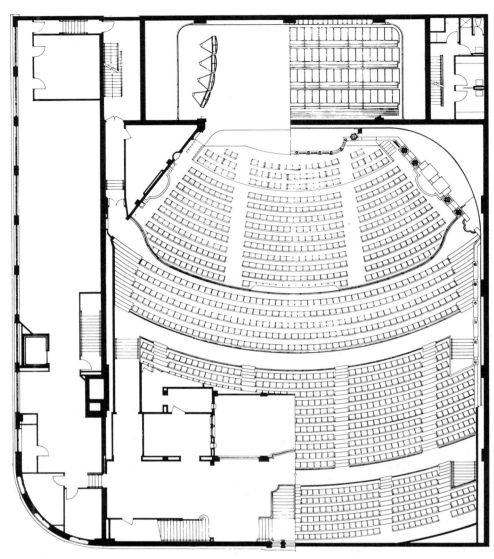

Figure 30. Carpenter Center for the Performing Arts, Richmond, Virginia. John Eberson, original architect; Marcellus Wright, Cox & Smith, renovation architect; Assembly Places International, renovation theater architect. Original completion, 1928; renovation completion, 1983, 2150 seats. Plan. Courtesy of Peter H. Frink.

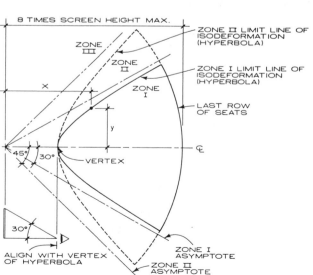

Figure 31. Viewing of a point of a screen. Reprinted by permission of John Wiley & Sons, Inc., *Architectural Graphic Standards*, C. G. Ramsey and H. R. Sleeper, 8th ed., 1988.

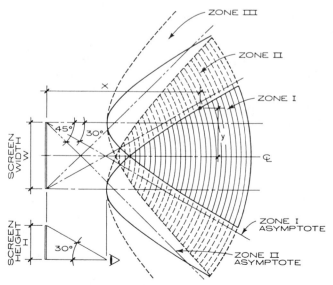

Figure 32. Viewing a flat screen. Reprinted by permission of John Wiley & Sons, Inc., *Architectural Graphic Standards*, C. G. Ramsey and H. R. Sleeper, 8th ed., 1988.

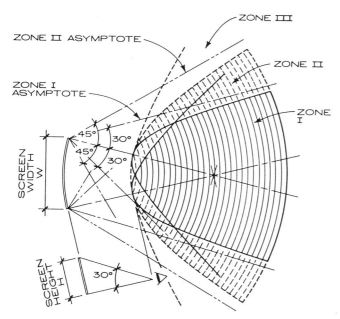

Figure 33. Viewing of a curved screen. Reprinted by permission of John Wiley & Sons, Inc., *Architectural Graphic Standards,* C. G. Ramsey and H. R. Sleeper, 8th ed., 1988.

Screen Projection

The minimum distance between the first row and the screen is determined by the maximum allowable angle between the sight line from the first row to the top of the screen and the perpendicular to the screen at that point. A maximum angle of 30–35° is recommended (Fig. 33).

The maximum distance between the screen and the most distant viewer (MDV) recommended is not more than eight times the height of the screen image. An MDV two to three times the screen width is preferred (Fig. 34).

Screen width is determined by use of the appropriate ratio for the screen width and height called the aspect ratio.

The overall shape of the ideal seating area for viewing a screen is fan shaped.

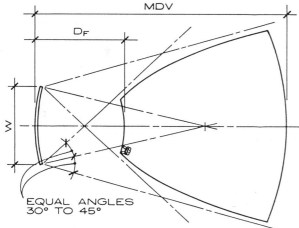

SCREEN PROJECTION

Figure 34. Plan showing screen relationships. Reprinted by permission of John Wiley & Sons, Inc., *Architectural Graphic Standards,* C. G. Ramsey and H. R. Sleeper, 8th ed., 1988.

Film Projection with Live Performances

Screen projection can work in an assembly envelope designed for live performances if the encirclement is not too great. The maximum size and location of the screen is determined by relating the isodeformation criteria to the limits of the seating.

BIBLIOGRAPHY

General References

C. G. Ramsey and H. R. Sleeper, *Architectural Graphic Standards,* 8th ed., John Wiley & Sons, Inc., New York, 1988.

G. C. Izenour, *Theater Design,* McGraw-Hill Inc., New York, 1977.

G. C. Izenour, *Theater Engineering,* McGraw-Hill Inc., New York, 1987.

M. Bieber, *History of the Greek and Roman Theater,* Princeton University Press, Princeton, N.J., 1939.

M. Forsyth, *Buildings for Music,* Cambridge University Press, New York, 1985.

S. Tidworth, *Theatres, an Architectural and Cultural History,* Praeger Publishers, Inc., New York, 1973.

A. Pildas, *Movie Palaces, Survivors of an Elegant Era,* Clarkson N. Potter, Inc., New York, 1980.

R. W. Sexton and B. F. Betts, *American Theatres of Today,* Vestal Press reprint, New York, 1977.

W. C. Young, *Documents of American Theater History,* Vol. 2, American Library Association, Chicago, Ill., 1973.

A. Nicoll, *The Development of the Theatre,* rev. 4th ed., George G. Harrap & Co. Ltd., London, Great Britain, 1961.

J. Mielziner, *The Shapes of Our Theatre,* Clarkson N. Potter, Inc., New York, 1970.

A. C. Ramelli, *Edifici per gli spettacoli,* Italy, 1956.

S. Joseph, *New Theatre Forms,* Theatre Arts Books, New York, 1968.

H. Schubert, *The Modern Theater,* Praeger Publishers, Inc., New York, 1971.

R. Aloi, *Architetture per lo spettacolo,* Ulrico Hoepli, Milan, Italy, 1958.

R. Aloi, *Theatres and Auditoriums,* Ulrico Hoepli, Milan, Italy, 1972.

R. Ham, ed., *Theatre Planning,* University of Toronto Press, Toronto, Ontario, Canada, 1967.

H. Burris-Meyer and E. C. Cole, *Theatres and Auditoriums,* Reinhold Publishing Corporation, New York, 1964.

F. Bentham, *USITT J.* **13**(2) (1977)

New Places for the Arts, a report from Educational Facilities Laboratories and the National Endowment for the Arts, Educational Facilities Laboratories, New York, 1976.

See also ACOUSTICAL DESIGN—PLACES OF ASSEMBLY; MUSIC HALLS

PETER H. FRINK
Assembly Places International
Philadelphia, Pennsylvania

THEME PARKS.   See AMUSEMENT PARKS

THEORY OF ARCHITECTURE

"The idea of *theory*," wrote A. C. Quatremère de Quincy in 1825, "differs from *practice* . . . in as much as it refers to the mental or intellectual activity that reasons or combines, rather than the bodily or manual activity that fashions or executes" (1). With the analytical precision indicative of French Neoclassical theory and this particular *secrétaire perpétuel* of the Académie des Beaux Arts, Quatremère de Quincy went on to differentiate three levels of theory: practical, didactic, and metaphysical. Practical theory, he explained, provides the architect with an historical record of what has been achieved in his art. Didactic theory instructs him in the rules and precepts of his profession. Metaphysical theory solicits knowledge or a "critique of a much more subtle nature." It governs not the rules but their sources; it drafts not the laws but investigates their spirit; it examines not the result but seeks the cause of the impressions we experience, "the means by which the art touches us, moves us, and pleases us" (2).

Although the idea of theory has engendered innumerable treatises, discourses, and manifestos throughout the course of Western architecture, it did at least offer, until the nineteenth century, a remarkable continuity in its historical development. In its oldest, classical meaning, architectural theory comprised a host of aesthetic, social, and practical concerns, ranging from conventions for proportions and use of the Orders to the rules of decorum governing the various building types, site layout, the building's interior organization, and such technological concerns as the type and method of construction, the selection of the material, its preparation, and workmanship. With the breakdown of this tradition in the last century and the attending technical specialization, architectural theory has more or less restricted itself to Quatremère de Quincy's third, and superior, branch of instruction, focusing less on the how of practice, and more on the why of architecture's compliance with or departure from norms. The rather close compass of theoretical issues debated prior to the twentieth century has given way to a host of competing ideologies; the decline of Modern theory in the last few decades has further exacerbated this trend.

Nevertheless, architectural theory manifests itself first and foremost as an historical problem, one that continues to return to familiar themes, issues of debate, and modes of expression. For the purpose of this article, theory will be considered in five periods of development: Theory in Antiquity and the Renaissance, The French Academic Tradition and Neoclassicism, Nineteenth-Century Theory, Modern Theory, and Post-Modern Theory.

THEORY IN ANTIQUITY AND THE RENAISSANCE

Architectural theory in the West begins with Vitruvius. *The Ten Books On Architecture* composed by this Roman architect, engineer, and artillery officer achieve their special importance first by the breadth of the undertaking, second, and more important, by the historical fortune of being the only architectural treatise to survive from antiquity. As such, it has been the primary authority in architectural thinking, setting the tenor of theory in the West for much of 1800 years.

Although it is the essential work in the development of this art, little is known of its author or the circumstances surrounding its publication. Vitruvius, the man who wrote, "nature has not given me stature, age has marred my face, and my strength is impaired by ill health," (3) appears historically only through a few, mostly self-abasing remarks scattered throughout the prefaces of the 10 books. Presumably born sometime around 84 B.C., he was by his own boast well educated in the liberal and fine arts (4), and seems to have traveled extensively in his youth, perhaps to Greece and Asia Minor. He served under Julius Caesar as a military architect, designing and building engines of war. The Ides of March temporarily left Vitruvius without a position, until Octavian reappointed him a few years later to his old command. Around 30 B.C. Vitruvius worked on restoring the water system of Rome and, shortly after Octavian's crowning as Augustus in 27 B.C., he received an architectural commission for a basilica at Fano. By this date, however, he felt slighted professionally and estranged from an increasingly opulent contemporary taste.

The 10 books of *De architectura* (*On Architecture*) probably were published separately, shortly before and after the commission at Fano. The reference in the preface of Book I to Octavian's defeat of Anthony and Cleopatra at Actium places the beginning of publication after 31 B.C. Vitruvius' mention of his age and ill health suggests the project was concluded not long after his basilica commission, possibly by 25 B.C. However, the scope of the effort and his impressive marshalling of facts allow us to surmise that the work was several decades in preparation. It was dedicated to Octavian as a guidebook to assist him in his ambition to rebuild Rome.

The treatise of Vitruvius certainly had its predecessors. Vitruvius himself refers to no less than 63, mostly Greek, works on architecture and related topics, beginning with a commentary on stage design by the Athenian Agatharchus from about 456 B.C. The Greek focus of the endeavor was not unusual for this date. As were his contemporaries Cicero and Varro, Vitruvius was part of what might be termed a first-century Greek revival—scholars attempting to graft Hellenic logical systems and terminology onto a Latin culture growing in political importance. The outline of *De architectura* conforms in only a small way with Vitruvius' division of architecture into three departments: building (Books I–VIII), fabricating timepieces (Book IX), and constructing machinery (Book X). Architecture as a high art is concerned principally with the design of temples and the rules for the Orders, although other important building types, such as forums, basilicas, theaters, and dwellings are given broad treatment. At the beginning of Book I Vitruvius separates the art into the realms of practice (*fabrica*) and theory (*ratiocinato*). The former is the manual activity associated with building and construction; the latter rationally demonstrates and explains conventions and proportional systems governing design.

The art's three main principles are strength (*firmitas*), utility (*utilitas*), and beauty (*venustas*). Strength encompasses the soundness of the foundation, the building's structure, and the selection of materials; utility concerns the convenient planning and social suitability of the edifice; beauty is the building's visual charm that arises chiefly out of proportional harmony. Beauty is further defined by six principles: order, arrangement, eurythmy, symmetry, decorum, and economy. These principles are often subdivided into three groups with order, eurythmy, and symmetry supplying the proportional criteria for design; arrangement dictating the correct planning and assembly of the work; decorum and economy clarifying the appropriate use of the Orders, the adaptation of the building to the site, and the correct management of materials.

Yet it is the first triad, *ordinatio, eurythmia,* and *symmetria,* to which commentators have been drawn most often because of their importance to ancient theory and Vitruvius' less than perspicuous rendering of their meaning. He defines order, for instance, as a quantitative concept giving "due measure to the members of a work considered separately, and symmetrical agreement to the proportions of the whole" through the selection of a module (5). Symmetry is the "proper agreement between the members of the work itself, and relation between the different parts and the whole general scheme, in accordance with a certain part selected as standard" (6). Eurythmy is the beautiful result achieved when the right module is chosen and the work is carried out according to the principle of symmetry. The ambiguity produced by the last two Greek terms is further compounded by the fact that at the beginning of Book III, Vitruvius introduces the Latin term proportion (*proportio*) that he defines in a way similar to symmetry, as "a correspondence among the measures of the members of an entire work, and of the whole to a certain part selected as standard" (7).

If Vitruvian aesthetics has sometimes bemused and even irritated later interpreters, his use of the human analogy for architecture, both to sanction architectural form and to establish proportional systems, has more often enchanted readers, particularly during the Renaissance. The third and fourth book of the treatise are devoted to the three Orders and their use in temples. He describes the Doric as the oldest of the three, taking its genesis on the Greek mainland and founded on the ratio of a man's foot to his height. The Ionic Order originated in the Ionian colonies of Asia Minor and imitated the slenderness of a woman. The Corinthian Order, based on the slighter contours of a young female, was invented in Corinth, he relates, when the architect Callimachus, in walking past the tomb of a maiden, was struck by the elegance of an acanthus plant growing up and around a basket that had been placed beside the tomb. Out of such gender distinctions grew an elaborate system of propriety restricting the various Orders to various building types and locations. Renaissance theory was built almost entirely on the codification of these principles.

One aspect of Vitruvian theory, however, that did not find universal acceptance by later classical theorists was his belief that proportional systems could and did change over time, and that it was the architect's task to modify a given proportional scheme to accommodate certain site restrictions. Vitruvius was aware, at least to an extent, of the optical adjustments used by the Greeks but, in the second chapter of Book VI, he goes beyond such enhancements to speak of the false judgments sometimes induced by optical effects, such as an oar in water that appears broken. To correct such visual problems, he encourages the architect to add and subtract dimensions whenever necessary to preserve the building's visual integrity. The question of the nature and relevancy of such modifications was debated during the Renaissance and at the start of the founding of the French Royal Academy of Architecture in 1671, yet it was not until the mid-eighteenth century that the implications of such a relativistic theory of beauty and proportion began to be recognized. This awareness in itself did much to undermine classical authority.

The influence of Vitruvius in antiquity appears to have been very slight. Only a few references to his treatise are known from imperial times, and it was not until the Carolingian period that the treatise enjoyed a measure of popularity, although mainly for its technical advice on such issues as mixing pigments, and building machines. The oldest existent manuscript of the treatise dates from around 850 A.D., from which time forward it was copied and passed around Europe through the monastic route. *De architectura* was certainly not lost during the Middle Ages, as it has often been stated. The archbishop of Rouen bequeathed a copy of the work to his cathedral in 1183; Vincent of Beauvais quotes Vitruvius on proportions; Petrach owned and annotated a copy of the work. The contemporary scholar Joseph Rykwert (8) has hypothesized a double architectural discourse between 1000 and 1500, with the text of Vitruvius being widely known to the culture of lords, clergy, and literati, and the geometry of Euclid being the principal guide to masons, carpenters, and others connected with building. Such interest, however, was only a prelude to the adulation Vitruvius received in the fifteenth and sixteenth centuries in Italy, beginning with Poggio Bracciolini's so-called discovery of the manuscript at the monastery of Saint Gall in 1414. By the end of the century the Renaissance would enshrine Vitruvius as the indisputable voice of classical antiquity.

The first major Renaissance theorist to rival Vitruvius in importance was Leon Battista Alberti (1404–1472), whose *De re aedificatoria* (*On the Art of Building*) was dedicated to Pope Nicholas V in 1452. Alberti, a papal secretary and *uomo universale* of the Renaissance, did not turn his attention to architecture until the mid-1440s, after he had composed the first Renaissance treatises on painting and sculpture, together with several other literary works. His interest was drawn to architecture, he notes in the preface to Book VI, after examining the sad condition of Roman monuments and the rather capricious state of architecture of his day, ignorant of the justness of ancient rules. His rather low opinion of Vitruvius' literary style (9), "What he handed down was in any case not refined, and his speech such that the Latins might think that he wanted to appear a Greek, while the Greeks would think that he babbled Latin," reflects more a frustration with the lack of clarity in Vitruvius' presentation than an effort to overturn the latter's precepts. Alberti even organized his treatise around the Vitruvian framework of *fir-*

mitas (Books II and III), *utilitas* (Books IV and V), and *venustas* (Books VI–IX).

Thus, Alberti sought to improve on the Roman author's effort to provide the Renaissance with a more coherent and logical basis for theory. Alberti's grounding of Renaissance architecture in the imitation of nature, his emphasis on its social or cultural importance, his definition of it as a professional discipline, and the pre-eminence he placed on beauty and harmonic proportions established the theoretical focus of the next four centuries. The new conception of architecture begins with his description of a building as "a form of body, which like any other consists of lineaments and matter, the one the product of thought, the other of nature" (10). The intent and purpose of lineaments "lies in finding the correct, infallible way of joining and fitting together those lines and angles which define and enclose the surfaces of the building" (11). "Beauty," notes Alberti in Book IV, "is that reasoned harmony of all the parts within a body, so that nothing may be added, taken away, or altered, but for the worse" (12).

Yet Alberti's most extensive treatment of beauty is presented in Book IX, where the cosmological underpinning of his theory becomes fully apparent. Since architecture, unlike the other fine arts, cannot imitate nature directly, it must do so by extrapolating the mathematical laws by which nature itself creates. The idea of beauty must therefore be joined to the notion of *concinnitas,* a rhetorical concept he borrows from Cicero (*Orator* xxiii), whose task and aim is "to compose parts that are quite separate from each other by their nature, according to some precise rule, so that they correspond to one another in appearance" (13). Within Alberti's metaphysics, the notion of concinnitas reads as a supersensuous idea transcending phenomenal reality, one that guides or controls nature's design through the demonstration of three qualities: number (*numerus*), outline (*finitio*), and position (*collocatio*). Number controls the addition or taking away of parts; outline governs their size and configuration; position defines the criteria for their correct placement. Experience or keen judgment on the part of the architect are insufficient in themselves to realize these qualities, and thus Alberti draws on the numerical symbolism of Plato's *Timaeus* to gather the harmonic ratios appropriate for architecture. Alberti's belief in an absolute numerical scheme for beauty and proportion was perhaps his most important contribution to Renaissance theory.

Alberti's effort was only the first in a line of Renaissance treatises to develop and refine similar ideas. Shortly after 1460 the Florentine architect Il Filarete (Antonio di Pietro Averlino Filarete, ca. 1400–1470) wrote his *Trattato di architettura* (*Treatise on Architecture*), most notable for its description of an ideal city. Between 1470 and the mid-1490s, Francesco di Giorgio Martini (1439–1501/2) wrote his *Trattato di architettura civile e militare* (*Treatise on Civil and Military Architecture*), based in part on Vitruvius and Alberti, and that developed especially the human analogy for architectural proportions. The first printed editions of the treatises of Vitruvius and Alberti were issued in 1486. The first illustrated edition of Vitruvius was prepared by Fra Giocondo in 1511, followed 10

years later by the first vernacular edition of Cesare Cesariano.

In 1537 Sebastiano Serlio (1475–1554) began publishing the first of the eight books he composed on architecture (only seven survive and only five had been translated into English). His aim was to assist and instruct the student in laying out the Orders. The same intention prompted the very influential *Regola delli cinque ordini d' architettura* (*Rules for the Five Orders of Architecture*) by Giacomo Barozzi da Vignola (1507–1573), published in 1562. Interest in Vitruvius culminated with Daniele Barbaro's annotated edition of Vitruvius' text in 1556, yet the Renaissance treatise that best synthesized ancient and modern ideals was *I quattro libri dell' architettura* (*The Four Books of Architecture*), published in 1570, by Andrea Palladio (1508–1580).

Originally trained as a mason, Palladio turned his interest to architecture after his spiritual adoption by the scholar Giangorgio Trissino in 1538. During the 1540s Palladio accompanied Trissino on a two-year sojourn in Rome, where Palladio was able to document classical and Renaissance monuments and gather enough material for two guidebooks. In the next decade he assisted Barbaro with his annotated edition of Vitruvius' *De architectura.* One of Palladio's last endeavors—the publication of Julius Caesar's *Commentaries* with 41 plates—bears witness to his love of classical grandeur.

I quattro libri dell' architettura broke no new theoretical ground. Rather, it was a synthesis of ideas from antiquity and the Renaissance, bringing together the precepts of Vitruvius (his master and guide) with the harmonic theory of Alberti, illustrated in the format made popular by Serlio and Vignola. Vitruvius, however, was more than simply a guide to Palladio; he was the oracle proclaiming the deepest secrets of ancient architecture—regularity, symmetry, proportion—the permanent measure of all values. For Palladio Roman greatness was synonymous with the notion of virtue, and harmonic proportions, as harmonic tones in music, sprang from the same universal laws that govern all creation. Palladio defined beauty as "the form and correspondence of the whole, with respect to the several parts, of the parts with regard to each other, and of these again to the whole; that the structure may appear an entire and compleat body, wherein each member agrees with the other, and all necessary to compose what you intend to form" (14) (Fig. 1).

If Palladio epitomized the Renaissance ideal in its grandest and most orthodox form, he also was poised historically at the point where the rule he espoused was rapidly giving way to the exception. Georgio Vasari, who was three years younger than Palladio, wrote *Dell vite de' più eccellenti pittori, scultori, ed architettori* (*Lives of the Most Excellent Painters, Sculptors, and Architects*) during Palladio's lifetime and praised Michelangelo, in particular, for breaking the bonds of academic measure, order, and rule. This burgeoning "self confidence" of the late sixteenth century, as Heinrich Wölfflin has described it (15), was one of the characteristics of the Baroque, the formation of which took place around the time of Palladio's death. The new sensibility was awakened and inspired by

Figure 1. *Villa Rotunda,* Andrea Palladio, Vicenza, Italy, 1566–1570.

the mass and scale of ancient works—their liberties and variations—rather than by their compliance with a fixed and uniform code. One need only to view the spatial dexterity and formal inventiveness of Gianlorenzo Bernini (1598–1680), Francesco Borromini (1599–1667), and Johann Bernhard Fischer von Erlach (1656–1723) to perceive the new artistic freedom enjoyed by baroque architects, intent on extending the horizon of their sources. In *Entwurf einer historischer Architektur (Plan of an Historical Architecture),* published in 1721, Fischer von Erlach reconstructs by way of historical summary not only the ancient architecture of the Jews, Egyptians, Syrians, Persians, and Greeks, but also that of the Arabs, Turks, modern Persians, Siamese, Chinese, and Japanese.

Together with this assault on orthodox Renaissance conventions, baroque architecture also tended toward what was in many respects a stricter geometrical and scientific determinism. Both aspects of this tendency—experimentation with form and a greater emphasis on a geometric approach to design—can be seen in the theory and organizational structure of the treatise *Architettura civile (Civil Architecture)* by Guarino Guarini (1624–1683), written sometime after 1660 but published posthumously in 1737. Guarini points out, on the one hand, the many variations in ancient and recent proportional schemes and encourages the architect to view form with an eye free of prejudice, to correct ancient rules, and to invent new ones. His infatuation with mathematics and its role in the methodology of design, on the other hand, conveys the new scientific demeanor taking root. The first book expounds the general principles of architecture in a crisp axiomatic fashion; the remaining four books have as their subject matter iconography, orthogonal elevations, orthogonal projections, and geodesy. The investigative spirit of the Galilean Revolution was clearly beginning to make itself felt in architecture. The Renaissance view of antiquity as an arcane treasury hermetically cloistering the timeless secrets of architecture was rapidly giving way in the late seventeenth century to the notion of progressive knowledge open to the future, one capable of adding to and improving ancient forms and proportions. The issues and

scope of this conflict were most extensively explored in a concurrent architectural debate beginning to take place in France.

THE FRENCH ACADEMIC TRADITION AND NEOCLASSICISM

The founding of the Royal Academy of Architecture in Paris in 1671 can be taken as the starting point of modern European theory and practice. Symbolically, the new academy represented, in line with the political and cultural ascendancy of France, a declaration of independence from the Renaissance tradition. In response to the perceived excesses of the baroque—architecturally, the academy's foundation reflected the tendency to provide a nationally sanctioned forum for the consolidation and rational reinterpretation of traditional conventions. The royal decision to establish such an entity around the time of the famous literary dispute concerning the superiority of the Ancients or the Moderns was also not fortuitous. The question of whether contemporary culture could match or even exceed classical accomplishments found its striking architectural parallel in the re-evaluation of Vitruvian and Renaissance theory.

The architectural debate in France was conducted by two remarkable antagonists. Nicolas François Blondel (1617–1686), a mathematician, engineer, and architect, was appointed the Academy's first director in 1671 with the mandate to codify academic theory in light of the abuses recently introduced into architecture by such baroque architects as Francesco Borromini. Claude Perrault (1613–1688), a famed surgeon, physicist, and architect of the east wing of the Louvre, was commissioned around the same time with the equally important task of preparing an annotated French translation of *De architectura* (Fig. 2). Perrault brought to his task not only the Cartesian method of doubt he had learned in his scientific pursuits, but also the conviction that contemporary architecture was marching along a path of development superior to ancient efforts and capable of further evolution. The doubts he raised concerning the classical tradition in his notes to the translation were elaborated on by him in the *Ordonnance des cinq espèces de colonnes* (1683), a work whose premises disputed the most sacred premises of classical and Renaissance theory.

In his *Ordonnance* Perrault proposed a new universal system for proportioning columns, dispensing with the complex fractional ratios of earlier modular systems. His new system was based on a smaller or *petit module* that would always be a whole number and thus could be committed easily to memory. Unlike his Renaissance predecessors, however, the ratios he proposed for the various Orders were not generated by an *a priori* harmonic system, but by taking the arithmetic mean of various historical examples. By such an approach, Perrault not only undermined the traditional cosmological basis for architectural proportion, but also severed its mathematical connection with such other arts as music. He specifically inveighed against the musical correlation on the basis of

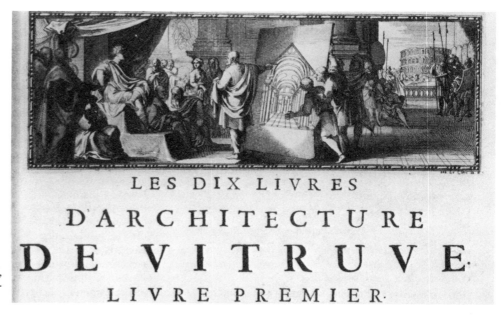

Figure 2. Frontispiece, Book I, Claude Perrault's French translation of Vitruvius.

his anatomical research into muscular movements, arguing that the eye and the ear were fundamentally different in their physiological operation. Perrault further denied the need for optical corrections, since the mind, he insisted, has the ability to correct distortions produced in perception.

The aesthetic basis of his theory was the distinction between positive and arbitrary beauty. The former was both a convincing and self-evident beauty, but was not centered around fixed and absolute standards for proportion. Rather, it resided in such qualities as the richness of the material, the magnificence and delicacy of its workmanship, and the measured correspondence of the parts to the whole. To the realm of "good taste" or arbitrary beauty Perrault delegated the proportional systems that had been the heart of classical theory. Since proportions had changed historically, Perrault argued, they were based more on custom than on any absolute standard of beauty.

As a practical illustration of his revolutionary position, Perrault introduced in his Louvre facade a new coupled-column Order, the pseudosystyle, that he said was inspired by the peristylar innovations of the third-century B.C. Greek architect Hermogenes (Fig. 3). Perrault spanned the enlarged space between the paired columns with a flat lintel or entablature, composed of small blocks of stone and held in place with a complex system of iron bars, not unlike a reinforced concrete system.

His antagonist Blondel was unimpressed both with what he regarded as the Gothic, or svelte, character of Perrault's Louvre colonnade and his seemingly excessive use of iron ties to hold the system in place. From his position as the pedagogue in charge of the first architectural institution in France, however, he was even less happy with the challenges Perrault had made to the foundations of classical theory.

Beginning with the first edition of his textbook, *Cours*

Figure 3. *The Louvre*, east wing, Paris, Claude Perrault, 1667–1674.

d'architecture (1675), Blondel set about refuting Perrault's views on optical corrections, proportions, and the relative nature of beauty. Although Blondel leaned toward the side of the Ancients in the concomitant dispute, he was nevertheless aware of the limitations of Vitruvius, and thus balanced Vitruvius' conceptual ambiguities with the more rational pronouncements of Vignola and Palladio. Cours d'architecture is, in fact, a comparative study of the best that classical and Renaissance theory had to offer, intelligently assembled and examined. Blondel held steadfast to the importance of optical corrections and the freedom this allowed the architect in design. A talented mathematician, he believed adamantly in the profound numerical relations governing all creation. Blondel also stressed the stable and constant principles of good architecture, and in this last respect he was much more successful than Perrault in setting the direction of academic theory in France. Over the next century the French Academy would enact his agenda and develop into the leading institution of its kind in Europe.

Yet the questions of theory that Perrault had raised through his writings and with his innovation of the Louvre colonnade did not entirely disappear, and were voiced with greater frequency throughout the eighteenth century, particularly after 1750. Already in 1702 Michel de Frémin published a small book entitled, Mémoires critique d'architecture, that both questioned the primacy of the Orders in architecture and praised the lighter, more rational structural system of Gothic churches. Four years later Jean Louis de Cordemoy, in Nouveau traité de toute l'architecture (1706), extolled the use of Perrault's petit module and the apreté (visual tension) and dégagement (lightness) of his Louvre colonnade. The broad window openings this system allowed, he argued, represented a major advance over what he termed the architecture en bas-relief or the Renaissance system of vaults, arcades, and applied pilasters. The contemporary historian Robin Middleton has termed this new aesthetic the Graeco-Gothic Ideal with its emphasis on combining the more slender, free-standing colonnade with the regular forms of early Christian and Greek models.

French theorists were not alone in questioning the premises of Vitruvian theory. Beginning in the 1730s the friar Carlo Lodoli (1690–1761) held regular peripatetic discussions on architecture in Venice, the theory of which is preserved in part in Andrea Memmo's Elementi di architettura Lodoliana (1786). In criticizing both Vitruvius and Perrault, Lodoli reasoned that the original error of ancient architecture was its very transposition of wooden forms into stone—thereby denying the material efficiency of either material. Harmonic proportions in his view were not the product of nature or a greater mathematical force, but merely a custom or blind belief in ancient authority. Moreover, the diversity of materials and their varying capacities to handle loads and stresses made it impossible to establish any definitive or absolute standards for proportion. Lodoli advocated instead an architecture that represented the poetic potential of the material.

Lodoli's search for a new basis for architecture took place on the eve of what can be described as the first great crisis of Western architecture. In 1753 a short manifesto appeared in Paris that also questioned the relevance of Vitruvian authority. The book was entitled, Essai sur l'architecture; its author was not an architect but a Jesuit priest, the Abbé Marc Antoine Laugier (1713–1769).

Laugier was an eminent orator and historian. As did his contemporary Jean Jacques Rousseau, Laugier possessed an unswerving faith in the primacy of reason and the natural goodness of man in his pre-societal condition. Reflecting on architecture through his readings of Perrault, Blondel, and Cordemoy, Laugier argued that architecture could only be reformed by discarding Vitruvian authority and returning to its first principles. For him this meant a return to the much simpler and uncorrupted principles of a proto-Greek architecture—the primitive hut—thereby purging this art of its later abuses. Along the grassy riverbank, he reasoned, natural man constructed his first shelter. He chose four fallen branches and raised them upright in a square plan. He laid four other branches horizontally across their tops, then he added others to form the pitch line of a roof. These three elements, the column, the entablature, the pedimental roof, defined for Laugier what was essential to architecture. Walls, doors, and windows he later allowed under the special category of licence. All other elements of the traditional architectural vocabulary, such as vaults, arches, pedestals, pilasters, niches, and certain decorative motifs, he dismissed as being capricious.

Laugier's proposals for a strict reform of architecture were really the product of two forces coming together in the middle of the eighteenth century. The first was a general reaction in France to the extravagance of the Rococo. The second was a new awareness and appreciation of the formal simplicity of Greek architecture and its fundamentally different formal vocabulary. The architecture of the Renaissance and French Classicism prior to 1750 had been modeled on Roman designs, presuming the supremacy of Roman art in the ancient world. Greece and its high culture were certainly known from literary sources, but few travelers had ventured to or gained entry into Ottoman Greece to record the remnants of its art. This situation changed quite suddenly around mid-century when Greece opened to Western travelers. In 1751 James Stuart and Nicholas Revett made the trip to Athens to begin their study of Attic works, resulting in the Antiquities of Athens (1762–1816). They were soon joined and in part preempted by their French rival David Le Roy, whose Ruines de plus beaux monuments de la Grèce appeared in 1758 (Fig. 4). In the same decade James Dawkins and Robert Wood visited Graeco-Roman ruins in Syria and Lebanon, producing The Ruins of Palmyra (1753) and The Ruins of Balbac (1757). The Greeks' colonial monuments in Sicily and at Paestum were also recorded in this decade, the latter by the French architects J. G. Soufflot and G. P. M. Dumont.

This burst of archaeological activity resulted in a fervent enthusiasm for all things Greek, and a more gradual process of experimentation with the Greek Orders and their differing proportions. Laugier, whose essay actually preceded many of these publications, found himself, together with David Le Roy, in the lead of this movement. The conventional language of architecture was the issue,

Figure 4. *The Parthenon,* Athens, ca 1750.

not archaeology. Response to the "Graeco-mania" came in the form of a series of publications produced by Italy's most talented artist and architect, Giovanni Battista Piranesi (1720–1778), who had been watching the shifting attitudes while teaching at the French Academy in Rome. In 1761 he published a lengthy rebuttal to Greek artistic supremacy, *Della magnificenza ed architettura di' Romani,* in which he argued that the Romans inherited their artistic culture not from the Greeks, but from the Etruscans, who were an older race than the Greeks and had perfected the arts and the science of engineering prior to the Greeks. The Frenchman Pierre Jean Mariette responded to Piranesi's thesis three years later with an article in the *Gazette littéraire de l'Europe,* in which he insisted that whatever the Romans achieved artistically was owed solely to Greek slaves. Piranesi replied in 1765 with two polemical works, in which he defended not only the honor of ancient Rome, but also the freedom of artists to draw from disparate sources to fashion what is, in essence, an eclectic solution.

This last issue, in fact, lay at the heart of the Graeco-Roman controversy. The rear guard defense that Piranesi had constructed had been intended to protect the tradi-tional Roman vocabulary of form and to preserve the creative license historically afforded the architect. He viewed Neoclassical reformers such as Laugier as extremists intent on reining the hand of the designer with their more sparing palette of Greek forms. Piranesi's defense, however, was short shrift at best, since in 1864 the German historian Johann Joachim Winckelmann (1717–1768) published his highly influential *Geschichte der Kunst des Altertums* (*History of Ancient Art*). He located the epitome of classical noble simplicity (and of ancient art) in the fourth-century B.C., and demanded an absolute (Platonic) conception of beauty. The strength of his idealist vision—the sublimity of great white masses gleaming atop the acropolis—was so persuasive as to propagate numerous Neoclassical imitations of Greek monuments. Sooner or later nearly every European and North American capital would be endowed with an array of such works.

Yet the implementation of Hellenic Neoclassicism would not truly materialize until about 1800 and, in the intervening decades of the eighteenth century, French architecture experienced one of its most formally rich and creative periods, suspended as it were between Greek and Roman alternatives. The Greek post-and-lintel system, for instance, recalled Perrault's now famed colonnade at the Louvre and, in the mid-1750s, something of a Perrault revival manifested itself, as seen in Jacques German Soufflot's Church of Ste. Geneviève (1756–1790), Pierre Contant d'Ivry's design for the Madeleine (1761), and the various works of Ange Jacques Gabriel, especially his buildings at the north end of the Place de la Concorde (1758–1775) (Fig. 5).

The theoretical basis for this revival, however, was not to be found in Perrault's *Ordonnance,* but rather in the important French concept of character, first raised in 1745 by German Boffrand in his treatise *Livre d'Architecture.* In developing the classical notion of decorum, Boffrand had employed the notion of character to refer to a building's general capacity to speak or articulate its purpose in an appropriate and elegant fashion. He suggested that a rapport with a spectator was initially established with the selection of the Order, but that a building was also capa-

Figure 5. Buildings on north side of the Place de la Concorde, Paris, Ange-Jacques Gabriel, 1758–1775.

ble of more distinct emotions through the formal development of the details. The architect's goal in delineating these nuances of meaning was not just to achieve beauty, but to set out a theme or set of themes within a clear framework.

Such a concept received further elaboration in the next few decades through the writings of Jacque Francois Blondel (1705–1774). In 1743 Blondel opened an architectural school on the Rue de la Harpe that later merged with the Royal Academy. In 1762 he was appointed as a professor to the Academy, and by this date was already known as the leading teacher in Europe. In six volumes, his encyclopedic *Cours d'architecture* (1771–1777) summarized academic theory at this important historical juncture. It not only reaffirmed the mythical origin of the Orders, their importance to architecture, and the absolute nature of beauty and proportion, but also embodied many of the reforms called for by the Graeco-Roman debate.

Blondel's lengthy section on character at the end of the first volume of *Cours d'architecture* derived from a paper he had read to the academy in 1766 entitled, "Essaye sur le caractère qui convient à chaque genre d'édifice." As with Boffrand, the Orders were defined as the first measure of magnificence to which a building can aspire, but Blondel went on to enunciate multifarious expressions, or imperceptible nuances, that evoke more subtle emotional characters—a list that extended over 30 pages and delineated such distinctions as the styles manly, virile, firm, light, elegant, delicate, rustic, naive, among many others. Again, the designer's task is to entertain and to move— élever l'ame du spectateur—also to create a composition that is new and original.

The expositions on character of Boffrand and Blondel promoted, in fact, the idea of an *architecture parlante*, by which architecture is construed primarily as an elocutionary art. This formulation was carried one step further by a work that appeared in 1780 entitled, *La génie d'architecture; ou, l'analogie de cet art avec nos sensations*. Its author, Le Camus de Mézières (1721–1789), wrote of the inexhaustible variation of moods and characters evoked by nature through its lines, forms, contours, and seasons, and of capturing these same sensations with poetic architectural forms. In defining architecture strictly as an emotive art, Le Camus de Mézières envisioned the architect as someone akin to a conductor or stage director, orchestrating a series of themes and counter-themes. He staunchly defended the idea of harmonic proportions in nature, and argued that their embodiment in architecture constituted the metaphysics of this art.

This high regard for the elocutionary capacity of form or an *architecture parlante* culminated with the theories of the two more prominent architects of this phase of Neoclassicism: Etienne Louis Boullée (1728–1799) and Claude Nicolas Ledoux (1736–1806). Both attempted a reconciliation of the academic tradition of absolute beauty with the expressive possibilities of character and form; both devoted the latter part of their careers to so-called visionary projects of extraordinary novelty and emotive power.

In this last respect they had important precedents in the ancient and modern schemes of classical grandeur composed by Piranesi and Marie Joseph Peyre in the 1750s. By the 1780s, however, new elements had entered into the formal vocabulary, not only Greek, but also Egyptian and even Gothic. This formal eclecticism—the possibility of which Piranesi had first suggested in his late essay *Diverse maniere d'adornare i cammini* (1769)—presented a serious challenge to academic authority. In this sense, the eschatological themes of many of Boullée's projects represented the impending collapse of an academic tradition that was exhausting the limits of its brilliant flowering.

Boullée was a pupil of J. F. Blondel and had enjoyed a moderately successful career that began in the 1750s with decorating, and later designing, Parisian hotels. He was best known, however, as a teacher, and around 1780 began work on a polemical and illustrative work to promote his aesthetic ideals. This unfinished treatise, *Essai sur l'art*, was ambivalent with respect to previous academic theory. On the one hand, he was willing to dispense with the primacy of the Orders and the importance of proportion in developing the theme of character. On the other hand, he remained adamant in his belief in the existence of absolute beauty and in the necessity to base architecture in nature. In commenting on the Perrault–Blondel dispute, Boullée rejected the relativism of the former in favor of the first principles for this art that he defined as the regularity and symmetry of form. As with Le Camus de Mézières's theory, the value of architecture resided in the sensation it produced, in the architect's genius in playing to the range of human feeling. Boullée called the effects of bodies the poetry of architecture; his highly rational and personal language of form consisted of cubes, spheres, cylinders, pyramids, and cones. These primeval forms constituted, as it were, the symbols of a transcendent order, the pre-existent harmony of man and nature presenting the highest value of art.

Ledoux's enigmatic treatise of 1804, *L'architecture considérée sous la rapport de l'art, des moeurs et de la législation*, proceeded from a similar ideology in its search for new symbolic and absolute conventions. Ledoux had achieved professional success in the 1770s and 1780s as the fashionable designer of glamorous urban residences, and as the inventive designer of the *barriéres* or toll houses surrounding Paris (Fig. 6). In 1771 he was also appointed the *Inspecteur des Salines* (or saltworks) for Lorraine and Franche-Comté, from which commission evolved his celebrated schemes for the utopian city of Chaux, a new industrial town, partially built, and based on the production of salt. In his many designs for the city of Chaux he brought the theory of character to its logical conclusion. Not only is every building marked according to its particular function or nature, but such a system is symbolically reinforced in plan, massing, and decorative appointments. In adapting motifs from various architectural vocabularies, Ledoux hoped to construct a universal formal language of gesture and emblem, and at the same time one that allowed infinite permutation. In addition to their compositional assurance, Ledoux's designs for Chaux exacted in their planning a specific social or functional value, supportive of the economic mode of production and style of living to be ordained. The inclusion of the

Figure 6. *Rotunda de la Villette,* Paris, Claude-Nicolas Ledoux, 1785–1789.

words morals and legislation in the title of his treatise underscores his view of the architect as the moral guardian engendering and distilling public conduct and thereby assisting economic efficiency. Such a quasi-positivistic attitude helped to push architecture toward its nineteenth-century formulation as a medium to represent or enhance cultural values, and later as a totalitarian instrument for behavioral control. At the same time, Ledoux's recycling and simplification of classical forms did much to erode the traditional meaning of their symbolism. His theory in this regard, while deist and grounded in the Enlightenment, points decidedly toward a purely functional conception of architecture, an idea that was to be more fully developed in the nineteenth century.

NINETEENTH-CENTURY THEORY

The new direction French theory would take in the nineteenth century was presaged by two works that appeared shortly after 1800. Two years into the new century the architect and engineer Jean Baptiste Rondelet (1734–1829) published the first volume of *Traité théorique et pratique de l'art de bâtir,* a work that is remarkable simply because it contains almost no theoretical discussion. Rondelet, who was famed for saving the collapsing church of Ste. Geneviève in Paris (now the Pantheon), was one of the first modern architects to argue that this art should emulate the science of engineering that was based on the principles of mathematics and physics.

Also in 1802, Jean Nicolas Louis Durand (1760–1834) began publishing *Précis des leçons d'architecture données à l'Ecole royale polytechnique* (1802–1805). Durand had been trained by Peyre, Le Roy, and Boullée, yet his book and the course on architecture he taught at the Ecole Polytechnique was without academic precedent. Not only did he dismiss Boullée's plea for character and expression in architecture, but he also rejected the normative value of Laugier's primitive hut and, in fact, denied architecture any transcendental justification. The classical Orders, he

argued, were not the essence of architecture; rules for proportion should be derived from the nature of the material and its use. Convenience, rather than beauty, was the reason for making architecture, thus the architect had two problems to solve: how to design and build a private building with the greatest convenience within a given budget; and how to design and build a public edifice with the greatest possible economy. The implementation of an economical solution, Durand further argued, pointed toward the use of simple and regular forms arranged symmetrically. To facilitate this process, Durand proposed a design method utilizing a grid, whereby columns could be located at intersections, walls along lines, and openings at the center of the module. In such a system, only the plan, elevation, and section were necessary to formulate the design; he further suggested an interchangeable typology of compositional parts that could be assembled or organized in various combinations. Although Durand's architecture was Neoclassical in its conception, it was, in fact, a closed syntactical system restricted only to the rule of its method and therefore able to accommodate any formal vocabulary. Economic factors, such as the injunction that maximum floor area be obtained with minimum perimeter construction, became the overriding criteria of design.

Durand's compositional methodology proved to be enormously influential throughout Europe, especially in Germany. It was, however, virtually ignored in France, where the newly formulated Ecole des Beaux Arts, organized in 1799 out of the remains of the Academy, attempted to recapture its lost standing under the sway of a Neoclassical orthodoxy that had overtaken Napoleonic France (Fig. 7). The conservative restoration of the Bourbons following Napoleon's defeat hardened this tendency and resulted in the appointment of A. C. Quatremère de Quincy (1755–1849) in 1816 as *secrétaire perpétuel* of the Académie des Beaux Arts.

Quatremère de Quincy, who had begun his career as a sculptor, was noted primarily for his dissertation on Egyptian and Greek architecture written in 1785 and for his stupendous *Encyclopédie méthodique: Architecture,* begun in 1788, and that contained, among other lengthy

Figure 7. *The Madeleine,* Paris, Alexandre-Pierre Vignon, 1807–1845.

articles, a 44-page discourse on the notion of character. Yet Quatremère de Quincy's theory was actually centered on a much different issue, derived in part from the normative rationalism of Laugier's primitive hut and, in part, from Winckelmann's grand vision of Hellenic Neoclassicism. Quatremère de Quincy's theory was predicated on three primordial types, the cave, the tent, and the hut, originating in the modes of living of hunters, shepherds, and farmers, and characteristically developed by the Egyptians, the Chinese, and the Greeks, respectively. Whereas the first two types lacked architectural possibility because of their massiveness or lack of permanence, the cabin was based on carpentry, joined solidity with variety, and offered a rich combination of parts capable of ornamental exploitation. However, wood in itself lacked sufficient monumentality, and thus these early constructions only raised themselves to the level of architecture when wooden forms were subsequently transposed into stone. Quatremère de Quincy argued that it was the specific elocutionary play of this transposition—*ce masque ingeniéux*—that lent architecture its essential artistic significance.

Yet Quatremère de Quincy's Neoclassicism, rooted in the eighteenth century, soon found resistance at the Ecole during the 1820s. The impetus to this unrest, ironically enough, was an impressive study Quatremère de Quincy had published on ancient polychrome sculpture in 1815 entitled, *Le Jupiter olympien, ou l'art de la sculpture antique considérée sous un nouveau point de vue*. In attempting to reconcile the dazzling reviews that classical writers such as Pausanias had given to the gold and ivory statuary of Phidias with the cooler, even hostile regard for these works by Neoclassical critics, Quatremère de Quincy emphasized the importance of color to the Greek artistic conception: initially to protect the wooden sculptures against the effects of weather and time, later as a means (sanctified by tradition) to relieve the coldness and monotony of large surfaces. What Quatremère de Quincy had hypothesized, in fact, was a general theory of polychromy for Greek art equally applicable to architecture. Thus when evidence began to accumulate in the 1810s and 1820s that paint had been extensively used on Greek monuments, efforts were also made to paint Winckelmann's white vision of antiquity in brilliant shades of color. In the 1820s, prize-winning students of the Ecole des Beaux Arts at the French Academy in Rome began sending back to Paris colored reconstructions of classical buildings, in open defiance of Quatremère de Quincy's more conservative view of the past. In Paris, the most vocal proponent for polychromy in antiquity was the architect Jacques Ignace Hittorff (1792–1867), who in 1822 undertook an archaeological tour of Sicily specifically to uncover painted monuments. In 1830 when Hittorff unveiled his polychrome reconstruction of a small heroum he had unearthed at Selinus, complete with its columns, entablature, walls, ceilings, and floors rendered in bright colors, a furious debate ensued. Not unlike the earlier Graeco-Roman debate, architectural polychromy was hardly the main issue in itself. It was simply the means seized by the younger generation, as were the Greek forms of the Neoclassical reformers, to flout academic authority and undermine the *status quo*. In their efforts to overturn the tenets of Neoclassicism, the advocates of polychromy in the 1820s and 1830s were most successful.

The rapid decline of Neoclassicism during these years left academic theory in France without a direction for the first time since its inception. One attempt to fill this void in France was made by those students who had sparked the rebellion in Rome, namely, Pierre François Henri Labrouste (1801–1875), Félix Jacques Duban (1797–1870), and Léon Vaudoyer (1803–1872). All were influenced by the humanitarian ideas of Saint Simon, the romanticism of Victor Hugo, and a historical conception that regarded architecture as the shell of human societies in successive stages of evolution. The classical monuments that had inspired generations of student *pensionnaires* before them were now less attractive than the early Florentine works of the Renaissance, colonial Greek monuments in Paestum and Sicily, and Etruscan ruins in Latium and Tuscany. Already in 1830 Vaudoyer was calling for an architectural revolution to bring design in harmony with the ideas of the present century and reflect the national character of France's institutions, customs, climate, and materials. In Duban's design for a new building to house the Ecole des Beaux Arts (1832–1840), he assembled motifs from the Colosseum and Cancellaria in Rome, and organized the site as a museum of French antiquities in an effort to instruct the student in architecture's development—a precondition for a new organic epoch of architecture (Fig. 8). Labrouste's Bibliothèque Ste. Geneviève (1843–1850) invoked not only a progressive functionalism with its fireproof construction, gas lighting, central heat and ventilation, and exposed cast-iron structure, but also a more literal *architecture parlante* with its exterior chiseled and painted with the names of those authors contained inside, depicting the intellectual evolution from mythic to scientific thought.

Another movement that emerged in France in the wake of Neoclassicism's collapse was the Gothic Revival. There interest in Gothic went back to Michel de Frèmin's praise of the style in 1702 for its lighter, more logical structural system, its space-saving attributes, and for ad-

Figure 8. *Bibliothèque Ste.-Geneviève*, Paris, Pierre-François-Henri Labrouste, 1842–1850.

mitting more natural light. Eighteenth-century designers, such as J. G. Soufflot, expressed similar sentiments, and even used Gothic as a rationale for the more slender profiles of their orders. Interest in Gothic architecture subsided with the increasing use of Greek forms, but returned with a flourish around 1830, spurred on by Victor Hugo's popular novel, *The Hunchback of Notre Dame*. Several preservation and antiquarian societies were formed in this decade. The first authoritative study of French Gothic architecture was Arcisse de Caumont's *Cours d'antiquités monumentales* (1830–1841).

The two most important French theorists of Gothic architecture were Jean Baptiste Antoine Lassus (1807–1857) and Eugène Emmanuel Viollet-le-Duc (1814–1879). Lassus was trained in the studio of Labrouste, but turned his attention to Gothic and in 1835 assisted in the restoration of Ste. Severin in Paris. Three years later he was appointed *inspecteur* to Duban's much discussed restoration of Ste. Chapelle, where he was soon joined by Viollet-le-Duc. In 1844 Lassus and Viollet-le-Duc won the competition for the restoration of Notre Dame in Paris (1844–1864).

Lassus wrote several scholarly works on Gothic monuments and the Middle Ages, but he was soon upstaged in this regard by the literary and creative endeavors of Viollet-le-Duc, who in a tour of Italy (1835–1836), expressed disappointment with the works of Palladio, Sansovino, and Vignola and, on returning to France, took up the Gothic cause as an assistant to the Commission des Monuments Historiques. Viollet-le-Duc worked first on restoring the Abbey church at Vézelay before assisting on Ste. Chapelle. His historical interest in Gothic resulted in the extraordinary 10 volume *Dictionnaire raisoné de l'architecture Française du XIe au XVIe siècle* (1854–1875) and the *Entretiens sur l'architecture* (1858–1872).

Although highly sympathetic to Gothic as the exemplar of rational architecture, Viollet-le-Duc's theory as it developed did not really call for a return to Gothic as a national style (Fig. 9). His interest in Gothic was mainly with its construction and the logical expression of its structural principles, but only insofar as these principles could be applied to nineteenth-century technologies and materials, such as iron trusses. A key notion in his theory was the idea of style that he defined in the *Dictionnaire* as "the manifestation of an ideal based on a principle" (16). Greek, Roman, and Byzantine architecture also had a logical guiding principle and therefore had style. In his analysis of a copper vessel in the sixth volume, *Entretien,* he defined the criteria for style as the clear indication of purpose, the selection of the appropriate material, its proper treatment, and the suitability of the object for the intended use. Throughout his writings he emphasized the importance of reason as the sole guide to architectural creation. At times he was materialistic in the importance he attached to the material itself, at the exclusion of other factors in the generation of form.

The decline of French academic authority following the French Revolution and the subsequent collapse of Neoclassicism as a viable style were not simply national events, but were indicative of a more general decline in the hegemony of French architectural theory throughout Europe. After 1800, both the United Kingdom and Germany began to pursue paths in theory increasingly separate from French developments.

The major British contribution to nineteenth-century architectural theory—the notion of the picturesque—had its basis in the eighteenth century. British reverence for the "picturelike" can be discerned in John Vanbrugh's 1709 memorandum concerning the preservation of ruins in the park at Blenheim, and in the gardens of Alexander Pope (at Twickenham, 1719) and William Kent (at Rousham, 1730; at Stowe, 1734). The notion was advanced as an aesthetic concept by Edmund Burke in *A Philosophical Enquiry into the Origin of Our Ideas on the Sublime and Beautiful* (1757). Burke denied absolute beauty and the importance of proportion in its formation, and shifted the experience of beauty from the mind to the senses, that is, to the physiological responses engendered by certain qualities of objects. As an aesthetic category distinct from beauty, Burke discussed the qualities of the sublime. Beauty resided in the sensations of smallness, smoothness, gradual variation, delicacy, clear and bright colors; the feeling of the sublime was evoked by power, darkness, solitude, vastness, infinity, magnitude, magnificence, and sad colors.

In a work published in 1794 entitled, *On the Picturesque as Compared with the Sublime and Beautiful,* Uvedale Price appended the concept of the picturesque as a third aesthetic category to Burke's system. Its qualities were roughness, variety, intricacy, and such accidental embellishments as weather stains and vines growing over walls. Richard Payne Knight further elaborated the concept in *An Analytical Inquiry into the Principles of Taste* (1805), in which he pleaded for England's return to the wild and unkempt, to the natural rather than the composed. As Knight's Gothic design for his castle at Downton (1772–1778) shows, the picturesque movement had aligned itself with Gothic architecture at an early date, and beginning in the nineteenth century began to form as a counter-movement to the Greek Neoclassicism of William Wilkins, Thomas Harrison, and others.

Figure 9. *Maison du Personnel,* Notre Dame, Paris, Eugène-Emmanuel Viollet-le-Duc, 1866.

The reason for the early popularity of Gothic architecture in England was the lead British scholars had taken in researching this style. John Carter (1748–1817) and John Britton (1771–1857) produced a number of books around the turn of the century that turned English attention to Gothic. Their efforts culminated in the second and third decades of the nineteenth century with two highly influential works: Thomas Rickman's *An Attempt to Discriminate the Styles of English Architecture* (1817) and August Charles Pugin's *Specimens of Gothic Architecture* (1821–1823). Yet the theorist who turned the movement into a crusade was Pugin's son, August Welby Northmore Pugin (1812–1852). The younger Pugin was a gifted artist first employed by Charles Barry to carry out the Gothic detailing of the Houses of Parliament. In 1836 he published his first of several books on Gothic architecture, *Contrasts; or, A Parallel between the Noble Edifices of the Fourteenth and Fifteenth Centuries, and Similar Buildings of the Present Day; shewing the Present Decay of Taste*. The result of his comparison, as evident in the title, was simple. The works of the Middle Ages were rewarding and full of Christian spirit; all modern works in the classical style were degraded and mean. In 1841 Pugin followed this work with *The True Principles of Pointed Architecture* that reduced design to two great rules: all features of a building should honor convenience, construction, and propriety; and all ornament should enrich the essential construction of a building. These nonstylistic premises, however, were infused with a zealous and impassioned moralism, equating the Gothic style, Roman Catholicism, and the English people with truth.

Pugin's fervid embrace of Gothic was actually the first salvo in a campaign, as British theory in the 1840s came alive with architectural debate, contemporaneously christened the Battle of the Styles. The youngest and perhaps the most progressive of the protagonists, Robert Kerr (1823–1904), published *The Newleafe Discourses on the Fine Art Architecture* in 1846, in which Ecclesiology (Pugin), the Royal Institute of British Architects (founded only in 1835), and professional training were singled out in chapters for special ridicule. Kerr, one of the founders of the Architectural Association, called for the end of all styles, more freedom for the designer, and an architecture based on suitability, economy, and command of the materials. The architect G. G. Scott (1811–1878) upheld the Gothic cause with *A Plea for the Faithful Restoration of Our Ancient Churches* (1850). He argued that modern architects should return to the Christian path and follow the style of the thirteenth century. Scott was opposed in this regard by the Renaissance advocates, James Fergusson and Edward Lacy Garbett. Fergusson, perhaps the most widely read English historian of the nineteenth century, adamantly opposed the "copyism" of the Gothic camp, and countered with a call for the "common sense" tradition of the Renaissance—a style in his view capable of further formal evolution (17). Garbett, in *Rudimentary Treatise on the Principles of Design in Architecture* (1850), arrived at similar position. He criticized the religious nationalism of the Gothic school and the stereotyped copies of eclecticism, because architecture in his view was primarily an expressive and poetic art. In a structural analysis of architecture's principles he rationalized three possible systems: the "depressile" trabeated system, the "compressile" arcuated system, and the "tensile" system of the future aligned with the steel truss. The problem, however, was that this new tensile style could not be created overnight, and as a temporary expedient Garbett urged the use of "Italianism" to satisfy contemporary needs (18).

Yet another theoretical direction was offered by the group of architects and artists aligned with Henry Cole and the *Journal of Design and Manufactures* (1849–1851). Cole had started his career as a civil servant and author of children's books. In the late 1840s he turned his attention to the arts and crafts. He founded the Art Manufactures guild, an association of artists with yearly exhibitions, and began a series of shrewd political maneuvers to take over the flagging Schools of Design, some 90 institutions throughout the United Kingdom charged with the task of raising the standard of British industrial design. Cole achieved his goal in 1851, but not before organizing the Great London Exhibition of 1851 and starting the *Journal of Design* with Richard Redgrave. Although the aim of the journal was to foster principles for industrial design, its articles were more often than not directed toward architecture and the problem of eclecticism in general. Owen Jones wrote a series of reviews on the Great Exhibition, and his effort to sketch propositions to correct contemporary artistic deficiencies led to his influential *Grammar of Ornament* (1856). Another regular contributor to the *Journal of Design* was Matthew Digby Wyatt, who wrote optimistically of the beneficial effects industrialization would have on art, and likened the Great Exhibition itself and the competition of commerce to the Olympic games of Greece. Wyatt also prepared the working drawings for Paxton's Exhibition Building and supervised its construction. Jones designed the interior color scheme.

The great nemesis to Cole, Redgrave, Wyatt, and Jones, and to Garbett and Fergusson for that matter, was the brilliant and eccentric John Ruskin (1819–1900). Ruskin is often cited as the heir to the cause of Pugin, but the artistic philosophies of the two men were basically different. Pugin at least tolerated some improvements technology could bring to daily life; Ruskin was an implacable foe to the machine and what he saw as its debasement of human labor and life. As a theorist on art, Ruskin's assertions varied from the trivial to the profound. His rather casual preference expressed in *The Seven Lamps of Architecture* (1849) for England's adoption of Venetian Gothic (over the Pisan Romanesque, early Gothic, and English earliest decorated) exemplifies the former tendency, while his transcendent theory of naturalism in art representing his thinking at its most sublime level, exemplifies the latter.

Ruskin's architectural theory was essentially a theory of ornament. He defined architecture as the art that "impresses on its forms certain characters venerable or beautiful, but otherwise unnecessary" (19). It is grounded in nature, the source not only of all decorative motifs, but also the spiritual wellspring nourishing and guiding the imagination of man. Nature is to be imitated, not literally but conventionally. Ruskin divided artists into two groups: those who alter and try to improve nature; and those who believe nature should improve them. All classically trained architects belong to the first category, whereas Gothic architects belong to the second. This theme is developed further in "The Nature of Gothic," the chapter of *The Stones of Venice* (1851–1853) published separately as a manifesto by William Morris in 1892. Ruskin claimed that Oriental, Egyptian, Assyrian, and Greek ornaments were servile, because their simplified geometrical forms had to be executed with great precision, thus enslaving the executing craftsmen. He denounced Renaissance ornament as a "wearisome exhibition of well-educated imbecility" (20). Only Gothic ornament was ethically acceptable to him, because its varying measurements, departures from symmetry, and diversity of forms allowed the artist to confer on the work his individuality and imperfection. Moreover, Gothic ornament was inventive. Whereas the classical tradition had developed only five Orders, Ruskin noted, "There is not a side chapel in any Gothic cathedral but it has fifty orders, the worst of them better than the best of the Greek ones, and all new; and a single inventive human soul could create a thousand orders in an hour" (21). Aside from the moral superiority of Gothic ornament, it also exhibited a full range of attractive visual attributes, such as savageness, imperfection, changefulness, grotesqueness, shadow, and polychromy. The ultimate aim of ornament for Ruskin was nothing less than spiritual transcendence, best exemplified, he believed, in the unnatural thinness of the statuary of Chartres. His theory in this regard was truly the glorious culmination of the English picturesque movement.

Ruskin's fervor kindled the flame of an entire generation of artistic reformers, chief among them William Morris (1832–1896). After leaving Oxford in 1859, Morris hired Philip Webb to design his Red House at Bexley Heath in Kent. Two years later Morris started the firm of Morris, Marshall & Faulkner, Fine Art Workmen in Painting, Carving, Furniture, and the Metals. Morris expounded his artistic theory in a series of lectures given between 1877 and 1894. A socialist politically, he called for art's return to the everyday, to pre-industrial methods of production, and for its basis to reside in craftsmanship rather than inspiration. Morris' activities coincided with the Queen Anne movement in the United Kingdom, and the emphasis on comfort and vernacular building as the starting point for modern domestic design. This trend would soon have extensive influence on the continent of Europe and the United States; its leading domestic architects were Richard Norman Shaw, Eden Nesfield, M. H. Ballie Scott, William Richmond Lethaby, and C. F. A. Voysey. Both Lethaby (1857–1931) and Voysey (1857–1941) continued with their so-called "free style" well into the twentieth century, in opposition to a conservative counter-tendency. Lethaby's writings, in particular, looked not only to Ruskin and Viollet-le-Duc, but also to the new developments unfolding in Germany after the turn of the century.

German theory in the nineteenth century shared many similarities with developments in the United Kingdom, particularly in its separation from French thinking around 1800. The leading architectural force in Germany at this time was David Gilly (1748–1808) who, in 1788,

moved his private architectural school from Stettin to Berlin and began an architectural program—inspired largely by the model of J. F. Blondel—that trained many of the most important architects of the next generation, among them Karl Friedrich Schinkel, Friedrich Weinbrenner, and Leo von Klenze. In 1797 he began the first German architectural journal, *Sammlung nützlicher Aufsätze und Nachrichten die Baukunst betreffend* (*Collection of Useful Essays and Reports Concerning Architecture*), that questions Vitruvian authority and took up the cause for a new Prussian style, inspired by the Hellenism of Winckelmann and Goethe. A regular contributor to the journal was David Gilly's son, Friedrich (1772–1800), who in his brief professional life eclipsed his father in importance in some respects.

The younger Gilly gained early prominence with his grand scheme for a monument to Frederick the Great in 1797. Over the next two years he traveled to France, England, and Southern Germany, filling sketchbooks (shortly passed down to Schinkel) with the latest trends. In 1799, one year before his untimely death, he began teaching perspective at his father's school. His influential sketches presented a classical architecture of robust elementary forms, drawing inspiration and formal motifs from Ledoux, Boullée, and John Soane. In his design for the monument to Frederick the Great, a Doric temple was set high on a massive substructure, flanked at one end by a columnar triumphal arch and at the other by four isolated obelisks. His project for a national theater (1798) drew on the first proposals of Peyre and de Wailly for the Odéon in Paris and Ledoux's theater at Besançon. Gilly's style is sometimes described as revolutionary classicism; his new Dorism, although supremely rational in its conception, was charged with great power and pathos.

Gilly's immediate heir was the great Karl Friedrich Schinkel (1781–1841), who in 1798 presented himself as a pupil to David Gilly after viewing the monument to Frederick. Schinkel soon moved into the Gilly household and, after the death of Friedrich Gilly, dedicated his life to carrying forward the younger Gilly's vision. Schinkel set out for the south in 1803, only to return to a Prussia that would soon be defeated by Napoleon in 1806. With the cessation of building activity, Schinkel began a career as a landscape painter of panoramas. He executed some interior designs for Queen Luise at the Schloss Charlottenburg in 1810 that led to a provisional appointment with the Prussian civil service, yet it was not until after Waterloo in 1814 that order, ambition, and financial means returned to the Prussian capital. A promotion within the civil service in 1815 allowed Schinkel to become, within a few years, the most prolific monumental builder in Germany.

Schinkel's theory is known from letters and citations recorded in diaries and notebooks. He planned to write a substantial textbook on architecture, but only fragments survive. His attraction to the ethical and aesthetic systems of J. G. Fichte, August Schlegel, and Friedrich Wilhelm Schelling impresses his language with an abstract, almost mystical meaning in his use of such terms as species and purposiveness (*Zweckmässigkeit*). The former concept represented for Schinkel the higher truth of nature and the human mind, the profound aim of art. The latter derived from Kant's third moment of beauty in the *Critique of Judgment*. For Kant it was a teleological concept signifying the intrinsic harmony or purposive wholeness of beautiful objects lacking an external purpose, not dissimilar to the Albertian notion of concinnitas. For Schinkel, purposiveness was the essence of architectural beauty, the rational unity or harmonious accord of the parts, when each part functions properly and exhibits its character.

Although Schinkel epitomized the best of late Neoclassical architecture, he was also preoccupied with the question of a new style and how it might be constructed. In one remarkable passage from his unfinished work on theory, he writes of his flirtation with an abstract style based simply on utilitarian purpose and construction that he rejected for its dry and severe result, its absence of the "historic and poetic" (22). He went on to outline the steps his age should take in pursuing a new style accommodating history: (*1*) determine what the age demands of architecture; (*2*) review history to see what forms have been used for similar purposes and which are suited to the present; (*3*) determine what modifications to these forms are necessary; and (*4*) consider how the imagination might produce from these modifications something totally new (23).

Schinkel was a transitional figure in the sense that he practiced his refined style at a time when this movement was losing its support throughout Europe. The leading adversary to Neoclassicism in Germany was the Karlsruhe architect Heinrich Hübsch (1795–1863) who, in his influential essay of 1828 entitled, *In welchem Style sollen wir bauen?* (*In What Style Should We Build?*), professed the intention to liberate architecture from the chains of classical antiquity. Hübsch sought to identify the objective parameters for a new style based on need, defined by a double purposiveness of convenience and solidity. A style, he felt, was best defined by its primary elements of roof and support; other factors affecting its development were local and traditional building materials, contemporary technological developments, climate, durability, and cultural aspirations. On the basis of these criteria, Hübsch embarked on an historical evaluation of the various styles and their suitability to modern needs. He eliminated all trabeated systems primarily because of poor stone selection in Germany, and was left with a choice between pointed- and round-arched (*Rundbogen*) systems. He opted for the round-arched system for a variety of reasons, among them the fact that it was both poetic and capable of further development. Although Hübsch's later architecture inclined toward a literal Romanesque, his designs of the late 1820s, such as the Finance Ministry in Karlsruhe, exhibited plain, exposed-brick facades with few historical trappings.

The title of Hübsch's book became a rallying cry in the 1840s, as typological eclecticism consolidated its position in Germany and the problem of history (that is, the need to sanction forms historically to legitimatize the cultural aspirations of a nascent German state) became more apparent. Almost everyone opposed eclecticism, especially those who championed a particular style as the basis for

further development. Thus the Düsseldorf architect Rudolf Wiegmann complained in 1841 that the present trend to build with Greek, Roman, Byzantine, Gothic, and Italian forms reduced architecture to the viewpoint of fashion and depicted an age that had lost its organic relation with its technology. Wiegmann advocated a national style and selected a modified Rundbogen. His principal Gothic antagonist was August Reichensperger, a politician and zealous follower of Pugin. In *Die christlich-germanische Baukunst und ihr Verhaltniss zur Gegenwart* (*Christian-German Architecture and Its Relation to the Present*), published in 1845, Reichensperger urged his countrymen to return to the path of the Middle Ages to find a new style.

The medievalism of Wiegmann and Reichensperger was countered by J. H. Wolff, who opposed the demand for a national style and advocated instead the eternal and the true—the classical in the spirit of Schinkel or Klenze (Fig. 10). In an 1846 address to an architectural congress in Gotha, he urged the foundation of a new style by uniting behind the principle of truth in architecture that he defined as honesty in construction and in the use of materials. In the same year, the theorist Karl Bötticher delivered his famous address to the Schinkelfest in Berlin, entitled, "Das Princip der hellenischen und germanischen Bauweise" (The Principle of the Hellenic and German Way of Building). Bötticher argued that the two major styles of his day, the Greek and the Gothic, were incapable of further evolution, since both were fully developed "space-covering" systems based on contrary static principles of trabeated and arcuated construction. For a new style to emerge, he argued, a new system of space covering must first appear, one that would embody a structural principle foreign to stone and be able to satisfy every spatial and functional need. This new material was iron; its principle was strength in tension. It was destined to produce a style, he believed, comparable in greatness to the Greek and Gothic.

Bötticher's prophetic address, however, was too precocious for a Prussian state only in the initial stages of industrialization. Moreover, the political unrest of 1848–

Figure 10. *Propylaeon,* Munich, Leopold von Klenze, 1846–1860 (first proposed 1817).

1849 in Germany quickly put an end to the enthusiasm of the 1840s for a new style. The cause of the unrest was widespread calls for a government of national unity and a constitution, a plea that was rejected by the Prussian monarch, Friedrich Wilhelm IV. The unrest that broke out in several cities was quickly suppressed, leading to a conservative reaction throughout the still independent German states.

One victim of the political events was Germany's leading architect and most important theorist of the nineteenth century, Gottfried Semper (1803–1879). Semper first gained prominence shortly after returning from his student tour of the south, when he participated in the polychrome debate of the 1830s in support of Hittorff's polychrome position. In 1834 Semper settled into a professorship at the Dresden Academy and quickly established a highly successful practice, beginning with his Renaissance-inspired Dresden Theater (1838–1841). His construction of a barricade for the Dresden uprising of 1849 abruptly forced him into exile in Paris, London, and Zürich.

Semper's architectural theory underwent many changes in its 35-year development. In his pamphlet on Greek polychromy of 1834 (just four years before his Dresden theater helped re-introduce Germany to the Renaissance) Semper decried the advent of eclecticism and proposed that "brick should appear as brick, wood as wood, iron as iron, each according to its own statical laws" (24). In his critique of the Great Exhibition of 1851 and the depreciating effect industrialization was having on art, Semper applauded the disintegration of art's traditional types (its historical language) and felt confident that capitalism would soon replace architecture's historical forms with new motifs based on the machine. Eight years later, however, he had reversed his position. In the prolegomenon to his major work on style, he sarcastically referred to those seeking to invent a new style as "materialists," "purists," "schematists," and "futurists," all of whom denied "some of the oldest traditions of architecture that are fully consistent with the logic of building and with artistic creation in general, and that have symbolic values that are older than history and that cannot possibly be represented by something new" (25).

These changes in Semper's thinking, however, were not arrived at casually. His theoretical search began with a work published in 1851 entitled, *Die vier Elemente der Baukunst* (*The Four Elements of Architecture*) that, in drawing on contemporary ethnographic research, postulated four elementary motives underlying architectural creation: walling, hearth-gathering, terracing, and making a structural framework. These motives were not static, but underwent continual development and formal variation under the conditioning factors of different materials, evolving technologies, and cultural forces. His work was carried forward 10 years later by his monumental study, *Der Stil in den technischen und tektonischen Künsten oder praktische Ästhetik* (*Style in the Technical and Tectonic Arts or Practical Aesthetics*), published in 1860–1863, that proposed to examine the premises of style in all its functional, material, technological, sociocultural aspects to gain insight into the source of current dilemmas.

Although Semper failed to complete his enormous endeavor, his analysis was always penetrating and incisive (Fig. 11). In his analysis of the walling or dressing motive (*Bekleidung*), for instance, Semper traced the idea of the spatial enclosure from its genesis in crude mats hung vertically as spatial dividers in primitive societies to the invention of textiles, later to the use of carpets as wall dressings hung over solid props. Eventually, the textile dressing evolved into other surrogate dressings, such as the textilelike alabaster panels found in Assyrian excavations of the 1840s. The most sophisticated use of the dressing theme in antiquity, for Semper, took place in classical Greece, where, in line with his polychrome conception of the Greek temple, paint became the new abstract sheathing, not just dressing the stone's appearance, but also masking its materiality and thereby letting it become pure form. Architecture's denial and transcendence of its real or material basis thus became, for Semper, its highest ideal. In this respect his theory differed markedly from the contemporary formulations of Ruskin and Viollet-le-Duc, but his thinking would be no less influential in establishing the basis for later developments.

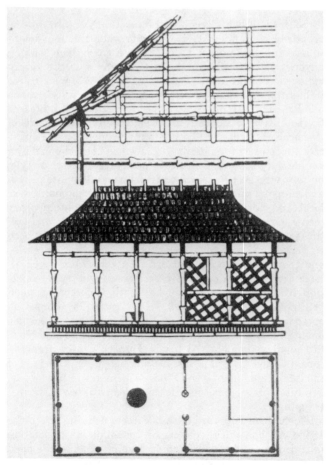

Figure 11. The "walling" motive as seen in an Indian hut from Trinidad on display at the Great Exhibition of 1851, from Gottfried Semper, *Der Stil,* 1860–1863.

MODERN THEORY

The first efforts to define a modern theory of architecture originated in Chicago and Vienna, under cultural conditions and circumstances as distinct as their geographical separation and respective landscapes might suggest. Chicago in the 1880s was an isolated boomtown on the edge of the great prairie, experiencing rapid growth and land speculation, and possessing the youthful intrepidity and ambition to rival the commercial centers of the East. Vienna, by contrast, epitomized the notion of the "old country," the historic capital of the Hapsburg Empire (dating back to 1278 A.D.), recently industrialized, yet with building codes and ordinances permitting little architectural experimentation. If the events in Chicago and the Midwest as a whole were a competitive result of a relatively broad circle of practitioners intent on finding a practical and visually pleasing solution to the highrise problem, the theoretical breakthrough in Europe was largely the result of a few individuals working separately yet drawing on the same sources.

The technical and aesthetic starting points for the developments in Chicago were William Le Baron Jenny's Home Insurance Building (1883–1885) and H. H. Richardson's Marshall Field Wholesale Store (1885–1887). The former building introduced into architecture the steel skeleton; the latter, with its bold vertical rhythm and simplified Romanesque massing, provided the aesthetic model to be emulated and refined.

Contemporary and subsequent developments proceeded at a brisk pace: Burnham and Root's Rookery (1885–1888), Adler and Sullivan's Auditorium Building (1886–1889), Jenney's Second Leiter Building (1889–1891), Burnham and Root's Monadrock Building (1889–1892), Adler and Sullivan's Wainright Building (1890–1891), Holabird and Roche's Marquette Building (1894), and Adler and Sullivan's Guaranty Building (1894–1895). Yet attempts to find the theoretical thread to unify this progressive de-historicizing of form (in Sullivan's case the passage from the taut classicism of the Auditorium Building tower to the filigreelike curtain sheathing of the Guaranty Building) will be unsuccessful. Certainly the organic metaphor attributed to Louis H. Sullivan (1856–1924) that form follows function provides little in the way of elucidation, since similar analogies had long enjoyed currency in nineteenth-century theory, and since Sullivan's buildings were hardly functional in any twentieth-century use of this term. Similarly, Sullivan's suggestion in his 1892 essay, "Ornament in Architecture," that architects refrain "for a period of years" from the use of ornament to resolve the problems of massing and proportion offers little insight into his art, since he argued in the same essay that "a decorated structure, harmoniously conceived, well considered, cannot be stripped of its system of ornament without destroying its individuality" (26). Moreover, Sullivan was first and foremost an ornamentalist, a careful student of such ornamental guides as Owen Jones's *The Grammar of Ornament* (1856) and V. M. C. Ruprich-Robert's *Flore Ornamentale* (1866–1876). Sullivan's late work, *A System of Architectural Ornament According with a Philosophy of Man's Powers* (1924), reveals ornament as the very germ of his transcendental philosophy.

Yet, despite the misunderstandings that have enshrouded for so long this talented and influential artist (in large part promulgated by Sullivan himself in his biographical and polemical writings), a quite different historical figure has begun to emerge in the past few years. The historian David Van Zanten has emphasized the importance of Sullivan's tutelage under the Philadelphia architect Frank Furness, and his distillation of progressive Beaux Arts ideals during his brief stay in Paris (27). The result is a highly individualistic artist maturing around 1890, attempting to mediate the exoticism of French Neó-Grec theory with a functionalist emphasis on truth in construction.

The same misunderstandings and disparity between polemical pronouncements and artistic practice can be seen in Sullivan's most gifted and loyal disciple, Frank Lloyd Wright (1869–1959). His theoretical maturity coincided with the development of Prairie Style around 1900 and, in a paper read to an architectural convention in the same year entitled, "The Architect," Wright called on his colleagues to bring forth a new architecture based on the materials and ideals of the new land, and dispense with the "archaeological dry bones" of the past. In the following year in his famous Hull House lecture, "The Art and Craft of the Machine," Wright referred to the machine as the catalytic agent of the new art, and technology itself as the indispensable partner in the future development of architecture. Yet Wright's great domestic advances over the earlier efforts by Bruce Price and McKim Mead & White were not as technological or machine-oriented as his statements suggest. They reside, rather, in his masterful exploitation of space in the open plan, the changed figure-ground relationship of the dwelling (produced by a visually strong base, horizontal fenestration, and low hovering roofs), the use of the hearth as an organizational tool in design, and the dissection or free manipulation of wall planes (Fig. 12). A close study of his early and highly inventive years, between the Winslow House (1893) and the Dana House (1901–1903), points to an intense and concerted effort to resolve a studied academism with a

Figure 12. *Frederick Robie House,* Chicago, Frank Lloyd Wright, 1908–1909.

looser vernacular tradition through a process of abstracting form and exaggerating conventional elements. In addition, Wright was certainly unique among architects in his study of non-Western artistic sources. As Neil Levine has observed, Wright and his experiments in the first decade of this century with fracturing images was without artistic precedent or parallel, unless one looks to the contemporary studies of Pablo Picasso and French Cubism (28).

The development of modern theory in Europe, although equally complex, is slightly easier to disentangle, if only because of the greater emphasis placed on theory. The architect Semper, in a state of near intellectual exhaustion in 1869, concluded his Zurich lecture "On Architectural Styles" with the admonition that the new style would have to await a new "world-historical idea" and, until that event took place, architects would have to be content with the "old" (29). Semper, however, was overly pessimistic in evaluating the present, for many of the components of this "world-historical idea" were already becoming apparent to his younger colleagues. The art critic Konrad Fiedler, in analyzing Semper's theory in his 1878 essay "Über Wesen und Geschichte der Architektur" ("On the Nature and History of Architecture"), suggested that the new architecture might be created simply by peeling away Semper's space-enclosing dressing and letting space itself become the new medium to be exploited. In an 1883 article, "Die Entwicklung des Raumes in der Baukunst" ("The Development of Space in Architecture"), the Viennese architecture Hans Auer called space, newly liberated by the spanning possibilities of iron, the soul of building. Ten years later the Leipzig professor August Schmarsow delivered his famous inaugural address, "Das Wesen der architektonischen Schöpfung" ("The Nature of Architectural Creation"), in which he also rejected Semper's art of the dressing and argued that architecture was purely and simply the creatress of space (*Raumgestalterin*) that should now be analyzed historically as feeling for space (*Raumgefühl*) (30). In the same year the Dutch architect Hendrik Berlage (1856–1934) delivered his important lecture "Bouwkunst en Impressionisme" ("Architecture and Impressionism"), in which he criticized the muddling with historical forms, urged the avoidance of excessive detailing, and emphasized the beauty of simple masses. Ten years later, in 1904, in a lecture given in Zürich entitled, "Gedanken über Stil in der Baukunst" ("Ideas on Style in Architecture"), Berlage attempted a quite explicit mediation of the theories of Semper and Viollet-le-Duc, and defined the new art of architecture as the creation of space.

The complementary idea to the concept of space in the formation of modern theory was the notion of pure form, that is, form as an abstract, nonhistorical element capable of artistic exploitation in itself. The basis for an aesthetics of form was an 1872 essay by Robert Vischer, "Über das optische Formegefühl" ("On the Optical Feeling for Form"). It expounded on a theory of visual empathy (*Einfühlung*), which he defined as the aesthetic enjoyment we feel in projecting our psychic feelings or sentiments into the artistic objects we contemplate. Vischer's theory of empathy was popularized in the 1890s by the psychologist

Theodor Lipps yet, even before that date, the notion began to work its way into architectural thinking. In 1886 Heinrich Wölfflin opened his doctoral dissertation, "Prolegomena zu einer Psychologie der Architektur" with the question: "How is it possible that architectural forms are able to express spirituality and feeling?" (31). Drawing on the psychological investigations of Vischer and others, Wölfflin argued for the importance of a collective feeling for form in artistic creation, pointing out that each period in history possesses its unique interpretation of this feeling. Another person investigating stylistic change and form, the Stuttgart professor Adolf Göller, published works in 1887 and 1888 in which he suggested that the beauty of form resided not in its ideal or symbolic content (the historical language of eclecticism), but rather in its abstract play of lines, light, and shade. The theories of Wölfflin and Göller were well known to German architects of this period; in 1889 the critic Cornelius Gurlitt reviewed Göller's theory for the Berlin architectural journal *Deutsche Bauzeitung*, and immediately pointed out its revolutionary implication—the possibility of a nonhistorical, abstract art.

In the same year the Viennese architect Otto Wagner (1841–1918) began to formulate his ideology of architectural modernity. In the 1889 preface to the first volume of *Sketches, Projects, and Executed Works*, Wagner denounced eclecticism in architecture for its consumption of millenia of styles, and for its childish convention of using specific styles for special purposes. After a somewhat incongruous acceptance of a certain free Renaissance as the only correct course for architecture, he quickly contradicted himself with the claim that the future style would be the *Nutz-Stil* (utility style), best exemplified in the newly constructed Eiffel Tower. Wagner's polemic, however, was in advance of his artistic practice. He had begun his career in 1863 and by 1889 was a moderately successful renaissance architect, whose practice consisted mainly of speculative apartment buildings. In the 1890s, concurrent with and perhaps spurred on by the events in Chicago, Wagner began an intensive search for new formal solutions and the theoretical basis to sustain them. In 1894 he was appointed to a chair at the Vienna Academy of Fine Arts and immediately reformed the curriculum to eliminate or downplay historicist training. Emboldened perhaps by the ideas and designs of such students as Joseph Olbrich, Max Fabiani, and Josef Hoffmann, Wagner began preparing the first manifesto to the new movement, *Modern Architecture* (1896).

The three principal themes of *Modern Architecture*— the ethical ruin of eclecticism, the plea for simplicity in the accommodation of modern needs, and the demand for a new style based on present technologies and methods of construction—hark back to the German eclectic debate of the 1840s, but the underlying conditions were fundamentally different. Wagner argued that the simple, practical, almost military approach is better suited to modern life because of its better, democratic, self-confident approach to everyday affairs: honoring comfort, cleanliness, and functional convenience. Dwellings should be bright, well ventilated, and appointed with simple, functional furnishings in harmony with the checkered breeches and leisure wear of the modern city's inhabitants. The heart of Wagner's theory is contained in the chapter "Construction," that begins with his criticism of Semper for making do with a symbolism of construction (primordial architectural motives such as the dressing) rather than construction itself as the starting point for architecture. Wagner expounded a rigorous artistic materialism, in which artistic forms only develop out of the construction and material, while new constructional materials and techniques, in turn, must give birth to new forms. He proposed that this new language of the engineer should replace the traditional historical language of architecture (Fig. 13).

Although Wagner's architecture never truly implemented his hardline aesthetics and—arguably—even utilized a symbolic constructional dressing alluding to the Semperian tradition, his book was eagerly read and discussed in other European capitals, and especially in Germany. Beginning in 1897 the Munich architect August Endell (1871–1925) published articles applauding the new trend toward practicality and the truthful expression of construction. Invoking the empathy theory of his former teacher Theodor Lipps, Endell called on the architect to become a form artist and investigate the psychological effects of certain lines and forms. In two books of 1901 and 1902, Henry van de Velde (1863–1957) exalted the new realism and attention to purpose. He argued that the sole criteria for modern design were reason and logic; absolute beauty resided in locomotives, bridges, and glass halls. Also in 1902 Hermann Mushesius (1861–1927), who had been living in London since 1896, published *Stilarchitecktur und Baukunst* (*Style–Architecture and the Art of Building*), in which he proposed an architecture based strictly on scientific objectivity (*wissenschaftliche Sachlichkeit*), abstaining from all decoration, and unconditionally correlating form and purpose.

The two culminating events for the Modern Movement prior to World War I in Germany were Peter Behrens' association with the Allgemeine Elektricitäts-Gesellschaft (AEG) and the founding of the Deutsche Werkbund, both occurring in 1908. Behrens (1868–1940) left the Darmstadt Colony and his Jugendstil period in 1903 to head the Applied Arts School in Düsseldorf; in joining the AEG in 1908 he affixed his Nietzschean vision of the future to the full acceptance of industrialization, producing in his Berlin Turbine Factory (1908–1909)—as he conceived it—the first temple to industrial power. Both Walter Gropius (1883–1969) and Ludwig Mies van der Rohe (1886–1969) received training in his office.

The Deutsche Werkbund attempted to enact a similar program on a grander scale. Muthesius returned to Germany in 1904 to take a position with the Prussian Board of Trade. Two years later at the German Exhibition of Arts and Crafts in Dresden, he aligned himself with Karl Schmidt and Friedrich Neumann in a coalition advocating the adoption of mass production for Germany industry. The Werkbund was conceived as a union of German artists and crafts firms dedicated to improving the quality of German products and enhancing Germany's position in world trade. Its high point was the Cologne Exhibition of 1914, displaying the famous buildings of Gropius and Meyer, van de Velde, and Bruno Taut, alongside the equally famous quarrel between Muthesius and van de Velde. Muthesius had prepared a ten-point program stressing the need for German industry to develop "types" or normative standards for German products and to accelerate mass production. Van de Velde countered with another program opposing any canon for standardization and defending the autonomy of the artist. Although Muthesius was forced to withdraw his program in the face of opposition from Gropius and others, the future was clearly on his side. A vision of this future could be gleaned in 1914 from the Futurists' drawings of the *Città Nuova* by Antonio Sant' Elia, prepared for the Nuove Tendenze Exhibition in Milan. Modern theory had made enormous strides in the 18 years since Wagner's publication, yet World War I abruptly brought this phase of the movement to an end.

Architectural theory between the two world wars is characterized by a consolidation and simplification of the modern tenets reached earlier, and by a score of competing ideologies operating within a limited theoretical range. The political and economic turmoil caused by the war sharply curtailed building activity until the beginning of the 1920s. Perhaps as a reaction to the nationalism that had brought about the war, a new spirit of international collaboration overtook the profession. Modernists of various persuasions united to maximize the effect of their agendas and reform the building codes and regulations inhibiting the realization of the new movement.

An early effort to define what was widely viewed as the new spirit of the times was the formation in 1917 of the Dutch De Stijl movement by a group of painters and architects, led by Piet Mondrian (1872–1944) and Theo van Doesburg (1883–1931). Their 1918 manifesto proclaimed a new consciousness of the age inclined toward the universal, and called for replacing the former cult of the individual with an international unity of art, life, and culture. In an effort to broaden the impact of the movement and its aesthetic agenda of primary colors and rectilinear lines, in 1921 van Doesburg embarked on a European tour, notable for his uninvited nine-month stay at the Weimar Bauhaus

Figure 13. The church of *St. Leopold Am Steinhof,* Vienna, Otto Wagner, 1904–1907.

and his collaboration with the Russian artist and theorist El Lissitzky. In Paris in 1923 van Doesburg and Cor van Eesteren exhibited their architectural conception of De Stijl principles with the use of models and orthogonal projections. In the same year another member of the group, Gerrit Rietveld, began work on his famous Schröder House in Utrecht.

The conclusion of the war in Germany spawned two architectural alliances, the Arbeitsrat für Kunst (Work Council for Art) and the Novembergruppe, that were both leftist in political orientation and were soon to merge into one movement. The 1918 manifesto for the Arbeitsrat für Kunst, written by Bruno Taut (1880–1938), called for the destruction of the monumental symbols of the past and the creation of large-scale housing projects in rural areas. In the following year the council organized "An Exhibition for Unknown Architects," for which Taut, Gropius, and Adolf Behne prepared the exhibition catalogue. Gropius urged architects, painters, and sculptors to destroy the professional *status quo* (the academies and professional organizations) and return to the crafts. The brutal suppression of the Spartacus League in Berlin a few months later, however, dampened similar public displays. In response to the conservative backlash, Taut circulated *"The Glass Chain,"* a private exchange of letters, sketches, and essays by members of the council. Taut published much of this correspondence in *Frühlicht* (Daybreak), first appearing as an addendum to a professional journal, later as an independent quarterly. Taut also summed up his ideas in his important book, *Die Auflösung der Städte* (*The Dissolution of the City*), published in 1920, in which he urged the breakup of cities and the return to an agrarian, handicraft-based economy.

Taut's plea very much influenced Gropius and became the first ideology for the architectural school known as the Bauhaus. The school had been founded in 1906 as the Weimar Arts and Crafts School, directed by van de Velde. He was forced to resign during the war as a foreigner in Germany, and governmental officials waited four years to name Gropius as his successor. Gropius restructured the Bauhaus and published a proclamation re-affirming the return to the crafts and the union of architects, painters, and sculptors. The first three years of the school's existence were dominated by Johannes Itten (1888–1967), a mystic who taught the famed introductory design course. Van Doesburg's visit in 1921 presented a major challenge to the original program, and Gropius, now under his influence, began to rethink the role of the school. In 1923 he announced a major reform, shifting the emphasis of the school from the crafts to the industrialization and mass production, thereby forcing Itten's resignation. The latter was replaced by the Hungarian László Moholy-Nagy (1895–1946), and the subsequent move of the Bauhaus to Dessau in 1925 strengthened its industrial commitment. One result of this commitment was Marcel Breuer's furniture designs, manufactured at the Bauhaus and sold on the commercial market. The Swiss architect Hannes Meyer (1889–1954) succeeded Gropius as the school's director in 1928 and attempted to implement a more socially conscious functionalism, known in Germany as *Neue Sachlichkeit* (the New Objectivity). By the date of his

forced resignation in 1930, the school had lost much of its initiative and survived its last years under Mies van der Rohe, until the Nazi government shut it down in 1933.

Of equal importance to the development of modern theory in the 1920s were the architectural works and writings of Le Corbusier, born Charles Edouard Jeanneret (1887–1966). Le Corbusier built his first house La Chaux de Fonds in 1905; before the war he taught at the local arts and crafts school and visited the leading architects in Paris, Berlin, and Vienna. In 1916 he moved to Paris and met the painter Amédée Ozenfant. Together, they evolved the philosophy of purism, an aesthetic based in Neoplatonism that was anticubist in conception and advocated the conscious refinement of existing types. In 1920, while working in a brickyard, Le Corbusier and Ozenfant founded the periodical *L'Esprit Nouveau*. Some of the essays that had appeared in this journal were republished in 1923 as *Vers une Architecture* (*Towards an Architecture*), bringing Le Corbusier international attention. In the same year he resigned his position in the brickyard and resumed his career as an architect.

Le Corbusier's theoretical development was multifaceted in its various aspects. As early as 1915 he worked with the engineer Max du Bois on a concrete slab system cantilevered off steel posts and intended for mass-produced housing that he called Maison Dom-Ino. By 1922 this concept had evolved into his *Maison Citrohan,* a box-like module system supported on two bearing walls with a two-story living area and sleeping loft. In the same year he exhibited the *Ville Contemporaine,* an elite capitalist city whose urban core consisted of 24 office towers surrounded by smaller residential highrises for white-collar workers.

This emphasis on an industrial solution to the housing problem was matched by his machine aesthetic, promulgated in *Vers une Architecture*. In this work he proposed the transference of assembly-line techniques to the housing industry and juxtaposed photographs of ships, airplanes, and automobiles with profiles of the Parthenon in a carefully orchestrated effort to sanction the new engineering language with artistic value. His specific theory was limited to his three remainders to architects: mass, surface, and plan. Three years later he further simplified and focused his message in *5 points d'une architecture nouvelle,* a very short manifesto intended to define the new architecture for the dwelling by (*1*) the use of *pilotis* to elevate the building off the ground; (*2*) roof gardens; (*3*) the free plan; (*4*) horizontal windows; and (*5*) the free design of the facade.

Le Corbusier's urban theory also influenced the creation of the Congrès Internationaux d'Architecture Moderne (CIAM) in 1928. Siegfried Giedion joined with Le Corbusier in organizing the first conference of 24 architects, meeting in Le Sarrez. The declarations of the first four conferences in 1928, 1929, 1930, and 1933 in many respects epitomized the direction of European theory in the 1920s. The aim of CIAM, as explained by Giedion in the 1950s, was to establish contemporary architecture's right to exist against antagonist forces in government and in official architectural circles, yet the polemics of the first several conferences was almost anti-architectural in their call for rationalization and standardization, industrialization, economics, optimum land use, and minimum living standards. The 1933 congress, that took place on a cruise liner sailing between Marseilles and Athens, produced the famous (and later infamous) Athens Charter, specifying the rigid functional zoning of cities into areas of dwelling, working, and relaxation, separated by greenbelts and connected with traffic arteries.

Although the Netherlands, Germany, and France dominated the course of modern theory on the continent of Europe, Italy, the United States, and the USSR also made important contributions. Artistic events in the last country proceeded at a particularly furious pace, as the USSR had to contend not only with the upheaval of the 1917 Revolution, but also with a delayed and rapid industrialization. The arenas for debate were the new schools and associations founded in the first few years after the revolution, among them ZHIVSKULPTARKH (Commission of Painterly-Sculptural-Architectural Synthesis), INKHUK (Institute for Artistic Culture), VKHUTEMAS (Higher Artistic and Technical Studios), Unovis (School of New Art), and Prolecult. The last was a revolutionary organization begun in 1906 to enhance proletarian culture, but that became especially active after the Revolution through the efforts of Vladimir Tatlin (1885–1953) and Alexander Rodchenko (1891–1956). It attempted to propagate the revolutionary message through theatrical productions, film, and graphic displays. Tatlin and Rodchenko even designed furniture and durable clothing for the workers.

ZHIVSKULPTARKH was the birthplace of the Soviet Rationalist movement, a group led by Nikolai A. Ladovsky (1881–1941) and Valdimir F. Krinsky (1890–1971). They were inspired by Cubism and by the work of the avant-garde artists Kasimir Malevich and El Lissitzy. Soviet Rationalism sought to create a suitable new language of architecture articulating spatial form. The experimental work of Ladovsky and Krinsky was carried on at both INKHUK and VKHUTEMAS, in what amounted to a psychological laboratory and design studio for the perceptual understanding of space and form. Rationalism was also the ideology behind ASNOVA (Association of New Architects), whose first major work was Konstantin Melinkov's geometrically complex USSR Pavilion, designed for the 1925 Paris Exposition des Art Décoratifs.

The aesthetic concerns of ASNOVA, however, were opposed by the Constructivist organization OSA (Association of Contemporary Architects), founded in 1925 by the Vesnin brothers and Moisei Ginzburg (1892–1946). The latter had formulated the theoretical thrust for architectural Constructivism in (1924) with Stil' i epokha (Style and Epoch). In the first half of this ambitious work, Ginzburg attempted a Wölfflinean analysis of stylistic change and its various cultural, environmental, and material contingencies, underscoring the historical inevitability of the new age of mechanization. The industrial and political revolutions, he argued, had centered architectural attention on housing and the socialist workplace. In the second part of the work, Ginzburg defined the meaning of Constructivism that he conceived not as a style but as a methodological stage in the creation of the new style, an intel-lectual framework by which one investigates the new material and technical determinants of form.

Italian theory in the 1920s existed almost as a countermovement to the socialist concerns of modern architects throughout Europe. Prewar Futurism had lost its momentum with the death of Sant' Elia in World War I. Benito Mussolini's installment in 1922 reflected the insular nationalism and conservatism in Italy that expressed itself architecturally with the classical Novecento, a group started by the architect Giovanni Muzio (b. 1893) and expounding the return to traditional architectural values. In 1926 seven graduates of the Milan Polytechnic announced the formation of the Gruppo 7, historically giving birth to Italian Rationalism and leading, in 1928, to the formation of the M.I.A.R. (Italian Movement for Rationalist Architecture). Rationalist architects, led by the talented Giuseppe Terragni (1904–1943), were influenced by Le Corbusier and the Russian avant-garde, yet sought a mediation of the past with the new engineer's aesthetic. The best of their productions, such as Terragni's Novocomum Apartment House (1928) and Casa del Fascio (1923–1936), rivaled and possibly eclipsed the achievements of northern Europe, but the movement began to lose force after 1930 in its competition with conservative factions to become the official Fascist style. The stripped-down Neoclassicism of the University of Rome (1932) signaled the victory of the so-called Stile Littorio (Lictorial Style).

Theory and practice in the United States in the 1920s lacked the critical intensity that was typical of European efforts. The two early exponents of Modernism, Louis Sullivan and Frank Lloyd Wright, had little influence on American architecture after World War I—the former with the collapse of his practice in the first decade of the new century, the latter with his voluntary withdrawal to Taliesin. The architecture of the tall building following the Chicago experiments of the 1890s returned to historicism, perhaps best represented by Cass Gilbert's Woolworth Building (1911–1913). After the war, Hood and Howell's Gothic scheme for the 1922 Chicago Tribune Competition re-affirmed this approach, winning out over alternative entries by such Europeans as Walter Gropius and Eliel Saarinen (1873–1950). The latter's design, however, did influence American architects, leading in the second half of the 1920s to the Art Deco movement or Moderne style, exemplified by the Chrysler Building (1928–1930), the Empire State Building (1929–1931), and Rockefeller Center (1932–1939).

Yet European Modernism was also beginning to have a more direct effect. In Los Angeles, two emigrés who had studied under Wagner, Rudolf Schindler (1887–1953) and Richard Neutra (1892–1970) were practicing a modern style. Schindler's Lovell Beach House (1925–1926), with its reinforced concrete structure and complex spatial composition, was remarkably in advance of Le Corbusier's much more famous villa designs of the late 1920s. Neutra's Griffith Park house for the same client, designed in 1927, combined a steel frame with a lightweight synthetic skin. Another European to have a decisive impact in the 1920s was William Lescaze, who teamed up with the American George Howe on the design of the Philadelphia Savings Fund Society Building (1929–1932) (Fig. 14).

Figure 14. *Philadelphia Saving Fund Society Building,* Philadelphia, George Howe and William Lescaze, 1929–1932.

The most important boost to Modernism in America, however, was delivered by the 1932 exhibition prepared by Henry-Russell Hitchcock (b. 1903) and Philip Johnson (b. 1906), entitled, "The International Style." Hitchcock and Johnson had traveled extensively in Europe in the 1920s and their exhibition and subsequent book by the same title was intended to introduce American architects to the recent European developments. The book, however, was more than simply a survey of European developments; it was a conscious effort to forge an apolitical ideology of Modernism, drawing back from the Neue Sachlichkeit positions of Hannes Meyer and Siegfried Giedion to accommodate American corporate practice. Its three aesthetic principles, volume, regularity, and the avoidance of ornament, implied a more thorough artistic logic. The treatment of a building as volume (rather than as mass), for instance, demanded flat roofs and that the exterior be treated as a smooth skin without recessions for windows. The stricture against decoration was based on the argument that craftsmanship had declined in the industrial age, therefore leading to the financial waste of such efforts. Decoration in the new era, Hitchcock and Johnson argued, had been replaced by attention to the detail.

The International Style was certainly one of the most influential books of the twentieth century, becoming a veritable bible for corporate designers after World War II. Its historical locus, written on the eve of the cataclysmic events in Europe, also enhanced its impact. Not only would many of the leading European representatives of Modernism shortly emigrate to the United States, but the ascending political and economic power of the new land would offer both the technology and financial capital to test the utopian theories.

POST-MODERN THEORY

The Modern revolutionaries of the 1920s and 1930s, defeated by the collective forces of economic depression, fascism, and world war, emerged as the undisputed victors in the 1950s. The most inventive of the "old" masters, Frank Lloyd Wright and Le Corbusier, entered re-invigorated, highly plastic phases of their careers: the former with the realization of the Guggenheim Museum (1956–1959, designed in 1943), and the latter with a bevy of colossal works, including his *Unités* at Marseilles (1947–1952) and Nantes (1952–1957), the chapel at Ronchamp (1950–1954), and the various buildings at Chandigarh (begun in 1950), and Ahmedabad (begun in 1950). Wright's and Corbusier's plasticism, however, represented only one aspect of a multifaceted Modernism that settled at the other extreme on the "almost nothing" glass and steel structures of Mies van der Rohe and the International Style. As a practitioner, Mies van der Rohe was one of the least active *avant-garde* architects of the 1920s, after making a somewhat hesitant conversion to the movement at the start of the decade. After taking his training under Peter Behrens during the AEG period, Mies established a quiet domestic practice in Berlin shortly before World War I. His association with the radical Novembergruppe in 1919 signaled a re-evaluation of his future aspirations; his two projects for glass towers in 1921 revealed the immediate influence of Paul Scheerbart's *Glassarchitektur* (1914). In 1923 Mies' thinking underwent another transformation with his involvement with the magazine *G*, edited by Hans Richter, Werner Gräff, and El Lissitzsky. Inspired by the experiments of the De Stijl group and the Russian Supremaist artist Kasmir Malevich, Mies began to explore the free plan. His direction of the Wissenhof Exhibition in 1927 affected his outlook once again, as he turned his attention to mechanization and standardization, popularized by the Neue Sachlichkeit movement. Yet he backed away from this position only a few years later. In his 1930 essay, "The New Era," Mies argued for an art without politics or ideology.

During these years his architectural production was sporadic, consisting mostly of housing. His first built masterpiece, the Barcelona Pavilion (1929), was hardly noticed. The taunt, symmetrical monumentality of his unbuilt design for the Berlin Reichsbank in 1933 was the first of a failed, five-year effort on his part to accommodate his aesthetics to Nazi sensibilities.

If Mies' portfolio before World War II did not presage his later international importance, he was not without his exponents. Hitchcock and Johnson in their travels to Europe had met and were attracted to Mies' work. In *The*

International Style they described Mies, together with Le Corbusier, J. J. P. Oud, and Walter Gropius, as one of the four leaders of the Modern Movement. Through the aegis of a number of American supporters, Mies accepted a position in 1938 as head of the School of Architecture at the Armor Institute of Technology (later Illinois Institute of Technology), and almost immediately began work on the planning and design of the new campus. A number of increasingly important projects followed the war: the Farnsworth House (1946–1951), the Promontory Apartments (1946–1949), Lake Shore Drive (1948–1951), Crown Hall at IIT (1950–1956), the Convention Hall project (1953–1954), and the Seagram Building (1954–1958, with Philip Johnson). By the date of this last work Mies had become the most influential architect in the United States, establishing a formalist vocabulary unsurpassed in its personal elegance and sensitivity to profiling and detailing.

Mies' minimalist vocabulary for the glass curtain also proved to have corporate appeal, not only for its economic restraint and transparent monumentality, but also for its very simplicity or capacity to be emulated and adapted to any site, city, or climate. The speculative buoyancy of the expanding capitalist societies in the 1950s was matched by a governmental penchant for large-scale urban redevelopment, carried out at the expense of the wholesale destruction of entire areas of the city. The New Brutalist exhibitions in Great Britain in the early 1950s, with their existential focus on the ravaged landscapes and the less fortunate "other half," depicted the downside to this tendency. Yet New Brutalist architects, such as James Sterling, paid tribute to the acknowledged masters of the profession, employing an idiom varying from the exposed glass and steel aesthetics of Mies to the Mediterranean vernacular of Le Corbusier.

The first orchestrated challenge to modern theory came not in the field of architecture, but in urban planning. In 1953 a group of young architects, led by Aldo van Eyck (b. 1918), Peter Smithson (b. 1923), and Alice Smithson (b. 1928), interrupted the CIAM meeting at Aix en Provence with an attack on the four functional categories of the Athens Charter: the separation by zoning of the activities of dwelling, work, leisure, and traffic. At the next CIAM conference in Dubrovnik in 1956, the group, now known as Team 10, presented urban studies that evaluated cities in terms of clusters, mobility, growth, change, and habitat. CIAM effectively dissolved under this criticism, and at a follow-up conference at Otterlo in 1959, sponsored by Team 10, van Ecyk drew on his own anthropological studies of non-Western societies to criticize modern architecture and urban design for its monotony and lack of identity, for its emphasis on what is different in our time rather than what is timeless to man. Such a criticism manifested itself in the 1964 plan of Giancarlo de Carlo (b. 1919) for Urbino that placed a new importance on the topography, preservation, and rehabilitation of the existing urban texture.

The late 1950s and early 1960s also saw an expansion of the formal limits of the International Style. The refined vernacular work of Alvar Aalto (1898–1976) in Finland, Jörn Utzen (b. 1918) in his Sydney Opera, and Oscar Niemeyer (b. 1907) in his many buildings in Brasilia reflected efforts to extend both the palette and the scale of Modernism. The various projects of Eero Saarinen (1910–1961)—the General Motors' Technical Center (1948–1956), the dormitories at Yale University (1958–1962), the TWA terminal in New York (1956–1962), and Dulles Airport in Washington (1958–1963)—display an assurance, but also a certain restlessness or uneasiness with the absence of a sustainable basis for design. Against this apparent calm of large-scale corporate and governmental practice, however, appeared an ever-exploding cadre of alternative ideologies, ranging from the futurist theories of Buckminster Fuller (1895–1987) to the poetic fantasies of Superstudio, the metabolic schemes of Kenzo Tange (b. 1913), and the methodological pursuits of the Hochschule für Gestaltung (HfG) in Ulm, and Christopher Alexander.

One of the most relentless critics of the architectural *status quo* (best exemplifying the transition from Modern to Post-Modern thinking) was Louis Kahn (1901–1974). Trained in a Beaux Arts classicism under Paul Cret in the 1920s, Kahn entered the profession just a few years ahead of the Great Depression. His lean years of the 1930s and 1940s consisted mainly of designing New Deal housing projects. During this maturation period he became familiar with the Dymaxion theories of Richard Buckminster Fuller, whose influence on Kahn was especially strong in the Philadelphia City Hall projects of the mid-1950s. A stay at the American Academy in Rome in 1950–1951 added another important classical dimension to his outlook, prompting his intense Socratic search for the essence and meaning of form. This search culminated in the late 1950s with his first major success, the Richards Medical Buildings at the University of Pennsylvania (1957–1961) (Fig. 15). In his later work for the Salk Institute (1959–1965), the Unitarian Church at Rochester (1959–1967), at Bangladesh (1962–1974), and at Ahmedabad (1962–1974) he proposed ever more primitive elemental compositions, bringing to Modernism what Paolo Portoghesi has described as a Copernican Revolution or a reversal of functionalist logic, so that form is not determined by function

Figure 15. *Richards Research Buildings,* University of Pennsylvania, Philadelphia, Louis I. Kahn, 1957–1964.

but becomes an *a priori* given in a dialectical tension with function, having transcendental value in itself (32).

Kahn's rigorous and elementary formalism had enormous influence in Europe in the 1970s, while his persistent questioning of modern conventions, inspired by examples of classical Rome, also nurtured a more critical attitude toward the premises of modern architecture. The intellectual heir to Kahn's quest in the United States was Robert Venturi with his *Complexity and Contradiction in Architecture* (1966).

The principal theme of *Complexity and Contradiction*—that orthodox modern architecture is doomed to failure (boredom) in its effort to impose a unitary logic incapable of accommodating human complexity—is carried out by Venturi under both cultural and populist analyses. In the first critique, Venturi leans heavily on the modern works of Le Corbusier, Aalto, and Kahn, together with a number of baroque examples, to argue that ambiguity can and should be accommodated within a conventional system. In this critique Venturi is less revolutionary and more mannerist in his approach. Yet, in the populist critique Venturi goes much further. His famous adage that "Our buildings must survive the cigarette machine," his plea for the acceptance of rhetorical or "honky-tonk" elements cut sharply into modern ideology and its underlying utopian values. For Venturi, this critique at times assumes a form of social protest against the system's misplaced efforts and monetary expenditure, for example, when he encourages the architect to use irony as an indirect means to register his "true concern for society's inverted scale of values" (33).

The critiques of Kahn and Venturi concerning the one-dimensionality of orthodox modern theory were but part of a much broader movement that took shape in the 1960s and 1970s, carried out in Europe under the banners of phenomenology, structuralism, semiotics, and Neo-Rationalism. The intellectual backdrop to many of these critiques were the philosophical, anthropological, and linguistic models of Martin Heidegger, Claude Lévi-Strauss, and Ferdinand de Saussure.

Aldo van Eyck's insistence on replacing the impersonal concepts of space and time with place and occasion, together with his concept of labryinthian clarity, helped to encourage the formation of the Dutch structuralist school, whose leading spokesman was Herman Hertzberger. With the design of such works as the Central Beheer (1974) Hertzberger argued for the use of polyvalent forms and spaces with the capacity to interact with the occupants; he also put forth the idea of a *musée imaginaire* to depict the unconscious, archetypal images existing in the collective memory—psychic needs that should be embodied in design. Structuralist theory in its broader formulation opposed the functional categories of CIAM and attempted to grasp "complex realities" as a whole; it demanded building forms capable of evolving over time, the use of small, discrete formal units able to be multiplied, and articulation in the building volume as well as in the overall urban pattern (34).

The linguistic models utilized by the structuralists also were applied to architecture in the 1960s and 1970s under the general theory of semiotics. This science is concerned with everything taken as a sign, generally classified into three rubrics: indexes (one-way street signs), icons (signs physically emulating their referents), and symbols (signs operating as conventions, such as a Doric Order on a bank). Another tripartite division separates the analysis of signs into pragmatic, syntactic, and semantic modes. The first treats the relation of signs to the interpreters; syntactics considers the relation of signs to one another; semantics concerns the relation of signs to the objects they represent. Architecturally, pragmatic analysis might deal with the psychological or sociological meaning of forms; syntactics analyses with the rules operating within the formal language itself, for instance, the relation of a column to a beam; semantics with the building in its context or cultural meanings.

In its purest form, semiotics is a neutral critical tool applied to architecture in an effort to understand better its working relationships and cultural significance. Initially, it was applied to architecture in a nonideological way, such as Umberto Eco's efforts to undertake a semiological examination of architecture in the late 1960s, culminating with his more general *Theory of Semiotics* (1976). Several essays in *Meaning in Architecture* (1969), edited by Charles Jencks and George Baird, reviewed various semiotic models and their appropriateness to architectural criticism. Geoffrey Broadbent has since utilized Norm Chomsky's syntactical notion of deep structures to propose a design methodology, analyzing buildings as containers of human activities, as modifiers of climate, as cultural symbols, and as consumers of resources.

In the 1970s, however, semiotics was more often employed actively as a means to critique modern theory or offer alternatives. The best-known effort in this regard is Charles A. Jencks' *The Language of Post-Modern Architecture* (1977) that proclaimed the death of the Modern era at 3:32 P.M. (or thereabouts), July 15, 1972—the minute the Saint Louis ghetto Pruitt-Igoe was unceremoniously dynamited by city officials. Jencks chided modern architecture, in particular the Miesian school of the International Style, for its univalence or reduction of the formal language to a few simplified (indexical) values, devoid of deeper levels of signification connected with ritual or metaphysics. He proposed in its place the pluralistic language of a multivalent architecture, incorporating in its eclecticism traditional and modern elements, vernacular and high art meanings. Another semiotic analysis of a different genre was Juan Pablo Bonta's *Architecture and its Interpretation* (1979) that studied the semiotic basis of both Modern and Post-Modern theory. One of the inherent contradictions of modern theory, in Bonta's view, was its self-imposed restriction to a neutral set of indexes (syntactic images such as an I-beam mullion) divorced from any social convention, thereby condemning itself to ever greater schematization or distortion in the course of its inevitable socialization (35).

If structuralism and semiotics represented efforts to bring outside models into architectural theory, the European Neo-Rationalist movement reflected an attempt to overturn modern theory by re-invoking canonic models from within the architectural tradition. The beginnings of Neo-Rationalism go back to the historical concerns of the

Italian Neo-Liberty school of the 1950s (Liberty was the Italian name for the Art Nouveau movement), led by Franco Albini, Ignazio Gardella, Aimaro Isola, and Roberti Gabetti. In what was, in essence, a prelude to the later debate, Reyner Banham sharply criticized this group in a 1959 *Architectural Review* article for its infantile regression and retreat from the principles of the Modern Movement. In the early 1960s, Neo-Liberty architects began to review critically the Italian Rationalist movement of the 1930s, and the first fruit of these labors was Aldo Rossi's *The Architecture of the City* (1966), a work that rivals Venturi's book of the same year as a seminal work of Post-Modern theory. Rossi's book is a sociopolitical analysis of urban form and typology, as well as a metaphysical study of the historical, geographical, structural, and cultural factors investing form with mnemonic vitality. The concepts of type and permanence are the pivotal notions for Rossi, forming the basis for his critique of functionalism's disdain for form's capacity to embrace many different values and uses. With his sketches and designs Rossi pursues, a rigid world with few objects, archetypal forms serving as a fixed reference yet capable of being animated with the phenomenological images they generate over time.

Neo-Rationalism expanded in the 1960s and 1970s to become the most visible (although diversified) movement in Europe through the Italian contributions of Carlo Aymonino, Vittorio Gregotti, Massimo Scholari, and Manfredo Tafuri, and with the efforts of architects of other countries, including Bruno Reichlin, Fabio Reinhart, Mario Botta, Mathias Ungers, Bernard Huet, Georgia Benamo, Christian de Portzamparc, Maurice Culot, and the Krier brothers. Leon and Rob Krier have been especially prominent in proposing new urban models and in criticizing CIAM tenets for destroying the historical texture of European cities. Anthony Vidler has termed their work "the third typology" because of its emphasis on formulating types for housing and the morphology of urban spaces. Leon Krier has suggested a political and architectural agenda calling for the physical and social conservation of historical centers, the use of urban space as the prime organizational element of the city, an emphasis on typological and morphological studies in design, the reconstruction of traditionally scaled streets, squares, and quarters, and a return to the primary elements of architecture, such as columns, walls, and roofs.

American debate in the 1970s and 1980s was less ideological and urban in its emphasis. The works of the New York Five (consisting of Richard Meier, Charles Gwathmey, Michael Graves, John Hejduk, and Peter Eisenman) were published in 1972 under a quasi-rationalist banner as a reinterpretation of the syntax of Giuseppe Terragni, Le Corbusier, and Theo van Doesburg (Fig. 16). Yet this prominent start was quickly followed by their dispersion and the subsequent individual flowering of the group's members. This chameleonic quality of American architecture, perhaps grounded in the devaluation of history and theory in architectural programs, also has its positive side in a certain vitality of pluralism and freedom of exploration.

Given the rapid commercial success and popularization

Figure 16. *San Juan Capistrano Library,* San Juan Capistrano, Michael Graves, 1980–1984.

of the Post-Modernists in the 1970s, it was almost predictable that the one conspicuous movement to emerge in the 1980s—Deconstruction—takes as its starting point the critique of Post-Modern historicism, that is, European Neo-Rationalism and American eclecticism. The sources of Deconstructionist theory range from the philosophical writings of Jacques Derrida to the Soviet *avant-garde* of

Figure 17. *Loyola Law School,* exterior stair detail, Los Angeles, Calif., Frank O. Gehry, 1981.

Figure 18. *Kate Mantilini Restaurant,* Beverly Hills, Calif., Morphosis, 1984–1986.

the 1920s, or more simply, to the desire to fracture the classicism and contextualism of Post-Modern theory (Figs. 17, 18). In Deconstruction Leon Krier's call for reconstruction meets its antithesis.

Although the tenets espoused by individual Deconstructionists—the creation of an architecture for alienated man, the dissolution of the limits of architecture, the revelation of the lived-in world as the disquieting space of accidents—suggest more the imminent breakdown of post-industrial society or an end to civilization altogether, they reveal something fundamental to the theoretical process. As with Dadaism or Surrealism, the dedication to the overt subversion of the norm, the willingness to flout existing rules and conventions in the search for the new and unseen (whatever its social, functional, or economic limitations) has always been an integral part of the critical development of art, the means by which art enriches itself and seeks out the new. Whereas some may view this critical process as iconoclastic, others, even from a position of skepticism, find intellectual nourishment in the freshness of the endeavor. The irony of this latest, but certainly not last, phase of the Post-Modern experience has been described by some critics as Neo-Modern, or as a return to the *avant-garde* ideologies of the 1920s. In this respect its recycling of forms and ideas is as old as theory itself.

BIBLIOGRAPHY

1. A. C. Quatremère de Quincy, Vol. II, *Dictionnaire Historique d'Architecture,* 2 vols., Paris, 1832, pp. 571–572. Revision of *Encyclopédie Methodique: Architecture,* 3 vols., Paris, pp. 1788–1825.
2. Ref. 1, Vol. II, p. 572.
3. Vitruvius, *The Ten Books on Architecture,* trans. Morris Hicky Morgan (1914), Dover Publications, Inc., New York, 1960, Book II, Preface, p. 4.
4. Ref. 3, Book VI, Preface, pp. 3–4.
5. Ref. 3, Book I, II.
6. Ref. 3, Book I, II.
7. Ref. 3, Book III, I.
8. J. Rykwert, *Res 3: J. Anthropology and Aesthetics* (1982), pp. 68–79.
9. L. B. Alberti, *On the Art of Building in Ten Books,* trans. J. Rykwert, N. Leach, and R. Tavernor, MIT Press, Cambridge, Mass., 1988, p. 154.
10. Ref. 9, Prologue, p. 5.
11. Ref. 9, p. 7.
12. Ref. 9, p. 156.
13. Ref. 9, p. 302.
14. A. Palladio, *The Four Books of Architecture,* trans. I. Ware (1738), Dover Publications, Inc., New York, 1965, p. 1.
15. H. Wölfflin, *Renaissance and Baroque,* trans. K. Simon, Cornell University Press, Ithaca, N.Y., 1975, pp. 23–25.
16. E. E. Viollet-le-Duc, *Dictionnaire raisoné de l'architecture Français de XIe au XVIe siècle,* 10 vols., Libraires-Imprimeries Réunies, Paris, 1854–1875, Vol. VIII, p. 479.
17. J. Fergusson, *History of Modern Styles in Architecture,* 3rd ed., New York, 1891, p. 115.
18. E. L. Garbett, *Rudimentary Treatise on the Principles of Design in Architecture,* London, 1850, p. 24.
19. J. Ruskin, *The Seven Lamps of Architecture,* Noonday Press, New York, 1977, p. 61.
20. J. Ruskin, *The Stones of Venice,* 3 vols., Peter Fenelon Collier & Son, New York, 1900, Vol. II, p. 160.
21. Ref. 20, Vol. III, p. 101.
22. K. F. Schinkel in A. F. von Wolzogen, ed., *Aus Schinkel's Nachlass,* 4 vols., Berlin, 1862, Vol. II, p. 211.
23. Ref. 22, Vol. II, p. 212.
24. G. Semper, *The Four Elements of Architecture and Other Writings,* trans. H. F. Mallgrave and W. Herrmann, Cambridge University Press, New York, 1989, p. 48.
25. Ref. 24, p. 195.

26. L. H. Sullivan, *Kindergarden Chats and Other Writings,* Witterborn, New York, 1976, pp. 187–188.

27. D. Van Zanten in Wim de Wit, ed., *"Sullivan to 1890," Louis Sullivan: the Function of Ornament,* Chicago Historical Society, Chicago, Ill., 1986, pp. 13–63.

28. N. Levine, *AA Files* **II**, 3–12 (1986).

29. Ref. 24, p. 284.

30. A. Schmarsow, *Das Wesen der architektonischen Schöpfung,* Hiersemann, Leipzig, 1894.

31. H. Wölfflin, "Prolegomena zu einer Psychologie der Architektur," *Kleine Schriften 1886–1933,* Benno Schwabe, Basel, 1946, p. 13.

32. P. Portoghesi, *After Modern Architecture,* Rizzoli, New York, 1982, p. 79.

33. R. Venturi, *Complexity and Contradiction in Architecture,* Museum of Modern Art, New York, 1966, p. 52.

34. A. Lüchinger, *Structuralism in Architecture and Urban Planning,* Karl Krämer, Stuttgart, 1981, p. 43.

35. J. P. Bonta, *Architecture and its Interpretation,* Rizzoli, New York, 1979, pp. 46–49.

General References

H. Auer, "Die Entwicklung des Raumes in der Baukunst," in *Allgemeine Bauzeitung,* Vienna, 1883, pp. 65–74.

H. P. Berlage, *Gedanken über Stil in der Baukunst,* Julius Zeitler, Leipzig, 1905.

H. P. Berlage, *Grundlagen & Entwicklung der Architektur,* Julius Bard, Berlin, 1908.

T. Buddensieg, *Industrielkultur: Peter Behrens and the AEG 1907–1914,* trans. I. B. Whyte, MIT Press, Cambridge, Mass., 1984.

J. Campbell, *The German Werkbund: The Politics of Reform in the Applied Arts,* Princeton University Press, Princeton, N.J., 1978.

U. Conrads, *Programs and Manifestoes on 20th-century Architecture,* MIT Press, Cambridge, Mass., 1975.

A. Endell, "Möglichkeit und Ziele einer neuen Architektur," *Deutsche Kunst und Dekoration* **I** (1897–1898).

A. Endell, "Formenschönheit und dekorative Kunst," *Dekorative Kunst* **2** (1898).

K. Fiedler, *Conrad's Fiedler's Essay on Architecture,* notes by V. Hammer, University of Kentucky, Lexington, Ky., 1954.

K. Frampton, *Modern Architecture: A Critical History,* Oxford University Press, Oxford, 1980.

J. Gadol, *Leon Battista Alberti,* University of Chicago Press, Chicago, Ill., 1969.

M. Ginzburg, *Style and Epoch,* trans. A. Senkevitch, MIT Press, Cambridge, Mass., 1982.

A. Göller, *Zur Aesthetik der Architektur,* Konrad Wittwer, Stuttgart, 1887.

A. Göller, *Die Entstehung der architektonischen Stilformen,* Konrad Wittwer, Stuttgart, 1888.

V. Gregotti, *New Directions in Italian Architecture,* George Braziller, New York, 1968.

W. Herrmann, *Gottfried Semper: In Search of Architecture,* MIT Press, Cambridge, Mass., 1984.

W. Herrmann, *Laugier and Eighteenth Century French Theory,* Zwemmer, London, 1985.

H.-R. Hitchcock, and P. Johnson, *The International Style,* W. W. Norton, New York, 1960.

C. A. Jencks, ed. with G. Baird, *Meaning in Architecture,* George Braziller, New York, 1969.

C. A. Jencks, *The Language of Post-Modern Architecture,* Rizzoli, New York, 1977.

C. A. Jencks, ed. with G. Broadbent and D. Bunt, *Signs, Symbols and Architecture,* John WIley, New York, 1978.

C. A. Jencks, ed., *Deconstruction,* An Architectural Design Profile, St. Martin's Press, New York, 1988.

L. Kahn, in H. Ronner et al., eds., *Louis I. Kahn: Complete Works 1935–74,* Westview Press, Boulder, Colo., 1977.

L. Krier, ed., *Rational Architecture: The Reconstruction of the European City,* Editions des Archives d'Architecture Moderne, Brussels, 1978.

M.-A. Laugier, *An Essay on Architecture,* trans. W. and A. Herrmann, Hennessey & Ingalls, Los Angeles, Calif., 1977.

Le Corbusier, *Towards a New Architecture,* trans. F. Etchells, Praeger, New York, 1960.

R. Middleton, "The Abbé de Cordemoy and the Graeco-Gothic Ideal: A Prelude to Romantic Classicism," *J. Warburg and Courtault Institutes,* **25**, 278–320 (1962); **26**, 90–123 (1963).

R. Middleton, and D. Watkin, *Neoclassical and 19th Century Architecture,* Harry N. Abrams, New York, 1980.

R. Middleton, ed., *The Beaux-Arts and nineteenth-century French Architecture,* MIT Press, Cambridge, Mass., 1982.

H. Muthesius, *Stilarchitektur und Baukunst,* Schummelpfeng, Mulheim and Ruhr, 1902 Kraus reprint, 1976.

A. Pérez-Gómez, *Architecture and the Crisis of Modern Science,* MIT Press, Cambridge, Mass., 1983.

N. Pevsner, *Some Architectural Writers of the Nineteenth Century,* Clarendon Press, Oxford, 1972.

A. W. Pugin, *Contrasts,* Leicester University Press, Leicester, 1973.

A. W. Pugin, *The True Principles of Pointed Architecture,* Academy Editions, London, 1973.

H. Rosenau, *Boulée & Visionary Architecture,* Academy Editions, London, 1976.

A. Rossi, *The Architecture of the City,* trans. D. Ghirado and J. Ockman, MIT Press, Cambridge, Mass., 1982.

J. Rykwert, *The First Moderns: The Architects of the Eighteenth Century,* MIT Press, Cambridge, Mass., 1980.

F. Schulze, *Mies van der Rohe: A Critical Biography,* University of Chicago Press, Chicago, Ill., 1985.

A. Smithson, *Team 10 Primer,* MIT Press, Cambridge, Mass., 1968.

A. Senkevitch, Jr., "Aspects of Spatial Form and Perceptual Psychology in the Doctrine of the Rationalist Movement in Soviet Architecture in the 1920s," *Via* **6**, 79–115 (1983).

S. Serlio, *The Five Books of Architecture,* Dover Publications, Inc., New York, 1982.

P. Singelenberg, *H. P. Berlage: Idea and Style,* Haentjens Dekker & Gumbert, Utrecht, 1972.

L. H. Sullivan, *The Autobiography of an Idea,* Dover Publications, Inc., New York, 1956.

L. H. Sullivan, *A System of Ornament According with a Philosophy of Man's Powers,* American Institute of Architects, Washington, D.C., 1924.

M. Tafuri with F. Dal Co, *Modern Architecture,* Harry N. Abrams, New York, 1979.

H. Van de Velde, *Die Renaissance im modernen Kunstgewerbe,* Paul Cassirer, Berlin, 1901.

H. Van de Velde, *Kunstgewerbliche Laienpredigten,* Herrmann Seemann, Leipzig, 1902.

D. Van Zanten, *Designing Paris: The Architecture of Duban, Labrouste, Duc, and Vaudoyer,* MIT Press, Cambridge, Mass., 1987.

E. E. Viollet-le-Duc, *Lectures on Architecture,* 2 vols. trans. B. Bucknall (1877–1881), Dover Publications, Inc., New York, 1987.

R. Vischer, "Über das optische Formgefühl," *Drei Schriften zum ästhetischen Formproblem,* Halle, 1927.

Vitruvius, *On Architecture,* 2 vols., trans. F. Granger, Harvard University Press, Loeb series, Cambridge, Mass., 1970.

O. Wagner, *Modern Architecture,* trans. H. F. Mallgrave, Getty Center for the History of Art and the Humanities, Santa Monica, Calif., 1988.

D. Watkin, and T. Mellinghoff, *German Architecture and the Classical Ideal,* MIT Press, Cambridge, Mass., 1987.

J. Wilton-Ely, *The Mind and Art of Giovanni Battista Piranesi,* Thames and Hudson, London, 1978.

F. L. Wright, in F. Gutheim, ed., *Frank Lloyd Wright on Architecture: Selected Writings 1894–1920,* Duell, Sloan, and Pearce, New York, 1941.

See also Architectural Press, U.S.; Bauhaus; Building Types; Criticism, Architectural; Ecole Des Beaux Arts; Media Criticism; Profession in Contemporary Society; Role of the Architect

Harry F. Mallgrave
Afton, Minnesota

THIRY, PAUL

The contemporary U.S. architect Paul Thiry (b. 1904), best known locally for introducing the seminal architecture of the European modernists to the Pacific Northwest in the mid-1930s, is known internationally for his regionalized modern houses and churches, campus buildings and plans, his participation with the Army Corps of Engineers in the design and planning of the Libby Dam in Montana, and his contribution to the planning and preservation of the United States capital as a member of the National Capital Planning Commission. Born in Alaska and receiving his architectural training at the University of Washington in the 1920s, when it, like other schools throughout the nation, was immersed in the beaux-arts, Thiry went abroad his third year to study in France at the École des Beaux Arts in Fontainebleau; he returned to Seattle in 1928 to receive his Bachelor of Architecture. The following year, he set up private practice, always working alone or at most with one or two other people.

Thiry began designing small, private residences, using the then conventional Tudor or colonial forms. Geared by his formal training to think in terms of the past, he was uninterested in and unimpressed by the new progressive work of Frank Lloyd Wright and the European modernists. When work dropped off during the Depression, Thiry again went abroad. This time he went to Japan where, staying in Wright's Imperial Hotel in Tokyo and meeting Antonin Raymond, his eyes were opened to the potentials

of the new direction. Raymond was by this time working in the idiom of the European modernists, whose austere forms were tempered by an influence of Wright (with whom Raymond had worked on the Imperial Hotel) and by Raymond's desire to accommodate traditional wooden structures of the Japanese. Thiry was highly impressed by the resulting synthesis: the plain surfaces, cubical forms, and sleek simplified rationalized approach of the one, with the grace, elegance, naturalism, and regional adaptability of the other. Leaving Japan after several months, Thiry continued on around the world, stopping off in France, this time to see Le Corbusier. He returned to Seattle, and in 1936 began designing in the then still radically new style of modernism. His formal stark cubical forms, white stuccoed walls, and flush unornamented surfaces were an abrupt departure from regional traditions, shocking local sensibilities accustomed to brick or wood, gently sloped roofs, picturesque forms, and Tudor or colonial styling.

Thiry was one of the first to introduce the new modernist forms to the Pacific Northwest. His was an international style-derived idiom, but one more Raymondian than Corbusian, bearing the influence of both Wright and the Japanese. Its aloof austerity was soon to soften still further under pressure from clients for more traditional elements, resulting in a regional variation of modernism particularly well suited to the Pacific Northwest: modern concepts of space, simple direct unhistoricized forms, ample use of large expanses of plate glass, but now conceived in natural unpainted wood and with gently pitched roofs.

Known primarily for his distinctively designed regionalized modern houses, churches, museums, libraries (including the State Library in the Washington State Capitol complex in Olympia), and university buildings, Thiry has also made a name for himself in city and regional planning. As chairman of the Seattle Planning Commission in the early 1950s and principal architect of the Seattle World's Fair from 1958 to 1962, Thiry was appointed member, then vice-chairman of the National Capital Planning Commission in the 1960s. This was an advisory committee set up to prepare and adopt comprehensive plans for the nation's capital. It was in this capacity he became embroiled in the controversy over whether to extend or preserve the West Front of the U.S. Capitol Building, opposing the national AIA, which favored preservation. As a planner, Thiry also played a significant role in the urban design projects for Seattle where he was an outspoken critic of the City Planning Commission's plans to erect an elevated freeway that blocked views of and access to the city's valuable waterfront. To his credit, Thiry resigned from the Commission in protest over its ill-advised decision.

In 1962, Thiry was retained as consulting architect for the Army Corps of Engineers' Libby Dam, a hydroelectric power project in northwest Montana. It was a noteworthy appointment in that rarely had an architect been involved in the development of such a project through all stages of its design. Thiry was responsible for drawing up the master plan as well as designing many of its subsidiary buildings. His major design goal was twofold: to accommodate visitors in a safe, comfortable, visually appealing way and to harmonize the large-scale engineered structure with the beauty of the natural terrain.

Recognized for his numerous contributions to architecture and planning on both a regional and national level, Thiry has been the recipient of numerous awards. Among them are AIA Fellow in 1951, chancellor of the College of Fellows in 1962, and, in 1965, an AIA citation for his work in community design.

MEREDITH L. CLAUSEN
University of Washington
Seattle, Washington

THOMPSON, BENJAMIN

Throughout his career Benjamin Thompson (b. 1918) has defied simple categorization. He is concerned equally with an almost styleless sense of tectonic integrity and with the enrichment of the urban environment. In 40 years of professional life he has been a founder of two substantial architectural practices; a teacher and head of an architectural school; a designer, importer, and marketer of furniture and furnishings; a successful restaurateur; and—through all these, often concurrent, careers—a fervent apostle of hope for U.S. cities.

Thompson characterizes his entry into the field of design as a "lucky chance"—a decision by default. Born in St. Paul, Minnesota, he was raised in an artistic environment and, at an early age, exposed to the vitality of European cities. His mother, Lynne Thompson, was a painter, writer, and early collector of modern art who encouraged her son's energetic drawing and painting.

After initial studies at the University of Virginia, Thompson transferred to Yale where he received a BFA in architecture in 1941. His architectural education was a product of uncertain times. U.S. architecture and architectural education were in transition—driven by new ideas from Europe, as well as by the realignment of U.S. social values, which accompanied the Great Depression and New Deal. At Yale, Thompson experienced the tension between an entrenched academic beaux-arts tradition and an emerging modernism. When he could, he focused his studies on socially oriented problems, such as schools for experimental education and farms utilizing innovative agricultural technology.

After graduating, Thompson served five years in the navy, first as an officer on a destroyer escort and later with the O.S.S. While on leave in Boston in 1944, he sought out Walter Gropius. In 1946, following his discharge, Thompson and a group of friends from his Yale days (Norman and Jean Fletcher, John and Sally Harkness, Robert McMillan, and Louis McMillen) invited Gropius to join with them in a new cooperative practice. They called it The Architects Collaborative, or TAC.

In his relationship with Gropius at TAC, Thompson enjoyed the tutelage of an idealistic, tolerant, worldly mentor. For him, TAC was a living demonstration of the worth of participation and teamwork. From its earliest days, a search for an appropriate architectural expression, based on an exploration of structure and materials, was part of TAC's response to each commission.

As TAC's projects progressed from smaller to larger, Thompson's work reflected an evolution of style based on an increasing familiarity with materials and a desire for greater tectonic integrity and regional expression. Thompson has always appreciated brick as a natural "craft" material that can lend texture, color, and humanity to a building because its basic module is scaled to the human hand and eye. The texture of brick (sometimes painted) became a counterpoint to the planar logic of structural concrete (often bush hammered to a stonelike surface) as a means for creating well-scaled buildings that were harmonious with their New England surroundings.

By the 1960s, Thompson had developed a rationalist vocabulary based on the inherent freedom of the two-way concrete waffle slab. Whenever possible this was exposed to view, both from below and on edge—where it frequently served, when required, as a de facto lintel for openings in external brick walls. All mechanical systems were either buried in the slab or carefully "zoned" within vertical and horizontal mechanical chases within oversize piers and above corridors. This expressively functional, structural vocabulary was very flexible. It allowed span variations and changes in configuration in response to programmatic and site considerations—all without sacrificing tectonic logic. It promoted a freedom of plan, space, and window-wall treatment; it provided for great flexibility in response to uneven terrain; and it encouraged the development of a compositional vocabulary based on dynamic asymmetry. Although this architecture inevitably partook, to an extent, of the dominant brutalism of its times, it always retained a remarkably consistent sense of humanity and scale.

Paralleling his increasingly refined sensitivity to site and context, Thompson began to develop a personal interest in the preservation of old buildings for new uses. In the late 1950s, he was asked to renovate eight eighteenth- and nineteenth-century dormitories within Harvard Yard—giving them new interior arrangements without visible exterior changes. In 1959, shortly after this early exercise in "historic rehabilitation," Thompson persuaded the university not to raze Boylston Hall, an 1857 granite academic building also in the Yard, but rather to remodel it. There, however, Thompson subtly juxtaposed new details—such as plate glass windows—with the historic fabric of stone arches and lintels.

In 1953, seven years after the founding of TAC, Thompson discovered another means through which he could shape the built environment. He launched himself into the world of interior design—and, as important, that of retailing—by opening a shop called Design Research (always known to cognoscenti as D|R). Thompson directed D|R from its beginnings in a Cambridge townhouse, through its expansion into showcase stores in New York (1964), and San Francisco (1965), and, finally, into a new, five-story, Thompson-designed, Cambridge headquarters in 1969 (Fig. 1)—a building that remains a landmark in both his own oeuvre and in the Harvard Square townscape. Thompson commissioned products from European craftsmen and designers such as Carl Auboch, Roberto Niederer, and Joe Colombo. And it was Thompson who, through D|R, introduced the United States to Marimekko fabrics and fashions from Finland. In the late 1950s and

Figure 1. Design Research, Cambridge, Massachusetts, 1969. Courtesy of Ezra Stoller.

the 1960s, D|R truly embodied the cultural awakening and growing visual sophistication of a generation of consumers. Because of D|R's close identification with Marimekko and Thompson's taste for unaffected design, D|R achieved a certain iconic status among the design conscious.

The entirely glass-walled D|R building, five floors of transparent shopping-as-theater, was Thompson's first exploration of the marketplace environment. It remains one of the most explicit statements of his belief in architecture as an unobstructive neutral container for the natural chaos and unpredictability of life. Ironically, a year after the construction of the Cambridge store, a hostile takeover forced Thompson out of D|R. His successor then rapidly overexpanded the chain into uncongenial markets and destroyed it.

Throughout this period, Thompson had also been teaching at Harvard's Graduate School of Design, and in 1963, Gropius selected Thompson to be his successor as chairman of the department. Thompson's goal during his four-year tenure was to actively relate professional design education to real social needs and to a concern for the natural and urban environments. He introduced a "real world" teaching methodology, emphasizing a knowledge of materials, a respect for the craft of construction, an understanding of the building's purpose, and a recognition of its true users. He brought teachers from varied disciplines into the design studios to convey a clearer sense of the real (as opposed to abstract and academic) tasks of architecture. He encouraged the design studio and the working office to intermingle, thus merging theory and practice into problem-solving exercises using real issues, people, and design procedures. Above all, Thompson encouraged humanist values. Across the country, in academic settings and at professional gatherings, he argued

against what he saw as a prevailing academicism in architectural design and a sterile impersonal attitude toward planning that was equally hostile to nature and to community patterns. He argued for quality, human scale, craftsmanship, compassion—and an elusive thing called joy.

In January 1966, Thompson left TAC to establish Benjamin Thompson & Associates—now usually known simply as BTA. He wanted to have more personal control over his work, so that it might better reflect his growing concern with the larger implications of architecture for the culture and spirit of cities, and for the diminishing quality of the natural environment. Born during the social upheaval of the mid-1960s, BTA's direction was strongly influenced by its times. Thompson believed that architects were too willing to bemoan central city blight and the devastation caused by urban renewal, while eschewing their own responsibility. He renounced the intellectualization of "inevitable" urban decay, arguing that the hard step was to lead, to suggest a way out, and that there had to be a vision of what could and should be. His 1966 essay, "Visual Squalor and Social Disorder," addressed the effects of the built environment on human behavior, and argued for an architecture of "joy and sensibility" as a norm for modern urban life.

It was an idea that grew into a thesis, now a vital part of every BTA undertaking. Thompson referred to his ideal as the "City of Man." It had to reflect human scale and involvement with social activity. Equally, it had to reflect an awareness of nature and things natural: of changing seasons, of orientation to water, and of places "intimate by day and radiant by night," where the "lovely unpredictability of life" would be nurtured and experienced on a daily basis. To make the City of Man more tangible, Thompson developed a triple-image slide presentation.

The use of three images was, in part, deliberately intended to avoid association with, and the dualities of, traditional academic comparative analyses. He also chose to accompany it with music, not a spoken text. It was an insightful, living, nearly life-size, collage of Thompson's favorite urban experiences.

The City of Man was evocative, but images could carry ideas only so far. Before there could be a reversal of urban decay, there had to be working examples: viable, true-to-life, functioning urban settings where these ideals could be demonstrated to work. Eventually, one of the key pieces began to coalesce in the very center of Boston. Thompson first reflected on the possibilities of Boston's Quincy Market buildings in the year BTA was founded. He studied the buildings, photographing them and pondering their potential uses. In early 1967, he went to the Boston Redevelopment Authority (BRA) with his vision for reviving the city's historic marketplace with food stalls, cafés, restaurants, and pushcarts, all operated by local merchants.

Although this was an unsolicited personal initiative, the BRA's initial response was favorable. When it then sponsored a developer–architect competition in 1970, Thompson's scheme was chosen. Six more years were to pass, however, before the renamed Faneuil Hall Marketplace finally reopened its doors in 1976, exactly 150 years after its original opening (Fig. 2). It was an immediate,

overwhelming commercial and popular success, with the highest gross sales per square foot of any retail development in the country at the time. And, perhaps almost as significant, it was a model of an historic rehabilitation by an architect of unimpeachable modernist credentials. In one sense, Faneuil Hall Marketplace demonstrated Thompson's theses on the continuity and integration of old and new design elements, refined since his experience at Boylston Hall. His restoration program provided for no historical "back dating." Instead, Thompson wanted to reveal the evolution of buildings over time, in response to growth, changing uses, and new techniques. This is most evident in the minimally detailed glass canopies projecting from the central building: they are the most transparent possible updating of prosaic early twentieth century canopies of glass brick. Less happy, in the eyes of both Thompson and the preservation community, was a BRA decision to remove 100 years of other more substantial and often elegant architectural accretions. Such preservation issues aside, however, here at last was a working prototype for a part of Thompson's vision of a revived urban life. Indeed, it might be argued that, with Faneuil Hall Marketplace, Thompson "invented," or at least brought to international attention, a new building type, which became known as the "festival marketplace."

Thompson's involvement at Faneuil Hall had another dimension as well. Together with his wife, Jane, he

Figure 2. Faneuil Hall Marketplace, Boston, Massachusetts, 1976–1978. Courtesy of Steve Rosenthal.

opened The Landmark Inn, a group of restaurants, including an outdoor café, occupying three floors at the end of one of the market buildings. That was not, however, the Thompsons' first such venture. Shortly after the loss of D|R they had opened Harvest, a modern bistro near BTA's office—because, as they said, Harvard Square needed a sophisticated neighborhood place for good lunches, as well as festive dinners and neighborly gatherings. After more than a decade, both ventures continue to flourish.

BTA has gone on to design and develop urban marketplaces in various cities, each responsive to its own special circumstances and each requiring a different form and design considerations. Among these are Harborplace in Baltimore (1980), South Street Seaport in New York (1985), Bayside in Miami (1987), Jacksonville Landing in Florida (1987), Century City in Los Angeles (1987), and Union Station in Washington, D.C. (1988).

South Street Seaport is the most complex of these projects. In marked ways it represents a transition into a new level of comprehensive urban design. BTA first prepared a master plan incorporating the existing streets and selected historic buildings within an 11-block area. This created the framework for private retail development within the urban seaport's "museum of the streets and sea." The pivotal connections between the old and new, between inland landmarks and historic ships, were the two new market halls. New Fulton Market is built, in part, over an existing fish market, on the original 1825 Fulton Market hall site. "Pier 17" is on a rebuilt pier in the East River.

The four-sided Fulton Market building was designed to look and feel right, without "donning a costume," by using timeless and styleless vernacular forms (hipped and ga-bled roofs, big "punched" windows, cable hung canopies) and traditional materials (granite, brick, corrugated metal). Pier 17 employs a comparable vocabulary of structural steel, glass, and bright red "corrugated iron," and has Pier 17 superimposed on it in huge, sign-painter serifed type. The "Pier 17" lettering is then punched through, as circumstances require, by window openings. Such graphic and typographic design has always been important to Thompson. His retail spaces are often enlivened with symbolic, graphic, and typographic *objets trouvés*. Even in the 1950s and 1960s, when orthodox modernists only used hygienic sans serif Helvetica, Thompson flaunted an enthusiasm for chunky serifed type faces.

In a more conventional setting, the Ordway Music Theater in St. Paul, Minnesota (1984) (Fig. 3), also reflects BTA's pursuit of romance, sociability, sensory pleasure, and human delight—all founded on unobtrusive technical competence. It is a good neighbor, mending St. Paul's urban fabric by filling in one edge of a park. And it creates a brilliant centerpiece for a growing cultural district.

Benjamin Thompson may have appeared a less-than-orthodox modernist in the 1950s and 1960s sometimes seeming, perhaps, a little conservative in his use of traditional materials and his concern for old buildings and contexts. Ironically, in the 1980s, BTA's work is equally unconventional because it so studiously eschews all explicit references to traditional architectural styles. Instead it unashamedly combines modern directness in its uses of materials with inspiration drawn from vernacular and contextual sources. Thompson's goals and collaborative method of design, rooted in his early association with Gropius, have remained consistent. They have only taken on a greater clarity and richness of vocabulary in the work of

Figure 3. Ordway Music Theater, St. Paul, Minnesota, 1985. Courtesy of Steve Rosenthal.

BTA. Having never accepted arbitrary rules of style, having held to the primacy of functional, sensory, and ethical issues, Thompson has steered a personal course. He has designed as a naturalist, with instinctive regard for the shape of the site, the animation of water, and the play of light and shadow, while always using materials with direct and elegant simplicity. Thompson believes that the "reading" of a building—the outward story of its structure, its layers of history, the tale it tells, what it does, and how it holds itself up—is the essence of architectural expression.

Since its founding, BTA's work has been recognized with, among other honors, 16 national and regional AIA Honor Awards and 3 Harleston Parker Awards for the best building in Boston. In 1987, BTA was selected for the highest corporate award of the AIA, the National Architectural Firm Award. Two years earlier, Thompson had received the Louis Sullivan Award in recognition of his long-term contribution to architectural design in brick and masonry materials. He has also been granted honorary doctorates from Colby College, The University of Massachusetts, and Minnesota College of Art and Design. Since 1966, he has been a Fellow of the American Academy of Arts and Sciences.

Now in its third decade, BTA continues moving toward Thompson's dream of building the City of Man, through increasingly comprehensive mixed-use city scale planning–design projects. Most of these relate to water and many are of a size (25–100 acres) beyond that normally undertaken by a single architectural firm. Cities such as San Diego and Buffalo have accepted BTA proposals to revitalize major waterfront sites. Similar commissions have come from European cities awakening to the potentials of neglected riverfronts and harbor edges, among them Amsterdam, Dublin, and London.

Typical of these sites, is London's Royal Victoria Dock: 90 acres of abandoned quays, warehouses, and factories facing a large impounded, constant-level docking basin, up to 80 m wide, separated from the tidal lower reaches of the Thames by locks. BTA's plan integrates places for people to live and work and to enjoy water sports, active recreation, and cultural events within a neighborhood-centered community. There are to be almost 2000 waterside dwellings on piers or facing canals, as well as three hotels, offices, light industrial buildings, small boat marinas, and a town center. At one end of the site, served by British Rail and a nearby expressway, is to be a metropolitan scale sports arena and adjoining exhibition hall.

For Dublin's Custom House Docks along the River Liffey, BTA has designed a vital new inner-city district around a similar, but more centrally located and better preserved, series of dock basins. It incorporates Victorian warehouses and storage vaults together with a major high-tech financial services center. Also included are three museums, a waterside hotel, services, shopping, eating, entertainment, and neighborhood residential clusters. Both the new and restored elements are carefully attuned to the dominant low scale and pervasive granite of Dublin's old center. The project enhances the city's economic base, its vitality, and its orientation toward the river.

With these comprehensive proposals, BTA is pioneering a new urban genre that goes beyond the scope of the earlier Faneuil Hall Marketplace and South Street Seaport. These new city districts, built of old and new elements, with a carefully controlled sense of scale, and on traditional street and site patterns, combine necessity and delight at a new level of diversity so that each city can be enjoyed as a City of Man.

BIBLIOGRAPHY

General References

B. Thompson, "Visual Squalor and Social Disorder—A New Vision of a City of Man," *Architectural Record* **145**(4), 161–164 (Apr. 1969).

B. Thompson, "The World around Us—Towards an Architecture of Joy and Human Sensibility," *Architectural Record* **142**(3), 153–158 (Sept. 1967).

B. Thompson, "Let's Make It Real," *Architectural Record* **139**(1) 107–120 (Jan. 1966).

B. L. Diamondstein, "Interview with Benjamin Thompson," in *American Architecture Now II,* Rizzoli International Publications, New York, 1985, pp. 212–221.

A. O. Dean, "Benjamin Thompson & Associates Receives AIA's Firm Award," *Architecture* **76**(1), 14–18 (Jan. 1987).

See also Adaptive Use; Preservation, Historic; The Architects Collaborative (TAC)

Dennis J. DeWitt
Benjamin Thompson &
Associates
Cambridge, Massachusetts

THORNTON, WILLIAM

Dr. William Thornton (1759–1828) is the second most important U.S. amateur architect, ranking behind his friend Thomas Jefferson (1743–1826). Like the "Sage of Monticello," he took up architecture as one pursuit open to a man of universal interests. He belonged, however, to a younger generation, that of Charles Bulfinch (1763–1844), the amateur who became a professional, and B. Henry Latrobe (1764–1820), the architect who transplanted the newly formed standards of professionalism from Great Britain. These four men dominate the history of U.S. architecture at the beginning of the nineteenth century and, in the small world of the young nation, their stories interlock. Thornton has to his credit having participated in the creation of two supremely important public buildings, the U.S. Capitol (1793–1829) and Jefferson's University of Virginia (1817–1826). His small oeuvre also includes two of the most remarkable neoclassic houses in the United States.

THORNTON'S BEGINNINGS

Thornton was born in the British West Indies but grew up in Great Britain. He studied medicine in Scotland, traveled on the continent, and moved in distinguished circles abroad. In 1786, he came to the United States to promote an enduring cause of his, the abolition of slavery and the creation of an African state for freedmen. He became a U.S. citizen and lived for a time in Philadelphia, the metropolis of the new country. In association with John Fitch, he began his lifelong interest in U.S. steamboats.

Thornton had been an amateur artist for some time, but he did not take up architecture until 1789. In that year, the competition to design a home for the Library Company of Philadelphia attracted him. After briefly studying from the available books, he submitted the winning design for Library Hall (executed, 1789–1790; demolished, 1887; facade recreated for the American Philosophical Society, 1956). Just at this time, a series of temple-fronted buildings brought a new monumentality to Philadelphia architecture. Library Hall, with a portico of marble pilasters set against its brick facade, was apparently the first urban building in this series. But the marble facades and freestanding porticoes of the next decade—at the first Bank of the United States (1794–1797), by Thornton's friend Samuel Blodget, Jr., and the Bank of Pennsylvania (1799–1801; demolished), by Latrobe— swiftly outshone Thornton's frontispiece. Along with most ambitious U.S. architecture of its period, Library Hall was a British provincial building that depended on outdated sources. Thornton still took the books and buildings of the defunct Anglo–Palladian movement (1710–1750) as standards, and he used ornament from the declining Adamesque phase (1760–1790) of the neoclassic movement. From such a naive and even dull beginning, he would mature into the creator of memorably inventive neoclassic designs.

Thornton returned to the family plantation in Tortola, British Virgin Islands (1790–1792) after marrying Anna Marie Brodeau of Philadelphia. His bride learned to supplement her husband's limited graphic skills, and she became one of the earliest female architectural draftspersons in the United States. In Tortola, Thornton worked on a universal system of spelling and a method of teaching the deaf to speak, both of which he published in 1793.

THE UNITED STATES CAPITOL

Thornton began his connection with the U.S. Capitol while he was in Tortola. A "Federal City" was to rise beside the Potomac, and in 1792 the commissioners of the city advertised a competition for the design of the national Capitol. Thornton made an unsophisticated design, the "Tortola Scheme," adapted from Anglo–Palladian country house ideas, and he brought this to Philadelphia, the nation's temporary capital city, four months after the deadline. Receiving permission to submit a design, he made a new one. In 1793, his unfinished drawings for this second scheme won the competition. The drawings vanished early on, and it is necessary to reconstruct Thornton's conception from his description (Fig. 1). The impractical features of the proposal betrayed his amateurism, whereas the design's boldly scaled use of classic antiquity represents a dramatic increase in imaginative power.

Figure 1. Project for West Front, U.S. Capitol, Washington, D.C., 1793. Reconstruction by Don A. Hawkins.

It seems likely that Thornton had already fallen—if only indirectly—under the influence of Jefferson, then the secretary of state. Jefferson was a determined man when it came to seeing his favorite architectural ideas realized. Between the early 1790s and the end of his presidency in 1809, his wishes reshaped numerous architects' conceptions for the Capitol, from Etienne-Sulpice Hallet to Latrobe. For instance, after Jefferson's idea of modeling the entire Capitol on the Pantheon in Rome proved unworkable, he wished the Capitol to imitate the Pantheon at least in part. Thornton's victorious design, in a striking departure from his former reliance on domestic prototypes, inserted into the middle of the Capitol something that sounds like a version of the Pantheon. Thornton meant this element as a secular temple that would have held a monument to George Washington and, probably, Washington's tomb.

Construction of the Capitol began in 1793, but to a plan that in reality was Hallet's, although it was officially seen as Thornton's design made more practical. Appointed a commissioner of the city of Washington, D.C. (1794–1802), Thornton moved there, where he lived for the rest of his life, and held various other government posts, notably as the first superintendent of the Patent Office (1802–1828). Meanwhile, a succession of architects erected the Capitol (1793–1829). At least three of them contributed profoundly to the form that the building took: Hallet (1793–1794); Latrobe, working first in collaboration with Jefferson (1803–1809) and then alone (1809–1812 and 1815–1817); and Bulfinch (1818–1829). Thornton seized opportunities to assert control over the design until the Latrobe–Jefferson period, when he angrily found himself an outsider to the building campaign. As finished, the Capitol owed only two elements to him, the wing elevations and the idea of a great central rotunda. (Thornton's cherished idea of devoting this space to Washington's tomb and monument was never realized.) Circumstances had grafted these elements onto a complex derivative of Sir Edward Lovett Pearce's Anglo–Palladian Parliament House in Dublin (1729 ff). The Irish building had given the world the model for a statehouse with wings, a domed core behind a temple portico, and a hall of debate with the curved seating of the classic theater, instead of two banks of straight seats.

THE OCTAGON, TUDOR PLACE, AND THE UNIVERSITY OF VIRGINIA

Problems of documentation complicate the study of Thornton's work. Of the other buildings connected with his name, three stand out, both for their quality and for the quality of the evidence.

In the late 1790s, Colonel John Tayloe III, member of a family of extraordinary architectural patrons, was determined to build a fine Washington townhouse. Studies for the house by both Thornton and Latrobe survive. Tayloe preferred Thornton's conception, which cleverly fitted a hexagonal house into an acutely angled site. Employing a device that had an Anglo–Palladian pedigree, Thornton used a cylindral bow to make the building turn the sharp corner. Unfortunately, the documents do not tell how far he participated in the creation of the house, traditionally called the Octagon (1799 ff; maintained as a museum by the AIA). The structure has a confusing facade (it indicates the presence of a *piano nobile* where none exists) and important Adamesque interiors.

For Thomas and Martha Peter, Thornton designed Tudor Place, their Georgetown house (ca 1810–1816), as a five-part villa of stuccoed brick, with end pavilions formed from earlier buildings. Like those for the Octagon, Thornton's studies for this house show him experimenting with varied room shapes, such as the ellipse and the apse-ended rectangle. However, the executed house has rectangular spaces, except for the portico on the garden front. This Doric porch is in essence a circular temple, or *monopteron*, inserted halfway into the main block, and the conception very likely came from a garden pavilion design that Sir William Chambers had published in his *Treatise* (1759 and later editions). Perhaps Thornton did not have optimal control over the execution of his design, but this villa forcefully embodies the neoclassic goal of architectural reform. Its animated composition, with its hollow, shadowy center, suggests Thornton's gift for picturesque design. Thornton's writings document his interest in the principles of the picturesque movement, which taught architects how to apply compositional ideas from landscape painting to architecture.

In 1817, Jefferson paid Thornton—and later, Latrobe—a high compliment. Jefferson asked for, and used, their ideas for the pavilions of the new school that would become the University of Virginia. Some of his friend's suggestions squared nicely with Jefferson's preferences, such as Thornton's recommendation of columns rather than piers for the covered walks. And Thornton's two elevations for pavilions, similar to an early project for Monticello, prompted Jefferson's design for his first pavilion, number VII. Unique among the pavilions, this one contributes its full share to one of the most distinctive effects of the Jefferson Lawn, its rich variety of facades. It seems appropriate that Thornton, a universal man first and foremost, made his last civic design for an institution dedicated to the values that had motivated him all his life.

BIBLIOGRAPHY

General References

C. E. Brownell and J. A. Cohen, *The Architectural Drawings of Benjamin Henry Latrobe,* Yale University Press, New Haven, forthcoming.

D. D. Reiff, "William Thornton," in A. Placzek, *Macmillan Encyclopedia of Architects,* Vol. 4, Free Press, New York, 1982, pp. 211–212.

E. Stearns and D. N. Yerkes, *William Thornton, A Renaissance Man in the Federal City,* American Institute of Architects Foundation, Washington, D.C., 1976.

CHARLES E. BROWNELL
University of Virginia
Charlottesville, Virginia

TILT-UP CONSTRUCTION

Tilt-up construction is a particular precast concrete technique in which wall panels are formed and cast horizontally on site and later "tilted up" to form the building perimeter. Although it has been used primarily in the construction of industrial and commercial buildings, there also exist several examples of tilt-up use for such diverse projects as multiunit residences, retail stores, waterfront clubs, and even churches. Several sculptures have also been made with the use of this technique (1).

An average tilt-up project is usually no less than 40,000 ft² ; however, some as small as 5000 ft² have been built cost effectively (2). Although most often used for single-story structures, panels have been stacked to realize multistory designs (Fig. 1). An average 6 to 8-in.-thick panel weighs approximately 25 tons and is on the order of 25 × 30 ft in size. Panels have been built as high as 60 ft and weighing twice this amount.

The advantages of tilt-up concrete construction are numerous, which accounts for its ever-increasing popularity. It is a fairly simple technique performed by minimally skilled labor and utilizing relatively inexpensive materials. Forming and finishing of the wall panels is more easily performed on the ground saving the cost of scaffolding. Tilt-up is an extremely efficient technology often making multiple use of building components. The building floor slab also serves as the casting surface for the wall panels. The panels themselves are bearing walls, support-

Figure 1. The Dunes Club at Amelia Island, Florida, displays the multi-level potential of tilt-up. Architect and contractor, The Haskell Company.

ing floor and roof loads as well as providing physical enclosure and serving as a medium for the final exterior finish.

Tilt-up also benefits from all the material advantages of concrete. Its plasticity allows for an almost unlimited variety of finishes: aggregate, stone, and tile insets; textured, and sandblasted are among the more common. Given a healthy dose of creativity, this quality can and has afforded many design opportunities. Concrete provides fire resistance at almost no additional cost. It also provides a fair measure of thermal resistance, which can be augmented by the use of lightweight concrete. Many designers have also taken advantage of a concrete wall's thermal mass to help temper the environment in passive-solar applications (3).

The success of any tilt-up project relies on a number of factors. Most important is a very thorough planning effort. By its nature, this technique interfaces with several trades. A coordinated and timely sequence is essential in realizing the full benefits of reduced construction time. Unlike more traditional precast concrete produced in a controlled factory environment, tilt-up must contend with weather conditions on site. This accounts for its relative popularity in warmer climates; ie, the southwest United States. The technique has, however, been used successfully in much colder climates, as far north as Canada. Related to this climate–weather sensitivity is the importance of selection and quality control of the concrete mix. It is advisable to have fair-sized sample panels erected on site under the proposed procedure. When the desired finish is reached in the sample panel, it then becomes the standard to which the project's panels are held. A consistent procedure is critical to achieving a reasonably even finish. As practiced today, the finished surface is cast face-down and, therefore, is not visible until much later when it is lifted. As a result, the sample panel is all the more important.

In summary, tilt-up can be described as an "evolutionary" concrete process utilizing the advantages of reduced forming and heavy equipment use to yield significant savings in cost and time. This technique requires from one-half to three-fourths the time required for comparable conventional construction methods. Projects as large as 700,000 ft^2 have been completed in as little as seven months (4).

HISTORY

Colonel Robert H. Aiken, who operated an engineering company in Illinois, is generally regarded as the originator of tilt-up concrete construction. He first used the concept, in the early twentieth–century, with simple retaining-wall construction. Aiken built walls on their side and then utilized a derrick to "tip" them into place.

> While this wall was lying upon the ground in process of construction, the thought occurred to me, while walking over it one day, that it would be possible to build the wall of a building in this way, leaving the proper openings for doors and windows, and tip it into place as the side of a house (5).

Figure 2. The Mess Hall at Camp Perry, Ohio.

The earliest buildings using this technique were several 5000 ft^2 barracks for the state of Illinois. Later, Aiken built a 6000 ft^2 factory in Zion City and a two-story munitions building for Camp Logan, both in Illinois. During this period, several refinements were made in this novel concrete technique. Probably most impressive among these early buildings is the two-story Mess Hall Building at Camp Perry, Ohio. Although it was a large building (measuring 192 by 132 ft) and despite its elaborate neoclassic detailing, this project was completed in one month's time (Fig. 2).

Colonel Aiken's tilt-up system can be described as following this sequence. Initially, a lumber platform is erected over a steel framework supported by jacks. This platform is set about 3 ft above the ground and immediately adjacent to the wall's final location. Door and window frames and any precast elements (eg, cornices and pilasters) are arranged in the form. The concrete pour then follows in a series of steps to facilitate the placement of the steel reinforcement. A special cement mixture is applied to finish the top of the slab, which will eventually be the exterior face of the building. After two days of curing, the wall is slowly tilted into position using a five-horsepower engine, which operates the platform jack screws (Fig. 3). The reoriented wall, now placed on the foundation, is temporarily braced during construction until the later final connections are made. The forming platform is relocated to the next position, modified for the particular wall panel, and the process begins anew. After several wall panels are raised to their final position, the walls are interlocked by encasing projecting reinforcing at the corners into a concrete column at each such junction.

Figure 3. A construction photograph of Colonel Aiken's tilt-up system.

The most impressive aspect of Aiken's technique is the speed with which these buildings were realized. The Camp Perry Building required about three days to mold and set each wall in place. Aiken designed an innovative, interlocking modular slab system for this two–story structure. With these technological advantages, the 47,000 ft^2 mess hall was completed in only 28 days.

Colonel Aiken believed that his new technique would institute a "new age of concrete" (6). He projected its use for structures of a dozen or more floors in height. He felt strongly that tilt-up could be used for various building types including housing. Thomas Edison shared Aiken's view that concrete could be used innovatively to provide low cost residential units (7). A patent was obtained by Halverson–Freichel in 1919. Despite such promising projections, the technique seemed to have fallen out of use until after World War II. Later patents in the 1950s were never tested or were declared null and void so that the modern-day tilt-up building system is nonpatented and in the public domain.

The availability of the modern, mobile crane breathed new life into tilt-up in the 1950s. Cranes replaced the lumber platform–jack screw assembly, allowing greater flexibility and economies with the technique. Its use started in California and the Sun Belt states where the climate is best suited to nearly year-round concrete construction. It has since spread to much colder climates and to many foreign countries. The modern-day technique differs from Aiken's method in several ways: (1) wall panels are typically cast on floor slabs, facedown; (2) cranes are used to tilt-up the panels, which requires special lifting hardware; and (3) the panels must be reinforced to withstand the unusual stresses of being lifted, unlike Aiken's continuously supporting platform. These and other items are discussed in greater detail in the following section.

MODERN-DAY TILT-UP PRACTICE

General Panel Design

There are a number of guidelines that should be followed when designing tilt-up panels to produce quality results. Panels should be the same size as each other, when possible, to realize the economies of tilt-up. This is especially important when the panels are required to be cast in stacks such as with a limited slab area. This also affects the lift rigging and the crane size. Openings should be centered in panel widths where possible. Panel joints need to be as far away from openings and major structural framing members as possible. The structural engineer for the building will usually establish these minimum dimensions. Vertical reveals are generally better than horizontal ones, because they do not weaken the panel at the area of maximum bending moment. When horizontal reveals are desired, it is better to locate them near the top or bottom of the panel than at the middle. It is usually more successful to emphasize panel joints than to attempt to conceal them.

Figure 4. A grid pattern with a "dimple" finish was used at the Christian Hospital Northeast in St. Louis, Missouri. Architect, Manske, Dieckmann & Kostecki.

Panel Finishes

Quite a variety of finishes are possible with the concrete tilt-up panels. Many are familiar with the commonly used exposed aggregate finishes. To achieve a more subtle aggregate exposure, often concrete panels are sandblasted (or water blasted) to reveal the color and textures of the internal stone aggregate. As with other types of concrete construction, an almost endless variety of textures are possible with the use of appropriate form liners or customized formwork. An unusual version of this involves the use of polyethylene sheeting over a gravel bed to yield a smooth, dimpled appearance (Fig. 4). Painting the tilt-up panels with a textured paint may be used for aesthetic or economic reasons. Although first costs are attractive, paint clearly requires regular renewal with attendant maintenance costs. It also does not take advantage of concrete's natural benefit as both structure and finish. Among the more costly finishes to consider are the use of natural stone cast into the face of the concrete panels. Anything from a rough-cut ashlar to a highly polished marble is possible (8).

Casting Slab and Formwork

An essential component of the tilt-up technique is the casting surface. Most often the building slab is used for this; however, other nearby large level surfaces are also possible. In any case, the casting surface must be a high quality finish as any imperfections will be telegraphed onto the wall panels cast on it. A sealer is typically used on the casting slab. Special chemical bond breakers are also necessary to ensure a clean separation between the lower slab and the wall panels cast on it. Given the technique's use of a crane for the lifting and setting of panels, the casting slab must be designed to accommodate the later weight and movement of such cranes. Another critical component of the slab's performance is based on the proper preparation and compaction of the grade below the slab. The project structural engineer will typically specify performance criteria based on the knowledge derived from a geotechnical engineer's analysis of the building site.

Modern tilt-up construction typically casts the exterior facade facedown. In accordance with the desired finish, the panels are thus formed onto the casting slab. Atten-

Figure 5. Panel formwork with reinforcement set in place.

Figure 7. Pouring and finishing of concrete panels.

tion must be paid to the most efficient location of panel formwork to facilitate later lifting and placement of the wall panels.

Steel reinforcement is placed per the engineering requirements of both lifting and in-place loads (Fig. 5). The building design structural engineer is responsible for the ultimate in-place loadings and designs the wall panels accordingly. A lifting hardware structural engineer takes the in-place design and ascertains which panel areas will require additional reinforcement to accommodate lifting stresses. When the analysis is complete, a set of panel shop drawings are prepared that locate lifting hardware (Fig. 6) and the additional steel reinforcement. The contractor, therefore, refers to both the building contract documents and the lifting hardware shop drawings while forming the wall panels.

An interesting variation to typical steel reinforcement bars involves the use of a "welded bar mesh." This technique, imported from Europe, uses a mesh fabricated from D4 to D14 steel reinforcement bars. Its primary advantage seems to be a potential for reducing labor time spent setting and tying rebar, thus speeding up a project schedule. Among welded bar mesh's disadvantages are its lim-

ited availability and its tendency to cause honeycombing when several mesh layers overlap. Furthermore, the lifting hardware engineers may be unfamiliar with this technique. Honeycombing can be typically controlled by properly vibrating the concrete. The other disadvantages will take some time for the industry to catch up on.

Concrete Pour

After having set the formwork and placed the steel reinforcement and lifting hardware, the contractor can begin to pour and finish the concrete (Fig. 7). Several characteristics of the concrete mix are worth noting. Obviously, the ultimate finish is dependent on the color and texture of the aggregate–cement components. Care must be taken, utilizing sample panels made under consistent procedures, in the selection of the proper concrete mix to yield the desired result. Quite often a high early strength concrete mix is used to ensure the requisite strength for lifting as soon as possible. Samples of the concrete are taken and tested regularly to verify that design performance criteria are met.

Given the fact that the exterior faces of the wall panels are hidden from view until they are lifted, quality control is critical. Among other things, this means ensuring an even distribution of the concrete to avoid honeycombing. The contractor must therefore, consistently and fully vibrate the concrete mix. This is particularly important in areas where the steel reinforcement is densely overlapped.

The Lifting Process

After the concrete panels have cured and the specified design strength has been achieved, the panels can be lifted into position. The company supplying the lifting hardware selects a rigging procedure appropriate to the shape, weight and strength of the concrete panels. If the panels have been properly designed by the project architect there should be little variation in the panel weights, thus allowing the most effective use of the crane capacity.

Figure 6. Detail of lifting hardware and related reinforcement.

Figure 8. Adjusting slings at the spreader bar to prepare for the lift.

Figure 9. Tilting the panel up.

Figure 10. Setting the panel in place and bracing it.

Similarly, consistency in the rigging procedure minimizes time spent making changes between panel lifts. In sequence, the contractor lifts each panel and moves it to its appropriate perimeter location, where it is plumbed and temporarily braced. The bracing type and placement, specified by the lifting hardware supplier, is designed according to several criteria including regional wind loading (Figs. 8–10).

Final Connections

In accordance with the particular requirements of the building design structural engineer, the final connections are made, tying the tilt-up wall panels to the balance of the structure. This typically consists of the following items, from the ground up:

1. Final plumbing and adjustments of the panels.
2. Anchoring of the panels to the foundation.
3. Pouring of the "slap strip" to fix the base of the panel. This strip is a 5–8 ft band along the building perimeter, left open to facilitate the placement of the wall panels.
4. Connections between panels, occasionally used to counter wind loads.
5. Structural connections for the transfer of the upper floors or roof structural components to the load-bearing wall panels.

With respect to item 2, it is noteworthy that the foundation may be of a continuous or pier nature. The pier foundations do seem to be more commonly used with tilt-up construction. The particular nature and frequency of the structural details vary according to the particular design employed by the project engineer (9).

In summary, the tilt-up technique has enjoyed a wider use as a result of the several advantages that it offers (Figs. 11–14). Among these are significant economies in both cost and time. Cost is reduced by the multiple use of the raised concrete wall as structural frame, enclosure, and exterior finish. The technique becomes more cost effective as the clear height to the underside of roof increases. This accounts for its widespread use for warehouses and other storage facilities. This technique also allows the use of very large panels, significantly larger

Figure 11. A traditional stone aesthetic was achieved by the use of a sophisticated pattern of reveals at the Grande Boulevard Mall in Jacksonville, Fla. Architect and contractor, The Haskell Company.

Figure 12. A unique high-tech image with an aerodynamic look characterizes the Hughes Aircraft Facility in Carlsbad, California. Architect, Krommenhoek/McKeown & Associates.

Figure 13. Tilt-up K-frames and wall panels were used by a creative design-build team to construct the Atlantic Winter Fair Complex in Halifax, Nova Scotia, within a seven-month period. Contractor, B. D. Stevens Ltd.

Figure 14. An intricately detailed portal for a recreational center shows the versatility of the tilt-up technique. Sculpture by David L. Engdahl, owned by Housing and Urban Development Department, City of Jacksonville, Florida.

than those possible with precast concrete. Thus, buildings can be erected considerably faster than with conventional construction methods, again yielding significant benefit to the project's owners. Finally, tilt-up lends itself to the "design build" approach where a coordinated procedure can improve over time with a team effort (10–12). Such an interplay of participants has great potential to refine and generally improve the quality of the tilt-up buildings produced.

BIBLIOGRAPHY

1. J. Varon, "Innovative Uses for Tilt-up Concrete," in R. E. Wilde, ed., *Tilt-up Construction,* Compilation No. 7, American Concrete Institute, Detroit, Mich., 1986, p. 20.

2. R. E. Spears, "Tilt-up Construction, Design Considerations—An Overview," in R. E. Wilde, ed., *Tilt-up Construction,* Compilation No. 4, American Concrete Institute, Detroit, Mich., 1980, p. 16.

3. The Burke Company, "Tilt-up Adapted to Solar Heating," in R. E. Wilde, ed., *Tilt-up Construction,* Compilation No. 4, American Concrete Institute, Detroit, Mich., 1980, p. 56.

4. Ref. 1, p. 18.

5. R. Aiken, "Monolithic Concrete Wall Buildings—Methods, Construction, and Cost," in R. E. Wilde, ed., *Tilt-up Con-*

struction, Compilation No. 4, American Concrete Institute, Detroit, Mich., 1980, p. 5.

6. Ref. 5, p. 4.

7. V. F. Leabu, "Discussion of the Article, 'Monolithic Wall Buildings—Methods and Construction Cost' by Robert Aiken," in R. E. Wilde, ed., *Tilt-up Construction,* Compilation No. 4, American Concrete Institute, Detroit, Mich., 1980, p. 12.

8. P. D. Courtous, "Architectural Esthetics of Tilt-up Panels," in R. E. Wilde, ed., *Tilt-up Construction,* Compilation No. 7, American Concrete Institute, Detroit, Mich., 1986, pp. 3–7. [See for additional information].

9. G. Weiler's, "Connections for Tilt-up Construction," in R. E. Wilde, ed., *Tilt-up Construction,* Compilation No. 7, American Concrete Institute, Detroit, Mich., 1986, pp. 11–15. [See for additional information].

10. W. D. Lockwood, "A Designer's View of Design/Build for Tilt-up," in R. E. Wilde, ed., *Tilt-up Construction,* Compilation No. 4, American Concrete Institute, Detroit, Mich., 1980, p. 19.

11. S. N. Hodges, Jr., "Tilt-up Construction Demands Team Effort," in R. E. Wilde, ed., *Tilt-up Construction,* Compilation No. 4, American Concrete Institute, Detroit, Mich., 1980, p. 71.

12. R. P. Foley, "Tilt-up Construction and the Designer-Contractor Team," in R. E. Wilde, ed., *Tilt-up Construction,* Compilation No. 7, American Concrete Institute, Detroit, Mich., 1986, p. 38.

General References

R. E. Wilde, ed., *Tilt-Up Construction,* Compilation No. 4, American Concrete Institute, Detroit, Mich., 1980. Reprint from *Concrete International: Design and Construction,* **2**(4) (Apr. 1980).

R. E. Wilde, ed., *Tilt-Up Construction,* Compilation No. 7, American Concrete Institute, Detroit, Mich., 1986. Reprint from *Concrete International: Design and Construction,* **2**(4), (Nov. 1982, Nov. 1984, Jan. 1985, and June 1986).

H. Brooks, S. E., *The Tilt-Up Design and Construction Manual,* HBA Publications, Newport Beach, Calif., 1988.

See also CONCRETE—GENERAL PRINCIPLES; INDUSTRIALIZED CONSTRUCTION; PRECAST ARCHITECTURAL CONCRETE

ANTHONY CONSOLI
Ellicott City, Maryland

MARK NEDZBALA
Columbia, Maryland

TIME-ADAPTIVE HOUSING

Time-adaptive housing defines an area of research and practice in architectural housing design that takes into account the constancy of change in lifestyle and living patterns. It recognizes that human time lines of living reflect a composite of personal and familial changes throughout a household's life cycle. These changes, in turn, have an impact on the necessity of change in personal place making. Thus time-adaptive housing emphasizes housing design that is responsive to the dynamics of life, thereby serving human occupancy on a time continuum in contrast to conventional design practice, which singularly addresses short-term programmatic needs. Within this reference, time-adaptive housing is also known as time-scaled housing and evolutionary housing. When implemented, time-adaptive housing reflects a conscious predetermination of design allowances that facilitates spatial and physical alterations in the dwelling to accommodate environmental response to changing household needs. Within this conceptual framework of responsive housing, there exist alternative proposals for achieving viable adaptive design solutions, with distinctions reflected in both method and degree of accommodation.

Addressing preplanned flexibility as an inherent attribute of the dwelling is not a new idea. Frank Lloyd Wright dealt with the issue of alterable environments in one of his Usonian residential structures, the Paul Hanna house, built in 1937. In the Hanna residence, he employed a unit system for building space. The floor plan, established on a hexagonal grid, is networked on these ordered lines to ensure consistent proportioning. It resulted in a spacious honeycomb plan that allows for interior flexibility and future expansion. Wright revealed that he was inspired by the intricate and complex shelter of the master builders, bees. He noted that the sociological structure and the activity within the beehive was demanding of a unit adaptable to the tremendous growth and vitality that flows from one generation of bees to another. Borrowing from nature, Wright employed the hexagon as the workable unit in a collaborative system where spatial units (rooms) could become time adaptive. Figure 1 shows an example where a change was made in the Hanna house several years after its original construction. The master bedroom was transformed into a library space with the removal of a few wall partitions. It is documented that its residents, the Hannas, who lived in the house throughout most of their lives, were very satisfied with their house and especially appreciated the way that it served all the changes their lives required (1).

In 1949, architect and designer Charles Eames designed his own residence with a concern for flexibility. The use of standardized industrial parts in the structure permitted alterability, in both its interior spatial organization and the building envelope (2). The off-the-shelf components were put together in a way that characterized a spatially ample open plan that allowed its owner a continuum of lifestyle changes over time. The time-adaptive attributes of this structure were remarkably demonstrated during the structure's planning and building process. Before its construction, the initial design was altered to reflect a change in both the building massing and its orientation, and although building materials for the original plan had already been ordered prior to these design alterations, these same materials were utilized to construct the revised design. The Eames house stands as an example of time-adaptive design in its effective manipulation of form, space, materials, function, and aesthetics.

The Dymaxion House prototype, designed by Buckminster Fuller in 1927 and built in the 1940s, was another effort to provide a residential environment that would anticipate change (3). In this instance, accommodation of

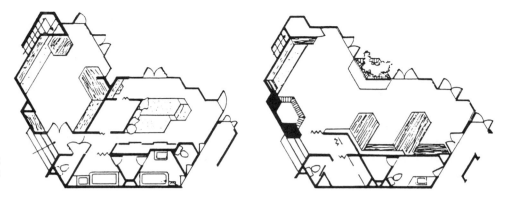

Figure 1. F. L. Wright—Hanna House bedroom wing. Original plan and adaptive alteration to library.

change within the living unit was centered on the replacement of obsolescent service components, while its spaces and building form remained relatively fixed. Its time-adaptive design relevance is found in its early implementation of the idea of planning and programming for change in the design process.

Whereas these early examples of time-adaptive housing are concentrated in single-family residences, architects of the 1960s in various European countries began applying the time-adaptive concept of design variability and flexibility to multifamily housing. The SAR (Stichting Architecten Research) Group, founded in the Netherlands in 1964, was organized to investigate improved methods of dealing with the design and construction of mass housing. Headed by N. J. Habraken, it introduced specific proposals outlining methods for the design of adaptable dwellings by means of "supports." The supports concept is based on the principle of user participation, where residents are actively involved in the housing process. As it was described by its proponents, "[t]he supports concept is one in which the dwelling is not a product to be designed and produced like other commodities of industry, but rather it is the result of a process in which the user can make decisions within a larger framework of communal services and infrastructure" (4). Within this dual sphere of decision making, the terms "support" and "detachable units" are defined: support involves decision making at the community level, and the detachable unit is that area over which the individual decides. Together they divide the dwelling and the larger structure into two groups of elements. The essential aim of the SAR Group in implementing the method within the Dutch community was to redirect the course of industrially produced housing to effect a more rationalized approach to housing production. This was an effort to minimize the growth of uniform and monotonous standardized building systems on the Dutch landscape in exchange for a built environment that would simultaneously reflect the aspirations of the community and those personal to the individual. Since its successful implementation in the Netherlands, the SAR method has been used in related applications elsewhere.

Another example of the application of time-adaptive design is seen in the Scandinavian experimental housing project built in 1966 in Uppsala, Sweden. Responding to consumer demand for housing units designed to accommodate comfortably a wide range of families with differing

lifestyles, ages, and spatial requirements, the building firm of Ohlsson and Skarne implemented a design that utilized a standardized shell and interior components, but allowed for flexible adaptation of the interior space by the tenants themselves. The experimental apartment building consisted of 16 units. A service wall was fixed between the units. Fixed also were the facade windows and interior columns located along the centerline of the exterior walls. All other interior components were designed to be movable by tenants, including room height partitions in 2 and 4-ft widths, door frame units, and room-height closet units. In addition, removable electrical service was attached to each door and wall element. Tenants living in this experimental apartment block were interviewed two years after their residence. It was found that most people were generally positive about their apartments' flexibility and the opportunities they provided for altering their living space. It was learned that residents changed their apartment plans in stages as they encountered shortages of space and realized the possibilities of the flexible system. Ultimately, a considerable number of spatial modifications were made to accommodate family needs. For the most part, it was found that the basic function of a room was changed on six different occasions by the average tenant. From the interview survey, a report produced by the Department of Building Function Study of the Lund Institute of Technology presents a visual documentation of each stage of the apartments' redesign. It contains interval drawings, which are able to capture the motion of the families' utilization of space over time. Each pattern of development was different, reflecting an overall physical expression of the families' internal dynamics (5).

In the 1970s, a vitalized interest in the subject was noted with studies undertaken in the United Kingdom and North America. In the United Kingdom, the work by architect Cedric Price entitled "Research on Housing, Parts 1 and 2" was published (6,7). He presented a study of "time-scaled housing" that implicitly depends on technology. In employing the principal tenets of technology (mass production, mobility, and planned obsolescence), Price introduces a component housing building system that is designed to conform to any site in any setting and to accommodate every type of residential activity. Its physical design comprises a collection of built modules that are formed from smaller building components. From this, a dwelling can be realized once its users interface and en-

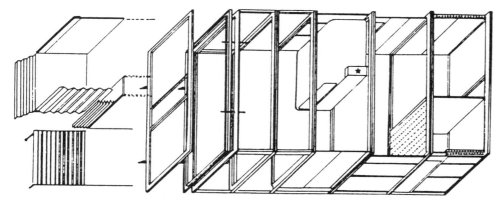

Figure 2. C. Price—Time-scaled housing system.

gage in the process of personalization and customization by fitting together and reorganizing the system's parts. This system can be seen in Figure 2. Price's work also presents an analysis of the economic advantage of allowing the houses to obsolesce when user interface ceases, thereby encouraging the concept of disposable housing (7).

Another time-adaptive design study, undertaken about the same time as Price's research, is Christopher Alexander's work on "Thick Wall Patterns" (8,9). It identifies two types of adaptation. One is mass adaptation, and the other is personal adaptation. The notion of mass adaptation addresses general populace needs, which Alexander sees as being served by "standardized" accommodation. His direct concern is with the second type, personal adaptation. He states that "[d]wellings must be designed in such a way that personal adaptation takes place as people live in them" (9). His proposal aims at contemporizing traditional conditions of times past, when, he believes, personal adaptation was more likely to occur, given the stationary nature of people and the handcrafted methods of place making. He asks the question, "What kind of house is both compatible with modern means of production and also capable of providing a high degree of personal adaptation?" (10). From this, Alexander proposes as a solution that houses be built with interior and exterior walls with thicknesses of 3–5 ft, constructed of a hand-carvable space frame. Floors would be similarly constructed, with a 2–3-ft depth. Figure 3 shows how a typical floor plan utilizing the thick wall material would be altered over time with different residents. This type of space frame would

allow for additive and subtractive alterations, where its residents could carve away or remove large sections at a time to serve all their functional and personalization needs. Its components, Alexander envisioned, could be readily purchased at a local hardware store.

Although implementation of Price's and Alexander's proposals suggests changes significantly apart from society's inclined mainstream manner and modes of domestic accommodation, their work serves to identify as middle-ground approaches two other investigations that have followed. In these subsequent studies, the time-adaptive design concept centers on the evolutionary pattern of implementation, reflecting, in contrast, a rather gradual process of integration into the ongoing activity of designing and building housing. Whereas the Alexander and Price studies offered distinct physical resolutions, these proposals forward a composite solution of design guidelines that allow immediate assimilation within the framework of existing residential design and building.

Andrew Rabeneck and David Sheppard, in their work with Building Systems Development in 1974, introduced an approach to adaptability that avoids earlier architect-inventor devices such as movable or carvable walls and convertible furniture in favor of simple planning spaciousness and ambiguous use spaces (11). The initial phase of their work focused on identifying the various limitations of accommodation in current design practice where its design intent concentrates on optimum function at minimum cost. This concern for spatial economy in design, they believed, results in spatial configurations that fit too tightly, are too functionally explicit, and as such, restrict evolutionary use patterns. In their examination of the typical organization of family units, they found that spaces designed and proportioned for single functions were unable to serve alternative uses. This is due, in part, to the design's inclusion of designated function-related fixtures, such as wardrobes, and window placement, which tends to reflect and fix a specific identity to each room's function. Other design constraints examined were the provision of only one living room/gathering space and general access to rooms by minimally proportioned circulation passageways.

From their observations, they formulated a series of design directives that would allow for adaptability. These were then translated into conceptual floor plans. Figure 4

Figure 3. C. Alexander—Thick wall patterns.

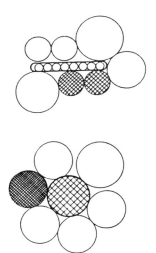

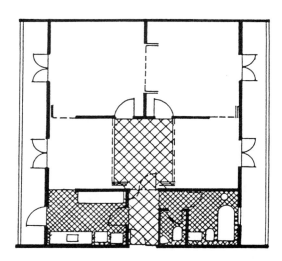

Figure 4. Rabeneck & Sheppard— Comparative spatial organization. Conventional linear vs time-adaptive planning.

identifies both how their conceptual organization of an adaptable unit differs significantly from that of conventional design practice and a floor plan that interprets these adaptive design guidelines. Their proposed design guidelines include directives that rooms be designed without prevalent visages of function, that room configurations be designed with the intention of facilitating multiple functions, and further, that the design provide for room-to-room potential with variable zoning. Another guideline holds that interconnection between rooms and doors and window placement are best predetermined in the design and building process so that later functional reorganizations are not hampered. Recommendations are made to enlarge the circulation space, whereby halls and vestibules would be large enough to serve as rooms between rooms. Other suggestions are that the equipment, service systems, and furniture not be constructed within the building fabric. The clear advantage of this is the minimizing of future alteration costs. Their summary statement on design planning for adaptability focuses on a minimized predetermination of pattern to provide for a maximized number of potential spatial organizations and functional uses with the aim of providing choice through ambiguity.

This notion of ambiguity has, in fact, significant historical importance in housing design, reaching as far back as the Mesopotamian hot climate country house, where the enclosed courtyard served as an extra functional use space that was accessible to and compatible with almost any room's function. Turn-of-the-century Victorian dwellings also displayed spatial planning in a fashion similar to that of the scheme outlined by Rabeneck and Sheppard. Typically, there is a degree of ambiguity in the general living spaces, where a front parlor or drawing room usually served equally as a gathering social space analogous to the current-day living room. Hallways were spatially generous, thus enabling some activity within these corridors other than general pass-through circulation. Spatial flexibility in the Victorian home typically included a sliding wall/door, which served to combine two spaces into one large room or to separate them into partitioned, private

areas. Room proportions were reasonably ample and facilitated multiple furniture organizations. Another design feature of the Victorian house was the dual staircase, which was common to most structures, as were the numerous exits. These design amenities explain how their recent conversions from single-family residences to multiple-unit accommodations were easily facilitated with reasonably limited construction alterations.

In 1984, a decade after the Rabeneck and Sheppard study, the Canadian Mortgage and Housing Corporation, Canada's federal housing agency, published an advisory document to promote sound planning and design. This work, "Internal Spaces of the Dwelling," presents a series of time-adaptive design guidelines (12). This research, based on 50 case studies of different living unit types, analyzes functional use and design variables within the unit spaces. A sequence of design qualities is presented for each of the various unit spaces common to every dwelling, including entrances/corridors, living rooms, dining rooms, kitchens, bedrooms, baths, and storage and utility spaces. In essence, the recommendation is that living units be designed with minimum pattern predetermination and that design features, in general, not inhibit choices of use. These decisions should rest with the occupants. The study also cautions that the dwelling should not be entirely adaptable, noting that certain areas require more flexibility, and others more permanence. The precedent question on which it developed its design guideline was, "How easily can this dwelling evolve with changing occupants and the passage of time?" To this end, these design directives were identified:

1. *Size.*
   - Rooms should be sized beyond minimum allowances to serve multiple functions.
   - Corridor spaces should be sized beyond minimum allowances to serve additional functions.
2. *Configuration.*
   - Square room configurations facilitate multiple furnishing organizations better than rectangular-shaped spaces.

3. *Organization.*
- Spaces should be designed to allow zoning alternatives, ie, with movable walls to expand or separate spaces.
- Room openings should be carefully located to permit multiple furnishing arrangements.

Within the brief history of time-adaptive housing's research and its prototypes, the recurring theme has been to view housing as a process, a perspective that may appear antithetical to the traditional static definition of a house as a secure and unchanging place of refuge from the outside world. In addressing this issue, the Illinois Institute of Technology (IIT) design prototype for the "House of the Future" illustrates that process-oriented (time-adaptive) housing affords innumerable possibilities that in the long run preserve and sustain domestic stability (13).

This project is the result of an interdisciplinary collaboration on the design of future housing systems investigating the possibilities of making housing more responsive to the needs of people through the use of technology. The computer in this prototype would serve as both a general household utility and a working tool in the design process. The future house would come as a kit of parts purchased to anticipate immediate and projected needs. These parts would change configuration as needs dictated. For example, on a daily cycle, component parts of the house could change to respond to changing activities or outside weather conditions. On a longer cycle, spaces could change with added or removed parts in response to material accumulations, family interest, or increases or decreases in family size.

The House of the Future uses a structural system that can be extended or reduced. Interior and exterior walls are movable and work with clip-on exterior modules, which enable alterations in both function and appearance. Utility cores can be moved about the house and reconnected to the utility infrastructure by way of a "deep floor" distribution system. The design objective in this adaptive dwelling is that it becomes an extension of its occupants, mirroring and assisting their interests and needs as they change in time (Fig. 5).

Figure 5. IIT house of the future.

Although the IIT House of the Future forecasts a domestic environment for future living, its programmatic focus and solution draw from current-day phenomena, including sociological trends as well as technological advances. In the first instance, current secular trends in domestic living patterns and arrangements are distinguishably different from those of the past and continue to be perpetuated over time. Today's societal cohabiting compositions are identifiably multivariate and continually changing. This, in effect, establishes a new directional focus on contemporary future dwelling design that inherently necessitates addressing issues of multidimensional changing needs, where the goal is to serve and satisfy dynamic response and accommodation. Adaptive dwellings designed with the mainstay attributes of alterability and flexibility afford a potentially viable solution for realizing and implementing a responsive environment.

Second, today's state of the art in design and building technology opens new avenues for design exploration within this area of investigation. Through the use of computer-aided design technology, proposals for alterable environments and user interface, in their layered design complexities of transfiguring space, materials, and form into numerous organizations, can be implemented to generate a variety of design alternatives. Additionally, today's advanced building technology has the capability to produce any level of building components and systems from small unit hardware elements to fully furnished modular living units (14).

Fusing design and technology to provide for functional changes in the adaptive domestic environment will similarly have an impact on design aesthetics. This suggests new parameters for design expression that are, in a way, analogous to artist Alexander Calder's design concept of the mobile. By setting artistic expression in motion, he gave it new freedom to move about space, creating and recreating new visual experiences for the observer. Time-adaptive housing, in its response to "living in motion," also offers an expanded dimension for visual experience when adaptive change occurs.

BIBLIOGRAPHY

1. P. R. Hanna and J. S. Hanna, *Frank Lloyd Wright's Hanna House, The Clients' Report,* MIT Press, Cambridge, Mass., 1981, pp. 53, 54.
2. B. J. Sullivan, *Industrialization in the Building Industry,* Van Nostrand Reinhold Co., Inc., New York, 1980, pp. 53, 54.
3. R. Marks, *The Dymaxion World of Buckminster Fuller,* Anchor Books, Garden City, N.Y., 1973.
4. N. J. Habraken and co-workers, *Variations, The Systematic Design of Supports,* MIT Press, Cambridge, Mass., 1976, p. 10.
5. K. J. Dominguez, "Redefining Residence for Altered Family Compositions," in *ACSA Annual Meeting Proceedings,* Vancouver, B.C., Canada, 1985, pp. 90–98.
6. C. Price, "Housing Research, Part I," *Architectural Design* **41**, 619 (Oct. 1971).
7. C. Price, "Housing Research, Part II," *Architectural Design* **43**, 24 (Jan. 1972).

8. K. J. Dominguez, "Design Technology and Dwelling Design: Perspectives and Prospects on the Time-adaptive Concept of Need and Accommodation," in *Proceedings of the 10th Triennial Congress of the International Council for Building Research Studies and Documentation,* Washington, D.C., 1986, p. 2792.

9. C. Alexander, "Thick Wall Patterns," *Architectural Design* **5,** 324 (July 1968).

10. *Ibid.,* p. 325.

11. A. Rabeneck and D. Sheppard, "The Structure of Space in Family Housing," *Progressive Architecture* **11,** 100 (Nov. 1974).

12. "Internal Spaces of the Dwelling," *Canadian Mortgage and Housing Corp.,* Ottawa, Ont., Canada, Cat. No. NH 17-25/1984E, 1984.

13. "House of the Future," *CRIT, AIAS,* 40–44, (1984).

14. K. J. Dominguez, "The Teaching of Time-adaptive Housing," in *ACSA Southwest Regional Meeting Proceedings,* Tulane Univ., New Orleans, La., 1985, pp. 24–29.

See also Behavior and Architecture; Eames, Charles; Fuller, R. Buckminster; Industrialized Construction; Physical and Mental Disability—Design for; Single—Family Residences; Single Parent Housing; Wright, Frank Lloyd

Karen J. Dominguez
Pennsylvania State University
University Park, Pennsylvania

TRAFFIC STUDIES.   See Parking and Traffic Circulation

TRAIN STATIONS.   See Transit Systems

TRANSIT SYSTEMS

The various modes of urban mass transportation on public routes are termed transit systems. Transit systems include buses, people movers, streetcars, light rail, rapid transit, and commuter and inter-urban railroad systems. The scope of this article is limited to the light rail and rapid transit systems and their hybrid variations. These systems have fixed guideways, require significant infrastructure in terms of line, stations and ancillary facilities, and are designed to transport large passenger volumes in urbanized areas.

Fixed Guideway transit systems may be classified by mode using the following characteristics:

1. *Right of Way.* The degree of separation between right of way and vehicular traffic is a primary determinant of potential speed and reliability of transit systems. Right of way is usually defined as uncontrolled, semi-controlled or fully controlled.

2. *Vehicle and Equipment Technology.* Light rail uses four, six and eight axle vehicles with a capacity of 80 to 270 passengers per vehicle. Car length ranges from 16 m to 29 m and can be articulated. Light rail is normally powered by overhead catenary systems to permit safe operation in non-exclusive right of way conditions.

   Rapid transit uses four axle vehicles varying in length from 14 m to 23 m. The vehicles are frequently coupled into "married pairs" of vehicles with an operator's cab at each end of the pair. The total passenger capacity of a vehicle varies from 100 to 250, seated and standing. Rapid transit is normally powered by a "third rail" adjacent to the tracks.

3. *Operation and Capacity.* Transit vehicles may operate in *consists* (trains) from one to ten vehicles. Modes using non-exclusive right of way seldom exceed three vehicles due to the necessity to stop within the space of city blocks without blocking cross streets.

   Passenger boarding may be accomplished by using street level, intermediate or high platforms. Street level boarding is normally used in light rail due to the uncontrolled right of way conditions. Intermediate and high level boarding which blocks pedestrian and vehicular crossing require semi-exclusive or fully controlled right of way. High level platforms permit more rapid boarding and decrease dwell time in stations and headways between trains, resulting in increased capacity. Increasing numbers of light rail vehicles are provided with movable steps, permitting boarding from either low or high level.

Although a wide range of transit modes is possible, most modes can be grouped into four classifications:

1. Light rail transit utilizes technology similar to streetcars with four axle or six axle articulated vehicles and overhead power distribution. Right of way is partially controlled. Vehicles are operated as individual units, normally with street level boarding areas.

2. Pre-metro defines a transitional mode between streetcars or light rail systems and rapid transit systems. Characteristics include increasing control of right of way, and the construction of underground stations with capacity for future rapid transit vehicles in congested areas. Often both single unit light rail vehicles and multiple unit rapid transit *consists* utilize the same right of way and stations. Stations may have split level or intermediate height platforms.

3. Light rail rapid transit utilizes rail equipment and systems in fully controlled right of way with a rapid transit operational approach providing multiple unit trains up to 300 feet in length and high level platforms.

4. Rapid transit systems operate exclusively on controlled right of way including aerial, surface and underground profiles. Train *consists* typically range from four to ten vehicles with a maximum length of approximately 750 feet. High platforms are pro-

vided to speed passenger boarding. The majority of rapid transit systems use rail technology and third rail power supply, but systems with rubber tire and overhead catenary technology are included in this mode. Most rapid transit systems use automatic train control and are capable of operating at minimum headways as low as 70 seconds.

HISTORY AND DEVELOPMENT

Rapid transit design and technology emerged from two very different origins in the nineteenth century: the steam locomotive passenger train, and the horse drawn street railway.

Urban steam passenger railways originated with the opening in 1863 of the London Underground Metropolitan Line. Insurmountable environmental obstacles to the operation of coal fired steam engines in cities led to designs for elevated urban railways by 1873 and to the exploration of alternative forms of propulsion, such as electric, pneumatic and cable systems.

Horse drawn street rail cars were first used in Baltimore in 1828. The advances of Thomas Edison and J. F. Sprague in electric motors led to the 1888 operation of the first large scale commercial electric streetcar system in Richmond, Virginia. Within the next few years thousands of miles of electric street railway were in operation worldwide.

The advances of Edison and Sprague in the United States were echoed in Europe by Werner von Siemens and others. By 1890 London became the first urban rapid transit system to be electrified. The common applications of electrification clouded many of the different characteristics of street railways and subway/elevated systems.

By the early 1900s underground electric railways were operating in Boston, Paris, New York and Budapest. In the first quarter of this century, streetcar lines expanded into inter-urban railways creating a light rail transit network of hundreds of miles in many areas of the United States. Before World War I more than 45,000 miles of streetcar and light rail track existed.

In the 1940s and 1950s the U.S. light rail systems deteriorated and lost patronage due to a variety of factors: poor maintenance and image, increasing car ownership, increasing acceptance of buses, inefficient operation and fare structures, and reduced reliability due to increased traffic congestion. All but a few of the U.S. light rail systems had disappeared by the mid-1960s. Systems in other countries were not abandoned as quickly as in the U.S., and they are slowly being replaced by rapid transit modes or upgraded in terms of right of way.

In the 1960s interest was rekindled in the importance of rapid transit systems as a vital component of urban transportation networks. Major cities around the world, such as San Francisco, Toronto, Montreal, Washington D.C., Munich, Milan and Stockholm, began constructing new systems; and cities with existing systems planned their expansion. Most recently, as the costs of rapid transit became prohibitive for all but the largest cities, light

rail transit has become a cost-effective mode for many cities.

PLANNING CONSIDERATIONS

Initial planning for new transit systems involves the survey of a sample of the residents of the proposed service area to determine factors such as travel habits and directions, economic status, employment, and attitude towards mass transit. The survey is used in conjunction with census information, traffic data, regional development statistics and other regionally accepted data to project trends over a 10 to 25 year period. This body of information, which is periodically revised, forms the basis for analyzing the expected patronage of alternative transit modes to a particular transit service area.

Early in the planning process it is essential to establish the relative importance of the benefits which can be expected from an investment in fixed guideway transit. These objectives are later used to evaluate modes and often include the following:

1. Attracting maximum ridership at minimum cost.
2. Minimizing long-term transit operating costs.
3. Reducing traffic congestion and the need for new roadway and parking construction.
4. Establishing an infrastructure as a guide or stimulus to future development.
5. Improving the quality and image of local mass transportation.
6. Reducing environmental pollution.

A fundamental component of any successful fixed guideway transportation system is service by other modes of transportation.

SYSTEM CONFIGURATION

Most urban areas consist of a high density central business district (CBD) or employment center surrounded by concentric circles of medium density residential areas. Beyond the historic residential districts are secondary suburban employment centers surrounded by low density residential areas.

The prototypical urban rail transit system consists of two or more lines which cross in the CBD and radiate through and sometimes past the suburban centers. The transportation corridor served by each rail line is geographically pie-shaped with high density and convenient pedestrian access to the line at the apex, and low density and poor access to the line as it radiates out of the city.

To serve the potential transit patrons in the widest portion of the corridor triangle, the transit line must either branch or other forms of transportation must feed patrons to the station by intermodal transfer. Some large systems, such as London and Moscow, construct radial transit lines which connect the branches and serve demand for inter-suburban travel.

Branching of transit lines to distribute service can be

observed in many mature rail networks. It has been applied in its most scientific manner in the Munich *U Bahn* where trunk lines typically support two secondary branches each of which support two tertiary branches. Another benefit of branching is that frequency of service is automatically balanced with patronage. Assuming a corridor with one trunk line and two tiers of branches, the frequency of service on the trunk line would be four times that of the branches.

Frequent branching is an expensive means of uniformly serving a corridor. It is more feasible in light rail systems than in rapid transit systems. The alternative method of serving low density suburban areas of a rapid transit corridor is to limit the branches and transport patrons to stations with alternative modes such as buses and light rail systems. Such intermodal facilities are always required at terminating stations to accommodate passengers from outside the local area who choose to commute by car or bus to the station. Since terminal stations, with their large parking facilities, are frequently sources of local traffic congestion, it is often advisable to give them direct access to freeway systems.

Linked pairs of transit corridors are preferable to lines which turn back in the CBD because they allow fewer and more flexible transfers between corridors, and they avoid the need for turn back and layover facilities in a high density area. To effectively balance through routing, pairs of corridors must be closely matched in patronage and frequency of service so that specific train sizes can serve both corridors.

The characteristics of the selected alignment and profile of a transit route through a transportation corridor are the primary determinants of service quality and cost. Factors which influence the decision can include the following:

1. Mode of operation and right of way control.
2. Availability and type of right of way.
3. Traffic and existing street patterns.
4. Density and type of surface development.
5. Geotechnical conditions.
6. Utilities and other subsurface development.

The mode of operation establishes the feasibility of an economical, at-grade alignment. Modes such as light rail which have uncontrolled or semi-controlled rights of way may be safely operated at grade in a variety of right of way conditions such as mixed traffic, separated median, pedestrian malls, parks, and adjacent to (or under) buildings. The controlled right of way required for rapid transit can sometimes be obtained at grade adjacent to railroads, and in expressway medians, but accommodation of existing traffic and development patterns normally leads to a grade separated solution—particularly in CBD locations.

Geotechnical conditions determine the feasibility of constructing subway profiles and the construction techniques which are appropriate in each specific situation. A high water table and poor geology may force consideration of surface or elevated profiles. If competent rock is found near the surface, the alignment normally drops to capital-

ize on the environmental benefits and economics of tunneling. The absence of rock normally leads to a relatively shallow cut-and-cover alignment.

Surface street and urban development patterns can often preclude the use of elevated or cut-and-cover construction. Grade separated stations are normally about 600 feet long and a minimum of 40 to 50 feet wide. Right of way to accommodate these facilities often can only be found in modern arterial streets. Cities such as London with pre-twentieth century development patterns frequently use the deeper earth or rock tunnel profiles to avoid surface disruption.

Utilities and other subsurface development are a major obstacle to cut-and-cover construction. Major utilities acquire easements and construct facilities in the same right of way that is attractive for transit. The maintenance and restoration or relocation of underground utilities in cut-and-cover construction is an expensive and time consuming process which exerts a strong influence on the alignment and profile of underground transit systems. Utilities may also affect surface alignments since it is not a good practice to align trackwork over other utility easements subject to future repair and excavation.

Station Location

The speed of a transit system is determined primarily by the frequency of stations, and secondarily by other factors such as dwell time, equipment performance and right of way characteristics. The spacing of stations must be balanced to permit maximum speed while providing enough stops to make the system convenient and attractive to patrons in the transit corridor.

Suburban lines with stations served by other transportation modes normally shorten travel time by having fewer stations, with relatively long distances (exceeding a mile) between stops. Lines in high density CBD locations normally provide frequent stops (less than $\frac{1}{2}$ mile apart) so that pedestrian access is no farther than a 5 to 10 minute walk from other modes of transportation. Only the largest cities can afford to invest in fixed guideway systems for both purposes. Most new transit systems include aspects of both situations.

The detailed location of transit stations involves the consideration of a complex set of issues including:

1. Availability of right of way for entrances.
2. Environmental impact on the community.
3. Proximity to other feeder modes such as bus and rail.
4. Proximity and attractiveness to patrons.
5. Relationship to existing development and future opportunities for development.

Stations in central business districts are normally linked to existing major centers of employment. Links often include direct connections to building complexes to make transit as attractive and convenient as possible in all weather conditions. Suburban stations generate high traffic demand and are best located adjacent to expressways and major arterial highways, with large sites to accommodate parking and drop-off facilities. It is common for transit to directly serve major institutional and recreational complexes—such as stadiums, convention centers and tourist attractions—as a public service even though their patronage may not justify stations.

FACILITIES ENGINEERING AND CONSTRUCTION METHODS

A wide range of engineering and construction techniques are employed to respond to the varied site, geological, and profile conditions of transit systems and the unique opportunities of each situation. The following techniques are frequently used on underground construction.

Cut-and-Cover

The most common form of underground transit construction is the open-cut method commonly called *cut-and-cover*. This technique involves excavation from the surface, construction within the open excavation, and backfilling. In urban sites this method is a complex operation involving traffic diversion, utility support and relocation, excavation support, underground construction, and backfilling. Figure 1 indicates the complexity of cut-and-cover construction at Washington's Union Station. The construction of this facility required underpinning Union Station, traffic diversion, utility relocation and support, and partial decking.

A number of variations of cut-and-cover construction involve alternative excavation support systems and decking. The most economical cut-and-cover technique is undecked construction in an open cut with sloped sides. This system is normally used only in open areas without traffic or utilities. Another economical system normally used un-

der streets is a "flexible system" of steel soldier piles and wood lagging. Bracing is provided by the deck beams and lagging, or tie-backs.

Semi-rigid excavation support systems include the many variations of slurry wall and secant pile construction. A common feature of all these systems is the placing of concrete in slurry supported trenches or holes. These systems are normally uneconomical unless the support can solve other construction problems such as underpinning and control of high ground water levels, or if the excavation support can also be designed as the permanent station structure.

Waterproofing of walls is a major consideration in all cut-and-cover designs unless the excavation is fully laid back to make the walls accessible. Because the exterior of station walls is inaccessible after construction, primary waterproofing depends on the integrity of the concrete and the treatment of construction joints. Additional protection can be provided by bentonite or membrane systems applied to the excavation support prior to construction. Waterproofing is extremely critical when the box structure is exposed as the station finish as in the Washington Metro. A common solution to water infiltration involves the construction of a cavity wall within the station to conceal leakage, to channel leakage and to create an easily maintained durable finish.

The cost of cut-and-cover station construction is directly related to the depth of the excavation, the quantity of the excavation, and the overburden supported. For this reason, cut-and-cover stations tend to be boxy in cross section and relatively shallow. Line structures are most economical as single boxes enclosing two or more sets of tracks. Therefore stations tend to have side platforms to avoid splitting of the line. To reduce loads, depth of overburden should be kept to the minimum, regardless of the

Figure 1. Cut and cover station construction with underpinning and traffic decking at Union Station in Washington, D.C. Courtesy of WMATA.

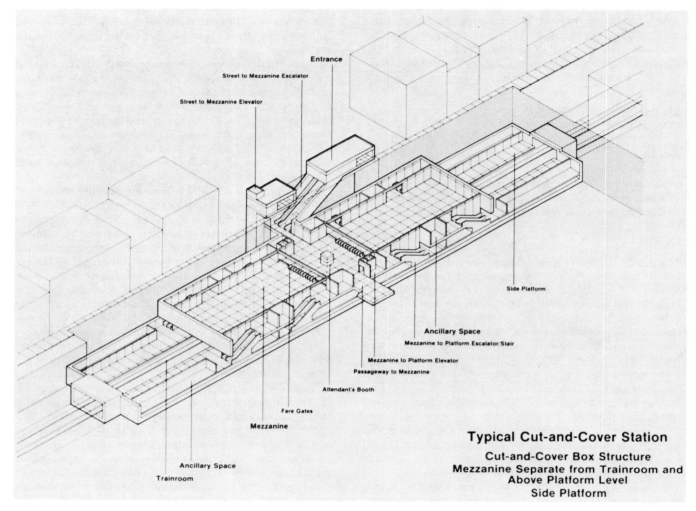

Figure 2. Diagram of a typical cut-and-cover station. Courtesy U.S. Department of Transportation.

depth of track profile. Although an eight foot depth of backfilled cover is typical in the presence of utilities, roof depths less than two feet below grade have been constructed when utilities are absent. Where geological and profile considerations create stations deeper than minimum requirements, it is economical to place the concourse and ancillary rooms within the station box on one or more mezzanines, as in Figure 2. Such mezzanines can seldom be completely filled, and unused space can simply be opened to the trainroom to improve passenger visibility and orientation, or it can be constructed for other uses such as joint commercial development.

Cut-and-cover stations are constructed both with clear span structures and with intermediate columns. Although box structures with columns appear more economical from an engineering standpoint, a clear span structure offers more freedom of movement and flexibility, equalizing value from both a construction and an operation standpoint.

Tunneled Line and Stations

Tunneled transit facilities are mined through underground headings rather than open excavations. Tunneled construction requires a series of regularly spaced, open-cut work shafts to provide ventilation, and space for the placement and removal of material and equipment. Tunnels may be constructed in either rock or soil using conventional mining techniques, or modern tunnel boring machines.

A mining technique which shows much promise is the so-called New Austrian Tunneling Method (NATM). The NATM uses a horseshoe shaped tunnel design, as indicated in Figure 3, to capitalize upon the natural load carrying abilities of the earth or rock. During excavation sensors are placed on the walls and ceiling to monitor the deformation of the rock as it adjusts to the loading. As deformation reaches predicted levels, tunnels are stabilized with shotcrete and wire mesh. If movement is

Figure 3. Installation of steel ribs and rock bolts using the new Austrian Tunneling method (NATM). WMATA, photograph by Phil Portlock.

greater than predicted, rockbolts and steel reinforcing ribs are installed, followed by additional shotcrete. A drainage felt and waterproofing membrane is installed over the shotcrete, and a finish liner is constructed of either shotcrete or unreinforced, cast-in-place concrete.

Tunnel construction is most economically used when sound rock is available relatively close to the surface. Tunneling is also used under other geological conditions when the surface and traffic disruption of cut-and-cover construction is unacceptable, or when adequate public right of way for alternative construction is unavailable.

The majority of tunneled stations use a multiple chamber design in which the various functional elements of the station—such as trainrooms, passageways and escalatorways—are housed in individual, small-diameter tunnels. (See Figure 4.) All multiple chamber tunnels normally follow the same sequence of construction. First, line tunnels spaced wide apart are driven through the alignment. Then trainrooms are enlarged from each tunnel. Cross

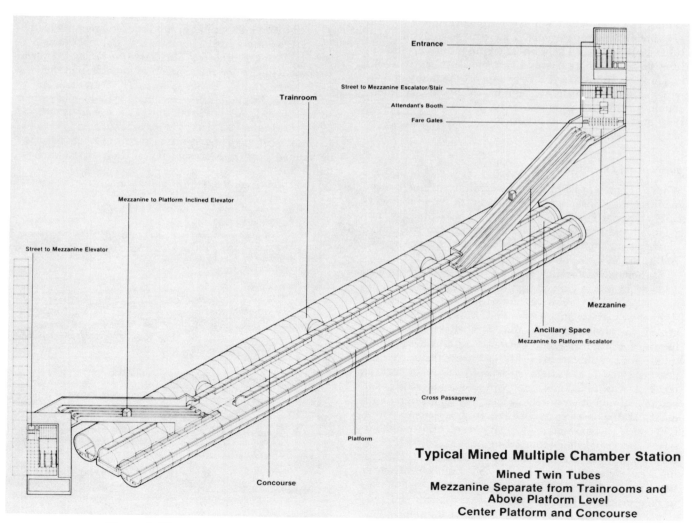

Typical Mined Multiple Chamber Station

Mined Twin Tubes
Mezzanine Separate from Trainrooms and
Above Platform Level
Center Platform and Concourse

Figure 4. Diagram of a typical mined multiple chamber station. Courtesy of U.S. Department of Transportation.

passages are constructed. Finally, escalatorways are constructed to the surface using a mixture of mining and open-cut techniques.

Single chamber mined stations require the enlargement of the initial two line tunnels into one large trainroom. This process is difficult and expensive but it yields benefits such as large, uncluttered, center-platform trainrooms which improve the operation, security, ventilation, and constructability of interior station components. Single chamber stations in earth normally require ground improvement techniques in advance of excavation to permit mining of the trainroom.

Station and tunnels are lined by a variety of systems including cast-in-place concrete, steel or cast iron, and, most recently, systems of rock bolting, shotcrete, steel mesh, and steel ribs, which may form both the temporary and permanent tunnel lining. Because they are mined, tunneled stations assume an arched form in cross section.

The depth of tunneled stations invites water infiltration due to hydrostatic pressure. Station finishes must be carefully designed to intercept leakage and channel it to sumps. The most common finish system provides a secondary "finish" liner in stations to serve as an umbrella over the trainroom. Secondary liners create a durable and attractive finish, conceal and divert moisture penetration, and provide an infrastructure to support the many components of station finish and equipment. Secondary liners should occupy minimum space (due to the cost of excavation) and allow accessibility to the primary liner for repairing major leaks.

Surface and Open Cut

Where permanent right of way is available, rapid transit facilities may be constructed most quickly and economically at grade. Track is laid using ties and ballast, within a fenced right of way. Surface facilities are frequently constructed on, or adjacent to, existing railroad easement and in the medians of major highways.

Stations at surface may have a concourse over, under, or adjacent to the transit right of way. Center platforms may be provided at relatively low cost if adequate width of right of way exists at stations. Platforms require weather protection consisting of canopies, or shelters. Figure 5 illustrates a large, at-grade station in a highway median.

At-grade rapid transit facilities have a utilitarian appearance due to a variety of exposed elements such as right of way fencing, signal equipment, electrification equipment and other ancillary facilities. In median alignments, traffic barriers may be required. In sensitive locations such as parks or low density residential neighborhoods the visual and acoustic impact can be reduced by choosing an open-cut alignment. With open cut, the profile is excavated to a depth slightly less than cut-and-cover construction. The cut material is either removed or used to create berms. The excavation is laid back, and relatively steep slopes are stabilized with landscaping. Open-cut stations are similar to those at grade, with concourses constructed as bridges over the excavated area.

Figure 5. Vienna Station, Washington, D.C. A center platform station in a highway median with acoustical barriers. WMATA photograph by Paul Myatt.

Elevated Alignment

Elevated lines are frequently used where grade separation is required, but where either geological conditions or excessive cost make underground construction infeasible. The best example is the Dade County Rapid Transit System in Miami, Florida, as illustrated in Figure 6. Aerial alignment has major environmental impacts, and in many respects they represent aesthetic rather than engineering or construction challenges. Designs must overcome major obstacles—primarily visual appearance and acoustical control. Aerial structures offer significant savings in construction cost over underground facilities, and these can be applied toward the resolution of their environmental handicaps.

To achieve public acceptance, it is essential that aerial

Figure 6. Government Center Station, Miami, Florida. A center platform aerial station integrated with high density urban development. Courtesy Metro Dade County, Florida.

alignments and profiles relate consistently to the surrounding street and development patterns. Meandering alignments and "roller coaster" profiles are visually disruptive in urban environments and should be avoided. Structures should be simple and consistent with relatively light colors which blend with the sky and reflect light under structures. Systems equipment (such as signals and power) must be carefully coordinated with structure.

The engineering of an elevated rapid transit line differs in many respects from underground construction. Lines are carried on girders supported by columns or bents with relatively long spans. Line structures are frequently separated structurally from stations to minimize vibration and simplify scheduling of construction contracts. Where each line is carried on an independent set of columns, the line can be split for center platform stations relatively easily. Elevated crossover structures can be relatively complex in appearance with a typical column placement. It is often advantageous to locate aerial crossovers adjacent to stations to minimize their impact. Station concourses are constructed under the alignment.

Right of way for elevated transit is most frequently found in the median of existing highways in areas of commercial zoning.

System Image

Modern rail transit systems must compete with the automobile for passengers who are accustomed to a high level of comfort and convenience. The most architecturally successful systems are those which uniquely express the image and culture of their population while successfully and efficiently fulfilling their primary function as a means of urban transportation. The best of these utilize architecture, engineering, construction methods, art and archaeology, and coordinated urban development to create an environment which is totally integrated with their surroundings.

A review of existing transit systems reveals that system image falls into three broad categories, with variations:

1. Utilitarian systems attempt to solve the transit problems with the most economical solutions at any given moment. Mexico City is an attractive utilitarian system.
2. Commercial systems relegate much of their design to the development process. The routes are aligned to capture the value of under-developed property. Stations are constructed to maximize the value of concessions, advertising, and direct connections to private buildings. In extreme examples, developers may design and construct the stations for the system. The Toronto system was conceived and constructed as a stimulus to concessions and joint development.
3. Public systems establish the highest standards of spaciousness, passenger comfort and convenience. Stations are designed as public monuments with quality materials and finishes. Concessions and pri-

vate development are carefully controlled or eliminated in these systems. Moscow, Washington D.C. and Montreal each have unique and high quality public systems.

Elements of Continuity

A second issue in system image is the decision of architectural continuity versus variety. Mass transit systems consist of a large number of diverse elements which must be organized to function and operate as a system.

System standardization attempts to simplify the design, construction and maintenance of a system. Those elements which are appropriately similar or identical in all stations are identified and their design is standardized, with minor variations, throughout the system. The standardization of these elements normally results in lower subsequent design costs, as well as the best possible control of the aesthetic and technical aspects of the system. Items frequently standardized include trainrooms, platform details, station furniture, lighting, fare collection equipment, ancillary rooms, vertical circulation elements, security and communications equipment, and graphics.

Elements of Variable Design

Station design may derive diversity from many sources. Appropriate opportunities for variety normally stem from station construction types, unique program requirements, and specific site characteristics. Each station should exploit the unique geometry of its profile and geology. Rock stations are deep with vaulted ceilings; cut-and-cover stations are shallow boxes. The most refined systems are those that use the appropriate station geometry for their construction type.

Other elements of variable design include the integration of surface and elevated structures with neighborhoods, the accommodation of site specific traffic and pedestrian traffic, and the use of variable finish materials where appropriate.

Station Design

Rapid transit stations are generally composed of four primary space components:

1. Trainroom or platform area.
2. Concourse or fare collection area.
3. Entrance structure.
4. Ancillary spaces (service rooms, substations and equipment rooms).

The relative location of these spaces varies and is determined by profile and site conditions. Their functions are frequently combined for economy.

The trainroom or platform area provides a space for passengers to wait, board or leave the trains. Its minimum length is determined by the train length. The minimum width is determined partially by station patronage and partially by safety considerations connected with the unloading of trains during peak hour emergencies. The trainroom normally has either a center platform or two side platforms, depending on the relationship between platform and tracks and the design of the adjacent line.

From an operational standpoint the center platform is more desirable because it provides a greater area to handle surge crowds, and it provides more direct circulation to and from the boarding areas. Economic considerations related to excavation and right of way often favor side platform configurations so that line and trackwork structures can run straight through stations—thus avoiding expensive flaring around center platforms. A cost-benefit analysis of the two platform arrangements must investigate the costs of station structures, line structures, and vertical circulation equipment to make an accurate assessment.

Special platform conditions include the following:

1. Twin tunnel stations have connected side platforms in each tunnel which effectively function as a center platform.
2. Stacked side platforms are used infrequently in alignments with limited horizontal width.
3. Terminal stations are almost always center platform to permit trains to layover and depart from either track without redirecting passengers.
4. Stations at branches in a line may often be designed with both side and center platforms, or multiple center platforms, to provide flexibility of operation with multiple trains.

Concourses provide space for fare collection equipment and associated passenger queuing space. The width of a concourse is determined primarily by station patronage, as this affects both the number of turnstiles and the width of the array. The fare collection array divides the concourse into the "free area," requiring no payment of fare, and the "paid area," which permits ticketed passage to the trainroom.

The length is determined by the programmed level of passenger comfort, the expected length of queues in both peak hour and emergency situations, and the space required for other equipment such as change and transfer machines and their associated queuing.

Many systems, particularly in Europe, use self service "honor fare systems" which are randomly checked by inspectors. Although honor fare systems require minimal concourse space for ticket vending, space for turnstile equipment is frequently constructed in case there is a need to install it in the future.

Concourses may be located at a mezzanine level between the street and platform level. However, they may also be located at grade or at platform levels for economy under certain site and profile conditions.

Entrance structures provide weather protection for street level stairs and escalators in underground systems. They are virtually a requirement in areas with severe weather conditions, but they may be eliminated in more temperate climates.

Ancillary or service rooms are the non-public spaces in transit stations which house equipment used for operational and maintenance functions. The following is a list of typical ancillary rooms:

- *DC Traction Substation (Vehicle Power)*
- *AC Electrical Switchgear and Distribution (Station and Site Power)*
- *Battery Room*
- *Mechanical Equipment Rooms (Fans and Shafts)*
- *Train Control and Communications Rooms*
- *Cleaner's/Trash Rooms*
- *Revenue Storage*
- *Telephone Rooms*
- *Toilets*
- *Fire Equipment Closets*
- *Elevator Machine Rooms*
- *Miscellaneous Equipment Storage Rooms*
- *Station Attendant Offices*
- *Emergency Stairways*

Vertical Circulation

Within each rapid transit station vertical passenger circulation is required to connect the station components on different levels. This circulation is provided by a system of stairs, escalators and elevators carefully tuned to patronage. The placement of these vertical circulation elements should promote simple, direct circulation patterns which are similar and easily recognizable throughout each transit system. The quantity of vertical circulation elements is determined by peak station patronage, the selected peak period level of service for design, and the balancing of various station components to maintain a consistent overall capacity in the station circulation system.

For passenger comfort, escalators are commonly provided for upward circulation. Stairs or escalators may be provided for downward circulation. As the vertical rise increases to 20 feet stairs become impractical as a means of normal circulation, although they are frequently provided for emergency egress. Stairs may be sized for future replacement by escalators if patronage increases are expected.

Transit escalators are best specified with 40 in treads to permit two way circulation when equipment is out of service. Speeds range from 90 to 120 fpm (feet per minute) in the United States, and up to 145 fpm on long escalators in other countries. In actual use, escalator capacities seldom exceed 120 passengers a minute. Escalators may be constructed to almost any height. There are many examples of transit escalators rising more than a 100 feet. High capacity elevators may often provide adequate capacity more economically than escalators in stations with 100 to 200 foot rises.

All transit stations are subject to occasional crush loadings under unusual conditions. It is essential in the operation of escalators to provide an open surge space at the ends of the newels, 20 to 30 feet in length to permit passengers to safely clear the moving portions of the equipment under crowded conditions. Escalators should always be monitored and shut down if necessary to prevent overcrowding.

Elevators are desirable in transit stations to accommodate elderly and handicapped passengers and to simplify normal station maintenance. For passenger security and flexibility, elevators should be adjacent to other vertical circulation elements. The use of glazed cars and hoistways enhances elevator security and makes them more attractive to patrons.

Inclined elevators (inclinators) are sometimes used at specific sites where deep stations under streets are served by long escalatorways. Inclinators eliminate the long narrow corridors which would be required to reach elevators and provide a common level of service to normal and handicapped passengers alike. Inclinators are relatively slow and expensive relative to elevators.

Station Furnishings and Equipment

Station environments must recognize human needs as well as system functional requirements. Many of these needs are met by station amenities which provide comfort, security or convenience to the user.

The lighting of transit stations is critical for safety, psychological comfort and reinforcing directional information. Platform edges, stair and escalator landings, and other walking surfaces require high level direct illumination to reduce hazards. As patrons enter underground stations, lower lighting levels are expected. Low level indirect lighting of walls and ceilings creates a more tranquil environment in crowded stations and enlarges the perceived size of underground stations. Illumination of key decision points and the maximum introduction of natural light reinforce directional graphics and enhance passenger orientation.

Transit stations require minimal furnishings. Benches are installed for waiting between trains. Trash and ash receptacles, properly serviced, will minimize maintenance. Most systems provide some sort of information and security stations—either in the form of a station attendant in an accessible booth or by locating passenger telephones and closed circuit TV cameras at regularly spaced intervals. Public address speakers allow operators to inform passengers of delays or changes in schedules. Public telephones can allow passengers to arrange rides or conduct business while waiting for trains. Some older systems place space for concessions in both free and paid areas to allow passengers a limited shopping opportunity. However, concessions in stations, even if carefully restricted, usually create increased maintenance requirements.

Graphics are provided to orient passengers within the system, assist and direct their circulation, identify various elements, call attention to hazards, and provide information on the station, transit systems, and city. To be effective, graphics should be uniform in placement, presentation and content. Information displayed in each sign should be simple and concise, limited to that required at each decision point. It must be integrated with the station design in size, color and message content with careful attention to adequate lighting. Types of graphics include directional signs which assist the orderly flow of patrons on the station; information graphics which orient patrons to the system operations and provide detailed information

on fares and the use of equipment; and identification signs which identify transit facilities and equipment.

Acoustic treatment is provided in stations to control and reduce noise from trains and equipment, reduce crowd noise, and provide good intelligibility for public address announcements. Good design restricts maximum trainroom noise to the range of 55 dBa without trains, and 80 to 85 dBa with moving trains. Maximum reverberation time should be limited to 1.2 to 1.5 seconds at 500 Hz. Since trains are the major noise source, maximum reduction is achieved by installing acoustic material adjacent to trackbeds. To control crowd noise and reverberation, it is desirable to treat approximately 30 percent of the walls and ceilings of public spaces with sound absorptive material possessing a minimum NRC of 0.75.

Station Area Development

It has long been recognized that a symbiotic relationship exists between transit stations and development. The railroad builders of the nineteenth century and the streetcar operators of the early twentieth century used transit as a means of stimulating development on their real estate holdings. The development near stations then increased patronage and contributed to the success of the transportation system.

Over the past two decades, the construction of new transit stations has generated explosive growth—particularly at suburban locations. The classic example is the Yonge Street line north of downtown Toronto where large clusters of office buildings surround every station. Systems in San Francisco, Washington, Atlanta and Baltimore are all experiencing similar development patterns. Figure 7 indicates station area development at the WMATA suburban Silver Spring station.

As public funding for transit systems is reduced, transit operators are seeking alternative sources of revenue from *value capture* mechanisms. The phrase value capture refers to the various methods by which a transit authority can share the economic benefits of publicly funded improvements which accrue to adjacent property owners.

The most common method of value capture is joint development in which a piece of adjacent property is devel-

Figure 7. Station area development in Silver Spring, Md. WMATA photograph by Larry Levine.

oped to the benefit of both the transit authority and a private party. Joint development usually occurs on property owned by the transit authority, such as a suburban parking lot, or a parcel which was used as a staging area.

Another method of value capture is a simple connection fee, in which a developer is permitted to construct a direct connection to the free area of the station for a fee.

Station cost sharing is a value capture mechanism being explored by many systems in the planning stages. Developers of adjacent parcels may either construct a station shell as part of a project, or contribute a portion of the cost of a new station to the transit authority. Cost sharing has been used effectively in New York City to finance the renovation of existing stations.

One of the most innovative forms of value capture is the establishment of special transit tax assessment districts around stations. Transit tax districts allow the funding of transit stations through taxation of property owners in the station area. Assessments can vary among districts and can take into consideration increases in property values, allowable density, station patronage, and distance from the station. The Southern California Rapid Transit District in Los Angeles, presently under design and construction, is the first major transit system in the United States to successfully use assessment districts in the financing of their stations.

CASE STUDIES

The following six case studies are examples of the best transit systems constructed in the past 50 years. All of these systems express the cultural, architectural and artistic character of the city in which they are constructed. These specific examples have been selected because they best represent an important philosophical direction in transit design.

Montreal Metro

The 16-mile Metro was opened in 1966 with 26 stations in conjunction with Expo '67. It now contains 53 miles and 55 stations on three lines with another seven miles of line and 13 stations under construction. The entire system is underground with 70 percent of the stations mined from rock due to favorable geological conditions. The Montreal Metro is well known for its rolling profile with deep dips between relatively shallow stations to enhance the acceleration and braking of the rubber tired trains. Daily ridership exceeds one million passengers.

The Montreal Metro is one of the best modern examples of the possibilities of a variable station design philosophy. Station designers are provided with performance criteria, standard equipment, and three standard trainroom designs for open-cut, earth tunnel, and rock tunnel. Beyond these standards, each station is designed to emphasize a unique image and concept and to present an individual appearance, particularly at the station entrance.

A ride on the Montreal Metro is a pleasant sensory experience of individual bright and colorful stations linked by an extremely smooth and quiet ride. The stations are frequently opened up into spaces of dramatic

Figure 8. Prefontaine Station, Montreal, Canada. A large skylight with perforated beams allows natural light to penetrate to the platform level. Courtesy of Karn Charuhas, Chapman & Twohey.

Figure 9. Radisson Station, Montreal Canada. Mezzanines within trainrooms maximize passenger visibility and orientation. Courtesy Communaute Urbaine de Montréal, Bureau de Transport Metropolitaine.

height to allow maximum penetration of natural light into the subway, as shown in Figure 8. Most are designed with mezzanines to permit maximum visibility and passenger orientation as in the Radisson Station, shown in Figure 9.

Mexico City

The Mexico City Metro System holds a construction speed record for modern transit systems. Its initial 26 miles and 46 stations which opened in 1970 were constructed in 40 months with the first segment operational just 2½ years after construction began. The network has been expanded to seven lines with a total of 66 miles and 186 stations. Five miles are under construction. The largely underground system was constructed in poor soils with "fast-track" scheduling, using both "laid back" and "slurry wall" cut-and-cover construction. Trainrooms are simple boxes kept close to the surface to minimize geological and ground water problems. Since the shallow depth prohibited mezzanine levels, concourses are located either at grade or at the trainroom level.

More than two million passengers ride the Metro each day, making Mexico City one of the world's most heavily utilized systems per mile. Ridership is growing at a rate of 11 percent a year with a one day record of 4.3 million riders. Passengers must queue to enter the more heavily used stations. For safety and economy, only stairs are used for vertical circulation. Automatic gates are utilized in stations to prevent overcrowding of trains, and regulate flow to the platforms.

The unique aspect of the system is its total expression of the cultural identity and history of Mexico City. Aztec design motifs are utilized in many of the stations as shown in Figure 10. Floor paving is polished marble. Cavity walls are finished in bright mosaics. More than 100 tons of archeological relics were discovered during excavation, and many are prominently displayed in stations along with Mexican art and large photographic panels of scenes relating to station locations. Music played over the system public address speakers adds to the festive and colorful Latin American atmosphere. Graphics were designed to create a pictograph or symbol for each station which is related either to a local landmark in the station vicinity or to the Aztec or Spanish meaning of the station name, as shown in Figure 11.

Stockholm *T-Bana*

The Stockholm system consists of a three-line, 66-mile network with 99 stations. An additional four miles are under construction. Underground construction includes both cut-and-cover and rock tunnel methods.

Stockholm's recently constructed rock tunnel stations on the *Jarva* and *Taby* are of significance because they express the construction of the station as the architectural finish. The stations are constructed in a competent layer of granite bedrock. Rock bolts and shotcrete provide both a temporary and a permanent station lining. Water infiltration is controlled by creating drainage channels within shotcrete using mineral fiber panels. In some stations the granite is left exposed as the permanent finish. The

Figure 10. Zaragoza Station, Mexico City. Courtesy of Karn Charuhas. Chapman & Twohey, Mexico City. Photomurals set into marble walls.

freeform shotcrete and granite tunnels create a cavelike subterranean environment. Each station is then embellished by artists who may choose either to paint the shotcrete lining or to sculpt and modify the space within the station (see Figure 12).

The Stockholm system is fully accessible to the handicapped. Concourses are commonly located at the surface and connected to trainrooms by long escalatorways. In many situations inclined elevators are installed adjacent to escalators and stairs.

Vienna *U-Bahn*

The Vienna underground system is master planned as a group of seven branching lines which will provide both radial and circumferential service when completed. Three lines, 20 miles, and 39 stations have been constructed. The underground is supplemented by both a streetcar system and a radial metropolitan railway system. The metropolitan railway design at the turn of the century by Otto Wagner is also a significant example of transit design.

The Vienna *U-Bahn* stations are models of the application of an industrial design philosophy to system interiors. The structural form of stations is determined by construction method and includes tunnel and cut-and-cover box construction. Within the varying trainroom structures the finishes have been developed with a single flexible, but visually consistent and economical, method of construction as shown in Figures 13 and 14.

Station interiors are designed as canopies generally protruding no further than the platform edge. The mate-

Figure 11. Mexico City. Line map with station name symbols. STC Subway, Mexico City. Courtesy of Cooper Hewitt Museum/The Smithsonian Institution/Art Resource.

Figure 12. T-Centrallen Station, Stockholm, Sweden. A shotcrete lining decorated by artists serves as the permanent station finish. Courtesy of Cooper Hewitt Museum/The Smithsonian Institution/Art Resource.

Figure 13. Stephansplatz Station, Vienna, Austria. A typical twin tunnel station. Courtesy of Karn Charuhas, Chapman & Twohey.

rials used are colored fiberglass panels with aluminum battens on a modular grid. All equipment and lighting is integrated into the station finish system. The floors are asphalt with precast edge strips.

Each station uses the same system of interior finishes. A unique graphic characteristic of the Vienna stations is that all station finishes on a given line reflect that line's identification colors. Where two or more lines share the same platform, this criterion produces some vivid station environments.

Washington Metro

The Washington Metro was master planned from its inception as a 101-mile, 86-station system serving the District of Columbia and six jurisdictions in Maryland and Virginia. Construction began in 1969 and the system became operational in 1976. The construction period for the complete system is projected to be approximately 30 years. Four lines with 61 miles and 60 stations have been completed.

The Washington Metro is recognized for the manner in

Figure 14. Reumannplatz Station, Vienna, Austria. A typical center platform station. Industrial design of station interiors integrates all components of furnishings and equipment. Courtesy of Austrian Press and Information Service.

Figure 15. Metro Center Station, Washington, D.C. The center transfer station in the Metro system clearly expresses its function as the intersection of two transit lines. WMATA photograph by Paul Myatt.

which engineering and architecture were integrated to produce a system of unparalleled continuity and elegance. The Metro is distinctive and dignified and, like all great transit systems, totally appropriate for its environment in the District of Columbia.

The varied topography produced a system constructed under almost every possible profile condition. Station construction types include multiple and single chamber rock, arched cut-and-cover, box cut-and-cover, open-cut, surface, elevated-on-embankment, and aerial.

The station designs are conceived as elements of a total system. Stations of similar construction types are almost identical, with monumental concrete barrel vaults for underground stations and gull wing or flat canopy structures at surface or elevated stations. Both the structural and the finish material is exposed concrete heavily textured with ribs and coffers as seen in the Metro Center Station, Figure 15.

The palate of materials was carefully limited by the designers to concrete, granite, bronze, stainless steel, tan brick, and *terra-cotta* paving.

The underground stations feature enormous single chamber trainrooms 30 feet high and 60 feet wide, with floating mezzanines. Platforms are 600 feet long. All primary station functions are contained within the trainroom. Passenger circulation areas are held several feet from the concrete walls to reduce vandalism and maintenance. The vaults are indirectly illuminated by concealed fluorescent lighting. Entrances are kept consistently low and discreet, with granite parapet walls enclosing escalators and stairs. A tall bronze pylon with the letter "M" announces each entrance.

Station facilities are air-conditioned and fully accessible to the handicapped by special glass enclosed elevators. A popular feature of the Metro is the flashing light in the platform edge.

Many of the suburban Metro stations are intermodal transportation centers with facilities for buses, van pools, parking and commuter rail.

Moscow Metro

The Moscow Metro system was opened in 1935 and was originally masterplanned for 87 miles and 82 stations. Moscow has steadily built the Metro system into one of the world's largest, with nine lines of 137 miles and 143 stations. An additional 11 miles are under construction. Stations are typically in deep tunnel—some more than 200 feet below grade. There is reportedly one mile of escalator shaft for each four miles of the system. The system carries more than 2.5 million passengers per day.

Moscow's 28 stations on the first two lines are the world's finest example of transit designed as a public monument. The stations have been called "Underground Palaces," and no other system in the world can compare to them in terms of grandeur, finish or passenger comfort.

Each station is designed differently, in a new classical style using the finest materials. Walls and paving are marble and granite in conjunction with mosaic and porcelain tiles. Escalator balustrades are polished oak and walnut. Enormous chandeliers and frescos can be seen on the ceilings.

Center platforms are used almost exclusively for passenger comfort and vary in width from 32 to 69 feet. Trainrooms feature high arched ceilings with a central waiting hall to separate passenger circulation and waiting from boarding activities. See the Komsomolskaya-Koltsevaya station in Figure 16, and the Airport station in Figure 17. Station entrances and exits are separated to minimize cross-circulation of passengers. The stations are air-conditioned, and the ventilation equipment changes the air eight to nine times an hour. Uniformed attendants are positioned throughout each station to provide information and directions to passengers.

Figure 16. Komsomolskaya-Koltsevaya Station, Moscow, USSR. Moscow's "underground palaces" offer the highest level of passenger comfort. Courtesy of WMATA.

Figure 17. Airport Station, Moscow, USSR. Courtesy of WMATA.

BIBLIOGRAPHY

General References

E. Abakumov, *The Moscow Subway,* Foreign Languages Publishing House, Moscow, 1939, pp. 5–24.

B. Bobrick, *Labyrinths of Iron, A History of the World's Subways,* Newsweek Books, New York, 1947, p. 325.

"Cooper Hewitt Museum" *Subways,* December 1977.

E. T. Myers, *Modern Railroads,* (May 1971).

L. Heder, ed., *Aesthetics in Transportation,* U.S. Dept. of Transportation, Cambridge, Mass., 1980.

W. Hinkel, ed. *U-Bahn-Bau in Wien,* Planen Bauen Wohnen und Umweltschutz, Wien, 1978.

L. H. Hock, M. J. Demetsky and M. R. Virkler, *Alternative Transit Station Designs,* National Technical Information Service, Springfield, Va., 1976.

Fortune, (December 1969).

Transit Journal **79**(6), 180 (June 1935).

Transit (October 1955).

R. Birger and co-workers, *The Stockholm Underground 1975,* Stockholms Ians Iandsting, 1976, pp. 62–102.

Mass Transit **11,** 16 (March 1984).

Ibid., **11,** 28.

Ibid., **11,** 43.

Mass Transit (November 1985).

S. F. Taylor, *Urban Transportation—Another Alternative: A World-Wide Survey of Light Rail Technology,* The Heritage Foundation, Inc., Washington, D.C., 1974.

Transit Journal **474,** 444 (Nov. 1938).

Transportation Research Board, *Light-Rail Transit: Planning and Technology, Special Report 182,* National Academy of Sciences, Washington, D.C., 1978.

Transportation Research Board, *Light-Rail Transit, Special Report 161,* National Academy of Sciences, Washington, D.C., 1975.

U.S. Department of Transportation, *Light Rail Transit, Technology Sharing: State-of-the Art Overview,* Transportation Systems Center, Cambridge, Mass., 1977.

U.S. Department of Transportation, *Study of Subway Station Design and Construction,* Urban Mass Transportation Administration, Washington, D.C., 1977.

W. Von Eckhardt, "A Rare Experience in Public Happiness," *The Washington Post,* Nov. 1969.

WABCO Mass Transit Center, *Rapid Transit Fact Sheet,* Westinghouse Air Brake Company, Pittsburgh, Penn., 1969.

ROBERT KARN
JOHN CHAPMAN
Karn Charuhas Chapman &
    Twohey
Washington, D.C.

TREES.   See SHRUBS AND TREES

TVA.   See TENNESSEE VALLEY AUTHORITY (TVA) ARCHITECTURE

U

UNGERS, OSWALD M.

Oswald Mathias Ungers was born in 1926 in Kaisersesch in der Eifel in what today is the FRG. He was the second of three children of a state employee. He went to school in the city of Mayen in 1932, and made his Abitur there in 1947. In 1945, he served in the German army and was a prisoner of war until 1946. From 1947 to 1950, Ungers studied architecture at the Technische Hochschule Karlsruhe, today Technische Universität Karlsruhe, which was then led by Egon Eiermann. He married in 1956 and has three children, one of whom is an architect.

In 1950, Ungers settled in Cologne, and opened his private practice there, which he still maintains. In 1963, he became a professor in the department of architecture at the Technische Universität Berlin, where he taught until 1968. In 1964, he opened an additional office in West Berlin. He was a visiting critic at Cornell University in 1965 and 1967. Ungers served as the chairman of the Department of Architecture from 1969 to 1975. He moved to Ithaca, N.Y. for the length of his term, and opened an office there in 1970. In 1975 he returned to his main residence in Cologne. Ungers is a professor at Cornell University; in addition, he was a visiting professor at Harvard University in 1973 and 1978, a visiting professor at the University of California at Los Angeles in 1974 and 1975, a Gastprofessor at the Hochschule für Angewandte Kunst in Vienna, and a professor at the Kunstakademie in Düsseldorf. He opened additional offices in Frankfurt am Main in 1976 and in Karlsruhe in 1983, both in the FRG.

Ungers has been a member of the Academia di San Luca in Rome since 1982. He also belongs to the Akademie der Wissenschaften in West Berlin, the American Institute of Architects, and the Bund Deutscher Architekten. His main awards include the Grosser Preis Bund Deutscher Architekten, 1987.

Ungers is one of the most important, influential, and controversial protagonists of the architectural discussion of the last decades, in both the international and German architectural scenes. His importance is based on the consistency, originality, and coherence of his writings and buildings. His striking role and his polarizing effect on the architectural panorama is based on the sharpness of his position, on the disruptive character of his work, and on the idealistic philosophical position Ungers developed in opposition to the basically materialistic modern movement.

Ungers's point of departure was given by his studies in the Karlsruhe school of architecture under Egon Eiermann. His early works reveal formal preferences developed from Eiermann, namely a tendency toward clear and simple geometric forms in floor plans and elevations, and the search for a formal language based on these. Examples of these are the Oderweg House in Cologne-Dünn-

wald and the apartment house Hültzstrasse in Cologne-Braunsfeld, both in 1951.

While Eiermann's architecture searched for both a constructively innovative and differentiated language, Ungers remained interested in a basically geometrical language, with preferentially massive, plastic bodies. His works of the mid-1950s show him developing from the simple bidimensional geometry of the early buildings to more three-dimensional compositions of cubes, prisms, and cylinders. The addition and penetration of these forms result in a highly dynamic and asymmetrical whole, which is supposed to correspond in its form to the building's functions, construction, and formal integration in the vicinity. Examples of this are the apartment house Mauenheimer Strasse in Cologne-Nippes (1957–1959) and the Werthmannstrasse Houses in Cologne-Lindenthal (1957–1958). Both are more or less normal buildings, with expressive appearances, but conventional in all aspects.

Ungers reached a high point in his work with his own house in Cologne-Müngersdorf (1958–1959). This building represents not only a synthesis of the developments of the decade, but a new step toward a growing complexity in his work and thinking. In this sense, it anticipates the theoretical statements made by Ungers in the manifesto written in 1960 with Reinhard Gieselmann "Zu einer neuen Architektur" ("toward a new architecture").

In this manifesto, which was published in 1963, the authors emphasize the cultural dimension of architecture. They speak about the essence of architecture as an art, about the necessity of assimilating the tradition to find the original, and about architectural form as an expression of the genius. They express their opposition to a view of architecture as technique, to the primacy of technique as a factor of architecture, and to any kind of "materialistic dictatorship of the methodics" and the resulting "formal uniformity and monotony." Ungers and Gieselmann confess their faith in a better architecture inspired on the building task and on the spirit of the site. They saw in their concepts a chance to cancel the separation of subject and object in the production of architecture and a way to the desired renewal of European architecture.

This manifesto was a critique on the commercial architecture in the 1950s, but not on the architecture of the modern movement as a whole. Ungers had not yet broken with the modern movement. In fact, the Ungers house is a good example of a modern building of its time, with its irregular, asymmetric, and dynamic composition of the masses and its exposed brickwork and concrete facade surfaces. Its formal language is clearly based on the inner organization of the building and on its construction. Ungers's way of integrating the house into its neighborhood was by repeating preexisting elements of the surroundings in his own design, as in the continuation of the pantile-covered roof of the neighbor's house onto his own,

Figure 1. House Ungers, Cologne-Müngersdorf, FRG, 1958–1959. Courtesy of Manuel Cuadra.

which elsewhere has a flat roof. Such a quotation was new, and such a solution should have become important in Ungers's design methods. In this case, however, it played a minor role (Fig. 1).

The 1960s signified a changing point for Ungers's career. He had been, up to then, a successful young architect with a great future, but with only small realizations. In the early 1960s, he became involved in the project for the Märkisches Viertel, a very large suburban housing estate in West Berlin. The Märkisches Viertel was supposed to become a model housing project in accordance with the principles of modern architecture. It became, with its anonymous high-rise housing silos, a symbol for the worst postwar developments in architecture and the most abhorrent of what was possible in the name of the modern movement. Ungers's reputation was severely hurt by the criticism of his participation in this project (Fig. 2).

From the mid-1960s to the late 1970s, Ungers built almost nothing, and increasingly dedicated his time to teaching in Ithaca, New York, and to theorizing. In these years, Ungers earned international success, particularly in the United States, and mainly because of his competition projects, such as that for Roosevelt Island, New York City (1975), which was not built but was widely published. Ungers's search for new ways out of his own dilemma corresponded to the search of other dissidents of the mod-

Figure 2. Märkisches Viertel housing estate, West Berlin, 1962–1967. Courtesy of Manuel Cuadra.

ern movement in the 1960s, such as the Italian rationalists. Thus, he suddenly received internationally the recognition he had lost in the FRG.

Ungers's contributions were initially on a theoretical level. They are summarized in his book *Die Thematisierung der Architektur, Architecture as Theme,* published in 1982 and 1983. This book is a compendium of Ungers's critiques of the functionalism of contemporary architecture and a proposal for a way out of the contradictions that the modern movement had accumulated in the last decades of generalized and undiscriminated expansion all over the world. The title, *Die Thematisierung der Architektur,* expresses both the idea of giving architecture a theme and of making architecture the theme of itself. In this book, Ungers insisted on seeing architecture primarily as an art, not just as an applied art, in not allowing architectural form to be a product of materialistic factors as are function and construction. In his antifunctionalistic view, architecture should have a theme, and this theme should be as independent as possible of the conditions of the material world. The search for a theme in accordance with the building task and the spirit of the site should be central in the design process.

In his book, Ungers presented five "themes" or motives for formal speculation. In accordance with his preferences, he did this in a poetic and plastic way, free from too much logic, with much room for speculation and for ambiguities, evoking images with the help of objects of art of preferentially Latin–Mediterranean origin or character, many by René Magritte, the Belgian surrealistic painter. His "themes" were as follows:

1. The theme of transformation, based on the idea of relating different forms by viewing them as aspects of originally the same element in different stages of development. For example, the gradual development of the column, a human invention, from the tree, an element of nature.

2. The theme of assemblage, based on the idea of relating contradictory elements to each other by confronting them and emphasizing their opposition.

3. The theme of incorporation, based on the idea of one element inside another, the one being respectively the other's interior or exterior. Both are at the same time individual elements and parts of a larger whole. As an example of this, Ungers cites Magritte's painting "L'importance des mervielles" (1927) showing a woman inside a woman and both of these women inside another woman; all three women seem to be one and the same.

4. The theme of assimilation, based on the idea that a new element becomes part of an old one, altering it, and being altered by it. A new whole appears, while the old whole survives. An example is Magritte's painting, "Le blanc-seing (carte blanche)," (1965) of a horse and rider crossing the forest, showing the interpenetration of the trees, the man, and the animal. They form a new whole, composed of the three elements, but this whole is more than the sum of the parts.

Figure 4. Alfred Wegener polar research institute, Bremerhaven, FRG, 1980–1984. Courtesy of Manuel Cuadra.

Figure 3. "Messehaus 9" and "Galleria" at the Frankfurt am Main fair, Frankfurt am Main, FRG, 1980–1983. Courtesy of Manuel Cuadra.

5. The theme of imagination, perhaps the most revealing one for Ungers's idealistic philosophy, based on the idea that all experimentation exists only in the imagination. An example is again Magritte and his drawing of an apple with the title "Ceci n'est pas une pomme," "This Is Not an Apple." It shows Ungers's consciousness of surrealism as the limit of idealistic ways of thinking, when the role of the purely mental is overemphasized.

When *Die Thematisierung der Architektur* was published, Ungers had already overcome the low mark of his career and was building more than ever in the FRG, including large public buildings. To the early works of this period belong the apartment house Schillerstrasse in West Berlin (1978–1979) and the Deutsches Architekturmuseum, the architectural museum in Frankfurt am Main (1979–1984). To the more consistent and mature realizations of the 1980s belong the Polarforschungsinstitut, a polar research institute in Bremerhaven; the Messehaus 9, the Galleria, and the Torhaus Gleisdreieck, ie, an exposition hall, its foyer, and a high-rise office building at the fairgrounds in Frankfurt am Main; and the Abwasserpumpwerk Tiergarten, a small pump plant in West Berlin.

The architecture of all of these buildings is based on recreating images related to the building task and desired spirit, by citing historical buildings, other constructions of a similar function, or regionally important buildings. In this sense, the Galleria (Fig. 3) is directly inspired in nineteenth-century passages, specifically in the more monumental Italian examples such as the Galleria Vittorio Emanuele II in Milano.

The architecture of the polar research institute, located in a West German North Sea port awakes, on a large scale, associations with ocean liners. On a small scale, the central part of the facade cites the traditional brickwork construction of the Bremerhaven region (Fig. 4).

The Torhaus, located at one of the main highway gateways of Frankfurt am Main, has, on a large scale, the appearance of a huge floodgate. In the treatment of the facade surfaces it seems to be Skidmore, Owing & Merrill's New York Lever House penetrating a Boullée-like massive prismatic body.

The pump plant in Tiergarten is reminiscent of nineteenth-century power plants, and the facade brings to mind a masonry construction of the same period (Fig. 5). In all of these buildings, Ungers creates strong images, which make evident what he fights for: the reevaluation of the cultural dimension of architecture and his understanding of architecture as a mainly intellectual and artistic discipline, based on the spirit of the building task and the site.

Figure 5. Pump plant Tiergarten, West Berlin, 1979–1987. Courtesy of Manuel Cuadra.

In his approach to construction, Ungers's works are characterized by his intention of evoking historical ways of building. He does not imitate old constructions. He builds using modern detail solutions, for example, the nonbearing brickwork cladding for the pump plant. Nevertheless, his language is not free of contradictions. Thus, the structural system of the Galleria is not an addition of arches, as it was intended to be, and as it seems to be, but a large shell, and the massive appearance of the Messehaus 9 obscures its prefabricated reinforced concrete skeleton construction. The Torhaus possesses the same structural system for the massive base and the transparent central body, and the closed massive facade is as inadequate for the offices behind it as the glass curtain wall is for the small service rooms behind it.

Such observations may not be seen as serious criticism of Ungers's work; they may appear far too banal compared to his achievements. On the other side, there are many absurd situations in Ungers's buildings resulting from a lack of consideration of the objective factors of architecture and from sacrificing functionally adequate solutions for formalisms, not to speak of his renunciation of the innovative potential of modern structural systems and building materials to the development of architectural form, for historicisms. Such situations show the limits of the validity of Ungers's approach to architecture. His concentration on the artistic dimension of architecture signifies a neglect of all of its other aspects. Ungers's buildings are convincing artistic alienations, even partially surrealistic, a mixture of poetics and banalities, apparently free of gravity and of the passage of time. However, it is questionable whether the generalization of a surrealistic attitude is justifiable in a discipline such as architecture with a social dimension.

Even for his adversaries, those "materialistic" architects who work within the modern movement, Ungers's achievements cannot be overlooked. For them, Ungers represents the challenge to attain, without renouncing the material world as their imagination's roots, what he has demonstrated to be still important for architecture: to be artistically intense.

BIBLIOGRAPHY

General References

O. M. Ungers and U. Kultermann, *Die gläserne Kette: Visionäre Architekturen aus dem Kreis um Bruno Taut 1919–1920,* catalog, Akademie der Künste, West Berlin, 1963.

O. M. Ungers and R. Gieselmann, "Zu einer neuen Architektur," in *Der Monat* (174), 96 (Mar. 1963). Also published in U. Conrads, ed., *Programme und Manifeste zur Architektur des 20. Jahrhunderts,* Bauwelt Fundamente 1, Bertelsmann, West Berlin, 1964, pp. 158–159.

O. M. Ungers and L. Ungers, *Kommunen in der Neuen Welt 1740–1971,* Kiepenheuer & Witsch, Cologne, FRG, 1972.

H. Klotz, *Architektur in der Bundesrepublik, Gespräche mit Günter Behnisch,* Ullstein, Frankfurt am Main, FRG, 1977.

O. M. Ungers, "Über das Denken und Entwerfen in Bildern und Vorstellungen," in M. Sundermann, ed., *Rudolf Schwarz,*

Akademie der Architektenkammer Nordrhein-Westfalen, Düseldorf, FRG, 1981, pp. 23–25.

O. M. Ungers, *Architettura come tema—Architecture as Theme,* Quaderni di Lotus, Milano, Italy, 1982. Also published as *Die Thematisierung der Architektur,* DVA, Stuttgart, FRG, 1983.

H. Klotz, "Oswald Mathias Ungers," in H. Klotz, ed., *Revision der Moderne: Postmoderne Architektur 1960–1980,* Prestel, Munich, FRG, 1984, pp. 297–321.

H. Klotz, "Oswald Mathias Ungers," in H. Klotz, *Moderne und Postmoderne: Architektur der Gegenwart 1960–1980,* Vieweg, Brunswick, FRG, 1985, pp. 215–242.

O. M. Ungers, *Bauten und Projekte 1951–1984,* Vieweg, Brunswick, FRG, 1985.

O. M. Ungers, "Die Komplexität der Architektur," in *Der Architekt* (9), 430–435 (Sept. 1987).

MANUEL CUADRA
Technische Hochschule
Darmstadt
Federal Republic of Germany

UNION INTERNATIONALE DES ARCHITECTES (UIA)

The Secretary General of the International Union of Architectes (UIA) has offices at 51 Rue Raynouard–75016 Paris, France. Founded in 1948, the UIA's mission is to represent all architects and to help set up activities on an international level between architectural organizations and architects of different countries. About 900,000 architects are represented by the member organizations. Activities with parallel nongovernmental organizations are designed to provide contacts with other disciplines, and the UIA also maintains contacts with intergovernmental institutions. The UIA is the only official architectural organization recognized by the Economic and Social Council of the United Nations, Geneva; the United Nations Industrial Development Organization, Vienna; the International Labor Organization, Geneva; the United Nations Educational, Scientific, and Cultural Organization, Paris; the World Health Organization, Geneva; and the United Nations Center for Human Settlements, Nairobi.

THE STRUCTURE OF THE UIA

The Assembly is the legislative body meeting every three years. It is made up of delegations from all national sections. The Council is the executive body and meets once a year. Members represent the five geographic regions: (*1*) Western Europe, (*2*) Eastern Europe and the Middle East, (*3*) the Americas, (*4*) Asia and Australia, and (*5*) Africa.

The Bureau is a select executive body that meets as needed between the Council meetings on matters not requiring the attention of the Council or Assembly. Members consist of the president, the secretary general, the treasurer, and the five vice-presidents representing the activities of the geographic regions. The Office of the General Secretariat is the UIA's administrative arm, which may attend to questions not specifically dealt with by one of the bodies of the union.

UIA PROGRAMS

In 1985, six programs were created: (*1*) Strengthening of the Profession, (*2*) Professional Training, (*3*) Development of Man and Society, (*4*) International Competitions for Architecture and Town Planning, (*5*) International Cooperation, and (*6*) Professional Development of Architecture. The last program includes work groups for urban and rural planning; work places and commercial spaces; habitat; public health; sport, leisure, and tourism; educational and cultural spaces; tropical construction; and heritage.

CONGRESSES

The world congresses attract between 5000 and 7000 architects and representatives of related disciplines. Meetings are held alternately in the geographic regions. The subject or theme of the world congresses have included the following:

1948, Lausanne, Switzerland. Architecture faced with its new tasks.

1951, Rabat, Morocco. How architecture is dealing with its new tasks.

1953, Lisbon, Portugal. Architecture at the Crossroads.

1955, The Hague, the Netherlands. Architecture and the Evolution of Building.

1958, Moscow, USSR. Construction and Reconstruction of Cities.

1961, London, UK, New Techniques and New Materials.

1963, Havana, Cuba. Architecture in Underdeveloped countries.

1965, Paris, France. The Training of Architects.

1967, Prague, Czechoslovakia. Architecture and the Human Milieu.

1969, Buenos Aires, Argentina. Architecture as a Social Factor.

1972, Varna, Bulgaria. Architecture and Leisure.

1975, Madrid, Spain. Creativity and Technology.

1978, Mexico City, Mexico. Architecture and National Development.

1981, Warsaw, Poland. Architecture–Man–Environment.

1985, Cairo, Egypt. Present and Future Missions of the Architect.

1987, Brighton, UK. Shelter and Cities—Building Tomorrow's World.

1990, Montreal, Canada. Cultures and Technology.

INTERNATIONAL COMPETITIONS, MEDALS AND PRIZES, PUBLICATIONS

The UIA sponsors international architectural competitions, providing review and advice on guidelines, jury selection, and publicity. The UIA also awards a Gold Medal and prizes selected by an international jury nominated by the UIA in such areas as town planning, improvement in the quality of human settlements, applied technology in architecture and criticism, and the teaching of architecture. The UIA publishes a monthly newsletter, reports of congresses, and informative materials.

Membership is restricted to National Sections (Table 1). However, limited participation is offered to firms, institutions, and individuals, in the category of subscriber participants.

Table 1. National Sections

Algeria	Jamaica
Argentina	Japan
Australia	
Austria	Kenya
	Korea
Bahamas[a]	
Bangladesh	Libya
Bolivia	Luxembourg
Brazil	
Bulgaria	Malaysia
Cameroon, United Republic of	Malta
Canada	Mexico
Republic of	Mongolia
Central America	Morocco
Costa Rica	
Guatemala	The Netherlands
Honduras	Nigeria
Nicaragua	North Korea
El Salvador	
Chile	Pakistan
China, the People's Republic of	Paraguay
	Peru
Colombia	Philippines
Cuba	Poland
Cyprus	Portugal
Czechoslovakia	Puerto Rico
Dominican Republic	Rumania
Ecuador	Scandinavia
Egypt	Finland
Fiji[a]	Norway
France	Denmark
	Iceland
Gabon	Senegal
GDR (East Germany)	Singapore
FRG (West Germany)	Spain
Greece	Switzerland
Hong Kong	Surinam[a]
Hungary	Syria
India	Tunisia
Indonesia	Turkey
Iraq	
Ireland	Uganda
Israel	UK
Italy	United States
	Uruguay
Ivory Coast	U.S.S.R. (*continued*)

Table 1. (*Continued*)

Venezuela	Zambia
Vietnam	Zimbabwe
Yugoslavia	

a Temporary members.

ROBERT T. PACKARD, AIA
Reston, Virginia

This article was based on information supplied by the UIA.

UNION OF SOVIET SOCIALIST REPUBLICS.

See SOVIET UNION ARCHITECTURE—SUPPLEMENT

UNITED STATES CAPITOL

Charles Pierre L'Enfant's 1791 plan for the capital of the United States reserved sites for "Grand Edifices" to house the functions and supply the symbols of the three basic components of the new democratic government: a "Congress House" (the Capitol) atop Jenkins Hill (now Capitol Hill), a "President's Palace" (the White House) connected to the Capitol by a wide avenue (Pennsylvania Avenue), and a Supreme Court building at what is now Judiciary Square, more or less midway between the other two. Quirks of history determined that the straight-line connection of the White House with the Capitol would be broken by the interposition of the Treasury Building, and that the Supreme Court Building, long delayed in its construction, should be a close neighbor of the Capitol. L'Enfant's plan for Washington, D.C., incorporated the classic concept of situating the seat of power on the "high place" (Greek: *acropolis*), a concept that also appealed to Renaissance classicism, particularly in the case of Michelangelo's redesign of the Capitoline Hill complex, the site of Rome's government-related buildings throughout the ages.

Early in 1792, the Commissioners of Federal Buildings for the District of Columbia announced a competition for the design of a capitol. The winner was to be awarded $500 and a city lot worth £100, and the runner-up was to receive $250. Dr. William Thornton, a professional physician and amateur architect born in the Virgin Islands, was awarded first prize even though his submittal was made, with the Commissioners' concurrence, after the deadline. The French-born architect, Stephen Hallet, whose submittal was initially accepted by the commissioners for additional study and refinement was instead declared the runner-up and, by way of consolation, was awarded $500 and the position of construction supervisor under Thornton. President Washington, who played a prime role in design review and architect selection, found Thornton's plan to have grandeur, simplicity and conve-

nience, while Thomas Jefferson admired its compact mass, interior layout and exterior beauty. After some revisions, Washington approved Thornton's design and, in a Masonic ceremony, laid the cornerstone on September 18, 1793.

As construction supervisor, Hallet found fault with Thornton's design, introduced construction changes reflecting his own ideas, and was dismissed in 1794. George Hadfield, a British-born architect succeeded Hallett in 1795 and served until 1798. Hadfield was followed by the Irish-born architect James Hoban, winner of the 1792 White House design competition. By 1800, the first part of the Capitol, the original Senate (north) wing, had been completed and President John Adams, the Congress, and the paraphernalia of government were moved from Philadelphia to the new capital city. George Washington remained intimately involved in the Capitol project until his death in 1799.

Benjamin Henry Latrobe, a British immigrant and professional architect–engineer, was appointed the second Architect of the Capitol by President Jefferson in 1803, succeeding Thornton, who had resigned in 1794. Latrobe served in that post until 1811, by which time he had carried out the construction of the original House of Representatives (south) wing and remodeled the interior of the original Senate wing. Thornton's plan for the bicameral Congress House was Palladian in spirit, consisting of a low domed rotunda, symmetrically flanked by the House and Senate wings, but by 1811, the main central feature had not yet been built; the wings were linked by a wooden passageway that was destroyed by British arson in the War of 1812 (August 24, 1814). Latrobe was reappointed Architect of the Capitol by President James Madison in 1815, remaining until late 1817. Congress was accommodated from 1815 to 1819 in temporary premises (the Old Brick Capitol, since demolished) on the site of the present Supreme Court Building. During his second appointment, Latrobe redesigned the damaged interiors of Thornton's original wings, changing the configuration of the House Chamber from elliptical to semicircular (present-day Statuary Hall) and producing the old Senate Chamber on the main floor and the old Supreme Court Room on the lower floor, both of which were carefully restored in the 1970s to their historic appearance as exhibits-in-place. Latrobe also left his mark on the exterior by widening the East Front portico (central portion) and setting it on a monumental base of broad stairs. That, combined with the elimination of similar stairs from the West Front (the Mall side), relocated the principal Capitol entrance from the west to the east, an anomaly because the "Grand Avenue" (Mall), the "President's Palace" (White House), and the implied future of the young country lay to the west. One of Latrobe's most unique contributions to the architecture of the Capitol was the introduction of the so-called American or Columbian orders; interior columns with ornamentation based on native motifs: ears of corn and leaves of tobacco (Fig. 1).

Following Latrobe, Charles Bulfinch, born in Boston and the architect of the Massachusetts and Connecticut statehouses, was appointed Architect of the Capitol by President James Monroe in 1818. Bulfinch completed La-

Figure 1. The "Corncob Column", designed by architect Benjamin Latrobe and carved from Aquia sandstone (Virginia freestone). Courtesy of the author.

trobe's designs for the east portico with its broad steps and for the Rotunda, producing a dome of copper-covered wood construction with a 24 ft (7.32 m) wide balustraded skylight and noticeably higher in profile than intended by Thornton and Latrobe. Bulfinch's design contributions also included revision of the west portico and extension of the West Front as well as terracing and landscaping, particularly on the west side. The office of Architect of the Capitol was abolished by an Act of Congress passed in 1828, and Bulfinch's services were terminated the following year.

The position of Architect of the Capitol went unfilled until 1851, when Thomas Ustick Walter of Philadelphia was appointed by President Millard Fillmore. From 1829 to 1836, the functions of that office were accomplished by the Commission of Public Buildings and Grounds, and from 1836 to 1851, Robert Mills, the Architect of Public Buildings discharged that responsibility. In 1850, the Senate's Committee on Public Buildings, chaired by Jefferson Davis, announced a design competition, for a prize of $500, for the extension of the Capitol. Enlarging the Capitol was necessary as a result of the increase among the membership and staff of Congress and in the volume of visitors to that institution. Mills, in a report on the situation, recommended sizable extension of the wings to provide for larger new legislative chambers, committee and audience rooms, and newly adapted spaces for the Supreme Court and the Library of Congress; he also proposed porticoes on the north and south, as well as a high

dome on an elevated peristyle drum over the Rotunda, similar to major domes in London (St. Paul's), Paris (the Church of the Invalides), and Rome (St. Peter's). The competition announcement permitted extension of the Capitol by additional wings on the north and south or by a separate and distinct building to the east, and promoted preservation of the general symmetry of the entire structure when complete. It also reserved to the committee the right to form a plan by using parts from the different submittals, for which they would proportionately divide the prize. That is what they did, directing Mills to develop a plan derived from the different submittals. President Fillmore, who had closely followed the Capitol expansion project, exercised the executive prerogative of plan approval provided by the legislation. He rejected Mills's plan and gave his cachet to Walter as Architect of the Capitol Expansion in order to carry out his competition concept.

The extensions effected during the 14 years of Walter's service (1851–1865) gave the Capitol its familiar, significant form. The horizontal extensions of the wings with their monumental porticoed House and Senate entrances on the East Front and the vertical extension of the high central dome produced a distinctive, easily recognized composition of mass and profile. His architecture was in sympathy with that of Latrobe and Thornton, maintaining dignity and harmony in its arrangement and propriety and sensitivity in its detailing. His design for the dome was an adventure in the emerging technology of cast-iron construction, utilizing the new structural material in open web ribs for both the inner and outer portions typical of Renaissance high dome construction. In addition to the main structural components, cast iron was also used for bracing frames, tie-rods, and the architecturally ornamental exterior and interior surfaces. The cast iron is painted white to match the exterior masonry. The height, measured from the East Front plaza, is 285 ft (86.87 m) and the diameter at its base is 135 ft 5 in. (41.28 m). The 19 ft 6 in. (5.94 m) high bronze "Statue of Freedom" by the U.S. sculptor Thomas Crawford (also responsible for the bronze entrance doors to the House and Senate wings and other Capitol statuary) was installed in late 1863 atop an iron globe surmounting the dome's lantern. In spite of the use of the Rotunda as a military hospital and the basement as a bakery, it was politically important to the government that the Capitol be symbolically completed during the Civil War as an affirmation of union and freedom.

Captain Montgomery C. Meigs, who following the war was responsible for the new Pension Building in Washington, was appointed by President Franklin Pierce's Secretary of War, Jefferson Davis, to be Engineer of the Capitol with special responsibilities in superintendence and finance. As such, he influenced a number of design improvements involving heating, ventilation, acoustics, and the central placement of the House and Senate Chambers in their respective new wings. Under Pierce's successor and Abraham Lincoln's immediate predecessor, President James Buchanan, and without the support of Davis as Secretary of War, the Walter–Meigs relationship became increasingly turbulent, resulting in Meigs's transfer in 1859. In 1862, the responsibility for extension of the Capitol was returned from the War Department to the Department of the Interior, and Thomas U. Walter resumed the functions of superintendent as well as architect. Following Walter's efforts to provide increased space for the Library of Congress in an extension of the central portion of the West Front, the Secretary of the Interior voided the construction contract and transferred Walter and his functions to the office of the Commissioner of Public Buildings and Grounds, which precipitated the resignation of the fourth Architect of the Capitol in 1865.

Under succeeding Architects of the Capitol in the late nineteenth and early twentieth centuries, modern services and conveniences were installed, for example, elevators (1874), fireproofing (1881), electric wiring (1900), and air-conditioning (1929). Separate congressional office buildings with interconnecting subway train systems were built, as was a separate Capitol Power Plant, to serve the ever-increasing complex on Capitol Hill.

The Library of Congress, which had been burned out of its central West Front location in 1851 and whose subsequent enlargement by Thomas U. Walter led to his resignation, finally received a building of its own. It was designed by the Washington architects John L. Smithmeyer, Paul J. Pelz, and Edward Pearce Casey and built in 1886–1897. The design was a highly ornate beaux-arts rendering of the Italian Renaissance style, and its volume was augmented by an adjacent annex in 1939 and the recently completed nearby James Madison Library Building. The Supreme Court, long a tenant in the Capitol and inheritor of the old Senate chamber for use as its courtroom, waited even longer for a building of its own. In 1935, on a site only one block east of the Capitol, the Supreme Court building was completed. A white marble beaux-arts Roman temple, it was designed by the eminent Cass Gilbert, architect of the U.S. Treasury Annex and several state capitols (Arkansas, Minnesota, West Virginia).

Frederick Law Olmsted, the foremost U.S. landscape architect–planner of the nineteenth century, was authorized by Congress in 1874 to develop plans for improvement of the Capitol grounds. Thomas U. Walter had, in his 1864 report to Congress, included such a plan for grounds development entailing acquisition of additional land immediately north and south of the Capitol building. Olmsted's designs brought formal order to the extensive grounds that had an informal, almost rural character before the construction of his improvements over the decade commencing in 1883. His work is mainly responsible for the impressive dignity of the surroundings, continuing to the present, in particular, the predominantly native plantings, the paved East Front plaza, and the West Front terraces and grand stairways of Vermont marble that replaced Charles Bulfinch's 1829 earth terraces. Olmsted also included a number of accessories and adjunct structures, such as walls, fountains, lampposts, bench shelters, even a grotto, designed with the assistance of Thomas Wisedell. The London-born Wisedell had been a member of the New York firm of Vaux and Withers; Calvert Vaux being Olmsted's associate in the 1857 design competition for New York's Central Park. In the spirit of the time, some of those architectural appurtenances lapsed from strict academic classicism, but the strength of Olmsted's grand concept has prevailed.

As late as 1874, Thomas U. Walter had presented plans for an extension of the central portion of the East Front, an idea he had proposed more than once during his tenure as architect. But it was not until 1958–1962 that an extension was accomplished, advancing the facade 32 ft 6 in. (9.75 m) and creating more than a hundred additional rooms. Within a decade of that event, plans were being considered for extension of the West Front, also. During the 1960s, as the facade masonry was visibly deteriorating, an even more visible system of wooden braces was erected, and as an accomplished fact, became part of the West Front. Through the 1970s and into the 1980s various design proposals were studied and debated, including advancing the facade to the edge of the terraces and excavating beneath them in order to gain additional space for Congress. In 1983, precipitated by actual breaking away of the exterior masonry, Congress appropriated funds for stabilization, restoration, and rehabilitation of the facade in its original location, which was completed in 1987.

An early favorite among building stones for public buildings in Washington was Aquia Creek sandstone, a form of Virginia freestone favored primarily because of its ready availability. Benjamin Latrobe had no illusions about the limitations of its structural properties, but the quarry was on the Potomac River only 40 mi downstream, and the stone was easily worked. He felt that columns of almost any size could be obtained, provided they could be transported. Charles Bulfinch found that the porous Aquia stone facing of the Capitol was seriously deteriorating and resorted to painting it in 1818 as a preservative measure. During the 1984–1987 restoration of the West Front, some of the original sandstone was discovered to have more than 30 coats of paint. Bulfinch-designed Capitol gateposts and gatehouses were constructed of Aquia stone ca 1820–1830 and were moved from Capitol Hill to Constitution Avenue, between 15th and 17th Streets, as part of the Olmsted relandscaping program. The warm color and delicate texture of those weatherworn structures have a haunting appeal, but the shortcomings of the stone as a material for monumental masonry are obvious. As interior masonry, the Aquia stone is seen to advantage in old parts of the Capitol, particularly in areas adjacent to the Rotunda and in the crypt; Latrobe used perfect pieces with notable success in his corncob and tobacco leaf columns. Various kinds of marble, granite, sandstone, and limestone from many domestic sources were used through the years in the construction of the Capitol; for instance, Maryland Seneca sandstone was used for the Rotunda floor and the center steps were built of Minnesota Rockville granite. Among the more recent projects, Georgia White Cherokee marble was used to cover the Aquia stone for the 1958–1962 East Front extension, and the 40% of the West Front Aquia stone deemed unsalvageable for stabilization or restoration was replaced with a similar Indiana limestone.

Fine art and ornamentation were constituent parts of the Capitol's architectural concepts from the outset. Artists responsible for the decorative sculptures and paintings were almost exclusively classically trained Italian natives. Consequently, the nature of the work was traditional, adhering to the academic conventions. By the

Figure 2. Aerial view of the United States Capitol showing the East Front and Dome in the foreground and the Mall in the background, leading to the Washington Monument and Lincoln Memorial. Courtesy of the Architect of the Capitol/U.S. Congress.

1840s U.S. sculptors were being given commissions, although Congress in 1817 commissioned paintings on Revolutionary War subjects by Colonel John Trumbull, who had been George Washington's aide-de-camp in that conflict. His four murals were installed, among others, on the walls of the Rotunda where the major painted decorations are the fresco—frieze 58 ft (17.68 m) above the floor, 8 ft 3 in. (2.52 m) in height, and 300 ft (91.44 m) in circumference, and the 4664-ft² (433.30 m²) mural, the "Apotheosis of Washington," covering the surface of the interior dome. The frieze and dome canopy mural were the work of Constantino Brumidi, an Italian painter who executed decorative paintings and murals in various corridors, rooms, and the Rotunda from 1855 until his death in 1880. His grisaille frieze, simulating relief sculpture and planned to depict American historical events from Columbus's landing to the California gold strike, was left unfinished. By 1888, Filippo Costagini completed eight panels based on Brumidi's sketches, but left some 32 ft (9.75 m) bare. Not until 1952, when Congress agreed on episodes (from the Civil War to the first airplane flight) to depict, did work resume on the frieze, this time by the U.S. artist Allyn Cox who was also responsible for cleaning it. Cox also cleaned and retouched the dome mural, which was completely cleaned and restored in 1988, returning it to its original 1865 appearance. The Capitol and its grounds constitute a veritable museum of public art, architectural and commemorative; much of the former is remarkable for its integration with and intensification of the mother art, and much of the latter is remarkable for its diversity of content and ingenuity of expression (Figs. 2 and 3)

Quite possibly the most pervasive U.S. icon, after the bald eagle and Old Glory, is the Capitol. The distinctiveness and powerful profile of its high dome, undiminished by the several extensions of the building complex beneath it, serve as an instantly recognized symbol of the nation and its capital city. The central Renaissance-style dome also served as architectural inspiration for many of the

ROOMS ON SECOND FLOOR OF THE CAPITOL

HOUSE SIDE

H–201, 202. House majority conference room
H–203, 204, 205, 206. Speaker
H–207. House reception room
H–208. Committee on Ways and Means
H–209, 310. Speaker
H–211. Parliamentarian
H–212, 213, 214. Members' retiring rooms
H–216, 217, 218. Committee on Appropriations
H–219. Republican Whip
H–221, 222, 223, 224. Cloakrooms
H–225. House Floor Library
H–226. House document room
H–227. Conference Room
H–228, 229, 230, 231, 232, 233. House Minority Leader
H–234. Prayer Room
H–235. Congresswomen's suite
H–236. Committee on Foreign Affairs

SENATE SIDE

S–206. Conference Room
S–207. Senators' conference room
S–208. Majority Leader
S–212. The Vice President
S–213. The Senators' reception room
S–214. Formal Office of the Vice President
S–216. Room of the President
S–218, 219. Official Reporters of Debates
S–220. Bill Clerk and Journal Clerk
S–221. Assistant Secretary
S–222, 224. Office of the Secretary
S–223. Secretary
S–225, 226. Cloakrooms
S–227. Republican Leader
S–228. Old Senate Chamber
S–233, 234, 235. Senate Disbursing Office
S–236. Comptroller

Courtesy of the Architect of the Capitol/U.S. Congress.

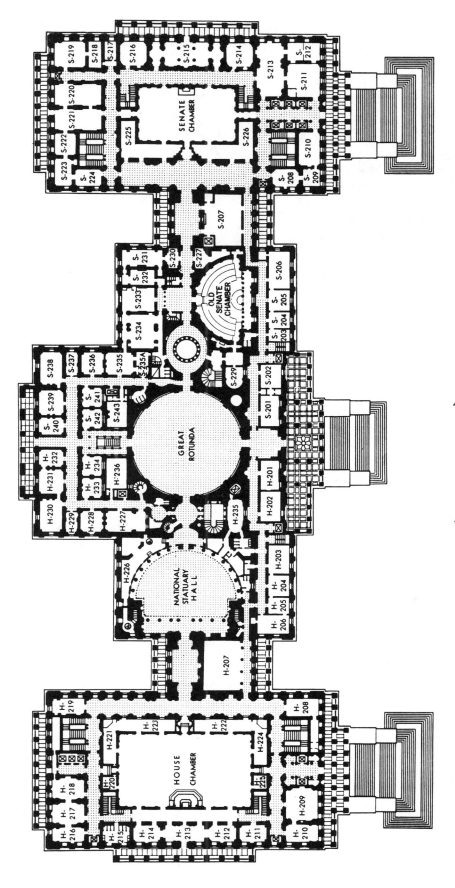

SECOND (PRINCIPAL) FLOOR PLAN

scale: 0 16 32 48 64 feet

1979

NORTH

UNITED STATES CAPITOL

Figure 3. Plan of the United States Capitol at main floor level, showing locations of the Rotunda, Old Senate Chamber, Old House Chamber (now Statuary Hall), the present Senate Chamber (north wing), and House Chamber (south wing).

state capitols built in the period between the Civil War and World War I. Pierre Charles L'Enfant's reference to Jenkins Hill as a pedestal waiting for a monument forecast the evolving appearance of a most effective architectural achievement, accenting the Washington cityscape and emphatically anchoring the extended vista of his "Grand Avenue," metamorphosed by the so-called McMillan Plan more than a century later into the Washington Mall. The initial adoption of a domed Roman classical revival style for the Capitol, inspired by an early admiration for the republican form of government, was faithfully followed through generations of alterations, additions, and other elaborations. By adherence to basic classical expression, typically articulated through variations on the recurrent theme of the Corinthian order, clarity of function and dignity in form were obtained.

An early intention for the Capitol was to serve as the tomb of George and Martha Washington, and a crypt was built below the central Rotunda for that purpose, but family insistence in 1832, the centennial of Washington's birth, that their remains not be moved from their cemetery at Mount Vernon determined that the Capitol should maintain its monumentality strictly on the basis of its functional symbolism and its architectural achievement, as it has.

BIBLIOGRAPHY

General References

L. Aikman, *We the People: The Story of the United States Capitol,* U.S. Capitol Historical Society, Washington, D.C., 1963.

U.S. Department of the Interior, Geological Survey, *Building Stones of our Nation's Capitol,* U.S. Government Printing Office, Washington, D.C., 1975.

G. Brown, *History of the United States Capitol,* 2 Vols., Da Capo Press, New York, 1970.

E. Cohen and F. Elias, "Restoring the U.S. Capitol West Front," *The Military Engineer* 77(501), 256–260 (July 1985).

L. Craig and the Staff of the Federal Architecture Project, *The Federal Presence: Architecture, Politics and Symbols in U.S. Government Building,* MIT Press, Cambridge, Mass., 1978.

Federal Writers' Project, *The WPA Guide to Washington, D.C.,* Pantheon Books, New York, 1983.

T. Hamlin, *Greek Revival Architecture in America,* Dover, New York, 1964.

H.-R. Hitchcock and W. Seale, *Temples of Democracy,* Harcourt Brace Jovanovich, Orlando, Fla., 1976.

Joint Committee on Printing, U.S. Congress, *The Capitol: A Pictorial History of the Capitol and of the Congress,* 7th ed., U.S. Government Printing Office, Washington, D.C., 1979.

F. Kimball, *Thomas Jefferson: Architect,* 2nd ed., Da Capo Press, New York, 1968.

H. Kirker, *The Architecture of Charles Bulfinch,* Harvard University Press, Cambridge, Mass., 1977.

P. F. Norton, *Latrobe, Jefferson, and the National Capitol,* Garland, New York, 1977.

F. L. Olmsted, Jr. and T. Kimball, eds., *Frederick Law Olmsted: Landscape Architect, 1822–1903,* Benjamin Blom, New York, 1970.

L. Wood-Roper, *F. L. O. A Biography of Frederick Law Olmsted,* Johns Hopkins, Baltimore, Md., 1983.

The Capitol Dome U.S. Capitol Historical Society, Washington, D.C. A quarterly newsletter. *Capitol Studies* U.S. Capitol Historical Society, Washington, D.C. A biannual journal.

Information articles and releases published periodically by the Office of the Curator (Art and Reference Division; Art and Reference Library; etc), Architect of the Capitol, Washington, D.C.

Architecture (The AIA Journal). Magazine of The American Institute of Architects, Washington, D.C.

J. WALTER ROTH, AIA
Alexandria, Virginia

UNIVERSITIES.   See CAMPUS PLANNING

URBAN DESIGN—SCALE AND ARCHITECTURE

Scale is a concept both subjective and imprecise. It relates to the physical world, yet it is often affected by abstract and nonconcrete influences such as culture and emotions. Dictionaries disagree on the word's meaning, which is understandable; they try to define words in as little text as possible. This article uses pictorial examples as a way of fleshing out a broad explanation of the concept of scale. Words alone are too limiting a medium for a full discussion of the subject of scale.

As applied to the urban environment, scale relates to open spaces (Fig. 1), interior space, enclosing surfaces, and buildings as objects. Elements affecting scale are pavements, wall surfaces and detail (Fig. 2), vistas and perspective, the velocity of the viewer, and perceptions of all sorts that have hard-to-define physical connections. As an illustration of a point affecting scale, a building might be cited that in itself is not urban, but that best illustrates an idea: the Belvedere in New York's Central Park is per se a building in a city, but its intrinsic scale is that of a

Figure 1. *Stockholm:* A market square carrying one scale in the market stalls and another tied to the enclosing buildings.

Figure 2. *Zurich:* A cozy old-city enclosed square with a fountain providing scale.

Figure 3. *Hydra:* A stepped alley, scaled for mule traffic.

"That pygmy elephant is so tiny."
"That balustrade is nicely in scale."
"Scale down that pylon. It's too monumental."
"Isn't that praying mantis gigantic?"

All of these phrases imply a unit of measurement not necessarily mentioned, anywhere from an ant to a pachyderm.

rural castle; it was purposely designed on a diminished scale to seem farther away than it actually is. The scale of the Belvedere has nothing to do with the Bowery or Broadway.

Within urban streetscapes, there is a variety of scale. Alleys (Fig. 3) speak a different language of space than sidestreets (Fig. 4), which in turn are different from thoroughfares. Residential streets are different from retail or industrial streets (Fig. 5). The scale of tree-lined streets (Fig. 6) is more often determined by the trees than the flanking structures. Boulevards (Fig. 7) begin to adopt a larger scale than that which would be implied by the frontal buildings themselves, as the viewer begins to see the larger city over the shoulders, so to speak, of the closer buildings. Parks have the scale of the country if they are large enough. When confined (Fig. 8), they work more as segments of similarly sized streets and boulevards. The foregoing set of generalities is admittedly subjective and arbitrary. They should stimulate the reader to go test them out personally.

Scale is, of course, a relative term. Consider these statements:

Figure 4. *London:* Row housing with scale-giving horizontal banding and trees.

Figure 5. *Athens:* A city street built out to the curb line, limiting the effective scale at street level.

Figure 6. *Autun:* Clipped trees shrink the scale of the surrounding plaza.

Generally, the unit of measurement for cities and their buildings is the human body, but not quite in the way that weight can be measured in kilograms or distance in miles. Le Corbusier is known for his Modulor illustration of a muscular man with huge hands (Fig. 9) as the benchmark for his buildings. Leonardo da Vinci is remembered for his spread-eagled man in a circle before that (Fig. 10), again a graphic reminder of a unit of scale.

Today, cities and their component buildings are much larger than any human and therefore are, in a sense, going to be automatically out of scale. However, scale has taken on a broader meaning than just how something relates to a 6-ft-tall anthropoid. Scale encompasses the relative size and form of elements within a composition as well (Fig. 11). Scale begins to encroach on the concept of proportion. Scale is elusive; one person's concept of something being in scale can be very different from another's, depending on both physical and cultural vantage points.

The concept of scale is nevertheless useful in attempting to describe a city, its buildings, streetscapes, and impact, indefinite though it may be. There is no better means for picturing the subjective aspect of the physical world, the truth that lies beyond feet and inches, population growth, and tax base. It is an essential working tool for

Figure 7. *Venice:* A water boulevard, its scale derived from the slow movement of gondolas.

Figure 8. *Salisbury:* Cedars of Lebanon and a Gothic cloister produce a perfect marriage of scale.

the sensitive designer, who is continually conscious of the relationship of elements both within and without a design.

Humanity began constructing shelter with the limitations of available natural materials and the strength in the human body. This can be seen in the structures of the remaining primitive societies on earth: huts of dried mud smeared over woven twigs, tents of animal skins stretched over bent saplings, domes made of blocks of frozen snow, vaults formed of curved bundles of reeds (Fig. 12), or rough shelters made of boulders piled into a hollow cairn. All of these techniques result in buildings whose every detail is observable with the naked eye and touchable. They all disappear into an environment that overpowers them visually, be it trees, rock outcroppings, snow glare, or just space on a large scale.

Artificial objects, even of the size of the HMS Queen Mary, seen on the horizon on the open ocean, or the stalagmite towers of downtown Atlanta, Ga., seen from 10 mi away, shrink into insignificance when compared to the enormity of nature's scale. The pedestrian would never think, while scurrying along Peachtree Street in the midst of a summer thunderstorm, that the city was related in scale to the anvil-topped thunderhead above. Seen from a Delta jet, the two can be in scale one to another. Point of view has a great deal to do with scale.

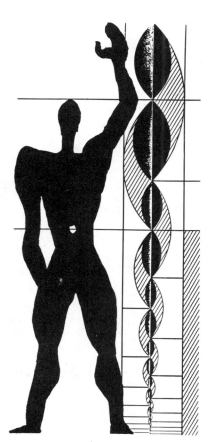

Figure 9. Le Corbusier's man-scale.

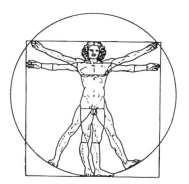

Figure 10. Leonardo da Vinci's man-scale.

Figure 11. *Positano:* A seaside town whose scale is diminished by both mountains above and space beyond.

SCALE IN GENERAL

Recognizable examples always make a point more clear. An analysis of a building known to many the world over, Frank Lloyd Wright's Marin County Civic Center (Fig. 13), should clarify the concept of scale.

This building sits among grassy hills dotted with live oaks. It straddles a col between two hills, spanning from crest to crest, much as a dam might joint the shores of a river. The building can be seen from a distance and has the ability to hold its own in the landscape, even though its radio mast (designed as a substantial architectural element in the composition) is not massive enough to be read from afar.

As one approaches, every increment of distance brings out a new recognizable part of the building's flanks and its

Figure 12. Model of primitive reed bundle construction (Stockholm Museum).

detail. It is equally strong on both sides of the "dam." There is an arch pattern reminiscent of Roman aqueducts, each horizontal layer of construction slightly smaller in scale than the one below. Balconies and *brise soleil* cast patterns that change during the day. Closer still, the fenestration patterns begin to appear, and the surface detail flags the attention. The entrance is inside a large tunnel arch at the center of the bottom level. As the visitor dismounts from a vehicle to enter, much as a Venetian doge might step onto his arch-covered landing from a gondola, there is a finely detailed Wright-designed wrought-iron gate to inspect. The scale has changed from that which fits nature's sweep to that which is looked at close up, in a sequence that registers only in hindsight.

The visitor climbs inside through a skylit atrium to the top floor, where it is possible to exit at grade at a rounded end of an apparently one-story structure. The metal roof is stepped and patterned, marked with regular globular finials to give yet another scale to what becomes a small intimate building, far removed from the hill-to-hill dam first seen. Truly, this product of Wright's genius has a working scale for nearly every possible vantage point.

Scale might have nothing to do with the impact of approaching this symbol of government from below, either in a car or walking up toward it from the parking area. It looms above, but not in an oppressive way. The unique detail takes it out of the historically heavy and forbidding character so common and familiar in this type of building. Wright was able to design a suitably governmental building, one that impresses and symbolizes the role of government, without employing Gargantua.

Mastery of scale in a building is displayed at the Dulles International Airport Terminal, designed by Eero Saarinen (Fig. 14). Its scale in space is even greater than that of the Marin County building, as the site is a wide, featureless plateau in Virginia. The massing and sculp-

Figure 13. *Marin County Civic Center:* Frank Lloyd Wright's flamboyant lesson in detail-controlled scale.

ture of it can be read from two miles away, as the visitor pops over a rise on the access highway onto the plateau. The small city of support buildings at Dulles have all been limited to simple gray boxes, the better to emphasize the terminal.

The outward-sloping piers and curved roof edges are soon discernible. Then, the mullion pattern appears upon swinging parallel to the building on approach. The sense of transparency becomes noticeable, in daylight and, sensationally, at dusk.

On arrival, having swung around to see the catenary section of the building as expressed on the west end, the visitor is struck by the bushhammered surfaces of the concrete piers and their slope, which overhangs the sidewalk and lends an imposing majesty of scale to the process of arrival.

Once inside, rather than the feel of an oversized concourse, as in Grand Central Station, the visitor is greeted by this wonderful miracle of space: a bellied ceiling which droops low in the center from high side supports. It is a very large space, and it could have been oppressive had all the area been covered by 12-ft ceilings. It could have been

Figure 14. *Dulles International Airport Terminal:* Eero Saarinen's masterwork in space-controlled scale.

out of scale with the people it serves if covered with a high vault. As it is, it is possible to read the full extent of the space without feeling squashed or ant sized. It is a most comfortable volume.

SCALE MANIPULATION TECHNIQUES

Enclosed Space/Open Space

The sense of enclosure of outdoor space influences scale. A closed courtyard such as those found in the Seville Alhambra (Fig. 15) allows small objects and patterns to be read in scale. Intricate geometrically patterned tiles, doors, and ceilings inlaid with thousands of fitted pieces of wood, vaults whose surfaces are dripping with cusps on cusps, and other such detail is not lost indoors and in enclosed courts.

Such detail would be lost and out of scale in Kew Gardens (Fig. 16), where the massing and large-scale sculpture of the greenhouses and pagoda in the open landscape count for more than any of the surface detail. Streets that open on one side, those facing bodies of water or open parks, pose a dual problem of scale to a designer, where detail is important on one sidewalk but massing counts from the opposite side. The Baltimore, Md., Inner Harbor comes to mind, where the buildings combine both strong massing and intricacies based on the sense of show business inherent in the development. City streets have always relied on the detail of marketing and signage for scale and interest, from the medieval streets of York (Fig. 17) to New York's Times Square.

Once a street passes a certain ratio of width to the height of flanking buildings, say, 3 : 1, nothing up in the air much matters to a person on the ground. When it is necessary to tilt one's head, rather than rotate the eyeballs to see a cornice line, the bottom of the canyon is the only important locale (Fig. 18).

Figure 15. *Granada:* The Alhambra's rooms and courts thrive on Moorish detail in fine scale.

Skyscraper Scales

A building can exist in three locales at once if it is tall enough and clustered with other tall buildings. Skyscrapers are somewhat like columns in that they can be termed as having three parts: base, shaft, and capital. When the scale gets very large, as in the Citicorp Building in New York (Fig. 19), the parts take on lives and scales of their own. The space at ground level at Citicorp has the scale of the street and the church that exists underneath the umbrella of the shaft overhanging above. It is not an intimate space, as the umbrella is so high overhead, but it accommodates humans. The shaft really cannot be read except from other surrounding shafts; it is just one tree trunk among tree trunks and it is possible to relate only to its bark, so to speak. Yet a cluster of skyscrapers seen from another angle develops a unique world where scale is theatrical and unrelated to reality.

The skyscraper skin that covers the Citicorp shaft has no scale, no element against which it can be measured. The shaft scale is its bulk within the observer's cone of vision, as seen from another building.

The capital or crown is that part of Citicorp visible from Brooklyn and New Jersey (Fig. 20), a sloping wedge so unique on the skyline that it cannot be missed. Its scale relates to the entire silhouette of Manhattan; it is a pristine piece of sculpture sitting on the rough masonry of the city.

Figure 16. *London:* Kew Gardens' buildings are in scale with the open space around them.

Figure 17. *York:* Medieval cities were built to the scale of carts.

Human Scale Overpowered

The Romanesque church facade of S. Michele in Lucca, Italy (Fig. 21), is intricately covered with columned arcades of small scale. The Cathedral at Pisa, Italy, is similarly decorated. However, the latter building sits in open space at some distance from the baptistry and the campanile with which it shares a compound. S. Michele has buildings in close conjunction on both sides. For all of the human-scaled elements on the facade, the scale of this building is that of the flanking buildings. There is no disguising its bulk under the circumstances.

It is necessary to get inside the block-on-block massing of Habitat in Montreal, Canada, (Fig. 22) for it to demonstrate a residential human scale, for the boxcar-sized precast concrete elements dominate the exterior.

Scale to Impress

Coming upon Salisbury Cathedral (Fig. 23) and upon Chartres from 10 mi away across field and farm are parallel experiences. The spired forms are immediately recognizable. They dominate the horizon. The closer one gets, the more impressive they become in relation to the towns they grace. Within the towns, the views are, of necessity, snatches seen over rooftops, becoming more and more angled upwards and laced with detail. Approaching on foot, the visitor's eyes continually jump back and forth between

Figure 18. *New York:* The scale of Wall Street is so confining that people have to look up for relief.

the spire and sculpture, from a huge scale to the human scale of the portico statuary. Yet the door they surround, the access to the interior space that was intended to suit the scale of God Himself, is again larger than life.

In its own way, the Grundtvig Church near Copenhagen, Denmark, (Fig. 24) makes a similar, singular, overpowering scale statement.

The multistory archways of Philip Johnson's AT&T Building in New York relate in scale neither to people nor to the street they face. The scale was chosen to let people know that the building houses an important corporate entity, as well as the gilded, oversized statue that formerly topped the company's headquarters.

Model-derived Scale

Some buildings, often those that were designed in model form, carry a no-scale surface with them, so that they change little as seen from 1000 ft distant or 6 ft away. Detail that cannot be added to white cardboard never get into the game. One design tool at the right hand of an architect is variety in the size of detail and surface break (Fig. 25). Different scales are expressed by these devices every bit as much as by varying bulk and overall dimension. Seen from varying distances, the lack of scaled detail makes a building confusing and, in some cases, dull.

I. M. Pei's East Wing to the National Gallery of Art in Washington, D.C. (Fig. 26), is not necessarily dull, but it is a good example of an exterior designed in model form. It was a sensationally elegant and convincing model. It fit in

Figure 19. *New York:* Ground-level of Hugh Stubbins's Citicorp Building, scaled to the street. Felt, but unseen without cocking one's head upwards, is the huge soaring bulk above.

Figure 20. *New York:* The midtown skyline shows a level array of stalagmites whose tips can be read as separate sculptures.

small scale, as a bird would see it, the classical axial relationships of the Mall, which could easily be read in the scale model. (They are impossible to see and sense on the ground.) The glazed skylights, built at model scale, became faceted jewels. The concept was irresistible. The model, a work of art in itself, convinced Congress of the rightness of the scheme and the value of funding it.

However, the finished museum has no exterior detail and therefore no intermediate scale to be read from across the street. There is an arresting veined stone skin that draws the attention at close hand. There are those grand skylights visible from several blocks away. But compared to the National Gallery designed by John Russell Pope, with its pilasters, moldings, and stringcourses, the East Wing stands naked and scaleless. Shadow-producing elements are, in any style, a valuable tool to the architect trying to control scale (Fig. 27). What may be lacking on the exterior of the East Wing is more than made up for inside. The interior is a most pleasant and successful space, of comfortable scale, where the architecture works with the art displayed.

Another Washington, D.C., building, the Pan-American Health Organization Building, was the result of an international competition, for which the design was worked out in model form. Thought of as a table piece, it is a nicely modeled volume of contrasting elements. However, the surface textures of both parts are so scaled as to read nearly the same way from across the Potomac as from across the street. It is possible to construct only a fraction of reality in a model.

Scale and Surface

In the southeastern United Kingdom, many older buildings are constructed of round, cannon-ball-sized pudding stones, found in the local chalk beds and the only local hard stone. Corners must be made of dressed stone imported from Normandy. The pudding stone is the right scale for one-story parish churches and such, but would be out of scale in Salisbury Cathedral (Fig. 28).

The reverse is also true. The heavy Volkswagen-sized stones of Mycenae in Greece would never fit the sophisti-

Figure 21. *Lucca:* S. Michele's facade of human-sized arcades.

Figure 22. *Montreal:* Habitat uses piled up block elements of such size as to lose residential scale.

cated delicacy of the temple of Nike on the Acropolis. Surface scale affects the image and feel projected by buildings (Fig. 29).

Unit block interlocking pavers, developed in Europe, are seen in the illustration of the quay at Oberwessel, Federal Republic of Germany, pictured in 1974 (Fig. 30). Since then, the product has come to the United States. It is now used everywhere and has supplanted many pavements because of its attractiveness and ease of installation. It is also a great scale giver in the urban United States, which has been overbuilt with asphalt and concrete, materials with no intrinsic texture or individual scale.

Conditions for Zero Scale

There is an enormous building at Cape Canaveral, Fla., in which space vehicles are assembled. It is probably at the outer limit of the practical enclosure of space, from both need and feasibility standpoints. When a three-stage rocket is placed inside, it may seem logical, but the scale is still beyond belief. If the rocket is removed, the empty volume staggers comprehension.

Victoria Station in London probably had the same impact in the nineteenth century as the Vehicle Assembly

Figure 23. *Salisbury:* The tall cathedral spire catches the scale of the countryside.

Building has today. Even with trains present, its space is hard to comprehend. Some things are just too big to be in scale with anything but themselves.

Wright conceived of a "mile-high" building for Chicago, Ill., in the late 1940s. So far, the tallest building humanity has been able to erect (exclusive of guyed aerial masts) is the Sears Tower in Chicago (Fig. 31). Building height limitations are more the product of economic justifications

Figure 24. *Copenhagen:* The Grundtvig Church is all out of scale with its neighbors because of its deceptive detail.

Figure 25. *Washington, D.C.:* The Watergate has intricately detailed balconies, which work to shrink the apparent scale of the project.

Figure 26. *Washington, D.C.:* The National Gallery East Wing interior has the scale of a theater, where patrons in motion are part of the show.

and ground-level access problems than of engineering considerations. A mile-high building, four times the height of the Sears Tower, would be completely devoid of scale on the upper level. There would not be anything to which it could relate in scale; no detail could be discernible. Often, it would just disappear into the clouds.

Lacking any element at all in the landscape, the sense of scale and distance becomes imprecise. In a vista across a half-frozen lake in Norway, with no people, boulders, trees, birds, or buildings in sight, the far shore could be perceived as being anywhere from half a mile to 30 miles away. This phenomenon is, of course, outside the experience of an urban population, except at night. Then, from high up in a Chicago condominium, or from a parador on a crag above Malaga, Spain (Fig. 32), the night scene is composed of spots of light and silhouettes with no identifying benchmark, beautiful but scaleless.

Downscaling

In Denmark, there is a child's delight called Legoland (Fig. 33), a town made entirely of Legos, little plastic, dimpled, interlocking blocks now in nearly every child's experience. The town's buildings and grounds are scaled

down to make children seem giant sized. The place teaches two lessons about scale:

1. The relationship of the individual Legos to the building they form; they disappear in the mind's eye.

Figure 27. *Wells:* Row house chimneys of elegant detail change the scale of the street.

Figure 28. *Madrid:* A rustic stone wall is in scale with and a great foil for these outdoor steps.

Figure 30. *Oberwessel:* Unit masonry paving with *Fräulein* scale.

2. The relationship between model buildings and people; the buildings remain scaled-down models. Adults do not change their sense of scale to accommodate the models.

Disneyworld, in Florida, contains a very interesting demonstration of scale. There, the designers concocted a village composed of what appear to be standard reproduc-

tions of Main Street-type buildings. They are mostly of nineteenth-century architecture, but they are all scaled down a fraction, not the drastic scale change at Legoland. At Disneyworld, the children sense the difference; it makes them seem bigger. Adults sense something is different, but exactly why is not clear. The doorways are still passable, and the buildings are still functional. It is a very effective and clever device in the service of entertainment.

Time and happenstance have produced such surviving antiquities as the Old Curiosity Shop in London (Fig. 34) and Paul Revere's House in Boston, Mass. The visitor gets

Figure 29. *Madrid:* A contemporary apartment house with scale-modifying detail.

Figure 31. *Chicago:* The Sears Tower is a scale-setting landmark for the entire city. The diagonals have no effect on scale.

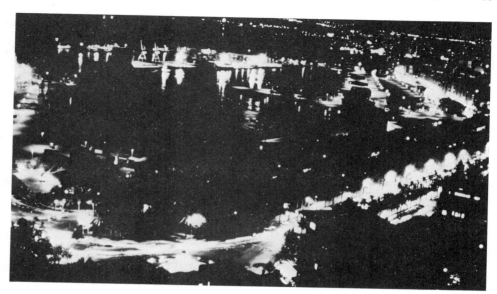

Figure 32. *Malaga:* Magical night vision from on high, with no scale.

the same sense of Lilliput from the dimensions of another era.

At Stourhead, United Kingdom, there is an artificial lake in a park, the handiwork of the renowned landscape architect "Capability Brown." Around the undulating shore, which hides its full expanse behind wooden points, are set several downscaled constructions: temples, bridges, and monuments. They all seem right in relation to the landscape, which provides no visual measuring stick. One has to walk directly up to one of these whimsical buildings to realize one has been fooled into thinking they are normal. As elements of scale themselves, they visually enlarge the impression of the size of the lake they border.

Scaling Up

A giant statue of Vulcan overlooks the city of Birmingham, Ala., a symbol of the steel-making industry there. It

Figure 33. *Legoland:* Denmark's downscaled gift to the world of children.

Figure 34. *London:* The Old Curiosity Shop, of Dickensian dimensions, is dwarfed by the flanking twentieth-century office building.

is so placed that one can see it best close by, rather than from a distance. It seems out of scale under those circumstances. The Statue of Liberty, having the entire New York harbor to relate to, comes off as being in scale.

The Lincoln Memorial is a monumental marble temple, and inside it is a monumental statue of Lincoln sitting in a monumental chair set against a huge stone wall. The scale is overblown on purpose and induces a sense of awe in any visitor. Everything there relates in scale except humans.

Somehow the Jefferson Memorial, across the Tidal Basin, although working in scale on the outside, fails in comparison to the Lincoln interior. Perhaps it is because the central, erect Jefferson statue, although overscaled like the Lincoln statue, shrinks as one circumnavigates it. One begins to compare Jefferson with the entire rotunda and not with oneself.

Some building types are intrinsically impressive and overscaled. The Roman Coliseum and any of the contemporary sports domes and stadia illustrate the effect of imposing size in a structure (Fig. 35). It need not be the exclusive property of government or religion (Fig. 36). Yankee Stadium, "The House that Ruth Built," had a definite influence on the success of the New York Yankees.

Scale and Foliage

Whether or not an open space in the city is soft with planting (Fig. 37) or all hard surfaced influences scale. Compare Pawley Park in Manhattan, with its tiny-leafed fronds of thornless locust trees overhead, with a similarly dimensioned hard-surfaced court such as the forecourt of S. Ambrogio in Milan, Italy (Fig. 38). Pawley Park is comfortable and in scale with tables, chairs, and people. S. Ambrogio is but a space to move through. It does not invite lingering. It is a creature of the church facade that dominates it.

Water also has a scale-altering effect (Fig. 39).

Figure 35. *Florence:* The large scale and forbidding masonry of a Pitti Palace influences attitude.

Scale and Speed

An interesting aspect of scale is related to the velocity of the viewer in space. In a city of walkers, such as downtown Munich (Fig. 40) or Cologne, Federal Republic of Germany, street furniture becomes not only useful, but important to scale: flower boxes and urns, fountains,

Figure 36. *Rome:* The monument to Vittorio Emmanuele II, overscaled to a fault, will outlast his place in history.

Figure 37. *Fairfax County:* Charles Goodman's Hollin Hills is a human-scaled suburban housing group that fits its woodland setting.

Figure 38. *Milan:* S. Ambrogio's stark Lombard Romanesque forecourt.

Figure 39. *Arhus:* A handsome Danish outdoor museum illustrates the expanding effect of water on scale.

Figure 40. *Munich:* A pedestrian-scaled centrum closed to cars, with suitable street furniture.

benches, and sculpture fit the scale of slow pedestrian movement. If people are in cars and in traffic, then the mezzanine level of the flanking buildings, the location of most urban mercantile signage, becomes important. The speed under those circumstances is still such that individual stores and content are recognizable. If those same cars are on an urban freeway going 55 mi/h, then the traffic signs become of necessity huge billboards in order to be read from several hundred feet away. Detail gets strung out horizontally, to be seen out of the corner of the eye.

There is a stretch of Route 50 in Rosslyn, Va., with a concrete retaining wall along the right-hand side of the inbound lane. The top of this wall undulates over a run of half a mile. It becomes almost a living thing, ropelike, as it slides by at high speed. To look at this wall from a stationary position gives no hint of its potential for compressing itself into 200 from 2000 ft under the influence of space—time.

Scale and Feeling

Scale can be manipulated to produce psychological impressions of power, awe, status, respect, and fear. The El Escorial site (Fig. 41) out from Madrid, Spain, was both a monastery and a palace. It is so huge and severe as to repel rather than attract. It is a building without planting on its approach side, and that sits on a wide, flat, paved parade ground gracelessly. Its scale is inhuman. It is necessary to go inside to get any sense that this building was occupied by people.

Figure 41. *El Escorial:* The size of this monstrous monastery-cum-palace makes the adjacent town seem puny.

The powerful Romanesque Cathedral at Durham, United Kingdom, is awesome from any vantage point. It has a far different feel, with its heavy but handsome piers and dim lighting, from King's College Chapel at Cambridge University, (Fig. 42), which is a symphony of floating late Gothic vaulting and glazed side walls. They have comparable nave volumes, yet they carry vastly different baggage in terms of scale. Durham produces awe; King's College Chapel uplifts.

Over the centuries, designers for the Roman Catholic Church have used the lessons of scale on emotions well, as witnessed by the buildings and urban setting of the Vatican (Fig. 43).

The United Nations grouping in New York was designed by an international committee of architects that included Oscar Neimeyer and Wallace Harrison. It was one of the few design committees ever that worked together constructively; it produced a fine horse instead of the expected uncoordinated camel. Not having to fill out a zoning envelope, as a commercial building would have required, the architects developed a scheme with elements that fit in scale not only the New York skyline, but also the open space retained on site. The juxtaposition of tall and low elements in the heart of the city is an example of the manipulation of scale to differentiate use from occupancy. The quality of materials and the statements made in the details set a scale fitting for the United Nations.

Scale and Roofed-over Space

There is a difference in perceived scale between similar interior and exterior spaces. If a roof is put over a railroad yard, which is what many early European stations did, essentially, the trains put into the station change the scale. It seems much larger than when seen in the open. In Milan, the covered street crossing Galleria Vittorio Emmanuele II (Fig. 44) is impressive with its enclosed height,

Figure 42. *Cambridge:* King's College Chapel is late Gothic with fine detail and a pleasant scale.

yet the enclosing mercantile buildings are not out of the ordinary in height. Their highly decorated fronts are particularly helpful in establishing the scale of the entire complex.

Verticality and Scale

Extreme height in buildings in the city works when that height is perceived to be in scale with the city itself. Such a building functions as a signpost in the sky. San Gimignano in Italy (Fig. 45) is a prime example of the use of relatively tall buildings to establish geographic position for someone on the ground. Every city these days seems to have some such landmark: communications towers in London and Toronto, the Washington Monument, the Eiffel Tower, the St. Louis Arch, and San Francisco's Transamerica Building. These all are visible down a city canyon or across cornices, providing a sense of location and city scale at the same time.

Tall urban buildings standing by themselves away from the downtown cluster pose a different condition of scale, although acting as landmarks (Fig. 46). Verticality in more modest structures can alter the perceived state of things (Fig. 47).

Figure 43. *Rome:* Bernini's fore-court has a grandeur of scale suitably in keeping with St. Peter's.

Figure 44. *Milan:* The Galleria Vittorio Emmanuele has sufficient height to carry off the deception that this covered arcade is a normal street.

Figure 45. *San Gimignano:* A town whose medieval family fortresses survive as landmarks in the sky.

Figure 46. *London:* Isolated Council Housing apartment towers have the scale of the city and not of the inhabitants.

Figure 48. *Washington, D.C.:* The romantic turrets of the Smithsonian allow it to hold up against the monumental scale of the Mall.

Figure 47. *Fairfax County, Va.:* The Author's Pohick Library uses mechanical towers to expand the scale and extend the reach of a one-story building.

Individual Places and Their Way of Affecting Scale

Traveling from one culture to another is a great teaching tool, particularly if the traveler becomes aware of scale differences between cultures. Illustrative of the different aspects of scale found in different locations are the following places:

1. Williamsburg, Va. This city is a re-creation/restoration of a pedestrian society, where excellent building detail was important to the population as it walked by, aware of every aspect of the buildings.

2. Washington, D.C. Washington is a horizontal city by law, full of parks and tree-lined streets, where urban scale is a local occurrence. Little of the downtown has any scale at all, with the office buildings all set flush with the property line and cut off at the height limit. The Mall is purposely gigantic in scale as a classical statement of grandeur (Fig. 48).

3. Boston, Mass. Before World War II, the Custom House Tower was the biggest sentinel around. It has now been swallowed up in new construction on a different scale. The John Hancock Building replaces the Customs

House as scale giver. Despite the big new buildings, Boston as seen from Cambridge is still a small-scale urban entity, as the riverfront is reasonably the same as before, dominated by brick townhouse backs.

4. Nantucket and Edgartown, Mass. These former nineteenth-century whaling towns were passed by in the Victorian industrial period and so demonstrate an authentic scale prevalent before steel, concrete, and automobiles. The pedestrian's world and people-scaled buildings predominate (Fig. 49).

5. Chicago, Ill. In contrast to New York City, which seems to hem one in, Chicago gives the feeling that the prairie is just a few blocks away down any side street. Chicago's canyons are incomplete; small buildings seen next to big buildings do not appear out of place. In New York, the three-story building looks forlorn. One thing these two giant cities have in common is that their skylines do not peak, as in other cities, with but a few tall buildings. That factor sets a unique scale when seen from out of town.

6. Savannah, Ga. Here is a city in scale with carriages rather than pedestrians. Its many parklike squares, stemming from Oglethorpe's initial eighteenth-century city plan, imply a faster pace than walking and a different scale of things. Three and four stories seem just fine in Savannah, whereas they are noticeably large in Edgartown.

7. Tallahassee, Fla. This growing capital city is losing its spreading live oak trees to progress and changing its scale in the process. The new skyscraper state capitol provides a signpost in the sky, but it also pokes a hole in the small town fabric and the scale of the city that surrounds it.

8. Lake Wales, Fla. Lake Wales is a typical country town that has upgraded its retail streetscapes with planting and street furniture, one-way streets, parking pull-

Figure 49. *Nantucket:* Main Street scaled to the pedestrian, with cobblestone paving and picket fences.

ins, new pavements of interest, and a pedestrian atmosphere. Not only is the place attractive, competing well with the "strip," but the scale of the town has changed as detail has become more important.

9. New Orleans, La. This city has a split personality as far as scale is concerned. The Vieux Carre is pedestrian scaled. Market Street is scaled for cars and intense business activity. The riverfront contends with the wide space of the Mississippi.

10. San Francisco, Calif. This is a place where hills have an effect on scale. The Coit Tower on one hilltop anchors an entire quadrant of the city into a residential scale. The Transamerica Building, by its unique shape, anchors the downtown. The suspension bridges give scale and definition to the city's shoreline. On the ground, it still feels like a large small town. The hills prevent that sense of endless metropolis (Fig. 50), and the bay shrinks all buildings that relate to the water.

Figure 50. *San Francisco:* The hills of the city shorten the apparent scale by limiting vistas.

11. Sienna, Italy. The piazza in the center of this essentially medieval city is one of a kind. It is treeless, sloping, paved, completely encircled, and open spaced (Fig. 51). The enclosing buildings are faceless except for the Palazzo Publico on the low side of the piazza. Attached to this town hall is a magnificent campanile, tall enough to dominate the open space before it. Bollards keep cars out of the infield. Pigeons are the main occupants of the space. At the time of the city's famed festival, the piazza is alive. Empty, it still works as an urban space, and that is because it is the perfect foil for the campanile, with which it is in scale.

Figure 51. *Sienna:* This treeless plaza is unique in that it sets off a secular public building rather than a church.

12. Pisa, Italy: Duomo, Baptistry, and the Leaning Tower. These are three lumps on a grassy tray. Being there is like walking around three models on a table. The observer is aware of the objects, but not the space between or around, as there is nothing to add scale except the three lumps themselves. There is plenty of surface detail, but the context seems to take scale away from people and give it to the buildings.

13. Venice, Italy. The Piazza San Marco has nearly the same elements as the piazza in Sienna, but feels vastly different. Its scale relates more to the flanking buildings than to its campanile. That is because of the way the space wraps around the campanile and opens up to the water, taking away some of the attention the tower commands on the ground.

14. Bergamo, Italy. The old city has a small but delightful piazza (Fig. 52), which is a space in full balance. Its elements are intricately interwoven and in scale one to another. As a public outdoor space, in scale with people, there is none to match it. Cars cross one side, but are kept out of the main space, thereby avoiding their presence as a scale giver.

15. Chichén-Itzá, Mexico. This is not so much an urban space these days (it used to be a Mayan city) as a place to experience a different sort of scale, one based on a combination of imposing building masses and the intervening distances of size. They work in harmony here. Were the buildings smaller, they would not relate. Were they closer together, they would crowd each other. Scale here relates to both space and buildings (Fig. 53).

16. Dinkelsbuhl, Federal Republic of Germany. This is a walled medieval town whose scale is influenced as much by history as by bricks and mortar. It is a pedestrian town,

Figure 52. *Bergamo:* Exquisite small piazza where everything is in perfect scale.

but one with a perimeter defense wall containing spaced stone towers. These are visible from every street and in all directions. Everything in town is in scale with those towers, and not the inhabitants. It is impossible to avoid the sense of enclosure.

17. Paris, France. The mammoth scale of public Paris is a legend. The Arc de Triomphe (Fig. 54) is in scale with the Champs Élysées and the Tuileries, thanks to the ego and drive of Prefect Haussmann. But they are all way past the point of relating to people. The Arc de Triomphe is one of the most deceptive things ever built. From a distance, it might appear to be no bigger than the Arch of Titus in Rome, four of which, stacked, could fit under the Paris arch.

Figure 53. *Chichén-Itzá:* Here, space and structure meet in scale.

Figure 54. *Paris:* The Arc de Triomphe and the Place d'Étoile are consistent with the royal scale of a Napoleon.

Figure 55. *Arcos de la Frontera:* An open space so scarce that tag substitutes for football and porches for playing fields.

The international journey through examples of scale just completed by no means exhausts the subject. Everyone will have, at one time or another, sensed that the urban context of the moment was just right or violently out of kilter, and scale probably has much to do with the feeling. It becomes a game to determine what, in a particular context, drives the scale, what is correct, and what is out of scale (Fig. 57). The rules are what one makes them.

18. Arcos de la Frontera, Spain. This is an ancient town crammed onto the top of a high butte, where the ground space is precious and buildings crowd each other. The visitor drives underneath the church buttresses to reach the town beyond. In this context, even a church porch becomes a playground (Fig. 55). Yet seen from afar, the buildings become inconsequential in comparison to the sheer cliffs on which the town rests.

19. Chester, United Kingdom. This place is an essay in half-timber construction (Fig. 56). The scale of the old town is established by the size of the patterns of tarred black timbers and white plaster infill, seen everywhere. One of these buildings, placed by itself in another context, would appear to be out of scale with itself, but in Chester, many variations of the same theme, side by side, all blend into a fit composition.

20. Athens, Greece. This city impresses with a hustle and bustle narrow street network, all clogged, with small-scale commerce spilling out of the shops. In the Plaka, there is no sense of a city with an ordered street system or public transportation network. To find order, and scale, one only has to raise one's eyes to the ever-present mass of the Acropolis. It gives stability and scale to the entire city, both physically and historically.

Figure 56. *Chester:* The half-timber capital of the world and very much in scale with itself.

Figure 57. *Capri:* Here, scale is what the viewer wishes it to be: vistas are endless, vantage points grand, and the water so transparent that the bottom of the sea is the limit of vision.

See also PLANNED COMMUNITIES; URBAN DESIGN—CREATION OF LIVABLE CITIES

EASON CROSS, JR., FAIA
Alexandria, Virginia

URBAN DESIGN: THE CREATION OF LIVABLE CITIES

The basic principle of urban design is disarmingly simple—the best city is that which provides the best experience of living. For the most part, it is proposed that those cities have proven most agreeable that are the most expressive of and responsive to their time, place, and culture; that are functional; that afford convenience; and that are rational and complete.

THE EXPRESSIVE CITY

It has long been recognized that to understand and appreciate any work of art one must first develop empathy for the time of its creation, the place, the cultural background, the materials and techniques available, the nature of the artist, and what he or she was trying to accomplish. So it is with all works of design—the fine arts and crafts, architecture, engineering, landscape architecture, and the plan layout of cities.

Time

The time of a city's creation, or being, has much to do with its nature. Pittsburgh, for example, was founded at the time of George Washington's explorations in the mid-1770s as a strategic fort at the confluence of two rivers and head of the Ohio (Fig. 1). Its plan layout was an eloquent statement of its purpose. One hundred years later, defense had become secondary to developing trade and river transportation. Accordingly, the walls of the fort were dismantled and new patterns of growth were formed along the rivers' edges and transmountain approach roads. With the materials at hand through mining and by barge, Pitts-

Figure 1. Fort Pitt at the Point.

Figure 2. Pittsburgh, Pa., "Hell with the lid off." Courtesy of the Carnegie Library.

burgh was soon to become a center for glass, iron, and steel manufacturing, a "hell-with-the-lid-off" city at the time of James Parton's visit in the 1860s (1) (Fig. 2). The transition from a manufacturing to business office center took another 100 years (Fig. 3). The next century will, no doubt, bring an equal transformation in response to changing needs and opportunities.

Place

A city's location is telling. Its position in relation to neighboring peoples may spell the difference between war, relative peace, isolated tranquility, poverty, or wealth. Proximity to routes of land or water transportation—to harbor, forest, agricultural lands, or minerals—has much to do with its character.

Such topographic features as hills (Rome), mountains (Darjeeling), prairie (Chicago), rivers (New Orleans), or lakes (Milwaukee) leave their indelible marks. Climate is also a function of place. Relative temperatures, precipitation, fog, frost, ice, and snow have direct effects on sensitive plan layout, as well as on architecture. The threat of a flood, earthquake, hurricane, or tornado is an obvious design consideration. Even such seemingly subtle factors as light quality and intensity, the direction of breezes, vegetative cover, and local coloration must be taken into account.

Subsurface conditions of place should not be ignored. Geologic structure and bearing may make the difference between a Venice and a Mont Saint Michel. Not as well understood are the tenets of geomancy—the tracing of subterranean lines of force and up-wellings of energy that were key, for example, to the location of prehistoric Stonehenge, the Cathedral of Chartres, and the plan orientation of ancient Kyoto. Often a glance is enough to reveal the design implications of place (Fig. 4).

Culture

Each culture throughout history has shaped its cities to meet not only its physical needs, but also to express the beliefs and ideals of its leaders. There have been, and are, restrictive taboos, demanding religious rites, and immutable inborn preferences and traditions. These beliefs affect such matters as favored locations, plan organization, abstract forms, and symbolism.

The distinctive mind-set of various ethnic groups and the effect on habitations and urban form have been de-

Figure 3. Pittsburgh in progress. Pittsburgh's evolution from fort to forge to present regional office center has spanned less than three centuries. Courtesy of the Carnegie Library.

Figure 4. "Falling Water," Pennsylvania. An integral part of the rocky woodland site and streaming waterfall, this expressive residence was designed by architect Frank Lloyd Wright—genius of place.

scribed (2). For example, traditionally the Egyptians have been imbued with a compulsive religious drive to extend body and mind as far as possible along a sacred processional line, which accounts for their axial ceremonial avenues and the symmetrical plan arrangement of their temples and homes.

The democratic Greeks have cherished their privacy and individual freedom. Their homes, entered by unpretentious doorways along narrow winding streets, open on private domains for family living. With lives attuned to the pantheon of their gods—Zeus, Apollo, Aphrodite, etc—their temples have been given positions of prominence, to be viewed from a variety of approaches. The Greek agora, or marketplace, temple grounds, towns, and cities are freely disposed. Delight is taken in sequential progression and revealment, as in the ascent to the Acropolis of Athens.

The medieval cultures of Europe produced compact walled and moated city–towns surrounded by open fields and forest. No precious measure of space was wasted in these bustling, utilitarian warrens. Yet each was unique in character as may be attested by visits to such vestigial cities as Amsterdam, Cologne, Geneva, Copenhagen, and Helsinki.

With the European Renaissance, free plan organization gave way to rigid geometry. Villas, palace grounds, and cities were designed to express the imperious dominance of the rulers of church and state. The powerful axis and cross-axis usurped the natural landscape and produced vast stretches of sterile nothingness, for no purpose but to impress. Versailles, the lavish pleasure ground of Louis XIV, the "Sun God," is but one example. The axial plan form, bilateral symmetry, and "wedding cake" architecture were to be adopted by the Western world as the ideal in urban and building design. Many believe that these architectural features have left their imprint on far too many U.S. cities (Figs. 5 and 6).

On the other hand, the Oriental cities of the Taoist, Zen–Bhuddist cultures have revered and deified nature. Homes, temple grounds, and cities have been fitted to the natural topographic forms and features with infinite care. Streets are meandering, tracing the ridges, valleys, and receptive cross-slopes. Rocks, streams, ponds, and groves are preserved to provide a setting of often breathtaking beauty. Chinese and Japanese planning and city design has been axial only in those rare instances where the Imperial will was to be made manifest, as in Peking's Temple of Heaven, or the Forbidden City. Elsewhere, for long centuries, delightful asymmetry and refreshing natural beauty have for the most part prevailed. The new burgeoning Western-style cities of China and Japan, however, show little regard for natural features—or for clean air, clear water, or sunlight. Shops, factories, homes, and apartments are crowded haunch to haunch along traffic-laden streets amid unprecedented pollution.

The traditional Moslem cities, with their Mecca orientation, their symbolic domes and spires, their bazaars and narrow shaded streets, the Scandinavian forest towns, the Spanish courtyard cities, and the African kraal–city compounds of a herder way of life, all have deep underlying reasons for being what they are and what they will largely continue to be.

These expressions of time, place, and culture are observable phenomena. Such design criteria must be understood and applied if the city, or any component thereof, is to succeed as a functioning unit.

Materials and Techniques

The history of architecture and city building can be traced progressively through the application of new materials and technical advancement. The wooden post and beam of primitive cultures found full expression in the stone columns and lintels of the Egyptian temple and in the segmented marble columns and architrave of the Parthenon. These elements epitomized the structural capabilities of their times.

It was with the corbeled arch of the Lion Gate in Mycenae (3) that architectural form broke through the limitations of the supported horizontal beam and began a transition that led to the Roman arch and then to the soaring Gothic arch (Fig. 7). Each new master cathedral designer of Gothic times introduced improved principles of construction, from the vaulted ceiling, to the clerestory, to the flying buttress.

In ecclesiastic and other structures, concrete and steel in their many variations opened new horizons. In the use of concrete, for example, the introduction of reinforcing, then spray application and prestressing were to extend the possibilities. In wood construction, new glues and preservatives, plywood, veneers, lamination, and innovative fastenings were developed. In metal technology, the framing of riveted steel members was followed by the introduction of welding, improved alloys, extruded shapes, the curtain wall, and the geodesic dome. Glass and plastics have undergone a similar development in manufacture and application.

Concurrently, in the field of transportation, recent decades have seen the evolution of vehicles from the wagon to the automobile, airplane, and interplanetary spacecraft. At the urban scale the changes include the parkway, the

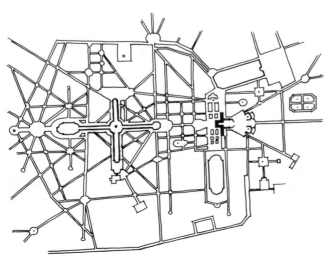

Figure 5. Plan of the Palace and Gardens of Versailles.

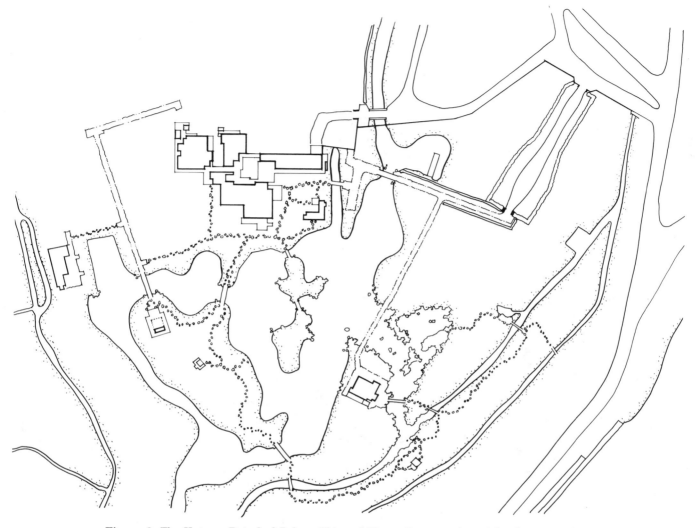

Figure 6. The Katsura Detached Palace. This and Figure 5 are two imperial palace grounds. These reveal not only the differing approaches to land planning, but also the philosophic orientation of the two cultures represented.

freeway, tiered parking decks, the subway, the skyway, and the whole range of rapid-transit innovations. Energy production and transmission too have undergone an exciting evolution in new types of fuel, new sources, new means and methods of distribution, and in the control of attending pollution.

Planning techniques have followed suit and point the way to new concepts and patterns of urban and suburban living. The comprehensive planning of city and region now embraces emerging ideas of zoning, growth control, environmental protection, and resource management. Each new material, technological advance, or design approach is soon applied to the improvement of the built environment. The challenge of each designer is to add by his or her lifetime work some significant contribution to the process.

The Designer

Historically, most cities of the world "just grew." Founded by chance at some amenable site, route crossing, or strate-gic location, they grew by agglomeration, first a cluster of shelters near a water source, then the connective paths that would soon become streets. Perhaps in time, a gated wall and fortification would arise. The siting of shops, marketplace, and all else would respond to immediate needs and conditions. Growth sometimes came by expansion of the town limits, but more often by compaction within the constricting walls—a grinding together by sheer force of urban dynamics.

It could be assumed that growth would be more efficient and life more pleasant if development were to follow a well-thought-out plan. It has been attempted by priests, astrologers, rulers, councils, and governments or governmental agencies and those in their employ. Currently in the United States, almost every governmental jurisdiction has its planning commission and department and has had them since the 1930s. This gives evidence that comprehensive planning is now considered to be a feasible and rewarding endeavor. In today's revved-up, burgeoning society it is considered to be essential.

As far as can be determined, Miletus, an ancient port

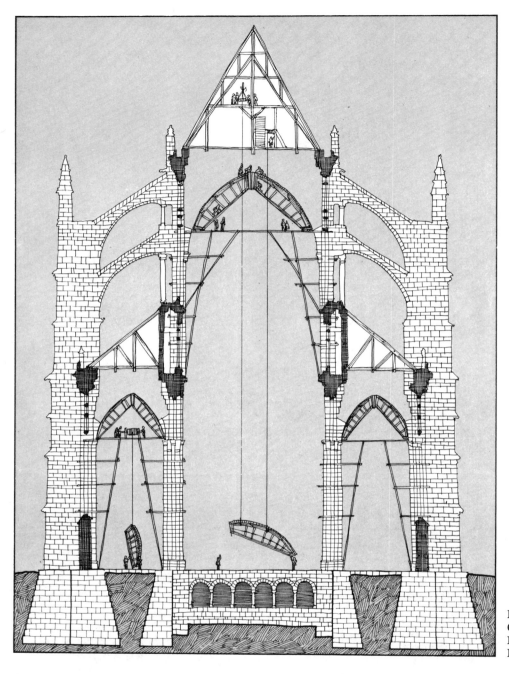

Figure 7. Cathedral drawing (4). Copyright 1973 by David Macaulay. Reprinted by permission of Houghton Mifflin Company.

on the coast of Asia Minor, was the first planned city. Its lucid outlines can still be seen, carved or worn into the underlying rock. At the base of a towering cliff is nestled one of the loveliest amphitheaters of the world. Hippodamos, the designer of Miletus, could not have foreseen, nor would have believed possible, the folly that was to spell the demise of this thriving harbor town. Thoughtlessly, the forest cover of the up-river headlands and watershed was cleared for lumber and farming, causing the whole of the topsoil mantle to be washed down on Miletus and out to the sea—leaving the city stranded miles from shipping lanes and overwhelmed by a swampy delta.

Since that time, many cities around the world have been planned, their diagrams preserved in libraries. Some

designs are no more than geometric doodles, but others give evidence of astute and inspired thinking. The outlines of many of these cities can still be seen *in situ* centuries later, giving structure to the present city form.

In most cases it can only be speculated as to the planners' goals. Kublai Khan, however, in setting out to create his great capital city of Cambaluc (later Peking) set down his goals and objectives. He called his scholar–advisers together, consulted with them, and described every aspect of the city's plan and construction—walls, gate towers, moats, reservoirs, streets, military installations, civic structures, temples, and marketplaces. As an example of the lofty thinking of this early planning team, it was decided that there should be no parks in Cambaluc. Rather, the whole of the city would be laid out as one great all-embracing garden–park of wooded hills, lakes, and waterways, with streets and buildings beautifully interspersed.

The goals of urban planning are probably much the same now as they were then, but life, and thus the factors to be considered, has become so complex that effective results can be achieved only by what have come to be called comprehensive planning procedures. These include, as a minimum:

Data gathering and recording.

Program development.

Exploratory studies.

Comparative analysis of the plan alternatives.

Testing and amelioration of projected environmental impacts.

Public hearings and response.

Adoption of a flexible conceptual plan and implementing guidelines.

The factors that need to be considered for urban planning will vary from time to time and place to place as conditions and needs differ. As a common denominator of most worthy design efforts, however, it is fair to surmise that all set out to maximize the possibilities and to provide the best possible living experience for present and future citizens.

THE FUNCTIONAL CITY

Cities come into being in response to human needs. They are judged according to the degree to which these needs are satisfied. In general terms, the human requirements are those of protection; shelter; food, air, and water; a healthful environment; gainful employment; trade; social intercourse; and some form of governance.

Protection

Throughout history, people have banded together for their mutual protection and safety. The first cities were no doubt little more than armed camps. The site chosen would be that which was most defensible, which provided water for daily use and siege, and which afforded materials for building the stockade or walls.

Defense in present times has assumed new forms and dimensions. The threat of nuclear attack would logically indicate the need for dispersed activity centers; low, stable building forms; extensive underground installations; and rapid point-to-point transport and transit. The consequences of warfare, however, have now become so utterly devastating that defense at the city level in fact seems almost futile. It has little apparent effect on urban design save in consideration of immediate shelter and ease of evacuation.

Protection also includes public safety from accident and crime. There is new emphasis on safer trafficways, pollution control, the elimination of slums, and the creation of a more salutary living environment.

Shelter

With cities soon to be the habitation of over 75% of the U.S. population, the need for improved shelter is evident. Yet in growing cities, housing is generally inadequate, archaic, and unaffordable. Clearly, new concepts of housing and community living are an unmet challenge of contemporary urban design. True modular construction, the application of innovative building materials, advanced techniques of fabrication, and the design of more complete and self-sufficient community groupings have yet to come into their own.

Food, Air, and Water

Historically, food for the cities was produced in surrounding farm plots, orchards, and vineyards. With improved means of transportation, preservation, and refrigeration, cities can now import food from around the world. Where possible, however, fresh produce from nearby farm fields and home gardens is clearly desirable. New types of geodesic growing houses, terraced roof gardens, and hydroponics give promise of "garden cities" far surpassing those that Ebenezer Howard envisioned.

The feeding of a city is no mean endeavor. A visit to the stockyards of Chicago, the Fulton Street fish market of New York, or Pittsburgh's produce yards in the early hours of the morning gives an idea of the dimensions of the problem.

With pollution control now taking effect, clean air for pleasurable breathing and healthful living seems again a reasonable possibility. Clear water, too—in faucets, aquifers, streams, and lakes—is technically feasible. Soil and water conservation programs, reforestation and afforestation, new approaches to water use, and waste treatment are all having their good effects.

The history of civilization can be traced in the migrations of people in search of potable water and their battles to obtain and secure the rights to an adequate supply. In the water-abundant United States, where the drawdown of subsurface aquifers is finally being noted, "enough" has come to mean all that one could possibly use or squander. In many cultures the family's daily water supply can be carried home in a jar on the head. Wasteful consumption has become so commonplace in the United States that second thoughts are not given to using some 30 gal to bathe or a gallon to brush teeth. It is said that a city's leaking hydrants and faucets could fulfill the essential needs of its inhabitants.

Environment

In viewing the city as a desirable place in which to live, it seems reasonable to equate the term environment with those conditions most conducive to optimum human well-being. These must satisfy not only the physical needs discussed, but also provide the visual, social, cultural, educational, recreational, and inspirational amenities. It is not enough that these be provided; they must also be made readily accessible.

The wonder and delight of Paris is in large part occasioned by the rich and tumultuous mix of people, goods, and amenities, all laced together by intriguing pedestrian walkways and pleasurable rapid transit. Montreal, in the Parisian tradition, and San Francisco, in its own way, also provide such an exhilarating environment for urban living. In these, as in all contemporary cities, there is always room for improvement, such as:

- The provision of an open space framework to separate, envelop, and refresh the various districts.
- More intensive urban activity centers of various types, complete with related housing, restaurants, shops, offices, and supporting services.
- Various means of pleasurable center-to-center interconnection.
- Pollution abatement. Clean air and water, sanitation, and relief from excessive noise, glare, and other forms of stress are fundamental to human well-being.

Gainful Employment

Most people work for a living. They are drawn to the city in search of opportunities to work at those occupations for which they have special aptitude. Urban areas are thus reservoirs of special skills and capabilities. Cities can draw on a whole region, or even worldwide sources, for materials and equipment. They are linked with air, land, and water transport networks for distribution.

In the traditional city–town, home was the workplace; with garden plot or vineyard just beyond the city wall, the family would produce the needed cheese, bread, wine, leather, shoes, or woven fabric, and sell the surplus. As certain products gained popularity the first floor of the dwelling would be converted to shop and the family moved to the rear or to the overhead loft.

With the advent of mechanization and industrialization, the dairies, mills, factories, and industrial plants were centralized, and except for the service trades, the workers were forced to commute or move to the industrial districts or company towns. Today things have changed again in regard to the types of employment, the nature of families, the means of communication and travel, and the ways of living itself.

In contemporary times, the types of skill in demand are as manifold and diverse as the profusion of new products. Families are smaller, less cohesive, more mobile, and multiskilled; members are employed wherever opportunities and aptitudes lead and public transportation will take them. Audiovisual–electronic communication now permits many to work from their homes and live where they will. The choice is usually one of lifestyle and amenity. For the reasons cited, the increasing trend is toward agreeable community living remote from major hubs of employment.

In any production center—from farm to fishery, artist colony, university, research park, or assembly plant— there are certain optimum conditions conducive to successful operation. Such centers are in themselves designed with care to provide the best possible facilities and relationships.

Trade

Commerce and trade are the city's lifeblood. From time immemorial the barter or sale of such commodities as salt, provisions, slaves, cotton, grain, livestock, furs, silk, pearls, and fabricated products has sustained or brought wealth to the cities of the world. Often the tendency is to associate cities with their articles of commerce.

Trade has much to do with city planning. Each center of commercial activity is, ideally, given the location, area, form, and supporting features to make it attractive and efficient. In this regard, the planners of U.S. cities have many lessons to learn.

The department store is an example of the importance of plan layout, routing, display, receiving, storage, delivery, customer comfort, and appeal. Industry can give instruction in the design of efficient systems.

European trade centers demonstrate the desirability of maintaining the integrity of the commercial street, of shops side-by-side on narrow ways without interruption at street level by uses or structures that destroy the continuity or dilute the intensity of the shopping experience. The Near East bazaars and those of the Orient demonstrate the value of compression; of generating excitement; of contributing sights, sounds, and smells; and of great variety and multiplicity of choice.

Most American grid cities, however, have an insensitive plan arrangement, with commercial districts sliced apart by wide trafficways, forced asunder by parking structures or compounds, and interrupted by monolithic banks, apartments, or office towers that blank out whole blocks at the pedestrian level of the shopping street. Some new suburban shopping centers are showing the way. To compete, the downtown must provide bazaarlike trade centers and intensive commercial compounds.

In the majority of U.S. cities, it is possible to find almost anything needed, with enough patience and money for cab fares. However, furnishing a home or even a room—or purchasing a Swedish lamp once seen and admired—can be utterly frustrating, because shops are so widely scattered in happenstance blocks defined by streets laid out for the wagon and buggy.

Social Intercourse

Humans are gregarious. At times they like to be together, to bustle, to jostle—or just to sit and watch as others go streaming by. For many city dwellers and visitors, shopping is the chief form of group interaction. Most people also enjoy meeting together for worship, lectures, concerts, theater, dining, sporting events, and other such group activities. Accordingly, proper cities provide cathedrals, performing arts centers, museums, and stadia as well as great department stores and restaurants. As the cultural and business center of the metropolitan region, the city is expected to provide the superlatives.

The measure of the livable city lies not only in the eminence of its structures, but also in the quality of the spaces that surround them, or are planned in between. Malls, squares, and plazas have universal appeal, especially if they are designed expressively to fulfill their purpose. Beyond these, a city is fortunate if it overlooks a

Figure 8. Toledo, Ohio. The city has rediscovered its waterfront and is assuming new form around river-related spaces. Courtesy of Sasaki Associates, Inc.

dramatic view, like Chattanooga and San Francisco, or is oriented to a waterfront, like San Antonio, Seattle, Chicago, and Toledo (Fig. 8). Perhaps even more fortunate is the city planned around a refreshing open-space system of parks, with interconnecting paths, bikeways, and parkways. There are few examples; however, Milwaukee is one and San Diego is another. All in all it can be said that the quality of life in a city is no better than the quality of its congregating spaces.

Government

All people have found the need for governance to hold them to some code of conduct or to some common cause. Historically, there has proved to be no one type of good city government. But Plato, in his *Republic;* Henry Adams (5); Lincoln Steffens (6), in the chronicles of his muckraking days; and Walter Lippman (7) have given valuable clues. The common elements are essentially as follows:

- Clear authority, derived of might, right of lineage, designation by a superior power, or more fortuitously by the will of the people governed.
- A compelling goal and objectives.
- A dynamic and flexible plan of action.
- Clear and equitable regulations.
- Authority of enforcement, uniformly exercised.
- The respect of the people.
- A sense by all citizens that they have a vote that counts.

No doubt the latter is one of the most important. The vitality of a city wanes when its people no longer believe that what they do or say matters. Conversely, the strength of a city depends on some mechanism by which the governed retain the spirit of individual contribution so directly evident in the old town meeting. This requires leadership integrity, a democratic approach to government, and the delegation of rights and decisions to the city by the state and nation.

Aside from providing for the needs of its people, the functional city must be considered in terms of its productive capacity; to thrive, its revenues must equal or exceed funds expended. In this context, production equates with not only products, materials, goods, and machinery, but with tourism and trade as well. The functioning city will function, not by chance, but because from broad concept to smallest detail it is planned that way.

THE CONVENIENT CITY

A city is composed of ways and places; places where people want to be or go, and ways by which to get there. Each is best planned to accommodate and express its anticipated function.

Places

Every activity has an appropriate kind of place. At a residential scale, for instance, there is the kitchen, dining area, terrace, garden, and child's play space. The homeowner will have opinions about what each kind of place should ideally be. So, too, with urban places such as the shopping mall, office park, civic plaza, and cultural center. The users will have their varied thoughts as to the character and qualities that they believe to be most desirable. These will vary with time, locality, and subjects, but gen-

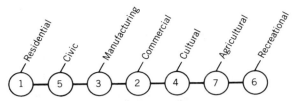

Figure 9. Here the diagrammatic land uses are aligned in a row without regard for interrelationships.

erally those places will be most successful that for the most users seem closest to the ideal. The qualities that affect the users include suitable size, shape, materials, texture, color, light quality, temperature, sound levels, symbolism, and furnishings.

Place designers strive to create not only the best possible place for each type of use, but also the most desirable approaches and the best fit with other use-areas and the surrounding visual and physical environs. It would follow that the merits of a city might well be judged by the quality of its various activity spaces. This is true, provided that accessibility and convenience are also considerations. These have to do with the matter of plan relationships.

Ignoring for the moment the influence of topography, it is possible to develop on a flat hypothetical plane various place-relationship diagrams for comparison. Within an urban region, the major land-use categories are generally considered to be residential, commercial, manufacturing, cultural, civic, recreational, and agricultural. In addressing their plan arrangement, there are many alternative possibilities (Figs. 9–12). If the disposition of the components were to be lineal as in Figures 9 and 10, it is obvious that the arrangement in Figure 10 would be preferable to the one in Figure 9. It would cause less disruption by through movement, would require less travel time, distance, and energy expended, and would provide the average citizen with a more pleasant visual experience in a normal day.

It can also be seen that a circular diagram as illustrated in Figure 11 would be better than the lineal, in that it would provide more direct cross-connection without the disruption of through-district movement. It is possible to move freely from the residential district to the shopping, civic, light industrial, or other areas.

This progression suggests the possibility of further diagrammatic plan improvement. For instance, the business district could be placed at the center surrounded by park,

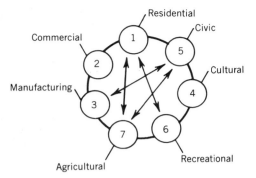

Figure 11. With circular disposition of major land uses, movement from one to another is clearly more efficient than the approaches in Figures 9 and 10.

recreation, and open space lands. Furthermore, the entire urban complex could be embraced by a delimiting matrix of farm fields, forest, or nature preserve. In this case, not only would all users enjoy verdant surroundings, but each area would have ready through-park access to the central business district. Residents could elect to live near workplace or other activity centers of their choice. The introduction of a partially subsurface rapid transit loop would complete the district linkage (Fig. 12).

In even such simple diagrams one can sense the possibilities of new approaches to metropolitan planning. Additional diagrammatic layouts can be conceived, such as the concentric plan, the satellite plan, the lobed plan, or com-

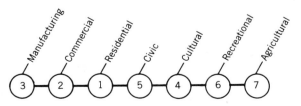

Figure 10. In this linear plan arrangement consideration has been given to creating a more logical sequence of movement from place to place.

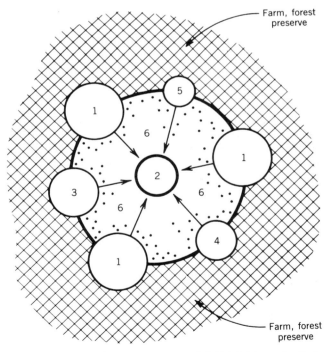

Figure 12. Here the major commercial district is centrally located. Access from the surrounding residential, civic, cultural, and manufacturing districts is direct and agreeable. 1, Residential; 2, Business (CBD); 3, Manufacturing; 4, Cultural; 5, Civic/government; 6, Park/recreation and open space.

binations thereof. If each major activity center were to be planned to include those supporting uses such as restaurants, services, and convenience shopping to meet daily needs, it can be seen that such concepts of place-relationship give promise of more pleasurable city living.

Topography should be a governing factor in the plan layout of a city. The abstract bubble diagrams described have validity only as a means by which to suggest and compare alternative relationships. Selected diagrams may then be arrayed in turn against a scaled map of the dominant topographic features of the city site to determine the feasibility of the superimposed diagrams and the degree of modification required to bring them, if possible, into harmony.

Often it becomes evident that a diagram cannot possibly work in the given terrain and must be discarded. Furthermore, the diagram may fit, but only with undue cost or stress, and the clarity of the plan and power of the landscape are both thereby diminished. At times, however, the exercise produces plan forms that sing in the landscape and sing in harmony. A compatible diagram evokes and dramatizes the full splendor of a superlative landscape setting. Such is the case in such memorable cities as Kyoto, Geneva, and Bogotá.

Urban planners have the opportunity to so diagram the ideal city plan for a given locality more often than it might be supposed. In long-term planning considerations, it is essential to explore and reexplore continually the optimum possibilities and to develop a program of phased transition toward the desirable goal. Once a "best case" conceptual plan has been determined for the region, then the more detailed design process can be initiated for each specific activity center. Here again, it is necessary to beware of the rigid master plan to which all that follows must strictly adhere. The best plan concept for any type of urban complex or subcomplex within it is that which provides a compelling design theme and guidelines, allows room for the exercise of individual choice and freedom of expression, and also provides the flexibility required for adjustment to changing conditions.

Fine use-areas and their developed three-dimensional volumes should be in all ways suited to their purpose. They should be compatible with and interrelate to adjacent structures. They should provide studied interconnection to related interior and exterior spaces. These areas should be responsive to climate, weather, sun, wind, and breeze, and they should be conceived as a contributing unit in the total extensional environment.

Experience has taught that for any urban activity center (urba-center) there are requisite conditions for successful performance. These are

- Demonstrated need; an adequate "critical mass" of potential users within the area to be served.
- Fixed area boundaries, to intensify the activity and preclude urban sprawl.
- A well-balanced mix of primary uses and supporting amenities.
- Separation of pedestrians and vehicles, that each may operate more safely, efficiently, and agreeably.

- Compatible relationships to the environs, to other development, and to the topographic features of the specific site.

Ways

The better ways, like the better places, are those best suited to their purpose. The nature of paths of movement will vary greatly with their type, which may range from the hiking trail to the bikeway, paved pedestrian walk, highway, transit route, canal, shipping lane, or airway. In their location and design, all such routes of passage or conveyance have many features in common. They are unifiers, providing point-to-point interconnection. They are dividers, with a tendency to become district limits or use-area boundaries, and if planned accordingly, this is often desirable. Unfortunately, paths of movement also have a tendency to split otherwise cohesive landscape, economic, or political entities. In the case of major travelways that disrupt natural systems or topographical features such as ridges, ravines, or rivers, costly tunneling or bridging is required.

The more successful routes tend to follow lines of least resistance. These are less disruptive, require less expensive site preparation and construction, and are more economical to operate. As routes of travel, they produce a sense of visual harmony and a resulting sense of pleasure in the user or observer. The abstract quality of a route's alignment is consistent with the desired characteristics of movement. The rate of speed, degree of comfort, viewing interest, and sequence of revealment are all largely determined by the pathway line.

All routes of movement have volumetric characteristics. As lineal spaces, each variable segment along the way is conditioned by size, shape, texture, color, sound, and light quality and by the type and degree of enclosure. In addition, the phenomenon of motion produces an evolving sequence of visual images. This involves variety, change, and progressions—all of which may be pleasurable if suited to the planned travel experience. Without exception, passageways are to be conceived in terms of safe, efficient, convenient, and pleasurable place-to-place travel.

Ascent of movement is attained at the cost of expended energy. Descent induces acceleration and often involves risk. A gently looping pathway, if harmoniously related to the topographic profile, is therefore usually preferred. In general, the milder the grade and the smoother the path or trajectory, the greater the efficiency, comfort, and controlled attainable speed.

The vertical profile as well as the plan or horizontal alignment should be considered. The near-level gradient is more desirable for fuel transmission lines and the transportation of goods because it is more economical in use, but it can often be achieved only at the cost of extensive grading or construction. In such cases, route selection favors the plain or the valley floor. Crossings of all types—streams (bridges), drainageways (culverts), ridges (cuts), valleys (fills or trestles), or other routes (overpass or tunnel)—should be avoided insofar as feasible.

Within an urbanizing region it is the transportation,

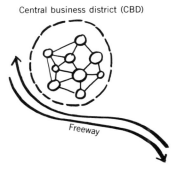

Figure 13. A compact and vital central business district. Within a theoretical central business district (see also Fig. 12), the circles represent major components such as banks, department stores, civic centers, shopping malls, or entertainment complexes. The connecting lines represent paths of circulation. A compact, cohesive center is vibrant and efficient.

transit, and transmission corridors that to a large extent establish the land-use patterns and thus the character of the landscape. In the alignment and three-dimensional design of pathways, therefore, the following considerations have telling significance.

- Freeways and arterial highways should surround rather than penetrate the metropolitan centers. When thoroughfares transect activity centers such as the central business district, the result may be disastrous, splitting the otherwise cohesive area and interposing heavy traffic loadings and frictions (Figs. 13 and 14).
- Metropolitan transportation corridors, combined whenever possible with transit and transmission rights of way, should provide direct interconnection between energy sources, production centers, and distribution terminals.
- Highways should be classified as to type and use—ranging from interstate freeways, to arterial park-

ways, circulation drives, scenic–historic byways, and truckways—and should be designed accordingly.

- Often multilevel, and always grade separated at intersections, highways should move between and around, but never through unified neighborhoods and communities.
- Where people could be affected by the quality of travel, not only should the gradient and surface treatment of the way be considered, but the visual surroundings as well. A moving vehicle is a multipoint viewing station. Much of what is learned about a countryside or metropolitan area is through observation along the traveled way. This leads to the premise that the routes to and through the city should be made as attractive as possible. Unfortunately, this has not always been achieved.
- A highway is a line of dynamic, often lethal, force. As such it should be so located and designed as to minimize hazard. On-grade crossings of high speed trafficways should no longer be condoned. Unlighted, they are extremely hazardous. With signalization and intermittent stop-and-go traffic movements highways are clearly inefficient; each such intersection reduces by half or more the related roadway capacity.
- Lines of transmission and distribution—as of energy, signals, fluids, or gas—are disruptive at best and too often leave ugly scars on the landscape through which they pass. By sensitive route selection, care in design, and consolidation of corridors, their negative impacts can and should be minimized.

The community or city in which the various paths of interconnection have been conceived in harmony with the built and natural landscape and each other is a pleasant place to be. It can be seen that only by astute planning and design can integrated systems of transport and transmission be brought into being (Figs. 15–17).

THE RATIONAL CITY

It was Descartes (9), father of the Age of Reason, who, in the days of chamber pot dumping from the balcony, proposed that there must be a better means of sewage dis-

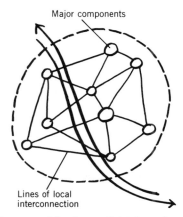

Figure 14. The central business district weakened, split, and dispersed. Dispersion of the elements, as by extensive on-grade parking areas or major thoroughfares, reduces the intensity and thus the advantage of being "downtown."

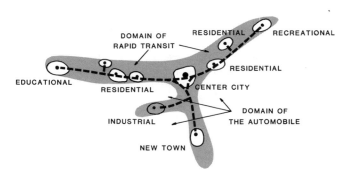

Figure 15. Transitways. Direct internal linkage of urban activity centers will be provided by rapid transit (rail, busway, and/or trams).

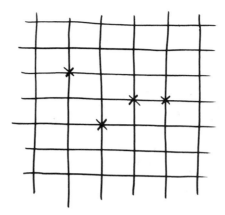

Figure 16. Highways. External access to the urban centers and supporting region will be provided by urban parkways (scenic freeways, without trucks). Transportation vehicles will move on their own independent routes.

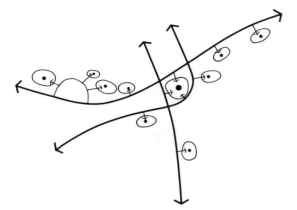

Figure 18. The conventional grid street pattern. Every intersection is a point of friction and potential accident.

posal. He was further convinced that there must be a more reasonable way of urban living than that which he was experiencing. He deplored the prevailing unquestioning willingness to accept the existing condition and set about to reexamine all aspects of life in his city and the city itself. He reaffirmed the belief of Hippodamus that a city with a well-conceived plan should be better in many ways than one resulting from haphazard growth.

It is possible that Descartes would approve of the fact that the need for comprehensive planning has finally been recognized in the United States, but he would no doubt find many accepted urban phenomena open to serious question. Among these are the grid plan block layout, the fronting of dwellings on trafficways, the omnipresent intrusion of vehicles, unlimited expansion, single-use zoning, pollution, and the lack of coherent city form.

The Grid

The purpose of a city layout in rectangles and squares is unclear. It is hardly for the sake of vehicular traffic move-

ment, for there is no less efficient or more-dangerous street or highway pattern than one imposing an intersection some 10 to 12 times in each mile. It is not for the convenience of the pedestrian, because children, adults, and the elderly must thereby negotiate hazardous trafficway crossings at the corner of every block. There is a better way (Figs. 18 and 19).

The Superblock. By simply doubling or trebling the length of each block, one-half to two-thirds of the intersections would be thereby eliminated, as would be the cost of building and maintaining the deleted roadways. It has been proven that automobile passage through two T-intersections can be accomplished with about one-eighth the number of fatalities, over the years, resulting from a full

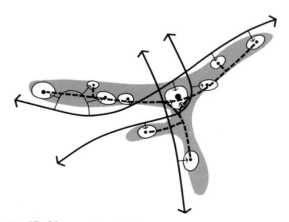

Figure 17. Movement and interconnection. The urbanizing regions of the future will be structured by integrated transit and transportation systems.

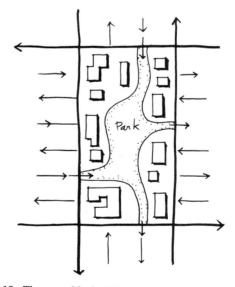

Figure 19. The superblock. Efficiency of movement is increased, hazard is decreased, and a parklike building setting is provided. By proven redevelopment techniques, large areas of constricted grid cities can be freed and revitalized. Such superblocks can well be freeform, and expanded to include an entire community or business office campus.

two-way crossing. This being so, it is evident that in residential areas where high speed through traffic is to be avoided, the superblock with alternating *T*s is obviously superior.

Parkway and Cul-de-sac. By all reason, the circulation roads within a city should be designed as moderate speed parkways with no facing homes or driveway entry cuts. Local cul-de-sac or loop residential streets should branch off at the sides no closer than 250 ft on center, whereby traffic circulation would be freer and more pleasant. Homes would face on quiet, low speed, undulating neighborhood frontage drives.

Arterial Beltway. Logically, higher speed roadways for transit or personal vehicles would be on wider parkways, without facing structures and with controlled access side streets no closer than 660 ft center to center. Such beltways would not penetrate the central business district or other activity centers, but would serve instead as open space separators and boundaries for the districts served.

Building Frontage

Most homes in most cities face directly on busy trafficways, exposed to the noise, fumes and danger. This is because most cities have ordinances requiring that residential properties be so platted as to front on public streets. The concepts of PUD (Planned Unit Development) and PCD (Planned Community Development) are relatively new. By PUD or PCD land-planning procedures, a local government may waive, for a sizable parcel, all or most development regulations, except density, coverage, and type of use, and review the evolving plans solely on the basis of projected performance. Dwellings can face on private motor courts or inward to pedestrian courtyards, gardens, or open park space. Few who have lived in such pleasant surroundings would opt for street living again. Not only residential structures but commercial, office, and institutional buildings as well can be clustered around such traffic-free courts, malls, or parklike campus meadows in neighborhoods planned to the side, and not astride, of arterial trafficways (Fig. 20).

Vehicular Intrusion

In many new towns and redevelopment areas, the automobile has been found to be undesirable and unnecessary. Acknowledging that the U.S. family is lost without its sets of "wheels," it is proposed that soon it will no longer be feasible to commute by personal automobiles from home to shop or office. With some 25–40% of downtown acreage now devoted to street right of way and parking, the essential intensity and ready interaction is sacrificed to the motorcar and its storage. Clearly, the more successful urban centers of the future will be relatively traffic-free, with automobiles garaged in subsurface levels or in peripheral compounds.

Vertical and horizontal circulation within such urban activity nodes will be provided by a whole new array of minitransit systems and people movers. The family auto-

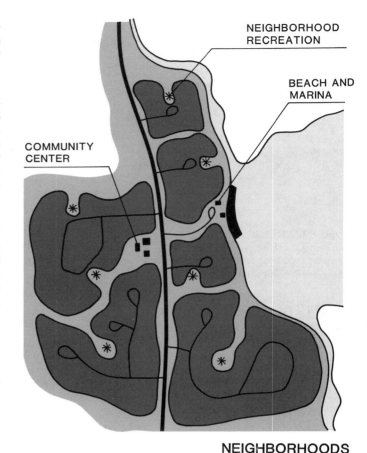

NEIGHBORHOODS

Figure 20. Neighborhoods. In the planning or replanning of cities, the reshaping of buffered neighborhoods, free from through traffic, is to be encouraged. Courtesy of Arvida Development Corporation.

mobiles will be restricted to intercity, rather than intracity, travel. In the hastening of this trend, prohibitive municipal parking fees, new types of rapid transit, park and ride, and compact transit-related communities will be compelling incentives.

Permissive Spread and Scatteration

Traditionally, the uncontrolled growth of U.S. towns and cities has been centrifugal, a spreading outward away from the obsolescence, decay, and high tax assessments of the core. With little deterrent and obvious benefits, the movement, which is slow at first, soon accelerates, then fairly explodes. With the coming of better roads and transportation it responds with leaps to the suburban fringes, then out into the open countryside. Each such outpost generates demands for more roads and services, which in turn disrupts the rural landscape, raises land values, and taxes the farmers off their farms.

Such unplanned and permissive scatteration has become so damaging a practice that numerous measures to preclude and correct it are now being studied and applied. They include regional-planning procedures, coastal protection, open space conservation, public land acquisition, resource management programs, scenic easements, protective taxation, and phased "contour" zoning.

A positive example of the benefits of controlled growth can be seen in the European countryside where in the main the old walled city limits have been assiduously maintained. Without the option of outward expansion, urban land values are sustained, vacant properties and obsolescence are virtually unknown, and urban living is animated. Beyond the town and city limits, farm fields, orchards, vineyards, and forest provide productive and refreshing surroundings.

Pollution

Pollution control may finally be coming into its own, no doubt because conditions have "bottomed out." The problem has become so shameful and repugnant that the public outcry has reached the ears of legislators. Pollution in any form will soon be recognized as a crime against society. When the facts are in, the case for clean water and air, freedom from debilitating noise and glare, and a healthful, attractive living environment will become irrefutably clear.

Urban Form

The U.S. city is amorphous, too often a shapeless conglomeration of rigid ways and static building blocks. It lacks recognizable and rational structure and has no coherent plan organization. At present, there seems to exist no clear concept of what a city should be. What is desired in these rapidly changing times is a redefinition of "city." Each city for its time, place, and people, must find its own direction. For only with clear and motivating goals can the ideal be visualized and given expressive form.

Problems

In the rational city those responsible should address the gamut of potential problems. Some of these problems seem as incidental as pests, rodents, strays, and impolite pets, others as remote as potential subsidence, landslides, earthquakes, or floods, any one of which can assume catastrophic proportions should they occur. Geologic instability is often related to sustained fresh water drawdown and the depletion of the underlying aquifers. This can result in soil shrinkage and, in coastal areas, salt water intrusion. Equally as drastic can be the collapse of abandoned shoring or columns in subsurface mine workings. Those who guide a city's growth and construction must proceed in full awareness of all such hazardous conditions. In this age of dawning computer technology the essential data, obtained over the years from many sources, can be readily stored and graphically arrayed until the essential base maps are up-to-date and complete.

Pollution, in its many aspects, can be insidious. Dirt, refuse, filth, obsolescence, and visual blight are easily detected and are eliminated by aggressive cleanup campaigns. Not so easily remedied is the progressive contamination of soils by airborne and waterborne chemicals, which in time reach levels of saturation that destroy vegetation and endanger human health. Stagnant air and in-

versions have become common plagues in most metropolitan regions. Recently, the added threat of acid rain has come to have even more alarming implications. Contaminated soils and earth fills polluted with toxic wastes can leach their poisons into underground reservoirs for miles around and for centuries to come.

In the teeming cities, a far more obvious problem is the breakdown of transportation and utility systems. Peak-hour traffic loadings and delays can be as vexing as peak-hour shortages and the soaring costs of energy and water. In the unconcerned, and thus irrational, city can be found the whole range of physical woes and abuses. Responsible planning and perceptive design are the only means by which chaos can be averted and a more agreeable way of city life created and maintained.

Opportunities

With comprehensive planning, the rational city could realize possibilities far beyond present dreaming. Plans should start with the preservation and protection of the existing natural features. Water resource management should at last be fundamental to all land planning and development (Figs. 21 and 22).

Streams, wetlands, water bodies, dominant topographic conformations, and areas of superior vegetative cover should be left intact as elements of an interrelated open space park preserve. The built environment should be planned to and around them, bringing people and nature into the best possible relationships. Unstable bearing

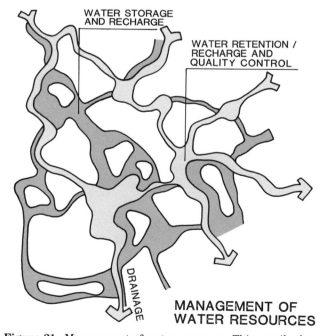

Figure 21. Management of water resources. This entails those procedures required to assure that the flow or discharge of water from a developed area into the receiving streams, basins, or aquifers is of quantity and quality equal to that accepted or withdrawn. Such procedures involve regulation of flows, storage, recycling, detention, recharge, and the preservation or installation of vegetative covers. Courtesy of Arvida Development Corporation.

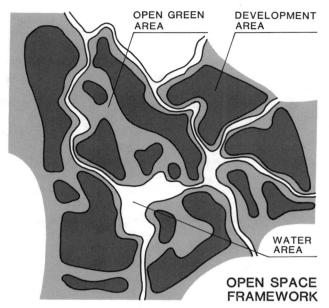

Figure 22. Open space framework. A further beneficial aspect of water management will be the preservation or creation of wetlands and meadows as wildlife habitat and recreation fields. Courtesy of Arvida Development Corporation.

strata and geologic faults should be avoided. Excavation and grading should be controlled by ordinance and the topsoil mantle conserved. Pedestrians, passenger vehicles, and trucks should be given their own separate and conducive pathways of movement. Trafficways, structures, and spaces should be sun, wind, and climate responsive. They should avoid floods, brace against storms, and use the cooling effects of vegetation, water, and channeled breezes.

Community plans should evince knowledge of natural systems and their tolerance. Land uses, densities, and floor area ratios should be so permitted as to impose no significant stresses by overloading. Residential, production, distribution, cultural, and recreation centers should be planned together as closely interrelated synergistic entities, conserving travel time, energy, and land.

Urban centers should be conceived as intensive business, trade, and cultural focal points. They should be created about multilevel transportation–transit nodes as hived pedestrian domains—domed, terraced, and interlaced with refreshing garden plazas and courts. Each such complex should be surrounded by low profile, lower intensity support facilities such as those providing convenience shopping, restaurants, supplies, and services. Beyond should be clustered the urban residential neighborhoods within and around open blue water and green parkland.

The suburban, rural, and outlying wilderness regions should be planned or replanned as a galaxy of towns, villages, communities, cohesive neighborhoods, and camps—each unique to its place, complete and embraced by fields, conservancy lands, lakes, waterways, and forest. The positive values of such a rational approach to land use and urban planning are obvious, and compelling.

THE COMPLETE CITY

A proper city is complete—a functioning organic entity. It can be compared to the human body in that it too is a body—with skeleton, veins, and arteries. It breathes, drinks, feeds, and gives off wastes. It grows, regenerates, and reproduces. It thinks and acts responsively, having mind and spirit. The good city, like a good person, is wholesome, animated, cultivated, and self-assured. It is of exemplary character and admirable mien. Like the human, the city has its *élan vital*—its driving force. It has a need to fulfill many vital functions. For a city to thrive it must be healthy not only physically, but economically, politically, and socially as well.

Physical Attributes

In the urban context, the term "organic" implies that the city, alive, will function and develop its evolving form and character in direct response to prevailing constraints and possibilities. It gives evidence of dynamic equilibrium—of all components working well together and in balance.

Economic

The economic viability of an urban metropolis depends on its ability to produce a surplus of long-term revenues over expenditures. That this is more difficult than it might seem is evinced by the fact that most cities are presently in dire financial straits. There are various reasons for this economic hardship. Some cities have outgrown their initial reason for being and have failed to find another. Some have exhausted their natural resources or are affected by external forces beyond their control. Other cities are slowed to a near standstill by constricted trafficways or outmoded transportation systems, and others have simply rotted away at the core in the wake of successive outward growth rings.

Obsolescence and vacancies breed all forms of urban problems. When a city is no longer healthful or safe, when it fails to provide more advantage than disadvantage, people leave—at least those who can leave, and unfortunately they are usually the productive ones. When contributing citizens move away, the tax yields are diminished, the needs become greater, and the problems exacerbated.

If there is a law of real estate economics it is this: the resident or entrepreneur will pay all possible to obtain a location that provides the most advantages at the least total cost, be it a city, a neighborhood, or a particular property. Advantages include such things as favorable environment, amenities, trade area, visibility, accessibility, and compatibility. Costs may include acquisition, development, rent, utilities, taxes, travel time, frictions, or energy expended.

Most cities fail simply because their present form is no longer suited to contemporary urban life. The old machine has broken down and overhauling is not enough. A new model is needed. Usually such a needed change is achieved only with new leadership and more astute management. There are new techniques and tools to help, such as urban renewal or redevelopment. These have proven highly effective when coupled with knowledgeable planning.

Political

No plan or proposal, however meaningful, can be effectuated except by political decision. The political machine is the mechanism by which communal opinion and public will can be transmuted into action. Political science is the understanding of the means by which this can be achieved. This system can be bad if the politicians are bad, because they are able to exploit the worst elements of a sinking city. Politicians, however, seem to be as good or bad as the electorate would have them, and enlightened voters seek enlightened political leadership. Enlightened leaders are the key to a city's improving status and advancement.

In order to work effectively as a citizen or as a planner–designer within the political framework, it has been found helpful to make several assumptions:

- Elected officials seek reelection, which is usually based on their performance.
- Given the opportunity, they seek to support proposals that are in the public good.
- When constituents question their leaders on any issue, the leaders need to be well informed.

It is therefore incumbent on any group or individual seeking favorable political action to make sure from the start that the facts and merits of the proposal are clear to those who are to make intelligent comments and decisions. Astute political leaders are keenly aware of the needs and opinions of their constituents. It is wise to seek the insight, guidance, and support of all possible contributors and build their ideas into the proposals to be presented.

The public agency is the working arm of government. In every department, the director and staff can bring to bear invaluable experience. They too have the need to be kept informed and are usually glad to contribute background information and advice throughout the planning process. In sum, politically, the successful plan is usually the one of which the decision makers and their advisers have been kept informed and to which they have made some positive contribution.

Social

The city can be compared to a hive of bees. Each type of bee—worker, soldier, drone, and queen—has its role, as does each individual. Without the bees and their activities, the hive has no meaning. The city too is meaningless except as a manifestation of the life of the people within it.

As an expression of bee society, the hive is an intricate marvel of efficient function. All relationships are well conceived and in balance. Observation of many such hives in nature reveals that without exception they are located near the base of resource—the flowers of orchard, field, or forest—and attuned to the sweep of the sun and play of the wind. The specific site of the hive is equally well considered. The fix in the crevice of a rock or in a hollow

trunk is selected to minimize natural constraints and to make optimum use of all possibilities.

When the colony outgrows the limits of a good working bee society, the hive is not enlarged to unmanageable size, converted to less efficient form, or abandoned. It is kept in use, with meticulous care, and a new bee community and hive is formed at another propitious location.

THE LIVABLE CITY

Looking ahead, it is proposed that most cities of the future will be distinguished by a long-range preservation, conservation, and development plan, with provisions for topographic restoration and reforestation. Their plan diagram and three-dimensional structure will express a more logical disposition of use areas that will intensify the activity centers, ring them with the required supply and service facilities, and provide for the creation of new or redeveloped residential neighborhoods within and around an interconnected open space system of in-city recreation lands, forest, and wildlife preserves. They will be blessed with direct and rapid multimodal transit, transportation interconnection of the urba-centers, and free linkage with their suburban–rural environs and the wilderness beyond (Figs. 23–25).

Cities of the future will conform with enlightened state, regional, and local governmental objectives. They will respond to the "want to be" of the land, preserve the integrity of the surrounding natural and constructed landscape, and conserve the ecological, agricultural, scenic, and historic superlatives. Future cities will impose no

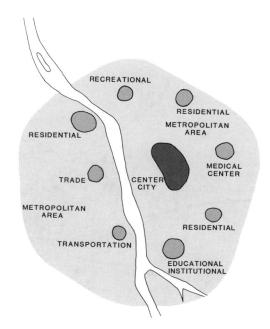

Figure 23. Urba-centers. The more livable cities of the future will be formed or reformed around intensive activity nodes or urba-centers. These will be planned and designed as interconnected satellites of the center city.

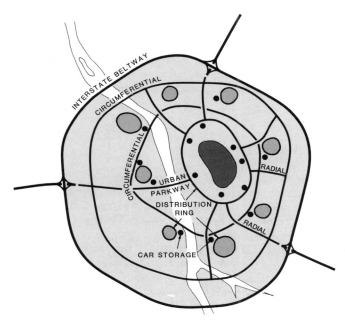

Figure 24. Transportation. The urban highways of the future will provide optimum access and efficient interconnection, with a minimum of disruption.

significant disruption to such natural systems as rivers, streams and drainage ways, fresh water aquifers, plant and animal communities, or the vital food chain. They will so address each topographical area and feature as to discover and reveal its highest qualities. These cities will accommodate and clearly express the functions to be served.

The notable cities of history will continue to be those that, to their users, seem expressive, functional, convenient, rational, and complete. That evasive quality called

beauty is also basic to urban design. The well-designed city must, above all, be beautiful. But, contrary to common understanding, beauty is seldom consciously contrived. It is never an ingredient to be added or is it to be misconstrued as mere decoration or effusive ornamentation. Beauty, the perceived harmonious relationship of all the elements, can only be inherent. It is that magical quality experienced when the total city and each of its components are perceived to be appropriate, in harmony, and in balance.

The ultimate test of urban design, as of all design, is its effect on the lives and experiences of its users. The ultimate city will be, for its time and place, the ultimate human habitation.

BIBLIOGRAPHY

1. J. Parton, "Pittsburgh," *Atlantic Magazine*, p. 21 (1868).
2. O. Spengler, *The Decline of the West,* Alfred A. Knopf, New York, 1962, pp. 100–102.
3. H. Gardner, *Art through the Ages,* 4th ed., Harcourt, Brace & World, New York, 1959, p. 96.
4. D. Macaulay, *Cathedral,* Houghton Mifflin Co., New York, 1973, p. 53.
5. H. Adams, *The Education of Henry Adams,* Vols. 1 and 2, Modern Library, New York, 1931.
6. L. Steffens, *The Autobiography of Lincoln Steffens,* Literary Guild, New York, 1931.
7. W. Lippman, *The Method of Freedom,* Macmillan, New York, 1934.
8. J. O. Simonds, *Earthscape, A Manual of Environmental Planning and Design,* Van Nostrand Reinhold Co., Inc., New York, 1986.
9. R. Descartes, *Discourse on Method,* trans. by P. J. Olscamp, Bobbs-Merrill, Indianapolis, Ind., 1965.

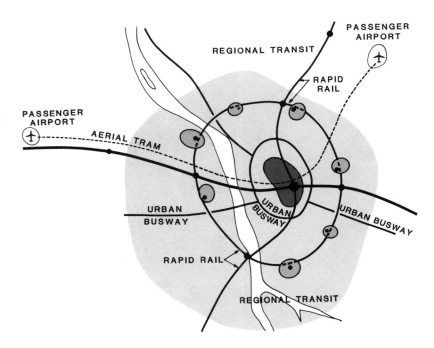

Figure 25. Transit. A system of interrelated transitways will loop freely through the metropolitan region, responding to the topographical features, providing direct access and linkage, and establishing the regional diagram. Modes will include innovative forms of air, rail, busway, subsurface, and waterborne travel.

General References

Refs. 5, 6, 7, 8, and 9 are good general references.

J. Barnett, *An Introduction to Urban Design,* Harper & Row, New York, 1982.

L. Benevolo, *The History of the City,* M.I.T. Press, Cambridge, Mass., 1981.

C. M. Deasy and T. E. Lasswell, *Designing Places for People,* Whitney Library of Design, New York, 1985.

S. Eisner and A. B. Gallion, *The Urban Pattern: City Planning & Design,* 5th ed., Van Nostrand Reinhold Co., Inc., New York, 1985.

A. B. Jacobs, *Looking at Cities,* Harvard University Press, Cambridge, Mass., 1985.

V. M. Lampugnani, *Architecture and City Planning in the Twentieth Century,* Van Nostrand Reinhold Co., Inc., New York, 1985.

L. Mumford, *The Culture of Cities,* Greenwood Press, Westport, Conn., 1981.

J. O. Simonds, *Landscape Architecture, A Manual of Site Planning and Design,* 2nd ed., McGraw-Hill Inc., New York, 1983.

A. W. Spirn, *The Granite Garden, Urban Nature and Human Design,* Basic Books, New York, 1984.

P. D. Spreiregen, *Urban Design, the Architecture of Towns and Cities,* McGraw-Hill Inc., New York, 1965.

A. Sutcliffe, *Towards the Planned City,* St. Martin's Press, New York, 1981.

A. Whittick, ed., *Encyclopedia of Urban Planning,* Krieger, Melbourne, Fla., 1980.

See also PLANNED COMMUNITIES (NEW TOWNS) R/UDAT REGIONAL URBAN DESIGN ASSISTANCE TEAMS; URBAN DESIGN: ARCHITECTURE AT URBAN SCALE

JOHN ORMSBEE SIMONDS, FASLA
The Loft
Pittsburgh, Pennsylvania

URBAN LAND INSTITUTE (ULI)

ULI-the Urban Land Institute is an independent research and educational organization whose members work with other land use professionals to make the best possible use of the land and development resources. ULI's purpose is to foster and encourage high standards of land use planning and development and to advance the public interest through education and research in land use. It is supported by membership dues and revenues from its various programs and grants from its own Urban Land Foundation.

History

ULI was founded in Chicago, Illinois, in 1936 as The National Real Estate Foundation for Practical Research and Education. In 1939, the name was changed to the Urban Land Institute. It became known as ULI; and, in 1969, the name was formally changed to ULI-the Urban Land Institute. Originally headquartered in Chicago, the Institute moved to Washington, D.C., in 1942.

Objectives

Within its broad statement of purpose ULI has the following objectives: to study and give interpretation to trends in land use as they relate to changing economic, environmental, and social needs; to define methods and techniques by which the private and public sectors can efficiently interrelate, effectively function, and successfully participate in the planning and development of the land; to evaluate and report on the policies and procedures of regulatory agencies; to act as a publisher and clearinghouse of educational information about land use; to foster and encourage educational activities and high standards of instruction in various fields of land use planning and development; to conduct educational review and analysis programs with reference to land use; and to maintain a membership representing the entire broad spectrum of private and public interests in land use education and research.

Membership Structure

In 1989, ULI had over 14,000 members and associates. The number of members is limited so as to maintain a balanced representation of backgrounds and skills among developers, professional services, public officials, academics and real estate financiers.

In 1942, the Community Builders Council was the first council formed as a means of organizing such a diversity of member interests. As of 1989, there were 19 councils covering the subjects of urban development/mixed use, commercial and retail, industrial and office park, community, residential, recreational, and small scale development, and the policy areas of national policy, development regulations, and development infrastructure and services.

Research

ULI conducts applied research on all aspects of land use and development. In 1989, $1.9 million was divided among six research program areas: development policy; housing and community development; nonresidential development; real estate finance; development economics and management; and transportation.

Education

In 1989, the education program receives $1.5 million funding which provides continuing education in the form of seminars, workshops, and a real estate development school. It supports programs at the university level with curriculum development, serves as a clearinghouse for teaching case studies, and facilitates faculty interchange. It also develops programs for public education.

Publications

Urban Land magazine which began publication in 1941, is the ULI's principal periodical. Members also receive *Land Use Digest, Inside ULI* and the annual *ULI Development Trends.* In addition, ULI publishes about 15

books each year and has over 100 titles in print. The flagship book series is the Community Builders Handbook Series. *The Project Reference File (PRF)*, which profiles 20 superior development projects each year, began publication in 1971 as a separate subscription service. Video supplements to selected *PRF*s were started in 1988.

Advisory Services

The ULI Panel Advisory Service was started in 1946 and offers public and private sponsors', the benefits of its members' experience help to solve a wide range of development problems. By 1988, ULI had conducted 165 assignments for a variety of clients ranging from private developers to units of government.

BIBLIOGRAPHY

General References

The following References can be obtained from ULI-the Urban Land Institute, Community Builders Handbook Series, Washington, D.C.

Business and Industrial Park Development Handbook, 1988.
Downtown Development Handbook, 1980.
Infrastructure Development, supplement series, 1989.
Mixed-Use Development Handbook, 1987.
Office Development Handbook, 1982.
Recreational Development Handbook, 1981.
Residential Development Handbook, 1980, 2nd ed., 1989.
Shopping Center Development Handbook, 2nd ed., 1985.
Working with the Community, supplement series, 1985.

See also PLANNED COMMUNITIES (NEW TOWNS); REGIONAL/URBAN DESIGN ASSISTANCE TEAMS (R/UDAT); URBAN DESIGN—ARCHITECTURE AT URBAN SCALE; URBAN DESIGN—CREATION OF LIVABLE CITIES

DAVID STAHL
FRANK SPINK
Urban Land Institute
Washington, D.C.

UREA FORMALDEHYDE.   See AMINO RESINS

URETHANES.   See FOAMED PLASTICS

V

VALUE ENGINEERING

Value engineering (VE) is an in-depth, creative approach to evaluating the basic functions of a facility, system, or process and identifying alternatives for achieving these basic functions at lower cost or increased revenues. Lower cost may be reduced initial capital cost, annual cost, periodic cost, or any combination of these. Increased revenues include those from operations such as paper mills, aquariums, and subway systems.

The VE methodology is concerned with asking

What is it?
What does it do?
What must it do?
What is it worth?
What does it cost?
What else will perform the same function?
What would that cost?

Its in-depth analysis separates it from cost-reduction techniques, which seek to reduce cost by using different materials or smaller quantities of materials or by eliminating some item in order to reduce costs to budgetary levels.

A question frequently asked is "Why do I need VE when I have my own designers to give me the most cost-effective design to meet my program requirements?" The answer to this question is examined in detail later in this article. In brief, the designers (or planners) are primarily concerned with providing the program requirements and completing the design within the required schedule. True, they are also concerned with evaluating the cost effectiveness of various systems to determine which system is best suited to meet the program requirements; however, the cost-effective analysis they perform is but a small segment of the VE process.

The VE team's main objective, on the other hand, is "How to provide the basic function at the lowest cost consistent with providing the program requirements." VE studies typically yield initial capital cost savings upward of 5%. Many yield 10, 20, even 30% and more. In addition, annual cost savings (operations, maintenance, energy, staffing, etc) can range upward of 5, 10, and 15%.

Another statistic related to the VE study is the ROI or return on investment. ROI is a ratio of the total dollars saved divided by the cost of the study. The average ROI appears to be running approximately 30:1 and higher. That is, 30 or more dollars saved for every dollar invested in the VE study. It should be pointed out that, although the cost of the VE study is usually paid for shortly after the study, the return (ie, the savings based on estimated construction cost) may not be realized until some time later. However, even under these conditions, the ROI would only decrease proportionately to the current interest rate between the time that payment is made for the VE study and the payments are made for the construction work.

HISTORY OF VALUE ENGINEERING

Value engineering had its origin during World War II at General Electric Company, where it was noticed that many of the substitute materials (forced by wartime shortages for war-critical materials) being used in equipment reduced costs, yet maintained, or in some cases improved, the performance of the product. At that time, Harry Erlicher, who observed many of these occurrences, thought that perhaps such substitutions in the product could be made in a methodical and deliberate manner rather than as a result of material shortages or other compulsory changes. Erlicher called on Lawrence Miles, who worked for him, and gave him the task of answering this question. Subsequently, Miles developed what is known today as value engineering. He called the system he developed value analysis. It produced the required result of reducing costs while retaining (or improving) the required functions of the product. The name was later changed to value engineering. In recent years, VE has gained popularity under several names, all of which are essentially synonymous. These are value engineering, value analysis, value management, and, more recently, value architecture. The terms value analysis and value management were favored by nonengineering professionals who found that the concept also could be applied to their disciplines.

Value engineering was employed by the Department of Defense in the early 1950s by the U.S. Navy's Bureau of Ships. In the 1960s, during Robert S. McNamara's term as Secretary of Defense, the VE program gained much wider popularity and was quite successful in reducing the costs to the military for many of their acquisitions; however, much of the VE performed for the Department of Defense at that time was on production items far beyond the design stage. Savings were significant, primarily because of large production quantities. Relatively little VE was done during the design stages. In more recent years, VE has grown in popularity in virtually every segment of industry and is employed primarily during the early design or planning stages when opportunities for changes are greatest and redesign (and the probability of delaying schedules) is relatively minor.

To date, and to the best of the author's knowledge, VE is in use in the following federal agencies: Department of Defense, Public Building Service of the General Services Administration, Naval Facilities Engineering Command, the Army Corps of Engineers, Department of Transportation, Health and Human Services, Veterans Administration, National Aeronautics and Space Administration, the

Environmental Protection Agency, and the National Institutes of Health.

In addition, many states and municipalities are employing VE on a mandatory basis. Private industry, developers, construction managers, and construction contractors are employing VE in their operations, as are consumer product, industrial product, military hardware manufacturing firms, and software firms. Value engineering appears to be growing at a rapid pace because of its history of successes and its relatively inexpensive cost to implement.

Use is also spreading to other countries such as West Germany, Japan, Taiwan, India, Korea, Saudi Arabia, Peoples Republic of China, South Africa, Belgium, Canada, Italy, and, most likely, many more that the author is not yet aware of.

DEFINITION OF VALUE ENGINEERING

Value engineering is an organized and methodological application of recognized techniques that seeks to identify the basic function(s) of a product or service and to provide the necessary function(s) at the lowest total cost, consistent with required performance, reliability, quality, maintainability, aesthetics, safety, fire protection, and other required parameters.

In this definition, the identification of the basic function is one of the prime tools in the VE methodology. To define the basic function clearly, only two words are used, a verb and a noun. This type of definition serves as a springboard, used during the creative idea session, to arrive at other means of achieving the basic function. For example, the basic function of a roof over an equipment storage facility may be defined by the following verb and noun: protect equipment. This implies that other systems may be employed that merely protect the equipment but are not necessarily a roof structure. On the other hand, if the function of the roof is defined as enclose space, other solutions might be more inclined to retain the roof structure. Therefore, the two-word definition of the basic function is of vital importance and should be selected with caution so as not to restrict the number of potential alternative solutions.

Value engineering differs significantly from standard cost cutting or cost-reduction techniques. Cost cutting normally consists of elimination or substitution of materials or components without necessarily maintaining the original function of the product or component. Value engineering seeks to achieve the required function at a lower cost. It also seeks to eliminate or reduce the cost of those functions that are secondary to the basic function.

Architecturally, VE seeks to reduce costs while maintaining the required architectural statements of, say, a building, both from the exterior and interior points of view. These are significant statements that the architect and interior designer have developed over a relatively long period of time and are based on input from clients, users, and owners and their own past experience. The contribution of these architectural statements to the community and the working environment are difficult to assess in monetary terms. Nevertheless, the monetary asset or value is there; only its magnitude can be questioned—not its existence. The asset to the community may include the following:

1. Enhancement of its image to encourage new businesses to locate their operations in that community or to help retain existing business in the community.
2. Enhancement of its image to generate or increase tourism to that community.
3. Stimulation of owners of existing buildings or businesses in the area to upgrade the architectural attractiveness of their premises.
4. Enhancement of its image for the pride, self-respect, and pleasure of the community members.

The value of the statement of the interior of a building can also include several areas:

1. Enhancement of employees' morale.
2. Increase in employees' efficiency and productivity.
3. Increase in employees' creativity.
4. Impressing visiting dignitaries, clients, or potential clients.

This is by no means intended to be an all-inclusive list of assets; rather, it is intended to illustrate the importance of the exterior architectural appearance and the interior design of a facility and to emphasize the recognition of this by the value engineer.

This does not mean to imply that VE suggestions are never addressed to the architectural statements. However, working with the architect and the interior designer, the VE team can often suggest modifications that

1. Enhance or maintain the aesthetics simultaneous with reduced costs.
2. Modify the aesthetics without impacting on the statement, while at the same time providing significant cost savings.

In addition, it is not unusual for the architect or the interior designer to request input from the VE team on a given problem area. The VE team itself is normally comprised of design professionals who have designed similar projects and can relate to the project. Thus, the VE team, working together with the architect and the interior designer, can make a significant contribution to the project.

TIMING OF THE VALUE ENGINEERING STUDY

The question often asked is "What is the best time to carry out a VE study?" In general, the answer is "the earlier the better." Often on large or complex projects, it is best to conduct more than one VE study—one early in the planning or design stage and one (or more) at later stages of design.

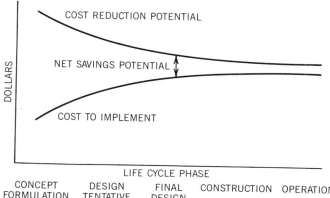

Figure 1. Life cycle phase.

Figure 1 illustrates typical curves for cost-reduction potential/cost to implement versus time. The cost-reduction potential decreases as a function of time primarily because more and more firm (and sometimes irreversible) decisions are made by users, owners, and designers simply because the project must move forward. There is normally a schedule to follow that requires decisions to be made at given points in time. Beyond these time/decision points, the potential for changes is significantly reduced. Also, some projects require that purchase orders be placed early for the long-lead items. When this occurs, the design must center around the long-lead items already ordered unless extenuating conditions arise.

The cost of implementation curve increases as a function of time for obvious reasons. As time progresses, more drawings and other contract documents are completed and more basic research into equipment and supplies has been accomplished. These may have to be revised if VE alternatives are adopted.

Opinions vary as to the optimum timing for a VE study on a project on which (1) only one VE study is to be conducted and (2) more than one VE study is to be conducted. To help make this decision, the following variables should be considered:

1. Complexity of the project.
2. The number of jurisdictions having input into the planning and design.
3. Background information such as environmental impact and political consideration.

Complexity of the Project. The more complex a project is, the more important it is to conduct an early study at either the concept stage or even at the scope-formulation stage. This helps to minimize the problems associated with modifying complex designs brought about by the VE study. If a second VE study is to take place, it should be sometime early in the preparation of plans and specifications, say, at the 25 to 35% stage. For larger projects, say greater than 50 or 100 million dollars, it may be advisable to include more VE studies at more frequent intervals. A minimum of 4 or 5 months should be allowed between studies to allow a sufficient amount of new design work to be accomplished so that the succeeding studies cover a significant amount of new work.

Number of Jurisdictions Having Input into the Planning and Design. To clarify the term number of jurisdictions, the single owner, designers, and single users are essentially one jurisdiction with three input sources. If, for instance, there is more than one owner or user, each represents an additional jurisdiction. If federal, state, county, city, or other regulatory jurisdictions require input or approval early in the planning and design stage, their impact on the VE process (and vice versa) must also be considered. In any event, a complex project with input and approval from various sources should be considered a candidate for having the first VE study at the scope stage of the project. Scope studies are normally very successful because modification to the scope at such an early stage is relatively easy to accomplish. Also, because modification to the scope involves the owners and users, costs savings are normally significant. See the section entitled "Who Has the Greatest Impact on Project Cost?"

VE studies after the scope study can concentrate on site utilization and the design details. There are other advantages to doing a VE study early in the planning or design stage, such as:

1. The planners, designers, owners, and users have usually tentatively, but not yet firmly, decided on such items as site utilization, building orientation, and building systems. This situation is more conducive to change because once a firm decision on which way to go is made, it is more difficult to suggest changes. It is better to work with the planners, designers, and the owners and users early on, rather than be faced with what may essentially be an irreversible system later on. They must make the final decision on all matters, but if the VE team can come in early enough, their input is more readily received and incorporated in the overall scheme before final decision making. It is well to repeat here that the VE team will include planning and design professionals who are also practicing consultants and who, for the most part, have been down the same road as the planners and designers of the project under construction. Therefore, they can relate their experience to the project and make significant contributions. On the other hand, they often feel reluctant to suggest VE design alternatives after the planning/

design is firmly in place because they are aware of the complexities of making changes at later stages of design.

2. There are many more options to evaluate at early stages of design. This is readily apparent from the above discussion. Often, it is mandatory that orders for long-lead items be placed early in the planning/ design stage. When they are ordered, options are narrowed and must center around the ordered items.

3. Redesign costs at early stages are relatively minor.

4. Potential for delaying schedules is minimal.

DESIGNER, OWNER, AND USER INVOLVEMENT IN THE VALUE-ENGINEERING STUDY PROCESS

The designers, owners, and users should be involved in the VE study process from start to finish; however, this involvement need not be, and seldom is, on a full-time basis. Having these cognizant and project knowledgeable personnel provide input at discreet times during the VE process helps the VE team better understand the overall mission (or function) of the project and to understand the planning and design of the project. This, in turn, assists in the formulation and development of viable design alternatives by the VE team.

Their involvement varies, depending on the project and the client. Normally, on the first morning of the VE study week, the designers give the VE team a project briefing. Typically, the VE team has already reviewed the project documents, having received them before the study. Therefore, the designers' project briefing on the first morning of the study fills in the missing blanks for the VE team. The owners should attend this briefing to provide their input on the project needs and constraints. The users should also attend this briefing to explain their requirements and details of their operations. During the VE study, members of the VE team should be permitted to contact any of these cognizant personnel on a one-on-one basis. Then, on the final day of the VE study, the same group of people attend a presentation of the VE team's ideas. This close working relationship provides insight for the designers, owners, and users on the details of each of the VE suggestions that facilitates poststudy evaluation of these suggestions.

In addition to the above, it may be advisable to have a prestudy orientation meeting with the designers, users, and owners to establish and define the agenda for the VE study week.

After the study is completed, a poststudy meeting is sometimes advisable and is held after the designers, users, and owners have reviewed the VE report submitted by the VE team leader. This poststudy meeting is designed to assist in the resolution of the VE suggestions.

WHO HAS THE GREATEST IMPACT ON PROJECT COST?

From Figure 2, it can readily be seen that the owners and the users have the greatest impact on project cost. They prescribe the design requirements, specifications, etc, that

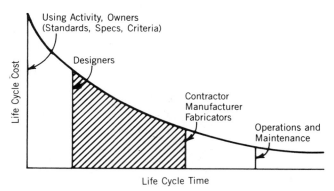

Decision Makers Versus Impact on Product Cost

Figure 2. Life cycle time. Decision makers versus impact on product cost.

in turn significantly impact on the cost. Regulatory agencies also have an impact on the project cost, but in the experience of the author, owners and users normally have the greatest impact on project cost.

Designers or planners have the next greatest impact on cost. They usually must operate within a relatively narrow range of budgetary costs. For instance, they normally perform cost-effective analyses of the various systems (structural, mechanical, etc) and suggest a given system based on life-cycle cost and other factors.

Construction contractors, in turn, have even less impact on cost, primarily because, for the most part, they are restricted to material changes, rerouting, size changes, etc. Again, these have a relatively small impact on project cost.

The operations and maintenance personnel normally have an even smaller impact on cost because they must operate (and maintain the facility) within the prescribed design. However, their impact can be enhanced by energy conservation and other relatively minor adjustments, which, over a period of time, do have a more significant impact.

QUALIFICATIONS OF THE VALUE ENGINEERING TEAM

Before defining team qualifications, it is well to discuss project complexity because team members' experience should be, in general, commensurate with the nature of the project. For example, a given project with complex architectural and structural systems requires an architect and a structural engineer with commensurate knowledge and experience. Conversely, a project with, for instance, straightforward electrical and civil concepts probably would not require these disciplines to be highly experienced. Hence younger, less experienced professionals could have the opportunity to serve on a VE team and truly enhance their own experience.

Another factor for consideration arises when, in the judgment of the person selecting the VE team, a relatively straightforward area of the design may be a prime candidate for a more complex system. Then, that team member should have experience and knowledge commensurate with the more complex design.

The theoretical approach to selecting team members for a VE study and practical economics can also create interesting complications. For example, a given VE study budget may be insufficient to exercise the theoretical approach to optimum benefits. If additional funding is not available, some compromise may be necessary. However, it is not the intent of this article to address these issues in detail, only to point out their existence.

For best results those participating in a VE study should

1. Have previously completed a 40-hour VE training workshop conducted by a Certified Value Specialist (CVS) whose training workshop has been certified by the Society of American Value Engineers (SAVE). (The Society of American Value Engineers specifies requirements for SAVE Certified Training Workshops and the requirements governing certification for CVS.)
2. Have several years experience in their discipline. It is not intended to define a precise number of years of experience; this is best left to those responsible for forming the team. Obviously, the team member's experience should be commensurate with the complexity of the project, as previously discussed.
3. Be totally objective in their participation on the VE team. Some VE team members, on some studies, are employees of firms who are competitive with the designers of the project. This type of situation requires total objectivity. Anything less may detract from the success of the VE study.
4. Not be a member of the incumbent design team. The reasoning being that there will be a tendency to be biased in favor of one's own design. This may have a negative impact on the other team members and the results of the VE study.
5. Have at least some knowledge of design and construction techniques peculiar to the geographic location of the project. It is advisable in some cases (but not necessarily all) that at least one member of the VE team possess this background. Paradoxically, often VE team members with either little or no background of local construction techniques contribute more to the study than those that do. This is simply because they do not know "what cannot be done!" Often what is normally not done in that particular area can in fact be done, and at a lower cost.
6. Finally, the VE team leader should be a CVS. It is a mandatory requirement that VE studies be conducted by a CVS for almost all the jurisdictions sponsoring value engineering studies.

COMPOSITION OF THE VE TEAM

Basically, the composition of the VE team should duplicate the disciplines of the design team; this includes spe-

cialties such as acoustics and planning. Their participation in the study should be approximately commensurate with the amount of work the project requires for that discipline. Some specialty disciplines may only be required on a part-time basis, whereas others will be needed on a full-time basis.

Again, no attempt is made here to create specific guidelines; rather, the professional judgment of those responsible for forming the VE team should bear that responsibility. Examples of VE team composition are

1. *Administrative or office building*
   CVS team leader
   Architect
   Structural engineer
   Mechanical engineer
   Electrical engineer
   Civil engineer
   Cost estimator
   Specialist discipline (part-time) such as construction manager, acoustical consultant, computer planner
2. *Wastewater treatment plant*
   CVS team leader
   Sanitary engineer, liquid treatment processes
   Sanitary engineer, sludge treatment processes
   Structural engineer
   Mechanical engineer
   Electrical engineer/instrumentation specialist
   Civil engineer
   Cost estimator
   Specialist disciplines (part-time) such as construction manager
3. *Hospital*
   CVS team leader
   Hospital planner
   Hospital architect
   Food-service specialist
   Materials management specialist
   Structural engineer
   Mechanical engineer (hospital experienced)
   Electrical engineer (hospital experienced)
   Civil engineer
   Geotechnical consultant
   Cost estimator
   Plus specialists as applicable (part-time) such as construction manager
4. *Solid waste disposal project in which wastes are being burned*
   CVS team leader
   Solid waste disposal specialist (full-time)
   Incinerator specialist
   Solid waste disposal planner
   Structural engineer

Mechanical engineer (solid waste disposal experience)

Energy recovery specialist (mechanical or chemical engineer)

Air emission control specialist

Construction manager

Electrical engineer (solid waste disposal experience)

Civil engineer

Cost estimator

Other specialists as applicable, such as department of sanitation planning construction specialist

Construction contractors have been included on studies with very successful results. These personnel provide in-depth consideration of construction techniques and problems sometimes not readily obvious to the design disciplines.

LEVEL OF EFFORT OF VALUE ENGINEERING STUDIES

Many attempts have been made to define the level of effort for VE studies with respect to the cost, complexity, or impact of a project. Only some very general guidelines for determining the level of effort will be presented here. The actual level of effort should be the responsibility of those planning the study. The following discussion presents the difficulty in defining specific levels of effort based on cost, complexity, or impact.

For instance, take two, five-story buildings of similar construction. One is 50,000 gross ft², the other 100,000 gross ft². Their respective costs are $6 million and $11 million. It takes basically the same level of effort to study each of these buildings, the reason being that they both have essentially the same elements. However, each element would produce different savings because of the difference in magnitude of the costs. This same reasoning applies to other structures as well as for buildings.

Another example: Consider a $20-million parking garage, a $20-million wastewater treatment plant, a $20-million theater, and a $20-million hospital. The construction costs of each of these projects is $20 million, but each requires a different level of effort and different specialty disciplines for obvious reasons.

The level of effort should consider the following:

1. Cost of the project.
2. Complexity of the project.
3. Complexity and impact the project has on the community, city, county, state, or federal regulations or other requirements.
4. The budget allocated for the VE study.

Normally, the level of effort for VE studies ranges from one 40-h study with one 5 to 6 person team, to several teams working simultaneously and meeting more than once during the planning or design stage. Larger projects are typically VE'd in smaller packages throughout the design stage. Refer to the previous section on "Composi-

tion of the VE Team" and the information above to determine the level of effort appropriate for an individual project.

VALUE ENGINEERING METHODOLOGY

VE methodology is a step-by-step process consisting of five phases, each of which produces written documentation of the information gathered or generated during the phase. This constitutes what is called the job plan. The five phases and a brief outline of each are

1. *Information Phase*
   Project familiarization
   Pareto's Law of Distribution
   Graphic function analysis
   Cost models
   Function analysis: Basic and secondary functions
                      Cost-to-worth ratio analysis
   FAST diagramming
2. *Creative Idea or Speculation Phase**
   Generation of VE ideas
   Various creative idea techniques
3. *Analytic or Judgment Phase**
   Evaluation of ideas generated from the creative phase
   Itemize advantages and disadvantages of each
   Selection of best ideas for development
4. *Development Phase*
   Development of cost savings with references
   Development of technical calculations with references
5. *Presentation/Proposal/Preliminary Report Phase*
   Verbal presentation of results
   Preliminary VE report
   Comprehensive description of as-designed item with sketches and cost
   Comprehensive description of VE alternative with sketches and cost
   Itemization of advantages and disadvantages

Information Phase

Project Familiarization. Typically, the first step in this phase commences on receipt of the project documents from the designers. Documents received may include drawings, estimated construction cost, basis of design, technical calculations, soils reports, catalogue cutouts of primary equipment, and correspondence pertinent to the project (ie, between designers, users, owners, regulatory agencies, public hearings, etc). These documents are first sent to the VE team leader, who distributes them to the team. Each team member reviews these documents for familiarization.

---

* The nomenclature of the phases varies from author to author.

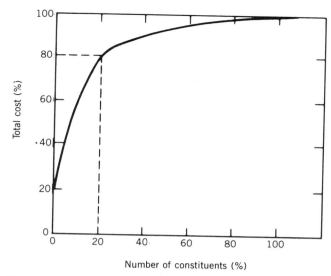

Figure 3. Pareto's law of distribution. Courtesy of U.S. Army Management Engineering Training Agency.

Various techniques are employed during this phase to help the VE team zero in on those areas of the project that have the greatest potential for savings. These are described in the following sections.

Pareto's Law of Distribution. One guideline used in helping to identify those areas with the greatest potential for savings is Pareto's Law of Distribution (Vilfredo Pareto, Italian economist, 1848–1923). As shown in Figure 3, the law illustrates that 80% of the cost of any facility system, etc lies in 20% of the components of that facility. To paraphrase this law, "Most of the cost of any facility, system, etc usually (but not always) lies in a relatively small number of components of that facility." Applying this law to the estimated construction costs of any project identifies a small number of areas on which the VE study focuses. The VE team does not ignore the other areas; they are evaluated, but not as much time is spent on them. Common sense dictates that the relatively large number of items that contain only a small portion of the costs would probably not yield savings commensurate with the length of time required to analyze the larger number of components. Hence, to maximize the efficiency of the VE analysis, it is important to concentrate on those relatively few areas that comprise the bulk of the costs.

Graphic Function Analysis. A practical application of Pareto's Law is perhaps best demonstrated in the VE methodology step termed graphic function analysis. This procedure plots, in bar chart form, the estimated construction costs of a project illustrating the component costs of the project to highlight high cost areas. For example, the following graphic function analyses illustrate the cost breakdown of a multi-activities building (ie, basketball, ballroom, banquet, stage theater, etc): Figure 4 illustrates the entire building cost summary. Note that 80% of the building cost is in 8 of 17 of the components. This is some-

what more than 20%; nevertheless, it demonstrates that "most of the cost lies in a relatively small number of components of the project." Figure 5 illustrates a breakdown of the highest cost item in Figure 4, namely, the special equipment. Here again, it shows that 80% of the cost of that subsystem lies in a relatively small number of components of the system. In Figure 6 the next highest cost item is the structural frame, which shows 80% of the cost in three of the nine components. Note that three components under $5000 were not plotted. Figure 7 is the next highest cost item, the exterior wall system, has 80% of the system cost in only one component.

Annual Cost Analysis. The graphic function analysis method just described is also applied to annual costs such as operations and maintenance (Fig. 8), energy, and annual staffing costs.

Cost Models. In addition to graphic function analysis, cost models are another tool in the VE methodology to assist the VE team in determining where best to concentrate their efforts; that is, which areas would have the greatest potential for savings. Basically, it represents a one-page summary of the cost estimate that identifies, at a glance, potential areas for savings. It also helps to uncover costs drivers in the project.

The construction of the cost model for a building, for example, proceeds as follows (Figure 9).

1. Costs extracted from the project's estimated construction cost are inserted in the appropriate broken line blocks of Figure 9.
2. Next, the building gross square footage is entered as indicated on Figure 9.
3. The top block of each discipline represents the total(s) under that discipline.
4. Next, the cost per gross square foot is entered as indicated for each discipline and each component within that discipline.
5. In addition, the percentage (compared to total building costs) of each discipline and component is entered as shown.
6. The next step requires some experience with previous building costs. The estimated worth of that component and discipline is entered as indicated. The difference between these two numbers represents the potential cost savings for that particular component. This sets a goal for the VE team. Hence, VE Goal/Worth is entered in the solid box.

Worth. For cost-modeling purposes, worth is often established by experience in past projects of a similar nature. This value must be selected with caution because too high or too low a worth can be misleading. Often, estimated costs by the designers of some components or materials are thought by the VE team to have unit costs either too high or too low. If so, this should be checked with the designers so that the costs are reflected accurately in the cost model and to establish a reasonable worth for that component.

Utilizing the cost model to its maximum potential re-

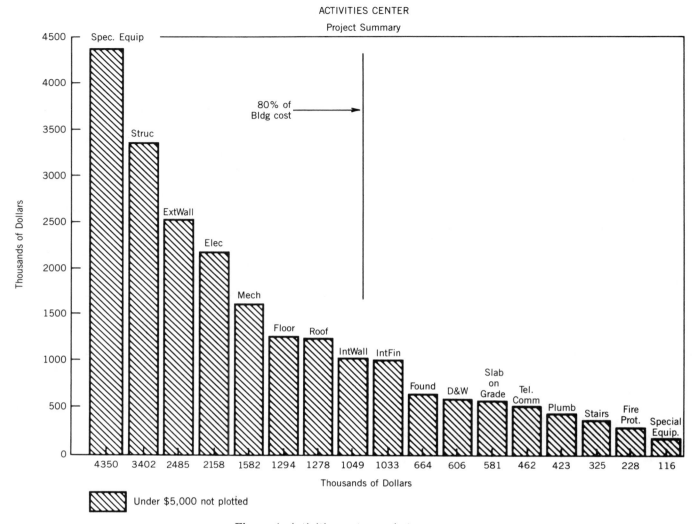

Figure 4. Activities center, project summary.

quires some experience and good judgement as does the use of any tool in any trade. The cost model of Figure 9 is that of a bus maintenance building. Evaluation of this model is as follows:

1. First, the total estimated building cost per gross square foot is evaluated against the worth. The results of this first analysis should indicate whether the cost per square foot is high, low, or within an expected range.
2. Next, each of the trades is evaluated in a similar manner to determine if each cost per square foot is high, low, or within an expected range.

The percentage of each discipline and system as a function of the total building cost is included in the cost models. The end result is that the VE team can better and more quickly isolate the high-cost areas with greatest potential for savings, which in turn helps to identify cost drivers.

The cost-model analysis is used in conjunction with the previously described graphic function analysis to help es-

tablish priorities of the creative idea (or speculation) phase described later. In addition, the following function analysis section and FAST diagramming section help define functions that aid in generating ideas during the creative phase and also provide additional information for establishing priorities.

Creativity Phase

Function Analysis: Basic and Secondary Functions. The determination of the basic and secondary function(s) of the project and its components is another step in establishing a foundation for the creativity session (ie, the listing of alternative ideas that will accomplish the basic function of the item under study).

Basic Function. The basic function defines the primary function of the component or item under study and is expressed in two words, a verb and a noun. The reason for defining the basic function is to facilitate the generation of alternative means to accomplish the basic function of the component or item under study. (This generation of ideas is accomplished during the creative idea phase discussed

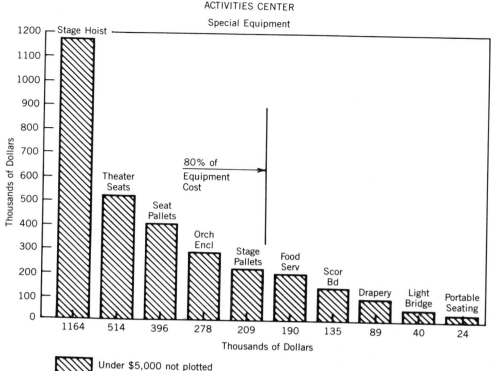

Figure 5. Activities center, special equipment.

later.) Also, the basic function should be described in broad terms to facilitate the generation of a large number of ideas. The following example is rather mundane but illustrates this concept quite well. For example, the basic function of a mousetrap might be stated as "kill mice." The generation of ideas following this definition would most likely be centered around ideas that kill mice. If the higher order (See the section on FAST diagraming for a definition of higher order.) function of a mousetrap were used, say "eliminate mice," then a whole new range of ideas are open because "eliminate mice" does not necessarily mean to kill them. That is, ideas could then include ways merely to eliminate mice. Therefore, using both verb–noun function definitions, "kill-mice" and "eliminate mice" produce more ideas that, in the final analysis,

would be more likely to produce more viable design alternatives.

This same concept can be applied to various structures. For example, the basic function of the roof of an equipment storage building might be defined as "cover space" or "enclose space." The ideas generated would most likely revolve around alternative roof materials. However, if the basic function of the roof was defined as "protect equipment," then ideas generated most likely would include omitting the roof and perhaps encapsulating or otherwise covering the material. In any event, the latter basic function widens the field for creative thinking.

Secondary Functions. To facilitate the defining of secondary functions, Table 1 illustrates a classic VE illustration of an ordinary lead pencil.

Table 1. Basic and Secondary Functions of the Components of a Lead Pencil
Item: Lead pencil. Basic function is "make marks."

Component	Function Verb	Noun	Basic	Secondary	Cost	Worth[a]
Graphite	Make	Marks	B		0.08	0.08
Wood	Holds	Lead		S	0.07	
Paint	Provides	Appeal		S	0.05	
Eraser	Removes	Marks		S	0.06	
Ferrule	Holds	Eraser		S	0.03	
Lettering	Provides	Identification		S	0.02	
Totals					0.31	0.08

[a] Worth is discussed under cost-to-worth ratios in next section.

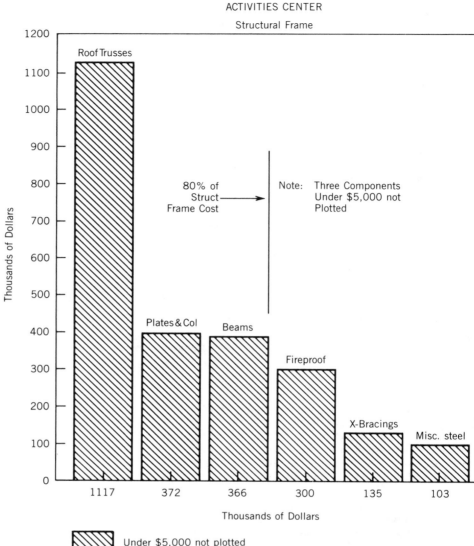

Figure 6. Activities center, structural frame.

Under $5,000 not plotted

The basic function of the pencil is to "make marks." The only component that performs this function is the graphite. Therefore, the graphite is identified as a basic function.

The other components provide other functions as shown but do not "make marks." Therefore, they provide secondary functions. Hence, any component of a system that provides functions other than the basic function of the system is considered a secondary function. This technique may be applied to any structure, system, or process.

Function Analysis: Cost-to-Worth Ratio Analysis. The cost/worth ratio is another tool in the VE methodology for determining those areas with the greatest potential for savings. To illustrate, Table 1 shows the total cost of the pencil to be $0.31. The cost of the component that provides the basic function (ie, the graphite) is shown to be $0.08. Therefore, the cost-to-worth ratio is 0.31/0.08 = 3.88.

The practical application of the cost-to-worth ratio lies in the hypothesis that the higher this ratio is, the greater the potential for savings. For example, if the VE study were to be conducted on a building, the components of the building would be broken down into functional areas such as roof, exterior walls, interior partitions, and electrical distributions. Each of these areas would then be broken down into its subcomponents and functionally analyzed (similar to the pencil). The resulting cost-to-worth ratio of each of the functional areas would then determine their potential for savings (Table 2).

In the above example, three basic functions are shown. For the particular building under study in this case, all three basic functions were applicable. Often, but not always, only one basic function is applicable. However, three are shown here to illustrate the point made in the previous section.

The cost-to-worth ratio of 4.99 indicates fairly good potential for savings. However, the cost-to-worth ratio of all the building's components (ie, exterior wall, interior parti-

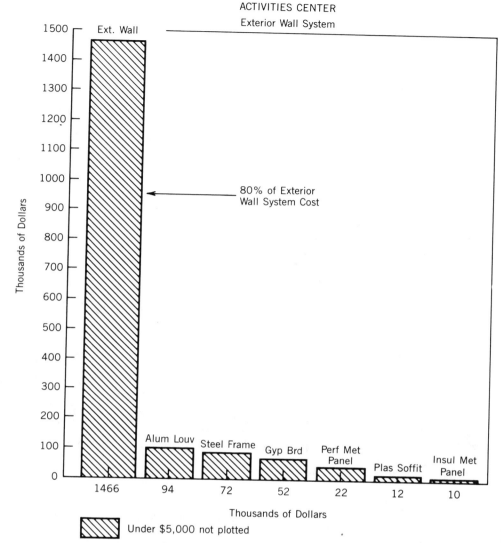

ACTIVITIES CENTER
Exterior Wall System

80% of Exterior
Wall System Cost

Thousands of Dollars

Ext. Wall

Alum Louv   Steel Frame   Gyp Brd   Perf Met Panel   Plas Soffit   Insul Met Panel

1466   94   72   52   22   12   10

Thousands of Dollars

Under $5,000 not plotted

Figure 7. Activities center, exterior wall system.

tions, HVAC, etc.) should be determined and compared with each other to determine relative degree of potential for each component. Note that the total cost of the component also influences potential for savings and should be a consideration when determining priorities.

Function Analysis System Technique (FAST Diagramming). The Function Analysis System Technique (FAST) diagramming illustrates the functional relationship of all the known functions of a system. It is first used in the information phase to help identify functions, then later, in

Table 2. Functional Analysis/Cost-to-Worth Ratio of a Roof System
Roof: Basic functions: Enclose Space, Preclude Environment, Protect Interior

Component	Function				Cost	Worth[a]
	Verb	Noun	Basic	Secondary		
Roof membrane	Enclose	Space	B		378,763	378,763
Insulation	Insulate	Space		S	410,327	
Light-weight roof fill	Channels	Water		S	66,535	
Flashing	Seals	Joints		S	6,516	
Roof decking	Supports	Load		S	1,026,387	
Totals					1,888,528	378,763

[a] Cost/Worth Ratio = 1,888,528/378,763 = 4.99

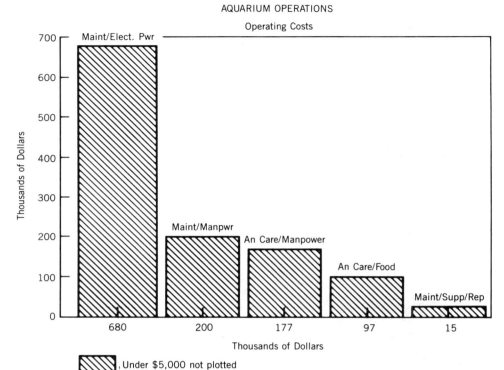

Figure 8. Aquarium operations, operating costs.

the creativity phase, to help generate VE ideas. FAST Diagramming was introduced by Charles Bytheway of Sperry-Rand, Univac Division, at the 1965 Society of American Value Engineers (SAVE) Convention.

This diagramming technique at first glance appears to be similar to PERT diagramming or flowcharting. However, the basic difference between FAST diagramming and these other diagramming techniques is that FAST diagramming is not time-oriented; it is function-oriented.

FAST shows pictorially the relationship of the functions of a product or service as it does the work it was designed to do. The verb–noun functions defined earlier are used, and the functions are arranged logically into a diagram using these guidelines:

1. Show the scope of the problem under study by two vertical dashed lines, one to the extreme left and one to the extreme right of the diagram (Fig. 10). Everything that lies between the two scope lines is defined as the problem under study.

2. The heavy horizontal line is the "critical path of functions" going from left to right across the scope lines.

3. On the critical path, only *required* secondary functions, the basic function(s), and the higher order function are included.

4. The higher order function lies to the immediate left of the left scope line.

5. The basic function(s) always lies to the immediate right of the left scope line.

6. All other functions on the critical path lie to the right of the basic function and will be required secondary functions.

7. All other secondary functions that the product or service performs lie either above or below the critical path of functions. These functions can be required secondary functions, aesthetic functions, or unwanted functions.

8. If the function happens at the same time and/or is caused by some function on the critical path, the function is placed below that critical-path function.

9. If the function happens all the time, the product is doing its work, such as an aesthetic function, and it is placed above the critical-path function to the extreme right of the diagram.

10. Specific design objectives that should be considered should be placed above the basic function and shown as dotted boxes.

11. To determine if the proper arrangement and relationships of the function are placed, two basic logic test questions must be met: How? Why?

    11a. As the critical path flows from left to right, the question "How" is answered.

    11b. As the critical path flows from right to left, the question "Why" is answered.

12. Only essential functions are included when constructing a FAST diagram.

13. All functions that lie on the critical path must take place to accomplish the basic function. All other functions on the FAST diagram are subordinate to the critical-path function and may or may not have to take place to accomplish the basic functions.

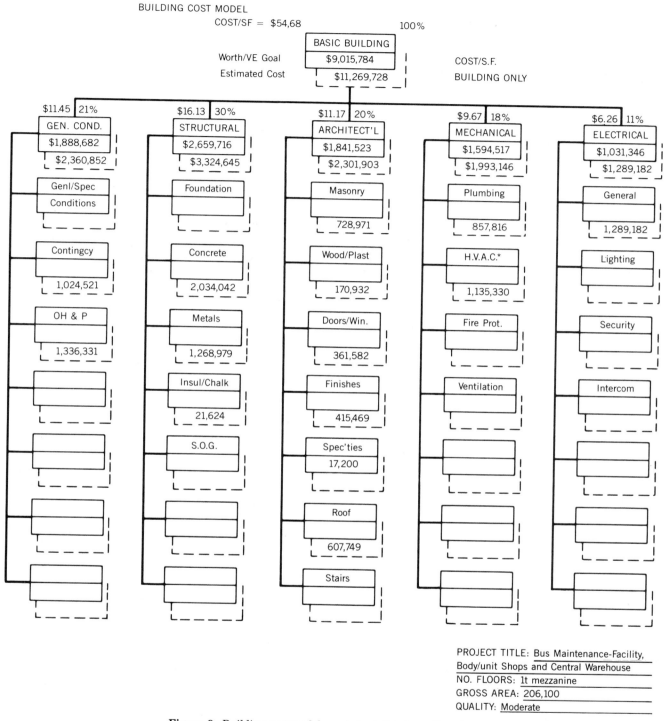

Figure 9. Building cost model, worksheet 2, information phase.

The best way to learn the FAST diagram technique is, of course, to use it on a simple example. Figure 11 is a simple example of the previously mentioned mousetrap.

In summary, the FAST diagram is a powerful technique that

1. Shows the specific relationship of all functions with respect to one another.

2. Tests the validity of the functions under study.

3. Broadens understanding of the project under study.

4. Aids in the generation of ideas during the creativity phase.

Creativity Phase

The objective of this phase is to generate a large number of alternative ways to accomplish the functions of the

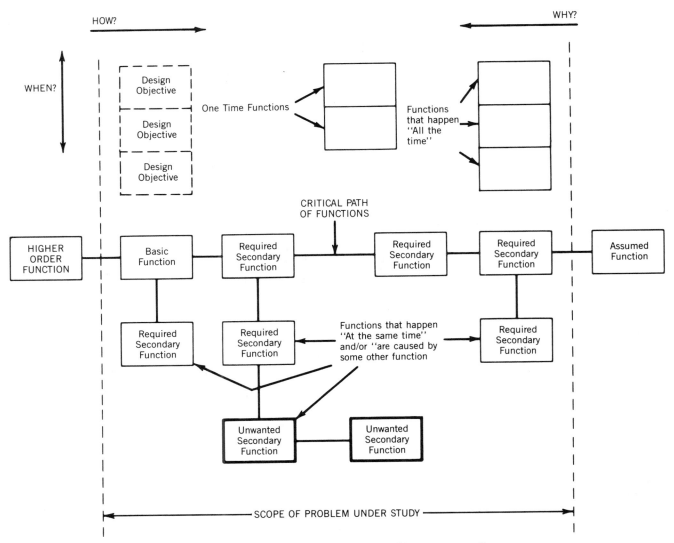

Figure 10. Scope of problem under study. Diagram convention.

items under study at lower cost. The ideas are normally written down on a form and numbered in consecutive order for identification. The methods used to generate these alternatives vary; however, the most commonly used method is to brainstorm ideas without evaluating them (until the next phase). In a typical brainstorming session all the participants of the VE study participate in the generation of ideas, not only in their own discipline area but in other disciplines as well. The aim of brainstorming in VE methodology is to generate a large number of ideas, even apparently ridiculous ideas that may violate client or user requests, design criteria, building codes, etc. It is important to also deviate from the normal solutions and include new and creative ideas. However, standard alternative design solutions will also be generated during the brainstorming session. It is also important that there be an uninhibited atmosphere with no criticism during this session. There should be an everything goes, everything is viable attitude until proven otherwise in the next phase.

This should not be interpreted to mean that the VE team will suggest a bunch of far-out ideas to the designer. It merely emphasizes the importance of having a free-spirited, uninhibited brainstorming session to generate a large number of ideas that create a higher probability of developing sound, viable design alternatives. For example, a creative brainstorming session may produce 150 to 200 ideas and more. However, after the next phase (analysis or judgment phase) described in the following section, there may be only 50 ideas remaining that the VE team judges to warrant serious consideration. After these 50 are evaluated in detail, and some technical or cost calculations are performed, there may be 30 or 35 VE alternatives that will be fully developed and presented to the designers, users, and owners.

Many VE contracts issued by government agencies (federal and state) require the VE effort to "challenge" established design criteria standards, user's requests or requirements, and, in some cases, local codes. In these

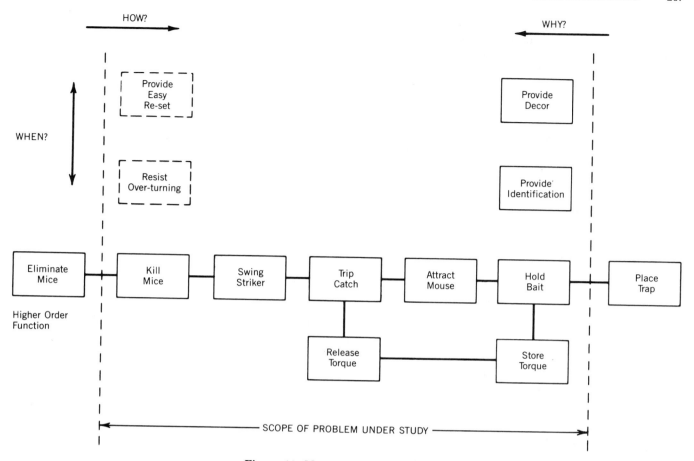

Figure 11. Mousetrap, FAST diagram.

situations, the brainstorming session should include challenges to the design criteria, etc. In many VE studies, these are the areas that produce the large portion of the savings.

Analysis or Judgement Phase

The process of weeding out the nonviable VE ideas and retaining the potentially viable ideas begins with the analysis phase. Here, consideration must include effects on functions, aesthetics, environmental costs, initial cost, and annual costs. Questions normally evaluated in detail for each idea include but are not limited to:

1. Will the idea perform the required function(s) and do so with reliability?
2. If there is a feature of the idea that is not viable, what can be done to change this feature such that the entire idea is viable?
3. Can it be combined with another idea to enhance its viability?
4. What are the potential initial capital savings—high, low, or moderate?
5. What are the potential annual cost savings—high, low, or moderate?
6. What are the environmental issues?

7. What are the nontechnical issues?
8. What are the problems associated with implementation of the VE alternative?
9. What would be the cost of implementation?
10. What is the probability of implementation?

The VE methodology offers several ways of selecting the more viable candidates for development in the next phase (ie, development). One method simply lists the advantages and disadvantages of each idea and assigns a numerical rating to each. For example, 10 might represent the top-ranked ideas, with lesser ranked ideas assigned lower numbers. Some of the ideas rated 10 at this stage of the process subsequently fall by the wayside after a brief analysis of cost or other factors. Conversely, other ideas initially ranked low sometimes turn out to be "10" ideas after detailed analysis. Therefore, it is important to analyze ideas closely and weed out the nonviable ideas before embarking on the time-consuming task of developing them, which comes in the next phase.

If a given idea, or a series of similar ideas, is judged to require a rather lengthy and detailed development, it is sometimes prudent to engage a more systematic evaluation of the idea(s) before attempting development. This approach, although somewhat time consuming, often saves more time in the end because it eliminates lengthy development of ideas that may prove to be nonviable when the final development calculations are made.

One systematic evaluation approach used is the weighted constraints chart method illustrated in Figure 12. The following steps are used in the development of the chart in an attempt to determine which HVAC system to develop in detail.

1. The ideas to be compared with the as-designed heating, ventilation, and air-conditioning system are listed in the left column.
2. The constraints are then listed across the top (ie, maintainability, future expansion capabilities, etc).
3. Next, the VE team discusses each of the constraints and then assigns a weight to each, indicating its relative importance. For example, first cost and operating cost were judged to be of the greatest concern (each was rated a 9 out of a possible high of 10). On the other hand, noise was judged to be of least concern (rated a 2).

Note: Although it is not intended to present a detailed discussion of the reasoning behind each of the VE teams decisions, as this would extend beyond the scope of this article, it is obvious that good engineering judgment must be exercised in order to have meaningful results.

4. The VE team then discusses the pros and cons of each of the four HVAC schemes and determines a

Weighted Constraints Chart

WEIGHT	7	8	9	9	2	5			
Constraints / IDEAS	Maintainability	Future Expan. Capab.	1st Cost	Operating Cost	Noise	Aesthetics	TOTAL	RANK	
Package in Bldg.	3/21	4/32	3/24	3/72	2/4	2/10	122	1	
Package on Slab	2/14	3/24	3/27	3/22	3/6	2/10	102	2	
Package on Roof	2/14	3/24	3/27	2/18	3/6	2/10	99	3	
As Designed Central Chiller	3/21	2/16	2/18	2/18	3/6	3/15	94	4	

4——Excellent 2——Fair
3——Good   1——Poor

Project _____

Date _____

Figure 12. Weighted constraints chart, worksheet 7, judgement phase.

relative weighting for each of the constraints. The weights are assigned as follows:

$$4 = \text{Excellent}$$
$$3 = \text{Good}$$
$$2 = \text{Fair}$$
$$1 = \text{Poor}$$

Note: None of the schemes were rated 4 (Excellent) or 1 (Poor) by the VE team.

5. Next, the constraint's weight is multiplied by the HVAC scheme's weight. For example, the package unit in the building was rated a 3 for maintainability, which was rated 7; the product is 21. This step is repeated until all the products of all the constraints and schemes are completed.

6. The totals for each scheme are then entered in the "total" column. The highest-ranked scheme in this analysis was the package unit inside the building because its total (122) was significantly higher than the other schemes. This scheme was therefore selected for development and subsequent presentation as a value engineering alternative design suggestion. Depending on availability of time, the VE team will sometimes develop the other remaining schemes, realizing that their judgment may not be in concert with that of the designers and users. The designers and users would then have several alternatives to the as-designed scheme to evaluate for possible implementation.

The weighted constraints chart can assume several other basic forms that assist the VE team in selecting those design alternatives with the greatest potential for implementation. It can also be used in succeeding phases (the development phase or the presentation phase) to help the VE team determine which ideas are the most viable candidates for consideration by the designers and users.

Development Phase

The alternatives remaining from the analytic phase are now developed in as much detail as practical. All calculations of initial and annual costs (energy, maintenance, staffing, etc) or replacement costs should list source references, assumptions, and conditions so that these may be checked by those who will be evaluating the VE suggestions. Finally, all technical calculations should also be source-referenced and include catalogue cut-outs where deemed necessary.

The development of costs should show the total costs of the as-designed system versus the VE suggested system. If this is not feasible, only the cost savings need be addressed.

Life-cycle costing (LCC) techniques are employed in development phase. The following brief example illustrates the LCC techniques.

A VE alternative suggestion was compared to the as-designed system. The conditions were

	As Designed	VE Alternative
Initial capital costs	\$3,000,000	\$3,300,000
Annual energy cost	\$ 200,000/yr	\$ 45,000/yr

The total life-cycle costs of each of the two systems (expressed in present worth cost[a]) is calculated as follows:

As Designed: $Pt = P1 + P2$
    where Pt = Total LCC
    $P1$ = Initial capital cost = \$3,000,000
    $P2$ = Present worth of the annual cost

Conditions: System economic evaluation life = 20 years
    Interest (discount) rate = 10%
    Annual energy escalation rate = 5%

The present worth ($P2$) of the annual costs at 10% discount and 5% annual escalation is calculated as follows:

$$P2 = A \times pwf$$

where A = annual energy cost = \$200,000
    pwf = present worth factor at 10% discount
        5% annual escalation
        20 years = 12.7178[b]

Therefore, $P2 = 200,000 \times 12.7178 = \$2,543,560$ and, $Pt = P1 + P2 = \$3,000,000 + 2,543,560 = \$5,543,560$

VE Alternative: $Pt = P1 + P2$ (using same procedures as for as-designed system above)

$$Pt = 3,300,000 + (pwf \times 45,000)$$
$$= 3,300,000 + (12.7178 \times 45,000)$$
$$= 3,300,000 + 572,301 = 3,872,301$$

[a] Present worth is defined as

1. A lump sum of money at a time regarded to be the present (ie, today's dollars).
2. The economic equivalent of a series of annual payments or annual income discounted back to present worth expressed as a lump sum of money in today's dollar.
3. The economic equivalent of a future expenditure or future income, discounted back to present worth expressed as a lump sum of money in today's dollar.

[b] From any present worth factor tables incorporating 10% discount with 5% escalation, 20 years.

Because the VE alternative requires an added \$300,000 investment, the payback time should be addressed. This may be accomplished using what is termed the Savings Investment Ratio (SIR); its equation is

$$SIR = \frac{\text{Present worth of the annual savings}}{\text{Present worth of the investment cost}} = \frac{P2}{P1}$$

When the present worth of the annual savings ($P2$) equals the present worth of the investment cost ($P1$), the equation equals 1 and is written as

$$SIR = 1 = \frac{P2}{P1}$$

Because present worth has already been discussed previously in this paper, the equation can be written as

$$SIR = 1 = \frac{A(pwf)}{300,000} = \frac{45,000 \ (pwf)}{300,000} = 1$$

Solving for pwf yields:

$$pwf = \frac{300,000}{45,000} = 6.666$$

The present worth factor table for 10% discount and 5% annual escalation is then checked to determine under what year pwf = 6.666 is closest. This number falls between the 8th and 9th year (6.5260 and 7.1839, respectively). Therefore, payback should occur in slightly over 8 years.

During the development phase, it is advisable to start formulating advantages and disadvantages to the VE alternative design suggestions. Stating the advantages helps those reviewing the VE suggestions to evaluate their viability. Stating the disadvantages establishes credibility of the VE team. It is to the VE team's advantage to state the disadvantages rather than have them pointed out by the reviewers.

Presentation and VE Report Phase

This phase, which concludes the VE job plan, consists of preparing and verbally presenting the VE alternative suggestions to the designers, owners, users, and other interested parties. Having everybody concerned with the project attend this presentation facilitates post-VE study review because it provides:

1. A firsthand comprehensive understanding of the VE alternatives.
2. An opportunity to question the VE team directly to enhance their understanding of the VE suggestions.
3. An opportunity to evaluate, firsthand, the qualifications of the VE team.
4. A forum for establishing rapport with all concerned parties. This creates an atmosphere conducive to a productive working relationship.

In summary, this approach facilitates post-VE study review and normally reduces the time required for evaluating of the VE report.

Following the verbal presentation, a written report is prepared which includes:

1. A comprehensive description of the as-designed system and the VE suggested alternatives and their associated costs. (Sketches are included where necessary.)
2. A list of the advantages and disadvantages of each VE alternative.
3. A general discussion of each VE alternative which presents the VE team's rationale for selecting and developing the alternative.
4. An estimate of the redesign time required for each VE alternative expressed in labor hours only.

The format of the VE report varies, but usually includes, in addition to the VE alternatives mentioned above, an introductory section that describes the project, identifies the VE team and other personnel connected with the study, and contains project data and details as necessary.

Post-VE Study Meetings. Depending on the project and the sponsor, the VE team sometimes attends poststudy meeting(s) to assist in determining the viability or implementability of the VE alternatives.

Final VE Report. Often the VE team is required to prepare a final report describing the disposition of each of the VE alternatives (ie, accepted, rejected, or pending further investigation). This type of information is valuable reference material for future VE studies.

BIBLIOGRAPHY

General References

A. J. Dell'Isola, *Value Engineering in the Construction Industry,* Construction Publishing Co., Van Nostrand Reinhold Co., New York, 1975.

C. Fallon, *Value Analysis to Improve Productivity,* John Wiley & Sons, Inc., New York, 1971.

General Services Administration, *Value Management Handbook,* PBS P 8000.1A, Oct. 31, 1978.

L. D. Miles, *Techniques of Value Analysis and Engineering,* 2nd ed., McGraw-Hill Inc., New York, 1972.

A. E. Mudge, *Value Engineering, A Systematic Approach,* McGraw-Hill Inc., New York, 1971.

W. J. Ridge, *Value Analyses For Better Management,* American Management Association, Inc., 1969.

U.S. Environmental Protection Agency, *Value Engineering Workbook for Construction Projects,* EPA-43019-76-008 (July 1976).

See also Diagnostics, Building; Estimating, Cost; Maintenance, Building; Preventive Maintenance

Edward J. Nichols
Ian Fraser
Alexandria, Virginia

VAN DE VELDE, HENRY-CLEMENT

Henry-Clement van de Velde (1863–1957) was an artist and architect active in Belgium and Germany. Identified with the art nouveau movement, his greatest fame occurred before World War I. Born in Antwerp, he studied painting at the Academie des Beaux Arts from 1881 to 1882, then went to Paris where he studied with Corolas Duran in 1883 and 1884, and became interested in the theories of pointilism. He participated in the formation of the group Als ik Kan (a club of luminist painters in Antwerp) and was admitted to the art group Les Vingt in 1888 where he met Paul Gaugin and William Morris.

He first exhibited with Les Vingt in 1889, where he became acquainted with the work of Seurat, Signac, and other French painters whose work was shown that year. Van de Velde experimented with neoimpressionism, and his painting "Woman at a Window" was exhibited in 1890. As a graphic artist he designed illustrations and ornaments beginning in 1892 and experimented with tapestries and furniture design. He was concerned with the unity of form and meaning in art, leading to a new decorative totality of the arts. He called for *un art nouveau*, perhaps the first use of that phrase (1894).

Van de Velde's reputation was largely based on his theoretical writings. Where the British arts and crafts movement was a reaction against machine-made ugliness, van de Velde sought a new aesthetic based on the nature of materials employed. William Morris had started manufacturing because he felt that artists were out of touch with ordinary life. Emphasis on craftsmanship was opposed to the machine made. Van de Velde thought that this was escapism of a romantic nature, and restated the issues in terms of learning from nature, seeking meaning and conscious beauty. Creation and production should be linked in logical design for mass production. In a long series of publications, van de Velde provided a theory to support art nouveau. In *Les formules* he discussed ornament, contrasting line and form. Line represented to him the realism of the engineer, and line derived from steel should reflect the ability of stretching in continuous curvilinear lines. Line was to be used to complement form (1).

Van de Velde's first experiments with architecture in 1896 were for his own house in Uccle, Belgium, where he applied his theories of aesthetics. In addition to designing the building, all of the furnishings and decoration were designed by him. Samuel Bing visited him and invited van de Velde to launch his new style at the 1897 Dresden Exposition. This first introduced art nouveau to Germany. He had the choice between decoration on flat surfaces and working out contrasts of three-dimensional forms, and by choosing the latter, van de Velde set the direction of his future work. This exhibit led to design of the new showroom in Paris, La Maison Moderne. The "Style Belge" received wide attention, and this shop brought together a group of artists and decorators with a common purpose.

In 1899, he was called to Berlin to direct the gallery "Hohenzollern Kunstgewerbehaus," for which he designed the facade as well as the interior fittings. Other Berlin shops designed by van de Velde in the art nouveau style included the Havana Company Cigar Store (1900) and the Haby Barbershop (1900). In 1902, he participated with several other architects including Peter Behrens in the Folkwang Museum at Hagen, to be opened as a permanent building with the Darmstadt Exposition of 1901. The interiors designed by van de Velde were successfully unobtrusive backgrounds for display, with careful control of decorated columns, friezes, and staircases. Some feel that was his most successful work in Germany, between his earlier interior decoration and his later architecture.

In 1902, van de Velde was asked to renovate the museum at Weimar and he went on to design the School of Applied Arts, which opened in 1908. By this time, van de Velde had moved away from art nouveau, and the school was a simple block with large windows and skylights in the studios. He stayed on to develop the radical curriculum. The success of the program led van de Velde to great fame and respect in Germany. While at Weimar, he designed the Esche House, Chemnitz (1903); the Leuring House, Scheveningen (1904); and the Central Hall for the Dresden Exposition of 1906.

Because van de Velde was not a German national, by 1915 it was necessary for him to leave Weimar, and he invited Walter Gropius to join the school. When the School of Applied Arts was disbanded later in 1915, Gropius made a proposal for the founding of a new educational institution, which eventually (1919) evolved into the Staatliche Bauhaus at Weimar.

Van de Velde was in wartime exile, and moved several times before settling again in Brussels in 1925. He continued to build occasionally throughout his long life; of note is the Kroller Muller Museum near Otterloo in the Netherlands, portions of which were not built until 1953.

BIBLIOGRAPHY

1. H. C. van de Velde, *Les formules de la beaute architectonique,* L'Equerre, Brussels, 1923.

General References

H. F. Lenning, *The Art Nouveau,* Martinus Nijhoff, The Hague, 1951.
P. Selz and M. Constantine, eds., *Art Nouveau,* The Museum of Modern Art, New York, 1959.
F. Russell, ed., *Art Nouveau Architecture,* Rizzoli, New York, 1979. See Chapt. 3 "Belgium," by M. Culot and Chapt. 7 "Germany," by I. Latham.

ROBERT T. PACKARD, AIA
Reston, Virginia

VAN EYCK, ALDO

The Dutch architect Aldo van Eyck was born in Driegergen, the Netherlands on March 16, 1918. He was educated in the UK at the King Alfred School, Hampstead, London, (1924–1932) and the Sidcot School, Winscombe, Somerset (1932–1935). His architectural education was at the Building School, The Hague, and the Eidgenossische Technische Hochschule in Zurich, where he completed his studies in 1943, the same year he married the architect Hannie van Roojen.

From 1946 to 1950 he worked in the Public Works Department in Amsterdam, and since 1952, in private practice in The Hague and Amsterdam. His partner from 1971 to 1982 was Theo Bosch, and since 1982, Hannie van Eyck-van Roojen. He was involved in the design of some 700 children's playgrounds with the Public Works Department in Amsterdam and in a wide diversity of building types, including public housing. A much-admired project was the Hubertus Home for single parents and children in Amsterdam (1975–1979) (1).

Aldo van Eyck's design approach is based on a concern for the individual and an understanding that buildings should be adaptable to uses other than those planned. In his statements, he has expressed a dislike for anonymous spaces and for ambiguous use of historic details favored by the postmodernists.

In 1947, van Eyck was named a delegate from The Netherlands to the International Congresses for Modern Architecture, better known as CIAM, which was founded in 1928 by Helene de Mandrot. CIAM's congresses and publications were a major influence on design and urban planning, including the historic Athens Charter (1933) concerning town planning. Many famous architects took part in the congresses, including Alvar Aalto, Walter Gropius, and Le Corbusier. The final congress of CIAM was in 1959 in Otterloo.

Van Eyck was active in the design discussions of CIAM. He has been a member of the progressive architectural group known as Team 10 since 1953. In addition, he has been a visiting critic and lecturer at a number of U.S. universities as well as in Europe and Singapore. He has been a professor at the Institute of Technology, Delft since 1968, and has been guest professor at the E.T.H. in Zurich and Paul Philippe Cret Professor of Architecture at the University of Pennsylvania in Philadelphia (1978–1983).

Van Eyck's work has been published and exhibited widely and he has won several first prizes in design competitions. He has received honorary doctorates from the New Jersey Institute of Technology (1979) and Tulane University (1979). He is also an Honorary Member of the Staatliche Kunstakademie, Dusseldorf (1979), a Member of the Royal Academy of Arts and Sciences, Belgium (1981), and an Honorary Member of the Bund Deutscher Architekten, FRG (1983). Van Eyck is an Honorary Fellow of the American Institute of Architects (1981).

BIBLIOGRAPHY

1. S. Doubilet, "Weaving Chaos into Order," *Progressive Architecture* **63**(3), 74–76, (Mar. 1982).

General References

A. L. Morgan and C. Naylor, eds., *Contemporary Architects,* 2nd ed., St. James Press, Chicago, 1987, pp. 940–942.

Robert T. Packard, AIA
Reston, Virginia

VENTURI, RAUCH AND SCOTT BROWN

Venturi, Rauch and Scott Brown (VRSB) is a Philadelphia firm that has had a significant influence on late twentieth-century architecture. The firm was founded in 1964 as Venturi and Rauch by partners Robert Venturi and John Rauch. They were joined in 1967 by Denise Scott Brown, who since 1960 had been collaborating with Venturi in teaching and the development of theory. In 1980, the firm became Venturi, Rauch and Scott Brown.

The firm's influence was first felt through the writings of Venturi and Scott Brown, beginning with Venturi's *Complexity and Contradiction in Architecture,* widely regarded as the seminal document of the postmodern move-

ment. Published in 1966, it is still in print and has been translated and published in nine languages.

In *Complexity and Contradiction,* Venturi issued his "gentle manifesto" against what he termed "the puritanically moral language" of late modernism. He asserted that the modernists had, in their revolutionary zeal, simplified and clarified architecture to the point of separating it "from the experience of life and the needs of society." While this simplification resulted in some beautiful buildings, the major result in the later years of modernism was a pervasive blandness or, as Venturi put it in his rewording of Mies van der Rohe's famous dictum, "Less is a bore" (1).

Instead, he called for "a complex and contradictory architecture based on the richness and ambiguity of modern experience." He continued (2),

> I am for messy vitality over obvious unity. I include the non sequitur and proclaim the duality. I am for richness of meaning rather than clarity of meaning. . . . I prefer "both-and" to "either-or," black and white, and sometimes gray, to black or white.

Perhaps the most influential aspect of the book was its exuberant embrace of historical example as a source for contemporary inspiration. Modernism had eschewed historical reference, asserting that the past was irrelevant to modern architectural concerns. Venturi, however, found rich lessons in the full range of the world's architecture, and illustrated his theories using examples from many periods and styles. This acknowledgment of the continuity of architectural experience helped bring about the rapprochement with the past that has been a major characteristic of architecture in the 1980s.

In 1972, Venturi, Scott Brown, and Steven Izenour published *Learning from Las Vegas,* in which they took the controversial approach of studying a form of building generally held in contempt, the commercial architecture of the highway "strip," as epitomized by Las Vegas. They believed that such vernacular architecture often demonstrated creative solutions to difficult problems and that "high-design" architects could learn important lessons from them.

Specifically, the book analyzed the use of symbolism on the strip as a basis for understanding symbolism as a significant element of architecture. On the strip, the large-scale, attention-grabbing signs became the most important design elements, adorning buildings that were little more than utilitarian sheds. The authors contrasted this "decorated shed" with the "heroic and original" structures of late modernism, which, to compensate for their ideology-imposed lack of ornament, were distorted in program and structure to become ornaments themselves. The authors concluded that the decorated shed, as a legitimate and relatively inexpensive response to modern conditions, had more relevance to the present world than the costly contortions of the modernist monuments (3).

> Architecture for the last quarter of our century should be socially less coercive and aesthetically more vital than the striving and bombastic buildings of our recent past. We architects

can learn this from Rome and Las Vegas and from looking around us wherever we happen to be.

Both *Complexity and Contradiction* and *Learning from Las Vegas* caused considerable controversy because of their challenge to the status quo, but they were embraced by a rising generation of architects who shared the dissatisfaction with the restrictions of orthodox modernism and were searching for valid alternatives. The books have remained in print and are still widely read in the United States and abroad. Venturi and Scott Brown have continued to develop and evaluate their theories in essays and addresses, and a number of these were collected in 1984 in *A View from the Campidoglio*.

As important as these theoretical investigations have been, however, the partners have always been first and foremost practicing architects and planners, and it is in the firm's work that their theories find realization and validation. The early work of the firm was as controversial as the writing, because it embodied the challenges expressed in the theory. The Vanna Venturi House (Fig. 1), for example, which Venturi designed for his mother in the early 1960s, broke many of the rules that modern architects were expected to follow: the facade contained applied ornament and historical allusion, especially in its broken pediment and traditional, multipaned windows; the symmetry of the plan was distorted to acknowledge and accommodate the functions of the various parts; and the house was painted an unorthodox green. In turn reviled and revered, it has become an icon of the postmodern movement.

The Guild House, an apartment building for the elderly built in 1965, offended because it did not try to be heroic, but rather was "ugly and ordinary" (4). It attempted to relate to the modest brick commercial and residential buildings around it. The tenants of the building were to be drawn from the surrounding neighborhood and the architects felt it was appropriate that the building reflect that neighborhood, rather than try to make an original architectural statement. This was achieved through the use of familiar (though subtly altered) elements such as red brick and double-hung windows. This concern for a building's context, unusual at the time but commonplace today, has been a hallmark of the firm's work from the beginning.

In urban planning, too, VRSB has made important contributions that have helped change conventional wisdom. In 1968, the firm, under the direction of Scott Brown, was retained to assist the Crosstown Community, a racially mixed area at the southern edge of Philadelphia's city center, in proposing alternatives to a planned expressway that threatened to obliterate the neighborhood. The resulting plan was developed in consultation with the residents themselves and was based on their needs and aspirations. It called for the enhancement, in practical, incremental steps, of what was already present in the community, rather than destroying the old and (maybe) replacing it with something "better," the prevailing planning philosophy of the time. The plan tried to show (5)

> that beauty could emerge from the existing fabric and that a not-too-apparent order should be sought from within instead of an easy one imposed from above. That piecemeal development need not spell disunity.

This philosophy is accepted wisdom today, and has informed the firm's subsequent planning efforts in such diverse communities as Miami Beach, Minneapolis, Memphis, and Mauch Chunk, Pennsylvania.

Although the firm has been closely identified in the public mind with postmodernism, the partners have, in fact, strived to stay clear of stylistic labels, and the firm's work shows a greater diversity than such designation might lead one to expect. This arises from a commitment to approach each project with an open mind, rejecting preconceptions and working to understand the traditions and needs of clients and users before arriving at design alternatives. Such an open process can lead to creative solutions that are at once appropriate and unexpected. At Philadelphia's Franklin Court (Fig. 2), for example, the

Figure 2. Franklin Court, Philadelphia, Pa. Courtesy of Mark Cohn.

Figure 1. Vanna Venturi House, Chestnut Hill, Pa. Photograph by Rollin La France.

Figure 3. Sainsbury Wing, National Gallery, London, UK. Miles Ritter, watercolorist; Gareth Schuh, delineator.

National Park Service wished to create a monument to Benjamin Franklin on the site of his long-demolished home. Research could not turn up enough evidence to allow an accurate reconstruction of the house, so the firm designed a series of ghost structures in steel that suggest the outlines of the house and its outbuildings. Although certainly an unconventional approach, the result is far more honest—and even profound—than a conjectural reconstruction could ever have been.

Over the years, the firm has maintained a strong practice, completing more than 400 designs and projects in cities and campuses throughout the United States and in Italy and Iraq. Current projects include major museums in Seattle, Wash., Austin, Texas, and La Jolla, Calif.; an extension, the Sainsbury Wing, to the National Gallery in London (Fig. 3); a new concert hall for the Philadelphia Orchestra; and projects for Princeton, Harvard, the University of Pennsylvania, UCLA, and Dartmouth. The firm's work has received extensive critical appraisal at home and abroad and has received over 70 major design awards, including, in 1985, the American Institute of Architects Architectural Firm Award, for having "so profoundly influenced the direction of modern architecture" (6).

BIBLIOGRAPHY

1. R. Venturi, *Complexity and Contradiction in Architecture,* The Museum of Modern Art, New York, 1966, p. 17.
2. Ref. 1, p. 16.
3. R. Venturi, D. Scott Brown, and S. Izenour, *Learning from Las Vegas,* MIT Press, Boston, Mass., p. xvii.
4. Ref. 3, p. 90.
5. D. Scott Brown, "An Alternate Proposal That Builds on the Character and Population of South Street," *Architectural Forum,* **135**(3) 44 (Oct. 1971).
6. "Venturi, Rauch and Scott Brown Wins the 1985 AIA Firm Award," press release, American Institute of Architects, Washington, D.C., Feb. 1, 1985.

General References

R. Venturi and D. Scott Brown, *A View from the Campidoglio: Selected Essays 1953–1984,* Harper & Row, New York, 1984.

S. von Moos, *Venturi, Rauch and Scott Brown: Buildings and Projects,* Rizzoli, New York, 1987.

DAVID A. DASHIELL III
Venturi, Rauch and Scott Brown
Philadelphia, Pennsylvania

VERTICAL TRANSPORTATION

Since earliest times people have searched for a practical way to transport goods vertically. By the Roman era, lifting devices consisting of a basket hauled up by a rope passed over a pulley were in use. In the Middle Ages various types of hoisting systems were common, including those powered by water as well as human- and animal-motivated systems (Fig. 1). In the Renaissance, Leonardo da Vinci, in his projects for machines, proposed gear trains composed of endless screws, related to the lifting jack (Fig. 2). This type of system was used in the 15th century for lifting heavy weights, ie, the straightening of the tower of the Podesta in Bologna (1).

Figure 1. Kyeser's elevator, ca 1400. Courtesy of Crown Publishers, Inc.

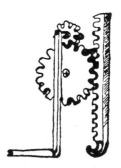

Figure 2. Lifting jack, ca 1500, Leonardo da Vinci. Courtesy of Crown Publishers, Inc.

Although these early elevators were used for transportation of people as well as goods, the problem of passenger safety had never been resolved. An example of this is an elevator developed in the 17th century for human transportation. This "flying chair" consisted of a chair, attached to a rope, that was free to move up and down in a shaft in the building in which it was installed. The chair was counterweighted by a lead block (2). Such flying chairs were used by members of several European royal families, and Louis XVI's daughter was involved in a serious accident on one of the chairs at Versailles (3).

In the first part of the 19th century a power driven elevator called a Teagle lift was developed in England (Fig. 3). The cab was counterbalanced, hoisted by ropes, and steam driven. By 1850 a similar type of system was introduced in the United States, but the real public awareness of elevator transportation came when an elevator was installed in the Crystal Palace Exhibition in New York City in 1853. This was the first safety elevator of Elisha Graves Otis, founder of the Otis Elevator Company.

As an employee of a bedstead manufacturing firm, Otis

had invented a safety device that would prevent the factory's freight elevator from falling should the hoisting ropes break. He then started his own business manufacturing safety elevators. The first demonstration of these elevators was at the Crystal Palace Exhibition (Fig. 4). The *New York Tribune* reporting on the machinery at the exhibition said "We may commence by referring to an elevator or machine for hoisting goods exhibited by E. G. Otis of Yonkers—which attracts attention both by its prominent position and by the apparent daring of the inventor, who as he rides up and down the platform occasionally cuts the rope by which it is supported" (4).

With the advent of elevator safeties, it became possible to operate safe passenger elevators. The first public passenger elevator was opened in a New York store, by its owner E. V. Haugwort, in 1857. This elevator traveled five floors, had a top speed of 40 ft/min (0.20 m/s), and was powered by steam engines.

The next major development in elevator technology came when, in 1872, W. Baldwin of Chicago designed the first indirect-acting hydraulic elevator. This type of elevator was capable of speeds of up to 600–700 ft/min (3–3.5

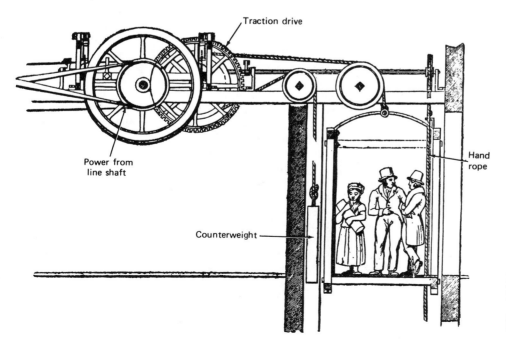

Figure 3. Teagle elevator, ca 1845. Reprinted by permission of John Wiley & Sons, Inc., *Vertical Transportation: Elevators and Escalators,* G. R. Strakosch, 2nd ed., 1983.

m/s). Combined with the Otis governor-operated safety device, introduced in 1878, safe stops at even higher speeds were possible, thus creating the most sophisticated elevator system of its time.

Safe, fast elevators made the upper levels of buildings as desirable to rent as those closer to the street and were instrumental in stimulating high-rise construction. In the late 1880s, cast iron and steel-frame buildings of 10 stories and more were being built in cities in the United States. All were served by elevators.

During this same period the forerunners of modern elevators were being developed. Before this time, electric elevators were powered by direct current, but in 1899 the Otis Company produced its first elevator powered by alternating current. In 1892, Otis introduced the first motor-generator set for controlling hoist motors, a system still in use today, and in 1893 a limited type of push-button elevator control was invented. The gearless traction elevator, which is now the standard for high-rise construction, was first introduced in 1904, but it was slow, continuous development over the next 80 years that eventually resulted in elevators with all the features commonly seen today.

Most of these advances were related not to the machines that power the elevator but to the controls and safeties that made passenger use more efficient. Until 1937, when automatic leveling of the cab was developed, (5) car and hoistway doors were retractable gates that enabled the operator to see the landing and level the cab manually. From 1937 until the late 1950s, gates were replaced with solid car doors that provided more protection for the car and for the hoistway. In the early 1920s a system was developed to close elevator gates automatically. Later, interlocking car and hoistway doors were developed, but attendant supervision was still required until door safeties were developed and installed in the 1950s (6). These safeties prevented premature closing of the doors, and their automatic retraction should they encounter an obstacle.

Most recent improvements in elevators have been in the electronics field, with introduction in the last 15 years of more sophisticated motion control systems and operations systems that instruct the elevator and oversee its operation. This aspect of elevator systems will be discussed at greater length later in this article.

Today, for the safety of the general public, elevator manufacture and installation in the United States is regulated by a national elevator code. Commonly referred to as ASME/ANSI A17.1, this code is in full the American National Standard Safety Code for Elevators, Escalators and Moving Walks written by the American National Standards Committee A17 on a Safety Code for Elevators. This code is superseded or augmented by local codes in some areas. For information on elevator codes that might be applicable in a given area, it is wise to contact the local, county, or state building code officials who have jurisdiction. When code issues are addressed in this article, unless otherwise stated, A17.1 will be the code referenced for elevator issues.

Access to buildings by the handicapped is a major issue related to elevator design and installation. American National Standard Code A117.1–1986, American National

(a)

Figure 4. (a) Otis' demonstration. Crystal Palace, N.Y., 1853 (b) Otis' patent sketch for a safety device. Courtesy of Archive United Technologies Corporation, Hartford, Conn.

Standard Specifications for Making Buildings and Facilities Accessible to and Usable by Physically Handicapped People, is the national code that addresses such issues and will be the code referenced in this article. As previously noted, this code too has been superseded or augmented in some jurisdictions.

All elevator systems are made up of essentially the same components (Fig. 5). The one component of the system that is often referred to as "the elevator" is in fact the car or cab—the passenger-handling part of the system. No matter what type of mechanical system is used to move the car from floor to floor, the car will appear essentially the same to the user, taking into account variations in the individual design of the car interior, which will be discussed later in this article. The only dissimilarities that might be discerned by an observant passenger are differences in speed of the moving car and a slightly different sensation as the car levels at the landing before the doors are opened. These are related to the operation of the systems that power the car.

The car moves from floor to floor in a hoistway or shaft. This specially designed space is intended to house the car and the mechanical components that hoist the car from

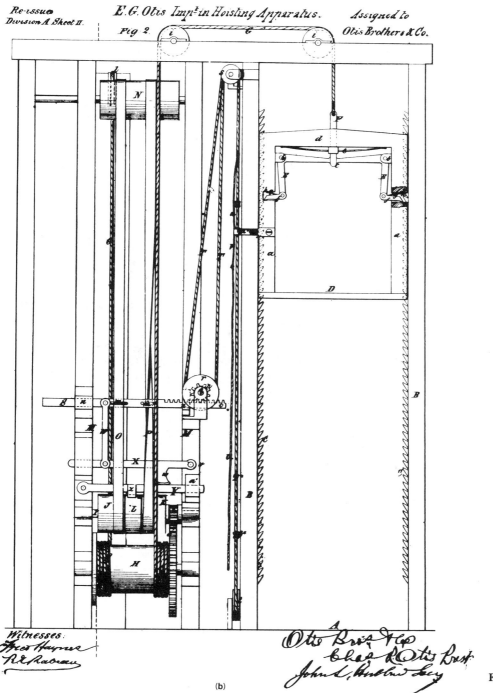

E.G. Otis Imp.t in Hoisting Apparatus. *Assigned to*
Otis Brothers & Co.

Fig 2

Witnesses:

(b)

Figure 4. *(continued)*

floor to floor. It is only accessible on a typical floor through the hall entrances that give access to the car. Under normal circumstances, the hall entrances will not open unless they are interlocked with a corresponding set of doors on the elevator car. An exception to this is when this automatic system is overridden by an elevator inspector needing access to the pit or top of the car.

At the top of the hoistway is the overhead or overrun space. This is the space beyond the last stop, above the top of the elevator car, that is intended to protect the elevator equipment and passengers in the unlikely event that the elevator should overrun its final stop. Below the final stop of the elevator in the hoistway is the pit. The pit contains buffers that limit the downward movement of the car and counterweights. Normal access to the hoistway is at this point, either by a door at the pit level or by a ladder from the level of the last stop. The vertical dimension of both the overhead space and the pit are determined by the height and speed of the elevator and vary considerably from system to system. This aspect of elevators will be discussed in more detail later in this article.

The distance from the lowest landing or stop of an ele-

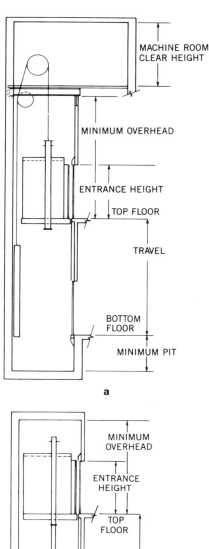

a

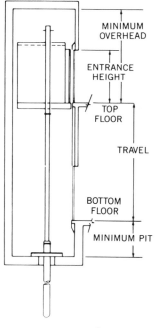

b

Figure 5. (a) Traction elevator (b) hydraulic elevator. Courtesy of Schindler Elevator Corporation.

vator to its highest landing level is usually referred to as its total travel. The number of total stops an elevator system can serve is a function of its maximum total travel.

Depending on the type of elevator system in use, the mechanical space will be adjacent to either the top or the bottom of the hoistway. This area is normally called either the elevator machine room or the elevator machine space.

Selection of a type of elevator is in most cases a selection of the type of mechanical characteristics that are most appropriate in a given situation. The considerations involve a number of features, including car size, weight capacity, speed, and cost. The two most common types of elevator systems available today are traction elevators and hydraulic elevators. These two elevator-system types differ greatly, not only in terms of the mechanical systems used to power them, but in terms of the features offered by each system.

The following description of system types is intended to outline systems that are produced commercially by a number of vendors. Each vendor makes a variety of pre-engineered elevators of each type, and there is a great deal of flexibility within a given range. Typically, elevator manufacturers work with engineering and design professionals and their clients to arrive at an elevator system that meets the demands of a given situation. For complex or unusual design conditions, an elevator consultant or elevator engineer may be employed to design a custom system. For most situations, however, an existing system can be identified to satisfy the design requirements.

As a general rule, hydraulic elevators are not capable of total travel of more than 70 ft (21.3 m). This, plus their slow speeds up to 200 ft/min (1 m/s) make them best

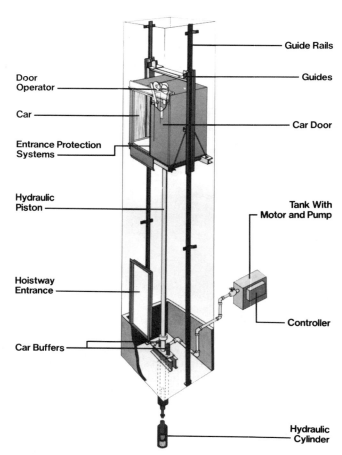

Figure 6. Hydraulic elevator with piston (hydraulic cylinder). Courtesy of Otis Elevator.

suited to low-rise applications. They are capable of lifting great loads and are frequently used as service and freight elevators in commercial applications. Because they do not require as much overhead and pit depth as traction elevators, they lend themselves to a variety of locations where traction elevators would not be appropriate.

Two common types of hydraulic elevator systems are commercially available today. The most common is the direct plunger driven from below (Fig. 6). This system is capable of the greatest speeds and the most total travel of the hydraulic elevators. The elevator car enclosure sits on a platform that is powered by a piston that extends as far into the ground as the elevator is required to rise vertically. Oil, under pressure from high-speed pumps located in the machine space, is forced under the piston and causes the car to rise. Single-piston (also called single-ram) load capacities are from 2000 to 20,000 lb (900–9000 kg), but multiple rams may be used to carry heavier loads. Multiple-ram applications include truck elevators and specialized heavy industrial uses.

Less common, but very useful for retrofitting low-rise residential and commercial structures or providing additional elevator service within a multistoried suite of offices, is the holeless hydraulic elevator (Fig. 7). This elevator operates on the same basic principle as the direct plunger-driven system except that the piston that raises and lowers the car is inverted, or manufactured in telescoping sections. The piston is located adjacent to the car in the elevator hoistway, allowing car movement without the obvious limitation of the piston extending several stories below the pit floor. At this time, this type of hydraulic elevator is limited to about 20 ft (6 m) of total travel, with three stops and a maximum speed of 125 ft/min (0.6 m/s).

In both types of hydraulic elevator the machine room is typically located directly adjacent to the elevator hoistway. However, the only connection between the piston and the pumps that pressurize the oil is an electrical conduit and the oil line. Therefore, it is possible to locate the elevator machine room remotely from the hoistway. This can be invaluable in retrofitting an existing building where available space is limited.

Elevators used in medium- and high-rise buildings are electric traction elevators, as are some residential elevators and dumbwaiters. Traction elevators work on a basic principle very different from hydraulic elevators. Instead of the elevator cab being pushed up from below, in a traction elevator the cab is hung from above using a series of wire cables called the elevator or hoisting ropes (Fig. 8). These cables pass through the top of the hoistway into the elevator machine space where they pass over the drive or traction sheave and reduce the unbalanced load which must be moved and stopped by the hoisting machine. Traction is obtained through the pressure of the ropes on the sheave, achieved through a variety of possible roping strategies involving secondary or deflector sheaves, an explanation of which is beyond the scope of this article. Simply stated, the ropes pass over the traction sheave and secondary sheave in a series of grooves and back into the hoistway where they are connected to the counterweight. The counterweight does exactly what its name implies, providing sufficient load opposite the elevator cab to cause friction at the traction sheave. The sheave, powered by the

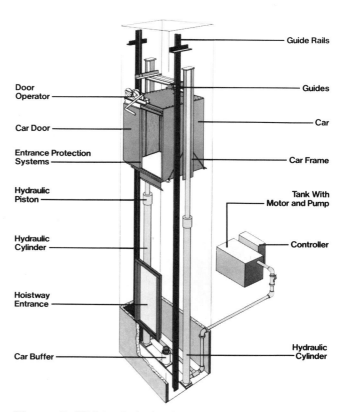

Figure 7. "Holeless" hydraulic elevator with telescoping plunger. Courtesy of Otis Elevator.

elevator motor or machine, can then use this friction to move the elevator cab up and down in the hoistway while the counterweight moves in the opposite direction with the least possible horsepower.

The counterweight is a stack of steel weights traveling in a frame to which the elevator cables are attached. It travels in guide rails that are attached to the hoistway wall (Fig. 9).

The car is protected from free-falling in the hoistway by the car safety. As noted earlier, Elisha Graves Otis' great contribution to the passenger elevator industry was his invention of a practical elevator car safety. The first Otis safety was an instantaneous type that stopped the car in case of slack or broken hoisting ropes. Sudden stoppage would be dangerous with higher speed elevators once the elevator had reached a certain rate of travel; therefore, Otis introduced the governor-type of safety device in 1878 (7). This type of safety is tripped when the car reaches a rate of speed faster than the maximum speed for which the system is designed. Once tripped, the safety gradually brings the car to a complete stop. Governor safeties are still in use today.

To allow occupied space below the elevator pit, a safety for the counterweight it also required. This horseshoe-shaped device can reduce the speed of the counterweight the same way the cab safety prevents overspeeding of the car, through friction. This device requires additional space in the hoistway, the implications of which will be discussed later in this article. In addition, an impact slab

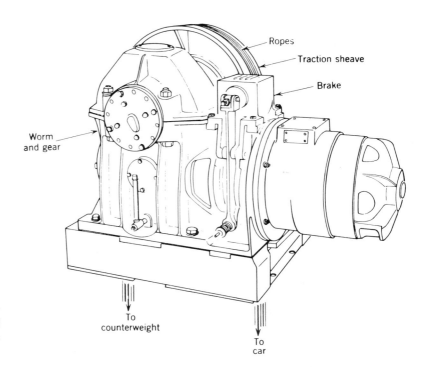

Figure 8. Geared traction machine. Reprinted by permission of John Wiley & Sons, Inc., *Vertical Transportation: Elevators and Escalators,* G. R. Strakosch, 2nd ed., 1983.

is required at the hoistway floor to further protect occupied spaces below.

It is possible to rope a traction elevator in such a way that the traction sheave and machine can be located beside rather than directly over the hoistway. The machine can be located at any level even below the lowest landing. In some instances the cables pass beneath the car frame rather than being attached to the top of the car. These are referred to as underslung or overslung elevators, a description of their roping. They are not recommended by most elevator manufacturers because the double length of cable required to travel to the top of the hoistway and back down to the hoisting machine is subject to stretching and wear, which lessen life expectancy and increase maintenance.

Like hydraulic elevators, traction elevators are available in two distinct operational variations—geared and gearless. And like hydraulic elevators, each type is appropriate for different applications.

In geared traction elevators a high-speed motor drives a worm and gear reduction unit that in turn drives the hoisting sheave described above. It is this geared drive that distinguishes this type of system. Pre-engineered systems are available that will carry 2000–4500 lb (900–2000 kg.) at speeds of from 200–450 ft/min (1.00–2.25 m/s). These comparatively low speeds make these systems unsuited to high-rise passenger applications, and, in fact, geared elevators are rarely used for buildings with more than 13 or 14 stops. However, two major advantages ensure the geared traction elevator its share of the market in midrise installations. First, the flexibility of worm/gear ratios, motor speeds, and roping arrangements make the geared systems practical for a wide range of speeds and loading requirements. Second, at this writing, the single biggest advantage of the geared system over gearless, in most applications, is the lower cost of equipment at the time of installation.

Gearless traction elevators are the standard type of elevator used in high rise, high-speed situations. They are generally applied at speeds from 500 to 1400 ft/min (2.5–7 m/s), though speeds up to 2000 ft/min (10 m/s) are in operation in commercial buildings; common capacities range from 2500 to 4000 lb (1100–1800 kg). These elevators are powered by a slow-speed dc motor that directly drives a large-diameter traction sheave. These systems are easy to maintain, dependable, and long lasting. In addition, their smoothness of operation makes them appropriate for situations that may not require great speed but where the sensation of effortless, elegant movement is desired.

All elevators, regardless of the way they are powered, have motion control and operations systems that control and instruct the motors that power the elevators. Motion control can be seen as a set of responses that are built into the mechanical system of the elevator itself. These responses are a function of the electrical system selected to control the motor operations. Because this selection will effect means and speed of door opening and closing, speed of the car in the hoistway, acceleration, deceleration, leveling, and stopping, and as a consequence be a factor in total elevator performance, it is worth mentioning here.

As previously mentioned, early elevators employed generator field control using motor-generator sets to provide direct current power for the motion control systems. These are commonly used today on both geared and gearless electric-traction elevator systems. Also in use on gearless traction elevator systems are more sophisticated solid-state electronic controls, silicon-controlled rectifiers to provide DC power, and more recently, variable frequency and variable voltage alternating current (AC) power. Hydraulic elevators and some slow-speed electric-traction elevators use relatively unsophisticated single- or two-speed alternating current as a motion control system, which accounts for their lower speeds.

However, as already stated, the motion control system

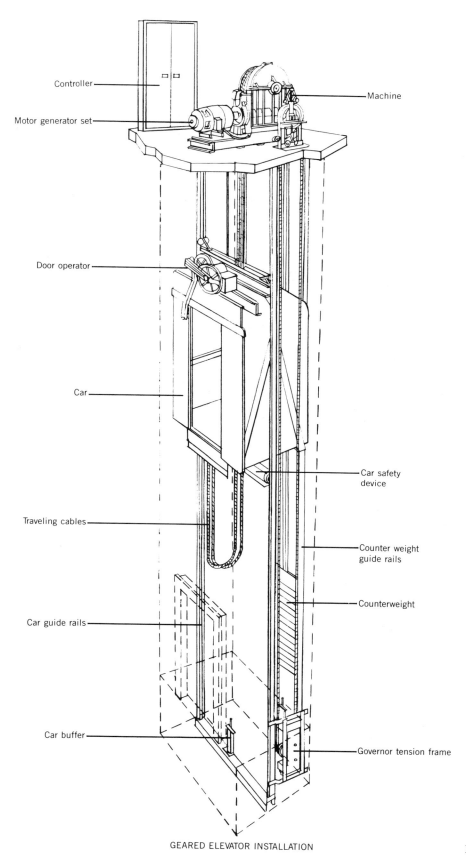

Controller

Motor generator set

Machine

Door operator

Car

Car safety device

Traveling cables

Counter weight guide rails

Counterweight

Car guide rails

Car buffer

Governor tension frame

GEARED ELEVATOR INSTALLATION

Figure 9. Geared elevator installation.

is a part of the pre-engineered elevator package and not an item over which the consumer has much selective control. Therefore, the speed and performance of the pre-engineered elevator system must be considered as a whole when the system is specified.

Elevator operations systems control the ability of the elevator to respond to demands for service. In early elevators these functions were performed by elevator operators. As speed of elevators increased, it became impossible for operators to respond quickly enough to stop elevators within leveling distance of floors requiring service, and leveling systems were developed. Elevator operators still performed the function of opening and closing both car and hoistway doors until the 1950s when a reliable system of door protective devices became available. These door protective devices prevented premature closing of the doors. Now these functions, and many more, are handled by the operations system.

The operations control system on new elevators is essentially a microprocessor network that gathers pertinent information from the elevator cars—passenger load, speed and direction of movement, calls originating in the car—and information being generated by other sources—calls from hall stations and direction, speed, and load of other elevators in the system. It is also able to take into account other programmable inputs—time of day, day of the week, parking strategies for idle elevators, time individual calls should wait before being answered, etc. It dispatches elevator cars in the most efficient way to meet the needs of the system on a minute-to-minute basis. Obviously, with the revolution that has been going on in the microprocessor industry in recent years, the sophistication of these systems has greatly increased. In fact, recent improvements in elevator performance are all related to the more efficient use of systems that were introduced in the early part of this century, through the more sophisticated controls available with microprocessors. Microprocessors are now being used to upgrade the responses of the motion control systems mentioned earlier and to identify and locate parts of the system in need of repair. Design professionals and their clients must be aware that the elevator system should not be tied into the overall building automation system, as this would make the elevators subject to the control of two systems instead of one and probably less reliable. Whatever specific features may be desired in an elevator control system, they should be identified early in the building planning process and specified in detail to ensure that the most appropriate total system will be provided for the building.

Two other kinds of vertical transportation, dumbwaiters and residential elevators, are important in both the design of new structures and the retrofitting of existing structures today. As they have become more economical in recent years, they have become more popular for a wide range of applications.

Dumbwaiters and residential elevators both travel in hoistways like full-size elevators and have certain requirements for pit and overrun space. They are not normally required to have separate machine spaces; often such equipment is located at the top of or adjacent to the bottom of the hoistway. They are available with either a geared traction lifting system, like the full-size elevators

already discussed, or a winding drum lift that operates on the winch system.

Dumbwaiters are defined by the national code as no more than 9 ft² (0.8 m²) in platform area and no more than 48 in. (122 cm) in height. Anything larger than this is considered to be an elevator or special materials lift. Dumbwaiters come as pre-engineered units in a variety of sizes, designed for different weight capacities and platform speeds. Drum-lift dumbwaiters, which have the most economical installation costs, can carry from 50 to 500 lb (23–225 kg) and usually travel at a speed of 50 ft/min (0.25 m/s). Most are designed for two or three stops, but some are capable of a total travel of 100 ft (30 m). Machines are usually located at the bottom of the hoistway when travel is limited (Fig. 10).

Traction dumbwaiters are nothing less than small traction elevators. They can carry up to 500 lb (225 kg) in load and are capable of speeds of up to 500 ft/min (2.5 m/s). Total travel on many units is virtually unlimited. Machines can be located at the top or the bottom of the hoistway. Despite higher initial costs, the speed and flexibility of this type of dumbwaiter would make it the obvious selection for a medium- to high-rise hospital or library.

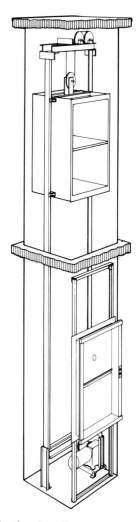

Figure 10. A dumbwaiter. Courtesy of Sedgwick Lifts.

Manual dumbwaiters are still available. By pulling on the dumbwaiter cable the user performs the function of the hoisting mechanism. Unfortunately, if this system does not prove to be satisfactory to the user, it cannot be upgraded to a power-operated system but must be totally replaced.

Residential elevators have many characteristics similar to those of the dumbwaiters. They have a maximum car platform size of 12 ft² (1.11 m²). However, cars are usually 8-ft (2.43-m) tall, like a full-size elevator. Drum-lift residential elevators travel at speeds up to 30 ft/min (0.15 m/s) and carry 450 lb (200 kg). Traction systems can carry up to 700 lb (315 kg) at 35 ft/min (0.17 m/s) or faster. Machine space locations are above, below or beside the hoistway.

In reviewing the different types of elevator equipment available, a variety of factors have been considered. The most important of these—speed and carrying capacity of the elevator—are among the items of information involved in determining the type, number, and size of the elevators most appropriate for a given application.

Speed appears to be a self-explanatory attribute. The faster an elevator travels, the more quickly it can deliver goods and people to their destinations. However, in lower rise buildings the truly critical factor is the floor-to-floor speed. This is a combination of the elevator's travel speed, and its acceleration and deceleration rates which are a function of the motion control system as well as the door opening and closing time. A high speed elevator will be unable to achieve its full speed in the distance between two floors; therefore its speed will be wasted on low- and medium-rise buildings. Speed therefore must be viewed in relation to the demands on the elevator system as a whole.

Capacity of the elevator must also be viewed as more than the simple ability of the machine to lift weight. The shape of the platform is important to its efficient handling of the goods it is intended to carry. For instance, a car designed to carry 3500 lb (1600 kg) may be shaped many different ways. Figure 11 shows one cab designed to carry passengers and one designed to carry a stretcher but also acting as a passenger elevator. Both carry the same load, but car A is a better, more efficient passenger elevator because the wider door and shallower configuration allow passengers to move more quickly in and out of the car. Therefore, consideration of capacity includes type and quantity of goods to be carried. For some standard recommended elevator capacities and platform areas see Table 1. The maximum size of a platform allowed for a certain loading is stipulated in the national elevator code and appears in column five of Table 1.

When designing an elevator system, not only do elevator speed and capacity need to be carefully analyzed but, in addition, it is very important to analyze unique individual building factors including population, building use patterns, overall number of stops, and floor-to-floor heights to develop the most efficient elevator system possible to meet the specific needs of the building. This process will be referred to as elevatoring.

There are many different theoretical approaches to this subject. Each elevator company and elevator engineer will have something unique in their approach that they feel makes their assessment of the elevator system most re-

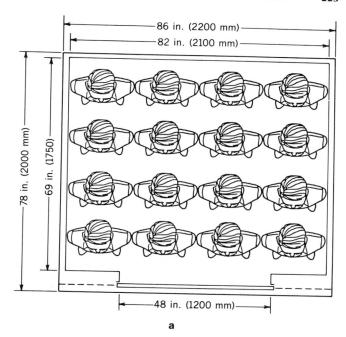

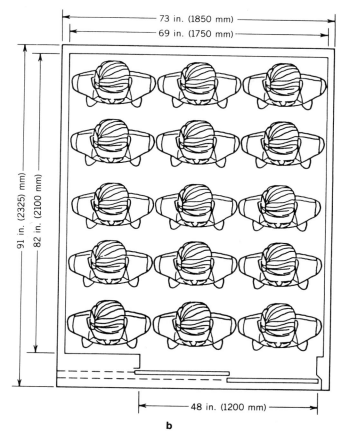

Figure 11. **(a)** Nominal loading, 3500 lb (1600 kg) "passenger-shaped" elevator **(b)** Nominal loading, 3500 lb (1600 kg) "stretcher-shaped" elevator. Reprinted by permission of John Wiley & Sons, Inc., *Vertical Transportation: Elevators and Escalators,* G. R. Strakosch, 2nd ed., 1983.

Table 1. Standard Recommended Elevator Capacities and Platform Areas

Inch/Pound Units

Capacity, lbs	Platform, in.		Car Inside, in.		Area, ft²	A17.1 Area Allowed, ft²	Observed Loading People[a]	Maximum Loading People[b]
	Wide	Deep	Wide	Deep				
2000	72	60	68	51	24.0	24.2	8	16
2500	86	60	82	51	29.0	29.1	10	19
3000	86	66	82	57	32.5	33.7	12	22
3500	86	75	82	66	37.5	38.0	16	26
3500 (alt.)	96	66	92	57	36.4	38.0	16	26
4000	86	82	82	73	41.6	42.2	19	28
4000 (alt.)	96	75	92	66	42.2	42.2	19	28
4500	96	82	92	73	46.6	46.2	21	33
5000	96	86	92	77	48.2	50.0	23	35
6000	96	99	92	90	57.5	57.7	27	41

Metric Units

Capacity, kg (lb)	Platform, mm		Car Inside, mm		Area, m²	Code Area Allowed, m²	Observed Loading People[a]	Maximum Loading People[b]
	Wide	Deep	Wide	Deep				
1200 (2640)	2200	1550	2100	1300	2.7	2.8	10	19 (16)
1400 (3080)	2200	1700	2100	1450	3.05	3.24	12	22 (18)
1600 (3520)	2200	1900	2100	1650	3.5	3.56	16	26 (21)
1600 (alt.)	2450	1700	2350	1450	3.4	3.56	16	26 (21)
1800 (3960)	2200	2050	2100	1800	3.8	3.88	18–19	29 (24)
1800 (alt.)	2450	1900	2350	1650	3.9	3.88	18–19	28 (24)
2000 (4400)	2450	2050	2350	1800	4.2	4.2	20	32 (27)
2250 (4950)	2450	2200	2350	1950	4.6	4.6	22	34 (30)
2700 (5940)	2450	2500	2350	2150	5.1	5.32	25	39 (36)

[a] Based on 2.3 ft² (0.22 m²) per person for 4000 lb and above.
[b] Based on 1.5 ft² (0.14 m²) per person.
Numbers in parentheses in the metric maximum loading column are established in European Code EN81.

sponsive to the actual conditions that will be encountered by system users. The following summary of factors considered in the elevatoring process is intended to provide a basis for understanding the processes and terms involved in most conventional elevatoring.

As an example of elevatoring it is probably most useful to start with a commercial application. Today virtually all commercial buildings constructed on more than one floor will have an elevator system of some kind. Commercial buildings house professional offices, stores, industrial plants, self-park garages, and, for the purposes of this article, will be assumed to include any function in which the building population has its arrival and departure concentrated during certain periods of the workday. This will subject the vertical transportation system to periodic peaks in both incoming and outgoing traffic. If the elevator system can be designed to accommodate these peaks it will perform normally adequately during nonpeak hours unless very unusual circumstances exist.

Accurate estimation of building population is the key to any successful elevator use plan. In an existing building requiring installation of a more updated elevator system, the owner should be able to determine building population per floor and elevator use resulting from tenant operation patterns with great accuracy. In the case of new construction, however, some assumptions must be made.

Office buildings can be divided into different occupancy classifications. First is the single-occupancy building. In this case a single owner/tenant occupies all floors of a building, providing a great deal of control over both the number of occupants per floor and their patterns of elevator use. For instance, although typically this type of building use would call for 12 to 18% or more of the building population to need incoming elevator service during the 5-minute peak directly preceding the time set for the start of work (8), in a single-occupancy building the owner/tenant could stagger work hours for different groups in the building population to reduce the peak load of the elevator system and possibly reduce the number or capacity of cabs required.

In the same way, a single tenant could determine the number of occupants per floor to be greater or fewer than would be indicated by a standard occupant per square footage calculation. Population in this type of building can be estimated on the basis of 120 ft²/person (11 m²/person), where the square footage is based on the net usable area per floor. In a very luxurious office setting the square footage allowed per occupant could be considerably higher than this; open-office settings could result in population densities of 100 ft²/person (9 m²/person). The more narrowly the occupant is able to estimate the probable use of building space, the greater the possible efficiency of the building's elevator system. It should be mentioned that there is some risk involved in tailoring any building to the specific needs of the immediate occupants if that would result in insufficient service for the building should the single occupancy change to a diversified building.

In a diversified building occupants are likely to be from different industries and would occupy various amounts of space within the building. This could result in the natural staggering of work hours lowering the impact of the incoming rush peak. Although this incoming peak would still occur, it may involve only 10–15% of the population as opposed to 12–20% in a single-tenant building (9).

Diversified building occupants are also calculated to require the greatest amount of square footage per person. This is due to the spatial inefficiencies caused by repetition of entrances, lobbies, reception areas, and support spaces. Normally, the population of a diversified building is calculated at 150 ft^2/person (14 m^2/person) of the net usable area in the building.

Within a single building there may be more than one type of occupancy. High-rise buildings with banks of elevators serving different groups of floors may have an area that is primarily diversified occupancy, a group of floors that have a single occupancy, and another group of floors that are residential. Obviously, the needs of all these user groups must be studied before the best elevator system can be designed.

This discussion of population and peak traffic for one building type should give an idea of the complexity of the issues involved in all types of population estimates for all building types. Because estimation of building population is so critical to proper design of the elevator system, if clear assumptions cannot be made it might be helpful to contact the local board of realtors for appropriate occupancy estimates in the area. Also, the local representative of one of the major elevator companies or an elevator consultant should be able to provide useful information from related experience.

In elevator speed and capacity and building population and user patterns we see the major components that will make it possible to design the elevator system for a building. With a few additional assumptions about floor-to-floor heights, lobby-level heights, and number of floors served, it is possible to proceed in determining what the system should be. The following is an example of elevatoring of a small suburban office building, see example below (10).

A. *Given:* Diversified offices, suburban location, investment-type building; 12,000 ft^2 gross per floor, 10 floors, 12-ft floor heights. Population: $12,000 \times 0.80 = 9600$ ft^2 net per floor @ 125 ft^2 per person = 77 people per floor.
Total population floors 2–10 = 693 people.
Assume: 10 passengers up per trip, elevators travel at 400 ft/min, 48-in. center-opening doors, floors 1 to 10, 12-ft floor-to-floor, $9 \times 12 = 108$ ft elevator rise
Probable stops: 10 passengers, 9 stops = 6.2, no highest call return

Time to run up, per stop: $\frac{108}{6.2} = 17.4$ ft rise per stop

17.4 ft at 400 ft/min = 6.1 s

Time to run down: $\frac{108}{1+1} = 54$ ft $\frac{(54 - 17.4) \times 60}{400} + 6.1 = 11.6$

Elevator performance calculations:
Standing time

Lobby time 10 + 0.8	= 10.8 s
Transfer time up stops 6.2 × 2	= 12.4
Door time, up stops (6.2 + 1) × 5.3	= 38.2
Transfer time, down stops 1 × 4	= 4.0
Door time, down stops 1 × 5.3	= 5.3
Total standing time	70.7 s
Inefficiency, 10%	= 7.1
Total	77.8 s

Running time

Run up 6.2 × 6.1	= 37.8
Run down 2 × 11.6	= 23.2
Total round-trip time	138.8 s

$$HC = \frac{(10 + 1) \times 300}{138.8} = 23.8 \times 4 = 95 \text{ people}$$

Percent HC: $77 \times 9 = 693$, $95/693 = 13.7\%$
Interval: $138.8/4 = 35$ s
Four 2500-lb elevators @ 400 ft/min required as a minimum.

B. If a single basement garage for 200 cars is added: 200 automobiles at 1.5 people per auto = 300 people = about 50% of building population. Therefore it is likely that elevators will travel to the basement every second trip.
Recalculate round-trip time: building B, floors 1 to 10
Additional time required for trip to basement garage
Stop at lobby—part of original round-trip

Run to basement, 10 ft	= 5.1 s
Transfer at B	= 4.0 s
Add door time B and 1, 2 × 5.3	= 10.6 s
Run up to 1, 10 ft	= 5.1
	24.8 s
Assume every second trip to B, 24.8/2	= 12.4 s

New round-trip time $138.8 + 12.4 = 151.2$ s

$$New HC = \frac{(10 + 1) \times 300}{151.2} \times 4 = 87 \text{ people}$$

New percent HC: $87/693 = 12.6\%$
New interval: $151.2/4 = 38$ s

The major elevator companies in the United States also provide an invaluable service to their clients by performing this type of analysis based on a set of criteria worked out in concert with the owner and his or her consultants. Called elevator or vertical transportation optimization studies, they consider essentially the same factors as the previous example of an elevatoring study in a more simplified form, see example below, and provide the designer and developer with system performance information in terms of the anticipated system performance potential before a user will be able to board the system (11).

Single-Group Up-Peak Elevator Optimization
Project: Lusby Office Building
Date: 03-28-1985
Building Data

Population	180
Lobby floor height	15 ft
Typical floor height	11 ft

Elevator Data

Door close time	3.5 s
Flight time (12-ft run)	4.3 s

Constraints

Minimum % HC up/5 min	12
% HC counterflow/5 min	1.5
% HC interfloor/5 min	.5
Maximum average interval	30 s
Maximum round-trip time	180 s
Minimum car capacity	3000 lb
Maximum car capacity	3500 lb
Max loading for 3000 lb	13
Max loading for 3500 lb	15
Geared (350 ft/min) option?	Y

Elevator Solution 1

No. of cars	Capacity	Speed	Floors Served	Passed	Car loading
8	3500	350	11	0	15

Up-Peak Performance

RTT	%HC			Interval
	Up	Cfl	Int	
150.0	12.1	1.5	0.5	18.8

High call reversal floor	10.7
Probable stops	8.4

Elevator Solution 2

No. of cars	Capacity	Speed	Floors Served	Passed	Car loading
8	3500	500	11	0	14

Up-Peak Performance

RTT	%HC			Interval
	Up	Cfl	Int	
137.8	12.3	1.5	0.5	17.2

High call reversal floor	10.7
Probable stops	8.1

Elevator Configuration

No. of cars	Capacity	Speed	Floors Served	Passed	Car loading
6	3500	500	11	0	15

Up-Peak Performance

RTT	%HC			Interval
	Up	Cfl	Int	
146.6	9.3	1.5	0.5	24.4

High call reversal floor	10.7
Probable stops	8.4

Elevator Solution 10

No. of cars	Capacity	Speed	Floors Served	Passed	Car loading
8	3000	1000	11	0	13

Up-Peak Performance

RTT	%HC			Interval
	Up	Cfl	Int	
128.4	12.3	1.5	0.5	16.1

High call reversal floor	10.6
Probable stops	7.8

As can be seen in the example above, the basic system requirements are tested against a variety of car configurations and speeds to arrive at the most ideal solution at the least cost.

Of this interval, about 60% is waiting time. Studies have shown that elevator users become impatient if waiting time in a commercial environment exceeds 40–50 s. If the average interval is computed to be 30 s, then half the users will wait 0 s and half will wait up to 60% of 60 s or 40 s. Other components of the interval include the door opening and closing times, car loading and unloading, and travel time between floors.

As can be seen, the less time required for waiting, the better users will be satisfied with the elevator system. This would seem to increase the temptation to provide more, faster elevators to reduce the waiting time for passengers. But elevator equipment is expensive to install and the space required for an additional elevator shaft and its lobby and support spaces will reduce the net rentable area on each floor it serves. All these factors must be considered by the building owner and his or her elevator and design consultants before a system is selected.

These calculations assume that all the elevators serving pedestrian traffic demands are available throughout the working day. The unstated implication is that a separate freight elevator will be provided to accommodate tenants who are moving, large-scale deliveries, and building service operations including renovation and redecoration of certain areas of the building. In the long term most building owners find that this additional initial investment proves to be worthwhile. In fact, many discriminating tenants are aware of the value of a separate freight elevator and are willing to pay the increased rent necessary to provide one. A freight elevator should ideally be at least 8 ft in one dimension to allow for the transportation of standard 4 ft × 8 ft building materials and furniture.

The first example, part B, raises another issue common in the elevatoring of commercial buildings and that is access to the parking garage. These parking garages are frequently located below the main lobby level. Obviously, as shown in the example, part B, requiring the elevator system to serve one floor below the lobby level does not greatly increase the service interval. For parking garages greater than one floor and serving the building population as well as people going to other destinations, the situation becomes much more complex. In this situation, many elevator cars will be filled on the parking levels, increasing waiting time for incoming passengers at the main lobby level. Some passengers from the parking levels will only travel as far as the lobby level, and some in-coming passengers will travel from the lobby level to the parking levels, preventing passengers boarding at the lobby level from being carried directly upward to their destinations and increasing their travel time. An additional consideration in this type of situation is security. In many office buildings there is security of some type at the main lobby level. If an elevator car travels directly from the parking levels to the office floors this security could be bypassed. For these reasons it is often recommended that parking levels be served by a set of dedicated elevators. Garage passengers then travel up to the main elevator lobby where they change to the elevators that serve the office building. Office building elevators can then be locked at night while still allowing the garage to operate independently.

The discussion thus far and the two examples of elevatoring given are based on critical levels of elevator use occurring during up-peak periods. They also assume an ability to understand this peak period by analyzing a 5 min segment of time. This is the conventional method for elevator system design. However, as computers and computer assisted design (CAD) systems become more readily available to design professionals, they may become powerful tools in more accurate assessment of system loads by using a supervisory computer program to compile simulation runs of the actual elevator system automatically. This technique could not only help select the best system configuration but also define the most appropriate computer control algorithm to oversee the operations control system (12).

Elevator system design for residential and hospital projects involves the same factors as those considered for commercial applications. There are many differences, however, in the demands that users will put on these different systems.

In residential applications, population figures are based on the number of bedrooms provided. Occupancy per bedroom will vary significantly between a low-income housing project and a "luxury" condominium. Peak traffic times may not be as easy to define in a residential situation. For instance, if most of the residents are working people, the elevator system will experience traffic peaks similar to a commercial building with down-peak rush in the morning the heaviest traffic period. Buildings with more children and nonworking parents or elderly people will see elevator use spread more evenly throughout the day. Hotels with frequent conventions should have the elevator capacity to serve up to 15% of the population in a 5-min period.

In general, people are more tolerant of increased elevator interval in a residential setting. Slower-speed elevators and side opening doors are frequently used in residential applications for increased economy. Residential buildings up to six stories in height with not more than 75 units can be served by one passenger elevator. Separate freight elevators are as desirable in residential settings as they are in commercial. Because of frequent moves, these elevators not only promote efficiency in the main elevator system but prevent unnecessary wear and tear on "public" cars.

Sleeping spaces should not be located next to elevator machine rooms or hoistways. If possible, these spaces should be isolated by mechanical shafts or stairs. If this is not possible, hoistways should be acoustically isolated.

All residential buildings should have at least one 68-in. × 51-in. elevator car to accommodate wheelchairs; codes may require more. In addition, some codes require one elevator car that will accommodate a mobile stretcher. This elevator could double as a freight elevator.

Hospitals present an almost bewildering array of situations with which the elevator system must be prepared to deal. First there is pedestrian traffic, made up of doctors, nurses, patients, outpatients, service personnel, and visitors, occurring in both directions throughout the day. Second, is the vehicular traffic, made up of patients on stretchers or in wheelchairs, service carts, portable equipment, etc. Third, is a system of automated supply carts and robots that serve certain sections of the hospital.

Although in small hospitals there is a temptation to combine pedestrian and vehicular transportation in one set of elevators, each system will be far more effective on its own. It must be remembered that vehicular elevators may be required to respond very quickly in life-threatening situations, a goal often difficult to achieve with an overcrowded mixed-use system. In addition, cars designed to accommodate a motorized hospital bed must have a 6500 lb (3000 kg) capacity, double what is required for a typical passenger elevator.

Beyond this, it is very difficult to generalize about elevator system design requirements for hospitals. Each facility, its traffic patterns, future expansion needs, and short- and long-term system requirements should be studied by design and hospital-care professionals to ensure the most efficient elevator system possible.

For the architect, the issues of elevator size, quantity, and location are integrated with the issues of entry, building organization, core factor, and floor-plate efficiency. The complexity and specificity of these factors in each design situation make it nearly impossible to generalize about the layout of elevators and lobby organization. However, there are certain industry standard practices that will apply in most typical commercial applications. Adherence to these standards will result in not only efficient organization of the hoistways themselves but adequate machine spaces and support areas both above and below the hoistways.

Most people have experienced a standard elevator lobby with between one and eight cars serving a mid- or high-rise building. One to three car groups normally occupy one hoistway and face a single-sided elevator lobby (Fig. 12a). Four to eight cars are normally housed in two or more hoistways facing each other with the typical elevator lobby located between the two (Fig. 12b). Eight is usually the maximum recommended number of passenger elevators to be served by one lobby. A greater number of elevators would require a lobby of such size that the average person would be unable to reach a car calling on the floor in the time that the car doors would remain open. As has previously been discussed, extending the time the elevator doors would remain open would result in inefficiency in the entire system. In addition, circulation becomes a problem as people leaving the main lobby must pass those waiting to load the elevators. A far better alternative is to use two remotely located cores of four or five elevators each, or zone the building into groups of floors served by banks of local and express elevators.

In general, the width of an elevator lobby should be at least twice the depth of the individual elevators it serves

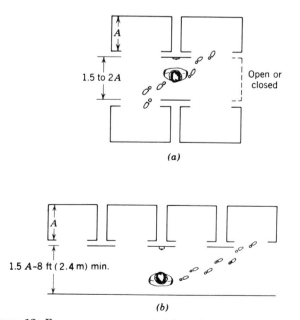

Figure 12. Four-car arrangements **(a)** preferred **(b)** acceptable. Reprinted by permission of John Wiley & Sons, Inc., *Vertical Transportation: Elevators and Escalators*, G. R. Strakosch, 2nd ed., 1983.

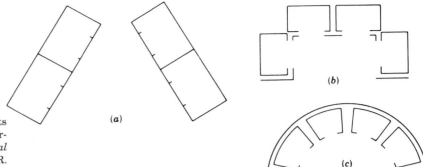

Figure 13. Unique elevator core arrangements (a) angle (b) alcoved (c) circular. Reprinted by permission of John Wiley & Sons, Inc., *Vertical Transportation: Elevators and Escalators,* G. R. Strakosch, 2nd ed., 1983.

but never less than 10-ft wide or greater than 14-ft wide. No person should be expected to travel more than 150 ft (45.72 m) to reach an elevator lobby on a habitable floor (13). Distances to elevators in parking garages, parking structures, factories, and warehouses may be far greater.

From a design perspective, odd numbers of cabs served by the same lobby are often difficult to deal with, primarily because they make the lobby itself more difficult to define as a space. Structural considerations usually make it difficult to space hoistway openings symmetrically, a consideration that will be discussed in more detail later. If a separate service or freight elevator is included in the design, it can sometimes reduce the requirements for passenger elevators, resulting in an even number of elevators served by the main lobby and an adjacent dependent service elevator lobby. All these factors should be considered in the elevator consultants analysis of building requirements and assessed by the designer to achieve the best combination of practical elevatoring and good architectural design.

Elevators may also be grouped in other arrangements such as in a curve, alcove, or square or with banks of elevators facing but not parallel to each other (Fig. 13).

When such a configuration is used, care must be taken to provide adequate waiting and circulation space at the main lobby and adequate machine space in the penthouse.

Many strategies have been devised to make elevator systems more efficient and responsive to specific building requirements. Most frequently seen are freight elevators with front and rear entrances. These double as passenger elevators during peak hours but can also be disconnected from group operation. The rear entrance typically gives access to the loading dock on the ground floor and service lobbies on other floors. In this type of arrangement the front and rear doors are not in operation at the same time and are controlled by separate car-operating panels.

Cars with front and rear entrances are also used when owing to expansion or modification a building has multiple landing levels. In this application, both front and rear entrances serve passengers and give access to different landing levels. For instance, entrance 3F may serve a floor at elevation +25.00 whereas 3R serves the next closest landing level at elevation +28.00 (Fig. 14). Both front and rear doors are served by the same car-operating panels. It should be considered that in this application each level will have an impact on the system the same as if it were

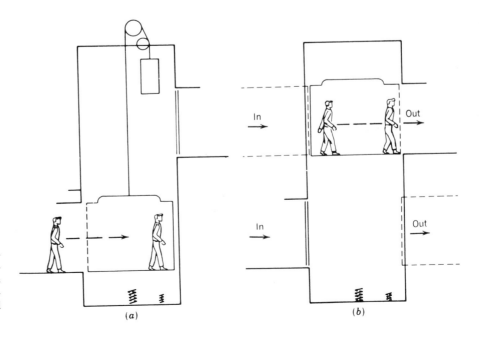

Figure 14. Pedestrian movement on elevators (a) transfer on (b) transfer off. Reprinted by permission of John Wiley & Sons, Inc., *Vertical Transportation: Elevators and Escalators,* G. R. Strakosch, 2nd ed., 1983.

an entirely separate floor, increasing the number of stops and the total requirements of the system.

Elevators can also be equipped with front and side entrances on the same car. These additional entrances can be used in the same way described for the front and rear entrance cars. However, this alternative is much more costly and two-speed doors must be used. An elevator manufacturer or consultant should be contacted before proceeding with a core configuration based on this cab design.

The concept of double-decker cars has also been experimented with, especially in very tall buildings such as the John Hancock Building in Boston and the Citicorp Center in New York. Two cars stacked on top of each other occupy the same hoistway, in theory doubling the capacity of the hoistway. One serves the odd floors and the other the even floors. Because the two elevators load simultaneously from two main lobby levels, these lobbies must be connected by escalators and shuttle elevators for the handicapped. A person entering either car at an upper level must be allowed to select any other floor as his destination. This, and an additional standing-time inefficiency due to the coordination of two elevator doors, increases the trip time in the system. Also, larger elevator machinery and greater hoistway dimensions are required to service the double cars. The positive and negative aspects of such a system must be studied carefully and weighed against both conventional and sky lobbies to decide which system will best serve the needs of the building population.

For extremely tall buildings, both modified conventional and sky lobbies frequently use alternative lobby strategies. In a modified conventional lobby the main lobby is served by two or more banks of elevators. The first serves the lowest group of floors as a bank of local elevators. The other elevators are express to a given floor, where they become local. Possible inefficiencies in this system are obvious. First, all the elevators require separate hoistway space on the lower levels; second, all elevator users must travel to the main lobby to transfer from one set of elevators to another.

Sky lobbies have been developed to reduce some inefficiencies encountered in the modified conventional lobby design. A building with sky lobbies can be seen as a series of shorter buildings stacked on top of one another. The shortest "building" is served by a bank of local elevators whereas shuttles carry passengers to mid- and high-zone sky lobbies where they transfer to local elevators to ride to specific floors. Systems can be designed so that the highest rise elevators in the lower banks serve the sky lobby level above. This gives passengers the ability to travel constantly either up or down in the system without returning to the main lobby to take a shuttle. In planning the building core and the floor-plate efficiency, sky lobbies give the designer the advantage of allowing similar elevator lobbies to be stacked one on top of another for each "building" (Fig. 15).

Some very tall buildings are also mixed-use buildings. The sky-lobby principle works well for such buildings because it is relatively easy to separate the elevator banks into functional groups. Building residents do not necessarily require access to office floors, and for security reasons the public would not be permitted on residential floors.

Considering the high quality of standard elevator systems, layouts, and technical support available from major elevator manufacturers, the most practical course of action when beginning the design process is to solicit their input, or that of a qualified elevator consultant, concerning the number, size, and speed of the elevators to best serve the project. Each elevator manufacturer will have slight variations in the systems, equipment, and layouts that they offer. Figure 16 shows information from a manufacturer on a hoistway layout for a pre-engineered elevator system. This type of information is available from all the major elevator companies, including Otis, Westinghouse, Montgomery, Dover, and Schindler-Haughton, and for the systems and configurations that they typically supply. Because of the variations in manufacturers' systems, there will be corresponding variations in hoistway requirements. However, it is possible to generalize about standard elevator layouts and hoistway design for the most standard types of elevators.

In the simplest terms an elevator hoistway is a hole in the structural slab that constitutes each floor of a building. In most cases a system of columns and beams will be required to support the slab edges at each side of the opening. Structural considerations of the building as a whole will determine exactly what size and shape will be required in these members. For the purposes of preliminary design in a typical medium- or low-rise building, it would be safe to assume that 8- to 12-in.-wide beams or shear walls surround the hoistways and columns at least 12-in.-wide may occur surrounding each group of two elevators (Fig. 17a). As in all structural issues, construction in seismic zones may have additional requirements. These structural elements cannot project into the clear hoistway space required for each car. As noted previously, these demands can make symmetry in a lobby served by an odd number of cars difficult to achieve (Fig. 17b).

The hoistway is surrounded by a 2-h fire-rated enclosure that in most cases is either an 8-in. concrete block wall or a steel stud and gypsum-board partition commonly called a shaft wall. Each of these shaft enclosures has advantages and disadvantages. Concrete block better sound isolates the hoistway from the surrounding floor and is considered by many people to be a superior backup material for stone facing, which is often used in elevator lobbies. Its major disadvantages are its increased cost over other systems and its slower erection time.

Gypsum drywall-cavity shaft wall consists of a stud-type known as a CH stud, two layers of ½-in. fire-code gypsum panels, and a 1-in. gypsum liner panel (Fig. 18a). This 3½-in. assembly is 2-h rated and applicable in most typical circumstances for heights up to 12 ft. The manufacturer recommends that a 5-in.-deep assembly be used at the front of the hoistway to allow space for elevator control and signal fixtures that project into the hoistway space when flush mounted in the wall (Figs. 18b and 18c).

This type of wall can be used as a base for mounting other veneer materials such as stone, wood paneling, or veneer plaster if care is used to select studs of sufficient size to carry the additional load. Although these assem-

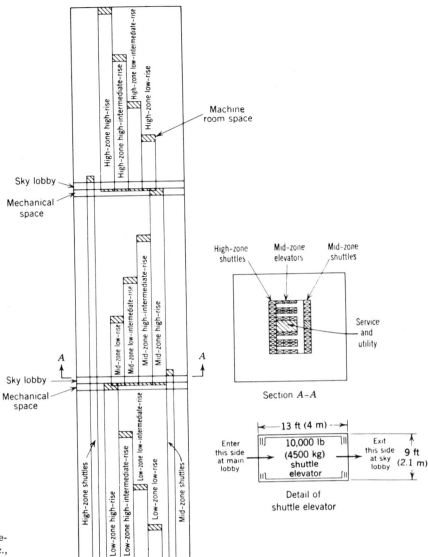

Figure 15. World Trade Center, New York. Reprinted by permission of John Wiley & Sons, Inc., *Vertical Transportation: Elevators and Escalators,* G. R. Strakosch, 2nd ed., 1983.

blies do not provide the same degree of sound isolation as concrete block, they are low cost and quickly erected.

Inside the hoistway enclosure wall is the rough hoistway opening. On the door side of the hoistway the finished sill projects into the rough hoistway. The dimension required varies, depending on the type of doors used. Single-slide and center-opening doors need 5 in.; two-speed and two-speed center-opening doors need 6½-in. of space for the finished sill (Fig. 19).

Single-slide, center-opening, and two-speed doors are the standard types of doors used on passenger elevators. Swing doors on the hoistway side are also permitted by code but are used almost exclusively for small personal elevators, such as those found in a private residence. This type of door is usually teamed with a manual gate on the cab.

An entirely different class of doors is frequently used in freight and industrial applications. These are vertical bi-parting doors or gates. As their name implies, these doors part in the middle, one section traveling up and the other down. They leave the entire width of the platform open for loading. These doors are so massive that it is usually preferred that they be motor operated; however, some sizes are available manually operated. These doors are not appropriate for passenger use because they lack the safety features built into typical passenger systems.

Elevator doors and frames are an important component of the 2-h-rated hoistway enclosure. They are 1½-h-rated assemblies, which when adequately attached to the 2-h-rated hoistway enclosure provide fire separation between the hoistway and habitable building floors. These doors are coordinated with similar doors on the face of the cab.

The space beyond the finished sill is called the clear hoistway. In general, a front-opening traction elevator with speeds up to 350 ft/min (1.78 ms) will require the following hoistway clearances: 8 in. (20.51 cm) either side

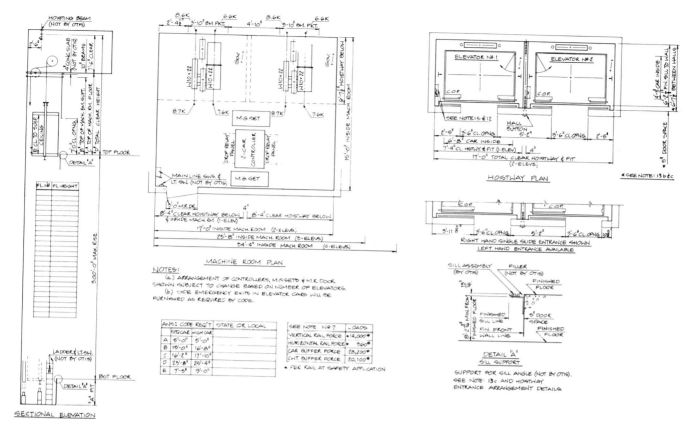

Figure 16. Manufacturers layout for a 2500 lb, 350 ft/min traction passenger elevator. Courtesy of Otis Elevator.

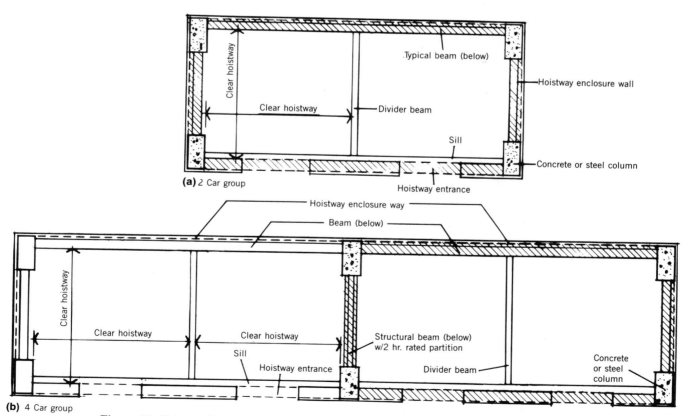

Figure 17. Hoistway layouts for similar pre-engineered elevator systems (a) 2 car group (b) 4 car group.

USG cavity shaft wall systems / SA-926

test data*

fire rating	fire-rated construction		description & test no.	acoustical performance		system reference
	detail & physical data			STC	description & test no.	
1 hr.	3⅛" wt. 8		Cavity Shaft Wall Gypsum Drywall—⅝" SHEETROCK brand FIRECODE "C" gypsum panels one side—1" USG gypsum liner panels set betw USG steel C-H studs 24" o.c.—panels appl to side opp liner panels & screw att—joints fin—fire rating also applies with IMPERIAL FIRECODE "C" Base and veneer finish surface—UL Des U469	N·A		A
2 hr.	3½" wt. 9		Cavity Shaft Wall Gypsum Drywall—2 layers ½" SHEETROCK brand FIRECODE "C" gypsum panels one side—1" USG liner panels set betw USG steel C-H studs 24" o.c.—panels appl vert to side opp liner panels & screw att—joints fin—rating also applies with IMPERIAL FIRECODE "C" Base and veneer finish surface—fire-tested both sides—U of C 4-2-75—UL Des U438	39 47	USG-750302 Based on 1" sound atten fire blankets in cavity— BBN-750706	B
2 hr.	3½" wt. 9		Cavity Shaft Wall Gypsum Drywall—½" SHEETROCK brand FIRECODE "C" gypsum panels—1" USG gypsum liner panels set betw USG steel C-H studs 24" o.c.—single layer panels ea side appl vert & screw att—joints stag on opp sides & fin— rating also applies with IMPERIAL FIRECODE "C" Base and veneer finish surface—fire-tested both sides—UL Des U467	N·A		C

(a)

details

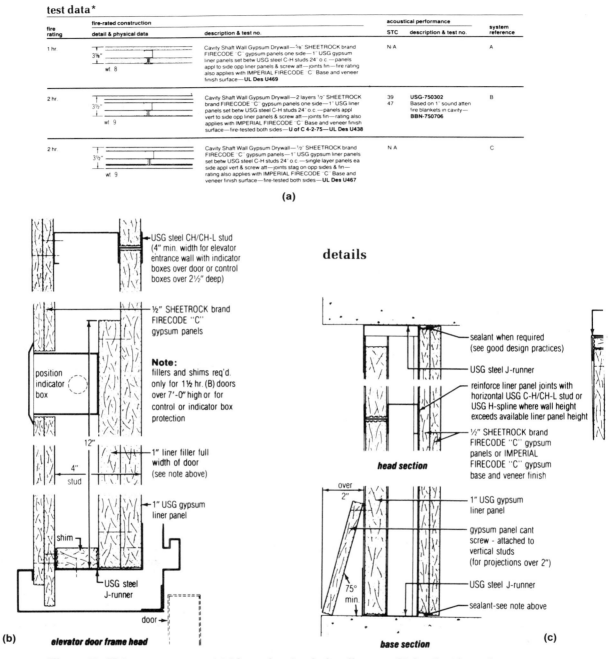

(b)

elevator door frame head

USG steel CH/CH-L stud (4" min. width for elevator entrance wall with indicator boxes over door or control boxes over 2½" deep)

½" SHEETROCK brand FIRECODE "C" gypsum panels

position indicator box

Note: fillers and shims req'd. only for 1½ hr. (B) doors over 7'-0" high or for control or indicator box protection

12"
4" stud

1" liner filler full width of door (see note above)

1" USG gypsum liner panel

shim

USG steel J-runner

door

head section

sealant when required (see good design practices)

USG steel J-runner

reinforce liner panel joints with horizontal USG C-H/CH-L stud or USG H-spline where wall height exceeds available liner panel height

½" SHEETROCK brand FIRECODE "C" gypsum panels or IMPERIAL FIRECODE "C" gypsum base and veneer finish

base section

over 2"

1" USG gypsum liner panel

gypsum panel cant screw - attached to vertical studs (for projections over 2")

USG steel J-runner

75° min.

sealant-see note above

(c)

Figure 18. Hoistway structures. (a) 2 h rated cavity shaft wall system (b) details, 2 h rated cavity shaft wall system (c) other details. Courtesy of United States Gypsum Company.

of the platform and 15 in. (43.58 cm) behind the platform (17 in. (43.58 cm) if counterweight safeties are used, which are required when occupied space occurs below the pit). A 1¼-in.(3.20 cm) running space separates the front face of the car from the edge of the finished sill (Fig. 20).

Elevators that operate at a higher speed will require more clearance at each side of the platform; elevators with speeds up to 700 ft/min (3.56 ms) will require 8½ in.

(21.79 cm) and those with speeds up to 1200 ft/min will require 9–10 in. (23–25.64 cm).

In some types of traction elevators the counterweight does not occur behind the platform. This is especially true for hospital elevators intended to carry stretchers, with their elongated cars, and all elevator cars with front and rear entrances. These elevators will require the standard 8-in. (20.51 cm) clearance on the side opposite the counter-

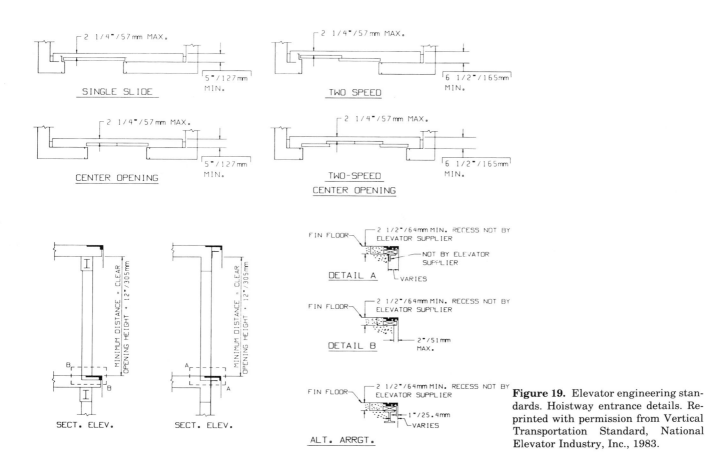

ELEVATOR ENGINEERING STANDARDS

1979 EDITION   TYPICAL PASSENGER AND HOSPITAL ELEVATOR
HOISTWAY ENTRANCE DETAILS

2 1/4"/57mm MAX.

5"/127mm MIN.

SINGLE SLIDE

2 1/4"/57mm MAX.

6 1/2"/165mm MIN.

TWO SPEED

2 1/4"/57mm MAX.

5"/127mm MIN.

CENTER OPENING

2 1/4"/57mm MAX.

6 1/2"/165mm MIN.

TWO-SPEED
CENTER OPENING

MINIMUM DISTANCE = CLEAR OPENING HEIGHT + 12"/305mm

B

SECT. ELEV.

MINIMUM DISTANCE = CLEAR OPENING HEIGHT + 12"/305mm

A

SECT. ELEV.

FIN FLOOR   2 1/2"/64mm MIN. RECESS NOT BY ELEVATOR SUPPLIER
NOT BY ELEVATOR SUPPLIER
DETAIL A   VARIES

FIN FLOOR   2 1/2"/64mm MIN. RECESS NOT BY ELEVATOR SUPPLIER
2"/51mm MAX.
DETAIL B

FIN FLOOR   2 1/2"/64mm MIN. RECESS NOT BY ELEVATOR SUPPLIER
1"/25.4mm
VARIES
ALT. ARRGT.

Figure 19. Elevator engineering standards. Hoistway entrance details. Reprinted with permission from Vertical Transportation Standard, National Elevator Industry, Inc., 1983.

weight and 1 ft-6 in. (46.15 cm) clearance on the counterweight side of the platform. Where no rear entrance is required, only 4 in. (10.16 cm) of space will be needed behind the platform. Front and rear doors will have similar space requirements at both ends of the platform. As previously noted, increased speeds will increase clearance requirements.

Another type of elevator that has a side-mounted counterweight is the observation elevator (Fig. 21). Most commonly used in atrium buildings or buildings with dramatic exterior views, these elevators are also found in shopping malls and racetracks. Design of this type of elevator is highly specialized, so an elevator manufacturer or elevator consultant should be contacted early in the design process to ensure adequate space allocation.

Hydraulic elevators have hoistway requirements similar to those of traction elevators except for one obvious difference. Because hydraulic elevators have no counterweights, they require only 2 in. (5.08 cm) of clearance behind the platform in the hoistway.

When more than one car occurs in a hoistway, the cars are separated by a 4-in. (10.16 cm) divider beam. This beam supports the rails at each floor level. If floors are more than 14-ft (4.26 m) apart, additional intermediate support may be required. As in all generalizations relating to structural issues, construction in seismic zones may have additional requirements.

By code, there may be a maximum of three elevators per hoistway. For configurations of elevator banks where more than three elevators are side by side, fire separation of one or more of the hoistways will be required. In banks of four elevators this is typically accomplished by inserting an 8-in. (20.32 cm) concrete beam or fire-rated steel beam of sufficient size to carry a 3½ in. (0.89 cm) 2-h fire-rated partition between the second and third elevator cars.

Elevator size is usually stated as a load-carrying capacity and a speed. Speed obviously affects clearances required in the hoistway. Elevator car size is a function of its rated load. Platform sizes may vary among suppliers owing to some of their particular design requirements; however, Table 1 gives some suggested industry standards for various capacity cars and their clear inside dimensions.

ELEVATOR ENGINEERING STANDARDS

1979 EDITION   ELECTRIC PASSENGER ELEVATORS
                         U.S. & S.I. UNITS
            RATED SPEEDS 100-350 FEET PER MIN./ 0.51-1.78 METERS PER SEC.

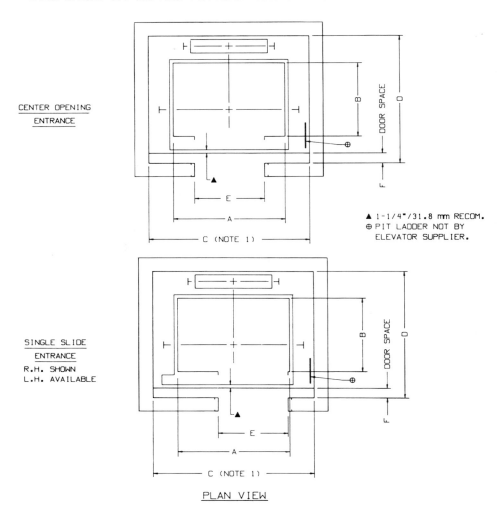

CENTER OPENING
ENTRANCE

▲ 1-1/4"/31.8 mm RECOM.
⊕ PIT LADDER NOT BY
   ELEVATOR SUPPLIER.

SINGLE SLIDE
ENTRANCE
R.H. SHOWN
L.H. AVAILABLE

PLAN VIEW

Figure 20. Hoistway plan requirements for passenger elevators with rated speeds of 100–350 ft/min. Courtesy of the National Elevator Industry, Inc., Elevator Engineering Standards.

To determine platform size from the clear inside cab dimensions, *Elevator Engineering Standards* gives the following rules of thumb:

To determine the approximate outside platform width: for passenger, hospital and freight elevators—add 4 inches (101.6 mm) to the "A" (car inside width) dimension.

To determine the approximate outside platform depth:

A. For passenger elevators center opening and single slide entrances, add 11 inches (279 mm).
B. For passenger and hospital elevators with two speed or two speed center opening entrances at one end only add 12½ inches (317.5 mm).
C. For hospital elevators with two speed front and rear entrances, add 21 inches (533.4 mm).
D. For freight elevators with front entrances only, add 7 inches (177.8 mm).

E. For freight elevators with front and rear entrances, add 10 inches (254 mm).

Note: The formula given above will provide approximate platform sizes. For exact platform dimensions, consult elevator supplier (14).

Vertical clearances required for different elevator systems are also related to the elevator's rate of travel or speed. The amount of overhead space, that is, distance measured from the elevation of the last stop to the underside of the machine room floor above, is calculated based on a variety of functional requirements of the space. This space provides room for equipment located on the roof of the cab and possible "refuge" for someone working on top of the cab while allowing for possible over travel and "jump" of the cab when the counterweight lands on its buffer (Fig. 22). Table 2 shows a calculation of required

ELEVATOR ENGINEERING STANDARDS

1979 EDITION   ELECTRIC PASSENGER ELEVATORS

U.S. & S.I. UNITS

RATED SPEEDS 100-350 FEET PER MIN./ 0.51-1.78 METERS PER SEC.

UNITS	RATED LOAD LB/kg	AREA ■	DIMENSIONS FEET & INCHES/MILLIMETERS					ENTRANCES FT-IN/mm		
			† A	† B	C	D	E	TYPE		F (MIN.)
APPLICATION - OFFICE BLDG., HOTELS, BANKS, RETAIL STORES, ETC.										
U.S.	2000	24.2	5-8	4-3	7-4	6-10	3-0	SINGLE	CENTER	5
S.I.	907.2	2.24	1727.2	1295.4	2235.2	2082.8	914.4	SLIDE ★	OPENING	127
U.S.	2500	29.1	6-8	4-3	8-4	6-10	3-6	SINGLE	CENTER	5
S.I.	1134	2.70	2032	1295.4	2540	2082.8	1066.8	SLIDE ★	OPENING	127
U.S.	3000	33.7	6-8	4-7	8-4	7-2	3-6	SINGLE	CENTER	5
S.I.	1360.8	3.13	2032	1397	2540	2184.4	1066.8	SLIDE ★	OPENING	127
U.S.	3500	38.0	6-8	5-3	8-4	7-10	3-6	SINGLE	CENTER	5
S.I.	1587.6	3.53	2032	1600.2	2540	2387.6	1066.8	SLIDE ★	OPENING	127
U.S.	4000	42.2	7-8	5-3	9-4	7-10	4-0	CENTER OPENING ★		5
S.I.	1814.4	3.92	2336.8	1600.2	2844.8	2387.6	1219.2			127

APPLICATION - APARTMENT HOUSES, SCHOOLS ETC.										
U.S.	1500	18.9	4-6	4-3	6-7	6-10	2-8	SINGLE	CENTER	5
S.I.	680.4	1.76	1371.6	1295.4	2006.6	2082.8	812.8	SLIDE ★	OPENING	127
U.S.	2000	24.2	5-8	4-3	7-4	6-10	3-0	SINGLE	CENTER	5
S.I.	907.2	2.24	1727.2	1295.4	2235.2	2082.8	914.4	SLIDE ★	OPENING	127
U.S.	2500	29.1	6-8	4-3	8-4	6-10	3-6	SINGLE	CENTER	5
S.I.	1134	2.70	2032	1295.4	2540	2082.8	1066.8	SLIDE ★	OPENING	127

★ THESE CAR DIMENSIONS AND ENTRANCE TYPES COMPLY WITH NEII "SUGGESTED MINIMUM PASSENGER ELEVATOR REQUIREMENTS FOR THE HANDICAPPED"- 1500 & 2000 RATED LOADS ARE FOR WHEELCHAIR ONLY.

■ MAXIMUM ALLOWABLE INSIDE CAR AREA IN SQ.FT./SQ.M., PER ANSI A17.1, RULE 207.1.   **Figure 20.** (continued)

Table 2. Calculation of Required Overhead Space for a Traction Elevator

Requirement	Example
1. Height of cab ceiling (note)	8 ft 0 in.
2. Space for lighting	1 ft 3 in.
3. Space between top of enclosure and bottom of crosshead	1 ft 0 in.
4. Depth of crosshead	0 ft 10 in.
5. Over travel	0 ft 6 in.
6. Counterweight buffer stroke @ 500 ft/min	1 ft 5 in.
7. Counterweight buffer jump	0 ft 8 in.
8. Rope stretch and counterweight buffer clearance (assume)	0 ft 8 in.
9. 2-ft clearance	2 ft 0 in.
	13 ft 40 in.
Distance from top landing served to underside of the top of the hoistway (slab or structure)	16 ft 4 in. (5000 mm)

overhead space for a traction elevator with a speed of 500 ft/min (2.5 m/s).

Elevator pit requirements consist of many of the same considerations as the overhead. Buffers for both the car and the counterweight are designed to stop the equipment if for some reason it travels beyond the lowest landing. The stroke of the buffer is a function of speed and defined by code (Table 3). Space is also required for the structure of the platform and guiding and compensating ropes (Fig. 23).

Figure 24 shows standard overhead and pit requirements for traction elevators operating at speeds from 100 to 350 ft/min (.5/1.77 m/s). For faster traction elevators dimensions will be increased.

Hydraulic elevators have slightly different requirements. Because there is no machine at the top of the hoistway, the overhead is significantly reduced. Space is still

Table 3. Pit Depths: Traction Elevators—Overhead Machines

	100	200	300	400	500	600	700	800
Speed (ft/min)	100	200	300	2	2.5	3	3.5	4
(m/s)	0.5	1	1.5	2	2.5	3	3.5	4
Depths								
With restrained rope compensation				8 ft 0 in. 1.6 m	8 ft 6 in. 2.6 m	9 ft 2 in. 2.8 m	9 ft 10 in. 3.0 m	10 ft 6 in. 3.2 m
With chain, free rope, or traveling cable compensation	5 ft 0 in. 1.5 m	5 ft 0 in. 1.5 m	5 ft 4 in. 1.6 m	7 ft 10 in. 2.4 m	8 ft 4 in. 2.5 m			
With reduced stroke buffer and either restrained rope chain, traveling cable, or free rope compensation			5 ft 0 in. 1.5 m	5 ft 4 in. 1.6 m	8 ft 0 in. 2.4 m	8 ft 6 in. 2.6 m	8 ft 6 in. 2.6 m	9 ft 2 in. 2.8 m
Buffer type	Spring	Spring	Oil	Oil	Oil	Oil	Oil	Oil

required for possible overrun and for refuge, but there is no machine beam to consider. Figure 25 shows the standard overhead and pit requirements for a hydraulic elevator traveling at speeds from 75 to 200 ft/min (.38–1.01 m/s).

Although machines for traction elevators may be located at the rear, side, or bottom of the hoistway, by far the most typical location is directly above the hoistway. The machine room floor is usually a 4-ft-6-in. (10.12–15.24 cm) slab placed directly on top of the machine beams. Minimum clearance, required by code, from the top of the machine room floor to the underside of the low-est obstruction above is 7 ft-6 in. (2.29 m). In a group of elevators the space over the hoistways and the associated lobby usually provides adequate space to house the equipment. Where more space is needed, the space between the hoistways, above the lobby, at the roof level can be used as a secondary elevator machine space (Fig. 26).

Equipment typically includes the hoisting machine and the electric elevator controller; a governor for safety application; a motor generator for any elevator of the generator field-control type; a floor-selecting device; and, for a group of three or more elevators, a group electrical controller (15). Access is required to all this equipment. Exact

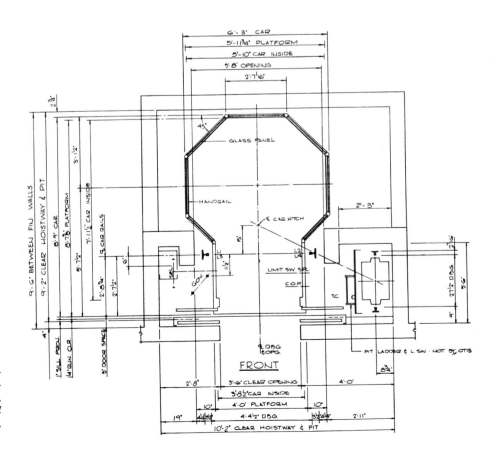

Figure 21. Sample layout of an observation-type elevator. Reprinted by permission of John Wiley & Sons, Inc., *Vertical Transportation: Elevators and Escalators,* G. R. Strakosch, 2nd ed., 1983.

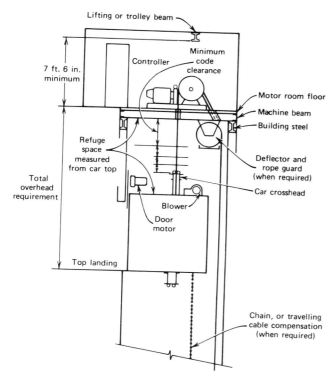

Figure 22. Pit and overhead space with chain or travelling cable compensation. Reprinted by permission of John Wiley & Sons, Inc., *Vertical Transportation: Elevators and Escalators,* G. R. Strakosch, 2nd ed., 1983.

clearances are established by the National Electrical Code.

The elevator machine room must be separated from the rest of the penthouse and can contain only elevator equipment. It must be accessible from habitable building space by a minimum 36–48-in. (91.44–121.92 cm) B labeled door leading to the machine room itself. You cannot pass though an elevator machine room to reach other parts of the building. Local codes should be consulted to determine if any other restrictions apply.

Elevator machine rooms must be ventilated and lighted. In areas prone to temperature extremes, machine rooms are heated and/or air-conditioned. The elevator manufacturer can provide a calculation of heat generated by the elevator equipment based on the speed of the elevators and the number of floors served to determine the temperature control required. Care must be taken to ensure that the location of any additional equipment in the machine room does not compromise the amount of space available for the elevator equipment itself. If space in the elevator machine area is limited in any way, it is best to contact an elevator supplier early in the design process to see in what way their standard layout can be modified.

Machine rooms for hydraulic elevators are usually located directly adjacent to the pit or the lowest landing level of the elevator. This room houses the oil tank, a pump to pressurize the oil, and the controller equipment. Clear headroom of 7 ft 6 in. (2.28 m) is required, and the

machine room must be separated from the surrounding space. Figure 27 shows a typical layout of a one- and two car hydraulic elevator hoistway and machine room.

The elevator hoistway, pit, and machine spaces are treated by code as one continuous space. Because this space is likely to interconnect every level of a building, it is also the most likely way a fire can spread from floor to floor. For this reason it is required that elevator hoistways be 2-hr-separated from the floors that they serve. In case of a fire, code requires that all elevators cease operation and return to the ground floor. Passengers on the elevators can then be evacuated and the elevators made available for use by emergency personnel. At least one elevator in a building must be powered by an emergency generator to allow fire fighters and other emergency personnel access to upper floors. In the case of hospitals and nursing homes with a great many bedridden occupants, elevators powered by the emergency generators can continue to be used to evacuate people under the supervision of fire control personnel.

A recent development in fire containment is the use of pressurized elevator shafts. A constant positive force or pressure of air is maintained in the elevator hoistway, making it difficult for fire or noxious fumes to spread into the hoistway and from there to other floors. This system requires fresh outside air pressurized by fans and carried in shafts adjacent to the hoistway throughout its length. The size of all these components is based on the size of the hoistway served and the number of stops in the system.

In a well-designed elevator system that provides smooth, efficient service with little interruption, the part of the system people are most likely to notice and remember is the elevator car. Within the confines of the limited space available, the design possibilities are endless. Many practical considerations must be taken into account when designing the car interior and specifying materials.

Elevator cars should, of course, be accessible to the handicapped. According to ANSI A117.1–1986, elevator cars must have a minimum depth of 51 in. (1295 mm), 54-in. (1370 mm) clear to the face of the door (Fig. 28). Door openings must be a minimum of 36 in (915 mm).

Some codes require that a car large enough to accommodate a stretcher be provided. It is possible that this car could double as a freight elevator.

In commercial buildings most elevator cars will have center-opening doors in the front only. The car operating panels may be located on either or both sides of the doors. Car position indicators are located above the door or directly above the car operating panel. When located above the car operating panel these indicators are usually digital. LED readout is recommended as most legible.

Most elevator manufacturers now produce standard control panels that comply with ANSI A117.1 for handicapped accessibility. This code requires that controls be located a maximum of 48 in (1220 mm) and a minimum of 35 in. (890 mm) above the floor (Fig. 29). These controls include the emergency alarm and emergency stop, which should be grouped at the bottom of the panel. In addition, it requires that tactile floor indicators and audible floor passing signals be provided for the sight impaired. ANSI

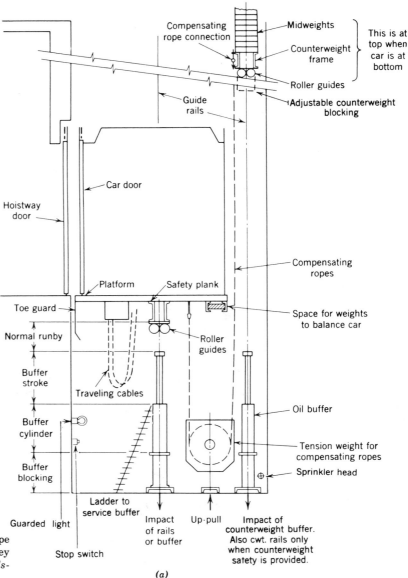

Figure 23. Pit construction and equipment with rope compensation. Reprinted by permission of John Wiley & Sons, Inc., *Vertical Transportation: Elevators and Escalators,* G. R. Strakosch, 2nd ed., 1983.

(a)

A117.1 and local handicapped codes should be consulted for additional accessibility requirements.

Several other components are frequently seen in elevator control panels. The emergency telephone may serve a different function in different elevator systems. In a small building with only a one- or two-car system the telephone may be a two-way telephone allowing a user trapped in an elevator to contact an elevator maintenance company. In a modern office building or hospital the telephone will likely be for use by emergency personnel only. By using this telephone a member of the emergency or fire-fighting team can keep in contact with the fire-control room or operations center. Some localities require that a phone jack be provided in the elevator car and that emergency personnel carry their own telephone handset. This precludes the possibility of tampering. Check local codes and

with local fire-control officials to determine exact requirements.

The front panel may also house a switch controlling the car lights and the fan. These are usually in a locked compartment or otherwise inaccessible to the general public. Also, a frame is usually provided for the elevator inspection form. The form itself or a statement explaining its whereabouts must be on display in the car at all times. The designer should consider the locations of all these elements to best control their appearance in the completed car.

In most elevator cabs, the front return panel, between the elevator door and the car side wall, is of the manufacturer's standard design. A swing-type front may be available. In this type of elevator return panel the entire panel is one hinged piece. Only the control buttons themselves,

ELEVATOR ENGINEERING STANDARDS

1979 EDITION

ELECTRIC PASSENGER ELEVATORS

U.S. & S.I. UNITS

RATED SPEEDS 100-350 FEET PER MIN./ 0.51-1.78 METERS PER SEC.

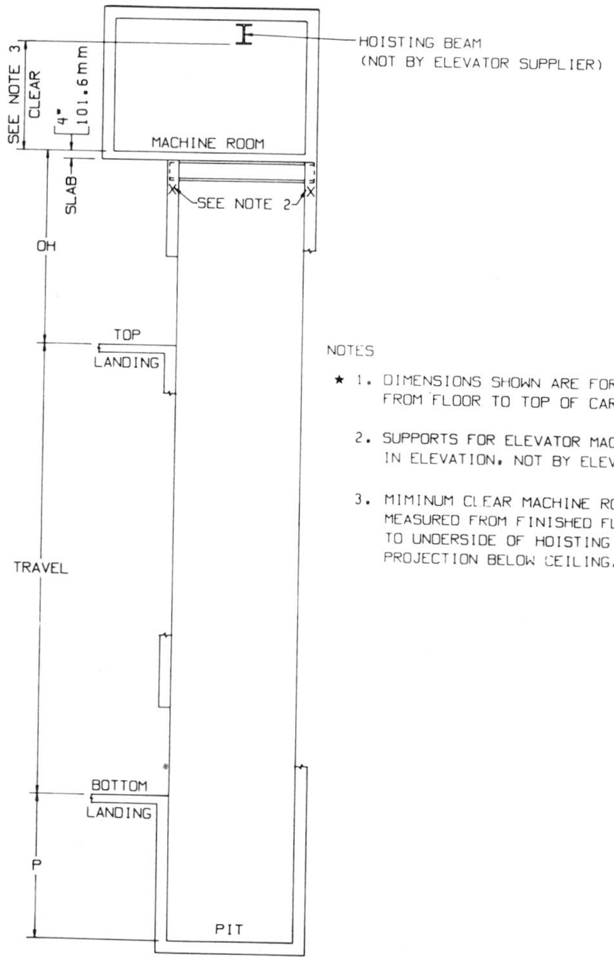

★ MIN. TOP OF MACHINE ROOM FLOOR "OH" FEET & INCHES/MILLIMETERS

UNITS	SPEED F.P.M.	SPEED M/S	1500 U.S.	680.4 S.I.	2000 U.S.	907.2 S.I.	2500 U.S.	1134 S.I.	3000 U.S.	1360.8 S.I.	3500 U.S.	1587.6 S.I.	4000 U.S.	1814.4 S.I.
U.S. / S.I.	100	.51	16-6	5029	16-6	5029	16-6	5029	16-6	5029	16-6	5029	16-6	5029
U.S. / S.I.	150	.76	16-9	5105	16-9	5105	16-9	5105	16-9	5105	17-0	5182	17-0	5182
U.S. / S.I.	200	1.02	16-9	5105	16-9	5105	16-9	5105	16-9	5105	17-0	5182	17-0	5182
U.S. / S.I.	250	1.27	16-9	5105	16-9	5105	17-6	5334	17-6	5334	17-6	5334	17-6	5334
U.S. / S.I.	300	1.52	16-9	5105	16-9	5105	17-6	5334	17-6	5334	17-6	5334	17-6	5334
U.S. / S.I.	350	1.78	16-9	5105	16-9	5105	17-6	5334	17-6	5334	17-6	5334	17-6	5334

RATED LOAD IN POUNDS/KILOGRAMS

MIN. PIT DEPTH "P" FEET & INCHES/MILLIMETERS

UNITS	SPEED F.P.M.	SPEED M/S	1500 U.S.	680.4 S.I.	2000 U.S.	907.2 S.I.	2500 U.S.	1134 S.I.	3000 U.S.	1360.8 S.I.	3500 U.S.	1587.6 S.I.	4000 U.S.	1814.4 S.I.
U.S. / S.I.	100	.51	5-0	1524	5-6	1676	5-6	1676	5-6	1676	5-6	1676	5-6	1676
U.S. / S.I.	150	.76	5-0	1524	5-6	1676	5-6	1676	5-6	1676	5-6	1676	5-6	1676
U.S. / S.I.	200	1.02	5-0	1524	5-8	1727	5-8	1727	6-0	1829	5-8	1727	5-8	1727
U.S. / S.I.	250	1.27	5-6	1676	6-0	1829	6-0	1829	6-6	1981	6-6	1981	6-6	1981
U.S. / S.I.	300	1.52	6-6	1981	6-6	1981	6-6	1981	6-6	1981	6-6	1981	6-6	1981
U.S. / S.I.	350	1.78	6-11	2108	6-11	2108	6-11	2108	6-11	2108	6-11	2108	6-11	2108

RATED LOAD IN POUNDS/KILOGRAMS

NOTES:

★ 1. DIMENSIONS SHOWN ARE FOR 8'-4"/2540 mm FROM FLOOR TO TOP OF CAR ENCLOSURE.

2. SUPPORTS FOR ELEVATOR MACHINE BEAMS AT X-X IN ELEVATION, NOT BY ELEVATOR SUPPLIER.

3. MINIMUM CLEAR MACHINE ROOM HEIGHT 7'-6"/2286 mm MEASURED FROM FINISHED FLOOR TO CEILING, TO UNDERSIDE OF HOISTING BEAM OR ANY PROJECTION BELOW CEILING.

HOISTING BEAM (NOT BY ELEVATOR SUPPLIER)

MACHINE ROOM

SEE NOTE 2

SLAB — 4"/101.6 mm

CLEAR — SEE NOTE 3

OH

TOP LANDING

TRAVEL

BOTTOM LANDING

PIT

P

ELEVATION

Figure 24. Elevator engineering standards. Electric passenger elevators, 1979 ed. U.S. & S.I. units, rated speeds 100–350 ft/min/0.51–1.78 meters/sec. Reprinted with permission from *Vertical Transportation Standards*, National Elevator Industry, Inc., 1983.

1979 EDITION   HYDRAULIC PASSENGER ELEVATORS
U.S. & S.I. UNITS
RATED SPEEDS 75-200 FEET PER MIN./0.38-1.02 METERS PER SEC.

1979 EDITION   HYDRAULIC PASSENGER ELEVATORS
U.S. & S.I. UNITS
RATED SPEEDS 75-200 FEET PER MIN./0.38-1.02 METERS PER SEC.

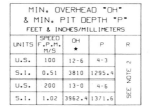

	MIN. OVERHEAD "OH" & MIN. PIT DEPTH "P" FEET & INCHES/MILLIMETERS			
UNITS	SPEED F.P.M. M/S	OH ★	P	R
U.S.	100	12-6	4-3	SEE NOTE 2
S.I.	0.51	3810	1295.4	
U.S.	200	13-0	4-6	
S.I.	1.02	3962.4	1371.6	

NOTE 1   CONSULT ELEVATOR SUPPLIER ON LIMITATIONS ON MAXIMUM TRAVEL.

NOTE 2   PROVISION FOR HYDRAULIC CYLINDER REQUIRES A 3'-0" X 3'-0"/914 X 914 mm SQUARE OPENING IN THE PIT FLOOR AND A WELL HOLE WITH DIMENSION "R" = (APPROX.) THE TRAVEL OF THE ELEVATOR PLUS 7'-0"/2134 mm.

NOTE 3   MINIMUM MACHINE ROOM SIZE FOR A SINGLE PUMP UNIT IS 7'-0" X 11'-0" X 7'-6"HIGH/ 2134 X 3353 X 2286mmHIGH.

RECOMMENDED MACHINE ROOM DOOR SIZE IS 3'-6" X 7'-0"/1066.8mm X 2133.6mm.

IT IS RECOMMENDED THAT THE MACHINE ROOM BE LOCATED ADJACENT TO THE HOISTWAY AND AT OR NEAR THE BOTTOM TERMINAL LANDING.

CONSULT ELEVATOR SUPPLIER FOR EXACT SIZE AND LOCATION.

LOCATION OF LIGHTING AND DISCONNECT SWITCHES SHALL BE IN ACCORDANCE WITH REQUIREMENTS OF ANSI A17.1 AND ANSI/NFPA NO. 70.

LOCATION OF SWITCHES ARE SIMILAR TO THOSE SHOWN ON ELECTRIC ELEVATOR MACHINE ROOM PLANS.

★   "OH" DIMENSION IS FOR 8'-4"/2540mm FROM FLOOR TO TOP OF CAR ENCLOSURE.

ELEVATION

Figure 25. Overhead and pit requirements, hydraulic passenger elevators with rated speeds of 75–200 ft/min/0.38–1.02 meters/sec. Reprinted with permission from *Vertical Transportation Standards,* National Elevator Industry, Inc., 1983.

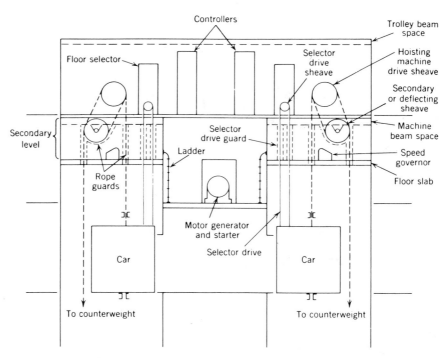

Figure 26. Cross section, elevator machine room. Reprinted by permission of John Wiley & Sons, Inc., *Vertical Transportation: Elevators and Escalators,* G. R. Strakosch, 2nd ed., 1983.

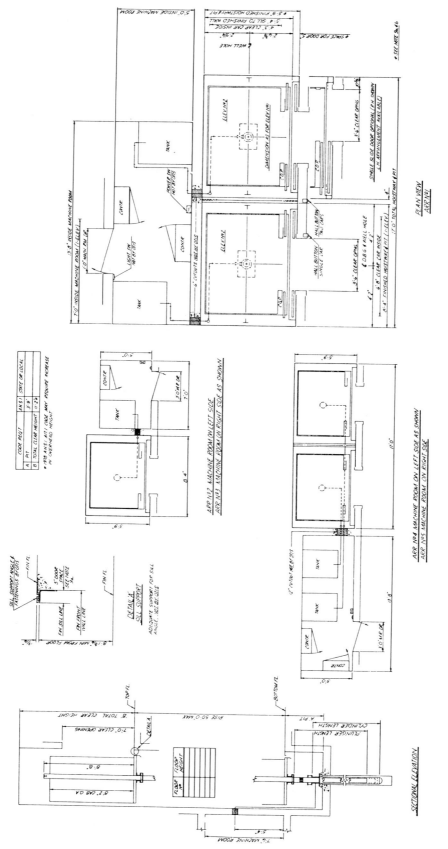

Figure 27. Manufacturers layout for a hydraulic elevator, capacity 2500 lb, speed 125 ft/min. Courtesy of Otis Elevator.

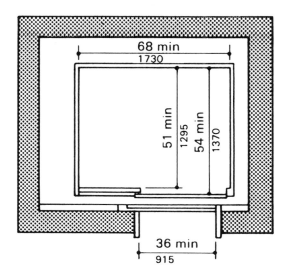

68 min
1730

51 min
1295

54 min
1370

36 min
915

NOTE: Elevator cars with a minimum width less than
that shown above, but no less than 54 in (1370 mm), are
allowed for elevators with capacities of less than 2000
lb. A center opening door application necessitates
increasing the 68-in (1730-mm) dimension to 80 in
(2030 mm).

Figure 28. Minimum dimensions of handicapped accessible elevator cars. ANSI A117.1, 1986.

the car position indicator, and a door for the telephone can be seen in an otherwise flush panel. More traditional is the return panel with applied or flush panels that are separate access panels for each functional component. These panels are usually of the same material as the elevator doors. Obviously, this is the highest use area of the

elevator car. Durability and ease of maintenance leads many designers to specify stainless steel, either polished or brushed. Manufacturers may have other standard finishes available that should be considered in the overall car design.

It should not be inferred that only the manufacturer's standard is available for any aspect of the car design. Elevator cars are made one at a time for specific installations and frequently by separate vendors who are subcontractors to the elevator manufacturers themselves. However, the more standard the car finishes are, the lower the cost. This is especially true of the front return panel or any operating or control panel because of electrical connections involved. The best course of action is to define the desired configurations clearly in the contract documents so that the various manufacturers' bids reflect the premium they require to provide a nonstandard design.

The other walls of the elevator car have fewer practical requirements. They can be covered in plastic laminate, carpeting, paneling, or any other material the designer deems appropriate for the car's use. Often designs consist of decorative panels hung on the structural car wall with a reveal and kick space in a different color or material. The only exceptions are as follows: materials used in the car must be 2-h rated and according to code must comply with burn test 1104, having a flame spread of 0–75 and smoke development of 0–450; walls should be in panels for ease of erection, repair, and maintenance; no real glass or mirrored glass may be used, although Plexiglas and mirrored Plexiglas may. In the case of observation or view elevators with exterior windows, laminated glass capable of withstanding testing without damage may be used. Check with local code officials and elevator manufacturers for additional information.

Warning signs are frequently required to be displayed within the elevator car. Size, color, and lettering style may all be specified by local fire code. During the design process it is wise to ascertain exact local standards.

When a passenger car will double as a freight car, it is customary to provide hooks around the top of the wall panels to hang grommeted protection pads during the elevator's use for freight hauling. The limitations of this system are obvious; often pads are lost, mishandled, or mis-

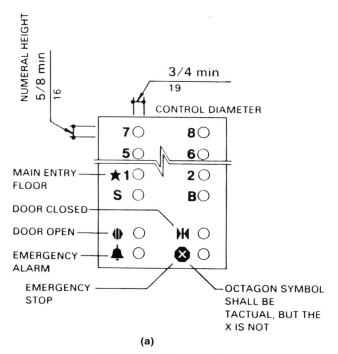

(a)

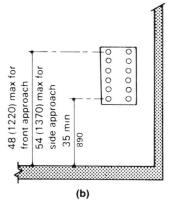

(b)

Figure 29. Car controls for handicapped accessible elevators (a) panel detail (b) control height. ANSI A117.1, 1986.

used in such a way that the walls of the car sustain damage anyway. The only absolute solution is inclusion of a separate freight elevator whenever possible. Pad hooks, when provided, can be designed to match car finishes and minimize visual impact.

Flooring materials are also open to the discretion of the designer. Probably the most frequently used material in commercial elevator cars is carpeting. Traffic is extremely high, so carpet will have to be replaced at frequent intervals as part of regular maintenance, but it is attractive and inexpensive and it can relate the elevator design to that of the lobby. Also used in commercial cabs is the tile or stone of the main lobby floor. When this type of flooring is being considered, special attention should be given to the required thickness, setting medium, and possible increased load in the car. Consult an elevator manufacturer or consultant before pursuing this alternative.

When talking about the ceiling of an elevator car, a distinction must be made between the finished ceiling of the car and the canopy above it. The canopy is the structural top of the car enclosure. Usually made of steel, it must be designed to withstand 300 lb (136 kg) on any area of 2 ft × 2 ft (610 mm^2) or 100 lb (45 kg) applied at any point without permanent deformation (16). Elevator equipment is located above this canopy. The amount of space required between the canopy and the finished ceiling depends primarily on the space required for the lighting system chosen. It should be noted that when elevator manufacturers and consultants talk about the height of an elevator car they are talking about the height of the canopy. The finished-ceiling height is a function of the car design.

The ceiling of the elevator car must be designed to respond to several important functional requirements. First, ANSI 17.1 requires that all cars be provided with ceiling emergency exits. The exit opening must have an area of not less than 400 in.^{2} (0.258 m^2) and must measure not less than 16 in. (406 mm) on any side (17). This opening must be unobstructed by elevator equipment both on top of and inside the elevator car.

Lighting is almost always provided in the ceiling of the cab. For safety reasons, exposed light bulbs are not allowed in elevator cars. Obviously, this places some restrictions on possible lighting design solutions. Some frequently used configurations include luminous or decorative ceiling panels covering an arrangement of fluorescent tubes, perimeter light coves housing concealed or protected incandescent fixtures, and a pattern of incandescent down lights with protective lenses or diffusers.

The minimum illumination permitted by code for passenger elevators is 54 lx and for freight elevators 27 lx. In addition, each elevator car must be provided with emergency lighting. Code requires that the intensity of illumination 4-ft (1219-mm) above the car floor and approximately 1 ft (305 mm) in front of the car operating device must not be less than 2.2 lx (18). The designer must incorporate emergency lighting into the design or risk the addition of surface-mounted battery-powered emergency lights to satisfy code officials.

Like elevator cars, elevator lobbies have a strong visual impact on the user and many functional require-

ments that must be satisfied by the designer. By far the largest component of the lobby design is the elevator hoistway door. As previously discussed, the hoistway door will have the same configuration as and will interlock with the car door, except in the case of the residential elevator that has a swing hoistway door and a gate on the car. It is important to note that the height of the opening of the car doors and the hoistway doors should be the same. This should be considered when the height of the car canopy is selected. Also, the designer should be aware that in many instances there will be a structural requirement for a beam at the front edge of the hoistway. Depending on the floor-to-floor height, this might compromise the space remaining for the hoistway doors.

When the designer would like the hoistway doors to appear to extend from floor to ceiling, especially in entrance lobbies or other floors with exceptionally high floor-to-ceiling heights, the solution is often a flush transom panel. Made of the same material as the door and in the same plane as the door, which is recessed from the plane of the wall, this panel visually extends the height of the door. In most situations, use of this type of door is limited by its added expense and additional hoistway depth is normally required when the transom panel is flush with the hoistway door panels.

Landing call buttons, or hall buttons, should be located as close to the center of the lobby as possible. If two are provided in, for instance, an eight-car grouping, they should be across from one another. This will give the people who have called an elevator an equal view of and equal access to any elevator that will serve the floor. Frequently, ashtrays are combined with call buttons to give people an easy way to dispose of lighted cigarettes before entering the elevator. Fully recessed ashtray modules are available from various manufacturers that can be modified to accept standard elevator call buttons. However, the designer should bear in mind that the depth of the recessed unit must not intrude on 2-h-rated hoistway enclosures. In other words, the finished wall surface must be located sufficiently beyond the fire-rated enclosure to accommodate the recessed ashtray. If this is not possible, surface-mounted units are available.

Hall or landing lanterns are the lights provided with each set of elevator doors. These lights show the direction of a stopping car as it approaches the floor. Where headroom permits, these are typically located above the door. Frequently they are located adjacent to the jamb near the head. This is especially true when there is a flush transom panel above the door. Because the panel is recessed flush with the door, location of the hall lanterns there might make visibility a problem (Fig. 30).

Most elevator manufacturers have standard designs for call buttons and hall lanterns in a range of standard finishes (Fig. 31). As previously noted, this should not discourage the designer from modifying or redesigning these fixtures to suit specific needs. However, this should be done in consultation with the elevator manufacturer to help reduce additional cost, delays in fabrication and poor design.

Manufacturers' standard designs conform to the requirements of ANSI A117.1 for accessibility of the handi-

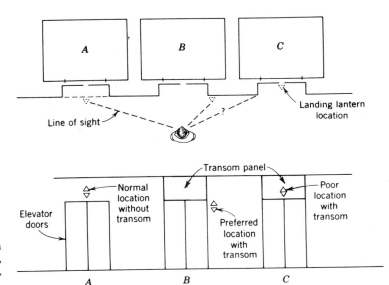

Figure 30. Landing lanterns should be located to be seen clearly. Reprinted by permission of John Wiley & Sons, Inc., *Vertical Transportation: Elevators and Escalators*, G. R. Strakosch, 2nd ed., 1983.

capped. Call buttons must be a minimum of ¾ in. (1.90 cm) in diameter and must be centered at 42 in. (106.68 cm) above the floor. The visual elements of hall lanterns must be at least 2½ in. (6.35 cm) in the smallest dimension and be mounted so that their centerline is at least 72 in. (1830 m) above the floor (Fig. 32). Audible signals and tactile floor designations are also required for the visually impaired. Check with local code officials for additional requirements.

Another component required in virtually all elevator installations is the hall or lobby warning sign. ANSI 17.1, the National Elevator Code, requires that a pictograph be posted over every corridor call station (Fig. 33). In the past, most local codes have required that similar verbal warnings be posted both at the call buttons and in the elevator car. Often requirements are specific as to size, color, and wording. Always check the requirements of local fire officials before proceeding with any elevator signage.

Requirements of the handicapped have stimulated the development of another category of vertical transportation systems that includes platform lifts and stair elevators. These systems are usually used when an existing structure is being retrofitted to accommodate the handicapped or when conventional elevators or ramps are impractical.

Platform lifts are small, self-contained lifts that will accommodate a single wheelchair. These lifts are typically used to overcome architectural barriers such as a flight of steps or a change of grade where there is insufficient room for a ramp. Platform size is 12 ft.² (1.12 sq. m), and total rise is from 3½ to 12 ft (1.06–3.6 m). These self-operated lifts are electrically powered and are appropriate for interior or exterior installations. Most are available as a standard package from the manufacturer with some flexibility as to finish. Required clearances and safety features vary according to lifting height (Fig. 34).

Another type of wheelchair lift is the inclined wheelchair lift. With this type of system a platform is carried on rails up the path of an existing stair. The rails must be supported on a separate structural frame from that sup-

porting the stair. Because the platform is pulled along the rails by cable like a ski-lift chair, it also has the ability to traverse landings, either straight or curved. These lifts have a maximum run of three full flights. When not in use, the wheelchair platform folds flat against the rails to minimize obstruction of the stair. These lifts may be used in both interior and exterior applications (Fig. 35).

A third common type of lift is similar to the inclined wheelchair lift except that it carries a chair instead of a wheelchair platform. These stair lifts are not intended to make buildings handicapped accessible but to assist those who have difficulty climbing stairs. Powered by a cable, these units are usually appropriate for one full flight of interior stairs only. Not all jurisdictions will allow any or all the platform lifts described. When retrofitting an existing building to accommodate the handicapped, it is best to consider all possible options—hydraulic elevators, wheelchair lifts, and ramps—and initiate a dialogue with local building, elevator, and fire-code officials to achieve the most appropriate design solution.

Other types of vertical transportation are available as standard systems from manufacturers, including inclined elevators, paternoster elevators or manlifts, industrial elevators, and various materials-handling systems. For additional information on these or on other specialized elevator applications, consult an elevator consultant or manufacturer.

Escalators and moving walkways are two similar types of vertical transportation systems that have become important components of our transportation network. They are found in airport, train, and subway terminals as well as in department stores, hotels, museums, convention halls, and sports arenas. In all these applications a system is required that will move large groups of people continuously from one point to another or along a path. This continuous movement of people is what distinguishes the function of an escalator from that of an elevator, which moves people in groups or batches. Most of the major elevator manufacturers also manufacture escalator systems.

Escalators are frequently preferred over elevators when visual access between spaces is desired or required,

Montgomery Fixtures & Signals A.P.D. Design

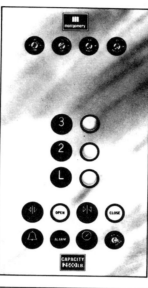

◄ Special Operation Key Switches

These special key switches operate devices such as fan, light & in-car emergency controls and are located in an individual panel above the car operating panel.

◄ Car Operating Panel

For HH-II and MX-3, the special operation key switches are mounted in the top of the car operating panel.

The car operating panel is located for accessibility to the handicapped. Emergency buttons are located 35" from the finished floor. Tactile markings are included to assist the handicapped.

The auxiliary car operating panel is an optional device, similar to the main car operating panel without the special operation key switches.

▲ Hall Lantern/Car Direction Sign

This fixture may be located in the hall, car door jamb or rear wall of the car. It may be of horizontal or vertical design for hall or rear car wall installation. The fixture indicates the direction the car will travel and includes an audible signal which sounds once for UP and twice for DOWN.

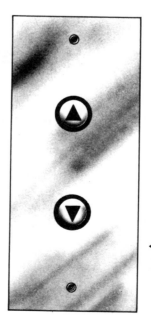

▲ Telephone Cabinet

The telephone cabinet is located below the main car operating panel. It is included when required by Code or specifications. The telephone instrument is not included.

◄ Hall Push Button Station

The hall push button station utilizes the same button design as used in the car operating panel and is located for accessibility to the handicapped.

montgomery®

ELEVATORS   ESCALATORS
POWER WALKS   POWER RAMPS

Montgomery Elevator Company
One Montgomery Court, Moline, Illinois 61265
Offices in principal cities of North America/Representatives Worldwide

Figure 31. Manufacturers standard elevator fixtures. Courtesy of Montgomery Elevators.

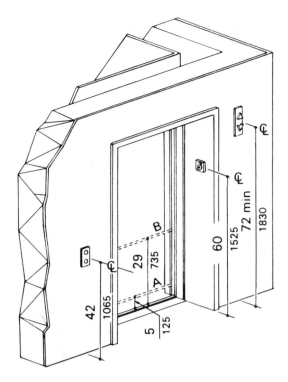

NOTE: The automatic door reopening device is activated if an object passes through either line A or line B. Line A and line B represent the vertical locations of the door reopening device not requiring contact.

Figure 32. Hoistway and elevator entrances for handicapped accessible elevators. ANSI A117.1, 1986.

as in a shopping mall or a multilevel office lobby. Escalators and moving walks are also important linkage devices directing people along a predetermined path between terminals or buildings and between disparate ground transportation systems. They may be used in both interior and exterior applications. The idea of requiring people to move on a predetermined path to access continuous up and down escalators is carried to an extreme in many retail situations where the customer must pass a maximum amount of goods on display to move vertically through the establishment.

The earliest type of escalator was the Reno escalator introduced in 1892 (19). This early escalator-type device was really a moving inclined ramp with fixed, cleated triangular platforms (Fig. 36). In 1900, the Seeberger flat-step escalator was introduced. It had flat treads but had to be entered at an angle to the escalator while the treads continued at the landing level and were returned under a diverter straight ahead. Otis manufactured both these types of escalators. In the 1920s the two types were combined into the type of escalator we use today, which has flat treads made up of interlocking cleats and combs and is entered and exited in a straight line with the moving treads (20). Except for some improvements in the depth of the support truss required, the only visible difference between the escalator of today and that of the 1920s is the availability of glass balustrades.

For all elevators having a travel of 25 ft (7.62 m) or more above or below the designated level, a pictograph as shown in Fig. 33 should be posted over each elevator corridor call station. The pictograph is 5 in. (127 mm) wide and 8 in. (203 mm) high.

301

Figure 33. Elevator corridor call station pictograph. ANSI A17.1, 1987.

In the 1960s moving walkways were introduced. These operate on the same principle as the escalator but have a single, flat, ramplike surface. They may be flat or inclined and, like the escalator, may be used in interior or exterior applications if they are correctly waterproofed.

In planning an escalator installation, the designer's primary concerns must be the type of path desired and the variability in the demand on the escalator system. In a department store, retail mall, or hotel, a designer is fairly safe in assuming that a single continuous up and down escalator, supplemented by elevators, will be adequate to meet transportation needs. The choice is then what kind of path to provide. The three most common arrangements are the parallel, the crisscross, and the stacked walkaround (Fig. 37). Because the landings all occur at the same end of the escalator, the parallel arrangement makes it easy for the user to change direction at any landing. It also provides for the least-congested flow.

The crisscross does not cause users any confusion about which escalator they should be entering to continue in the same direction. For this reason, it is considered by many people to be the safest arrangement. It also allows for safe intermingling of new passengers and those continuing on the system. It is often used in department stores because

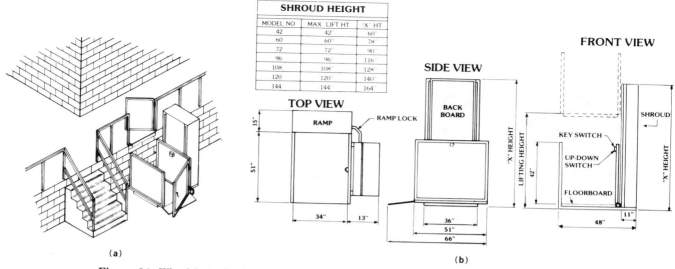

SHROUD HEIGHT		
MODEL NO	MAX LIFT HT	"X" HT
42	42"	60"
60	60"	78"
72	72"	90"
96	96"	116"
108	108"	128"
120	120"	140"
144	144"	164"

Figure 34. Wheelchair platform lift. (**a**) Interlocking safety gates (**b**) top, side, and front view. Courtesy of National Wheel-o-vator Company, Inc.

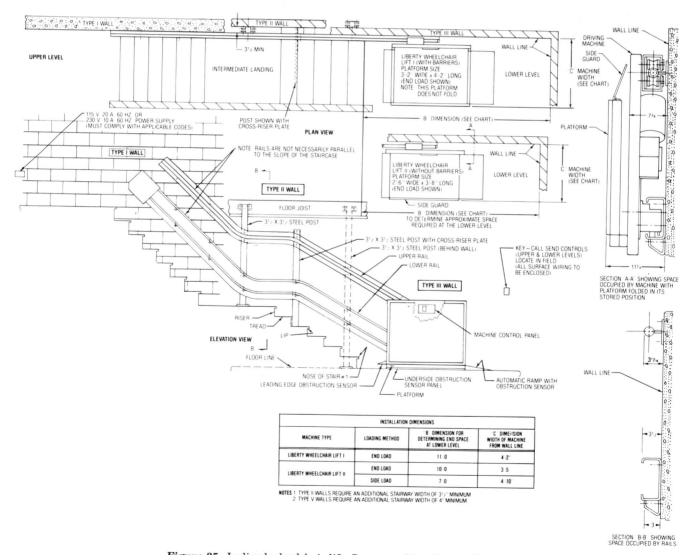

INSTALLATION DIMENSIONS			
MACHINE TYPE	LOADING METHOD	"B" DIMENSION FOR DETERMINING END SPACE AT LOWER LEVEL	"C" DIMENSION WIDTH OF MACHINE FROM WALL LINE
LIBERTY WHEELCHAIR LIFT I	END LOAD	11-0	4-2
LIBERTY WHEELCHAIR LIFT II	END LOAD	10-0	3-5
	SIDE LOAD	7-0	4-10

NOTES 1 TYPE II WALLS REQUIRE AN ADDITIONAL STAIRWAY WIDTH OF 3½" MINIMUM
2 TYPE V WALLS REQUIRE AN ADDITIONAL STAIRWAY WIDTH OF 4" MINIMUM

Figure 35. Inclined wheelchair lift. Courtesy of the Cheney Company.

Figure 36. "Reno" escalators. Courtesy of Otis Elevator.

of its efficiency in terms of space utilization and structural requirements.

The stacked walk-around is appropriate when the designer would like the escalator user to travel the longest path through that space to continue a multifloor trip. As previously mentioned, this has recently become a common device in department stores and shopping malls.

Multiple parallel escalators are most frequently seen when travel is not consistent and continuous but episodic. This is true in sports arenas and theaters where large groups of people congregate in an area at a fairly consistent rate over a period of time and then suddenly all desire to leave in the shortest time possible. In this situation a bank of escalators has several major advantages. First, by its sheer mass it will be highly visible to anyone entering the space. Second, when a larger than normal group wishes to travel in either direction, escalators can be reversed to accommodate the demand. Third, the large open landing at either end of the moving walk allows adequate room for people to congregate when waiting to enter the escalator or reorient themselves when leaving.

Because escalators do not meet the requirements of ANSI A117.1 to provide accessibility to the handicapped, virtually all escalator installations will be combined with an elevator installation of some kind. Determining the percentage of the building's users who will require or desire to use either system is a very difficult thing to quantify. Local codes may require a certain percentage of the population be served by an elevator system or it may be considered adequate to provide the bare minimum service for the genuinely disabled. Local elevator and escalator suppliers and consultants, along with local code officials, would be best qualified to determine the requirements of a specific building.

Escalators and moving walkways are rated according to nominal width and operating speed. In North America, nominal width is taken at about hip level. In Europe, it is at the level of the treads. Only two nominal widths are available for escalators: 32 in. (81.28 cm) and 48 in. (121.92 cm). A 32-in.-wide escalator allows only one passenger on a tread at a time; a 48-in.-wide escalator will allow two people to ride side by side. Perhaps more important, a 48-in.-wide escalator or moving walkway will allow one rider to pass a stationary rider. Capacities of escalators are theoretical and based on 1¼–2 passengers per tread. As Table 4 clearly shows, actual observed capacity is much lower than the hypothetical capacity. This should be taken into account by the designer of the system.

Escalators only come in two rated speeds in the United States, 90 ft/min (.45 ms) and 120 ft/min (.6 ms), although faster escalators are frequently used in European countries and the Soviet Union. Increased speed does not necessarily increase ridership if people are afraid to board the escalator. As speed increases, so should the number of flat steps at the top and the bottom of the escalator. Elevator manufacturers' standard is 1.67 steps. Strakosch recommends that this be increased to 2.67 steps for escalators with a speed of 120 ft/min (21).

The normal angle of incline for an escalator as established by the A17.1 code is within 1 or 2° of 30°. A 35° incline is allowed in Europe, but only at a speed of 90 ft/min (.45 ms).

A moving walkway may be either flat or inclined. The inclined segment may be at an angle of 1–15°; however, the walkway should begin and end with flat segments for level boarding and exiting (Fig. 38). Standard widths are 24 (61 cm), 32 (81.28 cm), and 40 in. (101.6 cm). Capacities are a function of speed, which in turn is related to the angle of incline (Table 5).

Once the location, width, and speed of an escalator is

Table 4. Escalator Capacities (30-in. Incline)

Width	Speed	Maximum Capacity Theoretical	Nominal Capacity Observed[a]
32 in. (600 mm)	90 ft/min (0.45 m/s)	425/5 min, 5000/h	170/5 min, 2040/h
	120 ft/min (0.6 m/s)	566/5 min, 6700/h	225/5 min, 2700/h
48 in. (1000 mm)	90 ft/min (0.45 m/s)	680/5 min, 8000/h	340/5 min, 4080/h
	120 ft/min (0.6 m/s)	891/5 min, 10700/h	450/5 min, 5400/h

[a] Based on one person every other step for 32-in. (600-mm) wide and one person per step for 48-in. (1000-mm) wide escalator.

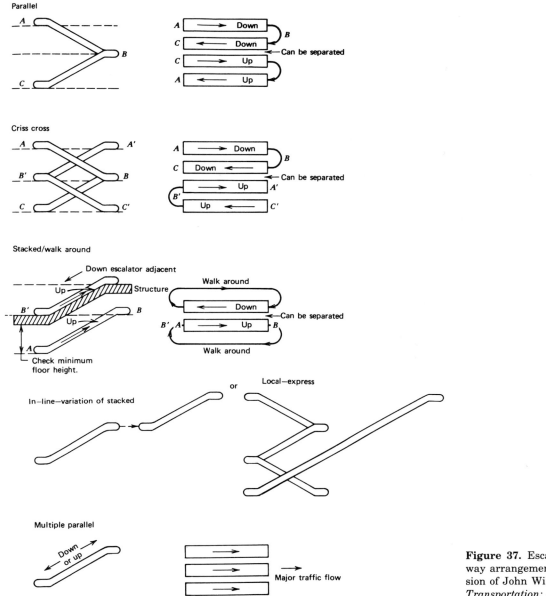

Figure 37. Escalator and moving walkway arrangements. Reprinted by permission of John Wiley & Sons, Inc., *Vertical Transportation: Elevators and Escalators,* G. R. Strakosch, 2nd ed., 1983.

Table 5. Moving Walkway Capacities, 40-in. (1000-mm) Nominal Width[a]

	Treadway Speed	Maximum Capacity Theoretical[b]	Nominal Capacity Observed[c]
0° incline	180 ft/min (0.9 m/s)	1200/5 min, 14,400/h	600/5 min, 7200/h
5° incline	140 ft/min (0.7 m/s)	932/5 min, 11,180/h	466/5 min, 5600/h
10° incline	130 ft/min (0.65 m/s)	867/5 min, 10,400/h	434/5 min, 5200/h
15° incline	125 ft/min (0.62 m/s)	833/5 min, 10,000/h	416/5 min, 5000/h

[a] Speed, angles, and capacities will vary with width. See A17.1 code.
[b] 2.5 ft^2 (0.23 m^2) of treadway per person.
[c] 5 ft^2 (0.46 m^2) of treadway per person.

PLANNING POWER WALKS/POWER RAMPS

Any arrangement or combination of horizontal and inclines, to a maximum of 12 degrees for almost any length can be provided.

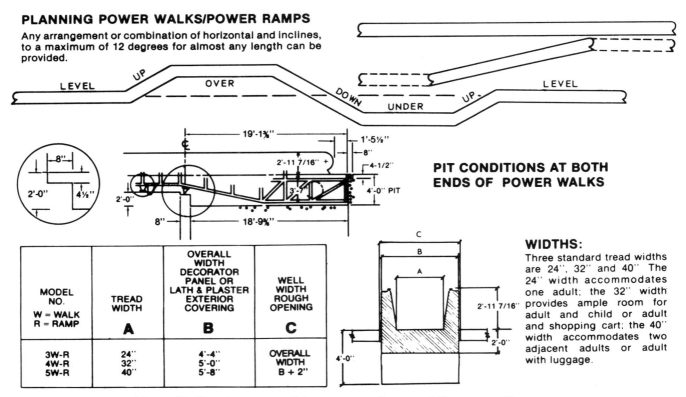

PIT CONDITIONS AT BOTH ENDS OF POWER WALKS

WIDTHS:
Three standard tread widths are 24", 32" and 40". The 24" width accommodates one adult; the 32" width provides ample room for adult and child or adult and shopping cart; the 40" width accommodates two adjacent adults or adult with luggage.

MODEL NO. W = WALK R = RAMP	TREAD WIDTH A	OVERALL WIDTH DECORATOR PANEL OR LATH & PLASTER EXTERIOR COVERING B	WELL WIDTH ROUGH OPENING C
3W-R 4W-R 5W-R	24" 32" 40"	4'-4" 5'-0" 5'-8"	OVERALL WIDTH B + 2"

Figure 38. Planning power walk/power ramps. Courtesy of Montgomery Elevators.

established, design is a fairly simple thing. The escalator is supported on a truss that spans from a structural beam above to a beam in the floor slab below. If a 32-in-wide (81.28 cm) escalator has a rise of more than 23 ft (7.01 m), or a 48-in.-wide (121.92 cm) escalator a rise of more than 18 ft (5.48 m), an intermediate support may be required. At the top end of the truss is usually the motor unit, although some manufacturers locate their drive motors along the truss. The pit area at the bottom provides room for the handrail to be reversed, the step return, and the step tensioning device (Fig. 39).

Both the pit area and the motor area need to be accessible. Normally this is accomplished by removing a hinged access cover that is provided as part of the escalator package.

Each escalator has two fixed work points, one at the top of the incline and one at the bottom. These points are located 1.73 × rise apart. The amount of space required between the work points and the structural supports, which are a part of the building itself, varies from manufacturer to manufacturer, depending primarily on the location of the motor unit (Figs. 40 and 41). If the manufacturer has not been preselected at the time an installation is laid out, the designer has no choice but to allow the

Figure 39. Escalator space requirements. Some escalators have the motor located at A. Reprinted by permission of John Wiley & Sons, Inc., *Vertical Transportation: Elevators and Escalators,* G. R. Strakosch, 2nd ed., 1983.

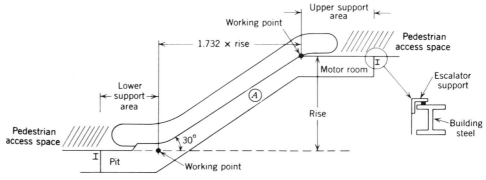

glass balustrade

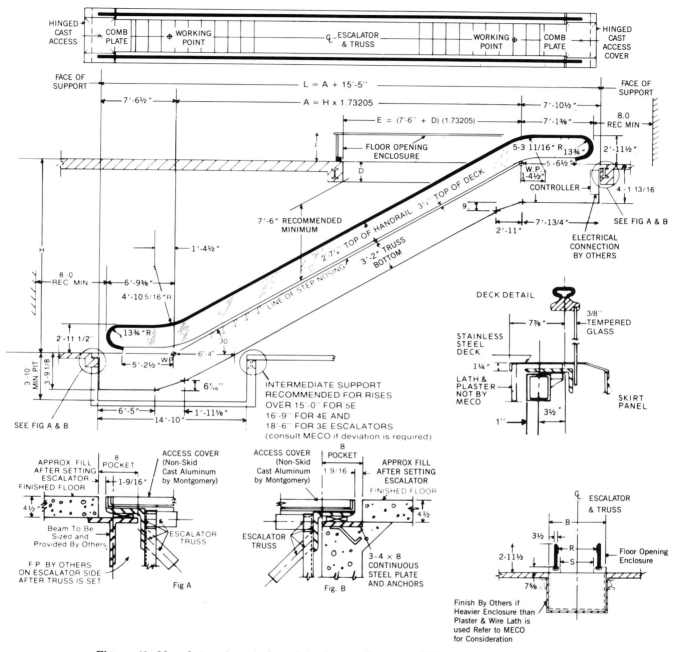

Figure 40. Manufacturer's typical escalator layout. Courtesy of Westinghouse Elevator Company, a division of Schindler Corp., Westinghouse is a registered trademark of the Westinghouse Electric Corporation, Trademark Licensor.

maximum required by any manufacturer and have any adjustments made during installation.

Table 6 gives some standard dimensions for horizontal space required by escalators. When considering the width and depth of the escalator, the designer should be aware that the dimensions usually provided by the manufac-

turer do not include finishes (Fig. 42). This finish is required to provide a 2-h rating. Adequate space should be allocated to permit this.

Aesthetically, a designer of escalators or moving walkways has few choices. The design of the treads and moving handrail is standard throughout the industry. In general,

Table 6. Horizontal Space Required. 30 in. Escalators[a]

Rise	Distance Working Point to Working Point	Distance Edge of Support to Edge of Support	
		1¼ Flat Steps	2¼ Flat Steps
10 ft (3.0 m)	17 ft 4 in. (5.3 m)	32 ft 2 in. (9.8 m)	34 ft 10 in. (10.6 m)
12 ft (3.6 m)	20 ft 10 in. (6.3 m)	35 ft 8 in. (10.9 m)	38 ft 4 in. (11.8 m)
14 ft (4.2 m)	24 ft 3 in. (7.4 m)	39 ft 4 in. (11.1 m)	41 ft 8 in. (12.7 m)
16 ft (4.8 m)	27 ft 9 in. (8.5 m)	42 ft 7 in. (12.9 m)	45 ft 3 in. (13.7 m)
18 ft (5.5 m)	31 ft 2 in. (9.5 m)	46 ft 0 in. (14.0 m)	48 ft 8 in. (14.2 m)
20 ft (6.0 m)	34 ft 8 in. (10.6 m)	49 ft 6 in. (15.0 m)	53 ft 2 in. (16.2 m)
22 ft (6.7 m)	38 ft 2 in. (11.6 m)	52 ft 11 in. (16.2 m)	55 ft 7 in. (16.9 m)
Distance from lower end support to inter-mediate support		15 ft 0 in. (4.6 m)	16 ft 4 in. (5.0 m)

[a] 32 in. (600 mm) and 48 in. (1000 mm) are the same.

the designer may select either glass or metal balustrades or balustrades clad in some other material such as plastic laminate. Also, the designer may specify the metal finish, either natural or painted, for exposed parts. The truss and soffits can be clad in whatever material is appropriate to the location in the building.

In the United States, standard escalator and moving walkway systems are manufactured by all the major elevator manufacturers. For more information on specific availability, consult either a manufacturer's representative or an elevator consultant familiar with local codes and installation practices.

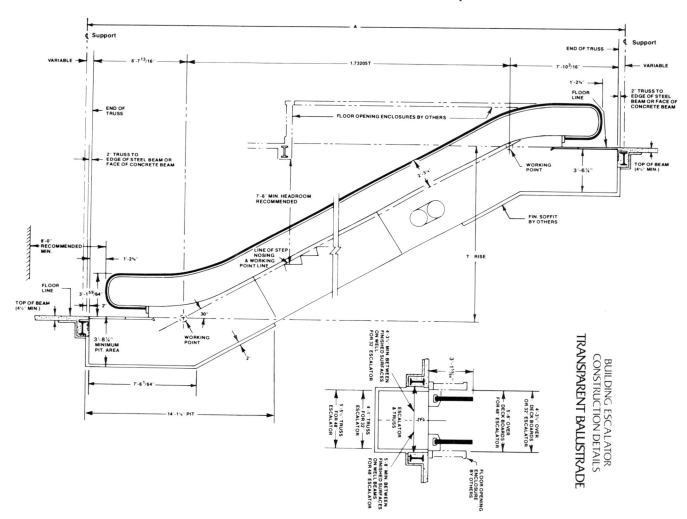

Figure 41. Manufacturers typical escalator layout. Courtesy of Montgomery Escalators.

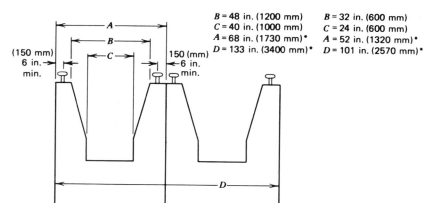

$B = 48$ in. (1200 mm) $B = 32$ in. (600 mm)
$C = 40$ in. (1000 mm) $C = 24$ in. (600 mm)
$A = 68$ in. (1730 mm)* $A = 52$ in. (1320 mm)*
$D = 133$ in. (3400 mm)* $D = 101$ in. (2570 mm)*

* Include a total of 4 in. (100 mm) on both sides for wall finish.

Figure 42. Escalator cross section. Reprinted by permission of John Wiley & Sons, Inc., *Vertical Transportation. Elevators and Escalators,* G.R. Strakosch, 2nd ed., 1983.

BIBLIOGRAPHY

1. M. Daumas, *A History of Technology and Invention,* Crown Publishers, Inc., New York, 1969, p. 23.

2. London Imperial College of Science and Technology, Electrical Engineering Department, J. S. Butler, et al., *Lifts and Escalators,* Imperial College Electrical Printroom Production, London, 1968, p. 2.

3. *Ibid.,* p. 2.

4. L. A. Peterson, *Elisha Graves Otis and His Influence on Vertical Transportation,* The Newcomen Society of England, Speech, 1949, p. 12.

5. Otis Elevator Company, *Tell Me About Elevators,* Otis Elevator Company, 1974, p. 17.

6. *Ibid.,* p. 25.

7. Ref. 5, p. 13.

8. G. R. Strakosch, *Vertical Transportation: Elevators and Escalators,* 2nd ed., John Wiley & Sons, New York, 1983, p. 227.

9. *Ibid.,* p. 227.

10. Ref. 8, p. 243.

11. Ref. 8, p. 227.

12. G. C. Barney and S. M. Santos, *Lift Traffic Analysis Design and Control,* Peter Peregrinus Ltd., UK, 1977.

13. Ref. 8, p. 166.

14. National Elevator Industry, Inc., *Elevator Engineering Standard Layouts,* National Elevator Industry, Inc. New York, 1979, preface.

15. Ref. 8, p. 166.

16. American Society of Mechanical Engineers, *ASME/ANSI A17.1, Safety Code for Elevators and Escalators,* American Society of Mechanical Engineers, New York, 1987, p. 58.

17. Ref. 14, p. 58.

18. Ref. 14, p. 62.

19. Ref. 8, p. 196.

20. Ref. 8, p. 196.

21. Ref. 8, p. 198.

General References

A comprehensive listing of elevator manufacturers, suppliers, consultants, and associations worldwide is *Elevator World*

Source published annually by *Elevator World* magazine, 354 Morgan Road, P.O. Box 6507, Mobile, Ala. 36606.

BETH D. BUFFINGTON, AIA
Washington, D.C.

VIOLLET–LE–DUC, EUGÈNE–EMMANUEL

Eugène–Emmanuel Viollet–le–Duc was born at the Rue Chabanais in Paris in 1814 and died in Lausanne in 1879. This complex, rebellious personality is known as architect, theoretician, author, and preservationist. His father was a civil servant and a scholar of sixteenth–century and earlier books. His mother was the daughter of a successful contractor. At the Rue Chabanais, Viollet–le–Duc's mother's sister lived on the third floor and her brother, the artist Eugene Delécluze, lived in the attic. Many famous people were entertained at the house including Stendhal, Prosper Mérimée, and Paul Louis Courier. Later, the family had an official home in a house on the grounds of the Tuileries Palace.

The young Eugène–Emmanuel and his brother Adolphe's education was supervised by their bachelor uncle, who placed them in a school at Fontenay. Eugène–Emmanuel was an unhappy student, and at Fontenay he learned his lifelong aversion to formal education. He joined his politically radical uncle in building the barricades of July 1830. He refused to enroll in the École de Beaux Arts because he felt that he would be forced into a mold. In 1832, when he was 18, his mother died, which drove him to intensive study, reading, drawing, and travel. His early love affair was broken off by the girl's family, who felt he was too young. At 19 years old, he married Elisa Tempier.

In August 1834, Viollet–le–Duc took a position teaching drawing at the École de Dessin (later the École des Arts Décoratifs), then a private school in Paris. Although he taught there intermittently until 1850, he left in 1835 for more than a year of travel in Italy, which he recorded in a group of over 450 drawings, watercolors, and sketches. On his return to Paris, he became interested in the medieval architecture of France. Victor Hugo's novel *The Hunchback of Notre Dame* was published in 1831, using the great cathedral as an integral part of the book. The book's popularity supported a new understanding of medieval building and greatly influenced public interest in the Gothic monuments of France.

In 1831, the new post of Inspector General of Ancient Monuments was created, and money was voted for preservation. The first inspector general was Ludovic Vitete, a friend of Viollet–le–Duc's uncle. In 1833, another family friend, Prosper Mérimée (later famous for his book *Carmen*), was named to the post, and by 1837 the Commission des Monuments Historiques was established, with Vitet a commissioner and Mérimée the secretary. In 1838, at age 24, Viollet–le–Duc was nominated "auditeur–supplant." In 1840 he was asked to prepare a report on the Ste. Madeleine church at Vézelay. Viollet–le–Duc took prompt action to preserve the building, which was restored 1840–1859. However, real fame came with his 1845 appointment, on the basis of a competition with Jean–Baptiste–Antoine Lassus, for the restoration of the Cathedral of Notre Dame in Paris. Large groups of workers were trained by Viollet–le–Duc, and many of them worked on later restoration projects. He designed the famous gargoyles and the flèche over the crossing. By 1849, Viollet–le–Duc wore the ribbon of the Legion of Honor, was appointed to many committees, and became one of three inspecteurs générals des Edifices Diocésains in 1853.

Viollet–le–Duc became close to the Imperial family of Napoléon III and his Empress Eugénie. He received the commission for the restoration of Pierrefonds, and managed private theatricals and fetes for the court. During this period, Georges–Eugène Haussmann was opening up the avenues of Paris. Although plans for the Paris Opera were begun in 1858 as a terminus of the Avenue del'Opera, the original architect was dismissed, and Viollet–le–Duc was approached. He recommended a competition for the design of the opera, which was eventually won by Jean–Louis–Charles Garnier, and completed in 1875. Viollet–le–Duc submitted his own designs for the competition, which are preserved in Paris (1).

Controversy continues about Viollet–le–Duc's role as preservationist. He is credited with work on the restorations of Ste. Chapelle in Paris, the walled town of Carcassonne, the cathedrals of Amiens and Reims, and countless other ancient structures throughout France. His approach was to study the evidence and then interpret the original appearance, resulting in much rebuilding, sometimes with added features that Viollet–le–Duc thought were consistent with the period of the buildings. This evocative approach still underlies one school of thinking about preservation.

At Saint-Sernin in Toulouse, Viollet–le–Duc planned changes to the exterior that involved a new roof as well as restoration of the apse, transepts, and nave to "a complete condition which may never have existed at any given moment" (2). Since 1979, a derestoration has been started. The question now is whether Viollet–le–Duc is not a part of the history of the buildings that he preserved. Without

his work, many old buildings would be in ruins, and the opinion of Viollet–le–Duc's work has improved in recent years.

In his writings, he brought a rational analysis to construction that has had a wide influence in architecture. His two most important publications are the *Dictionnaire raisonné de l'architecture française due XIᵉ au XVIᵉ siècle* (ten volumes, 1854–1868) and *Entretiens sur l'architecture,* published between 1858 and 1872. These books were found in the libraries of many nineteenth–century architects.

Viollet–le–Duc believed that all good architecture was based on a rational system of structure and organization reflecting the social conditions of the time and the building technology available. He recommended that the designer analyze what is pleasing by studying the masterpieces of the past and then make a similar analysis of the individual's own work consistent with the conditions and materials available. He promoted the use of cast iron in ways that influenced the younger designers in search of a new architecture for the times. However, his own work failed to live up to the promise of his theories.

The church of St.–Denys–de–Estree at Saint–Denis (1860) was probably typical of his own designs, where he created full–scale drawings of all capitals and carving. Critics find it an uninspired attempt at thirteenth–century Gothic style. Later scholars concentrate on Viollet–le–Duc's theoretical work. His rationalist concepts were known to have influenced such figures as Antonio Gaudi, Frank Lloyd Wright, Auguste Perret, and Ludwig Mies van der Rohe.

Viollet–le–Duc's role as preservationist was astounding for the number of famous monuments for which he was responsible. The new interest in Gothic was in opposition to the École des Beaux Arts. In 1863, a new constitution was proposed for the École, among the aims was an updated curriculum. At this time, Viollet–le–Duc had written a series of articles proposing a radical change in the education of architects. The government commission included some of his proposals for the reorganized curriculum, and Viollet–le–Duc was appointed Professor of History of Art and Aesthetics without approval of the academy. Student opposition was aroused by some of the new regulations, such as the one reducing the age of students eligible for the Prix de Rome from 30 to 25, and Viollet–le–Duc was booed at his first lecture. He persevered and achieved some success, but felt he should withdraw, and spent the rest of his life as a critic of the École des Beaux Arts.

Viollet–le–Duc valued independence of mind, and he had a real craving for being original. His attacks on institutions were not due to envy or disappointment, but were consistent with his self–view. He discovered architecture for himself. The key to his success was the logical analysis of Gothic work as a rational system. The analysis presented in the *Dictionnaire* was accompanied by elaborate plates analyzing the structural equilibrium of the work. Rather than aesthetic investigation, he emphasized the logical aspects of building. Only pure sculpture was permitted to be ornamental. His analysis is closely reasoned throughout his writing and accompanying plates. This ra-

Figure 1. Covered Market, Viollet–le–Duc, from *Entretiens sur l'architecture,* 1872. Courtesy of the American Institute of Architects.

tionalism is a product of the nineteenth–century, and Viollet–le–Duc's work must be read as a product of its time.

His second great work, the *Entretiens sur l'architecture* was published by A. Morel, Paris, between 1863 and 1872. The essays based on his lectures were carefully illustrated. This book was an application of the theories developed in the earlier work. This can be stated as leading from good architecture being rational to a need for a rational nineteenth–century architecture. He described the emotive power of architecture. He included a number of fascinating original designs to show how the nineteenth–century architect might adopt iron as a structural material. In his design for a covered market with meeting room above (Fig. 1), the concept of splayed iron columns was later applied in the 1895 École du Sacré Couer, Paris, designed by Hector Guimard. Viollet–le–Duc's search for a language of design fails to convince, but the theoretical basis remains as a foundation of twentieth–century design.

In later years, Viollet–le–Duc regretted his support of the Third Empire. He concentrated on writing, and by 1874, he resigned from the Service des Edifices Diocèsains and most of his restoration projects. Although serving as a counselor for Paris from Montmartre from 1874, he spent more and more time at his house in Lausanne and died there in 1879.

BIBLIOGRAPHY

1. *Viollet–le–Duc,* exhibition catalog, The Trust for Museum Exhibitions, Washington, D.C., 1987. Drawings are in the collection of Centre de Recherches sur les Monuments Historique, Ministere de la Culture et de la Communication, Paris.

2. E. E. Viollet–le–Duc, "Proportion," in E. E. Viollet–le–Duc, *Dictionnaire raisonné de l'architecture français du XIe au XVIe siècle,* Vol. 7, B. Bance, A. Morel, Paris, 1854–1868, p. 539.

General References

J. Summerson, "Viollet–le–Duc and the Rational Point of View," in *Heavenly Mansions and Other Essays on Architecture,* W. W. Norton Co., New York, 1963.

R. Middleton and D. Watkin, *Neoclassical and 19th Century Architecture,* a volume of the *History of World Architecture,* Electa Editrice, 1977. American edition published by Harry N. Abrams, New York, 1980.

H. R. Hitchcock, *Architecture: Nineteenth and Twentieth Centuries,* 4th ed., a volume of *The Pelican History of Art,* Penguin Books, Harmondsworth, UK, 1977.

E. E. Viollet–le–Duc, *Entretiens sur l'architecture,* An English translation was published under the title *Discourses on Architecture,* 2 Vols., Allen & Unwin, 1959. Another translation, of 1877 and 1881 was originally published by Sampson Low, Marston, and Searle and Rivington, London, and reissued under the title *Lectures on Architecture,* 2 Vols., Dover Publications, New York, 1987.

ROBERT T. PACKARD, AIA
Reston, Virginia

VISIONARY ARCHITECTURE

Visionary architecture is a term used to describe the theoretical writings and drawings published by several French architects of the late eighteenth and early nineteenth centuries. Other, later work consists of a wide variety of efforts that have been difficult to categorize. Concepts that have been applied to it include the bizarre, the fantastic, and the unique. Often the product of serious effort, examples can be taken from both folk and fine art.

About 1760, a group of French architects became active in planning a number of new building types. Many of these were proposals or studies that were not built, perhaps because of the immense scale of their plans. The influence of the Italian Giovanni Batista Piranesi (1720–1778) is evident in the French work. The work of Piranesi, who had wanted to be an architect, was restricted to drawing and architectural prints published in expensive books mostly sold outside of Italy. Piranesi was influenced in turn by the older Giuseppi Galli Bibiena (1699–1756), whose baroque architectural and perspective designs made for the Viennese and German courts were published in 1740.

The oldest of the French visionary architects was Etienne-Louis Boulée. The son of an architect, Boulée was born in Paris in 1728. Trained as a painter, his real interest was in architecture. By age 18, he was teaching at the École des Ponts et Chaussées. He received commissions to design a number of urban mansions (*hôtels*) and remodeled the chapels around the choir of the Church of St. Roch in Paris. His proposals for enlarging the palaces at Versailles and Saint-Germain en Laye and his design for a royal library failed because money was not available for these ambitious undertakings.

Boulée became a first-class member of the Royal Academy of Architecture in 1780, and was architect for the Comte d'Artois, brother to King Louis XVI. During the French Revolution, he became a member of the Institut de France, and taught at the École Centrales until his death in 1799.

Despite his successful early architectural career, Boulée is remembered for a series of drawings created in the decade before the French Revolution. The text accompanying the drawings appears to have been written at various times. The then-current artistic concern with nature was reflected in the creation of an *architecture des ombres* and an *architecture ensevelie*. This was also the post-Newtonian period, when the architect was challenged with establishing a relationship between the arts and science.

Boulée's proposals for buildings of far greater scale than was economically feasible were preserved by him, possibly as an aid to teaching. The chief characteristic of the architects of his time was a preference for large, simple masses, as shown in Boulée's design for a cenotaph for Newton (1784). The appearance of these buildings was meant to express clearly their use. The diversity of building types is indicated by the list of building designs included in *Architecture, essai sur l'art* (1). Its proposals included cenotaphs (cones, pyramids, and globes), an entrance to a cemetery, a chapel of the dead, city walls and gates, bridges, forts, a palace for a sovereign, capital buildings, a palace of justice, a national assembly hall, a metropolitan cathedral, a national library, and the remodeling of the palace at Versailles. The huge scale of the proposals was without regard to practicality and gave rise to the concept of visionary architecture.

Another architect, Claude-Nicolas Ledoux, was born at Dromans in 1736. He received a scholarship, but abandoned classical studies for drawing. He studied with painter Jean-Baptiste Pierre and later became a pupil of Jacques-François Blondel, an eminent professor of architecture at the Academie de l'Architecture. He designed a number of mansions (*hôtels*) in Paris beginning in 1750 and, with the patronage of Mme. du Barry, designed a chateau at Louveciennes in 1771. He was a respected teacher at the École des Ponts et Chaussées and became a member of the Academie de l'Architecture in 1762 and architect to Louis XV.

High estimates of cost and the originality of his style frightened away a number of prospective clients. He was named inspector of saltworks in Franche-Comte in 1774 and was commissioned to build a salt factory near the forest of Chaux, which he expanded in his writing to an entire model city. Only a small part of the construction was completed when work stopped in 1779. In 1784, he began construction of a new tax wall around Paris with toll gates or *barrieres*.

During the Revolution, he was arrested and barely escaped execution. By 1795, he was acting on design juries, and although he received no more commissions, he published his work, planned for five folio volumes. Two-thirds were published by Ledoux *"chez l'auteur"* in Paris in 1804 under the title *L'Architecture considerée sous le rapport de l'art, des moeurs et de la legislation* (2). Although he died in 1806, other plates were published in 1847. His work is typified by simplicity and grandeur. Fascinated by designs based on circles and squares, he did away with all ornament in favor of proportion and mass. The cosmological symbolism applied to his work at Chaux has attracted the most attention (Fig. 1).

A listing of some of the plates indicates the variety of building types and the application of his theories to actual

Figure 1. Maison des Directeur de la Loue. Courtesy of the Princeton University Press and The American Institute of Architects Archives.

and proposed projects. These include villas, mansions and chateaux, city gates for Paris, a tavern, bridges, an agricultural school, a prison, and a city plan of Chaux. For Chaux, Ledoux designed a hospice; a palace of concord; a house of union; a temple of memory; a house of communal life based on Rousseau's descriptions of an ideal society; a pantheon; a cemetery; a temple dedicated to love; a house of education; a marketplace; a saltworks; a cannon foundry; a cooper's workshop; the inspector's house at the source of the Loue; a workman's house for a father and three sons; houses for a stockbroker, a man of letters, the paymaster of Chaux, and a woodcutter; and barns. Some of these buildings are pure form studies, without ornament other than occasional free-standing sculptures. The result of Ledoux's work is a vision of a utopian agricultural community.

This free approach to theoretical design resulted in work that has attracted the attention of architectural scholars. Many examples of theoretical proposals for buildings that were not built have been analyzed for their contribution to architectural style and theory.

Other visionary work might better be labeled fantastic or bizarre. Examples of this include designs by artists, such as the work of James Wines and SITE for the Best Products Co. Folk art examples include Simon Rodis's Watts Towers in Los Angeles and Ferdinand Cheval's Palais Ideal, at Hautrives, France.

Architects whose built work has been analyzed in terms of the visionary or fantastic include Antonio Gaudi, Bernard Maybeck, Eric Mendelsohn, Paolo Soleri, Charles Moore, Bruce Goff, Frank Lloyd Wright, Robert Venturi, and Eero Saarinen.

BIBLIOGRAPHY

1. E. L. Boulée, *Architecture, essai sur l'art,* Bibliothèque Nationale, Paris, ms. 9153; H. Rosenau, London, 1953; P. de Montclos, Paris, 1968; transl., H. Rosenau, London, 1973.

2. C. N. Ledoux, *L'Architecture considerée sous le rapport de l'art, des moeurs et de la legislation, chez l'auteur,* Paris, 1804; Fasc. ed., Paris, 1961; Hildesheim, 1980; Ramee ed., 1847 Princeton University Press, Princeton, N.J., 1983.

General References

G. G. Bibiena, *Architectural and Perspective Designs,* Dover Publications, Inc., New York, 1964.

"Visionary Architects: Boulée, Ledoux, Lequeu," University of St. Thomas, Houston, Tex., Exhibition Catalogue, 1968.

G. B. Piranesi, *The Prisons (Le Carceri),* Dover Publications, Inc., New York, 1973.

J. M. Perouse de Montclos, *Etienne-Louis Boulée,* George Braziller, Inc., New York, 1974.

C. Jencks, *Bizarre Architecture,* Rizzoli, New York, 1979.

M. Schuyt, J. Elffers, and G. R. Collins, *Fantastic Architecture,* Harry N. Abrams, New York, 1980; *Phantastische Architektur,* DuMont Buchverlag, Cologne, FRG, 1980.

B. J. Archer and A. Vidler, *Follies: Architecture for the Late-twentieth-century Landscape,* Rizzoli, New York, 1983.

ROBERT T. PACKARD, AIA
Reston, Virginia

W

WACHSMANN, KONRAD

Konrad Wachsmann (1901–1980), architect and researcher, was born in Frankfurt-on-Oder, Germany, emigrated to the United States in 1941, and became a naturalized citizen in 1947. After completing his education in Berlin and Dresden, he worked briefly as designer and draftsman for Le Corbusier in Paris. Wachsmann was the architect for a prefabricated building company before opening his own office in Berlin from 1928 to 1932. After leaving Germany, he worked in Spain, Italy, and France. He was interned and then served in the French Army (1939–1941) before coming to New York. He arrived with a series of drawings of prefabricated structures and space frames, which attracted the interest of Walter Gropius.

Wachsmann collaborated with Walter Gropius in the development of the general panel prefabrication system in New York, from 1941 to 1949. He held several offices in the General Panel Corp., becoming chairman of the New York and Burbank company.

The effort to develop a prefabricated housing industry in the United States held great promise, but proved to be a failure by the 1950s. The dependence of a complete packaged system limited the use of common construction materials. They could not easily be integrated into the modular system. Issues of land use, transportation, and financing contributed to the failure of several efforts to provide prefabricated housing in the United States. This failure occurred despite government support. The present manufactured housing industry benefits from the lessons learned in the earlier efforts. An analysis of the early work is recorded in Gilbert Herbert's book *The Dream of the Factory-Made House: Walter Gropius and Konrad Wachsmann* (1).

In 1949, Wachsmann became professor and director of the Institute of Advanced Building Research, Institute of Design, at the Illinois Institute of Technology and later professor of architecture and director of the Building Institute from 1964 to 1972. He was in private practice in Chicago, Genoa, Italy, and Los Angeles from 1964 until his death in 1980.

His fame as teacher, writer, and researcher inspired a generation of students to think in unconventional terms about building. One product of Wachsmann's efforts was the Mobilar system of space frames. The connector between members was a particularly critical element that evolved through several stages. The Mobilar system was exhibited at the Museum of Modern Art in 1946. His book *The Turning Point of Building*, published in the United States in 1961, is a good record of his studies of connections in building (2). Although other products competed with the Mobilar system in the market, Wachsmann's pioneer role was clear.

In 1965, Wachsmann founded the University of South-ern California's Graduate Program on Industrialization. In his later years, he lectured and taught at universities in many countries. His support for industrialized construction was a 50-year effort.

Wachsmann believed that technology and art were not incompatible, and he wrote extensively on the freedom that technology could provide to the design process. Many of his projects were published in the press.

BIBLIOGRAPHY

1. H. Gilbert, *The Dream of the Factory-Made House: Walter Gropius and Konrad Wachsmann,* MIT Press, Cambridge, Mass., 1984.
2. K. Wachsmann, *The Turning Point of Building,* Reinhold Publishing Corp., New York, 1961. (Originally published as *Wendepunkt im Bauen,* Krausskopf Verlag, Wiesbaden, 1959.)

General References

R. Ward, Jr., "Toward Industrialization of Building" in *AIA Journal* **57**(3), p 33–43 (1972). A consideration of Wachsmann's work.

M. Emanuel, ed., *Contemporary Architects,* St. Martin's Press, Inc., New York, 1980.

ROBERT T. PACKARD, AIA
Reston, Virginia

WAGNER, OTTO

Otto Koloman Wagner (1841–1918) was an Austrian architect, engineer, and educator. During his lifetime the city of Vienna underwent substantial development, thereby initiating many urban planning concepts of the twentieth century. Wagner was an important figure in this arena.

In 1859, the liberal government undertook the development of Vienna by ordering destruction of the old city walls and the creation of the circle route around the old city, called the Ringstrasse. The development produced many governmental, cultural, and upper-class residential buildings. A feature of the residential development was the attraction of nobility and wealthy families to purchase luxurious apartment buildings as investments, reserving space for their own use.

In his early practice, starting in the late 1860s, Otto Wagner designed many apartment houses in the Ringstrasse area. As architect–entrepreneur, Wagner lived in the buildings himself until he would sell them to finance new ventures. In the Oestereichische Landerbank (1882–1884), he simplified the Renaissance style by emphasizing the horizontal lines on the street facade, bringing the windows to the face of the rear facade, and keeping the interior stairway in simple classic detailing. Despite these forward-looking devices, it would have been hard to predict his future development.

Criticism of the Ringstrasse development by Camillo Sitte was based on the failure to provide human-size squares. The social and psychological analysis of the use of urban spaces was a new element in the thought of the time, even though Sitte had no quarrel with the variety of historic styles evident in the Ringstrasse development. It was realized that the upper-class development had not improved the lot of the average citizen.

In 1890, Vienna annexed major suburban areas, and the opportunity made by this action led to an 1893 competition for the design of a suburban transportation system. Wagner submitted a winning design based on the concept of transportation as the key to growth. He proposed radial arteries and an outer circular route. Infinite expansion was the mood of the day. By winning the competition, Wagner moved into the center of the debate on urban-planning issues and, in 1894, was appointed professor of architecture at the Academy of Fine Arts. In teaching, writing, and development of the transportation system for the city, he moved into what has come to be called the modern movement.

With the assistance of younger men such as Joseph Maria Olbrich, Wagner designed bridges and stations for the rail system. This famous work led to consideration of engineering as a legitimate influence on the art of architecture, and the use of modern technology became a high priority. The stations are interesting in comparison to the work of Guimard for the stations of the Paris Metro (1899–1904). Wagner's work was more decorative. Two examples of Wagner's stations have been restored and erected in the Karlsplatz. One of them is used as an entrance to the newer underground, the other is a café.

In his book *Modern Architecture* (1895) (1), Wagner criticized the use of historic styles and called for a new style appropriate to the faster pace of modern society. He defined this need as a moral issue, calling on architects to be artists for their times.

The secessionist motto, "To the Age Its Art, To Art Its Freedom," was appealing to Wagner, and he and Olbrich were early supporters of this movement away from academic art. Modern urban man needed new forms and styles. Wagner's response was the search for new ideas in his buildings. His secessionist buildings include the Steinhof church (1904–1906), where modern materials and technologies were united with the symbolic forms of the church. This blending of two sources produced a strong environment using artists such as Koloman Moser for decoration and for window designs. He was proud to identify this church as giving better views and better sight lines than historic buildings and for less construction cost.

His Postal Savings Bank, built in two stages (1904–1906 and 1910–1912), allowed him another major effort at integrating new concepts into what was basically a utilitarian building. The granite and marble exterior walls were clearly expressed as veneer, with exposed bolt heads on the exterior, some of which are nonfunctional, but expressive of the concept. The success of the building depends on the integration of new materials, such as aluminum, and concepts of a public building fully integrated into the design. The main hall, suggestive of train station forms, was detailed with materials and fittings, which have been much admired. The glass barrel-vaulted ceiling of great simplicity was a remarkable achievement for that day. Some of his furniture designs for the Postal Savings Bank may still be found in the catalogs of furniture manufacturers and in museum collections.

The influence of Wagner on the younger designers such as Josef Hoffmann was considerable both as a professor and by the example of his work. Both Josef Hoffmann and Adolf Loos admired Wagner's work. Some 190 architects were educated under Wagner's direction at the Academy of Fine Arts.

Otto Wagner's late urban publications used Vienna as the example of urban issues, and his book *Die Groszstadt* (*The Metropolis*) was prepared for a conference at Columbia University in 1911 (2). As an urbanist, he welcomed growth; supported apartment living; recognized the use of traffic, water supply, and sewage as planning factors; emphasized the importance of the street; but was not sympathetic to the concept of the greenbelt around the city, which in fact was becoming a reality in Vienna. Wagner's utopian view of infinite expansion in an orderly manner represented a bureaucratic megalomania of scale. He recognized the need for employment outside the city center, and proposed each satellite community to contain manufacturing capability. Each city district would be about 100,000–150,000 inhabitants, with its own governmental structure.

Late in life, Wagner's output decreased. In addition to a simple apartment building at Neustiftgasse 40 in Vienna (1909), which has not survived in good condition, was his own house (1912) of simple geometric design. He continued planning for postwar Vienna until 1917.

Over his long career, Wagner rose to peaks of creative energy, which ensure his fame. It was left to the younger generation to carry on the ideas expressed in his work. The integration of historic forms into modern buildings using advanced engineering concepts were his great achievement. In international terms, Wagner's work is comparable in importance to the German Peter Behrens (1868–1940). The achievements of Auguste Perret (1874–1954) in France or Frank Lloyd Wright (1869–1959) in the United States are seen as more consistently at a higher level of creativity than the Viennese or German designers (3).

BIBLIOGRAPHY

1. O. Wagner, *Moderne Architektur: Seinen Schulern ein Fuhrer auf diesem Kunstgebiet,* Vienna, 1895, (*Die Baukunst unserer Zeit; Dem Baukunstjunger ein Fuhrer auf diesem Kunstgebeit,* 4th ed., rev. title, 1914) reprinted by Locker Verlag, Vienna, 1979.

2. O. Wagner, *Die Groszstadt: Eine Studie uber diese,* A. Schroll, Vienna, 1911.

3. H. R. Hitchcock, *Architecture: Nineteenth and Twentieth Centuries,* Penguin Books, Middlesex, 1977, pp. 455, 469.

General References

E. Godoli, "Austria: To the Limits of a Language: Wagner, Olbrich, Hoffmann," in F. Russell, ed., *Art Nouveau Architecture,* Rizzoli, New York, 1979, Chapt. 10.

H. Geretsegger and M. Peinter, *Otto Wagner, 1841–1918: The Expanding City and the Beginnings of Modern Architecture,* trans. by G. Onn, Rizzoli, New York, 1979.

H. Hollein, *Otto Wagner,* A. D. A. Edita, Tokyo, 1978.

C. S. Schorske, *Fin-De-Siecle Vienna,* Alfred A. Knopf, New York, 1980. Note especially Chapt. 2, "The Ringstrasse, Its Critics, and the Birth of Urban Modernism."

K. Varnedoe, *Vienna 1900: Art, Architecture & Design,* The Museum of Modern Art, 1986. Note the extensive bibliography.

ROBERT T. PACKARD, AIA
Reston, Virginia

Figure 1. A typical gypsum mine. Courtesy of USG Corp.

WALLBOARD AND PLASTER SYSTEMS

Gypsum is one of the oldest known building materials. It was used before recorded history as a plaster and decorative material. Gypsum is a nonmetallic rock found in nearly all countries of the world. Formations occur in massive beds varying from 2 or 3 feet to many feet in thickness.

Commercial gypsum is quarried or mined, depending on whether the rock is near the earth's surface or buried deep beneath it. It offers two great gifts—widespread abundance and remarkable fireproofing qualities.

Chemically, gypsum is $CaSO_4 \cdot 2H_2O$. In its pure form it is a white or light-colored mineral. Color variations range from shades of light gray, pink, dark gray, to black, depending on the type of sand, shales, or other minerals mixed with the gypsum. It has no odor and is neither acid nor alkaline. Hardness of gypsum is 2, which it defines on the Mohs scale in which talc, the softest mineral, represents 1 and the diamond, the hardest, represents 10. Its specific gravity is 2.3.

Gypsum is easily changed from its dihydrate form (gypsum mineral) to its hemihydrate form (plaster of Paris) and back to its dihydrate form as shown chemically:

$$CaSO_4 \cdot 2H_2O + Heat = CaSO_4 \cdot \tfrac{1}{2}H_2O + Water = CaSO_4 \cdot 2H_2O + Heat$$

gypsum   plaster of Paris   gypsum

This process is used to transform the mined gypsum mineral into a gypsum wall.

Gypsum mineral occurs in more crystal variations than any other mineral. Probably the most extensive collection of gypsum mineral samples and of the varied crystalline forms is on display at the USG Corporation Research Center, Libertyville, Illinois. Figures 1 and 2 show a typical gypsum mine and a quarry.

The primary manufacturers of gypsum products are listed below. Of these, the United States Gypsum (USG) Company is the largest.

U.S. Manufacturers
The Celotex Corporation
Centex American Gypsum Company
Domtar Gypsum America, Inc.
Georgia-Pacific Corporation
Gold Bond Building Products
   (A National Gypsum Division)
Pabco Gypsum
Republic Gypsum Company
Temple-EasTex, Inc.
United States Gypsum Company
   (A USG Corporation Subsidiary)
Windsor Gypsum, Inc.
Canadian Manufacturers
Atlantic Gypsum, Ltd.
Canadian Gypsum Co.
Domtar Construction Materials
Westroc Industries, Ltd.

Figure 2. A typical gypsum quarry. Courtesy of USG Corp.

CHARACTERIZATION OF PLASTER AND DRYWALL SYSTEMS

With the variety of plaster and gypsum drywall systems available today, it is difficult for architects or contractors to choose the system best suited to their job. One approach to this problem is to list and rate each system by its specific properties and benefits. Conventional plaster systems have for many decades been the best interior wall and ceiling finishes. They are considered superior to other products because they provide long-term systems performance, high impact resistance, and a truly monolithic abuse-resistant surface that can have either a smooth or textured finish. However, high cost has reduced their usage to jobs where greater cost can be justified, such as high-use public areas in hospitals, schools, and institutional buildings.

When gypsum drywall partitions and ceiling systems appeared in the early 1940s, cost and speed of erection became dominant factors. The previous benefits noted with the use of plaster systems, extreme hardness and total monolithic appearing surfaces, were less important in achieving marketability in most construction. Today, drywall systems technology has advanced to the point of providing a relatively smooth serviceable finish at the lowest possible, initial installed cost.

Veneer plaster systems were developed during the 1960s and early 1970s. These systems took advantage of the large-size gypsum panels used in drywall construction to improve speed of installation while providing more monolithic appearing, harder, abuse-resistant surfaces. Additionally, overall plaster thickness was reduced from the standard ½ in., associated with conventional plaster, to a mere ¹⁄₁₆ to ⅛ in. This was achieved by using high-strength forms of hemihydrate in the product formulations.

The difference in plaster thickness is accounted for by the fact that veneer plaster systems are either a single- or two-component method of finishing. The single-component system addresses joint reinforcement, joint and trim concealment, leveling, and finishing to provide aesthetics in a single coat of veneer plaster. On the other hand, the two-component method provides for reinforcement and leveling with a basecoat veneer plaster application, then applying a finish coat to this monolithic surface to achieve a superior finished appearance. The combination of the benefit of reduced thickness and high-strength material reduces drying time and provides a serviceable finish surface in less time.

Even though the initial cost of veneers is usually more than regular drywall, overall job cost can favor veneers owing to their faster finishing time. Drywall joint treatment and its required drying time before decoration can be started takes about 5 days. Single-coat veneer can be ready for decoration in as little as 48 h because unlike drywall, only a single drying cycle is required. This means that the builder can complete a unit 3 to 4 days sooner using veneer systems. On a large job, the builder can save substantial interest charges by reducing the time of the construction loan.

One other important consideration affecting appearance and performance of these systems is workmanship. The installation of framing, gypsum base, joint reinforcement, and perimeter relief are elements that must be carefully monitored. Proper technique for installing these elements and the effect on total systems performance and installed appearance will be discussed later and appear in material listed in the bibliography.

In summary, conventional plaster systems achieve a truly monolithic surface providing good abuse-resistance; gypsum drywall provides an acceptable wall and ceiling surface at the lowest cost. Performance cost and surface appearance of veneer plaster systems can be rated between that of conventional plaster and gypsum drywall systems.

PLASTER SYSTEMS

Conventional Plaster

Conventional plaster systems in all cases consist of a substrate, the surface that provides the rough form for the finished surface; a basecoat, usually ½–⅞ in. in thickness, which allows for leveling or forming of the surface contour; and the finish coat, which provides the necessary aesthetics for finished surface acceptance. Substrates to which conventional plasters are applied include gypsum and metal lath, masonry, and monolithic concrete interior surfaces.

Gypsum lath provides a rigid, fire-resistant base for the application of the gypsum plaster. The gypsum core of this lath is faced with a multilayer paper formulated to provide proper absorption to prevent plaster slide during application, resistance to sag, and positive bond of the basecoat plaster. The outer paper plys are made highly absorbent to draw moisture from the plaster mix uniformly and quickly to prevent sliding and allow the plaster surface to be leveled; the inner plys are treated, in manufacture, to form a barrier against water penetration, thus preventing early wetting of the gypsum core and subsequent sag of the gypsum lath. Face paper is folded around the long edges (forming a rounded edge), and the ends are square cut.

Gypsum lath is nail- or staple-applied to wood or nailable steel framing; clip fastened to wood framing, steel studs, and suspended metal grillage; or screw-attached to wood or metal forming and furring channels. When used with gypsum plaster, it provides assembly fire ratings up to 2 h. Securely attached, it adds lateral stability to the assembly. It is highly durable and provides exceptional bond strength to basecoat plasters, which together give excellent resistance to sound transmission. Resilient attachment further improves ratings, making assemblies suitable for party walls. Gypsum lath is available in ⅜- and ½-in.-thicknesses, 16-in.- or 24-in.-nominal widths, and various lengths.

Veneer Plaster

Veneer (thin wall) plaster combines the best attributes of both drywall and plaster systems. The combination of large size—48 in. (1.22 m) wide—and up to 14 ft. (4.267 m) veneer gypsum base, produced under ASTM Standard C-588, and high strength veneer plaster, manufactured to comply with ASTM Standard C-587, offers speed of erection, surface abrasion resistance, ease in decoration, versatility in texture finishing, and quick occupancy. Veneer plaster systems are becoming a large volume of business in the industry. This growing trend to veneer plaster systems is due to the advantages of easier and quicker installation, lower cost, lighter weight, and generally greater resistance to surface abrasion than for conventional plaster systems.

Fire ratings using the Type X gypsum base are comparable to or better than those for the traditional block-wall systems. This is also true of the sound transmission (STC) ratings. (Refer to the Gypsum Association Fire Resistance Design Manual.) Any fire rating achieved with Type X gypsum drywall is equally applicable to Type X gypsum base.

Single-coat veneer plaster finishes provide hard, durable surfaces not obtainable in ordinary drywall work and can offer the advantage of next-day decoration when breather-type paints are used. This provides a desirable, efficient means of interior wall and ceiling installation. Two-coat veneer plaster systems, although generally slightly more expensive than the single-coat systems, provide means to achieve the superior aesthetic quality of conventional plaster and maintain a high degree of system integrity.

A one-component veneer plaster system consists of one product, ready to be applied in a thin coat with only the addition of potable water. It should be applied using a scratch and double-back method of application, resulting in a finished thickness of from $1/16$ to $3/32$ in.

The surface can be troweled to a highly polished finish or, with the job addition of silica sand, it can be applied to achieve a float, swirl, Spanish, skip trowel, or other desired texture finish. The addition of sand allows the material to be texture finished; however, manufacturers' directions should be followed when adding sand if a premixed sand plaster is not used, or if a veneer specifically made for texturing is used.

Smooth finishes are more easily obtained over gypsum base, but can be achieved over other bases such as monolithic concrete coated with a quality plaster-bonding agent or over veneer basecoats applied to masonry block.

The two-component systems consist of separate veneer basecoat and finish materials. The reason for the existence of two-component systems is that many people in the industry hold a strong opinion that these systems offer a greater opportunity to achieve a uniform, monolithic, blemish-free surface comparable to conventional plaster.

Mixing in a 5-gal pail and a set time of less than 1 h are significant advantages of the veneer systems.

Ornamental Plaster

Ornamental plastering generally is divided into four areas:

1. Cornice work, both "run" and "stuck in place."
2. Enriched cornice work: combining a plain cornice

Figure 3. Running a cornice in place. Courtesy of USG Corp.

with cast ornaments attached to the face. This work is sometimes called "staff work."

3. Cast ornamental work.
4. Modeling and casting original work and reproducing them for mounting.

Each of these areas includes many types of ornamental work and specialized techniques. Shown in Figure 3 is an

Figure 4. Elaborate ornamental work. Courtesy of USG Corp. See also color plates.

example of running a cornice in place. Figure 4 is an example of a completed ornamental job.

Ornamental plastering is a vast field that provides unlimited ways to produce classic and unique decorations in all areas of construction. Many reference texts are available. Two of them are listed in the bibliography; they are *Plastering Skill and Practice* and *Plastering—A Craftsman's Encyclopaedia*.

GYPSUM PANEL PRODUCTS: DRYWALL

Gypsum board is a generic name for a family of panel products consisting of a noncombustible core, primarily of gypsum, with a paper surface covering the face, back, and long edges. A typical board application is shown in Figure 5.

Gypsum board is often called drywall or plasterboard. Its noncombustible core differentiates it from products such as plywood, hardboard, and fiberboard. It provides a monolithic surface when installed with a joint-treatment system.

Gypsum board products are readily available and easy to apply. They are the least expensive of wall-surfacing materials offering a fire-resistant interior finish. They satisfy a wide range of architectural requirements for design, application, performance, and availability. Ease of repair and adaptability to most forms of decoration add to its popularity.

Gypsum board is an excellent fire-resistive material. It is the most commonly used interior finish where fire resistance classifications are required. Its noncombustible core

contains chemically combined water that, under high heat, is slowly released as steam, effectively retarding heat transfer. Even after complete calcination, when all the water has been released, it continues to act as a heat-insulating barrier. In addition, tests conducted in accordance with ASTM Method E84 show that it has low flame spread, fuel, and smoke contribution factors. When installed in combination with other materials, it effectively protects building elements from fire for prescribed time periods.

Many types of gypsum board are available for all types of interior drywall construction. Developed as a result of specific requirements, gypsum board panels are mainly used as the surface layer of interior walls and ceilings; as a base for ceramic, plastic and metal tile; for exterior soffits; for elevator and other shaft enclosures; and to provide fire protection to structural elements.

Regular gypsum board is available in thicknesses of ¼ in. (6.4 mm) for use as a final layer for multilayer application or to cover existing walls and ceilings in remodeling; 5⁄16 in. for use primarily in mobile home construction; ⅜ in. (9.5 mm) principally for double-layer systems; ½ in. (13 mm) for most new single-layer construction and for double-layer construction where superior sound and fire ratings are required; ⅝ in. for use in higher quality single- or double-layer work; ¾ in. (19 mm) and 1 in. (25.4 mm) for special systems to be discussed under System Performance. Standard gypsum boards are 4-ft wide and from 8 to 14 ft long. Special lengths are available from manufacturers for orders of sufficient size. Some special widths are also available, but significant justification is generally necessary. Standard edges are shown in Figure 6. Of these

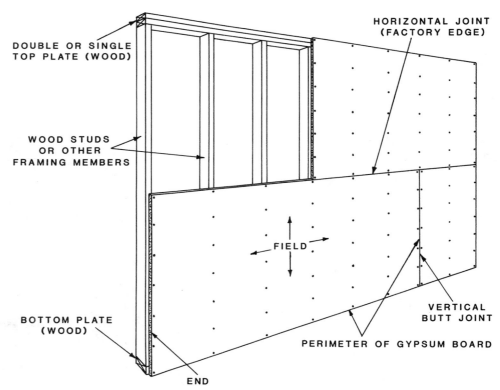

Figure 5. A typical gypsum board application. Courtesy of USG Corp.

DOUBLE OR SINGLE TOP PLATE (WOOD)

HORIZONTAL JOINT (FACTORY EDGE)

WOOD STUDS OR OTHER FRAMING MEMBERS

FIELD

BOTTOM PLATE (WOOD)

VERTICAL BUTT JOINT

PERIMETER OF GYPSUM BOARD

END

Gypsum Panel Products—Types of Edges

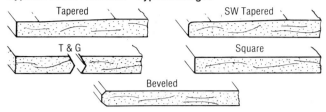

Figure 6. Types of gypsum wallboard edges. Courtesy of USG Corp.

edges, the tapered is by far the most preferred and most readily available.

Type X gypsum board is available in ½ in. and ⅝ in. thicknesses and has an improved fire resistance made available by special core additives and a more dense core. Type X gypsum board is used in most fire-rated assemblies and is available in the same width and lengths as is the standard board.

A board with an even greater fire rating, when used in approved assemblies is Sheetrock brand Firecode C gypsum panels available from the United States Gypsum Company, FRP from the Celotex Corporation and Firestop FS3 Celorock available from Georgia-Pacific Corp.

Predecorated gypsum board has a factory-applied decorative surface. The surfaces may be coated, printed, painted, or have a vinyl film. Panels laminated with a metal or cloth fabric surface are also available.

Several specialty panels are also available. They include

- Water-resistant gypsum board, which has a water-resistant gypsum core and water-resistant paper. This board serves as a base for application of wall tile or plastic finish panels in bath, shower, kitchen, and laundry areas. It is available with a regular or type X core and in ½-in. and ⅝-in. thicknesses.
- Gypsum coreboard, which is available as a 1-in.-thick (25.4-mm) solid coreboard or as a factory-laminated board composed of two ½-in. (13-mm) boards. It is used in shaft walls and laminated gypsum partitions, with additional layers of gypsum board applied to the coreboard to complete the wall assembly. It is available in 24-in. widths with a variety of edges.
- Gypsum sheathing, which is used as a protective, fire-resistive barrier under exterior wall-surfacing materials such as wood siding, masonry veneer, portland cement plaster, stucco, and shingles. It also provides protection against the passage of water and wind.
- Foil-backed gypsum panels, which are available with aluminum foil backing that provides an effective vapor barrier for exterior walls when applied with the foil surface against the framing. With a minimum of ¾-in (19 mm) enclosed air space adjacent to the foil, additional insulating efficiency may be achieved. This combination effectively reduces outward heat flow in the cold season and inward heat flow in the warm season. (Foil-backed gypsum board should not

be used as a backing material for tile, as a second face ply on a two-ply system, in conjunction with heating cables, or when laminating directly to masonry, ceiling, and roof assemblies because of the vapor-barrier action.)

- Gypsum base for veneer plaster, which is used as a base for thin coats of hard, high strength gypsum veneer plaster. This product is generally available in ½ in. (13 mm) and ⅝ in. (16 mm) thicknesses and is also available with an increased fire-rated type X core, and the high performance products previously listed.

INSTALLATION AND FINISHING: DRYWALL

Installation

Gypsum panels may be applied in one or two layers directly to wood framing members, to steel studs or channels, or to interior masonry walls with adhesive. Most construction is single-layer to surface interior walls and ceilings where economy, fast erection, and fire resistance are required. It is equally suitable for remodeling and for altering and resurfacing cracked and defaced areas.

Double-layer construction consists of a face layer of gypsum board applied over a base layer of gypsum board that is directly attached to framing members. This construction offers greater strength and higher resistance to fire and to sound transmission than single-layer applications. Double-layer construction when adhesively laminated is especially resistant to cracking and sag and minimizes fastener pops and joint deformation.

Gypsum boards are attached to framing by several methods, depending on the type of framing and the results desired:

- *Single nailing:* Conventional attachment for wood framing.
- *Double nailing:* Minimizes defects due to loose board.
- *Adhesive attachment:* A continuous bead of stud adhesive applied to wood framing plus supplemental nailing improves bond strength and greatly reduces the number of face nails needed.
- *Screw attachment:* Screws are excellent insurance against fastener pops caused by loosely attached board. Screws are recommended for wood-frame attachment and required for attachment to steel framing.

Specific attachment and fastener placement as recommended by the manufacturer should be followed to minimize finished job appearance problems. Single- and double-layer construction are shown in Figures 7 and 8. Many trim accessories are available for such functions as outside corner protection, expansion control, and window and door jamb protection.

Joint Systems

After installation of the board, it is necessary to reinforce the joints and to conceal the joints, fasteners, and inside

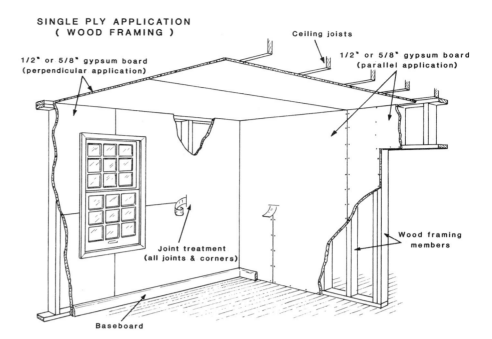

Figure 7. Single ply application. Courtesy of Gypsum Association.

corners. A reinforcing tape and joint compound are used for this purpose. This process produces the desired monolithic appearance. Joint tape is perforated paper, unperforated paper, or glass fiber scrim. It is made for use with ready mixed or job-mixed dry compounds. Precreased tape is available for corners and wall–ceiling intersections. Figure 9 shows a typical finished joint in steps.

Joint compounds are available in three general types:

1. *Taping:* Used to embed the tape as a first fill coat over metal trim and fastener or for laminating in double-layer construction.

2. *Topping:* A low-shrinkage, easily applied and sanded product recommended for second and third coats over taping and all-purpose compounds. Also used for simple texturing or skim coating. Not suitable for embedding tape or as first coat over metal corners, trim, and fasteners.

3. *All-purpose:* Used for embedding, finishing, simple texturing, and laminating. Combines single-package convenience with good taping and topping characteristics. Recommended for all general joint finishing and for repairing cracks in interior plaster and masonry not subject to moisture.

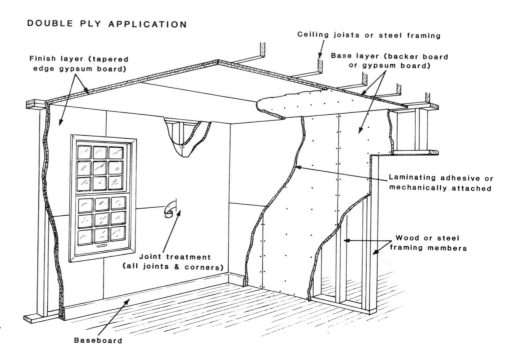

Figure 8. Double ply application. Courtesy of Gypsum Association.

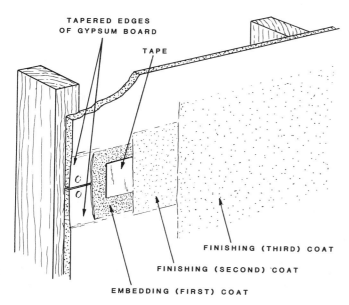

Figure 9. Finished joint showing steps. Courtesy of USG Corp.

The generally used joint compounds listed above are drying-type materials and must dry quite completely between coats. Also available are setting-powder compounds that permit same-day joint finishing and, usually, next-day decoration. These compounds are also ideal for heavy fills and are virtually unaffected by humidity. They provide low shrinkage and superior bond, which makes them excellent for laminating gypsum panels to gypsum panels, to sound-deadening boards, and to above-grade concrete surfaces. In addition, the compounds can be used for skim coating and for surface textures; also for filling, smoothing, and finishing interior concrete ceilings and concrete above grade; and for taping and finishing water-resistant panels under tile in bathroom wall areas. Other uses include finishing joints in exterior gypsum ceiling boards and presetting joints of veneer finish systems. They are available in a variety of setting times.

Finishing

Textures. Textures are applied to wallboard to give a desired finished look and to conceal minor surface defects. They must always be painted when used on walls, but are often left unpainted when used on ceilings. Textures vary from a simple sparse or fine spray to heavily sprayed materials that provide an acoustical advantage. They may be applied with a trowel or a roller or they may be sprayed. The desired finished look may be obtained with a trowel, roller, brush, sponge, or any other tool that will modify the applied material. A number of different finishes are available with the spray gun as the amount of spray, the viscosity of the mix, the type of nozzle, and the distance from the wall is modified.

Much of the texture work, including most trowel and roll-on textures, is done with the standard joint compound materials mixed to the special viscosity required for the job. In addition, many manufacturers provide specially formulated products designed to be simple textures, simulated acoustical patterns, and functionally acoustical. The spray texture materials are supplied in several different texture grains, the only difference being the size of the light-weight aggregate used in the formulation. Many of these materials may also be used over concrete, plaster, or wood. As specified by manufacturers, many of these materials may be blended with each other and with paints. A variety of products with many different characteristics are available from many different suppliers, hence a great deal of care must be used when choosing and applying this type of surface finish.

Paint. The most common finish of gypsum wallboard is paint. Most types of paint can be used if the surface has been properly prepared. Before finishing, any imperfections must be sanded and or repaired, joint compounds must be dry, and excessive dust must be removed from the surface. Before the final finish is applied, the surface should be sealed with a high-grade primer/sealer that is allowed to dry completely. The use of this sealer will minimize color and texture variations.

Paints may be applied with spray, brush, or roller. The final coat may be textured with a texture-type paint or by the addition of texturing material to the paint as directed by the many manufacturers of these products. If glossy paints are to be used or if severe lighting conditions are to be encountered, the following instructions should be followed to minimize suction, porosity, and other variations between the joint compound and the face paper surface.

After all irregularities have been eliminated and the joint treatment surfaces sanded or sponged where required, a thin skim coat of joint compound should be applied to the entire surface of the board. Caution should be taken to eliminate laps or tool marks in the skim-coating operation. The wall or ceiling surface should be lightly sanded or sponged where required to assure a smooth and even surface. A good quality alkyd or oil-based primer/sealer should be applied before decoration.

Specialty Finishes. In addition to paint and texture, gypsum board may be decorated with the application of paper, vinyl, or fabric wall coverings. The choice of materials and patterns is endless. Once again, the instructions of the supplier of the covering product are extremely important. Surface preparation and the adhesive are important for ease of application, quality of the job, and ease of removal for redecorating.

Construction Standards

Construction standards dealing with framing, fastener placement, and choice of product size and thickness can be found in "Sweet's General Building File" in *Architectural Graphic Standards,* or in manufacturer's literature such as the *Gypsum Construction Handbook* referenced in the bibliography.

Numerous assemblies that incorporate gypsum board and or plaster with wood or steel frame are described in various publications. After structural requirements have been met, the acoustical performance and the fire ratings are the factors of interest. Resistance to fire and to heat transmission are the most valuable characteristics of gypsum board. Many detailed construction assemblies have been defined and tested to take advantage of these properties. Gypsum board wall and ceiling systems effectively help control sound transmission when properly installed. As a result, many systems have also been designed and tested to take advantage of this characteristic. More than 100 tested assemblies with sound and fire ratings can be found in the Gypsum Association's *Fire Resistance Design Manual* and in the *Construction Selector* listed in the bibliography. These manuals describe numerous systems in detail.

System Performance

System performance relates to many small details of construction. The sources cited in this article provide all necessary information on common systems and on many special systems such as area separation walls, cavity shaft wall systems, and curtain-wall systems. When needs for these types of systems develop, one should take advantage of the work done by the manufacturers and the Gypsum Association.

STUCCO

Historically, stucco has been defined as a cementitious material used to provide a decorative finish for either exterior or interior surfaces. Today, the term stucco applies almost exclusively to portland cement based plastering materials used in exterior applications.

By definition, portland cements are hydraulic cements; they set and harden by reacting chemically with water. The process, called hydration, combines cement and water to form a stonelike mass.

The invention of portland cement (1824) is generally credited to Joseph Aspdin, an English mason. The first portland cement manufactured in the United States was produced in Coplay, Pennsylvania, in 1872.

Portland cement plaster is a combination of portland cement, lime, and aggregate mixed with water to form a plastic mass that will adhere to a surface and harden, preserving any form and texture imposed on it while in the plastic state.

Advantages attributed to portland cement based stucco include strength, fire resistance, rot and fungus resistance, color retentivity, and exceptional durability under weather cycles of wet and dry and hot and cold.

Today's "stucco" systems can be conveniently grouped into four categories:

Conventional Stucco

Portland cement stucco is applied in three coats over metal reinforcement, with or without a solid backing, to a total thickness of 1 in. The three coats in order of application are the scratch coat (nominal 3/8-in. thick), brown coat (nominal 3/8-in. thick), and the finish coat (nominal 1/8-in.

thick). Variations of this application address both wood frame (normally residential construction) and metal frame (commercial construction) assemblies and needs. See Figure 10.

In open-frame wood construction, an 18-gauge wire is stretched horizontally across the face of the studs about 6 in. apart. The wire is stretched by nailing or stapling it to every fourth stud and tightened by raising and lowering it and securing it to a center stud. The wall surface is covered next by a waterproof building paper or felt that is nailed over the wire strands. The line wire provides a back support to minimize bulging of the paper or felt between the studs when portland cement stucco is applied. Hexagonal wire mesh (stucco netting) is then applied over the waterproof paper backing or felt, using furring nails that hold the mesh out 1/4–3/8 in. from the framing members. Several types of metal reinforcement—diamond mesh, expanded rib, wire mesh—may be used. Some metal reinforcement is available that already has paper or polyethylene backing; this type can be used directly over the studs.

Gypsum sheathing and number 15 asphalt felt, or similar waterproof barrier, provide the backing for the sheathed frame construction assembly. Metal reinforcement is applied horizontally and attached through sheathing to the studs at intervals of not more than 8 in. with an approved nail or screw that holds the reinforcement at least 1/4 in. away from the sheating.

Two-coat work is common over solid masonry and cement surfaces that provide reasonably level surfaces and proper bonding properties to ensure long-term performance. Typically, an exterior stucco finish coat consists of white portland cement, lime, and silica sand, or a proprietary mix.

The final appearance can be varied by changing the size and shape of the aggregate in the finish coat, by adding color, by changing the consistency of the finish coat, and by the plasterer's skill in achieving various textures in the finish coat. Benefits of a portland cement stucco finish include ability to achieve varied finishes, low material costs, and minimum need for maintenance.

Hard-Coat Insulated Stucco

These systems can be applied over a variety of substrates, including gypsum sheathing and number 15 building felt and expanded polystyrene insulation board, or the basecoat may be applied directly over concrete block. The basecoat is typically reinforced with a woven wire mesh, referred to as "stucco mesh." Basecoat materials are portland cement based and typically contain low levels of dry polymer additives and chopped fiberglass strands for additional reinforcement. The basecoat is usually applied approximately 3/8 in. thick.

Various types of finishes may be used with these types of systems. Some manufacturers provide an integrally colored basecoat, requiring no additional finishing. The basecoat may also be painted or more commonly finished with a portland cement based finish coat similar to the conventional systems.

EXTERIOR LATH AND PLASTER

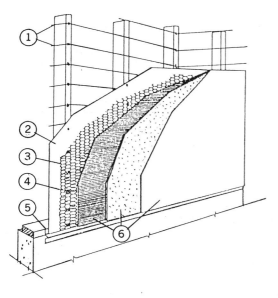

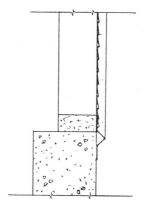

OPEN WOOD FRAME CONSTRUCTION

(1) Wire Backing[1]
(2) Building Paper[1]
(3) Wire Fabric Lath[1]
(4) Furring Nails[2]
(5) Drip Screed[3]
(6) Three Coats of Plaster (Scratch, Brown, Finish)

[1]Paper–backed wire fabric lath may be used omitting separate wire and paper.
[2]Self–furring lath may be used.
[3]Should be used with on–grade slab construction.
[4]Use control joints wherever possible.

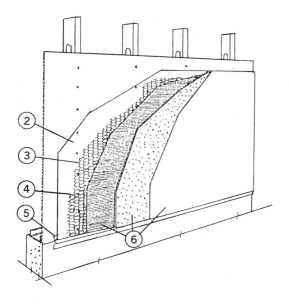

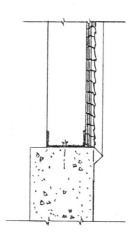

SHEATHED FRAME CONSTRUCTION (WOOD OR METAL)

Figure 10. Exterior lath and plaster. Courtesy of USG Corp.

Soft-Coat Insulated Stucco

These systems are applied over expanded polystyrene insulation board or mineral fiber or glass fiber. They are reinforced with glass/fiber mesh, over which a polymer modified portland cement basecoat is applied to a ⅛-in.

thickness. The basecoats typically contain a much higher level of polymer additives and are typically marketed as a liquid, to which portland cement is added on the job site.

Finishes for these systems are elastomeric-like and acrylic based and have a high resistance to cracking. System advantages include energy efficiency, color uniform-

Figure 11. Application of ceramic tile. Courtesy of USG Corp.

ity (the synthetic finishes provide color variety and uniformity superior to the other types of finishes), lightweight, and architectural freedom owing to the variety of shapes and reliefs that can be readily obtained using the lightweight insulation board base. These finish materials cannot provide for heavy relief or coarse heavy-textured finishes common with conventional three-coat-type systems.

CEMENT BOARD SYSTEMS

A relatively new development in both interior and exterior construction is the use of cement board systems. In these systems a board product manufactured with an aggregated portland cement core and reinforced on both face and back surfaces with polymer-coated, woven glass-fiber mesh serves as a backing much like the conventional portland cement stucco basecoat and metal reinforcement. In interior applications, the board is applied directly to framing; in exterior use a water barrier such as number 15 asphalt felt or Tyvek house wrap is installed before base application. Over metal framing, ½ in. rigid insulation board is required with thin stucco finishes. Boards are reinforced with a glass-fiber tape, and the entire surface, including joints, is treated with a proprietary polymer-modified portland cement board basecoat application before finishing. The basecoat precedes any finish selection and is applied approximately ¹⁄₁₆ in. in thickness.

On interior surfaces the cement board base serves as a highly water resistant, strong, lightweight, high performance backing for ceramic tile. Finishes for exterior ap-

plication include ceramic tile, thin brick, epoxy matrix stone aggregate surfacing, and manufacturer-supplied colored, elastomeric like acrylic based highly crack-resistant stucco-appearing finish coatings.

These systems provide a wide choice of architectural style, color, and texture while minimizing variance of cost and performance. Conventional application techniques make these systems ideal for all types of structures. In addition, the systems provide fire-resistance, weight reduction, and reduced heat transmission with insulation placed in the stud cavity. Figure 11 shows application of tile to a basecoated cement board surface.

BIBLIOGRAPHY

Concrete Information, Portland Cement Assoc, Skokie, Ill., 1980.

Construction Selector, SA-100/Rev. 1-88, USG Corporation, Chicago, Ill., 1988.

Design Data—Gypsum Products—Specifications. Recommendation, Standards and Uses of Gypsum Products, Gypsum Association, Evanston, Ill., 1986.

Fire Resistance Design Manual, Gypsum Association, Evanston, Ill., 1988.

Gypsum Board for Walls and Ceilings, Gypsum Association, Evanston, Ill., 1986.

Gypsum Construction Handbook, 3rd ed., United States Gypsum Company, Chicago, Ill., 1987.

Plastering—A Craftsman's Encyclopaedia, Butler & Tanner, Ltd., London, UK, 1976.

Portland Cement Plaster (Stucco) Manual, Portland Cement Assoc., Skokie, Ill., 1980.

F. Van Don Branden and T. L. Hastell, *Plastering Skill and Practice,* American Technical Society, Chicago, Ill., 1971.

Veneer Plaster Manual, International Association of Wall and Ceiling Construction/Gypsum Drywall Construction International, Washington, D.C.

See also INTERIOR PARTITIONS AND PARTITION COVERINGS; STUCCO, SYNTHETIC

RICHARD F. STONE
EDWIN J. JAKACKI
USG Corp.
Libertyville, Illinois

WARRANTIES, GUARANTEES.   See BONDS AND SURETIES

WASTE HANDLING.   See MAINTENANCE, BUILDING

WASTEWATER MANAGEMENT

WHAT IS WASTEWATER?

Wastewater is the flow of used water from a residence or community. The name is apt, for wastewater is actually

99.94% water by weight. The rest, 0.06%, is material dissolved or suspended in the water. The suspended matter is often referred to as suspended solids to differentiate it from pollutants in solution.

Wastewater, also known as sewage, includes everything that makes its way from the home to sewers, coming from toilets, drains, garbage grinders, bathtubs, sinks, and washing machines. The wastewaters from a single home that do not contain human wastes are referred to as grey water. Toilet wastes are referred to as black water.

Community wastewater also comes from three other sources: commercial, industrial, and storm and groundwater. Commercial wastewaters from office buildings and small businesses include both human wastes and water from cleaning or other minor processes. Industrial wastewaters may include large volumes of water used in processing industrial products. Storm water may enter through illicit connections of roof drains or by design in combined sanitary–storm sewer systems. Groundwater infiltrates into sewers through joints and cracks in pipes.

The wastewater components of major concern are those that will deplete the oxygen resources of the stream or lake to which they are discharged, those that may stimulate undesirable growths of plants or organisms (such as algae) in the receiving water, or those that will have undesirable aesthetic effects or adverse health effects on downstream water uses. The pollutants of concern are made up of both organic and inorganic materials.

Of the organics found in wastewater, a substantial portion consists of biodegradable materials—those that serve as food sources for bacteria and other microorganisms. These biodegradable substances include sugars, alcohols, and many other compounds that may find their way into sewers. The biological breakdown of these materials consumes oxygen. The amount of oxygen required to stabilize the biodegradable organics is measured by the biochemical oxygen demand (BOD) test. The higher the BOD, the more oxygen will be demanded from the water to break down the organics. This parameter is the most widely used measure of organic pollution applied to wastewaters. It is used in sizing treatment facilities and in predicting the effects of treated wastewater discharges on receiving waters. If the oxygen demand of the treated wastewater exceeds the oxygen resources of the receiving water, then the oxygen will be completely depleted and the stream or lake will become septic near the wastewater discharge point.

Because fish and many beneficial aquatic plants require oxygen to survive, the reduction of BOD becomes a major goal of all wastewater treatment plants. Some of the organics in wastewater are not biologically degradable and, thus, are not part of the BOD. Some of these nondegradable organics, such as pesticides, can have adverse long-term effects and can contribute to taste, odor, and color problems in downstream water supplies. The chemical oxygen demand (COD) test is used to measure the quantities of these materials present. The COD value also includes biologically degradable materials; therefore, the COD is higher than the BOD because more compounds can be oxidized chemically than biologically. Some of the COD-causing materials are organics that are very resistant to breakdown in the environment; they may be of concern where water is used for a municipal water supply downstream.

Wastewater contains bacteria and viruses that can transmit diseases. This consideration can be especially critical if the receiving water is used for recreation near the point of wastewater discharge. Thus, another important wastewater treatment concern is often the removal of as many pathogenic bacteria and viruses as possible before discharge of the wastewater. Because bacteria and viruses are of minute size, they can be enmeshed in suspended solids in the wastewater. The suspended solids can act as a shield to protect bacteria and viruses from contact with added disinfecting agents, hampering the disinfection process. Thus, removal of suspended solids is important to ensure good disinfection as well as to provide removal of some of the insoluble organic and inorganic pollutants.

Wastewater also contains two elements—phosphorus and nitrogen—that can stimulate undesirable growths of algae in lakes and streams. These algal growths can cause thick, green, scumlike mats that interfere with boating and recreation. They also may cause unpleasant tastes and odors in water supplies and operating problems in downstream water treatment plants and may exert a significant oxygen demand after the algae die. Where the uses of a receiving water may be adversely affected by algae, removal of phosphorus and nitrogen is of concern.

As noted earlier, municipal wastewater is usually 99.94% water; thus the concentrations of the pollutants discussed are very dilute. These concentrations are usually expressed as milligrams of pollutant per liter of water (mg/L). One mg/L of a pollutant is equivalent to 1 part of the pollutant (by weight) in 1 million parts of water—or, 1 part per million (ppm). One mg/L or 1 ppm, to put the terms in perspective, is equivalent to 1 min of time in 1.9 years or 1 in. in 16 mi. These statistics emphasize that wastewater treatment processes designed to remove a few mg/L of a pollutant are similar to sifting a haystack to remove the needle. However, the balance in nature for survival or death of fish depends on the presence or absence of only 2–3 mg/L of oxygen in the stream or lake, and undesirable growths of algae can be stimulated by a few tenths of a milligram of phosphorus and nitrogen per liter.

Typical concentrations of pollutants in raw, untreated, community wastewaters are as follows: BOD = 150–250 mg/L, COD = 300–400 mg/L, suspended solids = 150–250 mg/L, phosphorus = 5–10 mg/L, nitrogen = 15–25 mg/L, and total dissolved solids (TDS) = 400–500 mg/L.

TYPES OF WASTEWATER SYSTEMS

The traditional method of providing public wastewater facilities is to construct a system of gravity-collection sewers that conveys all the wastewaters from a town to a community treatment plant. This tried and proven central system is usually more cost-effective, because it is less costly to serve many people with one system than to serve each person individually. For scattered individual homes, however, such a conventional collection and treatment facility is often impractical because it becomes very costly to build the sewers needed to connect widely dispersed homes.

INDIVIDUAL HOME WASTEWATER MANAGEMENT

Individual home systems typically provide treatment of wastewater and then dispose of the treated wastewater on the site of the home. Approximately 25% of all housing units in the United States, dispose of their wastewater using on-site wastewater treatment and disposal systems (1). Although a wide variety of systems have been used, the most common is the septic tank/soil-absorption system. Unfortunately, on-site systems have sometimes been installed where soils are not suitable for conventional soil-absorption systems. Cases of contaminated wells and nutrient enrichment of lakes from near-shore development may occur when a soil-absorption system is installed in unsuitable soils.

Wastewater Characteristics and Modification

Wastewater characteristics affect the design of on-site treatment and disposal/reuse systems. The volume of wastewater to be treated is a critical parameter. Average wastewater flows from individual homes are about 45 gal per capita per day (170 L pcd). Often, in sizing systems a factor of safety is applied and flows of about 80 gal pcd (287 L pcd) are used. Several strategies have been used to modify wastewater characteristics: water conservation and resulting wastewater flow reduction, pollutant mass reduction, and on-site containment for off-site disposal. On-site containment can level out variations in flow rates that occur during the day. Each strategy reduces the volume or decreases the mass of key pollutants. The methods used include the following (1).

Elimination of Nonfunctional Water Use

- Improved water-use habits
- Improved plumbing and appliance maintenance
- Nonexcessive water-supply pressure

Water-saving Devices, Fixtures, and Appliances

- Toilet
  - Water-carriage toilets
    - Toilet tank inserts
    - Dual-flush toilets
    - Water-saving toilets
  - Nonwater-carriage toilets
    - Pit privies
    - Composting toilets
    - Incinerator toilets
    - Oil-carriage toilets
- Bathing devices, fixtures, and appliances
  - Shower flow controls
  - Reduced-flow showerheads
  - On/off showerhead valves
  - Air-assisted low-flow shower system
- Clothes-washing devices, fixtures and appliances
  - Front-loading washer
  - Adjustable cycle settings
  - Wash-water recycle features
- Miscellaneous
  - Faucet inserts
  - Faucet aerators
  - Reduced-flow faucet fixtures
  - Mixing valves
  - Hot-water pipe insulation
  - Pressure-reducing valves

Wastewater Reuse Systems

- Bath/laundry wastewater recycle for toilet flushing
- Treated toilet wastewater recycle for toilet flushing
- Combined wastewater recycle for toilet flushing
- Combined wastewater recycle for several uses.

Recently, the concept of segregating toilet wastes (black water) from the other household wastewaters (grey waters) for separate treatment and disposal has drawn attention. Segregating black water from other household wastewater by using a *nonwater-carrying toilet* could conserve water resources and reduce the volume and pollutant load discharged to on-site disposal systems.

After the toilet wastes are segregated and disposed of, the grey water must be handled. Grey water is relatively uncontaminated, compared with black water. Grey water, however, contains substantial quantities of physical and chemical pollutants as well as pathogenic organisms (2). Use of a septic tank—soil absorption system for grey water is an alternative to reuse. The reduced waste strength of the grey water may increase the life of a soil absorption field, but it is not known by what factor. Until further data are available, the Environmental Protection Agency (EPA) has recommended that grey water systems be designed as for typical residential wastewater (1).

Treatment Systems

The two major components of an on-site system are the treatment unit and the disposal system. Treatment options include: septic tanks and aerobic treatment units.

Septic Tanks. The septic tank is the most widely used on-site wastewater treatment method in the United States. Currently, about 25% of the new homes being constructed in this country use septic tanks for treatment before disposal of home wastewater.

Septic tanks are buried, watertight tanks that receive wastewater from a home, separate solids from the liquid, provide limited anaerobic digestion of organic matter, store solids, and discharge the treated wastewater to disposal (Fig. 1). Settleable solids and partially decomposed sludge settle to the bottom of the tank and accumulate. A scum of lightweight material (including fats and greases) rises to the top. The treated wastewater flows through an

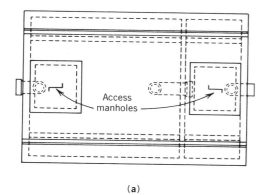

(a)

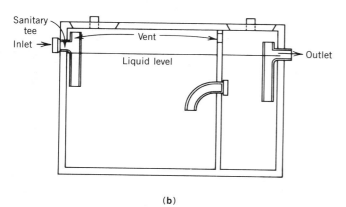

(b)

Figure 1. A typical two-compartment septic tank (**a**) plan; (**b**) longitudinal section.

outlet structure below the floating scum layer where baffles protect against scum overflow. Local regulatory agencies may require that the septic tank be located a specified distance from the home, water well, and water lines to reduce any risk of disease-causing agents reaching the water supply. These minimum separation distances are largely arbitrary and depend on the soil conditions. Many state and local building codes suggest separation distances that should be adhered to in the absence of any better information.

Septic tanks are usually purchased ready for installation and are normally designed in accordance with local codes. To ensure that the septic tank removes almost all settleable solids, most designs provide

1. A 24-h fluid retention time at maximum sludge depth and scum accumulation.
2. Inlet and outlet devices to prevent discharge of sludge or scum in the effluent.
3. Sufficient sludge storage space to prevent the discharge of sludge or scum in the effluent.
4. Vents to release accumulated gases.

A common septic tank design provides 300–450 gal (1140 to 1700 L) of tank volume per bedroom (1). Also, 250 gal (946 L) is often added when garbage grinders are used with septic tanks. Recent trends in septic tank design fa-

vor multiple, rather than single, compartmented tanks. When a tank is properly divided into compartments, BOD and SS (suspended solids) removal are improved. Figure 1 shows a typical two-compartment tank.

To provide access to inspect the inside of the septic tank, manholes should be provided. Manholes are usually placed over both the inlet and the outlet to permit cleaning behind the baffles. The manhole cover should extend above the actual septic tank to a height not more than 6 in. (15 cm) below the finished grade. The actual cover can extend to the ground surface if a proper seal is provided to prevent the escape of odors and accidental entry into the tank.

The most commonly used construction material for septic tanks is concrete. Virtually all individual-home septic tanks are precast. The walls have a thickness of 3–4 in. (8–10 cm), and tanks are typically sealed for watertightness after installation with two coats of bituminous coating. Care must be taken to seal around the inlet discharge pipes with a bonding compound that will adhere both to concrete and to the inlet and outlet pipe. Steel tanks have historically had short lives. Plastic and fiberglass tanks are very light, easily transported, and resistant to corrosion and decay. Although these tanks have not had a good history, some manufacturers are now producing an excellent tank with increased strength to minimize the chance of damage during installation.

The tank must be placed on a level grade and at a depth that provides adequate gravity flow from the home and matches the invert elevation of the house sewer. The tank should be placed on undisturbed soil so that settling does not occur. If the excavation is dug too deep, it should be backfilled to the proper elevation with sand to provide an adequate bedding for the tank. If the tank is not level, the inlet and outlet structures will not function properly.

A major advantage of the septic tank is that it needs very little routine maintenance because it has no moving parts. A well-designed and maintained concrete, fiberglass, or plastic tank should last for 50 years. Because of corrosion problems, steel tanks can be expected to last no more than 10 years. One cause of septic tank problems involves a failure to pump out the sludge solids when required. As the sludge depth increases, the effective liquid volume and detention time decrease. As this occurs, sludge scouring increases, treatment efficiency falls off, and more solids escape through the outlet. Periodic pumping of the tank is essential to long-term performance.

Tanks should be inspected at intervals of no more than every 2 years to determine the rates of scum and sludge accumulation. A long stick wrapped with rough, white toweling lowered to the bottom of the tank will show the depth of sludge and the liquid depth of the tank. The stick should be lowered behind the outlet device to avoid scum particles. After several minutes, the sludge layer can be distinguished by sludge particles clinging to the toweling. One should not climb into the septic tank because toxic gases can be present. If inspection programs are not carried out, a pump-out frequency of once every 3–5 years is reasonable. Special chemicals are not needed to start activity in a septic tank, improve operation, or to clean the tank.

Materials not readily decomposed (eg, sanitary napkins, coffee grounds, cooking fats, bones, wet-strength towels, disposable diapers, facial tissues, cigarette butts) should never be flushed into a septic tank. They will not degrade in the tank and can clog inlets, outlets, and the disposal system.

Aerobic Treatment Units. Aerobic treatment processes have received the greatest attention as an alternative to the septic tank based on more than 75 years' experience with this biological process in larger-scale applications (activated sludge process). In 1979, the National Sanitation Foundation (NSF) issued its Standard No. 40 on individual aerobic treatment units. It outlines criteria for evaluating such units and presents a procedure for testing and certification. Several states require NSF certification for aerobic units.

Aerobic biological treatment processes can remove substantial amounts of BOD and suspended solids that are not removed in septic tanks, can nitrify ammonia in the waste (under appropriate conditions), and can reduce pathogenic organisms. Despite these advantages, aerobic units are susceptible to upsets and have mechanical equipment that must be maintained.

The most common aerobic system promoted for individual home usage is the extended aeration process. Extended aeration is a modification of the activated sludge process. A high concentration of microorganisms is maintained in an aeration tank, followed by separation and recycling of all or a portion of the organisms back to the aeration tank. A variety of proprietary extended aeration package plants are available for on-site application. Figure 2 depicts two typical package-extended aeration systems. The process may be operated in a batch or continuous flow mode; oxygen is supplied by either diffused or mechanical aeration.

Extended aeration processes are more complex than septic tanks and require regular operation and maintenance. The plants may be buried or housed on site, but must be readily accessible. The aeration system requires power and generates some noise. Local codes may require certain setback distances. The process is temperature-dependent and should be insulated and covered in colder climates.

Aerobic unit performance is variable. Shock loads, sludge bulking, homeowner abuse or neglect, and mechanical malfunctions are among the most common reasons for poor performance. The uncontrolled loss of solids from the system is the major cause of effluent deterioration.

Most extended aeration package plants designed for individual home application range in capacity from 600 to 1500 gal (1270 to 5680 L), which includes the aeration compartment, settling chamber, and, in some units, a pretreatment compartment.

Some aerobic units provide a pretreatment step to remove gross solids (grease, trash, garbage grindings, etc). Pretreatment devices include trash traps, septic tanks, grinders, comminutors, and aerated surge chambers. The use of a trash trap or septic tank preceding the extended aeration process reduces problems with floating debris in

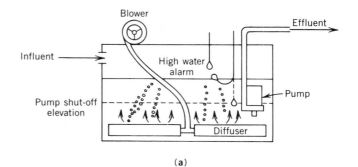

(a)

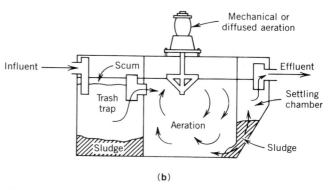

(b)

Figure 2. Examples of extended aeration package plant configurations (**a**) batch-extended aeration; (**b**) flow-through extended aeration.

the settling tank, clogging of flow lines, and plugging of pumps. Most aerobic units are supplied with some type of alarm and control system to detect mechanical breakdowns and to control the operation of electrical components. Electrical components are subject to corrosion and should be waterproofed and regularly serviced.

Typical on-site extended aeration package plants are constructed of reinforced plastics and fiberglass, coated steel, or reinforced concrete. The unit may be buried if there is easy access to all mechanical parts and electrical control systems, as well as appurtenances requiring maintenance such as weirs and air lift pump lines. Units may also be installed above ground, but should be properly housed to protect against severe climatic conditions.

Because of their maintenance requirements and variable performance, aerobic systems usually are not favored in areas where the soils are adequate for subsurface disposal of septic tank effluent. They have received attention when soils are inadequate as a treatment and disposal medium and when on-site wastewater systems that can discharge treated wastewater to surface waters are necessary. Septic tanks cannot produce a treated effluent quality adequate to discharge to a surface water.

Systems designed to discharge treated wastewaters to surface waters must produce a high quality effluent. The EPA has set concentration limits of 30 mg/L BOD_5 and 30 mg/L suspended solids for treatment plants that discharge to water courses. Lower concentrations may be required for scattered individual systems that discharge to small, intermittent streams. Bacteria counts will be limited, and limitations on nitrogen and phosphorus are likely for discharges to lakes or impoundments. Field experience with on-site aerobic treatment processes indicates that additional polishing of effluents with some type of filtration will be necessary before surface discharge to meet EPA requirements. If considering an aerobic system for surface discharge, local and state agencies (health department and pollution control agency) should be contacted to determine the acceptability of such systems and the effluent polishing (filtration, disinfection) requirements.

Disposal Methods

The most commonly used methods for disposal of wastewater from single dwellings and small clusters of dwellings may be divided into three groups: subsurface soil absorption; evaporation; and discharge to surface waters. Where site conditions are suitable, subsurface soil absorption is usually the best method of wastewater disposal because of its simplicity, stability, and low cost. Under the proper conditions, the soil is an excellent treatment medium and requires little wastewater pretreatment. Partially treated wastewater is discharged below ground surface where it is absorbed and treated by the soil.

Different types of subsurface soil absorption include trenches and beds, seepage pits, mounds, fills, and artificially drained systems. The type of subsurface soil absorption system selected depends on the site characteristics encountered. Critical site factors include soil profile characteristics and permeability, soil depth over water tables or bedrock, slope, and the size of the acceptable area. Where the soil is at least moderately permeable and remains unsaturated several feet below the system throughout the year, trenches or beds may be used. Trench and bed systems are the most commonly used method for on-site wastewater treatment and disposal (Figs. 3 and 4). Trenches are shallow, level excavations, usually 1–5 ft

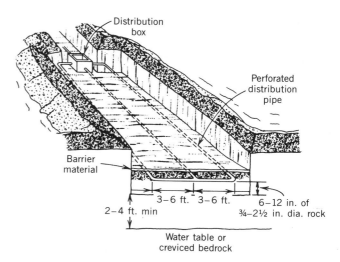

Figure 4. A typical bed system.

(0.3–1.5 m) deep and 1–3 ft (0.3–0.9 m) wide. The bottom is filled with 6 in. (15 cm) or more of washed crushed rock or gravel over which is laid a single line of perforated distribution piping. Additional rock is placed over the pipe, and the rock is covered with a semipermeable barrier to keep the backfill out of the rock. Both the bottoms and sidewalls of the trenches are infiltrative surfaces. Beds differ from trenches in that they are wider than 3 ft (0.9 m) and may contain more than one line of distribution piping. The bottoms of beds are the principal infiltrative surfaces.

Site criteria for trench and bed systems, summarized in Table 1, are based on factors necessary to maintain reasonable infiltration rates and adequate treatment performance over many years of continuous service. Reference 1 should be consulted for proper site evaluation procedures. Recommended rates of application in relation to soil textures and percolation rates are presented in Table 2. This table is only a guide. Soil texture and measured percolation rates will not always be correlated as indicated, owing to differences in structure, clay mineral content, bulk densities, and other factors in various areas of the country (1).

Conventional trench or bed designs should not be used for rapidly permeable soils with percolation rates faster than 1 min/in. (0.4 min/cm). Rapidly permeable soils may not provide the necessary treatment to protect groundwater quality. This problem may be overcome by replacing the native soil with a suitably thick (greater than 2 ft) layer of loamy sand or sand-textured soil.

Conventional trench or bed designs should also be avoided in soils with percolation rates slower than 60 min/in. (24 min/cm). These soils can be easily smeared and compacted during construction, reducing the soil's infiltration rate to as little as half the expected rate. Trench systems may be used in soils with percolation rates as slow as 120 min/in. (47 min/cm), but only if great care is exercised during construction.

Seepage pits are deep excavations designed primarily for lateral absorption of the wastewater through the side-

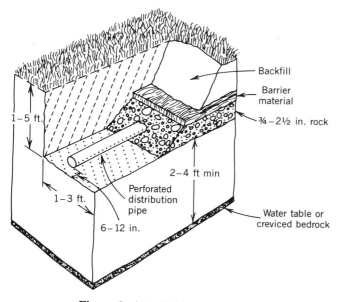

Figure 3. A typical trench system.

Table 1. Site Criteria for Trench and Bed Systems[a]

Item	Criteria
Landscape position[b]	Level, well-drained areas, crests of slopes, convex slopes most desirable. Avoid depressions, bases of slopes, and concave slopes unless suitable surface drainage is provided.
Slope[b]	0–25%. Slopes in excess of 25% can be used, but the use of construction machinery may be limited. Bed systems are limited to 0–5%.
Typical horizontal separation distances[c]	
Water supply wells	50–100 ft (15–30 m)
Surface waters, springs	50–100 ft (15–30 m)
Escarpments, manmade cuts	10–20 ft (3–6 m)
Boundary of property	5–10 ft (1.5–3 m)
Building foundations	10–20 ft (3–6 m)
Soil	
Texture	Soils with sandy or loamy textures are best suited. Gravelly and cobbley soils with open pores and slowly permeable clay soils are less desirable.
Structure	Strong granular, blocky, or prismatic structures are desirable. Platy or unstructured massive soils should be avoided.
Color	Bright, uniform colors indicate well-drained, well-aerated soils. Dull, gray or mottled soils indicate continuous or seasonable saturation and are unsuitable.
Layering	Soils exhibiting layers with distinct textural or structural changes should be carefully evaluated to ensure water movement will not be severely restricted.
Unsaturated depth	2–4 ft (0.6–1.2 m) of unsaturated soil should exist between the bottom of the system and the seasonally high water table or bedrock.
Percolation rate	1–60 min/in. (24 min/cm) (average of at least 3 percolation tests).[d] Systems can be constructed in soils with slower percolation rates, but soil damage during construction must be avoided.

[a] Ref. 1.

[b] Landscape position and slope are more restrictive for beds because of the depths of cut on the up-slope side.

[c] Intended only as a guide. Safe distance varies from site to site, based on topography, soil permeability, groundwater gradients, geology, etc.

[d] Soils with percolation rates < 1 min/in. (0.4 min/cm) can be used for trenches and beds if the soil is replaced with a suitably thick (> 2 ft or > 0.6 m) layer of loamy sand or sand.

walls of the excavation; they are used only where the groundwater level is well below the bottom of the pit, and where beds and trenches are not feasible.

One alternative for overcoming slowly permeable soils is to raise the absorption field above the natural soil by building the seepage system in a mound of medium sand (Fig. 5). This raises the seepage system above slowly permeable subsoil and places it in a dry, permeable sand. This technique has several advantages. First, the percolating liquid enters the more permeable natural topsoil over a large area and can spread laterally until it is absorbed by the less permeable subsoil. Second, the clogging zone that eventually develops at the bottom of the gravel

trench within the mound will not clog the sandy fill to the degree it would in the natural soil. Finally, smearing and compacting of the wet subsoil is avoided because excavation in the natural soil is not necessary.

The mound system consists of a suitable fill material, an absorption area, a distribution network, a cap, and topsoil. The effluent is pumped or siphoned into the absorption area through a distribution network located in the upper part of the coarse aggregate. It passes through the aggregate and infiltrates the fill material. Treatment of the wastewater occurs as it passes through the fill material and the unsaturated zone of the natural soil. The cap, usually a finer textured material than the fill, provides

Table 2. Recommended Rates of Wastewater Application for Trench and Bed Bottom Areas[a,b]

Soil Texture	Percolation Rate		Application Rate[c]	
	min/in.	min/cm	gpd/ft^2	Lpd/m^2
Gravel, coarse sand	< 1	< 0.4	Not suitable[d]	
Coarse to medium sand	1–5	0.4–2.0	1.2	49
Fine sand, loamy sand	6–15	2.4–6	0.8	32
Sandy loam, loam	16–30	6.4–12	0.6	24
Loam, porous silt loam	31–60	12–24	0.45	18
Silty clay loam, clay loam[e]	61–120	24–48	0.2[f]	8

[a] Ref. 1.

[b] May be suitable estimates for sidewall infiltration rates.

[c] Rates based on septic tank effluent from a domestic waste source. A factor of safety may be desirable for wastes of significantly different character.

[d] Soils with percolation rates < 1 min/in. can be used if the soil is replaced with a suitably thick (> 2 ft or 0.6 m) layer of loamy sand or sand.

[e] Soils without expandable clays.

[f] These soils may be easily damaged during construction.

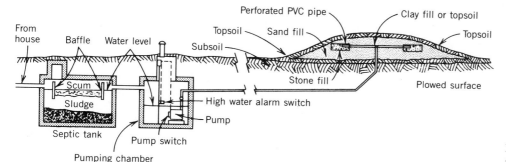

Figure 5. Cross section of mound system for problem soils.

frost protection, sheds precipitation, and retains moisture for a good vegetative cover. The topsoil provides a growth medium for the vegetation.

Another approach where subsurface disposal is not practical is the use of evapotranspiration (ET) beds. On-site ET disposal normally consists of a sand bed with an impermeable liner and wastewater distribution piping (Fig. 6). The surface of the sand bed may be planted with vegetation. Wastewater entering the bed is normally pretreated to remove settleable and floatable solids. An ET bed functions by raising the wastewater to the upper portion of the bed by capillary action in the sand and then evaporating it to the atmosphere. In addition, vegetation transports water from the root zone to the leaves, where it is transpired.

Based on experience to date with ET disposal for year-round single-family homes, approximately 4000–6000 ft^2 (370–560 m^2) of available land is typically required. The maximum slope at which an ET system is applicable has not been established, but use on slopes greater than 15% may be possible if terracing, serial distribution, and other appropriate design features are incorporated.

By far the most significant constraint on the use of ET systems is climatic conditions. The evaporation rate is controlled primarily by climatic factors such as precipitation, wind speed, humidity, solar radiation, and temperature. Recent studies indicate that essentially all the precipitation that falls on an ET bed infiltrates into the bed and becomes part of the hydraulic load that requires evaporation. Provisions for long-term storage of effluent and precipitation in ET systems during periods of negative net evaporation, and for subsequent evaporation during periods of positive net evaporation, are expensive. Thus, the year-round use of nondischarging ET systems appears to be feasible only in the arid and semiarid portions of the western and southwestern United States.

MUNICIPAL TREATMENT SYSTEMS

The alternatives for municipal wastewater treatment fall into three major categories (3):

- Primary treatment
- Secondary treatment
- Advanced wastewater treatment

The major goal of primary treatment is to remove from wastewater those pollutants that will either settle (such as the heavier suspended solids) or float (such as grease). Primary treatment will typically remove about 60% of the raw sewage suspended solids and 35% of the BOD. Soluble pollutants are not removed. At one time, this was the degree of treatment used by many cities. Now federal law requires that municipalities provide the higher degree of treatment provided by secondary treatment. Although primary treatment alone is no longer acceptable, it is still frequently used as the first treatment step in a secondary treatment system.

The major goal of secondary treatment is to remove the soluble BOD that escapes the primary process and to provide added removal of suspended solids. These removals are typically achieved by using biological processes, providing the same biological reactions that would occur in receiving water if it had adequate capacity to assimilate the wastewater discharges. The secondary treatment processes are designed to speed up this natural process so that the breakdown of the degradable organic pollutants can be achieved in relatively short time periods. Although secondary treatment may remove more than 85% of the BOD and suspended solids, it does not remove significant amounts of nitrogen, phosphorus, COD, or heavy metals, nor does it completely remove pathogenic bacteria and

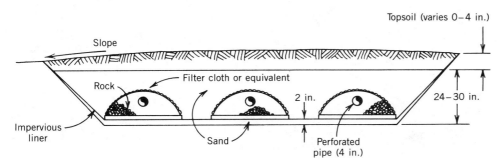

Figure 6. Cross section of typical ET bed.

viruses. These latter pollutants may require further removal where receiving waters are especially sensitive.

In cases where secondary levels of treatment are not adequate, treatment processes are applied to the secondary effluent to provide advanced wastewater treatment or further removal of the pollutants. Some of these processes may involve chemical treatment and filtration of the wastewater—much like adding a typical water treatment plant to the tail end of a secondary plant—or they may involve applying the secondary effluent to the land in carefully designed irrigation systems where the pollutants are removed by a soil-crop system. Some of these processes can remove as much as 99% of the BOD and phosphorus, all suspended solids and bacteria, and 95% of the nitrogen and can produce a sparkling clear, odorless effluent indistinguishable in appearance from a high quality drinking water.

Most of the impurities removed from the wastewater do not simply vanish, although some organics are broken down into harmless carbon dioxide and water. Instead, most impurities are removed from the wastewater as solids, leaving a residue called sludge. Because most of the impurities removed from the wastewater are present in the sludge, sludge handling and disposal must be carefully carried out to achieve satisfactory pollution control. Untreated sludge still consists largely of water—as much as 98–99%. Many treatment plants use a digesting process followed by a drying process for sludge treatment. Sludge digestion takes place in heated tanks where the sludge decomposes naturally and odors are controlled. Because digested sludge contains about 95% water, the next step in treatment is the removal of as much of the water as possible. Many small plants dry their sludge on open drying beds made up of sand and gravel. The sludge is spread on the bed and allowed to dry. After a week or two of drying, the residue is removed and used as a soil condi-

tioner or landfill. In some cases, the sludge is dewatered by mechanical devices that occupy much less space than drying beds.

Primary Treatment

Primary treatment removes from the wastewater those pollutants that will either settle out or float. As wastewater enters a plant for primary treatment, it flows through a screen. The screen removes large floating objects, such as rags and sticks, that may clog pumps and small pipes. The screens typically are made of parallel steel or iron bars with openings of about 0.5 in. (1.3 cm).

Screens are generally placed in a chamber or channel in an inclined position to the flow of the sewage for making cleaning easier. The debris caught on the upstream surface of the screen can be raked off manually or mechanically. The debris removed from the screen is usually buried in a landfill.

Some plants use a device known as a comminutor, which combines the functions of a screen and a grinder. This device catches and then cuts or shreds the heavy solid material. The pulverized matter remains in the wastewater flow to be removed later in a settling tank. After the wastewater has been screened, it passes into a grit chamber, where sand, grit, cinders, and small stones are allowed to settle to the bottom. The grit or gravel removed by the grit chamber is usually taken from the tank, washed so that it is clean, and disposed of by landfilling.

With the screening completed and the grit removed, the wastewater still contains suspended solids, some of which can be removed in a sedimentation tank. These tanks may be round or rectangular (Fig. 7), are usually 10–12 ft (3.1–3.7 m) deep, and hold the wastewater for periods for 2–3 hours. Wastewater flows very slowly

Figure 7. Circular sedimentation tanks.

through them, so that the suspended solids gradually sink to the bottom. This mass of settled solids is called raw primary sludge. The sludge is removed from the sedimentation tank by mechanical scrapers and pumps. Floating materials, such as grease and oil, rise to the surface of the sedimentation tank, where they are collected by a surface-skimming system and removed from the tank for further processing, usually in a sludge digester.

Secondary Treatment

The major purpose of secondary treatment is to remove the soluble BOD that escapes primary treatment and to provide further removal of suspended solids. A minimum of secondary treatment is now required for municipalities. In most cases, secondary processes are biological in nature and depend on bringing microorganisms into contact with the impurities in the wastewater so that they can use these impurities as food. The organisms convert the biodegradable organics into carbon dioxide, water, and cell material. This biological breakdown of organic material requires oxygen. The basic ingredients needed for secondary biological treatment are the availability of many microorganisms, good contact between these organisms and the organic material, the availability of oxygen, and the maintenance of other favorable environmental conditions (eg, favorable temperature and sufficient time for the organisms to work). A variety of approaches have been used in the past to meet these basic needs. The most common approaches are trickling filters, activated sludge, and oxidation ponds (or lagoons) (4).

Trickling Filters. A trickling filter consists of a bed of coarse material, such as stones, slats, or plastic materials, over which wastewater is applied in drops, films, or spray from moving distributors or fixed nozzles and through which it trickles to underdrains (Fig. 8). As the wastewater trickles through the bed, microbial growth occurs on the surface of the stone or packing in a fixed film. The wastewater passes over the stationary microbial population to provide the needed contact between the microorganisms and the organics. Trickling filters have long been a popular biologic treatment process. The most widely used design for many years was simply a bed of stones from 3 to 10 ft (1 to 3 m) deep through which the wastewater passed. The wastewater is typically distributed over the surface of the rocks by a rotating arm.

Bacteria gather and multiply on these stones until they consume most of the organic matter in the sewage. The cleaner water trickles out through pipes in the bottom of the filter. Rock filter diameters of up to 200 ft (60 m) are used. Trickling filters are not primarily a filtering or straining process as the name implies [the rocks in a rock filter are 1–4 in. (2.5–10 cm) in diameter, too large to strain out solids], but are a means of providing large amounts of surface area where the microorganisms cling and grow in a slime on the rocks as they fed on the organic matter. Excess growths of microorganisms wash from the rock media and would cause undesirably high levels of suspended solids in the plant effluent if not removed. Thus, the flow from the filter is passed through a sedimen-

Figure 8. Trickling filter treatment units with rotating distributors.

tation basin to allow these solids to settle out. This sedimentation basin is referred to as a secondary clarifier or a final clarifier to differentiate it for the sedimentation basin used for primary settling. To prevent the biological slimes from drying out and dying during nighttime periods when wastewater flows are too low to keep the filter wet continuously, filter effluent is often recycled to the trickling filter. Recirculation reduces odor potential and improves filter efficiency as it provides another opportunity for the microbes to attack any organics that escaped the first pass through the filter.

A typical overall efficiency of a trickling filter treatment plant is about 85% removal of BOD and suspended solids for municipal wastewaters, which corresponds to about 30 mg/L of suspended solids and BOD in the final effluent.

Activated Sludge. The activated sludge process is a biological wastewater treatment technique in which a mixture of wastewater and biological sludge (microorganisms) is agitated and aerated. The biological solids are subsequently separated from the treated wastewater and returned to the aeration process as needed.

The activated sludge process derives its name from the biological mass formed when air is continuously injected into the wastewater. Under such conditions, microorganisms are mixed thoroughly with the organics under conditions that stimulate their growth through use of the organics as food. As the microorganisms grow and are mixed by the agitation of the air, the individual organisms clump together (flocculate) to form an active mass of microbes called activated sludge. In practice, the wastewater flows continuously into an aeration tank (Fig. 9) where air is injected to mix the activated sludge with the wastewater and to supply the oxygen needed for the microbes to break down the organics. The mixture of activated sludge and wastewater in the aeration tank is called mixed liquor. The mixed liquor flows from the aeration tank to a secondary clarifier where the activated sludge is settled out. Most of the settled sludge is returned to the aeration tank to maintain a high population of microbes to permit rapid breakdown of the organics. Because more activated sludge is produced than can be used in the process, some of the return sludge is diverted or "wasted" to the sludge-handling system for treatment and disposal. In conventional activated sludge systems, the wastewater is typically aerated for 6–8 hours in long, rectangular aeration basins with about 1 ft³ of air injected uniformly along the length of the aeration basin for each gallon of wastewater treated (7500 cm³/L). Air is introduced either by injecting it into diffusers near the bottom of the aeration tank or by mechanical mixers located at the surface of the aeration tank. In some cases, oxygen has been injected instead of air, using covered aeration tanks.

The process is versatile because the design can be tailored to handle a wide variety of raw wastewater compositions and to meet a variety of effluent standards. Many variations of the basic activated sludge process described above have been developed for specific circumstances (4). The process is capable of producing a higher quality effluent than the trickling-filter process. A properly designed and operated activated-sludge plant removes essentially all soluble BOD. The secondary effluent BOD is made up primarily of the oxygen demand exerted by the suspended solids in the effluent. Typical effluent quality is 20–25 mg/L BOD and 20–25 mg/L suspended solids, although, with careful operation, the process has produced less than 10 mg/L BOD and suspended solids at some plants.

Figure 9. Aeration basin in activated sludge treatment plant.

Oxidation Ponds. Oxidation ponds (also called lagoons or stabilization ponds) are large, shallow ponds designed to treat wastewater through the interaction of sunlight, wind, algae, and oxygen. They account for about one-third of all secondary plants in the United States. About 90% of the ponds are used in towns with less than 10,000 people. Primary treatment is sometimes used as pretreatment, but the added cost is usually not justified. Typically, raw wastewater enters the pond at a single point in the middle of the pond or at one edge. Ponds are usually 2–4 ft (0.6–1.2 m) deep—at least deep enough to prevent weed growths but not deep enough to prevent mixing by wind currents. Shallow ponds are usually aerobic—that is, oxygen is present—through nearly all depths, except the anaerobic (devoid of oxygen) sludge layer on the bottom of the pond. Some ponds have been designed (and have worked well) with depths of 10–20 ft (3–6 m), where the anaerobic bottom zone becomes a greater portion of the overall system. The pond may have sufficient volume to accommodate from 15 to 60 days of wastewater flow, and it may be a fill-and-draw or continuous flow-through operation. Algae grow by taking energy from the sunlight and consuming the carbon dioxide and inorganic compounds released by the action of the bacteria in the pond. The algae, in turn, release oxygen needed by the bacteria to supplement the oxygen introduced into the pond by wind action. The most critical factor is to ensure that enough oxygen will be present in the pond to maintain aerobic conditions; if oxygen is insufficient, odor problems will occur. The sludge deposits from the pond eventually must be removed by dredging.

Ponds are sometimes designed with several cells in parallel to distribute the wastewater better and avoid localized zones of high oxygen demand caused by uneven deposits of sludges. Several smaller parallel cells also reduce the problems that can be encountered with wave action in large ponds. Ponds are sometimes placed in a series for highly polluted wastes or to permit use of the last pond in a series as a polishing step to provide higher removals of suspended solids. Pond effluent is sometimes recirculated to improve mixing in the pond.

To eliminate the dependence on algal-produced oxygen and to reduce the area required by the ponds, aeration equipment is sometimes installed in the pond to supply oxygen (Fig. 10). Such a system is called an aerated lagoon. Air can be supplied by a compressor that injects air into the pond through tubing installed on the pond bottom or by mechanical aerators installed at the surface of the pond. Aerated ponds are typically about one-fifth the size of a conventional oxidation pond and are a form of the activated sludge process. Aerated ponds are usually followed by a quiescent, second-stage pond to remove the suspended solids from the aerated-pond effluent.

Oxidation ponds usually meet secondary treatment requirements for removal of BOD, but they frequently fail to meet secondary requirements for suspended solids removal because of the presence of algae in the pond effluent. Much work has been done on various methods of removing these algae; the most promising alternatives to date are filtration through sand beds at low rates, filtration though a bed of rocks that may be a part of the dike

Figure 10. Aerated lagoon treatment system.

system, and a combination of chemical treatment of the pond effluent and settling.

The area required for this process depends on the climate, but typically ranges from 35 acres/million gallons per day (mgd) (37,500 m²/million liters/day) capacity for nonaerated ponds in warm climates to 85 acres/mgd (91,000 m²/million liters/day) in cold climates using conventional 4-ft-deep (1.2-m) lagoons.

Disinfection. Disinfection is the killing of pathogenic (disease-causing) bacteria and viruses found in wastewaters. The last treatment step in a secondary plant is the addition of a disinfectant to the treated wastewater. Chlorination (the addition of chlorine gas or some other form of chlorine) is the process most commonly used for wastewater disinfection in the United States. The chlorinated wastewater flows into a basin, where it is held for about 30 min to allow the chlorine to react with the pathogens. Chlorine is used primarily in two forms: as a gas or as a solid or liquid chlorine-containing hypochlorite compound. Gaseous chlorine is generally considered the least costly form of chlorine that can be used in large facilities, but it can cause safety hazards if not handled properly. Hypochlorite forms have been used primarily in small systems (less than 5000 persons) or in large systems, where safety concerns related to handling chlorine gas outweigh economic factors. Although there is concern about the formation of some by-products resulting from chlorination, the use of chlorine has proved to be a very effective means of disinfection of wastewaters.

An alternative to chlorine is ozone, which is widely used in Europe for disinfection of water supplies. Ozone is produced at its point of use by passing dry air between two high-potential electrodes to convert oxygen into ozone. Recent improvements in the technology of ozone production have bettered the reliability and economy of its generation. The advantages of using ozone are that it has the best germicidal effectiveness of all known substances, it adds dissolved oxygen to the wastewater, and it eliminates the by-products of chlorination that are of concern in some cases. The electrical generation of ozone is an energy-intensive operation. Ozone must be produced electrically as it is needed and cannot be stored.

ADVANCED WASTEWATER TREATMENT

Although secondary treatment processes, when coupled with disinfection, may remove more than 85% of the BOD and suspended solids and nearly all pathogens, only minor removals of some pollutants—such as nitrogen, phosphorus, soluble COD, and heavy metals—are achieved. In some circumstances, these pollutants contained in a secondary effluent are of concern. In these cases, processes capable of removing pollutants not adequately removed by secondary treatment are used for tertiary wastewater treatment (these processes are also called advanced wastewater treatment, or AWT). The following sections describe available AWT processes (5). In addition to solving tough pollution problems, these processes improve the effluent quality so that it is adequate for many reuse purposes and may convert what was originally a wastewater into a valuable resource.

Phosphorus Removal

Phosphorus sometimes disrupts the ecological balance of water by stimulating algae. To meet water quality standard, some cities must reduce phosphorus to low concentrations in wastewater discharges. In conventional wastewater treatment facilities, phosphorus is not removed to any appreciable extent. Available processes now allow for effective removal of phosphorus by relatively minor modifications to existing municipal wastewater treatment facilities.

In these processes, chemical coagulants—such as aluminum sulfate (alum), lime, or ferric chloride—are added. These coagulants cause the solids in the wastewater to clump together so they will settle out. The clumping together of solids (flocculation) is accelerated by slowly stirring the wastewater after the coagulants have been added. After flocculation, the wastewater enters a settling basin where the solids are settled out. If the proper amount of coagulant is added, the coagulant reacts with the phosphorus in the wastewater to convert it to an insoluble form that can be removed by settling, removing 90% of the phosphorus and suspended solids normally present in a secondary effluent.

The coagulant does not necessarily have to be added in a process downstream of the secondary process. Some plants add the coagulant to the raw wastewater as it enters the plant and remove the resulting solids in the primary clarifier; others add the coagulant to the aeration tank of an activated sludge plant, where it is mixed by the aeration process and the resulting floc is removed in the secondary clarifier; and others add the coagulant downstream in a separate tertiary process, including a third stage of settling.

Filtration

Filtration is the process of passing wastewater through a filtering medium, such as fine sand or coal, to remove suspended or colloidal matter. The goal of filtration in tertiary treatment is the removal of suspended solids from a secondary effluent or the effluent from the coagulation–sedimentation process. For example, the effluent from the tertiary coagulation and sedimentation typically will contain 3–5 mg/L suspended solids and 0.5–1 mg/L phosphorus. Efficient filtration can reduce suspended solids to zero and phosphorus to 0.1 mg/L or less. Filtration of secondary effluents without chemical coagulation (plain filtration) is also used. Typically, plain filtration will reduce activated sludge effluent suspended solids from 20–25 mg/L to 5–10 mg/L. Plain filtration is not effective on trickling filter effluents, because the trickling filter process is not as efficient in flocculating the microbes so that they are in a form readily removed by filtration.

Filtration of wastewater is typically achieved by passing the wastewater through a granular bed 30–36 in. (0.8–0.9 m) deep, composed of relatively small particles (less than 1.5 m). Wastewater is passed downward through the filter during its normal cycle of operation. Eventually, the filter becomes plugged with material removed from the wastewater and is then cleaned by reversing the flow (backwashing). The upward backwash rate is high enough that the media particles are suspended and the wastewater solids are washed from the bed. These backwash wastewaters (usually less than 5% of the wastewater flow treated) must be recycled to the wastewater treatment plant for processing. Filtration may be accomplished in open concrete structures by gravity flow or in steel pressure vessels (Fig. 11). The operation and control of the process may be readily automated.

Activated Carbon Treatment

Even after secondary treatment, coagulation, sedimentation, and filtration, the soluble organic materials that are resistant to biological breakdown persist in the effluent. The persistent materials are often referred to as refractory organics and are responsible for the color found in secondary effluent. Secondary effluent COD values are often 30–60 mg/L. The most practical available method for removing these materials is the use of granular activated carbon. Activated carbon removes organic contaminants from water by adsorption. The amount of carbon surface area available is the most important factor, because adsorption is a surface phenomenon. The activation of carbon in its manufacture produces many pores within the particles. It is the vast areas of the walls within these pores that account for most of the total surface area of the

carbon that makes it so effective in removing organics. After the capacity of the carbon for adsorption has been exhausted, it can be restored by heating the carbon in a furnace at a temperature sufficiently high to drive off the adsorbed organics. Keeping oxygen at very low levels in the furnace prevents the carbon from burning. The organics are passed through an afterburner to prevent air pollution. In small plants where the cost of an on-site regeneration furnace cannot be justified, it may be attractive to ship the spent carbon to a central regeneration facility for processing.

Granular carbon adsorption is achieved by passing the wastewater through beds of the carbon that may resemble a gravity filter or that may be housed in deep columns (20–25 ft or 6–7.7 m). These carbon beds usually provide 20–40 min contact between the carbon and the wastewater.

The degree of treatment provided before carbon adsorption can be varied, depending on the desired final effluent quality. Where very high degrees of treatment are required, secondary treatment, coagulation–sedimentation, and filtration usually precede carbon treatment. By combining these processes, a colorless, odorless effluent, free of bacteria and viruses, with a BOD of less than 1 mg/L and a COD of less than 10 mg/L, can be produced. To put this COD in perspective, several drinking water supplies in the United States have a COD of more than 10 mg/L.

Nitrogen Removal

In certain forms, nitrogen is one of the major nutrients supporting blooms of green and blue-green algae in surface waters. Nitrogen not only has nutrient value, but, in its ammonia form, can represent as much as 70% of the total oxygen demand of conventionally treated municipal wastewater. Ammonia nitrogen can be reduced in concentration or removed from wastewater by several processes.

Biological Nitrification–Denitrification. This process is the biological conversion of nitrogenous matter into nitrates (nitrification), followed by the anaerobic biological conversion of the nitrates to nitrogen gas (denitrification). The process is based on the principle that the nitrogen compounds found in raw sewage may be converted to the nitrate form in a properly designed secondary biological process (the nitrification process). These nitrates may then be removed by further treatment in the absence of oxygen. Under these anaerobic conditions, the nitrogen is released as nitrogen gas (the denitrification process). Because nearly 80% of the atmosphere consists of nitrogen, there is no air pollution associated with the release of nitrogen from the wastewater to the atmosphere. In some cases, carrying out only the nitrification portion of the process may be adequate. Nitrification is accomplished by providing oxygen in the amount required in the biochemical reaction to convert ammonia nitrogen to nitrate nitrogen, or roughly a 4.5 : 1 ratio of oxygen to ammonia nitrogen on a weight basis.

There are several alternative approaches to biological nitrogen removal. The most reliable performance has been found to occur when the first step of treatment is an

Figure 11. Pressure filter units, South Lake Tahoe, Calif. treatment plant.

activated sludge step, which oxidizes most of the raw wastewater BOD. The nitrification step can then be accomplished in a suspended growth system similar to the activated sludge process, in a fixed film system such as a trickling filter.

The denitrification step can be accomplished either in an anaerobic activated sludge system (suspended growth system) or in a fixed-film system. The high degree of biological treatment upstream of the denitrification process leaves little oxygen-demanding material in the wastewater by the time it reaches denitrification. The desired nitrate reduction will occur only as a result of oxygen demand being extended in the absence of oxygen in the wastewater. If denitrification is to be practical, an oxygen-demand source must be added to reduce the nitrates quickly. The most common method of supplying the needed oxygen demand is to add methanol to the denitrification process. The efficiency of biological nitrification–denitrification is usually 80–90% nitrogen removal.

Ammonia Stripping. This process removes gaseous ammonia from water by agitating the water–gas mixture in the presence of air. In practice, the process is based on the principle that nitrogen in the form of ammonium ions in secondary effluent can be converted to ammonia gas by raising the pH to high values. The gaseous ammonia can then be released by passing the high-pH effluent through a stripping tower where the agitation of the water in the presence of a large air flow through the tower releases the ammonia. The use of lime in coagulation–sedimentation permits simultaneous coagulation for suspended solids and phosphorus removal and the necessary upward adjustments of pH for the stripping process.

The three basic steps in ammonia stripping are: (1) raising the pH of the water to form ammonia gas, generally with the lime used for phosphorus removal; (2) cascading the water down through a stripping tower to release the ammonia gas; and (3) circulating large quantities of air through the tower to carry the ammonia gas out of the system. The towers used for ammonia stripping closely resemble conventional cooling towers. The concentration of ammonia in the off gas from the tower is very low—well below odor levels—and does not cause air pollution problems.

The major process limitation is the effect of temperature on efficiency. As the air temperature drops, efficiency also drops. For example, stripping removes about 95% of the ammonia in warm weather (21°C air temperature) but only about 75% of the ammonia when the temperature falls to 4°C. The process becomes inoperable as a result of freezing problems within the stripping tower when the air temperature falls very far below freezing.

Breakpoint Chlorination. In this process, chlorine is added to wastewater in such amounts that it reacts with ammonium nitrogen to form compounds that eventually are converted to nitrogen gas. To achieve the conversion, about 10 mg/L of chlorine must be added per mg/L of ammonia nitrogen in the wastewater. A typical secondary effluent ammonia concentration of 20 mg/L requires the use of about 1700 lb of chlorine per million gallons treated

(200 kg/million liters)—about 40 or 50 times more than normally used in a wastewater plant for disinfection only.

The facilities required for the process are simple. Wastewater (after secondary or tertiary treatment) flows into a mixing chamber where the chlorine is added and thorough mixing is provided. Because the large amount of chlorine used has an acidic effect on the wastewater, alkaline chemicals (such as lime or sodium hydroxide) may be added to the same chamber to offset this effect. The nitrogen gas formed by the reactions is released to the atmosphere. The process can achieve removal of more than 99% of the ammonium nitrogen. The chemical additions are monitored and controlled by a computer system, providing automated operation. The amounts of chlorine used provide very effective disinfection as well as nitrogen removal. Because the process is just as effective in removing 1 mg/L as 20 mg/L of ammonium, it can effectively be used as a polishing step downstream of other nitrogen removal processes. The low capital cost of the breakpoint process makes it attractive for this purpose.

Sludge Treatment and Disposal

In the process of purifying the wastewater, another problem is created—sludge handling. The higher the degree of wastewater treatment, the larger the residue of sludge that must be handled. Satisfactory treatment and disposal of the sludge can be the single most complex and costly operation in a municipal wastewater treatment system. The sludge is made of materials settled from the raw wastewater—such as rags, sticks, and organic solids—and of solids generated in the wastewater treatment process—such as the excess activated sludge created by aeration or the chemical sludges produced in some AWT processes. Whatever the wastewater process, there is always something that must be burned, buried, treated for reuse, or disposed of in some way.

The quantities of sludge involved are significant. For primary treatment, the sludge volume may be 0.25–0.35% of the volume of wastewater treated. When treatment is upgraded to activated sludge, the quantities increase by 1.5–2.0% of the volume treated. Use of chemicals for phosphorus removal can add another 1%.

Sludges withdrawn from the treatment processes are still largely water, as much as 97%. Sludge treatment processes are concerned with separating the large amounts of water from the solid residues. The separated water is returned to the wastewater plant for processing.

The basic functions of sludge treatment are

- *Conditioning.* Treatment of the sludge with chemicals or heat so that the water may be readily separated.
- *Thickening.* Separation of as much water as possible by gravity or flotation process.
- *Dewatering.* Further separation of water by subjecting the sludge to vacuum, pressure, or drying process.
- *Stabilization.* Stabilization or digestion of the organic solids so that they may be handled or used as soil conditioners without causing a nuisance or health hazard.

• *Reduction.* Reduction of the solids to a stable form by wet oxidation processes or incineration.

Although a large number of alternative combinations of equipment and processes are used for treating sludges, the basic alternatives are fairly limited. The ultimate depository of the materials contained in the sludge must be land, air, or water. Current policies discourage practices such as ocean dumping of sludge. If the sludge is incinerated, an ash residue remains. The sludge in some form will eventually be returned to the land.

Sludge Conditioning. Several methods of conditioning sludge to facilitate the separation of the liquid and solids are available. One of the most commonly used is the addition of coagulants—ferric chloride, lime, or organic polymers. Ash from incinerated sludge has been used as a conditioning agent. Chemical coagulants act to clump the solids together so that they are more easily separated from the water. In recent years, organic polymers have become increasingly popular for sludge conditioning. Polymers are easy to handle, require little storage space, and are very effective. The conditioning chemicals are injected into the sludge just ahead of thickening or dewatering processes and are mixed with the sludge.

Sludge Thickening. After the sludge has been conditioned, it is often thickened before further processing. Thickening is usually accomplished in one of two ways: the solids are floated to the top of the liquid (flotation thickening) or are allowed to settle to the bottom (gravity thickening). The goal is to remove as much water as possible before final dewatering or disposing of the sludge. The processes involved offer a low-cost means of reducing sludge volumes by a factor of 2 or more. The costs of thickening are usually more than offset by the resulting savings in the size and cost of downstream sludge processing equipment. Flotation thickening of activated sludge typically increases the solids content of activated sludge from 0.5–1 to 3–6%, greatly easing further dewatering. Gravity thickening of primary sludges can increase solids from 1–3 to 10%.

Sludge Stabilization. The principal purposes of sludge stabilization are to break down the organic solids biochemically so that they are more stable (less odorous and less putrescible) and more dewaterable and to reduce the mass of sludge. If the sludge is to be dewatered and burned, stabilization is not normally used. Many municipal plants do not use incineration, however, and rely on sludge digestion to stabilize their organic sludges. There are two basic digestion processes in use. One is carried out in closed tanks devoid of oxygen and is called anaerobic digestion. The other approach injects air into the sludge to accomplish aerobic digestion.

Many anaerobic digesters use a two-stage process. The sludge is normally heated by means of coils located within the tanks or an external heat exchanger. In the two-stage process, the first tank is used for the biological digestion. It is heated and equipped with mixing facilities. The second tank is used for storage and concentration of digested sludge and formation of a relatively clear liquid (supernatant) that can be withdrawn from the top of the tank and recycled to the treatment plant. The second tank may be an open tank, an unheated tank, or a sludge lagoon. Tanks are usually circular, are seldom less than 20 ft (6 m) or more than 115 ft (34 m) in diameter, and may be as deep as 45 ft (14 m) or more. As the organic solids are broken down by anaerobic bacteria, methane gas and carbon dioxide gas are formed. Methane gas is combustible and must not be allowed to mix with air or an explosive mixture may result. The digester gas containing methane is usable fuel and may be used for digester and building heating or as fuel for internal combustion engines that are used for pumping sewage, operating blowers, or generating electricity. An efficiently operating anaerobic digester converts about 50% of the organic solids to liquid and gaseous forms. The methane liberated has the potential to generate about 2100 kWh of electricity per year for every 100 people served.

Aerobic digestion is accomplished in open aeration tanks. Its most extensive use has been in relatively small activated sludge plants. The process can achieve about the same 50% solids reduction achieved in the anaerobic process, while offering advantages of being more stable in operation and recycling fewer pollutants to the wastewater plant than anaerobic digesters. It has the disadvantages of higher power costs and does not produce an energy source such as methane.

Composting primary and secondary wastewater sludges is a means of stabilizing sludge for reuse purposes. Sludge can be composted by mixing it with a bulking agent (such as wood chips or even refuse) and placing it in piles or windrows about 7 ft (2 m) high. Biological activity stabilizes the sludge and raises the temperature so high that most disease causing organisms are killed. After composting is complete (usually about 3 weeks), the material is cured for another month and then can be used as sludge conditioner. Establishing an adequate market for use of the composted product is the key to the success of this process.

Sludge Dewatering

The most widely used method for sludge dewatering in the past has been drying the sludge on sand beds (Fig. 12). These beds are especially popular in small plants because of their simplicity of operating and maintenance. They are usually constructed of a layer of 4–9 in. (10–23 cm) of sand placed over 8–18 in. (20–45 cm) of gravel. Sludge is drawn from the digester, placed on the sand bed, and allowed to stand until dried by a combination of drainage and evaporation. Drainage is collected in pipes beneath the gravel and returned to the wastewater plant for treatment. In good weather, the solids content can be increased to 45% (resembling moist dirt) within 6 weeks and can reach as high as 85–90%. Sand beds have sometimes been enclosed by glass, greenhouse-type structures to protect the sludge from rain and reduce the drying period. In small plants, the dried sludge is usually removed from the drying beds by hand; larger plants often use mechanical equipment. Although sand beds are simple to operate, the

Figure 12. Sand beds used for sludge dewatering.

Figure 13. Vacuum filter for sludge dewatering.

space requirements can be a disadvantage when secondary sludge is involved. Unless the beds are covered, the performance can be markedly affected by weather. With increased use of secondary treatment, the use of more compact and more controllable mechanical-dewatering systems is increasing. Such systems include vacuum filters, centrifuges, and pressure filters.

A vacuum filter basically consists of a cylindrical drum covered with a filtering material or fabric, which rotates partially submerged in a vat of conditioned sludge (Fig. 13). A vacuum is applied inside the drum to extract water, leaving the solids or filter cake on the filter medium. As the drum completes its rotational cycle, the filter cake is removed from the filter and the cycle begins again. The vacuum filter can be applied to digested sludge to produce a sludge cake dry enough (15–30% solids) to handle and dispose of by burial in landfill or by application to the land as a relatively dry soil conditioner. If the sludge is to be incinerated, it is not necessary to stabilize the sludge by digestion. In this case, the vacuum filter is applied to the raw sludge to dewater it. The sludge cake is then fed to the furnace to be incinerated.

Centrifuges are also a popular means of dewatering municipal sludges. A centrifuge uses centrifugal force to speed up the separation of sludge particles from the liquid. In a typical unit, sludge is pumped into a horizontal, cylindrical bowl rotating at 1600–2000 rpm. Polymers used for sludge conditioning also are injected into the centrifuge. The solids are spun to the outside of the bowl where they are scraped out by a screw conveyor. The liquid, or centrate, is returned to the wastewater treatment plant for treatment.

Pressure filtration is also an effective means of sludge dewatering that is finding increased use in the United States. In a filter press, sludge is dewatered by pumping it at high pressure through a filter medium that is attached to a series of plates. These plates are held together in a frame between one fixed end and one moving end. Sludge is pumped into the chambers between plates, so that the water passes through the filter medium and the solids are retained. Eventually, the pressure filter fills with sludge solids. Pumping of sludge is then discontinued, and the moving end of the press is pulled back so that the individ-

ual plates can be moved to dislodge the filter cake. After the cake is removed, the plates are pushed back together by the moving end and the cycle begins again. In a belt press, sludge is applied to a moving belt where a combination of drainage through the porous belt material and pressure is used to remove water.

Sludge Application to Land

Municipal sludge contains essential plant nutrients and useful trace elements of use as a fertilizer or soil conditioner. Before such use, the sludge is nearly always stabilized by digestion or some other process to control pathogenic bacteria and viruses and to minimize the potential for odors. Several alternative forms of the sludge can be used as fertilizer or soil conditioner: liquid sludge directly from the stabilization process, dewatered sludge, or dewatered and dried sludge.

Several cities apply liquid sludge to croplands. This practice has the advantage of eliminating dewatering costs, but the disadvantage of increasing the volume of sludge that must be handled and applied to the land. Such sludge is not used for root crops or crops consumed raw because of health considerations. It is frequently used for pastureland or corn, wheat, or forage crops. Smaller towns often haul the sludge in trucks that also spread the sludge on the land. Large cities usually find pumping the sludge through pipelines to the disposal site to be the cheapest method of sludge transportation.

To reduce the volume of material handled, dewatering is sometimes used before applying the sludge to the land. In small plants, sludge removed from drying beds is often stockpiled for use by the city or by local citizens. Larger cities may use mechanical dewatering systems, with the sludge cake hauled to the disposal site where it is plowed into the ground. Because of concerns over trace contaminants in sludge, the EPA has developed specific tests and procedures to determine the suitability of a given sludge for application to the land.

Sludge Incineration

If sludge use as a soil conditioner is not practical, or if a site is not available for landfill using dewatered sludge, cities may turn to the alternative of sludge incineration. Incineration completely evaporates the moisture in the sludge and combusts the organic solids to a sterile ash. To minimize the amount of fuel used, the sludge must be dewatered as completely as possible before incineration. If the sludge is dry enough, no fuel may be needed except to start the furnace. The exhaust gases from an incinerator must be treated to avoid air pollution. The EPA has developed standards that ensure that air quality will not be impaired by municipal sludge incinerators. The two most widely used sludge incineration systems are the multiple-hearth furnace and the fluidized-bed incinerator.

The multiple-hearth furnace is simple and durable and has the flexibility of burning a wide variety of materials. A typical multiple-hearth furnace consists of a circular steel shell surrounding a number of hearths. Dewatered sludge enters at the top and proceeds downward through the furnace from hearth to hearth, moved by the rotary action of rabble arms dried by a central shaft. Gas or oil burners furnish heat for start-up of the furnace and supplemental heat, if needed, to keep the temperature in the lower part of the furnace at 815°C or higher. The flue gasses may be passed through a scrubbing device to control air pollution. The fluidized-bed incinerator is a vertical steel cylinder filled with a bed of hot sand. Combustion air flows up through the bed of sand at a rate high enough to fluidize the sand. Dewatered sludge is injected into the fluidized sand where it is burned at 760–815°C. The sludge ash is carried out the top with the exhaust gases and is removed in the air pollution control process.

BIBLIOGRAPHY

1. *Design Manual, Onsite Wastewater Treatment and Disposal Systems.* U.S. Environmental Protection Agency, Washington, DC, October 1980.
2. *Alternatives for Small Wastewater Treatment Systems. On-Site Disposal/Septage Treatment and Disposal,* U.S. Environmental Protection Agency, EPA-725/4-77-011, Oct. 1977.
3. G. L. Culp, *Environmental Pollution Control Alternatives: Municipal Wastewater.* U.S. Environmental Protection Agency, Washington, DC, EPA-625/5-79-012, November 1979.
4. *Wastewater Treatment Plant Design: A Manual of Practice.* Water Pollution Control Federation, Washington, D.C. MOP 8, 1977.
5. G. L. Culp, G. M. Wesner, and R. L. Culp, *Handbook of Advanced Wastewater Treatment,* Van Nostrand Reinhold Co., Inc., New York, 1978.

See also PLUMBING SYSTEMS

GORDON L. CULP
HDR Engineering, Inc.
Bellevue, Washington

WATERPROOFING, DAMPROOFING SYSTEMS.   See MOISTURE PROTECTION

WATER SYSTEMS, STORAGE.   See PLUMBING SYSTEMS

WATER TREATMENT

OBJECTIVES OF WATER TREATMENT

The primary objective of water treatment for public supply is to take water from the best available source and to subject it to processing that will ensure that it is always safe for human consumption and is aesthetically acceptable to the consumer. For water to be safe for human consumption, it must be free of pathogenic organisms or other biological forms that may be harmful to health, and it should not contain concentrations of chemicals that may be physiologically harmful. To provide safe water, the treatment plant must be properly designed and skillfully operated. The task of furnishing safe water in the future may be more difficult in many instances because of the necessity of treating raw water of poorer quality.

The general requirements of an aesthetically acceptable water are that it be cool, clear, colorless, odorless, and pleasant to the taste; also, it should not stain, form scale, or be corrosive. Treatment plants must be designed to produce water of uniformly good quality despite variations in raw water quality and plant throughput. Because the consumer is interested in the quality of the water at his tap rather than that at the treatment plant, precautions must be taken to preserve water quality in the distribution system.

This article provides a brief overview of a complex topic. For a complete treatment of the subject, the reader is referred to reference 1.

FEDERAL REQUIREMENTS FOR WATER TREATMENT

On December 16, 1974, President Gerald Ford signed into law the Safe Drinking Water Act (SDWA), which was recorded as Public Law 93-532 (PL 93-523). This act gave the Environmental Protection Agency (EPA) the authority to control the quality of the drinking water in public water systems through the development of regulations or by other methods. One of the requirements of the law was that National Primary Drinking Water Regulations be promulgated, establishing maximum contaminant levels to prevent the occurrence of any known or anticipated adverse health effects with an adequate margin of safety. Table 1 shows these standards as they existed in 1986.

In answer to what was perceived as public concern about drinking water quality, Congress passed a sweeping set of amendments to the 1974 SDWA in June 1986. Prior to this, the EPA had established the allowable concentrations for the contaminants in Table 1 and published a list of 83 contaminants for which it felt allowable concentrations should be considered. Congress brushed aside any further deliberation on the list and dictated by law that

Table 1. The EPA's 1986 National Primary Drinking Water Regulations

Constituent	Maximum Contaminant Level
Arsenic	0.05 mg/L
Barium	1 mg/L
Cadmium	0.010 mg/L
Chromium	0.05 mg/L
Fluoride	Varies with temperature
Lead	0.05 mg/L
Mercury	0.002 mg/L
Nitrate as N	10 mg/L
Selenium	0.01 mg/L
Silver	0.05 mg/L
Sodium	Analyze one sample per year plant at entry to distribution system for surface waters and once every three years for groundwater systems
Ra-226 and -228	5 pCi/L
Gross alpha activity (including Ra-226 but excluding radon and uranium)	15 pCi/L
Beta and photon radioactivity (detailed studies must be made if the gross beta activity exceeds 50 pCi/L)	4 mrem/yr
Corrosivity	Measure pH, calcium hardness, alkalinity, temperature, and total dissolved solids, and calculate the Langlier index for a midwinter and a midsummer sample each year for surface sources and for one sample per year for groundwater systems
Total coliforms	1. One per 100 mL, average of all samples in a month measured by the membrane filter technique 2. One per 100 mL in more than 5% of the samples measured by the membrane filter technique
Turbidity	1. 1 ntu,[a] average of all samples in a month as measured at entry points to the distribution system 2. 5 ntu, average of two consecutive days as measured at entry points to the distribution system
Endrin	0.0002 mg/L
Lindane	0.004 mg/L
Methoxychlor	0.1 mg/L
Toxaphene	0.005 mg/L
2,4-D	0.1 mg/L
2,4,5-TP (Silvex)	0.01 mg/L
Total trihalomethanes	0.1 mg/L, 12-month running average of quarterly samples, each quarterly sample consisting of at least four individual samples

[a] May be 5 ntu under certain conditions.

all 83 (Table 2) be regulated by 1989: nine by June 1987, 40 in the next 12 months, and the rest in the third year. EPA substituted seven contaminants (Table 3) for the first 83 contaminants specified by Congress. The first nine included eight volatile organic compounds (VOCs) and fluoride. Congress also directed the EPA to add 25 additional contaminants to the list every three years, with no limit on the number of additions.

The 1986 amendments require that all supplies (well waters included) be disinfected and that all surface waters be filtered, unless stringent criteria for exemptions are met. The related regulations also specify exacting performance requirements for water treatment and distribution facilities, specify the treatment technology to be used for each contaminant, require the use of low-lead pipes and solders, and increase the monitoring requirements. Congress removed the EPA's latitude in enforcing the standards. Previously, the EPA could assess fines of up to

$5000 per day for willful violations. If the State did not act on such violations, the EPA had the authority, but was not required, to initiate action against the violator. Under the amendments, the maximum fines were increased to $25,000 per day whether the violations are willful or not. If the state does not act within 30 days of notification by the EPA, the EPA must initiate action. The reader is advised to contact the State water supply agency to obtain a copy of the most current EPA regulations, which will evolve over a period of several years as a result of the 1986 SDWA amendments.

SOURCE DEVELOPMENT

The alternative sources of water are surface water, groundwater, and the conjunctive use of both. The source selected is a key factor in determining the nature of the

Table 2. Contaminants for Which Standards Were To Be Established by the EPA from 1987 to 1989

Volatile Organic Chemicals

Trichloroethylene	Benzene
Tetrachloroethylene	Chlorobenzene
Carbon tetrachloride	Dichlorobenzene(s)
1,1,1-Trichloroethane	Trichlorobenzene(s)
1,2-Dichloroethane	*trans*-1,2-Dichloroethylene
Vinyl chloride	1,1-Dichloroethylene
Methylene chloride	*cis*-1,2-Dichloroethylene

Microbiology and Turbidity

Total coliforms	Viruses
Turbidity	Standard plate count
Giardia lamblia	Legionella

Inorganics

Arsenic	Molybdenum[a]
Barium	Asbestos
Cadmium	Sulfate
Chromium	Copper
Lead	Vanadium[a]
Mercury	Sodium[a]
Nitrate	Nickel
Selenium	Zinc[a]
Silver[a]	Thallium
Fluoride	Beryllium
Aluminum[a]	Cyanide
Antimony	

Organics

Endrin	1,1,2-Trichloroethane
Lindane	Vydate
Methoxychlor	Simazine
Toxaphene	PAHs
2,4-D	PCBs
2,4,5-TP	Atrazine
Aldicarb	Phthalates
Chlordane	Acrylamide
Dalapon	Dibromochloropropane (DBCP)
Diquat	1,2-Dichloropropane
Endothall	Pentachlorophenol
Glyphosate	Picloram
Carbofuran	Dinoseb
Alachlor	Ethylene dibromide
Epichlorohydrin	Dibromomethane[a]
Toluene	Xylene
Adipates	Hexachlorocyclopentadiene
2,3,7,8-TCDD (Dioxin)	

Radionuclides

Ra-226 and -228	Gross alpha particle activity
Beta particle and photon radioactivity	Radon
Uranium	

[a] Substitute contaminants were adopted by the EPA in June 1987; see Table 3.

Table 3. EPA Substitutions, June 1987

Out	In
Zinc	Aldicarb sulfoxide
Silver	Aldicarb sulfone
Sodium	Ethylbenzene
Aluminum	Heptachlor
Molybdenum	Heptachlor epoxide
Vanadium	Styrene
Dibromomethane	Nitrite

general advantages and disadvantages of the alternative sources are discussed below.

SURFACE WATER SUPPLIES

Surface waters usually can be obtained without the need for pumping normally associated with groundwaters (or with less costly pumping than groundwaters require). It is also usually possible to define the quantity and quality of a surface supply at a lower cost than that associated with exploration of a groundwater supply.

The quality of lake water is not as consistent as that of groundwater, but is more consistent than that of river water. The turbidity of river water may change rapidly during a heavy rainstorm or from runoff due to melting snows. Lake water quality may change from wind-generated currents or when thermal stratification occurs. If a lake freezes over, the dissolved oxygen may be depleted in portions of it, with the result that the bottom deposits become anaerobic and many compounds become soluble. Many lakes and reservoirs have substantial quantities of iron, and occasionally manganese, in their bottom deposits. Normally, they are of no particular importance to water engineers because they are oxidized and precipitated, or chelated, with organic compounds. However, when the bottom deposits in the relatively shallow areas of the lake become suspended because of wind-induced currents, these deposits can enter the intakes. Significant changes in water quality can also occur when lakes "turn over" as temperature gradients change in the fall and spring.

Whereas groundwater often can be used with a minimum of treatment, often requiring only disinfection, most surface waters require chemical coagulation, sedimentation, filtration, and disinfection to make them suitable for use as public water supplies.

required purification, transmission, and storage facilities. The supply must provide a reliable quantity of water for the long-term needs of the community, and preferably will have a quality that minimizes the amount of treatment required. A detailed evaluation of all alternative sources should be made to compare the yield, reliability, quality, treatment, collection, and distribution costs. Some of the

GROUNDWATER SUPPLIES

When available in sufficient quantity, groundwater is often the preferred source. Most is clear, cool, colorless, and quite uniform in character. Underground supplies are generally of better bacterial quality than surface water, but may be more highly mineralized. Adequate natural protection of groundwater involves purification of water by infiltration into the soil, percolation through underlying material, and storage below the groundwater table. Also, groundwater is usually more uniform in temperature than surface water.

Groundwater sources also have some disadvantages. The cost of pumping groundwater may be greater than that of pumping surface water. Unless there are good geological data on the area, exploration to define the quality and quantity of groundwater could be expensive and speculative. Some groundwaters are highly mineralized and contain large quantities of iron, manganese, sulfates, chlorides, calcium, magnesium, and other elements that are expensive to remove. Some groundwaters are high in color. Elements such as iron and manganese are held in solution at low pH values in the aquifers because of the presence of carbon dioxide. Once the water is pumped to the surface, the free carbon dioxide is liberated, and the ferrous and manganous ions precipitate out of the solution. If the groundwater is overpumped, its quality can change significantly as water from other formations flows into the system.

All groundwater withdrawal points should be located a safe distance from sources of pollution. Sources of pollution include septic tanks and other individual or semipublic sewage disposal facilities, sewers and sewage treatment plants, industrial waste discharges, land drainage, farm animals, fertilizers, and pesticides. Where water resources are severely limited, groundwater aquifers subject to contamination may be used for water supply if adequate treatment is provided.

Because many factors affect the determination of safe distances between groundwater supplies and pollution sources, it is impractical to set fixed distances. Where insufficient information is available to determine a safe distance, the distance should be the maximum that economics, land ownership, geology, and topography permit. If possible, a well site should be located at an elevation higher than that of any potential source of contamination. The direction of groundwater flow does not always follow the slope of the land surface, so the slope of the water table should be determined from observation wells.

DECIDING ON THE TREATMENT REQUIRED

The next section of this article describes treatment techniques. This section provides an overview of the types of treatments needed to remove various contaminants.

Turbidity

EPA regulations require low levels of turbidity to allow for effective disinfection. In the current draft of the regulations required by the 1986 SDWA amendments, the turbidity of filtered water must be maintained at less than 0.5 turbidity units 95% of the time. The effective method for turbidity removal is chemical coagulation and filtration; and in highly turbid waters, sedimentation is also needed.

Iron and Manganese

Water containing iron and manganese is objectionable to consumers because precipitation of these metals causes the water to turn yellow-brown or black. This rusty-colored water causes yellow-brown stains in plumbing and disagreeable tastes in drinking water and beverages and stains laundered clothing. Water containing less than 0.1 mg/L iron and 0.05 mg/L manganese is not objectionable to the average customer.

The most common method of removing iron and manganese is to oxidize the iron and manganese by aeration (or chemically) and then filter the oxidized precipitates out of the water.

Taste and Odor

Odors are caused by the volatile substances in water, and tastes are caused by dissolved materials. Dissolved inorganic compounds are detectable by taste, but are odorless. Taste and odor are closely related and often are difficult to distinguish because taste is easily masked by olfactory sensations. Many processes are used to remove taste and odor: chlorination, ozonation, potassium permanganate treatment, aeration, and activated carbon treatment.

Bacteria, Viruses, and Other Pathogens

Effective removal of viruses, bacteria, and other pathogens (such as *Giardia* cysts) require optimization of the combination of chemical coagulation, sedimentation, and filtration, coupled with addition of adequate amounts of disinfectant such as chlorine or ozone. The EPA requires that all systems provide 99.9% inactivation of *Giardia* cysts and 99.99% of enteric viruses and publishes guidelines on the nature of treatment needed for varying raw water conditions.

Organic Chemicals

As evident from Table 2, many of the regulated contaminants are organic in nature. Many of these are of concern as suspected carcinogens. The VOCs can be removed by aeration, most effectively by running the water through a packed tower. The nonvolatile organics are usually removed by adsorbing them onto activated carbon.

Inorganic Chemicals

The technique for removal of the various regulated inorganic compounds vary from compound to compound. Table 4 summarizes the most effective methods for several major contaminants.

Table 4. Most Effective Methods for Removal of Inorganic Chemicals in Primary Drinking Water Regulations[a]

Contaminant	Most Effective Methods
As^{3+}	Chemical clarification (oxidation prior to treatment required) Ferric sulfate, pH 6–8 Alum, pH 6–7 Lime
As^{5+}	Chemical clarification Ferric sulfate coagulation, pH 6–8 Alum coagulation, pH 6–7 Lime
Barium	Lime clarification, pH 10–11 Ion exchange
Cadmium	Ferric sulfate clarification, above pH 8 Lime clarification
Cr^{3+}	Chemical clarification Ferric sulfate, pH 6–9 Alum, pH 7–9 Lime
Cr^{6+}	Ferrous sulfate clarification, pH 7–9.5
Lead	Chemical clarification Ferric sulfate, pH 6–9 Alum, pH 6–9 Lime
Mercury, inorganic	Ferric sulfate clarification, pH 7–8
Mercury, organic	GAC
Nitrate	Ion exchange
Se^{4+}	Ferrous sulfate clarification, pH 6–7 Ion exchange Reverse osmosis
Se^{6+}	Ion exchange Reverse osmosis
Silver	Chemical clarification Ferric sulfate, pH 6–9 Alum, pH 6–8 Lime

[a] From reference 2.

TREATMENT TECHNIQUES

Pretreatment

Surface water supplies, whether from rivers or reservoirs, often contain impurities or characteristics that may best be removed prior to conventional water treatment. Two of the most commonly used pretreatment methods are screening of surface water for removal of general debris and presedimentation of river water for removal of suspended silt load.

In rivers or lakes where the water transports debris such as leaves, branches, logs, and similar objects, it is necessary to provide screening facilities before water is withdrawn for treatment. When substantial amounts of debris are present, mechanically cleaned screens should be considered.

Protective bar racks are often placed upstream of mechanical moving screens as barriers to logs, large fish, and other similar objects that could cause damage or are not suitable for removal by a screen. These bars may be spaced 3–4 in. (76.2–101.6 mm) apart, and inlet velocities are less than 0.25 ft/s (76.2 mm/s). They may be fixed in place with no provision for cleaning because they are not intended to collect material, but merely to prevent entry of large material.

Sedimentation as a unit process is discussed later. Presedimentation is a pretreatment process for control of silt load on subsequent treatment units. It is unnecessary to use presedimentation for reservoir supplies because the reservoir accumulates the silt. Therefore, presedimentation as a unit process is associated almost solely with river supplies and, more specifically, only with those river supplies that carry heavy silt loads.

COAGULATION AND FLOCCULATION

Coagulation

Impurities in water often cause it to appear turbid or colored. These impurities include suspended and colloidal materials and soluble substances. Because the density of many of these particles is only slightly greater than that of water, agglomeration or aggregation of particles into a larger floc is a necessary step for their removal by sedimentation. The process that combines the particles into larger flocs is called coagulation.

Impurities that can be removed by coagulation include turbidity, bacteria, algae, color, organic compounds, oxidized iron and manganese, calcium carbonate, and clay particles. Coagulation has been shown to be effective for the removal of color and other organic constituents in water using iron (Fe) and aluminum (Al) salts. Al(III) and Fe(III) are the salts used most frequently to coagulate colloidal material in water treatment.

Synthetic organic polymers can be effective coagulants or coagulant aids. Polymers are long-chain molecules comprising many subunits, called monomers. Cationic polymers can be effective in coagulating negatively charged clay particles. Anionic particles generally are ineffective coagulants for negatively charged clay particles. When anionic polymers are used in conjunction with another coagulant, such as alum, their coagulating effectiveness is increased.

Dosages of only 0.5–1.5 mg/L of cationic polymer frequently are sufficient to achieve coagulation. In contrast, 5–15 mg/L of alum is often needed to obtain similar results. Other important differences between the uses of polymers and metal ions are sludge quantities and dosage control. The use of alum or ferric chloride can result in copious volumes of sludge that must be handled, whereas the additional sludge quantity is negligible when a polymer is used. There is a narrow range of optimum polymer dosages. Overdosing or underdosing results in restabilization of the colloids. The control method for polymer feed systems must be precise and reliable to give satisfactory performance.

RAPID MIXING

The rapid mixer is used to provide complete and thorough mixing of the coagulant and the raw water. Typically, the rapid mix unit is the initial process in a water treatment plant. The mixing, or blending, is required to force multiple contacts between each of the colloidal particles and the products of the coagulation process. Proper design of the rapid mixer can result in low coagulant doses and improved aggregation during flocculation.

Many devices for rapid mixing, including baffled chambers, hydraulic jumps, mechanically mixed tanks, and in-line jet blending, have been used. The mechanically mixed tanks, which are typically termed "completely mixed" or "back-mixed" units, have been the most commonly used devices. These tanks have been typically designed for detention times of 10–30 s and velocity gradients (G) in the range of 200–1000 s^{-1}.

FLOCCULATION

The flocculation process aggregates destabilized particles into larger and more easily settleable flocs. This process typically follows rapid mixing. Destabilization results from chemical reactions between the coagulant and the colloidal suspension, and flocculation is the transport step that causes the necessary collisions between the destabilized particles.

The following types of mechanical mixing devices are typically used in water treatment flocculation:

- Paddle or reel-type devices.
- Reciprocating units (walking beam flocculators).
- Flat-blade turbines.
- Axial flow propellers or turbines.

Typical units are shown in Figure 1.

Paddle units rotate at low speeds (2–15 rpm). Their design is based on limiting the top speed of the paddle farthest from the center axis to 1–2 ft/s. Walking beam flocculators are driven in a vertical direction in a reciprocating fashion. The unit contains a series of cone-shaped devices on a vertical rod. The cone devices impart energy to the water as they move up and down, thereby creating velocity gradients.

Turbines are flat-bladed units connected to a disk or shaft. The flat blades are in the same plane as the drive shaft. The blades can be mounted vertically or horizontally and typically operate at 10–15 rpm.

SEDIMENTATION

The two principal applications of sedimentation in water treatment are plain sedimentation and sedimentation of coagulated and flocculated waters. Plain sedimentation is used to remove solids that are present in surface waters and that settle without chemical treatment, such as gravel, sand, silt, and so on. As discussed earlier, it is used as a preliminary process to reduce the sediment loads in the remainder of the treatment plant and is referred to as "presedimentation." Sedimentation also is used downstream of the coagulation and flocculation processes to remove solids that have been rendered more settleable by these processes. Chemical coagulation may be geared toward removal of turbidity, color, or hardness.

A common practice is to follow flocculation with sedimentation in order to reduce the load of solids applied to filters. A large portion of the solids can be removed from the water by gravity settling following coagulation and flocculation. As discussed later, the development of coarse-to-fine filters, through the use of mixed-media or dual-media filters, means that much heavier loads of suspended solids can be filtered at reasonable head losses than could be handled in the past using single-medium fine-to-coarse sand filters. This makes it possible to consider direct filtration (without settling following flocculation) in an increasing number of situations. However, there remains a need for sedimentation in waters that are too turbid for direct filtration or that require other chemical treatment (softening) prior to filtration.

A variety of basin shapes and configurations have been used for settling. Figure 2 shows cross sections of circular and rectangular settling basins. The main design criterion is the overflow rate (throughput rate in gallons per day divided by the plan area of the settling zone). Typical overflow rates for alum floc are 350–550 gpd/ft^2 (0.59–0.93 m/h) and for lime floc are 1400–2100 gpd/ft^2 (2.37–3.56 m/h). The higher rates are used in warm waters, and the lower rates in cold waters. Modern sedimentation basins are equipped with sludge collection and removal mechanisms to eliminate the need to shut down for cleaning.

In the 1960s, an approach was developed that allows the capacity or efficiency of many existing settling basins to be improved. This approach uses the "tube settling" concept. A series of shallow (about 2-in deep) 2-ft long tubes inclined at 60 deg can be installed in modules in existing basins to increase clarifier rates by 2–4 times.

Steeply inclined tubes can be used in either upflow solids contact clarifiers or horizontal flow basins to improve the performance and/or increase the capacity of existing clarifiers. Of course, they can also be incorporated into the design of new facilities to reduce their size and cost. Capacities of existing basins can usually be increased by 50–150% with similar or improved effluent quality. The overflow rate at which tubes can be operated is dependent on the design and type of clarification equipment, character of the water being treated, and desired effluent quality.

The shape of a basin determines how the tube modules can be most efficiently arranged to utilize the available space. The best arrangement may be determined strictly by the basin geometry once the tube quantity is established. Of course, other factors must also be considered. For example, it is desirable to locate the tubes as far as possible from areas of known turbulence or locate them to take advantage of an existing effluent laundering system. In circular basins, the tube modules are often placed in pie-shaped segments, as can be seen in Figure 3.

FILTRATION

Water filtration is a physical–chemical process for separating suspended and colloidal impurities from water by

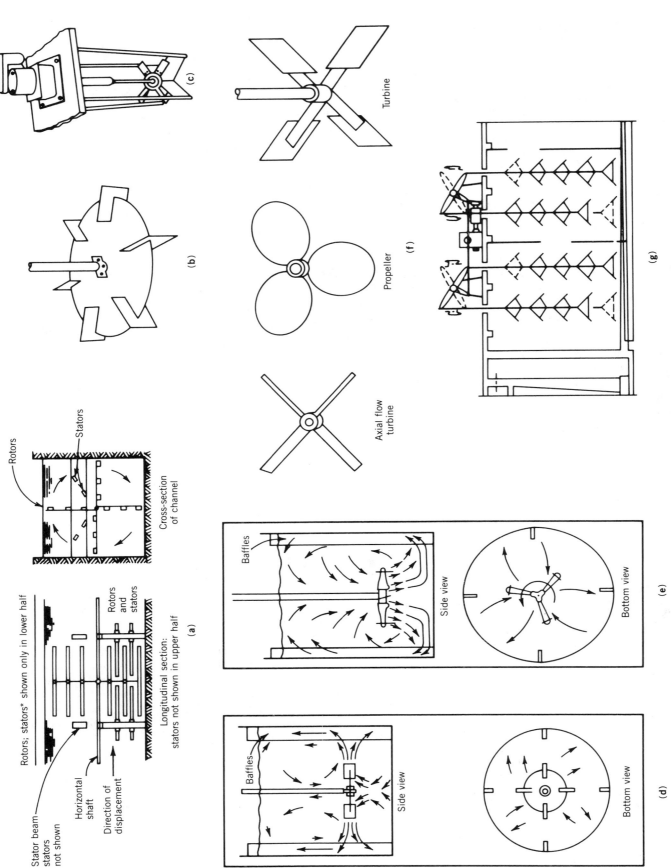

Figure 1. Typical flocculation units (**a**) paddle type with rotors and stators; (**b**) plate turbine type; (**c**) axial flow propeller type with straightening vanes; (**d**) schematic and radial flow pattern in baffled tank; (**e**) schematic of axial flow pattern in baffled tank; (**f**) basic impeller styles; (**g**) walking beam flocculator.

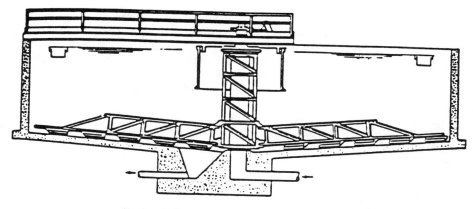

Circular clarifier, center-fed with vertical inlet discharge.

(a)

SLUDGE DISCHARGE LINE

Rectangular sedimentation basin with flight and chain sludge removal system.

(b)

Figure 2. Typical settling basins (a) circular clarifier, center-fed with vertical inlet discharge; (b) rectangular sedimentation basin with flight and chain sludge removal system.

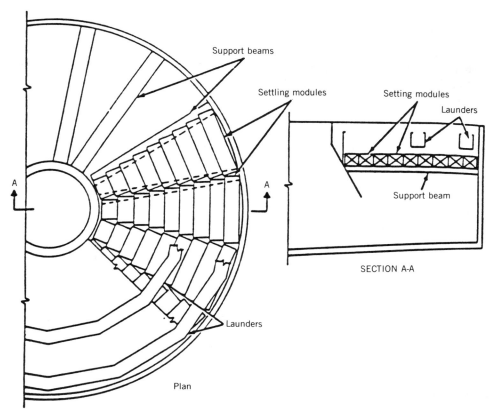

Support beams

Settling modules

Setting modules

Launders

Support beam

SECTION A-A

Launders

Plan

Figure 3. Illustrative tube installation in circular basin.

passing it through a bed of granular material. There are several ways to classify filters. They can be described according to the direction of flow through the bed, that is, as downflow, upflow, biflow, radial flow, horizontal flow, fine-to-coarse, or coarse-to-fine. They may be classed according to the type of filter medium used, such as sand, coal (or anthracite), coal–sand, multilayered mixed media, or diatomaceous earth. Filters are also classed by flow rate. Slow sand filters operate at rates of 0.05–0.13 gpm/ft^2 (0.12–0.32 m/h); rapid sand filters operate at rates of 1–2 gpm/ft^2 (2.44–4.88 m/h); and high-rate filters operate at rates of 3–15 gpm/ft^2 (7.32–36.6 m/h). The rate of filtration is only one factor (and a relatively unimportant one) affecting filter effluent quality. Chemical dosages for optimum filtration, rather than maximum settling, as well as other variables are much more important than filtration rate to the production of good water. Coagulation and filtration are inseparable. They are actually closely related parts of the liquid–solids separation process. Because most water plants utilize sedimentation for a preliminary gross separation of settleable solids between coagulation and filtration, the crucial direct relationship of coagulation to optimum filterability often has been overlooked. Filters may also be classified by the type of system used to control the flow rate through the filter, such as constant rate, declining rate, constant level, equal loading, and constant pressure. Constant rate filtration is the most popular control system in the United States.

Another characteristic is pressure or gravity flow. Gravity filter units are usually built with an open top and constructed of concrete or steel, whereas pressure filters are ordinarily fabricated from steel in the form of a cylindrical tank. The available head for gravity flow usually is limited to about 8–12 ft (2.44–3.66 m), but may be as high as 150 psi (1033 kPa) for pressure filters. Because pressure filters have a closed top, it is not easy to inspect the filter media. Further, it is possible to disturb the media in a pressure filter by sudden changes in pressure. These two factors have tended to limit municipal applications of pressure filters to treatment of relatively unpolluted waters, such as the removal of hardness, iron, or manganese from well waters of good bacterial quality.

Filters are highly efficient in removing suspended and colloidal materials from water. Impurities removed by filtration include turbidity, bacteria, algae, viruses, color, oxidized iron and manganese, radioactive particles, chemicals added in pretreatment, heavy metals, and many other substances. Because filtration is both a physical and a chemical process, there are a large number of variables that influence filter efficiency.

Filter efficiency is affected by the following properties of the applied water: temperature, filterability, and the size, nature, concentration, and adhesive qualities of suspended and colloidal particles. Cold water is notably more difficult to filter than warm water, but usually there is no control over water temperature. Filterability, which is related to the size and adhesive qualities of the suspended and colloidal impurities in the water, is the most important property.

Some properties of the filter bed that affect filtration efficiency are the size and shape of the grains, porosity of the bed (or the hydraulic radius of the pore space), arrangement of grains (whether from fine-to-coarse or coarse-to-fine), depth of the bed, and head loss through the bed. In general, filter efficiency increases with smaller grain size, lower porosity, and greater bed depth. Coarse-to-fine filters contain much more storage space for material removed from the water than fine-to-coarse filters and permit the practical use of much finer materials in the bottom of the bed than can be tolerated at the top of a fine-to-coarse filter.

Hydraulic throughput rate also affects filter efficiency. However, within the range of 2–8 gpm/ft^2 (4.88–19.5 m/h), the rate is not nearly as significant as other variables to effluent quality. In general, the lower the rate, the higher the efficiency. All other conditions being equal, a filter produces a better effluent when operating at a rate of 1 gpm/ft^2 (2.44 m/h) than when operating at 8 gpm/ft^2 (19.5 m/h). However, a given filter may operate entirely satisfactorily at 8 gpm/ft^2 (19.5 m/h) on properly prepared water, yet fail to produce a satisfactory effluent at 1 gpm/ft (2.44 m/h) when receiving improperly pretreated water. With good filter design, the optimum throughput rate is a matter of economics rather than a question of safety.

The efficiency of filters in bacterial removal varies with the applied load of bacteria, but with proper pretreatment, it should exceed 99%. Bacterial removal by filtration, however, should never be assumed to reach 100%. The water must be chlorinated for satisfactory disinfection. Coagulation, flocculation, and filtration remove more than 98% of polio virus at filtration rates of 2–6 gpm/ft^2 (2.44–14.6 m/h), but complete removal is dependent on proper disinfection.

The turbidity of the effluent from a properly operating filter should be less than 0.1 ntu. With proper pretreatment, filtered water should be essentially free of color, iron, and manganese. Large microorganisms, including algae, diatoms, and amoebic cysts, are readily removed from properly pretreated water by filtration.

DISINFECTION

In the United States, the number of outbreaks of diseases identified as waterborne has dropped steadily following the introduction of chlorination of potable water. Of course, improvements in other water treatment procedures (flocculation, filtration, etc) have contributed to the decrease in waterborne disease, but disinfection is, and will remain, the most important treatment process for the prevention of such disease. In recent years, concerns over the long-term health effects of some byproducts of disinfection, especially chlorinated organic compounds, have surfaced. Federal drinking water standards now regulate the amounts of these byproducts through a limitation on trihalomethanes (THMs).

The most common type of disinfectant used for municipal water systems is chemical oxidants, such as chlorine (Cl_2), bromine (Br_2), iodine (I_2), ozone (O_3), and chlorine dioxide (ClO_2). Ozone is also used, especially in Europe. In some small systems, uv radiation has been used.

Chlorine

Chlorine is used primarily in two forms: as a gaseous element or as a solid or liquid chlorine-containing hypochlorite compound. Gaseous chlorine is generally considered the least costly form of chlorine that can be used in large facilities. Hypochlorite forms have been used primarily in small systems (for fewer than 5000 persons) or in large systems where safety concerns related to handling the gaseous form outweigh economic concerns. Chlorine gas is a respiratory irritant, with concentrations in air of 3–5 mg/L by volume readily detectable. It can cause varying degrees of irritation of the skin, mucous membranes, and respiratory system, depending on the concentration and duration of exposure. In extreme cases, death can occur from suffocation.

It is important to know the relative resistances of viruses, bacteria, and cysts to chlorine to be certain that a chlorination practice will be adequate. There are wide differences in the susceptibility of various pathogens to chlorine. Waterborne pathogens, in order of disinfection difficulty, generally are bacteria < viruses < cysts, and the difficulty increases in sewage or water contaminated with sewage. The destruction of pathogens by chlorination is dependent on the water temperature, pH, time of contact, degree of mixing, turbidity, presence of interfering substances, and concentration of chlorine available. Chloramines formed if ammonia is present are much less effective disinfectants than free chlorine. Lower pH and higher temperatures increase disinfection efficiency.

Contact time is an important variable. The EPA has published guidelines on the amount of contact time needed as a function of chlorine residual (2). The product of the chlorine residual (milligrams per liter) and contact time (minutes) is called the "CT" value.

The EPA's CT values for achieving 90% inactivation (the level of added disinfection needed to achieve overall 99.9% inactivation for waters that have had effective pretreatment by coagulation and filtration) of *Giardia lamblia,* one of the more resistant pathogens, are shown in Table 5 for various disinfectants and pH and temperature conditions.

Table 5. CT Values for Achieving 90% Inactivation of *Giardia lamblia*

	pH	0.5°C	5°C	10°C	15°C
Free chlorine[a]	6	60	40	30	20
	7	90	60	40	30
	8	130	90	60	50
	9	170	120	90	60
Ozone	6–9	1.5	1	0.8	0.7
Chlorine dioxide	6–9	27	17	13	9
Chloramines (preformed)	6–9	1270	730	630	500

[a] CT values vary, depending on the concentration of free chlorine. Indicated CT values are for 2.0 mg/L free chlorine.

Ozone

Ozone is a more potent disinfectant than chlorine. The advantages of using ozone are its high germicidal effectiveness, which is the greatest of all known substances, even against resistant organisms such as viruses and cysts, and its ability to ameliorate many problems of odor, taste, and color in water supplies. In addition, its potency is unaffected by pH or ammonia content.

Ozone must be produced at its point of usage because of its short half-life, about 40 min at pH 7.6. It is generated by passing dry air between two high-potential electrodes to convert oxygen into ozone. Improvements in the technology of ozone production have improved the reliability and economy of its generation. The development of dielectric ozone-resistant materials has simplified the design and operation of ozone generators; in addition, new electronic designs have increased the efficiency of ozone production.

Ozone does have disadvantages. Because it must be produced electrically as it is needed and cannot be stored, it is difficult to adjust treatment to variations in load or to changes in raw water quality with regard to ozone demand. As a result, ozone historically has been found most useful for supplies with low or constant demand, such as from groundwater sources. Moreover, although ozone is a highly potent oxidant, it is quite selective and by no means universal in its action. Some otherwise easily oxidized substances, such as ethanol, do not react readily with ozone.

In many ways, the desirable properties of ozone and chlorine as disinfectants are complementary. Ozone provides fast-acting germicidal and viricidal potency, commonly with beneficial results regarding taste, odor, and color. Chlorine provides sustained, flexible, controllable germicidal action that continues to be beneficial during distribution. A combination of ozonation and chlorination has proven to provide effective water supply disinfection.

UV Radiation

Electromagnetic radiation, in wavelengths from 240 to 280 nm, is an effective agent for killing bacteria and other microorganisms in water. A low-pressure mercury arc enclosed in special uv-transmitting glass emits between 30 and 90% of its energy at a wavelength of 253.7 nm.

Uv disinfection systems can be either sealed from the water or open to it. Lamps are placed above the water at the apex of the parabolic reflectors, which typically are aluminum. Because of its open nature, the system can permit contamination and damage. Tubular reactors are most common in water treatment because they are sealed and operate under pressure. Multiple lamp reactors are used to increase throughput. The units generally contain lamps that are positioned parallel to the flow of water through the unit.

The biocidal dose of uv energy depends on the intensity of the absorbed uv energy and the time of interaction. This dose is a function of the following factors:

- The energy input from the uv source.
- Energy dispersion, based on distance from the source.
- The depth of the fluid between the organisms and the uv source.
- The absorptivity of the fluid.
- Losses and reflection of uv light within the contactor.

Also, the repair of uv-damaged nucleoproteins can occur in the dark.

Uv light disinfection does not produce a residual. If a residual is required, a second disinfectant must be used. Current technology is limited to the use of uv light in small systems.

ACTIVATED CARBON TREATMENT

Activated carbon adsorption is the most effective and reliable water treatment process available for the removal of a broad spectrum of organic substances dissolved in water. When organics that are not readily adsorbed constitute a water quality problem, other treatments may be used in place of carbon, or carbon usage may be supplemented by other processes, such as air stripping.

In the past, the principal reason for the use of activated carbon treatment was to control taste- and odor-causing organics. This was mainly for aesthetic rather than public health purposes. To control tastes and odors in water, the carbon dosage requirements are low, and the necessary contact times short. This set of circumstances permitted the application of powdered activated carbon (PAC) rather than granular activated carbon (GAC). The use of PAC was advantageous because in most cases it could be used with no changes or additions to existing treatment facilities other than the installation of powdered carbon storage and feed equipment. Contact time was provided in existing settling basins, and the spent carbon was removed in existing rapid sand filters and disposed of along with the settling basin sludges.

Over the past 15 years, there has been a tremendous proliferation, in number, variety and quantity, of complex organic chemicals used for agricultural, industrial, and domestic purposes. Many of these substances eventually find their way into sources of public water supply. Even in very low concentrations, many of these compounds have toxic, carcinogenic, mutagenic, or teratogenic properties that may produce long-term insidious health effects in water consumers.

Development of this extensive array of new synthetic organic chemicals has been paralleled by the development of new, sophisticated, and extremely sensitive equipment that can detect and measure minute concentrations of these synthetic organics in water. Monitoring capability has progressed rapidly from parts per million to parts per billion, parts per trillion, and beyond.

Compared with the requirements for taste and odor removal, the dosage and contact times are much greater for removal of synthetic organic compounds. This difference in carbon removal efficiency dictates the use of GAC rather than PAC. When GAC is used for taste and odor

control, it is possible to add a shallow bed (1 ft or less) of GAC on top of an existing sand filter, or to substitute a properly sized and graded bed (24–36 in.) of GAC in lieu of the fine media in a rapid sand filter, with satisfactory results. However, experience has demonstrated that such shallow beds of GAC generally are unsuitable for removal of natural or synthetic organics for other control purposes. Deeper beds and longer contact times are necessary for economic, efficient removal of these trace materials. The majority of new installations are separate deep-bed GAC contractors. The contactors may be located in the treatment process train, either ahead of or following plant filters. When GAC contractors are located after the filters, they will be either downflow or an upflow–downflow series configuration in order to avoid the leakage of carbon fines that is common to all upflow carbon beds.

GAC empty bed contact times of from 15 or 45 min are required for most installations. The time to be provided for a particular supply depends on the characteristics and concentrations of the organics to be removed and the other properties of the water to be treated.

Most water treatment plant installations of GAC involve the construction and use of on-site reactivation facilities. One exception is small plants using less than 200 lb of carbon per day (91 kg/d), which can economically use carbon on a once-through, throwaway basis. Another is plants that use between 200 and 1500 lb/d (91 and 681 kg/d) of GAC. Such plants might consider central off-site carbon reactivation if the cost of hauling would permit economical operation.

PAC has been used successfully for more than 50 years to remove taste and odor from public drinking water supplies. In this type of use, PAC dosages usually are in the range of 1–5 mg/L, although dosages as high as 20–30 mg/L have been used in some places for short periods of time when taste and odor problems were severe. PAC is commonly used on a one-time, throwaway basis, with no attempt at recovery or reuse.

The principal benefit of PAC in water treatment is the removal of taste and odor. In some waters, PAC may also remove color or organics that otherwise would interfere with coagulation or filtration.

Removing VOCs

Synthetic VOCs are increasingly being detected in drinking water sources, and particularly in groundwaters once thought to be pristine. Unlike THMs, these compounds are not disinfection byproducts, but are pollutants entering groundwater aquifers through improper storage and handling of chemicals or wastewater disposal activities. They are named VOCs because of their distinctive common property of high volatility with other organic substances such as pesticides.

The presence of VOCs in groundwater poses a threat to one of the nation's most important resources. Approximately 80% of all public water supplies in this country rely on groundwater resources for potable water, and about 96% of all water used for rural domestic purposes (individual home water supplies) is obtained from groundwater. Of the first nine contaminants regulated by the EPA as a result of the 1986 SDWA amendments, eight were VOCs.

VOCs are seldom detected in concentrations greater than a few micrograms per liter in surface waters because the compounds do not occur naturally and are relatively volatile. However, surface water subject to wastewater discharges may contain elevated concentrations of organic solvents during periods of ice cover, when volatilization of these solvents is restricted.

Rather than using treatment to remove the VOCs, the long-term interests of both the water purveyor and the consumer are best served by making available an uncontaminated source. The strategies available for accomplishing this goal are primarily management strategies. They include:

- Elimination of the contaminant source.
- Containment of the contaminant.
- Location of a new water supply source.
- Blending of existing water supply source.

Management strategies have the potential advantage of low capital cost, but they are not always implementable, and treatment must be used.

Other than some reduction resulting from incidental evaporative losses, conventional water treatment consisting of coagulation, sedimentation, filtration, and chlorination has been found to be largely ineffective in reducing the concentration of VOCs. However, because of the generally hydrophobic nature of VOCs and their tendency to partition into other phases, they can be removed by aeration, adsorption, or a combination of these processes.

Aeration is a unit process in which water and air are brought into contact with each other for the purpose of transferring volatile substances to water (gas absorption) or from water (air stripping). The latter process, air stripping, is applicable to VOC control and has been effectively used in water treatment to remove hydrogen sulfide and carbon dioxide and also to remove certain taste and odor-producing compounds. Although the use of air stripping solely for the purpose of controlling trace organics is a relatively new concept in the drinking water industry, for removal of many VOCs it is a cost-effective alternative to adsorption.

Numerous types of aeration devices have been developed in which air stripping can occur. These alternatives may be classified into three general categories:

- Diffused aeration, which involves the injection of air into water.
- Spray aeration, which involves the injection of water into air.
- Waterfall aeration, which involves the cascading of water over media, forming droplets or thin films of water to contact the air.

These techniques are shown in Figure 4. The most efficient method is the packed tower.

Iron and Manganese Removal

Groundwaters generally require treatment for iron and manganese removal much more often than surface waters; only rarely does free-flowing surface water require such treatment. Iron and manganese are dissolved in groundwater supplies by the action of carbon dioxide on carbonate-bearing minerals.

There are many methods used for the removal of iron and manganese in public water supplies. The primary method involves oxidation, precipitation, and filtration. Other methods include ion exchange, stabilization, and lime softening. Specifically, chemicals and methods for controlling iron and manganese include:

- Aeration, precipitation, and filtration.
- Chlorination or chlorine dioxide oxidation, precipitation, and filtration.
- Potassium permanganate oxidation, precipitation, and filtration.
- Ion-exchange (zeolite) softening.
- Manganese–zeolite filtration.
- Stabilization or sequestering.
- Lime softening.

The most common method of removing iron and manganese from water supplies involves aeration, precipitation, and filtration. Simple aeration converts ferrous bicarbonate to insoluble ferrous hydroxide.

The rate of oxidation of Fe(II) by oxygen is slow under conditions of low pH. Aeration of water low in dissolved oxygen and high in carbon dioxide tends to raise the pH slightly because carbon dioxide is easily removed by aeration. Reaction rates are fairly slow at a pH of less than 7, and a pH of 7.5–8 may be required to complete the reaction within 15 min. In some cases, 1 h or more of contact time may be needed to complete the reactions. Organic iron is not removed by aeration. Frequently, another strong oxidizing agent, such as chlorine or potassium permanganate, is required to oxidize and then remove this type of iron.

Sufficient detention time must be provided for oxidation and flocculation of iron and manganese compounds. The kinetics of water supplies vary, and field testing is required. Filtration is always required for final removal of iron and manganese compounds. Sedimentation basins are rarely provided, unless required for other reasons. Detention tanks suffice for reaction/flocculation basins.

FLUORIDATION/DEFLUORIDATION

Fluoride is required for the formation of bones and teeth, and fluoride ions are essential to the normal growth and development of humans. Research over many years has shown that the addition of controlled amounts of fluoride to a water supply provides effective reduction in the incidence of dental decay. Generally, a fluoride level of about 1 mg/L is considered optimum. At fluoride levels below 1 mg/L, some benefit occurs, but the reduction in the dental

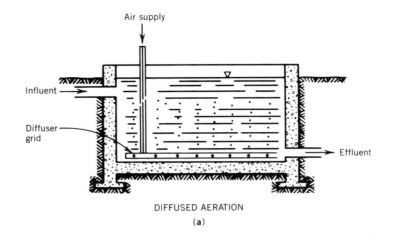

DIFFUSED AERATION

(a)

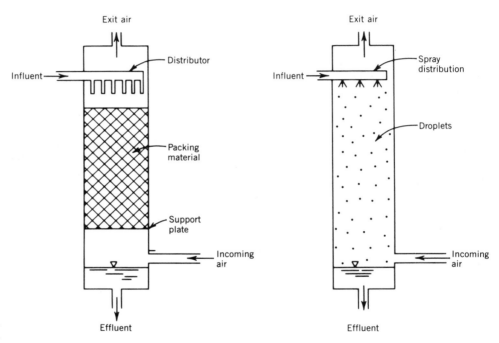

Figure 4. Schematics of air stripping equipment **(a)** diffused aeration; **(b)** waterfall aeration (packed tower); **(c)** spray aeration (spray tower).

WATERFALL AERATION (PACKED TOWER)

(b)

SPRAY AERATION (SPRAY TOWER)

(c)

caries is not great, and it gradually decreases as the fluoride level decreases. High concentrations of fluoride can cause mottling (discoloration) of teeth. When the fluoride level exceeds about 1.5 mg/L, any further increase does not significantly decrease the incidence of decayed, missing, or filled teeth, but does increase the occurrence and severity of mottling.

In water naturally high in fluoride, defluoridation is required. Because water with fluoride concentrations of less than 0.7 mg/L do not have appreciable dental significance, they are generally referred to as "naturally fluoridated." For drinking water with fluoride concentrations below 0.7 mg/L, controlled fluoridation is used to increase the concentration. The process of fluoridation is now practiced in approximately 5000 communities, serving over 80 million persons. The three most commonly used fluoride compounds in water treatment are sodium fluoride (NaF),

sodium silicofluoride (Na_2SiF_6), and fluosilicic acid (H_2SiF_6). Sodium fluoride is the most commonly used.

Fluoride must be injected into all of the water entering the distribution system. If there is more than one supply point, separate fluoride feeding installations are required for each water facility. In a well system, the application can be in the discharge line of each pump or in a common line leading to a storage reservoir. Fluoride can be applied in a treatment plant in a channel or line from the filters or directly in the clearwell. Whenever possible, it should be added after filtration to avoid possible losses due to reactions with other chemicals. Of particular concern are coagulation with alum and lime-soda softening. The fluoride injection points should be as far away as possible from the addition of chemicals that contain calcium because of the insolubility of CaF.

When excessive amounts of fluoride occur naturally,

defluoridation is required. Two methods of defluoridation have found practical application. One involves passing water through defluoridation media such as bone meal, bone char, ion-exchange resins, or activated alumina. The second involves the addition of chemicals such as lime or alumina prior to rapid mixing, flocculation, and sedimentation in a waterworks for the removal of fluoride only or the concurrent removal of fluoride and other ions (eg, calcium and magnesium for water softening).

SOFTENING

Hardness in water is due principally to calcium and magnesium ions. The use of the term hardness originates from the characteristics of the reaction products of soap and the hardness-creating ions. A hard, insoluble, gritty curd is produced that prevents the formation of a lather until sufficient soap is added to react with all of the hardness ions. Hard water increases consumption of soap and may have an adverse effect on clothing and other articles being cleansed. Hardness can also shorten the life and decrease the efficiency of pipes, fixtures, and heating and cooling systems, and water with a high hardness concentration is unsuitable for use in many enterprises, such as laundries, canneries, power plants, ice plants, railroads, and industries using boilers. There are definite economic penalties associated with the use of hard water.

It has been well demonstrated that lime softening of all the water for a community is not only more economical, but also provides better quality water for most purposes than can be obtained from individual domestic or industrial softeners, except where a water of zero hardness is required in a particular industrial application. For general evaluation of relative hardness, the hardness ratings are given in Table 6.

The perception of satisfactory hardness varies in different locations throughout the country, as influenced by the hardness of locally available sources of water supply. For example, people living in New England, where natural waters are soft, might consider a hardness of 100 mg/L excessive, whereas residents of the Midwest or Southwest with naturally hard water sources might consider such a hardness to be satisfactory.

The cost of water softening is generally not considered justified when the hardness of the source of the water supply is less than 150 mg/L. Public water supplies usually are not softened below 30–50 mg/L because softer waters are corrosive unless treated with an alkali. Magnesium hardness concentrations greater than 40 mg/L are undesirable because of the potential for magnesium hydroxide scale formation in domestic hot water heaters.

Table 6. Hardness Ratings

Rating	Hardness, mg/L as CaCo$_3$
Soft	Less than 50
Moderately hard	50–150
Hard	150–300
Very hard	More than 300

To gain the aesthetic and financial benefits of soft water, communities with hard water supplies generally have used either the lime-soda softening process or the cation-exchange process. Economic factors generally limit cation exchange to small water systems.

The main function of a lime-soda softening plant is to remove hardness constituents by first converting them to insoluble precipitates and then separating the precipitates from the water by settling and filtration. Hydrated lime (in small plants) or slaked quicklime (in large plants) is added to the water to react with carbon dioxide and calcium bicarbonates to form insoluble calcium carbonate, with magnesium bicarbonates to form insoluble calcium carbonate and magnesium hydroxide, and with any other magnesium compounds to form insoluble magnesium hydroxide plus soluble calcium sulfate and calcium chloride. If necessary, soda ash is then added to reduce hardness further by precipitating the remaining magnesium hardness, noncarbonated calcium following lime addition hardness, and nonsettled calcium carbonate. Prior to softening, some preliminary pretreatment may be advisable if

1. Raw water turbidities exceed 3000 ntu at times.
2. The raw water has a high concentration of free carbon dioxide (more than 10 mg/L).
3. The raw water is high in organic colloids of a type that impedes crystallization of calcium carbonate.
4. The raw water quality is highly variable over short periods of time.
5. Recalcining of sludge is to be practiced.

Otherwise, the clarification and softening process trains can be combined. Basically, the applicable design standards for mixing, flocculation, and sedimentation are the same for the lime-soda process as for conventional clarification. When the softening and clarification processes are combined, the clarification criteria should govern.

Following lime softening, it is necessary to lower the pH. This is most typically done through recarbonation. The term recarbonation refers to the addition of carbon dioxide to lime-treated water. When carbon dioxide is added in high-pH lime-treated water, the pH is lowered, and the hydroxides are reconverted to carbonates and bicabonates. Thus the term recarbonation is descriptive of the result of adding carbon dioxide to water.

The basic purpose of recarbonation is the downward adjustment of the pH of the water. Properly done, this places the water in calcium carbonate equilibrium and avoids problems of deposition of calcium scale that would occur without the reduction in pH accomplished by recarbonation. In waterworks practice, the carbon dioxide is added to the water ahead of the filters in order to avoid coating the grains of the filter media with calcium carbonate, which would eventually increase the grain size to the point where filter efficiency would be reduced. In waterworks, it is also important to lower the pH of the lime-treated water to the point of calcium carbonate stability to avoid deposition of calcium carbonate in pipelines.

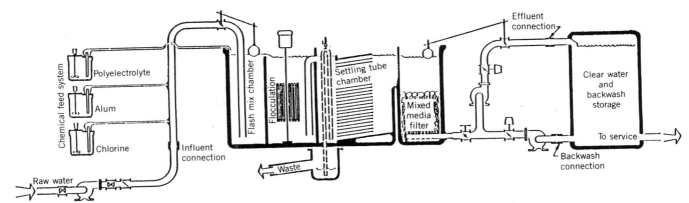

Figure 5. Flow diagram of a type A package plant.

PACKAGE PLANTS FOR SMALL SYSTEMS

Small water treatment systems have a unique set of requirements that distinguish them from larger facilities. These particular requirements are related to the problem of treating water to achieve the same quality as in larger community water systems, but distributing costs over a much smaller customer base. As drinking water quality standards become more stringent, costs increase, further compounding these problems. An economical alternative to the high costs of conventional treatment for small systems is a package plant. Package plants are available within the size range of 0.01–2 million gallons per day (mgd) (0.038–7.6 ML/d).

Package plants can be used to treat water supplies for communities as well as recreational areas, state parks, construction camps, ski resorts, remote military installations, and other locations where potable water is not available from a municipal supply. Several state agencies have mounted package plants on trailers for emergency water treatment. Their compact size, low cost, minimal installation requirements, and ability to operate virtually unattended make them an attractive option in locations where revenues are insufficient to pay for a full-time operator.

The package plant is designed as a factory-assembled, skid-mounted unit generally incorporating a single tank or, at most, several tanks. A complete treatment process typically consists of chemical coagulation, flocculation, settling, and filtration. Package water treatment plants are available from several manufacturers in a wide range of capacities, incorporating a complete treatment process. Design criteria used for these package plants vary widely. Some manufacturers adhere closely to accepted conventional design practices such as 20–30-min flocculation time, 2-h sedimentation time, and rapid sand filters rated at 2 gpm/ft² (4.88 m/h). Other manufacturers have utilized new technology, including tube settlers and high-rate dual- and mixed-media filters, to reduce the size of plants and extend the capacity ranges of single factory-assembly units. The sizable reduction in package plant tankage has greatly increased the capacity attainable in single truck-transportable units. For example, using tube settlers and mixed-media filters, a single factory-assem-

bled, truck-transportable package unit can be built with a capacity of 1 mgd (3.79 ML/d). Following conventional design criteria, a plant of the same physical dimensions would produce less than 0.25 mgd (0.95 ML/d).

A flow diagram for a package plant incorporating these newer techniques is shown in Figure 5. Plants of this type are manufactured in capacities from 10 gpm (0.63–6.3 L/s) to 1400 gpm (12.6–88.4 L/s) by MicroFloc Products of the Johnson division of the UOP Co.

In early 1980, this same package plant manufacturer introduced a new concept in package water treatment plant design, utilizing an upflow filter of low-density plastic bead media, termed an adsorption clarifier, followed by a mixed-media filter for final polishing. The adsorption clarifier package plant utilizes the hydraulic energy of incoming water to mix chemicals and provide flocculation. These package units are very compact and are available in capacities ranging from 350 to 4200 gpm (1.91 to 22.89 ML/d).

Before selecting a package plant for a particular application, a potential user must be certain that it can produce the required quality and quantity of water from the proposed raw water supply. Package plants (especially those employing high-rate unit processes) characteristically have limitations related to the quality limitations of the raw water supply. These limitations must be recognized when considering a package plant. For example, such factors as low raw water temperature, high or flashy turbidity, excessive color, or atypical coagulant dosages (higher than expected based on normal turbidity levels) may influence the selection and rating of a particular package plant. Under certain conditions, on-site pilot tests may be justified and warranted to verify the suitability of a package plant. This is especially important because many of the new package plant designs employ high-rate, short-detention-time unit processes that require close control in order to perform effectively.

BIBLIOGRAPHY

1. Culp, Wesner, and Culp, *Handbook of Public Water Systems,* Van Nostrand Reinhold Co., Inc., New York, 1986.
2. *Manual of Treatment Techniques for Meeting the Interim Pri-*

mary Drinking Water Regulations, U.S. Environmental Protection Agency, Washington, D.C., EPA 600/8-77-005, May 1977.

GORDON L. CULP
HDR Engineering, Inc.
Bellevue, Washington

WEESE, HARRY

Born in Evanston, Illinois, in 1915, Harry Mohr Weese has been a prominent architect in Chicago and nationally since the 1950s. A career in architecture was suggested to him at the age of 10 by his banker father, who considered it a good combination of business and art. Weese attended MIT for three years, Yale for one, and finished at MIT in 1938, earning a Bachelor of Architecture. He then received a fellowship to study city planning with Eliel Saarinen at the Cranbrook Academy in Bloomfield Hills, Michigan. He later called this creative community a "springboard to reality with working artists and architects." Among his fellow students were Charles and Ray Eames, Harry Bertoia, Florence Knoll, and Eero Saarinen. After a six-month stint at the Chicago office of Skidmore, Owings and Merrill (SOM), Weese opened a practice with Benjamin Baldwin, a colleague from Cranbrook, in 1941. When World War II broke out, he enlisted in the Navy and served as an engineering officer on a destroyer until 1945. Weese returned to the architectural world with a year at SOM, and in 1947 established a private practice in Chicago. By 1986, Harry Weese & Associates (HWA) had 42 employees in the original Chicago office and a total of 85 in branches in Washington, D.C., Miami, Los Angeles, Dallas, and Singapore.

Weese's early practice produced some exemplary modernist houses. He was later to design more spatially sophisticated homes for a Canadian island vacation compound and for his own family weekend retreat. In 1950, Eero Saarinen introduced him to Irwin Miller of Cummins Engine Co., who was to develop Columbus, Indiana, as an architectural showplace. Weese and his firm went on to design many buildings for Irwin Miller and the community, becoming the best represented architect in Columbus. His most noted building there is the First Baptist Church, built in 1965 (Fig. 1). Sited on a rise of ground, the building's low brick walls and peaked slate roofs give a first and lasting dramatic impression silhouetted against the sky. It stands unequivocally as an ecclesiastic symbol. According to the architect, the square plan derives from Le Corbusier's monastery at La Tourette in France, while the segmented brick walls are reminiscent of Alvar Aalto. These two architects are the influences Weese most often specifically acknowledges; in both he sees an identification with nature that has had a lasting impact on his own work. As he has stated, "Nature is design."

Weese's relationship to the various schools of Chicago architecture is more ambiguous. Some critics claim that he is a link between the first Chicago School exemplified by Louis Sullivan and the resurgence of Chicago under Mies van der Rohe; others contend that he constitutes a third Chicago all to himself. Weese believes that architects should incorporate the best of the old with the new, and he borrows from all of the city's rich architectural past. In the tradition of Chicago's nineteenth-century vernacular architecture, he has used brick bearing walls for urban housing since 1952. In the Hyde Park Redevelopment, HWA and I. M. Pei reintroduced traditional city planning concepts and the townhouse. Weese adapted the Chicago School bay window as a prominent design motif in the 1955 residential high-rise at 227 East Walton

Figure 1. First Baptist Church, Columbus, Indiana, 1965. Photograph by Balthazar Korab.

Street. The famous maxim of Louis Sullivan, "Form follows Function," was sympathetic to Weese's training at MIT, where functionalism was ascendant, and Weese became a self-avowed functionalist. He likes his buildings to grow from the inside out. Weese's debt to the Chicago vernacular tradition and the Chicago School results in designs that respect their architectural context, a principle that has guided him throughout his career. He said to critic Paul Heyer, "We must respect the valid existing environment while building what is appropriate to present needs." (1)

Weese brought this concern for the surrounding environment, both physical and cultural, to his first international commission, the U.S. Embassy in Accra, Ghana, completed in 1959. The building is raised on tapered concrete piloti to protect walls of louvered native mahogany from termites. The design is a creative response to Ghanian vernacular architecture. In addition, the piloti, with overhang, double roof, and shaded louvers, are a sophisticated response to extreme environmental conditions.

Another prominent early building was the Arena Stage Theater, built in Washington, D.C., in 1962. The nation's first prominent repertory theater-in-the-round is expressed in binuclear form with auditorium, entry link, and support facilities. The shape of the theater is a reflection of the stage geometry itself, with the box seats protruding from outside walls. Inside, lighting apparatus, catwalks, and stage engineering are expressed as functional aesthetic. The success of Arena Stage led to many other commissions for performing arts halls. Among these are the Milwaukee Center for the Performing Arts (1969), housing two small and one large auditoriums; the Grand Rapids Convention Center (1980), seating 2500; and several other smaller theaters for universities.

From the late 1950s through the mid-1970s, HWA did a great deal of planning and designing for expanding colleges throughout the United States. The firm developed and built master plans for Cornell College and Drake University in Iowa, and Reed College in Oregon. HWA created entire collegiate communities such as St. Louis's Forest Park Community College and Lake Michigan College in Benton Harbor, Michigan. The firm built the South Lower Campus Complex and Elvejhem Art Center for the University of Wisconsin; libraries at the University of New York and at the University of Massachusetts; and science facilities at the University of Colorado, Beloit College in Wisconsin, and a half of a block at Mayo Clinic in Rochester, Minnesota.

In the Terman Engineering Building at Stanford (1977), Weese tried to foster both a humanistic environment for its users and a rapport with the original nineteenth-century university architecture. The L-shaped building encloses a reflecting pool on two sides. Its many windows ensure that every space within the building has natural light and a view of the surroundings. Sliding shutters protect against sun glare, and the building is largely cooled by natural ventilation. The building's beige stucco panels and red tiled roof respond to the original sandstone and tile buildings of the university. HWA did the same at the University of Colorado in Boulder.

In 1966, HWA was awarded the contract for the design of the new Washington, D.C. Metro system, a 100-mile, light-rail network. For the first time, an architect was hired to design a complete system as an equal to the engineers. HWA had the unique first-time opportunity in the United States to produce a system-wide design. Weese contributed wide-reaching innovations. The first concern was for the people who were to use the system. The single-tunneled stations with high coffered vaults, and without space-breaking columns, have proved to be safe and graffiti-free and are a source of civic and national pride. Following the subsequent establishment of a Washington office, the firm became recognized in the transit field, attracting additional system commissions in Buffalo, Miami, Los Angeles, and Dallas.

Weese applied his technical ingenuity to large office buildings. The Time-Life Building (1968), a 30-story tower in Chicago, was his first major office building. Critics have called it Weese's most Miesian building, although it explores additional terrain. The underlying concrete structure has a skin of Cor-Ten steel and bronze glass, with prominently inverted spandrels. The indented spandrel panels at every story, combined with the windows, add a strong horizontal emphasis and pay homage to the original Chicago School. The Time-Life Building was perhaps the first U.S. office building to use tandem elevators. The monumental bilevel lobby derives its form from these elevators, with their two stacked cabs serving alternate floors. This system efficiently transports the large number of rush-hour employees.

For the Mercantile Bank in Kansas City (1975), HWA devised a novel fire protection system that circulates liquid coolant through the building's structural steel columns. Weese solved a number of unusual problems in Chicago's Metropolitan Correctional Center, a high-rise, minimum-security detention facility completed in 1978 (Fig. 2). The triangular floor plan allows individual perimeter cells, each with an efficient slit window, yet assures adequate internal common space. He elaborates on the triangular floor plan concept in 200 S. Wacker, an office building in Chicago (Fig. 3). This aluminum and mirror glass structure is composed of two triangular towers of different heights joined to form a trapezoid, which effectively exploits the site.

HWA also utilized unorthodox shapes in high-rise housing, experimenting with multifaceted facades to produce the greatest volume for the least perimeter. These "inside–outside" plans also make the most of internal space planning and external views. A housing project for the U.S. Embassy in Tokyo (1982) is a gentler innovation (Fig. 4). The compound includes three-stepped apartment towers and a series of townhouses. To mitigate the overfamiliarity that results from the inhabitants both living and working together, careful attention was given to create a sense of privacy. In the often chaotic visual environment of Tokyo, the design has internal cohesion, yet responds to much of the particular Japanese sense of material, texture, and lifestyle.

Harry Weese's willingness to curb his own design creativity to preserve older buildings is unique in an architect of his stature. Hailed by *Time* magazine in 1974 as the "Preservation Man," he fought to save and renovate some

Figure 2. Metropolitan Correctional Center, Chicago, Illinois, 1978. Photograph by Hedrich-Blessing.

amusement parks, more marinas, shops, and cafés under a raised Lake Shore Drive, and even new islands in Lake Michigan. Weese's persistence has paid off with concrete results. In the late 1970s, he catalyzed an urban renaissance in the South Loop area of Chicago. With a small group of architects and developers, he bought a series of loft buildings called Printing House Row and helped turn them into apartments and retail space. The area has become a thriving new neighborhood, with trendy shops and restaurants, and is even healthy enough to support proposed new construction by HWA. Weese also masterminded Wolf Point Landings, a riverfront community at the bend of the Chicago River, consisting of a cold-storage warehouse already converted to lofts, four riverside homes in construction, and planned apartment buildings, hotel, and marina.

Harry Weese & Associates received the prestigious AIA Firm of the Year Award in 1978. Weese's personal

of Chicago's most noted monuments. His most publicized rescue was the Adler and Sullivan Auditorium Theatre, which in the mid-1960s had been abandoned for 20 years and was awaiting destruction. Weese insisted that he could renovate it at a fraction of the projected cost, and in 1968, the Auditorium was reopened, restored to its original 1887 gold-leaf grandeur. Other restorations include the Field Museum, Newberry Library, and Orchestra Hall in Chicago, as well as the St. Louis Post Office. Even his offices reflect his concern for the coexistence of the old and the new; since 1966, HWA has inhabited a remodeled nineteenth-century warehouse in a formerly depressed area of downtown Chicago.

Weese's interest in preservation extends to a concern for the active life of the city as well as for its individual buildings. Since the 1950s, when he decried the middle class exodus to the suburbs, Weese has tried to spark an urban revival in Chicago. A disciple of Daniel Burnham, he has plans to extend the original Burnham plan, turning Chicago's lakefront into a giant pleasure garden, with

Figure 3. 200 South Wacker, Chicago, Illinois, 1981. Photograph by Bill Hedrich/Hedrich-Blessing.

Figure 4. U.S. Embassy Housing, Tokyo, Japan, 1982. Photograph by HWA.

honors include Chicagoan of the Year for 1978 (awarded by the Chicago Press Club) and the Distinguished Service Award from the Chicago Chapter of the AIA in 1981. He holds honorary degrees from Northwestern University, Catholic University of America, Columbia College, and DePaul University. Weese was a member of Citizen's Advisory committees under Presidents Johnson and Nixon, and in 1974, President Ford nominated him for a six-year term on the National Council of the Arts. He has been an architectural consultant for two mayors of Chicago and is currently active as a member of the Design Arts Committee for the National Council on the Arts. He also was a pivotal jury member in the Vietnam War Memorial competition.

Although Weese's buildings are famous for not conforming to a uniform or predictable style, they spring from an underlying depth of conviction. His constant respect for context, whether architectural, historical, or social, gives his work its own idealistic consistency.

CATHARINE WEESE
Harry Weese & Associates
Chicago, Illinois

WEIDLINGER, PAUL

Born in Budapest Hungary, in 1914, Paul Weidlinger began his engineering training at the Technical Institute in Brno, Czechoslovakia, where he received a B.S. in 1934. He then entered the Swiss Polytechnic Institute in Zurich, receiving an M.S. in 1937. Weidlinger left Zurich for Paris, where he worked as designer in Le Corbusier's office until the outbreak of World War II, when he departed

for Bolivia. As Director of Engineering for the Sociedad Constructura Nacional (1939–1942) and Chief Engineer of the Bureau of Reclamation (1942–1943), Weidlinger oversaw the design and construction of large public works projects, including a massive concrete dam. In 1943, Weidlinger came to New York, where he entered the office of Fellheimer and Wagner as a structural engineer.

Beginning with his first U.S. publication, "Architecture and Reinforced Concrete" (1), Weidlinger established his reputation as a brilliant and innovative solver of difficult architectural engineering problems. Of particular note during this period of professional development was his collaboration with Konrad Wachsmann on the development of Wachsmann's long-span truss systems.

He was, in the early 1950s, one of the first to explore the structural and architectural uses of aluminum, particularly the development of the aluminum curtain wall for high-rise buildings. Additionally, his proposal (with Mario Salvadori) for long-span lightweight concrete shell structures and a self-supporting concrete stadium (project, 1950) were the subject of considerable interest in the early 1950s.

In 1949, Weidlinger founded Weidlinger Associates in Washington, D.C., as an engineering firm specializing in the design of architectural structures. From the beginning, the firm pioneered in the field of structural engineering for buildings. Among the most innovative of its designs were the design of the first satellite communications antenna, Telstar, and other steerable antennas for Bell Laboratories; the Reader's Digest Building in Tokyo, built to withstand the violence of seismic events, yet at the same time maintaining an image of "the traditional Japanese qualities of lightness and grace in modern materials of concrete and steel" (2); the brutalist, exposed concrete design of Marcel Breuer's Whitney Museum in New

York; and the parabolic-shelled Priory Church in St. Louis, Mo. (1962). In 1958, the firm developed the MEBAC theatre, the first application of an air-inflated, lens-shaped membrane roof, 145 ft in diameter. In order to better understand the motion of building, the Weidlinger firm developed a methodology for analyzing the elastic–plastic response of structures under dynamic loads (1963). The firm was also a pioneer in the development of the use of the computer to solve increasingly complex structural problems.

The firm also evolved. In 1954, Salvadori formed a separate division to solve problems in applied mechanics. In 1962, the firm became a partnership. In 1976, a third division, civil engineering, emphasizing bridge design, was added. Weidlinger Associates is now a partnership of consulting engineers with its headquarters in New York City and branch offices in Cambridge, Mass.; Chesapeake, Va.; Menlo Park, Calif.; Orlando, Fla.; and Brussels, Belgium. The distinguishing characteristic of the work of Weidlinger Associates is the close cooperation between its engineering design division and its applied science division. This close link has allowed them, with the active assistance of computers, to take a leading role in several aspects of structural engineering and applied mechanics. In particular, this has permitted them to perform pioneering work in structural design and research.

In high-rise building design, Weidlinger's scheme for Eero Saarinen's CBS building in New York (1962) made it the first reinforced concrete high-rise office building erected in New York. A 1966 U.S. Steel Company-sponsored study of high-rise steel office buildings resulted in the development of the flame shield concept, which eliminated the need for fireproofing deep spandrel beam webs. This feature became the most distinctive element of New York's One Liberty Plaza, the first high-rise to use this concept. In 1975, the firm developed the shear field panel concept, an extremely efficient system of wind bracing for high-rise steel structures, using precast concrete panels with window openings on the facade of the skyscraper. By incorporating both the enclosure and the wind bracing functions directly into the facade, it combined the structural advantages of a tube structure with the economic advantages of prefabrication. This type of innovation resulted in designs for such buildings as the Georgia Pacific Headquarters in Atlanta, Ga., and One Financial Center in Boston, Mass.

In long-span designs, the firm maintained a distinctive lead. After MEBAC, it developed a fabric and tripod steel arch system to cover the Tropical Forest Pavilion at the Franklin Park Zoo in Philadelphia, Pa. In the mid-1970s, the firm also proposed a fabric-covered megastructure for a General Services Administration (GSA) office building and another fabric-covered stadium for Saudi Arabia. In 1975, a seven-acre tension structure was proposed for a zoo in Boston. In the area of long-span trusses, the firm is best known for the design of the Philip Morris manufacturing plant in Richmond, Va., the Birmingham-Jefferson Civic Center Coliseum (1973), and the Marriott Marquis Hotel (1985) in New York City. Its most recent ventures have included the design of the space frame for the Jacob Javits Convention Center in New York (1987). The firm is currently beginning work on a new transportation center at John F. Kennedy Airport that will serve as a hub to existing terminals and a people mover system.

In bridge design, the firm is best known for its competition-winning 1965 Great Belt Bridge project to cross a three-mile strait between the Danish islands of Zealand and Funen. This was the first application of a tubular, self-anchored, prestressed concrete suspension bridge. Its two unique and interdependent features were a cylindrical prestressed shell that was to act as the stiffening girder and a self-anchoring cable system. The girder was a suspended tube through which the traffic was to run. The civil engineering division has more recently been involved in the rehabilitation of large suspension bridges, including the Manhattan and Bronx Whitestone Bridges in New York and the Benjamin Franklin Bridge in Philadelphia.

Weidlinger Associates' prominence in the field has encouraged it to produce, besides the Great Belt Bridge, several visionary proposals in various engineering fields and building types. One of its more visionary proposals was for a floating airport, or FLAIR, commissioned by the Institute for Defense Analysis (1969). To be located offshore in as much as 600 ft of water, this platform would serve as a turning point for transatlantic flights, alleviating the congestion at existing airports in the New York area.

Another strength of the firm is in the development of protective structures under blast loadings. The firm was responsible for the design of many bomb-resistant hangars at U.S. Air Force bases and has gone on to develop guidelines for protective design of new embassy buildings. As special consultant to the State Department, it developed design criteria that afford maximum protection from terrorist attack.

On a more pacific bent, the firm has also provided engineering support services to major artists, including Dubuffet, Picasso, and Noguchi, for the design and placement of large-scale sculptures. At the General Electric Headquarters Building, the Daily News Building, and the National War College, the firm has honed and polished its skills in the restoration of landmark buildings.

In recognition of Weidlinger's distinctive gifts as an engineer, he was awarded the Frank Brown Medal by the Franklin Institute in 1986, and in 1985 the American Institute of Architects conferred an Institute Honor on the firm.

BIBLIOGRAPHY

1. P. Weidlinger, "Architecture and Reinforced Concrete," *Pencil Points,* **24,** 58 (Aug. 1943).
2. "History of Weidlinger Associates," Weidlinger Associates, New York.

General References

Reference 1 is a good general reference.

"Cooperation Between Architects and Engineers," *Progressive Architecture/Pencil Points,* **27,** 81–86 (June 1946).

"Concrete Construction," *Encyclopedia Americana,* Vol. VII, New York, The Americana Corp. 1947, pp. 465–474.

"Welding, Its Implications and Applications, Part I," *Progressive*

Architecture, 79, 29–81 (June 1947); "Welding, Its Implications and Applications, Part II," **29**, 78–81 (July 1947).

"Aluminum as a Structural Material, Part I," *Progressive Architecture* 77 (Sept. 1948); "Aluminum as a Structural Material, Part II," *Progressive Architecture,* (Oct. 1948).

"Tomorrow's Structural Theory," *Architectural Forum,* **91,** 104 (Aug. 1949).

"Implications of Lightweight Aggregates," *Architectural Record,* **106,** 149 (Nov. 1949).

"A New Approach to Safety of Buildings," *Architectural Record,* **112,** 29 (Oct. 1952).

"Aluminum Curtain Walls in the USA," presented at the *Symposium on Aluminum in International Architecture,* (Aug. 23, 1957).

"Design Principles," *Encyclopedia Britannica,* Architectural Engineering Section, Vol. 2, Encyclopedia Britannica Co., New York, 1962, p. 275D/E/F.

"Preliminary Design for Multistory Steel Structures," *Architectural & Engineering News Digest* 57, 67–69 (Aug. 1963).

"Temperature Stresses in Tall Reinforced Concrete Buildings," *Civil Engineering,* 58–61 (Aug. 1964).

"A Look at the Future of Structural Design," *Architectural Record,* **138,** 172–174 (Jan. 1965).

"Structural Requirements of a Building," *Building-Research,* 2(3), 5 (May–June 1965).

"Floating Airport," *Ocean Industry* (May 1970).

"Una Nuova Concezione per lo Studio del Contraventamento di Edifici Alti in Acciaio," *Acciaio,* 525–528 (Oct. 1971).

See also SALVADORI, MARIO

STEVEN BEDFORD
Middlebury, Connecticut

WELDED CONNECTIONS.   See STRUCTURAL STEEL

WEST AFRICAN VERNACULAR ARCHITECTURE

TRADITIONAL RURAL DWELLINGS OF WEST AFRICA

The recovery of vernacular domains and the emergence of a renewed interest in traditional architecture in the past decade have coincided with a growing awareness of the social and environmental defects of standardized technology. Much has been written to criticize both the Enlightenment myth of progress and its opposite, the nostalgia for lost values. If, in the United States and in Europe, there is a need among architects to move beyond modernization and its emphasis on optimized technology, in non-Western countries, there is imperative to work out the paradox of how to benefit from modernization while at the same time returning to the wisdom of traditional ways of building.

The built environment of hundreds of ethnic groups throughout Africa presents an impressive variety of adapted design principles and building techniques that belie the widespread image of the primitive hut readily attributed to rural Africa. A fuller understanding of the fundamental constituents of architecture such as type, space, form, function, and the concept of dwelling may be gained through the study of traditional habitations, which materialize the collective perception of a society of men's and women's place in the universe and the relationship they develop with their physical, sociologic, and spiritual environments. However, the great variety and diversity of rural dwellings as well as of beliefs and practices in Africa make it very difficult to write about African architecture as a whole. This comprehensive view limits its area of survey to the region of West Africa, which extends south of the Sahara desert, including Mauritania, Mali, Burkina Faso, Niger, and the coastal countries of Senegambia, Guinea-Bissau, Guinea, Sierra Leone, Liberia, Ivory Coast, Ghana, Togo, Benin, Nigeria, and Cameroon.

Before examining the types of dwellings and the skills and knowledge of local materials involved in West African traditions of building, it is necessary to offer an insight into some aspects of the cultural context that produces and is generated by this architecture. Despite the vast and complex range of culture-types within this region, there are recognizable common characteristics that make it possible to advance a few generalizations likely to promote a better understanding of the integrity of African built environments.

THE CULTURAL CONTEXT

The House as Sign of Community

Building, as one of the primary texts for handing down a tradition and presenting a view of reality, is a group solution to habitation problems—communally worked out, reaffirmed, and readapted accordingly by each generation. However, the practice, carefully transmitted from one generation to another, provides not a rigid framework for conformity but basic tools for creativity. Many foreigners coming to Africa have described the villages as a collection of similar houses. Yet these houses strongly bear the individual imprint of those who live in them; no two houses look alike in a village despite the similar materials, plan, and spatial organization they share. Every owner participates in the design process; building, maintaining, and adjusting one's house is part of one's rhythm of life. That task is shared by the whole family, if not by the entire village, as in cases of fire or natural disaster. It functions as a social regulator, strengthening the cooperative spirit, stimulating creativity, and performing an educational role.

The house is a manifestation of a community identity. Knowledge of the model is not in the possession of a specialist but of all the members. Size, layout, relation to site, aesthetic quality, and technique and order of construction are determined according to principles honored by everyone through collective assent. The house is the most personal of ethnic traits. Wherever they go, immigrants bring their architecture with them, so that it is not unusual, for example, to find two or three types of house in a village whose segmented heterogeneous communities present a cultural and linguistic diversity due to migration. Home should convey a sense of familiar ground, in symbolic as well as functional terms. Knowing that all the houses of one's community conceal a single plan, that none will disorient the visitor who is a member of the community, welcomes as well as maintains feelings of ethnic solidarity. Form in this context ignores dissension and division. Singularized chiefly by each builder's and dweller's particularities, architecture is at once personal and communal; it materializes the community's unity as it also marks the difference between one group and another.

The House as Materialization of the Spoken Word

"There where the African man is, religion is" wrote the philosopher John Mbiti (1) who affirmed that African traditional societies do not know of any areligious man. Such a concept of religion should, in fact, not be understood in terms of an institution that provides clear distinctions between what is sacred and what is secular and opposes the spiritual aspect of life to its material aspect. More integral to the everyday behavior of a person or a community, the religious vision of the world in African contexts is, as A. Hampate Ba states, "the bond between man and the spoken word" (2). The universe is perceived in terms of forces in perpetual motion—"a vast cosmic unity [within which] everything is connected, everything is bound solidly together; and man's behavior both as regards himself and as regards the world around him (the mineral, vegetable, animal world and human society) is subject to a very precise ritual regulation, which may vary in form with the various ethnicities and regions" (3). The African people are thus said to carry religion with them wherever they go, whatever they do: in the fields where they sow and harvest; in a beer gathering; in a funeral ceremony; in a music interaction; in the telling of stories; in the making of potteries; in the weaving of cotton; or in the building-as-dwelling process that punctuates the rhythm of their lives.

All history is myth. "A mythical approach lies at the origins of every nation's history" remarks Boubou Hama and J. Ki-Zerbo: "every history starts off as religious history" (4). Oral traditions, also known as the religions of the Spoken Word, engage men and women in their total beings, speaking to them according to their understanding. They are at once "religion, knowledge, natural science, apprenticeship in a craft, history, entertainment, recreation" for, "speech is the externalization of the vibrations of forces, [and] every manifestation of a force in any form whatever is to be regarded as its speech. That is why everything in the universe speaks: everything is speech that has taken on body and shape" (5). The bond between dwelling and dweller in this context means a spiritual, dynamic perception of architecture in which every single humanmade object, every piece of land, every environmental presence vibrates with life and is likely to act on every human's existence. If the village, the house, all settlements in Africa have the quality of human-the-maker, human-the-speaker written all over them, this never physically appears as a result of human control over nature, but more as an interaction with nature's vital spirit

or its descending on the community. The human dimension, the human scale, and the human touch of this architecture, which are the qualities commonly admired by foreigners and valued by urban architects attempting to put tradition to use in contemporary practice, remind above all that the relation of men, women, and building does not necessarily have to be one of oppression and submission (as often seen in modern societies); it can be one of mutual vulnerability.

The House as Site of Fertility: Earth and Water

In a world view where everything is intimately linked together, and where a remarkable rapport exists between humans and their surroundings, all acts are bound to reverberate on one another. To settle down in a specific place, to enclose space, and to define a precise locality is, as one may say, to stop the free flow of the spirit of the earth. It is to leave a mark on the body of mother earth and to make an impression on the landscape.

Such an act of alteration entails acts of pacification (most often carried out with the mediation of the local custodian of the earth), for the earth is not a mere piece of land to live on and abuse to one's liking, but an awe-inspiring living complex by which life springs and to which life returns (at death). One tampers with it at one's own peril, hence the necessity to take long-term views of habitats. Settlement involves a disruption of natural order because clearing the forest, enclosing open land, plowing, and digging are acutely felt by the people as affecting the forces of the earth. In traditional communities, not only the materials could not be plundered from the land, but they are used only according to their availabilities, that is to say, in such quantities and in such periods of the year as to cause minimal harm to the surroundings. Permanence and security are not gained through the durability of the building materials, but through the maintaining, expanding, and renewing of the buildings by the family over generations. The relationship of people with their built environment is a continuous relationship of participation rather than of mere use. This, most likely, is the force in perpetual motion that creates the bond between building and dwelling, between man and the spoken word.

"Who spoils one's word spoils oneself" says the African adage. To build is a religious act. It is to partake in the primal myth of creation, in which "God shaped man out of earth and water" as explained by the Dogon sage Ogotemmeli (6). Air, earth, water, and light are the four fundamental elements that account for the beginnings of the world and the making of men and women in West African mythology. They are also the very elements made manifest in the concept of building, which is an act of establishing a habitable world in the midst of primeval "wordless" disorder (the Yoruba call habitable land, *ile aiye* or House of the World. Houses, like humans, are created out of small balls of earth taken from the earthen fabric of the ancestor's body; they are both said to be earthborn and earthbound. In Yoruba (Nigeria), Nuna (Burkina Faso), Tamberma (Togo), and Dogon (Mali) myths, for example, the first men and women were all molded from clay and were given life by God's breathing into their ears. A Tamberma custodian of the earth thus relates the process of child conception (7):

> He [the ancestor] uses this ball to make the child. Earth is for strength. This earth is mixed with clay because clay is both elastic and resistant. The water used to moisten the earth is the blood. Stones in the earth are the bones. For breath, he made a hole and blew air into it.

The water–earth relation is also, as seen earlier, one of essentially similar importance in Dogon cosmology. According to Ogotemmeli, "The life-force of the earth is water. God moulded the earth with water. Blood too he made out of water. Even in stone there is this force, for there is moisture in everything" (8). If water here is the divine seed whose penetration into the womb of the Earth resulted in the birth of the Pair Nummo (the essence of God or Water, the two spirits of opposing sex who were at the origin of the ancestors of men and women), breath is Nummo in motion, the vapor that constituted speech and the moisture (water-word) Nummo brought down to their Mother in the fibers with which they clothed her, giving thereby a language to the Earth and putting an end to the disorder of the universe (9). Furthermore, Nummo is light for, as Ogotemmeli also explained it (10):

> if Nummo is water, it also produces copper. When the sky is overcast, the sun's rays may be seen materializing on the misty horizon. These rays, excreted by the spirits, are of copper and are light. They are water too, because they uphold the earth's moisture as it rises. The pair excrete light, because they are also light.

The substance of the Dogon man's and woman's creation may thus be summed up as: water, the divine seed, indispensable to the molding of clay, and the spoken word, or fertilizing word, whose passage through a woman's body maintains the moisture necessary for procreation. (It comes in from a bisexual aperture, the ear, and goes directly to the female sexual parts, where it encircles the womb as the copper spiral encircles the sun.) The water-word theme linked to the process of procreation and birth is commonly found in the primal myths of other peoples of West Africa, most strikingly in those of the Fali (Cameroon, 11), the Mande (Mali, Senegal, 12), and the Ashanti (Ghana, 13). It is also a theme recurrently encountered in the concept of dwelling of a number of groups within this region of Africa. The house image conveyed through available recorded material is often that of a world recreated from the womb of the earth; one whose well-being and fecundity lies both in its symbiotic relation to the breath of nature (or the operative force of the male and female/water and earth principles) and its ability to experience the properties of, hence the energies in, the earth.

Water is integral to the notion of dwelling; this pervades every aspect of West African building tradition and is reflected in the smallest everyday detail of people's lives. Water availability is usually considered one of the critical factors in the choice of a site of any settlement. If, in nomadic architecture, people's displacements are effected in response to climatic conditions and natural resources available to their livestock—of which water is directly or indirectly most important—in sedentary architecture, people often choose to live close to a source of water or to fields for farming. Each source of water has its own spirits, and villagers' knowledge of their community's territory entails knowledge of the locations of the major watercourses, lakes, and rivers far beyond their home base, whether they have been to these places themselves or not. Examples of well-known water deities fears and credited with creation (or endowed with fertility power) are those of the river Tano in Ghana and the Ivory Coast or of Lake Bosomtwe in Ghana and the spirits Zin and Zin-kibaru among the Songhay of Niger. These deities have widespread worship, far beyond the rivers that bear their names. In daily existence as well as in the process of building, the task of fetching and carrying the water necessary for sustenance and for the molding of clayey soil in early construction always devolves to women. Men collect the earth (by digging it, breaking it, and gathering it in small piles), and women provide the water. One factor that remains crucial in the preparation process for building is the correct proportions of water to earth that give it the right consistency. The particles need to cling together without becoming either too runny or too dried up. The Tamberma call such proper mixture of earth and water *titati,* or "moist earth." Furthermore, if the men lay out the foundation, erect the walls, effect the carpentry and the roofing, it is again women who complete the house by plastering the walls, decorating them, and adding all the built-in features that furnish the spaces and thereby organize them in their precise, various functions. In its making process as well as in its structural details, the house is the site where the male and female principles constantly interact.

A good finish coating is both aesthetically (spiritually) and functionally important. Commenting on this question, Tamberma builders make it clear that beauty "depends on both the architect and the plasterers. If he knows how to build well and if the house [woman] knows how to do it well they will say that the house is beautiful when they walk by" and her "arranging it well" means that "the house will last" (14). It is also at coating time that the walls may be painted. The coating is sometimes sprinkled with a decoction of locust-bean pods (*Parkia biglobosa*) that dries into a waterproof finish. Extra-finely crushed laterite usually painted over the coating mixture before applying the decoction gives the walls their reddish, terracotta color. This color can yield many interpretations as to its meaning; one that seems most relevant here is the one that commonly equates red earth to the color of the sun, of blood, hence of the newly born. Among the Bwa (Burkina Faso) for example, a man born again to his community during the rite of initiation must go naked, his body painted with red earth (15). Among the Tamberma, the ideal time to construct a new house is the year in which the men's or the women's initiation begins again after its 4-year cycle. The "new red" of the new house, in conjunction with the "new men" or "new women" is an event of particular significance to the villagers.

The house, like the human body, is cyclically born again to the family inhabiting it. It is dressed, colored, and beautified by adornment marks. Mural decorations belong to the domain of women's creations. The wall designs are either painted, incised, or molded as bas-reliefs. They cover exterior walls, especially the facades looking out to the courtyards, and are most often found around the frame of doorways and on interior walls and built-in furnishings. Each design motif bears a name and has its own repertoire of significations whose articulation depends on the overall context in which it is located. Some of the motifs commonly encountered, for example, among the Kassena and Nankani (Burkina Faso) include horizontal triangles, triangles or lozenges filled with alternate oblique hatchings, vertical straight lines, vertical zigzag lines, half circles, which come in countless variations as signs of calabashes, filed teeth, triangular amulets, guinea corn, furrowed field, water, and potteries (most of them being objects of particular significance to a woman's realm of activities); these geometric designs are furthermore often juxtaposed with figurative designs such as those of the cane, the hoe (usually molded on the sides of women's doorways), the serpent coiling back on itself or girding the center of the wall surfaces, flowing from one facade to the other or extending around the circumference of a dwelling unit (Fig. 1). Despite their great variety of design, composition, and quality (going from abstract or semi-abstract to highly figurative designs), these motifs, when apprehended in their wholeness, all converge to insist on the life-giver image of the house as human body and on its symbols of fertility and longevity (16).

As commonly observed, the most important shrines to a family within a community are usually those devoted to the earth, water, and the fertility of women. This is often also reflected in certain architectural features of the house. The place where water is to be found is likely to be one of its pivotal points. On entering the dwelling unit of a

Nuna (Burkina Faso) woman, for example, the visitor immediately finds himself or herself in front of a red varnished pot that contains drinking water. Where it is placed is a built-in feature whose shape and bas-reliefs represent furrow patterns and the breast, womb (the pot of water itself), and feet of a woman. Of high significance are its placement—always facing the entrance door and thereby exposed to the only source of light in that space—the care given to the sculpturing and finishing of the figure, and the wealth of its associative connotations: male–female, water–earth rapport of fecundity; woman–water-carrier and water-giver; woman–life–nurturer and childbearer; red like the color of the newly born and the house walls; ready for sowing and productive like the prepared, furrowed field. This, in sum, is the sight that welcomes the visitor to whom water is always given first on arrival.

Another example worth mentioning here is the Joola (Senegal) impluvium house, a most striking and elaborate architectural form of earth building (Fig. 2). The house is built around an inner court with an inwardly inclined roof whose compelling visual effect has never failed to impress foreign observers. The interpretations yielded by the combination of this roof shape and the open, circular ground space it defines are numerous; but none of them seems satisfactory when isolated on its own. By the name given to this type of dwelling, it is commonly assumed among researchers that if the house is built that way, it is because of a question of function: the funnel-shaped roof and the round court serve to collect the rainwater, hence the many names such as interior court, pit, tank to catch rainwater, or rain vessel given to this central opening, which varies in size with each house and takes on as many faces (from a courtyard to a mere spot of light) as there are houses of this type. However, many devices for collecting

Figure 1. Nankani, Burkina Faso. A woman's flat-roof dwelling unit. Note the low arched doorway to her indoor spaces. To the left is the outdoor cooking area roofed with millet stalks, whose access is gained by striding over the low entrance wall. A serpent-decorated ridge girds the center of the wall surfaces.

Figure 2. Joola, Senegal. Impluvium dwelling, axonometric cutaway. (**1**) main entrance veranda; (**2**) interior circular veranda; (**3**) court; (**4**) water jar; (**5**) hearth; (**6**) enclosed granary; (**7**) bed; (**8**) backyard veranda; (**9**) bathing enclosure; (**10**) backyard.

rain water are possible, as observed among other groups of people. Why then, have the water fall in the center of the house so as to have it evacuated outside the house again through an earthen trough? This is a question that remains open to speculation, and is probably not relevant to the context of "a vast cosmic unity" worldview. Whatever the interpretation advanced, there are a few factors that can be considered here. This interior open space changes from one house to another, hence the impossibility to give it a fixed function: as an interior court, it offers a place for family reunion, for rest and conversation (people like to sit around the light source): more defined by the roof however, it also serves as a time clock (women's daily activities evolve around it and are influenced by the quality of the light available); finally, it is the very place where each household's jar of drinking water is located: people come into contact with the sunlight or the moonlight when they have access to the water.

The House as Basis for Regeneration: Social Viability Through Children and Ancestors

A mythical, social, and functional grasp of the water–earth rapport is in a way fundamental to the understand-

ing of the mutual dependency, in West African architecture, between light and darkness, outside and inside, and between the world of the living and that of the deceased. Foreigners visiting the houses in Africa have consistently wondered at the lack of light of their interiors. The scarcity of openings on the roofs and on the walls as well as their small sizes make it very difficult if not impossible for a person from the outside to see inside. To have access into the interior realms of a house is to undergo a change, both physical and spiritual. Blindness is bound to occur when one steps in from the bright outside sunlight. The progress into the inside of a house is a progress into its darkness. Insight, figuratively speaking, always entails moments of blindness. To advance, one must go sightless during the time it takes to adjust one's eyes and as one crosses the immaterial (light/darkness) threshold that links the social to the personal.

Abrupt transition from light to dark marks the daily rituals of the acts of entering and exiting. Architecture promotes an awareness of dwelling as social intercourse. Penetration into the house entails a renewal of contact with the Earth spirit of fecundity, therefore a renewal of life-force resources; it is a pause for retreat and revitalization as well as for procreation. The flow of progress carries on its course and, taking a new lease on life, goes hand in hand with the necessity to leave death and to bring new lives into the community. This is further materialized in architecture by the great importance given to the physical appearances of doors and entranceways. Strong emphasis is commonly laid on the placement, shape, size, adornment, symbols, and/or constitution of the entrance door, which forms a site for rites of passage and is also indicative of the status of the house—the hierarchic rank of the occupant within the family as well as within the community. Striking examples may be found, for example, in the architecture of the Massa (Cameroon); the Moba and the Konkomba (Togo); the Bisa, the Mossi, the Kassena, the Nankani and the Kusasi (Burkina Faso), whose peculiar doorways are all equipped with a screen wall with heights varying from one group to the other. Characteristic of the system of entry that gives access to the woman's dwelling unit among the three last groups, is the low, arched doorway framed by a ridge that projects beyond the outer walls of the room. Usually measuring less than a meter high, the doorway requires that one stoop down, head for the dark in this position, then, immediately on entering, stand up halfway to stride over a small semicircular wall (Fig. 3). The doorway thus created not only protects the inhabitants from visual indiscretion, allowing them to retreat and look out without being seen, it also requires that the act of entering and exiting only be done with a marked change of body position. It is bound to slow down outsiders' access into the interior and to discourage all intrusions (a man does not enter a woman's space without notifying her of his presence, or without her consent). Furthermore, besides marking the entrance as the pas-

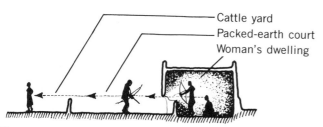

— Cattle yard
— Packed-earth court
— Woman's dwelling

Figure 3. Nankani and Eastern Kassena, Burkina Faso. Section through a woman's dwelling space. The low screening wall of the doorway protects the interior from rain and wind as well as from wild animals. In the past it served as a necessary defensive purpose, allowing the inhabitants squatting inside to have a direct view to their front courts and to the cattleyard. They can thus see without being seen.

sage from the social to the personal, such system of entry also speaks for a concept of the house that belongs to a wider cultural context, in which each dwelling is a materialization of the continuous bond between the living members of a family and its departed ones. Rites of separation and reintegration, or of purification and incorporation related to pregnancy, childbirth, adultery, and death are performed at the entrance of the house. Among the Nankani, for example, the passage through the low circular wall of the doorway marks the different stages of childhood in a person's life. To be properly incorporated into the family group, a child should not be taken out of his mother's room until it can crawl over the wall by itself. Among the Kassena, the final departure of a woman is made explicit by knocking a piece off the top of this screen wall at the doorway of her room. The woman has left this world through the doorway to another world. The unceasing to-and-fro movement of coming and leaving takes on, hereby, all its significance, for the necessity to demarcate a world from and within another is one whose meanings operate on a multitude of levels. As an act of ordering, such necessity prevails, whether these worlds are those of the living within the dead, the visible within the invisible, the past or the future within the present, the inside within the outside, or the familial within the communal; and vice versa.

Both children and ancestors are commonly referred to as "builders up of a compound." (As will be seen further on, the compound or extended family house is constituted by several individual dwelling units inhabited by kin households.) The viability of the family depends on both its guardians and its perpetuators. The presence of the dead is strongly felt by the people; they are everywhere, in the courtyard, in the village, in the field; they are talked to and invoked in case of need and they are kept well-informed on the events within the community. Ancestors' advice is sought in every decision that concerns the well-being of the house or the village. Their responsibility toward their descendants and the community does not end with their departure from life, for death usually means incorporation into the council of ancestors and the afterlife world. Their role among the living continues therefore to be a protective one; their sponsorship is solicited both when a child is born to the family and when a new house is constructed. Access into the house is only gained with the acknowledgment of their presence; and they may grant or refuse entry to those who populate their world. Ancestral shrines (in the forms of conical earthen pillars or mounds) are therefore usually set up in front of the house portal or at the compound entrance. The western orientation of the main entrance frequently encountered in West African dwellings has been given several explanations. Among those available, certain refer to the wind, rain, and terrain topography factors. However, for the Tamberma, it is said that the house is so oriented because it has to face the village of the Sun and as a villager explains, "the dead people are in the west, therefore the doors of our houses face west so that they can return there" (17).

The sign of a family's wealth and prosperity does not lie in the large size of the rooms of the dwelling units within the compound. It shows, rather, in the very number of rooms and of dwelling units. The larger the family, the quantitatively grander the house. "A damaged house," as an African saying goes, "is a damaged family." Family and house often bear the same name. The concept of wealth and of power deriving from the people rather than from landed property or from the extent of conquered land is one that is manifest in many aspects of African dwelling and in the social organization of the compound. In many instances, such as among the Kusasi (Burkina Faso) or the mountain peoples of northern Cameroon, the compound grows with each new wife or each daughter-in-law who joins the family. It spreads further as they become mothers, for a woman having no offspring usually possesses only one room. As soon as she gives birth to a child, however, she may expect to have a second room built at the beginning of the next dry season. Modifications are then made to expand her unit within the unity of the compound. To have progeny is to continue to build and to have a house "that lasts." A man who has no children, says the Nankani, is often laughed at or pitied because if he were to die, "they would break down [his] house and plant tobacco in it" (18). Thus, a beautiful compound is one whose dwelling units keep on multiplying, just like a well-to-do family is one whose members keep on proliferating. Longevity in building, as seen earlier, is a concept that derives from participation or from the joint effort of the people—children and ancestors of the earth who are the guarantors of continuity.

"To draw up and then return what one has drawn—that is the life of the world" explained Ogotemmeli, who referred here to the coming and going action of the sun, its making the waters of the earth rise and descend again in rain (19). It is neither the sun nor the earth, neither light nor darkness that constitutes life, but the interactive movement of both. The house, like the womb of the earth, lives and is ready to produce life when its force converges with that of the sun. It is said that if light is the lifeblood of a space, darkness can be called its soul. The smaller the opening of an enclosure, the stronger and more precise the light. The darker the space, the brighter the light perceived. Of importance in many West African earth dwellings is the location in the roof of sources of light (if any) other than the one led in from the doorway. Apertures formed by means of broken-bottom pots stuck into the terrace roof at construction time, or moulded on the very top as in the domical Musgum houses (Fig. 4), they function both as skylight and as smoke exhaust. A light coming in on the side from a large opening in the wall is much more diffuse than one that strikes from a small one on the top with its beam sharply penetrating the interior of the house and varying its vertical inclination according to the time of the day. Darkness bears a strong luminous quality in a space thus lit by a single powerful shaft of light or by several as in a row. Such a shaft appears even more dramatic as the light intermingles with the cooking smoke escaping through the same opening at certain periods of the day. When one penetrates into the dim, fresh interior of the house, such a sight is likely to induce a quiescent state of mind and to inspire one to collect oneself, for this is again an instance of nature's vital force descending on the community.

It is not unusual to encounter houses that are built

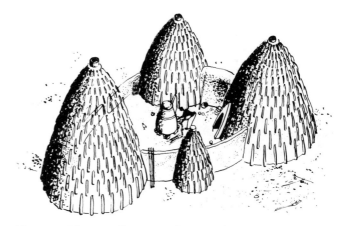

Figure 4. Musgum, Cameroon. Compound constituted by conical shell structures linked to one another around an interior courtyard by connecting walls.

precisely to incorporate the daily movements of the sun in its journey across the sky. The selective way in which the sun enters a house is a factor of common importance in architecture and the Joola impluvium house is one among many possible examples. It is said that the Tamberma build their house as a sanctuary they dedicate to the Sun (*Kouiye*). Each house is thus oriented toward the setting sun so that at dawn the sun begins its itinerary by touching the woman's central bedroom: at noon it strikes through the *tabote* or "house hole" located on the terrace roof of the entrance or cattle room, and associated with the sun at its zenith; and then at dusk it enters the house portal to speak with the family ancestors whose shrines facing the entrance of the house, that is to say, facing west is alignment with the Sun's village, are by this time bathed with sunlight. The *tabote* hole, which is the locus of the house's life and vitality, is as the Tamberma put it, "made so that the Sun . . . looks at the ancestors by this hole and communicates with them." This daily contact is necessary, for the ancestors will always ask the Sun for health. Women, whose bedrooms located on the terrace also face west, will descend to the cattle room under the very *tabote* hole to secure the Sun's blessings when they are about to give birth or to bring new life into the sanctuary (20). One of the characteristics shared by the Birifor and the Lobi (Burkina Faso) houses is their frequent architectural inclusion of an ancestors' room within their interiors. This room, occupied solely by the numerous statuettes that represent the ancestors, is usually of selective access. Situated in the furthest interior of the compound, it is the place where, by a single terrace roof opening, the sun directs its rays inside while one after the other, the council of ancestors take turns to speak to the sun, keeping in touch with it from dawn to dusk.

The House as Cosmos: Gender, Anthropomorphism, and Social Organization

The creation of houses is similar to the creation of humans. The house, like the human body, is made according to principles that regulate the world. It is conceived as a model of the universe. Each part possesses all the characteristics of the whole, and the small, which is accessible to all the human senses, always mirrors the large. Each living thing partakes in the tradition of the Spoken Word. Despite the location, form, structure, and function that determine its specificity, what constitutes its link to every other thing around it are precisely the energies it houses and generates, or the relations it weaves within the order of the universe. All architectural space, be it a granary, a house, a sanctuary, or a village, is a macro-microcosm whose lucidity helps to situate humans within their environmental context and to heighten their awareness of the laws of nature as infinite mutual dependencies within a vast continuum of rapports.

A well-known example of the human cosmic house in West African architecture is the Dogon dwelling whose ground floor is perceived as representing the earth and the terrace roof heaven. It symbolizes at once the union of God and the Earth and that of man and woman. The entrance room is the man with the outside door as his sex. The central room and the store rooms on each side of the building constitute the woman who, lying on her back with outstretched arms and with the communicating door open, is ready for intercourse. The ceiling of this central room being the man still, the beams, his skeleton, and the four poles, the couple's arms, the image is that of a man and a woman together whose breath finds its outlet through the opening above the hearth located in the room at the back of the central room. Concordantly, the Dogon village structure should, ideally, also reproduce the order of the universe through that of the human body. It should extend from north to south like the body of man lying on his back. Like the hearth (air and water) in the house, the smithy (metal and fire) is located in the north or at its head. To the east and the west, round houses for menstruating women are the hands of the village, whereas the family houses in the center are its chest and belly. The grindstone and the foundation altar are its sex and other communal altars further south, its feet. Within the village, each quarter, treated as a complete whole and a separate entity, should be arranged in the same way as the village. Such features are certainly not unique to the Dogon, and striking similarities may be found in the village layout of the Taneka (Benin). Here, the district also mirrors the order of the agglomeration in its entirety, and the 4 parts identified in the village also correspond to 4 anatomic parts of the body. The village ideally lies along an east to west axis (21). Again, among the Fali (Cameroon), the house shows in its founding structure the woman lying on her back, and in its superstructure, the man who fecundates her. The earthen masonry—female element—is topped by the straw-and-wood roofings, which is sustained by pillars—all male elements (22). The house is the site of union for the male and female principals. It is the sign of man and woman in the act of creation.

Because the creation of the first human beings has its parallel in the creation of houses, the composition of the house is usually likened with that of the human body: the earth is the flesh; the water, the blood; the stones, the bones; the plastered surface of the walls, the skin; and the air or smoke, the breath. The naming of spaces in traditional West African architecture does not usually refer to their function such as cooking, living, or sleeping. It refers, in many instances, to the various parts of the body. Those most important are the head, the belly, the sexual organ, the limbs, the jawbone, and the inion, which are considered the most important bones of the body in this context. Thus, the entrance doorway by means of which one enters the interior of the body-womb-house is frequently known as "the mouth." The kitchen, which contains the hearth and is often the starting point for the building of a house, is called "head of the house." The woman's space is usually perceived as the woman's womb and its round entrance, her sex. Thus, it is said that an infertile house is one whose door remains closed. The term used to designate the woman's space (dina) among the Eastern Kassena, for example, carries with it that of a woman who has borne a child (na). The Fali kitchen is said to convey the image of a man with his eyes, shoulders, clavicles, arms, back, and feet, and whose presence is tripled with each of the three main pillars that sustain the family house. A more complex image, which includes the man's chest, belly, navel, penis, and testicles as well as the woman's features (doubling those of the man in their different attributions), is given to the overall composition of the house and its detailed symbolism. The Tamberma house presents another elaborate variant to this image. Features tightly associated with different component parts of the house include the eyes and ears (openings on the wall); the teeth (grindstones); the mouth, tongue, and lips (the front portal, the lintel above it, and the rim of the entranceway roof); the navel, arteries, and testicles (earthen lines and conical extensions above the door); the knees (wooden entrance hooks); the stomach (egg-shaped granaries); the penis (terrace gutter); and the anus (gutter at center back of the house). Slightly different from the Dogon house in its symbolism of the universe, the Tamberma house bears three levels of the world within its interior: the ground level, which stands for the underworld; the terrace level for the earth; and the granaries level for the sky. Its house plan retraces the position of a woman lying prone, head to the east, feet to the west; a position whose orientation is similar to that found in the Dogon house. Here, the head of the house lies in the cattle room alcove (called jawbone), which, situated next to the kitchen and leading to the terrace roof, is considered to be the focus of wisdom and fortune in the house and a referral point for its major constructional phases at the beginning (23).

Whatever aspect one may choose to look at in African architecture, one is led back to the primordial act of creation and to the fundamentals of building as living. To understand is to create. Awareness of the origins of humans is, in fact, never dead knowledge, and what is thought to be primordial or original is always reactivated and multiplied. Moving from births to births or from departures to departures, the cycle of life and death repeats itself in every facet of the concept of dwelling. Each making is a way of relating. The spatial and social organization of the house in this context is, again, a setting into motion of the male and female interactive forces. Where dwelling is a continuous movement of mutually dependent principals, the house is both the result of gendered activities and their generator. Gender shapes space and is in turn shaped by its arrangements. The gender divide varies widely from one cultural zone to another and, as observed, it pervades all aspects of village life. One of the forms it also takes, for example, concerns the repartition of space and of responsibility. In many West African compounds, the outside of the house is perceived as being the men's area of motion, whereas its inside remains the women's domain. The area immediately outside the main entrance is defined as a male area; it is the place in which the senior man's daytime arbor is located. Here the men receive their visitors, and people from different parts of the region gather to attend such rituals as the funeral ceremony. A man is usually not seen inside the house except at meal times or until after sunset. He is expected to be outside most of the day, and one of the places where he is most likely to be found if needed during the dry season months, when he is not working in the fields, is at the village tree or the so-called palaver tree. This is the place where the men of the entire community meet to discuss judicial, administrative, and agricultural matters. It is, like the male pillars that constitute the sustaining force of a house, the referral point of a village. In certain instances, it takes the form of a symbolically elaborate structure, such as the *togu na* among the Dogon. This setting for the men's meetings and collective decision is worth noting here, for *togu na,* which means "the great shelter" or "the mother shelter," is also referred to as "the house of words" or "the men's house," and women do not set foot on it.

The inside of a compound is the ground where most of the women's activities occur. Studies of the building evolution within the compound show, in many cases, that even in societies where the patrilinear system dominates, men used to—many still do today—share the same dwelling unit with their wives. In instances where the man has more than one wife, he will alternately live with each of them, but he does not necessarily have a separate room of his own. The compound is thus composed of dwelling units that correspond to the number of wives within the large family. As long as the man still fulfills his role as impregnator, he remains with his wife(ves) within the compound. However, when with age he is no longer in a position to do so, he may decide to move to a unit, with or without his senior wife, that is situated adjacent to the main entranceway. This site of comings and goings is the point of transition not only between the familial and the external worlds, between life and the afterlife, but also between the woman's and the man's domains. Thus it is highly significant that the oldest of the living dwell at the threshold of the compound, in between the outside and the inside, in a space of transition that is constructed so that it remains in contact with family life while looking on to the outer worlds. The gender divide eases out as older women and men no longer participate directly in the procreation process, having already fulfilled their duty to the community in this matter. Gender taboos that previously apply to them while they were still capable of bringing out new lives are no longer effective, and it is not unusual to see older people performing activities reserved for their opposite sex. Old women and men, highly respected in a system where seniority is valued, can encroach on the gender line as their role comes closer to that of their ancestors and takes on a protectively mediator character.

The term compound in the context of West Africa usually designates a plural entity formed by a number of households primarily organized on the basis of agnatic descent, cultivating separately and/or collectively the family farmland, and residing in the same composite habitation. The compound therefore houses anywhere from four to more than a hundred members whose lineage can be traced to a male ancestor. (Matrilinear communities are also encountered in West Africa, but they are not common.) Several generations of fathers and sons form this dwelling group, also known as the joint or extended family. An organization within a predominantly patrilinear system of kinship, it is usually constituted of several close male agnates, their wives and their children. The cohesion of the group is maintained through the mediation of the oldest male member of the joint family, known as head of the compound, and the supervision of his senior wife. Although she is responsible for the well-being of all the women within the compound and therefore for all the activities occurring within her domain, he superintends the out-goings and in-comings of the entire compound. Such a role is acknowledged by the frequent construction of a daytime arbor that faces the entrance from the outside and provides the senior man with a place to carry out his duty as guardian of the family. Determining the allocation of dwelling spaces for the collectivity, the building of new units, and the destruction of older ones, he also makes the final decision as to whether a newcomer can incorporate into the compound community, and he undertakes to marry all its members. As the priest of all family shrines, he maintains close communication with the ancestors—the custodians of the laws and customs of the cultural group and is therefore trusted for his ability to transmit their words and decisions to the rest of the family while also influencing them in their intervention. If the decisions concerning the overall progress of the family belongs to this senior man, it is, again, to the senior woman that the women's role of guardians of the tradition devolves. "Everything the little Moore says, he has learnt it under the tent" goes a saying (in nomadic societies, the tent is set up by the woman). Of common place are expressions like "I sucked it at my mother's breast" or "I have it from Our Mother" to relate what has been passed down by the elders. The same system of mediation prevails on the larger scale of the village. No land can be cleared for a new field, no compound erected, no grave dug without the intervention of the custodian of the earth whose collaboration is indispensable. This custodian belongs to the lineage whose ancestor was the first settler of the territory currently occupied by his descendants. Placing himself under the protection of the local Earth deity he, as a founding member of the community, has the responsibility to intercede for the villagers with the earth spirits who give them the resources to live. Such a position is not based on a relationship of authority, for the custodian is obeyed but does not give orders. His role is to maintain the continuity of the link between humans and the forces of nature.

THE BUILDING TYPES

The house is one of the most visibly personal traits of a cultural group. To each group then, corresponds a different type of dwelling. When one travels across Africa, the architecture, which may change in a short radius of 15–20 km, is the very sign that immediately indicates whether one is in a different territory and cultural area or not. A broad classification of rural West African architecture according to form and building material makes it possible, however, to distribute this architecture into three main basic types on which a great number of variations occur. Each of the types in question may be considered to correspond to a specific climatic zone; for cultural and physical factors inevitably interact, and climate and soil certainly remain significant in the choice of house forms and of building materials. The first type commonly encountered inside and at the borderlines of the Sahara desert are the tent and shell structures. The second type may be found in the savanna grass and woodland belt whose width approximates 600 km south of the Sahara. It includes a wide variety of earth buildings whose common feature is the flat terrace roof. The third type, which also exists in the second climatic zone mentioned, prevails on the coastal and inland tropical belt that spreads from Senegal to Cameroon. It includes a variety of cylindrical and rectangular dwellings whose shared characteristic is, with a few exceptions, the conical or saddle-back thatch roof.

Tent and Shell Structures

In the northern part of the Sahel belt, within the edge of the southern Sahara, the climate is semidesertic. Shrubs are scarce, and short grass grows in abundance after a light seasonal rainfall. The population is mainly composed of nomadic and seminomadic groups who repeatedly move from one place to another, depending on natural resources for their livestocks. Their transhumant lifestyles necessitate that their dwellings be freestanding, lightweight, easily dismantled and reassembled, and anchored to the ground by means of removable poles. Erected with a minimum of wooden supports, these dwellings are usually shaped in aerodynamic forms, which can withstand winds and sandstorms, compensating thereby for the lightness of their structures. The tent material varies from one geographic location to another in accordance with aesthetic and climatic exigencies such as heat, rain, and the absence or availability of vegetation. It may be made from the hide of goat, cow, or camel; with woven animal's hair; with thatch, woven, or plaited mats; or with heavy textiles. Nomadic life makes no long-lasting impression on the landscape; people receive from nature whatever they can find and they leave the land almost the way they found it. Furthermore, in the nomadic notion of dwelling, humans and animals are so utterly dependent on each other for their subsistence and their homemaking that if the displacements of the nomads are effected because of their animals, the animals are often either the direct suppliers for the prime building materials of the tent or they are the ones who carry the tent on their back as the group moves from place to place.

The Tuareg Tent. The Tuareg, one of the major nomadic groups of West Africa, occupies a vast area of the western Sahara. They are encountered in Mauritania and Mali as well as in Niger. Their settlements comprise anywhere from two dozen to no more than four or five tents, often set up according to seasonal wind directions. During the hotter months of the year, the physically ideal location for the tent is on the heights of a sand dune where it benefits from the cooling breeze. During the colder months, however, the better location remains that behind the sand dune, in a depression zone. Accordingly, the tent is equipped with adjustable flaps so that the interior is kept warm and is protected from cold winds and heavy sandstorms when these are tied down to the peripheral poles; it is opened to ventilation when they are flipped up over the tent. The space within the tent is organized into subspaces. The multifunctional living space, sometimes defined by a mat on the cleared ground, is adjacent to the bed, which is usually placed on the side of the axis of the tent, especially in rectangular dwellings (Fig. 5). All utensils and belong-

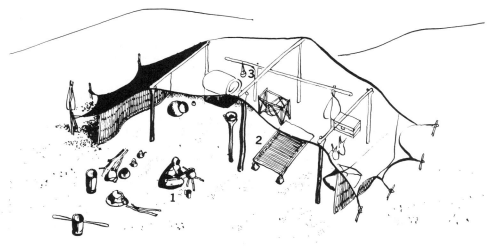

Figure 5. Tuareg dwelling, Mauritania. Tent built on a rectangular plan. **(1)** cooking area; **(2)** bed; **(3)** storage.

ings are kept against the tent walls. Thus, the hanging of reed mats (these also serve to close the tent all around at night) and the storage of objects on the sides and/or in the back of the tent delimitate the interior boundary of the tent. Cooking is done outside, in front of the tent where a small stone hearth and a quern or a mortar are located. Decoration is the very element that demarcates the inside world of the family from the outside world of the desert. Almost every object, every surface (interior roof and walls, leather, bed, tent poles, ridge poles, calabashes, wooden bowls, gourds, and other kitchen utensils) inside the tent is carefully adorned with colored, carved, and braided work. Although variations are numerous, the type of structure most commonly encountered is the frame composed of three sets of two vertical poles, each set being spanned by a ridge pole. The tent fabric, usually made of skin vellum, is spread over the three sets and then stretched and attached to lateral anchoring sticks.

The Fulani Dwelling. To the south and west of the Tuaregs live the Fulani, seminomadic and transhumant pastoralists who are mainly occupied with cattle-raising. Widely known under the name of Fulani, they are also variously referred to by their neighbors as the Fulbe, the Fula, the Fulaabe, the Fulanke, and the Peuhl. They occupy a vast territory that spreads along the southern Sahara border and across 13 states of Africa, all the way from Senegal to Chad. Fulani settlements are of variable importance in size; the dwellings are distributed in a radius extending from less than 500 m to several kilometers. Often coexisting with other agriculturalist groups in an area, the Fulani lead life-styles that involve both transhumance and sedentarism. The prevailing type of their architecture is the dome-shaped thatch dwelling, of which the half-peanut-hull form, encountered for example among the Peuhl of the Ferlo desert in Senegal, is a variant. The frame made so as to bring about such womblike shapes is constituted by means of easily bent acacia bush and flexible young tree branches assembled into a tight trellis. Woven thatch is then laid over the frame and occasionally covered with a braided net to hold it in place in the case of strong winds. Inside the dwelling a platform for storage is set against the wall on one side and the children's bed usually on the other side. The couple's bed is placed opposite to the entrance, which is the only source of light. The doorway is low and small and often marked with braided work; the bed and platform are raised on wooden supports covered with mats. Here one of the most important features inside the dwelling is the woman's collection of earthenware jars and pots, of calabashes and calabash lids neatly displayed on the platform, piled one on top of the other, or hung from the domic roof with braided string constructions, all in order of decreasing size. These vessels store food and plant medicines such as milk, millet, peanuts, baobab tree leaves, pods, tree bark, and various other ingredients. The lids, the wooden bowls, as well as the gourds and calabashes that are used for carrying, drinking, and marketing milk, are often ornamented with elaborate patterns. Very lightweight and easily packed one inside the other whenever they need to be carried along, the collection of gourds and calabashes,

which are hard-shell fruits widely grown in the tropics, constitutes the woman's prized personal possessions. As symbols of her milking and life-giving capacity, they reflect the woman's status of "being a Fulani," just as the cattle represents the man's wealth and status in the society. The form of the Fulani dwelling is, in this context, above all the form of an overturned calabash.

Flat-Roof Earth Dwellings

Earth buildings whose common attribute is the flat terrace roof may be found in a zone south of the Sahara that extends across Mali, Burkina Faso, and northern Senegal, Ivory Coast, Ghana, Benin, Togo, Nigeria, and Cameroon. Here, longer annual rainfall with a high degree of variability fosters the growth of a savanna woodland vegetation and makes crop production possible. The alternation between a wet and a dry season, the availability of clayey soils, and the farmer's sedentary mode of life favors a type of dwelling that accommodates both the climatic factor (dryness and humidity; heavy rains, in addition to cold winds and intense heat) and the agricultural factor (storage space, preserving the annual crop and dwelling spaces reinforcing farming groups).

Settlement. The village, like the compound, is defined by the relationship among its inhabitants. The link between the people is usually what makes up a quarter and an agglomeration. With this in mind, it is easier to understand why foreigners traveling in Africa often have difficulty in seeing a village in what they perceive only as scattered homesteads. Although nucleated villages are no exceptions, the types that form the majority in this area are the semidispersed and dispersed settlements. Even if the physical demarcation between quarters or between agglomerations may not be evident at first sight, a grasp of the overall extent of a village allows one to distinguish the difference of distances between compounds, which extend anywhere from a few dozen to a few hundred meters in an average radius of a kilometer or more. Villages are constituted of loosely grouped family habitations, and the constellation of these groupings is actually what represents a quarter. With a few exceptions—such as among certain Bobo (Burkina Faso) communities where villages are fortified, or among the Kapsiki or the Goude (northern Cameroon) where villages are strategically protected by a system of plant fortification erected in response to a need for defense due to historical contingencies—the boundaries of the village are hardly perceptible and so are, at a smaller scale, those of a compound's territory. They usually correspond with the boundaries of the cultivated land, but can also be delimited by edible fruit trees, which serve as referral points and are prominent landmarks in the sub-Saharan landscape. At night, however, the limits of a village are perceived differently, for people consider then that they stop at the walls of the compounds.

Arbor and Granary. Two features that remain characteristic of the compounds within this savanna grass and woodland belt are the senior man's arbor and the granaries. This arbor serves as a daytime place for the senior man to rest, to receive the visitors as well as to supervise the incoming and outgoing movements of the compound. Built with a simple post-and-beam system that is covered with straw or millet stalks, it is positioned to face the entrance way at the same time as it allows the inside onlooker to have a view of the neighborhood. In instances where the settlements are more densely grouped, this arbor is set up for each quarter, instead of each compound. Thus, each village may have several quarter-arbors in addition to the collective one shared by the entire male community. It is worth noting that these arbors come in the form of a simple platform raised on wooden logs whenever they are shaded by a large tree and do not need to be covered by a straw or millet-stalk roofing.

Millet and sorghum are the two major staples grown in the area, and their annual preservation requires that spe-

cial accommodation be provided. Here the presence of the granaries takes on its full significance; their function is to house the basic foods or the source of energy for the family. As container and giver of life and as guarantor of continuity, the granary, like the house, is often conceived in the image of the world. Its access is reserved and its construction calls for both skill and care. As architectural features, granaries are frequently presented in the most thoroughly decorated or most powerful forms. Such are, for example, the earth granaries among the Songhay (Niger) that are moulded as towering, giant-sized potteries; those among the Konkomba (Ghana, Togo) whose womblike figures stand on three or four legs; those among the Puguli (Burkina Faso) that rise like voluminous ink bottles (Fig. 6); or those among the Tamberma (Togo) that

Figure 6. Puguli homestead, Burkina Faso. Cutaway axonometric; only the courts are outdoor and uncovered (**1**) raised adobe sloping area where a small granary or clay pots are stored; (**2**) cooking and storage space that women sometimes use for resting; (**3**) packed-earth open court enclosed by a high wall; (**4**) raised sloping area where large water or guinea-corn beer jars are stored; (**5**) entrance corridor where goats used to be kept at night; (**6**) main space of each unit (**7**) cooking fireplace whose smoke serves to protect the granary; (**8**) granary; (**9**) small granary for corn, millet, or peanuts; (**10**) man's space (**11**) elder man's space erected as a second story on top of the terrace roof; (**12**) ladder.

Figure 7. Tamberma dwelling, Togo. The egg-shaped granaries on the sides are here almost entirely covered by the thatch roofs.

are shaped like large ostrich eggs (Fig. 7). All granaries are raised above the ground on stones or on a foundation of posts to avoid dampness and rodents. They are built either with mats covered with clay on one or both sides, or with coiled rings of earth overlaid with a coat of the same material mixed with straw, lime, or cow dung. Granaries are filled before they are sealed; they are frequently topped with conical thatch roofs, especially when they are not provided with a drainage device for the rainwater. Openings giving access to the inside foods are made either on the top or on the side, in which case a small window opening is cut into the wall and sealed off or closed with a door. The design and placement of the granaries vary according to each group and to both the practical and symbolic functions they bear within the family. The family granaries—also designated as the man's granary, because they are entrusted to the senior man who is responsible for the distribution of the grain in the compound—are the largest in volume; hence they often stand in the central cattle kraal of the compound or immediately outside the compound, within its exterior confines. In a few instances, such as among the Puguli, the Dagari, and the Lowiili (Burkina Faso), they are incorporated in the interior of the homestead and are built at the time of construction. As women's responsibility is not to disseminate the grains, but to transform them into life-giving force, their personal granaries usually contain foods other than the basic crops, such as nuts and peas. These are the cultures women tend on their own in the peripheral vicinity of the compound. With a few rare exceptions such as among the Dogon, women's granaries are placed inside their own dwelling spaces. They often come in ovoidal forms and in much smaller sizes, their diameters rarely exceeding 1.5 m (see Fig. 6).

Building Materials and Techniques. Finding the best soil is crucial to earth building. Too much clay tends to make the construction expand when it is wet and to contract and crack when it is dry. Too much sand, on the other hand, makes it liable to crumbliness and erosion in dry climatic condition. The soils in this area of Africa are generally most suitable, for their silt content is low and, as mixtures

in varying proportions of sand and clay, they are readily available for construction. The use of adobe (sun-dried earth and straw) in the building of houses is gaining popularity in many parts of the world. Its revival, as it is well known, is due to its ability to store energy and stabilize temperature, as well as its aesthetic potential for sculptural forms. In a culture where wealth is equated not with the size of estate but with the number of family members, a house built with local resources can also be easily extended as the family increases, without involving great costs.

Before building a compound, the plan with the placements and perimeters of the rooms is marked on the ground, using as a measuring unit the human body and its extensions. A shallow foundation trench is then usually dug at about no more than 10–20 cm deep. The walls are erected according to two basic techniques: the hand-molding of earth courses and the use of adobe sun-dried bricks. In the first method of construction, clods of kneaded soil mixed with water are flattened out into a continuous band that covers the perimeter of the space enclosed. This band measures approximately 25–50 cm high and 20 cm thick. While building this first course, the men smooth both the outer and inner surfaces with their hands and occasionally form small earth cones at 40–60-cm intervals on its top so as to anchor the following layer. A variant of this technique is the use of small rolls of earth whose width is no larger than that of a forearm (8 cm). In this case, the resulting thinness of the wall is compensated by the appropriate small size of the space enclosed or the curvilinearity of its form. This is, at a larger scale, the technique used by women when modeling pottery. Walls are erected through the superimposition of courses of earth. The first courses, which define the boundaries of a dwelling unit or of a homestead and its composite spaces, should be left to dry and harden before the second courses can be added on top. The time needed for each source to dry depends on the soil quality and the climatic condition, as well as the thickness of the walls. When the walls are thin, as in the case just mentioned, openings are cut into them only after the masonry is completed. In the second method of construction, the sand-and-clay earth may be mixed with straw or with fine laterite gravel to form the building material. Each brick is compacted by hand or, more commonly, in a bottom- and topless wooden frame that is removed afterward while the brick is left in place to dry under the sun. Laid in courses and cemented with layers of adobe in the construction process, these bricks are usually molded in rectangular blocks. However, bricks in the form of circular cones with a diameter of 5–15 cm at the base and laid in adobe mortar are also encountered among the Hausa in Niger and Nigeria. The Dogon houses in Mali make use, on the other hand, of rubbles embedded in adobe (Fig. 8)—a primary building material that belongs to the area but is otherwise not commonly used in savanna architecture. Whether the walls are built with earth courses or with adobe bricks, they are plastered on the inside, or on both sides in the case of adobe brick or stone houses, with a mixture of earth that contains manure or has a larger proportion of straw. Microbial products usually help to bind particles, and the fermentation

Figure 8. Dogon cliff-dwellings, Mali.

Characteristic of a major building type of sub-Saharan architecture, the flat earthen roof is a feature that also distinguishes the life style of its inhabitants. A multifunctional place, it used to play a prominent part in people's daily lives. If in the past it served a strategic purpose, providing a circulation and meeting place that overlooked the village distant surroundings, today it still retains its daily practical function as terrace. People dry foods, condiments, and clothes; they thresh millet; and they sleep on the terrace during warmer nights. In the construction process of the roof, beams are spaced at no more than 1 m apart. The gap between every two beams is bridged with a series of wooden sticks more than a meter long. On top of these sticks and in an opposite direction, smaller pieces of dead wood are then laid before they are covered with adobe. The roof is tamped just like the floor of the house by women with a wooden beater. While doing so, women may add a variety of products to reinforce the surface's resistance, a preventive device necessitated by the sporadic but torrential rains that come pouring down for 10 or 11 weeks around late April and early May. The most common additives are manure (mainly cow dung), ashes, soil taken from anthill or termite mounds, fine laterite gravel, or various decoctions such as the one prepared with locust-bean pods mentioned earlier. Besides being a water sealer, the last-named also gives the surface a polished, varnishlike quality. Generally, room walls are built at a level higher than the roof surface to form low enclosing parapets. This not only serves to delimit the terrace spaces parallel to those of the rooms underneath (each household thus has its own terraces), it also provides a means to anchor the beams more firmly and to prevent cracks from developing at the junction points of two independent rooms. Furthermore, such a method of roof construction offers a solution to the problem of water leakage between adjacent rooms as it requires that drainage devices be provided for each terrace space. In other words, each room is conceived so that its rainwater can be collected and evacuated on one of its exterior sides, allowing thereby its other side walls to be built adjacent to those of another room while eliminating the critical problem of water infiltration. This accounts for the wide range of varieties and of possibilities in composition (or rooms associations) and form encountered in West African flat-roof dwellings. The terrace-roof system is a versatile system in which square, circular, and ovoidal spaces easily intersect with one another to form complex, elaborate house plans and volumes that are unique to this type of sub-Saharan architecture. A vertical expansion of the dwelling is also made convenient with this system because a second-story room can, for example, be erected for the elder man above his wife's room in accordance with certain societies' customs (Fig. 6), or for the children and for the storage of the household's belongings as among the Dogon (Fig. 10). Also peculiar to the terrace roof is its light and ventilation system. As mentioned earlier, pots with their bottoms broken off are stuck in the adobe at construction time (Fig. 6) in places where openings may serve both as skylight and as smoke exhaust. When it rains, each opening is covered again with the severed bottom, thereby keeping the inside space safe from rainwater.

of these organic elements strengthens the material used to plaster the walls. The finish coating protects the walls from weather damages while it also fulfills an aesthetic function. It can be reinforced with a decoction of locust-bean pods (*Parkia biglobosa*) that dries into a waterproof finish. Or it can be decorated with imprinted motifs whose patterns are created by pressing repeatedly two segments of corncobs, pebbles, or sticks on the coating while it is still soft. These motifs spread the flow of rainwater into smaller streamlets, preventing thereby a localized erosion of the walls (see Fig. 1).

Structural Systems. The walls are either erected on a shallow foundation of approximately 20 cm deep or on no foundation at all. They are built according to two basic structural systems: (1) the solid bearing-wall system with wall thicknesses approximating 50 cm (Fig. 9); and (2) the post-and-beam system (Fig. 6), which allows for much thinner, therefore more flexible, nonbearing walls and prevents the roof from collapsing in case the rain saps the wall footings. Other systems include combinations of these two, and the "roof-with-no-wall" structure of the conical shell houses encountered among the Musgum in northern Cameroon (Fig. 4). These bell-shaped houses are built up in a ring with thin walls that support themselves without any wooden framework or reinforcing posts and are embossed all over on the exterior for both functional and aesthetic considerations.

Figure 9. Tuculor dwelling, Senegal, cutaway axonometric. The perforated facade is here detached from the house for an informative purpose. It normally stands in the hatched and darkened area of the drawing.

Dwelling Design. The erection of contiguous rooms call for three types of dwelling designs: *1*) the conglomerate type, which may or may not have exterior courts, but is usually conceived with ladders leading to the roof either from the outside (Fig. 6) or from the inside; *2*) the closed courtyard type, where all the dwelling units open onto an interior central court functioning both as connective–distributive space and as an area for granaries and/or cattle

Figure 10. Dogon dwelling, Mali, cutaway axonometric. (**1**) village path; (**2**) main access to the compound; (**3**) secondary access; (**4**) vestibule or main dwelling space of the elder man and woman; (**5**) granary; (**6**) vestibule; (**7**) terrace roof; (**8**) storage; (**9**) children's bedroom; (**10**) opening for light and cooking smoke.

(Fig. 11); *3*) the semi-open courtyard type, where dwelling units are dispersed and loosely linked to each other by enclosing walls or fences. These walls define with the dwelling walls the shape and limit of the main interior court, which fulfill the same functions as those just mentioned previously (Fig. 12). This third type of dwelling design is common to both flat-roof and thatch-roof compounds to be discussed further on.

A last but not least prominent trait of flat-roof dwellings is the constitution of the women's units. They usually stand out in a compound as being the most sculptural and elaborate in terms of form and the most thoroughly decorated on the outside as well as the inside. Women play an important role in the continuity of tradition, and it is, indeed, usually the senior women's dwellings that are most likely to retain their richly adorned or carefully fin-

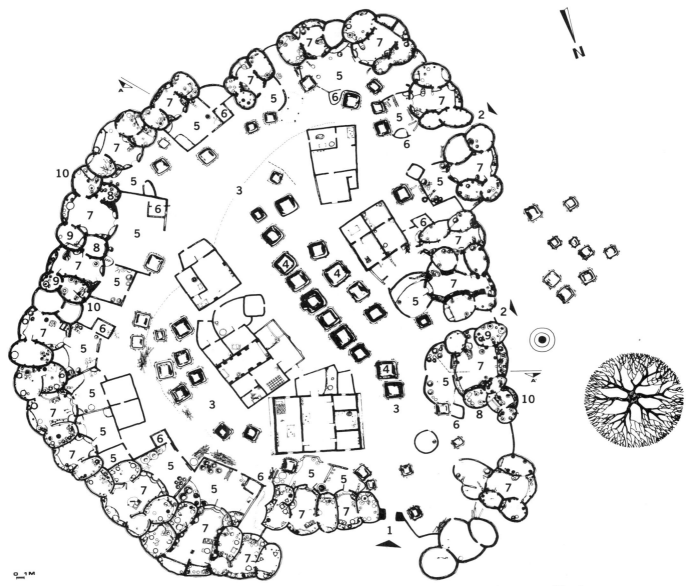

Figure 11. Lela, Burkina Faso, compound plan. (**1**) main access; (**2**) secondary accesses; (**3**) cattleyard; (**4**) granaries; (**5**) tamped courts; (**6**) bathing enclosure; (**7**) main living space; (**8**) storage; (**9**) fish-smoking space; (**10**) cooking space.

ished traditional architectural features. A woman's unit usually houses a grinding stone, a small granary, diverse family belongings, her collection of potteries and calabashes, and the sleeping mats. It is therefore often equipped with built-in furnishings (niches, seats, platforms, shelves, shea-nut containers, for example) that are carved in and molded once the walls and floors are completed. In contrast with the bareness and plainness of the man's or the young newly married couple's units, the woman—mother's unit not only bears more complex features in its interiors, it is also composed of at least two basic spaces on which a number of variations may be found: the living and sleeping space where daily activities are carried out and the cooking space. Smaller in size, the latter is usually located furthest toward the interior, away

from the entrance door that gives access to the adjacent living-sleeping room (Fig. 13). Its role, however, is not secondary, as it houses the hearth and is often symbolically referred to as the head of each woman's dwelling, as discussed earlier. In many instances, a second outdoor cooking space may be built in addition to the indoor kitchen just described. Connected to the indoor spaces but accessible only from the outside, such outdoor cooking space is often partly enclosed and occasionally covered on the top with millet stalks that shelter it from the sun. The indoor kitchen is here used only for cooking during the rainy season, whereas for the rest of the year it is used for the simmering of sauces and for fish or meat smoking, which requires a smaller, long-lasting fire. When the kitchen is an element separated from the woman's room,

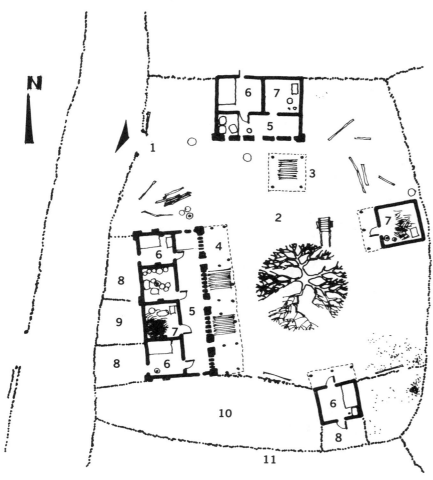

Figure 12. Tuculor dwelling, Senegal plan. (1) access gate; (2) court; (3) daytime arbor; (4) thatch-roof veranda; (5) intermediary space for resting, cooking, and taking one's meals mostly during the rainy season; (6) bedroom; (7) storage; (8) storage and bathing enclosure; (9) toilet; (10) cattle enclosure; (11) wooden stick fence.

it may take on a communal function, like among the Soninke (Senegal, Mauritania, and Mali). It is then situated toward the center of the compound and is built as a collective indoor space where all the women of the compound install their stone hearths for inside cooking. These may be moved outside the communal kitchen during the dry season. Each woman's dwelling unit generally opens onto a small packed-earth area or court that delimits the household's territory and gives access to the central court or cattle kraal. Not infrequently, the unit also incorporates a storage space and/or a reception space designed as an antechamber.

Three examples of flat-roof dwellings are introduced here to give a better idea of the many possibilities this architecture offers: the Dogon, the Tuculor, and the Lela dwellings. Reproduced in plans and axonometrics, they are selected for their representative differences in settlement, topographic situation, mode of construction, and space forms. Other supplementary drawings and photographs show an example of hand-molded courses technique (Figs. 6 and 7); the complex constitution of a Nankani women's dwelling (Figs. 1 and 13); and the courtyard stone house in Oualata, Mauritania (Fig. 14).

The Dogon Cliff-Dwelling. Settlements of the Dogon along the rocky Bandiagara cliffs in Mali are seminu-

cleated; they are relatively dense, each homestead being separated from the other only by a narrow alley or by a few meters of strips of rock (Fig. 8). The villages insinuate themselves against the face of an escarpment with a drop of about 200 m. Their cosmologic and anthropomorphic configurations as well as those of the houses have already been discussed earlier. Each compound is composed of a number of quadrate dwellings, each distinguished by the single round tower that constitutes the cooking space. Each dwelling belongs to a household and is located, according to the space available, as close to the dwelling of the man's father as possible. The man's and the woman's granaries are erected in the interval space between two dwellings (Fig. 10). Access to the interior of the compound is generally gained through a rectangular vestibulelike room (Fig. 10). This reception space is equipped with a wooden or adobe bench where the visitors can sit and talk without interfering in the interior life of the compound. It is also the place to which the senior man moves when his age no longer allows him to fulfill his procreative role; he thus takes on the more marked responsibility of guarding the compound by situating himself, as we have seen earlier, in an area of transition between the worlds of the living and the dead members of the family. The dwelling is built with two stories. Access to the ground floor is again through a small vestibule space or antechamber,

Figure 13. Nankani woman's dwelling unit, Burkina Faso. This unit is part of a ring of units that encloses the cattle courtyard (see also Fig. 18). (**1**) antechamber to the man's space; (**2**) outdoor cooking space; (**3**) sleeping and storage space; (**4**) semi-circular wall facing the entrance to the living space; (**5**) open exterior cooking area; (**6**) millet stalks; (**7**) cattle kraal; (**8**) packed-earth court; (**9**) sheep pen; (**10**) indoor cooking space.

whose entrance doorway is located at a right angle with the doorway leading to the central living-sleeping space. Having the two doorways not aligned with one another helps to preserve the intimacy of interior life (Fig. 15). It is in this vestibule space that the grindstone is installed, so that women can benefit from the light and ventilation while grinding. The adjacent living and sleeping space, which usually contains an adobe bed and a series of clay pots set against its walls, leads to two narrow storage spaces along its sides. It also gives access to the cylindrical cooking space whose smoke escapes through a large opening situated on the second story and terrace roof level (Fig. 10). The storage spaces, on the other hand are usually devoid of openings to the exterior. The upper story is reached by a stepped forked tree trunk usually propped against the outside wall, close to the entrance doorway of the vestibule. This story includes the multifunctional terrace, which leads to either other storage rooms on both sides or a children's bedroom above the vestibule. The dwelling walls are constructed with rubble embedded in adobe and plastered also with a coat of adobe. The bearing-wall and the post-and-beam systems found in the central room are combined here to complement each other.

The Tuculor Dwelling. Settlements of the Tuculor living on the banks of the Senegal river in northern Senegal are also nucleated. Built contiguous to each other, the compounds are mostly composed of several independent buildings (Fig. 12). These buildings are usually dispersed in a lot whose shape depends on each individual case and is delimitated by an enclosure made of wooden sticks. Each dwelling comprises a series of three adjacent spaces (Figs. 9 and 16). First is a veranda covered with an in-

Figure 14. Moor village of Oualata, Mauritania. Inside courtyard and ornamented entrance to a woman's dwelling space on the left.

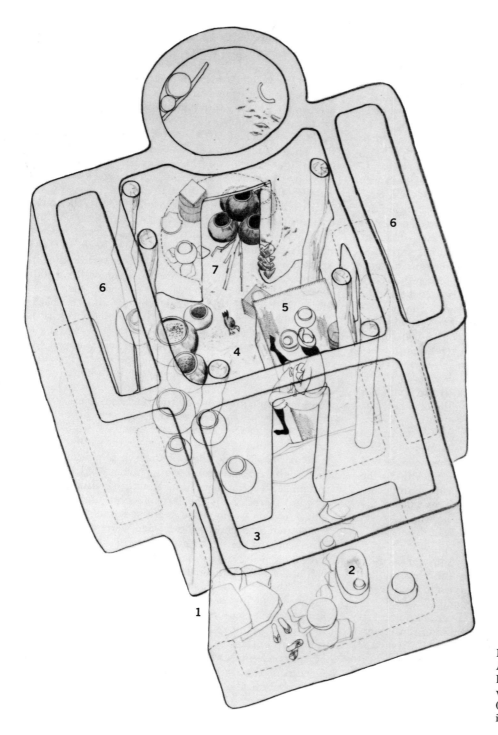

Figure 15. Dogon dwelling, Mali. Axonometric of the ground floor level. (1) door; (2) grindstone; (3) vestibule; (4) main dwelling space; (5) adobe bed; (6) storage; (7) cooking area.

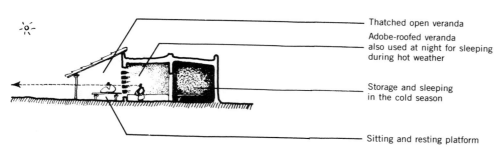

Thatched open veranda

Adobe-roofed veranda also used at night for sleeping during hot weather

Storage and sleeping in the cold season

Sitting and resting platform

Figure 16. Tuculor, Senegal. Section showing the three main dwelling spaces.

325

clined thatch roof that projects beyond the flat roof of the building, leaning on it on one side for support and resting in the front on wooden posts and beams. Underneath this veranda, platform beds raised on wooden supports are commonly found; people sit, rest, and receive their visitors there. On entering the central doorway of the dwelling, one finds oneself next in a corridorlike space whose width corresponds to the length of an adobe platform bed set against the walls on one side of the room. This intermediary space for circulation gives access to the sleeping and storage rooms behind it and, in many cases, to a series of fenced courts in the back where the toilet and bathing area are located (Fig. 12). During the rainy season, the corridor space or antechamber is also used for cooking. It is well-lit and well-ventilated by the mosaic of perforations that punctures the wall facade of the dwelling and allows those inside to maintain visual contact with the outside while providing them shelter from the sun and heat (Fig. 17). Carefully adorned with molded reliefs and elaborate patterns, the Tuculor facade is both aesthetically and functionally a remarkable feature. The successive spatial order of the dwellings units—the veranda, the antechamber, the sleeping and storage rooms—contribute to create an intimacy gradient that provides the inhabitants with a choice of spaces of varying degrees of privacy. The same holds true for the range of functions to which these spaces can adapt in accordance with the changing climatic conditions. For example, during the dry, hot season, people may prefer to sleep in the veranda at night, but as the temperature lowers, they will move to the antechamber, then to the more protected sleeping rooms further inside. Cooking is also done in both the veranda and in the antechamber as the portable iron hearth can be moved around accordingly. The dwellings are mainly constructed with the bearing-wall technique, except for the veranda roof, which is partly supported by wooden posts and beams.

The Lela Dwelling. Unlike in the two previous cases, the Lela settlements are situated in the central, flat mainland of Burkina Faso; they are thus composed of compounds built at about 150–300 m apart and dispersed over a distance that may stretch beyond several kilometers. Each compound is constituted by a number of contiguous dwelling units built so as to encircle a central courtyard or cattle kraal. The overall form of the compound is generally either circular or ovoidal (Fig. 11). Each dwelling unit belongs to a household; each has its own packed-earth court and is placed under the responsibility of the man in charge of the household, also known as "head of the court." The spatial organization of the compound reflects both the close interrelation of the inhabitants and their self-sufficiency. If the leadership of the compound lies in the hands of the "head of the compound" or senior man, all family responsibilities do not solely fall on him. They are distributed among the household heads, and the role of the senior man, like that of the central courtyard in the compound, is to connect, coordinate, and mediate. A main entrance leads into the inside of the compound; in some instances, one or two side entranceways may also exist, but they function more as shortcuts, giving direct access

to the fields, to the nearby well, or to other places that are frequented on a daily basis. The large central court usually accommodates a number of family granaries; in the case of the compound presented here, it also accommodates a few recent constructions that have not been incorporated with the others on the periphery of the compound. A crown of dwelling units delimitates both this periphery by its exterior walls and the central courtyard by the low walls of its packed-earth courts. As transitional realms, the central courtyard can be considered to be a link between the exterior of the compound and its interior, whereas the packed-earth court can be viewed as a link between the outdoors and the indoors. Enclosed by a low wall that is connected to the dwelling unit, the packed-earth court constitutes a locus for social interaction and is the place where daily activities expand from inside the unit. It accommodates a bathing enclosure, a cooking hearth, and in many cases, a set of jars for millet beer preparation (Fig. 18). Access to the inside of the dwelling unit is through its single doorway, which is itself accessible only through the exclusive opening of the packed-earth court. Each dwelling unit is commonly constituted as a cluster of at least four spaces: the large living and sleeping space; the indoor cooking space; the sauce-simmering and fish- or meat-smoking space; and the storage space. More than one storage space may be found adjacent to the indoor cooking space, and a space to keep the goats at night may also be incorporated, usually located immediately to the side of the entrance doorway. The main living space contains the woman's grinding stone and has elaborate features built in the walls and floor, such as raised adobe edges that serve as platform, bench, and shelf; carved adobe seats, niches and buttressing columns. Sleeping mats hung from the ceiling during the day are unrolled on the bare floor at night. Once the length of this living space is crossed, one gains access to the storage and main cooking spaces on one side and to a sauce-cooking space on the other. The latter is equipped with a smoking device necessary for the preservation of fish and meat. The construction of the dwellings makes use of the post-and-beam system, hence the erection of thin, nonbearing walls that are built-up in courses with hand-molded clods. Sometimes the walls of the main living and sleeping space of the unit are reinforced by the carved-in buttressing columns mentioned earlier instead of the wooden posts and beams, but this is not a constant feature in the construction. The predominant post-and-beam system allows more flexibility in the shaping and combination of spaces. Here the cylindrical rooms within and between the clusters intersect with each other to form a solid, interlocked honeycomblike structure along the perimeter of the compound.

Thatch-Roof Dwellings

Cylindrical or rectangular dwellings whose shared characteristic is the thatch roof may be easily found in the savanna grass and woodland area, but they prevail in the tropical rain-forest belt that spreads along the Atlantic coast, from southern Senegal to southern Cameroon. In the former zone, compounds made up of cylindrical earth

Figure 17. Tuculor dwelling, Senegal. Variations on perforated facades with or without thatch-roofed veranda.

or stone dwellings topped with conical thatch roofs and linked to one another by enclosing walls are common to many ethnic groups. These cylindro-conical earth dwellings may occasionally also be juxtaposed with flat-roof units within the same compound. Of commonplace to the tropical zone are rectangular dwellings with saddle-back

thatch roofs whose presence may be partly attributed to a different climatic condition (longer rainfalls, heat and humidity) that requires constant means of ventilation and to the availability of wooden building materials that lead more easily to straight alignment. The settlement patterns of the thatch-roof dwellings are similar to those of

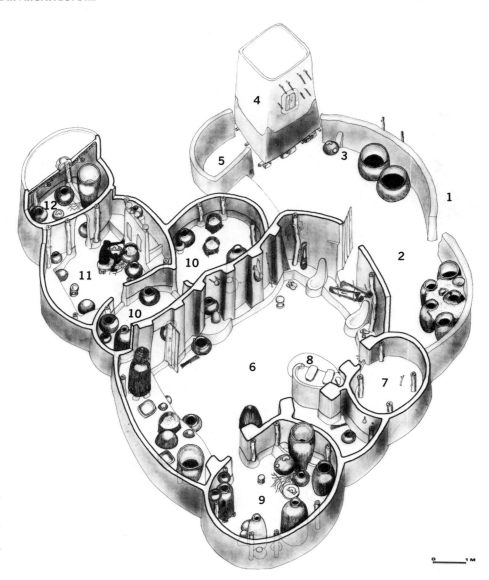

Figure 18. Lela, Burkina Faso. Cutaway axonometric of a woman's dwelling unit. (**1**) cattleyard; (**2**) tamped court; (**3**) exterior cooking area; (**4**) granary; (**5**) bathing enclosure; (**6**) main living space; (**7**) goat pen; (**8**) grinding stone; (**9**) fish-smoking area; (**10**) storage; (**11**) cooking area; (**12**) shea-nut roasting area.

the flat-roof habitations. The villages may seem more concentrated, but nucleated settlements are rare and the majority is constituted by a constellation of quarters, which is in turn formed by a number of loosely grouped compounds. The closer one moves to the rain-forest belt, the more yam (a tuber staple), rice, cassava, and maize cultivations are likely to take over the millet-sorghum grain-growing activities of the savanna belt. Therefore, the means of storage change accordingly and they no longer occupy a prominent role, as some of these staple crops can either be stacked or stored on the plant and used only as required. Large adobe grain containers are not encountered in the area; one may find, instead, smaller storage enclosures that are incorporated at the base of the roof or in the ceiling of the dwelling, as among the Bamileke (Cameroon, Fig. 19) and the Joola (Senegal, Fig. 2).

In the humid rain-forest zone, the walls of the dwellings are often erected with either wattle-work (Fig. 20), wood posts, stems of giant ferns, bamboo, or raphia to facilitate air circulation. They are also erected in adobe and reinforced with an interior armature of bamboo or palm-frond wattles that prevents rapid rain deterioration. Of exception here is the stone used as building material among the Bassari of Southern Senegal whose cylindro-conical dwellings are constructed with walls of laterite boulders plastered on the inside with adobe (Fig. 21). By their fabrication as well as by their numbers, the thatch roofs are often indications of the family's or the inhabitant's stature. A prominent architectural feature, they may, as in some cases, slope down to about half a meter from the ground, sheltering almost completely the adobe walls (Fig. 22) and remaining thereby the most visible part of the dwellings from the outside. Both the conical and the saddle-back roofs are constructed with their eaves projecting beyond the walls to deflect rain water; they are made of thatch, palm, or banana leaves. Their shapes usually correspond to that of the dwellings' plans. When the walls are built on a circular plan, the form of the roof is

Figure 19. Bamileke dwelling, cutaway axonometric. (1) bamboo wall covered with adobe; (2) hearth; (3) bed; (4) storage.

conical. When they are erected on a square or rectangular plan, however, the roof is either saddle-backed, pyramidal, or, more rarely, hipped (Fig. 23). Of exception is the Bamileke house (Cameroon), which has a conical roof resting on square walls. In this case, the roof is prefabricated with an armature that is supported by a pyramid struc-

Figure 20. Bassari, Senegal. Dwelling with walls made of wattle-work.

Figure 21. Bassari compound, cutaway perspective. (1) main access; (2) court; (3) day time arbor; (4) hearth; (5) enclosed cooking area; (6) sleeping and storage space; (7) storage room; (8) storage platform.

ture attached to two circular platforms, a small one on the top and a larger one on its base (Fig. 19). Roof shapes may, in turn, influence the form and arrangement of the dwelling spaces. Thus, although many variations in house shapes are possible in this building type, they are usually

Figure 22. Fulani dwelling, Guinea and Senegal, cutaway perspective. (1) hen pen; (2) main entrance; (3) court; (4) cooking area; (5) main living space; (6) peripheral veranda/storage; (7) storage; (8) hearth; (9) bathing enclosure.

Figure 25. Konkomba dwelling, Togo.

Figure 23. Ashanti dwelling, Ghana. **(1)** entrance; **(2)** court; **(3)** covered cooking area; **(4)** hearth; **(5)** sleeping and storage space; **(6)** main living space; **(7)** bathing enclosure.

not constructed as composite forms as with flat-roof dwellings. Instead, they remain separate free-standing structures, because waterproof connections are difficult to achieve between two or more thatch roofs and it is more practical to cover a singly shaped space with a conical thatch roof than to try to adapt the roof to a complex shape that results from a combination of several spaces. The Joola (Senegal) impluvium house (Fig. 2) provides an interesting exception on which a number of variants exist among the different groups of the same people. Here, a number of flat-roof adobe units are nested below a single, two-sloped circular thatch roof whose inward inclination, as mentioned earlier, gives it the shape of a funnel when seen from the interior.

Three structural systems prevail in the thatch-roof building type. In the first system, which is also the most widespread one, the conical roof is supported by rafters directly embedded in the adobe walls (Fig. 24) or tied to

the load-bearing wood or bamboo uprights of the walls. In the second system, the hipped (Fig. 23) or saddleback roof rests on peripheral beams that are fixed on top of the adobe side wall or fastened to a series of load-bearing poles. Finally, in the third system, which is also the less common one, the saddle-back roof reposes on posts and beams that are set in anchoring mounds molded on top of an adobe ceiling (Fig. 2). Compounds are usually formed by free-standing dwellings assembled around an interior courtyard (Fig. 25) or dispersed in a space physically delimitated by enclosure walls or fences. Because the dwellings are constructed as single spaces, the kitchen is usually erected as a building that remains separate from the sleeping place. The storage facility is often a structure raised on posts and beams and incorporated in the ceiling of the dwelling. The day-time arbor positioned in flat-roof houses outside and in the front of the compound is, in the architecture of the forest zone, either nonexistent or it is situated inside the compound court.

The Konkomba Dwelling. The Konkomba live in northern Ghana and Togo, along the banks of the Oti river and on the Oti plain. They are grain farmers, and their staple crops are millet and sorghum, but they also grow yams, which constitute the basic nourishment for part of the year. Reflecting this mixed pattern of cultivation, their settlements, which are situated close to the limit between the savanna woodland and the rain-forest zones, provide a

Figure 24. Kusasi, Burkina Faso. Section through a dwelling showing rafters resting on top of the adobe circular wall.

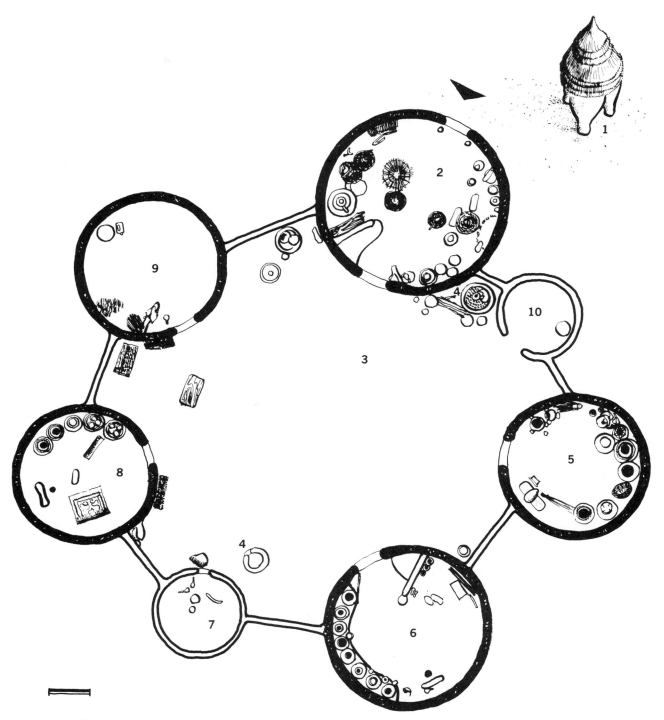

Figure 26. Konkomba, Togo, dwelling plan. (**1**) granary; (**2**) vestibule; (**3**) court; (**4**) hearth; (**5**) cooking space; (**6**) couple's dwelling; (**7**) hen pen; (**8**) children's room; (**9**) guest room; (**10**) bathing enclosure.

good example of the thatch-roof, cylindrico-conical building type that is encountered in both zones, with only a few variations in the compound plan and the wall materials. Konkomba villages are usually small, both in number of compounds and in population. They are semidispersed, unlike the settlements of their neighbors, the Tallensi

and the Dagomba, which are very dispersed in the first case and tightly nucleated in the second case.

Konkomba compounds are, accordingly, small in scale; they usually comprise an average of four to eight cylindrical buildings laid out in a circle and linked to each other by surrounding walls (Fig. 26). This irregular circle of dwellings encloses a large internal courtyard whose packed-earth floor also defines the limit of the compound's interior. One of the most striking features of Konkomba architecture is its large three-, at times four-legged adobe granaries whose jar- and womblike figures stand out as being both half-human and half-pottery. The number of legs may correspond to that of the divider walls inside the granary; for the legs, which are molded into the latter's surface are actually built up of stones placed under the center of gravity of each of the compartments formed by these divider walls. The adobe granaries usually contain grains. Other granaries made of large woven baskets supported by wooden posts, raised above the ground and roofed with thatch are also used to store ground nuts and unthreshed sorghum and millet. Yams may be accommodated in one of the compartments of the adobe grain granary or they may be stored in the woven granaries. There is, in other words, no special yam-storage facility. In most cases, these granaries are placed outside the compound, in its immediate vicinity. However, it has also been observed that in the compound of a lineage elder, the adobe granary stands alone and apart from the others, at the entrance to this elder's reception space or antechamber.

Access to the compound is gained through a large cylindro-conical building that is opened on both sides, serving thereby as a connection space between the exterior and the interior of the compound. This antechamber is a reception area in which agricultural and fishing tools are stored as well as jars that contain peanuts and water. During the day, people may choose to carry out a number of activities related to farming or food gathering here. At night, this space can be used to keep one or two cattle, or a small number of sheeps and goats. The doorway of the antechamber is often made with its jambs molded out so as to accommodate conical built-in laying places for hens. The entrance is the site of fertility rites and symbols. The dwellings within the compound are divided among the wives (in a polygamous household), each having her own sleeping space, her wet-season kitchen, occasionally her storage room, her outdoor cooking hearth and bathing enclosure (Fig. 26). Each room is constituted as a separate thatch-roof cylindrical building. Adobe built-in edges along the peripheral wall serve as banquettes or as platforms on which storing jars are placed and piled up against the wall. The building technique used in Konkomba architecture is the hand-molding of coiling earthen courses described earlier in the methods of construction for flat-roof dwellings. More characteristic of this architecture, however, is the finished treatment of the walls whose surfaces are plastered and whitened with a wash in which the lime obtained from ground shells of the Oti riverbanks is added to the usual cow dung. Porthole entrances cut into the walls of the rooms after their completion require that access into these rooms only be gained by striding over the part of the wall forming the raised threshold. A wall partition (approximately 1.5 m high and 1.2 m wide) erected against the peripheral wall and close to the entrance opening functions as a screening device, so that a person standing outside in the courtyard cannot look into the inside of the room. The exterior as well as interior wall surfaces of the dwellings remain in certain cases bare, whereas in others they are lavishingly adorned with painted patterns and figures (Fig. 25).

The Fon Lake-Dwelling. The Fon houses of Ganvie, a lake-dwelling village situated on the northwestern shore of Lake Nokwe in southern Benin, furnish an interesting example of a rectangular, saddle-back thatch-roof building type whose walls and floors provide ample inside ventilation and appropriate resistance to constant high humidity. More than 10,000 people live in this settlement, which can only be reached by boat, for no bridge, road, or dam connects it with the shore. Even within Ganvie, the streets between the houses are water, and the inhabitants rely on the pirogue as the only means of transportation. Here, the staple food is fish, as the people live solely by fishing and by trading their smoked fished for manioc, yams, or millet that are cultivated by their neighbors on the banks of the lagoon.

Fon lake-dwellings are built on platforms that rest on stilts and can be seen raised 1.5 or 2 m above water level during the dry season, when the water is low. At high water, as in the rainy season, however, the pirogues can be led right up to the door of the house. The stilts supporting the platform and forming the house corner posts are imputrescible tree trunks driven deep into the bottom of the lake. Palmyra fronds and raphia constitute the main building materials; tied together entirely with liana barks or raphia fibers, they provide the construction with an average durability of about 20 years. The grass roof has a noteworthy curved ridge and a remarkable thickness that protects from the rain and sun. The type of dwelling that prevails is composed of three spaces: the platform outdoor space that leads to two indoor spaces—the large living and cooking room and the usually smaller sleeping room (Fig. 27). Tools and belongings are generally stored on overhangs that are either fastened to the roof structure itself or to the side walls at the roof base of the dwellings. Not only see-through walls and floors are made so as to facilitate air circulation, but the living room is also designed with two opposite openings—the entrance door and the back door or back window—that provide maximal cross ventilation. Thus, it is also in this room that cooking is done; the cooking hearth, placed on one side and toward the back, is made of adobe, although in some cases, it is also constituted of a mere basket plastered with a thick layer of clay.

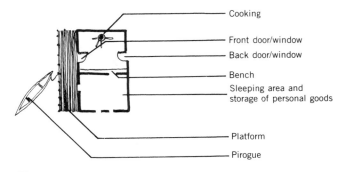

Figure 27. Fon, village of Ganvie, Benin. Schematic plan of a dwelling.

The Joola Impluvium Dwelling. The impluvium house is an exceptional example of a rain-forest architecture that combines both the flat-roof and the thatch-roof building types. It is an architecture that has been in use until recently among the N'gen, G'Ban, and Dida of Ivory Coast and among the Ibo and Yoruba of Nigeria. Today, the only traditional impluvia that are still inhabited in rural West Africa are those encountered in Joolaland in Senegal. The elders who occupy them with their families call attention to the fact that these houses require a large collective manpower for their complex, elaborate workmanship, and that such labor has become more and more difficult to obtain if not entirely impractical because of the massive depopulation of the countryside that accounts for the absence of young men in the villages. In 1980, only about 15–20 impluvia were still standing in Joolaland.

The Joola live in the Lower-Casamance region of Senegal that lies between Gambia and Guinea-Bissau. They are known as skilled rice growers, palm wine collectors, fishermen, and builders. Rice is their staple diet and rice-growing, with its rituals, ceremonies, and authentically perfected techniques, is a regulating activity in Joola village life. The architecture, rich and diversified, bears witness to the people's complex cultural heritage and social organization. There are at least five different types of Joola dwellings, of which the impluvium is one. Or, one can also say alternatively, that a number of variants to the Joola dwelling exist, in which only a few constants are recognizable. Worth mentioning here are the use of the same building material and technology, the similar conception of an attic space for rice storage and, more importantly, the combination of a composite house form with a unifying thatch roof. The strong sense of autonomy within communal life that has long been attributed to the Joola is thus reflected in the house structure. The impluvium dwelling may be described as a small circular fort constituted by a number of individual units built in a ring around an internal court, and covered with a double-crown thatch roof: one encircling the lower part of the roof, the other forming the upper crown and sloping inwardly like a funnel (Fig. 2). The size and shape of the opening that results from this funnel-shaped roof correspond, as previously described, to those of the inner court of the dwelling.

Access to the interior of the impluvium is gained through a small multifunctional veranda in front of the main entrance, which is often marked by a pair of rounded pilasters. Each unit within the impluvium is built as a compact, flat-roof adobe construction that usually consists of a sleeping room, a small storage room equipped with its own door, and an attic space for the storage of rice and other goods. Each household generally occupies two units; one for the man and one for the woman. The man's unit is often less complex than that of his wife; it may come as a single space with the attic but without the storage room. Each woman has her own hearth placed outside the room, against the wall that faces the inner court. Mounds molded on top of the adobe roofs of the units serve as anchoring devices in which forked tree trunks are firmly set so as to install a post-and-beam system that supports the overall thatch roof while remaining independent from the load-bearing walls. Such an intricate roof setup provides the advantage of constant air circulation, thereby preventing the adobe roofs and walls from storing the sun's heat. By having the thatch roof slope inwardly, projecting beyond the walls of the units, a well-ventilated circular veranda is created along the walls that face the inner central court. Each unit opens therefore on the interior to this veranda space where women do their cooking and carry out their daily chores; where the family members sit or rest on the long wooden benches placed against the wall; and where they have access to the drinking water. Each unit also opens on the exterior to a more personal veranda whose access is only through the dwelling interior. In certain instances, a small sleeping room for a young man may be annexed to the unit in the veranda space. This veranda, in turn, gives access to an outdoor personal court enclosed by a fence made with palm ribs. Here people usually prepare palm wine, and store straw, potteries, and other objects not in daily use. This is also the place where a bathing enclosure is commonly installed.

West African architecture, like other traditional rural architecture around the world, is to be used and to be seen. Every house here is at once a tool, a work of art, and a place of worship. It is built to shelter, to protect, to prolong existence, to give aesthetic pleasure, to erect a stage for social play, to promote communion with ancestors and deities, as well as to respond to the forces of nature. Neither merely a means to an end nor an end in itself, it is both an environment to live in and to live with.

BIBLIOGRAPHY

1. J. Mbiti, *African Religions and Philosophy,* Heinemann, London, 1969, p. 39.
2. A. Hampate Ba, "The Living Tradition" in *General History of Africa,* Vol. 1, UNESCO, Heinemann, and University of California Press, Berkeley, Calif., 1981, p. 167.
3. Ref. 2, p. 171.
4. B. Hama and J. Ki-Zerbo, "The Place of History in African Society" in ref. 2, p. 46.
5. A. Hampate Ba, ref. 2, p. 168, 170.
6. M. Griaule, *Conversations with Ogotemmeli,* New York: Oxford University Press, for the International African Institute, 1965, p. 140.
7. S. P. Blier, "Architecture of the Tamberma," Columbia University Ph.D dissertation, 1981, p. 238.
8. Ref. 6, p. 19.
9. Ref. 6, pp. 19–20.
10. Ref. 6, p. 19.
11. J-P. Lebeuf, *L'Habitation des Fali.* Hachette, Paris, 1961.
12. G. Dieterlen, "The Mande Creation Myth" in Elliot P. Skinner, ed., *Peoples and Cultures of Africa,* Doubleday/Natural History Press, New York, 1973.
13. G. Parrinder, *African Mythology,* Hamlyn, Verona, Italy, 1967.
14. Ref. 7, p. 105.
15. J. Capron, *Communautes villageoises Bwa,* Musee de l'Homme, Paris, 1973.

16. J-P. Bourdier and T. T. Minh-ha *African Spaces. Designs for Living in Upper Volta,* Holmes & Meier, New York, 1985, pp. 142–191.

17. Ref. 7, p. 184.

18. R. S. Rattray, *The Tribes of the Ashanti Hinterland,* 2 Vols. Oxford University Press, New York, 1932; reprinted 1969, p. 196.

19. Ref. 6, p. 108.

20. Ref. 7, pp. 128–133.

21. T. M. Shaw, "Taneka Architecture and Village Structure in Northwestern Benin," Columbia University Ph.D dissertation. 1981, pp. 70–71.

22. Ref. 11, pp. 519–526.

23. Ref. 7, pp. 267–271.

General References

S. Denyer, *African Traditional Architecture,* African Publishing, New York, 1978.

J-C. Froelich, *Les Montagnards paleonigritiques,* ORSTOM/ Berger-Levrault, Paris, 1968.

R. Gardi, *Indigenous African Architecture,* Van Nostrand Reinhold, New York, 1973.

M. Griaule, and G. Dieterlen, *Le Renard Pale,* Musee de l'Homme, Paris, 1965.

R. Lecoq, *Les Bamileke,* Editions Africaines, Paris, 1953.

L'Habitat au Cameroon, by the Architecture students of L'Ecole Superieure des Beaux-Arts, Paris, editions de l'Union Francaise, 1952.

A. Maillard, *Habitat Cote d'Ivoire,* Centre de Recherches Architecturales et Urbaines, Abidjan, Ivory Coast, (n.d.)

J. C. Moughtin, *Hausa Architecture,* 1985. Ethnographica, London.

J. Nicolaisen, *Ecology and Culture of the Pastoral Tuaregs,* The National Museum of Copenhagen, Copenhagen, Denmark, 1963.

P. Oliver, ed., *Shelter in Africa,* The Overlook Press, Woodstock, N.Y., 1977.

L. Prussin, *Architecture in Northern Ghana,* University of California Press, Berkeley, Calif., 1969.

C. Seignobos, *Nord Cameroun, Montagnes et hautes terres,* Editions Parentheses, Roquevaire, France, 1982.

T. Spini, and G. Antongini, *Il Camino degli antenati. I Lobi dell' Alto Volta,* Editori Laterza, Rome, 1981.

See also ADOBE CONSTRUCTION; HOT WET CLIMATE, BUILDING IN; NOMADIC ARCHITECTURE

JEAN-PAUL BOURDIER,
TRINH T. MINH-HA
Berkeley, California

THE WHITE HOUSE

The official residence of the President of the United States, called The White House in recognition of its distinguishing color, is located on Pennsylvania Avenue, Northwest, in the monumental core of the capital, Washington, D.C. More than living quarters for the nation's First Family, The White House is an extended complex providing offices and support facilities for the President and staff, special spaces for state occasions, and adjacent landscaped grounds in abundance to accommodate public visitation and celebrations.

In 1791, Thomas Jefferson, President George Washington's Secretary of State, envisioned an orthogonal street plan for the capital city of the newly founded United States. In that plan, a President's House and a Capitol building site were linked by public walks, anticipating the idea of the Mall. That same year, L'Enfant produced, upon the request of President Washington, a plan that featured an array of intersecting diagonal avenues superimposed on a rectangular grid of streets. Two of the principal intersections were to accommodate a President's Palace and a Congress House, linked by a Grand Avenue, which became the Washington Mall. L'Enfant's idea for the President's House, set in a President's Park, included a main section with detached L-shaped office wings forming open courtyards and totaling some 700 ft (213.36 m) in length.

George Washington, who as an eighteenth century gentleman was well aware of architectural conceits, but who as an experienced surveyor was concerned with the practical, felt that the President's House should be compact and complete, but capable of receiving expansions that would provide architectural enhancement. Jefferson, who as a devoted amateur had studied the architecture of classical antiquity, absorbed the principles of grand residential design expounded by Italian Renaissance master Andrea Palladio. As ambassador to France, he had also been profoundly impressed by the great contemporary mansions in Paris, so he campaigned for a design that would transcend simple utility and achieve architectural distinction befitting its purpose. In fact, Jefferson was so concerned that he submitted an anonymous entry in the design competition, held in 1792: a compact domed palazzo resembling Palladio's Villa Capra.

The competition was won by James Hoban, an Irish architect practicing in Charleston, S.C., who had already come to Washington's attention. His design, for which he was awarded $500 by the Commissioners of the District of Columbia, appears to have been based on Leinster House (Dublin, 1745), the Palladian palace designed for the Duke of Leinster by Richard Castle. Originally conceived by Hoban as a three-story structure, the President's House was eventually built with four levels: a basement opening to the south, serving as a ground floor and now featuring a Diplomatic Reception Room; a first floor (State Floor) at the grade of Pennsylvania Avenue, now used for ceremonies, public receptions, and tourist visitation; a second floor, now used for family and guest quarters; and a third floor, adapted from the balustraded attic in 1927, providing additional family bedrooms, sitting rooms, a sun room, and storage space. Acting with dispatch in order to ensure that the city of Washington would indeed be the capital of the United States, the President promptly approved Hoban's design. Within three days following the close of the competition, the Commissioners had Hoban under contract, and he had staked out the building on the site. The exterior walls and roof were completed by the end of 1798, but the interior finishing constantly lagged.

Jefferson, during his presidency, had Superintendent

of Public Buildings Benjamin Henry Latrobe prepare designs for extended east and west wings in the form of low terrace and pavilion constructions to provide spaces for supporting service facilities and executive offices. These recalled Jefferson's own Palladian arrangement of "dependencies" at Monticello, the country mansion he had designed for himself in Piedmont, Va. He also had Latrobe prepare designs for extended central porticos: a rectangular porte-cochere on the north (Pennsylvania Avenue) (Fig. 1), and a semicircular veranda on the south (the President's Park). Latrobe retained his position under President James Madison, but was not able to complete intended grounds development and interior decoration programs before his termination as Superintendent and the catastrophic burning of the President's House by the British during the War of 1812.

Aquia Creek sandstone, a Virginia freestone, was extensively used in the earliest public buildings of Washington, but because of its fragility, it was sometimes painted. The President's House, which had been popularly referred to as the "White House" even before the turn of the nineteenth century, was painted following its burning by the British on August 24, 1814, thus concealing smoke stains on the facades. Investigation of the east facade in the early 1980s revealed 32 coats of paint accumulated over the years. Stabilization and reconstruction were well along by 1815 under Hoban, the original architect. In the interest of saving time, he replaced the brick masonry structure with timber in parts of the interior and, because of the increasingly rapid depletion of the Aquia quarries, he used Seneca Creek sandstone from nearby Maryland. Eventually, marble from quarries on both sides of the Potomac River, north of the city, was used. At various times, the President's House was called the President's Palace or Mansion, the Great House, and the Castle. In early 1818, following its repair, it was officially named the Executive

Mansion by President Madison. It was officially renamed the White House by an act of Congress early in the administration of President Theodore Roosevelt.

The first hundred years of its existence saw the development of the Executive Mansion from Washington's preferred compact and complete core to an extended building complex incorporating Jefferson's terrace–pavilion wings and L'Enfant's plan to accommodate executive offices in a series of closely associated structures. By the end of the 1930s, the initial central portion, with public rooms downstairs and private apartments upstairs, had been essentially completed and adorned by the two great porticos; Jefferson's wings had been built, and the part of the President's Park immediately adjacent on the south side had been landscaped with beds and flowers. By midcentury, Andrew Jackson Downing, the most prominent U.S. landscape architect of the time, had prepared plans for the grounds as part of his romantic concepts for the Mall and, in particular, the environs of the red sandstone Smithsonian Building.

In the 1830s, a rudimentary central heating system was installed in the Executive Mansion. In the 1840s, the system was extended and, also, gas illumination was supplied for the house and the grounds. In the 1850s, Thomas U. Walter, the Architect of the Capitol, updated the interior, and city water was brought in. During this period, bathrooms were built: President Andrew Jackson had a cedar trough bathtub, and Millard Fillmore had one of mahogany lined with zinc, which Rutherford B. Hayes replaced with a modern one in 1881. In the last decade of the century, electricity was added to the improvements.

Through the second half of the nineteenth century, greenhouses and conservatories were built in profusion atop Jefferson's west terrace wing, and by 1870 his east wing was taken down to be replaced by a successor structure, designed by Alfred B. Mullett, architect of the State,

Figure 1. The north facade of the White House features a dignified classical portico favored by Thomas Jefferson. Courtesy of the National Park Service, U.S. Department of the Interior.

War and Navy Building (now the Old Executive Office Building). A plan prepared by the staff of the Office of Public Buildings and Grounds on the centennial of the design of the original President's House (1892) proposed a block-long continuous structure, never built, of more greenhouses and conservatories on the south and enclosing a square private garden court framed by the 1792 mansion on the north, with a new historical art wing on the east (opposite the Treasury Building) and an official wing on the west, facing the State, War and Navy Building.

The Columbian Exposition of 1893 in Chicago, Ill., celebrating the quadricentennial of Columbus's discovery of the New World and the District of Columbia Centennial in 1900 produced significant impacts that would affect the Executive Mansion in the twentieth century. The Columbian Exposition reinstated the classical spirit in architecture that had been compromised by Victorian eclecticism. The District of Columbia Centennial produced proposals that would rededicate Washington to the planning principles that inspired L'Enfant. These paved the way for the production in 1902 of a plan prepared under the direction of the U.S. Senate's District Committee Chairman, James McMillan. The plan, traditionally referred to as the McMillan Plan, directly affected the development of the Mall, the President's Park, and associated areas of monumental Washington, and would continue to affect the federal city and its environs through the establishment of a permanent Commission of Fine Arts.

Architect Charles Follen McKim, partner in the firm of McKim, Mead and White, a key figure in the Columbian Exposition, and a member of McMillan's Senate Parks Commission, was commissioned in 1902 to rehabilitate the White House. The comprehensive scope of the work made it necessary for President Theodore Roosevelt and his family to move out. Roosevelt did not want to be out of the house for more than a few months, nor would he permit drastic architectural changes. In addition to external and internal improvements to the structure and spaces of the mansion itself, the greenhouses and conservatories on the west were removed and replaced by an Executive Office Wing, and Jefferson's other terrace to the east, which had been removed during Mullett's involvement, was replaced by the East Gallery, providing a public entrance capable of handling visitors in large numbers. During World War II, the east wing was extended again for increased office space and security provisions. In the mansion, the structural timbers placed by James Hoban following the 1814 burning were replaced with modern masonry and steel construction; utility systems were updated; new reception rooms and support facilities were installed in the basement; the State Dining Room was enlarged on the first floor; office spaces were converted to family uses; and the overall decor was generally harmonized, in keeping with a trend to return to the historical period of the nation's founding.

Theodore Roosevelt, whose time restrictions for the project were more faithfully observed than his constraints regarding retention of the interiors and conservatories, was pleased with the work and its timely completion. He expressed to Congress his desire that the White House,

like Washington's Mount Vernon and Jefferson's University of Virginia, should henceforth be preserved. It is ironic that, by the express direction of the Executive and the Congress, neither the White House nor the Capitol has been placed on the National Register of Historic Places, apparently as a means of their retaining absolute authority and complete control over those properties.

White House expansions and improvements continued well into the twentieth century. In 1927, the need to replace a severely deteriorated roof resulted in the conversion of the attic into a new third floor, yielding additional residential and service space. Like Theodore Roosevelt a quarter century earlier, President Calvin Coolidge had to find temporary quarters during the construction. During the long tenancy of Franklin D. Roosevelt, the White House underwent numerous incremental alterations and additions, but in 1946, when his successor, Harry S. Truman, proposed adding a new wing to the Executive Office Building, Congress refused to appropriate the necessary funds. A year later, Truman proposed building a balcony from the second-floor family quarters within the columned perimeter of the monumental south portico (Fig. 2). In that way, the desire of the folksy man from the Midwest for a homey back porch would be satisfied. A special appropriation by Congress was not required, and despite objections by the Commission of Fine Arts and the press, the tenacious President accomplished his objective. Despite his wish to enjoy his residency in the White House, Truman was destined to live across Pennsylvania Avenue in Blair House, the presidential guest house, during much of his time in office. The historic early nineteenth-century Blair–Lee houses, together with somewhat later contiguous residential properties, are now used by the White House and State Department for state occasions and as guest quarters for eminent visitors. Following decades of deterioration, the properties were extensively remodeled and redecorated in the mid-1980s.

Structural weaknesses observed in 1946 prompted another comprehensive overhaul of the White House. Hoban's earlier timber replacements to support the second floor had not been supplanted by McKim's 1902 project,

Figure 2. The south facade of the White House, with a portion of the President's Park in the foreground. Truman's balcony addition to the massive portico is restrained, but evident. Photograph courtesy of J. Walter Roth, AIA.

and incremental modernization programs after that further weakened the structure. Between 1949 and 1952, following some three years of preliminary investigations, the White House was, in effect, gutted. The renovation was under the direction of staff consultant architect Lorenzo Simmons Winslow, with the involvement of architect William Adams Delano (responsible for the 1934 Post Office Building in Washington's Federal Triangle and for President Truman's balcony), a distant cousin of Franklin Roosevelt. The relatively new third-floor structure, of modern construction, and the original exterior walls were saved, but an entirely new, independent structure of steel and concrete was built within and under that envelope. Additional basement levels were excavated for new utilities and service spaces. Although architect Winslow recommended retention of historic materials and reuse of historic motifs, much of the existing fabric was wasted, and many details were sacrificed to expediency. By present-day preservation standards and restoration practices, the 1952 rehabilitation represents a lost opportunity to achieve a sensitive result; otherwise, the project was a notable engineering achievement.

Through the two centuries of its existence, the White House has hosted a considerable number of occupants, who have left their marks to varied degrees on the building, its finishes, and its furnishings. Changes were continually taking place, some minor and marginal, and others quite comprehensive and conscientious, but it was not until the administration of President John F. Kennedy that such activities were conducted by professional curatorial staff with the assistance of advisory committees. Special subcommittees were formed to carry out specific projects, such as stocking a White House library. The White House Historical Association was chartered in 1961 for educa-

Figure 3. A 1974 aerial view of the White House, looking northwest. The Old Executive Office Building (formerly the State, War and Navy Building) is to the west; Pennsylvania Avenue and Lafayette square are to the north; the Treasury Building is to the east; and the President's Park is to the south. Courtesy of the National Park Service, U.S. Department of the Interior.

tional purposes, to issue publications, and to acquire historical furnishings. The collection of paintings, dating back to 1800, is large and varied, containing portraits of the Presidents and other historical personages and subjects and representative works of notable artists. The furnishings and appointments in the public and state rooms, down to the table settings, are tantamount to a collection of a museum of applied art.

In spite of perennial campaigns by presidential candidates running against bureaucracy and promising to reduce the number of federal government employees, White House staff and costs continue to increase. Much more than a residence for the First Family, the White House is a historic landmark receiving special conservation care, a major tourist attraction suffering the impact of a constant flow of sightseers, an elaborate urban park, an extensive office building, a complicated communications center, and a concentrated security installation. Its various components are under the jurisdiction of diverse government agencies. The National Park Service (Department of the Interior) tends the grounds and maintains the mansion. The Public Buildings Service (General Services Administration) is responsible for the office wings and Executive Office Building. Elements of the Department of Defense staff the mess facilities, communication centers, and limousine services. The Secret Service operates security facilities.

In recent years, much attention has been given to physical and electronic devices as deterrents to terrorist attacks. During 1983–1987, at a cost of almost $7 million, East Executive Avenue, the two-way, two-blocks long city street between the White House and the Treasury Building, was converted into a pedestrian park, ostensibly to accommodate the long lines of tourist visitors who formerly had to queue along a narrow sidewalk, but actually as a security measure to remove the possibility of a high-speed vehicular approach from an exposed flank.

Theodore Roosevelt's Executive Office Building, on the west side of the White House, was intended by its architect as an interim measure to get offices out of the second floor of the mansion (Fig. 3). It was almost doubled by President William Howard Taft in 1909–1910, less than 10 years after its initial completion. Twenty-four years later (1934), during the first term of Franklin Roosevelt, the Executive Office Building's space was tripled. This was accomplished by converting attic space, adding basement space, and extending the first floor as a terrace–pavilion. Architect McKim's intention to keep his 1902 Executive Office Building unobtrusive, if not temporary, was respected by Eric Gugler, Franklin Roosevelt's choice as design architect. Gugler's minimal concept also received the approbation of the Commission of Fine Arts.

Subsequent initiatives to increase executive office space by adding to the Executive Office Building, such as that by Truman in 1946, have been avoided in a number of ways. The State, Navy and War Building, now called the Old Executive Office Building, was annexed to house the offices of the Vice President, the Secret Service, and others. New executive office buildings were constructed, and historic buildings around Lafayette Square, on the north side of Pennsylvania Avenue, directly opposite the

White House, were restored or reconstructed. Various other buildings neighboring the complex, such as the small but convenient Winder Building (1847–1848) (originally privately built for lease to the government), were occupied. So the White House is much more than a mansion for the First Family, and even more than a President's Palace: a verdant pause in a busy metropolis, it is the focus of a cluster of assorted buildings, symbolizing the continuity and pervasiveness of a national and democratic government.

BIBLIOGRAPHY

General References

J. N. Pearce, *The White House: An Historic Guide,* White House Historical Association, Washington, D.C., 1962 *et seq.*

D. J. Lehman, (*Old*) *Executive Office Building: General Services Administration, Historical Study No. 3,* U.S. Government Printing Office, Washington, D.C., 1970.

Washington—The Design of the Federal City, National Archives Publication, No. 73-1, General Services Administration, Washington, D.C., 1972, pp. 12, 13, 76.

H. N. Jacobsen, F. D. Lethbridge, and D. R. Rosenthal, W. J. Cox, eds., *A Guide to the Architecture of Washington, D.C.,* 2nd ed., McGraw-Hill Inc., New York, 1974.

L. Craig and the Staff of the Federal Architecture Project, *The Federal Presence: Architecture, Politics and Symbols in U.S. Government Building,* MIT Press, Cambridge, Mass., 1978.

W. Ryan and D. Guinness, *The White House: An Architectural History,* McGraw-Hill Inc., New York, 1980.

E. L. Templeman, *The Blair Lee House: Guest House of the President,* EPM Publications, McLean, Va., 1980.

The Federal Writers' Project, *The WPA Guide to Washington, D.C.,* Pantheon Books, New York, 1983.

W. Seale, *The President's House, A History,* White House Historical Association and The National Geographic Society, Washington, D.C., 1986, 2 vols.

See also U.S. CAPITOL

J. WALTER ROTH, AIA
Alexandria, Virginia

WHITE, SANDFORD.   See MCKIM, MEAD & WHITE

WINDOWS

The collective deployment of windows in buildings is called fenestration. This refers to openings of one kind or another covered by transparent or translucent membranes. The word has its origins in antiquity, when, in Latin, the word *fenestra* was synonymous with what is now called a window: an opening in a wall to admit air and light. The contemporary French word for window, *fenêtre,* reflects these origins. Following the development of theories of architectural order, fenestration came to mean not only windows themselves, but their disposition and compositional arrangement in a building facade or wall. This is the sense in which the word is used today in architecture.

In understanding the architectural and technical origins of windows, it is of some interest that the term fenestration is used also in the contemporary study of human anatomy, referring to parts of the inner ear and of the vascular system, where thin skin membranes are stretched over delicate bonework or some other structure. Fenestration is also used in entomology to refer to transparent spots in the wings of certain insects. These nonarchitectural uses of the term fenestration refer to the ways in which people devised windows before the advent of glass and framing systems for glazing. Dried and cured animal skins, stretched over lightweight wood frames or simply draped over natural or manmade openings, were probably the earliest form of window.

For as long as people have constructed shelters, they have faced the problem of letting some parts of the outdoor environment in, while keeping other parts out; windows, as mediators between the insides and the outsides of buildings, are one of the principal architectural means for doing this. In any case, as they are now known, windows have distant origins, possibly reaching back even to the reasons for which one cave was chosen for a dwelling over another, simply on the basis of available openings for sunlight and air.

Through time, many varying demands have been placed on fenestration and builders have gone to great lengths to devise new ways to meet these design challenges. In contemporary buildings, windows and their appurtenances are expected to satisfy more requirements than perhaps any other single building component and may be subjected to the most demanding uses. Furthermore, the demands placed on windows are not static; fenestration must be designed to respond throughout the day and over the course of the seasons to the varying demands of climate, occupant needs and desires, and changes in architectural tastes.

Today, windows can be thought of as operable parts of a building envelope; in this sense, they must perform many interrelated and sometimes conflicting functions, including:

- Providing sunlight, when it is available and desired.
- Providing visual and audial privacy, while admitting sunlight.
- Admitting ventilating air and cooling breezes, when they are wanted.
- Insulating and protecting against harsh cold, driving winds, and wind-driven rain.
- Permitting regular, easy operation by building occupants.
- Providing unobstructed access to desirable views.
- Affording a measure of economy, durability, and maintainability.
- Affording security against vandals, burglars, and intruders.
- Contributing to a building's architectural order and character.

The requirement that windows contribute to an overall sense of architectural order and character has at times overshadowed almost all other considerations. Indeed, until freed of prior constraints by the technology of modernism in the early twentieth century, the designers and makers of buildings devised theories of window placement and window-making that related little to their more functional attributes (Fig. 1).

However, even the classical architectural orders and later refinements by Palladio and others owed much of their nature to what was then known about building materials and the technology for making buildings. The proportions of the Palladian order, after all, are not unrelated to knowledge at the time about how to carry brick structurally, how to make glass, and how to manufacture frames capable of carrying glass.

A tremendous range of highly distinctive window configurations has emerged over time, to the extent that a complete, illustrated glossary of window types and window-related terms would require space and effort well beyond the scope of this article. Among the terms that would have to be included in such a listing are bay windows (angular or curved projections filled by fenestration); bow windows (curved in plan, sometimes projecting beyond the plane of the wall); casement windows (made of metal or timber with the long dimension of the sash hung vertically opening inward or outward); Chicago windows (a distinctive configuration, predominant in Chicago during the first half of the twentieth century, in which a full structural bay is occupied by a fixed central pane of glass, flanked by two smaller operable panes); clerestory, or clearstory, windows (fixed or operable glazing placed well above the viewing plane in a space or a room, usually to admit daylight); dormers, French windows, lancets, lattice windows, and many others. Table 1 lists the range of materials from which windows are now made and discusses their attributes. Table 2 suggests various window configurations and their properties.

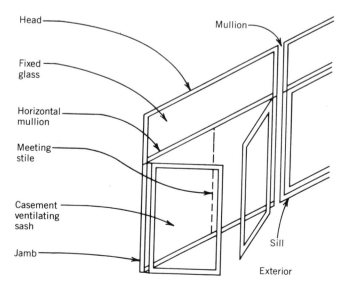

Figure 1. Window nomenclature. Reprinted by permission of John Wiley & Sons, Inc., *Architectural Graphic Standards,* C. G. Ramsey and H. R. Sleeper, 8th ed., 1988.

Table 1. Materials for Making Windows

Window Type	Advantages	Limitations
Solid wood	Wood is a good thermal insulator; custom shapes and sizes possible; "natural" or historic appearance possible; can be painted a variety of colors; very durable factory coatings are available.	Components are subject to expansion with moisture; requires painting and other care at regular intervals; thicker frame and sash than metal windows.
Solid aluminum	Wide choice of colors for coatings; lightweight; some flexibility in shapes and sizes; very low maintenance; variety of extruded sections available for frame and sash members.	Unless thermally improved (with a "break" in the frame between inside and outside), subject to heat loss and condensation; custom shapes and sizes not possible; for strength, must be thicker than steel; when coated, frame has shiny appearance.
Vinyl-clad wood	Combines strength of wood and durability of vinyl; very low maintenance; very strong; stock sizes only, but available with good trim and fitting kits to fit various openings.	Limited choice of vinyl colors, especially in darker ranges; custom shapes and sizes not possible; vinyl can be broken by accidental blows, but is repairable.
Vinyl-clad aluminum	Durable and strong; better thermal properties than unclad units; very low maintenance.	Limited choice of vinyl colors, especially in darker ranges; can be expensive; no custom shapes or sizes; unhistoric, shiny appearance from vinyl.
Aluminum-clad wood	Very strong and durable; wider range of colors available; some flexibility in sizes and shape.	Heavier than plain wood or metal; subject to moisture penetration at aluminum seams and joints unless very well made; unhistoric appearance and "thick" frame and sash.
Steel	Thin, very strong; flexibility in shapes and sizes; wide range of color choices; lower maintenance than wood.	Not very common for residential use, but possible; can be expensive; requires periodic painting; unless thermally "broken" and well insulated, subject to conductive heat loss moisture condensation.
Solid vinyl	Very durable; few components subject to moisture retention or decay; good insulator; wide variety of color choices available.	Can be expensive; may not be appropriate in appearance for older or historic homes.

If prescriptions for fenestration and windows were bound inextricably with what were then thought to be the timeless ways of making buildings, it followed that orthodox architectural modernism quickly seized on the window as a prime area of expressive opportunity and a suitable object for the full force of architectural iconoclasm. Whole building envelopes became "windows," dissociated by the steel frame and glass curtain wall from the normal limits of fenestration—small openings in vast, load-bearing, otherwise opaque walls—to become walls entirely

Table 2. Window Characteristics

Window Types	Opens 100%	Diverts inflowing air upward	Deflect drafts	Rain protection while partly open	Screen, storm sash easy to install	Easy to wash	Easy to operate over an obstruction
Horizontal sliding					●	●	
Double hung					●		
Double hung (reversed)					●	●	
Casement (out)	●		●		●		●
Casement (in)	●		●		●	●	●
Pivoted (vertical)	●		●			●	●
Pivoted (horizontal)	●	●	●	●		●	
Top hinged (out)	●			●	●		
Bottom hinged (in)	●	●	●	●		●	●
Fixed sash							●
Jalousie	●	●		●			●

Source: National Institute of Standards and Technology.

made of glass. It is unclear in many buildings where window ends and wall begins, or whether there is any wall at all.

Throughout the Western world, the early proponents of a new, modern architecture—Gropius, Garnier, Wright, LeCorbusier, Reitveld, Wagner, and many others—sought and found new ways to break from the constraints of the punctured structural bearing wall. Windows wrapping around corners, whole expanses of uninterrupted glass panes—in short, glass and glass block doing things in combination with other materials that had never before been done—represented unprecedented attitudes toward spatial definition and architectural composition.

As the twentieth century progressed and an international style emerged from the roots of modernist theory and dogma, the technology of the curtain wall kept pace. Developed to a high art form and state of technical perfection by such internationally active architectural firms as Skidmore, Owings & Merrill, the steel and glass curtain wall became an earmark of urban and suburban building alike, relegating mere "windows" to houses and lesser nonresidential buildings. Only recently, and in limited ways, have windows as such returned to larger-scale buildings.

The development of float glass, plate glass, and tempered safety glass was spurred in part by demands within the automotive industry, but was also fueled by shopkeepers' interest in making ever-larger storefront displays of merchandise. The new glasses made such applications safer, less expensive, and more sturdy; they also helped to open an entirely new realm of technical and expressive potential for commercial, industrial, and institutional architecture.

The glass curtain wall—held in place by high-strength steel and aluminum components affixed to an independent structural system—seems a natural outgrowth of the glassmaking industry's intensive search for ways to make pieces of glass that became stronger, larger, and freer of visual distortions. Making glass for building applications and making windows have become very different, separate enterprises.

In the meantime, however, some window manufacturers have flourished, growing substantially from their origins in local mills serving regional markets. Window manufacturing is now a highly developed, relatively concentrated industry with national sales and distribution organizations. The advent of new paints, coatings, and claddings has moved the industry from the realm of sim-

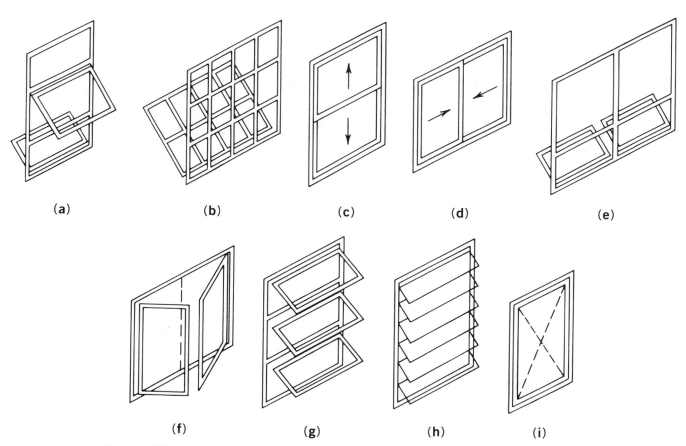

Figure 2. Window types (a) projected; (b) security; (c) double hung; (d) sliding; (e) combination; (f) casement; (g) awning; (h) jalousie; (i) pivoted. Reprinted by permission of John Wiley & Sons, Inc., *Architectural Graphic Standards*, C. G. Ramsey and H. R. Sleeper, 8th ed., 1988.

ple millwork and glazing to highly automated, factory-based production methods.

The windows in most residences built today are likely to be constructed from vinyl and other plastics, wood, glass, and metal; gone are the heavy counterweights and complex, often cumbersome pieces of sashwork that characterized "production" windows earlier in the twentieth century. Replacing them are a wide variety of options for hardware, claddings, dividers, and glazings.

Window sizes, shapes, and configurations are available in more variations than ever before, even in the United States, where, for nearly 200 years, double-hung units seemed to have gained an unshakable place in residential construction. Today one can choose from stock offerings of sliding and fixed windows, casements, awnings, hoppers, vertically and horizontally pivoted, single-hungs, double-hungs and many combinations of all types (Fig. 2). Furthermore, many manufacturers are now able to make windows of custom design at costs only slightly above the costs of stock units.

It is little wonder, perhaps, that many people have turned against the hermetically sealed steel-and-glass skyscraper. Buildings may be among the vehicles that best provide links with history and, as some have argued, even the primordial past. Also, windows that open and close, and that can be adjusted to suit conditions and preferences, provide a vital link between people and their outdoor surroundings. Perhaps modernist architects went too far in altering—or even eliminating—windows in order to express the freedoms supposed to follow from automation and mass production. Far from becoming the promised vehicle for social good and universal access to wealth, modern building technology, for many, seems to have imposed a brand of joyless tyranny.

In any case, continuity with history, in an age of discontinuity, has taken on a new importance that has not left the realm of architecture untouched. Thus, some present-day practitioners of architecture have returned to the broader, classical notion of windows and fenestration, as part of a larger movement involving reexamination of premodern precepts and the development of postmodern sensibilities.

The question may be: Now that the technical means are available to do virtually anything, what is the desired result? For some contemporary architects, the answers in part involve a return to the use of windows on very large buildings, which earlier would more likely have been built out of some system of glass-and-curtain-wall. These postmodern buildings take advantage of advances in the technology of window manufacture, using windows as essential elements in redefining architectural orders.

Even if few of these newer architectural compositions really come to a full circle in meeting the stylistic conventions and architectural successes of their historic antecedents, they are at least buildings in which windows—once again—are clearly windows.

BIBLIOGRAPHY

General References

H. E. Beckett, *Windows: Performance, Design and Installation,* Van Nostrand Reinhold, New York, 1974.

V. Clery, *Windows,* Penguin, Jonathan-James, New York, 1978.

B. P. Lim, *Environmental Factors in the Design of Building Fenestration,* Applied Science Publishers, Inc., London, 1979.

W. A. Shurcliff, *Thermal Shutters and Shades,* Brick House Press, Andover, Mass., 1980.

Sweet's Catalog Files. Volume 1, Product Selection Data, McGraw-Hill Information Systems Company, New York, 1988.

D. P. Turner, ed., *Window Glass Design Guide,* The Architectural Press, London, 1977.

See also ACRYLICS; ALUMINUM; ENVELOPES, BUILDING; GLASS FILMS; GLASS IN CONSTRUCTION; LIGHTING—DAYLIGHTING; SEALANTS

THOMAS VONIER, AIA
Washington, D.C.

WOMEN IN ARCHITECTURE

WOMEN IN ARCHITECTURE IN THE UNITED STATES

In 1891, the first woman graduated from Cornell University with a degree in architecture. A decade later Sophia Hayden graduated from the Massachusetts Institute of Technology. From these beginnings in the nineteenth century the number of women in the architectural profession grew to 50 by 1910. At that time half of the architecture programs in the U.S. openly denied admission to women. Well into the twentieth century, most of the country's universities maintained strict quotas restricting the admission of female students. These restrictions were relaxed only during times of male student shortage, ie, World Wars I and II.

A pioneer woman architect, Louise Blanchard Bethune (1856–1913), was the first woman to become a member of the AIA and also the first Fellow in 1888. Theodate Pope Riddle (1868–1946), another pioneer, hired faculty members to tutor her privately. She was the first woman to become a licensed architect in both New York and Connecticut and in 1926 was appointed to the AIA College of Fellows. In 1951, prevailing prejudices and overt action against women entering the architectural schools were expressed in writing by the dean of Harvard's Graduate School of Design. He wrote that professional education was wasted on women who would end up abandoning their career in favor of raising a family.

Pietro Belluschi, the dean of MIT's School of Architecture wrote in his essay of 1955, "The Exceptional One," "I know some women who have done well at it, but the obstacles are so great that it takes an exceptional girl to make a go of it. If she insisted upon becoming an architect, I would try to dissuade her. If then she was still determined, I would give her my blessing that she could be that exceptional one." Many other outstanding women architects forged ahead despite these great obstacles and became role models for the generations to follow. The women's movement in the 1960s and 1970s with its Supreme Court backing of civil rights legislation modified such overt expressions of prejudice in the schools and in employment.

During the earlier periods, for a woman to receive the necessary education, mentorship, and apprenticeship required to become an architect, she needed substantial financial reserves in addition to exceptional drive and perserverance. For example, Julia Morgan (1872–1957), was unable to obtain architectural education in the United States. She studied engineering at Cornell then had to travel to Paris to receive her architectural training at the Ecole des Beaux Arts.

The relatively small but growing numbers of women in architecture continually reveal that the ability to juggle time and major responsibilities of home, raising large families, and career can be amazing. These remarkable women are also recognized by their peers for outstanding architectural contributions.

ADVANCES OF WOMEN IN ARCHITECTURE

There has been an exponential increase in the number of women in architecture and their professional recognition in the final decades of the twentieth century. Quotas have been removed from school admission policies and women now comprise 20%–50% of the students in architecture schools. Affirmative action policies have provided a small percentage of government work to be awarded to minority and women owned businesses. The awards have aided these women in maintaining their own practices.

In May, 1988 the number of women Corporate members (licensed architects) in the AIA had increased to approximately 2100 which is equivalent to 4% of its total membership. Due to multiple state registrations it is difficult to determine the total number of licensed architects in the U.S. but an estimate would be twice the number of AIA Corporate members, or approximately 4200 registered women architects. Women's outstanding contributions to the profession have been recognized by fellowship in the AIA; 39 women have been inducted into the College of Fellows between 1867–1986.

The civil rights movement of the 1970s resulted in Supreme Court decisions against discrimination because of one's color, national origin, or sex, and supported affirmative action policies which provided women architects with a very small portion of government contracts. This enabled the increasing numbers of women who owned architectural firms to sustain a practice and encouraged many architectural schools to add women to their faculties. Women have fared somewhat better in auxiliary areas such as interiors, public relations, programming, and have even moved into other design fields of landscape architecture and graphic design.

Undaunted by the lack of role models and mentors, women have formed their own networks of associations in architecture, the first such organization was formed in St. Louis in 1918. Similar networks exist today under names such as, The Association of Women in Architecture, The Organization of Women in Architecture, Atlanta, Austin, Houston, College Station Tex., Denver, Washington, D.C., Chicago, Los Angeles, Minneapolis, New York, Roanoke, and San Francisco.

FOREIGN BORN AND TRAINED

In the United States many of the women in architecture are foreign born and trained. The Philippines, South America, and Europe appeared to encourage more women students than the U.S. did prior to the Women's Movement. Some notable examples are Fani Hansen (Bulgaria), Susan Torre (Argentina), Rosaria Pomelli (Italy), and Denise Scott Brown (born in Africa, educated in South Africa and Europe). In many of these foreign countries, women are repressed personally and socially but are able to work and advance without prejudice in their profession.

WOMEN IN ARCHITECTURAL FIRMS

Two surveys by the AIA of women employees in architectural firms in 1974 and 1981 revealed a majority of women experienced discriminatory practices in school and later at work. There were incidents promoted by coworkers, contractors, and superiors with work assignments and professional growth into managerial positions. Despite these negative responses, seven out of ten would choose architecture again if they had the option of changing careers.

BIOGRAPHIES OF WOMEN ARCHITECTS IN THE UNITED STATES

It would be impossible to list all the outstanding women architects in this summary, who despite formidable barriers have made a positive impact on their profession. As of 1989, with the exception of Lutah Maria Riggs and Mary Colter, these women are still living and practicing architects.

Elaine Carbrey, AIA. Elaine Carbrey earned her B.Arch. at Louisiana State University, her professional affiliations include the AIA and the AICP. She is Vice President and Head of the Planning Department of Gruen Associates in Los Angeles, involved with planning communities in several states and in foreign countries such as Antigua and Indonesia. Ms. Carbrey has participated as Project Manager or Principal Planner in many city and regional planning projects, including: The Westwood Village Specific Plan and Environmental Impact Reports, Los Angeles; The Central Phoenix Development Plan, designed to assist the city in realizing its potential as a major urban center in the Southwest and to provide an overall framework to guide public and private investments; Waterwood, a balanced, water oriented new town in east-central Texas which will contain public marinas, a yacht club, luxury resort hotels, lakefront and golf course condominiums, a marina village with restaurants, entertainment and specialty shops, plus complete community facilities and services in the areas of health, education, commerce, and recreation to accommodate an ultimate planned population of 25,000.

Ann Chaintreuil, AIA. Ann Chaintreuil received her M.Arch. at Syracuse University. She worked in the summers during her school years for local architecture firms.

Chaintreuil spent a year at the Architectural Association in London and also worked for a Boston firm before returning to Rochester where she was given valuable mentorship from the principal. She admits that "mentorship" is difficult for women to receive, most protege roles being reserved for men. She is a partner in the firm of Macon/Chaintreuil in Rochester. Two of her credits are the Max Loenthal building for Rochester Institute of Technology and the National Institute for the Deaf in Rochester, N.Y.

Mary Jane Colter (1869–1958). Although born in Pittsburgh, Mary Jane Colter considered St. Paul, Minn. where her family settled when she was eleven her hometown. Her interest as a child in art persuaded her to hide her Sioux drawings when her mother burnt all Indian articles in their home to prevent the spread of smallpox which at that time permeated the surrounding Sioux territory. Mary's love for Indian art influenced her work both in architecture and in decoration. Three years after high school, after the death of her father in 1886, she persuaded her mother and sister to send her to art school in San Francisco thereby enabling her to support them by teaching art. Her knowledge of architecture was acquired through an apprenticeship in a local architect's office. At that time there were few certified architects (1100 in the U.S., California did not begin licensing architects until 1901) and apprenticeship was the accepted way of fulfilling the desire to become an architect. Sharing the prevailing design philosophy of California architects who rejected the European model in favor of a style reminiscent of the old southwest, Mary Colter became one of the strongest proponents of that revival.

After several years of teaching she was approached by the Fred Harvey Company which operated the restaurants and hotels of the Santa Fe Railroad. They needed a "decorator who knew Indian things and had imagination" and Mary Colter supplied that need for the next forty years. Starting as the decorator for the Indian Building (part of the Alvarado Hotel designed by Charles F. Whittlesey) in Albuquerque, she went on to design the Hopi House constructed by Hopi builders of indigenous wood and stone at the Grand Canyon in 1902. Other Grand Canyon projects followed: Bright Angel Lodge, Phantom Ranch, the Lookout, Hermit's Rest, and the Watchtower. Her phenomenal interest in Indian Art was instrumental in producing a special architectural style with unusual and beautiful interiors in the many hotels and gift shops she designed. The proof of Mary Colter's exceptional work lies in the extraordinary buildings she created as an integral part of the magnificent Grand Canyon.

Natalie De Blois, FAIA. After graduating from Columbia University with a B.Arch. at the end of World War II, a time when architecture was about to awaken, Natalie De Blois obtained employment with the New York office of Skidmore, Owings and Merrill. Her abilities were quickly recognized and she was promoted to the ranks of Participating Associate and awarded a Fulbright Fellowship to study at the Ecole des Beaux Arts in Paris.

Natalie De Blois was responsible for the design of a remarkably large number of major and often award winning projects including the Terrace Plaza Hotel, Cincinnati, Ohio; the Ford Motor Company Office Building, Dearborn, Mich.; the Bank of Fort Worth, Fort Worth, Tex.; the Great Southern Life Insurance Company, Houston, Tex.; the Consular–Amerikahaus Buildings for the U.S. State Department in Frankfurt, Dusseldorf, Bremen and Stuttgart, Germany; the Connecticut General Life Insurance Headquarters, Bloomfield, Conn.; the Union Carbide Corporate Headquarters, the Lever House, and the Lincoln Center for the Performing Arts Library–Museum in New York City.

In 1961 Natalie De Blois transferred to the Chicago office of SOM where she worked as Participating Partner for the next 13 years. The list of major designs to her credit is impressive and includes the Equitable Life Assurance Building, Chicago, Ill.; Boots Pure Drug Company Headquarters, Nottingham, England; Overbeek Office Building, Rotterdam, Holland; Horizon House Apartments, Fort Lee, N.J.; and the International Bank for Reconstruction, Washington, D.C.

After devoting three decades to the SOM firm, De Blois decided to relocate to Houston to work with the 3D/International firm. Her designs included the Riyadh Inter-Continental Hotel extension, Saudi Arabia; the Williams Center Forum, Tulsa, Okla.; and the Seafirst Fifth Avenue Plaza Office Building, Seattle, Wash.

Since 1980 Natalie De Blois has taught on the architecture faculty of the University of Texas at Austin and served as a visiting lecturer or instructor at the University of California, Berkeley; University of Southwest Louisiana, Lafayette; University of Oklahoma, Norman; and the University of Houston, Tex.

Katherine (Kate) Diamond, AIA. Although Kate Diamond was born in the U.S., lived in Chicago and completed high school in Southern California, she studied architecture at the Technion in Israel. She served also as an officer in the Israeli Air Force Corps of Engineers where her duties included designing military and other government buildings. On her return to Los Angeles she became a designer and marketing architect in a medium sized firm where she designed several award winning buildings including the Otto Nemenz International Office Building, The Park Beyond the Park office project, and the conversion of a historic munitions factory into the multifunctional family center for the U.S. Air Force. In 1985 she formed a partnership in Siegel, Sklarek, Diamond AIA, Architects as Partner-in-Charge of Design. Her designs reflect her experience as a Research Assistant on a project studying architectural applications of complex morphology. She calls her design philosophy "Sculptured functionalism" because it combines a commitment to user responsive architectural solutions with an equal interest in architecture as sculpture. Projects to her credit are the Lawndale Civic Center Expansion, the Student Services Building addition at the University of California, Irvine, Tarzana Storage Facility, Jefferson Elementary School and Commonwealth Elementary School in Los Angeles. (Fig. 1).

Figure 1. Commonwealth Elementary School. Courtesy of Rogers.

Sarah P. Harkness, FAIA. Major projects require team efforts and Sarah Harkness has made an outstanding contribution to collaborative efforts. The design of women architects shows no discernible architectural style, but as Harkness says "We hope there is a difference. We need it: the man-made environment is close to disaster."

Sarah Harkness received her architectural education at the Cambridge School of Architecture and Landscape Architecture, an all women's school staffed by many professors from Harvard's Graduate School of Design. The Cambridge School of Architecture was the professional learning campus for many notable women from 1917–1942 when its existence was terminated by its parent school, Smith College.

She was a founding partner in 1946 of The Architects Collaborative (TAC) in Cambridge, Mass., with her husband John Harkness and her good friends, Norman and Jean Fletcher and Walter Gropius. Their system of collaborative decision making resulted in sharing design experience with a high level of quality, expertise, and responsibility on all projects propelling the phenomenal growth of TAC to a multinational corporation.

Her credits include the North Shore Community College, Beverly, Mass.; the Olin Arts Center, Bates College, Lewiston, Maine; the Fox Lane Middle School, Bedford, N.Y.; and the Schlechter Auditorium, Dickerson College, Carlisle, Pa. The award winning Bates College Library was designed to functionally and visually relate to its predecessor with a brick exterior and pitched roof, consistent with the character of the campus yet encompassing a dramatic upbeat four–story elevation facing the large scale quadrangle (Fig. 2). Energy conscious design and humane environments are prominent in her many school and university projects.

Jane Hastings, FAIA. Jane Hastings, founder of The Hastings Group, has maintained her own practice in Seattle, Washington for over a quarter century. She has purposely kept the firm small to assure personal attention to every project. Her practice is substantially single–family residences (Fig. 3) with notable exceptions: the Ventilation Building of the Mercer Island First Hill Lid; the I–90 Bridge Approach; the Flaming Geyser Bridge Design; and

Figure 2. Bates College Library. Courtesy of Phokion Karas.

Figure 3. The Karrow residence. Courtesy of Robert Nixon.

the restoration of Imogen Cunningham Hall on the University of Washington campus.

Hastings' concern for energy efficiency predates the energy crisis era of alarm and was evident when she was the architect for several solar homes and remodels. She has dealt successfully with the environmental factors and severe climates of sites as diverse as Kodiak, Alaska; cascade ski areas; and beaches assailed by gale–force winds.

After receiving her architectural education at the University of Washington, Jane Hastings gained valuable experience as an employee of several architectural firms on a variety of building types such as: industrial, manufacturing, educational, housing, office, theater, sports, museum, and laboratory facilities. Like many other women architects, she has been involved extensively with professional, civic, and educational activities, such as National Director of the AIA and Vice President of the International Union of Women Architects. She has served as a member of: the Council of Design Professionals; the city of Seattle Landmarks Preservation Board and the Design and Construction Review Board for the Seattle schools, and has taught on the faculty of the University of Washington and the Seattle Community College.

Jane Hastings' tradition of quality architectural design has been recognized locally and nationally with awards and publications spanning 20 years over two continents. Her designs have been published in: *House Beautiful, House and Garden, Sunset Magazine, The Seattle Times, The AIA Journal, Sunset Books, House and Home,* and in Japanese publications.

Andrea P. Leers. Andrea P. Leers is a graduate of Wellesley College and received her M.Arch. from the University of Pennsylvania. Like many other women architects, she formed a professional partnership with her spouse. After the marriage ended she successfully continued the practice and retained such notable clients as: the Massachusetts Port Authority; the Hebrew College, Brookline, Mass.; Wheelock College, Boston; Tufts University, Medford, Mass.; and the Arlington Massachusetts Housing Authority. Ms. Leers has been a member of the architecture faculty at Harvard, MIT, and Yale.

Laurie Mutchnik Maurer, FAIA. Laurie Maurer received her architectural education at Pratt Institute in Brooklyn, New York where she graduated with honors. After gaining a few years of experience with Philip Johnson Associates and Marcel Breuer & Associates she opened an office in partnership with her husband. In addition to a successful architectural practice Maurer finds time for continuous, extensive professional and public service and teaching on the faculty of Pratt Institute.

Laurie Maurer's architectural service and public service activities include: AIA Director, N.Y. region; Affirmative Action Committee; Task Force on Women; liaison to the National Council for Interior Design Qualifications; New York State Association of Architects, Task Force on Illegal Practice; AIA Design Award Jury member; work on the Advisory Committee/Parks Recreation and Cultural Affairs; and with the Mayor's Panel Committee.

In addition to these professional and public service ac-

Figure 4. Maurer's office. Courtesy of Becket Logan.

tivities, Laurie Maurer has served on numerous panels serving women and the architecture profession. She works in a historic section of Brooklyn in offices designed and owned by Maurer and Maurer (Figs. 4 and 5).

Julia Morgan (1872–1957). Julia Morgan, unable to gain acceptance into a school of architecture, studied engineering at Berkeley and then went on to the Ecole des Beaux Arts, Paris where she was the first woman to be accepted into the architecture program. Upon her return, she became the first woman to be licensed in California and established a practice that produced many notable buildings, ie, the tourist attraction, San Simeon, otherwise known as the Hearst Castle in San Luis Obispo, Calif.

Morgan hired engineers, designers, and office staff to carry out her prolific designs of about 800 architectural projects. Always caring for her employees, she kept them on payroll during the depression. Showing attention to detail, she personally visited the construction sites to check contractors, materials, and craft workers.

Large-scale works to her credit include several early buildings, Mills' College, Oakland, the Asilomar Conference Center near Monterey; the Herald Examiner's newspaper plant, Los Angeles; and group housing and recreational facilities for YMCAs in the West and Hawaii. She also designed many churches, schools, and women's clubs. Julia Morgan demonstrated a pragmatic approach to architecture listening carefully to the voices of both clients and users.

Lutah Marie Riggs, FAIA (1896–1984). Lutah Marie Riggs, a pioneer in her profession graduated from the University of California, Berkeley in 1919 and established a practice in Santa Barbara, Calif. Her career spanned several decades and her devotion to quality products resulted in numerous outstanding residential and commercial projects such as the Lockwood Cabin at Lake Arrowhead, Calif., the Vedanta Temple and expansion to the El Paseo historic complex, both in Santa Barbara. Ms. Riggs was active on the Santa Barbara AIA and served as both Commissioner and member of the California State Board of

Figure 5. Maurer's office. Courtesy of Becket Logan.

Architectural Examiners. Lutah Riggs became the first woman in California to become a Fellow of the AIA.

Denise Scott Brown. Denise Scott Brown was born in Zambia, educated in South Africa, traveled to England, and finally to the United States. Her passion for architecture, particularly urban planning, propelled her to obtain a Master of City Planning and a M.Arch. from the University of Pennsylvania. Uniting architecture and planning she influenced environments and many students. Her powerful theories suggest that social, economic, political, and aesthetic concerns be treated as a whole and design of buildings or neighborhoods should not be governed by merely functional or other narrow design parameters.

Denise Scott Brown taught on the architecture/planning faculty at an impressive number of schools, including: the University of Pennsylvania, Oberlin, Yale, Rice, UCLA, and UC Berkeley. She often had to fight for tenure or for the title "professor." "I became successively more bellicose." Her voice and influence has been heard on jury and selection panels throughout Europe, U.S., and Africa.

Denise Scott Brown has effectively combined career and family life by working with her husband. Her first husband Robert Scott Brown was killed in an auto accident. She later married Robert Venturi, FAIA. They are partners in the firm Venturi, Rauch and Scott Brown. She enjoys the challenge of working on small but difficult urban problems that entail requirements for social planning, democratic processes, incrementalism and pragmatism with concerns for preservation and economic viability. Her work has been honored with an impressive number of awards from such organizations as, The National Endowment of the Arts, the Pennsylvania Historical and Museum Commission, and the American Planning

Association, Eastern Pennsylvania Chapter. Notable projects to her credit include: A study of Fairmount Park, Philadelphia; Washington Avenue, Miami Beach; the Princeton Design Study; and the Strand Planning Study, Galveston, Tex.

Margot Siegel, AIA. Margot Siegel, born in Germany, moved to New York City as a young child where she attended Hunter College High School, a public school for gifted achievers. After receiving her B.Arch. (1955) from Pratt Institute in Brooklyn Siegel moved to Southern California where she worked for several architects including A. Quincy Jones, FAIA. In 1972 she ventured into her own practice with residential projects to facilities for non-profit organizations such as the United Way, YWCA, NCJW, and facilities for public agencies such as the U.S. Navy, the V.A., and SCRTD. Other projects include commercial clients in the entertainment industry, and the design of three exposed concrete utilitarian buildings at Los Angeles International Airport: the Cooling Tower (Fig. 6), Cogeneration Facility and Central Utility Plant Expansion. After practicing for 14 years as a sole proprietorship, in 1985 she formed Siegel Sklarek Diamond A.I.A. Architects, a partnership, with Norma Sklarek, FAIA and Katherine Diamond, AIA, as a wholly women owned and managed firm. The firm's clients include several municipalities, three campuses of the University of California, and the Los Angeles Unified School District. Margot Siegel's design philosophy is to be responsive to the needs and budget of the client with consideration given to the users.

Cathy Simon, FAIA. After earning a B.A. from Wellesley College, Cathy Simon attended the Harvard Graduate School of Design where she obtained a M.Arch. From

Figure 6. Cooling tower at Los Angeles International Airport. Courtesy of Margot Siegel.

1974–1985 Ms. Simon worked in the office of Marquis Associates in San Francisco where she became a principal of the firm in 1978 and then Head of the Design Studio.

Cathy Simon has taught on the faculty of U.C. Berkeley and the Women's School of Planning and Architecture at U.C. Santa Cruz. She has efficiently managed an architectural career, teaching, public and professional service a long with a husband and daughter. Her architectural works have been recognized by awards including: the Canadian Architect Award for the Tropical Center at the Stanley Park Zoo; H.U.D. Special Recognition for the Rosa Parks Senior Apartments; the American Institute of Steel Construction Award of Excellence of the Primate Discovery Center, San Francisco Zoo; S.F./AIA Honor Award for the Rosa Parks Senior Apartments; the C.C./AIA Firm Award; the C.C./AIA Merit Award for the Design Professional's Insurance Company; and the California Preservation Foundation Design Award for the Chambord Apartments.

Her architectural works are on several college and university campuses including: a Humanities building and Hygiene Science addition for Bard College, Annandale-on-Hudson, N.Y.; Shields Library, U.C., Davis; and the Elena Baskin Visual Arts Studios, U.C., Santa Cruz, California.

Some commissions were obtained by winning open competitions. Her designs are eminently responsive to each project's program as evidenced by the Primate Discovery Center in the San Francisco Zoo. Designed to house seventeen species of endangered monkeys in seemingly free and natural settings, this zoo represents a new approach to enjoying and learning about animals. The soaring atria are aesthetically composed of curved, vaulted arches, reaching 56 ft at their apex and covered in vinyl covered steel mesh. The landscaping is naturalistic with each primate species in its own environment: the aquatic Macaques have a waterfall; the three smallest monkeys are in glazed showcases; the tallest atrium with its tall trees accommodates the Columbuses; Mandrills have their mound in a concrete moat; Patras have their grasses; and the nocturnal Owl monkey is housed behind glass in a dark room lighted by a blue light similar to moonlight while being observed from an almost totally darkened room. The facility also includes a learning center in a glass–walled exposition space roofed by three descending glass–walled arches. This primate center succeeds in being a place for conservation and management of animals and for entertainment and education of the public (Fig. 7).

Norma Merrick Sklarek, FAIA. Overcoming the double hurdle of being black and female, Norma Sklarek received her education at Barnard College and Columbia University's School of Architecture. She was the first black woman to become a licensed architect in New York, California, and the United States and the first black woman to be honored by Fellowship in the AIA.

Ms. Sklarek had the opportunity to work on major building projects, gaining experience with sophisticated engineering systems with Skidmore, Owings and Merrill in New York City, Gruen Associates, as Director of Architecture, and Welton Becket Associates, as a Vice President and Project Director. Projects to her credit include: the Oakdale Shopping Center, Minneapolis, Minn.; Park Center Commercial Complex, San Jose, Calif.; Fox Plaza, San Francisco (Fig. 8); San Bernardino City Hall, Calif.; and the U.S. Embassy, Tokyo, Japan.

Like many other women in architecture, Ms. Sklarek

Figure 7. Primate Discovery Center. Courtesy of Kirk Gittings.

Figure 8. Fox Plaza, San Francisco. Courtesy of Morley Baer.

has been able to balance a full family life with active architectural pursuits outside of her office practice. She has done professional renderings in tempera, taught for a number of years at UCLA on the graduate architecture staff, and has been a guest lecturer at the universities of: Hampton Va., Columbia N.Y., Southern Los Angeles, Iowa State, and Howard in Washington, D.C. She has held positions on the Board of Directors of the LA/AIA, CC/AIA and the USC Architectural Guild.

Norma Sklarek has served for many years as Commissioner to the California Board of Architectural Examiners and as Master Juror for NCARB, grading the Design and Site Planning licensing papers. She served as a technical advisor for the 8th ed. of the *Architectural Graphic Standards*. She was a principal in Siegel Sklarek Diamond A.I.A. Architects. Norma Sklarek is now with the Jerde Partnership.

Virginia Tanzmann, AIA. After graduating from Syracuse University School of Architecture with a B.Arch. in 1969, Virginia Tanzmann moved to Southern California for her internship and worked in various architectural capacities. Later, she was the architect for the Southern California Transit District directing the work for their widespread maintenance and operating facilities, including both in–house and consultant provided services.

She founded Tanzmann Associates, a firm with an average staff of twelve. Their projects include master and site planning, programming, special studies, new construction, renovation and rehabilitation, and interiors and graphics. Tanzmann's project types include educational, governmental, religious, medical, industrial, office, retail, transportation, and residential facilities. Some notable examples are: library and law offices for the Center for Law in the Public Interest, Hollywood Bowl Master Plan, Los Angeles, Calif.; Seismic, Fire and Life Safety Improvements; Florwood Manor and Condominiums, 44 units, Hawthorne, Calif. Their private clients include: Buena Park Mall, Fredrics of Hollywood, The Helene Curtis Corp., and the American Heart Association.

Anne Griswold Tyng, FAIA. After obtaining a liberal arts education at Radcliffe, Anne Tyng studied architecture at the Harvard Graduate School of Design. Throughout her professional career Ms. Tyng maintained a passionate interest in mathematics and its relationship to proportion and architecture. This eventually drew her to the University of Pennsylvania where she earned a Ph.D. in architecture with a thesis titled, "Simultaneousness, Randomness and Order." Anne Tyng worked with Louis Kahn for three decades and saw their three person office grow to an average staff of ten and their projects receive worldwide recognition for geometric forcefulness.

Beverly Willis, FAIA. Strikingly individualistic in her architectural background is Beverly Willis, an artist and fresco painter, who did not study architecture at an accredited university. Nevertheless, she became licensed and moved into positions of leadership in the architectural community of San Francisco and in the AIA. To the question, "Why did you become an architect?" Beverly Willis responded, "The idea and ideals of architecture make the culture of our era. I am part of that."

Beverly Willis organized the architect/builder team of Olympia and York, the Marriott Corporation, Beverly Willis Architect and the Zeidler-Roberts Partnership that won the international competition for the rights to design/build the Yerba Buena Gardens, a 22 acre mixed-use complex in San Francisco. Together with the Zeidler-Roberts Partnership and Laurence Halprin, Landscape Architect, she master planned the site and developed its conceptual design adopted by San Francisco in 1983.

Ms. Willis was the architect for the first building in the United States designed exclusively for the use of a ballet company. The San Francisco Ballet Association building is located prominently in the performing arts area of the San Francisco Civic Center along with the opera and symphony buildings (Fig. 9).

A worldwide interest in the adaptive re-use of old brick buildings and the revitalization of blighted downtown areas was kindled by the works of: Willis on the rehabilitation and restoration of two buildings in the Jackson Square area in the 1950s and 1960s, William Wurster's renovation design of the Ghiradelli Square, and Joseph Esherick's renovation design of the Cannery. Her distinguished smaller projects include Margaret Hayward Park Recreation building, the River Run Vineyard residence,

Figure 9. San Francisco Ballet Association Building. Courtesy of Peter Aaron/Esto.

the Shown and Sons Winery, and the Owl Ranch Poolhouse, all in Napa Valley.

In addition to a number of design awards from various components of the AIA, the state of California and national and regional Builder's Associations, Beverly Willis was the recipient of the Phoebe Hearst Gold Medal for service to the city of San Francisco and received an honorary Doctorate of Arts from Mount Holyoke College. Her work and writings have been published nationally in books, magazines, and newspapers including: *Progressive Architecture, Architectural Forum, Home, House and Home, Sunset, Savy, Ms., Working Woman, The New York Times,* and *The Christian Science Monitor.*

Zelma Wilson, FAIA. Zelma Wilson studied art at UCLA, architecture at U.C. Berkeley and then received her B.Arch. from the University of Southern California. After working for the Los Angeles Planning Department, she obtained valuable experience in the offices of DMJM, Victor Gruen Associates, R. M. Schindler, and Raphael Soriano prior to opening her own office in Ojai, Calif. As her practice grew Wilson acquired two partners and changed the firm name to The Ojai Group.

Ojai's projects started with houses and grew to institutional work, churches, and private schools. Wilson believes that women bring to architectural concerns that which is not addressed by their male counterparts because women are by nature, nurturers and have a greater concern for the potential users. Zelma Wilson has won professional recognition with AIA Chapter Honor awards and received AIA Fellowship for outstanding contribution to the profession in the areas of design, education, and community participation.

INTERNATIONAL WOMEN ARCHITECTS

Argentina

Flora Manteola, Architect. An architecture graduate of the University of Buenos Aires, Flora Manteola is cur-

rently a professor and coordinator of the university's Department of Design Disciplines. She has been a partner in the Buenos Aires based firm of Manteola, Sanchez Gomez, Santos, Solsona, Arquitectos for over twenty years.

Josefa Santos, Architect. Josefa Santos, like her partner Flora Manteola graduated from the University of Buenos Aires. Ms. Santos is a member of the Board of Directors of the Professional Council of Architecture. Their firm Sanchez Gomez, Santos, Solsona, Arquitectos has been published extensively in leading architectural journals in Argentina, Brazil, U.S., Japan, Italy, and Switzerland. They have been awarded over thirty first prizes in competitions and a large number of honorable mentions. Their projects span a wide range of building types from industrial to manufacturing, such as Papel Prensa, a paper manufacturing complex; the Argentina Television Color production center (ATC); and the Fate Tire Factory with employee housing. Commercial projects include the UIA Tower, the Prourban Tower (Fig. 10), institutional buildings, recreational facilities, banks, schools, health care facilities ie, the Clinica Juri, a plastic surgery clinic, multi–unit residences, low, medium, and high income single–family residences, and mixed–use complexes ie, a community in Buenos Aires with 2100 terraced housing

Figure 10. Edificio de Oficinas Torre Prouban, Argentina. Courtesy of Manteola, Sanchez Gomez, Santos, Solsona Arquitectos.

units including a retail center, health care facility, church and recreational facilities, and the Manantiales, Punta del Este in Uruguay (Fig. 11), a terraced one–to–four–story housing community with a spacious plaza and retail center.

Australia

Although 30% of the architecture students in the Australian universities are female only 5% actually complete the program with a professional architecture degree. The majority of the women students opt for allied fields such as urban planning, landscape architecture, or interiors. At present, about 3% of the registered architects of Australia are women.

Brit Andresen. After graduating with a B.Arch. from the University of Trondheim in Norway, Brit Andresen worked, became registered, and joined the Architectural Associations of the ARCUK in the United Kingdom and the state of Queensland, Australia. In addition to her architectural practice in Brisbane, she has served on architecture faculties of: the University of Queensland, St. Lucia and UCLA, Los Angeles. She has been a visiting critic at the School of Architecture at Malta University, the Portsmouth School of Architecture and the Bristol School of Architecture in England.

Brit Andresen has won prizes in architectural competitions in Norway, England, Iraq, and Australia for projects as diverse as libraries, housing, and museums. She has a professional architectural partnership with her husband, Michael Keniger.

Canada

One-third of Canada's architects are in Ontario where the total number of women in the Ontario Association of Architects has grown from 1% in 1960 to about 6% in 1988. Over the past decade a number of women have been recognized with fellowship in the Royal Architectural Institute of Canada for their outstanding contribution to architecture. Several have also been elected as Fellows of the Royal Institute of British Architects.

Pamela Cluff, FRAIC, FRIBA. Pamela Cluff is the principal in charge of design in the firm of A. W. Cluff and P. J. Cluff. In the early years her firm's practice consisted of

Figure 11. Manantiales, Uruguay. Courtesy of Manteola, Sanchez Gomez, Santos, Solsona Arquitectos.

schools, residences, and commercial projects. Later the work concentrated on health facilities, specializing on issues related to the elderly and disabled, psychogerontology, criminology rehabilitation, and social development.

Lily Inglis, RIBA, FRAIC. Lily Inglis, born in Milan, Italy, continued her education in England, then immigrated to Canada where she became involved in the protection and preservation of the historic heritage of buildings in Kingston, Ontario. She is a member of the Ontario Association of Architects and has been involved in the restoration and adaptive re–use of older buildings.

Phyllis Lambert, PhD. ENG. HON, FRAIC. Phyllis Lambert studied architecture at Yale University and received a M.Arch. from the Illinois Institute of Technology. She teaches Urban History at Concordia University and has won recognition for her work in the field of conservation and restoration on projects in Canada and noteworthy projects as the Biltmore Hotel in Los Angeles and the Ben Ezra Synagogue in Cairo, Egypt. As founder and Director of the Canadian Center for Architecture, Phyllis Lambert is building a research center to house an extensive collection of architectural books, manuscripts, drawings, and photographs.

Christine Perks, ARIBA, FRAIC. Christine Perks was born in Poland but received her education in Montreal graduating from McGill University with a B.Arch. She worked in private practice for several years in Bermuda, in the office of George F. Eber in Montreal, as project architect on two buildings at Expo '67, and in Alberta and Toronto before returning to Ottawa. She is the Director of the Facilities Development Division, Department of External Affairs, in charge of the management of physical planning, design, and construction of buildings and multi–use complexes required in support of Canada's integrated foreign operations.

Helga Plumb, M.Arch., FRAIC. Helga Plumb was born in Austria but received her architectural education in Canada at the University of Toronto. She has worked in Massachusetts, Alberta, and Toronto and has been on the faculty or a visiting professor at the Technical University of Nova Scotia, the University of Toronto, Harvard University, and Waterloo University. Award winning projects to her credit include the Joseph Shepard Office Building, the Tom Longboat Junior Public School and the Oaklands condominiums and town houses.

China

The percentage of women in practice in the People's Republic of China and in China's architectural schools is approximately 30%. In 1987 the Beijing Architectural Design Institute had 213 qualified architects, 34% of whom were women. Many of these women have won competitions, commissions, and awards for outstanding designs on major projects. A woman's Architectural Association in Beijing has 116 members.

Huang Hui, Architect. Huang Hui graduated from the architecture department of Tsin Hwa University in 1961. A senior architect with many outstanding buildings to her credit, she has recently won the prize for Excellent Design from the Ministry of Urban and Rural Construction and Environmental Protection for her outstanding design of the Beijing High School #4. The environment she designed for the classrooms is creative, original and particularly conducive to study.

Qui Xiuwen, Architect. Since graduating from Tsin Hwa University in 1965, Qiu Xiuwen has worked in the government office of the Ministry of Urban and Rural Construction and Environmental Protection.

Zhai Zongfan, Architect. Zhai Zongfan graduated from the architecture department of Chong Qing University in 1947. Outstanding projects to her credit include the National Sports Center, General Stadium and Swimming Gymnasium in Pakistan and the National Library in Beijing, the largest library in Asia, although massive in size, retains the traditional Asian architectural flavor (Fig. 12). A large skylighted atrium in the National Library is furnished with landscaped potted plants and benches (Fig. 13).

England

Eva Jiricna, Architect. Eva Jiricna studied architecture and civil engineering in Prague. She moved from Czechoslovakia to London in 1968 where she worked for the firm of Louis de Soissons on many large scale, major building projects until 1980. It was however, in interior design that she received wide recognition particularly for the Lloyds of London Building on which she headed the interiors team in the office of Richard Rogers & Partners. In 1985 she went into partnership with Kathy Kerr and pioneered the concept of "less is more" using a palette of black and white, metallic ceilings and walls, and occasional bright yellow accents.

In her firm of Jiricna Kerr Associates, Jiricna has blended modernism and "high tech." This unusual style was utilized in a very practical way in the remodeling of Harrods' Department Store in London. Movable walls allow departments to expand or contract, the partitions also

Figure 13. National Library, Beijing. Courtesy of Zhang Guang Yuan.

function for display are constructed of vacuum–formed aluminum and sprayed with automotive metallic paint. The vertical posts, painted a bright yellow, also serve as electrical conduits. Halogen uplights, suspended extruded aluminum ceilings, mirrored panels, and a black floor of reconstituted granite tiles result in a distinctly personal style.

Finland

Scandinavian countries have been world leaders in women's rights. Finland in 1906, was the first European country to grant women suffrage and the right to political office. By the last decade of the nineteenth century, women were admitted into the Finnish university and into its architecture program, only through special permission upon application for "exemption from her sex."

The turn of the century saw women in Finland being accepted as full–time regular students into the architecture program and expressed sophisticated democratic ideas with a government reform which gave every tax paying citizen the right of involvement into the decision making of his home town. The twentieth century has seen the percentage of women in architecture, a traditionally male field, steadily grow to 33% or 500 women out of a total of 1500 Finnish architects.

Elsa Arokallio, 1892–1982. Elsa Arokallio designed many schools including the Hagman School in Helsinki which attracts visitors even today. Her Kauhava barracks were designed with a strict and elegant classicism.

Marta Blomstedt, 1899–1982. Together with her architect husband, Marta Blomstedt achieved functionalism's most central monuments, the Pohjanhovi Hotel and the Kannonkoski Church. After the death of her husband, Blomstedt designed many other impressive buildings including post offices, a magazine publisher's building, and many houses.

Figure 12. National Library, Beijing. Courtesy of Zhang Guang Yuan.

Elsi Borg, 1893–1958. Elsi Borg designed interiors, furniture, book illustrations, and greeting cards. Her architectural accomplishments included hospitals and military buildings.

Signe Hornborg, 1862–1916. Signe Hornborg was the first professionally trained woman architect in Finland. She graduated from the Polytechnic Institute of Finland as an "extra student," the term given to part–time students, since women were not admitted as full–time students at that time.

Italy and France

Gae Aulenti, Architect. Gae Aulenti, an Italian architect, was the winner of an invited competition to transform an abandoned hotel and train station (designed by Victor Laloux and built in 1900) Gare d'Orsay into a museum, Musee d'Orsay. On this project Ms. Aulenti functioned as design architect with the French architectural firm, ACT as the associate architect. The museum efficiently accommodates 25,000 visitors per day. Her design succeeded in achieving a high quality of light, air, and acoustics. It has been criticized for its strange combination of post–modernism with unseemly materials and forms such as metal bridges with massive structural supports and stone staircases adorned with lightweight aluminum panels. Prior to this monumental assignment, Gae Aulenti's portfolio included showrooms, offices, apartments, stage sets, and exhibition and furniture design.

Solange D'Herbez De La Tour. Born in Bucharest, Rumania, Solange D'Herbez De La Tour received a B.S. in architecture from the University of Bucharest and then graduated as an urbanist and town planner from the Polytechnical School of Bucharest. She opened an office in Paris, France in 1950 where she designed many projects including over 5000 apartment units, cultural and public buildings, university sports buildings, day nurseries, elementary schools, hospital projects, and town planning for new cities. Solange D'Herbez's accomplishments in bringing world wide appreciation of the role of women in architecture was recognized by the AIA by their election of her as an Honorary Fellow. She founded the Union Internationale Des Femmes Architects (UIFA) which recognized women architects throughout the world and offered them opportunities for an international exchange of ideas, concerns, initiatives, and friendships. As of 1988 there are over 57 countries represented with members from all continents, races, and religions.

India

The percentage of women in India's architecture schools has increased steadily from 10% in 1970 to 50% in 1987. There are two notable architectural firms with husband and wife partners: Satnam & (wife) Namita Singh in Chandigarh and Akhila (wife) and Rarikumar in Madras. Another exceptional architectural partnership was formed by two sisters, Brinda Somaya and Ranjini Kalappa.

Ranjini Kalappa. After receiving a B.Arch. from J.J. College of Architecture at Bombay University, Ranjini Kalappa attended Pratt Institute in New York where she received a M.Arch. A few years of experience in New York offices prepared her for the return to her native Bombay where she and her sister opened their firm, Somaya and Kalappa.

Brinda Somaya FIIA. Following in her sister's footsteps, Brinda Somaya graduated from J. J. College of Architecture at the Bombay University with a B.Arch., studied at Smith College, then returned to India and formed an architectural partnership with her sister.

Somaya and Kalappa. Brinda Somaya and Ranjini Kalappa completed their architectural education and apprenticeships in India and in the United States, formed their own architecture and interior design firm in Bombay, later married and each raised two children. Since they have always worked, they firmly state, "Work is an inseparable part of our lives and much hard work and sacrifice have gone into our career." They have received many prestigious commissions including 5–star hotel complexes, exclusive homes, swimming pools, and factories. The West End project on an 18 acre site in the city of Bangalore involves a new 120 room addition, renovation of 100 rooms, new restaurants, swimming pools, a health club, and meeting and convention halls. Other projects to their credit include the Holiday Inn, a 200 room hotel at Bangalore where a stained glass atrium is protected from the elements by a double roof floating 70 ft above the floor level, dominating the hotel interior by day with its soft reflected light and by night by its dramatic impact; the TATA Electric Company's Swimming Pool and Stadium complex in which the possibility of leakage was reduced by elevating it with a series of terraces; a school and training center for spastics at Bangalore; TATA Electronic Development Services Factory near Bangalore is planned to accommodate both human needs and technical requirements. Their architecture is contemporary, but at the same time relates to other buildings in Delhi which are often Lutyens or Moghul style. Without adopting these traditional styles Somaya and Kalappa like to think that their designs relate to these older styles and reflect the socio–economic issues of the 1980s.

Japan

From 1982–1986 the percentage of women in Japan's architecture schools has steadily increased from 2.5%–3.3%. The educational requirements and years of schooling parallel that of schools in the United States. There are two categories of certified architects: First Class certificate holders are qualified to design and obtain building permits for all sizes and types of projects, 2.8% are women; Second Class certificate holders are limited to small scale buildings. Japan's Architectural Association's (JAA) membership of approximately 7000 has fewer than 1% women members.

Masako Hayashi, Architect. Masako Hayashi has won recognition and acclaim for her outstanding residential

Figure 14. House on a cliff. Courtesy of Osamu Murai.

Figure 15. House interior. Courtesy of Osamu Murai.

designs. She is the first women to receive the highest prestigious Architectural Institute of Japan Award, conferred on persons who have contributed to the enhancement of Japan's architectural culture and public well being. She has also been internationally recognized with Honorary Fellowship in the AIA. Her residential designs create the best possible houses in very limited space with innovative use of building materials, simple, clear cut expression, and bold space utilization (Figs. 14 and 15).

Itsuko Hasegawa, Architect. Itsuko Hasegawa is the first woman architect in Japan to win a large institutional building design award. This prestigious competition was for the Shonandai Cultural Center. After graduating from the School of Architecture, Kantogakuin University she worked in the office of Kiyonori Kikutake then studied and worked at the Tokyo Institute of Technology before establishing her own firm. In 1986 she received the annual award of the Architectural Institute of Japan, the annual award of the Japan Inter–Design Conference, and first prize in the Shonandai Cultural Center Design Competition, now under construction. Hasegawa designed dramatic, unique houses in which she has decreased the volume of each room and achieved savings on the air conditioning. The terrace features a pergola, in summer it

can become an outdoor room and in winter serves as a passive energy greenhouse accumulating solar heat. Structurally, her houses are a combination of wood and steel framing. Each house has an individual spatial form with different combinations of curvilinear and straight shapes. Hasegawa states, "I like to permit the occupant to live outdoors. My design of such an outdoor room gives the house not only a sense of spatial extension but a sense that the architecture is part of the natural environment." (Fig. 16).

Norie Kikutake, Architect (1929–1988). Norie Kikutake studied architecture at the University of Tokyo, high–rise construction in Mutoh Lab, and design and criticism in Kishida Lab as an assistant to professors. After her marriage to architect Kiyonari Kikutake they opened a studio/office. Kikutake started her career as a practicing architect with Sky House, Izumo, and other major works. Ever curious about the unknown, she participated in various international conferences, made many friends, and was loved for her reserved but warm personality. Norie Kikutake lived an intellectually and aesthetically full life in her role as an architect and mother of two daughters and one son (Fig. 17).

Mexico

Among the contemporary, prominent women architects in Mexico are Margarita Bartiloti, Josefina Basail, Marga-

Figure 16. Shonandai Cultural Center in Fujisawa, Japan. Courtesy of Kokumei Furudate.

Figure 17. Sky House, 1958, night view. Courtesy of Yukio Futagawa.

rita Chavez de Caso, Virginia Isaac, Yolanda Snaider, and Sara Topelson de Grinberg.

Sara Topelson de Grinberg, Architect. After graduating from architecture school at the Universidad Nacional Autonoma de Mexico (UNAM) in 1971, Sara Topelson de Grinberg took graduate studies at UNAM in Contemporary Architecture and later in the Evolution of Space in Mexico, at Politecnico National in the Theory of Architecture, at the Instituto Nacional de Bellas Artes on the History of Arts in Mexico.

In private practice since 1973, Topelson de Grinberg's credits include the architecture of many housing, educational, industrial and residential projects. She has served as a professor on the faculty of the Universidad Nacional Autonoma de Mexico, the Universidad Anahuac, and the Universidad Autonoma Metropolitana teaching courses as diverse as Aesthetic Theory, History of Architecture, Urban Design, Design Workshop, and Mathematics. Sara Topelson de Grinberg has also been very active with architectural societies and associations locally and internationally.

Union of Soviet Socialist Republics

The architectural profession with its creative and technical demands is viewed by many in the Soviet Union as a profession that requires an extraordinary amount of personal dedication and self sacrifice often displacing family life. Nevertheless, the percentage of women in the architecture schools today has grown to approximately 50% and the percentage of women architects practicing today in the USSR is about 30%. Many of the woman architects hold positions of responsibility where they contribute to urban planning, landscape architecture, interior design, and the design of individual building projects.

BIBLIOGRAPHY

General References

S. Ahuja, *Indian Architect & Builder,* Oct. 1987 pp. 80–95.

D. Dietsch, "Women at Columbia: A Century of Change," *Progressive Architecture* **63**, 22–23 (June 1982).

B. Dinerman, "Women in Architecture," *Architectural Forum* **13**, 50–51 (Dec. 1969).

D. Favro, "Women in Architecture," *Architecture and Planning UCLA* 17 (Fall 1987).

"Four fine fellows," *AIA Journal* **52**, 86–87 (Sept. 1969).

V. L. Gratton, "Mary Colter, Builder upon the Red Earth," *Northland Press* Flagstaff, Ariz., 1980.

S. P. Harkness, "Solar Design: State of The Art," *Northeast Sun* (Feb. 1985).

R. F. Hodgon, "Influences, Positive and Negative on Women Entering the Profession," *AIA Journal* **66**, 43–45 (Aug. 1977).

S. Holmes Boutelle, "Berkeley Houses by Julia Morgan," *Berkeley Architectural Heritage Assoc.*

"Japan" *GA Global Architecture* no 20.

"Missed Connections," *Architectural Record* (March 1987).

M. Miyawaki, "Masako Hayashi," *Japan Architect* **53**, 44–53 (July 1978).

L. Gilbert, G. Moore, *Particular Passions,* pp. 311–323.

R. Reif, "Fighting the System in the Male Dominated Field of Architecture," *The New York Times* 60 (Apr. 11, 1971).

"Surveying the Role of Women in the Profession," *AIA Journal* **61**, 9 (June 1974).

A. Temko, "Environmental Design," *San Francisco Chronicle* 6 (Mar. 7, 1983).

S. Torre, *Women in American Architecture: A Contemporary Perspective,* 1877.

A. G. Tyng, "Architecture Is My Touchstone," *Radcliffe Quarterly* (Sept. 1984).

M. J. Wade, *Horizon* **31**(4), 33 (May 1988).

"Women Architects Seek Wider Role in Profession, End to Discrimination," *Architectural Record* **153**, 36 (Apr. 1973).

"Women in Architecture," *Engineering News-Record* **1**, 13 (Apr. 1959).

NORMA SKLAREK, FAIA
The Jerde Partnership
Los Angeles, California

WOOD. See INDIVIDUAL ARTICLES.

WOOD IN CONSTRUCTION

This article presents general information about wood, within the framework of specific information about forestry, lumber manufacture, and the use of lumber products in construction. The emphasis is on those aspects of the process which directly or indirectly affect the strength, appearance, or performance of wood in construction.

THE NATURE OF WOOD

Wood is a unique building material because it is natural—the only major structural material that is organic in origin. In addition, because wood is a building material produced by nature, it is a renewable resource. Most of the actual "production" of wood is accomplished within the tree itself, by itself. Because of this there is little human control over it beyond changing its shape once the "production" has ended. To take full advantage of wood as a building material, it is necessary to recognize its organic nature—with its resulting limitations and strengths—and to work within those parameters.

Wood is made up of living cells which collectively become wood fibers and, as such, form the structure of the tree. Because cells are the basic components of wood, an understanding of these basic building blocks is fundamental to an understanding of the use of wood in construction.

Wood Cells

Tree cells, which transport and store food from the leaves and moisture from the soil, are composed primarily of cellulose and lignin; their round and rectangular tubelike forms give wood its structural efficiency and high strength-to-weight ratio. Their fibrous, tubular form also allows the cell walls to deform under force so that fasteners such as nails and screws can be readily driven.

Most tree cells are oriented with their longitudinal axis up and down the tree, but both hardwood and softwood trees also have some cells that radiate from the center of the tree toward the outside, or the bark. These so-called radial cells conduct moisture radially across the tree, and vary greatly in size depending on the species. The largest radial rays, a collection of radial cells, are easily visible in some hardwood species. They can also be identified during the seasoning of large logs or timbers. The surface cracks (called seasoning checks) which form during the wood seasoning process occur along these radial rays.

In a living tree the cells contain moisture and the outer layers of the tree are saturated with it. This moisture in trees or freshly cut lumber is commonly known as sap. A distinction may be made between sap which is located in the cell cavities (called free water), and sap which is located in the cell walls (bound water).

The moisture content of wood is referred to as a weight relationship—the weight of the moisture in relation to the oven-dry weight of wood fiber. It is generally expressed as a percentage. For example, when the free water has left the cell cavities but bound water is still held in the cell walls, the weight relationship of moisture to wood fiber in most softwood species is about 28%.

Because most tree cells are long and slender, and follow the linear axis of the tree, shrinkage as a result of bound water leaving the tree cells is primarily measurable in the width and thickness of sawn lumber. Longitudinal shrinkage of structural framing is so slight as not generally to be a consideration when estimating dimensional change as a result of seasoning.

In addition to the moisture and nutrient transporting longitudinal and radial cells, some softwoods also have resin canals. These conduits for resin are often visible in softwood species such as pine, spruce, Douglas fir, and larch.

Pitch, which forms on the surface of some softwood species, is a mixture of resin and turpentine. While the presence of pitch can be nothing more than a nuisance when lumber is used for structural purposes, it can present problems if allowed to appear on the surface of paneling or millwork. Consequently, drying practices have been developed to minimize this problem.

One of the principal factors in the strength and workability of wood is the density of the cell fiber. Generally speaking, low density wood fiber is easier to cut or machine than high density fiber. Dense trees of the same species are in general physically stronger than less dense trees within the same species, and dense species are in general stronger than less dense species. The terms softwood and hardwood have no relationship to density, as both groups exhibit a wide range of species density.

Wood density is generally expressed as specific gravity, with the average specific gravity of most softwood species falling between 0.30 and 0.65. Design value tables in building codes and structural design manuals recognize the importance of specific gravity in relationship to nail, bolt, and plate holding capacities. Because of this, they group species in relation to their specific gravity when assigning fastener holding values.

TREE STRUCTURE

Sapwood/Heartwood

Figure 1 shows a cross section of a living tree, from the outside to the inside—bark, cambium layer, light colored sapwood, sometimes darker colored heartwood, and pith.

New growth on a tree occurs at the cambium layer. Each year a living tree adds several new layers of wood

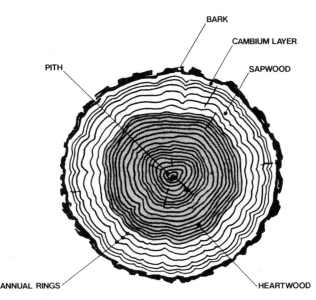

Figure 1. Cross section of a log showing its layers from pith to bark.

cells to its exterior, and these new cells become what is called sapwood. The thickness of the sapwood layer varies with species and growing conditions. As the tree grows larger, it no longer needs its entire trunk for the transfer of moisture and nutrients, and when this happens the inner layers of sapwood change and become heartwood. The principal function of this centrally located heartwood is mechanical support of the tree. The transition from sapwood to heartwood is also accompanied by the formation of extractives in the cell walls of the heartwood. These extractives play an important role in the decay resistance of some species. Extractives, including tannins, resins, and oils, are not a part of the wood structure, but contribute to its color and properties. They can be removed, depending on the base of the extractive, by solvents such as water, alcohol, or acetone.

Sapwood is not generally resistant to decay. The type and quantity of extractives trapped in the cells of the heartwood produce decay resistance in a species. In attempting to tell the two apart, heartwood is usually the darker of the two. That, regrettably, is only a general rule, because some colorless extractives in the heartwood of a few species are toxic to decay-causing fungi. Consequently color by itself is not necessarily an indicator of decay resistance.

Although sapwood has a much higher moisture content than heartwood, it generally releases moisture more readily and is somewhat less dimensionally stable than the more difficult-to-dry heartwood.

As has been discussed, sapwood and heartwood do not behave the same. Similarly, the wood fiber that is formed adjacent to the pith (Fig. 1) also behaves differently from the surrounding, more mature wood. All new layers of tree cells occur on the outside of a tree so the pith and the first few rows of cells adjacent to the pith are representative of the young, rapidly developing tree. The material in this "early tree zone" is referred to as juvenile wood. Juvenile wood is not as dimensionally stable as the more mature portions of the tree.

An understanding of a tree's growth characteristics also helps in visualizing where in the tree certain grades of lumber are most often found. For example, in dense forests softwood trees seek light with their uppermost branches, while the lower branches, having lost their function, wither and fall off. This creates long branchless sections in trees' lower portions, and it is from these branchless—and hence knotless—portions that the knot-free grades are generally found.

Earlywood/Latewood

Figure 1 also shows evidence of the growing cycle of the tree, commonly referred to as annual rings. The rings are a record of the changing needs of the tree and the effect of climate on the density of wood fiber.

In spring the demand for moisture and nutrients is high, leading softwoods to produce large diameter, thinwalled cells. The resulting wood is called earlywood. Then, later in the year when the demands decrease, the new cells are smaller and more thickly walled, producing latewood. Because of its thicker, stronger cells, latewood

is generally darker and easily distinguishable in most trees. Earlywood and latewood are sometimes also called springwood and summerwood but these terms are somewhat misleading in suggesting an exact correlation of seasons to cell structure.

Understanding the difference between earlywood and latewood may prove valuable when selecting grades or sorting lumber for individual uses. Because latewood is denser than earlywood, it will not take stain as readily as springwood. On the other hand latewood is more abrasion resistant than earlywood, so it should be used when selecting material which will receive heavy wear, such as stair treads.

Because latewood is harder and smoother than earlywood, brittle paint may peel from its surface more readily than from earlywood. If the bands of latewood are narrow, as they are in some species, or if the bands are perpendicular to the surface to be painted, then the paint may span the latewood and last longer than it would on species with wide latewood rings or on lumber which is not cut with the annual rings perpendicular to the face to be painted.

Many finish grades are cut from the tree to take advantage of the differences in earlywood and latewood. These techniques will be discussed under Manufacture.

NATURAL CHARACTERISTICS

A number of factors affect the use of wood in construction. These factors may be natural characteristics, or they may be the result of a characteristic developed during the manufacture of the product. In either case, these characteristics affect the strength and visual quality of the finished product and must be understood by anyone involved in wood construction.

Knots are probably the most common characteristic in lumber. They are that portion of a limb located within the body of a tree. While variations in structural properties may vary slightly, depending on the type and location of the knot involved, it can be said that knots in both finish and structural grades reduce the quality of the grade as they grow larger.

Knots are caused by new layers of wood cells growing around limbs. A variation of this is that new layers growing over a dead limb have a different end result from cells surrounding living fiber. If the limb is already dead, it probably will not be physically attached to the tree fiber as it is surrounded. In most cases the knot will become loose as the lumber dries out and shrinks away from it. Intergrown or live knots, on the other hand, are firmly fixed to the wood fiber and are rarely dislodged.

A variety of external forces can also cause characteristics in wood. Decay-producing fungi can enter a tree as a result of storms or attacks by birds and insects. White speck, honeycomb, burls, peck, grub holes, and exaggerated loss of bond between the annual rings due to pitch pockets may all be the result of accidents, insects, or birds.

Checks and shakes are local wood fiber failures or weaknesses which may occur in either finished lumber or the tree. Checks, which occur parallel to the growth rings, are the result of outer fibers of the tree or lumber drying more rapidly than the inner fibers. Shakes are lengthwise separations between and parallel to the annual growth rings. Shakes may be the result of an injury to the tree or may occur when the tree is felled, causing fiber separation as it hits the ground.

Compression wood is abnormal wood that forms on the underside of leaning or crooked softwood trees. It is characterized by hardness, brittleness, and a relatively lifeless appearance. Compression wood is not allowed in structural grades.

Slope of grain is one of the natural characteristics which has a great deal to do with the mechanical properties of wood.

While the list of natural grading characteristics is a long one, heavily and colorfully embellished by lumber industry terminology, most grade rule books and other literature provided by lumber industry trade associations contain descriptions and in some cases pictures of these characteristics to guide the specifier or user in grade selection.

TYPES OF TREES

The term hardwood is generally used to describe deciduous trees, trees that lose their leaves. Softwoods are conifers, trees that keep their needles all year. In reality the hardness or softness of wood fiber has little to do with whether a tree has needles or leaves. From a botanical standpoint the distinction between the two groups is that hardwood seeds are enclosed (angiosperms) and they have a leaf and a flower. The softwoods have exposed seeds (gymnosperms), usually in a cone, and with few exceptions have needles which remain all year.

Commercially available softwoods are in general easily nailed and shaped with conventional hand tools. These characteristics, combined with their relatively high strength-to-weight ratio, account for their wide use in both finish and structural design. While some of the hardwoods are used structurally, they are most generally desirable for furniture, flooring, cabinet works, and paneling. Because this article is directed at wood use in construction, the remainder of the discussion will generally be limited to the softwood species.

PHYSICAL AND MECHANICAL PROPERTIES

Trees, and the fiber from which they are formed, have both physical and mechanical properties. Physical properties have to do with the structure of the wood—its abrasion resistance, machining characteristics, resistance to decay, hardness, and weight. Mechanical properties have to do with the wood's ability to resist forces and deformation. Mechanical properties generally relate to structural characteristics, while physical properties generally relate to finish or visual uses. A complete description of the physical and mechanical properties of the U.S. softwood species would be impossible within the context of this article, but several general statements can be made.

The heartwood of redwood and the cedars is decay resistant; that, combined with good paintability, makes these species desirable for decks, siding, and trim. Many of the western pines, such as sugar pine and ponderosa pine, have excellent machining properties and are commonly used for windows and moldings. Southern pines and ponderosa pine receive chemical treatment easily and well. All softwood species can be used structurally, but the predominant structural species are Douglas fir, southern pines, larch, hemlocks, tamarack, spruces, true firs, and some of the northern and western pines such as lodgepole, red, and jack. All of the softwood species are suitable for paneling, subject to local availability in the desired patterns and grades.

GROWING REGIONS

Trees exist as part of a complex collection of living things known as a forest. The trees may be deciduous, coniferous, or a combination of both, depending on the climate.

Forests can develop wherever minimum summer temperatures average 50°F and the minimum rainfall is about 8 in. Above these limits, combinations of tree species make up forest types of varying complexity. Where one type ends and the other begins is difficult to determine but, generally speaking, four softwood growing regions have commercial importance in North America.

Canada has a wide variety of species, but the great majority of that country's softwood production is limited to the spruces, pines, and true firs. The northeastern region of the continental United States has many of the same species as Eastern Canada, and in addition produces some hemlock, tamarack, and eastern white pine.

The moist softwood-producing region of the coastal northwest provides species such as redwood, cedars, Douglas fir, hemlock, and sitka spruce. The moist winds off the Pacific Ocean provide a unique temperature climate for these species. These forests are also perhaps the most spectacularly beautiful in the world. Heading inland in the northwest, the pines, true firs, larch, and other spruces begin to predominate.

The various southern pine species thrive in the temperate zone from Virginia to east Texas. The southern pines grow quickly in this region, with a large volume of the lumber in this production being second or third generation growth.

Obviously the lumber species indigenous to a region will dominate the local lumber market if availability and cost are the only considerations. In some cases, however, the unique physical or mechanical properties of a species may result in distribution and availability beyond its regional boundaries.

Some forests grow pure stands of a single species, while others produce a species mix. These latter are usually harvested and manufactured into lumber together, resulting in lumber identified as a species combination. Spruce-pine-fir, hem-fir, and southern pine are all examples, with southern pine actually being any combination of four southeastern pines.

The average age of timber stands in North America has gone down since logging began. The amount of clear lumber from old-growth timber is limited; its harvesting is strictly controlled. The resource base has changed since the early part of the century, and present forest management practices have brought about more effective use of younger but still mature trees, along with much less waste in the process.

LUMBER MANUFACTURE

Lumber manufacture proceeds from the forest through the distribution point. In general terms, the process involves taking a tree and cutting it, drying the pieces, surfacing them, assigning a grade to them, and finally shipping the end product to its destination. Various manufacturing practices directly affect the availability, size, characteristics, and quality of the final product.

Cutting

In the forest, the faller first fells the tree and "bucks" it to length. The length of the logs is limited by the capabilities of the equipment hauling them and by the mill that manufactures them into lumber. After being felled the logs are brought to the mill where they are sorted by species, size, and quality.

As a log enters the mill the bark is removed by hydraulic or mechanical means and the log is fastened to a carriage. The carriage thrusts the log through a stationary bandsaw blade; the carriage and bandsaw together are called the headrig. The quality and variety of lumber produced are governed by the judgment and skill of the headrig sawyer. Based on his own experience and on lumber orders, he saws the lumber into the best possible assortment of grades, thicknesses, and widths (Fig. 2). Modern technology and the use of scanners and computers are also coming to play an increasingly important role. How the bandsaw blade is oriented with respect to the growth rings, knots, and other characteristics changes the character and grade of the resulting piece.

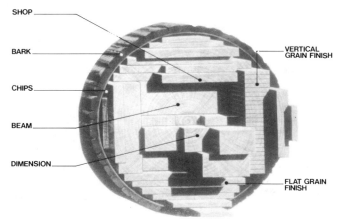

SHOP

BARK

CHIPS

BEAM

DIMENSION

VERTICAL GRAIN FINISH

FLAT GRAIN FINISH

Figure 2. This method of cutting is called "sawing around the log." The sawyer took six cuts from Side 1, then turned the log to begin sawing Side 2. The same procedure was followed with Sides 3 and 4 until a 16-inch square timber remained. It can be reduced as shown or marketed as a timber 16 inches square.

The sawyer understands the tree growth characteristics and cuts the highest valued pieces from the lower and outer portions of the tree. The old limb structure remaining near the center of the log is revealed as knots as the saw cuts deeper into the log. "Knotty" grades of lumber will generally come from smaller trees or the center part of an old growth tree. The log will be cut into smaller pieces by resawyers operating other saws in the mill. "Timbers" of high quality may also be cut from the outer portion of large trees (Fig. 2). If the center of the tree (the heart pith) is not part of the cross section of the piece, it is described as free of heart center (FOHC). The result is a piece with no juvenile wood, fewer radial cells in its cross section, and therefore less tendency toward checking, twist, and bow.

The edgerman next cuts the piece to width. The amount of wane—absence of wood from the edge of a piece—is determined at this point and limited by grade.

After edging the lumber is trimmed. A trim saw—a series of circle saw blades set at two-foot intervals—is used to trim the ends and cut out any undesirable sections of the piece. Random length shipments and lumber availability in multiples of 2 ft can be traced to this step in the manufacturing process.

Drying

After cutting, the decision to dry lumber or manufacture it as unseasoned is made. One factor in the decision is market preference. In markets close to producing regions, there is some preference for unseasoned lumber because of its cost advantage and characteristic ease of nailing. In areas more distant from the producing region, higher freight costs for shipping the heavier unseasoned lumber become a factor, and dry lumber is preferred.

The species and its dimensional stability may also affect the decision to dry or not. Douglas fir, for example, is generally more stable in the green state than hem-fir or southern pine, which are more commonly dried.

The end use requirements are perhaps the major determining factor in deciding whether or not to dry. The more critical the application, the closer the tolerances, and hence the lower the moisture content to which the product will generally be manufactured. Lumber intended for paneling and trim will usually be manufactured to lower moisture contents than general purpose boards or framing lumber.

As previously noted, wood is made up of cells that are full of water at the time of harvest. Wood cells are constantly giving off or taking on water from their environment in an attempt to reach equilibrium moisture content. Because of this, the equilibrium moisture content changes with temperature and relative humidity, and therefore varies depending on climate. One of the goals of seasoning is to dry the lumber as close to the equilibrium moisture content as possible, thereby minimizing the amount of dimensional change after the material is in place.

Wood is seasoned by air drying or kiln (sometimes pronounced "kill") drying. Air drying takes advantage of the natural tendency of wood to reach an equilibrium moisture content. Lumber is usually stacked and stickered (spacers placed between the pieces), oriented to the prevailing winds, and allowed to dry naturally.

Kiln drying accelerates the natural process by using higher temperatures and controlling relative humidity in an enclosed structure called a kiln. Either method is capable of achieving the desired moisture content levels, so industry standards do not distinguish between the methods of drying.

As wood dries, the outer fibers dry more rapidly than the inside core. The fibers shrinking around a wet core can result in across-grain stresses and thus cause seasoning checks. Warp and splits can also develop during the drying process but are limited in the final lumber product by grading rules. Air drying, which is a slower process, can reduce the amount of stresses induced and thereby reduce the number of seasoning characteristics. The high heat process of kiln drying, on the other hand, has the advantage of killing insects and larvae that may be in the wood. This process is also recommended whenever resinous species are to be used for exposed finish applications. The problem of bleeding pitch is eliminated by crystallizing or "setting" the pitch through kiln drying these species for a sufficient period of time at high temperatures.

Regardless of the method used, drying lumber to industry standards helps to stabilize less stable species, to arrest the growth of decay fungus and to make the wood immediately suitable for finishing. Decisions about the method of drying, the level to which wood should be dried, and even whether to dry it or not, are all related to the end use application of the lumber product.

Surfacing

Surfacing is the next step in the process. The lumber may be left rough; have a circle saw texture; bandsaw texture; or be surfaced smooth by a planer or sander. The kind of surfacing done is described in terms of sides and edges to be surfaced. S4S, for example, means surface four sides. See Table 1.

If a board being surfaced is scant in thickness at some point along its length, a manufacturing characteristic called a skip may occur. A roller burn may develop if the piece jams and the feed roller rubs in one place. These characteristics affect appearance but do not reduce the strength of the piece.

Lumber sizes in the U.S. are given as nominal dimensions in inches. At the time a piece of lumber is first sawn from the log it may approach those dimensions. During further manufacture, however, resawing, resurfacing, and seasoning diminish the size considerably, resulting in an actual dimension substantially less than nominal.

The lumber industry produces two sizes of dimension lumber, depending on moisture content: a "dry" size and a slightly larger "green" size. Once the unseasoned size reaches 19% moisture content, it will be approximately the same size as the dry. Because in actual practice some variations may occur between green and dry sizes, they should not be mixed during construction even though their structural properties are the same. Table 2 indicates green and dry sizes at the time of manufacture.

Grading

After surfacing, lumber is graded. Lumber grading ensures that the buyer will receive pieces of each grade with the same range of characteristics, strength, and appearance, regardless of origin. Grades also provide the buyer or user with a dependable measure for determining the value of the lumber under various market conditions. Grading lumber makes it possible to assign design values to it and predict its performance levels.

In 1970 the National Bureau of Standards, in cooperation with softwood lumber producers, distributors, and users, established a voluntary standard for sizes, grades, and inspection practices for softwood lumber. It is known as Voluntary Product Standard PS 20–70, the American Softwood Lumber Standard.

An important part of this Standard is its provision for the organization and functions of the American Lumber Standards Committee. Lumber conforming to the basic minimum size and grade provisions of the American Lumber Standards, and graded under rules approved by the Board of Review of the American Lumber Standards Committee, are generally recognized by building code agencies as approved for building code acceptance.

All major building codes require that lumber that is used structurally be properly identified by a certified grading agency. The usual method is a grade stamp, which amounts to a quality control mark and contains the following information.

1. The logo—a registered trademark of the grading agency.
2. A mill name or number identifying the origin of the product.
3. The moisture content designation at the time of manufacture.
4. The species or species combination.
5. The grade name or number.

These five pieces of information can be seen on any approved grade stamp. Figure 3 illustrates the layout of the

Figure 3. How to read a grade stamp. (1) Logo of the inspecting agency, in this case Western Wood Products Assn., certifying inspection of the piece. The logo shown is a registered trademark. (2) Mill identification. Firm name, brand or assigned mill number. (3) Grade designation. Grade name, number or abbreviation. (4) Species identification. Indicates species by individual species or species combination. (5) Condition of seasoning. Indicates condition of seasoning at time of surfacing: S-DRY—19% maximum moisture content; MC-15—15% maximum moisture content; S-GRN—over 19% moisture content (unseasoned).

Table 1. Standard Lumber Sizes/Nominal and Dressed[a]

Product	Description	Nominal Size Thickness, in.	Nominal Size Width, in.	Dressed Dimensions Thicknesses and Widths, in. Surfaced Dry	Dressed Dimensions Thicknesses and Widths, in. Surfaced Unseasoned	Lengths, ft
Dimension	S4S	2	2	1½	1⁹⁄₁₆	6 ft and longer in
		3	3	2½	2⁹⁄₁₆	multiples of 1 ft
	Other surface combinations are available.	4	4	3½	3⁹⁄₁₆	
			5	4½	4⁵⁄₈	
			6	5½	5⁵⁄₈	
			8	7¼	7½	
			10	9¼	9½	
			12	11¼	11½	
			Over 12	Off ¾	Off ½	
Timbers	Rough or S4S (Shipped unseasoned)		5 and Larger	Thickness, in. ½ Off Nominal (S4S)	Width, in.	6 ft and longer in multiples of 1 ft

				Dressed Dimensions (Dry) Thickness, in.	Dressed Dimensions (Dry) Face Width, in.	Lengths, ft
Decking	2 in. (Single T&G)	2	5	1½	4	6 ft and longer in
			6		5	multiples of 1 ft
			8		6¾	
			10		8¾	
			12		10¾	
	3 and 4 in. (Double T&G)	3	6	2½	5¼	
		4		3½		
Flooring	(D&M), (S2S & CM)	⅜	2	⁵⁄₁₆	1⅛	4 ft and longer in
		½	3	⁷⁄₁₆	2⅛	multiples of 1 ft
		⅝	4	⁹⁄₁₆	3⅛	
		1	5	¾	4⅛	
		1¼	6	1	5⅛	
		1½		1¼		
Ceiling and Partition	(S2S & CM)	⅜	3	⁵⁄₁₆	2⅛	4 ft and longer in
		½	4	⁷⁄₁₆	3⅛	multiples of 1 ft
		⅝	5	⁹⁄₁₆	4⅛	
		¾	6	¹¹⁄₁₆	5⅛	
Factory and Shop Lumber	S2S	1 (4/4)	5 in. and wider except 4 in. and wider in 4/4 No. 1 Shop and 4/4 No. 2 Shop	¾ (4/4)	Usually sold random width	4 ft and longer in multiples of 1 ft
		1¼ (5/4)		1⁵⁄₃₂ (5/4)		
		1½ (6/4)		1¹³⁄₃₂ (6/4)		
		1¾ (7/4)		1¹⁹⁄₃₂ (7/4)		
		2 (8/4)		1¹³⁄₁₆ (8/4)		
		2½ (10/4)		2⅜ (10/4)		
		3 (12/4)		2¾ (12/4)		
		4 (16/4)		3¾ (16/4)		

[a] Abbreviated descriptions appearing in the size table follow: S1S—surfaced one side; S2S—surfaced two sides; S4S—surfaced four sides; S1S1E—surfaced one side, one edge; S1S2E—surfaced one side, two edges; CM—center matched; D&M—dressed and matched; T&G—tongue and grooved; rough full sawn—unsurfaced lumber cut to full specified size.

Table 2. Dimension/Stress-Rated Framing Lumber 2 × 2 Through 4 × 16

Light Framing 2 × 2 through 4 × 4	Construction Standard Utility	This category for use where high strength values are not required, such as studs, plates, sills, cripples, blocking, etc.
Studs 2 × 2 through 4 × 6 10 ft and shorter	Stud	An optional all-purpose grade limited to 10 ft and shorter. Characteristics affecting strength and stiffness values are limited so that the "stud" grade is suitable for all stud uses, including load bearing walls.
Structural Light Framing 2 × 2 through 4 × 4	Select structural No. 1 No. 2 No. 3	These grades are designed to fit those engineering applications where higher bending strength ratios are needed in light framing sizes. Typical uses would be for trusses, concrete pier wall forms, etc.
Structural Joists and Planks 2 × 5 through 4 × 16	Select structural No. 1 No. 2 No. 3	These grades are designed especially to fit in engineering applications for lumber 5 in. and wider, such as joists, rafters, and general framing uses.

grade stamp used by one grading agency. The arrangement of this information varies with the agency.

Shipping Practices

When lumber is shipped from the manufacturing plant, the amount of protection it receives depends on the moisture content of the material, the grade level, and the destination.

Unseasoned lumber is usually shipped unprotected from the weather by truck, flatcar, or ship. If a long journey is expected, as in the case of products for export, or if the material is to be stored at its destination for an extended period of time, an anti-stain treatment is often applied.

Dry lumber in the upper grades is usually wrapped in a protective material or shipped in an enclosed boxcar. The goal is to minimize moisture regain, and to keep the stock bright and clean during transit.

Most lumber products used in construction will be shipped in lengths of 8–20 ft. The availability of longer lengths is limited. Structural products are generally available in units of a single length, whereas appearance products are usually part of a random length unit.

Exceptions to these rules are usually special order situations calling for more lead time and a premium price.

Storage and Handling

When lumber products are delivered to a destination, it is important that they be properly stored and carefully handled. Proper practices will protect the wood from water, sun, and damage due to handling.

Unseasoned lumber should be stored so it can dry slowly and uniformly. This can usually be accomplished by stacking unseasoned material with spacers between the pieces (called stickering), thus allowing air to circulate around the pieces. In addition, the lumber should be protected from hot sun, which can cause uneven drying stresses and result in warpage.

Lumber products that have already been dried should be protected from moisture regain. Paper wrapping and solid stacking discourage damp air from circulating around the lumber, and reduce moisture pick-up from the surrounding environment. Dry lumber products are commonly protected by storage in sheds.

General handling practices should include storing lumber up off the damp ground, protected from sun and rain. Plastic wrapping should be avoided because it can trap moisture in the lumber stack. Lumber should also be neatly stacked where it can stay clean and be easily reached without damage.

TYPES OF LUMBER

Working within the framework of the Voluntary Product Standard, softwood lumber producers in the United States produce lumber which falls within three overall categories. While there is some overlap in end use, a wide range of grades, species, and sizes can be classified as follows:

1. *Structural lumber.* This lumber is generally 2 in. (nominal) or more in thickness, and has working stresses assigned to it. Designers can use these assigned working stresses to calculate lumber for engineered applications.
2. *Yard lumber.* Lumber manufactured in these grades is not generally used in an engineered application. Siding, shelving, trim, and sheathing are all generally fabricated from yard grades.
3. *Factory and shop lumber.* This material is produced or selected primarily for remanufacture. Manufacturers use these grades for doors, windows, cabinets, furniture, or industrial uses. This lumber is not generally stocked in retail lumber yards for consumer use.

Structural Lumber

As previously noted, structural lumber is distinguished from other lumber categories because working stresses (design values) are developed for each size, grade, and species. (These design values are computed by the grade rules writing agencies responsible for the species being analyzed following the American Society for Testing and Materials (ASTM) standards). Resulting design values are then reviewed by the American Lumber Standards Committee, in accordance with the American Softwood Lumber Standard (PS 20-70), before publication or submission for inclusion in the building codes.

Lumber design values included in the grade rule books, building codes, or the National Design Specifications (NDS) for Wood Construction (published by the National Forest Products Assn.) show design values for single species as well as species groupings. Because structural grades are evaluated primarily for their strength and stiffness, trees with similar mechanical properties that may be harvested in the same growing region can be marketed together. For example, any combination of California red fir, grand fir, noble fir, Pacific silver fir, white fir, or western hemlock may be contained in one shipment under the name hem-fir. Similarly, an entire shipment made up of only one of these species would still be assigned the same design values as any combination of the species grouping.

Knots are only one of many natural grading characteristics but they are one of the most important when assessing the structural integrity of a piece of lumber. Ratios have been developed which relate the strength of lumber with knots to the strength of a piece without them. The knot is not considered to add any physical strength to the piece.

Slope of grain can be a result of three things: sawing lumber from a tree at an angle to the length of the tree, cutting lumber from a crooked tree, or twisted (spiral) grain. Depending on its origin, slope of grain can be considered either a natural tree characteristic or a characteristic developed as a result of the manufacturing process. Slope of grain is expressed as a ratio of the deviation from the edge to a particular measurement of length. For example, if the grain moves away from the edge of a piece of lumber a distance of 1 in. and this occurs within 15 in. of length, the slope of grain is said to be 1 in 15.

Slope of grain is an important grading characteristic and one that can potentially cause confusion in the marketplace. When an untrained person compares a piece of lumber with maximum knot size allowed for grade to a piece with the maximum slope of grain per grade, few would pick the maximum knot size piece of lumber as being of equal grade. In fact, the slope of grain grading is just as important as knot size in analyzing the physical properties of structural grades.

GRADES

Given the vast number of species, grades, and sizes available, designers could easily be overwhelmed if it were not for a unifying factor for structural grades. That unifying factor for softwood lumber grades is called the National Grading Rule. All visually graded structural lumber that is 2–4 in. (nominal) thick and at least 2 in. wide (called dimension lumber) carries the same grade names when produced in North America (Table 3).

The majority of the structural uses and sizes are covered under the dimension lumber category but some other size categories and grades are subject to special consideration.

Heavy timbers are 5 in. thick and thicker (5 × 5 and larger). There is some similarity across the country between grade names and grading characteristics, but there are also some regional differences. A specifier must be familiar with the locally available species and grades so that the most advantageous grade and species can be chosen when dealing with these larger structural grades.

Two special types of structural grades of lumber—machine stress-rated (MSR) and end or edge glued—also fall within the size categories of dimension lumber and deserve special consideration.

Machine stress-rating is a mechanical method by which the stress-rating of dimension lumber is determined from a measurement of its stiffness, or modulus of elasticity. Research has shown that a direct relationship exists between the bending stiffness of a piece of lumber and its breaking strength or modulus of rupture. Because the only way to determine the modulus of rupture is to break the piece, the next best thing is to determine the board's stiffness and then predict the modulus of rupture. A regular program of sampling and testing to failure assures that the modulus-of-rupture modulus-of-elasticity relationships are correct.

Provided the proper adhesives and quality control procedures are maintained, end or edge glued structural lumber can be used interchangeably with normal solid sawn dimension lumber. The manufacture of structural glued dimension lumber has become common practice due to increased interest in more efficient use of logs and demand for special and long lengths not always available in solid sawn material. Glued products, manufactured from short lengths of dry wood, also have excellent dimensional stability characteristics.

It is important to note that any list of grade names or species is not a catalog, allowing a buyer or specifier to pick and choose in anticipation of immediate local availability. Marketing practices for structural grades of lumber vary depending on growing regions, shipping costs, and regional preferences, and there is no way to explain those differences thoroughly within the scope of this article. Buyers and specifiers needing assistance would do well to contact local lumber trade associations for specific information.

Table 3. Average Shrinkage Values, Green to Oven Dry Moisture Content[a]

Species	Width		Thickness	
	Percent[b]	Constant	Percent[b]	Constant
Douglas Fir–Larch	7.6	0.00281	4.1	0.00152
Hem-Fir	7.9	0.00293	4.3	0.00159
Western Cedars	5.0	0.00185	2.4	0.00089
Pine				
Idaho White	7.3	0.00299	5.0	0.00205
Lodgepole	6.7	0.00248	4.5	0.00167
Ponderosa	6.2	0.00231	4.8	0.00180
Sugar	5.2	0.00213	3.1	0.00127
Spruce, Engelmann	6.6	0.00244	3.4	0.00126

[a] Typical Shrinkage Calculations: $S = D \times M \times C$

where S = shrinkage in in.
    D = actual dressed dimension in in. (thickness or width)
    M = percent of moisture change
    C = constant for species used (from table)

Example:
Floor joist, 2 × 10, Douglas fir–Larch, dry. Dressed width is 9¼ in., at time of manufacture (maximum 19% moisture content). E.M.C. to be 8% in use.
D = 9.25 in.
M = 11 (19–8%)
C = 0.00281 (width)
S = 9.25 × 11 × 0.00281 = 0.2859 (9/32) in. shrinkage per joist.
Next compute wall plate shrinkages, adding to floor joist shrinkage, times the number of floors for the total building shrinkage factor.

[b] Percent values are for shrinkage from green to oven dry.

MOISTURE STANDARDS

Lumber, when left to its own natural acclimation process, will dry down to a moisture content which relates to its seasonal and regional environment, usually somewhere between 5 and 18%.

Some structural lumber is manufactured green (unseasoned) and left to acclimate naturally at the lumber yard and during construction. As noted earlier, local preferences and species influence the availability of seasoned versus unseasoned framing lumber. But regardless of local preferences, the thickest seasoned structural grade generally available is 2 in. thick. Framing lumber more than 2 in. thick is sold unseasoned.

Most species of structural lumber are dried in a kiln, but the method of seasoning is only identified on the grade stamps of the southern pines. The grade stamps for all other species only indicate one of the three conditions of seasoning—15% at the time of surfacing, 19% at time of surfacing, or surfaced while unseasoned. Structural lumber merely marked "Dry" or "S–Dry" is seasoned to a maximum moisture content of 19% or less. Lumber seasoned to 15% maximum moisture content is grade stamped MC 15 or, in the case of southern pines, KD 15.

The wide variety of end uses for yard grades dictates a wide range of moisture standards. Yard grades that are to be used as wall or roof sheathing can be purchased dry or unseasoned, based on the same standards as the structural grades. Species and knotty grades appropriate for shelving and paneling may be purchased in lots in which the moisture content of the majority of the pieces is 15% or less, with none of the pieces above 19%.

The premium grades, holding the highest value, are given the appropriate amount of care during seasoning. Most grading agencies note that the maximum moisture content of dry premium grades will be 15% and that the vast majority of the pieces (75–80%) shall not exceed 12%.

Lumber to be used for paneling, siding, or trim, which has been seasoned down to this 12% level, will be quite stable. The interior environments in most structures in the continental United States maintain wood at a moisture content somewhere between 8 and 15%. Paneling or trim which is installed at 12% moisture content would be subject only to normal seasonal dimensional changes and consequently performs very satisfactorily.

Just as with grade mixes, marketing practices involving seasoning require knowledge of the local market.

MATERIAL SELECTION

The actual decision to use wood in construction is directly affected by building type. For structural application the building codes regulate how and where a structural element can be used. Occupancy type, fire ratings, height, and area restrictions all must be considered in the selection and assembly of structural wood systems.

Wood systems include light frame construction, platform and balloon frame, post and beam, and heavy timber. In addition, some construction systems combine the advantages of wood-based components with other materials. The list of component options includes solid sawn, finger-jointed, and machine stress-rated lumber; solid and laminated decking; trusses with lumber, metal, and plywood webs; and various laminated veneer lumber products.

Wood components can be assembled as part of the system in various ways. The kind of connection and the stresses acting on it will affect the choice of a connector. The options include traditional joinery (glue, nails, screws, or bolts), and nailing plates, timber connectors, tension rods, and a wide range of mass produced metal hangers, connectors, and hold downs for every conceivable application.

Loading and span capabilities of systems vary, so in addition to code conformance, the wood component or system must also meet the structural requirements of the application. For example, a greater load or longer span usually results in a larger, deeper member with stronger connections.

Connection design considerations such as nail withdrawal resistance and plate holding power become more critical as systems are more precisely engineered or the structural redundancy of a system is reduced. When designing with wood it is important to remember that these properties vary from species to species.

If the structural system is to be exposed, then the visual characteristics of the wood become an important consideration. Because structural grades of lumber are graded primarily for strength rather than appearance, special care may be needed to get the desired effect. Knot size, seasoning checks, splits, wane, and surface texture can all be limited through specifications. Generally speaking, higher grades will have smaller and fewer characteristics. Obviously the type of connectors used will also influence appearance and can be selected to contribute visual interest.

Wood siding, paneling, and trim are available in a wide range of patterns for use both indoors and out, and for residential and commercial applications. When selecting a pattern, care should be taken to assure that it is compatible with the species, grade, conditions of seasoning, climate, and end use.

Caution should always be exercised when success is copied out of context. For example, wide trim boards installed in the desert southwest may not be as desirable as they were on the building in the northwest. And the dark roughsawn paneling that looked so nice in the lightwell at the shopping center might seem stark and foreboding in the room with the small windows on the north side of the house.

Visual effect should only be the starting point in the material selection process. The dimensional stability of the species should be considered, and any compromise in quality or moisture standards should be balanced by a more conservative approach in pattern selection, product face width, architectural protection of the surface, or grain orientation. Also, because budget can seldom be ignored, design problems should be analyzed and as many plusses as the money will allow should be chosen.

To assure dimensional stability, a narrow pattern which allows for some movement, such as a channel or bevel should be selected (Fig. 4). Vertical grain material experiences less face width dimensional change than flat grained pieces, but is only available in the premium categories. If a wide pattern and flat grain are necessary, then the material must be well seasoned and acclimated to the environment prior to installation. A stable species should be selected; proper installation should be ensured and a protective finish applied.

Because the cost of the material and time frame of the project will be affected by the local availability of the lumber or wood components selected, proximity to a material source makes a selection realistic.

The versatility of woods allows it to be used in all aspects of construction, but the best results are achieved when requirements are clearly established, options evaluated, and strengths and limitations fully considered.

DETAILING

Wood, when properly used in construction, can provide satisfactory service for hundreds of years. (A house in

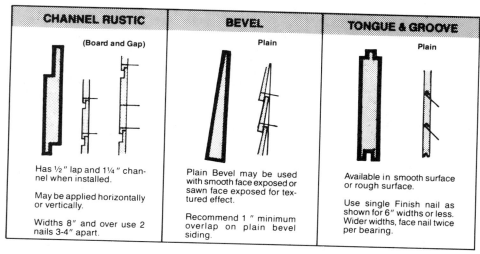

CHANNEL RUSTIC

(Board and Gap)

Has ½″ lap and 1¼″ channel when installed.

May be applied horizontally or vertically.

Widths 8″ and over use 2 nails 3-4″ apart.

BEVEL

Plain

Plain Bevel may be used with smooth face exposed or sawn face exposed for textured effect.

Recommend 1″ minimum overlap on plain bevel siding.

TONGUE & GROOVE

Plain

Available in smooth surface or rough surface.

Use single Finish nail as shown for 6″ widths or less. Wider widths, face nail twice per bearing.

Figure 4. Profiles of three commonly used siding types and recommended nailing patterns for the best results.

Massachusetts, believed to be the oldest wood frame structure in the United States, dates back to 1637.) A long service life is the result of careful planning and detailing which begins with design and specification and continues on through the construction process. An understanding of wood's natural characteristics, appreciation of its attributes, and respect for its limitations allow it to be used with confidence in a wide range of construction applications.

Shrinkage

Shrinkage and swelling considerations are unique to wood-based products. Dimensional change is related to moisture content and is not to be confused with expansion and contraction, which are heat related.

Softwood species have minimal longitudinal shrinkage characteristics, so the need for length considerations can be eliminated. Design considerations for shrinkage should be applied to thickness and width of horizontal members, and the cumulative effect this has on floors should be recognized. Shrinkage is normally uniform in structures using platform frame construction throughout. However, the use of a system with continuous vertical bearing members will create differential shrinkage, which must be given special attention.

Detailing large expanses of interior and exterior drywall, paneling, and siding could cause the finish surface to buckle at each horizontal floor level because of the effects of multistory dimensional change. Consequently, expansion joints or slip-joint details are often used at each floor level to allow for shrinkage. The amount can be approximated using a formula similar to the one in Table 4.

Table 4. Characteristics of Woods for Painting and Finishing

Softwood	Weight at 8% Moisture Content, lb/ft^3	Ease of Keeping Well Painted (I = Easiest, V = Most Exacting)	Resistance to Cupping (1 = Best, 4 = Worst)	Conspicuousness of Checking (1 = Least, 2 = Most)	Color of Heartwood (Sapwood is Always Light)	Degree of Figure on Flat-Grained Surface
Cedar						
Alaska	30.4	I	1	1	Yellow	Faint
California incense	24.2	I			Brown	Faint
Port-Orford	28.9	I		1	Cream	Faint
Western redcedar	22.4	I	1	1	Brown	Distinct
White	20.8	I			Light brown	Distinct
Cypress	31.4	I	1	1	Light Brown	Strong
Redwood	27.4	I	1	1	Dark brown	Distinct
Products overlaid with resin-treated paper		I		1		
Pine						
Eastern white	24.2	II	2	2	Cream	Faint
Sugar	24.9	II	2	2	Cream	Faint
Western white	27.1	II	2	2	Cream	Faint
Ponderosa	27.5	III	2	2	Cream	Distinct
Fir, White	25.8	III	2	2	White	Faint
Hemlock, Western	28.7	III	2	2	Pale brown	Faint
Spruce	26.8	III	2	2	White	Faint
Douglas-fir (lumber and plywood)	31.0	IV	2	2	Pale red	Strong
Larch, Western	38.2	IV	2	2	Brown	Strong
Lauan (plywood)		IV	2	2	Brown	Faint
Pine						
Norway (red)	30.4	IV	2	2	Light brown	Distinct
Southern (lumber and plywood)	38.2	IV	2	2	Light brown	Strong
Tamarack	36.3	IV	2	2	Brown	Strong

Lateral Forces

Wood frame construction, using shear walls and roof diaphragms, provides superior performance against high load forces resulting from wind or seismic conditions. Wood can carry short term stresses far above normal, giving it a high margin of reserve strength. One of wood's greatest advantages is in diaphragm applications.

Because an engineered diaphragm's ability to transfer loads effectively is directly related to the adequacy of the connectors, the system requires the application of a specific design method and imposes strict detailing requirements for fasteners and connectors. Attention should be given to rafter-to-ridge beam connections, trusses-to-wall or rafters-to-wall, wall system to wall system at floor levels, and wall-system-to-foundation connections.

Timber Connections

The performance of wood construction is often connector-dependent. The quantities and sizes of connectors needed depend on the loads to be carried as well as the size of the member, but the actual detailing of the connector is really more a matter of common sense than of technical expertise.

Large wood members will shrink, but proper detailing will allow for that. Long rows of bolts and connectors at the top and bottom of a member should be avoided because they can cause tension perpendicular to the grain of the wood and may result in splitting at the bolts. Connections which allow some movement across the width of a member are preferred.

Notching should be avoided because it reduces the effective shear strength of a wood member. It also makes the member vulnerable to tension stresses perpendicular to the grain of the wood.

Wood is not as strong in tension perpendicular to the grain as it is in tension parallel to the grain, so loads should be suspended from the tops of wood members to avoid inducing tension stresses. If the loads are light, they can be fastened above the neutral axis, although this should be avoided when possible.

Connections can be detailed to avoid collecting moisture by including weep holes, separating wood from concrete with bearing plates, and protecting them from the weather as much as possible.

Solid sawn timbers, dry joists, and glue-laminated beams are all manufactured to different moisture content levels. If combined in the same system, their differential shrinkage should be considered and connections detailed accordingly.

Heavy Timber

Building codes have provisions for heavy timber building types in which exposed members detailed to designated sizes are afforded a one-hour fire rating. This is because, in a fire, timbers char on the exposed outer surfaces, thus insulating the core from heat and reducing the rate of burning of the timbers. As a result, the undamaged portion of the cross section retains its strength and stiffness properties.

Exposed heavy timber sizes may be used in light frame wood buildings to meet one-hour fire resistance requirements if detailed in accordance with the National Evaluation Board Report No. NRB–250.

The report recognizes the weak link in an assembly exposed to fire to be the metal connector. However, if the connection is detailed so it is protected from fire exposure by 1.5 in. of wood, fire rated gypsum board, or other approved coating, a one-hour fire rating is achieved.

Firestopping/Draftstopping

Firestopping and draftstopping details are required by the building codes for wood construction. Firestopping prevents movement of flame and gases to other areas of a building through small concealed passages such as floors, walls, and stairs. Draftstopping prevents it through larger passages such as attic spaces and floor assemblies with open-web trusses.

Decay

Control of decay is achieved primarily through proper detailing. Such detailing provides positive site and building drainage as well as ventilation and condensation control in enclosed spaces. It should also include adequate separation of wood members from moisture sources to prevent excessive absorption. Wood which is naturally durable or pressure-preservative-treated should be used where adverse conditions exist.

FINISH GRADES

As previously noted in this article, yard lumber is used primarily for nonengineered applications such as siding, shelving, sheathing, and trim. Factory and shop lumber is produced and selected primarily for remanufacture into windows, doors, cabinets, etc, and as such, beyond the brief discussion below, is not a proper subject for this article.

Finish grades and yard grades are unique in construction because of the minimal influence on them by building codes. The previously discussed structural grades are rigidly controlled due to concern for structural adequacy. But because siding and paneling do not involve personal safety, there is a great deal more freedom involved in these finish grades, a freedom which also includes drawbacks.

Unlike structural grades of lumber in which the distinctions are by design value, finish grades are categorized according to appearance, and distinctions are based on visual and performance criteria. Color, grain pattern, durability, paintability, workability, and dimensional stability are more important considerations than strength and stiffness (Table 1). Similarly, natural and manufacturing characteristics in the wood are evaluated in terms of their effect on appearance. The size, number, and quality of the grading characteristics are considered, and their combined effect on appearance determines the grade.

How the lumber is cut from the tree greatly affects its appearance and performance properties. For example, the wood's proximity to the outermost portion of the tree affects its durability. If cut from the outer sapwood, it will be less decay resistant. Closer to the center it will be more durable but it will also be likely to have more knots. Vertical grain lumber—a piece with its face perpendicular to the growth rings—exposes more dense latewood and is therefore more abrasion-resistant as well as dimensionally stable. Flat grained material cut tangentially to the growth rings results in a visually interesting grain pattern, but is more susceptible to cupping if not properly seasoned.

Different end uses of both flat and vertical grain lumber have led to the development of different sawing techniques. Quartersawing, used primarily in hardwood manufacture, produces all vertical grain material. Plainsawing is a more efficient method, which produces a high yield mix of vertical and flat grain. Plainsawing also allows larger pieces to be cut.

Several general statements can be made about softwood finish grades manufactured in North America. The premium quality grades, those with few blemishes, are often referred to as "select" or "finish" grades, and the select and some of the finish grades have names like "C" select or "D" select, with the C grade being a better grade than the D.

The knotty types of grades are found in a wide range of categories including, but not limited to, classifications such as common, knotty, and board grades. Quite often these knotty categories have a number grade, *i.e.* "No. 2 Common," with the small numbers being the better grades.

INSTALLATION AND FINISHING

After species, grade, and pattern selection have taken place, proper installation will help maintain the desired visual effect. The basic goals for installation of finish carpentry materials, whether interior or exterior, are to secure the material in place and to minimize dimensional change.

Preconditioning and Moisture Control

Wood shrinks and swells with changes in moisture content. To minimize dimensional change after installation, siding, paneling, and trim should be installed at a moisture content that matches its environment as closely as possible. "Knotty" grades can have a higher moisture content than the "clear" grades. When installed in an environment dryer than the lumber itself, the material can be expected to shrink. This shrinkage can be minimized by preconditioning finish carpentry materials before installation.

Good practice calls for stacking the wood in the place where it will be installed, protected and with spacers between layers, for a week to ten days before application. Interior construction which contains moisture, such as plaster or drywall, should be dry before the paneling or millwork is delivered, and concrete or block walls should be waterproofed or a vapor barrier put in place before wood products are installed.

Moisture penetration or vapor condensation behind siding and paneling can cause swelling of the back side, resulting in cupping and other performance problems. To help maintain a dry wall assembly, proper flashing and venting details should be installed, along with a vapor retarder on the warm side of the insulation.

Priming and Sealing

Material which has been properly seasoned, stored and handled can still pick up moisture after installation, so wood in high moisture areas should be protected. Extra protection can be given by priming or prefinishing all sides, edges, and ends after preconditioning and before installation. Prefinishing can also minimize objectionably unfinished lines where joints open up due to face width shrinkage.

"Back priming," as it is sometimes called, is especially important when siding products are installed over rigid foam insulation. Condensation between the insulation and the unfinished siding can cause swelling of the backside of the siding resulting in cupping. Back priming moderates this effect.

Siding performs better when installed over building paper. The paper can also help to buffer the rapid temperature swings associated with siding installed over rigid foam products.

Nailing

Nailing is perhaps the single most important part of proper installation of wood products, both inside and outside the structure. The idea is to fasten the material securely in place without restricting dimensional change across the width of the piece. Excessive or improper nailing which restrains natural movement can result in splitting. Recommended nailing diagrams allow for movement in a variety of ways, depending on the pattern selected.

Methods of nailing include "blind" and "face nailing." Blind nailing is used for narrower widths of tongue and groove type patterns, with the nails being concealed by each succeeding piece during installation. Face nailing is used for wider patterns and those that do not lend themselves to blind nailing. For interior applications, nails are commonly countersunk and the holes filled in with putty or wood filler.

Non-corrosive nails should be used for exterior or high humidity interior applications. They include stainless steel, high tensile aluminum, and hot-dipped galvanized nails. Aluminum should not be used with pressure-treated products, and electro-coated galvanization should be avoided.

For exterior applications, nails should be long enough to penetrate into a wood base 1.5 in., or 1.25 in. with a ring or screw shank. Nailing is suggested over staples to achieve the necessary withdrawal resistance. For vertical applications this may require blocking or furring in addition to wall framing. Building codes require that the spacing of framing or blocking shall not exceed 24 in. on center.

Finishing Considerations

Wood has the ability to accept and retain a wide variety of finish coatings. Decisions about interior coatings are limited only by the imagination and the recommendations of the coating manufacturer.

When selecting coatings for exterior applications the options are still quite varied, but construction practices, climate, architectural considerations, and detailing start to play equal roles with product selection in the expected life of the coatings.

Viewing older buildings is a good way to learn about the effects of weather and design considerations on wood exteriors. Southerly and westerly exposures, and walls which are subject to batterings by winter storms, are usually weathered the worst. Walls without overhangs and drip caps at windows and doors do not perform as well as those that have both. When water or snow are allowed to splash on or accumulate against exterior walls, the lower portions lose their coatings more quickly. These are all architectural considerations that should be included in the design process. Caution should always be used when trying to adapt architectural decisions across climatic zones.

As previously mentioned in this article, paint and stain adhere to earlywood better than they do to the more dense rings. Vertical grain grades, which expose narrower bands of latewood to the surface to be coated, offer a better opportunity for the coating to span the latewood than do flat grained boards.

Generally speaking, cedars and redwoods maintain coatings the best. Idaho white pine (also referred to as western pine) and sugar pine follow closely behind, the true firs and hemlocks are next, with Douglas fir and the southern pines being the most difficult of these to maintain when exposed to weathering (Table 1).

The grade of wood used and the type of finish desired are the major influences in choosing the final coating. For example, knots are difficult to paint over; when a semi-transparent or transparent finish is used, and knots are allowed to be part of the character of the finish, they are no longer a difficulty. Roughsawn or resawn lumber surfaces are particularly good for use with non-film-forming types of finishes.

A critical factor in determining the service life of the coating is the moisture content of the wood at the time of coating. Simply put, the coating should be applied when the wood has reached a moisture content that closely approximates what it will be at the same time next season.

Natural Finishes

On a cyclical basis, there is a resurgence of "leaving it natural," either as an attempt to eliminate maintenance or to develop an architectural character. Some structures left to weather naturally have sidings which have kept the weather out since the turn of the century.

The difficulty is that some people want siding not only to keep the weather out but to look a particular way as well. Stating it slightly differently, these people usually want fewer weathering characteristics than could be expected if the siding and trim were protected to some de-

gree. When structures are left to weather naturally, surface checks can be expected to develop and cracks may occur. The grain rises as it becomes wet and then dries out again, and boards may cup or warp due to unequal drying on the sides of the piece. Unequal weathering at protected versus unprotected exposures for long periods of time also causes unequal coloring.

If these types of physical changes are accepted and understood, "leaving it natural" may be an option for some situations. But most building owners do not find the majority of these changes acceptable and opt for a protective coating. An "almost natural" solution is the use of commercially available bleaching oils or stains which simulate the graying process and also include a water repellent and possibly a fungicide and/or mildewcide as well. While this type of process is not maintenance free, it can simulate the natural look while minimizing some of the weathering characteristics which building owners may find objectionable.

GLOSSARY

Air Dried. Lumber which has been dried in the open air.

American Lumber Standards (ALS). The American Lumber Standards Committee, established by PS–70 (The American Softwood Lumber Standard) with members representing consumers, distributors, architects, builders, users, and producers, are appointed by the U.S. Secretary of Commerce to oversee the implementation of lumber standards in the United States.

Annual Ring. Annual increment of wood growth, consisting of earlywood and latewood, as seen on a cross section. Same as growth ring.

Anti-stain Treated. Lumber or other wood product treated with any one of a number of various chemicals to prevent staining caused by exposure to weather and to inhibit growth of wood-staining fungi.

ASTM. American Society for Testing and Materials, Philadelphia, Pa.

Balloon Framing. A framing system in which joists are fixed to vertical studs running the full height of the building, from the ground sill or plate to the head plate supporting the roof rafters.

Band Saw. A saw consisting of a continuous piece of flexible steel, with teeth on one or both sides, used to cut logs into cants and also to rip lumber.

Bevel Siding. A lumber pattern with a flat face, a thin edge, and a thick edge.

Bound Water. Water associated with cell-wall material in wood.

Bow. A deviation flatwise from a straight line drawn from end to end of a piece, measured at the point of greatest distance from the straight line; it does not include short kinks.

Boxed Heart (BH). The term used when the pith falls entirely within the four faces anywhere in the length of a piece.

Bucker. A person who saws felled trees into logs.

Burl. A large wartlike excrescence on a tree trunk; it

contains the dark piths of a large number of buds which rarely develop; the formation of a burl apparently results from an injury to the tree.

Cambium. A thin layer of tissue between the bark and wood that repeatedly subdivides to form new wood and bark cells.

Cants. Large planks or timbers cut on the head saw for further sawing elsewhere.

Cell. A general term for the structural units of plants including wood fibers, vessel members, and other elements of diverse structure and function.

Cellulose. The carbohydrate that is the principal constituent of wood and forms the framework of the wood cells.

Checks. A separation of the wood, usually occurring lengthwise of a piece across the rings of annual growth; these are usually a result of seasoning.

Circular Saw. A round saw having cutting teeth on its perimeter. Originally common as a head saw in sawmills, it has been largely replaced by band saws. Circular saws remain widely used as trim and cutoff saws.

Clear (CLR). A term describing the higher grades of lumber—sound, relatively free of blemishes.

Commons. A term describing the ordinary grades of knotty lumber.

Compression Wood. Abnormal wood that often forms on the lower side of branches and of leaning trunks of softwood trees. Compression wood is identified by its relatively wide annual rings, usually eccentric, and its relatively large amount of summerwood, usually more than 50% of the width of the annual rings in which it occurs. Compression wood shrinks excessively lengthwise compared to normal wood.

Conifers. The botanical group of trees having needles, or scalelike leaves, and cones; they are usually "evergreen."

Cup. A curve in a piece across the grain or width of a piece; it is measured at the point of greatest distance from a straight line drawn from edge to edge of a piece.

Decay. Decay is disintegration of wood due to the action of wood-destroying fungi. The words "dote" and "rot" mean the same as decay.

Deciduous. Trees that lose their leaves. Usually broadleaved and usually classified as hardwoods.

Design Value. A measurement of strength in lumber, involving six different properties of wood. These are: fiber stress in bending (F_b), tension parallel to grain (F_t), horizontal shear (F_v), compression parallel to grain (F_c), compression perpendicular to grain ($F_c\perp$), and modulus of elasticity (E).

Dimension. A term generally applied to framing lumber when the nominal size is 2 in. thick and 2 or more in. wide. The National Grading Rule for Softwood Dimension Lumber defines "Dimension" as lumber from 2 to 4 in. thick and 2 in. and wider.

Dimensional Stability. The ability of a material to maintain its original dimensions under variations of temperature, moisture, and physical stress.

Durability. A general term for permanence frequently used to refer to the degree of resistance of a species or an individual piece of wood to attack by wood-destroying fungi under conditions that favor such attack; the term "resistance to decay" is more specific.

Earlywood. The portion of the annual growth ring that is formed during the early part of the growing season. It is usually less dense and mechanically weaker than latewood.

Extractives. Substances in wood, not an integral part of the cellular structure, that can be dissolved out with hot or cold water, ether, benzene, or other relatively inert solvents.

Factory Lumber. Lumber intended to be cut up for use in further manufacture; it is graded on the basis of the percentage of the area which will produce a limited number of cuttings of a specified, or a given minimum, size and quality.

Faller. A person who cuts down trees in a logging operation.

Finger-Joint. A way of joining pieces of lumber by machining them on the ends and bonding them together with glue. The joint is similar to slipping the fingers of two hands together. Also called end-joint or glue-joint.

Finish (Lumber). A term indicating the higher grades of lumber—sound, relatively free of blemishes.

Flat Grain (FG) (Slash Grain (SG)). Lumber sawn approximately parallel to the annual growth rings so that all or some of the rings form an angle of less than 45° with the surface of the piece.

Free of Heart Center (FOHC). Applied to lumber sawn to exclude the heart center or pith of the log.

Fungus. A parasitic plant that feeds on wood. Some fungi cause decay, stain, or mold in wood.

Gradestamped. Applied to lumber when its grade is indicated with an official stamp impression.

Green Wood. Unseasoned wood.

Hardwoods. The botanical group of trees that are broad-leaved; the term has no reference to the actual hardness of the wood. Angiosperm is the botanical name for hardwood.

Head Rig. The primary saw in a sawmill operation on which logs are first cut into cants before being sent on to other saws for further processing.

Heart, Heartwood. The wood extending from the pith to the sapwood, the cells of which no longer participate in the life process of the tree. Heartwood may be infiltrated with gums, resins, and other materials which usually make it darker and more decay-resistant than sapwood.

Honeycomb. Pits or spots in wood caused by fungi. It develops in the living tree and does not develop further in wood in service.

Intergrown Knot. A knot partially or completely intergrown on one or two faces with the growth rings of the surrounding wood.

Joist. Pieces (nominal dimensions 2–4 in. in thickness ×5 in. and wider) of rectangular cross section graded with respect to strength in bending when loaded on the narrow face; used as supporting members under a floor or over a ceiling.

Kiln Dried (KD). Lumber which has been dried under conditions of controlled temperatures and humidities in a dry kiln.

Knot. That portion of a branch or limb that occurs in a piece of lumber.

Latewood. The portion of the annual growth ring that is formed after the earlywood formation has ceased. It is usually denser and mechanically stronger than earlywood.

Machine Stress-rated (MSR Lumber). Lumber that has been evaluated by mechanical stress rating equipment; each piece is non-destructively tested and marked to indicate the modulus of elasticity. MSR lumber is also required to meet certain visual requirements.

Millwork. Generally refers to wood remanufactured in millwork plants; it includes such items as inside and outside doors, windows and door frames, blinds, porch-work, mantels, panel-work, stairways, moldings, and interior trim. It does not include flooring, ceiling, or siding.

Modulus of Elasticity (MOE). The relationship between the amount a piece deflects and the load causing the deflection determines its stiffness. Factors affecting the MOE are grade, size, span, and species.

Modulus of Rupture (MOR). A measurement of the load required to break a particular size and length of lumber.

Moisture Content (MC). The moisture content of wood is the weight of the water in wood expressed as a percentage of the weight of the wood from which all water has been removed (oven dry). Moisture is removed from lumber either by air drying or by use of special drying kilns.

National Grading Rule (NGR). The general rule covering grade strength ratios, nomenclature, and descriptions of grades for dimension lumber conforming to the American Lumber Standards. Regional rules prepared by a rules writing agency must conform to the National Grading Rule for dimension lumber to be certified as conforming to American Lumber Standards.

Nominal Measure. Is "board measure" contents of lumber when calculated from measurements of named sizes; same as gross measure.

Old Growth. This refers to timber in or from a mature, naturally-established forest. Old growth trees have grown during most if not all of their individual lives in active competition with their companions for sunlight and are relatively free of knots.

Over-dry Wood. Wood completely dried until it is without any moisture content.

Pattern (PAT). Any one of a number of shapes or configurations to which lumber may be worked.

Peck. Pockets or areas of disintegrated wood caused by advanced stages of localized decay in the living tree; it is usually associated with cypress and incense cedar. There is no further development of peck once the tree is felled.

Pitch. An accumulation of resin.

Pitch Pocket. An opening extending parallel to the annual rings of growth usually containing, or which has contained, pitch (either solid or liquid).

Pith. The small soft core occurring in the structural center of a log.

Plain Sawn. Refers to lumber sawn so that the annual rings form angles of 0° to 45° with the surface of the piece.

Platform Framing. A framing system in which the vertical members are only a single story high, with each finished floor acting as a platform upon which the succeeding floor is constructed.

Pre-finished. Refers to lumber, plywood, molding, or other wood products with an applied finish coating of paint, stain, vinyl, or other material.

Pressure Treating. Refers to a process of impregnating lumber or other wood products with various chemicals, such as preservatives and fire retardants, by using high pressure to force the chemical into the structure of the wood.

Quarter Sawn. Refers to lumber sawn so that the annual rings form angles of 45° to 90° with the surface of the piece.

Random Length (R/L, RL). Refers to lumber containing an assortment of lengths. A random length shipment should contain a fair assortment of the lengths being produced by the manufacturer.

Remanufacture. Reworking larger pieces of lumber into smaller pieces.

Resin. Inflammable, water-soluble, vegetable substances secreted by certain plants or trees, and found inside the wood of many coniferous species. The term is also applied to synthetic organic products related to the natural resins.

Rough Lumber. Lumber as it comes from the saw which has not been further surfaced or machined; lumber which is not dressed.

Sap. All the fluids in a tree (special secretions and excretions, such as gum, excepted).

Sapwood. The layers of wood next to the bark, usually lighter in color than the heartwood, one-half inch to three or more inches wide that are actively involved in the life processes of the tree. Under most conditions sapwood is more susceptible to decay than heartwood; and, as a rule, it is more permeable to liquids than heartwood. The sapwood of a given species of tree, however, is not essentially weaker or stronger than its heartwood.

Seasoning. Removing moisture from green wood to improve its serviceability.

Second Growth. Refers to timber that has grown after the removal by any means of all or a large portion of the previous stand, usually young trees. It also refers to wood assumed to have grown in a forest after removal of any large part, or all, of a previous stand.

Select (SEL). A term describing the higher grades of lumber—sound, relatively free of blemishes.

Shake. A lengthwise separation of the wood which occurs usually between or through the rings of annual growth.

Shop Lumber. Lumber intended to be cut up for use in further manufacture; it is graded on the basis of the percentage of the area which will produce a limited number of clear cuttings of a specified, or a minimum, size and quality.

Shrinkage. Decrease in size of wood due to decrease in moisture content.

Skip. An area on a piece that failed to surface.

Slope of Grain. This is a deviation of the fibers from a straight line parallel to the sides of a piece.

Softwoods. The botanical group of trees that have needle or scalelike leaves and are evergreen for the most part—cypress, larch and tamarack being exceptions. The term has no reference to the actual hardness of the wood—"softwoods" are often referred to as conifers, and botanically they are called gymnosperms.

Spiral Grain. A type of growth in which the fibers take a spiral course about the bole of a tree instead of the normal vertical course; the spiral may extend right-handed or left-handed around the tree trunk.

Split. A lengthwise separation of the wood due to the tearing apart of the wood cells.

Springwood. The portion of an annual growth ring which forms during the early part of any season's growth; usually less dense, weaker mechanically, and lighter colored than summerwood.

Sticker. Sticks of wood used to separate lumber in stacking.

Structural lumber (STR). Lumber cut chiefly from the middle portion of the log between the sap and the pith; it is high strength construction lumber.

Stud. Used for framing interior or exterior wall sections of a building, usually a $2'' \times 4'' - 8'$ or precision end trimmed from 8' stock. However, other light framing sizes may also be used for studding.

Summerwood. The portion of the annual growth ring that is found during the latter part of the yearly growth period; it is usually more dense and stronger mechanically than springwood.

Surfaced Dry (S–Dry). Lumber dried to 19% or less moisture content.

Surfaced Green (S–Grn). Unseasoned lumber, with moisture content in excess of 19%.

Surfaced Lumber. Lumber which has been planed or sanded on one or more surfaces.

Swelling. An increase in size of wood due to increase in moisture content.

Timbers. Lumber 5 inches or larger in least dimension; generally used in heavy construction.

Tongue and Groove (T&G). Lumber that has been worked with a tongue on one edge of each piece and a groove on the opposite edge to provide a closely matched joint when fitting two pieces together.

Trim Saw. A set of saws, usually circular, used to cut lumber to various lengths by lowering individual blades to make contact with the lumber as it passes beneath the saws on a moving chain. Trim saws also cut out defects and improve recovery.

Twist. A distortion caused by the turning or winding of the edges of a board so that the four corners of any face are no longer in the same plane.

Vertical Grain (V.G.). Another term for edge grain—annual rings at an angle of 45° or more to the wide face of a piece of lumber.

Wane. Bark or lack of wood from any cause on the edge or corner of a piece.

Warp. Any variation from a true or plane surface; it includes crook, bow, cup, twist, or any combination thereof.

White Speck. Small white pits or spots in wood caused by the fungus *formes pini*. It develops in the living tree and does not develop further in wood after it has been processed.

Yard Lumber. Lumber of those grades, sizes, and patterns generally intended for ordinary construction and general building purposes.

BIBLIOGRAPHY

General References

E. Allen, *Fundamentals of Building Construction, Materials and Methods,* John Wiley & Sons, Inc., New York, 1985.

American Institute of Timber Construction, *Timber Construction Manual,* John Wiley & Sons, Inc., New York, 1985.

ASTM D245-81, Establishing Structural Grades and Related Allowable Properties for Visually Graded Lumber, American Society for Testing and Materials, Philadelphia, Pa.

ASTM D2555-81, Establishing Clear Wood Strength Values, American Society for Testing and Materials, Philadelphia, Pa.

D. E. Breyer, *Design of Wood Structures,* McGraw-Hill, Inc., New York, 1980.

W. M. Harlow and E. S. Harper, *Textbook of Dendrology,* McGraw-Hill, Inc., New York, 1969.

F. B. Hoadley, *Understanding Wood,* The Taunton Press, Newton, Conn., 1981.

R. J. Hoyle, Jr., *Wood Technology in the Design of Structures,* Mountain Press Publishing Co., Missonla, Mont., 1978.

E. Lucia, *Head Fig, Story of the West Coast Lumber Industry,* Overland West Press, 1965.

National Design Specifications for Wood Construction, National Forest Products Association, 1986.

Panshin and DeZeeuw, *Textbook of Wood Technology,* 3rd ed., McGraw-Hill, Inc., New York, 1970.

Random Lengths Publications: Terms of the Trade. 1978.

M. Reed, *Residential Carpentry,* John Wiley & Sons, Inc., New York, 1985.

U.S. Department of Agriculture, Forest Service: Wood Handbook, Agriculture Handbook No. 72. U.S. Government Printing Office, Washington, D.C.

U.S. Department of Agriculture, Forest Service: Wood Frame House Construction, Handbook No. 73, U.S. Government Printing Office, Washington, D.C.

U.S. Department of Agriculture: Miscellaneous Publications, Atlas of U.S. Trees, No. 1146, U.S. Government Printing Office, Washington, D.C.

U.S. Department of Agriculture, Forest Service: Wood as a Structural Material. The Pennsylvania State University (1980).

U.S. Department of Commerce & National Bureau of Standards: American Softwood Lumber Standard PS 20-70. U.S. Government Printing Office, Washington, D.C.

Western Woods Use Book, 3rd ed., 1985; *Lumber Terminology & Invoice Procedure,* 1977; *Product Use Manual,* 1981; *Wood Frame Design,* 1984; all published by Western Wood Products Association; Portland, Oregon.

See also Architectural Woodwork; Construction Systems; Glued Laminated Wood (Glulam); Hardware—Rough and Finish; Termites—Control by Soil Poisoning; Wood Flooring; Wood Framing; Wood—Structural Panel Composites; Wood Treatment

Don E. Wallace
Gunnar Brinck
Western Wood Products
Association
Portland, Oregon

WOOD, STRUCTURAL. See Wood in Construction; Wood Framing—Supplement; Wood, Structural Panels

WOOD—STRUCTURAL PANELS

Structural wood panel systems are used in dozens of commercial, residential, and industrial construction applications. Structural panels feature versatility and excellent structural performance. They are economical and available in a variety of grades and thicknesses. This article includes descriptions of structural wood panel grades and specifications and installation recommendations.

COMPOSITION AND MANUFACTURE

The structural wood panel industry has evolved from the manufacture of a single product (plywood) to a much broader industry that produces a wide variety of panels for many different applications. Plywood, manufactured to numerous application specifications, still represents a large portion of the structural wood panel industry. Other types of structural wood panels include waferboard, oriented strand board (OSB), and structural particleboard.

Standard structural wood panels of all compositions are manufactured in thicknesses ranging from ¼ to 1⅛ in. Thicker panels can also be manufactured on special order. Standard dimensions are 4 × 8 ft, although some mills can produce longer panels for special applications such as commercial roofs.

Plywood

Plywood is made up of thin sheets of wood called veneers or plies. Logs to be used in plywood production are first debarked and cut to panel length. The logs are then placed on a large lathe. Veneer is peeled or unrolled from the logs, much as paper towels are unwound from the roll. The veneer sheets are trimmed to panel size, which is typically 4 × 8 ft. Next, the veneers are arranged in layers, which are in turn assembled crosswise to each other and bonded under heat and pressure with resin adhesives. The strength of the wood goes with the direction of the grain. By alternating directions of the grain in the layers, strength is achieved in both the length and width of the panel.

Originally, structural plywood was made entirely from Douglas fir and was used only for doors, drawer bottoms, and automobile running boards. Now, dozens of different tree species from all over North America are used in plywood production, and the end uses have mushroomed to a broad range of domestic and foreign applications. Douglas fir is still one of the most common species used in plywood production, along with the southern pines (loblolly, longleaf, shortleaf, and slash) (Table 1). Principal uses of plywood and other structural panels include walls, floors, roofs, roof decks, siding, wood foundations, concrete forming, materials handling, truck and rail car siding, cabinets, and furniture.

Waferboard, OSB, and Structural Particleboard

Nonveneer structural wood panels include waferboard, OSB, and certain classes of structural particleboard. Nonveneered panels are composed of reconstituted wood wafers, flakes, or particles. They can be manufactured from a broader range of tree species. U.S. Forest Service research indicates these panels use almost 90% of a log, compared to 40% for lumber. Particleboard is a resin-bonded panel made of small, randomly oriented particles. Waferboard is a resin-bonded panel of larger waferlife flakes. OSB is composed of cross-laminated, compressed layers of mechanically oriented, resin-bonded wood strands.

Composite Panels

Composite panels are produced by bonding reconstituted wood cores, instead of veneers, between conventional veneer face and back plies. Composites look and act much like conventional all-veneer plywood and may be used in many typical plywood applications.

PRODUCT AND PERFORMANCE STANDARDS

Some grades of veneer panels are manufactured under the detailed manufacturing specifications or under the performance testing provisions of U.S. Product Standard PS 1-83 for Construction and Industrial Plywood, developed cooperatively by the plywood industry and the U.S. Department of Commerce. Other veneered panels, however, as well as an increasing number of performance-rated panels, are manufactured under the provisions of American Plywood Association (APA) performance criteria for specific designated construction applications. APA is a nonprofit trade association that represents 80% of U.S. structural panel manufacturers. As well as providing grade and species information, the trademark on APA performance-rated panels includes recommendations for end use and maximum support spacings.

Grade Designations

Construction and industrial panel grades are generally identified in terms of the veneer grade used on the face and back of the panel (eg, A-B, B-C) or by a name suggesting the panel's intended end use (eg, APA Rated Sheathing, APA Rated Sturd-I-Floor). Veneer grades define veneer appearance in terms of natural unrepaired growth characteristics and allowable number and size of repairs that may be made during manufacture. The highest-quality veneer grades are N (available only on special order) and A. The minimum grade of veneer permitted in exterior plywood is C. D-grade veneer is used only in panels intended for interior use or applications protected from exposure to permanent or severe moisture.

Exposure Classifications

There are four exposure durability classifications. Exterior panels have a fully waterproof bond and are designed for applications subject to continuous exposure to the weather or to moisture. Exposure 1 panels, identified in Table 2 under PS 1 as interior-type with exterior glue, are highly moisture-resistant and are designed for applications where the ability to resist moisture during long construction delays or exposure to conditions of similar severity is required. Exposure 1 panels are made with the same

Table 1. Classification of Species

Group 1	Group 2	Group 3	Group 4	Group 5
Apitong	Cedar, Port Orford	Alder, red	Aspen	Basswood
Beech, American	Cypress	Birch, paper	bigtooth	Poplar, balsam
Birch	Douglas fir 2[a]	Cedar, Alaska	quaking	
sweet	Fir	Fir, subalpine	Cativo	
yellow	balsam	Hemlock, eastern	Cedar	
Douglas fir 1[a]	California red	Maple, bigleaf	incense	
Kapur	grand	Pine	western red	
Keruing	noble	jack	Cottonwood	
Larch, western	Pacific silver	lodgepole	eastern	
Maple, sugar	white	ponderosa	black (western poplar)	
Pine	Hemlock, western	spruce	Pine	
Caribbean	Lauan	Redwood	eastern white	
ocote	almon	Spruce	sugar	
Pine, southern	bagtikan	Engelmann		
loblolly	mayapis	white		
longleaf	red			
shoftleaf	tangile			
slash	white			
Tanoak	Maple, black			
	Mengkulang			
	Meranti, red[b]			
	Mersawa			
	Pine			
	pond			
	red			
	Virginia			
	western white			
	Poplar, yellow			
	Spruce			
	black			
	red			
	sitka			
	Sweetgum			
	Tamarack			

[a] Douglas fir from trees grown in the states of Washington, Oregon, California, Idaho, Montana, and Wyoming and the Canadian Provinces of Alberta and British Columbia are classed as Douglas fir 1. Douglas fir from trees grown in the states of Nevada, Utah, Colorado, Arizona, and New Mexico are classed as Douglas Fir 2.
[b] Red meranti is limited to species having a specific gravity of 0.41 or more based on green volume and oven dry weight.

exterior phenolic resin adhesive used in exterior panels. However, because other compositional factors (such as in the lowest grade of veneer (D) permitted in plywood panels) may affect bond performance, only exterior panels should be used for permanent exposure to the weather or moisture. Exposure 2 panels (identified as interior-type with intermediate glue under PS 1) are intended for pro-

tected construction applications where only moderate delays in providing protection from moisture may be expected. Interior panels that lack further glue-line information in their trademarks are manufactured with interior glue and are intended for interior applications only. Exterior and exposure 1 panels are the most common.

Table 2. PS 1 and Performance-rated Panel Exposure Durability Designations

PS 1 Designations	Performance-rated Panel Designations	Recommended Use	Typical Applications
Exterior	Exterior	Permanent exposure to weather or moisture	Exterior siding, soffits, fences, decks, planters, storage buildings, concrete forms
Exposure 1 (interior/exterior glue)	Exposure 1	Prolonged temporary exposure to weather or moisture	Roof and wall sheathing, roof overhangs
Interior/intermediate glue[a]	Exposure 2[a]	Brief temporary exposure to weather or moisture	Sheathing, if quickly covered
Interior/interior glue[a]		Protected from weather or moisture	Cabinets, furniture, built-ins, shelving

[a] Not commonly available.

Species Group Number

Plywood manufactured under U.S. Product Standard PS 1-83 may be made from over 70 species of wood. These species are divided according to strength and stiffness properties into five groups. Group 1 species are the strongest and stiffest, Group 2 the next strongest and stiffest, and so on. The group number appearing in an APA trademark is based on the species used for face and back veneers. Some species are used widely in plywood manufacture, and others rarely. Local availability should be checked if a particular species is desired.

PANEL TYPES AND APPLICATIONS

Sheathing

Plywood sheathing panels are unsanded grades designed for residential and other light-frame roof sheathing, subflooring, and wall sheathing applications. They include panels designated under PS 1 as C-D Interior with exterior glue (popularly called CDX), C-C Exterior, Structural I and II C-D Interior, and Structural I and II C-C Exterior.

Sheathing panels usually bear the notation "sized for spacing." This indicates the panel has a +0, −1/8-in. dimensional manufacturing tolerance for length and width. Although structural wood panels exhibit excellent dimensional stability, panel edges and ends should be spaced slightly when installed to allow for any expansion caused by moisture absorption.

Flooring

In flooring applications, structural wood panels can be used in several configurations. Touch-sanded single-layer floor panels are designed for residential and other light-frame single-floor applications. The panels are a combined floor system, serving both as subfloor and underlayment. Some finish flooring, such as carpet and pad, can be installed directly on the smooth panel surface. For resilient nontextile flooring, such as tile or linoleum, veneer-faced panels with a sanded face should be specified.

Single-layer floor panels are manufactured with either square or tongue-and-groove edges. Tongue-and-groove panels have the advantage of eliminating the need for blocking beneath panel edges for support. Most single-layer panels are tongue-and-groove and have a net face width of 47½ in., although manufacturing practices vary.

Exterior Siding

Plywood sidings, including APA 303 siding, are exterior panels manufactured with a variety of surface patterns, most of them developed for optimum performance with stain finishes. Patterns include brushed, rough-sawn, kerfed, channel groove, reverse board-and-batten, medium-density overlay (MDO), and Texture 1-11. Siding panels are available in a variety of strength and appearance grades. Depending on the species, type of repair, finishing, etc, premium appearance products may be found in all grades. Certain grades, however, may be difficult to obtain in some areas. It is necessary to check with the supplier before specifying.

In addition to their primary use as exterior siding on all kinds of residential, commercial, institutional, and industrial structures, plywood siding panels are used for a variety of other indoor and outdoor applications, including paneling, fencing, soffits, chimney enclosures, and wind screens. Following are descriptions of siding styles.

1. *APA Texture 1-11.* This is special APA 303 siding with shiplapped edges and parallel grooves 1/4 in. deep and 3/8 in. wide; grooves 4 or 8 in. on center (oc) are standard. It is manufactured with scratch-sanded, overlaid, rough-sawn, brushed, and other surfaces.

2. *Kerfed Rough-sawn.* This is siding with a rough-sawn surface with narrow grooves providing a distinctive effect. It has long edges shiplapped for a continuous pattern. Grooves are typically 4 in. oc.

3. *Rough-sawn.* This siding is manufactured with a slight rough-sawn texture running across the panel. It is available without grooves or with grooves of various styles, in lap sidings, and in panel form.

4. *MDO.* This siding is available without grooving, with V grooves (spaced 6 or 8 in. oc usually standard); or in Texture 1-11 or reverse board-and-batten grooving.

5. *Brushed.* Brushed or relief-grain textures accent the natural grain pattern to create striking surfaces.

6. *Channel Groove.* This siding has shallow grooves typically 1/32–1/16 in. deep and 3/8 in. wide, cut into faces of 3/8-in. thick panels, 4 or 8 in. oc. Other groove spacings are available. It is shiplapped for continuous patterns.

7. *Reverse Board-and-batten.* This siding has deep, wide grooves cut into brushed, rough-sawn, coarse-sanded, or other textured surfaces. The grooves are about 1/4 in. deep and 1–1½ in. wide, spaced 8, 12, or 16 in. oc. It provides deep, sharp shadow lines. Long edges are shiplapped for a continuous pattern.

Sanded and Touch-sanded Plywood

Panels with B-grade or better veneer faces are always sanded smooth in manufacture to fulfill the requirements of their intended end uses, applications such as cabinets, shelving, furniture, built-ins, etc. Sheathing panels are typically unsanded since a smooth surface is not a requirement of their intended end use. Other panels, such as underlayment, require only touch sanding for sizing to make the panel thickness more uniform.

Specialty Panels

Specialty grades include panels designed for specific applications such as concrete forming or marine use or for applications with specific performance requirements.

High-density Overlay. High-density overlay (HDO) is a plywood panel manufactured with a hard, semiopaque resin–fiber overlay on both sides. HDO is extremely abrasion-resistant and is ideally suited to punishing construction and industrial applications such as concrete forms, industrial tanks, work surfaces, signs, agricultural bins, exhaust ducts, etc. HDO is also available with a skid-resistant screen-grid surface and in Structural I or II. It has an exterior exposure durability classification.

Medium-density Overlay. Medium-density overlay (MDO) is a plywood panel manufactured with smooth, opaque, resin-treated fiber overlay, which provides an ideal base for paint on one or both sides. MDO is an excellent material choice for shelving, factory work surfaces, paneling, built-ins, signs, and numerous other construction and industrial applications. MDO is also available as a siding with a texture-embossed or smooth surface on one side only and in Structural I or II. It has an exterior durability classification.

Marine. Marine-grade plywood is designed for marine applications, especially where bending is required, as in boat hulls. Marine-grade panels are manufactured with the same glue-line durability requirements as other Exterior-type panels, but with more restrictive veneer grade (B or better) and species requirements. Marine-grade panels are made only with Douglas fir or western larch and have an exterior exposure durability classification.

Plyform Classes I and II. Plyform is a highly reusable APA proprietary panel designed specifically for concrete form applications. It is an exterior-type panel with both faces made of sanded B-grade veneer and is mill-oiled unless otherwise specified. Two classes of Plyform can be manufactured: I and II. Plyform Class I, the stronger, stiffer, and more commonly available, is limited to Group 1 faces, Group 1 or 2 crossbands, and Group 1, 2, 3, or 4 inner plies. Class II is limited to Group 1 or 2 faces (Group 3 under certain conditions) and Group 1, 2, 3, or 4 inner plies. Plyform can also be manufactured with HDO surfaces or with Structural I veneers and glue line. HDO Plyform's hard, smooth, abrasion-resistant surface is resin-bonded to the plywood and does not require oiling. Structural I Plyform, specially designed for engineered applications, is the stiffest and strongest type of Plyform. Plyform panels have an Exterior exposure durability classification.

Plyron. Plyron is an all-veneer APA proprietary panel manufactured with a hardboard face on both sides. It is available in interior or exterior type. Interior Plyron may be ordered with a standard, tempered, smooth, or screened hardboard surface and is manufactured with D-grade veneer, except for the ply directly beneath the hardboard surface, which must be C-grade. Exterior Plyron is available with a tempered, smooth, or treated surface and is manufactured with C-grade veneer throughout. Plyron provides an extra-smooth, paintable, and long-wearing surface ideal for work benches, fixtures, built-ins, cabinets, doors, concentrated load flooring, and other industrial applications.

Decorative Panels. Decorative panels can be manufactured in both interior and exterior types and with rough-sawn, brushed, grooved, or striated faces. Common interior applications include paneling, accent walls, built-ins, counter facings, and displays. Exterior decorative panels can be used for siding, gable ends, fences, and other outdoor applications.

TREATED PLYWOOD

Fire-retardant-treated Plywood

Plywood pressure-impregnated with fire-retardant salts is available, and further information may be obtained from the American Wood Preservers Association.

Pressure-preservative-treated Plywood

With proper treatment, plywood may be used in a variety of underground and exposed applications, including permanent wood foundations, cooling towers, water troughs, bulkheads, piers, and floats. Plywood used in these demanding applications is impregnated with preservative salts under high pressure. The waterborne salts, typically ammoniacal copper arsenate (ACA) or chromated copper arsenate (CCA) are forced into the wood in a special high-pressure chamber. The wood is then redried to a specified moisture content of 19% or less, and the preservatives become chemically bonded with the wood cells. The salts are permanently trapped in the structure of the wood and protect the plywood from fungi, termites, and decay. When building with pressure-preservative-treated wood, all surfaces that will be underground or in water should be treated. This is best achieved by having wood materials cut to size before treatment. Plywood and lumber pieces that are cut or drilled after treatment must be field-treated by repeated brushing, dipping, or soaking. For some applications, other preservatives, such as creosote and pentachlorophenol, may be used.

STRUCTURAL PANELS IN USE: AN OVERVIEW OF APPLICATIONS

The low in-place cost, versatility, good looks, and strong structural performance of plywood and other structural wood panel systems presented here make them suitable for a variety of applications. In residential construction, remodeling, commercial construction, and specialized industrial uses, architects and builders often specify structural wood panels. The following summaries are brief descriptions of primary panel applications.

Residential Construction

Structural wood panels are used extensively in home construction. Key uses include floors, walls, roofs, exterior siding, permanent wood foundations, and interior built-ins such as storage cabinets and shelves. In mobile homes, structural panels are used for siding, roofs, floors, ridge beams, and even the foundations on which the homes are placed.

Commercial Construction

In offices, stores, churches, and other commercial and public buildings, structural wood panels are used in roof deck construction, wall sheathing, and floors. Plywood is also used for concrete forming in road and bridge construction and sewer and water projects. Engineering research for commercial construction methods continues, with emphasis on wind-resistive panel roof systems, heavy load-bearing floors, and efficient concrete-forming applications.

Industrial Applications

Industrial applications of structural wood panels include pallets, crates, bins, and other materials-handling devices; transportation equipment such as truck trailers and rail cars; and plant repair and remodeling. Plywood is used for materials-handling equipment because it is strong, durable, and economical. Specialty panel products, such as fiber glass-reinforced plastic overlaid panels, are well suited for truck trailers and vans and other demanding industrial applications where attractive, all-weather materials are needed.

Home Repair and Remodeling

This broad category of structural panel applications includes room additions; home repairs; do-it-yourself projects such as toys, games, shelving, and indoor and outdoor furniture; and a variety of other home projects. Panel selection is as diverse as the category and depends on performance requirements, exposure to weather, and finishing and appearance needs.

SPECIFICATION AND INSTALLATION

Once the performance requirements of the application are identified, structural panels can be specified on the basis of their intended use and required characteristics. All panels that have any edge or surface permanently exposed to the weather are classed as exterior. One exception is plywood used for permanent wood foundations, which may be interior-type with exterior glue, provided it is pressure-preservative-treated in accordance with the treating and drying provisions of the AWPA Standard C22. Exposure 1 (or interior with exterior glue) should be specified for applications where prolonged but temporary exposure to the weather or moisture is required. Open soffits or roof sheathing exposed on the underside may be any panel classed as Exposure 1 (or interior with exterior glue) where appearance is not a principal consideration.

Panels for Roof Sheathing

Sheathing permanently exposed to weather is classed as Exterior. Sheathing should be installed with the long dimension of the panel across supports, except where noted, and with the panel continuous over two or more spans (Fig. 1). In some cases, the long dimension of the panel may be parallel to the supports if the panel has adequate thickness. Panel clips, tongue-and-groove panels, or lumber blocking can be used between joists to provide edge support. Panel end joints should occur over framing. Spacing of 1/8 in. at panel ends and edges should be allowed, unless otherwise recommended by the panel manufacturer.

APA PANEL ROOF SHEATHING

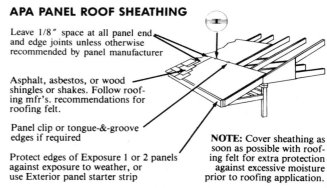

Leave 1/8″ space at all panel end and edge joints unless otherwise recommended by panel manufacturer

Asphalt, asbestos, or wood shingles or shakes. Follow roofing mfr's. recommendations for roofing felt.

Panel clip or tongue-&-groove edges if required

Protect edges of Exposure 1 or 2 panels against exposure to weather, or use Exterior panel starter strip

NOTE: Cover sheathing as soon as possible with roofing felt for extra protection against excessive moisture prior to roofing application.

Figure 1. Structural Panel Sheathing. Courtesy of the American Plywood Association.

Panels should be nailed 6 in. oc along the edges and 12 in. oc at intermediate supports; when supports are spaced 48 in. oc or more, nails should be spaced 6 in. oc at all supports. Engineered shear walls and diaphragms may require additional nailing. For panels 1/2 in. and less, 6d common nails should be used, and 8d for greater thicknesses, except that when panels are 1 1/8 in., 8d ring-shank or 10d common nails should be used. Equivalent fasteners may be specified.

Panels for Floors

Subflooring. Subflooring should be installed with the long dimension of the panel across supports and with the panel continuous over two or more spans as shown in Figure 2. Panel end joints should occur over framing. Spacing of 1/8 in. at panel ends and edges should be allowed, unless otherwise recommended by the panel manufacturer.

Panels should be nailed 6 in. oc along the edges and 10

APA UNDERLAYMENT OVER APA RATED SHEATHING SUBFLOORING (Double Floor)

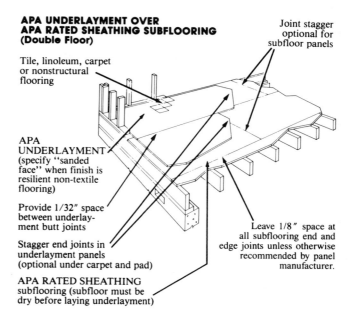

Tile, linoleum, carpet or nonstructural flooring

Joint stagger optional for subfloor panels

APA UNDERLAYMENT (specify "sanded face" when finish is resilient non-textile flooring)

Provide 1/32″ space between underlayment butt joints

Stagger end joints in underlayment panels (optional under carpet and pad)

APA RATED SHEATHING subflooring (subfloor must be dry before laying underlayment)

Leave 1/8″ space at all subflooring end and edge joints unless otherwise recommended by panel manufacturer.

Figure 2. Underlayment Over Sheathing Subflooring. Courtesy of the American Plywood Association.

in. oc at intermediate supports with 6d common nails for ½-in. panels and 8d for greater thicknesses. Where panels are 1⅛ in. thick and supports are 48 in. oc, nails should be 8d ring-shank or 10d common and spaced 6 in. oc at all supports.

Combined Subfloor-Underlayment (Under Carpet and Pad). This should be installed with the long dimension of the panel across supports and with the panel continuous over two or more spans (Fig. 3). Panel edges should be tongue-and-groove or supported on 2-in. lumber blocking installed between joists. It is necessary to protect against damage until the finish floor is installed. Panel end joints should be staggered. They should occur over framing. Spacing of ⅛ in. at panel ends and edges should be allowed, unless otherwise recommended by the panel manufacturer. For nailed floors, panels should be nailed 6 in. oc at the edges and 10 in. oc at intermediate supports, except that when supports are spaced 48 in. oc, nails should be spaced 6 in oc. at all supports.

For panels ¾ in. thick or less, 6d ring- or screw-shank nails should be used, and 8d for thicker panels. With 1⅛-in. panels, 10d common nails may be used if supports are well seasoned. End joints should be filled and thoroughly sanded. (This step may not be necessary under some carpet and structural flooring products, so it is necessary to check with the flooring manufacturer.) Any surface roughness, particularly at joints and around fasteners, should be lightly sanded.

Field-glued Floors. If nonveneer panels with sealed surfaces and edges are used, only solvent-based glues should be used; this should be checked with the panel manufacturer. A continuous line of glue on the joist and a continuous or spaced line of glue in the grooves of tongue-and-groove panels should be applied. It is necessary to use 6d ring- or screw-shank nails spaced 12 in. oc at panel ends and intermediate bearings. Major model building codes accept 12-in. spacing with glue, but some local codes may require closer spacing. When panels thicker than ¾ in. are used in glued floors, the same fastener schedule as for nailed-only construction should be used.

Underlayment (Over Subflooring). Underlayment should be applied just prior to laying the finish floor, and damage must be protected against until the finish floor is installed. Panel end joints should be staggered with respect to each other, and all joints should be offset with respect to the joints in the subfloor (Fig. 2). Panel ends and edges should be butted to a close but not tight fit (1/32-in. space). Panels should be nailed 6 in. oc along the edges and 8 in. oc each way throughout remainder with 3d ring-shank nails for thicknesses ½ in. or less and 4d for ⅝ and ¾ in. or with 16 gauge staples at 3 in. oc along panel edges and 6 in. oc each way. The staple length must be sufficient to penetrate at least ⅝ in. into, or completely through, subflooring. End joints should be filled and thoroughly sanded. (This step may not be necessary under some carpet and structural flooring products, so it should be checked with the flooring manufacturer.) Any surface roughness, particularly at joints and around fasteners, should be lightly sanded.

Panels for Walls and Soffits

Spacing of ⅛ in. at panel ends and edges should be allowed, unless otherwise recommended by the panel manufacturer (Fig. 4). Panels should be nailed 6 in. oc along the edges and 12 in. oc at intermediate supports with 6d common nails for panels ½ in. and less and 8d for greater thicknesses. Engineered shear walls and diaphragms may require additional nailing. Diagonal bracing is not required, nor is building paper, except under stucco.

Plywood Siding

Spacing of ⅛ in. at panel ends and edges should be allowed, unless otherwise recommended by the panel manufacturer (Fig. 4). Panel siding should be nailed 6 in. oc along the edges and 12 in. oc at intermediate supports with 6d nonstaining box, casing, or siding nails for panels ½ in. and less and 8d for greater thicknesses. If siding is applied over nonstructural sheathing thicker than ½ in., the next regular nail size should be used. Nonstaining box nails should be used for siding installed over 1-in. thick foam insulation sheathing. Lap siding should be nailed 4 in. oc at vertical joints and 8 in. oc along the bottom edge. For plywood ⅜ in. thick, 6d nonstaining box, casing, or siding nails should be used, and 8d for thicker panels.

Diagonal bracing is not required with panel siding. Lap siding should be applied only over nailable panel or lumber sheathing. Building paper may be omitted if the vertical joints in the plywood panel siding are shiplapped or covered with battens (except for grooved sidings applied horizontally), or if the siding is installed over panel sheathing. All panel edges should be sealed. For panels to be painted, the sealer can be paint primer; for panels to be stained, the sealer should be a water-repellent preservative compatible with the finish.

APA RATED STURD-I-FLOOR
(Single Floor)

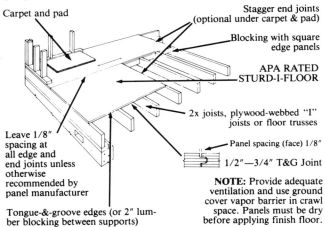

Carpet and pad

Stagger end joints (optional under carpet & pad)

Blocking with square edge panels

APA RATED STURD-I-FLOOR

2x joists, plywood-webbed "I" joists or floor trusses

Panel spacing (face) 1/8"

1/2"—3/4" T&G Joint

Leave 1/8" spacing at all edge and end joints unless otherwise recommended by panel manufacturer

Tongue-&-groove edges (or 2" lumber blocking between supports)

NOTE: Provide adequate ventilation and use ground cover vapor barrier in crawl space. Panels must be dry before applying finish floor.

Figure 3. Single Floor Construction. Courtesy of the American Plywood Association.

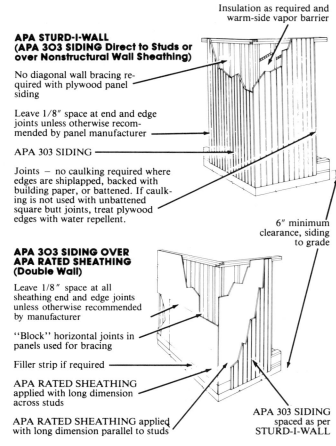

APA STURD-I-WALL
(APA 303 SIDING Direct to Studs or over Nonstructural Wall Sheathing)

No diagonal wall bracing required with plywood panel siding

Leave 1/8″ space at end and edge joints unless otherwise recommended by panel manufacturer

APA 303 SIDING

Joints — no caulking required where edges are shiplapped, backed with building paper, or battened. If caulking is not used with unbattened square butt joints, treat plywood edges with water repellent.

Insulation as required and warm-side vapor barrier

6″ minimum clearance, siding to grade

APA 303 SIDING OVER APA RATED SHEATHING
(Double Wall)

Leave 1/8″ space at all sheathing end and edge joints unless otherwise recommended by manufacturer

"Block" horizontal joints in panels used for bracing

Filler strip if required

APA RATED SHEATHING applied with long dimension across studs

APA RATED SHEATHING applied with long dimension parallel to studs

APA 303 SIDING spaced as per STURD-I-WALL

Figure 4. Wall Construction and Plywood Siding over Sheathing. Courtesy of the American Plywood Association.

Soffits

Panels should be nailed 6 in. oc at each end support and 12 in. oc at intermediate supports with 6d nonstaining box, casing, or siding nails for panels ½ in. and less and 8d for thicker panels. For 1⅛-in. textured panels, 8d ring- or screw-shank or 10d common smooth-shank nails should be used (Figs. 5 and 6).

Hot-dipped or hot-tumbled galvanized steel nails are recommended for most siding applications. For best performance, stainless steel nails or aluminum nails should be considered. Galvanized fasteners may react under wet

OPEN SOFFITS

Shim at each rafter for flush joint at change of panel thickness

Any appropriate APA Exterior or Exposure 1 grade of adequate thickness (15/32″ or more) to prevent protrusion of roofing nails or staples at exposed underside and to carry design roof load. Where appearance is important, specify APA EXT.

APA RATED SHEATHING

Long dimension

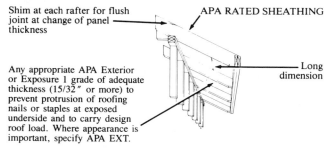

Figure 5. Open Soffits. Courtesy of the American Plywood Association.

CLOSED SOFFITS

APA RATED SHEATHING

Protect edges of Exposure 1 or 2 sheathing against exposure to weather

Continuous screened vent or louvered vent

Leave 1/8″ space at all panel end and edge joints. Support all panel edges.

Long dimension

Any appropriate grade of APA EXT plywood for soffit

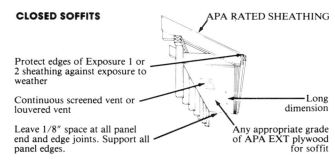

Figure 6. Closed Soffits. Courtesy of the American Plywood Association.

conditions with the natural extractives of some wood species and may cause staining if left unfinished. Such staining can be minimized if the siding is finished properly or if the roof overhang protects the siding from direct exposure to moisture and weathering.

Treated Plywood Panels

FRT plywood should be pressure-treated in accordance with AWPA C27.

Pressure-preserved plywood should be pressure-treated in accordance with AWPA C9 with creosote, pentachlorophenol, or waterborne preservatives as required for coastal water, soil or water, above-ground exposure, respectively. All treated plywood used in permanent wood foundation systems should be certified by the preservative treater as complying with the treating, drying, retention, and penetration requirements of the AWPA Standard C22 and should be appropriately marked attesting such compliance. Plywood treated with waterborne preservatives should be dried after treatment to a moisture content of 18% or less.

Panels for Concrete Forming (CSI Division 3)

A plywood thickness should be used that is sufficient to support concrete at the temperature and rate poured; forms should be securely braced and shored to prevent displacement and to support construction loads safely.

Specifications for Panel Painting and Decorating (CSI Division 9)

Preparation of Surfaces. *Exterior Panels.* Panels to be exposed outdoors should have all edges sealed. With paint, the sealer should be a liberal coat of exterior house paint primer. With stain, the sealer should be a water-repellent preservative compatible with the finish coat.

All Panels. Holes and cracks should be filled with putty or plastic wood (except for rustic-type panels intended for stain finish). After drying, the panels should be sanded lightly in the direction of the grain of the face veneer. Any tree pitch or sap spots should be first touched up with a sealer where the finish is paint.

Application of Finish. Brush, roller, or spray application should be specified; brush application gives the best performance.

1. *Exterior Panels—Painted.*
   - *First Coat.* This should be an exterior stain-blocking primer as recommended by the manufacturer of the finish coat (may be tinted). The quantity recommended by the paint manufacturer should be applied.
   - *Second Coat.* This should be a top quality exterior acrylic latex house paint designed for use with primer; color as selected. Two top coats provide better performance.

2. *Exterior Panels—Stained.*
   - *First Coat.* This should be a top quality exterior penetrating semitransparent oil stain where grain show-through is desired or a heavily pigmented solid color oil or all-acrylic latex stain where the grain is to be masked; color as selected. It should be applied in one or two coats, as recommended by the manufacturer.
   - Semitransparent stain should be used where color differences in the wood, or between the wood and repairs, are not objectionable. A brush-out test on a sample of the siding containing color-contrasting characteristics is recommended to assure that the finished appearance will be acceptable.

3. *Interior Panels—Painted.*
   - *First Coat.* This should be a stain-blocking primer as recommended by the manufacturer of the finish coat.
   - *Second Coat.* This should be a latex–emulsion top coat designed for use with primer; color as selected. Two top coats can be used if needed to cover.

4. *Interior Panels—Color Tone.*
   - *First Coat.* This should be a stain and companion sealer mixed to a selected color (or sealer and then stain applied separately).
   - *Second Coat.* This should be an interior satin varnish (additional coats can be applied as desired for depth of luster).

5. *Interior Panels—Light Stain.*
   - *First Coat.* This should be a pigmented resin sealer (wiped off when tacky).
   - *Second Coat.* This should be a clear resin sealer.
   - *Third Coat.* This should be a tinted undercoat, thin enamel, pigmented sealer, or light stain applied thinly and wiped to the desired color depth; color as selected.
   - *Fourth Coat.* This should be an interior satin varnish (additional coats can be applied as desired for depth of luster).

TIPS FOR STORAGE, HANDLING, AND FINISHING

Proper storage, handling, and finishing techniques can ensure optimum long-term performance of structural wood panels. In storage and handling, the edges and ends of panels, especially tongue-and-groove floor and shiplapped siding panels, should be protected. Panels to be moved by forklift are placed on pallets to bunks to avoid damage by fork tines. Panels to be transported on open truck beds should be covered with standard tarpaulins. For open rail car shipment, lumber wrap should be used to avoid extended weather exposure.

Whenever possible, panels should be stored under a roof, especially if they will not be used immediately. Sanded and other appearance grades should be kept away from open doorways, and the top panel in a stack should be weighted to avoid any possible warpage from humidity. If moisture absorption is expected, the steel banding on the panel bundles should be cut to prevent edge damage.

Panels to be stored outside should be stacked on a level platform supported by 4 × 4-in. stringers or other blocking. The panels or platform should never be left in direct contact with the ground. At least three full-width supports should be used along the 8-ft length of the panel, one centered and the others 12–16 in. from each end.

The stack should be covered loosely with plastic sheets or tarps. The covering at the top of the stack should be anchored, but kept open and away from the sides and bottom to assure good ventilation. Tight coverings prevent air circulation and, when exposed to sunlight, create a greenhouse effect, which may encourage mold formation.

APA 303 siding should be edge-sealed (both blind and exposed edges) to minimize the possibility of water staining or mildew. Sealing is easiest when panels are stacked. New edges of panels cut to fit should be resealed. The type of sealant recommended depends on the finish treatment to be used on the siding.

Once installed, panels should be protected as soon as possible. For example, subflooring is protected by installing roof sheathing, roof sheathing with finish roofing material, underlayment with plastic sheeting or finish flooring, etc. Enclosing the structure as quickly as possible, keeping panels dry before attaching other materials (such as underlayment or finish flooring), and assuring adequate ventilation, particularly in attics and crawl spaces, can prevent many costly problems and callbacks.

In addition to the structural wood panel products and applications described here, there are many other specialty products and tested applications. Some of these include fiber glass-reinforced plastic (FRP) panels for industrial applications, construction systems for noise transmission control, wind-resistive roof systems, home energy-saving systems, and industrial floors.

BIBLIOGRAPHY

General References

APA Product Guide: Grades & Specifications, Form J20, American Plywood Association, Tacoma, Wash., Dec. 1988.

APA Design/Construction Guide: Residential & Commercial, Form E30, American Plywood Association, Tacoma, Wash., Feb. 1989.

APA Panel Basics Correspondence Course, Form D850, American Plywood Association, Tacoma, Wash., Mar. 1985.

APA Product Guide: Preservative-Treated Plywood, Form Q220, American Plywood Association, Tacoma, Wash., July 1988.

Research Report 132: Plywood in Hostile Environments, Form Z820F, American Plywood Association, Tacoma, Wash., Apr. 1986.

See also ADHESIVES; CONCRETE FORMING; GLUED LAMINATED WOOD (GLULAM); WOOD FRAMING; WOOD IN CONSTRUCTION

MARILYN LEMOINE
American Plywood Association
Tacoma, Washington

WOOD TREATMENT

Wood is by nature a durable material. However, in many cases it must be treated with chemicals to protect it from destruction caused by rot, insects, fire, or water. Figure 1 shows extensive decay on a 2 in. × 4 in. (40 mm × 90 mm) wood member. Wood has good natural resistance to weak acids and alkalies, and it can be treated to resist chemical corrosion.

The surface of wood weathers to a grey patina by exposure to light, moisture, and air. Stains and paints are used to prevent this natural coloration. In countries like Japan, where wood is not traditionally painted, residential buildings have subtle brown and grey colors that may look drab to western eyes. This low-maintenance approach allows wood siding in Japan to last longer than painted wood. Layers of paint resist insect attack, but they also tend to trap moisture against the wood's surface. This encourages fungal growth. Wet and dry and cold and hot cycles cause swelling and contraction of the dead wood. This in turn creates opportunities for fungi to attack. Usually, the words "rot" or "decay" signify fungal growth and the resulting destruction to wood members. Chemical wood treatment can prevent or kill living fungi, insects, or ma-

rine borers. Changing moisture content is a key factor in wood decay. Barring attack by insects or marine borers, wood that is always under water or that is always dry has an almost unlimited life span. Wood can become infested with and promote the growth of certain insects, bacteria, and fungi that, although not causing structural damage, can cause allergies and disease in people. Legionnaire's disease is caused by organisms living in buildings. Since these do not cause structural damage, they are not discussed here.

This article deals with the causes, prevention, and treatment of structural damage due to fire or living organisms. After a brief historical introduction, this article surveys the various types of wood decay with treatment suggestions for each type. Second, there is a technical discussion of treatment processes and chemicals used and then a look at building codes and organizations related to wood treatment worldwide. Last, there is a section on construction practices to resist wood deterioration. These suggestions summarize good practice in the use of wood as a permanent building material.

HISTORICAL SURVEY

Trial-and-error experiments throughout history have resulted in wood construction details and maintenance strategies to preserve wood for long periods of time. These methods were successful enough that it was only the use of large quantities of wood, first in ships, then in railroad ties, and later in electric and telephone utility poles, that created the chemical wood treatment industry. These uses subjected wood to rapidly alternating wet and dry cycles. When kept at a low moisture content and protected from sun and rain, wood is a practically permanent material. Sycamore coffins made of untreated wood have lasted since the 12th Dynasty in Egypt (2000–1788 B.C.) (1). Many early civilizations, including the Greek, Roman, and Chinese, placed stone blocks under wooden columns to help prevent contact with the ground and its vegeta-

Figure 1. Extensive decay on 2″ × 4″ pine stud.

tion. The Greeks used oils from olive, juniper, and cedar trees as wood preservatives. Pliny the Elder wrote that "[t]imber well smeared with cedar oils does not suffer from maggots or decay." Small holes were also drilled into the wood, and oil was poured into them. Early Baltic peoples charred timbers and used them for marine pilings.

The rapid decay of timber in UK warships (40 acres of oak forest was needed to build one 70-gun warship) caused concern and investigation into decay prevention. In 1590, 100 ships of the Spanish Armada were destroyed by shipworms in the West Indies. Copper sheathing helped prevent destruction to the exterior, but interior dry rot problems continued. The Netherlands had severe problems with timbers used in dikes and marine structures. Still, it was not until the late nineteenth century that the railroad's use of large amounts of wood in contact with the ground created the mass-production wood treatment industry. The life span of a wood tie was increased from 12 years in 1900 to over 35 years today. The first successful attempts at wood preservation in the United States were not made on account of the scarcity of wood, but because of the high cost of replacing it after it had deteriorated. Several wood treatment processes were actually in use years before they were patented. In 1705, mercuric chloride (corrosive sublimate) was used by a German named Holmberg (2). William Crook obtained a wood preserving patent in 1716 for a mixture "one part of which is the oyle or spirit of tar." Later, in 1767, De Boissieu used mercuric chloride. Copper sulfate was recommended by De Boissieu and Bordenave. It was not until 1832 that a U.S. patent was granted to Kyan for the use of mercuric chloride salt, which became known as Kyanizing. In 1839, a patent was granted to the Frenchman Boucherie for copper sulfate treatments on living trees. In keeping with this trend of use before legal recognition by patent, zinc chloride was recommended by Thomas Wade in 1815, and later, in 1838, Sir William Burnett obtained a patent. His process became known as Burnettizing. Coal-tar and creosote methods have a long history. In 1836, Franz Moll obtained a patent for an injection method. G. Fletcher boiled wood paving blocks in dead oil of coal tar and laid them in the yard of the New Orleans Gas Light Co. in 1872. They absorbed 20 lb oil/ft^3 (320 kg/m^3). When seen 30 years later, they were perfectly preserved. In 1874 in Germany, a method of treating railroad ties with zinc chloride and creosote was developed, but not until 1902 in Germany did Max Reuping develop an economical method of creosote treatment. The year 1904 saw the formation of the American Wood Preservers Association (AWPA). The U.S. Forest Product Laboratory (USFPL) began systematic tests of treated and untreated wood posts in contact with the soil in 1908 (3).

CAUSES OF WOOD DECAY

Wood treatment is necessary when the moisture content of the wood is between 20 and 60% at temperatures between 37 and 104°F (3 and 40°C). Stagnant air and darkness promote decay. Fungi such as dry rot, wet rot, brown rot, and cellar rot decompose cellulose and hemicellulose

rapidly under damp conditions. Bacteria rarely cause decay. Insects can infest wood and destroy it. In dry wood, the main pests are ambrosia beetles, longhorn beetles, powder-post beetles, deathwatch beetles, carpenter bees, carpenter ants, and termites. In marine locations, wood is attacked by gribbles, mollusks, teredos, and marine borers, especially *Limnoria,* a small crustacean related to lobsters and shrimp, but only 0.063–0.125 in. (1.5–3 mm) long. To protect wood from attack, insecticides, fungicides, and obnoxious creosotes are applied to the wood and allowed to penetrate. Organic solvents, water-based salts, and tar oils may be used. These preparations can be very effective. However, over long periods of time (more than 30 years), many of these chemicals may be attacked by microorganisms or may leach out of the wood. One of the most effective long-term preservatives, creosote, has carcinogenic properties and is restricted in use. Pentachlorophenol and the inorganic arsenicals have also been restricted in the United States. The U.S. Environmental Protection Agency (EPA) has extensive documentation on the health effects of wood preservatives (4,5). Wood treatment helped by proper architectural detailing is the best method to create permanent wood structures.

For organisms to attack and destroy wood, there are four requirements for growth. These are food (this may be the wood itself or something associated with the wood), suitable moisture (the moisture content should be in excess of 20%), suitable temperature (the temperature extremes should be mild, 41–104°F (5–40°C)), and oxygen (this will always be present unless the wood is completely submerged in water or unless it is below the ground-water line). Signs of decay are sawdust, insect droppings, or insect wings. The wood can also be inspected by jabbing it with a pointed knife or awl. Healthy wood should produce long slivers. Decayed wood may crack or crumble or be soft and mushy. Decayed wood tends to lift in short lengths and break suddenly without splintering. Another test is to tap the wood and listen to the sound. Hollow or dead sounds may indicate internal damage. Special sonic devices have been used to measure the passage of sound through utility poles. For more detailed inspections, bioassay can be used to determine the organisms responsible. Usually, this is done from a wood core. X-ray inspections have been done on large, important structures. Many types of organisms destroy wood.

Bacteria

Bacterial attacks rarely cause enough damage to significantly reduce wood strength; some species stimulate fungal growth, whereas others may inhibit it. Bacteria can attack and break down preservatives such as creosote and pentachlorophenol (6). A bactericide may be necessary to prevent attacks on these wood preservatives.

Fungi

Robert Hartig (1894), the father of forest pathology (7), first demonstrated that fungi were the main cause of wood decay. Fungi destroy more wood than any other organism. Fungi and wood preservatives interact in many ways. Fungal hyphae are threads of cells that invade wood along the same pathways that preservative solutions take. Preservative deposits in the wood first delay the initiation of colonization and then retard the rate of hyphal growth. Last, they slow the rate of cell wall lysis or destruction. It is the structure of the cell walls that ultimately gives wood its strength. The cell walls are mainly composed of lignin. The ability to attack lignin is a prerequisite for wood-destroying organisms. The rate of decay is related to the degree of concentration of preservative. Hyphae produce secretions that can degrade preservatives. An external nutrient source is probably important in helping the invading fungus. Some preservatives, like copper naphthenate and tri-*n*-butyltin oxide in standard concentrations can still be invaded by fungal hyphae. Stag's horn fungus (*Lentinus lepideus*) is tolerant of creosote and is widespread in nature. *Fusarium oxysporium* can break down fluorochrome arsenate dinitrophenol (Wolmanizing), creosote, and copper chromium arsenate (8). Many types of molds or stains (Fig. 2) do not destroy wood's structure. Where appearance is not critical, these nondestructive molds and stains are allowed by building codes. White pocket, white speck, or dote is a common, harmless fungus that lives on softwoods. After the wood is cut into boards, the fungus ceases to grow or spread. All but the highest grades of lumber allow some white speck.

One of the most destructive groups of fungi is dry rot. These fungi are characterized by cotton-wool-like masses in damp conditions or, in drier conditions, a grey skin with yellow or lilac patches. Stable indoor environments are best suited to dry rots. These fungi usually cause more damage and are harder to eradicate than wet rot. Dry rots cannot colonize very damp wood. Once established, they create their own moisture. Their name comes from the fact that they can live and grow in dry wood. Decay usually takes place out of sight and is caused by hyphae, or threads, which can get as thick as a pencil. Decay can be detected by the softness of the wood when probed with a pencil or awl. The wood may also have a wavy texture. Decayed wood may be cracked at right angles to the grain in a cubic pattern. The wood has a dry, powdery texture and a brown or light grey color. Dry rot typically refers to *Merulium lacrymans* in Europe and *Poria incrassata* in North America. Solutions to dry rot infestation include removing the source of moisture and drying out the wood and building completely. The fungi then stop growing, but do not die. Infested wood and 1–1.5 ft (300–500 mm) of the adjoining wood should be removed and burned. Professional treatment of diseased wood can save it in place by drilling holes at an angle to the grain and repeatedly filling these with preservative. Noncombustible surfaces in the vicinity of the attack should be sterilized with a blow torch until hot to the touch and then treated with a dilute solution of sodium pentachlorophenate or sodium orthophenylphenate. Remaining unaffected wood should receive two to three coats of preservative, and new wood should be treated by a high-preservative-retention technique such as a vacuum pressure method. Dry rot is like a contagious disease that may spread from small begin-

Figure 2. Moldy decay on rafter.

nings. Inspectors should be aggressive in looking for small signs of future rot.

The other principal group of fungi that destroy wood is wet rots. These fungi are most active in woods of 30–40% moisture content, although they can survive down to 21% moisture content. Some wet rots are white and produce lintlike pockets. Other types discolor wood to a reddish brown or brown. The hyphae are not thick like some dry rots and may be pale yellowish or violet. Usually, the decay is internal and invisible on the surface, except when fruiting bodies are produced. Some of these growths may look similar to mushrooms (Fig. 3). Two typical wet rot species are *Coniophora cerebella* (cellar rot) and *Paxillus panuoides*. To combat wet rot, the source of moisture should be removed. Rapid drying kills the fungus. Wood with structural damage should be replaced, but lightly decayed wood can be treated adequately with a fungicide–insecticide preparation. Adjacent surfaces do not need to be sterilized as with dry rot. Replaced wood should be treated with a long-lasting preservative.

Termites and Other Insects

Many types of insects eat or live in wood. Ambrosia beetles, round-headed and flat-headed borers, and powder-post beetles can get into freshly cut wood and cause considerable damage. Some beetles stay in the wood developing slowly, only to emerge a year or more after the wood is dry. It is difficult in these cases to tell when infection has first occurred. Freshly cut wood should be sprayed with approved chemical solutions to prevent both insect and fungal infestations. Powder-post beetles of the species *Lyctus* cause the most damage to hardwood lumber. Eggs are laid in wood pores, and larvae burrow through the wood, leaving 0.063–0.083-in. (1.6–2-mm) tunnels packed with a fine powder. Damage is indicated by holes left on the surface as the winged adults emerge. Several types of powder-post beetle attack seasoned pine. Some experts feel that the powder-post beetle attacks only the sapwood of hardwoods and for only 10 years after the tree has been harvested (9). Manufactured items are often damaged before sale. The new owner may not discover the damage until much later. Paint and varnish prevent infestation, but they do not kill existing beetles. These may continue to attack the wood even though it is painted, oiled, waxed, or varnished. A 3-min soaking in an insecticide containing petroleum oil solution can stop infestation and prevent attack of lumber up to 1 in. (25 mm) thick. Sterilization of greenwood by steam at 130°F (55°C), or of wood with lower moisture content at 180°F (82°C), for 2 h is effective at stopping infestation.

Carpenter ants are black or brown. Some are giant-sized when compared with other ants. They do not eat the wood, but instead use it for shelter. Their burrows can be recognized as pinholes that go across the grain. Although not as destructive as termites, if left undisturbed for a few years their tunnels can become enlarged enough to make wood replacement necessary. They are most frequently found in porch columns, porch roofs, window sills, and sometimes the wood plates in foundation walls. Damp wood is desirable to carpenter ants. They need high humidity during the early stages of life. Precautions against termites also work for carpenter ants. Small infestations can be treated by dusting with an approved insecticide. Carpenter bees can also burrow into wood. Like carpenter ants, they only use the wood as a home. Exposed exterior rafter ends are a favorite home.

Termites are one of the most notorious insects. They can cause extensive damage in short periods of time. These insects look superficially like ants in size, appearance, and colony behavior. The termite body does not have the ant's tiny wasplike waist. Its body is formed in one piece. A single ant wing is about the length of its body or less, whereas a termite's wing may be over twice as long

Figure 3. Mushrooms (fungi fruiting body) on oak log.

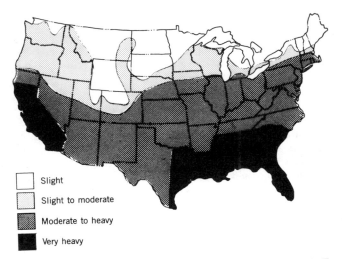

Slight

Slight to moderate

Moderate to heavy

Very heavy

Figure 4. Termite distribution map of the United States (10). □, Slight; ▨, slight to moderate; ▩, moderate to heavy; ■ very heavy.

as its body. There are two types of termites: subterranean termites and dry-wood or nonsubterranean termites.

Subterranean termites require access to soil moisture. They maintain contact with the moist soil by building tubes to the wood. Freezing temperatures kill them, so major infestations are limited to warm climates with few freezing days (Fig. 4). The workers cause most of the damage. At certain seasons, male and female winged forms occur. These swarm and then shed their wings. Sometimes they are called flying ants, but not all flying ants are termites. A good precaution is to collect some of the insects and verify them as termites before spending money on eradication. Subterranean termites are not transmitted through purchased lumber, but enter buildings through ground nests. They construct galleries that follow the wood grain, but may not be visible from the surface (Fig. 5). An awl, ice pick, or knife is an effective instrument in probing wood for termite damage. The hazard of infestation is greatest in basementless buildings with concrete slab foundations or poorly drained and ventilated crawl spaces. The best protection is to prevent access to the building. Foundations should be of concrete or sealed

Figure 5. Extensive termite damage may be hidden beneath these signs of tunneling.

masonry. The soil should also be treated. Formosan termites have appeared in the United States. They are more active and voracious than native species, but they seem to respond to conventional termite treatments.

Nonsubterranean (dry-wood) termites cause less destruction than subterranean termites. Severe damage is restricted to southern California, southern Florida, and Hawaii. They reproduce slowly, but a few years of activity is enough to destroy wood structural members. They are generally similar to other termites. Unlike with subterranean termites, infested wood can spread these termites into new construction. Paint or preservative treatment can prevent entrance of dry-wood termites. Fumigation kills existing termites, but because it does not leave a residue, it does not prevent future attack. Dusts or liquid insecticides can be forced into termite nests. This is generally more expensive than fumigation, but it is also more effective.

Once insect damage is noted, treatment should occur as soon as possible and should be repeated after a few years. Seriously infested wood should be removed and burnt. Insecticides can be injected into insect holes to kill eggs and larvae. Insecticides should be liberally brushed onto the wood surface and into all joints and cracks. Powerful insecticides can be harmful to humans and animals (11). When first applied, they may be a fire hazard. In the United States, professionals are required to handle the more powerful insecticides. Tents may be placed over entire buildings in order to fumigate them. This is a common method used in severe cases of infestation.

Marine Borers

Marine organisms can be destructive to wooden ships and harbors. During the California gold rush of 1849, a large harbor was created in San Francisco Bay. By 1857, it looked "like a forest without leaves." There were 800 abandoned ships. Whole wharves were destroyed by shipworms. Replacements to the wharves also failed. In 1889, creosote treatment was initiated, and in 1905, concrete began to be used. More destruction of wood wharves occurred in 1925. There are two main types of marine borer. *Limnoria* and *Sphaeroma* are one type. These crustaceans burrow close to the surface. *Limnoria* are 0.125–0.167 in. long (3–4 mm). *Sphaeroma* are 0.5 in. long (13 mm) by 0.25 in. wide (6.5 mm) and resemble the common sow or pill bug. They do less damage than *Limnoria* and can sometimes be found in fresh water. The other main type is shipworms. They are the most destructive of marine borers. The species *Teredo* and *Bankia* are referred to as shipworms. The species are similar in appearance and have a free-swimming stage. Upon settlement into the wood, they develop into a new form. The head grows into a pair of boring shells, which enlarge rapidly. The tail or siphon stays in place at the entrance to the burrow. As the animal grows, it always fills the burrow. The siphon circulates water through the shell-lined burrow. The burrow itself acts as the animal's shell. When crowded together, burrows are only a few inches long (100 mm). When not crowded, burrow and animal can get to be from 1–4 ft long (300–1200 mm). Pholads are relatively rare wood-boring mollusks that resemble clams. They enter the wood through a small entrance hole and grow larger as they burrow. Their maximum size is normally 2.5 in. long (64 mm) with a 1-in. (25-mm) diameter. They are found in tropical waters like the Gulf of Mexico. All woods may be attacked. Azobe, ekki, greenheart, jarrah, kasikasi, manbarklak, opepe, pyinkado, teak, totara, and turpentine are relatively immune from attack, although resistance varies depending on local conditions. There are many methods of prevention and protection from attack. Concrete or plastic sleeves may be applied, as *Limnoria* tunnel only in the top 0.75 in. (20 mm) of wood. If they are denied access to the surface, they do not attack the wood. These methods should not be used for fender piles that will be rubbed by ships. Existing piles can be wrapped. The wrapping creates a layer of stagnant water that kills any borers that may be living in the wood. Chemical treatments with creosote may not be successful against *Limnoria*. Creosote is still the best chemical treatment for marine applications. Creosoted piles should last 15–30 years, depending on the integrity of the coating. Pilings should not be braced below the high-water line. Cutoffs, bolt holes, and framing should be treated with hot creosote. A dual treatment of creosote or creosote–coal tar and Chemonite (ammoniacal copper arsenite) has proven somewhat effective against *Limnoria tripunctata* (gribble), which are devastating in warm intertidal waters. Plywood hulls can be covered with a protective membrane of glass fiber-reinforced plastic membrane. This is effective against marine borers. Plastic should not be applied to wood previously treated with oil base preservatives since it does not stick to the oil. During World War II, unsuccessful attempts were made to electroplate wood piles.

TREATMENT PROCESSES

There are three main reasons for decay in preservative-treated wood. One is substandard treatment of the wood. This occurs when insufficient preservative is absorbed or injected into the wood. The second is removal of these chemicals by leaching or by microorganisms. Last, certain types of fungi have acquired resistances to common preservatives. Wood treatment companies must pick a process that allows sufficient concentrations of a chemical to penetrate the wood deeply enough to discourage decay. The cost and depth of penetration of the chemical into the wood are the primary distinctions among preservation processes. All treated wood members should be stamped or tagged to identify the type of process used. The EPA also requires handouts warning against breathing or ingesting sawdust from cutting treated wood. Carpenters may unknowingly poison themselves by cutting stacks of treated lumber day after day.

One main treatment process type uses pressure. These pressure process techniques require placing the wood inside a pressurized container and applying preservative chemicals. Typically, milled lumber is loaded onto a railroad car and rolled into a long steel cylinder. In the full cell process, preservative is forced into both cell walls and cell cavities. This results in a high retention of preservative. Creosote used in marine structures has been applied

this way. Water-based preservatives and fire retardants can be applied with the full cell process. The large amount of preservative used in this process usually stains the wood and may cause drying problems. Where dry wood with deep penetration of preservative is required, the empty cell technique is used. Pressurized air is first forced into the wood. Chemical preservatives are then applied. When the pressure is released, the entrapped air forces the preservative from the cell cavities, but leaves it in the cell walls. This method leaves less preservative in the wood to cause staining and difficulty in painting. Some woods may be cut with knives to depths of 0.75 in. (20 mm) to help penetration by the preservative.

The other principal treatment technique does not use pressure. Nonpressure processes range from simple brush or spray applications every two or three years to steeping wood in tanks for several days. Fence posts may be treated in open tanks heated to 175–195°F (80–90°C). The wood is kept at this temperature for several hours and is then allowed to cool, during which time it absorbs the preservative. This gives protection comparable with that from pressure treatment, but it is usually limited to use in fence posts. Organic solvent-type preservatives are often applied by a brief immersion of the wood in the solvent. Small sections of wood may be dipped for as little as 10 s. Large sections may require many minutes. Wood in stacks can be sprayed with preservative. These methods are limited to woods that easily absorb preservative. Woods vary considerably in their ability to absorb preservative. Hardwoods such as oak, mahogany, and teak absorb only a small amount of preservative after prolonged treatment. Yellow pine can easily absorb preservative. Nonpressure processes are generally unacceptable in exterior conditions or near the soil. They may provide a cost-effective means of treatment for wood that is generally protected from decay by proper architectural detailing.

Wood may also be treated in place. Some preservative chemicals require periodic application. Typically, the wood is brushed with the chemical, which soaks into the wood. Insect holes may be packed with cotton balls soaked in preservative. Wood may be cut and injected with chemicals. Existing poles can be treated by digging out soil at the base and brushing with preservatives. The poles are then wrapped with asphalt paper or polyethylene in order to help retain the chemicals. A typical mixture used on poles is 15% creosote, 10% penta, and 15% sodium fluoride.

WOOD PRESERVATIVE CHEMICALS

Wood preservative chemical treatments have been developed on a trial-and-error basis over hundreds of years. By their nature, they are poisonous to life. Historically, they have caused unexpected health problems. When green railroad ties were treated with a dry powder containing salt, arsenic, and mercuric chloride, "the arsenic and corrosive sublimate effloresced from the ties. Cattle came and licked them for the sake of the salt and they died, so that the track for ten miles was strewn with dead cattle." In the United States, the EPA has investigated the use of many preservative chemicals. A rule was issued in February 1985 banning over-the-counter sale to consumers of compounds containing creosote, pentachlorophenol, and arsenic. Some of these chemicals have also been linked to cancer.

Oil Types: Creosote and Creosote Mixtures

Creosote-type preservatives are some of the oldest and most effective preservatives. Unfortunately, they produce strong odors and are not paintable. There is some evidence that they may be carcinogenic to people with long-term exposures. Creosotes vary widely in chemical composition. Like bitumens in roofing, they are a petroleum residue with a complex chemistry consisting mostly of aromatic hydrocarbons (naphthalene, methylnaphthalene, fluorene, anthracene, pyrene, etc) and some tar bases (pyridines, quinolines, acridines, etc). Creosotes that are mixtures of both high- and low-boiling-point distillates tend to be the best wood preservatives. Because of this complex and variable chemistry, creosotes tend to be classified by source and type of solution.

The amount of creosote oil retained in the wood is usually measured in pounds per cubic foot, expressed in pounds (English system only). Block flooring might have 6 lb (96 kg/m^3), telephone poles 10 lb (160 kg/m^3), and marine pilings 16–24 lb (260–380 kg/m^3).

Anthracene oils are coal-tar distillates with a higher specific gravity and boiling point than coal-tar creosote. They have the same advantages and disadvantages as coal-tar creosote, but less material is lost to evaporation during application. Coal-tar creosote is a black or brownish oil made from coal tar. It is an effective wood preservative against most organisms. It is insoluble in water and has a low volatility. It is easy to apply, and the depth of penetration is easily measured. When first applied, creosote can be a fire hazard. It has a strong, unpleasant odor and is not paintable. It is normally used outside for posts and poles placed in the ground or water. Creosotes derived from wood, oil, and water gas have the same properties as coal-tar creosotes, but are less effective. Creosote solutions are typically mixtures of 50–80% coal-tar creosote and coal-tar or petroleum oils. They have the same properties as coal-tar creosotes, but are less effective. Crystal-free coal-tar creosote is similar to coal-tar creosote, but its crystal-forming materials have been removed. This makes application by brush or spray easier. This also results in some reduction in effectiveness.

Organic Solvent Types

Copper naphthenate is a mixture of petroleum oils and 5–30% copper naphthenate. It gives wood a greenish or dark color with protection similar to that of pentachlorophenol. It is ineffective against marine borers. Pentachlorophenol is one of the most common preservatives. There are many standard formulations of pentachlorophenol for specific situations. A 5% solution of pentachlorophenol in petroleum oils and a 2% solution in creosote are common preparations. These provide a high degree of decay protection from fungi and termites. Pentachlorophenol provides little protection from marine borers. Its odor is acceptable,

and it is paintable. After the solution has dried, the wood is no more of a fire hazard than untreated wood. Water-repellent preservatives are typically mineral spirits and 10–25% nonvolatile materials of which not less than 5% is pentachlorophenol. These preservatives retard moisture changes in the wood, but unless thoroughly applied have little water-repellent value. They provide good protection against decay and insects, but cannot be used in contact with the ground or continual dampness. They should have not less than 0.045% copper-8-quinolinolate where food will come in contact with the wood.

Water-base Types

Acid copper chromate (Celcure) is normally 31.8% copper oxide and 68.2% chromic acid. Copper sulfate, potassium dichromate, or sodium dichromate may be substituted for the copper oxide. Its advantages are good protection against decay, insects, and marine borers. Treated wood can be painted, and there is no objectionable odor. The wood can be in contact with the ground or water. The degree of impregnation depends on the use required. Ammoniacal copper arsenite (Chemonite) is approximately equal amounts of copper oxide and arsenic pentoxide with about 2% acetic acid. Copper hydroxide may be used instead of copper oxide, and arsenic trioxide can be substituted for arsenic pentoxide. The wood can be in contact with the ground. In harsh conditions, high penetration and retention of preservative is necessary. These chemicals provide good protection from decay and termite attack and against marine borer attack where pholad-type borers are not present. Chromated copper arsenate (CCA) preservatives form a family with three different types, called Types I–III. These contain varying proportions of chromium trioxide, copper oxide, and arsenic pentoxide. Substitutions can be made. Sodium or potassium dichromate may be used instead of chromium trioxide. Copper sulfate, basic copper carbonate, or copper trioxide can be substituted for copper oxide, and arsenic acid or sodium arsenate may be used for arsenic pentoxide. Type I compounds provide excellent protection against fungi, termites, and the marine borers *Limnoria* and *Teredo*. The wood can be in contact with the ground. Types II and III offer good protection from decay and insect attack. They can be painted and have no objectionable odor. These types can be used in contact with the ground or water. Chromated zinc arsenate is 20% arsenic acid, 21% sodium arsenate, 10% sodium dichromate, and 43% zinc sulfate. The wood can be in contact with the ground, but not water. It provides good protection from decay and termites. The surface is paintable and has no objectionable odor. Chromated zinc chloride is typically 80% zinc oxide and 20% chromium trioxide where zinc chloride may be used instead of zinc oxide and sodium dichromate can be used for chromium trioxide. These provide good protection under dry conditions and are moderately effective when in contact with the ground. The chemicals leach out of the wood and should not be used under harsh conditions. Chromated zinc chloride (fire retardant) is 80% chromated zinc chloride, 10% boric acid, and 10% ammonium sulfate. This preservative provides good protection from decay and insects and also provides good fire-retardant characteristics. Preservative retentions of 1.5–3 lb/ft^3 (24–48 kg/m^3) should be used. This preservative should not be used in contact with the ground or water since it leaches out from the wood. Fluorochrome arsenate phenol is 22% fluoride, 37% chromium trioxide, 25% arsenic pentoxide, and 10% dinitrophenol. Sodium pentachlorophenol may be substituted for dinitrophenol. Sodium or potassium fluoride may be used for fluoride. Sodium chromate or dichromate may be used for chromium trioxide, and sodium arsenate can be substituted for arsenic pentoxide. These preparations should not be used in contact with the ground or water when good protection is required. They do provide good protection against fungi and insects when used above ground. One common proprietary process is Wolmanizing. Wolman salts were first developed by K. H. Wolman in Germany. They were introduced into the United States in 1921. The original formula was 85% sodium fluoride, 10% dinitrophenol, and 5% potassium bichromate. Zinc metal arsenite is 60 parts arsenious acid and 40 parts zinc oxide with enough acetic acid to maintain preservatives in solution. The wood can be used in the ground, but generally is not recommended for contact with water. This preservative provides good protection against decay and insects. It can be painted and has no objectionable odor.

CORROSION-RESISTANT CHEMICALS

KP resin is a phenolic resin solution that gives wood a high degree of acid resistance. Treatment is limited to southern pine, hard maple, cativo, and kempas. The wood retains its natural color. Treated wood should not be exposed to alkaline solutions, aniline, chlorine gas, strong bleaching solutions, or strong oxidizing acids.

Asidbar is a black coal-tar composite treatment that gives wood a high degree of acid resistance. It is used on southern pine and Douglas fir. The chemicals tend to soften and expand above 130°F. Treated wood should not be exposed to acetate solvents, benzene, benzol, ethers, trichloroethylene, xylene, or xylol.

FIRE-RETARDANT CHEMICALS

Combustion of wood occurs in three steps. First, the wood is heated to the decomposition point. Then, the wood changes into flammable gases. These gases ignite. The flames spread the fire to more wood. The burned wood turns to charcoal, which seals and protects the inside of wood beams or logs. Heavy wood timber maintains its strength longer than unprotected steel. Fire can cause concrete to spall and lose strength. Wood can be a good material to resist fire damage. Small wood members are not thick enough to build a thick charred layer and need to be protected with fire-retardant chemicals.

In some construction locations, building codes allow fire-retardant-treated wood to be classified as noncombustible. The use of wood in these locations may result in shorter construction times and less total weight. This, combined with lower material costs, can result in lower project costs. Fire-retardant-treated wood has been mar-

keted since World War II. Good fire retardants tend to be water-soluble, possibly because they react with the wood at a molecular level. For instance, boric acid powder is much less effective than a solution of boric acid. Fire retardants are usually inorganic salts that react with each other at temperatures below the kindling point of wood. Combustible vapors released by the wood react with the fire retardant byproducts to create water and carbon dioxide. The water and carbon dioxide help smother the fire. Some fire retardants help create a tight charcoal layer that restricts or slows combustion. Fire retardants that reduce the rate of flame spread may be the most helpful in reducing fire damage. Smoke, the product of incomplete combustion, is more prevalent in fire-retardant-treated wood. When wood is completely burned, it produces only water, carbon dioxide, and carbon. Fire retardants change and complicate this process, leading in some cases to obnoxious smoke. Smoke inhalation is the leading cause of death from fires. The type of smoke and rate of smoke production are important factors in the selection of fire retardants.

In the United States, all fire-rated materials have an Underwriters Laboratories Inc. (Northbrook, Illinois) label and rating. When used in exterior locations, care should be taken that the fire retardant has been tested by a standard such as ASTM D2898 to ensure that the retardant will not leach out in the weather. Termite and decay protection can be included in fire-retardant-treated wood. This wood can also be made paintable.

Commonly used chemicals are monoammonium phosphate, diammonium phosphate, ammonium sulfate, sodium tetraborate (borax), boric acid, and zinc chloride. One nonproprietary formulation that has worked well in laboratory tests is sodium silicate solution, kaolin, and water (12).

Non-Com fire-retardant-treated wood is for interior use where the relative humidity is less than 80%. Inorganic salts that react chemically with the wood to reduce flammable vapors are used. A protective char forms on the wood, allowing thick members to retain their strength. Wood with Non-Com treatment has an Underwriters Laboratories rating of FRS. If painting is required, the wood must be dried to a maximum moisture content of 12%. Treated wood cannot be used outside and should be stored at the job site so as to be protected from the weather either indoors or on raised platforms covered with tarpaulins or polyethylene film.

NCX fire-retardant-treated wood can be used outside. Monomeric resin solutions are used. These are cured by kiln drying, after which they are not affected by outdoor weather. Wood with NCX treatment has an Underwriters Laboratories rating of FRS. NCX-treated wood should be used where appearance is important. Clear architectural finishes can be applied without problems. Treated wood may darken slightly, but the wood's basic hue will remain unchanged. Sticker marks may show after drying. Underwriters Laboratories allows milling of some species after drying. The wood should not be used in contact with the ground.

Intumescent paint is used to describe certain fire-retardant coatings. These products slow the progress of a fire by forming a protective foam. In many cases, the charred foam can be scraped off, and the underlying wood repainted. Heat-sensitive ingredients in the fire-retardant paints begin to intumesce (swell) at 300°F (150°C). The resulting foam, hundreds of times thicker than the original paint film, slows the fire, reduces smoke, and delays the buildup of toxic gases. Intumescent coatings may be used either in strategic places or throughout a building. These coatings are especially recommended for corridors or areas leading to fire exits. They are available in colors or clear with scrubbable surfaces (13).

CODES AND ORGANIZATIONS

The building codes address treated lumber in two situations. One is in fire-resistant assemblies (construction). The current editions of the *Fire Resistance Directory* and the *Building Materials Directory* of Underwriters Laboratories are the definitive sources for this information. The other use is in prevention of decay. Wood used in decay prone locations must be treated or of naturally resistant species. These are usually limited to heartwoods of baldcypress (tidewater red), redwood (*Sequoia sempervirens*), black locust, black walnut, and eastern red cedar (Table 1).

Table 1 ranks the decay resistance of many woods. The natural variation within species makes this an uncertain proposition at best. In this table, decay is meant to include that caused by both fungi and insects. Some species are resistant to fungi, for example, but are eaten by termites. Therefore, the table's rankings represent the average resistance to decay by either insects or fungi of an average tree. Variations in names for the same tree are separated by a slash.

The *Manual of Recommended Practice* of the AWPA contains standards for specific preservatives and application techniques. Quality control standards are published by the American Wood Preserves Bureau (AWPB). Treated lumber typically has a stamp giving the specific AWPB standard followed, such as AWPB LP-22, which is pressure treatment with a water-based preservative suitable for ground contact.

There are many international organizations involved in wood protection and preservation. The International Union of Forest Research Organizations (IUFRO) has a working group on wood protection. Its objectives are to assess the present state of knowledge in the field of wood protection and to summarize worldwide current research; to indicate the areas of needed research and their relative priorities; to provide assistance in international standardization on methods of testing and application of wood preservatives; and to arrange for and participate in international conferences. The International Research Group on Wood Preservation (IRGWP) is another organization. Its objectives are to gather information on the biology of wood decay; to gather information on climatic nutrient factors; to contribute to fundamental principles, standards, methods, and means; to compare results on an international basis; and to investigate the relationships between preservatives, treatment methods, and species. The European Committee for the Homologation of Wood Preservatives is composed of representatives of European countries. Its aim is to arrive at common standards of acceptance and approval of wood preservatives. This committee complements the work of the IUFRO, mentioned above. The Comité Européenne de Coordination des Normes is concerned with unified methods for testing wood preservatives.

CONSTRUCTION PRACTICES TO RESIST WOOD DETERIORATION

1. Place no untreated wood within 8 in. of direct contact with the ground. Place it higher in humid climates.
2. Avoid any accumulation of moisture from condensation, from plumbing or air conditioner leaks, or from the soil.
3. Provide adequate ventilation beneath buildings.
4. Remove all stumps or wood debris from beneath or near buildings.
5. Provide adequate soil drainage so that building foundations stay dry.
6. Use only seasoned wood that is entirely free from decay.
7. Use only wood that has less than 20% moisture content (dry).
8. Use fire-retardant-treated wood where building codes or life safety considerations suggest noncombustible materials.
9. Condition soil within 4 ft of foundations in order to kill present and future termites.
10. Allow for visual inspection of wood structures. Crawl spaces around foundations can save the inspector from having to tear up finish materials in order to look for signs of rot.
11. External joinery such as door and window frames where water can accumulate should be sloped to drain and should be constructed of treated lumber.
12. Modern woods tend to contain more sapwood than in the past. Sapwood is especially susceptible to decay. Treated wood may be good insurance in hard-to-repair or critical locations.
13. A fairly wide roof overhang of 2 ft (600 mm) with gutters and downspouts that are kept unclogged protects adjacent walls and foundations. If gravel beds at the drip line or other strategies are used to keep water from splashing onto walls, gutters and downspouts can be eliminated.
14. Soil should be graded to slope away from building foundations. Water should never be allowed to stand near building foundations.
15. Use only lumber cut from trees that have been felled recently. Fallen dead trees contain more active fungi and insect larvae than standing trees.

Table 1. Relative Decay Resistance of Heartwoods[a]

Common Name	Marine Borer Resistance	Region of World	Notes[b]	References
Excellent				
Afrormosia/kokrodura	Good	West Africa	R	14, 15
Baldcypress, old growth		North America	R, D&T	14
Catalpa		North America		14
Cedar, eastern red		North America	R, D&T	
Cedars (most)		North America	D	14
Greenheart	Good	South America		14, 15
Iroko/Mvule		Africa		14, 15
Jarrah/eucalyptus	Good	Australia		14, 15
Juniper		North America		14
Lapacho	Poor	South America		14
Lignum vitae		Central America		14
Locust, black		North America	R, D	14
Mulberry, red		North America	R	14
Osage, orange		North America	R	14
Pyinkado	Good	Southeast Asia		15
Redwood, sequoia		North America	R, D&T	14
Teak	Excellent	Southeast Asia	R	14, 15
Walnut, black		North America	R, D	14
Yew, Pacific		North America	R	14
Very good				
Apamate		Central America		14
Cedar, Spanish		Central America		14
Cherry, black		North America		14
Chestnut, sweet (American)		North America		14
Courbaril		Central America		14
Cypress, Arizona		North America		14
Encino/oak		Central America		14
Goncalo alves		Central America		14
Kapur		Southeast Asia		14
Mahogany, American		Central America		14
Meranti, dark red		South Pacific		14
Mesquite		North America		14
Oak, bur		North America		14
Oak, chestnut		North America		14
Oak, gambel		North America		14
Oak, Oregon white		North America		14
Oak, post		North America		14
Oak, white		North America		14
Peroba de campos		South America		14
Primavera		Central America		14
Rosewood, Brazilian		South America		14
Sassafras		North America		14
Good				
Andiroba		South America		14
Angelique	Fair	Central America		14, 15
Apitong gurjun/keruing yang	Good	Southeast Asia		14, 15
Avodiré		West Africa		14
Douglas fir (dense)		North America		14
Gola		West Africa		14
Honeylocust		North America		14
Karri, eucalyptus		Australia		14
Larch, western and Japanese		North America		14
Laurel		South America		14
Mahogany, African/khaya		West Africa		14
Mahogany, almon		Philippines		14
Mahogany, bagtikan		Philippines		14
Mahogany, red lauan		Philippines		14
Mahogany, tanguile		Philippines		14
Pine, ocote		Central America		14
Pine, southern yellow (dense)		North America		14
Santa Maria	Poor	Central America		14
Sapele		West Africa		14
Tamarack		North America		14

(*continued*)

Table 1. (*continued*)

Common Name	Marine Borer Resistance	Region of World	Notes[b]	References
Tamarack		North America		14
Walnut, European		Europe		14
Fair to poor				
Alder		North America		14
Ashes		North America		14
Aspens		North America		14
Balsa		Central America		14
Banak		Central America		14
Basswood		North America		14
Beech		North America		14
Birches		North America		14
Buckeye		North America		14
Butternut		North America		14
Capirona		South America		14
Cativo		Central America		14
Cottonwood		North America		14
Elms		North America		14
Firs, true		North America		14
Gum, black		North America		14
Gum, tupelo		North America		14
Hackberry		North America		14
Hemlocks		North America		14
Hickories		North America		14
Jelutong		Southeast Asia		14
Limba		West Africa		14
Lupuna		South America		14
Magnolia		North America		14
Mahogany, mayapis		Philippines		14
Mahogany, white lauan		Philippines		14
Maples		North America		14
Mersawa/palosapis		South Asia		14
Oak, black		North America		14
Oak, red		North America		14
Obeche		North America		14
Obeche/samba/wawa		West Africa		14
Paraná pine (not a pine)		South America		14
Pines[c]		North America		14
Poplars		North America		14
Ramin/melawis		Southeast Asia		14
Sanda/cocal		South America		14
Seraya, white		North America		14
Spruces		North America		14
Sterculia, yellow		North America		14
Sweetgum		North America		14
Sycamore		North America		14
Virola/cuangare		South America		14
Willows		North America		14

[a] All sapwood is either nondurable or perishable.

[b] R, Wood with highest natural resistance to decay; D, wood with natural resistance to decay according to the *Uniform Building Code;* D&T, wood with natural resistance to decay and termites according to the *Uniform Building Code.*

[c] All other pines not mentioned previously.

BIBLIOGRAPHY

1. H. F. Weiss, *Preservation of Structural Timber,* McGraw-Hill Inc., New York, 1916, p. 9.

2. G. M. Hunt and G. A. Garratt, *Wood Preservation,* McGraw-Hill Inc., New York, 1938.

3. *Wood Handbook,* Agriculture Handbook No. 72, U.S. Forest Products Laboratory, USGPO, Washington, D.C. 1974, p. 18-10. See table 18-2 for test results.

4. C. Langley, project manager, *Wood Preservative Pesticides,* *Creosote, Pentachlorophenol, and the Inorganic Arsenicals, Position Document 4,* Registration Division, Office of Pesticide Programs, Office of Pesticides and Toxic Substances, U.S. Environmental Protection Agency, Washington, D.C., 1983.

5. *Federal Register* **49**(136), 28,666–28,689 (July 13, 1984). Notice of intent to cancel with comments.

6. W. Liese, *Biological Transformation of Wood by Microorganisms,* Springer-Verlag, New York, 1975, pp. 118–121.

7. D. D. Nicholas, ed., *Wood Deterioration and Its Prevention by*

Preservation Treatments, Vol. I, *Degradation and Protection of Wood,* Vol. II, *Preservatives and Preservative Systems,* Syracuse University Press, Syracuse, N.Y., 1973. The principal reference is to Vol. I, p. 7.

8. Ref. 7, Vol. I, p. 200. See table 5.1 for fungi tolerant to wood-preserving chemicals.

9. S. A. Richardson, *Protecting Buildings, How to Combat Dry Rot, Woodworm, and Damp,* Davis & Charles, London, 1977, p. 110. Interesting personal experiences.

10. R. H. Beal, J. K. Mauldin, and S. C. Jones, "Subterranean termites, Their Prevention and Control in Buildings," *U.S Department of Agriculture Home & Garden Bulletin* Vol., 64, USGPO, Washington, D.C., 1986.

11. D. P. Morgan, *Recognition and Management of Pesticide Poisonings,* 3rd ed., U.S. Environmental Protection Agency, Washington, D.C., 1982.

12. Ref. 3, p. 15-9.

13. H. B. Olin, *Construction: Principles, Materials, & Methods,* The Institution of Financial Education, Chicago, Ill., 1975, pp. 216–218. General work.

14. Ref. 3, pp. 1-5–1-38 and tables 3-10 and 3-11.

15. *NavFac DM-2.5, Structural Engineering, Timber Structures,* Naval Facilities Engineering Command, U.S. Department of the Navy, Alexandria, Va., USGPO, Washington, D.C., May 1980, table 1.

General References

H. B. van Groenou, H. W. L. Rischen, and J. Van den Berge, *Wood Preservation During the Last 50 Years,* A. W. Sijthoff's Uitgeversmaatsch Appij N.V., Leiden, the Netherlands, 1952. General work.

W. Liese, ed., *Biological Transformation of Wood by Microorganisms,* Springer-Verlag, New York, 1975. Technical papers.

H. L. Edlin, *What Wood Is That?,* Viking Press, New York, 1977. Good guide to wood species recognition that includes 40 actual samples.

A. Everett, *Materials,* Mitchell's Building Construction, John Wiley & Sons, Inc., New York, 1978. General work.

C. Hornbostel, *Construction Materials,* John Wiley & Sons, Inc., New York, 1978. General work.

H. E. Desch, revised by J. M. Dinwoodie, *Timber, Its Structure, Properties, and Utilization,* 6th ed., Timber Press, Forest Grove, Oreg., 1981. College text.

R. W. Meyer and R. M. Kellogg, eds., *Structural Uses of Wood in Adverse Environments,* Van Nostrand Reinhold Co., New York; 37 detailed symposium articles.

See also PEST CONTROL; TERMITES—CONTROL BY SOIL POISONING; WOOD IN CONSTRUCTION.

JAMES H. FITZWATER, AIA
Design Automation
Houston, Texas

WORKING DRAWINGS

Producing a set of working drawings that adequately and accurately represents a building project requires careful consideration of how the information will be organized, represented, and what methods will be used to create and reproduce it.

DRAWING REPRODUCTION

Until the mid-1960s, the common method of reproducing working drawings was to lay the transparent original on a sheet of paper coated with a light-sensitive substance. In a process similar to making a photographic contact print, the pair of sheets was exposed to an intense light. The linework on the original drawing would prevent the light-sensitive coating directly behind from being exposed. This paper was then fixed by a solution of ammonia and water. The exposed areas of the coated paper turned a dark blue and the coating on the unexposed areas was washed away creating a white linework image of the original. These prints with a dark blue background, were known as blueprints and a set of working drawings was commonly called a set of blueprints. Because making blueprints required water and bulky equipment, only large architectural and engineering firms had the volume of work to justify having their own facilities; smaller firms had to use off-site facilities provided by vendors.

In the 1960s, a dry ammonia process was developed that used ammonia vapors to treat the exposed print paper. Diazo prints could be processed with a desktop sized printing machine that made it possible for firms and individuals to make their own prints from the original drawings. Although the blueprinting process is no longer used, a set of working drawings is still referred to by many people as blueprints.

DRAWING ORGANIZATION

A set of working drawings should be organized according to the basic sequence of work and according to the major disciplines involved.

Title Sheet Site Drawing: vicinity map, legends, abbreviations

Architectural: plans, elevations, sections, details, schedules

Structural: plans, details, schedules, notes

HVAC: plans, schedules, notes

Plumbing: plans, fixture schedules, riser diagrams, notes

Electrical: plans, panel diagrams, fixture schedules, notes

Landscape: plans, paving details, plant material schedules, details

BUILDING PLANS

Plan drawings are primarily used to convey location and layout information about a building project. These drawings indicate the overall layout of building spaces, the location and extent of building materials, building components, assemblies, furniture, and fixtures. Plans are also used to key the view of other types of drawings such as elevations, sections, and details. Depending on the scope of the project and its complexity, information may be divided among several types of plan drawings such as wall and partition layouts, ceiling plans, roof plans, casework, furniture layout, finishes, and color schemes.

Floor Plans. Floor plans provide information about laying out the building. Dimensions are used to locate walls and partitions, doors, windows, stairs, louvers, equipment, casework, and other components that are part of the built structure. The plans generally indicate the extent of building materials and finishes (Fig. 1).

Ceiling Plans. Ceiling plans show the extent and layout of ceiling finishes and systems including the layout of fixtures installed in the ceiling such as lights, HVAC grilles, access panels, sprinkler heads, and speakers (Fig. 2).

Roof Plans. Roof plans primarily show the layout of the roofing systems, drainage flow, and locating various roof accessories such as skylights, vents, drains, antennae, and walkways (Fig. 3).

ELEVATIONS

Elevations are used to show vertical information about wall surfaces, ie, the extent and type of materials, location of openings, and other components attached to walls.

Exterior Elevations. Exterior elevations generally show the appearance of exterior facades indicating the layout of exterior materials, location and arrangement of openings, the location of items attached to the exterior walls, ie, downspouts and exterior lighting (Fig. 4).

Interior Elevations. Interior elevations show the location and arrangement of interior finish materials, openings, architectural trim, and items attached or built into the wall (Fig. 5).

SECTIONS

Sections, along with elevations are primarily used to show the vertical layout and arrangement of the primary building features and components.

Building Sections. Building sections show the vertical layout of floors, ceilings, and roofs indicating the different configurations of interior spaces (Fig. 6).

Wall Sections. Wall sections are used to show the important construction features of typical walls including footings, floor connections, location of window sills and heads, and arrangement of materials composing the wall (Fig. 7).

DETAILS

Details are large scale drawings, either plans or sections, showing the exact relationship and connections between different building components and materials, ie, how a window frame fits into an exterior wall, the connection between a column and beam, or how wall mounted plumbing fixtures are supported (Fig. 8).

NOTES

Notes are text information that further describe the graphic information on the drawings. Notes are used to indicate materials, fastening methods, sizes, layout requirements, and other information that cannot be clearly described graphically (Figs. 1–8).

DIMENSIONS

Although drawings are generally drawn to specific scales, the level of accuracy is generally not sufficient for estimating or construction purposes. Therefore, dimensions are provided to accurately indicate the location and size of building components both horizontally and vertically. Dimensions are used extensively on plans, elevations, sections, and details (Figs. 1–8).

SCHEDULES

Schedules are used to indicate the variety of types, styles, materials, and finishes associated with building components such as doors and windows that are used extensively throughout a project. The formation is generally presented in a tabular format. The information is keyed to the drawings using a standardized notation such as door number, room number, or window type. Working drawings for most building types include schedules for doors, windows, partitions, room finishes, hardware, and often louvers, casework, and lighting fixtures.

Door Schedules. Door schedules indicate the different types, sizes, and finishes of doors in the project (Fig. 9).

STRUCTURAL DRAWINGS

The structural drawings include foundation drawings, in addition to plans of the structure of the building. Many engineers use computers to assist in sizing the structural members. The selected structural system affects the appearance of the drawings. Details include connections, framing of openings, and provisions for the support of heavy loads and special conditions. Integration of the structural system into the building may require adjustment of the architectural drawings to provide adequate structural support and required clearances for mechanical and electrical systems. For simple buildings, the information may be included on the architectural drawings.

MECHANICAL AND ELECTRICAL DRAWINGS

The drawings for mechanical (HVAC and plumbing) and electrical work are developed at the same time as the architectural and structural drawings. Often the architect provides plan templates for use by the engineers. Coordi-

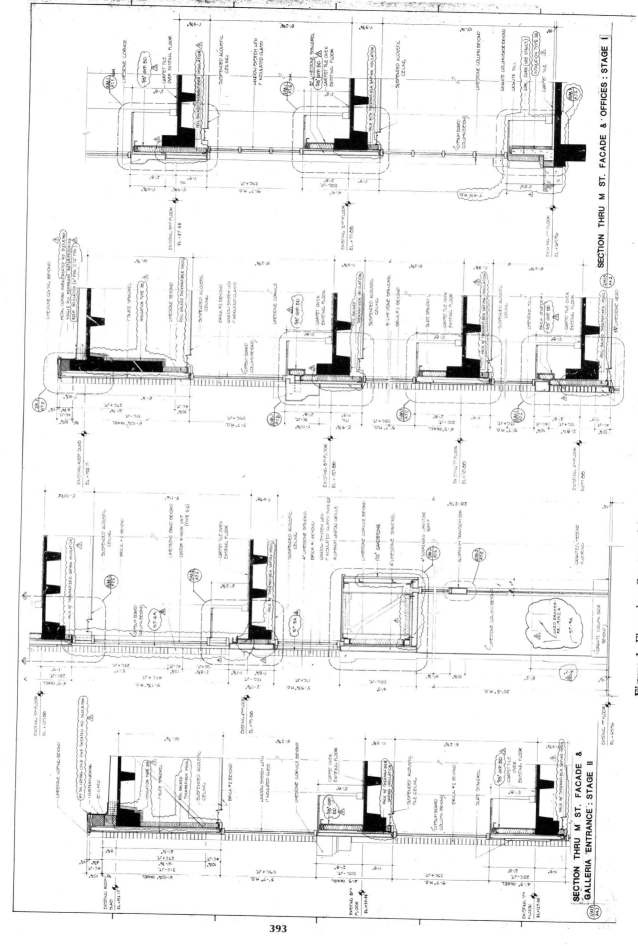

Figure 1. Floor plan. Courtesy of Geier Brown Renfrow Architects and Segretti Tepper Architects, PC.

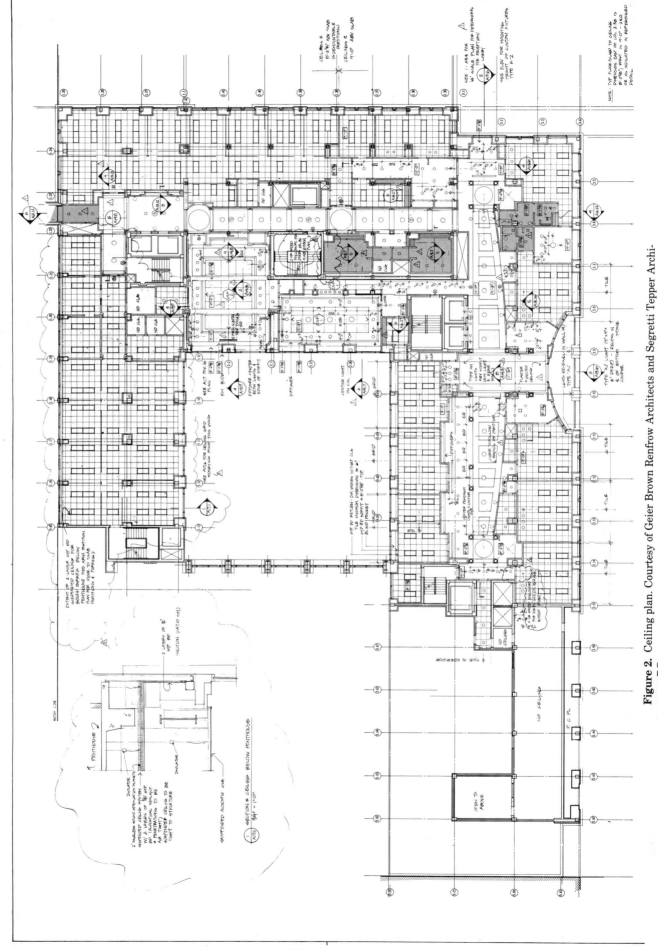

Figure 2. Ceiling plan. Courtesy of Geier Brown Renfrow Architects and Segretti Tepper Archi-

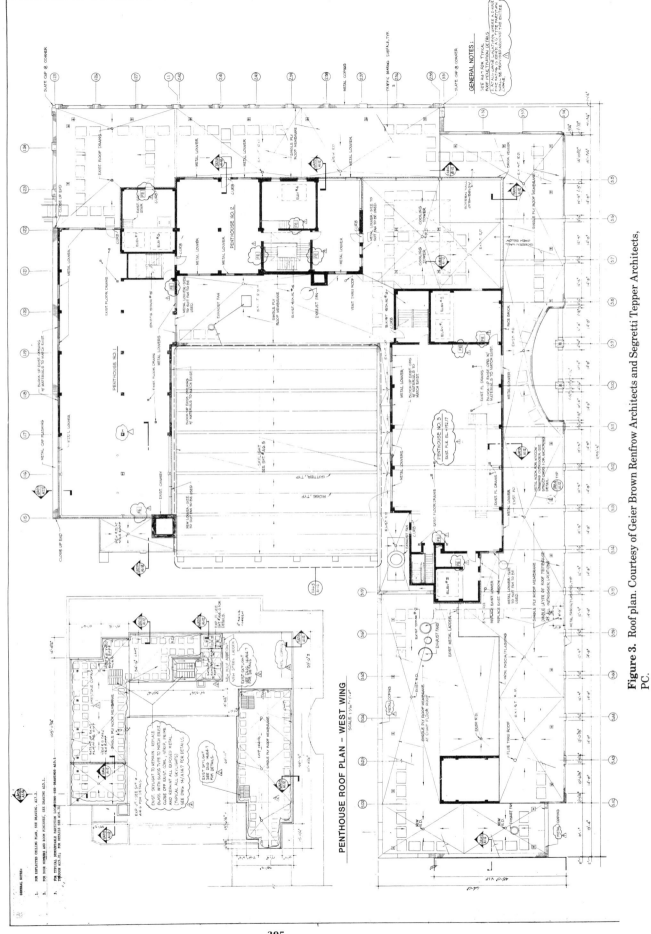

Figure 3. Roof plan. Courtesy of Geier Brown Renfrow Architects and Segretti Tepper Architects, PC.

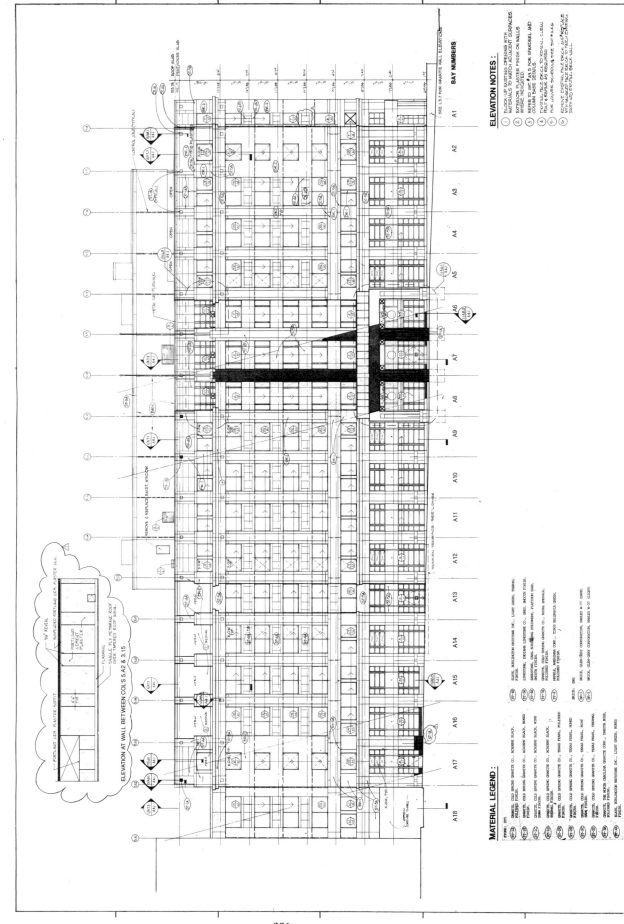

Figure 4. Exterior elevation. Courtesy of Geier Brown Renfrow Architects and Segretti Tepper Architects, PC.

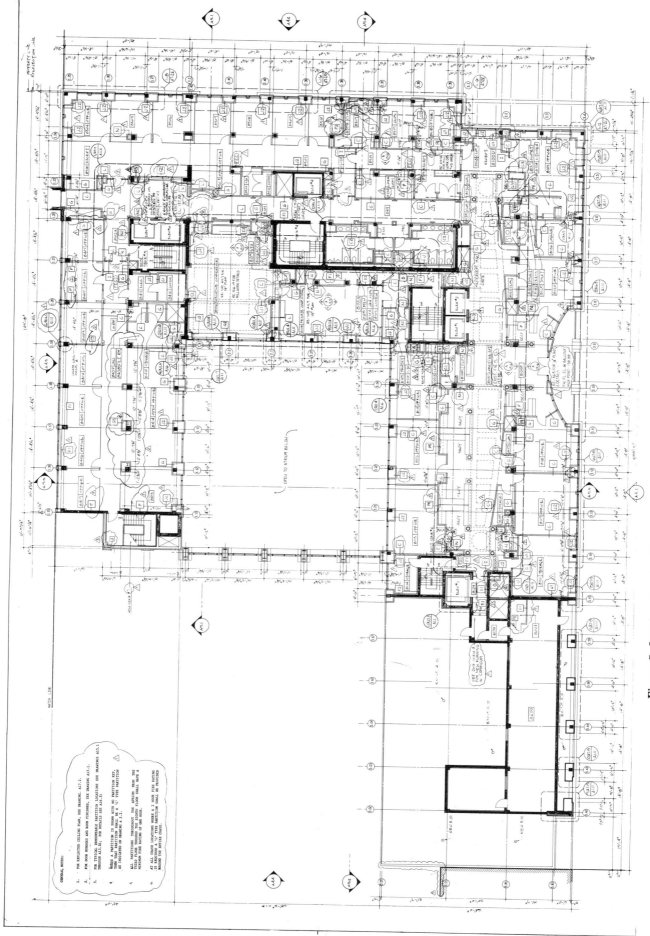

Figure 5. Interior elevation. Courtesy of Geier Brown Renfrow Architects and Segretti Tepper Architects, PC.

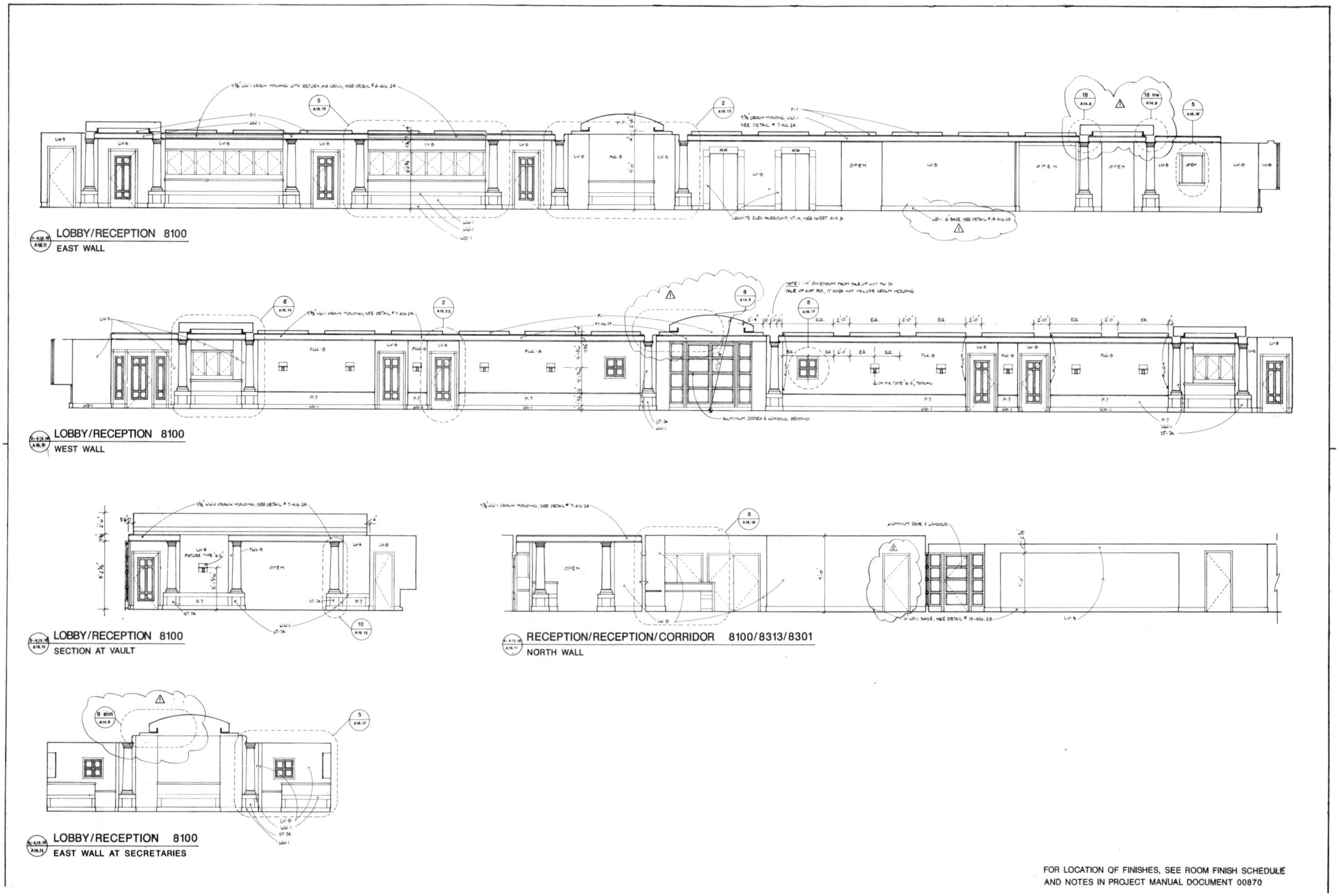

LOBBY/RECEPTION 8100
EAST WALL

LOBBY/RECEPTION 8100
WEST WALL

LOBBY/RECEPTION 8100
SECTION AT VAULT

LOBBY/RECEPTION 8100
EAST WALL AT SECRETARIES

RECEPTION/RECEPTION/CORRIDOR 8100/8313/8301
NORTH WALL

FOR LOCATION OF FINISHES, SEE ROOM FINISH SCHEDULE
AND NOTES IN PROJECT MANUAL DOCUMENT 00870

Figure 5. Cont.

398

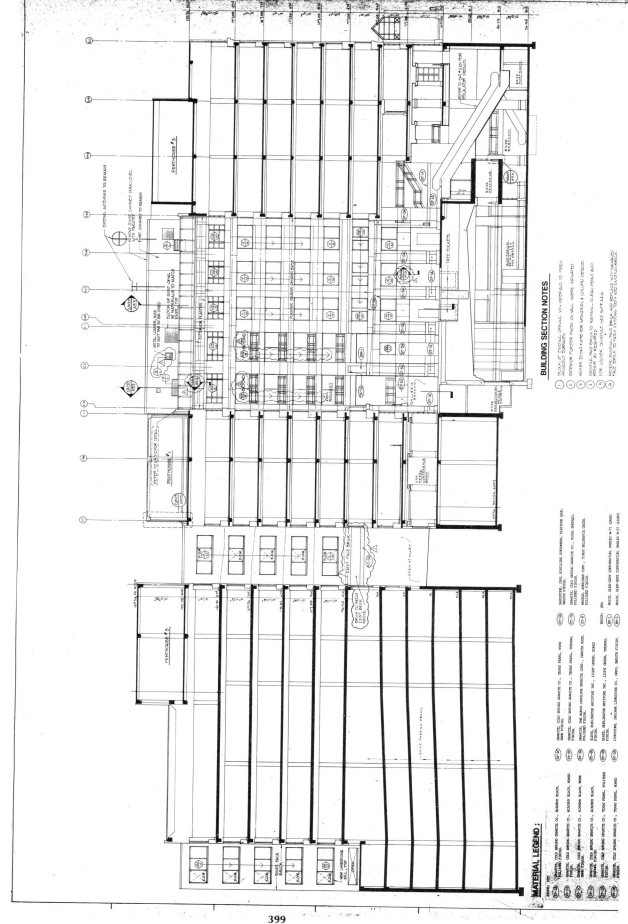

Figure 6. Building section. Courtesy of Geier Brown Renfrow Architects and Segretti Tepper Architects, PC.

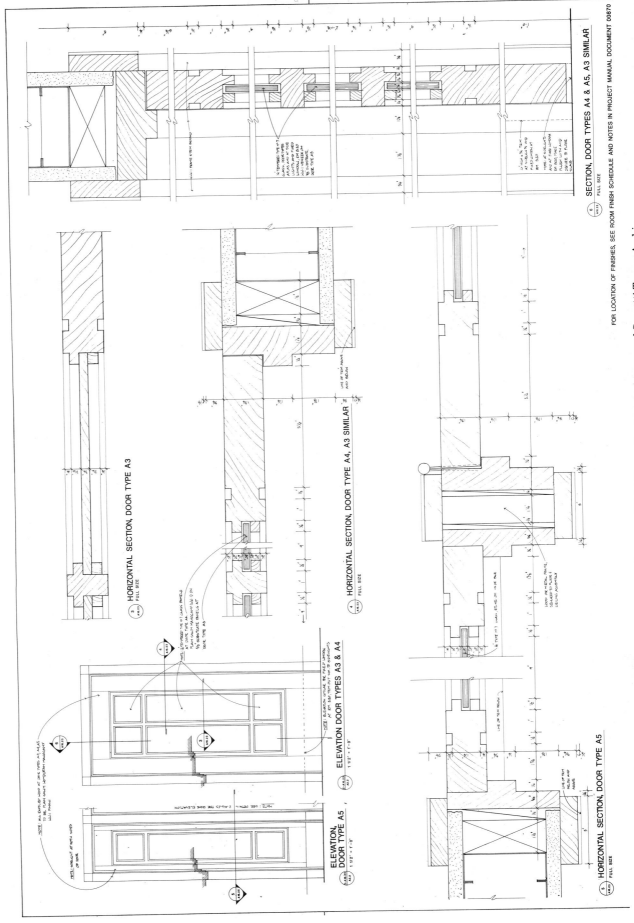

Figure 7. Wall sections. Courtesy of Geier Brown Renfrow Architects and Segretti Tepper Archi-

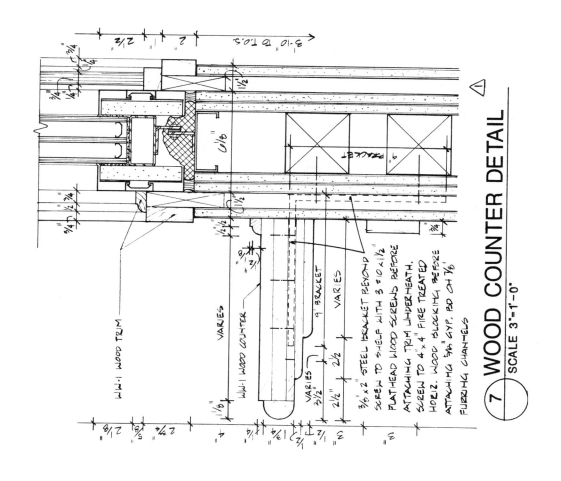

7 WOOD COUNTER DETAIL
SCALE 3"=1'-0"

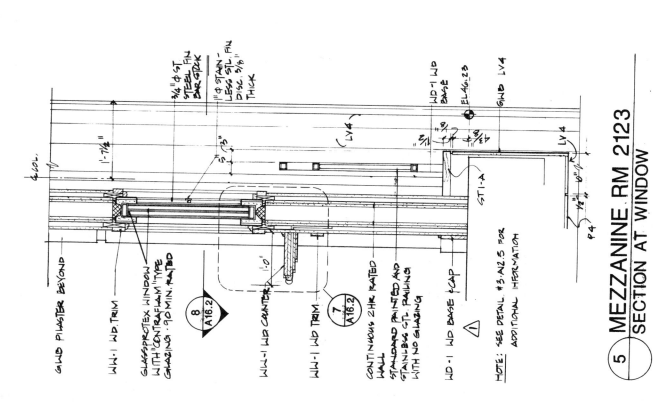

5 MEZZANINE RM 2123
SECTION AT WINDOW

Figure 8. Details. Courtesy of Geier Brown Renfrow Architects and Segretti Tepper Architects, PC.

DOOR SCHEDULE							
DOOR NO.	TYPE	SIZE		FIRE RATING	HARD-WARE	FINISH	DETAILS/REMARKS
		WIDTH	HEIGHT				
2001	A	3'-0"	8'-0"	3/4 HR.	HW5	PTD. P2	
5003	A	3'-0"	8'-0"	3/4 HR.	HW5	PTD. P2	
6003	A	3'-0"	8'-0"	3/4 HR.	HW5	PTD. P2	
7001	D	6'-0"	8'-0"	3/4 HR.	HW8	PTD. P2	
7002	A	3'-0"	8'-0"	3/4 HR.	HW5	PTD. P2	
7003	D	6'-0"	8'-0"		HW4	PTD. P2	SECURITY SYSTEM
7003A	A	3'-0"	7'-0"		HW2	PTD. P2	
7003B	E	6'-0"	7'-0"		HW7	PTD. P2	
7003C	A	3'-0"	7'-0"	3/4 HR.	HW4	PTD. P2	
7003D	A	3'-0"	7'-0"		HW2	PTD. P2	
7003E	A	3'-0"	7'-0"	3/4 HR.	HW4	PTD. P2	
7004	C	3'-0"	8'-0"	3/4 HR.	HW6	PTD. P2	SECURITY SYSTEM
T1	A	3'-0"	8'-0"		HW1	PTD. P2	TEMPORARY
T2	A	3'-0"	8'-0"		HW1.	PTD. P2	TEMPORARY
8004	A	3'-0"	8'-0"		HW5	PTD. P2	
917	A	3'-0"	8'-0"		HW5	PTD. P2	
5000	G	6'-0"	8'-3½"		HW10	CLEAR ANODIZED	WITH PAIR OF SIDELIGHTS 6/A18 , 2/A18
5001A	EXIST	EXIST	EXIST		HW11	EXIST	
5001B	EXIST	EXIST	EXIST		↓	EXIST	
5004	C	3'-0"	8'-0"	—	HW1	PTD. P2	
5004A	A	3'-0"	8'-0"	—	HW2	PTD. P2	
5005A							
5005B							
5006							
5007							
5008							
5008A							
5010							
5011							
5012							
5014							
5016							
5017							
5018							
5019							
5020							
5021	↓	↓	↓		↓	↓	
5022	A	3'-0"	8'-0"	—	HW2	PTD P2	
5023	A	3'-0"	8'-0"	—	HW1	PTD P2	
5024							

Figure 9. Door schedule. Courtesy of Geier Brown Renfrow Architects.

nation of work by engineering consultants and the architect occurs during preparation of the working drawings. Special layouts are included for major equipment. Adequate space for ducts and risers, location of electrical closets, and communications equipment are allowed for on the architect's drawings. Considerable information on equipment can be given in tabular form (see Table 1). Depending on the building, plumbing drawings show water supply, waste lines, (including special treatment for toxic wastes), vents, valves, and piping, fittings for sprinkler systems, and other special systems. Computerized building management systems are frequently installed in larger buildings.

Determining the proper scale for a drawing is a function of the extent and detail of information that must be shown. A site location drawing might be at the smaller scales (1:500 to 1:2000 (1 in. = 50 ft to 1 in. = 200 ft)). Site drawings would be drawn to somewhat larger scales (1:200 to 1:500 (1/16 in. = 1 ft to 1 in. = 50 ft)). Depending on the size and shape of a building, floor plans, elevations, and building sections showing the entire building are usually drawn at scales of 1/16 in. to 1/4 in. = 1 ft (1:200 to 1:50). Partial floor plans of complicated elements such as bathrooms and stairs may be drawn at larger scales up to 1 in. = 1 ft (1:10). details are drawn at scales ranging between 1 in. to 3 in. = 1 ft (1:10–1:5), or even full size.

Legends are used to indicate standard graphic representations for commonly used building materials and components (Fig. 10).

GRAPHIC CONVENTIONS

Table 1. Comparison of Drawing Scales

Scales for use with Metric Drawings	Scale Ratio	Scales for use with Conventional Units
1:5	1:4	3″ = 1′0″
1:10	1:8	1½″ = 1′0″
	1:12	1″ = 1′0″
	1:16	¾″ = 1′0″
1:20		
	1:24	½″ = 1′0″
	1:48	¼″ = 1′0″
1:50		
	1:96	⅛″ = 1′0″
1:100		
	1:192	1/16″ = 1′0″
1:200		
	1:384	1/32″ = 1′0″
	1:480	1″ = 40′0″
1:500		
	1:600	1″ = 50′0″
	1:960	1″ = 80′0″
1:1000		
	1:1200	1″ = 100′0″
1:2000		
	1:2400	1″ = 200′0″

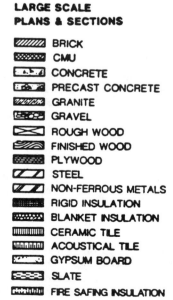
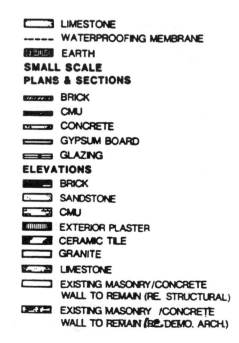

MATERIAL INDICATIONS

LARGE SCALE PLANS & SECTIONS
- BRICK
- CMU
- CONCRETE
- PRECAST CONCRETE
- GRANITE
- GRAVEL
- ROUGH WOOD
- FINISHED WOOD
- PLYWOOD
- STEEL
- NON-FERROUS METALS
- RIGID INSULATION
- BLANKET INSULATION
- CERAMIC TILE
- ACOUSTICAL TILE
- GYPSUM BOARD
- SLATE
- FIRE SAFING INSULATION

- LIMESTONE
- WATERPROOFING MEMBRANE
- EARTH

SMALL SCALE PLANS & SECTIONS
- BRICK
- CMU
- CONCRETE
- GYPSUM BOARD
- GLAZING

ELEVATIONS
- BRICK
- SANDSTONE
- CMU
- EXTERIOR PLASTER
- CERAMIC TILE
- GRANITE
- LIMESTONE
- EXISTING MASONRY/CONCRETE WALL TO REMAIN (RE. STRUCTURAL)
- EXISTING MASONRY/CONCRETE WALL TO REMAIN (RE. DEMO. ARCH)

Figure 10. Materials legend. Courtesy of Geier Brown Renfrow Architects and Segretti Tepper Architects, PC.

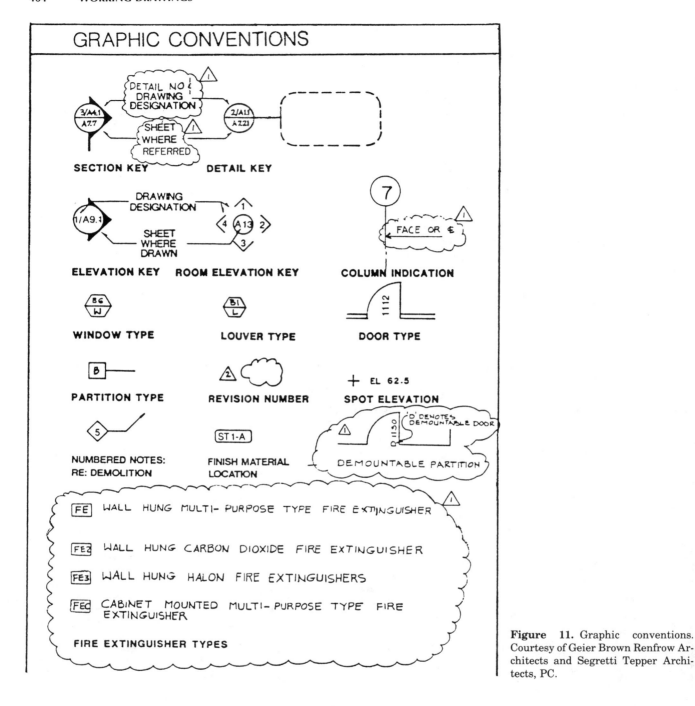

Figure 11. Graphic conventions. Courtesy of Geier Brown Renfrow Architects and Segretti Tepper Architects, PC.

GRAPHIC STANDARDS

Adherence to various symbols and other notational standards is necessary to make a set of working drawings function together and consistent in presenting information. Industry accepted conventions have emerged that would be followed except in those instances were there are none or the existing conventions are inappropriate. Creating new conventions for the sake of individuality is generally not helpful to those who must use the working drawings. Working drawings contain so much information that

is unique to the project, the use of industry recognized standards makes the drawings easier to read (Fig. 11)

DRAWING COORDINATION

Correct coordination of information is a major factor in producing a useful set of working drawings. The same or similar information shown on different drawings must agree and be consistent. The drawings produced by each discipline must agree with those produced by others and provide the necessary supporting detail. A major problem is the coordination of information contained in the project specifications. Items and conditions described in the specifications must be adequately described on the drawings.

BIBLIOGRAPHY

General References

O. A. Wakita, R. M. Linde, *The Professional Practice of Architectural Drawings,* John Wiley & Sons, Inc., New York, 1984.

W. P. Spence, *Architecture·Design·Engineering·Drawing,* McKnight Publishing Company, Bloomington, Ill., 1979.

See also CONSTRUCTION DOCUMENTS; DRAFTING, ARCHITECTURAL; RENDERINGS, ARCHITECTURAL

DENNIS B. BROWN, AIA
Washington, D.C.

WREN, SIR CHRISTOPHER

Christopher Wren was born in 1632 to a highly placed clergyman of the Church of England, who was knowledgeable in science and architecture, and who became Dean of Windsor. His uncle Matthew had also been Dean of Windsor and later became Bishop of Ely. He received a then-traditional early education in the classics, in spite of the outbreak of civil war in 1642, and began studies in astronomy and physiology. He graduated from Wadham College, Oxford University, with a B.A. and, in 1653, an M.A. degree. After four years in research as a Fellow of All Souls College at Oxford (eventually receiving a doctorate of civil laws in 1661), Wren became Professor of Astronomy at Gresham College, London, writing that geometry and arithmetic were ". . . the only Truths that can sink into the Mind of Man void of all Uncertainty" (1).

Meanwhile, he had received no formal instruction in architecture, but taught himself through an inquiring study of Italian and French treatises and pattern books, including that of Vitruvius, exploring the relationship between immutable natural laws that could be expressed mathematically and their interpretive application to artistic design through mutable rules. Before 1660, he had prepared a treatise on "New Designs Tending to Strength, Convenience and Beauty in Building." It was not until 1665 that Wren undertook his only architectural visit abroad, where he met with some leading French and Italian architects, including Bernini, during an eight-month stay in France (1).

In 1661, Wren participated in the founding of the Royal Society, left his Gresham post to return to Oxford as Savilian Professor of Astronomy (serving until 1673), and was sought after for scientific and architectural advice. He was consulted by King Charles II on the design of the fortifications of Tangier and, as a result, was offered the post of Surveyor General of the Royal Works upon the death of the incumbent, a position Wren held from 1669 to 1718. Bishop Sheldon of London consulted him on the bad structural condition of the old St. Paul's Cathedral and com-

missioned him to design the Sheldonian Theatre (ca 1664–1669) at Oxford, which made substantial use of his mathematical and structural talents. Also in 1661, his uncle commissioned a new chapel for Pembroke College, Cambridge, which was completed in 1665 as Wren's first work of architecture.

Following the Great Fire of 1666, which had hopelessly damaged most of the City of London, Wren proposed within 10 days an ideal plan for the City calling for straight streets, etc, which was deemed impractical. Later, however, he was active in establishing new safety regulations for buildings and, significantly, was busy as the chief architect for the rebuilding of over 40 parish churches, developing the single steeple ". . . large enough for a good Ring of Bells . . ." as an important British urban design and architectural element, which had considerable later influence in the United States (2). His principal work, the evolutionary design and construction of the new St. Paul's Cathedral, started soon after 1670 (although he had proposed a reconstructed dome for the former edifice shortly before the fire) and was eventually completed in 1711. In 1698, he became Surveyor of Westminster Abbey.

His significant work for the Church of England; for the Crown (under four sovereigns), including the Hampton Court Palace enlargement (1689–1700) and the Greenwich Naval Hospital (1696–1716); and for academia, including the Library for Trinity College at Cambridge (1676–1684) consumed most of his effort, and he also advised friends and colleagues on architectural matters. He worked with the finest building materials and craftsmen on all of his projects (3).

He was knighted ca 1673, was President of the Royal Society from 1681 to 1683, and entered Parliament in 1685, serving in the House of Commons intermittently for a total of about three years (through 1702) from several residence districts. He was interred in St. Paul's in 1723, his marker bearing the legend, in Latin, "Reader, if you seek his monument, look around you."

BIBLIOGRAPHY

1. K. Downes in A. K. Placzek, ed., *Macmillan Encyclopedia of Architects,* Vol. 4, The Free Press, New York, 1982, pp. 419–433.

2. L. Milman, *Sir Christopher Wren,* Duckworth and Co., London, 1908, including Appendix K by Wren regarding the parish churches.

3. B. Fletcher, *A History of Architecture on the Comparative Method,* 16th ed., B. T. Batsford Ltd., London, 1954, p. 812**.

General References

L. Weaver, *Sir Christopher Wren, Scientist, Scholar and Architect,* Charles Scribner's Sons, New York, 1928.

S. Sitwell, *British Architects and Craftsmen,* 4th ed., B. T. Batsford Ltd., London, 1948.

R. Dutton, *The Age of Wren,* B. T. Batsford Ltd., London, 1951.

J. Lindsey, *Wren, His Work and Times,* Philosophical Library, Inc., New York, 1952.

M. S. Briggs, *Wren the Incomparable,* George Allen & Unwin Ltd., London, 1953.

V. Fuerst, *The Architecture of Sir Christopher Wren,* Lund Humphries, London, 1956.

W. Yust, ed., *Encyclopedia Britannica,* Vol. 23, Encyclopedia Britannica, Inc., Chicago, Ill., 1961, pp. 803–804.

J. Summerson, *Sir Christopher Wren,* Archon Books, Hamden, Conn., 1965.

B. Little in J. M. Richards, ed., *Who's Who in Architecture,* Weidenfeld and Nicholson, Ltd., London, 1977, p. 346–350.

J. Summerson, *Georgian London,* Penguin Books, New York, 1978.

J. Summerson in P. W. Goetz, ed., *The New Encyclopedia Britannica,* Vols. 10 and 19, Encyclopedia Britannica, Inc., Chicago, Ill., 1980, pp. 760 and 1020–1024.

K. Downes, *The Architecture of Wren,* New York, 1982.

C. Wren Pevoto, *Sir Christopher Wren, His Life and Works: A Bibliography,* Vance Bibliographies, Monticello, Ill., 1984.

RALPH WARBURTON, FAIA,
FASCE, AICP
University of Miami
Coral Gables, Florida

WRIGHT, FRANK LLOYD

If there is any one architect about whom the proverbial John Q. Public knows something, it is surely Frank Lloyd Wright. People who have not read a word of his writings do not hesitate to invoke his name. Many who are not the least bit familiar with the principles of organic architecture crave to live in a home designed by him. Simon and Garfunkel have even sung about him. It is no exaggeration to say that there is something of the legendary about Frank Lloyd Wright. Further, Wright was a legend of sorts even in his own time. In no small part, this was due to Wright's flair for self-promotion and scandal-ridden personal life, as is made clear in a recent biography of Wright, *Many Masks* (1). But Wright's genius and originality played a much greater role in the creation of the Wright legend.

Wright's beginnings (he was born in 1867) were not especially promising. His father was a talented minister, more notable for his setbacks than his accomplishments. The family warmth that Wright would later seek to reflect, and create, in his early prairie houses simply was not present in his own home. Nor was rootedness, another desideratum of the mature Wright, a distinguishing feature of his childhood. By the time Wright was seven, he had moved a number of times. His record as a student at the University of Wisconsin, Madison, was hardly an inspiring one. There is a notion that Wright was predestined to become a great architect and that the cathedral prints his mother hung over his crib provided him with early inspiration. This myth has recently been laid to rest (2). No one doubts, however, that the Froebel blocks that Wright's mother gave him to play with greatly inspired the budding architect.

Nonetheless, after a stint with the architectural firm of Joseph Silsbee, well known for its work in the Queen Anne style, Wright signed up as a draftsman with the indomitable Louis Sullivan. The latter, admittedly, was more noted for his commercial than for his residential architecture. He was also more given to ornamentation than the young Wright. Still, Sullivan left an indelible imprint upon his assistant. Although Wright would break with Sullivan after a few years and not speak with him for many more years, he always remained in the older man's debt. It was Sullivan who taught Wright that the form of a building should express its underlying function. Largely because of Sullivan, Wright early on developed a contempt for the beaux-arts architecture that was so popular in the late-Victorian United States. It was Sullivan who compelled Wright to recognize that architecture was as much a social manifestation as it was an art. Most of all, Sullivan provided an example of daring, creativity, and independence of thought.

Sullivan, of course, was not the only influence on Wright. His Unitarian upbringing undoubtedly had some effect on both his views and his work. When Wright lived in the prosperous Chicago suburb of Oak Park, Ill., near the turn of the century, he was in close touch with a number of Unitarian ministers. One such minister, William C. Gannett, wrote a book that made a powerful impression on Wright. Gannett's *The House Beautiful* (1897) made a bold plea for simplicity and gracefulness in housing design. The Unitarian influence on Wright was not limited to housing, as Oak Park's Unity Temple (1906) and the much later Unitarian Meeting House (1947) of Madison, Wis., attest. To Wright, all architecture was "a sermon in stone." He truly believed there was a realm of the divine within nature and that it was the architect's duty to capture it, even if that meant spitting against the wind. It is a small wonder then that Wright has been dubbed a "minister of reform" (3).

The Orient also exerted a profound influence on Wright. Japanese art made its U.S. debut at the 1876 Centennial. Seventeen years later, Japanese architecture would have its turn when the Ho-o-den Palace was put on display at the Chicago World's Fair. Wright was undoubtedly familiar with these examples, but his own attachment to things Japanese did not become apparent until his trip to Japan in 1905. The young architect became quite taken with Japanese printmakers, who in his eyes caught the essence of natural materials in rare and beautiful fashion. But he was also enamored of Japan's architecture. The Ward Willitts home (1902) of Highland Park, Ill., clearly betrays the influence of Japan. So too, of course, did the Imperial Hotel (1922) in Tokyo, a seemingly indestructible edifice, which survived a severe earthquake during the 1920s only to be demolished years later. One commentator has gone so far as to suggest that the prairie style with which Wright distinguished himself in the early years of this century could more accurately be termed the Japanese style.

That is a slight exaggeration. Wright's prairie style was fashioned in the main as an indigenous U.S. response to what he perceived as an architectural wasteland. Just as his contemporary, John Dewey, rebelled against the classical tradition in philosophy, Wright lashed out at the neoclassical hegemony in architecture. Such architecture, Wright held, was hopelessly derivative and shamefully un-American. That is to say, it was more reflective of the Renaissance than it was of the U.S. physical and cultural landscape. The architecture of the Renaissance, according to Wright, was little "but the bare bones of a life lived and dead" (4). Even the genuine article Wright viewed suspiciously. As if to drive home the point that the Greek way was not, or rather should not be, the American way, Wright added that Greek architecture was itself largely a sham. Admiring though he was of Greek sculpture and the Minoan architecture of the island of Crete, Wright believed that the more typical work of the Hellenistic period was insufficiently sensitive to the natural environment and largely indifferent to the importance of using native materials. What was more, form had no real connection with function in the architecture of the ancient Greeks. Their architectural efforts were, in a word, "pagan poison" (5).

The architecture of the late nineteenth-century United States, of course, was not purely a copy of the classical and Renaissance. But there was enough of the old wine in the new bottles to horrify Wright. (The work of McKim, Mead and White comes to mind most immediately.) He was especially aghast at the cornice, which in his mind symbolized all that was false and meretricious in architecture. Cornices slapped nature in the face, but served no useful function whatsoever. They were dangerous to boot. Perhaps even more significantly for Wright, the cornice "had much—much too much—foreign baggage in its train, ever to be allowed to come back to America (6).

The note of cultural nationalism sounded here is reminiscent of Ralph Waldo Emerson, the transcendentalist sage who had made a similar plea for an American literature in the age of Andrew Jackson. The similarity is probably not fortuitous because Wright read and admired Emerson. (The appendix to Wright's *The Living City* is a piece on the virtues of farming by the Concord intellectual (7).) But if Wright was insisting that the United States emancipate itself from its European fetters, he was also suggesting, in the vein of progressive historian Frederick Jackson Turner, that the Midwest no longer look to the Eastern seaboard for inspiration. With its closer ties to Western Europe, the East had at least some justification for its aping of the old. The Midwest had no such excuse.

Enter the prairie style. It is perhaps best to delineate the architectural features of this style before enunciating the doctrine behind it. Those who make the pilgrimage to Oak Park are struck by, among other things, the wide doorways and freely circulating rooms, the neat and lengthy exterior trim, and the amount of window space, not to mention the overhanging eaves and gently sloping roofs. Each of these served a wider purpose. The open plan reflected Wright's long-standing aversion to boxiness. ("The box is a Fascist symbol," Wright stated with characteristic hyperbole during an interview in the early 1950s (8).) The trim gave a certain unity and continuity to the Wright homes, and the expanded fenestration invited na-

ture inside. The eaves provided shelter from the outside world, a principal concern of Wright's during the Oak Park years. Wright's preoccupation with privacy was even more evident in the entrance to his homes; they were often exceptionally difficult to locate. It should be noted that at this stage in his career Wright was more interested in familial than in individual privacy. To many a sensitive soul in this period of rapid and often jarring social change, the nuclear conjugal family was indeed a haven in a hostile world, to use Christopher Lasch's term (9). Wright captured the warmth and intimacy of the family environment with his sensitively designed fireplaces; the hearth, in his eyes, was the perfect symbol for family togetherness. Perhaps harmony within the home was more aspiration than actuality for Wright, as several of his own marriages would be racked by scandal and intrigue.

Other aspects of Wright's prairie style work merit attention. The gently sloping roofs for which he is so famous intentionally captured the contours of the prairie. "The horizontal line," Wright insisted, "is the line of domesticity" (10). This was a significant statement, given that Wright saw himself primarily as an architect of the home. But there was more to the prairie style than horizontal lines. A critic put it well in saying that "Wright took the fashionable American house of the early nineties, with its high-pitched roof and spindly chimneys, its numerous dormer windows and its crazy turrets and towers, and brought this wild, shambling, pseudo-romantic creation, half Pegasus and half spavined selling plater, down to earth" (11). A Wright biographer has noted that the architect spoke frequently of "marry [ing]" his homes "to the ground" (12). This earth-hugging quality of Wright's early domestic architecture reflected his desire to integrate home and nature, as did his use of earth tones within the home. The itch to integrate went further, however. For not only was the house never to be treated in isolation from the external environment, but also furnishings in the household were not to be viewed apart from one another or apart from the home. Thus Wright built furniture into the house as much as was feasible. Moreover, he insisted on using native materials in their natural form for both the exterior and interior of a home. For one, such a tack would cut costs considerably. More importantly, though, homes built with such materials would have the stamp of authenticity upon them. Besides, Wright queried his audiences, why paint wood when its beauty lies in its natural essence, not in its bastardization? This then was the meaning of organic architecture. Needless to say, it was applicable to much more than the U.S. prairie.

There are two splendid domestic monuments to Wright's organic architecture. The first, which harks back to the Oak Park years, is the Robie House (1907) (Fig. 1). It has been described as "one of the seven most notable houses ever built in America" (13). With its gracefulness, its links to the natural environment, and its sense of wholeness, the Robie House is the perfect embodiment of the prairie style. The other home was designed and built in the thick of the Depression and is at or near the top of the list. This is, of course, the Edgar Kaufmann residence (1936) at Bear Run, Pa., otherwise known as Fallingwa-

Figure 1. Frederick Robie House, Chicago, Illinois, 1909. Courtesy of the American Institute of Architects.

ter. It would be hard to improve on a Wright biographer's enraptured hymn to this masterpiece (14):

> In its startling departure from traditional modes of expression, [Fallingwater] revealed an aspiration for freedom from imposed limitations, and in its successful partnership with the environment, it was a guidepost to humanity's proper relationship with nature. Fallingwater was also a resolution of dichotomies. At the same time strikingly substantial and dangerously ephemeral, it is securely anchored to rock and ledge, but seems to leap into space. . . . Fallingwater is a study in opposites—motion and stability, change and permanence, power and ephemeralness—that make the human condition a paradox of welcome adventure and anxious uncertainty.

Organic architecture implied much more than the reform of architecture. Indeed, as Wright fashioned it, it meant the reform of the entire society. Or, to put it another way, Wright hoped to reform society through architecture. He even went so far as to suggest that his homes would have a positive effect on the divorce rate. (He never specified how long it would take for his buildings to produce such a beneficial effect.) Certainly, Wright believed he could have a salutary impact on the workplace. His justly renowned Johnson Wax Building (1936) in Racine, Wis., was calculated to improve the morale and productivity of the employees there (Fig. 2). Apparently, it had precisely that effect. No less ambitious was Wright's effort to construct a utopian city.

It has been stated that Wright belonged to "the anticity party in American thought" (15). Here, Wright had plenty of company, for hostility to the city has run like a red skein through our culture. Thomas Jefferson, whom Wright greatly admired in spite of the former's toleration of cornices, saw the city as a cancer sore upon the body politic. Twentieth-century U.S. architects were scarcely more nuanced in their view of cities. "The modern city," Wright often quipped, "is a place for banking and prostitution and very little else" (16). Considering his rather dim view of bankers (an animus he shared with Henry Ford), it is a wonder that he bothered to draw a distinction here. In any event, Wright saw the typical U.S. (and presumably European) city as overgrown, overcrowded, and ex-

ceedingly impersonal. For him, the modern city was, in a word, unnatural. But Wright was not any more pessimistic about cities than Karl Marx was about capitalism. Marx held that capitalism bore the seeds of its own destruction, but that human agency should accelerate the inevitable. Wright believed that the demise of the U.S. city was ineluctable and that he could provide a gentle assist.

Wright reserved his choicest epithets for New York City. His ire was especially aroused there by the abundance of skyscrapers, "an exaggerated superconcentration that would have shocked Babylon" (17). Not only did skyscrapers engender congestion and pollution, but by blocking out sun and light, they turned Manhattan into a perpetual "City of Night." Worst of all, the skyscraper "has no higher ideal of unity than commercial success" (18).

Antipathetic to the city though he was, Wright at the same time took advantage of what urban environments had to offer. Virtually all of his books, for instance, were published in New York City. If not enamored of urban civilization, Wright nonetheless was fond of urban diver-

Figure 2. S. C. Johnson Co. Administration Building, Racine, Wisconsin, 1950. Courtesy of the American Institute of Architects.

sions (19). His most memorable urban structure, the Guggenheim Museum (1957), completed just two years before his death, is situated in the middle of Manhattan. About as emphatic a rejection of post-and-beam architecture as is possible, the Guggenheim imaginatively blends structural solidity with visual fluidity. It has been said of it that the viewer is constantly kept "on the road" (20). The city that Wright so despised, ironically enough, now has as a major landmark one of the architect's most daring creations.

Against the specious unity of New York City (and lesser cities) Wright counterposed his own urban vision. Wright's Broadacre City was hardly a city in the conventional sense of the term. Yet it cannot be gainsaid that his ideal city possessed characteristics that were urban as much as they were rural and/or suburban. Perhaps it is misleading to use the standard terminology in describing Broadacre. It was more akin to a "new town" than to either city or suburb. The Jeffersonian aspect of Broadacre City was apparent at the outset. Just as Jefferson had hoped that every American would have a vine and fig tree, Wright dreamed that each would be guaranteed an acre of land. Not unlike his idol, Wright fervently wished that most men and women would be able to grow their own food. In the Broadacre scheme, citizens of different social classes would rub elbows much more than was usual in the United States, and much more, for that matter, than they would have in Wright's earlier blueprints for planned communities. Aesthetic considerations, not surprisingly, were paramount. Industry was an integral part of Broadacre City, but it had to be light, and clean. Utility wiring was required to be underground. Most important of all for Wright, though, the new city would avoid the bane of centralization.

Wright's individualistic vision has had its detractors, of course. Broadacre paid insufficient attention to mass transit in the eyes of many city planners. But this omission should have surprised no one. Wright strongly believed, after all, that the automobile was "the advance agent of decentralization" (21). Perhaps with the Broadacre vision in mind, it has been asserted that Wright "had great faith in the democracy of the free enterprise system" (22). Such a statement misses the distinctive nature of Wright's political vision.

Wright may have been to some extent the inspiration behind Howard Roark, the architect-protagonist of Ayn Rand's cult classic of the 1940s, *The Fountainhead*. But his individualism bore little resemblance to the novelist's laissez-faire utopia. To be sure, Wright and Rand both harbored an elitist disdain for the mobocracy. Yet the architect countenanced a far greater degree of government intervention in society than Rand. As a young man, Wright listened with rapt attention to the quasi-populist utterances of William Jennings Bryan. Still later, during the Progressive era, Wright befriended Robert LaFollette, the very avatar of progressive reform and the foe of monopoly everywhere. (It should be noted that all natural monopolies in Broadacre City were to be publicly, that is to say, governmentally, owned.) During the 1930s, Wright backed Franklin Roosevelt's semicollectivist New Deal, although he broke with the President over the coming of the war. Wright's sympathy for Roosevelt's domestic aims had many sources. Perhaps the rough similarity of Roosevelt's Greenbelt towns to Broadacre City was one of them. Finally, in sharp contrast to those who worshipped at the shrine of St. Ayn, Wright distrusted the profit motive. So disgusted was he with it, in fact, that he briefly became a Stalinist fellow traveler in the late 1930s.

A profound antiauthoritarian streak remained within him, however. It surfaced in the 1940s with his stout defense of conscientious objection, and it reappeared in the following decade with his fierce denunciation of McCarthyism. In more subtle ways, this facet of Wright was present in his architecture as well. It is instructive that Wright completed only one government building within the United States. That structure, the Marin County Civic Center (1959), just north of San Francisco, Calif., slammed the door on the dome, which Wright regarded as both pretentious and autocratic (Fig. 3). Significantly, those wings at the building devoted to the coercive aspects of government (ie, law enforcement) were eclipsed by those portions of the center that emphasized public service. This was individualism, but with a difference. It certainly had little in common with the individualism of the Randian right.

Figure 3. Marin County Civic Center, California, 1959. Photograph by Stephen A. Kliment. See also color plates.

If not the stereotypical rugged individualist, then was Wright a modernist? He is often lumped with Walter Gropius, Le Corbusier, and Mies van der Rohe as one of the master builders of modern architecture (23). Wright's work appeared alongside that of the above-mentioned architects in the International Style Exhibition at the Museum of Modern Art in 1932. Both Wright and the modernists wanted, and put into place, an architecture expressive of the modern age. Both stressed the interdependence of form and function. Gropius acknowledged Wright's influence on him, but Wright did not return the compliment. (Tom Wolfe provides an amusing sketch of Wright's antipathy towards Gropius in *From Bauhaus to Our House* (24).) However, several of Wright's homes in the Los Angeles area, in particular the 1927 La Miniatura, suggest the influence of cubism, surely an integral component of architectural modernism in the 1920s. Still, we cannot dismiss Wright's own protestations that organic architecture was not coterminous with modern architecture. In his mind, the work of the modernists was cold, sterile, and impersonal. Moreover, they turned their backs on nature, whereas Wright rushed to embrace it. As architects who were more at home in the modern city, they produced buildings with more of an urban cast than did Wright. The latter's Usonian homes, in fact, were conceived as a self-conscious response to Le Corbusier's Citrohans. The circles and hexagons of which Wright became increasingly fond late in life might have been an attempt to escape from what he viewed as the iron cage of modern architecture. Finally, there was little sense of irony in Wright's work. The same cannot be said of the modernists, and especially of their postmodernist successors. Wright admittedly paved the way for modernism in architecture, but he emphatically distanced himself from that movement.

Wright can be criticized on a number of counts. For one, he relished playing the role of the misunderstood and neglected genius even as he was being showered with accolades by his profession. For another, he failed to realize that the decline of the city, which he cheerfully prophesied on a number of occasions, did not necessarily augur well for U.S. civilization. It certainly did not augur well for the more impoverished inhabitants of U.S. urban areas. There were also some tensions in Wright's thinking that were never adequately resolved. Wright always claimed to be speaking for the community as a whole, and yet he consistently, and sometimes brazenly, flaunted his independence of it. More importantly, Wright never squarely faced the question of whether it was possible to have an organic architecture in a society that was itself hardly organic. And finally, Wright never explained just how to arrive at his prized destination, Broadacre City. Wright's blithe indifference to questions of power and politics suggested most Americans would be left behind at the station.

Whether burying him or praising him, it must be conceded that Wright remains a paradoxical figure. A rebel in both his public and private life, Wright still designed many buildings that assumed a woman's place was in the home. Although Wright was an individualist by temperament, the learning environment at his Taliesin North and West was scarcely calculated to foster genuine individual-

Figure 4. Taliesen West. Photograph by Peter H. Bickford. See also color plates.

ity (Fig. 4). For all his love of the land, Wright built only one house for a farmer during his long and productive career. He was a functionalist whose own furniture made him "black and blue." He preached a gospel of organic architecture, and yet his building designs for Baghdad in the late 1950s were remarkably inorganic. He was a critic of what is called "grandomania," although he sometimes displayed that trait himself. He was an arch foe of the skyscraper, but just before his death he began designing a mile-high structure for the state of Illinois. His Usonian homes were meant for people with relatively low incomes, but they sold most frequently to professionals with rather high incomes. He despised conspicuous consumption, but now that he is dead his homes have become status symbols. Last, he wedded an appreciation of new technology with a notion of community that bordered on the nostalgic. The description of Wright as "a nineteenth-century man using twentieth-century methods" was surely on the mark (25).

Frank Lloyd Wright has indubitably left his mark on this age. But it is not merely the mark of an architect. Speaking before an audience in London during the late 1930s, Wright stated that "[e]very great architect is—necessarily—a great poet" (26). Whether or not this is true of every great architect remains a matter of debate. There are few, however, who will not see in that statement an apt description, perhaps the most apt description, of Wright himself.

BIBLIOGRAPHY

1. B. Gill, *Many Masks: A Life of Frank Lloyd Wright*, G. P. Putnam's Sons, New York, 1987, *passim.*

2. *Ibid.,* p. 28.

3. R. M. Crunden, *Ministers of Reform: The Progressives' Achievement in American Civilization*, Basic Books, Inc., New York, 1982, pp. 134–138.

4. F. L. Wright, *The Future of Architecture,* New American Library, New York, 1953, p. 129.

5. *Ibid.,* p. 138.

6. *Ibid.,* p. 131.

7. F. L. Wright, *The Living City,* New American Library, New York, 1958, pp. 251–255.

8. Ref. 4, p. 29.

9. C. Lasch, *Haven in a Heartless World: The Family Besieged,* Basic Books, Inc., New York, 1977.

10. Ref. 4, p. 191.

11. L. Mumford, *The Brown Decades: A Study of the Arts in America, 1865–1895,* Dover Publications, Inc., New York, 1971, p. 76.

12. R. C. Twombly, *Frank Lloyd Wright: His Life and His Architecture,* John Wiley & Sons, Inc., New York, 1979, p. 136.

13. *Ibid.,* p. 384.

14. *Ibid.,* p. 278.

15. M. White and L. White, *The Intellectual Versus the City: From Thomas Jefferson to Frank Lloyd Wright,* Harvard University Press and the MIT Press, Cambridge, Mass., 1962, pp. 4, 189–199.

16. Ref. 12, p. 324.

17. Ref. 4, p. 169.

18. Ref. 4, pp. 170, 180.

19. H. Muschamp, *Man About Town: Frank Lloyd Wright in New York City,* the MIT Press, Cambridge, Mass., 1983, *passim.*

20. V. Scully, Jr., *Frank Lloyd Wright,* George Braziller, Inc., New York, 1985, p. 31.

21. Ref. 4, p. 192.

22. C. Jencks, *Modern Movements in Architecture,* Penguin Books, New York, 1986, pp. 135–136.

23. P. Blake, *The Master Builders: Le Corbusier, Mies van der Rohe, Frank Lloyd Wright,* W. W. Norton & Co., New York, 1976.

24. T. Wolfe, *From Bauhaus to Our House,* Farrar, Straus & Giroux, New York, 1981, pp. 52–53.

25. Ref. 12, p. 414.

26. Ref. 20, p. 11.

General Reference

P. Hanna and J. S. Hanna, *Frank Lloyd Wright's Hanna House, The Client's Report,* Architectural History Foundation, New York, MIT Press, Cambridge, Mass., 1981.

BARRY D. RICCIO
University of Illinois at
Urbana-Champaign
Urbana, Illinois

WRITTEN EXAMINATION PROCESS.   See REGISTRATION EXAMINATION PROCESS—ARCHITECTS

WURSTER, WILLIAM WILSON

Imagine San Francisco without Ghirardelli Square or the Bank of America headquarters. Such are the major imprints that architect William Wilson Wurster left on the Bay Area landscape. Imagine the University of California at Berkeley without the College of Environmental Design. This, too, might have been the case were it not for the influence of educator William Wurster, one of America's most renowned architects.

William Wurster's career spanned half a century, from the mid-1920s until his death in 1973. Born in Stockton, California, in 1895, Wurster graduated with honors in architecture from the University of California in 1919. He began his career working for architects in San Francisco and Sacramento, spent time traveling in Europe and in the Philippines, and then worked for the firm of Delano and Aldrich in 1923–1924. Returning to California, Wurster opened his own architectural office in 1926. For the first several years, his work consisted primarily of small houses, and he was soon doing 50–80 per year.

Among Wurster's most noteworthy projects during this early period was the design of Stern Hall, the first women's dormitory at Berkeley, constructed in 1942 and quite a novelty at the time. Designed in collaboration with Corbett and MacMurray of New York, this building housed 90 women students on four acres of eucalyptus groves overlooking the Berkeley hills in one direction and the Golden Gate in the other. To the architects' credit, they sent a questionnaire to every women's college in the United States, asking about dorm room sizes, study halls, bathroom and laundry facilities, and so on, and incorporated their findings into their scheme. The building was carefully configured to reflect the slope of the hillside site. One of its principal design features was an open-sided stair tower, a detail used in many of Wurster's smaller scale houses. Cantilevered balconies at the end of projecting wings provided a convenient environment for sunbathing. The building elicited praise among the architectural community for breaking with tradition in several ways. Its bold interior color scheme (red, chartreuse, yellow, and a glowing blue) marked a radical departure from the norm (1). Furthermore, it was neither Gothic nor Colonial in style, as had been the trend in the late 1920s when many college campuses were booming. Indeed, it eschewed all conventional stylistic approaches (2).

Among Wurster's other more notable nonresidential projects during this early period was the Yerba Buena Club. This temporary structure housed a Women's Club and the Decorative Arts Exhibit, both part of the 1939 Golden Gate International Exposition on Treasure Island in San Francisco Bay.

Wurster's work in the area of housing won him wide acclaim. As one critic in the *Architect and Engineer* put it back in 1941, "His buildings all have simplicity and restraint which produce an extremely fresh quality. . . . Believing that houses should be merely a backdrop for the life within and the landscape without, rather than a dominant note in themselves, his plans are evolved with a generous open quality which, combined with extensive use of glass areas, creates an enlarged sense of space even in his smaller houses. The interiors repeat again the same qualities" (3).

After 16 years of practice in 1942, having completed the design of 5000 units of war housing, Wurster decided to return to school and enrolled at Harvard to study city planning. His decision to become a student after running a successful practice was considered foolish at the time. Colleagues wondered what planners could possibly have to teach architects. However, Wurster's own experiences made him a strong proponent of adult education, something taken for granted today, as a method of "breaking down the barriers between the professions" (4). In his usual fashion, Wurster kept himself more than busy, enrolling in summer courses at Massachusetts Institute of Technology, and eventually accepting a position as design critic at Yale.

From 1944 to 1950 he served as dean of the School of

Architecture and Planning at MIT, and subsequently from 1950 to 1959 chairman of the Department of Architecture at the University of California, Berkeley. Wurster's influence was profound. Among his major accomplishments was the hiring of nontraditional new faculty members, such as Kevin Lynch at MIT and Garrett Eckbo and Christopher Alexander at Berkeley. Wurster was instrumental in forming a new, multidisciplinary academic community linking sociology and building programming, economics and design, and drawing upon mathematics, aesthetics, science, and ethics (5). His philosophy recognized the interdependence of the design professions and the necessity for architecture to consider the environment as a whole (6). An outgrowth of that philosophy was the establishment of U.C. Berkeley's College of Environmental Design (CED) in 1959, which ultimately linked the disciplines of architecture, landscape architecture, and city planning all under one roof; Wurster served as dean of CED from 1959 to 1963. In the 1960s the College of Environmental Design moved to newly constructed Wurster Hall, a building that symbolizes Wurster's contribution as an educator. It was designed by Vernon DeMars, Joseph Esherick, and Donald Olsen, architects whom Wurster had assembled to teach at Berkeley.

His marriage in 1940 to Catherine Bauer (1905–1964), a noted planner and writer, was long lasting. A graduate of Vassar College, her association with architecture critic Louis Mumford helped steer her toward a career in housing. She was an advocate of human-scale public housing through her writing, lobbying, public administration, and teaching (7). Her book, *Modern Housing,* published in 1934, articulated her views on housing reform (8). She

worked closely with Wurster for many years and served as a professor of city planning at the University of California. She died in 1964 while on a hiking trip in the mountains near San Francisco (9,10,11).

In 1943 he formed a partnership with Theodore Bernardi and Donn Emmons in the firm known as Wurster Bernardi and Emmons. The office was unusual as far as architectural offices go. As Wurster himself put it (3, 12),

> For a time, the office was like a series of small offices, each composed of a junior and senior draftsman. Each team had several jobs. On one job the senior would do the drafting and the junior would write the specifications—then they would reverse. The same was true of supervision. Except for the very first meeting I have always tried to have one of this team, or both, present at every conference with the client. This, I found, saved time and gave a sense of reality to the team. As I have always thought of the office as a training ground, it gave a fine experience to the men when the time came for them to go on their own.

His professional work in the San Francisco Bay area soon grew in size and stature. Although he continued his small-scale residential work, he also received several major commissions. Three San Francisco works stand out in particular: the Golden Gateway Redevelopment project, Ghirardelli Square, and the Bank of America headquarters. Completed in 1967, Golden Gateway is a massive project occupying the site of a former picturesque produce market (Fig. 1). Wurster Bernardi and Emmons, along with DeMars and Reay and consulting architects Anshen and Allen, won the Golden Gateway project through a

Figure 1. Golden Gateway Center, San Francisco, Calif., Wurster, Bernardi and Emmons, Inc., Architects. Photograph by Roger Sturtevant.

Figure 2. Ghirardelli Square, San Francisco, Calif., Wurster, Bernardi and Emmons, Inc., Architects. Photograph by Roger Sturtevant.

major design competition. A mixed-used downtown project, it combined 794 high-rise apartment units, 38 townhouses, and connecting plazas with a lower level of shopping arcades and parking. It is next to Embarcadero Center, another mixed-used facility of offices, shops, restaurants, and a hotel. Although the townhouse design was praised for its detailed street furniture, paving patterns, ground covers, trellises and wood fences, the project as a whole has engendered some criticism for elevating so many uses above the street and for what some view as an imperfect integration with the cityscape (13).

By contrast, a project which has received worldwide accolades is Ghirardelli Square, a complex of nineteenth-century brick warehouses and factories that was transformed into specialty shops and quality restaurants atop a 300-car subterranean parking facility (Fig. 2). Wurster Bernardi and Emmons worked with landscape architect Lawrence Halprin and Associates on this endeavor. Opening in the mid-1960s, this project was a trailblazer for future adaptive use projects around the country, such as Fanueil Hall in Boston and Union Station in St. Louis. Situated on an extremely sloping site with panoramic views of the Golden Gate and San Francisco Bay, Ghirardelli Square can perhaps best be described in the architect's own words (14):

> A series of levels and spaces, the plaza draws visitors into its center through two main entrances and allows them to radiate outward via walkways, ramps, stairs, decks, and balconies to mezzanines and upper building levels. The plaza has a fountain, trees, tubs of flowers, benches, table umbrellas, etc. The new buildings continue the spirit of the old with bay windows, domes, clerestories and lights, all specially designed. Signing, regarded as a key to the character of the square—induced in part by the huge old sign that identified the factories for many years—was also custom-designed and fabricated for particular functions. Lights like those of the retained factory sign outline the old buildings and a landmark tower.

Recipient of a 1966 honor award from the American Institute of Architects, Ghirardelli Square won praise from the awards jury (14):

> A highly successful urban development employing old buildings and open spaces for new uses. Its qualities of gaiety, liveliness and color make it a delightful addition to the San Francisco scene. . . . New and old features are happily blended. The view over the bay is preserved and enhanced; parking is inconspicuous and accessible. In terms of esthetics, economics, convenience, and cheerful vitality, Ghirardelli Square shows what can be done by careful rehabilitation of significant older buildings in the center of the city.

Even today, Ghirardelli Square is undoubtedly one of America's most successful urban open spaces, not only meeting but exceeding the criteria spelled out by William Whyte in his well-known study of successful plazas and streetscapes (15).

Perhaps the most visible of Wurster's work is the world headquarters for the Bank of America (Fig. 3). At 52 stories and 770 ft high, this building was the tallest in the American West when it opened in 1969 at a cost of $85 million, and it remains San Francisco's tallest skyscraper. A separate two-story glass pavilion sits on a corner of the site, housing the bank's main office building. Underneath is a concourse with shops, a 200-seat amphitheater, restaurant, and parking for 400 cars. A restaurant with a panoramic view crowns the top of the skyscraper. Wurster Bernardi and Emmons and Skidmore Owings and Merrill, with Pietro Belluschi as consultant, were the architects. Once again Lawrence Halprin and Associates were the landscape architects. Among the key decisions by the architects were that (1) the building should be dark in color (dark red granite, with a polished, highly reflective surface and bronze tinted glass), and (2) it should not be an austere, rectangular box. Both decisions have been subject

Figure 3. Bank of America World Headquarters, San Francisco, Calif., Wurster, Bernardi and Emmons, Inc., Architects. Photograph by Ezra Stoller.

the "Manhattanization" of San Francisco. To combat the boxlike image, the building uses bay windows throughout, a strong element in the San Francisco vernacular, which affords greater views, light, and floorspace. One might argue whether or not the bay window reproduced at this large a scale is even perceivable to the average pedestrian on the street. Nonetheless, the building was praised for its fine craftsmanship, precision, and attention to detail, features rarely seen in office buildings of the day (16).

Wurster designed many more works that can be described here, but among the more impressive commissions were the Center for Advanced Studies in the Behavioral Sciences (1955) and the Medical Plaza (1959) at Stanford University; Strawberry Canyon Recreation Center on the Berkeley campus (1959) (Fig. 4); and the U.S. Consulate Office Building in Hong Kong (1959). He also wrote numerous scholarly articles and professional publications (17). Among Wurster's many distinctions were his memberships on the National Capitol Park and Planning Commission in Washington (1949–1950); the Architectural Advisory Panel of the State Department's Foreign Building Office (1958–1963); and the State of California's Capitol Building and Planning Commission (1959–1967). He was also a fellow of the American Institute of Architects, the American Academy of Arts and Science, Boston; the Royal Academy of Fine Arts, Copenhagen; and the National Academy of Design. In 1969, he received a gold medal from the American Institute of Architects in recognition of his distinguished service to the architectural profession. As the journalists commented (6),

> Mr. Wurster's selection for the 1969 Gold Medal recognizes a unique contribution in the development of an American architecture. His early independence of other styles and forms, his nondogmatic approach to design, his simplicity and directness were a break with the past which, when it happened in the late 1920s, was quickly recognized as long overdue. In breaking with the past, Wurster found more basic sources of architectural design—the people and their ways of living and the land with its particular characteristics. But this regional approach, unlike other regional architectures, produced no style, no personalized forms. It offered principles, broad in concept, universal in application—principles that have had great influence on architects.

to criticism. The dark color was justified as a way of diminishing the building's scale when seen from a distance. It also allowed walls rather than windows to be the strong pattern-making element. However, the building's dark color is incompatible with the light, pastel colored cityscape which surrounds it, and its sheer massiveness and height continue to evoke strong controversy and fears of

Figure 4. Strawberry Canyon Recreation Center on the Campus of UC Berkeley, Wurster, Bernardi and Emmons, Inc., Architects. Photograph by Ernest Braun.

BIBLIOGRAPHY

1. S. Carrighar, "A Woman's Impression of the New Girls' Dormitory at Berkeley," *Architect and Engineer* **151**, 12–21, 31 (Dec. 1942).

2. "William Wurster Portfolio," *Architectural Forum* **79**, 45 (July 1943).

3. J. L. Johnson, "Work of W. W. Wurster and His Office," *Architect and Engineer* **144**, 16 (Mar. 1941).

4. "Wurster to be Gold Medalist," *Progressive Architecture,* **50**, 27 (Feb. 1969).

5. R. Montgomery, "William Wurster—Environmentalist," *Progressive Architecture* **55**, 26 (Feb. 1974).

6. "William Wurster to Receive AIA 1969 Gold Medal," *Architectural Record* **145**, 36 (Feb. 1969).

7. C. K. Bauer, "The Dreary Deadlock of Public Housing," *Architectural Forum* **106**(5), 140 (1957).

8. C. K. Bauer, *Modern Housing,* Houghton–Mifflin, Boston, 1934.

9. S. Cole, "Catherine Krouse Bauer," in B. Sicherman, ed., *Notable American Women: The Modern Period,* Belknap, Cambridge, Mass., 1980.

10. "Woman Hiker Dead: Aided Three Presidents on City Planning," *New York Times* 40 (Nov. 24, 1964).

11. E. L. Birch, "Bauer, Catherine K.," in Adolf K. Placzek, ed., *Macmillan Encyclopedia of Architects,* vol. 1, Free Press, New York, 1982, p. 154.

12. Ref. 2, p. 46.

13. Moore, Charles W. "In San Francisco, a Renewal Effort Based on Civic Pride Falls Short of Expectation." *Architectural Forum* **123**, 58 (July–Aug. 1965).

14. "1966 AIA Honor Awards: Ghirardelli Square, San Francisco." *AIA Journal* **46**, 46 (July 1966).

15. Whyte, William H. *The Social Life of Small Urban Spaces,* Washington, D.C.: Conservation Foundation, 1980.

16. "The Sculptural Expression of Tradition in San Francisco (Bank of America World Headquarters)." *Architectural Record* **148**, 126 (July 1970).

17. "Architectural Versatility in the Work of William Wilson Wurster: A Selected Bibliography." Architecture Series: Bibliography: A-1159. Monticello, Ill.: Vance Bibliographies, 1984.

General References

E. L. Birch, "Wurster, William Wilson," in Adolf K. Placzek, ed., *Macmillan Encyclopedia of Architects,* vol. 4, Free Press, New York, 1982, pp. 450–451.

W. W. Wurster, "College of Environmental Design, University of California, Campus Planning, and Architectural Practice," an interview conducted by S. B. Riess, Regional Oral History Office, The Bancroft Library, University of California, Berkeley, Calif., 1964.

See also Adaptive Use; Urban Design—Architecture at Urban Scale; Urban Design—Creation of Livable Cities

Kathryn H. Anthony
University of Illinois
Champaign, Illinois

Y

YAMASAKI, MINORU

Minoru Yamasaki (1912–1986) was a U.S.-born architect of Japanese descent. His unique interpretation and expression of architectural form during the era of modernism in the United States establish his place in U.S. architecture. Like his contemporary, Edward Durell Stone, Yamasaki sought to bring to the modern movement elements of historicism and a human scale. His work was considered controversial by those who found it decorative, ornamental, and self-indulgent. Yamasaki strived to create environments that could provide historical perspective and meaning.

His most successful device for accomplishing relevance in his work was to develop historical allusion through the use of ornamentation. Yamasaki pursued this ideal in a time when structural purity and the tenets of the international style were adhered to by most of his colleagues. A characteristic feature of Yamasaki's work is the fragmentation of the wall into an apparent fabriclike screen, which conceals the structural members. Umbrella walls, metal grilles, and axial plans with gardens and pools contribute to the impression of historically contrived elegance that was typical of Yamasaki's later designs. Much of Yamasaki's work was greatly influenced by international travel in his early career and direct confrontation with historically significant sites and buildings. References to the Gothic style are prevalent in his work, and he used it to express his respect for history and tradition, human scale, and machine technology. Yamasaki was concerned with humanity's place within architecture, an idea ignored by many of his contemporaries. He deplored architecture that regarded occupants as an extension of the machine.

Yamasaki admired the work of Mies van der Rohe, most particularly the Seagrams Building in New York, stating that "Mies showed us that machine-made buildings can be as beautiful as the hand-made buildings of the past." What he disliked was the repeated unconscious replication of the Miesian style by his contemporaries.

Born the son of poor Japanese immigrant parents in Seattle, Wash., Yamasaki's early life was much like that of other Japanese boys in his neighborhood. His time was divided between school and working at various jobs to help support his family.

While still in his early teens he determined that architecture was to be his ultimate career goal. This decision was greatly influenced by a visit from an architect uncle from Japan. The architectural drawings shown to him by his uncle made a great and lasting impression on Yamasaki, and he resolved that he too would become an architect. After successfully completing high school, Yamasaki enrolled in the architecture program at the University of Washington, Seattle. To pay for his education, he worked five grueling summers in Alaskan fish canneries for $50 per month. In 1934, Yamasaki graduated with honors.

Yamasaki traveled to New York City to enroll at New York University and find employment in one of the famous architectural firms. The Great Depression had a strong economic hold on the country, and it was difficult to find work. Yamasaki worked at various jobs, even resorting to work as a dish wrapper for a Japanese import firm. He finally found employment in the drafting rooms of a number of successful large offices: Shreve, Lamb, and Harmon (architects of the Empire State Building, New York, 1932), Harrison and Abramovitz (architects of Rockefeller Center, New York, 1930), and Raymond Loewy Associates. He gained considerable technical ability and skill and ultimately became Chief Draftsman of 100 people.

During his 10 years in New York, Yamasaki grew considerably as a designer. It was during this time that he met and married his wife, who was studying piano in New York.

In 1945, Yamasaki accepted the position of Chief Designer with the office of Smith, Hinchman and Grylls in Detroit, Michigan, assuming responsibility for a staff of 600 draftspersons.

While there, he met Eero Saarinen. Smith, Hinchman and Grylls and Saarinen's firm were collaborating on the General Motors Technical Center project. He was most impressed with the energy and intensity that Saarinen brought to his work.

In 1951, Yamasaki made his architectural debut. Along with two former colleagues, George Hellmuth and Joseph Leinweber from Smith, Hinchman and Grylls, he accepted an independent commission to design the Lambert-St. Louis air terminal. The design proposal sought to create a significant gateway to the city. It set a new precedent for the design of airport terminals. The vaulted thin-shell construction technique allowed for column-free interior spaces with ready adaptability for expansion. It is of interest to note that Eero Saarinen's work on the Kresge Auditorium at the Massachusetts Institute of Technology, Cambridge (1953) was accomplished at the same time. It is possible that both schemes were inspired by the styling studio display showroom at the General Motors Technical Center.

In 1954, Yamasaki suffered a near fatal ulcer attack, which he attributed to his rapid work pace. Perhaps his personal drive was fueled by a sense of ethnic inferiority. After recovering, he became involved with a project to design the U.S. Consulate complex in Kobe, Japan. Yamasaki traveled to Japan, leaving the United States for the first time.

He continued around the world on his return trip, making stops in India, the Middle East, and Europe. The impressions made upon him during this trip were profound and affected his design philosophy during the rest of his long career.

In 1955, Hellmuth withdrew from the partnership and

Figure 1. McGregor Memorial Conference Center, Wayne State University, Detroit, Michigan, 1955. Courtesy of the author.

the firm continued as Yamasaki, Leinweber and Associates. During this time, Yamasaki took on his first design project since returning from his extensive trip around the world.

The McGregor Memorial Conference Center, Wayne State University, Detroit (Fig. 1), reflects the concept of the building as a gateway (similar to the Lambert-Saint Louis airport terminal), and connecting point, between the university and the community. Yamasaki demonstrated in this building a developing philosophy that moved close in spirit to that of European Gothic. Although the landscaping and site planning have clear Oriental overtones, the pointed arch configuration of the building structure became Yamasaki's most consistent and powerful design theme. He used this structural theme to achieve a visual effect that went beyond the structure itself.

1956 marked the completion of the Pruitt-Igoe housing project in St. Louis, Missouri. This large-scale award-winning project was built by the St. Louis Housing Authority using local and federal funding. Successive and extensive budget cuts eventually produced a bare-bones facility that was occupied by a segment of the local population for which the original project was not designed. By 1974, vandalism had made the buildings virtually uninhabitable. The project was closed and demolished later that same year. Pruitt-Igoe's destruction was perhaps the greatest disappointment in Yamasaki's career and stands as a milestone in recent architectural history. Many consider its destruction the end of the modern movement.

Yamasaki designed the Reynolds Metal Building in Detroit in 1959. The building was compared to Stone's

U.S. Embassy in New Delhi, India, which Yamasaki had visited.

Much of Yamasaki's work was accomplished in the 1960s, including the U.S. Science Pavilion for the Seattle World's Fair of 1962, the Civil Air Terminal in Dhahran, Saudi Arabia, the North Western National Life Insurance Company building in Minneapolis, Minnesota, and the Sanctuary of the Synagogue at Glenore, Illinois.

The Michigan Consolidated Gas Company in Detroit and the IBM Office Building in Seattle were proving grounds for Yamasaki's commission to design the two 110-floor towers for the World Trade Center in New York. The design of a structural system for such a large-scale building was a large obstacle to overcome. The solution was surprisingly simple and had already been tested on the IBM Office Building in Seattle. The 208-ft wide facade developed for the twin towers became a unified steel lattice with vertical columns 39 in. on center, providing lateral resistance to wind loads, etc. This left the interior office space column-free. The floor trusses, which were 33 in. in depth, transferred the interior floor load 60 ft to the building core and outside wall.

The problem of vertical circulation was solved by using a combination of express and local elevator banks. This system required fewer elevators, reducing the demand for circulation space and allowing 75% of the total floor space to be used for occupancy.

Yamasaki was a very productive and innovative architect. He challenged the international style and, for many of his contemporaries, provoked controversy over his individualistic but consistent approach to design. It is likely that he will be best remembered for his design for the World Trade Center and for his sincere belief in an architecture that is responsive to technology and yet still acknowledges the condition of humanity.

BIBLIOGRAPHY

General References

P. Heyer, *Architects on Architecture,* Walker and Co., New York, 1966.

CLARK LUNDELL, AIA
Auburn University
Auburn, Alabama

Z

ZERO LOT LINE DEVELOPMENT. See CLUSTER
DEVELOPMENT AND LAND SUBDIVISION

ZOOS

A zoo, or zoological garden, is a place where wild and sometimes domesticated animals are exhibited and studied in captivity. Generally, zoos exhibit only three classes of the vertebrate phylum: Aves, Mammalia, and Reptilia. Aquariums concentrate on marine vertebrates and also invertebrates. Insectariums exhibit another phylum, the arthropods. New trends to present more complete exhibits of ecosystems, the biotic and abiotic components, are also beginning to include the other four kingdoms: Prokaryotae, Protista, and Fungi.

Architectural design in the zoo can be described by four basic issues. From the broad to the specific, these are the history of the zoo, the modern zoo, exhibit design, and the exhibit animal.

The history of the zoo reflects the history of humanity's changing attitude towards the environment. Two forms of animal collections can be described: the menagerie (2500 BC–1828 AD) and the zoological garden (1828–present). The distinction is one of intent. A zoo is established for scientific and educational purposes, and a menagerie is not. The menagerie evolved in three stages: the ancient collections for pleasure, worship, and domestication; the medieval collections for study and as symbols of power; and the Renaissance and Baroque collections for pleasure and study, which were marked by an aggressive rationalism in their organization. From these early beginnings, the zoo has developed in two stages: the early or transitional zoo at the turn of the century and the modern zoo, the contemporary result of scientific and technological advances.

The second basic issue in architectural design of the zoo is the form and philosophy of the modern zoo, its purposes, its types, and its design concerns. Inside the zoo is the third basic issue, exhibit design. This consists of restraint techniques and materials; the programmatic needs of the animal, the keeper, and the visitor; and conceptual ideas in design. Inside the exhibit, the fourth issue in architectural design is the captive animal-client. The specific needs of each animal are assessed by the zoo biologist or curator. However, for the architect or designer, a general understanding of the animals' spatial, physical, and behavioral needs is critical.

THE HISTORY OF THE ZOO

The Ancient Menageries

The cave paintings in Lascaux of 10,000–15,000 years ago represent one of humanity's first attempts to capture wild animals. This pictorial collection of red deer, wooly rhinos, wild horses, and bison, beautifully and accurately portrayed, was part of a magical bond between the hunter and the hunted. Although this was not a menagerie in the physical sense, it was an attempt by primitive humanity to collect and manipulate the unpredictable forces of nature, to possess and control some power of the animals in the world.

Gradually, as humanity settled, some animals became domesticated, for example, the sheep 8000 years ago and the dog 6000 years ago. In India, the elephant was domesticated 2500 years ago. At this time also, Queen Hatshepsut of the 18th Dynasty in Egypt maintained a "garden of acclimation" in hopes of domesticating other animals, like the oryx, the addax, and the cheetah. Descriptions of the physical nature of this and other early collections are scarce, but recent archaeological evidence from Mesopotamia suggests that large predators were kept in pits, more gentle animals in fenced paddocks, small mammals and birds in bar cages, and fish and waterfowl in large basins or ponds. It seems reasonable to assume that this was true for menageries all over the ancient world.

Important collections, however, were not always for domestication. The Ling-lu or "garden of intelligence" in the Honan province of China was started in about 1100 BC by Emperor Wen Wang of the Chou Dynasty, who is said to be the author of *I Ching*. This garden was approximately 1500 acres (600 hectares) and contained mammals, birds, and fishes. It survived for several hundred years as a collection for pleasure and meditation.

Wild animals throughout history have not only been domesticated and studied, but also worshipped. Animal cults, and the assignment of symbolic and mythological powers to various animals, were common in all ancient societies. Because of this religious significance and the great cost of collecting and maintaining wild animals, ancient menageries were restricted to possession by the royalty. The Akkadians, Sumerians, Assyrians, Babylonians, and Persians all had considerable animal collections. It was not until the *paradeisos* of the Greek city-states between the sixth and fourth centuries BC that wild animals were exhibited strictly for the public. These walled gardens of wild animals were collections for public pleasure and stock for homage and gifts. Aristotle (384–322 BC) wrote his *History of Animals* listing 300 species, based on these collections as well as on the animals sent to him by Alexander the Great from his travels and conquests. Aristotle's idea of the "Scala Naturae," and "great chain of beings," was to dominate humanity's attitude towards animals for the next 2000 years. This chain was a hierarchy of life forms from the simplest and most humble to the complex and most important, culminating in humanity.

In the Roman era, animals were considered primarily for their usefulness or their entertainment value. Wild animals were collected mostly for the arena (Fig. 1). The

Figure 1. Colosseum, Rome, 80 A.D., detail showing underground cages for arena animals. Mechanical elevators brought the animals up to the arena (1).

gladitorial games involved thousands of wild animals and men, for which there is ample documentation. For example, the Emperor Trajan, in celebrating the Dacian victory in 106 AD, "used up" 11,000 wild beasts and 10,000 men in the games. Yet there were also individuals at this time who were scientifically interested in wild animals, notably Pliny the Elder (23–79 AD), who wrote 37 volumes on natural history. Wild, unusual, and fictitious animals were a large part of contemporary mythology, and it is interesting to note that Pliny believed in the cyclops and was certain they lived in the middle of the earth, somewhere under Italy or Sicily. Another notable Roman, Marcus Terentuis Varro, also had scientific interests and kept a large aviary near Monte Cassino, in about 120 AD. He, like his friend Lucius Lucullus, kept exotic birds for pleasure and for food. Both men had their dining rooms in their aviaries (Fig. 2).

The Medieval Menageries

In the medieval age, humanity's attitude towards animals returned to one of rampant symbolism and superstition, like that of primitive humans. The collections of animals in the bestiaries were part fact and part fantasy. The bestiaries were books based on ancient Greek and Roman texts that described and illustrated numerous animals (real and imagined) as examples of Christian beliefs. These books were plentiful and popular. However, as they were copied over the centuries, the information became less and less accurate.

In general, the feudal system of the Middle Ages limited commerce, trade, and travel. Although there were some traveling fairs and menageries, these consisted of few animals, mostly bears and game birds. Exotic animals were difficult to collect, transport, and maintain, and as in the ancient menageries, the possession of several wild and ferocious animals was a symbol of great power. Charlemagne (742–814) was able to establish three large menag-

Figure 2. Aviary of Marcus Varro, Monte Cassino, 120 A.D. An interpretation by Pierro Ligorio, of the dining room and aviary (2).

eries. The Great Caliph of Bhagdad, of *One Thousand and One Nights* fame, gave him the only elephant seen in Europe since the Roman Empire.

It was with the impetus of Charlemagne's monastic reforms that the Saint Gall Benedictine monastery in Switzerland produced one of the most remarkable cellular organizations for the housing of wild animals. Charlemagne had ordered the bishops and abbots of his realm to establish animal parks on monastery lands. At Saint Gall in 819, animal barns and pens were laid out in consistent orthogonal modules based on Christian symbolism and ratios. This animal collection was quite large and included bears, deer, pheasants, and marmots, among others. Most monastic menageries of this period were smaller, consisting only of indigenous species. The more common monastic menageries later became the models for many royal hunting parks.

The menageries of unusual and exotic animals still remained primarily possessions of the royalty. Henry I in the UK (1110–1135) had a menagerie at Woodstock, which was eventually moved to the Tower of London, where it remained until the opening of the London Zoo in 1828. In France, Phillip IV had a menagerie in the Louvre in Paris. Probably the most incredible menagerie ever amassed was that of Kublai Khan, described by Marco Polo in 1320. This collection at Kambaluk (present-day

Beijing) was so immense that it required 10,000 keepers to maintain it. Large collections of exotic animals remained a prerogative of the royal and the wealthy for the next five centuries, but changes in commerce and travel increased the variety of menagerie denizens.

The Menageries of the Renaissance and the Baroque

With the development of the lateen rig, the sternpost rudder, and the compass in the fifteenth century, transoceanic voyage was made possible in all weather and year round. This was especially important after the fall of Constantinople in 1453, which made overland trade with the Far East more difficult. The result was the beginning of world exploration. In 1519, Hernando Cortés landed in Mexico and discovered Montezuma's menageries, one at Tenochtitlan and another at the scientific center of the Aztec empire, Tezcuco. These incredible collections contained thousands of animals as well as unusual people—hunchbacks, dwarfs, bearded ladies, albinos, and others (this, though, is not the first instance of a human menagerie. The Medici Cardinal, Hippolyte, was one among others to have such a collection). The Aztec menageries were set in groves of ancient trees, with pens made of bronze bars for wild animals and several large, sunken basins for fish, reptiles, and poisonous snakes, in addition to numerous ponds for waterfowl. During the Spanish siege of 1521 at Tenochtitlan, Montezuma's menagerie was butchered and eaten by the 300,000 starving people of the city. The buildings were demolished soon after by the conquering Spanish soldiers.

The exploration and exploitation of the New World brought a variety of wealth to the European continent and with it a stimulus for new ideas. The Renaissance shifted attention from the heavenly to the humanly. The attitude towards animals and nature changed from medieval mysticism and apprehension to rationalism and domination. Humanity became the center of the universe and imposed its intellectual will upon the world. This was expressed in urban and landscape designs as symmetry and geometric order. The Neugebaude menagerie of Emperor Maximi-

lian II in 1569 is an example of this metric style of the humanity-over-nature order (Fig. 3). The menagerie was erected next to the old imperial hunting lodge at Ebersdorf near Vienna and was called Das Neugebaude (the new building). It is now part of the Vienna central cemetery. The original menagerie was a square garden marked by four large towers at the corners. In 1587, Emperor Rudolf II employed the architect Ferrabosco, who added an outer wall, punctuated by 10 little towers. Later, partisans of the Hungarian Revolution destroyed parts of Das Neugebaude and strangled some of the animals. Emperor Karl V then renewed the menagerie collection and had it moved to Schönbrunn. This application of an orthogonal grid on the landscape and vertical stakes of towers, where presumably one could look down on the ravenous animals, reflects the ideologies of the Renaissance. Humanity controls nature and by rational powers has dominion over the earth.

The spirit of the Renaissance evolved and found exuberant expression in the Baroque era. Rene Descartes (1596–1650) proposed a mathematical philosophy that required the imposition of systematic intellect upon the disorder of nature. This idea inspired much of the period's grand designs. The monumental incarnation of this belief was the park at Versailles, designed by André Le Nôtre from 1661 to 1668. Louis XIV kept animals there for decoration and bred them for the hunt in the Menagerie du Parc (Fig. 4). This menagerie was located to the northwest of the Grand Canal and was approached by waterways. The animals were kept in paddocks that radiated from a large central pavilion. This was the first time animals had been arranged and integrated with rare flora; previously, the animals had been scattered throughout parks or paddocks. Originally, the public was allowed to see the animals, but too much damage ensued, and afterwards only members of the court were permitted.

Versailles was the expression of the Baroque in France. In Vienna, the menagerie at the Belvedere Palace shows the same stylistic gesture of radiating views out into the landscape (Fig. 5). This menagerie was begun by the Bavarian garden engineer Girad in 1700. Prince Eugene of

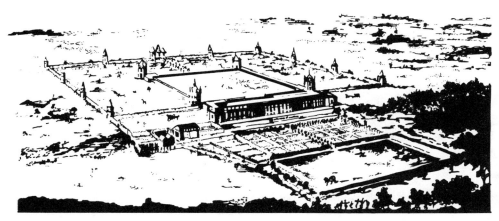

Figure 3. The Neugebaude Menagerie, Austria, 1587. Perspective view (3). Courtesy of Rheinisches Landesmuseum, Bonn.

Figure 4. Versailles, Menagerie du Parc, 1668. Perspective view (2).

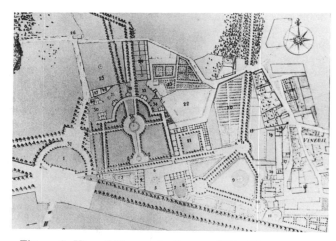

Figure 6. Vinueil Menagerie, France, 1700s. Plan view (2).

Savoie housed his animals there after designs by Lukas von Hildebrandt. The wedge-shaped paddocks extended from a fountain at one end of the palace. Each sector was separated by walls, with housing for the animals located at the back. The gardens of the paddocks were rigidly designed with lawns and pools of various shapes. The fronts of the enclosures were framed by statuaries and elaborate grillwork.

In contrast to these menageries dominated by a single design idea, ie, the radiating plan, the menagerie of the Prince of Conde at Vineuil had a variety of elements that were developed over time (Fig. 6). This collection of the early eighteenth century consisted of many parts, which in their site organization resemble the plan of Hadrian's villa near Tivoli in the second century BC. Views of the Vineuil menagerie, its grottos, statues, and animal enclosures, were printed on a French card game and show the marvelous variety of garden spaces constructed there.

Garden designs of this period were reflections of various cultural attitudes. In the UK, Lancelot Brown was

developing the romantic school of landscape design with his work at Blenheim Palace in 1758. Indigenous animals were free to roam the grounds in bucolic serenity and were kept out of the formal gardens by the "ha-ha," or sunken fence. In Austria, Emperor Franz I developed Schönbrunn near Vienna as an animal garden for his wife, Marie Theresa.

Schönbrunn had been the private deer preserve of the Hapsburgs. The plan of the menagerie (Fig. 7) was a sophisticated version of the Baroque radial plan seen at Versailles and Belvedere Palace and is remarkably similar to the plan of the hunting lodge at Karlsruhe of 1715. The Schönbrunn paddocks are inscribed in a circle. Originally enclosed by a wall, the animals could be seen only from the center (in 1884, Emperor Franz Josef had the surrounding wall removed). The pavilion was added seven years after the plan had been established. The walls of the hexagonal pavilion were covered with orange plaster and

Figure 5. Belvedere Palace Menagerie, Austria, 1700. Perspective view (2).

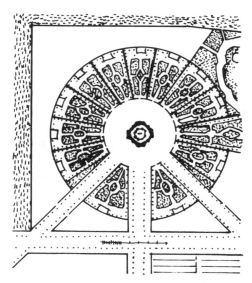

Figure 7. Schonbrunn Menagerie, Austria, 1752. Plan view (4).

set upon an elevated terrace lawn surrounded by a circular gravel walk. The Empress would have breakfast there and look out into the paddocks. Once again, the Renaissance and Baroque notions of humanity as the center of the universe were made incarnate, and the animal world was gathered around its feet.

Interestingly, in 1772, Empress Maria Theresa sponsored important innovations in prison design, with the construction of the Maison de Force at Ackerghem, near Ghent. This house of correction, designed by Malfaison and S. J. Kluchman, featured more humane treatment and housing of prisoners. The plan was based on the same principles as the menagerie—the central court was for the guards, and the radiating paddocks were separated by the walls of cell blocks and thus segregated into courts for women criminals, vagrants, men criminals, etc. The concerns of housing captive criminals and captive animals are in many ways analogous, but aside from this comparison, the menagerie at Schönbrunn, opened to the public in 1765, is important today as the oldest continuous animal collection.

These menageries of the seventeenth and eighteenth centuries provided wonderful opportunities for scientific investigation. In Sweden, Carolus Linnaeus (1707–1778) had access to the Royal Menagerie. This was a time when the explorers of Africa and the New World were constantly returning with previously unknown species of animals and plants, and it was in this stimulating environment that Linnaeus devised our present system of nomenclature for biological species. This was also the time of people like Georges-Louis Leclerc Bufon (1701–1788), who germinated the idea for the theory of evolution. Humanity's attitude towards animals was beginning to change from Aristotle's "Scala Naturae" and the belief in a specific and divine creation of all things to an understanding of the common process of adaptation for all life

forms. On the broader societal level, attitudes were also changing. The plight of the working class in the polluted industrialized cities created a new demand for parkland and recreation, and everywhere it was a time of significant political upheaval.

After the French Revolution in 1789, the animals in the King's menagerie at Versailles were either butchered or moved to the public Jardin des Plantes in Paris. This botanical collection had been set up in 1662 by Louis III in order to systematically study the plant life indigenous to Europe as well as specimens brought back from world explorations. This taxonomic approach was then also applied to the animal collection. Although the plan of the animal collection was laid out in a more natural arrangement than the original formal gardens (Fig. 8), the organization of the animals was into categories, with areas for reptiles, birds, and mammals. With the establishment of the animal collection at the Jardin des Plantes, the stage was set for the first zoo.

The Transitional Zoo

The last 200 years have seen a change from the prevalence of monarchical governments to parliamentary governments. Consequently, (royal) private animal collections have largely given way to public collections. New ideas and scientific concerns have also altered the forms and roles of zoological collections. Probably the most outstanding influence was Charles Darwin's publication of the Origin of Species in 1859. This work eventually shifted scientific emphasis from the static nature of categorization and taxonomy to the dynamic concept of evolution and the changing influences of the environment. Subsequently, the form of the early zoo changed from the "postage stamp" exhibits (one or two of every kind) to the modern zoo, with thematic exhibits of habitats, behavioral or morphological adaptations, etc. There has also been a

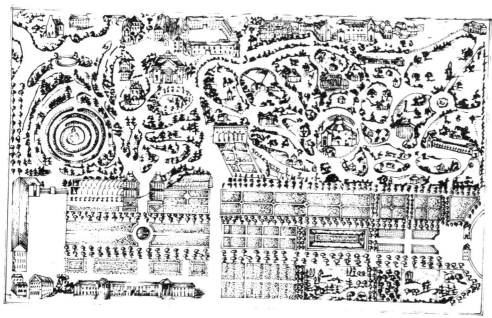

Figure 8. Jardin des Plantes, Paris, 1780s. Plan view (5). Courtesy of Bibliotheque Centrale, Paris.

change in the purpose of animal collections. What had been menageries are now zoos. Purpose is the essential difference between a menagerie and a zoo: a zoo has an educational objective, and a menagerie does not. Today's zoo evolved from the early menageries and in fact is a recent development. The Jardin des Plantes had a pivotal role in this evolution. There had been other collections in history that were established for scientific or educational reasons, but these were the exception. At the Jardin des Plantes, the directors did not originally have a scientific interest in the animals. They were forced to house the animals that had been confiscated from aristocratic and traveling menageries. This was in conflict with their botanical interests and their finances, and it was some time before they adjusted to their new roles.

The first animal collection begun especially for educational purposes was founded with the enthusiasm of Sir Thomas Stamford Raffles and the London Zoological Society in 1828, setting aside 36 acres (14 hectares) in Regent's park for the London Zoo. Raffles was a statesman and a zoologist, perhaps known best for founding the colony of Singapore. He died before he could see his dream realized, but the London Zoological Garden rapidly became popular. Actually the word "zoo," abbreviated from "zoological garden," was not coined until 40 years later, in a dance hall song about the London Zoo written by Hugh Willoughby Sweny: "The OK thing to do, on a Sunday afternoon, is to toddle in the zoo."

The directive in the London Society Charter was for the "advancement of zoological and animal physiology and the introduction of new and curious subjects of the animal kingdom." Even the London Zoo had remnants of the menagerie form, and in fact exhibited the hippopotamus Obayasch with its Arab keeper in 1851.

However, the London Zoological Society was responsible for a number of important contributions. It hired a full-time architect, Decidimus Burton, and in 1849 constructed the first reptile house. This was a wooden structure that had skylights made up of small panes of glass set in frames between the rafters. After the development of the cast iron process in 1865, the improvement of the cast plate process for glass, and the innovative design of the Crystal Palace for the Great Exposition of 1851 in London's Hyde Park, construction materials and techniques changed. The new Reptile House in 1899 was larger, with an iron structure and two strips of continuous skylights in the central hall.

Other new buildings included the first aquarium in 1853 and the first insectarium in 1889. At the London Zoo, as at the other early zoos, the particular needs of the animals were not yet well understood. Concern for appearance guided architectural designs and usually followed contemporary fashion (particularly neoclassical) or the exotic vernacular of the animal's home country.

The London Zoo today is one of the most respected zoological institutions in the world. It has several outstanding achievements in zoo biology, research, and publications as well as several well-known buildings. Among these structures are the Penguin Pool and the Gorilla House by Tecton (completed in 1933), the Snowdon Aviary designed by Lord Snowdon, Cedric Price, and Frank

Newby in 1965, and the Elephant and Rhino Pavilion designed by Casson, Conder and Partners in 1965.

Another important early zoo was the Berlin Zoo, established in 1844. By 1869, at an incredible pace, several buildings had been constructed: the elephant house, the lion house, the antelope house, a deer house, a monkey house, aviaries, three restaurants, a pump house, refrigeration units, and a viewing tower. Possibly the most well-known building was the Hindu elephant house designed by Ende and Brockman. The exterior was brightly colored with yellow, blue, and brown tiles on the domes. The interior was elaborately decorated. Unfortunately, the zoo was heavily damaged during the bombing of World War II, and this building was destroyed. The elephant house, like the other buildings, reflected the power and grandeur of imperial Germany. The buildings were exquisite reproductions of various exotic styles, meant to suggest the architecture of foreign lands.

The image of any public building constructed at this time was vitally important. The École des Beaux Arts tradition strongly influenced the design approach everywhere. In light of this stylistic pressure, a wonderful project was designed in 1908 by Gustave Loisel, the author of Ref. 2, and V. Desire Bessin. This project was a building for carnivores that combined a classical facade and plan organization with a mountainous hill and running stream (Figs. 9 and 10). This building was to be placed on a northeast–southwest axis. Along the sides of the building (the hill), visitors could look across the running water and see lions, tigers, and other large cats. The transverse section was developed to allow the animals to move in and out of the building over a keeper's corridor. There were small cages in these corridors for raising live food for the carni-

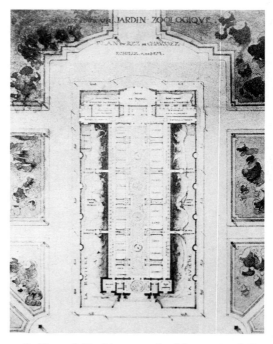

Figure 9. Plan of "Architecture des Menageries Colline pour Logement de Carnivores" (2).

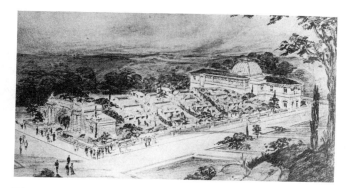

Figure 10. Cut-away perspective of "Architecture des Menageries Colline pour Logement de Carnivores" (2).

Figure 11. Stellingen Zoo, Germany, 1910. View of gate (6).

vores. The ingenuity of the section, the clarity of the plan, and the richness of the outdoor exhibit, with the hillside and stream, made this project unique. It was, however, only a project; the first moated enclosures built were those at the Stellingen Zoo near Hamburg.

The zoos built in this early stage were built in a period when public recreation was an important issue. In the past, insane asylums had been public places where for a small price (as with their contemporary menageries) people could go in and watch the inmates. At about the time of the establishment of animals at the Jardin des Plantes, madhouse reforms stopped this practice, but the need for public recreation remained. The polluted, congested cities created a demand for the natural greenery of parks. Even cemeteries were used like parks for family gatherings and outings. The early zoological garden easily filled these needs for nature and recreation. In the United States, zoos were begun later than in Europe and were first established in the era of P. T. Barnum. This created competition for the interest and revenue of the public and somewhat diluted their scientific objectives, but resulted in some picturesque zoos.

It was this variety of social pressures and cultural attitudes that gave the early zoos their specific character. Gate entrance designs demonstrated these differences. The London Zoo, located in Regent's park and in a country dominated by the natural landscape school, presented a kind of vegetal gate, shrouded by trees. The Berlin Zoo of imperial Germany built an imposing Baroque edifice of elaborate style and at great expense. The entrance to the Philadelphia Zoo in the United States, begun in 1874, was somewhat Victorian. The entrance to the Stellingen Zoo was strikingly similar to a gateway design by Leque in the 1790s for a hunting park and had a distinctly circuslike image (Fig. 11). Yet it was the ideas first demonstrated at the Stellingen Tierpark that began the era of the modern zoo.

THE MODERN ZOO

The modern zoo began with the moat enclosures built at Carl Hagenbeck's Stellingen Zoo in 1910. Hagenbeck was an animal trader and trainer. it was his realization that if an animal cannot jump or cannot climb or swim, then a physical barrier does not have to be bars, cages, or pits, but that dimension that the animal cannot cross. Moats were used to enclose the larger animals and thus keep them at ground level with the visitors. A similar technique, the ha-ha, had been known before, but it was Hagenbeck's innovations that revolutionized exhibit design.

With the contemporary developments in reinforced concrete at the turn of the century, natural organic forms were created and manipulated to form moats, mountains, and enclosures. By the juxtaposition of enclosures, one behind another, yet separated by moats, animals could be exhibited together as they might be seen in the wild. Predators like lions were seen behind their prey, ostriches and zebras, but were kept isolated from them. This device was called a panorama and was eventually copied by zoo directors around the world. Hagenbeck was thorough in his effort to recreate the foreign character specific to the lands of his animals; he even included native people in some exhibits, such as Lapps with their reindeer and tents and Egyptians with camels, as well as Masai, Japanese, and others. By contrast, other early zoos had merely imposed an architectural symbol of the indigenous civilizations, to the point of housing storks in chalets and elephants in Hindu temples. Although the Stellingen Zoo was not specifically scientific, it was this intention to reproduce the realistic qualities and aspects of an animal's natural environment in a fashion that responded to the physical abilities of the animal that began the modern zoo.

In addition to the new approach to animal exhibition seen at the Stellingen Zoo, other influences have affected the form of the modern zoo. Technological and scientific advances have altered the design and role of the zoo today. Among the technological influences was the advent of the gasoline car, patented by George Seldon in 1895, which changed the location and organization of zoos. Early zoos were situated near railroad stations. As the cities grew, these zoos became difficult and expensive to modernize or expand. The car eliminated these site constraints by making suburban and rural locations possible. Gradually, as the car became more available to more people in the 1940s, drive-through wild animal parks were begun. The Marquess of Bath, together with a circus man, Jimmy Chipperfield, created the first drive-through animal park.

Their motivation was not scientific, however; the park was in answer to a $3 million tax bill on an inheritance of 9000 acres (3600 hectares). For an admission price, the public could see a beautiful park full of lions from its cars. Many other parks have followed, and in general they should not be confused with the wild animal parks associated with mainstream zoos, whose parks are for conservation and research, not for financial investments.

Other technological influences, the invention of the Kodak camera in 1884, and later the marketing of television sets after World War II along with the beginning of color transmission in 1953, changed one of the basic roles of the zoo, to show animals. Whereas before the only reliable way to see a wild animal accurately was at the zoo, today any number of photographs or films can render this visual information. This has profoundly changed public expectations of the zoo experience. Before, it was enough just to see what the animal looked like. Today, people expect not only to see the animal, but also to see what the animal does (climb, fly, swim, etc).

Scientific investigations have also helped to create the modern zoo. As early as 1896, Robert Garner put forth impressively modern ideas for the housing of apes, based on observations of physiology and behavior. Research in animal nutrition, pathology, behavior, anatomy, reproduction, and physiology has provided a wealth of information that today guides the design of the modern zoo, its exhibits, and its methods of animal husbandry.

Scientific studies and interest, together with the negative side of technological advances (pollution, exploitation, and waste), have given conservation and research imperative roles in the modern zoo. This recognition of and concern for the wilderness came as early as 1903 in the UK with the establishment of the Society for the Preservation of the Wild Fauna of the Empire. During the period of the world wars, economic struggles overshadowed zoological concerns, but zoology reemerged in 1948, with the charter for the International Union for the Conservation of Nature. In 1961, the World Wildlife Fund was established for the prevention of animal extinction. Along with these efforts, zoos formed organizations and regulatory procedures to respond to the growing concerns for animal welfare and survival. Among them are the American Association of Zoological Parks and Aquariums (1924); the Washington Convention of 1973, which measures and regulates trade in endangered species; and the International Species Inventory System (ISIS) (1974).

Purpose

The modern zoo serves basically four purposes: recreation, education, research, and conservation. Recreation is the oldest role of animal collections and is still a significant part of the zoo as a public institution. It is public attendance that is largely responsible for a considerable portion of the zoo's funding. Education of the public, to increase its interest in and appreciation of the animal world and the complexity of the biosphere, is now becoming a principal objective for all zoos. A variety of activities, programs, and publications exist for the benefit of the zoo visitor. It is by this communication of knowledge and concern that zoos can hope to continue with public support. Research, another role of the modern zoo, was originally limited to taxonomic or comparative anatomy or pathology. Today, research with zoo animals also includes ethology (animal behavior), comparative medicine, and comparative physiology. Examples of promising studies include work with capybaras for compounds to combat leukemia and with armadillos to fight leprosy.

Conservation is another important function of the zoo today. It has been estimated that half of all the species of plants and animals alive today will be extinct by the year 2100. The wilderness not only is being depleted of wild animals, but is also itself being replaced, altered, or destroyed by humanity's encroaching technology.

One unique response to the roles of research and conservation is the Frozen Zoo at the San Diego Zoo in California. Started by Kurt Benirschke, the Frozen Zoo consists of living tissue that is frozen in liquid nitrogen and maintained at a constant temperature of $-250°F$ ($-112°C$). Samples of gametes (unfertilized eggs or sperm cells), embryos, and fibroblasts (skin cells) are kept for breeding and research. Using this technique, gene pools can be increased, and by procedures involving surrogate mothers, wild stock can be increased.

Some conservation efforts have economic interests, as in providing a gene bank for hybrid food sources, eg, the "beefalo." However, conservation in the zoo is primarily for three reasons: to restock the wild; to provide a repository for animals that are, or are nearly, extinct in the wild; and to provide a self-perpetuating stock for the zoos. Some examples of successful conservation efforts are the nenes (Hawaiian geese), the European wisent or bison, Prjevalsky's horse, and many rare game birds.

Zoo Types

Currently, there are more than 900 zoos worldwide, and 450 in the United States alone. Financially, there are three options for the establishment of a zoo. These are the national zoo, eg, at Washington, D.C., or Vincennes, Paris; the municipal zoo, eg, at Frankfurt, FRG, or Bern, Switzerland; or a private zoo, eg, the Basel Zoo (a joint stock company), the Zurich Zoo (a cooperative society), or the London Zoo (a scientific society).

The arrangement of the animal collection is another aspect of zoo type. There are essentially eight categories:

Systematic. This arrangement is functionally the easiest for maintenance and animal husbandry, in which similar animals are grouped together. It can emphasize the differences between groups, but can also become monotonous for the zoo visitor.

Taxonomic. This is a selective zoo that groups species that are zoologically related.

Zoogeographic. This is organized into groups according to their continent of origin.

Ecological/Habitat. This exhibits only species of a certain habitat, eg, polar, desert, forest.

Regional. This is a subset of the ecological zoo, but is limited to the species indigenous to the geographical region of the zoo.

Popularity. This is a system of organizing the animal collection based on the popularity of the exhibit and activities, eg, monkeys near a peanut stand and flamingos near the entrance.

Behavioral. This is the most recent arrangement for zoos, eg, aquatic, nocturnal, arboreal.

Universal. This is a selective combination of the above categories. It is a representative cross section of the vertebrate animals of the world and is the most common zoo type.

Design Concerns

Probably the most significant factor in determining the design or character of any zoo is the site. The climate of the site, its topography, and its soil conditions (for fauna and flora, drainage, and building foundations) have the most profound influence on the choice of zoo type, exhibit size and design, circulation, and image of the zoo. Climate also affects the visitor population. In seasonally changing environments, winter is often a slow time for zoos. A recent project by Perry, Dean, Hepburn and Stewart Architects, for the Franklin Park Zoo in Boston, Massachusetts, is based on a response to this issue of climate. The project is a linear organization of exhibits that are layered for an indoor winter and an outdoor summer concourse (Fig. 12). There is also a lower level for parking and service.

The nature of zoo design is in many ways similar to that of urban design, and many of the master plan elements are the same. In the past, zoo designs have reflected styles and philosophies of urban spaces and landscape designs. The City Beautiful Movement in the United States, which started with the Columbian Exposition of 1893, is also an instance of urban planning ideas influencing zoo designs. In particular, the site plan of the Chicago Zoological Park in Brookfield, Illinois, started in 1926, as well as that of the Bronx Zoo begun in 1899 incorporate a grid of paths, with neoclassical buildings and special elements that punctuate the cross-axes and express the tenets of the City Beautiful Movement (Fig. 13). The strength of these organizational devices creates a center or main space for the zoo visitor.

Site planning strategies also include building types and location. Common building requirements for a major modern zoo include (9): a first-aid station, administration buildings (libraries, archives, lecture halls, meeting rooms, research laboratories), restaurants, an animal hospital, an education building, an animal food warehouse, a central food kitchen, buildings for works and maintenance operations (transportation equipment, etc), a children's zoo, zoo shops, parking, and gardens. The zoo staff generally consists of administration and office personnel, maintenance workers, curators (the staff biologist in charge of acquisition and transfer of surplus animals, establishing standards for animal care and housing, and supervising animal care personnel), keepers (those directly responsible for animals and their cages), veterinarians (responsible for all phases of animal health and preventive care), and variable staffs of paid and volunteer personnel and promotional societies.

Some of the various concerns in zoo planning are utilities, security systems, insulation from noise and pollution, and the response to environmental regulations such as those that prevent storm runoff from animal paddocks from entering public storm sewers and streams without first being treated or those pertaining to the disposal of massive amount of animal manure on the site.

Other master plan elements deal more directly with the visiting public. Information systems and circulation are two of these. Information systems include lectures, signs, maps, brochures, and guidebooks as well as tape-recorded messages, films, zoo guides, and seminars. These are important because information about the zoological and botanical collections is critical to an enjoyable and meaningful zoo visit. Signage is perhaps the most obvious method of conveying information in the zoo. Consistency of sign style and placement help to orient the visitor and unify the impression of the whole zoo. In zoos that regularly have international populations, signs should be in several languages. Expediency is essential in sign design, especially in exhibit labeling. In Hodge's 1978 Demographic Study of Zoo Visitors, it was found that only 5.8% of visitors read labels. Of these, family groups stay at an exhibit longer than peer groups. Adults stay an average of 50 seconds, and do not revisit exhibits. Children stay only 35 seconds, but tend to revisit exhibits. This implies that the label or sign must have an appropriate amount of

Figure 12. Franklin Park Zoo Project, Boston. Sectional views (7). Courtesy of *Architectural Forum.*

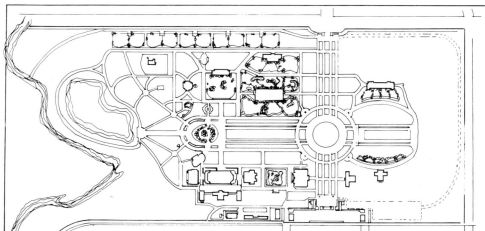

Figure 13. Brookfield Zoo, Chicago, 1934. Plan view (8). Courtesy of the Chicago Zoological Society.

information, be attractive, and be interesting because it may only have between 35 and 50 seconds to give its message. The ratio of sign information to the magnitude generated by the exhibit animal is another aspect that deserves consideration in label design. Animals that are more active or unusual stimulate a desire to know more about them. Interest is also relative to visual features and details of the exhibit enclosure and is influenced by whether or not the animal is a zoo regular (an elephant, lion, bear, monkey, etc).

The communication of information about the animal and its place in the environment can be accomplished in a variety of ways, by signs, films, slides, demonstrations, lectures, etc. A design by Venturi, Rauch, and Scott Brown for a children's zoo at the Philadelphia Zoo (Fig.

14) proposes some new ideas for involving the visitors in finding out about the animal. The design includes oversized exhibits, periscopes, and the development of different spatial character and details for the visitor. In addition, magnetic rings worn by the children trigger recordings for various displays and exhibits. This suggests that not only is the animal world wonderfully diverse, but so are the possibilities for information systems.

The other design factor most affecting the zoo visitor is circulation. Circulation design determines not only the sequence of exhibits, but also their quality and extent, as any parent of tired children can testify. As zoos have grown in size, particularly with large wild animal parks, pedestrian access has become more limited. Responses to this problem include moving sidewalks, buses, trains, and

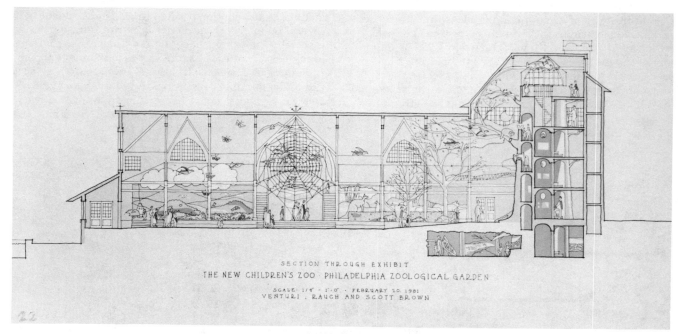

Figure 14. Philadelphia Zoo, Children's Zoo, 1981. Sectional view. Courtesy of Venturi, Rauch and Scott Brown.

monorails. Mechanized transportation has advantages and limitations. Certainly, it is easier on the foot-weary, but the pace, direction, and sequence are all beyond the control of the individual. For the zoo staff, however, it provides an opportunity to control or direct the visitor's impressions. Animals are sometimes trained to be active when the monorail or bus passes by. Tour guides prepare verbal information about the animals and can illustrate ideas by the sequence or timing of the trip. With mechanized mobility, visitors can see more of the zoo, but it is a controlled view, and the designer can screen or hide unattractive features. This occurs at the Bronx Zoo in New York on the Bengali Express monorail ride, from which visitors look out on one side only, and the high-rise buildings of the city are kept behind them and out of sight. This helps create the impression of being out of the city, in a foreign land with the animals.

Methods of circulation can determine not only the views, but also the visitor's appreciation or impression of the animal resident. At the Vincennes Zoo in Paris, visitors can travel vertically to the top of a viewing tower, look out upon the zoo, and see elephants from above. At the Thoiry Wild Animal Park, also in France, visitors can drive their cars through the park, where elephants are free to roam and often come close enough to put their trunks inside the cars in search of handouts. At the Bronx Zoo, elephants can be seen from the monorail, but there are also elephant rides available. These options obviously give the visitor different impressions of an animal's size, movements, smells, and, perhaps, personality. Together with information systems, the different methods of transportation and circulation have a variable ability to affect the zoo visitor.

INNOVATIONS AND TRENDS

Most zoos today are conscious of humanity's threat to the wilderness and wildlife. The roles of recreation, education, research, and conservation are acknowledged by all the major modern zoos. Emphasis on conveying knowledge and appreciation of the animal world governs most exhibit design and zoo planning. Innovations in zoo planning and architecture are directed towards these roles and objectives.

Although there have been new ideas in exhibit design, enclosure techniques have not varied much. Exhibit designs generally strive for naturalistic enclosures, providing for more of the animal's temporal, physical, and spatial needs, even to the point of supplying rain showers in tropical exhibits (eg, the Tropic World Exhibit at the Chicago Zoo).

The attitude towards architecture in the zoo is, generally speaking, to "green it out," to minimize the visual impact of the building in the landscape by submerging it and screening it with vegetation. This has pros and cons, but it is the common approach of zoo directors today. Yet an unusual suggestion for zoo architecture has been offered by the Cambridge Seven Group, in a project for the Boston Zoo. This project provides an answer to the problem of the megalopolis, that is, the problem of a diminishing countryside and the heightened need for city dwellers to experience some aspect of the natural world. The project would be located in the heart of the city, featuring a 12-story structure that recreates various microclimates for a wide range of exhibits (Fig. 15). In designing this project, the same architects produced another new idea in zoo architecture, that of modular design, demonstrated in the Special Exhibits Building project. This concept would integrate solar design with a modular building enclosed in a space frame, which would allow for horizontal or vertical expansion or contraction of any exhibit. The interior columns were designed to be hollow-core ducts supplying the four corners of each module. This flexibility would be extremely useful, as the demands for size change with the needs and availability of the animals.

In addition to these innovations in zoo design is a proposal to broaden the scope of the zoo program. This is the Biological Centre for Canberra, proposed to the Australian government in 1965. The intention was to present humanity's relationship to the biological world—plants, animals, and microorganisms. Exhibit themes would include population dynamics, the importance of microorganisms, genetics, natural selection and evolution, possible life on other planets, medicines, use and misuse of pesticides, and conservation, among others. With the aid of infrared viewers, microscope projections, and closed-circuit television, the visitor could be exposed to a new variety of life forms, as well as to the usual zoo animals. Noting that there may be as many as five taxonomic kingdoms, Prokaryotae (one-celled organisms lacking a membrane-bound nucleus, eg, bacterium or blue-green algae), Protista (mostly unicellular organisms with a membrane-bound nucleus, eg, protozoans), Fungi, Plantae, and Animalia, this proposal could illustrate many of the current ideas in scientific thought and help fill the widening gap between scientific and public knowledge.

EXHIBIT DESIGN

Inside the zoo, exhibit design involves basically three issues: animal restraint, programmatic concerns, and conceptual design. Animal restraint serves three purposes: to protect the animals from one another, to protect the public from the animals, and to protect the animals from the public. More harm is done to zoo animals by the visiting public, often resulting in serious injury and death, than might be imagined. By the use of signs, handrails, shrubbery, flower beds, and other features, zoo and exhibit designers attempt to prevent this kind of problem with the public. The other aspects of animal restraint, its materials and methods, have a long history and consist of a variety of barriers (eg, moats, glass, bars, etc).

The programmatic issues are the criteria established by the needs of the animal, keeper, maintenance worker, and visitor. The conceptual aspect of exhibit design refers to the importance of communicating knowledge about the animal.

Animal Restraint

The first method used to contain a wild animal was the pit used to capture it. Pits, especially for bears, were popular

PROPOSED DOWNTOWN ZOO

1 Typical Exhibit Space
2 Typical Public Gallery and Ramp
3 Typical Staff and Mechanical Space
4 Paddock Area for large mammals
5 Aviary, walk-through bird exhibit
6 Auditorium
7 Laboratories and Staff Offices
8 Entrance Bridge from Tremont Street
9 Rooftop Terrace Restaurant
10 Boylston Street

NOTE:

The visitor enters the building lobby (8), proceeds to the roof (9) by elevator, and then descends by ramps and galleries (2) through the sequential exhibits (1) in a continuous downwards flow.

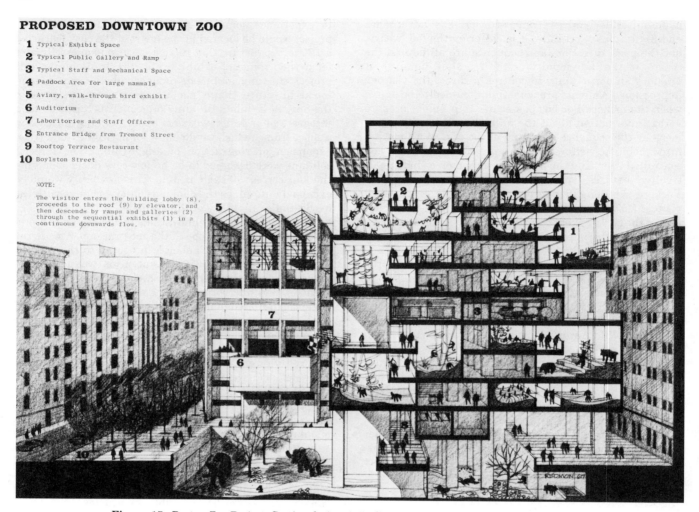

Figure 15. Boston Zoo Project. Sectional view (10). Courtesy of Cambridge Seven Associates.

in many cities up until the nineteenth century. The first enclosures on grade consisted of stout palisades of softwood. Animal visibility was not good with the numerous thick members. With the availability of cast iron, wrought iron, and later steel, fewer and thinner members could be used to make bars for cages. Bar cages remained the most common method of restraining wild animals up until this century. Even in uncommon circumstances, bars were used for restraint, as in the polar bear and seal exhibit at the Menagerie at Helsingfors, where bars were set in a natural body of water and so provided an inexpensive source of fresh water for these aquatic mammals (Fig. 16).

Bar cages were often combined with solid walls of brick or stone. These structures were usually massive and imposing, incorporating bars with spiked tops that were intended to deter, if not kill, any animal that tried to escape. The spikes also added to the fearsome impression of the beast inside. In contrast, other cages, especially for monkeys and birds, were often delicately detailed. Glass for animal enclosures became practical after the invention of plate glass in the 1840s. It was used to exhibit small mammals, reptiles, and fish.

Reinforced concrete was another material that was used more after modern developments at the turn of the century. The first broad application was at the Stellingen Zoo in 1910, to create mountains, grottos, and moats on what had been a potato field.

The first instance of a moat enclosure did not actually use the moat as a barrier, but as an enclosure. After the invention of gunpowder in the fourteenth century (in Europe), the medieval city moat was no longer functional for defense and so was modified to keep wild deer and pigs. Another historical technique for enclosing animals was the ha-ha. This method, popularized in the eighteenth century, kept animals in apparent freedom by submerging the barrier or fence in a trough below the eye level of the observer. The first modern moated enclosure, based on the same principle, was constructed at the Stellingen Zoo. This exhibit technique was not fully appreciated by other zoos for almost 50 years. There were some other early examples, such as the Mappin Terraces at the London Zoo (1913) and some exhibits at the Vincennes Zoo, but these were unusual. With a moated enclosure, animals could be seen without any visual obstructions, in outdoor settings more like their native habitats, and in larger enclosures

Restoration, Historic Kiplin Hall, North Yorkshire, England. Built 1623 by George Calvert, First Lord Baltimore. Restoration of house and gardens by Martin Standcliffe, RIBA, assisted by the School of Architecture, University of Maryland.

Science and Technology Centers Technology and Innovation Center, Hallmark, Inc., Kansas City, Missouri.

Science and Technology Centers Cité des Sciences et de L'industrie Parc de la Villette, Paris, France. Architect: Adrien Fainsilber.

Soviet Union Architecture Catherine the Great Palace, Leningrad. Courtesy of Nancy Block.

Soviet Union Architecture Church of the Resurrection of the Saviour on the Blood, St. Petersburg (1883–1907) Alfred A. Parland. Courtesy of Nancy Block.

Soviet Union Architecture Teremok cottage at Talashkino, outside Smolensk (1887) Sergei Y. Maliutin. Courtesy of Anatole Senkevitch.

Theaters and Opera Houses   Radio City Music Hall, New York, New York. Courtesy of George A. Le Moine.

Theaters and Opera Houses   Im Hof der Residenz, Munich, Germany. Courtesy of Eckebrecht/Bavaria.

Theaters and Opera Houses   Paris Opera, Paris, France. Courtesy of Jacques Moatti/Explorer.

Wallboard and Plaster Systems Ornamental plaster. Courtesy of U.S. Gypsum Corp., Libertyville, Illinois.

Wright, Frank Lloyd Marin County Civic Center, California, 1959. Photograph by Stephen A. Kliment.

Wright, Frank Lloyd Taliesen West, outside of Scottsdale, Arizona. Photograph by Peter H. Bickford.

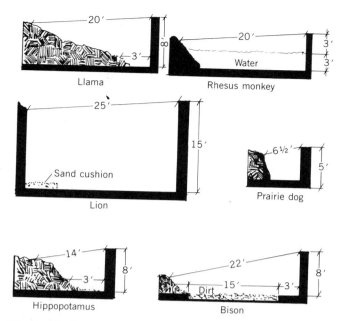

Figure 17. Moat section (11). Courtesy of The Zoological Society of London.

Figure 16. Menagerie D'Hoegholmen at Helsingfors. Two views (2).

that allowed for more natural groupings of animals. These exhibits could also be layered to provide a juxtaposition of animals.

Today, moated enclosures are common. Dry moats must be made with soft humus, peat, or gravel and a means of egress to prevent fractures and further stress in case the animal falls in. With provisions for getting in and out of the moat, it is important that the moat not become a living space for the animal. This leads to the psychologically bad condition of looking down on the animal, as in the primitive pit. Water moats are another design option, although there are some problems associated with them. The water must be kept clean. If the water freezes over, monkeys can walk across and escape; ungulates may try to walk on the ice, but can slip and fall. Drowning is another problem that has occurred in zoo history.

The dimensions of the moat, the breadth and height, are based on the physical ability of the animal to jump or climb. Some animals are better candidates for moated enclosures than others. Large cats, like mountain lions or cheetahs, that are good climbers and jumpers are generally not kept in moated enclosures. Heavy-bodied animals like lions, tigers, bears, elephants, rhinos, and giraffes are more easily contained in moated exhibits. Other such animals include cattle, gazelles, deer, bison, zebus, elands, ostriches, and tapirs as well as smaller animals like anteaters, raccoons, otters, peccaries, wolverines, and cranes. Water moats can be used to exhibit baboons, spider monkeys, gibbons, macaques, lions, tigers, and other animals. In addition to being dry or wet, the configuration of the moat is also designed specifically to the animals' physical

abilities. Shape, material, and slope are variables that determine the effectiveness of a moat (Fig. 17).

The moat is a barrier in the horizontal plane. Other restraint techniques rely on vertical elements. Careful attention must be given to the design of these elements to ensure that the restraint barrier does not become a visual barrier as well. Examples include fencing (chain-link, weld-mesh, electrified), vertical wires set in tension frames, mesh (link or welded), steel cables, and a variety of glass and plastics (Figs. 18 and 19).

There are some obvious problems with glass as an enclosure material. Strength is easily accomplished with laminates, but reflections and glare can be serious visual obstacles. Reflections and glare can be reduced or eliminated by slanting the glass, using a brighter light in the exhibit than in the visitor's space, or using dark surfaces in the visitor's area. Plastics also present a problem as an enclosure material because scratches on the surface can affect visibility. Both materials, glass and plastics, offer protection for the animal from airborne germs and infections. This is especially important for animals that are susceptible to human sicknesses, like gorillas and orangutans. However, both materials can inhibit sound transmission, which may affect the visitor's full understanding of the animal, eg, in seeing a gorilla beat his chest, but not hearing anything, or in seeing the red throat sac of the siamang inflated, but not hearing any accompanying sounds.

In all exhibit materials, four properties are desirable: innocuousness (avoiding poisonous stains or finishes, exposed glass wool insulation, etc); resistance to wear and tear from abrasion, chewing, or excretion; easy maintenance; and normal durability (resistance to weather; structural and mechanical worthiness). The problem of exhibit materials is an important and complex one, Con-

Figure 18. National Zoo, Washington, D.C., Great Flight Cage. Exterior view.

Animal restraint can also be accomplished by other, nonmaterial methods. Perhaps the oldest method, although not always possible or practical, is domestication. This is appropriate in children's zoos, where llamas, horses, sheep, and elephants, for example, are exhibited in close contact with the visitors. Environmental characteristics can also be manipulated to enclose wild animals. For instance, most birds prefer not to fly into darkness; therefore, if the visitors' area is darkened, and there are no places to perch, the birds will not fly into, or alight in the visitors' area (Fig. 20). Reptiles, which are imperfectly homoiothermal and cannot regulate their body temperatures, will not trespass areas that are maintained at temperatures that are unpleasant for them and so can be contained without visual barriers.

For mixed exhibits, it is possible to enclose animals by varying the qualities of the landscape. Animals will not remain in, or fight for, land that does not suit them. By developing different characters of vegetal enclosure and different environmental elements (water, rocks, brush, etc), a variety of species can be kept in the same exhibit, but in separate areas.

Programmatic Concerns

In the design of animal enclosures, there are four kinds of clients: the animal, the keeper, the maintenance worker, and the visitor. The animal has spatial, physical, and behavioral needs (see The Animal) as well as basic physiological requirements for appropriate temperature, humidity, ventilation, and lighting. Animals need access to sunlight, or its equivalent, in varying amounts. Ultraviolet and infrared (to bask in) are used for this purpose in some instances. The exhibit space should also be suitable

stant wash water and urine on concrete can significantly reduce its structural life and cause serious damage to other materials by corrosion. Such factors, in addition to the animal's strength and ingenuity, must be considered in detailing animal exhibits.

Figure 19. National Zoo, Washington, D.C., Great Ape House by Wilkes and Faulkner. Exterior view.

Figure 20. An example of a change in light levels as a barrier technique.

to the animal's morphology. The enclosure need not be cubical, but can utilize or express organic forms and provide a wonderful opportunity for the designer to respond to the variety of animal forms. The Rhinoceros and Cattle Egret exhibit at the Zurich Zoo, designed by R. Zurcher in 1963, is an example of this kind of sensitivity. The doorway for the rhinoceros is round, and the floor is undulating, which fits the animal's form and movements.

Considering the floor and substrate, an appropriate choice of materials is essential for an animal's health and well-being. The continuously growing hooves of the ungulates need a rough, abrasive surface to wear them down. The soft feet of pacing animals, like lions or tigers, do not. Materials and their connections are essential considerations in exhibit design. An enclosure for an animal that can pull over 500 lb (225 kg) or weighs over 2 tons (1.8 t) is detailed much differently than an enclosure for an animal with the size and strength of a shrew.

The keeper's needs are another programmatic concern for the designer. Washing out cages requires plenty of high-pressure hot water, efficient drainage, and ventilation. The job of cleaning the cages demands that the animal either not be a threat to the keeper or be removed during the process. This usually involves "shift" cages. A shift cage is one into which animals can be transferred while the keeper cleans the enclosure. In a line of cages, this allows the keeper to shift a row of animals to accommodate cleaning. Other procedures require "squeeze" cages to restrain the animal, generally for transportation or for medical attention. These cages consist of an enclosure with adjustable sides that squeeze together and prohibit large body movements of the animal. Often the squeeze cage is incorporated into the animal's normal enclosure, eg, its sleeping den, so that during moments of medical necessity or during the stress of being transported the squeeze cage does not add to the animal's anxiety.

The job of the maintenance worker also affects the design program of an exhibit. The electrical, mechanical, and plumbing components of an exhibit must be designed to facilitate maintenance. Instances where light bulbs, vents, or drains must be repaired or replaced should not involve unnecessary procedures or stress to the exhibit animal.

The visitor's needs obviously determine some of the qualities and details of the animal enclosure. Good visibility of the animals, with suitable exhibit design and information about them, on labels, signs, films, or recordings, is important for a meaningful exhibit. In the effort to assure a satisfying experience for the public, some designers have implemented designs based on rotating exhibits. The weasel exhibit at the Apple Valley Zoo in Minnesota is an example. Visitors there always see an active, playful weasel in the exhibit because, at certain intervals, the weasel on exhibit is changed with one off exhibit, and therefore the animal is always fresh and eager to explore its new surroundings.

Other ideas have been developed to enhance the zoo visit. Films seen before the exhibit, sound effects, animal demonstrations, and "zoo labs" for the public are a sample of the variety available.

Conceptual Design

Exhibit design in the modern zoo has a responsibility to communicate information about the zoo animal. The morphology and the behavior of the wild animal are only a part of the exhibit experience. There are opportunities in the design arrangement, and sequence of exhibits to illustrate themes or concepts found in nature. The imagery and perception of the enclosure are educative and have a marked effect on the public's appreciation of the animal. Perception of the animal is also affected by the relative position of the viewer (12). Looking down on an animal puts the viewer in a dominant position, perhaps less disposed to learning or respect, and is psychologically bad for the animal.

Aside from relative positions, the image of the restraint technique and the degree of proximity affect the visitor's perception of the animal to varying degrees. A crocodile behind spiked bars appears more ferocious than one behind a glass wall. The degree of proximity, how close the visitors are and how much of the same environment they and the animals share, can also affect the perception of the animal. Barriers can prevent the exchange of thermal, acoustical, and physical characteristics that help explain the exhibit animal's particular adaptations. This can be especially true for aquariums, where only visual information passes beyond the exhibit enclosure. Yet the conceptual design can overcome the feeling of separateness. A fine example of this is the Baltimore Aquarium's Coral Reef Exhibit. In this, the visitor enters the top of an elliptical donut and is led down a winding ramp in the middle of the reef exhibit tank. The fish swim around the donut in the same stratification that exists in the wild. Predators (sharks) are kept separate in a tank at the bottom. The impression of being surrounded by fish is augmented by taped sound effects. Other aquariums have achieved the same effect in different ways. The Shark Encounter at Sea World in Orlando, Florida, uses a moving sidewalk through a transparent tunnel 118 ft (36 m) long that is stretched across the bottom of the shark tank. The sharks glide hauntingly above and around the visitors.

Absolute physical separation is often achieved by glass barriers for reasons of health or safety, but the impression of separation can be dramatically reduced by the use of the same materials, textures, colors, and light levels in the exhibit and in the visitors' area. An especially good illustration of this possibility exists at the Sonora Desert Museum in Arizona (Fig. 21). Here, the visitor descends into tunnels under the desert floor to see the subterranean exhibits of indigenous animals (who also have free access to outdoor enclosures). The visitor is transported into the natural environment of the animal and gains an immediate appreciation of the qualities of its habitat.

Exhibits that do not rely on barriers between visitors and the animals offer a different perception of the animal and its world. Thermal, acoustic, and other environmental qualities are shared. Some species, especially birds, can be exhibited this way. The exhibit design is usually made as realistic as possible, thus presenting a wonderful chance to see the animals in their natural setting and to appreci-

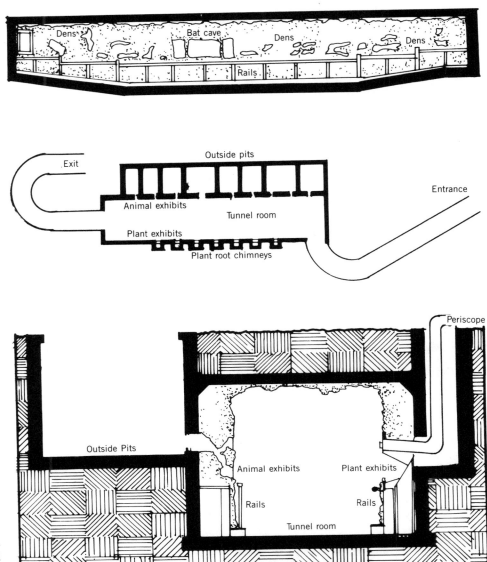

Figure 21. Sonora Desert Museum, Arizona. Plan and sectional view (13).

ate their adaptations, coloring for instance, where the pale underside of flying birds seen against the sky or the brown, textured backs of turtles seen against the rocky banks of streams make them less conspicuous. Finding the animals in this kind of exhibit is frustrating for some, adventurous for others. An unusual example of this kind of exhibit is in the Baltimore Zoo in Maryland. Inside the zoo's perimeter fence, wild sheep, llamas, and deer are allowed to roam free; visitors then come upon these animals unexpectedly, which adds to the delight of seeing them free.

The conceptual aspect of exhibit design can integrate the type of animal restraint and the qualities of the exhibit enclosure to interpret or express some feature of the animal or its habitat. The Snowdon Aviary at the London Zoo, designed by Lord Snowdon, Cedric Price, and Frank Newby in 1965, is an example. It is a marvelous tension structure, which in some ways is analogous to the tension structure of birds that is necessary for flight. This large aviary has a difficult site, but utilizes the changes in its topography; a visitor's large walk is cantilevered, suspending the visitor in the exhibit space. The Elephant and Rhino Pavilion, also at the London Zoo, was designed by Casson, Conders and Partners. This building's conceptual inspiration seems to have guided the creation of its form. The massing of the building and its textures are meant to suggest a herd of elephants at a watering place, and inside the imagery is carried further with interior lighting and structure.

Problems can arise when the concept is misguided or misplaced. The Penguin Pool at the London Zoo, designed by Tecton in 1933, is an example. This structure follows closely a project for a theater design by Meyerhold and Lissistky in Moscow (1928). The elliptical pool has a planar ramp that spirals down the center. Although lovely in its form, it is not suited to penguins, but is now under preservation order for its striking design.

THE ANIMAL

Inside the exhibit is the most important client for the zoo architect, without which there would be no zoo. The living animal represents the basic unit of the animal collection. It is estimated that 4,500 species of mammals, 8,590 of birds, 5,000 of reptiles, 2,900 of amphibians, 23,000 of fish, and 765,257 of insects have been identified. In the average zoological collection, there are roughly 15 categories of animals exhibited (14):

> Small mammals (rodents, marsupials, monotremes, etc).
>
> Primates (monkeys and apes).
>
> Mammal predators (great cats, otters, members of the dog family, etc).
>
> Bears.
>
> Seals and sea lions.
>
> Vast ungulates (elephants, rhinos, hippopotamuses, and tapirs).
>
> Large ungulates (giraffes, horses, zebras, camel, deer, cattle, antelope, okapis, hyraxes, and the pig family).
>
> Sheep and goats.
>
> Penguins.
>
> Large flightless birds.
>
> Small birds (parrots, pigeons, hummingbirds, etc).
>
> Water birds.
>
> Birds of prey (vultures, condors, eagles, etc).
>
> Game birds and bustards (pheasants, cranes, bustards, etc).
>
> Reptiles (snakes, crocodiles, alligators, monitors, etc).

Even with this great array of animals, most zoos rarely exhibit more than 1000 different animals in any year. The trend in zoos today is away from the postage stamp zoo and towards natural groupings of animals in more natural settings. The resultant animal collections therefore consist of fewer species and more specimens. In this regard, the major zoos have begun to specialize in various animals, breeding and maintaining animals that for one reason or another adapt particularly well to the climate, facilities, or treatment at the specific zoo. Quite often, this specialization is aimed at preserving endangered species or species extinct in the wild. Farms and parks for breeding and research are set aside for just this purpose. Some examples include the San Diego Wild Animal Park of the San Diego Zoo, and the Whipsnade Zoo of the London Zoological Society. The National Zoo in Washington, D.C., also has a breeding farm, located in Front Royal, Virginia, for maintaining several endangered species, and the New York Zoological Society has perhaps the largest breeding

and research facility at St. Catherine's Island off the coast of Georgia.

At present, in 750 zoos worldwide, there are more than 162,874 mammals, 256,413 birds, and uncountable others in captivity. Only a portion of the animals in these zoos are received from captive breeding efforts. Birth in the collection is just one method of animal acquisition for zoos. There are five other possibilities: exchanges, purchases, gifts, direct collecting expeditions, or the voluntary actions of animals (that fly or wander into zoo grounds). Because of the enormous complexity and multiple chance factors of breeding or buying wild animals, a computer-based system has been established at the Minnesota Zoo, near Minneapolis. This system, ISIS, was begun in 1974 and has 150 participating zoos. It contains statistics on the birth, age, sex, location, sale, loan records, and death of over 90,000 animals. With this service, zoos can organize breeding and management measures to ensure or increase the present supply of wild animals and plan for the demands of the future.

Just as important as animal supply is animal husbandry. Research is constantly providing new ideas and insight concerning the detailed requirements and management of particular exhibit animals. This information is accessible in the publications and journals of the various zoological societies. For exhibit design, there are three general topics that are of consequence. These are the animal's spatial, physical, and behavioral needs.

Spatial Needs

In the wild, an animal and its environment can be seen as a living system; the animal contributes to the cycling of materials and energy in its ecosystem. Within the various ecosystems are numerous habitats (or biochores), which are collections of niches having the same geographical and climatic characteristics, eg, the forest floor or the tundra surface. The niche (or biotope) is the specific terrain of an animal. Within the niche are spatial and physical elements particular to each animal. The home range is a spatial quality of the niche that is made up of the animal's regular movements and activities (Fig. 22). It is a number

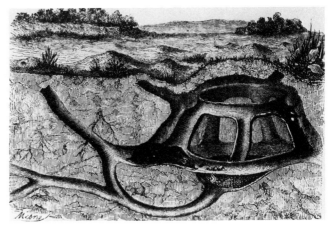

Figure 22. Mole habitat. Schematic sectional view (15).

Table 1. Examples of the Extent of Territory in the Wild[a]

Species	Locality	Approximate Size	Authority
Howler monkey	Panama	300 acres	Carpenter
Cougar	California	20 mi^2	Leopold
Lion	Kruger National Park	13 mi^2	Bigalke
Giant panda	Chinese Tibet	1 mi^2	Schafer
White-tailed eagle		2 mi^2	Alverdes
Mute swan		0.5 mi^2	Heinroth
Lizard	Cuba	37 yd^2	Evans

[a] Ref. 16. Courtesy of Dover Publications.

of points and settings that are linked by paths. All animals, aquatic, terrestrial, arboreal, or subterranean, have a home range. This corresponds to our own notion of a home range, a general limit of familiar places within which we feel comfortable.

The territory is an area inside the home range that is "fenced" and defended by the animal, yet is shared with other species that do not threaten its mates or resources. The size of a territory is relatively constant for each species and is generally proportional to the size of the animal and its food supply (Table 1). Carnivores usually have larger territories than herbivores because their food source is neither abundant nor constant in one place. Another factor determining the size of an animal's territory is the limitations of its fencing techniques; scent markings, visual displays, or acoustics are effective only at certain distances. The size of a territory can be either permanent or temporary, depending on the animal and its circumstances.

These two classifications of space in the wild, the home range and especially the territory, are of particular importance in designing the size and character of a zoological exhibit. They are also important in correcting the popular misconception that the wild animal has been taken from its idyllic freedom in the wild. Animals are in fact prisoners in space and time, confined by geographical distribution, physical barriers (like mountains and rivers), temperature and humidity, and food resources. Animals cannot move freely in and out of the terrain or habitat to which they are adapted.

In addition to the physical and physiological barriers, there are powerful psychological barriers created by the relationships between animals, a phenomenon regarded by some as the most significant factor affecting behavior in the wild. This relationship is governed by the "flight distance" and is another aspect of the animal's spatial environment. Flight distance is the distance between animals, or between animals and humans, at which the animal feels threatened and will take flight. This distance varies with the species and the circumstances. In the wild, it can be as much as 600 yd (540 m) for some animals under stress. This amount of space would obviously be impractical to reproduce in the zoo. However, by the gradual acclimation of the animal to human presence, this distance can be reduced. The size of an exhibit enclosure is then based on a reasonable flight distance that allows animals to establish a comfortable distance between themselves and visitors or other animals. These spatial criteria, a suitable home range and/or territory that can be marked and defended and the attention to an appropriate dimension for maintaining a suitable flight distance, are an intrinsic part of exhibit design.

Physical Needs

Within the niche are physical as well as spatial elements that are significant to the wild animal. These constitute fixed points in the animal's world. Just as a human has specialized areas for eating, bathing, sleeping, excretion, and food storage, so does the animal. These significant places are returned to again and again and represent a space–time pattern, as described in ref. 16. Excretion zones (localized or diffuse), breeding grounds, observation posts, wallowing holes, dust baths, basking areas, and scratching posts are all examples of these physical (and spatial) elements or fixed points in time and space (Fig. 23). The nest or den is also an important physical element. This animal architecture can be incredibly sophisticated or extremely simple (18,19). Often, there are several nests, some more secure than others, that are used only in emergencies.

The physical elements are part of the qualitative details of exhibit design. It has been suggested that these features are in fact more important provisions for the animal's exhibit space than an increase in exhibit size. Whatever the physical elements, they have specific meaning to the various animals and must be designed accordingly. For example, to a rhinoceros water is to wallow in, for a tapir it is to swim in, for a raccoon it is a shallow puddle to wash food in, and for beavers it is a running stream to build in. An understanding of the variety of physical elements and their relative meanings in the animal's natural environment provides the basis for exhibit design.

Figure 23. Zebra and termite mound scratching post (17). Courtesy of Dover Publications.

Behavior

The characteristics of an animal's behavior, social or individual, are also essential in the process of designing zoo exhibitions. An animal society organizes itself to provide conventional competition among members. This function relates to the control of population according to food and other resources available. By knowledge of this social organization in the wild, the zoo can design and plan for appropriate ratios of sex, age, and number of specimens. In the exhibit of a group of animals, the social organization will have an alpha animal, the leader, and an omega animal. Design details should then provide places of refuge for the omega or any other animal during serious confrontations to avoid unhealthy stress or injury.

In groups, some species tolerate physical contact with conspecifics, and some do not. Some tolerate contact with other species, like the cattle and cattle egret. In mixed exhibits, biological rank is a critical issue. Biological rank is a system of dominance that governs behavior among species. For example, the lion feeds on a carcass before the jackal, which feeds before the vulture. It also operates among similar species; the roe deer is subordinate to the chamois, which is subordinate to the ibex. In mixed exhibits, this hierarchy or ranking governs the animal's behavior and also indicates a similar need for places of refuge and cover for the lower-ranking animals in times of stress.

Other behavioral characteristics of animals are more intrinsic to the individual, although the behavior may hold for all of the species. Circadian rhythms, the effect of celestial time as a biological regulating mechanism, have particular consequences in exhibit design. Nocturnal animals are active at night and require reversed lighting cycles if they are to be seen active during the day. Crepuscular animals (active in the early morning and evening) and diurnal animals (active at day) do not present the same problem, although for the visitor it can make the difference between an interesting exhibit and a less interesting one, ie, an active animal or a sleeping one. Some animals' metabolic rhythms, in particular of hibernation and estivation, can also have implications for exhibit design that must be taken into account. Behaviors relating to daily existence (eating, sleeping, etc) are all parameters of which the knowledgeable exhibit designer is conscious. Some animals that feed high in the trees in their natural habitats should have their food placed high in their enclosures, and not on the floor; others must have places to hoard their food before eating it. The list of particulars is innumerable.

The animals' movements, or locomotion, can dramatically affect the design of an exhibit. This is obviously true in the case of seals, sea lions, and manatees, but is also true for other animals. The recent design for the World of Birds by Morris Ketchum, Jr. and Associates at the Bronx Zoo is based on this idea (Fig. 24). Birds should not be kept in enclosures that have sharp or tight corners because flight then becomes dangerous. Their solution was to design enclosures that had no corners. This created shapes that are normally difficult to accommodate in plan, but by the clustering of these exhibits, themes could be developed for the educational benefit of the public.

Behavior is an important component of the contemporary philosophy of exhibit design, which is to exhibit not just the animal, but also what the animal does. Methods are being experimented with to encourage the animal's natural behavior. By keeping the animal active, the detrimental affects of boredom can be mitigated. In an unstimulating environment, animals redirect their frustrations and energies towards themselves, often resulting in problems like pathological social and sexual behavior, self-mutilation, and stereotypy.

One method to provide stimulation and encourage activity is behavioral engineering, or operant conditioning (21). This involves a variety of techniques designed to teach the animal certain acts, which are then rewarded. The Panaewa Rain Forest Zoo in Hilo, Hawaii, employed this idea in its tiger exhibit. The tiger was encouraged to

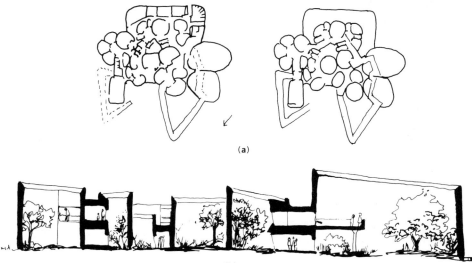

(a)

(b)

Figure 24. Bronx Zoo, World of Birds Exhibit Building. (**a**) Plan and (**b**) sectional views (20). Courtesy of *Architectural Forum*.

Figure 25. Copenhagen Zoo, Honey Tree (22). Courtesy of Jeremy Cherfas.

pounce upon its prey, a mechanical rabbit. Photocells would detect the tiger, and a chunk of meat would be delivered as a reward. This demonstrated for the public one of the natural acts of a tiger, stalking and pouncing, and at the same time provided an interesting and eventful exercise for the tiger. The honey tree in the bear exhibit at the Copenhagen Zoo (Fig. 25) is another instance in which natural behavior (a bear climbing a tree for honey) is rewarded and thereby repeated or learned.

There are many examples of this kind of system for encouraging animal behavior; however, there is some resistance to the idea of mechanized stimulation of animal behavior (23). Given the psychological component of the animal's interaction with its territory, natural furnishings in the exhibit can be used to increase spatial complexity and thus enrich the normal behavior of the exhibit animal. These natural objects can be temporary or permanent, stationary or mobile. By being natural (eg, leaves, sand, etc), they can increase the authenticity of the exhibit, informing the visitor more about the animal. The objection to natural substrates and objects is one of hygiene, and the risk of disease and parasites. Yet with the development of antibiotics and better veterinary care, this may be less of a problem in the future.

Altogether, attention to the spatial, physical, physiological, and behavioral aspects of the animals' world; con-

siderations of construction, materials, and cost; and the programmatic input of keepers, maintenance workers, and visitors establish the criteria necessary for good exhibit design and inspiration.

BIBLIOGRAPHY

1. L. B. Dal Maso, *Rome of the Caesars,* Bonechi, Rome, 1974, p. 78.
2. G. Loisel, *Histoire des Menageries de L'Antiquité à Nos Jours,* Vol. 1, Henri Laurens, Paris, 1912.
3. *400 Jahre Zoo,* Rudolf Halbelt, 1976, p. 29 Rheinsches Landesmuseum, Bonn.
4. D. Hancocks, *Animals and Architecture,* Praeger Publishers, New York, 1971.
5. *Guide Pittoresque Jardin des Plantes,* Bibliotheque Centrale, Paris c. 1915.
6. J. Cherfas, *Zoo 2000—A Look Beyond the Bars,* British Broadcasting Corp., London, 1984, p. 38.
7. "The Franklin Park Zoo," *Architectural Forum* (128) (May 1968).
8. *Guidebook, Chicago Zoological Park, Ill.,* Chicago Zoological Society, Chicago, Ill., 1936.
9. J. Fisher, *Zoos of the World—An Outline of Wild Animals in Captivity,* The Natural History Press, New York, 1967.
10. Ref. 4, p. 191.
11. R. Bigalke, "The Use of Moats in Zoological Gardens," in C. Jarvis and D. Morris, *International Zoo Yearbook,* Vol. 2, London Zoological Society, London, 1960.
12. J. C. Coe, "Design and Perception: Making the Zoo Experience Real," *Zoo Biology* **4,** 197–208 (1985).
13. W. H. Carr, "Tunnel in the Desert," The Sonora Desert Museum; Educational Series #2, Tucson, Arizona, 1957, pp. 18, 19.
15. B. Rudolfsky, *The Prodigious Builders,* Harcourt Brace Jovanovich, New York, 1977.
16. H. Hediger, *Wild Animals in Captivity—An Outline of the Biology of Zoological Gardens,* Dover Publications, New York, 1964.
17. H. Hediger, *The Psychology and Behavior of Wild Animals in Zoos and Circuses,* Dover Publications, New York, 1955.
18. D. Hancock, *Master Builders of the Animal World,* Harper & Row Publishers, New York, 1973.
19. K. Von Frisch, *Animal Architecture,* Harcourt Brace Jovanovich, New York, 1974.
20. *Architectural Forum* (130), 86–91 (June 1969).
21. H. Markowitz, *Behavioral Enrichment in the Zoo,* Van Nostrand Reinhold Co., New York, 1982.
22. Ref. 6, p. 151.
23. M. Hutchins, D. Hancocks, and C. Crockette, "Naturalistic Solutions to the Behavioral Problems of Captive Animals," *Der Zoologische Garten,* 28–41 (1984).

General References

References 2, 4, and 6 are good general references.

H. Hediger, *Man and Animal in the Zoo,* G. Vevers and W. Reade, trans., Delacorte Press, New York, 1969.

P. Batten, *Living Trophies,* Thomas Y. Crowell Co., New York, 1976.

Lord Zuckerman, *Great Zoos of the World—Their Origin and Significance,* Westview Press, Boulder, Col., 1980.

K. Sausman, ed., *Zoological Park & Aquarium Fundamentals,* American Association of Zoological Parks and Aquariums, Wheeling, W.V., 1982.

International Zoo Yearbook, London Zoological Society, London, published annually.

LYNNE IADAROLA
Chevy Chase, Maryland

SUPPLEMENT TO THE ENCYCLOPEDIA

By the time the page proofs have been read and returned to the publishers, six years will have been spent in compiling this Encyclopedia. Recruitment of authors began as the word list, or subjects to be covered, was developed. After several months drafts of articles arrived and the review process was under way.

The original intent was to publish all volumes of the Encyclopedia at one time. We recognized, however, that the advantages of publishing serially would outweigh the drawbacks, and permit all those involved to concentrate on one volume at a time. This also permitted the authors some flexibility in article titles.

It did, on the other hand, raise the problem of dealing with a handful of articles which missed their deadlines. In some cases, a change in the title (such as Architectural Fees to Remuneration) allowed us to include the article in a later volume.

This did not work in all cases, however. Therefore, some articles that missed the publisher's deadline, along with new topics that emerged after the initial word list was compiled, suggested to us the idea of incorporating this important material in the form of a Supplement, which we decided to place in this fifth (last) volume of the Encyclopedia.

ADAM, ROBERT AND JAMES

Robert and James Adam were among the few who gave their name to a style of architecture and interior design. The Adam style was predominant in England from about 1760 to 1776, and later in Scotland. The international influence of their work is reflected in the design of architects, Samuel McIntire and Charles Bulfinch of the United States.

The fashion for work of the Adams was based on the decorative freedom they brought to classic detailing. It represents a relief from the colder and more formal Palladian work of an earlier generation. A number of the large Jacobean country houses were modernized to make them acceptable to the age of "sensibility." The delicate, decorative Adam style fit this market to perfection. Planning of elaborate color schemes is an integral part of the Adam design, recorded in careful drawings.

The Adam brothers were the sons of the noted Scots architect William Adam (1689–1748) and Mary Adam nee Robertson (1699–1761). In addition to Robert (1728–1792) and James (1732–1794), their older brother John (1721–1792) and younger brother William (d. 1822) were also architects. There were also six daughters in the family.

Born in Kirkcaldy, Scotland, Robert Adam attended the Edinburgh High School and matriculated at Edinburgh College (now University) in 1743. His education was interrupted by the rebellion of 1745, and he joined his elder brother John as apprentice in his father's office. His father died 2 years later, and the brothers took over his commission for the building of Hopetoun House in West Lothian. The house for the first Earl of Hopetoun was built from 1699–1703 to the design of Sir William Bruce, remodelled by William Adam and, beginning in 1750, by his sons.

In 1754, Robert left for a 4-year Grand Tour in the company of Charles Hope, younger brother of the Earl of Hopetoun. In early 1755, Robert Adam was in Rome, where he met Charles-Louis Clérisseau at the French Academy. Clérisseau had also been a friend of the young William Chambers. Robert drew continuously, under the instruction of Clérisseau, and some 3000 drawings from the Italian journey are preserved in the Soane Museum in London. These included a number of architectural fantasies that were indicative of Robert Adam's search for a freer style than that of his present day England. Another companion was the artist Giovanni Battista Piranesi (1720–1778).

In 1757, Robert Adam went to the Dalmatian coast to visit the ruins of Diocletian's palace at Spalato. In a 5-week period, the palace was measured and drawings were made that were eventually published in 1764 under the title *Ruins of the Palace of the Emperor Diocletian, at Spalato in Dalmatia*. Publication in London had been delayed by Robert Adam until the enthusiastic reception given the 1762 publication of James Stuart's and Nicholas Revett's *Antiquities of Athens* had somewhat faded.

On his return, rather than going to Edinburgh, Robert opened his office in London in 1758. The influences on Adam included the earlier Palladian style represented by Lord Burlington (Richard Boyle, 1695–1753) and William Kent (1685–1748); current work in Paris, which he had visited on his way to Italy and had seen in books; and the monuments of antiquity and the Renaissance work that he had studied in Italy. Robert Adam's personal style was enriched by the major increase in published sources and in his own travel sketches. Throughout his life, Robert Adam delighted in drawing. Many of his drawings have been preserved in London's Soane Museum and other collections.

His chief rival in London was Sir William Chambers, who enjoyed the patronage of Lord Bute and who tutored the Prince of Wales, later George III, in architecture. Robert Adam set out to compete on equal terms, calling his brother James and two of his sisters, to join him in London. He was soon involved with work at Hatchland, Surrey, for Admiral Edward Boscawen, who also arranged for Robert Adam to design the Admiralty Screen in Whitehall, London, Robert's first independent architectural commission.

Throughout the 1760s, Robert and James Adam became famous for their interior designs to update existing country houses. Representative work of the first 10 years include:

Harewood, Yorkshire
Croome Court, Worcestershire
Compton Verney, Warwickshire
Kedleston Hall, Derbyshire
Boxwood, Wiltshire
Osterly Park, Middlesex
Syon House, Middlesex
Mersham-le-Hatch (first completely new house)
Lansdowne House
Newby Hall, Yorkshire
Luton Hoo, Bedfordshire
Kenwood, now in the County of London

Syon House is representative of their work. The original structure was a Jacobean house; the new work was within the shell. The large suite of new rooms was completed, but the proposal for a central rotunda in the internal court was not built. The hall is rectangular with an apse at one end. One end leads to an oval anteroom, the other to an anteroom with free-standing columns forming a square shape within a rectangle. The biggest challenge was the Jacobean long gallery, only 14-ft wide, for which Robert designed a series of pilasters, fireplaces, and decorative plasterwork incorporating painted decorations. Although constructed over a number of years, the variety and quality of the interiors was the first of their projects selected for publication in their books.

Lansdowne House was another important commission given to the Adams by Lord Bute and later Lord Selbourne (famous for negotiating the treaty that ceded independence to the American colonies). Lord Selbourne was later named Marquess of Lansdowne, which gave the name to the house. The sequence of rooms was impressive. A portion of the house was destroyed, and two of the interiors were bought for museums in the United States. The drawing room, now in the Philadelphia Museum of Art, has undergone recent restoration, returning the colors of the room to the original scheme (1).

The need for skilled workers to execute the interiors resulted in the Adam brothers training and employing large numbers of sculptors, painters, plasterworkers, furniture makers (including Thomas Chippendale), and metalworkers (Matthew Boulton). Although many careful drawings were produced for these interiors, many of the workers were artists in their own right, and particularly in the early work were used by the Adams with only some direction. At the peak of the operation, some 3000 workers are thought to have been employed by William Adam and company, of which the four Adam brothers were directors. Many projects were executed over several years, and trained workers would move from one house to another as work required.

Financial problems occurred with their speculative building project the Adelphi (1768–1772), a group of some 11 large townhouses involving embankment of a section of the Thames. Although financially ruinous, this was an important urban type that was taken up by others such as John Wood and his son in the Circus and Royal Crescent at Bath.

Later projects included townhouses in London, such as 20 St. James Square, 20 Portman Square, and the demolished Derby House in Grosvenor Square, known from drawings. In each of these the formal grouping of rooms for entertaining set new standards and successfully integrated rooms of varying shape and size in elegant sequence. The exteriors were simple, with classic detailing of shallow relief; interiors were elaborately decorated.

The Adams' architectural work is best demonstrated in the late work, such as Edinburgh University (1789) and the Register House, Edinburgh, built in the 1780s to designs of 1772. Robert Adam also used his romantic castle style at Culzean Castle (1777–1790) with its pseudo-Gothic exterior and its not at all Gothic interiors. Robert Adam died in 1792, and James in 1794.

After the failure of William Adam & Co. in 1801, assets were sold by the auction house of Christie's, London, in 1818 and 1821. Sir John Soane acquired the collection of the Adam's drawings in 1833. The published literature on the Adam brothers is extensive.

BIBLIOGRAPHY

1. T. Fisher, "Adam's Eve," *Progressive Architecture* **67**, 9, 145 (Sept. 1986).

General References

G. Beard, *The Work of Robert Adam,* John Bartholemew and Sons Ltd, Edinburgh, 1978; Bloomsbury Books, an imprint of Godfrey Cave Assoc. Ltd., new ed., under license from John Bartholemew & Sons, Ltd., London, 1987.

R. Oresko, ed., *The Works in Architecture of Robert and James Adam,* Academy Edition, London, and St. Martin's Press, New York, 1975.

J. and A. Rykwert, *Robert and James Adam, the Men and the Style,* Electa Editrice, Milano, 1984. Published in Great Britain by Collins, 1985, and in the United States by Rizzoli, New York, 1985.

J. Summerson, *Architecture in Britain 1530–1803,* 5th ed., Pelican History of Art, Penguin Books, Harmondsworth, UK, 1969.

Robert T. Packard, AIA
Reston, Virginia

CONCRETE—ADMIXTURES, CURING AND TESTING

Concrete is the only building material manufactured on the job and, as in any manufacturing process, close quality control at every stage of concrete production is vital. Only then will the end product, the hardened concrete, incorporate the desired properties, expected to give long, satisfactory service.

The use for which the concrete is intended determines the particular properties required. To attain concrete with these desired properties, many factors must be considered. Selection of materials and mix proportions, operations such as mixing, handling, placing, compacting, finishing and curing; and jobsite conditions such as temperature, humidity and wind—all play an important part. Each of them must be taken into consideration and then closely controlled (1).

In efforts to produce stronger, more durable concrete, members of the construction industry have studied and experimented with concrete, developing standards, specifications and manufacturing, and testing procedures toward that end. Those engaged in this work have included architects, engineers, producers of concrete ingredients and chemicals for admixtures, and representatives of testing agencies and laboratories. Many organizations such as the American Concrete Institute, Portland Cement Association, Expanded Shale Clay and Slate Institute, National Institute for Standards and Technology, ASTM, ANSI, and engineering departments at state and private universities have also played a major role.

The results of this research over the years have produced admixtures which increase the quality of concrete under a variety of conditions; developed curing procedures which ensure the concrete develops its full potential strength; and established field and laboratory testing procedures providing vital information to designers, contractors, and users of concrete structures.

ADMIXTURES

Admixtures for concrete are designed to aid in the control of a number of conditions encountered in the production of concrete. Compressive strength, flexural strength, watertightness, durability, and resistance to wear are some of the more common qualities that can be improved through the use of admixtures (1).

Table 1. Recommended Air Content Percentage

Nominal Maximum Size of Coarse Aggregate (in.)	Exposure	
	Mild	Extreme
⅜ (10 mm)	4.5	7.5
½ (13 mm)	4.0	6.0
¾ (19 mm)	3.5	6.0
1 (25 mm)	3.0	6.0
1½ (40 mm)	2.5	5.5
2 (50 mm)	2.0	5.0
3 (75 mm)	1.5	4.5

AIR ENTRAINING

Air entraining admixtures disperse small air bubbles in the concrete, which improves the concrete's resistance to freezing and thawing and to scaling by deicing chemicals. Recommended total air contents are shown in Table 1 for different exposure conditions and for maximum size of aggregate.

The advantages of air entrainment in concrete are generally well understood. In the freshly mixed or plastic state, air entrainment improves workability; increases slump; produces a more cohesive mix; reduces segregation, settlement shrinkage, and bleeding; and sometimes permits the use of less well-graded aggregate. Also, air entrainment in hardened concrete improves weatherability; increases watertightness and resistance to damage from freezing and thawing, deicing, scaling and sulfate resistance; and reduces the weight of concrete.

It is the control of this air content in air-entrained concrete that is probably one of the most difficult and most frustrating problems that the ready-mix concrete producer has to deal with. At times, concrete that shows acceptable air content in actual field tests of concrete in the freshly mixed state, later appears to have problems with weathering. Upon microscopic examination of hardened concrete, the air void system shown is inadequate.

In the typical non-air-entrained concrete, the heavier materials settle to the bottom of the slab, forcing the lighter material to the top. Channels are formed by the lighter bleed water displaced by the settlement of the heavier aggregates. In the wintertime, water enters these channels, freezes and expands, causing disintegration of the concrete.

Difficulties with Entraining and Maintaining Air Content

Actually, it is a well known fact that some concrete mixtures are known for their difficulty to entrain and maintain the required air content. Generally, these problem concrete mixtures contain either large amounts of fine materials, high carbon-content fly ash, high alkali cements, low mortar content placed at low slumps or at high concrete temperatures, or superplasticized concrete.

Today, however, with the introduction of a new multicomponent air-entraining admixture, it is possible to create an effective air void system in concrete which consists of a sufficient number of very stable, small, disconnected, closely-spaced air bubbles. The advantages to concrete include a greatly improved stability of entrained air; an improved air void system in hardened concretes; and an improved ability to entrain and retain air in low-slump concretes, concretes containing high carbon-content fly ash, concretes containing large amounts of fine material, concretes using high alkali cement, high temperature concretes, concretes with extended mixing times, and concretes containing high range water reducing chemical admixtures (superplasticizers).

Quality Control Testing

Obviously, with acceptable aggregates, the amount and quality of air entrainment in concrete is the prime determinant in achieving durability. Therefore, frequent checking of the air content should be a common practice on jobsites (2).

HOT AND COLD WEATHER CONSTRUCTION

Hot and cold weather construction requires that additional precautions be taken to ensure proper curing of the concrete. High temperatures accelerate the hardening of concrete and more water is needed to maintain the consistency of the mix and more cement is required to prevent a strength reduction due to the added water. Chilled water or ice may be used to reduce the temperature of the aggregates, and admixtures can be used to retard the initial set. Hot weather construction begins at temperatures ranging from 75°F to 100°F.

Generally in cold weather, heat must be provided to keep the concrete above 40°F during placing and the early stages of curing for a period of 7 days. Protection against freezing may be necessary for up to 2 weeks. This is accomplished by covering the concrete with plastic sheets and heating the interior space with a portable heater called a salamander. Type III and IIIA cement, low water-cement ratio, accelerator type admixtures, and steam curing can be employed to reduce the time the concrete must be protected. Concrete should never be placed directly on frozen ground. Fresh concrete that was frozen during curing should be removed and replaced because frozen concrete containing ice crystals has very little strength.

Hot Weather Concrete

The ACI Committee 305 on Hot Water Concreting published a report ACI 305R–77, later revised in 1982 which provides designers and contractors with much information on this subject. It defines hot weather and its effects on concrete. George R. Burg, a member of the committee, lists the following undesirable effects in the absence of special procedures:

1. Accelerated setting time.
2. Increased water demand.
3. Decreased strengths.
4. Greater tendency to crack or craze.

5. More difficulty in achieving proper volume of entrained air.

6. Difficulty with normal handling, finishing, and curing.

7. Reduced durability due to increased water demand and cracking.

8. Increased rate of slump loss.

Recently, other factors have complicated hot weather operations. They should be considered and compensated for, along with climatic factors, and may include:

1. Greater use of finely ground cement which increases rate of hydration.

2. Greater use of concrete with high compressive strengths, requiring higher cement contents.

3. Design of thin concrete section with corresponding greater percentage of steel.

4. Increased size of concrete delivery trucks.

5. Requirements for movement of large volumes of low slump concrete over greater horizontal and vertical distances.

6. Increased use of concrete pumping equipment.

7. Increased use of conveyor belts.

8. Economics necessary to continue work in extremely hot weather.

Greater care and effort is required to produce, transport, and place concrete under conditions of high temperature, low humidity, and high winds. The need for overall cooperation and organization of the concrete construction team is increased during hot weather.

Committee recommendations include the use of cold water or ice for mixing water, prohibition on additional water (retempering) on delivery, and the use of retarding admixtures, meeting ASTM C494 requirements which, if carefully controlled, can ameliorate the effects of the elevated temperature.

Cold Weather Concrete

The ACI Committee 306 has met for over 25 years and issued reports on the effects of concreting in cold weather. One of the early reports "Recommended Practice for Cold Weather Concreting" was issued in 1966 and withdrawn in 1978 at which time the Committee issued a new report, revised in 1983 and has released a Standard Specification for Cold Weather Concreting (ACI 306.1–87). In this specification cold weather is defined as a period when for more than three successive days the average daily outdoor temperature drops below 40°F (5°C). Concrete placed during these conditions will not reach its designed or expected strength. Measures to offset this loss of strength include:

1. Heating the ingredients of the concrete; ie, cement, aggregate, and mixing water.

2. Temporary enclosure of the area of the pour and introduction of heat to the area.

3. Addition of accelerating agents such as ASTM C494.

4. Use of Type III portland cement meeting requirements of ASTM C150.

5. Addition of 100 lb/yd^3 (59 kg/m^3) cement.

However the addition of the strength accelerating agent may introduce a new problem. This material contains calcium chloride which, if improperly used, may reduce the ultimate strength of the concrete and cause an electrolysis condition to develop which may cause oxidation of reinforcing steel. Hence producers of the accelerating agents now have available such agents which do not contain chlorides.

ACI Specification 306.1–87 notes that detailed procedures for production, transportation, placement, protection, curing, and temperature monitoring of concrete during cold weather shall be submitted to the architect/engineer.

CURING AND PROTECTION

Two physical properties have a very pronounced effect on the final compressive strength attained by concrete—temperature and the rate at which the water used in mixing is allowed to leave the concrete. The optimum temperature for curing concrete is 73°F.

In the ACI Committee 308 report 1981, revised 1986, *Standard Practice for Curing Concrete,* curing is defined as maintaining a satisfactory moisture content and temperature in concrete during its early stages so that desired properties may develop. The strength and durability of concrete will be fully developed only if it is cured properly. Where ambient conditions of moisture, humidity, and temperature are sufficiently favorable other action may not be required.

Curing Methods and Materials

Water Curing. The use of ponding, sprays, steam, or saturated cover materials such as burlap or cotton mats, rugs, earth, sand, sawdust, and straw or hay.

Ponding or Immersion. The most thorough method used sometimes for slabs for bridge floors, culverts, pavements, flat roofs, in situations where a pond can be created by a dike at slab edge.

Fog Spraying or Sprinkling. An effective curing method in situations where runoff can be controlled and water supply is adequate.

Sealing Materials

Plastic film—0.004 in. (0.10 mm) thickness meeting ASTM C171 (1.3.1.7).

Reinforced paper—Two layers of Kraft paper with bituminous adhesive meeting same ASTM as above.

Liquid Membrane—Forming curing compounds complying with ASTM C309 (1.3.1.9). Compounds of waxes, natural and synthetic resins of high volatility at atmospheric temperature.

Cold-Weather Protection and Curing. Air-entrained concrete should not be allowed to freeze and thaw in a saturated condition before developing a compressive strength of 3500 psi (24 MPa); must comply with ACI Committee 306 (1.3.2.4).

Hot-Weather Curing. This curing must comply in accordance with ACI Committee 305 (1.3.2.3).

Mass Concrete Curing. Mass concrete is a volume of cast-in-place concrete large enough to require measures be taken to cope with the generation of heat and volume change to minimize cracking. It may occur in piers, abutments, dams, heavy footings, and similar massive constructions. Such measures may include: use of low cement content; use of a pozzolan or other mineral admixture; cooling the concrete materials; use of ice instead of mixing water; use of embedded cooling pipes in the concrete; and use of low heat cement. Such procedures are described in ACI Committee 207 (1.3.2.1).

Other Construction Requiring Curing

Precast units
Vertical slipform construction
Shotcrete
Refractory concrete
Cement paint, stucco, and plaster
Shell structures
Insulating concrete
Concrete with colored or metallic surfaces

TESTING

Concrete testing is performed both in the field at the construction site and in engineering laboratories. Laboratory testing may be to determine the quality of samples prepared in the field or may be a part of research projects to further the knowledge of the behavior of concrete. For this latter purpose beams, columns, slabs, and assemblies are cast under rigid quality controls and then tested, often to failure to provide valuable information on concrete materials, effect of admixtures, methods, and types of reinforcing, concrete placing and curing methods and such techniques as prestressing and posttensioning. In addition to these stress tests other techniques such as striking concrete surfaces with a hammer, known as a delamination survey may provide a trained technician with information about the density of in-place concrete, and petrographic and spectrographic analysis can reveal the presence of a variety of substances which may affect the strength and durability of the sample of concrete in question.

On most cast-in-place concrete structures the specifications require tests be performed on samples of the concrete as it is being placed.

Sampling Fresh Concrete ASTM C–172

Sample the concrete at two or more regularly spaced intervals during discharge of the middle portion of the batch. Do not obtain samples from the very first or last portions of the batch discharged. Samples should be obtained in as short a time as possible, but in no instance

shall it exceed fifteen minutes. A sample of at least one cubic foot is required for strength tests. Smaller samples may be used for routine air content and slump tests.

Sample by repeatedly passing a receptacle through the entire discharge stream or by completely diverting the discharge into a sample container (wheelbarrow).

Transport the sample container to where the fresh concrete tests are to be performed or where test specimens are to be molded. The sample shall be combined and remixed with a shovel the minimum amount necessary to ensure uniformity.

Start tests for slump or air content, or both, within five minutes after obtaining the final portion of the composite sample. Start molding specimens for strength tests within fifteen minutes after fabricating the composite sample.

Slump Test ASTM C–143

The purpose of the test is to determine the consistency of fresh concrete and to check uniformity of concrete from batch by means of a guide standard.

The procedure is as follows:

1. Dampen the mold (slump cone) and place it on a flat, moist, nonabsorbent (rigid) surface. It shall be held firmly in place during filling by the operator standing on the two foot pieces. From the sample of concrete obtained in accordance with the instructions above, immediately fill the mold in three layers, each approximately one-third the volume of the mold. Rod each layer with 25 strokes of the tamping rod. Uniformly distribute the strokes over the cross section of each layer. Rod the second layer and the top layer each throughout its depth so that the strokes just penetrate into the underlying layer (Figs. 1a–1c).

2. In filling and rodding the top layer, heap the concrete above the mold before rodding is started and keep excess concrete above the top of the mold during the entire rodding operation. After the top layer has been rodded, strike off the surface of the concrete by means of screeding and rolling motion of the tamping rod. Remove the mold immediately from the concrete by raising it carefully in a vertical direction. Raise the mold a distance of 12 inches in five seconds by a steady upward lift with no lateral or torsional motion. Complete the entire test in two and one-half minutes (Figs. 1d and 1e).

3. Immediately measure the slump by determining the vertical difference between the top of the mold and the displaced original center of the top surface of the specimen (Fig. 1f).

Making Compression Test Specimens ASTM C–172

Specimens are made and tested for either of two reasons: (1) to check the adequacy of mix proportions for strength or as a basis for acceptance, or for quality control, (2) to determine when to remove forms or when a structure may be put into service.

Mold specimens promptly on a level, rigid, horizontal surface, free from vibration and other disturbances, at a place as near as practicable to the location where they are

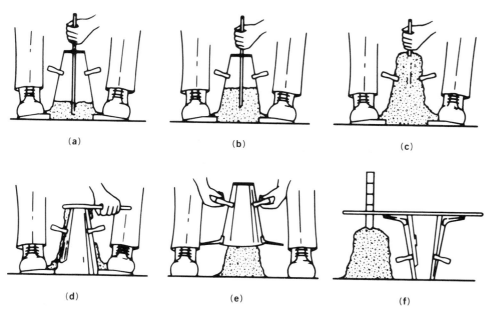

Figure 1. (a) Tamp 25 times; (b) tamp 25 times into first layer; (c) tamp 25 times into second layer; (d) strike off, clear excess; (e) lift evenly upward; (f) measure slump.

to be stored during the first 24 hours. If it is not practical to mold the specimens where they are to be stored, move them to the place of storage immediately after being struck off. Avoid jarring, striking, tilting, or scarring the surface of the specimens when moving to a safe place.

Place the concrete into the molds using a scoop. Select each scoopful from the sample, as obtained in the outline above, to ensure that it is a representative sample of the batch. Move the scoop around the top edge of the mold as the concrete is discharged in order to ensure a symmetrical distribution of the concrete and a minimum segregation of the course aggregate within the mold. For concrete with a slump of three inches or above, the following procedure should be used:

1. Place the concrete in the molds in three layers of approximately equal volume. Rod each layer with the rounded end of the rod 25 times, distributing the strokes uniformly over the cross section of the mold. When rodding the second and third layer, allow the rod to penetrate about one-half inch into the underlying layer. After each rodding operation, tap the sides of the cylinders lightly to close any voids (Fig. 2a–2c).

2. After consolidation, finish the top surfaces by striking them off with the tamping rod or with a trowel or float (Fig. 2d).

3. When curing, cover the specimens immediately after finishing with a nonabsorptive cover or plate to

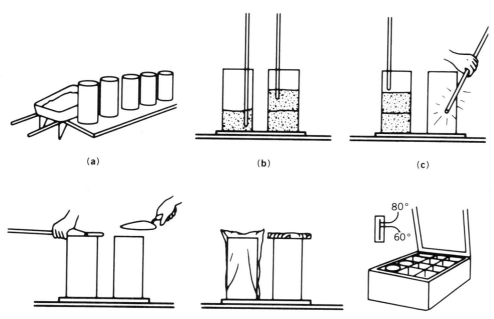

Figure 2. (a) Prepare site to cast free from vibration; (b) fill ½ and tamp, fill ⅔ and tamp; (c) fill to overflow and tamp, tap sides; (d) screed off excess, trowel top; (e) plastic cover, board cover, and identify cylinders; (f) cure first 24 hours.

prevent evaporation of water from the unhardened concrete. During the first 24 hours after molding, store all test specimens under conditions that maintain the temperature immediately adjacent to the specimens in the range of 60 to 80 degrees and prevent loss of moisture from the specimens (Fig. **2e** and **2f**).

4. After the 24 hour on the job curing period, the cylinders shall be transported to the laboratory for testing in a container that will keep them from excessive vibration or bumping so as not to damage the green specimens.

5. At the end of the test curing time, usually determined to be 7 or 28 days, the outer cylinder is removed and the concrete cylinder is placed in a press. The point at which the cylinder fails in compression is registered on a gauge in pounds, and the strength of the concrete is calculated in pounds per square inch.

Reports of these cylinder tests are furnished to the project architect and structural engineer. When such reports indicate concrete with strength below design requirements additional testing and/or corrective action may be initiated.

Other Applicable Tests

In addition to the slump test and the cylinders prepared for compression testing jobsite tests can be performed to determine air content by pressure method ASTM C–231 or by volumetric method ASTM C–173 and unit weight ASTM C–138.

A less frequently used test is to prepare rectangle of concrete, 6 × 6 by 20 in. (152 × 152 by 508 mm) for a beam flexural strength test. These tests are described in a booklet, *Testing Freshly Mixed Concrete* (3).

BIBLIOGRAPHY

1. *Concrete Performance Data Handbook,* Master Builders, Division of Martin Marietta Corporation, Cleveland, Ohio, 1983.

2. G. R. Burg, *Concrete Products,* Master Builders, Cleveland, Ohio, October 1985.

3. G. R. Burg, *Testing Freshly Mixed Concrete,* Master Builders, Division of Martin Marietta Corporation, Cleveland, Ohio.

General References

Concrete Construction is a magazine for architects, engineers, contractors, and suppliers of materials and equipment providing sound technical information on all facets of concrete construction from residential to high-rise.

See also COLD DRY CLIMATE, BUILDING IN; COLD WET CLIMATE, BUILDING IN; CONCRETE—ARCHITECTURAL; CONCRETE FORMING; CONCRETE—GENERAL PRINCIPLES; HOT DRY CLIMATE, BUILDING IN

JOSEPH A. WILKES, FAIA
Annapolis, Maryland

FLOORING, WOOD

In the Middle Ages flooring began to be used—rough-hewn planks, shaped by broad ax and foot adz. Many examples exist, throughout the world, of floors that have been in daily use for the last 800 years. With the early machine years came finer milling and the ornate parquets—many patterns still in use today.

Many species of wood, both softwoods and hardwoods, have been used for flooring in building types including residential, commercial, institutional, and educational.

The most commonly used wood is oak, both red and white. Maple has long been the standard material for gymnasium floors because of its hardness. It provides a durable, nonsplintering surface with good finishing and maintenance qualities.

Other hardwoods more rarely used because of their higher cost have included beech, birch, black locust, cherry, pecan, and walnut.

Softwoods including varieties of pine, fir, hemlock, spruce, and larch have been used for flooring in the U.S. since colonial times and although less frequently used today still find application in residences and restoration of historic monuments.

STRIP OAK FLOORING PEAKED IN 1956

The oak flooring industry grew at a steady pace with its singular product being strip flooring of various dimensions. Later, some small portion of strip was made into unit block parquet. Also there was some production of wider planks. In the late 1930s a small amount of factory-finished flooring began to appear.

Following World War II, oak floors were used in the vast majority of homes built during the boom years of the 1950s. New products began to appear as factory-finishing expanded. New plywood technology contributed to oak-plywood block flooring. Basement houses used strip over diagonal solid boards or over the newly available plywood subflooring. Construction in the southern states was joist and subfloor system over a crawl space and strip again was the choice. The apartment industry also boomed with solid strip block and the plywood laminated block installed in hot asphalt-type mastic over thousands of acres of concrete.

All this activity resulted in Oak Floor Industry realizing its peak production year in 1956 with 47 manufacturers operating 243 flooring machines producing 1 billion 400 million feet of product.

TYPES OF WOOD FLOORING

Table 1 shows the species and grades of wood used as flooring indicating the industry organization, dimensions of the materials produced, and notes related to the producer associations.

1. Flooring can be manufactured from practically every commercially available species of wood. In the United States wood flooring is grouped for market-

Table 1. Typical Grades and Sizes of Boards by Species or Regional Group[a]

GROUP	INDUSTRY ORGANIZATION	GRADE	THICKNESS	WIDTH		NOTES
Oak (also beech, birch, pecan, and hard maple)	National Oak Flooring Manufacturers' Assoc.	Quarter Sawn: Clear Select Plain Sawn: Clear Select No. 1 Common No. 2 Common	$3/4''$, $1/2''$ Standard; also $3/8''$ $5/16''$	Face $1^1/2''$ $2''$ $2^1/4''$		This association grades birch, beech, and hard maple. First Grade, Second Grade, Third Grade, and "Special Grades." Pecan is graded: First Grade, First Grade Red, Second Grade, Second Grade Red, Third Grade.
Hard maple (also beech and birch) (acer saccharum—not soft maple)	Maple Flooring Manufacturers' Assoc. Inc.	First Grade Second Grade Third Grade Fourth Grade Combinations	$3/8''$, $12/32''$ $41/32''$, $1/2''$ $33/32''$ $53/32''$, $5/8''$	Face $1^1/2''$ $2''$ $2^1/4''$ $3^1/4''$		Association states that beech and birch have physical properties that make them fully suitable as substitutes for hard maple. See manufacturer for available width and thickness combinations.
Southern pine	Southern Pine Inspection Bureau	B & B C C & Btr D No. 2	$3/8''$, $1/2''$ $5/8''$, $1''$ $1^1/4''$, $1^1/2''$	Nom. $2''$ $3''$ $4''$ $5''$ $6''$	Face $1^1/8''$ $2^1/8''$ $3^1/8''$ $4^1/8''$ $5^1/8''$	Grain may be specified as edge (rift), near-rift, or flat. If not specified, manufacturer will ship flat or mixed grain boards. See manufacturer for available width and thickness combinations.
Western woods (Douglas fir, hemlock, Englemann spruce, Idaho pine, incense cedar, lodgepole pine, Ponderosa pine, sugar pine, Western larch, Western red cedar)	Western Wood Products Association	Select: 1 & 2 clear- B & Btr C Select D Select Finish: Superior Prime E	$2''$ and thinner	Nominal $3''$ $4''$ $6''$		Flooring is machined tongue and groove and may be furnished in any grade agreeable to buyer and seller. Grain may be specified as vertical (VG), flat (FG), or mixed (MG). Basic size for flooring is $1'' \times 4'' \times 12'$; standard lengths $4'$ and above.
Eastern white pine Norway pine Jack pine Eastern spruce Balsam fir Eastern hemlock Tamarack	Northern Hardwood & Pine Manufacturers' Association	C & Btr Select D Select Stained Select	$3/8''$, $1/2''$ $5/8''$, $1''$, $1^1/4''$, $1^1/2''$	Nom. $2''$ $3''$ $4''$ $5''$ $6''$	Face $1^1/8''$ $2^1/8''$ $3^1/8''$ $4^1/8''$ $5^1/8''$	The various species included in this "Lake States Region" group provide different visual features. Consult manufacturer or local supplier to determine precisely what is available in terms of species and appearance.

Darrel Downing Rippeteau, Architect; Washington, D.C.

[a] Reprinted by permission of John Wiley & Sons, Inc., *Architectural Graphic Standards*, 8th ed., 1988. Courtesy of C. G. Ramsey and H. R. Sleeper.

ing purposes roughly according to species and region. There are various grading systems used with various species, and often different specifications for different sized boards in a given species. For instance, nail size and spacing varies among the several board sizes typically available in oak.

2. Information given here should be used for preliminary decision making only. Precise specifications must be obtained from the supplier or from the appropriate industry organization named below.

3. Several considerations in wood flooring selection and installation are applicable industrywide.

4. Table 1 includes typical grades and sizes of boards for each species or regional group. Grade classifications vary, but in each case one can assume that the first grade listed is the highest quality, and that the quality decreases with each succeeding grade. The best grade will typically minimize or exclude features such as knots, streaks, spots, checks, and torn grain and will contain the highest percentage of longer boards. Grade standards have been reduced in recent years for practically all commercially produced flooring, hence a thorough review of exact grade specifications is in order when selecting wood flooring.

5. End matching gives a complete tongue and grooved joint all around each board. Board length is reduced as required to obtain the matched ends.

Strip Flooring. Figure 1 shows details of sizes and patterns. Strip flooring, either hardwood or softwood, is tongue and groove (T&G) on long edges as well as ends

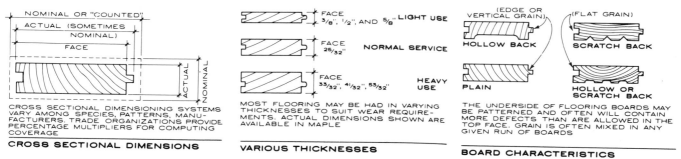

Figure 1. Sizes and patterns of strip flooring. Reprinted by permission of John Wiley & Sons, Inc., *Architectural Graphic Standards*, 8th ed., 1988. Courtesy of C. G. Ramsey and H. R. Sleeper.

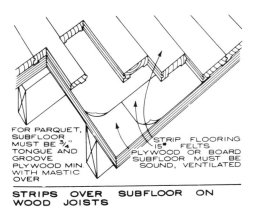

Figure 2. Strip flooring on wood frame construction. Reprinted by permission of John Wiley & Sons, Inc., *Architectural Graphic Standards,* 8th ed., 1988. Courtesy of C. G. Ramsey and H. R. Sleeper.

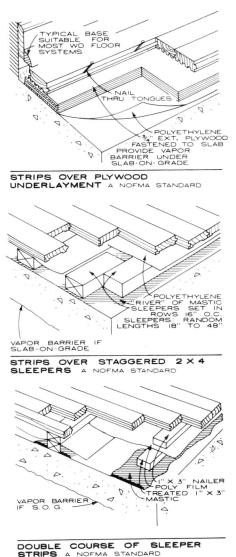

Figure 3. Strip flooring nailed to wood sleepers attached to concrete slab. Reprinted by permission of John Wiley & Sons, Inc., *Architectural Graphic Standards,* 8th ed., 1988. Courtesy of C. G. Ramsey and H. R. Sleeper.

(end matched) to produce best results. It can be installed over boards or plywood or other panel composite subfloor by nailing through the tongue, by hand nailing, or by machine nailing, often using special deformed shank nails for greater holding power (see Figs. 2 and 3).

Special installation systems providing positive attachment to concrete slabs may employ steel splines locking strips together or metal channel runners with clips (see Fig. 4).

Parquet Flooring. Parquet flooring, using many varieties of hardwoods in many colors and patterns, was installed in the most elaborate palaces, government buildings and residences throughout Europe and other parts of the world during the 19th century. Some, with restoration, are in use today (see Fig. 5). In more recent times the interest in parquet flooring has produced a variety of new materials and sizes most suitable for installation with mastics on plywood subflooring in wood frame construction or directly on slabs in concrete construction (see Fig. 6).

Wood Block Flooring. End-grain wood blocks in thicknesses up to 4 in. have been used in industrial buildings for many years. Covered with bituminous pitch, this ma-

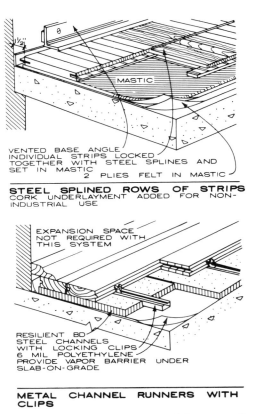

Figure 4. Strip flooring over concrete slab construction using metal splines and metal channel runners with clips. Reprinted by permission of John Wiley & Sons, Inc., *Architectural Graphic Standards,* 8th ed., 1988. Courtesy of C. G. Ramsey and H. R. Sleeper.

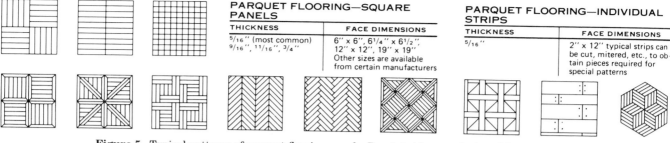

<table>
<tr><th colspan="2">PARQUET FLOORING—SQUARE PANELS</th></tr>
<tr><th>THICKNESS</th><th>FACE DIMENSIONS</th></tr>
<tr><td>5/16″ (most common)
9/16″, 11/16″, 3/4″</td><td>6″ x 6″, 6¼″ x 6½″,
12″ x 12″, 19″ x 19″
Other sizes are available
from certain manufacturers</td></tr>
</table>

PARQUET FLOORING—INDIVIDUAL STRIPS	
THICKNESS	FACE DIMENSIONS
5/16″	2″ x 12″ typical strips can be cut, mitered, etc., to obtain pieces required for special patterns

Figure 5. Typical patterns of parquet flooring panels. Reprinted by permission of John Wiley & Sons, Inc., *Architectural Graphic Standards*, 8th ed., 1988. Courtesy of C. G. Ramsey and H. R. Sleeper.

terial provides a durable, comfortable, and nonstatic surface. After years of wear, the surface can be sanded smooth and refinished for more years of service. In nonindustrial uses the pitch coating is replaced by a urethane finish (see Fig. 7).

INSTALLATION

Wood flooring is visually attractive and provides an excellent wearing surface. However, wood requires particular care in handling and installation to prevent moisture attack. Minimize moisture attack on wood floors by avoiding

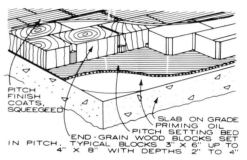

Figure 7. Wood block flooring set in mastic with pitch coating for industrial use. Urethane coating for nonindustrial use. Reprinted by permission of John Wiley & Sons, Inc., *Architectural Graphic Standards*, 8th ed., 1988. Courtesy of C. G. Ramsey and H. R. Sleeper.

proximity to wet areas. Installation should occur after all "wet" jobs are completed. All the permanent lighting and heating plant should be installed to ensure constant temperature and humidity.

Expansion and contraction is a fact of life with most wood flooring. Perimeter base details that allow for movement and ventilation are included in the details above. Moisture control is further enhanced by use of a vapor barrier under a slab on or below grade. This provision should be carefully considered for each installation. Wood structures require adequate ventilation in basement and crawl space.

Wearing properties vary from species to species in wood flooring and should be considered along with appearance. In addition, grain pattern will affect a given species wearability. For instance, industrial wood blocks are typically placed with the end grain exposed because it presents the toughest wearing surface. The thickness of the wood above tongues in T & G flooring may be increased for extra service.

Because of the varying properties of different species of wood to be used for flooring, it is recommended that installers follow closely the instructions of the manufacturers and call on their representatives if questions arise.

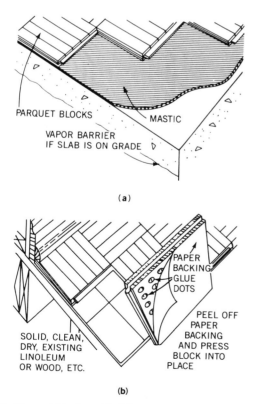

Figure 6. Parquet blocks set in (a) mastic and (b) pressure-sensitive "do it yourself" prefinished panels. Reprinted by permission of John Wiley & Sons, Inc., *Architectural Graphic Standards*, 8th ed., 1988. Courtesy of C. G. Ramsey and H. R. Sleeper.

ASSOCIATIONS AND STANDARDS

National Wood Flooring Association, 11046 Manchester Rd., Kirkwood, MO 63122

National Oak Flooring Manufacturers Association, 8 North Third Street, Memphis, TN 38103

Maple Flooring Manufacturers Association, 60 Revere Drive, Northbrook, IL 60062

American National Standard for Laminated Hardwood Flooring, ANSI/HPMA LHF, 1987

Hardwood Plywood Manufacturers Association, P.O. Box 2789, Reston, VA 22090

See also CERAMIC TILE; MOISTURE PROTECTION; RESILIENT FLOORING; RUGS AND CARPETS; TERMITE CONTROL BY SOIL POISONING; TERRAZZO; WOOD IN CONSTRUCTION; WOOD, STRUCTURAL PANELS

JOSEPH A. WILKES, FAIA
Annapolis, Maryland

FRAMING, WOOD

Wood-frame buildings have been built in the United States since the early settler days. Many of these buildings continue to serve the function for which they were originally intended: homes, churches, barns, schools, etc.

Historically, the sizes and types of wood material assembled to form the framing of a building were chosen on the basis of the craftsmen's experience and judgment. The twentieth century, however, has seen the development of scientifically-based engineering principles that guide nearly every step in the choice and assembly of materials in order to produce a safe wood-frame structure. These principles are contained in building codes that must be understood and properly applied.

TYPES OF WOOD FRAMING

The three most commonly used methods of wood-frame construction in the United States are post-and-beam, balloon, and platform. These three methods of construction are differentiated on the basis of how the structural elements of the building are assembled.

Post-and-beam construction consists of large structural members that are assembled on top of a foundation system and interconnected to form the framework of the building. Non-structural panels are assembled and installed between the structural framework to form the building enclosure.

Balloon construction is used in buildings with two or more stories. The structural elements consist of nominal 2-in.- (5.1-cm-) thick dimension lumber in the form of studs and joists. Full height studs extending in one piece from foundation to roof are erected to form the exterior shell of the building. The floors are then installed by connecting them to the wall structure.

Post-and-beam and balloon framing are rapidly disappearing as methods of construction, although post-and-beam framing remains popular for crawl-space framing in the Northwest and in coastal areas.

The most commonly used approach to wood framing is platform construction, in which the structural elements consist of nominal 2-in.- (5.1-cm-) thick dimension lumber in the form of studs and joists. After the foundation is built, the joists and sheathing for the first floor are assembled, forming a platform on which to continue working. The walls of the first floor are assembled, erected on the platform, and interconnected to form the framework of the first-floor enclosure. If the building is to contain another floor, the joists and sheathing for the next level are assembled on top of the wall framing to form another platform. Again, wall framing is assembled, erected on the platform, and interconnected. Ceiling joists and roof framing are erected on top of the walls of the uppermost floor platform.

The material presented in the remainder of this section describes the process and materials used in platform construction and is based on Ref. 1. The discussion begins with foundation systems, moves on to floor and wall systems, and closes with roof systems.

FOUNDATIONS

The foundation system must be capable of supporting the wall, floor, roof, and other building loads. It must also be level and square since it forms the base for the entire superstructure.

In buildings with basements, the foundation system consists of a footing and a foundation wall. The footing forms the base on which the wall rests and serves to transmit the superimposed load to the soil. A typical foundation wall footing, illustrated in Figure 1, is rectangular in cross section. As a general rule the depth of the footing is equal to the thickness of the wall it supports; its width is twice the width of the supported wall. The required dimensions of the footing for a specific building are a function of the bearing capacity of the soil and of the load imposed by the building. These required dimensions are usually specified in the local building code.

The foundation wall forms an enclosure for the basement; it carries the wall, floor, roof, and other building loads; and it forms the base on which wood framing rests. The most common materials used in the construction of foundation walls are cast-in-place (poured) concrete or concrete block. Steel or wooden forms must be erected on top of the footing to hold the liquid concrete to form the foundation wall as illustrated in Figure 2. After the concrete is placed, and while it is still in a plastic state, anchor bolts are inserted in the top of the wall at 8-ft (2.44-m) intervals. The anchor bolts serve to attach the floor framing to the foundation wall. Concrete block foundation walls are laid directly on the footing, as illustrated in Figure 3. The blocks in the top course are solid to form a cap interrupting the vertical migration of moisture, radon, and termites. Anchor bolts, to which the floor framing is attached, are inserted between the blocks at 8-ft (2.44-m) intervals as the blocks are laid. The thickness of poured concrete and concrete block foundation walls ranges from 8 to 12 in. (20.3 to 30.5 cm), depending on the height of the soil outside the wall. The thickness is commonly dictated by local building codes. Both poured concrete and concrete block foundation walls require water-

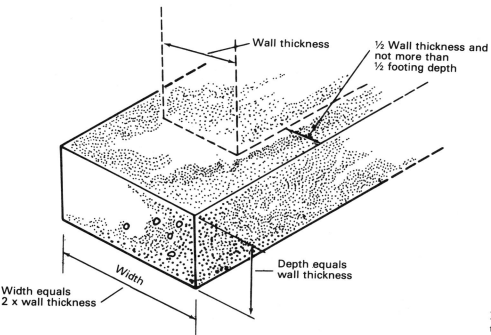

Wall thickness

½ Wall thickness and
not more than
½ footing depth

Depth equals
wall thickness

Width

Width equals
2 x wall thickness

Figure 1. Concrete footing. Courtesy of National Association of Home Builders.

proofing treatment. In addition to the waterproof coating, concrete blocks are first coated with a cement-mortar coating to seal and smooth the outer wall surface.

Concrete is usually used to finish the floor of basement foundation buildings. Structurally, the floor keeps the soil pressure from pushing in the bottom of the foundation walls. Sewer and water lines serving the building and basement floor drains should be installed first. Next, 4 in. (10.2 cm) of compacted gravel and a 6 mil polyethylene film should be placed. Finally, a 3½-in. (8.9-cm) concrete slab should be poured.

Crawl-space foundation systems consist of a footing

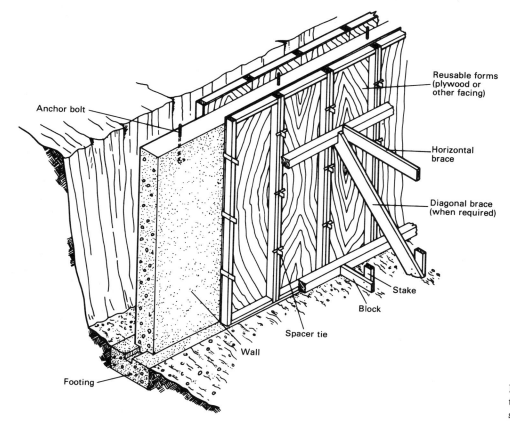

Anchor bolt

Reusable forms
(plywood or
other facing)

Horizontal
brace

Diagonal brace
(when required)

Stake

Block

Spacer tie

Wall

Footing

Figure 2. Poured concrete foundation wall. Courtesy of National Association of Home Builders.

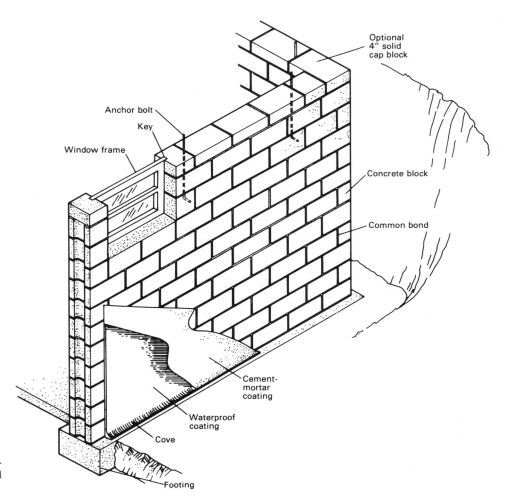

Figure 3. Concrete block foundation wall. Courtesy of National Association of Home Builders.

and foundation wall constructed in much the same manner as basement foundation walls. A crawl-space foundation may be chosen because of the presence of a high water table or because of the cost since a crawl-space foundation avoids the cost of excavation for a basement. Excavation is generally confined to the perimeter of the structure and to a depth adequate to place the footing below the depth of frost penetration. In northern states and in Canada, frost penetration may be 4 ft (1.2 m) or more. The height of the crawl-space wall should be adequate to provide 18 in. (45.7 cm) between ground level within the crawl space and the underside of floor framing members. Further protection from moisture of the floor framing members should be provided in the form of adequate ventilation of the crawl space and installation of a vapor retarder on the ground, as illustrated in Figure 4.

Both basement foundation walls and crawl space foundation walls can be constructed using pressure-treated lumber and plywood. The pressure-treated wood foundation system illustrated in Figure 5 offers some unique advantages: electrical wiring is readily installed; insulation may be installed between the studs; and standard interior wall finish materials are easily nailed over the studs. Other advantages include suitability for construction in cold weather; potential for prefabrication; and

fewer tradesmen to coordinate since carpenters build and erect the foundation panels.

Slab-on-grade foundation systems combine the footing, foundation wall, and ground floor into one system. In cold climates where the ground freezes to any appreciable depth the footing for the slab-on-grade foundation system must be set below the frost line. A poured concrete or concrete block foundation wall, or stem wall, is constructed on top of the footing as illustrated in Figure 6. The stem wall should extend at least 8 in. (20.3 cm) above finished-grade level. Sewer and water lines are installed within the perimeter of the foundation and a 4–6-in.-(10.2–15.2-cm-) thick layer of well tamped gravel or crushed stone is then installed and covered with a vapor retarder such as 6-mil polyethylene sheet. Rigid-board insulation, such as polystyrene, should be installed either under the floor slab, as illustrated in Figure 6, or on the outside of the stem wall, as illustrated in Figure 7. Finally, the concrete floor slab is placed with a minimum thickness of 3.5 in. (8.9 cm). An alternative form of the slab-on-grade foundation and floor system is illustrated in Figure 7. In this illustration the functions of the footing, stem wall, and floor slab are performed by a continuous concrete structure placed in one continuous pour. Steel reinforcing rods and wire mesh add strength to the con-

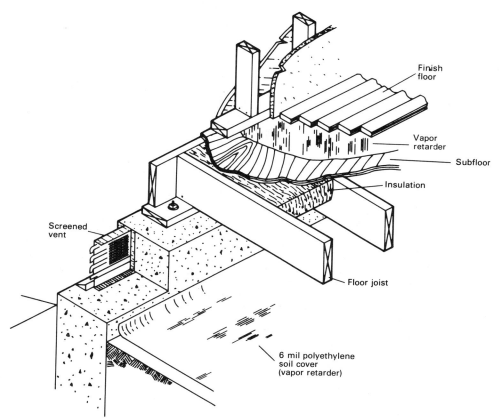

Finish
floor

Vapor
retarder

Subfloor

Insulation

Screened
vent

Floor joist

6 mil polyethylene
soil cover
(vapor retarder)

Figure 4. Crawl-space vent and soil cover. Courtesy of National Association of Home Builders.

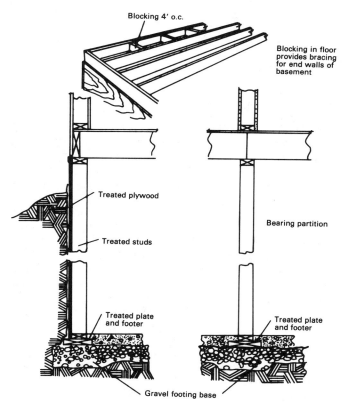

Blocking 4' o.c.

Blocking in floor
provides bracing
for end walls of
basement

Treated plywood

Bearing partition

Treated studs

Treated plate
and footer

Treated plate
and footer

Gravel footing base

Figure 5. Pressure-treated wood foundation. Courtesy of National Association of Home Builders.

crete and minimize cracking. The combined floor slab and footing foundation system are appropriate in warmer climates that are not subjected to deep frost penetration.

FLOOR FRAMING

Floor framing in buildings with basement or crawl-space foundation systems consists of columns or posts, beams, sill plates, joists, and floor sheathing. Assembled on a foundation, they form a level, anchored platform for the rest of the house. They also serve as a strong diaphragm to keep the lateral earth pressure from pushing in the top of the foundation wall.

A wood-frame floor system should be anchored to the foundation to resist wind forces acting on the structure. This anchorage is usually provided by the sill plate that is attached to the foundation by anchor bolts, as illustrated in Figure 8. An alternative, used in the absence of a sill plate, is to attach metal straps, embedded in the foundation, directly to the floor joists. In the case of a pressure-treated wood foundation, the top plate of the foundation wall serves as the sill plate. Adequate anchorage of the floor system is usually provided by toe-nailing the floor joists directly to the top plate of the foundation wall, although steel strapping may be added.

In coastal areas subjected to high winds and in those parts of the country prone to earthquakes, special anchoring of foundations and floor systems may be required by local building codes. An exceptionally strong framing sys-

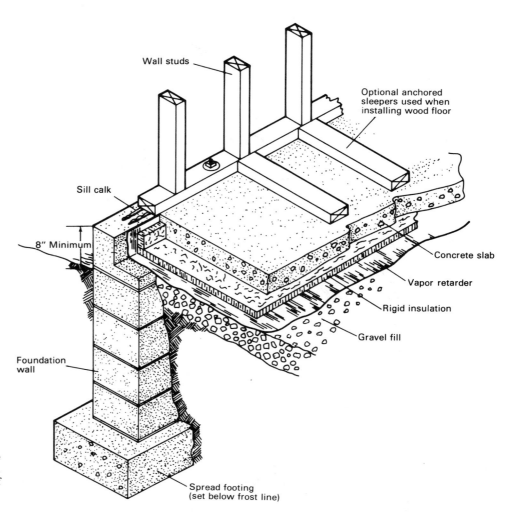

Figure 6. Independent concrete slab, foundation wall, and footing. Courtesy of National Association of Home Builders.

tem developed by the U.S. Forest Products Laboratory is the truss-frame system described in Ref. 2.

Center Beam and Support

Wood-frame floor construction typically employs a beam or girder of wood or steel to provide intermediate support for the first floor. In two-story construction the center beam generally supports the second floor as well. In the two-story case, a load-bearing wall on the first floor positioned directly over the center beam supports the second floor and transmits the load of the beam below. For maximum benefit in reducing floor joist spans, beams and bearing walls should be located along the center line of the structure.

The center beam usually bears on the foundation wall at each end and is supported at intervals along its length by columns or posts. The spacing of the columns or posts is adjusted to the spanning capability of the beam for a particular design load. The bottom of the supporting posts should rest on square footings whose dimensions are determined by the bearing capacity of the soil and the superimposed load. The height of the posts or columns should be adjusted so that the top of the supported beam is level with the top of the foundation wall or anchored sill plate on which the floor joists will be installed.

Floor Joists

In the most simple method of floor framing, the joists bear directly on top of the wood or steel center beam and the anchored sill plate. Floor joists and the wood used in the center beam should be dry lumber (15–19% moisture content) to minimize shrinkage and associated floor settling. To safeguard against settling, it is possible to equalize the depth of wood at the beam and at the outer wall by installing the beam on top of the foundation wall or anchored sill plate. The joists are then installed perpendicular to the beam, using metal joist hangers or supporting ledger strips as illustrated in Figure 9. The outer ends of the joists rest on the foundation wall or sill plate. This method of joist installation has the added advantage of providing more basement headroom or more height above ground level in crawl spaces.

Floor joists are selected primarily to meet strength and stiffness requirements. Strength requirements depend on the load to be carried. Stiffness requirements place an arbitrary control on deflection under load. Stiffness is also important in limiting vibrations from moving loads, often a cause of annoyance to occupants.

Wood floor joists are generally of 2-in. (5.1-cm) nominal thickness and 8–12-in. (20.3–30.5-cm) nominal depth. The size required depends on the loading, length of span,

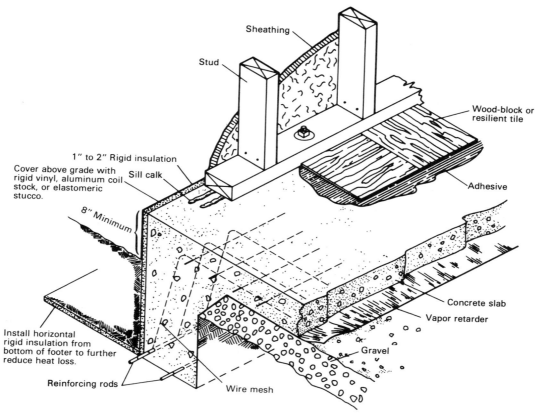

Figure 7. Combined floor slab, foundation wall, and footing. Courtesy of National Association of Home Builders.

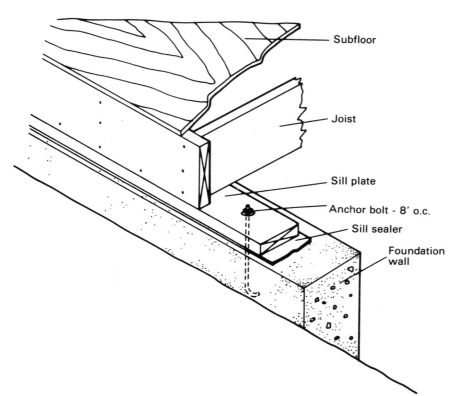

Figure 8. Anchoring floor system to poured-concrete foundation wall. Courtesy of National Association of Home Builders.

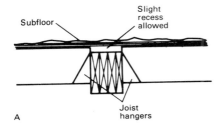

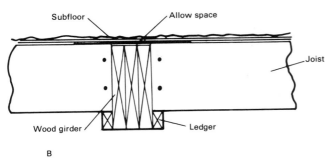

Figure 9. Joist butted center beam **(a)** supported by joist hangers; **(b)** supported by ledger strips. Courtesy of National Association of Home Builders.

spacing between joists, and species and grade of lumber used.

Alternative materials used for floor framing are manufactured components. An engineered floor truss may be purchased from a local truss fabricator. Given the antici-

pated loads to be supported and the required span, the truss fabricator will design and produce the desired number of floor trusses. Each floor truss consists of a top and bottom chord and web members. The chords and web members are interconnected by metal plates. In general, the height of the floor truss will be greater than a solid wood joist. A second alternative is a plywood-web floor joist resembling a steel I-beam in cross section.

The header joist, or band joist, used across the ends of floor joists has traditionally been the same size as floor joists. One function of the header joist is to brace the floor joists temporarily in position prior to application of the floor sheathing. It also helps to support stud loads in conventional framing, where wall studs do not necessarily align with floor joists. With careful planning, however, each wall stud should bear directly over a floor joist, as illustrated in Figure 10. In this aligned construction, the header joist may consist of nominal 1-in.-thick (2.54-cm-thick) header.

Bridging

Bridging between floor joists is no longer required by any of the major model building codes in normal house construction, ie, spans not exceeding 15 ft (4.6 m) and joist depth not exceeding 12 in. (30.5 cm). Even with tight fitting, well-installed bridging there is no significant transfer of loads after the sheathing and finish floor are installed. Bridging also increases the likelihood of floor squeaking.

Floor Openings

Large openings in the floor, such as stairwells and fireplaces or chimneys, usually interrupt one or more joists.

Figure 10. Vertical alignment of framing members simplifies framing and transmits loads directly through structural members. Courtesy of National Association of Home Builders.

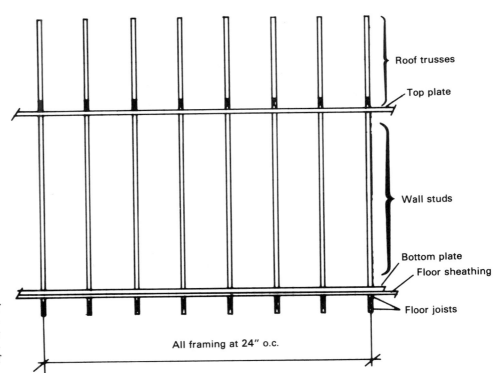

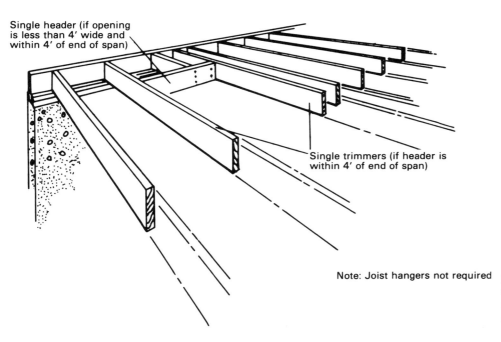

Single header (if opening is less than 4' wide and within 4' of end of span)

Single trimmers (if header is within 4' of end of span)

Note: Joist hangers not required

Figure 11. Floor opening framed with single header and single trimmer joists. Courtesy of National Association of Home Builders.

Such openings should be planned so that their long dimension is parallel with the joists, in order to minimize the number of joists that are interrupted. The opening should not interrupt the center beam or the bearing partition that supports the upper floor.

A narrow floor opening that starts within 4 ft (1.2 m) of the end of the joists is illustrated in Figure 11. A single header is installed between the standard floor joist serving as the trimmer joist on one side of the opening, and the trimmer joist that has been installed to form the proper opening width. The interrupted joist is the tail joist and is nailed to and supported by the header. A single header is adequate for openings up to 4 ft (1.2 m) wide; a double header should be used for openings from 4 to 10 ft (1.2 to 3 m) in width. Tail joists in excess of 6 ft in length should be attached to the header with metal joist hangers. As a general rule, if a double header is required, the trimmer joists on both sides of the opening should also be doubled, as illustrated in Figure 12.

Floor Framing at Projections

The framing for wall projections such as bay windows, wood chimneys, or first- or second-floor extensions beyond the wall below should consist of the projection of the floor joists as illustrated in Figure 13a. The projection usually should not exceed 24 in. (61 cm).

Projections at right angles to the length of the floor joists also should be extensions not exceeding 24 in. (61 cm). A doubled joist should be located back from the wall at a distance about twice the width of the overhang. The joist blocks forming the overhang should be attached to the double joist with metal joist hangers.

Cutting Floor Joists

It is sometimes necessary to cut, notch, or drill joists to conceal plumbing pipes, heating ducts, or electrical wiring in a floor. Joists and other structural members that have been cut or notched can sometimes be reinforced by nailing a reinforcing slab to each side or by adding an additional member. Notching of top or bottom of the joists should only be done in the end one-third of the span and not more than one-sixth of the depth of the member. When greater alterations are required, headers and tail joists should be added around the altered area in a fashion similar to any other floor opening. The chords and web members of a floor truss should never be cut, notched, or drilled.

Floor Sheathing

In the past, double floor construction consisting of a subfloor and finish floor or underlayment has typically been employed. However, where carpet and/or resilient floor covering are used throughout, a single layer of tongue-and-grove plywood, designed as a combination subfloor and underlayment, may be applied directly to floor joists. Flakeboard or oriented strand board and other reconstituted wood panel products are used for this purpose.

In addition to nailing, floor sheathing should be attached to the joists with a construction-grade adhesive. Glue-nailing of the floor sheathing will increase floor stiffness and/or allowable span of the floor system and can eliminate or reduce loose nails and squeaks, which can otherwise develop with even a small amount of joist shrinkage.

EXTERIOR WALL FRAMING

The floor framing and floor sheathing provide a working platform for construction of the wall framing. The term wall framing usually refers to exterior walls rather than interior partitions, and it includes vertical studs, horizon-

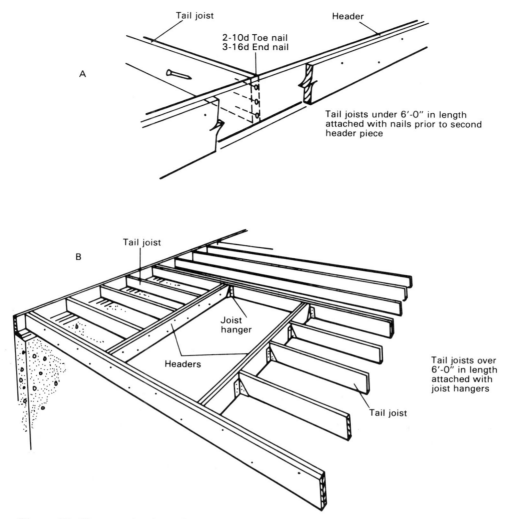

Figure 12. Floor opening framed with double headers and trimmer joists. Courtesy of National Association of Home Builders.

tal members such as top and bottom wall plates, and window and door headers, as illustrated in Figure 14.

Wall framing members are generally 2 × 4-in. (5.1 × 10.2-cm) studs spaced 16 in. or 24 in. (40.6 cm or 61 cm) on center, depending on vertical loads and the support requirements of the covering materials. An alternative is the use of 2 × 6-in. (5.1 × 15.2-cm) lumber to provide space for greater amounts of insulation. Headers over windows and door openings in load-bearing walls consist of doubled 2 × 6-in. (5.1 × 15.2-cm) or deeper members, depending on the span of the opening.

In platform construction, the wall framing members are cut to length, arranged on the horizontal platform, and connected together. Before erection, corner bracing in the form of let-in bracing as illustrated in Figure 14, steel X-strapping, or a 4 × 8-ft (1.2 × 2.4-m) sheet of structural sheathing should be installed to prevent racking and to maintain squareness of the wall section. The entire section is then tilted up, plumbed and braced, and fastened to the floor system by nailing through the bottom plate and floor sheathing into the floor joists.

An industrialized approach to platform construction involves the production of wall sections in a factory-based assembly-line process. The factory-produced wall panels are hauled to the construction site and erected.

In areas subject to hurricanes or high winds, it is often advisable, and frequently required by local building codes, to fasten the wall and floor framing to the anchored foundation sill plate. This fastening may be provided by nailing wall sheathing to the sill, floor joists, and wall studs. An alternative is to use steel straps, as illustrated in Figure 15.

Several arrangements of studs at outside corners can be used in framing walls. A two-stud corner as shown in Figure 16 uses the least lumber, provides the necessary strength, and provides more space for insulation than other configurations. Support for wallboards is provided by installing metal wallboard backup clips.

Window and Door Framing

The members used to span over window and door openings are called headers or lintels. As the span of the opening

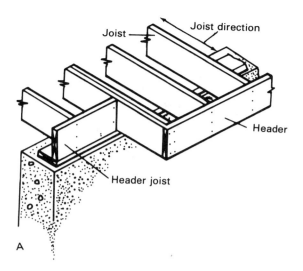

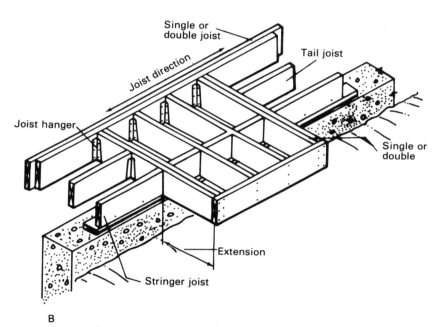

Figure 13. Floor framing at wall projections **(a)** continuation of floor joists; **(b)** projections perpendicular to floor joists. Courtesy of National Association of Home Builders.

increases it is necessary to increase the depth of the members to support the ceiling and roof loads. Local building codes frequently specify the species, size, and grade of lumber for various width openings under different load conditions.

An alternative header assembly called a plywood-box header is illustrated in Figure 17. This header design provides space for insulation, and the potential for shrinkage associated with a solid lumber header is almost eliminated. Plywood ½ in. (1.27 cm) thick may be nailed or glue-nailed to framing members to form the plywood-box header. The plywood may be applied to the inside, outside, or both sides.

Exterior Wall Sheathing

Exterior wall sheathing is the covering applied over the outside wall framework of studs, plates, and window and door headers. It forms a base on which the exterior finish can be applied. Certain types of sheathing and methods of application can give the building great rigidity, eliminating the need for special corner bracing. Sheathing also serves to reduce air infiltration and, in certain forms, provides significant insulation. Some sheet materials serve both as sheathing and finish siding, eliminating the need for separate sheathing and siding layers.

Types of wall sheathing include wood boards, insulating fiberboards, plywood, wafer board, oriented strand board, particle board, composite panels or reconstituted wood cores between veneer facings, foil-faced laminated paperboards, gypsum boards, and a variety of rigid-formed plastic boards with and without facings.

Sheathing paper may be installed over the sheathing material to aid in controlling air infiltration and to resist the entry of water in liquid form. The sheathing paper should, however, allow the movement of water vapor.

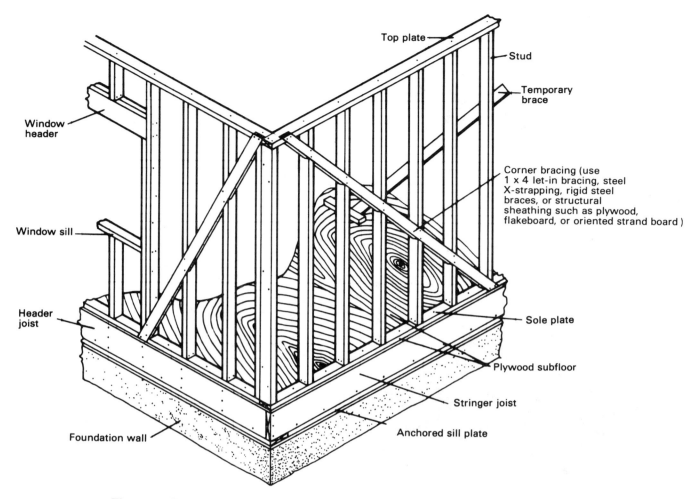

Figure 14. Wall framing with platform construction. Courtesy of National Association of Home Builders.

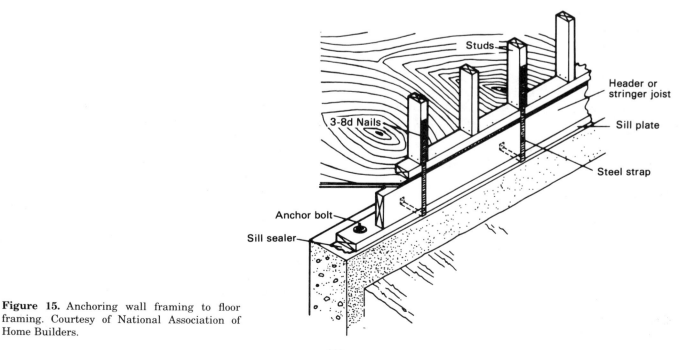

Figure 15. Anchoring wall framing to floor framing. Courtesy of National Association of Home Builders.

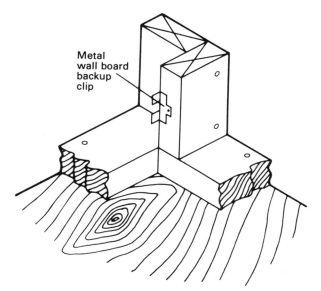

Figure 16. Two-stud corner with metal wallboard backup clips. Courtesy of National Association of Home Builders.

When a building is to be covered by stucco or masonry veneer, a sheathing paper such as asphalt-felt paper should be installed regardless of the sheathing material. Ordinarily, however, sheathing paper is not used over plywood or other water-resistant materials except around window and door openings to resist air infiltration.

Air-infiltration-barrier sheet materials resist the passage of moving air but allow water vapor to escape. These air-infiltration-barrier sheets may consist of a variety of products, ranging from non-woven fabrics to perforated plastic membranes. They can be used in all parts of the country but are particularly effective in cold and/or windy climates.

Interior Partition Framing

Most interior walls do not support a vertical load and are therefore referred to as partitions. The exception is the center, load-bearing wall in two-story construction. Such interior load-bearing walls are constructed in the same manner as an exterior wall.

Interior partitions consist of studs, top and bottom plates, and horizontal headers over door and other openings. Since the partitions carry no structural load, double top plates and structural headers over openings can be eliminated and replaced with single framing members.

Interior partitions should be fastened to exterior walls and other interior partitions with which they intersect. A mid-height block installed between the studs of the intersected wall or partition can be used to attach the end partition-stud. The metal wall board backup clips illustrated in Figure 16 should be installed to support the edge of the interior wall finish material. The bottom plate of the partition should be nailed to the floor sheathing without regard for floor joist location or direction.

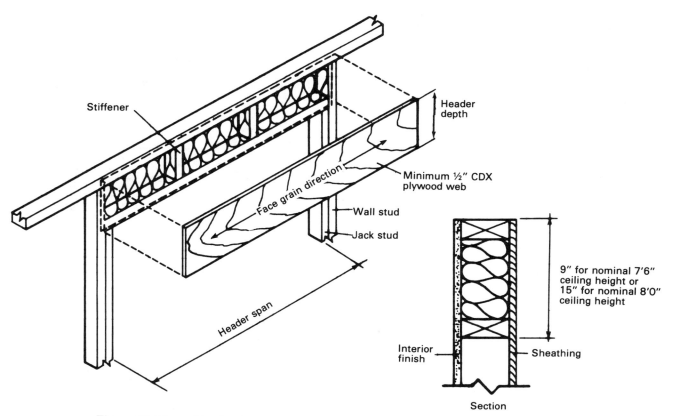

Figure 17. Plywood-box header for window and door openings. Courtesy of National Association of Home Builders.

UPPER-STORY FRAMING

Upper-story floor joists are installed on top of the walls and partitions below. The edge floor joists and header joists are toe-nailed to the outer edge of the top wall plate of the exterior walls. Extensions of the upper-story floor to create an overhang are framed as previously described. Floor openings, floor sheathing, exterior walls, and interior partitions are constructed in the same manner as described for the first story.

CEILING AND ROOF FRAMING

Roof frames provide structural members to which roofing, vents, and finish ceiling materials may be attached and within which insulation materials may be placed. The most commonly built roofs are made with triangular roof trusses designed and produced in a factory. Some common truss designs are illustrated schematically in Figure 18. The top and bottom chords of roof trusses are fastened together with steel plates and reinforced with interior web members that are connected to the chords by other steel plates. Wood trusses can span up to 50 ft (15.2 m) and are designed to require support only at the two ends of the bottom chord.

Trusses are transported to the construction site and erected on top for the wall framing either by means of a crane or manually. The most critical aspects of erecting the trusses are establishing their vertical and horizontal alignment and securely bracing the trusses until the roof sheathing is attached. Temporary braces should be used to prevent sudden gusts of wind from knocking down the trusses. Once all trusses have been erected, permanent bracing, according to the truss manufacturer's instructions, should be installed. In hurricane areas, twisted steel tie-down straps are recommended to secure the truss firmly to the exterior wall.

Ceiling Joists and Rafters

In lieu of manufactured trusses, roofs can be framed on site using rafters and ceiling joists. This method is usually more expensive and time-consuming than using prebuilt trusses.

Ceiling joists serve the same function as the bottom chords of a truss; they support ceiling finishes and serve as tension members to prevent the bottom of the roof rafters

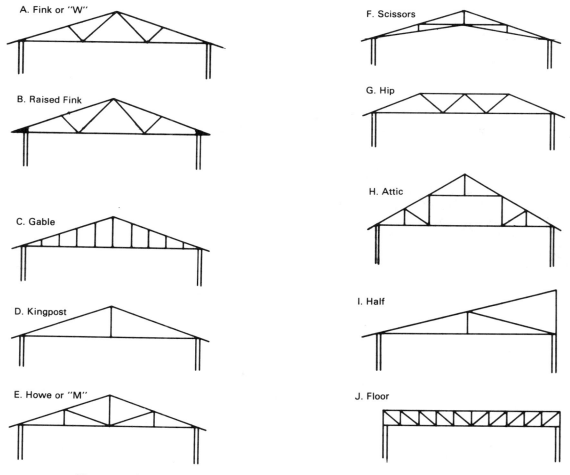

Figure 18. Common truss designs. Courtesy of National Association of Home Builders.

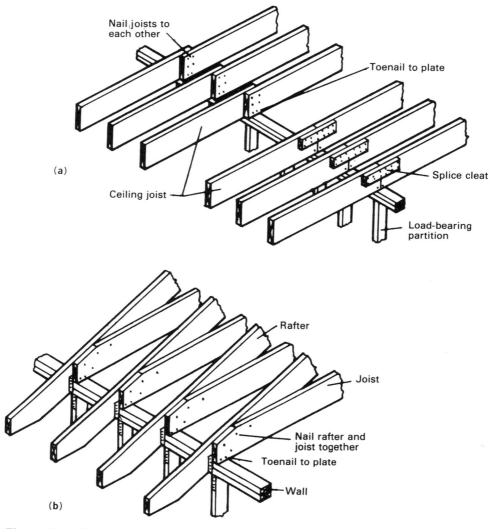

Figure 19. Ceiling joist connections at (**a**) center bearing wall; (**b**) exterior wall. Courtesy of National Association of Home Builders.

and tops of the exterior walls from spreading outward. Ceiling joists are installed to span from exterior walls to load-bearing interior walls as illustrated in Figure 19. When possible, the interior walls should be located to allow use of standard lumber lengths such as 12, 14, or 16 ft (3.7, 4.3, or 4.9 m) or longer. Usually, ceiling joists require 2 × 6- or 2 × 8-in. (5.1 × 15.2- or 5.1 × 20.3-cm) material, but correct sizes for various conditions are designated in local building codes.

Rafters should not be erected until ceiling joists are fastened in place, since the outward thrust of the rafters may push out the exterior walls. Rafters are usually precut to length, with proper angles cut at the roof ridge and eave and with notches cut to rest on the top plates of the exterior walls. Vertical studs for the end walls are notched to fit under and past the end rafter and connect to the top plate of the end wall. A ridge board, usually a 1 × 8-in. (2.5 × 20.3-cm) member for 2 × 6-in. (5.1 × 15.2-cm) rafters, provides support and a nailing area for the rafter ends. When roof spans are long and slopes are flat, it is common practice to install a collar beam between opposing rafters. Steeper slopes and shorter spans may also require collar beams, but only between every third rafter pair. Collar beams can be 1 × 6-in. (2.54 × 15.2-cm) material. If the space under the rafters is to be finished as in a 1½-story house, the collar beams should be of 2 × 4 in. (5.1 × 10.2-cm) material and installed between every rafter pair since the collar beams will serve as ceiling joists for the finished space. A schematic of typical rafter framing is shown in Figure 20.

Roof Variations

The triangular ends of a pitched-roof building are called the gable ends. It is sometimes desirable to provide an extension of the roof beyond the gable-end wall. This extension is called a gable overhang or rake overhang. Special framing is required to support the rafters at the end of the roof extension (fly rafters) if in excess of 12 in. (30.5 cm).

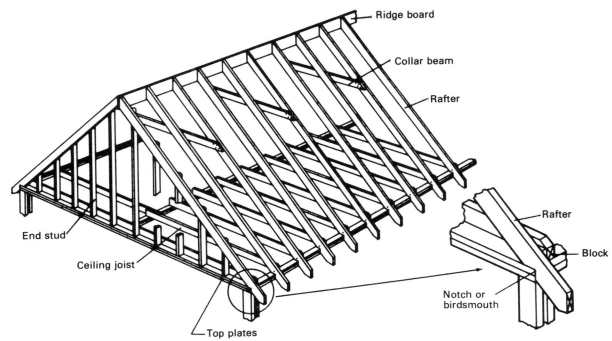

Figure 20. Typical rafter framing for pitched roof. Courtesy of National Association of Home Builders.

In L-shaped buildings, roof trusses are erected on one rectangular section and roof sheathing is applied. Roof trusses are then installed on the adjoining rectangular section. The remaining roof segment between the roof ridges must be manually framed. A ridge board is cut and installed to join the two ridges. Valley boards are cut and installed on top of the sheathing from the ridge to the eave. Valley rafters are then cut and installed at the proper spacing between the ridge and valley boards.

Other special roof framing is required for the installation of skylights and windows serving the attic space. These windows may be installed in either a gable dormer or a shed dormer, as illustrated in Figure 21.

Sloping ceilings are often used in contemporary interior design. These ceilings can be created by using scissors trusses in the roof framing (Fig. 18) or with single-member roof framing in which the rafter serves as the support for both roof sheathing above and ceiling covering below.

The rafter ends bear on walls or beams at different elevations.

Flat or low-pitched roofs, sometimes known as shed roofs, can take a number of forms. Roofs of this type require larger framing members than do steeper pitched roofs because they carry both roof and ceiling loads. A major concern in flat-roof construction is the increased likelihood of roof leaks.

Roof Sheathing

Roof sheathing is the covering applied over roof rafters or trusses to give racking resistance to the roof framing and to provide a surface for the attachment of the roof covering. Plywood and wafer board or oriented stand board are the most commonly used sheathing materials. In some low-pitched or flat roofs, solid wood decking is used as the sheathing material. Regardless of the material, sheathing must be thick enough to span between supports and to provide a solid base for fastening the roofing material.

COMPLETING CONSTRUCTION

Much work remains in the construction process after wood framing and sheathing of floors, walls, and roof are completed. The exact sequence may vary but, in general, proceeds as described below.

Stairs, windows, and doors are installed as framing progresses. The roof covering is applied soon after the roof sheathing is installed to protect the inside of the building. Applicable plumbing, electrical, heating, and cooling systems are installed as soon as the building is closed in. The next steps involve installation of exterior siding, interior

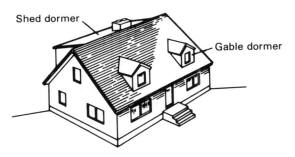

Figure 21. Pitched roof with gable and shed dormer. Courtesy of National Association of Home Builders.

wall coverings, kitchen and bath fixtures, and moldings. Painting is performed on the exterior wood surface as soon as is practical; interior painting is performed before adding the finishing touches. Finally, decorative items such as light fixtures, floor coverings, and cabinetry are added.

GLOSSARY

Anchor Bolt. A bolt to secure a wooden sill plate to concrete or masonry floor or foundation wall.

Apron. The flat member of the inside trim of a window placed against the wall immediately beneath the stool.

Bay Window. Any window space projecting outward from the walls of a building, either square or polygonal in plan.

Beam. A structural member supporting a load applied transversely to the member.

Bearing Partition. A partition that supports any vertical load in addition to its own weight.

Bearing Wall. A wall that supports any vertical load in addition to its own weight.

Bridging. Small wood or metal members inserted in a diagonal position between the floor joists at midspan to brace the joists.

Built-up Roof. A roofing composed of three to five layers of asphalt felt laminated with coal tar, pitch, or asphalt. The top layer is covered with crushed slag or gravel. Generally used on flat or low-pitched roofs.

Collar Beam. A nominal 1- or 2-in.- (2.54- or 5.1-cm-) thick member connecting opposite roof rafters at or near the ridge board. Collar beams serve to stiffen the roof structure.

Column. 1. In architecture, a vertical supporting member, circular or rectangular in section, usually consisting of a base, shaft, and capital. 2. In engineering, a vertical structural compression member that supports loads acting in the direction of its longitudinal axis.

Construction, Frame. A type of construction in which the structural parts are wood or depend on a wood frame for support. In codes, if masonry veneer is applied to the exterior walls, the structure is still classified as frame construction.

Corner Brace. A diagonal brace placed at the corner of a frame structure to stiffen and strengthen the wall.

Cornice. Overhang of a pitched roof at the eave line, usually consisting of a fascia board, a soffit for a closed cornice, and appropriate moldings.

Cornice Return. The underside of the cornice at the corner of the roof where the walls meet the gable-end roof line. The cornice return serves as trim rather than as a structural element, providing a transition from the horizontal eave line to the sloped roof life of the gable.

Crawl Space. A shallow space below the living quarters of a basementless house, normally enclosed by the foundation wall.

Dormer. A roofed projection from a sloping roof, into which a dormer window is set.

Eave. The lower margin of a roof projecting over the wall.

Fascia. A flat board, band, or face, used by itself or,

more often, in combination with moldings, generally located at the outer face of the cornice.

Flashing. Sheet metal or other material used in roof and wall construction to keep water out of adjoining parts of the structure.

Fly Rafters. End rafters of the roof overhang supported by roof sheathing and lookouts.

Footing. A concrete section in a rectangular form, wider than the bottom of the foundation wall or pier it supports. With a pressure-treated wood foundation, a gravel footing may be used in place of concrete.

Foundation. The supporting portion of a structure below the first-floor construction, or below grade.

Framing, Balloon. A system of framing in which all exterior wall studs extend in one piece from the sill plate to the roofplate.

Framing, Platform. A system of framing in which floor joists of each story rest on the top plates of the story below or on the foundation sill for the first story, and the bearing walls and partitions rest on the subfloor of each story.

Frostline. The depth of frost penetration in soil. This depth varies in different parts of the country.

Gable. The portion of the roof above the eave line of a double-sloped roof.

Gable End. An end wall having a gable.

Girder. A large or principal beam of wood or steel used to support loads at points along its length.

Header. 1. A beam placed perpendicular to joists, to which joists are nailed in framing for chimneys, stairways, or other openings. 2. A wood lintel.

Hip. The external angle formed by the meeting of two sloping sides of a roof.

Hip Roof. A roof that rises by inclined planes from all four sides of a building.

I-beam. A steel beam with a cross section resembling the letter I. I-beams are used for long spans as basement beams or over wide wall openings, such as a double garage door, when wall and roof loads are imposed on the opening.

Joist. One of a series of parallel beams, usually 2 in. (5 cm) thick, used to support floor and ceiling loads, and supported in turn by larger beams, girders, or bearing walls.

Ledger Strip. A strip of lumber nailed along the bottom of the side of a girder, on which joists rest.

Let-in Brace. A nominal 1-in.- (2.54-cm-) thick board applied diagonally into notched studs.

Lintel. A horizontal structure member that supports the load over an opening such as a door or window; also called a header.

Lookout. A short wood bracket or cantilever to support an overhang portion of a roof, usually concealed from view by a soffit.

Lumber, Boards. Lumber less than 2 in. (5.1 cm) thick and 2 or more in. wide.

Lumber, Dimension. Lumber from 2 in. (5.1 cm) to, but not including, 5 in. (12.7 cm) thick and 2 or more in. wide. Including joists, rafters, studs, plank, and small timbers.

Lumber, Pressure-treated. Lumber that has had a preservative chemical forced into the wood under pressure to resist decay and insect attack.

Masonry. Stone, brick, concrete, hollow tile, concrete block, gypsum block, or other similar building units or materials or a combination of the same, bonded together with mortar to form a wall, pier, buttress, or similar element.

Millwork. Building materials made of finished wood and manufactured in millwork plants and planing mills. It includes such items as inside and outside window frames and doorframes, blinds, porchwork, mantels, panel work, stairways, molding, and interior trim. The term does not include flooring or siding.

Nonbearing Wall. A wall supporting no load other than its own weight.

On Center (oc). The measurement of spacing of elements such as studs, rafters, and joists, from the center of one member to the center of the next.

Oriented Strand Board (OSB). A panel composed of layers, with each layer consisting of compressed strandlike wood particles in one direction, and with layers oriented at right angles to each other. The layers are bonded together with a phenolic resin.

Partition. A wall that subdivides spaces within any story of a building.

Perm. A measure of water vapor movement through a material (grains per square foot per hour per inch of mercury difference in vapor pressure).

Pier. A column of masonry, usually rectangular in horizontal cross section, used to support other structural members.

Pitch. The measure of the steepness of the slope of a roof, expressed as the ratio of the rise of the slope over a corresponding horizontal distance. Roof slope is expressed in the inches of rise per foot of run, such as 4 in 12.

Plate. *Sill plate:* A horizontal member anchored to a masonry wall. *Sole plate:* bottom horizontal member of a frame wall. *Top plate:* top horizontal member of a frame wall supporting ceiling joists, rafters, or other members.

Plumb. Exactly vertical.

Rafter. One of a series of structural members of a roof designed to support roof loads. The rafters of a flat roof are sometimes called roof joists.

Rafter, Valley. A rafter that forms the intersection of an internal roof angle. A valley rafter is normally made of double 2-in.- (5.1-cm-) thick members.

Rake. Trim members that run parallel to the roof slope and form the finish between the wall and a gable roof extension.

Ridge. The horizontal line at the junction of the top edges of two sloping roof surfaces.

Ridge Board. The board placed on edge at the ridge of the roof, into which the upper ends of the rafters are fastened.

Sheathing. The covering, typically plywood or insulation board, used over studs or rafters of a structure.

Sheathing Paper. A building material, generally paper or felt, used in wall and roof construction as a protection against the passage of air and water.

Sill. 1. The lowest member of the frame of a structure, resting on the foundation and supporting the floor joists of the uprights of the wall. 2. The member forming the lower side of an opening such as a doorsill or windowsill.

Soffit. The underside of an overhang cornice.

Soil Cover (Ground Cover). A light covering of plastic film, roll roofing, or similar material, used over the soil in crawl spaces of buildings to minimize the movement of moisture from the soil into the crawl space.

Span. The distance between structural supports such as walls, columns, piers, beams, girders, and trusses.

Stud. One of a series of slender wood or metal vertical structural members placed as supporting elements in walls and partitions (plural: studs or studding).

Subfloor. Boards or plywood laid on joists, over which a finish floor is laid.

Toe-nailing. Driving a nail at a slant with the initial surface, to permit it to penetrate into a second member.

Tongue and Groove. Boards or planks machined so that there is a groove on one edge and a corresponding projection (tongue) on the other edge, thus allowing a number of such boards or planks to be fitted together. "Dressed and matched" is an alternative term with the same meaning.

Truss. A framed or jointed structure, composed of triangular elements, designed to act as a beam of long span; each member is usually subjected to longitudinal stress only, either tension or compression.

Truss Plate. A heavy-gauge pronged metal plate that is pressed into the sides of a wood truss at the point where two more members are to be joined together.

Underlayment. A material placed under flexible flooring materials such as carpet, vinyl tile, or linoleum to provide a smooth base over which to lay such materials.

Valley. The internal angle formed by the junction of two sloping sides of a roof.

Vapor Retarder. Material used to retard the movement of water vapor into walls. Vapor retarders are applied over the warm side of exposed walls or as a part of batt or blanket insulation. They usually have a perm value of less than 1.0.

BIBLIOGRAPHY

1. G. E. Sherwood and R. C. Stroh, eds., *Wood Frame House Construction*, National Association of Home Builders, Washington, D. C., 1988. A comprehensive guide to wood-frame construction from excavation to finishing. Includes special topic sections on concrete, lumber grades, decay and termite protection, noise control, pressure-treated wood, and all-weather construction.

2. *Truss-Framed Construction*, NAHB Research Foundation, Rockville, Md., 1984. A manual of design and construction for the truss-frame system that combines roof truss, floor truss, and wall studs into a rigid unit frame.

General References

APA Design/Construction Guide: Residential and Commercial, American Plywood Association, Tacoma, Wash., 1979. Designed as a handy reference manual for panel specifiers and users. Contains information on panel grades plus APA specifications for floor, wall, and roof systems.

APA Product Guide: Grades and Specifications, American Plywood Association, Tacoma, Wash., 1984. A useful reference for structural wood panel users, specifiers, dealers, and distributors. Illustrates and explains APA trademarks appearing on panel products.

All-Weather Wood Foundation, American Plywood Association, Tacoma, Wash., 1978. Describes and illustrates construction of an all-weather wood foundation with either a full basement or crawl space. A list of other information sources is included.

FHA Pole House Construction, 2nd ed., American Wood Preservers Institute, McLean, Va., 1975. An updated edition of an FHA publication first issued in 1969. Describes a variety of ways to effectively use pole frame designs.

Manual of Lumber- and Plywood-Saving Techniques for Residential Light-Frame Construction. NAHB Research Foundation, Rockville, Md., 1971. Most of the information in this manual relates to floor and wall construction and, to a lesser extent, roof construction. Intended for code officials, building inspectors, builders, subcontractors, and others concerned with cost-effective use of lumber and plywood.

NAHB Research Foundation, *Reducing Home Building Costs with OVE Design and Construction,* National Association of Home Builders, Washington, D.C., 1977. Describes a practical series of optimum value engineered (OVE) cost-reducing techniques covering each stage of home building.

Insulation Manual: Homes and Apartments, NAHB Research Foundation, Rockville, Md., 1979. Provides information on the proper installation, use, economics, and benefits of insulation, and guidance on other energy-conserving techniques for designing and building homes.

NAHB Research Foundation, *Off-Center Spliced Floor Joists,* Research Reports Vol. 4 National Association of Home Builders, Washington, D.C., 1982. A manual on the design, fabrication, and installation of off-center spliced floor joists.

NAHB Research Foundation, *Plywood Headers for Residential Construction,* Research Reports Vol. 5 National Association of Home Builders, Washington, D.C., 1983. A manual on the design, fabrication, and installation of plywood box headers.

NAHB Research Foundation, *Residential Concrete,* National Association of Home Builders, Washington, D.C., 1983. Provides guidelines for ordering ready-mixed concrete. Admixtures such as accelerators, retarders, plasticizers, and superplasticizers are discussed. Extensive illustrations are provided on form building, jointing, and basement leakage control.

All-Weather Wood Foundation System: Design, Fabrication, and Installation Manual, National Forest Products Association, Washington, D.C., 1982. Part I of this three-part manual addresses structural design, detailing, and material specifications for architects, engineers, draftsmen, and builders. Part II covers quality fabrication of the foundation. Part III deals with installation methods. Parts II and III are particularly useful to builders and fabricators of treated-wood foundations.

U.S. Department of Housing and Urban Development and U.S. Department of Labor, *All-Weather Home Building Manual,* compiled by NAHB Research Foundation, Guideline 4, U.S. Government Printing Office, Washington, D.C., 1975. Written for the home builder, this manual describes practices that permit construction to continue in cold, wet, or hot and dry weather.

See also FOUNDATION SYSTEMS; GLUED LAMINATED WOOD (GLULAM); INDUSTRIALIZED CONSTRUCTION; INTERIOR PARTITIONS AND PARTITION COVERINGS; MOISTURE PROTECTION; TERMITES—CONTROL BY SOIL POISONING; WINDOWS; WOOD IN CONSTRUCTION; WOOD, STRUCTURAL PANELS; WOOD TREATMENT

ROBERT C. STROH
NAHB Research Center
Upper Marlborough, Maryland

INTERIOR PARTITIONS AND PARTITION COVERINGS

PARTITIONS

The word partition derives from the Latin verb *partire* (to divide). The meaning of the word has not changed. A partition is something that divides or separates, such as a wall dividing a room or a septum of a plant structure. Partitioning is the act of dividing, separating, compartmenting, enclosing.

The common usage of the term in construction today usually defines a dividing wall within a building. This may mean any building component that separates one space from another. The word partition does not convey whether the divider of the space is load bearing, transparent, perforated, solid, nonbearing, or other possibilities that make up categories of partitions.

Herein common categories of partitions found in building construction are addressed. The partition category is followed with commentary on how the partition is typically utilized and its expected performance.

PARTITION CATEGORIES

In an attempt to categorize partitions, they have been divided into the following types: screen (allowing passage of air and light); transparent or translucent (allowing passage of light, not air); opaque (preventing passage of air, light, sound, and other items); operable (selectively preventing passage of air, light, and sound); and temporary (muting or controlling passage of air, light, and sound).

Screen partitions typically allow passage of air and light. They refer to a construction whose function is solely to separate, shelter, or conceal. Screens do not support loads. Screening material is usually mounted on framework and can be movable or fixed. Screens can be made of mesh material or grillage allowing free passage of air, or of transparent, translucent, or opaque materials such as fabric, glass, paper, metal, wood, or plastic that can be paneled and mounted on a frame. Interior screen partitions are typically not full height. Exterior screens traditionally refer to the framed metal or plastic mesh mounted on frames.

Transparent or translucent partitions permit the passage of light, but not air. Transparent partitions permit a clear view beyond and admit light. Translucent partitions admit light without a clear view. Glass, plastic materials, paper, fabrics, and thin-cut diaphanous stone can be utilized for light-pervious partitions. Typically this type of partition is supported by its framework.

Opaque partitions do not permit the passage of light or air. Opaque materials can be solid structural units, assemblages of materials, or nonstructural materials used to block light, air, sound, temperature differences, radio waves, and a host of other items that may require control. Opaque partitions are one of the largest and most familiar category of partition. This includes wood- and metal-stud partitions with a variety of finishes, wood panels, and masonry construction. Opaque, nonstructural partitions range from opaque glass to movable walls.

Operable partitions are a special category that provide a temporary division of space. They are not structural and may need to be made of flexible or partially transparent material. Operable partitions may be left open or closed depending on the functional criteria of the space. The ability to easily change room sizes and configurations affords flexible utilization of spaces.

Temporary partitions include demountable walls, movable screens, system furniture panels, and other materials that can serve as dividers of space to suit immediate needs.

PARTITION PERFORMANCE CRITERIA

Partitions are designed to fulfill particular requirements. If spaces are divided for functional differences there are criteria that will most likely influence the selection of a partition category or type. Criteria that are typically used in the specification and design of partitions include the following: use separation; acoustic separation, including sound transmission, sound absorption, and noise-reduction coefficients; visual separation; fire and smoke separation; air separation; temporary separation; sensory separation (anechoic chambers); separation and protection from elements and intrusion, including weather (mainly exterior consideration), radio-wave frequencies, radiation (x-ray), ultraviolet filtration; security and protection from intrusion and attack, including sensor device construction, ballistic and forced entry protection; aesthetics; durability and maintenance; cost of labor and materials.

PARTITION ASSEMBLY

Herein five types of partition assemblies in common use are addressed.

Internally Framed Partition Assembly

This is an assembly with an internal rigid structure covered with a material that meets the performance and aesthetic criteria of a project. Examples can range from familiar wallboards on wood or metal studs to mud plastered onto sticks.

This type of assembly is the most flexible and is widely used. Vertical supports (studs) are spaced at intervals to minimize the cost and weight of the structure. The intermittent structural spacing also leaves an air space that affects performance assessment. Modular wood stud or metal framing members, which are most commonly used, are relatively lightweight, with good tensile and compression properties.

A concealed, internal structure permits a complete range of utilization of almost all coverings and surface finishes available. Unlimited combinations of stud depth, secondary framing members, bracing and finish surfaces are available. This is significant for assemblies requiring specific controls for fire resistance, air-pressure control, acoustics, heat gain and loss, security, etc.

Externally Framed Partition Assembly

Partitions with a rigid external structure or framework have inset material panels. This system is more limited than the internally framed assembly. Framing members are exposed, thereby requiring a finished appearance for both the structure and the panel material.

The structure dimensions are set by the height and load requirements. Panel thickness is set by the limits of the structure and cannot be totally responsive to all performance criteria.

The most common example of this assembly type is a glazed curtain wall. Other examples include marble panels set in frames, shoji (paper) screens and less conventional materials such as chain-link-fencing fabric. Panel materials are typically thin and include glass, paper, wood panels, metal panels, screen materials, and thin-cut stone. The thickness of the panel material determines the overall performance of the partition for sound, fire, security, durability, and other pertinent criteria. Cost, performance, and size considerations limit the finish materials available for this assembly type.

Solid Assemblies with Integral Finishes

The simplest assembly type utilizes one material for the structure and the finish. Materials in this category must be self-supporting and acceptable as an interior finish material. Most materials in this category have been in use since early civilization and include concrete, stone, brick, block, structural tile, adobe, and logs.

Because these assemblies are monolithic or homogenous materials, the performance characteristics are more limited than framed assemblies. Massive thickness is one characteristic that creates limits through weight and cost. Homogeneity also provides an uninterrupted medium for sound and thermal energy transmission. These materials are typically very strong, durable and, with the exception of logs, highly fire resistive and can have additive finishes that increase their performance.

Operable Partitions

An operable partition may be a single or a series of sliding panels, a lift-up divider, or a pleated accordion-type partition that folds into a compact closed position.

Operable partitions can be made from large panels hung from ceiling tracks, allowing the panels to be moved from a closed position where they form a partition, to an open position where they have been removed from the room. The panels typically slide into a stacked or accordion position. Operable partitions are facilitated by the control provided by a floor track.

These partitions have been developed to provide significant reduction of sound transmission. Recent new developments include fire rated operable partitions that serve as smoke- or fire-alarm-activated rated separations.

Operable partitions include accordion-type partitions that are also hung from overhead tracks and fold back in accordionlike pleats.

Temporary Partitions

Temporary partitions are transportable panels, screens, or framed glass that serve as temporary dividers or definers of space. The modular office panel that was initiated in the late 1960s has proliferated into the office partition standard of the 1970s and 1980s.

Modular office furniture or systems furniture provide partition panels that mount into a framework or are self-supporting and attach together for support. In some systems the panels are part of the furniture pieces that stack or link together. The partition panels are typically not ceiling height and are made of a composite core finished with metal, plastic, fabric or wood. Vision panels are made with glass or a transparent plastic such as acrylic or polycarbonate.

Demountable partitions are nonbearing partition panels, usually prefabricated, that can be installed, used, and then removed and reinstalled in another location. Demountable partitions infer full-height installations. Manufacturers have developed the prefabricated panels with a variety of prefinished surfaces, including glazing, wallpaper-covered drywall, sound-absorbent fabric-covered panels, and washable units with plastic laminate surfaces.

Demountable partitions can be field fabricated from drywall and metal studs, if during the initial installation attention is paid to the metal track connections. Demountable partitions cannot achieve the air-pressure seal, required by certain specialized facilities, of full-height conventional partitions. However, demountable partitions are not regarded as fixed assets and may be an inspired business choice for rapidly changing office operations.

Other temporary partitions include decorative wood- and fabric-covered screens. Curtains and drapes may serve as temporary partitions where the requirement for privacy is not permanent and only visual.

Exhibition furnishings and showroom partitions are usually fabric covered or have a similar surface that permits the mounting of displays. This variety of temporary partitions has quite specific display requirements. Exhibit partitions usually are higher than eye level and visually screen one exhibit from another. They must be easily demountable into smaller transportable pieces. Exhibit and displays must be stable enough to support hung exhibits and withstand impact from viewers. Safety requirements stipulate a flame-spread rating for exhibit and display materials.

PARTITION COVERINGS OR INSET MATERIALS

Coverings

Materials used to cover a partition are usually called wall coverings. The term refers to an exposed material attached to a substrate or directly to a structural component or, in certain instances, the structural component is the exposed material. Wall coverings can be applied to exterior or interior surfaces. In this article, coverings for interior surfaces are addressed.

Wall coverings were developed to enhance the performance of building materials to protect humans from the elements. In the most basic sense this included resistance to wind, water, fire, and temperature extremes while providing a habitable space. As humans became more sophisticated in their utilization of materials, the durability, structural soundness, and appearance of the materials gained importance. Today new construction materials and systems are continually being developed, with the constant goal of improving material performance. The basic requirement of protection from natural elements has been expanded to include noise, seismic forces, toxic materials, fumes, and smoke. Consideration of comfort, visual appearance, historic authenticity, life safety, cleanliness, product liability, maintainability, and life cycle value are now included in the material selection process.

Materials used since prehistoric times co-exist with manufactured synthetics. Here materials that are today commonly employed as interior wall coverings are listed and the uses of some as exterior wall coverings are briefly discussed. The material heading is followed by a commentary on how the material is typically utilized and its expected performance. Also, simple materials, those found and used in their natural state, and complex materials requiring assembly or mixture to be utilized, are covered.

Performance Criteria. The selection criteria for wall-covering materials includes the following.

- **Strength**—the ability to withstand natural and other external forces including:
- Thermal expansion and contraction—the change in length or volume that occurs in a material when heated or cooled.
- Impact resistance—the ability of a material's surface to resist a sudden blow.
- Indentation—the proclivity of a material to yield to an impact; an inlet or dent in a material's surface.
- Hardness—the firmness and yield response of a material to impacts.
- Structural properties—counteraction to natural static forces.
- Shear strength—the ability of a material to resist deformation or pull apart in parallel planes; the maximum shear stress that a material can sustain.
- Tensile strength—the ability of a material to resist the state or condition of being pulled; the maximum tensile stress that a material can sustain.
- Compressive strength—the ability of a material to resist the state or condition of being compressed or shortened by a compressive force; the maximum compressive stress that a material can sustain.
- **Safety**—the provision of materials that protect and do no harm to occupants.
- Fire resistance—the ability of a material or assembly to maintain a set temperature on one side, to not fail structurally or enflame for a specified period of time, under conditions of standard heat intensity. Fire re-

sistance of materials and assemblies is determined through standardized testing by the American Society for Testing Materials (ASTM).

- Flame-spread rate—the rate at which fire develops in a material. A low rate means a slow spread of flame. American Society for Testing Materials (ASTM) performs the material tests and determines the ratings.
- Combustion products—the by-products from combustion.
- Smoke—particulate matter from combusting materials. Smoke obscures visibility during a fire, and contains particulate matter and lethal toxic gases. A low smoke-development rating is preferred in areas where visibility is essential in exiting. ASTM performs the tests and determines the ratings.
- Toxic fumes—gases are one of the by-products of combusting materials. Carbon monoxide, hydrogen cyanide, nitrogen dioxide, and hydrogen chloride are lethal. There is no standardized testing for toxic fumes. The National Building Code (BOCA) and the Uniform Building Code (UBC) have toxicity requirements, but no verifiable test method.
- **Durability**—the ability of a material to sustain hard wear and continued use.
- Resistance to wear—the ability of a material to sustain wear and appear as new.
- Abrasion resistance—the ability of a material to resist repeated rubbing and scuffing.
- Tearing–splitting–cracking—the ability of a material to resist tearing, splitting, and cracking due to wear, temperature differences, incidental building movement, and humidity changes.
- Defacement resistance—the ability of a material to resist deliberate damage, or sustain damage and be easily cleaned or repaired.
- Chipping—the ability of a material's surface or a coating to resist chipping.
- Scratching—the ability of a material or a coating to resist scratches.
- Graffiti—the ability of a material to sustain graffiti damage and be cleaned.
- Fading resistance—the ability of a material or coating to resist fading from exposure to uv light.
- Chemical resistance—the ability of a material or coating to resist damage from applied corrosive chemicals.
- Microbial–bacterial resistance—the ability of a material to resist development of environments conducive to microbial life forms. In some cases materials can be treated with an antimicrobial agent that actively kills microbial life forms. However the process used in this treatment may expose plant workers to carcinogens.
- Vermin control—the ability of a material to resist vermin infestation. Vermin include insects and small rodents.
- Mildew resistance—the ability of a material or coat-

ing to resist and not support mildew and fungal decay.
- Humidity–moisture absorption characteristics—the ability of a material or coating to maintain dimensional stability or adhesion in high humidity or moisture conditions.
- **Material Compatibility**—the materials and coatings in contact with each other are compatible and do not damage each other.
- Chemical interaction—the ability of a material that comes in contact with another to chemically affect it.
- Galvanic action—the interaction of dissimilar metals causing a current flow between metals that results in corrosion.
- Discoloration—the interaction of materials or coatings with each other, or the affect of adjacent activities or elements resulting in discoloration or staining of materials or coatings.
- Coating adhesion—the ability of a coating to remain as originally placed.
- Softening—the deterioration of a coating by loss of hardness.
- Emulsification—the dissolution of a coating.
- Lifting–flaking—the delamination or adhesion loss by a coating.
- Thermal expansion—the movement of a material due to temperature changes; dimensional stability of a material.
- **Comfort:**
- Acoustic properties.
- Sound transmission—does the material transmit sound energy?
- Sound absorption—does the material absorb sound energy?
- Noise reduction coefficient—the combination of sound reflection and sound absorption.
- **Functional Utility:**
- Usefulness—is the material appropriate for the intended use?
- Function—does the material fulfill its intended function? That is, is there visual privacy, light reflectivity, display, and durability?
- **Aesthetic Considerations**—materials must fulfill the intangible requirement of aesthetic taste. This requirement will always be subject to personal interpretation. Generally, materials should be selected as appropriate to the use and in harmony with the overall design intent of a project.

MASONRY

Masonry is the term applied to the assembly of building units. The units are conventional materials that can be bonded together in a pattern with mortar. This includes a variety of formed, cast, carved, and baked rectangular shapes.

The word mason originated from the stone and bricklayers who formed the Freemason societies in the Middle Ages. Masonry has come to refer to any unit that can be constructed by a mason.

Masonry units can be solid or hollow, made of baked clay or shale (terra-cotta tile, bricks, adobe), ceramic veneer, cast or natural stone, clay tile, glass block, gypsum block, concrete block, and concrete bricks. Unit masonry is typically manufactured in sizes easily handled by a single mason.

The partition assemblies utilizing mortar include internally framed structures using masonry veneers, solid assemblies using masonry as veneer or as the whole partition material, and occasionally thin veneer stone set into a framed assembly.

Stone

Stone is a natural mineral solid material that forms the earth's crust. Stone or rock is composed of one or more minerals and has three basic classifications: igneous, metamorphic, and sedimentary. The hardest stones are typically found in the igneous class, represented by granite or gneiss. The metamorphic classification examples include marble and slate. Sedimentary rock examples include shale, travertine, limestone, and sandstone.

Stone has been utilized as a wall structure and a wall covering since prehistoric times. Stone is durable, dense, and aesthetically appealing with natural texture and veining.

Stone has been used as structure and as an applied exterior or interior wall covering. Stone can be embellished with carved decorations or laid in patterns that enhance its use as an aesthetic wall covering. Some thin-cut marbles are transparent, and other types of stone can be carved to form screens. As a quality material, stone is one of the most prized and expensive wall coverings in use today. Marbles and granites grace the lobbies and facades of many institutions and office buildings.

Stone has always been a labor-intensive material. This makes stone an expensive material. Fortunately increases in the cost of labor have paralleled new efficiencies in quarrying procedures and construction techniques.

Stone constructed as a structural wall or as a veneer facing is usually laid in a pattern. Standard stonework patterns include: uncoursed fieldstone or rubble, uncoursed ledgerock, coursed rubble stone, uncoursed squared stone, coursed ashlar-running bond, random coursed ashlar, random broken course ashlar, and river bed stone. Stone veneer applications require bonding, within the masonry pattern or with triangular metal ties. Coursed stone can be reinforced with steel. Stone is a material with little tensile properties and considerable compressive strength.

Nonstructural stone is typically a thin veneer application with slabs cut in 1½–¼ in. thicknesses. Stone wall coverings are supported by structural steel or solid masonry in high applications or backed by wood or metal studs in lower height interior applications.

Thin-cut stone can be natural cleft that leaves the split textured face of the stone or finished with honing, a smooth surface with a matte texture, polishing for a slick mirrorlike finish, or rubbing to remove all or part of the natural graining of a cleft face. Thin stone set in mortar may absorb the moisture and appear mottled until the mortar dries.

Building stone is noted for permanence and durability. Stone wall coverings effectively protect against wind, water, and fire. Stone is not flammable, and in general has excellent performance characteristics for strength, wearing, resistance to defacement, mildew, vermin, moisture absorption, and general stability.

With the proper sun orientation, thick stone walls can provide a heat absorbing mass, creating a time lag in thermal transmittance. This can be effective for passive solar designs and in the construction of fireplaces and stove surrounds. However stone is dimensionally affected by thermal expansion and contraction. Selection of supporting materials, compatible with the physical characteristics of stone is important in the selection of stone finish.

Airborne pollutants, water and other chemicals can deteriorate exposed stone. Some types of stone, such as sandstone or travertine are porous, or the finish surface stains easily, as in marble, requiring fillers and sealers. The selection of a stone wall covering requires matching the appropriate type of stone with the application. Due to its density, stone is effective in reflecting airborne sounds. Stone will transmit solid-borne sound energy and it is not sound absorptive.

Stone has a thermal resistance, an R-value, of .08/in. thickness (for limestone). Fieldstone has an average weight of 144 PCF. Granite has a density of 160 PCF.

Brick

Brick as an interior wall covering is a durable, attractive material. Because it is resistant to defacement of all varieties, including graffiti, when the face brick has been sealed or glazed, brick is an attractive low maintenance alternative for high abuse facilities. Aesthetically, brick provides scale, texture, natural color, and subtle patterns. Brick masonry is a labor-intensive and therefore costly material, making brick selection a choice for long-term value.

Brick has considerable compressive strength, making it an appropriate choice for structural partitions and partitions selected for security purposes. Brick masonry ranges from 100 to 130 PCF. Tensile properties can be enhanced with steel reinforcing and bonding patterns.

Brick has been thoroughly tested in fire-resistive assemblies. Four inches of solid brick has an ultimate fire resistance of 1¼ h, 8 in. has a fire resistance of 5 h; and 12 in. has a fire resistance of 10 h. This makes brick a safe choice for fire protection. Brick as a finish surface can be backed by standard brick, block, concrete, steel, or wood studs.

Brick is not a sound absorbent material, however, its density causes it to effectively reflect airborne sound. Brick walls transmit structure-borne sound energy unless isolated. A 4-in. brick wythe has an STC value of 45. A 10-in. brick wall with a 2-in. air cavity has an STC value of 50.

The thermal properties of brick masonry have significant design implications. One hundred linear feet of masonry will expand approximately .43 in. at 100°F. Brick exposed to a source of heat is not dimensionally stable. This applies to both interior and exterior applications. Expansion and contraction relief must be addressed in brick masonry design.

As with stone, brick walls can be utilized as heat absorbers and radiators in passive solar situations and in fireplace and stove designs. Brick thermal resistance is low considering current requirements. Adding insulation, air space, and other insulative materials to a brick assembly increases the R value considerably. A solid 8-in. brick wall has an R-value of 2.1; a 10-in cavity brick wall has an R-value of 3.0.

Concrete Masonry Units

Concrete brick and block have physical properties similar to brick. Block has good compressive strength but is not as crush resistant as brick. Block is less dense than brick with an 8-in. wide block weighing ca 35–55 PSF compared to an 8-in. wide brick weighing 69–79 PSF. Its larger size, less costly ingredients, and manufacturing process makes block considerably less costly and not as labor-intensive as brick. Block does not have brick's refined surface appearance, texture, and color quality. Standard block has an open porous texture that requires filling to receive surface coatings. Block can be cast with resinous facings for a smoother finish surface. Splitting concrete bricks and solid blocks produces a rough texture that mimics a natural finish. Block material can be cast into shapes and sculpted for striking patterns or pierced units that permit air passage and that can serve as screens.

Block is a durable, relatively maintenance-free interior wall surface. Block, properly filled and sealed with a surface coating, provides an integral interior surface for a brick–block exterior wall. Block resists defacement, abrasion, and chipping. It can be damaged by impact.

Block partition assemblies are tested for fire resistance and rated with an equivalent thickness, ET rating. Block ET for a pumice aggregate block is 4.7 in. for a 4-h rating, ET for a cinder or slag aggregate block is 5.9 in. for a 4-h rating. Interior block partitions are effective fire rated separations that weigh and cost less than brick, stone, and concrete.

Acoustically, block is similar to other masonry products, being dense and sound reflective. However, block can be manufactured as an acoustic unit. Blocks are cast with vertical slotted faces where the interior cavity acts as a sound resonator. Absorption rates can be increased when absorbent material is placed in the cavity. A lightweight 8-in. CMU block wall has an NRC of .40–.45 and an STC of 49–52. Paint reduces the NRC value.

The thermal characteristics of concrete block are again similar to other masonry products, except that the cores of the hollow units can be filled with insulative materials. Filling the cores with perlite can increase the resistance of an 8-in. block from R 2.18 to R 5.03.

Cast Stone

Cast or artificial stone is a mixture of stone chips or fragments embedded in a molded block of mortar, plaster, or cement. The finish surface is treated to simulate a ground, honed, polished, or rusticated finish. The physical properties of cast stone are similar to other manufactured masonry products such as brick and concrete masonry. Cast stone is a less costly alternative to stone.

Terra-Cotta and Clay

Modern architectural terra-cotta can be extruded or handmade. The machine extruded product is commonly known as ceramic veneer. Both handmade terra-cotta and ceramic veneer are available in a wide variety of colors. Ceramic veneers are usually exterior wall panels of 18 in. × 30 in. or 20 in. × 27 in.

Terra-cotta tile units are also known as structural clay tile. The units are extruded rectangular hollow forms. The tile units have 12-in. × 12-in. faces and thicknesses of 2, 3, 4, 6, 8, 10, and 12 in. Units 6-in. wide or less have one cell, whereas larger units have two cells.

Clay-tile units are constructed in bond patterns similar to other unit masonry materials. Clay tile was commonly used bonded with brick and CMU blocks and finished with plaster. In the past 40 years, clay-tile use has virtually disappeared as a partition material. This is due to many factors including the intensive and costly labor used in the manufacture and construction of clay-tile units, and the popularity of different partition assemblies such as concrete masonry and wood or metal studs with gypsum wallboard.

Clay tile varies in weight from 65 PSF for a 12-in. hollow tile to 34 PSF for a 4-in. hollow tile. Clay-tile units have a fire resistance rating of 3 h for a nominal 6-in. glazed or unglazed two-cell 25% cored tile unit, or a 1 h rating for a 4-in. glazed or unglazed tile with a core not exceeding 30% and plastered ¾ in. thick on one side. Clay tile can be load bearing and nonload bearing. Both can be utilized as furring and fireproofing. Similar to other manufactured masonry products, clay tile has good compressive properties along with the drawback of brittleness.

Thermal and acoustic properties are similar to other unit masonry products. Durability and maintenance characteristics are again similar to other masonry products. Aesthetically, clay tile is extremely flexible with a myriad of colors and glazed finishes available. Clay tile can be manufactured with chemical-resistant finishes and constructed with chemical-resistant mortars. Stack-bonded hollow clay-tile units have been utilized as screening partitions.

Adobe

Adobe is a soil with a high diatomaceous (type of clay) content. When mixed with water the soil becomes plastic, allowing molding into bricks. Adobe bricks are large sized (±8 in. × 16 in. × 10 in.) rough shapes that have been sun dried.

Adobe is primarily utilized in the desert areas of the United States as an interior and exterior wall material. Excessive wetness will erode and dissolve the adobe clay. Interior adobe is generally finished with plaster. Typically, adobe partitions are units laid in courses of solid running bond.

The physical properties of adobe are comparable to the

prior listed unit masonry products with the exception that it is not as permanent a material, particularly when deluged with water. Adobe is indigenous to desert areas, making the material readily available and relatively inexpensive. The large-size units reduce the labor cost for construction.

The choice of interior adobe partitions follows from the selection of adobe for the exterior construction materials. Adobe masonry provides thick, rough walls. This is ideal for thermal time-lag heating and cooling, which is more than appropriate in a desert climate.

Glass Block

Glass block is the term given to a class of glass building materials that are utilized as masonry units. Glass blocks are made from two pieces of pressed glass fused together. The hollow center is partially evacuated. This provides a dead air space.

Glass block is manufactured with imprinted designs and patterns on both sides of the glass surfaces. The glass can be clear, frosted, tinted, and solar reflective. Most units have texture and distortion that permit the passage of light without relinquishing visual privacy.

Standard block units are 3-7/8-in. thick by varying widths, or 6, 8, or 12-in. square. A thin 3-1/8-in. unit is available. Glass block is usually laid in a stack bond pattern with uniform mortar joints of 1/4 in.

Glass block was introduced in the 1930s and was limited to front door sidelights or was used in lieu of windows in industrial buildings. The intent was to utilize light without the security problem of large glass panes. The popularity of glass block waned for many years until the recent upsurge in use as an interior partition material. Glass block is a low maintenance material with a light emitting advantage. The security afforded by small glass units has always been an attractive feature of glass block. The material is also durable, resisting abrasion and defacement.

Glass block does not support much more than its own weight. As a glass it is a brittle material with compressive strength and little tensile or ductile properties. Similar to brick, glass blocks can be constructed in curvilinear shaped partitions and interspersed with other masonry materials.

Glass block has low fire-resistive ratings. Its acoustic properties are essentially the same as brick. To prevent sound transmission, structural isolation needs to be considered.

Preventing solar transmission has been addressed in the more recent block products that include tinted and solar reflective units. Clear blocks with smooth surfaces are being used for passive solar collection. Special light-diffusing units have been developed to provide glare free daylight.

WOOD

There is frequent interior use of products manufactured for exterior applications. These materials are commonly used as interior wall coverings.

Wood boards used in the construction of walls can be

the sheathing substrate, as well as the exterior or interior wallcovering.

Wood used for interior wall paneling and trim needs to be free from warping with a fine grain and texture, hard and clear of defects or knots. Interior wood may be left with a natural finish or painted. Woods that are best suited for natural finish have rich grains and include oak, birch, cherry, maple, mahogany, beech, ash, sycamore, walnut, and teak. Wood that is better suited for painting usually is smooth with uniform texture, moderate hardness, and includes ponderosa pine, sugar pine, poplar, northern and Idaho white pine.

Siding and trim used in moist areas or exterior locations must be resistant to decay, able to receive and hold paint, virtually free from warp with good weathering characteristics. The wood traditionally used for these applications is clear cedar, redwood, and cypress. These woods can remain natural or be enhanced with clear preservatives. If these woods are painted it is critical to paint both sides to maintain dimensional stability and to retain the paint. Kiln dried boards at a stabilized moisture content will perform better and retain finishes.

Siding can be installed horizontally in the following board styles: Flush pattern tongue and groove; V-Joint tongue and groove which has medium shadow patterns; bevel siding which can be plain laps or a rabbeted bevel for defined joint; shiplap which includes a plain board and a V rustic for articulated joints; beaded boards and simple drop or German siding which has a distinctive shadow line. Vertical siding accommodates the following styles: Flush pattern tongue and groove, V-Joint tongue and groove, channel rustic, board and batten, board and board, batten and board and plowed fascia. Natural finish board sidings are frequently utilized as low maintenance interior surfaces that have distinction.

Shingles can be installed in the following patterns: staggered, fish scale, diamond, sawtooth, and chisel. Shakes have a more random appearance and are usually installed similar to a staggered shingle pattern. Pattern shingles are not in common use and would be costly to install and provide.

Solid wood is subject to warp and shrinkage, moisture induced fungi, insect infestation, and is flammable. Boards can be kiln dried, preservative- and fire-retardant-treated. Wood boards may have densities up to 18–22 PCF with thermal resistance (R) of 2.44 to 2.64 per inch thickness. Shingles weigh less and have higher R values.

Plywood

Plywood is the name given to a structural wood product which consists of three or more thin layers of wood laminated together with a permanent moisture resistant wood glue. Plywood wood species should have similar shrinkage requirements. To achieve this specification plywood usually consists of an odd number of layers. Plywood becomes a thin structural wood panel that is dimensionally stable. It is able to host hardwood veneers for paneling and rough construction grades for formwork.

Plywood is manufactured in exterior and interior grades. Exterior grade glues are fully waterproof and the exterior veneers are a higher grade of wood than interior plywood. Plywood is also manufactured with cores of solid wood lumber and of particle board. Plywood is a nailable material produced in 4 × 8 ft and 4 × 10 ft panels, with or without tongue and groove edge joints.

Plywood wallcoverings include wall sheathing, which is a superior construction technique providing greater stiffness and racking resistance than boards. Plywood panels are available as flush panels (Medium Density Overlaid MDO) without grooving, with V grooves, with board and batten patterns on rough sawn veneers, channel groove vertical siding pattern, brushed or relief grain textured surface panels, Kerf cut rough sawn panels and texture 1–11, a vertical grooved style of panel with ship-lapped edges. Wood veneers used for exterior grade plywood include Douglas fir, redwood, cedar, southern pine, lauan, and other weather resistant species.

Plywood panels are available as flush panels ready for paint or other wall treatment, textured panels similar to the vertical grooved patterns for the exterior plywood and fine veneer panels for stained or clear finishes. Hardwood veneer panels can have the veneer flitches assembled to be book matched for maximum grain continuity, slip matched where the grain pattern is constantly repeated or random matched with a deliberate mismatch of the veneers. Interior panels should be assembled according to the American Wood Institute (AWI) custom grade. Plywood also comes prefinished with plastic laminates, vinyl sheets, stone, sand, or other materials mounted to the exterior face of the plywood sheets. Plywood clear finished veneers are made of the complete range of wood that is available for satin or clear finishes.

Thin lightweight modular panels can be enhanced with the finest veneers. Plywood is dimensionally stable, free from warping. As a wood product it is still flammable and affected by exposure to weather and insect damage, but to a far lesser degree. Plywood can be preservative- and fire-retardant-treated. The glues used in bonding plywood are not inert. The vapors released from the glues contribute to airborne pollutants. Plywood has not been singled out as a danger although it has been cited as contributing to allergic reactions. Plywood has a thermal (R) value of 1.24 for a 1 in. thickness. Plywood panels weigh a consistent 34 PCF. Compared to solid wood, plywood is relatively inexpensive.

Particle Board

Particle board is a class of building boards formed from wood chip particles and a binding high performance glue. This board is frequently used as interior prefinished (plastic laminate, vinyl) panels providing a nailable substrate. The particle material is also formed into siding shapes and trim shapes making a nailable, paintable product less subject to warp movement. Particle board made of cedar chips is used to partition storage closets.

Particle board is a dimensionally stable wood product. It has the same advantageous physical properties of plywood and some composites of the structural strength. It is manufactured in different densities for varied applications. Particle board being made of waste pieces, is a less expensive material than unprocessed wood or plywood.

The binding glues in particle board, similar to plywood, release vapors and contribute to indoor air pollution. Particle board has to be laminated with a veneer material to have a finished appearance. The boards can be treated for moisture and fire retardance.

Particle board has a density per cubic foot ranging from 37 PCF to 62.5 PCF. The thermal resistance per 1 in. thickness ranges from an R of 1.85 to 0.85.

Cork

Cork is a resilient material from the bark of the cork oak tree. This bark is characterized by its granular appearance and resiliency. Thin veneer layers are cut from the bark to produce a wall covering material. The veneers are bonded with a synthetic resin and backed to form boards or tiles. Cork is finished with wax. Cork boards are porous and are adversely affected by humidity and moisture. This material which realizes its resiliency from millions of small trapped air spaces, is a good insulative material.

Cork is fairly durable for normal wearing conditions. Deliberate defacement will permanently damage the material. It is frequently used as tackable display boards. The surface durability can be increased with clear sealers and coatings. However these coatings will decrease the natural acoustic absorptivity of cork. The material is naturally resistant to vermin and mildew. Cork is not a fire rated material although it could be treated with a fire retardant. A 1 in. thickness of corkboard weighs 0.58 PSF.

PLASTER AND GYPSUM MATERIALS

Plaster is a composition of lime cement, sand, and water. Additions to the composition can include fibrous materials such as perlite, and wood fibers to increase bond strength. Plaster is used as a finish surface material on partition assemblies, from solid masonry to wood or metal stud framed walls.

Plaster is mixed with water to form a plastic malleable material that is applied to a substrate such as gypsum board, metal lath, or masonry units. Plaster is traditionally applied in three coats: the first, or scratch coat, bonds to the substrate material, the second, or brown coat, levels the coating and the final coat provides a finish surface. Modern developments to plaster include higher strength and quicker bonding that can reduce the number of coats required. The most widely used plaster material is calcined gypsum.

Gypsum is utilized in plaster, plasterboard, wallboard, and gypsum partition blocks. Gypsum is a non-combustible material that can be manufactured as thin boards and as building units. Manufactured gypsum products can serve as finished surfaces, making this a safe, lightweight, easy to construct and finish building material.

Gypsum plasters are available in ready mix products for all purpose installations, acoustical plasters to meet sound absorption needs, gaging plasters combine with lime putty to vary the setting time and strength, molding plaster is used for molding or casting and Keene's cement is a high density plaster. Gypsum plasters can be applied to the same substrates (board, lath, block) as other plasters.

Plasters have moderate compressive strength properties ranging from 700 psi to 2000 psi. Tensile strength is quite low with strengths of 150 psi to 400 psi. Plaster density ranges from 120 PCF to 42 PCF depending on the filler materials.

This is a material with low thermal resistivity. An inch of cementitious plaster has an R of 0.20, an inch of gypsum plaster has an R of 0.67. In a partition assembly plaster will contribute positively to the overall partition thermal rating. Plaster will expand and contract significantly with changes in temperature. Sufficient expansion relief joints must be provided when plaster is subject to temperature changes.

Plaster is a completely inorganic material making it incombustible, rot- and vermin-proof. It does have a tendency to crumble when exposed to wearing or moist conditions, unless the plaster composition is adjusted to resist such adverse conditions. Plaster will not hold up to impacts or scratching, chipping defacement. Mildew is supported by moist plaster and moist conditions should be avoided.

Graffiti can damage a plaster surface and is not easily removed. Plaster is a relatively simple material to repair, with damaged areas cut away and patching plaster blended over the damaged surface or hole. Plasters crack and spall when their supporting substrate warps, settles or deforms from loading conditions.

A material of choice for fire protection, plaster does not support flames. Plaster does not release toxic fumes, although it does cure over time releasing harmless vapors. Examples of fire resistance include a 2-hour rating for structural members achieved with 1 in. of gypsum plaster of ¾# metal lath and a 4-hour rating with 1½ in. of plaster on ¾# metal lath.

Plaster can provide good acoustic control with special mixes of sound absorbent acoustic plasters. A plaster surface can be manipulated through the mix to be either sound reflective or sound absorbent. Plaster with a dense mix can effectively contribute to a partition assembly controlling airborne sound. Plaster with an acoustic mix plastered on an isolated assembly can assist in the control of structure-borne sound.

Aesthetically plaster is a multidimensional material. True to its name it has no form, plaster can be flat or curved, smooth, rough, textured, molded, hard, or soft. Plain plaster and lath is an elegantly simple finish surface. It has the ability to smooth over imperfections, round curves and conceal dimensional discrepancies. The finishing techniques for plaster include surface textures and integral coloring. Plaster also serves as a ready substrate for a multitude of other finishes including paint, tile, marble, plastic, textiles, and paper.

This is a readily available material made up of natural components. The appearance of the finished plaster does depend on the quality of the installation. Installation is more labor intensive than plasterboard/gypsum drywall making the cost of plaster markedly higher than board products.

Gypsum Drywall

Gypsum drywall or wallboard is a basic building product consisting of paper surfaces bonded to a core material of calcined gypsum. The gypsum is sandwiched between two sheets of specially treated paper forming a ribbon of board. After the gypsum has set, the board is cut into regular sheet sizes. Gypsum boards are manufactured in 4 or 8 foot widths and 8, 10, 12 and 14 foot lengths.

Boards are used in thicknesses of ¼ in. for multi-layer or resurfacing applications, 5/16 in. utilized in modular buildings and mobile homes, ⅜ in. used similarly to ¼ in. for repairs and resurfacing laminations, ½ in. widely used as a finish for standard height partitions or as part of a multi-layered assembly, ⅝ in. used for better quality installations, higher walls or areas requiring more rigidity and strength. ⅝ in. is a standard thickness for fire rated assemblies, and 1 in. boards which are utilized for shaft wall linings or areas needing solid assemblies. Boards are formed with eased or tapered edges that permit a filled or taped joint, concealing the joint in the finished product. If joints are not properly taped cracks will appear at the joint. Tapering also allows the installation of protective metal corner beads. The beads receive a hard plaster compound which levels the board to the corner.

Gypsum boards are produced in the following categories:

Regular—surface boards for walls and ceilings.

Type X—boards with improved fire resistance from core material additives. Available in ½ in. and ⅝ in. thicknesses.

Predecorated—boards produced with an applied wallcovering of paper, vinyl, vinyl coated paper.

Water-resistant—boards with a water resistant gypsum core and moisture repellent paper. Water resistant boards can also be treated for fire resistance.

Backing board—a base layer board for multilayered assemblies.

Coreboard—a thick (1 in.) board for shaft walls or solid assemblies.

Sheathing—a board produced to resist fire, moisture, and serves as a substrate for exterior materials, tiles, and masonry veneers.

Gypsum lath—a substrate board that serves as a base for plaster.

Foil backed—boards produced with an aluminum backing providing a thermal resistive vapor barrier.

Gypsum drywall boards have an abundance of uses as described above. Drywall boards have become the primary wall surfacing material in this country on the basis of improved installation techniques. Boards are nailed, screwed and/or glued to structural framing members. In conditions where substrates are not level multiple layers and leveling furring should be used. Joints, nails, and screw locations should not be visible in the finish drywall surface. The horizontal application of boards is recommended over vertical because boards are stiffer and stronger in the long dimension, the amount of joint work is less and joint imperfections are minimized. Supports should be spaced 16 or 24 in. on center.

Gypsum drywall boards are similar to plaster in their moderate compressive strength. Due to the paper coverings, the tensile strength of drywall is better than plaster. A relatively light building material, gypsum drywall board weighs 2 PSF. Additives of vermiculite, perlite, and fibers of glass or minerals increase fire resistance, glass and wood fibers increase strength and reduce weight.

The molded core of solid gypsum is incombustible and nonflammable. Gypsum boards are a choice fire-rated material. 5/8 in. Type-X gypsum board applied to both sides of a stud partition will have a 1-hour fire resistance rating. Double layers will provide a 2-hour rating. Three layers of 1/2 in. Type-X boards can provide a 3-hour rating and 5/8 in. Type-X with 2 in. of gypsum tile can provide a 4-hour fire resistance rating.

Gypsum board is dimensionally stable. It is durable and resistant to cracking, impacts, scratching, vermin, and moderate wear. Boards can be damaged by forceful impacts and willful defacement. Special care should be taken in moist or wet areas. Water resistant board can be utilized as a base for ceramic tile, but the actual board should not be directly exposed to moisture. Even covered with tile, the cut edges of water resistant drywall can wick moisture into the core if the tile bedding or grouting fails. Moisture will deteriorate the core material and can mildew the paper surface.

Acoustically gypsum drywall is a hard reflective surface to airborne sound. The board will transmit structure-borne sound energy. The finish surface of the drywall boards can be treated with sound absorbent materials, soft textiles, fabric covered foams, and even formed foam shapes that will create an anechoic effect if all surfaces are treated the same. STC and NRC ratings will vary with the number of board layers, the use of resilient clip attachments, the spacing/isolation of structural elements. These factors all will influence the sound transmission or noise controlling ability of a drywall assembly.

Thermal conductivity is relatively high, making thermal resistance fairly low. A 1/2 in. gypsum drywall board has an R of 0.36, a 5/8 in. board has an R of 0.41. Foil backing can increase the thermal resistance.

Gypsum drywall surfaces can be left smooth to receive paint or sheet wallcovering or a textured surface can be applied. Texturing can be achieved with thin plaster coatings, specialty thick paint materials or with a textured wall covering. Boards of gypsum drywall can serve as a base for tile, masonry veneers, metals, wood panels, plastic, vinyl, paper, mirrors, and other materials. Boards can be inset panels in an external frame or gypsum core boards can form a wall. This is a readily available material, installed in prefabricated modular sizes. All of these factors make gypsum drywall an attractive moderate cost building finish material.

Mud

Mud is earth mixed with water to form a malleable substance that can be applied to a surface. Mud varies with composition of soil. Clay soils provide more cohesive mud than sandy soils. Mud is used as an exterior and interior wallcovering. Typically utilized to increase the performance of log, stone, adobe, sod, and other simple structural types. Mud was possibly the first applied wallcovering used in conjunction with other simple materials. Mud has been in use since prehistoric times.

Mud is in common use today throughout the world, particularly in Third World countries where manufactured materials are expensive and not available. Mud can and is used in combination with adobe, sod, thatch, reeds, logs, and other low cost, indigenous, available building materials. Mud was a predecessor to plaster and mortar prior to the discovery of lime/gypsum based cement.

Mud applied to a rough structure closes gaps between structural units, increases resistance to wind and water, acts as a bond similar to mortar and provides a relatively smooth finish. Mud is readily available and has little cost. As an earth material mud is not flammable and has insulative properties. Mud may not be hygienic and can contain harmful elements. Mud is not durable, it erodes with rain and moisture, although it can be re-applied with small cost. It performs better in dry climates.

Packed dry mud of a 115 PCF density has an approximate thermal resistance of .20 per 1 in. thickness. Mud with a sand composition exceeding a 120 PCF will have an R of less than 0.19 per 1 in. thickness.

GLASS

Glass is a hard, brittle, usually transparent substance made by fusing one or more oxides of silicon, boron, or phosphorus with basic oxides, (sodium oxide, calcium oxide), followed by rapid cooling to prevent crystallization. Many different chemical compounds are used to affect color, durability, strength, and other physical properties.

Glass is formed primarily through the float process, where molten glass is poured onto a bed of liquid tin, forming a thin flat ribbon of glass. The glass is annealed, (controlled cooling), then cut into desired shapes. This process produces high optical quality glass with parallel surfaces. Float glass is produced clear (colorless, transparent) or mixed with additional metallic oxides produces heat-absorbing glass.

Float glass can be manufactured from thicknesses of 3/32 in. up to 1 1/4 in. in sheets ranging from 48 × 84 in. up to 120 × 204 in. The older process produces plate or rolled glass. This process forms molten glass between two rollers set at a desired thickness. The glass is annealed, cut and then ground and polished on both sides to produce a uniformly thick piece of glass. This process produces flaws such as seeds, bubbles, cracks, and sand holes. The rolled process is mainly utilized for stained, patterned, and wire glass.

Stained glass is colored by the addition of metallic oxide pigments. Patterned glass is produced by rollers with a surface pattern, imparting the pattern on the glass as it rolls through. Stained and patterned glass is used primarily for aesthetic affects. Wired glass is produced by placing a woven wire fabric in the molten glass prior to rolling. Both patterned and wired glass can be colored. The wire fabric prevents the glass from falling apart after being broken. Wired glass is utilized in areas requiring security or safety.

The types of glass available for use in partitions include heat-treated glass, insulated glass, laminated glass, reflective glass, and opaque glass. These types of glass are produced by treating manufactured glass.

Heat-treated Glass. Heat-treatment increases the tensile strength of glass. Heat treated tempered glass, which fractures into small non-jagged pieces upon impact, reduces the possibility of injury.

Insulated Glass. Insulating glasses are factory assembled glass panes with a sealed air space between panes. The air space limits and reduces the transmission of heat or sound energy. Insulated glass is primarily an exterior product with interior applications when temperature and sound control between spaces is desired.

Laminated Glass. Laminated glass is produced by sandwiching layers of transparent plastic between panes of glass and heating under pressure to form a single laminated unit. The plastic prevents the glass from shattering. Laminated glass is used in applications requiring safety, security, solar, and sound control. Multiple laminations of glass can produce a glass unit that can resist bullets, or when thick enough, grenade or assault rifle attack. Glass can be further processed by etching, chipping, or sandblasting to create different effects.

Reflective Glass. Reflective or mirrored glass is backed with a coating of silver, aluminium, or a metal oxide on one surface. The coating makes the glass reflective. Mirrored glass is usually opaque although it can be manufactured to be mirrored to one side and transparent to the other. Two way mirrors have specific uses where unnoticeable observation is required for experiments or security purposes. Mirrors are used at times to cover whole wall services, expanding the visual appearance of a space.

Opaque Glass. Opaque glass is created by fusing a ceramic color onto a glass panel. Opaque glass is commonly used in exterior applications as spandrel glass. Interior use of opaque glass as a finished wall surface has little application to date.

Glass is in common use as a partition material allowing light and visual communication while limiting sound or air transmission. The partition assemblies that utilize glass include internal frames where glass is introduced in small units as viewing windows, externally framed partitions where glass may be the body of the partition providing sound and air separation with visual transparency and in temporary partitions to provide viewing or transparent sections. Glass framing materials are usually wood or metal with synthetic gaskets, glazing sealants, and compounds. The structural stability of a glass partition is dependent on the anchoring of the frame and the amount of edge support or bite the frame provides the glazing.

Glass may also be translucent, mirrored, colored, or patterned to provide design effects. The glass framing pattern can also provide visual interest and design opportunities. Glass has many desirable, aesthetic, and psychological qualities. Closed interior rooms can borrow light from adjacent spaces making the rooms less oppressive. Small spaces can appear enlarged with strategic placement of transparent or mirrored walls. Glass panels permit visual interaction and a sense of community in an office without physical interaction. Mirrored and special glass panels also permit surveillance in security applications.

As a hard material, glass is fairly easy to maintain. Oils and other common dirts are easily washed away. Most graffiti will not adhere to glass. Untreated glass is fragile, making it susceptible to breakage vandalism.

Glass is a brittle material with low tensile strength. Heat treatment can increase the tensile strength of glass. Glass is relatively heavy with 1/4 in. plate weighing 3.28 PSF, 1/2 in. plate weighing 6.56 PSF, 5/8 in. insulating weighing 3.25 PSF and 1/4 in. wire glass weighing 3.5 PSF.

Untreated glass is a safety hazard, that shatters into jagged shards when broken. Because glass is transparent and can be mistaken for an opening, it is critical, (and usually a model code requirement) that full height interior glass partitions have tempered or other safety glass. Glass used in exit areas is specified under building codes.

Glass is not flammable and it is not stable when subjected to temperature extremes. Plain glass will shatter in high heat fires. Glass in fire rated assemblies has to be wired and is limited to 100 square inches. Check the applicable model code for proper use of glass in fire rated partitions.

Glass is conductive, permitting easy transmission of sound and heat energy. Glass can be manufactured to resist heat flow with the introduction of captive air spaces or plastic laminations. Acoustic qualities can be achieved with laminated and double-paned glass and enhanced with the framing gasket detail. Interior clear glass thermal properties are illustrated with the following examples: R of 1.36 for an 1/8 in. thick single pane of flat glass. R of 2.17 for doubled glazed 1/8 in. panes with a 1/2 in. air space, R of 2.63 for triple glazing with 1/4 in. air spaces. Acoustic values of glass vary by thickness with an STC of 23 for 1/8 in. float glass, STC of 31 for 1/2 in. float, STC of 32 for 1 in. insulating up to an STC of 38 for 5/8 in. laminated glass. Heat treatment, thickness, color, reflectivity all affect the R and STC values. Glass is readily available and can be installed without intense labor. Per square foot area, glass compares favorably with the cost of other partitioning materials.

CERAMIC TILE

Ceramic tile is a finish surfacing material applied to a completed partition assembly or floor. This section will address wall applications of tile. Tiles are applied to substrates of gypsum drywall, plaster, plywood, brick, terracotta, or concrete block masonry with a cementitious bedding surface or adhesive.

Tile is classified by density and measure of absorption. The classifications include impervious, vitreous, semivitreous, and nonvitreous, with absorption rates of .05% or less for impervious, 3% for vitreous, 7% for semivitreous and over 7% for nonvitreous tiles.

Tile may be unglazed, made from a homogenous mixture of clay, silica, flint, and kaolin. The color and texture of unglazed tiles is uniform throughout the tile. This is important for surfaces subjected to abrasive wear. Glazed tiles are ceramics that have an additional hard-fired finish. Glazes are available in a variety of colors, mottled and stippled textures, gloss, lustrous or matte sheens. Special glazes can be added for abrasive finishes or glazes can be fired at higher temperatures for chemical resistant properties.

Ceramic tile used in wall applications is usually glazed. Glazing makes a tile surface slick, resistant to dirt and graffiti, easy to clean and maintain. Unglazed ceramic mosaic tile can also be used. Paver and quarry tiles are usually reserved for flooring. Glazed wall tiles are usually $4\frac{1}{4} \times 4\frac{1}{4}$ in., 4×6 in., 6×6 in., 8×8 in. Ceramic mosaic tiles are usually 1×1 in., 1×2 in. and 2×2 in. Trim tiles are manufactured to form finished corners and edges. Wall tiles can be set in patterns or the tiles are fired with machine or handpainted patterns or decorations. Colored or patterned tile can form contrasting borders or accent patterns. Tiles can be assembled to form large pictures. A computer generated graphics program is available that can transcribe photographic images into glaze colors to formulate any image desired.

Ceramic tile can be set in conventional mortar beds of $\frac{3}{4}$ in. $+/-$ or thin-set in organic adhesives, dry-set mortars, Latex-Portland cement mortar, furan mortar or conductive dry-set mortar. Grouting materials include sand-portland cement, dry-set grout, latex-portland cement grout, mastic, furan, and epoxy grouts. The quality of a tile installation is dependent on the setting bed being appropriate to the underlying structure and to the intended use.

Ceramic tile can be manufactured with carbon to serve as a conductor. This is usually a floor application where static electricity is not desired. Ceramic tile is a hard, durable finish when installed correctly. Tile resists wear and usually outlives other building elements. This makes tile difficult and costly to remove in renovations. Ceramics resist abrasion and surface defacements, making tile an appropriate choice in high abuse areas. Tile will shatter or chip under hard impact, particularly if the setting bed does not support the tile uniformly. Ceramic mosaic and other hard fired tiles are more durable than glazed surface tiles with soft fired clay.

Tile is not flammable and can be used in a fire resistive assembly. Soft fired clay will absorb moisture, fail and shatter if subjected to temperature extremes, including fire. Hard fired tile set properly is moisture resistant. Some tile grouts are susceptible to mildews and must be carefully selected if the application is constantly moist. Glazed wall tile is easily cleaned and can be subjected to harsh chemical disinfectants and cleaning agents. These properties make tile a safe choice in areas requiring hygienic conditions such as kitchens, health and food service facilities, and bathrooms.

As part of an assembly, ceramic tile will increase the density and weight of a wall. Glazed wall tile weighs 3 PSF and unglazed ceramic mosaic tile weighs 2.5 PSF. Tile is an acoustically hard, reflective surface best utilized in areas requiring ease of maintenance, where reflective sound is not critical.

Ceramic tiles provide a wealth of colors and texture to the palette of a designer. As a modular unit, they automatically give an interior scale. Tiles are manufactured world wide, making the product readily available in a wide range of prices. Tile setting is labor intensive which makes the material costly in comparison with other finishes.

PAINTS AND COATINGS

A coating is defined as a covering layer, or a material layer which is applied to a surface to protect, seal, smooth, conceal, preserve, or decorate the substrate. Coatings are usually in a liquid form. Paint is a film, layer, or coat of pigment applied to the surface of an object. It can be defined as any liquid material that obscures or modifies the applied surface when it dries or solidifies into a film.

Paint or coatings with pigments contain two materials, vehicles which are liquid carriers and pigments, which are the coloring and concealing agents. The liquid vehicle has two components, a volatile or solvent such as mineral spirits or water and a non-volatile or binder. The volatile component facilitates the paint application and through evaporation allows the paint or coating to become a film. Conversely it will dissolve the film material and can be used to adjust the viscosity of the mixture. The nonvolatile component or binder is the portion of the paint film that binds the particles of pigment to the film surface.

Pigments can be natural, synthetic, organic, and inorganic. The concealing power of a pigment varies with the type of pigment. Dark pigments are more effective in obscuring a substrate than light pigments. Fading results from pigmentation instability. Blues and greens are more susceptible to ultraviolet caused fading.

The main differences in the properties of paints and coatings is a factor of the binder characteristics. Binders used in building coating materials include:

Alkyds. Alkyds which are oil-modified resins. These are versatile, used in exterior and interior applications on wood, gypsum drywall, plaster, and other painted surfaces including epoxies if sanded first. It is available in flat, semigloss, low lustre, and high gloss finishes. Alkyds are durable, nearly odorless, and require a primer on most surfaces.

Epoxy. Epoxy, which provides tile like hardness and high adhesion come in two varieties, an epoxy ester and a two-component epoxy resin. The two-component epoxy is a heavy duty chemical resistant formula used in industrial applications. The epoxy ester is easier to apply and provides more chemical resistance than an alkyd. Epoxies can be applied to tile, metal, porcelain, fiber glass, concrete, and wood. Epoxy paints will not adhere to latex, alkyd, or oil paint. These paints are hard to use, difficult to cleanup, and have odors and fumes.

Epoxy Coal-tar. Epoxy coal-tar which is a two-component epoxy with a coal tar modification is used in wet areas and for resistance to liquid chemicals.

Inorganic Binders. Inorganic binders are used in conjunction with anticorrosive paints to provide high resistance to moisture.

Latex Binders. Latex binders are the most widely used water-based paints. Latex polymers include poly(vinyl acetate), acrylic, and butadiene–styrene. These polymers are quick drying with little odor. Latex paints are used primarily on gypsum drywall, plaster, masonry, and wood. Latex will adhere to surfaces painted with flat oil or latex, it has difficulty adhering to alkyd and high gloss surfaces. Almost any paint can be applied over latex. Latex is less durable and less washable than oils or alkyds.

Oil Binders. Oil binders, particularly linseed oil is the primary binder for exterior paints and metal primer paint. Oil binders are durable under normal conditions, they are not resistant to abrasion or chemicals. Oil adheres well to bare wood and surfaces painted with latex, alkyd, or oil. It does not adhere to wall paper, drywall, or masonry. It is durable and can withstand washing. Oil emits a strong odor and is thinned with equally strong smelling turpentine or mineral spirits. Oil based paint can take 2–3 days to dry.

Oil Alkyd Binders. Oil alkyd binders are a linseed oil and alkyd mixture that provides that positive qualities of both materials. Oil alkyd dries faster and retains a high gloss luster.

Oleoresinous Binders. Oleoresinous binders are a heat processed mixture of hard resins and drying oils. Increased resin strengthens the chemical resistance and the hardness of the coating compared to an oil binder. Resin also can increase gloss luster and improve adhesion, drying, and durability.

Phenolic Binders. Phenolic binders are a synthetic product. Phenolic paints can be clear or pigmented and are used as protective topcoatings on metals in humid or completely wet conditions.

Rubber-based Binders. Rubber-based binders include chlorinated rubber which is solvent thinned. It has high resistance to water, water vapor, strong acids and alkalies, and corrosive chemicals. It is an appropriate coating for masonry, concrete, floors, and areas that will be under water. Rubber-based coatings are available in flat and low luster finishes, with few color choices. It is quick drying, expensive with a strong odor. Latex, oil or alkyd paint can be applied over rubber-based coatings. Oil based paint will not adhere to this type of coating.

Silicone Alkyds. Silicone alkyds combine silicone and alkyd resins. These coatings have excellent gloss and color suitable for metal surfaces. It is a durable finish resistant to high temperatures.

Urethane. Urethane is available in three finishes, single component oil-modified, moisture-curing and a two component system. Urethanes are applied to bare wood, and over latex, alkyd or oil paints. Oil-modified urethane can be used as a spar varnish or as a tough surface finish. Moisture curing urethane is flexible with a high resistance to chemicals and water.

Vinyl Coatings. Vinyl coatings are copolymers of vinyl acetate and vinyl chloride. Vinyl is very thin requiring multiple coatings. With good resistance to weather they are used on exposed metal surfaces.

Cement Coating. Cement coating is a mixture of portland cement, water, pigment and a water repellent. Cement paint is used to resurface masonry or concrete and is frequently used in basement areas. It takes 2 days to cure and forms a poor base for other finishes.

Special Purpose Paints

Special purpose paints include fire retardant and fire resistive paints. Fire retardants resist flame spreading on combustible surfaces. Fire resistive coatings can provide rated protection from 1–2 hours. These paints are either intumescent (swells or foams when heated) or subliming mastics. Other special coatings include mildew and heat resistant paints.

Some paints can provide special effects such as flecked multicolored latex paint that gives the appearance of fabric. This can conceal surface defects and can be repaired easily. Sand finish and textured paints dry with a rough finish. These paints are usually latex or alkyd based and conceal surface defects and drywall seams. Painting over these surfaces will present some difficulty requiring more paint or complete removal. Transparent finishes are used to protect and tone wood or preserve polished metal surfaces.

Varnish. Varnish provides a clear tough finish for wood. It can also be used to protect painted surfaces. Varnish is produced in alkyd, phenolic, polyurethane, epoxy, and moisture-cured urethane. Alkyd is the least durable and the urethanes are the most durable varnishes. Most paints do not adhere to varnish with the exceptions of oil and alkyd, if the varnish is thoroughly roughened.

Shellac. Shellac is an alcohol solution of a lac resin. Lac is derived from a tropical insect. It is an inexpensive quick drying clear or red-brown coating for bare, bleached, or stained wood. It cannot be used over other finishes and it can be easily damaged by water.

Stain. Stain consists of pigment in an oil, water, or alcohol liquid. Oil based stains are the most common. Stains tone and enhance wood grain by being absorbed into the pores of the wood. Once stained the wood can be left bare, oiled, waxed, or coated with varnish. There are products that combine stain and varnish that must be used with care as they streak easily and are not as durable as a varnish coating.

Bleach. Bleach is used to lighten dark or discolored wood. Bleach chemicals are corrosive and must be used with care. Bleach is scrubbed into the wood rinsed and dried. The process can be repeated. Bleach raises the wood grain, requiring sanding and refinishing. Chlorine laundry bleach is commonly used.

Fillers. Fillers are used to smooth imperfections in wood grain and marble veining. Filler can be natural or colored to match the filled material. Fillers are thinned with solvents and once applied, leave a satin smooth finish. Filler is not protective and can be sealed with varnish or paint.

Coatings and Paints

Coatings and paints are selected to provide improved performance of a substrate material. The performance requirements include; protection from rot or corrosion, improved appearance, improved sanitation, better illumination, safety and fire protection. Coatings including paint protect a surface by sealing and covering, thereby preventing moisture penetration, chemical and fume corrosion, ultraviolet radiation deterioration, and providing abrasion resistance. Coatings also can make a material more dimensionally stable by preventing moisture penetration. Paint and coatings assist in overall maintenance by protecting materials from dirt and making surfaces easier to clean.

Color and luster are the aesthetic choices when selecting a coating. Color is a personal preference. Luster or gloss affects appearance and durability. The three most widely used paints: latex, alkyd, and oil are produced in flat, semigloss, and high gloss lusters. High gloss paints are the most wear resistant with a greater amount of resin than low luster finishes. High gloss paints should be considered for areas subject to heavy use and frequent cleaning. Food service areas, health care facilities, kitchens, bathrooms, laboratories are appropriate areas for high gloss finishes. Flat paints with low luster are recommended for areas that do not require frequent washing. Low luster finishes reduce light glare and present a softer appearance.

Coatings and paint affect material durability, maintenance, thermal transmission, acoustic performance, and fire resistivity. When heat transmission and acoustic performance is critical the coating on the material surface must be entered into the calculations, ie, acoustic block performance is negatively affected by paint. The finish coating on a material requires as much consideration as the selection of the material.

OPERABLE PARTITIONS

Operable partitions are manufactured in two main types: Folding accordion partitions and operable walls. Folding partitions include finished particle board solid panels that are hinged together with vinyl hinges. The panels range from 5 in.–12 in. in width by ¾ in. thick and can accommodate heights up to 12 ft. The partitions operate by folding accordion fashion against a wall or into a pocketed

stack. The partition slides along on steel ball bearing wheels on an overhead simple metal track. Panels can be finished with plastic laminate, vinyl, or fabric wallcovering. Panel partitions are used for visual privacy only and do not provide sound transmission control. The finishes can be selected to comply with required flamespread ratings.

Accordion partitions in the simplest version are finished with heavy duty vinyl fabric attached to a steel framework that keeps the fabric rigid and accommodates the accordion folding action. The partitions operate on a single heavy duty overhead track on ball bearing steel wheels. The vinyl covers are seamed with concealed joints. The covers are heavy duty vinyl fabric with a synthetic backing. The vinyl usually meets class A flame spread ratings. This type of partition is designed for acoustic and visual privacy. The top and bottom of the partitions have vinyl seals which can be adjusted at the bottom. The formed steel framework is attached to steel panels lined with acoustic absorbent material. The end posts are equipped with foam lined sound seals and latches. This type of partition may weigh approximately 2 lb per linear foot without special acoustic treatment and over 5 lb per linear foot with acoustic treatment. With acoustic treatment the panels achieve an STC of 39–40. These partitions can also be finished with a sound absorbent material such as carpet achieving NRC ratings between 0.55–0.85. These partitions can operate manually or with electric power and can cover widths up to 60 ft and heights up to 27. The partitions fold into a relative small stack depth of approximately 2 in. of stack depth per linear foot of partition. The partition track is usually straight but the partitions can accommodate curved conditions and conditions where several partitions join together in L, T, or X joints to divide a large room into many smaller areas.

Similar construction is found in fire resistive accordion folding partitions where the panels and components are all roll formed steel for their noncombustible properties. These partitions are heavier and can attain an STC of 44.

Operable walls are constructed of large panels that are manufactured in thicknesses of 2, 3 and 4 in. corresponding to the acoustic and height of the wall. The panels come in heights ranging from 8–44 ft with many interim heights available. Operable walls can cover widths up to 132 ft.

Standard panel widths do not exceed 48 in. Panels frames are constructed in 14 or 16 gauge steel with a lighter gauge (20, 21) steel skin finished with corrosion resistant primers. The panel skin is welded to the frame for a strong unitized construction. The panels are then covered with a finish material.

Finish materials include reinforced vinyls, acoustical non-woven carpet, wallcovering and upholstery fabric, painted steel, and wood veneer. Finishes are typically factory laminated to the steel panels. Each panel has an acoustic seal at each edge which is concealed when the panel is fully extended. The joining edges of the panels are equipped with steel astragals to maintain closure. The top seals are usually extruded vinyl that maintains continuous contact with the ceiling to prevent acoustic transmission. Bottom seals are again vinyl and can be sweeps or automatically operating seals that drop into place when the panels are fully extended.

Suspension systems consist of heavy gauge or case hardened steel with steel or reinforced nylon carrier or bearing trolleys. The tracks can curve or run straight. The panels fold in a zig zag fashion into a stack. Large panels require 4–6 in. of stack depth with additional depth required for jambs.

Acoustical ratings for larger panels range from 46–55 STC and up to a 0.90 NRC. Operable walls can be rated fire partitions. A 1 hour rating is possible. The walls come equipped with operating exit doors to maintain means of egress. One company manufactures a rated wall that is alarm activated and can serve as an operable fire wall to limit and compartmentalize fire and smoke.

Temporary and Demountable Partitions

Demountable partitions are used where building program requirements are constantly changing, requiring personnel and their corresponding spaces to be altered. Demountable partitions consist of rigid panels which can include drywall, mineral fiber, glass fiber, or particle board. One type of system uses individual panels that mount to a steel spline at the edge. The panels can be finished with acoustically soft materials such as fabric or with hard surfaced washable materials such as plastic laminate. Panels also can be self supporting constructed with a rigid frame covered with a metal skin. View panels with transparent glazing can be constructed for these systems.

Special insulated panels with metal skins and foam insulation cores are used for temperature controlled cold and warm rooms. These are designed as demountable panels secured in top and bottom tracks. In the spline system there are several alternatives where an individual steel spline is attached to a wall structure which could be conventional metal studs, masonry, or drywall. The demountable surface is reusable. In another system a demountable stud is constructed with a spline attachment for the demountable panels.

The self supporting panels which are finished on both sides are mounted into a framework of pre-finished metal track or the panels come equipped with an adjustable seal at the bottom and top of the panel. Some of the manufactured track is designed to be a chase for power and communication cables and wiring. Demountable partitions can have excellent sound transmission control and sound absorption characteristics. Panels average about 40–50 STC and 0.40–0.85 NRC.

Most panels are constructed with fire resistive materials meeting flame spread requirements. Demountable partitions do not achieve fire ratings. Demountable partition materials have to be durable and strong to accommodate being erected and demounted several times over the life of a panel. The metal finished panels have more durable finish surfaces which can be repainted if necessary. The fabric finished panels can be refinished if the fabric becomes unacceptably worn or dirty.

Demountable partitions are a fast growing segment of the building material market. These partitions address flexibility and expansion issues for an uncertain and changing business market. Demountable partitions also are considered to be furnishings with different accounting and tax implications.

PLASTICS

Plastic is a term used to describe any ductile malleable material. Chemically it is a large class of organic compounds synthesized from hydrocarbons, proteins, cellulose, polymeric substances, and resins. Plastic materials are capable of being molded, extruded, cast, or fabricated into various shapes or filaments.

Plastics represent an evergrowing segment of building materials, those most commonly used as wallcovering materials include plastic laminates, vinyl wallcoverings, vinyl sidings, plastic glazing materials, hard plastic boards, and soft foamed plastics. Plastic materials are prime ingredients in paint, adhesives and synthetic textiles.

Plastics have two main categories:

Thermoplastics. Thermoplastics which are plastics that can be softened by heating and hardened by cooling in a temperature range suited to the plastic. Thermoplastics can be molded or extruded. Thermoplastics can sustain being heated and cooled repeatedly without a change in chemical composition. Thermoplastics include ABS plastics, (butadiene, styrene), acrylics, cellulosics, fluorocarbons, nylon, polycarbonate, polyethylene, polypropylene, polystyrene, poly(vinyl chloride), and Saran.

Thermosets. Thermosets which are plastic materials, once set by heat are no longer malleable. The material has chemically changed due to heat, chemical reaction to catalysts, ultraviolet light, or another action that results in an unchangeable state. Thermosets include alkyds, epoxy, melamine, urea, phenolic, polyester, silicon, and urethane.

Wallcovering and Wall Glazing

Wallcovering and wall glazing materials include polystyrene, vinyls, poly(vinyl chloride), poly(vinyl flouride), polyester, melamine, phenolic, acrylic, polycarbonate, and polyurethane. Paint, sealant, insulations, vapor barriers, internal sandwich panel materials all employ plastic materials that are part of a partition assembly.

Polystyrene. Polystyrene is polymer derived from styrene. It is a hard, brittle, thermoplastic material with good dimensional stability. Polystyrene can be molded and extruded. It has excellent electric insulating qualities and good optical clarity as a film. Common products include grilles, diffusers, glazing film, and insulation board.

Vinyl. Vinyls are a class of plastics containing acrylics, vinyl, and styrene polymers. Poly(vinyl chloride) (PVC) and poly(vinyl fluorides) (PVF) are both thermoplastic materials with wide building material use. PVCs are rigid and flexible with high resistance to ultraviolet aging, wear and abuse. PVC is a component in vinyl wallcoverings, vinyl siding to name a few, and as a coating material. PVF is a high crystalline plastic widely available as a tough film. It is used as a tough coating laminated to other materials, (plywood, vinyl, particleboard, steel, foil) as a protection. It has high resistance to abrasion and it is resistant to stains.

Polyester. Polyester is a thermoset resin that can be reinforced with glass fibers. It is a tough material, resistant to ultraviolet light, temperature changes, and weather. It can be blended to be rigid, flexible, as a fabric, or resilient. Polyester can resist breakage, most chemicals and water. It is sometimes utilized as a protective coating or as part of another material or fabric.

Polyethylene. Polyethylene is a thermoplastic material from an ethylene polymer. It can be manufactured in different densities. Polyethylene is usually translucent, flexible, even at low temperature, resilient and tough. It is resistant to most chemicals, water, and oils. It is not dimensionally stable with a high thermal expansion and it does fail under ultraviolet light, thermal, and physical stress. Polyethylene is most familiar as a sheet material used as temporary glazing, air, and vapor barriers.

Melamine. Melamine is a hard, durable, and dimensionally stable thermoset plastic usually combined with formaldehyde. It is resistant to most chemicals, abuse, and heat. Melamine compounds incorporate fillers of cellulose, minerals, processed fabric, glass fiber or combinations of fillers. Melamines have almost a limitless range of colors and patterns. Melamines can be molded imitating other materials or processed in sheets for laminating to base materials such as particle board, plywood, or other compounds or plastics.

Phenolic. Phenolic plastic is a thermoset material consisting of resins from a condensed phenol (aldehyde with phenol or cresol). Phenolics are strong, durable, abuse, electrical, and heat resistant. Phenolics have limited colors and can serve as a laminate base for other plastics such as melamine. These melamine/phenolic laminates, both high pressure and low pressure, provide a common wall covering which is easy to clean, resists abrasion, is dimensionally stable, and comes in a wide range of finish colors and patterns. Bakelite which made the familiar black telephone set, is also a phenolic plastic.

Acrylic. Acrylics are thermoplastic materials formed from an acrylate polymer. Acrylics are usually transparent dimensionally stable materials that resist weather, breaking, fading, discoloration, and chemicals. Acrylic plastics have good structural properties and can be used as glazing, casework, and furniture. As glazing, acrylics have superior acoustic and thermal transmission properties. Interior applications can prevent the accidental shattering which occurs with glass. However, acrylics do scratch and can be difficult to maintain if soiled or dusty conditions are prevalent.

Polycarbonate. Polycarbonates are thermoplastic resins with high strength, resistance to weather, noncorro-

sive chemicals, electricity, and staining. It serves as a glazing material with 87% light transmittance, resistant to abuse, water, and humid conditions. Polycarbonates can be laminated to a thickness that can resist ballistics.

Polyurethane. Polyurethanes are typically thermosetting resins that can be produced rigid or flexible as a solid dense material or a foam. It is a lightweight tough material with resistance to water, mildew, rot, and chemicals. It can be made flameproof. Polyurethanes can also be thermoplastic which have excellent toughness, resisting abrasion, impact, oil, and grease. Polyurethanes can be manufactured with other plastics to produce wallcoverings with anechoic properties. (NRC ranging from 0.36–0.96)

In general plastics have high thermal expansion and contraction rates. While this property has disadvantages in detailing for movement and allowing for distortion in large sheets it does have an advantage in a plastics ability to resist stress concentrations. This same property assists in the durability factor for many plastics. Plastics are now being produced with high resistance to ultraviolet deterioration, weather, abrasion, and impact resistance. Plastic use as interior glazing and door glazing prevents shattering accidents. Plastics are not susceptible to chemical corrosion or electrolytic action. Some plastics are subject to dissolution with solvents. One method of bonding sheets of acrylic uses a solvent that melts the joining surfaces together. Some plastics are easily damaged by scratching or cutting.

Safety

Fire safety has been a major concern with the use of plastics. All plastics, which are made of organic materials, can burn. Many plastics are self-extinguishing once an igniting flame has been removed. Thermoplastic materials will soften and melt when exposed to high heats. A critical factor in the selection of a plastic material is the ease of ignition. Plastics can be manufactured with a wide range in degree of flammability. Flame spread ratings must be reviewed before selecting a plastic wallcovering.

Another safety issue is the release of toxic fumes. Some plastic compositions are unstable and constantly deteriorate releasing fumes. Urea-formaldehyde foams were banned as insulative materials due to this problem. Considerable investigation, including testing, should be made if uncommon and untested plastic materials are considered for wallcovering materials. With the discovery of health problems linked to interior airborne pollutants more testing data is needed to make informed selections of plastic materials. Plastic materials requiring scrutiny include wallcoverings, laminate adhesives, general adhesives, sealants, and coatings.

Plastics have considerable creep behavior. Most materials exhibit some elastic behavior within certain stresses. Plastics, particularly thermoplastics exhibit creep over time whether loaded or not. This phenomenon increases at elevated temperatures. To avoid failures creep and loading behavior must be calculated when using plastics.

METAL

Metal is a class of elements characterized by a distinct luster, malleability, ductility, thermal and electrical conductivity, and a capability for forming positive ions. Metals used in partitions typically are framing members of internally supported and externally framed walls. Metals can be used as the wallcovering or skin of a partition. This use includes thin sheets of metal attached to a substrate or self supporting formed metal. Metal used as a wallcovering will either be flat sheet metal or formed sheet metal. Metal can be processed into threads and woven as fabric.

Sheet metal is made by shaping either hot or cold metal by pressing it between two rollers set at a selected thickness. Rolls may be flat or another shape accommodated by the rollers. Forming is the process of pressing metal into a shape by a mechanical operation, not using machine tools such as hammering or die-pressing.

Metals are joined through different processes. Some processes are limited to certain metals. Common joining procedures include welding, soldering, brazing, bolting, and riveting. Adhesives can also be used for laminations and seaming.

Bolting and riveting attaches two sheets together with bolts or rivets. Rivets form a permanent connection. Welding joins metal through the application of heat, pressure and at times, a filler material. This process fuses the adjoined sheets and filler. Welding uses different processes including carbon arc, electric arc, fusion, gas, forge, and resistance. Welding requires knowledge of the material reactions and can cause changes to the strength and ductility of the metal. Brazing is a process where a molten filler is used to join metals. Brazing temperatures are lower than welding temperatures. Soldering is similar to brazing. Soldering filler temperatures are lower than brazing fillers. Since the temperatures are low, fusion of the material does not occur and the joint is weaker than the base metals making secondary joint reinforcement advisable. Adhesion attaches two metals with an applied adhesive, joints may be reinforced by crimping and interlocking. Structural metals, typically steel and aluminum are welded and bolted, sheet and decorative metals (aluminum, copper, brass, lead) are soldered and brazed. Riveting and adhesives are used in all types of metal, usually in thin sheets.

The metals frequently used for sheet wallcovering include steel, aluminum, aluminum alloys, copper, copper alloys, lead, tin, brass, and bronze. Metals can be finished through several processes. Metals produced without an overcoating can be finished mechanically through blasting, which produces a mottled or steel shot surface, polishing or buffing which produces a smooth, bright or shiny finish, etching where acidic or alkali chemicals etch the metal surface to obtain a random patterned effect, grinding which produces an even texture and hammering which produces continuous indentations providing a mottled texture.

Unprotected metals corrode and oxidize, which is the gradual dissolution of the metal into the atmosphere, water, or soil. Metals also deteriorate through a process known as electrolytic corrosion. When dissimilar metals are in contact with each other and an electrolyte such as water galvanic action occurs deteriorating and corroding the more susceptible metal. Avoiding this type of corrosion requires insulating one type of metal from the other to prevent contact. Metals prone to galvanic action in descending order of resistance are stainless steel, copper, lead, tin, nickel, iron, steel, zinc, and aluminum. Interior applications must consider electrolytic corrosion since moisture condensation is a given condition.

Metals can resist corrosion and oxidizing with protective coatings:

Aluminum. Aluminum can be protected by anodizing, organic coatings, and enameling. Anodizing is a controlled electrolytic process where negatively charged oxygen anions combine with the aluminum forming a coat of aluminum oxide. Colors can be integrally obtained in the anodic process and there are several types of anodizing. Organic coatings include fluorocarbon resins, plastisols, and siliconized polymer coatings. These coatings are essentially plastic films which have approximately 20 years of use. Organic coatings can receive pigments to provide colors. Porcelain enamel coatings are vitreous (glass) inorganic coatings bonded to aluminum at high temperatures. Porcelain enamels can be mixed to provide colors.

Copper. Copper can be chemically colored or finished with acidic processes. This typically provides a patina which prevents further deterioration. Copper can receive organic coatings, laminated film coatings, and vitreous enamels. For example, enamel over hammered copper is a finish that can be smooth, rich in color with depth and texture.

Steel. Steel can receive organic and enameled coatings with the exception of stainless steel. Stainless steel is a corrosion and rust resistant material of an iron base alloy containing chromium. The corrosion resistance is provided by chromium. Steel can also be protected with a metallic coating of zinc. This process is called galvanizing and inhibits corrosion. Steel can receive other metallic coatings such as aluminum, brass, copper, chromium, and terne metal. These processes combine the finish properties, such as the natural corrosion resistance of aluminum, of the applied metal and the strength of steel.

Metal sheets are typically used as solid sheets, formed pans and ribs or as laminated sandwich assemblies:

Solid Metal Sheet. Solid metal sheet can be thin gauge or heavy gauge. Thin metals require uniform support or forming. Metal sheets in partition construction are usually attached to a supporting structure or frame and used as a durable protective finish. Heavy gauge sheet steel is in frequent use for ballistic and radiowave protection. Lead-coated steel is used to restrict radiation, ie, in hospital X-ray rooms. Heavy gauge sheets are welded in place. Thin sheets are used for their attractive appearance, low maintenance, and resistance to abrasion, defacement, and graffiti. If the sheets are too thin or the finish too soft, metal can easily dent or scratch.

Formed Pans. Formed pans or sheets can be self supporting over a span. These metal shapes can be a facing or a complete wall. Formed metal can create interesting textures and is more resistant to denting or scratching. However the choice of finishes is limited when compared to sheet metal. Corrugated metal panels have made a definitive design resurgence with some of the new stylistic approaches to architecture. Formed sheets can include pressed lead which can provide decorative patterned wall coverings.

Laminated Metal. Laminated metal panels are composites with metal surfaces bonded to a core material. Laminated panels can have insulative cores that have good thermal and acoustic properties. Metal skinned panels are used for operable and demountable partitions. The metal surface can be treated with any type of finishing appropriate to the particular metal. This affords a wide range of finish appearances, textures, colors, and patterns to a designer.

Metals are resistant to moisture, defacement, and abrasion, Metals are relatively easy to maintain on interior partitions. The most frequent damage is incurred by denting. Metals have excellent tensile and compressive structural properties. They are typically dense, tensile, ductile materials. Aluminum weighs 165 PCF, brass 526 PCF, copper 556 PCF, lead 710 PCF, steel 490 PCF, stainless steel 500 PCF. The ability of metal to be thin, strong and attractively finished affords it a singular advantage as a building material.

Metals are not flammable and are stable materials that do not release toxic fumes. However, metals will lose strength and melt under high temperatures. Structural metals require protection from fire to prevent structural failures. Finish metals meet most flame spread requirements for interior finishes unless an applied coating is flammable.

Acoustically, metals are hard materials that reflect airborne sound energy. Due to the reflective and dense properties of metals they are excellent when used to control airborne sound. With structural isolation, steel and lead lined steel can effectively control air and structurally transmitted sound energy. Perforated metals backed with absorbent materials or metal faced with sound absorbent materials can be effective sound absorbents.

BIBLIOGRAPHY

General References

J. S. Stein, *Construction Glossary,* John Wiley & Sons, Inc., New York, 1980.

H. J. Rosen, *Construction Materials for Architecture,* John Wiley & Sons, Inc., New York, 1985.

J. R. Riggs, *Materials and Components of Interior Design,* Reston Publishing Company, Inc., Reston, Va., 1985.

Time-Life Books, *Paint and Wallpaper,* Time-Life Books Inc., Alexandria, Va., 1977.

Time-Life Books, *Walls and Ceilings,* Time-Life Books Inc., Alexandria, Va., 1977.

Time-Life Books, *Roofs and Sidings,* Time-Life Books Inc., Alexandria, Va., 1977.

Time-Life Books, *Masonry,* Time-Life Books Inc., Alexandria, Va., 1977.

C. G. Ramsey, H. R. Sleeper, *Architectural Graphic Standards,* 8th ed., John Wiley & Sons, Inc., New York, 1988.

J. H. Callander, *Time Saver Standards,* McGraw-Hill Inc., New York.

Drywall Construction Handbook, United States Gypsum, Chicago, Ill.

Lathing and Plastering Handbook, United States Gypsum, Chicago, Ill.

Sweet's Catalog File, McGraw-Hill Information Services Company, New York, 1989.

S. Whiton, *Interior Design and Decoration,* J. B. Lippincott Company, New York, 1974.

J. Feirer, G. Hutchins, *Carpentry and Building Construction,* Chas. A. Bennett Co., Inc., Peoria, Ill., 1981.

C. M. Harris, *Dictionary of Architecture and Construction,* McGraw-Hill Inc., New York, 1975.

J. Leckie, G. Masters, H. Whitehouse, L. Young, *Other Homes and Garbage,* Sierra Club Books, San Francisco, Calif., 1976.

The Readers Digest Encyclopedic Dictionary, The Reader's Digest Association, 1967.

B. Rudofsky, *Architecture without Architects,* Doubleday Inc., New York, 1964.

K. Clark, *Civilization,* Harper & Row, New York, 1969.

I. MacHarg, *Design with Nature,* Natural History Press, the Falcon Press, Philadelphia, Penn., 1969.

J. Bronowski, *The Ascent of Man,* Little, Brown and Company, Boston, Mass., 1973.

See also ADOBE CONSTRUCTION; BRICK MASONRY; CONCRETE MASONRY; GLASS IN CONSTRUCTION; PAINTS AND COATINGS; WOOD IN CONSTRUCTION; WOOD, STRUCTURAL PANELS

SARA P. O'NEIL-MANION, AIA
Bethesda, Maryland

METRIC SYSTEM

"SYSTEM INTERNATIONALE" (SI) UNITS IN ARCHITECTURE

Architects have experienced little problem in using (SI) units of length, area, volume, liquid volume, mass, time, and temperature (Table 1).

SI UNITS IN ENGINEERING

Engineering calculations may be addressed in two ways. The first is to adopt the SI units and formulas based on these units. The second, sometimes used when computerized programs based on conventional units exist, is to convert the results of calculations to SI units. Conversion

Table 1. SI Units Used in Architecture

Unit	Symbol	Acceptable Equivalent
Length		
Meter[a]	m	
Millimeter	mm	0.001 m
Kilometer	km	1000 m
Micrometer	m	0.000 001 m
Area		
Square meter	m²	
Square millimeter	mm²	
Square kilometer	km²	
Hectare	ha	1 ha = 10,000 m
Volume		
Cubic meter	m³	
Cubic millimeter	mm³	
Liter[a]	L	
Milliliter	mL	
Cubic Centimeter	cm³	
Mass		
Kilogram	kg	
Gram	g	
Metric ton[b]	t	1 t = 1000 kg
Time[c]		
second	s	
minute	min	
hour	h	
day	d	
month		
year	a	
Temperature[d]		
	°C	1°C = 1.8 °F

[a] The spellings "metre" and "litre" are preferred by ASTM.
[b] U.S. short ton (2000 lb) = 0.907 185 metric ton (t).
[c] The international standard for writing time is given by h/min/s on a 24-h day. The date is expressed as year/month/day.
[d] Freezing water temperature of 32°F is expressed as 0°C.

requires good judgment in the rounding of numbers. Conversion tables are easily found, as in the introductory pages of the Encyclopedia.

THE INTERNATIONAL SYSTEM OF UNITS

The term SI refers to the French "System Internationale." The international system (SI) is a logically developed system of measurement where the interrelationships between units are simply expressed. The symbols in use are international in application (Table 2). The United States is a notable exception in its continued use of conventional units. However, the use of SI units in the United States is not unusual in many industries, and is encouraged by the demands of international trade.

Table 2. SI Units

Quantity	Unit	Symbol
Base Units		
Length	meter[a]	m
Mass[b]	kilogram	kg
Time	second	s
Electric current	ampere	A
Thermodynamic temperature	kelvin	K
Luminous intensity	candela	cd
Amount of substance	mole	mol
Supplementary Units		
Plane angle	radian	rad
Solid angle	steradian	st
Derived Units With Compound Names		
Area	square meter	m²
Volume	cubic meter	m³
Density	kilogram per cubic meter	kg/m³
Velocity	meter per second	m/s
Angular velocity	radian per second	rad/s
Acceleration	meter per second squared	m/s²
Angular acceleration	radian per second squared	rad/s²
Volume rate of flow	cubic meter per second	m³/s
Moment of inertia	kilogram square meter	kg·m²
Moment of force	newton meter	N·m
Heat flux density	watt per square meter	W/m²
Thermal conductivity	watt per meter kelvin	W/(m·K)
Luminance	candela per square meter	cd/m²
Derived Units With Special Names		
Frequency	hertz	Hz 1/S
Force	newton	N kg·m/s²
Pressure, stress	pascal	Pa N/m³
Work, energy, quantity of heat	joule	J N·m
Power	watt	W J/s
Electric charge	Coulomb	C A·s
Electric potential	volt	V W/A
Electrical capacitance	farad	F C/V
Electric resistance	ohm	Ω V/A
Electric conductance	seimens	s 1/Ω
Magnetic flux	weber	WB V·s
Magnetic-flux density	tesla	T Wb/m²
Inductance	henry	H Wb/A
Temperature	degree Celsius	°C K
Luminous flux	lumen	lm cd·sr
Illumination	lux	lx lm/m²
Activity	becquerel	Bq 1/s
Absorbed dose	gray	Gy J/kg
Non-SI Units Used With SI		
Minute		min
Hour		h
Day		d
Nautical mile		n mile
Knot		kn
Kilometer per hour		km/h
Revolution per minute		r/min
Degree (angle)		°

Table 2. (*Continued*)

Quantity	Unit	Symbol
Minute (angle)		'
Second (angle)		"
Kilowatt-hour		kW·h

a The spelling "metre" is preferred by ASTM.

b "Weight" is the commonly used term for "mass."

Some common prefixes used for multiple units include deka (10 times), hecto (100 times), kilo (1000 times) and mega (one million times). Small unit prefixes include deci (1/10), centi (1/100), milli (1/1000) and micro (one millionth of).

POTENTIAL BENEFITS OF CONVERSION TO SI UNITS

Although the United States building industry is conversant with the concepts of modular grids and dimensional coordination, further benefits have been attained by a general conversion to SI units. In particular, rationalization of product and equipment sizes allow simple integration into the built structure. An effort has been made to standardize dimensional notation, particularly for computerized drawings.

ISSUES OF CONVERSION

Currently no estimated target date exists for total world conversion to the SI system.

Experience in countries that have converted to the SI system suggests that the initial need is to rewrite codes and standards using SI units. This is a legal necessity, and in some countries the change has been legislated.

Considerable work has been done in the United States to allow the SI system to be used in construction. However, until a large proportion of U.S. construction is specified with SI units, voluntary conversion of that industry will not occur.

In the United States, educational materials provide opportunities for familiarizing students with SI units, and public awareness is simplified because of the United States rational monetary system.

BIBLIOGRAPHY

General References

S. Braybrooke, ed., *AIA Metric Building and Construction Guide,* John Wiley & Sons, Inc., New York, 1980.

ROBERT T. PACKARD, AIA
Reston, Virginia

MOISTURE PROTECTION

Moisture penetration into structures has always been one of the most common problems with many causes. Construction technology has produced a variety of solutions to prevent or correct these defects. In addition to the obvious damage to interior surfaces, building equipment, and furniture, water intrusion may cause adverse health problems in the form of mildew and molds. There have been instances of electrical fires caused by moisture entering electric vaults, transformers, and switch gear.

DEFINITIONS

Dampproofing. Dampproofing refers to provisions made to prevent moisture from entering a wall, foundation, or slab on grade. The term is applied to materials with low permeability. The difference between dampproofing and waterproofing materials are in their perm ratings. Dampproofing materials have a one or more perm rating.

Waterproofing. Waterproofing refers to provisions made to prevent water from entering a building enclosure. The term is applied to materials with very low permeability under hydrostatic conditions. In cases of deep foundations with below grade occupied spaces, a waterproofing system can be specified to withstand 50 feet of head.

Water Table. Water table refers to the below grade standing water elevation, which may vary over time as a result of climatic conditions.

Condensation. Condensation refers to the change of state of water vapor to a liquid form. When air carries a maximum amount of water vapor, the condition is described as saturated, or 100% humidity. The amount of water vapor which can be in the air increases with temperature.

Surface Water. Surface water refers to water traveling over the surface of the ground. A strata of impervious soils can trap water above the strata, complicating foundation design.

Moisture Protection. Moisture protection is a generic term referring to systems used to keep water out of a building.

WATER IN BUILDINGS

The sources of water include rain, snow and ice, surface water, ground water, high water tables, condensation on surfaces or in the enclosure. This article does not address water problems caused by operating sprinkler systems, or internal flooding caused by breaks in water lines, etc.

Climatic variations have resulted in different approaches to solving water problems. Common building materials have been tested to determine their characteristic behavior under exposure to moisture. Variations in temperature cause materials to expand or contract at various rates. The joints in construction provided to accommodate this movement are likely areas for water infiltration. Most materials used in construction are not impervious to moisture, and capillary action may occur. The remainder of this article will discuss detailing and materials used to control moisture penetration.

SYSTEMS

The roof surface in most climates is the most critical for moisture control. Proper flashing to other materials such as at roof edges, against walls, or for roof penetrations is a necessary part of the roofing system. Control and expansion joints in roofing need separate attention. Because of the temperature differential between the building interior and the surface of the roof, the release of water vapor is a necessary part of the design. Techniques include venting of the roof insulation at the perimeter or by use of roof vents. In wood construction, edge vents or cap vents are needed for a successful roof installation.

Water runoff from the roof is normally collected in gutters and downspouts. The quantity of water runoff may be calculated on the basis of rainfall experienced at a specific site (see Tables 1 and 2).

Severe damage can occur if the downspouts are not kept clear of debris, particularly if downspouts are built into masonry walls. A rule of thumb for residential buildings is to allow 100 sq. ft of roof area per 1 sq. in. of downspout.

In typical winter conditions in much of the United States, attention should be given to the use of waterproof membranes at the perimeter of the roof under roofing shingles to prevent leaks resulting from ice dams.

A historic problem for masonry walls has been walls exposed to wind driven rain. Attempts to seal the exterior of the wall have not been particularly successful. Many of the leaks can be traced to cracks between the masonry unit and the mortar joint. In freezing areas, the saturated masonry may spall. Efflorescence appearing on the surface of masonry has also been a problem. Solutions are found in proper selection of masonry materials and detailing of the masonry, such as the use of cavity walls. The theory of wall design is to collect water which has penetrated the outer surface and to lead it out of the wall through weep holes. This theory applies to metal curtain walls, as well, and study of successful walls will show attention to wind driven rains. The wind forces experienced on high-rise structures are much greater than low buildings. Thermal differences between sunlit and shaded surfaces add to the stresses on the wall.

Openings in the wall require careful detailing. For in-

Table 2. Downspout Sizes

Type	Area sq. in.	Nom. Size in.	Actual Size in.
plain	7.07	3	3
round	12.57	4	4
	19.63	5	5
	28.27	6	6
corr.	5.94	3	3
round	11.04	4	4
	17.72	5	5
	25.97	6	6
corr.	3.80	2	1¾ × 2¼
rect.	7.73	3	2⅜ × 3¼
	11.70	4	2¾ × 4¼
	18.75	5	3¾ × 5
plain	3.94	2	1¾ × 2¼
rect.	6.00	3	2 × 3
	12.00	4	3 × 4
	17.81	5	3¾ × 4¾
	24.00	6	4 × 6

stance, condensation may collect on glass and metal surfaces, and the connection between frame and wall require sealing. Flashing at the sill of door and window openings is good practice to allow any water striking the surface of the opening to exit without damage to the wall. In cold climates, thermal separated frames and double or triple glazing can be used to limit condensation problems.

GROUND SURFACE

The point at which the wall meets the ground or other horizontal surfaces is a vulnerable area for water infiltration. Backfilling against foundation walls should not break through the dampproofing or waterproofing. Materials used for backfill should be free of such deleterious materials as expansive clays, trash, rocks, or organic materials. Compaction should be adequate to prevent settlement, but not so much as to cause damage to the foundation wall or impede drainage. On the modified Proctor density scale, 85 to 88 is proper compaction. Surface water should be kept away from the walls by sloping surfaces away from the wall. A gravel strip adjacent to a wall may be used to control splashing, through wall flashing slightly above the exterior grade is desirable with masonry walls. If interior floor spaces are below grade, attention must be paid to dampproofing or waterproofing to avoid water moisture penetrating the walls and slabs.

FOUNDATIONS

Modern foundation materials include concrete, concrete masonry units, or possibly pressure treated wood. Since World War II, several products have been developed to secure damp proof construction, or waterproofing when high water tables require it.

In general, these products form two groups. The first is designed to remove water from the ground in close proximity to the foundation wall. The products include footing drains (French drains) below the lowest floor, of clay tile,

Table 1. Downspout Capacity

Intensity in in./h Lasting 5 min.	Sq. ft Roof/ sq. in. Downspout
2	600
3	400
4	300
5	240
6	200
7	175
8	150
9	130
10	120
11	110

porous concrete, or perforated plastic pipe. Protected by a geotextile cover and free draining granular material, the footing drains remove water near the wall. A positive out-flow from such drains are part of an effective system. In some situations, under-slab drainage systems may be used to reduce water pressure.

An alternate wall system is to use foundation mats designed to allow any water to drain off the wall rapidly, collected in the footing drainage piping. These wall products include woven or mat surfaces which prevent small soil granules clogging the drainage passages. The wall mats are placed over a membrane layer applied to the foundation wall. The filter fabric can be extended to cover the footing drain to keep the water flowing freely.

The second function of foundation moisture protection materials is to prevent moisture from entering the building wall. This is achieved by applying various impervious materials to the structural foundation. Historically this might have been tar, but now is more likely to involve adhesives and sheet materials. Depending on ground conditions, these products may require slab and wall treated to form a continuous surface. In areas of hydrostatic pressure, this may require special slab design with a second slab over the membrane. In some locations, such provisions may be limited to elevator pits, sump pumps, and other low lying spaces (Fig. 1).

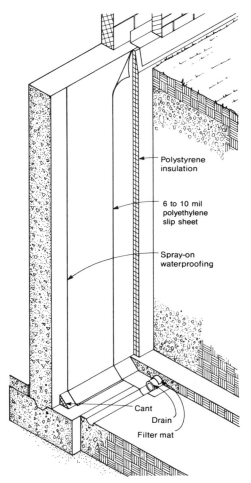

Figure 2. Spray-on waterproofing.

It is possible to improve water resistance of concrete by the addition of admixtures, but the more general practice is to use the exterior coating systems. Penetration of the wall by utility lines must be carefully sealed. Materials for this use would include sprayed-on bentonite, or liquid-applied rubbers and urethanes. Areaways must be provided with drainage provisions, and be kept clear of debris. The materials selected should be able to bridge cracks in the foundation, and be flexible to movement in the foundation wall over time.

SELECTING BELOW-GRADE WATERPROOFING

Since the only opportunity to install these systems is during construction, they should be specified with care. The surface to receive the waterproofing materials should be smooth. Concrete block should be parged. Sprayed on or trowelled materials require less attention to uniformity of surface than the sheet membranes (Fig. 2). A protection board is frequently placed over sheet membranes to protect them during backfill operations. When the exterior of the foundation wall is to be insulated, the insulation should be on the outside of the dampproofing membrane. Joints and seams require sealing using glue or mechanical bonds, although heat-welded seams are superior under

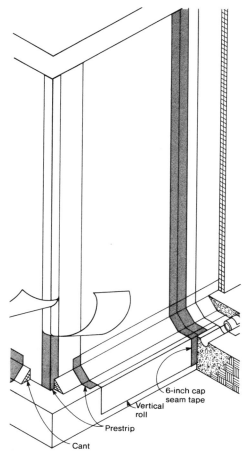

Figure 1. Sheet membrane waterproofing.

hydrostatic pressures. Compatibility of components is important, particularly if polystyrene insulation is placed over liquid applied urethanes or asphaltic rubbers. The solvents may degrade the insulation. Some materials will react to chemicals in the soil. For instance, bentonite clays will not perform well in the presence of salt or saline soils. Soils may be tested for compatibility with a selected system.

Materials used include betonite clays, asphalts, rubberized asphalts, butyls, polyethylenes, urethanes, cementitious products and auxillary materials such as mastics, sealants and tapes. Many proprietary products are composite in nature, and should be selected on the basis of the site conditions and installation requirements. The problem of controlling leaks in existing building foundations has led to the use of cementitious parging materials containing iron filings, which in the presence of moisture rust and expand the parging, sealing off leaks.

HISTORIC PRESERVATION

Builders of the past did not have adequate knowledge about moisture protection. Typical damage to old buildings includes wood, where mold growth and decay result from dampness. Brick damage may be caused by freezing moisture which cracks or spalls brick. Surface salts are a sign of a moisture condition in the wall. Other materials, such as sandstone, limestone, mortar, stucco, and plaster can be effected because the calcium content is water soluble, other stones fare better. Iron, steel, tin, and zinc may deteriorate in contact with moisture if not properly painted or protected. Rusting and corrosion are signs of moisture infiltration. Interior surface finishes in historic structures may be damaged by damp walls which cause paint blisters, and separates finishes from the walls.

Considerable remedial work has resulted in recommended approaches to historic buildings. The United Kingdom and the Federal German Republic are good sources for information and techniques, and The National Park Service in the United States has several publications of use for preservation of existing buildings.

INSULATION AND VAPOR BARRIERS

Thermal comfort is attained when the environment surrounding the individual can remove the bodily heat and moisture at the rate at which they are being produced. The relatively restricted range of conditions which are comfortable means an indoor temperature between 70°F and 80°F and not less than 20% nor more than 60% relative humidity, for lightly clad sedentary adults. Changes in clothing, activity, and air velocity increases the range of comfort. To achieve these conditions in most climate areas, modern buildings are insulated. The difference between outside conditions and interior comfort means that under some conditions, dewpoint temperatures may occur in the wall. For this reason, vapor barriers are introduced into the wall construction. Placement of vapor barriers in the wall is determined by analysis of climate and construction.

Under extreme conditions, water vapor can be added or subtracted from the interior air. In times of high relative humidity, condensation may occur on cool surfaces, with the possibility of molds and mildew. Increased ventilation can be provided, and water vapor can be lowered using a dehumidification system.

BIBLIOGRAPHY

General References

ASHRAE Handbook of Fundamentals, American Society of Heating, Refrigerating and Air Conditioning Engineers, New York, 1985.

T. B. McDonald, "Selecting Below-Grade Waterproofing," *Architecture* **77** 12 (Dec. 1988).

The NRCA Roofing and Waterproofing Manual, 3rd ed. National Roofing Contractors Association, Rosemont, Ill., 1989.

C. G. Ramsey, H. R. Sleeper, *Architectural Graphic Standards,* 8th ed., John Wiley & Sons, Inc., New York, 1988.

B. M. Smith, *Moisture Problems in Historic Masonry Walls: Diagnosis and Treatment,* U.S. Department of the Interior, National Park Service, Preservation Assistance Division, undated.

See also Cold Dry Climate Construction; Cold Wet Climate, Building in; Concrete—Admixtures, Curing and Testing; Diagnostics, Building; Foundation Systems; Hot Dry Climate Construction; Hot Wet Climate, Building in; Mechanical Systems; Paving Systems, Asphalt; Roofing Materials

Robert T. Packard, AIA
Reston, Virginia

QUANTITY SURVEYING

Quantity surveying is the title given to the profession on cost estimating and related services as defined in the United Kingdom and much of the rest of the world. The training is formal and apprenticeship is rigorous, involving four years of university and a further two years of working directly under a senior quantity surveyor. A salient feature of quantity surveying is the preparation of a complete bill of materials. This bill is given by the quantity surveying firm to all interested contractors, and the owner pays for the service. The bill of materials becomes part of the construction contract and is the basis for the progress payments and valuation of extra work. For example, the quantity survey sheets for a particular trade may include the name of the project, the quantity survey item number, a description of the work, quantity, unit of measure (number, area, volume, etc.), and a blank for entering cost.

Each subcontractor preparing a bid for his or her phase of the work saves the time required to take off quantities with greater assurance of the quantities' accuracy. The bidding process takes less time, effort and bids can be more competitive.

Quantity surveying is not generally practiced in the United States, but there is some interest in the process in the construction community. Computerization of the process is a logical way to increase the quantity surveyor's efficiency.

See also CONSTRUCTION DOCUMENTS; ESTIMATING, COST

RECREATIONAL FACILITIES

This article deals generically with the wide range of indoor and outdoor recreational facilities. As activities vary to an infinite degree, so do their facilities. Therefore, the infinite activities or functions dictate the facilities or spaces and their requirements.

PUBLIC-SECTOR OWNERSHIP

Recreational facilities can be identified in a variety of ownership categories and can be classified in varied levels of service to the market users. Public-sector ownership of facilities, which are most often visualized when reference may be found in any governmental jurisdiction, is made to recreational facilities.

Local Parks

Throughout urban, suburban, and rural environments, there can be several types of parks: those performing an ornamental use, those that provide for recreational uses, and those that serve an environmental purpose.

Local Ornamental Parks. Ornamental areas may be considered as any space that is looked at and passively enjoyed by the public. There are four basic types of ornamental parks: Open spaces, monument spaces, landscape spaces, and sitting spaces. Open spaces can include outdoor site facilities such as bandshells, gardens, and fountains. Such spaces may be called squares, alleys, malls, intersections, cul-de-sacs, plazas, and ways. Monument spaces can include sculptures, memorials, flagpoles, and related types of tributes. Landscape spaces can include gardens, fountains, and plazas. Sitting spaces can include seating arrangements, kiosks, and gardens.

Local Recreational Parks. Recreational parks are any space where activity of more than a passive nature is conducted. Various features can be found in the play space of a local recreational park, including apparatus, play lawns, sandboxes, play pools, and paved game areas.

Neighborhood Parks

Most neighborhoods have at least one neighborhood park within a three- or four-block walking distance of every home. The actual number of parks will depend on the accessibility of people and availability of suitable land. The quantity and quality of such recreational facilities and features within the park will depend on the size of the population and its particular needs. A neighborhood park or recreation area may include a playground, a play building, and/or play fields.

Neighborhood Play Area. The neighborhood play area within the park is oriented to the children. It includes a playground with play sites or play station groups such as play-field area; play surfaced area; play craft area; play court area; play apparatus area with a toddler yard, early childhood yard, and childhood yard or play units, and a play building with playrooms, which is the basic indoor recreation facility for which architects are responsible.

Neighborhood Recreation Area. The neighborhood recreation area within the park is oriented to adults and can include a park recreation ground with recreation sites (recreation station groups) such as recreation fields (junior ballfields), recreation craft area, recreation surface area, recreation courts, accessory service units, and a park recreation building with recreation rooms of various types.

Subcommunity or Community Parks

Groups of neighborhoods may have recreation parks that contain playgrounds, play buildings, recreation grounds, and recreation buildings. In addition, there may be specialized recreation facilities, such as roller-skating rinks, junior ballfields, and service sites for maintenance, repair, and storage, and specialized recreation structures, such as shelters, play mobiles, and service structures (Figs. 1–4).

Municipal Parks

Municipal governments have recreation parks that include park play areas with playgrounds and play buildings for children and park recreational areas with recreation grounds for adults and recreation buildings for adults and other age groups (Figs. 5–7).

Educational recreation facilities include school park complexes at either active schools or surplused schools. These are used as nature centers, arts centers, day-care centers, or other education-related facilities (Fig. 8). Cultural recreation facilities include museums, theaters, libraries, and auditoriums. Institutional recreation facilities include facilities of governmental, housing, or hospital use that often contain recreation facilities of various types.

Regional Parks

Clusters of municipalities may have recreational parks with areas set aside for municipal as well as regional use, with generalized and specialized recreation facilities as diverse as natatoriums, stadiums, gymnasiums, and observatories (Figs. 9–13).

Local Environmental Parks

Parks may be considered those spaces that have some ecological sensitivity and contain natural features for protection and conservation.

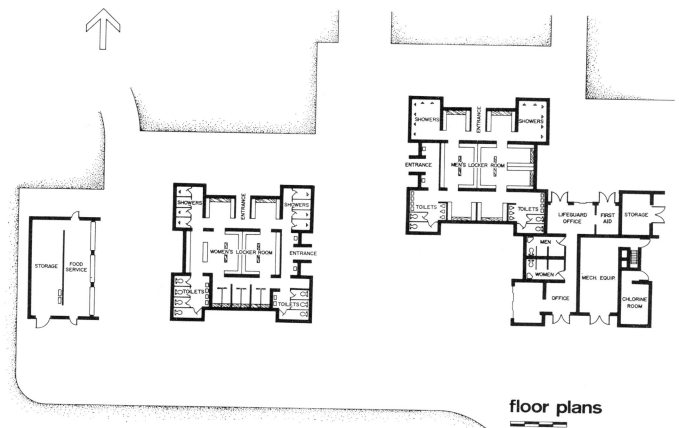

floor plans

0' 4' 8' 12' 16'

Figure 1. Floor plan, public bathhouse, Clarkstown, N.Y. Courtesy of Ward Associates.

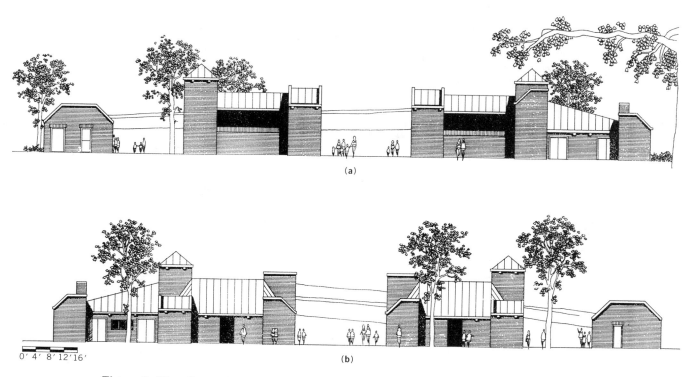

(a)

0' 4' 8' 12' 16'

(b)

Figure 2. Elevation, public bathhouse, Clarkstown, N.Y., (**a**) front view; (**b**) pool side view. Courtesy of Ward Associates.

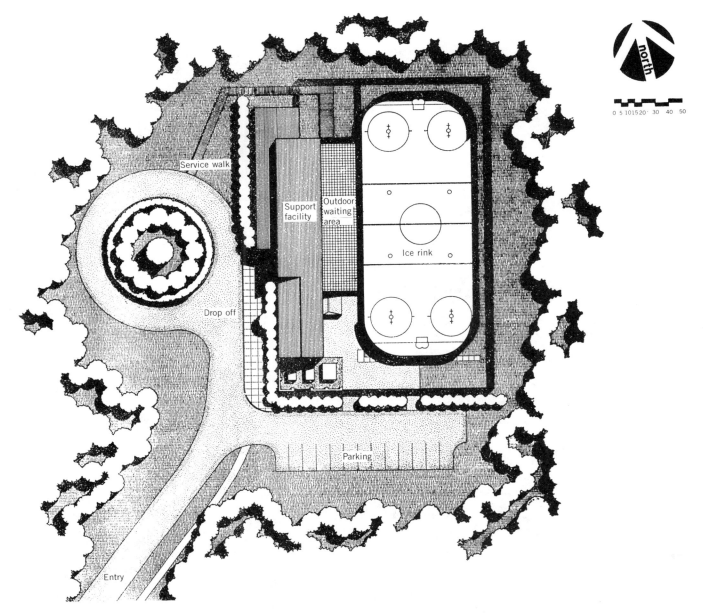

Figure 3. Site plan, public ice rink, Huntington, N.Y. Courtesy of Ward Associates.

PRIVATE-SECTOR OWNERSHIP

The private sector ownership of facilities is often overlooked when considering recreation facilities.

Industrial Recreation Facilities

Major industrial companies often maintain some recreation facilities. These may be specialized sites, such as athletic fields, picnic areas, and even resort camps, and specialized structures, such as auditoriums, recreation lounges, libraries, and meeting rooms. Many plants have established nurseries for children of workers in order to get the labor force involved in recreation pursuits. Some

utility companies have planned excellent facilities; however, these are primarily for public use as per Federal Power Commission requirements (Figs. 14–16).

Commercial Recreation Facilities

Commercial establishments throughout the country cooperate and collaborate with counties and cities in providing facilities on certain lease or rental arrangements to the public. In turn, county and city parks and recreation systems should afford complemental and supplemental facilities for use by commercial enterprises, particularly by hotels and motels. Commercial recreation facilities include:

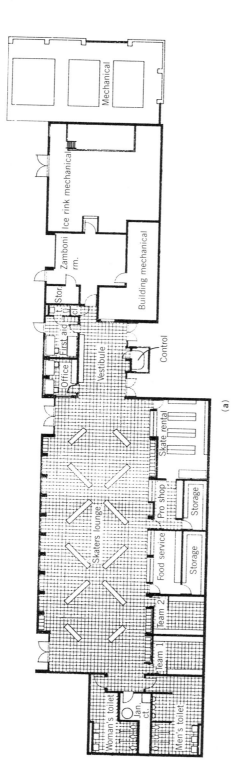

(a)

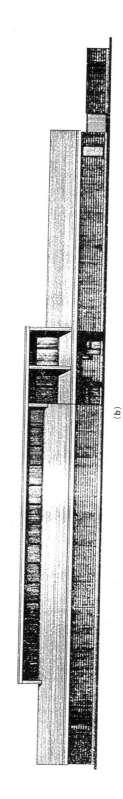

(b)

Figure 4. (a) Public ice rink floor plan; (b) front elevation, Huntington, N.Y. Courtesy of Ward Associates.

495

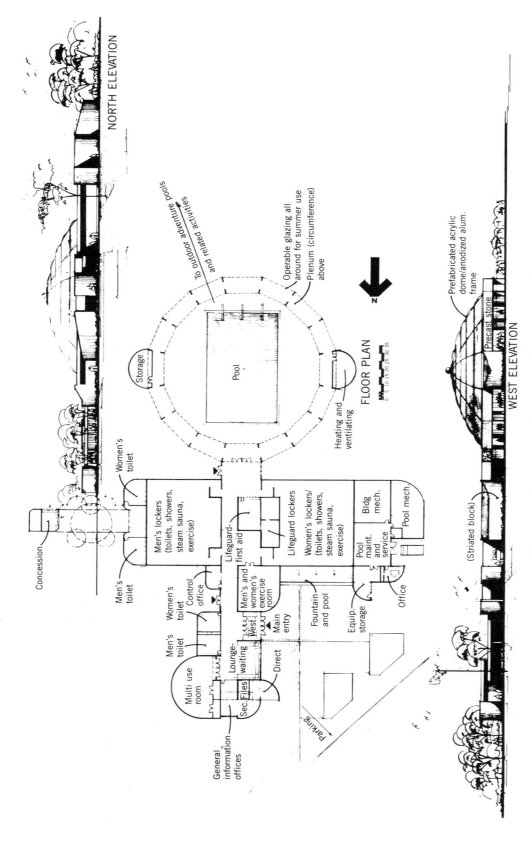

NORTH ELEVATION

Concession

Men's toilet

Women's toilet

To outdoor adventure pools and related activities

Operable glazing all around for summer use

Plenum (circumference) above

Storage

Pool

N

FLOOR PLAN

0 5 10 15 20 25 30 35

Heating and ventilating

Women's toilet

Men's toilet

Men's lockers (toilets, showers, steam sauna, exercise)

Lifeguard-first aid

Lifeguard lockers

Women's lockers (toilets, showers, steam sauna, exercise)

Bldg. mech.

Pool mech.

Pool maint. and service

Office

Control office

Men's and women's exercise room

Fountain and pool

Equip. storage

Women's toilet

Multi use room

Lounge-waiting

West.

Sec. Files

Main entry

Direct

Parking

General information offices

Prefabricated acrylic dome/anodized alum. frame

Precast stone

(Striated block)

WEST ELEVATION

Figure 5. Floor plan, public community center/pool, Hempstead, N.Y. Courtesy of Ward Associates.

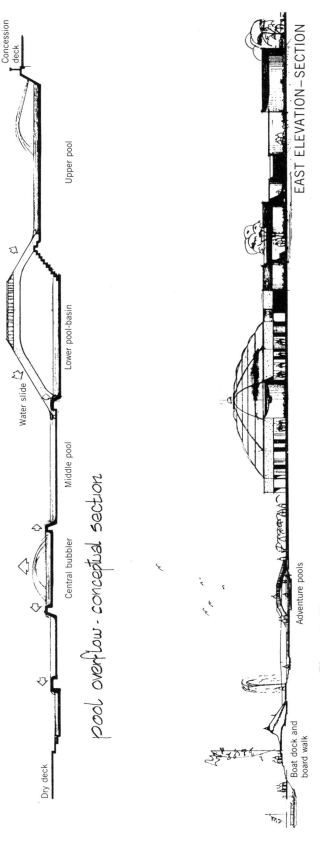

Figure. 6. Elevation, community center/pool, Hempstead, N.Y. Courtesy of Ward Associates.

pool overflow - conceptual section

Concession deck

Upper pool

Water slide

Lower pool-basin

Central bubbler

Middle pool

Dry deck

EAST ELEVATION–SECTION

Adventure pools

Boat dock and board walk

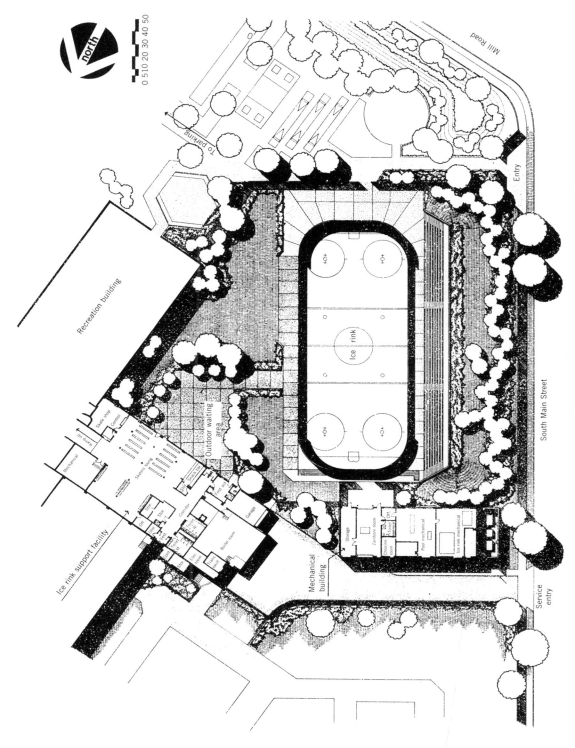

Figure 7. Site plan, public community center/ice rink, Freeport, N.Y. Courtesy of Ward Associates.

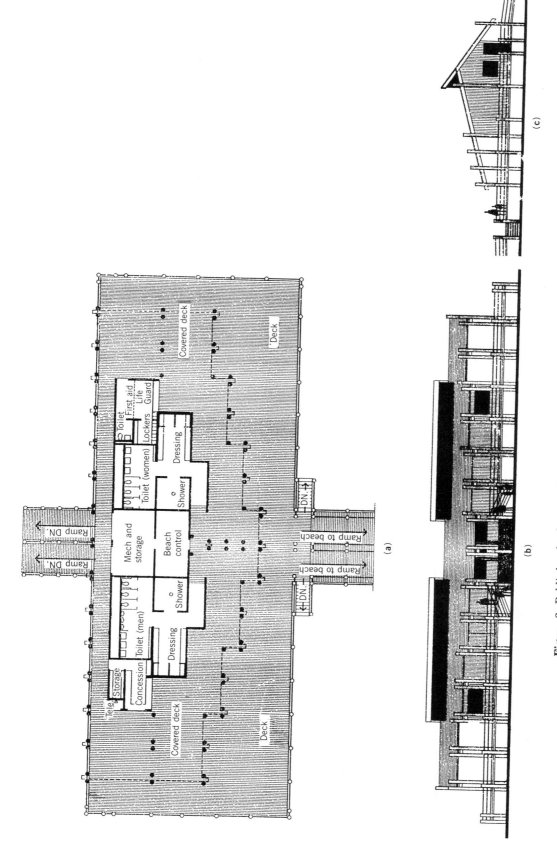

Figure 8. Public beach administration building (**a**) floor plan; (**b**) front elevation; (**c**) side elevation, Cold Spring Harbor, N.Y. Courtesy of Ward Associates.

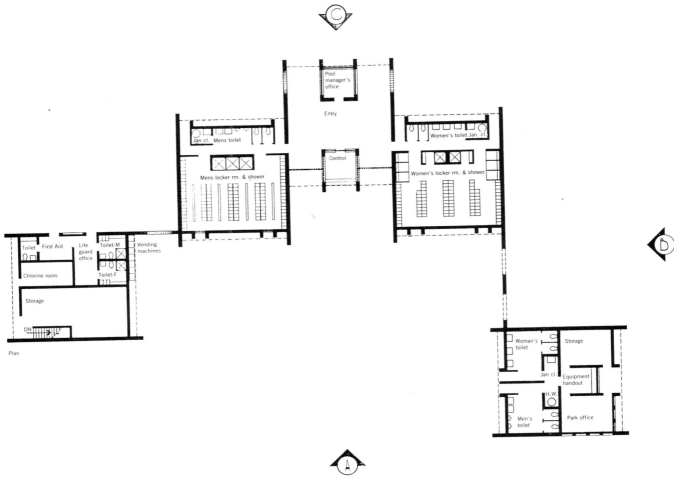

Figure 9. Floor plan, public recreation hall/bathhouse, Hempstead, N.Y. Courtesy of Ward Associates.

Amusements operations
    Kiddie rides
    Theme parks
    Carnivals
    Circuses
    Rodeos
    Fun houses
    Concessions, such as shooting galleries
Sports establishments
    Bowling alleys
    Golf driving ranges
    Ice-skating rinks
    Roller-skating rinks
    Ski centers
    Swimming pools
Entertainment Houses
    Drive-ins
    Theaters
    Movies
    Night clubs

Noncommercial Recreation Facilities

Noncommercial membership establishments throughout the country should also work in conjunction with counties and cities in providing recreational facilities. Some examples of noncommercial or other not-for-profit organizations and facilities they could sponsor are listed here.

Sports clubs
    Swimming pools
    Tennis courts
    Boat basins
    Golf driving ranges and courses
    Hunting and fishing grounds
Fraternal organizations
    Camp grounds
    Playing fields
Social clubs
    Dancing clubs
    Orchestral clubs

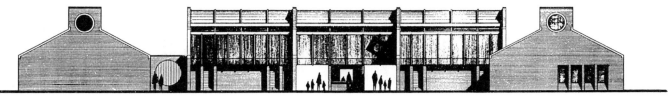

Elevation-"A"

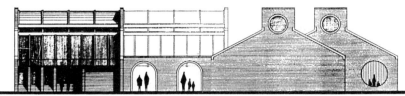

Elevation-"B"

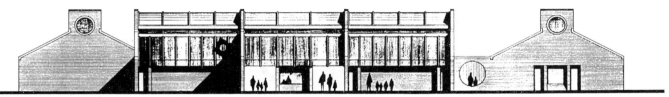

Elevation-"C"

Figure 10. Elevation, public recreation hall/bathhouse, Hempstead, N.Y. Courtesy of Ward Associates.

Glee clubs
Discussion clubs
Special-interest clubs
Camera clubs
Stamp clubs
Arts and crafts clubs

Agricultural Recreation Facilities

Because the country contains some of the most beautiful and fruitful agricultural lands in the world, every effort should be made to preserve them from other development. While being preserved, they can also be used for leisure-time activities such as demonstration farms, vacation ranches, and open spaces.

Some farms and ranches have been developed as vacation retreats that provide a break from the usual routine for rest as well as for work. Also, the farm, its equipment, and its animals can attract residents as well as tourists. Plow, seed, and harvest time also call for occasions and festivities that attract outsiders.

Residential Recreation Facilities

Every home or apartment subdivision should be considerate of the local interests of its future residents. Some fine examples of developments already exist just outside the cities. It has become obvious that the utilization of existing property features in the design of golf courses, community centers, country stores, pools, playgrounds, and play fields help sell a development.

The quasi-public-sector ownership of facilities are sometimes viewed as social agencies, although a majority of their use is for recreation.

Organizational Recreation Facilities

Voluntary organizations, working in cooperation with governmental recreation agencies, can encourage provision of services that might otherwise be lacking while avoiding duplication of effort with governmental programs.

The following types of semipublic agencies provide recreation facilities:

Community Chests
Neighborhood Associations
Youth Service Organizations
Scouting Groups
Community Service Organizations
Chambers of Commerce

Spiritual Recreation Facilities

All churches, synagogues, and other houses of spiritual worship have facilities serving the overall needs and interests of their community's constituents. Such centers of worship contain multipurpose rooms, auditoriums, gymnasiums, gardens, courtyards, courts, and other facilities that can be used for recreation.

HISTORY

Recreation is an outgrowth of ritual, ceremonial, military, and spiritual celebrations that have existed for thousands of years and have always had accompanying facilities. Coliseums, stadiums, plazas, gardens, and a host of facilities can still be found throughout the world.

In the last 300 years in the United States, the recreational facility has changed considerably. It has emerged into the array of variations described in the introduction. However, the most common type of recreation facility is the "center," sometimes called the Youth Center, the Rec Center, the Neighborhood Center, or the Community Center. The perception of this type of recreation facility is today almost universal. However, it has also changed over the years.

In the Colonial period, the tavern served as the center or focal point of recreation. It was male- and adult-oriented. However, when town halls made their appearance in the Revolutionary period, the scene shifted to a more formalized environment with a large assembly hall and smaller meeting or anterooms. It remained male- and adult-dominated for more than a hundred years. The home remained as the female and youth recreation environment. However, when the one room schoolhouse emerged from the roving home tutor era, the activity shifted from the home to the school for children as well as for women. The schoolhouse became more accepted for a range of personal or group activities. As the school grew into four rooms and then eight rooms, and the outhouse moved inside, assembly and play spaces moved inside and

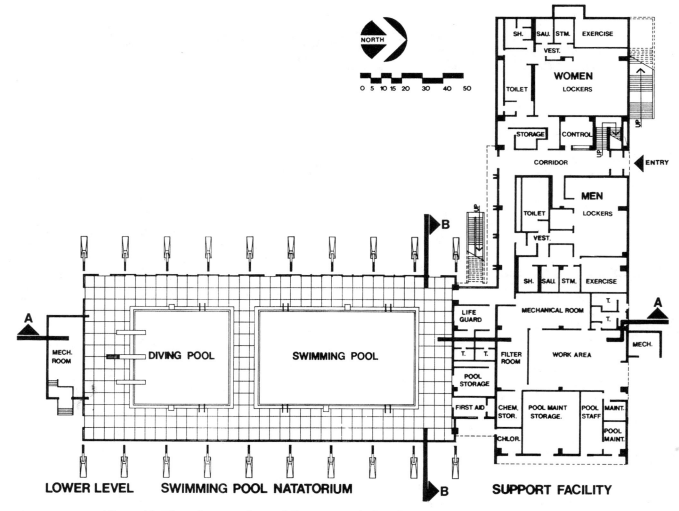

Figure 11. Floor plan—1st floor, public recreation hall/pool complex Hempstead, N.Y. Courtesy of Ward Associates.

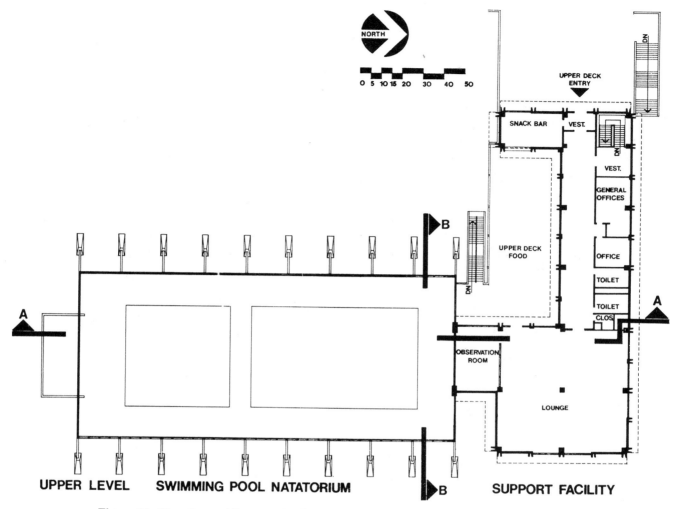

NORTH

0 5 10 15 20 30 40 50

UPPER DECK
ENTRY

SNACK BAR | VEST.

UPPER DECK
FOOD

VEST.

GENERAL
OFFICES

OFFICE

TOILET

TOILET

CLOS

OBSERVATION
ROOM

LOUNGE

UPPER LEVEL   SWIMMING POOL NATATORIUM   **SUPPORT FACILITY**

Figure 12. Elevation, public recreation/hall/pool complex, Hempstead, N.Y. Courtesy of Ward Associates.

emerged as year-round facilities. As the environment changed from rural to urban, the exterior architecture and building materials changed and became more substantial. It was soon recognized that the more formal process of education was separate from the informal process of recreation. Therefore, industry, charitable groups, and entrepreneurs soon developed separate community spaces.

The community center as a facility invariably involved an indoor structure supported by certain special outdoor facilities. The concept evolved from the traditional Y's neighborhood settlement houses and recreation centers found in the South, where the only sound building was the brick gymnasium, to a multiuse facility.

ROLE OF THE COMMUNITY CENTER

A community center, which is developed and operated by a municipality, should complement other community facilities such as the schools, churches, synagogues, Y's,

and other social agencies, rather than duplicate their activities or facilities. In essence, the center should fill any void that exists in the community for certain social, recreational, cultural, and other services. Today, the community center is often found as the key element in a complex along with a school, a library, and a town hall. It has numerous subelements, including such indoor facilities as a senior citizen's suite, child-care suite, youth suite, adult games suite, and a fitness suite. The outdoor facilities might include fields, courts, pools, and rinks.

The community center must be dedicated to meeting the general and special needs of all residents, the young and the old, the disadvantaged as well as the advantaged, and the physically and mentally handicapped. Thus, its services extend to the total community rather than a single neighborhood or special group. It could be considered a multipurpose facility to serve all needs.

A profile of a community center usually reflects its general functional requirements, spatial arrangement, architectural embellishment, and operational involvement. Principles of planning and designing a center are summarized as follows:

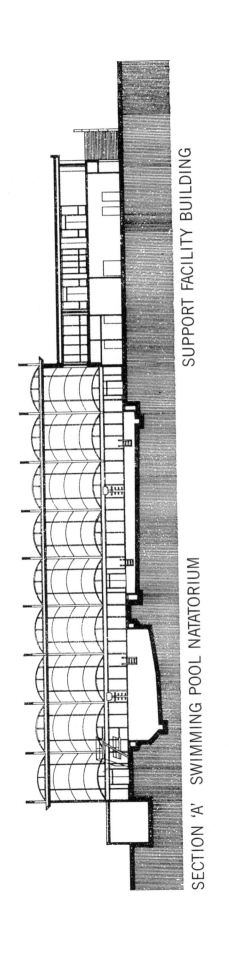

SECTION 'A' SWIMMING POOL NATATORIUM

SUPPORT FACILITY BUILDING

0 5 10 15 20   30   40   50

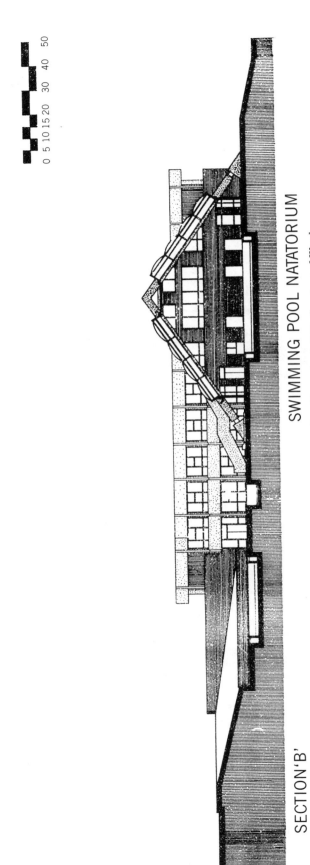

SECTION 'B'

SWIMMING POOL NATATORIUM

Figure 13. Elevation, public recreation hall/pool complex, Hempstead, N.Y. Courtesy of Ward Associates.

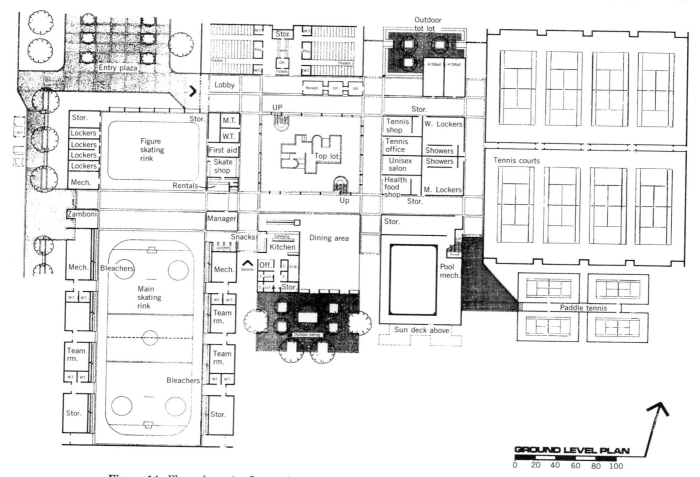

Figure 14. Floor plan—1st floor, private tennis/ice center, West Haven, Conn. Courtesy of Ward Associates.

- Be reflective of the educational and recreational programs.
- Be based on a user analysis and site analysis.
- Be as centrally located as possible to serve all sectors.
- Be beautiful and attractive, a distinct asset.
- Be a place where children, unaccompanied by parents, will be completely safe.
- Be a facility that provides a wide range of services needed.
- Be a place for people to come to for participation in a variety of activities.
- Be a year-round facility.
- Be of a low noise level for surrounding residents.
- Be accessible to adequate parking for users of the center.
- Be reflective of the needs and interests of the residents.
- Be of a design character complementing the surrounding area.
- Be available for use by civic and youth groups and other organized community groups that need space to conduct their activities.

- Provide new services or improve and expand those already existing, without detracting from other services.
- Be primarily of service to the needs of the general population of the service area rather than a particular sex, age, or problem in the neighborhood.
- Be reflective of the kind of program desired, as well as required.
- Be reflective of the concept of the multiple use and receive due consideration in the planning process.
- Be planned by people who will be affected by the facility, particularly with the professional staff and consultants.
- Be located as influenced by a master plan and program of the community or the school system.
- Be inclusive of activities meeting the needs and desires of the people and accurately determined as a part of the planning stage.
- Be of a design reflective of cooperation between educational programming-researching experts, planning groups, designing-engineering firms, and administrators.
- Be implemented by a construction system managed

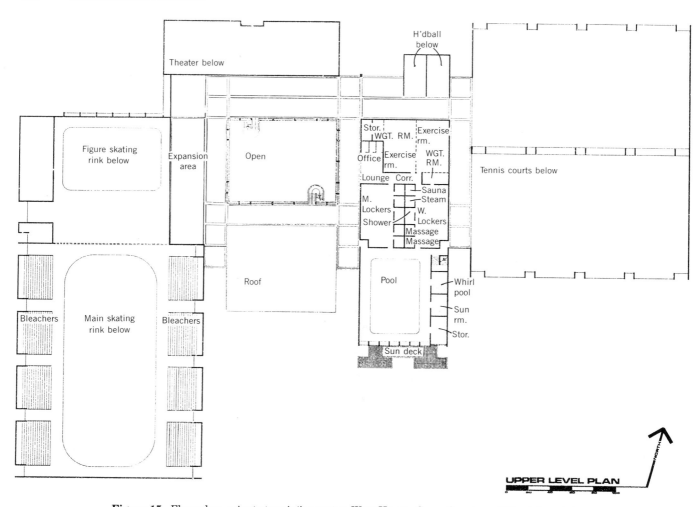

Figure 15. Floor plan, private tennis/ice center, West Haven, Conn. Courtesy of Ward Associates.

by a chief administrative official responsible with a clear-cut plan of procedure to guide his or her actions.

- Be located where it will receive maximum use.
- Be reflective of maximum flexibility of design in order to easily effect change if future requirements so dictate.
- Be planned to achieve maximum safety and security of all participants and provide a pleasant environment.
- Be in compliance with all local and state laws and other regulations, including professional standards.
- Be considerate of capital and operational maintenance costs including energy and labor, in the planning process.

CONTEMPORARY RECREATION FACILITY DESIGN

Facility design is predicated on a sound program or specification. The practical use of specifications is often thought to be applicable only to construction. However, as a pre-

lude to any description of the types and elements of recreation facilities, a review of the other specifications that are necessary in the total development process is required. With the increased emphasis on new recreation facilities, it is important that a summary of the various phases of development be reviewed. Each of these phases necessitates a specification of sorts. In the development process, such important services as the following are required:

Researching-planning
Designing-engineering
Constructing-furnishing
Marketing-promoting
Maintaining-supervising
Organizing-administering

It is obvious that there is more to the establishment, development, and management of a recreation project than the construction phase. The construction specification is most comprehensive in the diversity and complexity of materials, methods, and machinery employed in the variety of tasks that must be engaged in to construct a project. There are other types of specifications to be considered.

An initial major type of specification that capsulizes the requirements of the recreation facility researching-planning effort is the study design specification. This sets forth the requirements to be included in the finished report. Sometimes in school facilities it is called an education specification; other times a master plan and program. The education specification is completed by a study process that involves a comprehensive analytic procedure. The education specification in turn is a document that sets forth the requirements for the architect/landscape architect and engineer team. This specification is usually prepared by a researcher-planner or programmer in conjunction with the architectural team.

The second major type of specification is the facility design specification. This sets forth the requirements to be included in the finished document, which is called the construction specification. The construction specification is completed in concert with plans and details. It sets forth the requirements for the manufacturer to supply and the contractor team to construct. This specification is usually prepared by designer-engineers.

A third type of specification addresses the requirements of the managing-operating effort. This sets forth the requirements, sometimes called an administration/operation specification or manual, for the administrators and operators to manage the facility. This operation specification is usually prepared by the manufacturer/contractor and designer/engineer.

The age-old precept that form follows function is reflected in the necessity for the program statement to be completed before embarking on a construction specification. That a structure might be beautiful, but not successful unless it works, also is reflective of the necessity for an operations specification to ensure the implementation of what was intended.

When park or school facilities are to be used by children and adults of a neighborhood or community for recreation or education, additional facilities may be required to meet local needs and desires of the people. The list of "optional" facilities should be studied carefully in relation to the required social, intellectual, or physical activity

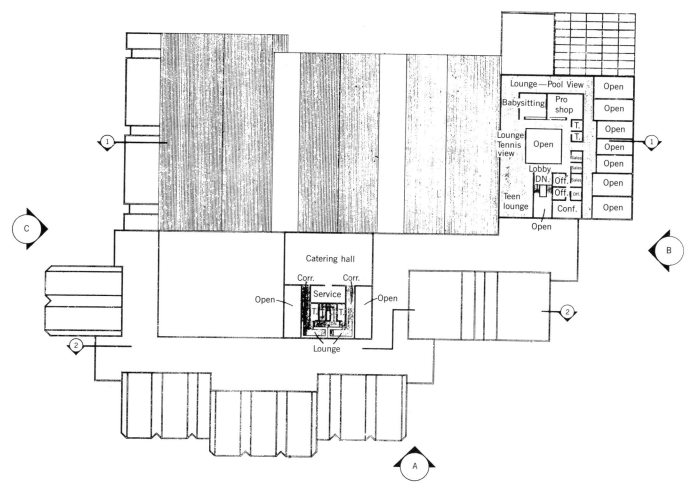

Figure 16. Pool plan, private tennis/ice center, West Haven, Conn. Courtesy of Ward Associates.

program and to the inter- or intramural involvement of others beyond the market area. It should be borne in mind that the program and activities determine the nature and quantity of area and facilities needed.

The following illustration of the utilization and composition of a universally perceived recreation center facility will highlight the essential and optional elements.

ESSENTIAL SPACES

The following outdoor facilities are suggested.

Hard-surfaced Area (Multi-use Area)

Delineation of Activities. Space may be required for tennis, basketball, handball, volleyball, badminton, paddle tennis, shuffleboard, roller skating, ice skating, dancing, outdoor shows or concerts. The size would vary depending on the capacity projected.

Description of Facilities. This area could be provided with all-weather hard-surfaced material such as asphalt or concrete. In locations of 40° north latitude where natural ice skating is a possibility, the surface should be nearly level, with a pitch of no more than 2–3 in. to permit flooding. A 6 in. curb should encompass the area to facilitate the retention of water. It is not always necessary to fence in the area. However, if tennis courts are to be included as part of the layout, fences should be placed the required distance behind the end lines of the courts. A range of court activities can be laid out on such a surface.

Fields

Delineation of Activities. Safety zones should be provided around and between fields and game areas, plus space for walkways, spectators, and landscaping. A minimum of 50% of the actual space required for installation of the facilities should be added to the total. Space should also be provided for parking cars and for access roads.

Description of Facilities. This area is an open turfed area that contains certain specific sport areas that are acceptable for a variety of uses. Separate distinct areas for boys and girls are usually desirable. The basic or dominate sport areas are noted below. Other activities that may be conducted on the same space during other seasons are also noted. Playing stations are those specific dimensioned areas established by the rules of the game.

Boy's Area	Typical Size, ft	Typical Total Ft²	Typical Acres
Softball diamonds (spring) (2) soccer field (fall) (1) or speedball or lacrosse or touch football fields (4)	400 × 220	88,000	2.1

Girl's Area	Typical Size, ft	Typical Total Ft²	Typical Acres
Softball diamonds (spring) (2) field hockey (fall) (1)	280 × 400	112,000	2.7
Archery range (fall or spring) (1) bait and fly casting (1)	100 × 150	15,000	0.36
Areas Common to Girls and Boys			
Multiple station golf driving range	50 × 100	5,000	0.12

Core support or service facilities may include snack bar, bike rack, storage, drinking fountain, bleachers, buffers, flagpole, seats.

Indoor facilities that are found in a building complex are also numerous but may include these suggested spaces.

Gymnasium (Multi-use area)

Delineation of Activities. Basketball, volleyball, badminton, roller skating, dancing, and related activities could be contained in such a space, the size depending on the capacity or the number of games to be played at a time.

Description of Facilities. This area could contain a synthetic surface as opposed to the frequently used hardwood floors. This would allow for activity use of a different type. However, it should be cautioned that the floor materials, of which there are at least 14 different manufacturers, should be able to accommodate the different activities.

Game Room

Delineation of Activities. Table games, floor games, and dancing should all be taken into consideration.

Description of Facilities. This area could contain a carpeted surface, resilient flooring, or hardwood.

Combatant or Wrestling Room

Delineation of Activities. Facilities for karate, judo, and other martial arts, as well as various wrestling activities, should be provided.

Description of Facility. This room must be set up for mats of various impact ratings, plus have walls free of protrusions and hazards.

Aerobics or Dance Area

Delineation of Activities. Aerobics, calisthenics, jazzercise, ballet, and other movement programs must be planned for.

Description of Facility. This area must have synthetic flooring, mirrors, wall bars, and special sound and light effects.

Exercise or Fitness Area

Delineation of Activities. Rowing, exercycling, universals, nautilus, free weights, and other equipment programs could be conducted.

Description of Facility. This area must have carpeted flooring, mirrors, wall patterns, and special light and sound effects.

Crafts Area

Delineation of Activities. Clay sculpture, woodworking, metal work, and other activities could be conducted.

Description of Facilities. This area must have sinks, cabinets, kilns, heat lamps, and other facilities for craft work.

Arts Area

Delineation of Activities. Oil paints, charcoal, watercolors, inks and other media may be used.

Description of Facilities. This area must have studio lighting, display areas, easels, sinks, storage racks, and other facilities.

OPTIONAL FACILITIES

The optional facilities listed here may be part of the required facilities in certain school or park situations.

It is important to recognize that additional space must be provided for placement of park or school buildings, parking space, walkways, access roads, service roads, and landscaping. The exact amount needed will depend on the design of the park or school (campus, cluster, or traditional type), topography of land, the efficiency of use, and other factors.

Outdoor Facilities	Space Required, Acres
Baseball diamond	2.0
Football field with 1/4-mile track	3.0
Golf driving range	4.0
Putting green	0.25
Artificial ice-skating rink	0.75
Outdoor swimming pool	0.05
Skiing area	1–10
Outdoor rifle range	2–5
Bait-casting area	1–2
Field archery area	5–10
Separate tennis courts (2 courts)	0.36
Separate handball courts (4 courts)	0.12

Indoor Facilities	Space Required, Sq. ft.
Senior room	1,200
Pre school or playroom	950
Natatorium	30,000
Sauna and steam	800
Stress test room and laboratory	1,500
Tennis court (min. 2)	10,370
Racquetball court (min. 2)	1,360
Handball court (min. 2)	1,360
Indoor rifle range (min. 4 firing pts)	1,616
Stage	3,070
Assembly hall	12,600
Meeting room	950
Indoor track	231,800

CORE SUPPORT OR SERVICE SPACES

Core support or service spaces include offices, public restrooms, locker rooms, coaches rooms, trainer and treatment rooms, concession or snack facilities, storage rooms, and phone and vending areas.

Another example of recommendations for the number of indoor facilities for physical activities in either education or recreation are predicated on the following computations, which have been advocated by the education profession:

- Enrollment to be served—1500
- Average size of physical activities classes—40
- Number of physical activities classes to be scheduled—38
- Number of periods of physical activities per week per user—3
- Total number of classes to be accommodated—(3 × 38) = 114
- Number of days per week (5) divided into 114 = 22.8
- Number of periods of physical activities per day = 6
- Number of teaching or playing stations required 22.8 ÷ 6 = 3.8
- 3.8 is rounded out to 4 teaching or playing stations.

It is usually desirable to add one teaching or playing station for general competitional use (intramurals, intermurals). This will raise the number of teaching stations to five. A teaching or playing station is an area where a class of 30 to 40 students and a teacher or leader may carry on an activity during a school period.

The recreation facilities that are represented by sports, fitness, and other education and recreation programs consist of so many kinds that it is impossible to provide a detailed checklist for each facility. However, it may be helpful to illustrate a typical checklist for a physical activities facility.

- Number of teaching and playing stations determine the size of the gym needed and whether one or two gyms will be required and the nature of the other teaching stations such as swimming pool and special exercise rooms.
- Location in regard to site and balance of the school or park plant access and shared use.
- Dimensions of all areas such as locker rooms, showers, and gyms to afford safe circulation.
- Height of gym ceiling and other teaching or service areas conform to activity.
- Material for floor covering in gym conforms to activity.
- Finishing on walls conform to activity.
- Treatments of acoustics relate to capacity of use.
- Requirements for lighting reflect actual foot candles of illumination desired at eye level for activity.
- Requirements for heating, air conditioning and ventilating reflect the capacity of use.
- Space for storage conforms to the activity requirements.
- The space for office and other core or support facilities reflects type of use.
- Requirements for spectators and type of seats—rollaway or fixed-type bleachers. Consider size, permanency, and capacity.
- Type of apparatus and the floor, wall, and ceiling mountings to accommodate specific types of apparatus as required.
- Requirements for lobby or foyer size reflect the public use.
- Type of basketball backstop to be used—swing up, roll-away, or fixed—determined by other space uses.
- Location and number of bulletin boards, fire extinguishers, and drinking fountains reflect the type of use.
- Type of folding partitions, screens, or net curtains reflect the type of use.
- Locations of wainscot and eyebolts in wall are considerate of use.
- Type of floor finish in halls and lobbies is considerate of use.
- Location and type of court markings on floor reflect activities required.
- Type of special electrical fixtures, such as special wiring for public address system or television, and electrical load reflects type of use.
- Location of exit doors, both within building and those leading to outdoor playing fields, reflect use and control patterns.
- Location of locker room and its peak load and average daily load are considerate of different use areas.
- Required storage lockers or baskets area sized and in sufficient quantity.
- Number of dressing lockers required (size and number) for type of use.

- Recommended floor material in locker and shower rooms for sanitary and safe conditions.
- Height of locker-room ceiling is adequate to prevent abuse.
- Special dressing facilities for handicapped is considered.
- Location and number of drains; color of walls; air temperature; number of shower heads, drinking fountains, and toilets; widths of aisles; number and size bulletin boards and mirrors; and size of the toweling room is considerate of type of use.
- Requirements for drying-room equipment and laundry equipment is considerate of use.
- Size of towel-issue room, equipment-issue room, pro-shop, etc. is considerate of use.
- Amount of illumination required throughout the locker room, activity rooms, halls, and public spaces must be adequate.

The more detailed the data specified above, the better. Inevitably, there will have to be compromises; nevertheless, this should not occur at the initial stage of preparation of the researching-planning specifications.

BIBLIOGRAPHY

1. J. R. Hoke, Jr., *Architectural Graphic Standards,* John Wiley & Sons, New York, 1988.
2. R. Flynn, *A Site Design Process,* The Athletic Institute & American Alliance for Health, Physical Education, Recreation & Dance, Reston, Va., 1985.
3. G. E. Fogg, *A Guide for Planning The Field House as a College or School Physical Education Facility,* National Recreation & Park Association, Arlington, Va., 1986.
4. A. Petersen, *The Design of Outdoor Physical Education Facilities for College and Schools,* Bureau of Publications, Teachers College, Columbia University, New York, 1963.
5. J. Delamater, *Planning Facilities for Athletics, Physical Education, and Recreation,* Bureau of Publications, Teachers College, Columbia University, New York, 1963.
6. M. Nelischer, *Handbook of Landscape Architectural Construction,* Landscape Architectural Foundation, Washington, D.C., 1985.
7. J. DeChiara and L. Koppelman, *Time Saver Standards for Site Planning,* McGraw-Hill Inc., New York, 1978.
8. E. E. Seelye, *Data Book for Civil Engineers—Design,* John Wiley & Sons, New York, 1960.
9. T. Walker, *Site Design and Construction Detailing,* PDA Publisher, 1978.

See also Campus Planning; Elementary Educational Facilities; Secondary Schools; Swimming Pools

Arthur H. Mittelstaedt, Jr., Ed.D.
Ward Associates P.C.
Bohemia, New York

REGISTRATION OF PROFESSIONALS IN CONSTRUCTION

Licensing has a profound effect on the professions it regulates. In addition to establishing the minimum standards for entry into a profession, licensing laws delineate the scope of the profession, define exempt individuals and services, and control interstate and corporate practice. Of the more than 800 different occupations and professions that are licensed in at least one state, only about 60 are regulated in a majority of the states (1). Architects and engineers are among the last group.

Regulation of professions and occupations is one of the police powers of the states, ie, it is based on the need to protect the public health, safety, and welfare. The type of regulation the state imposes varies depending on the characteristics of the occupation, the client–consumer group, and the impact of the occupation on public safety. Practice regulation, the strictest form of regulation, means that only those individuals who meet the legislated criteria may perform the services of the profession. Licensure is used in some states to denote practice regulation, but may also be used as an umbrella term to describe all types of occupational regulation. Under title laws, sometimes called certification laws, only the use of the title is restricted to those individuals who meet the established standards; individuals who do not meet those standards may not use the title but may continue to perform the services. Many practice laws also include provisions restricting use of the title. In almost all 50 states architects and engineers are regulated by practice laws.

Because of the increasing number of professions and occupations that are regulated or seeking regulation and because of the costs associated with regulation, in the last 20 years state legislators have been taking a harder look at the justification for state intervention. "Sunset" laws in many states now require periodic reviews of regulatory boards to ensure that they are fulfilling their public protection role; more recently, "sunrise" laws have begun to mandate review of the need for state regulation according to established criteria before legislation to regulate the profession or occupation can even be introduced. The Federal Trade Commission and the U.S. Department of Justice have also become active in scrutinizing regulations and challenging both criteria for licensure and restrictions of practice that in their judgment do not serve a public protection goal. As in the health professions and other industries, the design professions have been affected by this trend. On the one hand, long-established boards regulating architects and engineers have had to demonstrate their effectiveness in protecting the public safety (including by stepping up enforcement activities) to obtain re-authorization through sunset, and state board regulations regarding advertising or other competitive practices have been discarded in many instances. On the other hand, emerging professions seeking licensure, such as interior design, have encountered roadblocks in the rigorous sunrise procedures of some states.

ARCHITECTS

By 1940, boards to regulate architects had been established in almost 90% of the states, and since 1951 architects have been licensed in all 50 states. Only a few of the laws are title laws; most restrict the practice of architecture to those individuals who meet the mandated criteria. Standard requirements for architectural licensing as promoted by the National Council of Architectural Registration Boards (NCARB) and incorporated into most state laws consist of an accredited degree, a structured internship, and passage of the NCARB examination. Legislative guidelines for architectural licensing laws are also published by the NCARB. The NCARB definition of architecture, which has been incorporated into many architectural licensing laws, is:

> . . . services, hereinafter described, in connection with the design, construction, enlargement, or alteration of a building or group of buildings and the spaces within and surrounding such buildings, which have as their principal purpose human occupancy or habitation. The services referred to in the previous sentence include planning, providing preliminary studies, designs, drawings, specifications, and other technical submissions, and administration of construction contracts.

Exemptions in architectural laws are defined in two categories: structures and individuals. While exemptions vary greatly from state to state, types of individuals that are commonly exempt in state laws include employees of licensed architects who are working under the direct supervision of the licensee, federal government employees, and licensed engineers performing architectural services that are incidental to the practice of engineering.

Exemptions for structures may be codified by building or structure type, use, cost, or size. Types of structures that are most commonly exempt from architectural practice laws include single-family residences and farm buildings. Buildings intended only for the use of the owner and not for public assembly or use are also frequently excluded from the acts, as are nonstructural renovations or alterations. Exemptions by size range from blanket exemption of buildings–structures of not more than 500 ft^2 to exemption of specified types of structures up to 20,000 ft. Size exemptions may also be defined by number of stories, number of living units, or cubic feet. In addition, structural exemptions may also be overlapping: that is, an exemption for single-family residences may not apply if the building exceeds a square-footage limitation or involves certain types of construction; similarly, buildings for public assembly may be excluded from coverage under square footage exemptions. While exemptions defined by building cost are still incorporated in some states' laws, many are being replaced by square footage exemptions to prevent inflation or fluctuations in the economy from reducing or otherwise affecting the intended scope of the exemption.

Architectural licensing is on an individual basis. Nevertheless, architectural services are usually performed and offered to clients within some kind of business or corporate context. Licensing laws, therefore, also regulate the corporate practice of architecture. Most such restrictions are included in the architectural licensing laws and regulations, but in some states are delineated within separate professional corporation or business corporation statutes.

As with other exemption provisions, corporate practice restrictions are not uniform in all 50 states. On the one hand, almost half permit architects to practice virtually without restriction within any type of corporate structure. On the other hand, about 12 states require that at least one owner, whether a partner, principal, or director, be a licensed architect. At the most restrictive end of the spectrum are the state laws, in over 12 states, that require a specific percentage—often one third—of the directors, principals, partners, shareholders, etc., to be licensed architects. Many of these laws also specify that a total of two thirds of the directors or owners of the firm or corporation must be licensed professionals, whether architects, engineers, or other design professionals.

However, regardless of restrictions on corporate practice, all 50 statutes specify that a licensed architect must be in direct control and responsible charge of the performance of architectural services and that the corporate structure cannot shield the individual from liability. This principle of individual responsibility for practice lies at the heart of state licensure.

ENGINEERS

State regulation of professional engineers in the United States dates back to the early 1900s. Requirements for licensure as an engineer follow the pattern of education, training, and examination. The standard education requirement common to the statutes is a degree accredited by the Accreditation Board for Engineering and Technology or an equivalent as determined by the state boards. The licensing examination for engineers in most states is the two-part test administered by the National Council of Engineering Examiners (NCEE), which consists of an examination in the fundamentals of engineering and an examination in the principles and practices of engineering. Unlike architectural licensing laws, which have no intern category, engineering laws include a classification of engineers-in-training or intern-engineers. Requirements for the in-training category usually include completion of the education requirement and passage of the examination on the fundamentals of engineering.

In addition to overseeing the engineers' professional examination, NCEE has promulgated a model licensing law to promote uniformity among the states. As defined in the NCEE model law, engineering encompasses

> . . . any service or creative work, the adequate performance of which requires engineering education, training and experience in the application of special knowledge of the mathematical, physical and engineering sciences to such services or creative work as consultation, investigation, evaluation, planning and design of engineering works and systems, planning the use of land and water, teaching of advanced engineering subjects, engineering surveys and studies, and the review of construction for the purpose of assuring compliance with drawings and specifications; any of which embraces such services or

work, either public or private, in connection with any utilities, structures, buildings, machines, equipment, processes, work systems, projects, and industrial or consumer products or equipment of a mechanical, electrical, hydraulic, pneumatic or thermal nature, insofar as they involve safeguarding life, health or property, and including such other professional services as may be necessary to the planning, progress and completion of any engineering services (3).

Virtually all engineering licensing laws require a licensed professional engineer to be in responsible charge of the performance of engineering services. Most laws do not impose additional requirements beyond specifying individual responsibility for services; in other words, the majority of the engineering laws do not restrict corporate practice provided that a licensed professional is in responsible charge of services. However, some do impose percentage-of-ownership requirements such as those included in provisions regulating the corporate practice of architects. From one or more to one half or two thirds of the directors or shareholders are required to be licensed.

Less than one third of practicing engineers are licensed under state statutes. The percentage reflects the great number of engineers who practice within industry or another branch of engineering that does not require licensure; occupational exemptions for engineers employed within industry or government are common to most of the state laws. Exemptions for licensed architects performing engineering that is incidental to the practice of architecture are also frequently included in the engineering laws. All 50 states do, however, require engineers who are in private practice and in responsible charge of engineering services to be licensed. The practice of land surveying is regulated under separate statutes in most states.

LANDSCAPE ARCHITECTS

The practice of landscape architecture has existed as a recognized profession since 1899. The first state board regulating the profession of landscape architecture was established in California in 1954. To date, almost half of the states have enacted practice acts for landscape architects, and over 15 have passed laws restricting the use of the title landscape architect.

Because landscape architecture as a profession is newer to state regulation than the professions of architecture and engineering, requirements for licensure for landscape architects have not achieved the level of uniformity among the states that is common to architecture and engineering licensing laws. Requirements for licensure as a landscape architect however do generally include a combination of education and experience as well as passage of the Uniform National Examination prepared by the Council of Landscape Architectural Registration Boards. The definition of landscape architecture also varies somewhat from state to state. One of the more comprehensive definitions is included in the Florida law regulating the practice of landscape architecture:

> (a) Consultation, investigation, research, planning, design, preparation of drawings, specifications, contract documents

and reports, responsible construction supervision, or landscape management in connection with the planning and development of land and incidental water areas where, and to the extent that, the dominant purpose of such services or creative works is the preservation, conservation, enhancement, or determination of proper land uses, natural land features, ground cover and plantings, or naturalistic and aesthetic values; (b) The determination of settings, grounds, and approaches for and the siting of buildings and structures, outdoor areas or of other improvements; (c) The setting of grades, shaping and contouring of land and water forms, determination of drainage, and provision for storm drainage and irrigation systems where such systems are necessary to the purposes outlined herein; or (d) The design of such tangible objects or features as are necessary to the purpose outlined herein (4).

As in the professions of architecture and engineering, laws governing landscape architects also control the corporate practice of the profession, but retain the principle of individual control and responsibility by the licensee. While the movement to achieve state regulation of landscape architects has for the most part been successful, it has also encountered setbacks resulting from the current antiregulation trend in the states. Two landscape architects' boards have been eliminated under sunset review; one, in Oregon, has since been re-authorized, but efforts to reenact the Colorado board, which was abolished in 1977, have so far been unsuccessful.

INTERIOR DESIGNERS

Unregulated prior to 1982, interior designers are now actively seeking enactment of state registration laws. Following a four-year effort, the first title law for interior designers was enacted in Alabama in 1982. The law defines interior design as services

. . . in connection with the design, utilization, furnishing or fabrication of elements in interior spaces in buildings, homes, and related structures. Such services include, but shall not be limited to, the following: programming the functional requirements for interior spaces; preparing analyses of user needs; planning interior spaces; preparing designs, drawings and specifications for selection, use, location, color, and finishes of interior materials, equipment, furnishings and furniture; and administering contracts for fabrication, procurement or installation in connection with such designs, drawings and specifications (5).

Three additional states have since enacted title laws for interior designers: Connecticut (1983), Louisiana (1984), and Florida (1988). The Florida law defines exempt interior decorator services and includes the interior designers in a joint board with architects, both for the first time. The District of Columbia passed a practice act licensing interior designers in 1986; although not yet in effect, proposed regulations for the law were published in July 1988 and the law is expected to go into effect during the 1989 calendar year. Altogether, in the past years, legislation to regulate interior designers has been discussed or introduced in almost 30 states.

Criteria for registration vary in the laws and the proposed legislation; for example, not all require an accredited degree, but most include a combination of education and training in interior design and passage of the examination developed by the National Council for Interior Design Qualification (NCIDQ), a council of interior design professional societies established in 1972. The Council also publishes model title legislation; the model includes an accredited degree, passage of the NCIDQ examination, and some professional experience as prerequisites for registration. As with most professions, the impetus for seeking state regulation and for establishing uniform standards and qualifications for interior designers has come primarily from the professional societies, chiefly the American Society of Interior Designers and the Institute of Business Designers.

ISSUES AND TRENDS IN STATE REGULATION

Among the clear trends in state regulation of the construction industry design professions is the continuing movement toward uniformity in state licensing law provisions, especially toward standardization of requirements for entry into the professions. Differences in state laws, especially in provisions relating to exemptions and corporate practice, will not disappear, however, as state regulators continue to stress the need for tailoring laws to respond to specific local and geographic conditions. Incorporation of stronger enforcement provisions in state laws and an increase in enforcement activity, both in relation to licensees and nonlicensees, will also continue as state boards must increasingly demonstrate the effectiveness of the laws' protection of the public health, safety, and welfare.

A difficult issue that will require continued attention is the question of the overlap of practice areas among the design professions. While these issues have been effectively addressed in some instances by incorporation of dovetailed exemptions in the state laws, eg, the use of the incidental services exemptions, and by reliance on the individual licensees' professional judgment in not performing services for which they are not qualified, differences in the laws' definitions of scope of practice and exempt areas of practice continue to cause confusion. Increased enforcement activities by the states have also focused attention on the grey areas of overlapping practice among the professions. This issue may be further complicated in the future by requests for licensure from other specialized disciplines within the design industry.

These important issues in state regulation—uniformity, scope of practice, enforcement, and the emergence of specialized disciplines—are not peculiar to the design professions, but are common to all of the regulated professions. They therefore will need to be addressed by state regulators and the professions within the overall framework of the state regulatory process and with primary consideration for the public-protection purpose of licensure.

BIBLIOGRAPHY

1. F. S. Berry, "State Regulation of Occupations and Professions," *The Book of the States,* 1986–1987 ed., Vol. 26, The Council of State Governments, Lexington, Ky., 1986, p. 379.
2. *National Council of Architectural Registration Boards Legislative Guidelines and Model Law,* NCARB, Washington, D.C., 1985, revised 1987, p. 1.
3. *National Council of Engineering Examiners Model Law,* Washington, D.C., 1988, revision, p. 4.
4. *Florida Statutes, 1988, Chapt. 481, Part II, 481.303(6).*
5. *Code of Alabama,* Title 34–15A–1(3) (Acts 1982. No. 82–497, Sect. 1).

General References

Architectural Licensing: Summary of State Statutes, The American Institute of Architects, Washington, D.C., July 1981 (1989 ed. available in December 1989).

Landscape Architecture and Professional Registration Laws, American Society of Landscape Architects, 1983.

National Council of Architectural Registration Boards Legislative Guidelines and Model Law, NCARB, Washington, D.C., revised June 1985.

National Council of Architectural Registration Boards Member Boards Requirements Chart, July 1988.

National Council of Engineering Examiners Model Law, Washington, D.C., 1988, revision.

State-by-State Summary of Engineering Corporate Practice Laws, National Society of Professional Engineers.

State-by-State Summary of the Requirements for Engineering Registration, National Society of Professional Engineers, 1985.

See also CONSTRUCTION LAW; EDUCATION, ARCHITECTURAL; INTERIOR DESIGN; LANDSCAPE ARCHITECTURE; NATIONAL COUNCIL OF ARCHITECTURAL REGISTRATION BOARDS; REGISTRATION EXAMINATION PROCESS, ARCHITECTS

NANCY SOMERVILLE
The American Institute of
Architects
Washington, D.C.

REGULATIONS—ZONING AND BUILDING CODES

Zoning ordinances and building codes are legal limitations on construction enforced under the police powers of the state. Although in most cases, the regulations are minimum standards, in effect they become the normal standards for construction. The development of regulations is a continuing process, and they are updated on a regular basis. Many examples can be cited of the need to upgrade the safety of older buildings. All codes refer to standards developed by others, and by reference become a part of the code.

The model code organizations publish a series of codes. Typical are separate codes for mechanical, plumbing, fire prevention, existing buildings and others. Many of the standards for fire safety are developed and published by the National Fire Protection Association (NFPA) under the general heading of *National Fire Codes.* Among the most widely known NFPA publications are the *Life Safety Code* and the *National Electric Code.*

There are three major model code organizations in the United States. These are the Building Officials and Code Administrators International, Inc. (BOCA), International Conference of Building Officials (ICBO), and the Southern Building Code Congress International, (SBCCI). Although attempts to arrive at a single United States code have not been successful, the Council of American Building Officials (CABO), a joint venture of the three major United States model code agencies, works to achieve consistency of requirements in code language.

It is important to determine the codes, including date of issue, for each location, since the various states or communities will vary in which model code is in force. In addition, local ordinances may modify the requirements of the codes. Some cities prepare their own codes to meet higher safety standards. It is possible that a building code may conflict with the requirements of other regulations, and in these situations, the more restrictive language is usually acceptable. For unresolved issues, the building officials in the community will make a decision. For government construction, the local building code may be superseded by other regulations.

Other national regulatory organizations affecting construction include the Consumer Products Safety Commission, the Environmental Protection Agency (EPA) and the Occupational Safety and Health Administration (OSHA).

ZONING ORDINANCES

Zoning refers to the legal designation of land for specific uses. In the United States, the legal right to enforce zoning is reserved to the States, and may be delegated to a governmental area or community. Zoning is adopted by ordinance, and includes a zoning map of the affected area.

Zoning represents the physical aspect of master plans recorded on a zoning map. Regional planning agencies may be established to address larger scale issues, to be reflected in local zoning ordinances. Rural areas may not have zoning ordinances other than limitations imposed by the State. The city of Houston, Texas, was one of the few U.S. cities to develop without zoning.

Zoning is enforced by formal review of development proposals and site plans submitted to governmental review agencies. Such groups as planning commissions, boards of zoning appeals, land restoration (sanitary landfill) boards, architectural review boards, health care advisory boards, and other groups such as tree commissions may review and rule on submitted plans. A change or variance of zoning normally requires public hearings before a ruling is made. Zoning decisions may be appealed to the board of zoning appeals, which may involve further public hearings. The courts have clarified the legal standing of zoning decisions.

A typical zoning ordinance may address general requirements such as limit of jurisdiction, uses previous to the ordinance, and what is exempt from the ordinance. Zoning districts define approved land uses, and normally include residential, commercial, and industrial uses. Some ordinances contain provisions for planned unit development districts. Further restrictions may apply, described as overlay districts for historic areas, natural resources, airport noise districts, central business district sign controls, highway corridor controls, etc.

The zoning ordinance may define areas of varying density for each use. A typical section of the zoning ordinance includes a definition of the zone, permitted uses, uses requiring special permits, special exception uses, and limitations on use. Once these requirements are met, the zoning ordinance describes the minimum lot size, maximum building height, yard requirements, and other structures on the property.

Common terms defining bulk of a building include the angle of bulk plane taken from the front lot line, and in the case of plane of measurement for structure with parallel exterior walls is further defined as the minimum distance between structures. Each district use can specify a differing angle of bulk plane. As an example, a high-rise suburban office building might have the following yard requirements:

1. *Maximum building height.*
   Any approved increase would require larger yards.
2. *Minimum yard requirements.*
   Front yard, specified angle of bulk plane but limited by width of the right of way of a street.
   Side yard, not required, but if provided, of a minimum width.
   Rear yard, angle of bulk plane, usually less stringent than the front yard.

A regulation contained in many zoning codes regulates the mass of the building by regulating the total square footage to the lot area. This is known as the floor area ratio (FAR).

The maximum density expressed as dwellings per acre applies to residential buildings, and the requirements for open space as a percentage of lot size is specified for all zones. Additional regulations are cross referenced in the appropriate zoning district description.

A major area of concern is parking, loading zones, and private streets. Parking requirements relate to the use and bulk of the building, and in suburban areas may require parking structures for maximum development of the property. Signage, trees, landscaping, and screening are other areas for zoning consideration. Special standards for air pollution, fire and explosion hazard, radiation hazard, liquid and solid waste, and noise control may apply to development.

Exceptions to zoning provisions may include increased height credit for adjoining air rights purchased for this purpose. Other special property uses might be air rights over highways or public transportation such as trains, subways, etc. Intense development such as regional shopping malls may be exceptions to normal zoning requirements. Information to be shown on plan drawings is specified in the ordinance. Fees are required for review, and for large projects may be substantial.

In areas of rapid growth, delays in the approval process may occur, and economic pressures for rapid change may be placed on the planning process. Zoning has a major economic impact on land values and taxation. A change of zoning may represent substantial profit to the owner.

BUILDING CODES

The purpose of building codes is to insure public safety, health and welfare as affected by building construction. This purpose includes structural strength, adequate egress, sanitary equipment, light, ventilation, and fire safety. The codes attempt to secure safety to life and property from hazards incident to the design, erection, repair, removal, demolition, or use and occupancy of buildings, structures or premises.

History

Building codes date to antiquity. The first recorded example is included in the Code of Hammurabi dating from the 18th century B.C. Laws concerned building and land ie, should a building collapse and death occur, the builder was to be put to death.

Roman building regulations which have survived include some relating to fire safety. Building regulations can be traced through canon law of the medieval church, and in the Germanic codes. New codes of law, such as the Code Napoléon had wide influence. An example of provisions states that if a building should fall, whether in whole or in part, within 10 years of its construction because of bad workmanship or poor soil, the architect and workmen are financially liable for the loss. In London, after the great fire of 1666, new laws prevented the use of wood framing in houses. English common law was operative in the American colonies, and codes applied in the Spanish and French colonies. A landmark law was the New York City housing code of 1867. The first zoning ordinance was passed in New York City in 1913.

The years since have seen a proliferation of building regulations throughout the country. The national model code groups were organized to rationalize building regulations. The earliest of these was the Building Officials and Code Administrators (BOCA) International, Inc., founded in 1915. The first edition of the *BOCA National Building Code* was published in 1950.

Currently, the model codes are reissued every three years. Intermediate changes are published annually. Jurisdictions may specify the date of the edition in force in an area, requiring specific adoption of later editions of the code. The following text is derived from the BOCA National Building Code, 1987, copyright 1986 by the Building Officials and Code Administrators, International, Inc. 4015 West Flossmoor Road, Country Club Hills, Ill. 60478. Selected material published by agreement with the author. All rights reserved. This edition differs from earlier editions by its organization.

Preliminary information includes a sample ordinance for adoption of the 1987 BOCA National Building Code by individual local authorities, and a guide to the use of the code.

Article 1—Administration and Enforcement

After a state, county or community government adopts one of the model codes, it generally applies to all construction within the jurisdiction. Included in the code adoption is a requirement for a review and approval process by a public building official and his staff. Records are kept, permits issued, orders given, and the building official may issue rules to protect public health, safety and general welfare. Typical rules might relate to the local climate of the area or more stringent requirements than included in the code.

Codes require that the contract documents shall be prepared by architects and engineers licensed to practice in the state. The professionals shall sign and seal the documents submitted for review.

The fees charged for review and approval are specified by the jurisdiction. The building official has the right of inspection in cooperation with police, fire, and health departments. Violations of the code may result in prosecution. Special inspections, such as those of elevator installations, are also a responsibility of the building official and his staff.

Appeals to decisions of the building official and his staff may be made to a five member Board of Appeals consisting of architects, engineers, and builders or building superintendents, each appointed by the jurisdiction. Appeals are made at public hearings, and decisions of the Board are made by resolutions with certified copies sent to the parties affected. Aggrieved parties may appeal to the courts for correction.

An important control of compliance with the code is the certificate of use and occupancy. A new building may not be used or occupied in whole or in part until the certificates have been issued. Similar regulations apply to alterations, pre-existing buildings which predate adoption of the code, or to changes in use and occupancy. Temporary certificates may be issued to allow occupancy before the final work is complete if public safety provisions are acceptable. Certificates specify the use, type of construction, maximum live load, occupant load and any special conditions.

Unsafe structures may be condemned by the building official, and vacant buildings sealed. If unsafe conditions are noted by inspection, the building official will serve a written notice specifying the corrective actions needed. The owner of a building who has been served with an unsafe order may demand the appointment of a Board of Survey if the owner feels the requested corrections are in error. Refusal to comply may result in legal action. In emergency situations, the building official may order occupants out of the building, and temporary safeguards put in place. Streets may be closed if necessary.

Article 2—Definitions

Each model code includes a section of definitions of terms which have important bearing on the interpretation of code provisions. By reference, definitions included in plumbing, fire protection, and mechanical codes are incorporated in this section. An example of a definition is given:

Use group: The classification of a building or structure based on the purpose for which it is used as listed in Article 3.

Use Group A	assembly
Use Group B	business
Use Group E	educational
Use Group F	factory and industrial
Use Group H	high hazard
Use Group I	institutional
Use Group M	mercantile
Use Group R	residential
Use Group S	storage
Use Group U	utility and miscellaneous

Article 3—Use Group Classification

Each of the use groups are further defined in Article 3. In addition, mixed use and occupancy uses are defined, and uses not described will be assigned the use group which it most nearly resembles.

Article 4—Types of Construction Classification

Construction classification relates to the fire safety of the construction systems used. 5 types are defined, of which 2 are described as noncombustible, 2 as noncombustible/combustible and 1 as combustible, as shown in Table 1, [1].

Article 5—General Building Limitations

This section of the code defines limits of area and height, and modifications allowed under certain conditions. There is provision for buildings of unlimited area for some uses, provided with fire suppression systems, and with requirements for fire rating of exterior enclosure illustrated in Tables 2 and 3 [2, 3].

Other sections of this article relate to awnings and canopies, temporary structures, and requirements for physically handicapped and aged for most use groups. Historic buildings and districts may be relieved of code provisions with the approval of the Board of Appeals.

Article 6—Special Use and Occupancy Requirements

This section contains provisions for covered mall buildings, high-rise buildings, hazardous production materials (HPM) facilities, and membrane structures. Other provisions define requirements for mezzanines, open well (atrium) spaces, open parking structures, and garages. Also included are provisions for institutional facilities, bleachers, grandstands and folding or telescopic seating, motion picture projection rooms, screening rooms and sound stages, rooftop heliports, stages and platforms, and airport traffic control towers. Other uses with restrictive regulations include facilities for combustible dusts, grain processing and storage, explosion hazards, flammable and

Table 1. Fireresistance Ratings of Structure Elements (in hours)[j]

Structure element[a]		Type 1 — 1A	Type 1 — 1B	Type 2 Protected — 2A	Type 2 Protected — 2B	Type 2 Unprotected — 2C	Type 3 Protected — 3A	Type 3 Unprotected — 3B	Type 4 Heavy timber[c] — 4	Type 5 Protected — 5A	Type 5 Unprotected — 5B
1 Exterior walls	Load-bearing	4	3	2	1	0	2	2	2	1	0
		← Not less than the rating based on fire separation distance (see Section 906.2) →									
	Nonload-bearing	← Not less than the rating based on fire separation distance (see Section 906.2) →									
2 Fire walls and party walls (Section 908.0)		4	3	2	2	2	2	2	2	2	2
		← Not less than fire grading of use group—(see Table 902) →									
3 Fire separation assemblies (Sections 313.0, 910.0 and 913.0)		← Fireresistance rating corresponding to fire grading of use group—(see Table 902) →									
4 Smoke barriers (Section 911.0)[g]		1	1	1	1	1	1	1	1	1	1
5 Fire enclosures of exits, exit hallways and stairways (Section 816.9.2, 910.0)[b]		2	2	2	2	2	2	2	2	2	2
6 Shafts (other than exits) and elevator hoistways (Section 910.0, 915.0)[b]		2	2	2	2	2	2	2	2	1	1
7 Exit access corridors[f,g]		1	1	1	1	1	1	1	1	1	1
		← Note d →									
8 Separations	Tenant spaces[f]	1	1	1	1	0	1	0	1	1	0
		← Note d →									
	Dwelling unit[f]	1	1	1	1	1	1	1	1	1	1
		← Note d →									
	Other nonbearing partitions	0	0	0	0	0	0	0	0	0	0
		← Note d →									

Structure element[a]		Type 1 — 1A	Type 1 — 1B	Type 2 Protected — 2A	Type 2 Protected — 2B	Type 2 Unprotected — 2C	Type 3 Protected — 3A	Type 3 Unprotected — 3B	Type 4 Heavy timber[c] — 4	Type 5 Protected — 5A	Type 5 Unprotected — 5B
9 Interior bearing walls, bearing partitions, columns, girders, trusses (other than roof trusses) and framing (Section 912.0)	Supporting more than one floor	4	3	2	1	0	1	0	see Sec. 405.0	1	0
	Supporting one floor only or a roof only	3	2	1½	1	0	1	0	see Sec. 405.0	1	0
10 Structural members supporting wall (Section 912.0)[g]		3	2	1½	1	0	1	0	1	1	0
		← Not less than fireresistance rating of wall supported →									
11 Floor construction including beams (Section 913.0)[h]		3	2	1½	1	0	1	0	see Sec. 405.0[c]	1	0
12 Roof construction, including beams, trusses and framing, arches and roof deck (Section 914.0)[e,i]	15′ or less in height to lowest member	2	1½	1	1	0	1	0	see Sec. 405.0[c]	1	0
				← Note d →							
	More than 15 but less than 20′ in height to lowest lowest member	1	1	1	0	0	0	0	see Sec. 405.0	1	0
		← Note d →									
	20′ or more in height to lowest member	0	0	0	0	0	0	0	see Sec. 405.0	0	0
		← Note d →									

[a] For increased fireresistance rating requirements in special high hazard uses involving a higher degree of fire severity and higher concentration of combustible contents, see Section 600.2. For fireresistance rating requirements for structural membranes and assemblies which support other fireresistance rated members or assemblies, see Section 912.1.

[b] For reductions in the required fireresistance rating of exit and shaft enclosures, see Sections 816.9.2 and 915.3.

[c] For substitution of other structural materials for timber in Type 4 construction, see Section 1702.2.

[d] Fire-retardant treated wood permitted, see Sections 903.5 and 905.3.

[e] For permitted uses of heavy timber in roof construction in buildings of Types 1 and 2 construction, see Section 914.4.

[f] For reductions in required fireresistance ratings of exit access corridors, tenant separations and dwelling unit separations, see Section 810.4 and 810.4.1.

[g] For exceptions to the required fireresistance rating of construction supporting exit access corridors and smoke barriers, see Sections 910.6 and 911.2.

[h] For buildings having habitable or occupiable stories or basements below grade, see Section 807.3.1.

[i] 1 foot = 304.8 mm.

[j] Copyright by the Building Officials & Code Administrators International, Inc.

Table 2. Height and Area Limitations of Buildings[j]

Height limitations of buildings (shown in upper figure as stories and feet above grade), and area limitations of one or two story buildings facing on one street or public space not less than 30 feet wide (shown in lower figure as area in square feet per floor).[a]

N.P.—Not permitted
N.L.—Not limited

	Type of Construction									
	Noncombustible					Noncombustible/Combustible			Combustible	
	Type 1		Type 2			Type 3		Type 4	Type 5	
	Protected[b]		Protected		Unprotected	Protected	Unprotected	Heavy Timber	Protected	Unprotected
	1A	1B	2A	2B	2C	3A	3B	4	5A	5B
A-1 Assembly, theaters	N.L.	N.L.	5 St. 65' 19,950	3 St. 40' 13,125	2 St. 30' 8,400	3 St. 40' 11,550	2 St. 30' 8,400	3 St. 40' 12,600	1 St. 20' 8,925	1 St. 20' 4,200
A-2 Assembly, night clubs and similar uses	N.L.	4 St. 50' 7,200	3 St. 40' 5,700	2 St. 30' 3,750	1 St. 20' 2,400	2 St. 30' 3,300	1 St. 20' 2,400	2 St. 30' 3,600	1 St. 20' 2,550	1 St. 20' 1,200
A-3 Assembly Lecture halls, recreation centers, terminals, restaurants other than night clubs	N.L.	N.L.	5 St. 65' 19,950	3 St. 40' 13,125	2 St. 30' 8,400	3 St. 40' 11,550	2 St. 30' 8,400	3 St. 40' 12,600	1 St. 20' 8,925	1 St. 20' 4,200
A-4 Assembly, churches[d]	N.L.	N.L.	5 St. 65' 34,200	3 St. 40' 22,500	2 St. 30' 14,400	3 St. 40' 19,800	2 St. 30' 14,400	3 St. 40' 21,600	1 St. 20' 15,300	1 St. 20' 7,200
B Business	N.L.	N.L.	7 St. 85' 34,200	5 St. 65' 22,500	3 St. 40' 14,400	4 St. 50' 19,800	3 St. 40' 14,400	5 St. 65' 21,600	3 St. 40' 15,300	2 St. 30' 7,200
E Educational[c,d]	N.L.	N.L.	5 St. 65' 34,200	3 St. 40' 22,500	2 St. 30' 14,400	3 St. 40' 19,800	2 St. 30' 14,400	3 St. 40' 21,600	1 St. 20' 15,300	1 St. 20' 7,200
F Factory and industrial[h]	N.L.	N.L.	6 St. 75' 22,800	4 St. 50' 15,000	2 St. 30' 9,600	3 St. 40' 13,200	2 St. 30' 9,600	4 St. 50' 14,400	2 St. 30' 10,200	1 St. 20' 4,800
H High hazard[e]	5 St. 65' 16,800	3 St. 40' 14,400	3 St. 40' 11,400	2 St. 30' 7,500	1 St. 20' 4,800	2 St. 30' 6,600	1 St. 20' 4,800	2 St. 30' 7,200	1 St. 20' 5,100	N.P.
I-1 Institutional, residential care	N.L.	N.L.	9 St. 100' 19,950	4 St. 50' 13,125	3 St. 40' 8,400	4 St. 50' 11,550	3 St. 40' 8,400	4 St. 50' 12,600	3 St. 40' 8,925	2 St. 35' 4,200
I-2 Institutional, incapacitated	N.L.	8 St. 90' 21,600	4 St. 50' 17,100	2 St. 30' 11,250	1 St. 20' 7,200	1 St. 20' 9,900	N.P.	1 St. 20' 10,800	1 St. 20' 7,650	N.P.
I-3 Institutional, restrained	N.L.	6 St. 75' 18,000	4 St. 50' 14,250	2 St. 30' 9,375	1 St. 20' 6,000	2 St. 30' 8,250	1 St. 20' 6,000	2 St. 30' 9,000	1 St. 20' 6,375	N.P.
M Mercantile	N.L.	N.L.	6 St. 75' 22,800	4 St. 50' 15,000	2 St. 30' 9,600	3 St. 40' 13,200	2 St. 30' 9,600	4 St. 50' 14,400	2 St. 30' 10,200	1 St. 20' 4,800
R-1 Residential, hotels	N.L.	N.L.	9 St. 100' 22,800	4 St. 50' 15,000	3 St. 40' 9,600	4 St. 50' 13,200	3 St. 40' 9,600	4 St. 50' 14,400	3 St. 40' 10,200	2 St. 35' 4,800
R-2 Residential, multi-family	N.L.	N.L.	9 St. 100' 22,800	4 St. 50' 15,000[f]	3 St. 40' 9,600	4 St. 50' 13,200[f]	3 St. 40' 9,600	4 St. 50' 14,400	3 St. 40' 10,200	2 St. 35' 4,800
R-3 Residential, one and two family	N.L.	N.L.	4 St. 50' 22,800	4 St. 50' 15,000	3 St. 40' 9,600	4 St. 50' 13,200	3 St. 40' 9,600	4 St. 50' 14,400	3 St. 40' 10,200	2 St. 35' 4,800
S-1 Storage, moderate	N.L.	N.L.	5 St. 65' 19,950	4 St. 50' 13,125	2 St. 30' 8,400	3 St. 40' 11,550	2 St. 30' 8,400	4 St. 50' 12,600	2 St. 30' 8,925	1 St. 20' 4,200
S-2 Storage, low[g]	N.L.	N.L.	7 St. 85' 34,200	5 St. 65' 22,500	3 St. 40' 14,400	4 St. 50' 19,800	3 St. 40' 14,400	5 St. 65' 21,600	3 St. 40' 15,300	2 St. 30' 7,200
U Utility, miscellaneous	N.L.	N.L.								

[a] See the following sections for general exceptions to Table 501:
  Section 501.4 Allowable area reduction for multi-story buildings.
  Section 502.2 Allowable area increase due to street frontage.
  Section 502.3 Allowable area increase due to automatic fire suppression system installation.
  Section 503.1 Allowable height increase due to automatic fire suppression system installation.
  Section 504.0 Unlimited area one-story buildings.
[b] Buildings of Type 1 construction permitted to be of unlimited tabular heights and areas are not subject to special requirements that allow increased heights and areas for other types of construction (see Section 501.5).
[c] For tabular area increase in buildings of Use Group E, see Section 502.4.
[d] For height exceptions for auditoriums in buildings of Use Groups A-4 and E, see Section 503.2.
[e] For exceptions to height and area limitations for buildings of Use Group H, see Article 6 governing the specific use. For other special fireresistive requirements governing specific uses, see Section 905.0.
[f] For exceptions to height of buildings for Use Group R-2 of Types 2B and 3A construction, see Section 905.2.
[g] For height and area exceptions for open parking structures, see Section 607.0.
[h] For exceptions to height and area limitations for special industrial uses, see Section 501.1.1.
[i] 1 foot = 304.8 mm; 1 square foot = 0.093 m^2.
[j] Copyright by the Building Officials & Code Administrators International, Inc.

Table 3. Percent Reduction of Area Limits[a]

No. of Stories	Type of Construction		
	1A & 1B	2A	2B, 2C, 3A, 3B, 4, 5A, 5B
1	None	None	None
2	None	None	None
3	None	5%	20%
4	None	10%	20%
5	None	15%	30%
6	None	20%	40%
7	None	25%	50%
8	None	30%	60%
9	None	35%	70%
10	None	40%	80%

[a] Copyright by the Building Officials & Code Administrators International, Inc.

Table 4. Fire Grading of Use Groups[a]

Use Group		Fire Grading in Hours
A-1	Assembly, theaters	3
A-2	Assembly, night clubs	3
A-3	Assembly, recreation centers, lecture halls, terminals, restaurants	2
A-4	Assembly, churches	1½
B	Business	2
E	Educational	1½
F	Factory and industrial	3
H	High hazard	4
I-1	Institutional, residential care	1
I-2	Institutional, incapacitated	2
I-3	Institutional, restrained	3
M	Mercantile	3
R-1	Residential, hotels	2
R-2	Residential, multi-family dwellings	1½
R-3	Residential, 1- and 2-family dwellings	1
S-1	Storage, moderate hazard	3
S-2	Storage, low hazard	2

[a] Copyright by the Building Officials & Code Administrators International, Inc.

combustible liquids storage, liquified petroleum gas facilities, mobile units, paint spraying and spray booths, radio and television towers, antennae, swimming pools, and temporary structures.

Article 7—Interior Environmental Requirements

This section of the code addresses light and ventilation. The use of natural light is defined, to be matched by artificial lighting if natural lighting is not available. Similarly, natural ventilation called for may be replaced by following provisions of the mechanical code listed in the appendices. Minimum room dimensions are given, and ventilation requirements for roof rafter and attic areas, and crawl spaces defined. Courts used for lighting and ventilation have minimum dimensions, and access for cleaning. Similar requirements are listed for rear yards. Window cleaning safeguards are required for buildings over four stories or 50 feet where windows must be cleaned from the outside. Sound transmission control in residential buildings are to meet Sound Transmission Class (STC) ratings given, and appropriate standards referenced for testing of walls, partitions, and floor/ceiling assemblies.

Article 8—Means of Egress

Requirements for egress are based on the occupant load ranging from 3 sq. ft per person for standing space to 300 sq. ft per occupant for storage areas, mechanical equipment rooms. Location of exits, capacity of stairways, doors, ramps, corridors, and number of exits are defined. Components of exit facilities are defined in considerable detail including exit signs and lighting.

Article 9—Fire Resistive Construction

Table 4 shows the fire hazard classification by use group [4].

Testing requirements are based on standards referenced in the appendices. Requirements for exterior walls and exterior opening protection, fire walls, party walls and openings through them, fire separation walls, and smoke barriers are important sections. Fire resistance of structural members, requirements for fire ratings of floors, roofs, ceiling assemblies apply to the type of construction. Roof construction, including roof structures, is a separate section. A large part of the article relates to fire rated vertical shafts, fire doors, windows and shutters, fire dampers and the use of plaster to achieve fire resistance. Firestopping, draftstopping, and permissible combustible materials are clarified. Decorative material, exterior trim, ratings for thermal and sound insulating materials, construction of plenum spaces, and smoke and heat vents are specified. Restrictions on single-family residential construction are also listed.

Article 10—Fire Protection Systems

Fire suppression systems are required for most buildings other than one and two family houses with exceptions for small buildings. Since fire potential varies with the hazard, the code establishes three classes, as shown in Table 5 [5].

The various types of suppression systems are specified with reference to appropriate standards: water, foam, carbon dioxide, halogenated, dry chemical and wet chemical. Standpipe systems, fire department connections, water supply, and yard hydrants are described. Fire protective signaling systems, automatic fire detection, and smoke control systems are described as supervision centers as specified in NFPA standards listed in the appendices. Approved portable fire extinguishers are also described as required for certain functions, such as commercial kitchens with exhaust hoods.

Article 11—Structural Loads

This article describes the safe loading on structure, defining live loads, dead loads, and concentrated loads. The lowest live load per square foot is 20 lb in unoccupied attics, to 250 lb for sidewalks and vehicular driveways subject to trucking and heavy storage facilities. In an office building, the office space is rated at 50 lb except for corridors (100 lb) and file and computer rooms (80 lb). Contruction should allow for concentrated loading, in of-

Table 5. Guide for Suppression System Selection[b]

Hazard	Water Sprinklers or Spray 1004.0 to 1006.0	Foam 1007.0	Carbon Dioxide or Halogenated 1008.0 to 1009.0	Dry Chemical 1010.0	Wet Chemical 1011.0
Class A fire potential	X	X	X	X	X
Class B fire potential	X	X	X	X	X
Class C fire potential	X		X		
Special Fire Hazard Areas[a]					
Aircraft hangars	X	X	X	X	
Alcohol storage	X	X	X	X	
Ammunition loading	X				
Ammunition magazines	X				
Asphalt impregnating	X	X			
Battery rooms			X		
Carburetor overhaul shops	X	X	X	X	
Cleaning plant equipment	X	X	X	X	
Computer rooms	X		X		
Dowtherm	X				
Drying ovens	X		X	X	
Engine test cells	X	X	X		
Escalator, stair wells	X				
Explosives: manufacturing, storage	X				
Flammable liquids storage	X	X	X		
Flammable solids storage	X				
Fuel oil storage	X	X			
Hangar decks	X	X			
High piled storage in excess of 15 feet in height	X	X			
HPM use facility:					
Fabrication areas (Ordinary Hazard Group 3)	X				
Service passages (Ordinary Hazard Group 3)	X				
Separate inside HPM storage rooms without dispensing (Ordinary Hazard Group 3)	X				
Separate inside HPM storage rooms with dispensing (Extra Hazard Group 2)	X				
Egress corridors (Ordinary Hazard Group 3)	X				
Hydraulic oil, lubricating oil	X		X		
Hydroturbine generators	X		X		
Jet engine test cells	X	X	X		
Library stacks	X		X		
Lignite storage and handling	X				
Liquefied petroleum gas storage	X				
Oil quenching bath	X	X	X	X	
Paints: manufacturing, storage	X	X	X	X	
Paint spray booths	X		X	X	
Petrochemical storage	X	X	X		
Petroleum testing laboratories	X	X	X		
Printing presses	X		X		
Rack and palletized storage in excess of 12 feet (3658 mm) in height	X	X			
Range hoods	X		X	X	X
Reactor and fractionating towers	X				
Record vaults	X		X		
Rubber mixing and heat treating	X				
Service stations (inside buildings)	X		X		
Shipboard storage	X		X		
Solvent cleaning tanks		X	X	X	
Solvent thinned coatings		X	X	X	
Switchgear rooms			X		
Transformers, circuit breakers (outdoors)	X				
Transformers, circuit breakers (indoors)	X		X		
Turbine lubricating oil	X	X	X	X	
Vegetable oil, solvent extraction	X	X			

[a] Within buildings or areas, so classified, as to require a suppression system.
[b] Copyright by the Building Officials & Code Administrators International, Inc.

fices, 2000 lb. Impact loads are critical where moving equipment is used, as for elevators, and for grandstands where lateral sway bracing in necessary. Special loading must be accommodated in structural design. Examples given include retaining walls, hydrostatic uplift, construction and erection loading, guardrails, and handrails. Roof loading involves wind, snow, and seismic forces. The code contains a series of maps defining snow, wind, and seismic zones. The code defines required calculations for use in structural design.

Article 12—Foundation Systems and Retaining Walls

The code controls foundation design and construction, with regard to safe support of loading in addition to weight of the foundation. The code requires investigation and testing of soil bearing capacity to establish allowable loading. Rock bearing, depth of footings below grade to avoid freezing and other common conditions. Footing design includes design load, lateral loads, earthquake loads, vibratory loads, and varying unit pressures. Timber footings and wood foundations are allowed for one or two family structures if the wood is properly pressure treated in accordance with standards referenced. Steel grillage, concrete footings, masonry unit footings, mat, raft and float foundations, pier and piles are controlled. Allowable loading on piles is described, and controls are placed on steel, concrete-filled steel pipe and tube, cast-in-place, precast concrete, timber composite piles and caisson piles.

Foundation walls, and retaining walls are controlled. The code requires waterproofing, dampproofing, and footing drains for basements and below grade spaces on walls and under slabs, with certain exceptions.

Article 13—Materials and Tests

The article requires testing for materials not listed in the code. Used materials may be reused if they meet code requirements. The code official may require testing for safe loading, strength, durability, maintenance, and performance. Fire tests may be required. Standards exist for most building products, but new materials and assemblies will be tested. Approvals shall be in writing, with conditions as defined in the code. Articles 14 through 20 govern materials, design, construction, and quality for buildings.

Article 14—Masonry

The masonry article describes brick, structural clay, tile, glazed masonry units, concrete masonry units, terra cotta, natural and cast stone, mortars, and grouts for masonry construction. Masonry wall construction, bonding, lateral bracing, chases and recesses in bearing walls, and waterproofing of chases are required provisions. Corbeled and projected masonry is limited. Provisions are made for bearing on hollow masonry unit walls, and reference is made to standards for engineered unreinforced masonry, reinforced masonry, and unreinforced masonry. Use of structural glass block is defined. Isolated piers and dry-stacked, surface bonded masonry walls are allowed.

Article 15—Concrete

Concrete considerations include seismic design provisions, materials used, quality of concrete. The standards of the American Concrete Institute (ACI) are referenced for all concrete work, and ASTM standards for ready mixed concrete. Sections cover formwork, embedded pipes and construction joints, details of reinforcement, concrete-filled pipe columns, shotcrete, and minimum slab thickness.

Article 16—Gypsum and Plaster

In general, this section requires compliance with listed standards of the American Society for Testing and Materials (ASTM). This covers interior lathing and gypsum plaster, cement stucco lath and plaster, gypsum board, and gypsum board and plaster systems.

Article 17—Wood

The National Forest Products Association "National Design Specification for Wood Construction" establishes structural wood and connections standards. Wood systems and materials controlled by code include heavy timber, light wood framing including sheathing, stressed skin panels, glued-laminated timber and built up wood construction, fiberboard, plywood, and particle board. Pressure-treated wood use is specified in the code.

Article 18—Steel

Steel materials and use is referenced to the American Institute of Steel Construction (AISC) "Specification for the Design, Fabrication and Erection of Structural Steel for Buildings" or the AISC "Load and Resistance Factor Design Specification for Structural Steel Buildings." The code addresses formed steel construction, open web steel joist construction, reinforcing steel, cast steel, cast iron; and special steel and steel cable structural systems. Many standards listed in the appendices relate to these products and systems, as referenced in this article.

Article 19—Lightweight Metal Alloys

This section concerns aluminum, but other metals are covered. Appropriate standards of the Aluminum Association (AA) are referenced.

Article 20—Plastic

Approved materials include light-transmitting plastics and foam plastics. Concerns are strength, durability, sanitation and fire resistive attributes of plastics used.

Article 21—Exterior Walls

This article addresses general construction requirements, referring to other articles, and includes a section on flood-resistant construction, ratproofing, weather protection, wall panels, metal, masonry, thin stone and tile and structural glass veneers.

Article 22—Vertical and Sloped Glass and Glazing

This section concerns glass supports, dimensional tolerances, wind load, safety and sloped glazing, and skylights. Limits are placed on the use of plastic glazing, glass in handrails and guardrails, glazing for racquetball and squash courts.

Article 23—Roofs and Roof Coverings

Limitations on use of various roofing products are included in this article. Roof coverings are classified in three classes of fire safety plus unclassified materials suitable for one or two family residential units. Wood shingles, asphalt shingles, flashing, fastening, light transmitting plastic roof panels are specifically addressed.

Article 24—Masonry Fireplaces

This article describes fire safety aspects of masonry fireplace construction, and structural support of the chimney.

Article 25—Mechanical Equipment and Systems

The code includes by reference the National Mechanical Code. Specific requirements include drying rooms or dry kilns, waste and linen handing systems, refuse vaults, dust, stock and refuse conveyor systems, medical gases and oxygen systems.

Article 26—Elevator, Dumbwaiter and Conveyor Equipment, Installation and Maintenance

The code includes by reference the *Safety Code for Elevators, Dumbwaiters, Escalators and Moving Walks*, published by the American Society of Mechanical Engineers (ASME). Specific building code requirements relate to maintenance and accidents, existing elevator installations, alterations, power elevator operation, hoistway enclosures and venting, elevator opening protection, emergency signals and signs, manlifts, industrial lifts and loading ramps, automotive lifts, conveyors, and escalator fire safety.

Article 27—Electrical Wiring, Equipment and Systems

The building code includes by reference *the National Electric Code* published by the National Fire Protection Association (NFPA). Specific code requirements include inspection and tests, temporary use, need for permits and inspection, defective wiring, additional loads in existing buildings, emergency electrical systems, and power standby systems.

Article 28—Plumbing Systems

The building code includes by reference *the National Plumbing Code* published by BOCA. Additional code requirements include sewer and water supply data, permits and certificates of approval, water supply systems, existing buildings and installations, plumbing fixture surrounds, and private sewage disposal systems.

Article 29—Signs

Permits are required for the erection of signs. The provisions regard proper support and safety of exterior signs. Maintenance, bonds and liability insurance are required. Lighted signs are to be certified in compliance with the NFPA National Electric Code.

Article 30—Precautions During Building Operations

This article addresses permits, tests, inspection and maintenance of equipment, and safeguards on the construction site. Special provisions are made for existing buildings, protection of public and workers, demolition and excavation, empty lots to be filled to level of the street, and capping of utility connections.

Requirements are included for retaining walls and partition fences, storage of materials, removal of waste material, and protection of adjoining property. Scaffolds, hoists, stairways and ladders, temporary lighting, fire and health hazards, welding safety precautions, and sanitation facilities regulations are described. The last section concerns resolution of disputes caused by acts of the building official.

Article 31—Energy Conservation

The provisions in this section are covered in more detail in the *Model Energy Code* published by the Council of American Building Officials (CABO) referenced in the appendices. In general provisions comply with ASHRAE 90A: Energy Conservation in New Building Design. Code provisions address exterior building requirements, electrical and mechanical systems and water heating. There is a provision for alternative systems which meet the energy consumption for a building of the same size as defined by code regulations.

Article 32—Repair, Alteration, Addition to and Change of Use of Existing Buildings

Concerns in this section of the code relate to fire safety, and evaluation of existing buildings. Code conformance is required for buildings where unsafe conditions exist, or where changes in use occur. A minimum requirement is to provide for the handicapped, even if no other changes are required. Evaluation of existing buildings is on the basis of building scores and evaluation formulas.

List of Appendices

Appendices list referenced and related standards, as well as information on unit dead loads, unit working stresses for ordinary materials and recommended fastening schedules. Metric equivalents have been added as an appendix to the model codes.

CONCLUSION

The increased technical complication of construction has resulted in a continuous annual review of the model building codes, which can no longer be considered in a fixed state. Refer to *An Architect's Guide to Building Codes &*

Standards for the revision process for each of the model codes. The need for building research is a necessary adjunct to the code process. Review of long standing provisions suggest that some basic assumptions are being rethought. Computer programs have been developed to assist in code searches, and it can be expected that more automation will enter into code writing, compliance and review.

BIBLIOGRAPHY

1. *The BOCA National Building Code*, 1987 ed., Building Officials & Code Administrators International, Inc., Country Club Hills, Inc., pp. 56–57.
2. *Ibid.*, pp. 62–63.
3. Ref. 1, p. 63.
4. Ref. 1, p. 168.
5. Ref. 1, pp. 208–209.

General References

An Architect's Guide to Building Codes & Standards, The American Institute of Architects, Washington, D.C., 1988.

The BOCA National Building Code, Building Officials & Code Administrators International, Inc., Country Club Hills, Ill.

Standard Building Codes, Southern Building Code Congress International (SBCCI), Birmingham, Ala.,

Uniform Building Codes, International Conference of Building Officials (ICBO), Whittier, Calif.

See also Acrylics; Adaptive Use; Aluminum; Atrium Buildings; Baths; Brick Masonry; Cold Wet Climate, Building in; Concrete—Architectural; Concrete Forming; Concrete—General Principles; Concrete—Lightweight Aggregates; Concrete Masonry; Concrete—Posttensioning; Concrete—Prestressed; Concrete—Admixtures, Curing and Testing; Construction Industry; Electrical Equipment; Electrical Principles; Electrical Systems; Envelopes, Building; Fireplaces; Fire Safety—Life Safety; Flood Plains, Coastal Area Construction; Foamed Plastics; Foundation Systems; Glass in Construction; Kitchens, Residential; Mechanical Systems; Moisture Protection; Movement of People; Pest Control; Plastics; Plumbing Systems; Polycarbonates; Precast Architectural Concrete; Preservation, Historic; Restaurant and Service Kitchens; Roofing Materials; Seismic Design; Signing—Environmental Graphics; Solar and Energy Efficient Design; Steel In Construction; Structural Steel; Vertical Transportation; Wallboard and Plaster Systems; Wood in Construction; Wood, Structural Panel Composites

ROBERT T. PACKARD, AIA
Reston, Virginia

RESTAURANT AND SERVICE KITCHENS

Food service is unique as a large industry because it combines both the service and the manufacturing sectors of industry. Whereas most goods are manufactured at one place, sold at a second place, and consumed in a third place, the modern hotel, restaurant, or institutional food operation accomplishes all three of these functions in one place. As an added challenge, food service people must handle a perishable product served to an ever-changing number of people. To manufacture, sell, and serve a perishable product to be consumed on the premises to a changing number of people requires highly specialized equipment and dedicated, hard-working people.

The hospitality industry has demonstrated a steady pattern of growth over the past 40 years. The number of restaurants, fast-food chains, and hotels continues to increase, together with the number of meals eaten out of the home by each person in the United States. The pattern of increase has been a 1–1.5% increase per year of out-of-the-home meals for the past 20 years. The public shows little apparent resistance to paying for the convenience of eating a meal away from home, even when the economy is on a downswing. Although several years in the 1970s and 1980s saw no net growth, the food service industry as a whole showed a rising trend in food sales in hotels, restaurants, and institutions over the long term.

This growth requires owners and managers of all types of food service facilities to construct new food outlets and to renovate their existing operations on an ongoing basis. Even during the recession of 1982, construction and renovation projects in many food companies continued at a brisk pace. Large corporations such as Marriott, Hyatt, Sheraton, McDonalds, Burger King, and others continued to add food facilities and to renovate old ones during such periods. Even in the best of times, owners and managers are faced with the need to control increased energy, labor, and operating costs while continuing to maintain high standards of quality for their guests. The steady growth of the food service industry combined with a need to control costs through more efficient facilities has created a continuing demand for well-designed food operations.

HISTORY

Dining away from home has a proud history. There were wayside inns that fed the traveler even in ancient times. On a different level, there have been the feeding of industrial and office workers, school and college food service, and fine dining in restaurants and hotels. Fast-food, health-care food service, and numerous other dining segments of the food service industry are far removed from the wayside inn. Mass feeding away from home has always required special equipment and supplies and methods of efficient and economical operation.

The food service equipment business began in sheet metal shops. These firms had among their personnel workers experienced with cooking and serving food as it was done in Europe. Many were chefs who came to the United States and saw an opportunity to develop a kitchen equipment business based on their European experience. Thus most of the early firms had sheet metal shops as the foundation of their business.

Food service was simple in the early 1800s and was patterned after basic home feeding. Because restaurants had to produce food in volume, there was a need for worktables and large sinks that would allow ample work space. Large copper-jacketed kettles, heavy iron skillets, *bains marie* (hot water containers for keeping food hot), and similar equipment that would be judged primitive by today's standards were the prevailing standard.

During the early years, kitchen equipment firms not only built the equipment, but also planned the kitchen layouts and installed every item of equipment. Over the years, equipment was constantly improved for greater efficiency. Also, it was made more attractive through the use of copper and blue steel in designs that made each firm's products distinctive and easily recognizable.

At first, kitchen equipment was custom-made and built as heavy as possible to withstand hard wear. In time, standards were developed as to size, weight, and construction to meet service requirements. This standardization made possible volume production that reduced costs and assured quicker deliveries.

Mass-production manufacturing provided greater production efficiency through standardization. Equipment could be sold to a dealer below what it would cost the dealer to make it.

At the start, there was some resistance by dealers to this loss of their manufacturing volume. Some dealers responded by improving their own production methods and continued to manufacture their own products. Eventually, dealers came to accept the reality of lower costs and faster deliveries and began buying from manufacturers such items as ranges, dishwashers, jacketed kettles, mixers, etc, each of which carried the manufacturer's brand.

In the early 1900s the principal kitchen equipment firms were located in the East. They were able to make installations almost anywhere in the country, although they stayed mainly east of the Rocky Mountains. Often, they were called upon by customers in distant cities who knew these firms from past experience and wanted their equipment and services for other locations. There were also a few kitchen equipment firms west of the Rockies and on the Pacific coast that provided similar service to their customers.

EARLY FOOD SERVICE EQUIPMENT COMPANIES

Listed below are brief historical sketches of some of the firms that laid the foundations of the food service equipment industry.

L. Barth & Co. Leopold Barth started his business in New York City in 1868 with a pushcart selling kitchen utensils. He opened a basement store in Manhattan dealing in pots, pans, and crockery. His son Harry joined the firm and expanded the line to include hotel and restaurant equipment and supplies. The L. Barth Co. opened the first full-line dealership and installed many food service facilities in New York and in the eastern part of the United States.

W. F. Dougherty and Sons, Inc. W. F. Dougherty started his firm in Philadelphia, Pa., in 1852. His son William took over the firm and engaged in selling and some manufacturing of equipment. The firm installed many large and complex kitchens, such as those of the Columbia Presbyterian Medical Center in New York City and the Pennsylvania State Farm Show at Harrisburg. The Harrisburg installation was the largest food facility under one roof in the world at the time of its installation.

Straus-Duparquet. X. F. Duparquet came to the United States from France in 1840 and opened a kitchen equipment shop in 1852 in New York City. Many of the pieces of equipment, such as ranges, coffee urns, cast-iron kettles, and refrigerators, were manufactured by the company. After a few years, the firm became the Duparquet, Huot & Moneuse Co. The firm prospered, selling equipment in Europe and the United States, but during the Depression was sold to a large dealer in New York, Nathan Straus & Co.

Albert Pick & Co. This once-great firm was founded in 1857 as Pick, Block & Joel, a supply house that catered principally to saloons. Albert Pick, Sr. joined his uncle's firm in 1893 and introduced many innovations to the company's operations. Then, in 1900, he and several associates acquired financial control of the company and changed its name to Albert Pick & Co. The firm was located in Chicago, Ill.

The great hotel boom of the 1920s led to further expansion, with salespersons covering 34 states selling equipment, supplies, furniture, and furnishings. The company backed them with a large kitchen engineering staff and several factories producing kitchen equipment, wood fixtures, silverware, and refrigerators.

In 1926, Pick acquired the John Van Range Co. and then L. Barth & Co. of New York. The crash of 1929 brought the end of the hotel boom, and the end of the merged Pick-Barth soon followed.

Ruslander & Sons, Inc. This firm started as a partnership in 1888. The name was A. S. Ruslander & Son, and it was located in Buffalo, N.Y. It manufactured hand-hammered copper cooking utensils. In 1904, E. M. Statler, of Statler Hotel fame, prevailed upon Levi Ruslander, son of A. S., to develop and manufacture a line of custom-built kitchen equipment for hotels and restaurants. In appreciation, the firm enjoyed a considerable volume of business from the Statler Hotels for many years thereafter.

The company has continued to grow and prosper under the direction of Harold S. Ruslander, the third generation. He has been active in industry betterment, and also was active in the early years with the National Sanitation Foundation (NSF) and the development of the Food Facilities Course at Cornell University.

John Van Range Co. John Van started business in Canada in 1837. He moved to Cincinnati, Ohio, in 1847. His principal products were wood- and coal-burning stoves for domestic and commercial use and a line of army ranges. The company developed the steel range, which replaced the cast-iron range. Later, it added portable bake ovens, coffee urns, hand-hammered copperware, kettles, and other items.

At the height of its operations, the company had offices in six major cities. The company was acquired by the Albert Pick and Pick-Barth operation, an arrangement which continued until 1932, when the company reverted to its original operation.

FOOD SERVICE EQUIPMENT ASSOCIATIONS

Food Service Equipment Industry, Inc. (FSEI). In 1933, the National Industrial Recovery Act (later called the NRA) was passed. It required every industry to organize and to draft its own code of operation. This was to be supervised by a government administrator. A Chicago attorney, Henry S. Blum, who did considerable work with hotels and restaurants, notified the Chicago dealers about this NRA requirement. He suggested they organize as an industry rather than run the risk of having the government assign them arbitrarily to a category that would not be properly representative of them.

A national meeting of food service equipment dealers was held in Chicago in June 1933. They formed FSEI to comply with the NRA requirements. Officers were elected, and an Illinois charter was granted. After 14 months (in May 1935), the NRA was declared unconstitutional by the Supreme Court. At that time, FSEI had about 150 members. When the NRA went out of existence, about 50 members resigned. In 1946, FSEI began its cooperation with the NSF to develop and maintain industry standards of sanitation, encouraging the use of corrosion-resistant materials and establishing fabrication practices that would make equipment easier to clean and improve from a sanitation point of view. More than 300 manufacturers now operate according to these standards, and their equipment bears the NSF seal of approval.

In 1957, in cooperation with food service consultant J. Earle Stephens of Stephens-Bangs Associates, FSEI helped establish a food facilities engineering course at Cornell University's School of Hotel Administration, under the direction of H. B. Meek. The purpose was to train people for the kitchen equipment field. From 1958 to 1971, this grew to a series of successful courses under the direction of O. Ernest Bangs. He was succeeded by Paul Broten. Facilities engineering is now an integral part of the school's curriculum so that all graduates may have a better understanding of kitchen equipment problems.

National Association of Food Equipment Manufacturers (NAFEM). In 1948, a group of manufacturers organized NAFEM. In its early years, NAFEM was concerned with problems of distribution, trade shows, credit policies, and other matters referring to its business with dealers. The headquarters was first in the East, but was later moved to Chicago, where NAFEM's affairs were handled by a trade association management firm. NAFEM is now recognized as a leader among associations in the food service equipment field.

Food Facilities Consultants Society (FFCS). This society was organized in 1955 under the leadership of Fred Schmid, one of the country's top consultants, and others who felt the need to establish standards in the plumbing, designing, and engineering of all types of public feeding facilities. The organization was first named the Food Facilities Engineering Society. The current name was adopted in 1969.

One of the conditions of membership in the FFCS is that no member have any connection with the manufacture or sale of products. Thus there is no competition with fabricators or dealers on jobs planned by members of the society.

International Society of Food Service Consultants (ISFSC). The strict membership requirements of the FFCS (limited to independent consultants) eliminate kitchen engineers working for food service equipment dealers, manufacturers, or other firms. Recognizing the need for a professional organization for such people, Harry R. Friedman, a Florida kitchen designer, helped form such an organization in October 1957.

Food Service Consultants Society International (FCSI). In 1980, the FFCS and ISFSC were merged to form FCSI. FCSI now includes a broad range of consulting professionals, engaged in food facilities design, management advisory services, interior design, and other special areas of expertise related to the food service industry. The international office of the society is located in Seattle, Wash.

National Sanitation Foundation (NSF). The NSF was conceived by Walter F. Snyder in 1944. His first efforts were with the food and beverage industries.

In 1948, in cooperation with the University of Michigan School of Public Health, Snyder, representing the NSF, invited 250 representatives from various branches of industry and an equal number of regulatory agencies to meet at the university.

This started the foundation on its long road of standards development. Such standards were to assist manufacturers in planning the design and manufacture of items that would be sanitary and easily cleaned. Each group conducted meetings over a long period of time to establish standards acceptable to public health officials, sanitarians, and industry.

The NSF is now located in its own building in Ann Arbor, Mich., where it has offices and testing laboratories. Its efforts have made great contributions to better health and sanitation, and the NSF seal of approval is a recognized standard throughout the entire food service equipment industry.

PRELIMINARY PLANNING

The Scope of a Project

The size and complexity of the project greatly influence the design approach taken by the architect, owner, or manager. If the project involves only the layout of a new hot food production area for an existing restaurant, the approach used and the planning process are fairly simple. If the project entails the construction of a new restaurant or the complete renovation of an existing facility, the planning process becomes more difficult. And if the project includes the construction of a new facility that is to serve as the prototype for a chain or franchise, the planning process is even more complex.

The scope can be divided into three levels of complexity, each of which requires different individuals' involvement and different amounts of planning time. Determining the scope of the project is an important first step before the planning begins.

Level I
Scope. At this level, the project involves no more than the selection of a principal piece of equipment or the replacement of a small area of a food facility.

Level II
Scope. The project is the construction of a new food facility or a major renovation of an existing facility. The scope and complexity of a new facility can be easily underestimated. At Level II, the planning process for a major renovation may be even more complex than for building a new facility because of the difficulty of dealing with existing walls, structural members, utilities, and space and the demolition of parts of the existing structure. Moreover, decisions must be made about which pieces of existing equipment should or could be used in the newly renovated facility.

Persons Likely to Be Involved. These include architects/engineers, the owner or manager, a food service facilities design consultant, and an interior designer.

Planning Time. A Level II project can take from two months to two years to plan, depending on the size of the project and availability of funds.

Level III
Scope. The development of a chain or franchise prototype, in addition to the considerations relating to Level II projects, involves a corporate strategy, a well-researched marketing plan, complex financial planning, and a strong management team. The food facility design at Level III must fit the needs of the menu, market strategy, and financial package that is being developed by the corporation.

CONCEPT DEVELOPMENT

It is not unusual for a person to consider a new restaurant, or in fact to open a new restaurant, without knowing what type of food facility would have the best chance of succeeding. The potential entrepreneur may have some investment money, a location or theme in mind, and a great amount of enthusiasm for the food business, but may not have really thought through the total concept of the operation. Concept development, applied to the food service industry, means planning a menu, a decor, and a method of serving food in harmony with an identified market to achieve a profitable operation. For the corporation, concept development should also include a strategy for growth and financial return on investment.

Hotel Food and Beverage Concept Development

The development of a food service concept for hotels has evolved in recent years from a philosophy that considered the food and beverage department as a necessary evil to the modern idea that the food and beverage department is an important profit center. Some large hotels have food and beverage sales of over $35 million per year, which exceeds the room sales and creates in management a high expectation of profit from these two departments.

The Hilton Hotel, in Atlanta, Ga., has developed a concept for its first-class rooftop restaurant that goes beyond the idea of food service as a profit center. The restaurant, called Nikolai's Roof, was conceived as a luxury dining room and was marketed to the city of Atlanta as well as to the hotel guest. The decor was exquisite, the food was planned to include a great amount of showmanship, and the entire theme captured the imagination of the residents of the city. The concept was developed with such success that the guests of the hotel had great difficulty getting reservations to dine. The idea that a hotel restaurant would be so overcrowded with guests from the community that it could not serve the guests of the hotel would have been unthinkable in the early days of hotel keeping in the United States. Nikolai's Roof restaurant is an excellent example of the execution of a hotel dining concept that complements the hotel itself and draws a significant number of guests from the community.

Hotel managers have known for many years that hotel restaurants must have certain desirable features if they are to be successful. Some of these features are adequate parking, a unique theme or decor (differing from that of the hotel itself), strong promotion of the restaurant to the community, and a distinctive menu and method of service.

The developers of hotel properties, and in some cases hotel chains, have used outside consultants and outside management companies to create specialty restaurants that are unique and can be successfully marketed to both the hotel guests and the community.

Restaurant Chain and Fast Food Concept Development

The basic ideas developed by Dave Thomas, Chairman of the Board of Wendy's, that led to the formation of Wendy's are presented as an illustration of a fast-food concept.

- Wendy's was to produce a "cadillac" hamburger with a tremendous number of available condiments.
- It limited the menu to the smallest number of items possible and would prepare only a few food items extremely well.
- It created an image that was different from that of the largest competitors. In the case of Wendy's, distinctive features included an old-fashioned nostalgic theme, carpet on the floor, service personnel to clear the tables, marketing to adults, and a hamburger larger in size than the competition's at a lower price per ounce.

The concept development of Wendy's was more comprehensive than that for a single restaurant. The franchise strategy was carefully thought out to create a balance between company-owned stores and franchised stores. In 1970, only two stores were open, both company owned and operated. By 1975, 83 company-owned stores and 169 franchised stores were in operation. A ratio of 30–40% company-owned stores to 60–70% franchised stores permitted a balance of control and greater financial return from company-owned properties.

The Wendy's concept of development included a limited menu, strong market penetration, attractive facilities and decor, corporate control of quality, and planned expansion.

Restaurant chain concept development often follows the same pattern as the Wendy's example, although usually the growth is much less dramatic. Gilbert/Robinson, Inc. and Continental Restaurants, Inc. are two examples of successful restaurant chains that have developed multitheme restaurant concepts. These two companies have several different themes, and each restaurant is promoted in the name of the theme rather than the corporate name. For instance, Continental Restaurants has a series of restaurants named J. Ross Browne's Whaling Station, with a heavy emphasis on seafood. The company also has a series of restaurants called Mountain Jack's that promote prime rib and steaks. The development of these restaurant concepts through excellent marketing, well-planned menus, and good design comes about through the efforts of a sophisticated management team.

Institutional Concept Development

Institutional food service is usually conceived as a service to an organization and most often has a not-for-profit philosophy. Most institutional food operations are expected to break even, and all are expected to budget and operate within well-defined ranges of cost, so that they do not become a financial burden on the organization they serve. In some cases, the institutional food operation is expected to make a profit and to pay for all of its direct and indirect operational costs.

The development of an operational concept for an institution is often ignored, and this is usually a serious mistake. The institution must accurately interpret its market and must sell its products, even when the food is indirectly paid for by the customer. For instance, in hospital food service, an unattractive meal presentation in the patient's room may result in a dissatisfied and complaining patient, and possibly adverse health effects. In a college or university dining hall, a comprehensive concept of service and decor can greatly influence financial success. Attractive cafeteria service or a "scramble" design, for example, can increase the popularity of a college food service operation. A dining facility operated by a corporation for its employees should also have a well-planned concept and decor. The ability of a corporate food service operation to attract employees may influence the degree of subsidy that a company is willing to contribute to the operation.

Individual Restaurant Concept Development

The client who most frequently comes to the architect or the food facilities design consultant for help with concept development is the individual restaurant owner. The restaurant owner typically organizes a corporation composed of a small number of local businesspeople and then begins to develop a concept that will eventually become a free-standing restaurant. The success or failure of the venture often rests on how well the concept is put together during the planning stage and how well the plan is followed.

The Five M's of Concept Development

The successful food services operation combines the following elements of concept development:

- Menu.
- Market.
- Money.
- Management.
- Method of execution.

Menu. The menu has a tremendous influence on the design and success of a good operation. In design and layout considerations, these are just some of the factors determined by the menu:

- Amount of floor space.
- Type and size of seating.
- Method of designing service areas.
- Dishwashing area size and machine capacity.
- Type of cooking equipment.
- Capacity of each piece of cooking equipment.
- Size of refrigeration and storage areas.
- Number of employees.
- Selling price of food.
- Amount of the investment.

Market. Early studies are important before proceeding with the construction of a food facility. The basic marketing questions that must be answered are:

- To whom is the food operation being marketed?
- Is the market large enough to generate sales and produce a profit?
- How will the market be identified?
- What method will be used to communicate to this market?
- Will the potential customer want or need the food product?
- Will a quality assurance plan be developed that will encourage the customer to return because of superior service and/or product quality?
- Will internal marketing successfully sell the customer additional services or products after he/she arrives at the food facility?

A classic mistake that has been made by several large corporations and by numerous individual restaurant operators is to conduct the market analysis and then fail to follow the results. There are several cases in which extensive marketing feasibility studies were conducted by outside marketing firms, but the owners and managers made their decisions on gut feelings rather than from the hard data derived from the study.

Even owners (or potential owners) of food operations who have no marketing background can conduct their own market research, with guidance and common sense. Do-it-yourself marketing and the limitations of this approach are discussed later in this section.

Money. The proper capitalization of a food facility must include funds for:

- Planning costs.
- Building construction or renovation.
- Equipment (fixed).
- China, glassware, and utensils.
- Furniture and fixtures.
- Decor.
- Operating costs.

These funds must be identified and committed before serious planning can begin. In concept development, the commitments may not be made in the early planning stage because the costs are not yet known. Therefore, the planning for capital funds is a two-step process:

1. The financial needs are estimated, and sources of financial support are contacted to determine the possibility of obtaining investment funds.
2. After concept development has taken place, preliminary designs and construction estimates have been made, and market research has been completed, financial commitments can then be made by lenders and investors.

Management. The quality of the management of the food service operation is the most important element in achieving success. The following are typical questions to be addressed by the owners:

- Who will operate the food facility?
- What kind of food experience and educational background must this person have?
- Who will assist this management person in covering the long hours that are usually required to operate a food service facility?
- What kind of pay will this person receive?
- Will this person be rewarded in some way for excellent sales and profit results?
- How will the owners set operational policies and communicate these to the management staff?

The answers to these questions determine the organizational structure and the kind of management team used to operate the food facility.

The successful restaurant often is owned and operated by one person whose personality and personal greeting become a part of the guests' dining experience. On the other hand, the management of a food and beverage facility of a hotel may be under the control of more than one person, and usually is part of a more complex organizational team. In this case, the policies and procedures of the food facility are described in an operations manual so that many different persons can manage under the same management policy.

Method of Execution. The last step in concept development involves operational matters. Certain decisions about operating methods must be made during the concept development phase on matters such as production methods, control systems, and personnel.

Production Methods. Will convenience foods or traditional scratch cookery be used? This decision has a great influence on the size of refrigerated and dry storage areas and on the size of the kitchen. Production methods also determine the number of employees in the kitchen and the skill level of these employees.

Control Systems. Food and beverage controls involve many different parts of the facility, and planning for these controls before the project is under construction is strongly recommended. The following areas of control should be carefully considered:

- Cash control.
- Sales analysis.
- Guest check control.
- Food production forecasting.
- Storeroom and refrigeration control.
- Backdoor security.
- Labor control.
- Purchasing and receiving control.
- Quality control.
- Portion control.

Personnel. The development of financial feasibility studies cannot begin until the amount of labor is known. The employee schedules, operation hours, staffing patterns, staff benefits, skill levels, and level of supervision of employees must all be decided before serious development of the food facility begins. As part of its concept development, the fast-food industry bases its low labor costs on the use of hourly unskilled labor scheduled to work short periods of time. Part-time employees are scheduled to work busy periods. The traditional eight-hour day is seldom used in the fast-food industry, except for supervisors and managers. The use of part-time employees in fast-food restaurants has also significantly reduced the cost of benefits. The use of part-time employees was carefully thought out as part of the concept development in the fast-food industry.

The Go/No-go Decision

After completing market and financial feasibility studies and presenting these to bankers and potential investors, the owners can make a good judgment as to the potential success of the food facility project. Further contacts with zoning boards, liquor license agencies, and other municipal groups bring the project to a point of decision. The accumulation of the data contained in the feasibility studies, together with encouragement or discouragement from lenders, investors, and municipal agencies, leads the owner to the first go/no-go decision. In other words, if the project looks financially sound, the market is identified, a need for the food services exists, and the capital is obtainable, then the decision to go can be made.

If one or more of the elements of the go/no-go decision are uncertain, then there are three alternative courses. The first is to correct the problem area that has been identified. Is the facility too large? Are the labor costs too high? Is the menu wrong for the market? Is the competition too strong in the immediate trading area?

The second option is to abandon the project and look for another place to invest the funds. The third alternative is to delay the decision until the final go/no-go decision. This alternative is financially risky because to progress from this point costs money for food service facilities design consultants, architects, lawyers, accountants, and other professionals.

The following section describes some of the professionals needed to ensure a successful food service project.

Design and Planning Professionals

Preliminary planning needs to be accomplished on most projects with those who are trained as professional planners. The alternatives to the engagement of professional planners for the renovation or construction of a food service facility are

- To buy a franchise package that has been planned by a large corporation. A high percentage of successful food operations have been opened through franchising because of the excellent guidance available before construction and the tested management methods that are imposed by the franchising company.
- To purchase or lease an existing facility and "do it yourself." This alternative is often chosen and is one of the reasons for the high bankruptcy rate for restaurants.
- To construct a food facility with the help of a building contractor, a small amount of money, and a great amount of enthusiasm. This alternative is also often chosen and often results in failure.
- To plan food services facilities with the service of an architect, but without the use of a food service facilities design consultant. This alternative is frequently selected in an effort to save money. The architect may design the food facility in his or her own firm or ask an equipment dealer to submit a layout. This alternative can cost the client many thousands of dollars in poor layout, improper equipment selection or inefficiency in operations.

Cost Justification for Professional Planners

How much will it cost to retain an architect or food service facilities consultant, and how can the cost of these services

be justified? These are questions frequently asked by those who are contemplating a major food service project. These same questions are also asked by the restaurateur or food service director who is thinking of refurbishing a department in the kitchen or rearranging a service area. To answer these questions, the prospective owner or manager should consider the cost of a single piece of kitchen equipment. A double-deck convection oven might cost approximately $5,500, or a walk-in refrigerator/freezer may cost $15,000–25,000, depending on the size and finish. A hood over the range section of a medium-sized kitchen may cost $30,000–45,000, depending on the size, construction, and features specified. If the cost of the hood is calculated by the foot, the cost is

$$\$30,000 : 20\text{-ft hood} = \$1,500 \text{ per linear foot}$$

A compact arrangement for the equipment under the hood could save 4 or 5 linear feet of hood construction. The correct size and shape of the walk-in refrigerator/freezer could reduce the needed refrigeration and floor space by 20%. Selection of the correct amount of oven capacity and the most efficient use of floor space occupied by a compact oven could reduce the size of the kitchen. In this example, the savings to the client might be

Hood	$ 6,000
Walk-in: 20% × $20,000	$ 4,000
Oven: One compact convection rather than two	$ 5,500
Savings in floor space: 70 ft² × 100/ft	
(construction cost)	$ 7,000
Total Savings	*$22,500*

The fee for the food service facilities consultant is usually computed on an hourly basis and often ranges between 6 and 10% of the cost of the equipment. On a food service project with equipment costs of $200,000, the fee would be between $12,000 and $20,000. As illustrated in the example, it takes few errors in a kitchen design to waste this amount of money. The financial loss that comes about through poor design in labor, maintenance, and other operational costs cannot easily be estimated. The loss of funds through a failure to develop proper specifications, resulting in the purchase of equipment at a high price, is also difficult to estimate.

The value received from a professional food facilities design consultant can be summarized as follows:

- Savings in operational costs as a result of layout and design efficiencies.
- Savings in equipment costs as a result of proper selection.
- Savings in construction costs as a result of the efficient use of space.
- Savings in purchase price as a result of properly written specifications and bid documents.

Professional Planners

The scope of the project, as described earlier in this article (Level I, II, or III), requires different professional people to assist in the planning. The specialists who are usually associated with the development of a food facility are

Specialists	Scope of Project		
	Level I	Level II	Level III
Food service facilities design consultants		X	X
Architects	X	X	X
Engineers	X	X	X
Interior designers		X	X
Bankers		X	X
Lawyers		X	X
Accountants		X	X
Equipment dealers	X	X	X
Manufacturers' representatives	X		
Realtors		X	X
General contractors		X	X
Subcontractors	X	X	X

Some of the professional people who play an important part in the planning process are discussed below. (Other specialists are consulted on specific planning aspects, but do not play a central role.) The food service facility design consultant's role is described in some detail below.

Architects

The professional architect is licensed to practice in the state where he or she works. The architect should be selected carefully because of the complexity of the process of designing, bidding, and constructing a commercial building. Architects are often specialists in one segment of the construction industry, such as home or industrial or commercial structures. Experience in working with large commercial buildings is important in working on a food facility. It is advisable to examine buildings that the architect has designed and to talk with those buildings' owners to gain insight into the quality and detail that can be expected from the architect.

The architect is the person primarily responsible for the design, preparation of specifications, engineering, bidding, construction, and acceptance of a new building or renovated facility. He or she usually engages other professional people, such as engineers, to handle the electrical work, plumbing, heating and air conditioning, structure, and other special aspects of the project.

Interior Designers

For a new facility, the interior design should be discussed first with the architect to determine whether or not this service is included in the architectural fees. If it is not included, the owner must then decide whether or not to use an outside interior designer or the architect. Often, the architect selects all interior building finishes, and an interior designer selects the furniture, draperies, and wall hangings.

One excellent method of finding a good interior designer is to find a restaurant, hotel interior, or institutional food operation that the owner feels is especially attractive and then find out who designed it. Another method is to have several interior designers submit preliminary design sketches and then select the one whose work appeals to the owners. The designer should be told that the presentation to the owner must be done without obligation and that he or she will be competing with other design firms. The fee arrangements should be presented in writing at the time of the presentation.

The interior designer selects floor finishes, wall colors and finishes, fixtures, furniture, graphics for walls, and lighting. Samples and choices of color schemes are submitted by the designer until the client is satisfied with the layout and atmosphere or feel of each room. The designer then writes the specifications, prepares bid documents, and oversees the installation. Some design firms provide furnishings as well as design services.

Summary

A food facilities design project, regardless of its scope and complexity, must start with a preliminary plan. If the owner or manager follows the planning method suggested, a successful food facility is not necessarily guaranteed, but the chances of its success are greatly enhanced. The preliminary planning process should include

- *Careful consideration of the scope and complexity of the project.* This enables the selection of an appropriate planning team. If the project is simply a replacement of equipment, the team will be small or perhaps consist of only the food facilities design consultant and the manager. If the scope involves large-scale renovation or construction, a larger group of professional people will be drawn into the project.
- *Concept development.* For hotels, restaurants, and institutions this is now recognized as an important planning stage. It includes consideration of menu, market, money, management, and the method of execution of the plan.
- *Feasibility studies.* Marketing and financial feasibility studies are often requested by bankers, investors, and others before financial commitments can be made. For large projects, these may be conducted by professional accounting firms; in other instances, the owners or managers may want to undertake them themselves. A go/no-go decision to proceed with the project should be made only after the marketing and feasibility studies have been completed.
- *Design and planning professionals.* The services of these necessary members of the team should be viewed by the owner as a good financial investment.

FOOD SERVICE DESIGN

With the tremendous expansion in the use of consultants throughout the economy in recent years, the demand for a high quality of service has become pressing. In response to this need, professional associations have been formed to establish performance criteria for membership and create a code of ethics that members are expected to follow. FCSI is such an association, having established itself as a recognized group of professionals in the field of food service design and consulting. Membership requirements are set at a high level, and the members are expected to have years of experience in designing and coordinating small and large food service projects. The complexities of food service design have forced the design consultant to broaden the scope of services offered. The most demanded types of service the consultant provides are described below.

Master Planning

Approaching the development of food service facilities haphazardly, without making a careful study of the long-range goals, can lead to inefficiency of operation and waste of capital funds. A master plan should be written for the food service that includes alternative locations and different types of services. A master plan usually examines long-range growth, evaluates the market to be served, and incorporates space and architectural considerations.

Systems Recommendations

Systems are defined as series of interacting parts (subsystems) that must be considered to achieve the most satisfactory and efficient results. For example, in food services, ware-washing systems are developed that include delivering the dishes to the ware-washing area, scraping soiled dishes, transporting the dishes back to service areas, washing pots and pans, and sanitizing large carts. These systems may involve conveyors, dish machines, pot and pan machines, cart washrooms, dish carts, and many other pieces of expensive equipment. Because of the large amount of both capital and operating funds involved in such a system, a careful study should be made of the best systems to use. Tray delivery systems for hospitals, fast-food systems, and warehouse/food delivery systems are examples of complex food service systems that usually involve the services of a food service facilities consultant.

Financial Evaluations

The feasibility studies discussed earlier may be a part of the consultant's work on a food service project. Consultants are also often requested to conduct evaluations of existing food operations. An evaluation of the financial condition of the food service is usually the most important part of the management advisory or operations analysis work conducted by the consultant.

Design Programming

A prerequisite to design development of food service facilities is a narrative discussion describing how a particular project food service system is intended to operate. The consultant's specific objective is to highlight space and labor usage and its cost in a manner that clearly defines the flow of goods and services through the proposed plan solution. The following topics are, in many cases, covered in this type of program document:

- Objective of the food service operation.
- Types and numbers of persons to be served.
- Hours of facility operation.
- Basic staffing requirements.
- Type(s) of menus to be served.
- System selected for serving.
- Handling and storage systems for food and supplies.
- Area requirements for production and service.
- Preliminary food/beverage service equipment gross budget estimate.

Operations Consulting

The consultant's services are solicited when the owner/operator is having problems. The most common analyses include:

- Space utilization analysis to increase seats, turnover, or production/storage capacity.
- Layout and equipment efficiency and effectiveness analysis.
- Control and security system organization, to reduce costs and losses.
- Marketing/menu assistance, to increase customer counts.
- Operations concept assistance, to ensure optimum use of facilities.

THE DESIGN SEQUENCE

A planning model or design sequence used by both architects and food facilities design consultants breaks down the process into the following sequential functions:

1. Proposal and client contact.
2. Feasibility.
3. Programming.
4. Schematic design.
5. Design development/engineering.
6. Bidding and awarding the contract.
7. Construction and coordination.
8. Inspection/acceptance.
9. Implementation and training.

It should be noted that the feasibility and implementation and training functions are usually performed by a food service facilities design consultant rather than an architect.

The following outlines the food facilities design consultant's role in the traditional design sequence listed above (Fig. 1).

Proposal and Contract

The architect or client will wish to explore with a consultant what services are provided and the cost of those services. The food facilities design consultant usually meets

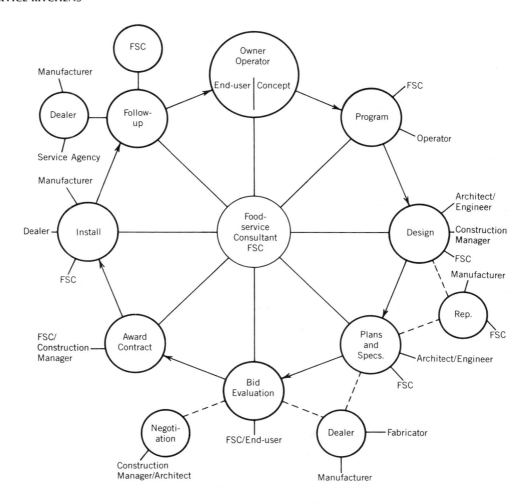

Figure 1. Design sequence.

with the client to discuss the project, to determine the scope, and to gather enough information to prepare the proposal. Often, there is no charge for this first step. However, if out-of-town travel is required and the evaluation of the project will take more than one day, a fee might be charged for the initial meeting. The proposal is written for three primary purposes:

1. To establish (sell) the credentials of the food facilities design consultant.
2. To describe the work to be accomplished.
3. To set the fee.

FCSI has adopted a standard client contract, which is available from the FCSI headquarters in Seattle. A typical list of the items included under "work to be accomplished" from the files of Birchfield Foodsystems, Inc. is shown below.

Work To Be Accomplished

1. The consultant must meet with the architect, client, and other personnel to review preliminary plans for the new facility.
2. The consultant must meet with the architect and

mechanical engineers to review schematic drawings to ascertain the adequacy of space and to determine the characteristics of the available utility services.
3. The consultant must present preliminary drawings for the food services areas in 1/8-in. = 1-ft scale as often as necessary until the architect, client, and other members of the project team are satisfied with the design.
4. The consultant must develop a 1/4-in. = 1-ft scale drawing of the kitchen, serving areas, and support food services areas indicating the placement of the equipment.
5. The consultant must furnish to the architect, engineers, and client specification sheets of standard catalog equipment recommended for purchase and develop utility requirements for each piece of equipment.
6. The consultant must develop elevation drawings for the principal fabricated equipment.
7. The consultant must prepare a 1/4-in = 1-ft scale drawing indicating plumbing and electric spot connections for each piece of equipment and the utilities for each piece of equipment.
8. The consultant must review shop drawings and

mechanical drawings prepared by the successful kitchen equipment contractor and other contractors and work with the client in seeking agency approvals for the design.

9. The consultant must inspect the installation of the kitchen and food service equipment and prepare a list of all items that do not meet the specifications.

10. The consultant must submit equipment guarantees and manuals to the client and demonstrate to the employees the proper operation of each piece of equipment. It is also necessary to meet with the manager and supervisors to explain the design.

The above is an excerpt from a proposal prepared by Birchfield Foodsystems, Inc. for furnishing design services.

BASIC DESIGN PRINCIPLES

Although there are significant differences in the physical layouts, menus, and methods of service of various food facilities, there are some design principles that can be followed by a food facilities designer in any case. These principles lead to efficiency and a pleasant workplace for the worker, but do not lead to one particular layout. Prototype restaurants of the three leading hamburger chains are quite different in layout, each for its own reasons, but all follow a set of design principles.

A common misconception about design is that there is only one right way to lay out the equipment and arrange the space. There are, in fact, many designs that would be acceptable and workable for the same facility. A competent designer approaches a facilities design project knowing that there are many variables that affect the design, and in each project a different set of variables prevails. Each food facility is treated as unique, with its own design problems to be solved.

The Principle of Flexibility and Modularity

The use of heavy-gauge stainless steel in the construction of kitchen equipment is almost universally accepted by the food service industry. Stainless steel does not rust, is easy to clean, is not porous, and does not easily wear out. Stainless steel has the major fault of being very inflexible. In other words, a stainless steel table in the kitchen has a great amount of permanence, and the table cannot be modified easily to accommodate a change in the design. If, for instance, a work area 14 ft in length were required, the principle of flexibility would lead the designer to specify two tables, one 6 ft long and one 8 ft long. These two lengths would permit a rearrangement of the kitchen without the necessity of cutting the table to accommodate a new design. This illustrates a design principle that includes component parts that can be rearranged as changes occur. The change might be the result of new management, different methods of service, a new menu, or a new preparation method. Designing for change is a part of the principle of flexibility.

In the dining area, flexibility can be achieved by the use of dividing, movable walls. In the service area, the

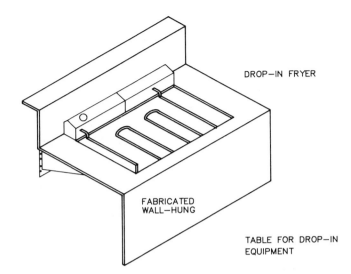

Figure 2. Modular drop-in fryer.

space can be divided to accommodate both table service and buffet service.

An inflexible construction that was popular in the past was the construction of concrete pads for kitchen equipment. These bases were used in place of legs for refrigerators, ovens, or other heavy pieces of equipment to eliminate difficult-to-clean areas under the equipment. The problem with these bases was that as the equipment was replaced or the kitchen was rearranged, the bases were then the wrong shape or were in the wrong spot. A concrete base is difficult to eliminate and almost impossible to move. Concrete bases have been used infrequently in recent years in commercial kitchens.

Modularity is a concept in design in which the space and equipment have standardized sizes and functions. For example, in the construction industry, doors are modular because they are sized according to an industry standard. Reach-in refrigerators in the food service industry usually are modular in size and function. In a free-flow or scramble cafeteria, the service components should be modular so that the service lines can be easily changed as menus and customer tastes change. Modular range sections are quite common and permit the designer to select from many types of equipment and arrange it in a smooth and continuous line up. The use of "quick disconnect" utility lines that permit inexpensive changes and that allow easy disconnection of the equipment are an excellent example of flexibility and modularity. The modular pieces can be designed for off-the-floor installation, with the entire range section mounted on legs for ease of cleaning. In future years, if a piece of equipment needs to be replaced, the modular unit can be removed without disturbing other pieces of equipment (Fig. 2).

The Principle of Simplicity

In designing a food facility, the designer is well advised to keep it simple. Food services facilities invite clutter, and clutter leads to poor sanitation and confusion in the work areas, as well as an environment that customers may find uncomfortable and overcrowded.

The principle of simplicity should be used in every design project. Some examples of this principle are:

- Clean uncluttered lines for range sections.
- Simple wall-hung tables in areas where a heavy grease or soil condition exists.
- The use of modular or drop-in cooking equipment that eliminates corners, edges, and unnecessary undershelves or overshelves.
- The elimination of wheels on equipment that will seldom be moved.
- The elimination of utility connections that penetrate the floor (rather than the wall behind the equipment), creating dirt pockets and clutter.
- The selection of a piece of equipment without accessories, if the accessories are not really needed.
- Convenient waiter stations near the serving area in the dining room.
- The arrangement of tables in the dining room to create natural and comfortable aisle space for waiters and guests.

Examples of the violation of the principle of simplicity exist in many restaurant kitchens. For instance, large stainless-steel equipment stands for fryers and grills sold by equipment manufacturers are expensive and difficult to clean. A better solution is a simple, flat stainless-steel table with drop-in fryers and grills. This saves thousands of dollars in the original installation and makes the cleaning process much simpler for the employees.

The Principle of Flow of Materials and Personnel

The movement of food through a food services facility should follow a logical sequence beginning with receiving and ending with waste disposal. Since both receiving and waste disposal usually occur at the back dock of a food operation, the food moves through the food facility in a circle, as illustrated in Figure 3.

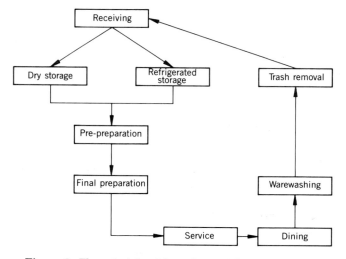

Figure 3. The principle of flow of materials and personnel.

The following are examples of some flow considerations in design:

- The movement of employees from one section of the kitchen to another.
- The flow of dishes through the dishwashing system and back to the service area.
- In a restaurant, the flow of customers from the entrance to the cocktail lounge and/or to the main dining room.
- In a cafeteria, the flow of customers from the entrance, through the service cafeteria, to the dish dropoff point.
- The flow of raw food ingredients through the main traffic aisles of the kitchen to the preparation area.

It is helpful for the designer to diagram the flow patterns on the preliminary floor plan, showing the movement of customers, food, dishes, trash, and garbage. If these flow lines are color coded, the patterns are then much easier to see and understand, and assist the designer in arriving at a design solution that accommodates the proper flow of materials and personnel.

The Principle of Ease of Sanitation

In virtually every type of facility, more employee labor hours are spent cleaning the food operation than are spent preparing the food. A food facility designed with sanitation in mind can be cleaned more quickly and easily and thus require fewer labor hours for this aspect of operation. Some examples of sanitation design considerations are described below.

Building Finishes. Structural glazed tile on the walls is the most desirable finish because it is easy to clean and resists damage from carts and other objects that strike the wall surface. Ceramic tile is an easy-to-clean surface and can be purchased in colorful patterns that make the kitchen a pleasant place to work. Epoxy paint on concrete block is the least expensive acceptable wall finish, but turns brown around areas that are exposed to high heat. The painted surface is also easily chipped by rolling equipment. The use of bright colors in the kitchen improves the general appearance of the space and encourages cleanliness. Quarry tile is the standard floor finish for the industry because it does not wear, is grease resistant, and is less slippery than other floors when wet.

Wall-hung Equipment (Off the Floor). The use of equipment that is attached to the wall, eliminating the use of legs, makes for an excellent sanitation design. It is desirable to use equipment racks that have a limited number of legs so that space is created under the equipment for ease of cleaning.

Garbage Disposals. These are used in work areas to facilitate waste disposal.

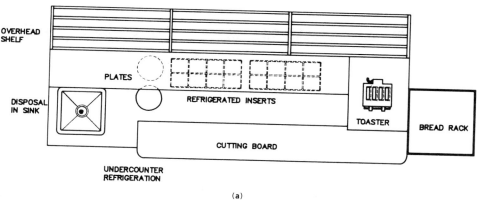

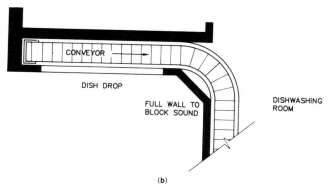

Figure 4. (a) Well organized sanitary sandwich production unit (b) sanitary system for removal of soiled dishes.

Self Storage Design. Portable shelving systems and open shelving under tables can be cleaned easily (Fig. 4a and b).

The Principle of Ease of Supervision

Many hotels and food service institutions built during the 1920s and 1930s had vegetable preparation areas that were remote from the main kitchen or separated by partitions and were therefore difficult to supervise. The open type of design, which is now preferred, allows the supervisor to oversee the production areas more efficiently. The elimination of walls and partitions also permits workers to move and communicate with each other more easily and tends to reduce the number of people needed.

The separation of production areas by floor level violates the ease of supervision principle not only by increasing the amount of supervision needed, but also by creating cumbersome flow patterns between the floors. The designer should avoid separating the production areas by floor whenever possible.

It is often desirable to put half walls under hoods and between work departments. A 4-ft half wall provides separation, but does not block the view. Half walls are helpful as

- Places to attach wall-hung equipment.
- Sanitary means of locating utility connections.
- Methods of containing spilled water (around stock kettles).

The Principle of Space Efficiency

As the costs of building construction and maintenance rise, designers are constantly striving to incorporate space-saving ideas into their work. In this case, necessity can be turned to advantage: space savings are translated into space efficiency in the design of small, well-equipped food facilities work areas.

The principle of space efficiency can, of course, be carried to the extreme. Small efficient kitchens can be a pleasure to use, but kitchens that are too small can be unpleasant for the cooks and kitchen workers. How can the designer know the difference between a small and efficient kitchen and one that is too small? Providing the following components helps to ensure that each section of the kitchen has the necessary equipment and storage space to enable the employees to work efficiently:

- A work surface (table).
- A sink.
- A cutting surface.
- Storage for utensils.
- Storage for pans.
- Storage for raw ingredients.
- Storage for the finished product.
- Proper aisle space for movement.

If each work area includes the above desirable features and the work area is arranged efficiently, the food facility is space efficient (Fig. 5).

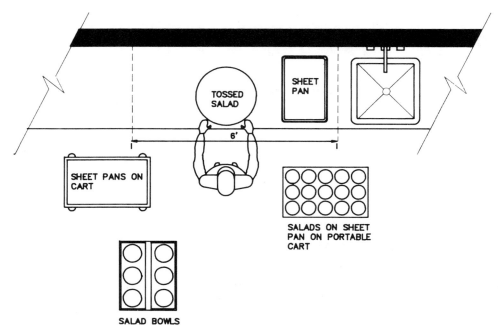

Figure 5. An efficiently arranged work station.

FOOD SERVICE DESIGN CONSIDERATIONS

Sufficient Work Space

There are many different work spaces that must be considered in the overall design of a food facility. The amount of space needed by a dishwasher is far different from the amount of space needed by a waiter at a beverage station. In the dishwasher's situation, the worker moves back and forth, stooping, gathering carts and racks, and performing other tasks that require a considerable amount of space. The waiter may need only enough room to pass by a beverage station and pick up a coffee pot or glass of milk en route to the dining room.

The information provided below on work space can be used as a general guideline. It is no substitute, however, for a commonsense evaluation of the unique requirements of any given food service facility. The amount of space that an individual worker needs is influenced by

- The number of people working in the space.
- The amount and type of equipment.
- Whether or not the equipment doors swing into the aisles.
- The type of food being processed.
- The amount of space needed for storage.

Aisle Space

The aisle spaces needed in each work area are listed.

Description of the Space	Aisle Width Needed, in.
Single aisle, limited equipment	30–36
Double aisle, limited equipment	42–54
Single aisle, protruding equipment	42–54
Double aisle, protruding equipment	54–66
Aisle with little traffic	36–48
Aisle with much traffic	48–72

An example of a double aisle with protruding equipment is shown in Figure 6.

As noted in the preceding list, the width of major traffic aisles should range between 4 and 6 ft. A major traffic aisle is used for the movement of people and material from storage to production areas or from production areas to the point of service. A piece of equipment with a protruding door should never be located in a major traffic aisle that is only 4 ft wide. An aisle 6 ft wide can accommodate a refrigerator door or other protruding equipment.

It is important that the aisles be the proper sizes because they have a significant influence on the total size of the food facility. If the aisle is too narrow, the employees have a difficult time working in the space. If the aisle is too wide, the employees are required to take many extra steps during the day, and fatigue and low productivity result (Fig. 6).

Standards for Work Surfaces

The NSF lists, in Standard Number 1 (revised June 1984), the following descriptions of materials that may be used for food service equipment.

The three types of surfaces and the materials that may be used are:

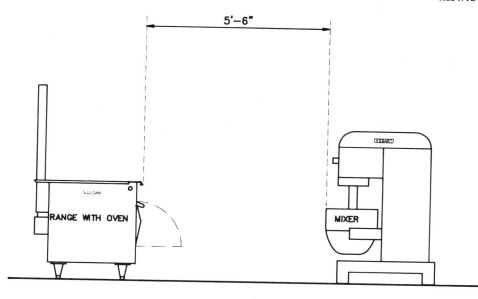

Figure 6. Standard aisle space for double aisle, protruding equipment.

Food Contact Surfaces. Surface materials in the food zone must be smooth, corrosion resistant, nontoxic, stable, and nonabsorbent under use condition. They must not impart an odor, color, or taste or contribute to the adulteration of food.

Splash Contact Surfaces. These must be smooth, easily changeable, and corrosion resistant or rendered corrosion resistant with a material that is noncracking and nonchipping.

Nonfood Contact Surfaces. These must be smooth and corrosion resistant or rendered corrosion resistant.

Work surfaces should be arranged within easy reach of the worker. Table tops are often 30 in. wide in production areas because the average worker can reach out only 30 in. from a standing position. The height of the working surface should permit the worker to chop or do other hand work without stooping over. The height of a work surface must be adjusted for the height of the worker and the type of material that is placed on the work surface. A thick cutting board, for instance, raises the surface height by as much as 1.75–3 in.

The standard used by most designers for the height of a work surface is 34–37 in. If a work area will be used for heavy, bulky objects, a lower height should be selected. Some height variations can be created for the worker by the use of mats on the floor, cutting boards on the table, or adjustable table feet.

The amount of space needed from one side of a work surface to the other depends on the size of the objects being worked on and the layout of the work area. For example, if standard 18 × 26-in. sheet pans are used as trays for holding individual tossed salads, space is needed for empty bowls, bulk tossed salad, empty sheet pans, and sheet pans filled with salads. In this example, 6 linear feet is used by the worker, even though the worker cannot reach that far from one position (Fig. 5).

The most important concept for the designer in good workplace layout is to think through all of the steps in a process and then provide a space for the food and equipment needed to carry out these steps. For instance, a sandwich makeup table in a cold food production area needs:

- Storage for plates.
- Refrigerated storage for food.
- Storage for bread.
- A utensil drawer or rack.
- A cutting surface.
- A toaster.
- Refrigerated compartments for condiments.
- A sink with hot and cold water.
- A garbage disposal or can.
- A pick-up area for waiters.

A pizza makeup table satisfies most of these requirements. It has many refrigerated compartments, a wide cutting surface, and space for many of the other pieces of equipment needed (Fig. 7).

Properly Designed Equipment

The NSF has established standards for constructing food service equipment that are primarily concerned with safety and sanitation. The reader can consult NSF publications, which are available from NSF at a small cost.

Availability of Materials Handling Tools

The lifting of heavy objects by food service workers leads to accidents and personal injury. Materials handling tools and equipment that can greatly reduce or eliminate worker injury include forklift trucks, hand forklift trucks (mules), carts, hand trucks, portable receiving ramps, and skate wheel conveyors.

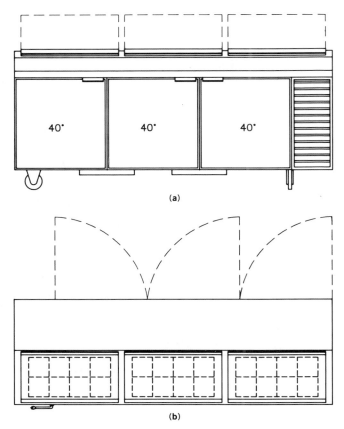

Figure 7. (a) Pizza table designed into a sandwich work station (b) pizza table designed into a sandwich work station.

The materials handling tool that is most frequently used for assembling ingredients in the kitchen is a simple cart. The cart is often abused by the worker through heavy use and the dropping of full cases of food onto the top shelf. The designer should specify the heaviest cart possible (600–1000-lb capacity) to prevent damage and abuse.

Forklift trucks are usually for use in large food service warehouses, but the hand-operated forklift is frequently used in the storerooms and kitchens of medium-sized and large food service operations. Hand-operated forklifts raise the pallets of food a few inches off the floor, permitting easy transport to a freezer or storeroom. Hand trucks are simple L-shaped two-wheeled devices that permit the worker to balance a stack of case goods on two wheels and to move the stack in or out of storage.

Receiving ramps and skate wheel conveyors permit the movement of materials from one level to the next without lifting. Receiving docks are the wrong height for some of the different types of delivery trucks that bring goods to receiving areas. A portable receiving ramp constructed of lightweight aluminum is helpful in solving the height variation problem. Motorized load-leveler devices are often designed into the ramp to solve this same problem. Motor-driven belts, dumbwaiters, and elevators are also used to transport materials from one level to the next.

Adequate Lighting

The standard measure of light is the footcandle. One footcandle is equal to the amount of light from a standard candle that strikes a 1-ft^2 surface from a distance of 1 ft. The farther away a light is placed from the surface to be lighted, the lower the number of footcandles. For this reason, lighting needs to be spaced at small intervals in a food production area. The following chart should be used as a guide in selecting the proper light levels for food facilities.

Space	Footcandles
Kitchen work area	30–40
Classroom	40–50
Cashier	50–60
Storeroom	10–15
Landing platform	20–25
Building entrance	10–20
Bathroom	10–30
Hotel, general areas	10–20
Accounting and bookkeeping	100–150
Food service dining rooms	
fast food	40–50
moderate price	10–20
high price	5–15

In service areas that are seen by the public, one effective means of lighting is to provide a high intensity of light on the food and low intensity for the main part of the room. High-intensity lighting for food display is illustrated in Figure 8.

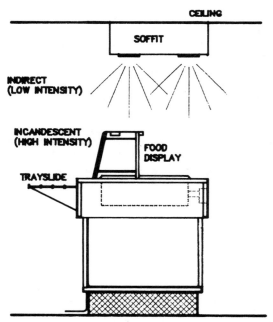

Figure 8. Lighted service counter under the sneeze guard and in the soffit.

Control of Noise Levels

High noise levels are unpleasant for the worker in a food service facility. It has been demonstrated in industrial settings that excessive noise causes fatigue, accidents, and low productivity in a direct relationship to the volume of the noise. Some techniques that help to reduce noise in a food service facility are:

- Sound-deadening materials sprayed onto the underside of all tables and counters.
- The separation of areas (other than production) in the food facility department, especially ware-washing. The construction of walls between the kitchen and ware-washing areas restricts noise transmission.
- Designing conveyors to create a sound barrier between dish dropoff points and ware-washing.

An illustration of the components of a sound barrier that might be used in a self-busing application for a restaurant or cafeteria is provided below:

- Acoustic ceilings that are grease and moisture resistant.

- Carpeting in dining rooms in the seating areas.
- Carpeting on the walls in dining areas; this is an excellent wall finish because it not only absorbs sound, but takes the punishment of chairs and tables, which often scars wood or paint wall finishes.
- Double doors between the dining room and the kitchen.
- Background music in both the public areas and the back of the house (kitchen, ware-washing, and service areas).
- Remote refrigeration compressors.

SPACE ANALYSIS

It is the design consultant's job to determine the space requirements for each section of the food service facility before the actual design can begin. This early but difficult estimate of space is achieved by gathering basic data about the nature of the planned food operation. Once this information has been obtained, the space requirements of each functional part of a food service facility are analyzed (Fig. 9). The areas that need to be considered are the following:

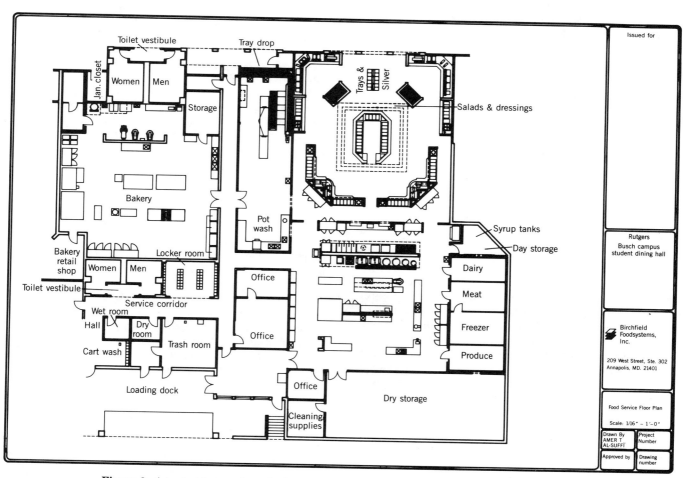

Figure 9. A typical large volume food service design with self-service scramble cafeteria, kitchen, and bakery.

Receiving
Storage
    dry storage
    paper and cleaning supplies storage
    refrigerated storage
    utensil and cleaning equipment storage
Office
Preparation areas
    preparation
    hot food preparation
    cold food preparation
    final preparation
Bakery
Employee locker room/toilet
Service areas
Dining rooms
Ware-washing

BIBLIOGRAPHY

General References

I. S. Anoff, *Food Service Equipment Industry,* Cahners Publishing Co., Boston, Mass., 1972.

Foodservice Equipment, NSF Standard No. 2, National Sanitation Foundation, Ann Arbor, Mich., 1976.

L. H. Kotschevar, *Food Service Planning,* 2nd ed., John Wiley & Sons, Inc., New York, 1977.

R. D. Ley, *Foodservice Refrigeration,* CBI Publishing Co., Boston, Mass., 1980.

A. C. Avery, *A Modern Guide to Foodservice Equipment,* CBI Publishing Co., Boston, Mass., 1980.

J. C. Birchfield, *Design & Layout of Foodservice Facilities,* Van Nostrand Reinhold Co., Inc., New York, 1988.

See also HOTELS; KITCHENS, RESIDENTIAL; RESTAURANTS

JOHN C. BIRCHFIELD
Birchfield Foodsystems, Inc.
Annapolis, Maryland

RESTORATION, HISTORIC

The art and science of building restoration encompasses a wide range of activities from highly technical research and reproduction of materials, finishes, and building methods by qualified professionals to replacement of these elements by interested owners of old buildings. It presumes a knowledge and inclusion of methods used by historians, archaeologists, and skilled craftsmen in wood, masonry, metal, as well as paints and the varieties of finishes. It requires a degree of skill and perseverance not usually needed in new construction, and for this reason, may be more costly in execution.

DEFINITION OF TERMS

Restoration. Architecturally used, it means putting back as nearly as possible into the form it held at a particular date or period in time. Its accomplishment often requires the removal of work which is not of the period. The value of a restoration is measured by its authenticity.

Preservation. The stabilizing of a structure in its existing form by preventing further change or deterioration. Preservation, since it takes the structure as found, does not relate to a specific period in time and is, architecturally, the most intellectually honest treatment of an ancient monument.

Reconstruction. The re-creation of a building from historical, archaeological, and architectural documents and other evidence, often highly conjectural. Parts of buildings which are restored often must be reconstructed because original work has been removed or changed; this detracts somewhat from the accuracy and possibly from the intellectual honesty of the restoration.

HISTORY

The ever-present problem confronting the architect, restorer, or sponsor, which must be resolved through a careful evaluation, is the reason for undertaking the project at all and the result which is desired. It may be assumed that the fundamental reason for preservation is to bequeath to the future a reliable representation of the architecture of the past. The nineteenth century English restorationists who earned for themselves the reputation of vandals sincerely believed that all old buildings should be returned to that particular period in history which they themselves thought had been the most important. They often revealed great imagination and scholarly understanding of a past architecture, but in superimposing their ideas on older buildings which had been modernized from generation to generation through the years they changed or destroyed forever some of the best examples of eighteenth century English architecture.

USE AND EXHIBITION OF RESTORED BUILDINGS

The use to which the restored building is put should be as compatible as possible with the intention of the original builder and designer (Fig. 1). Thus it is logical to restore a courthouse for that use if there exists a need for a courthouse of that size in that location. A residence, large or small, will be best preserved if continued in use as a residence. (The Society for the Preservation of New England Antiquities, for instance, has worked out a number of leasing arrangements which provide for the use and exhibition of buildings by private individuals. The agreement insures their preservation in perpetuity while serving the dual purpose of public education and private accommodation.)

Structures which cannot continue to be used for their original purpose will, through their room arrangement, size, and location suggest other modern uses which may prove to be adequate economically. Offices, shops, information centers, society headquarters, country clubs, little theatre groups, and many other functions may be considered; the list is endless.

The problem of establishing a use to which an old

Figure 1. Kiplin Hall, North Yorkshire, England, built in 1623 by George Calvert, First Lord Baltimore. Restoration of house and gardens by Martin Stancliffe, RIBA, assisted by the School of Architecture, University of Maryland, College Park, Md. Photograph courtesy of David P. Fogle. See also color plates.

building may be put after its restoration is actually not unlike that confronting an investor in any commercial enterprise except that the latter has a particular type of building and use in mind and can make an evaluation on that basis. The potential sponsor for a restoration project, on the other hand, may find it necessary to investigate the entire field of human endeavor before reaching a decision. Analysis of possible uses should be determined on fundamental guidelines:

1. The historical or architectural importance of the structure: national, state, local; important individual, important event, other social significance; a unique architectural example of a period, the work of a great architect.

2. The size of the structure and the disposition of its rooms.

3. The location of the structure: city, town, or country; accessibility to people; availability of supporting or auxiliary facilities.

Guided by these basic considerations the economic potential may be evaluated.

REQUIREMENTS AND HISTORIC VALUE

While making a study of possible uses for the building, consideration must be given to the consequent requirements and possible effect on the historic value of the architecture as it still exists in original form. For example, an old structure which has been entirely changed on the inside during the course of its history and retains practically no original work, may be worthy of restoration on the exterior only, permitting complete latitude for the redesign of the interior. This may be particularly true of a building which has no special historical significance. On the other hand, it is sacrilegious to destroy original period interior work, in a building rich in social history, to effect the alterations required for a modern use. In such a case, only those uses should be considered as can be reasonably

well accommodated within the existing arrangement of rooms, without changing their architectural character.

An early determination of the possible use to which a building may be put is essential to guide the direction and scope of the architectural examination. There is no formula which will provide an instant solution to the policy which should guide the preservation of any monument, each must be studied, investigated, researched and evaluated. The actual work done must not ever be capricious but should always be fully authenticated if the finished work is to have full value. Figure 2 is an example of restoration in progress.

At this stage it may be found that certain suggested uses will be unacceptable because of the inability of the old structure to accommodate the mechanical equipment required without serious damage to its architectural character. The fact that many people are interested in specific times and events has influenced the sponsors of most restorations to select particular periods in time for restorations. The ethics of restoration to some selected time in history may be open to debate, but it has not been often that a building in this country has been preserved exactly as found.

Figure 2. Hotel Chalfonte, Cape May, New Jersey. A national historic landmark site, restoration in progress. Photograph courtesy of David P. Fogle.

The last and perhaps most elusive determination which will become a part of the program for a restoration is the date or period in time to which the building is to be restored. The selection should be made on the basis of complete research, historical, archaeological and architectural. Paradoxically the date selected will also indicate to a degree the extent of the architectural and archaeological investigations. Both of these examinations will destroy some of the existing features and it is obviously better to preserve *in situ* as much of the work of the selected date as possible.

A tentative date may be selected after a study of the preliminary research of the historian and superficial examinations by the archaeologist and architect. At this stage it is reasonable to suppose that the historical characters or events associated with the building are known, and many of the architectural features will have been identified. It should be possible to make reasonable conjectures as to some specific physical features of architectural importance which existed at the time the events of history took place. Such a determination will make it possible to avoid disturbing much of the fabric which dates from the date tentatively selected.

It will be found in some cases that the importance of the architecture will outweigh that of political or personal history and the tentative date will be selected accordingly. Conversely in some houses the preservation should be directed to unusual or significant architectural features of a different period.

In projects where architectural character is of primary importance the interests of architectural authenticity will be given precedence: no work dating from or before the period to be restored should be removed in the course of the architectural investigation or restoration. On the other hand, if the presentation of the building is to emphasize historical persons or events, the authenticity of anything but the surface visible on the date selected will be of less importance. A careful reconstruction may be as valuable as a setting for the presentation of history as a restoration even though the patina of age is removed and replaced by a modern finish.

ARCHITECTURAL RESEARCH

The objective of architectural research is to determine the character and date of a building and all its parts. This will include identifying the several periods of its construction and of all modifications, additions, and changes that have been made, as well as the order of their occurrence. It should provide the information on which to base recommendations for a restoration period or date.

Background material to be studied must include:

1. Historical and archaeological reports for documented dates of initial construction, and of all subsequent changes or additions, pictures, descriptions, bills of materials, artifacts, and all references to the activities of the owners and builders.
2. Precedent buildings, those of the same or approximate date in the immediate vicinity, as well as those in areas of similar culture and background which might have had an effect on the design, methods of construction, or craftsmanship employed in the erection of the subject building.
3. Builders' and carpenters' handbooks known to have been available to the architect, "undertaker" (as the builder or contractor was often called in the eighteenth century), owner, and all modern published books which are illustrated with photographs and measured drawings showing dated examples of buildings of the period.

OTHER REQUIREMENTS

The goals to be achieved must be clearly described. This means that the skills and capacities required of the craftsmen engaged should be spelled out. It is not enough to specify that the work shall be in accordance with normal or good trade practices. The craftsmen must be highly trained in modern trade practices, but must also have an interest and skill in the methods and practices used by the craftsmen of the period of the restoration. Of particular importance are the trades of the brick mason, stonemason, rough carpenter, joiner (or finish carpenter), cabinet maker, painter, and plasterer.

Specifications for brick or masonry mortar are of special importance and must be so written that the resulting work will look like that of the period of the original builder. This may mean that the specification for brick mortar will call for oyster shell lime and a specific grade and color of sand; or, after experimentation, it may be found that a ready-mixed mortar with admixtures of ground oyster shell and a certain sand will produce the desired appearance. The specification must call for the results to be achieved and suggest means to achieve them. (The contractor must frequently be charged with the responsibility of experimenting until acceptable results are achieved.) The bricks in important work may have to be handmade in order to match original work. This may involve the erection of a brick kiln, the provision of special wood for burning therein, and all the incidental processes of opening a pit, digging clay, puddling, molding, and drying the bricks before burning them. In addition to all this the craftsmen needed to operate the plant must be found or trained.

All exposed woodwork or millwork must be fabricated so that its final appearance will be that of the work of the period of the restoration. This may mean that the specifications will mention the type of saw to be used in making boards—circular or band or even, in some cases, cut by hand with a pitsaw, rived or handhewn with broad axes or adzes. Finished trim should not show the mill marks caused by the knives in the planing mill, but if the work is sanded as required to achieve a good modern finish, it may be too smooth for restoration work. Cautions must be included against ghosted mill marks made by knives out of balance since these defy removal by sanding. Hand planes leave an identifiable mark on finished woodwork, particularly in broad areas like paneling, whether the work is finished natural or painted; hand planing will be necessary for reproduction of such work.

The type of nails and hardware required for any ancient building will certainly require a specification differing from that used in modern practice. The use of proper hardware, both rough and finished, is one of the most important details of a restoration. Hinges, locks, keepers, holdbacks, nails, etc., of various periods and differing localities exhibit characteristics which must be reproduced for authentic restoration. No single detail is more likely to damage an otherwise excellent job than the use of hardware which is wrong for the place or period.

Painters, in addition to being able to lay on paint without the usual sags, runs, or holidays, must be capable of mixing pigments and matching colors from wet to dry and dry to wet (there is a difference and great skill and patience is required). They must also be skillful in removing paint, coat by coat, to determine a sequence of repaintings or to clean old work entirely and prepare a surface for new paintwork. They must be capable of doing graining, stippling, and other finishes not normally used today.

CONCLUSION

Restoration in recent years has been assisted by federal, state, and local programs which provide technical and financial assistance. The National Historic Preservation Act of 1966 established the National Register of Historic Places to identify "sites, buildings, objects, districts, and structures significant in American history, archaeology, and culture," creating an important incentive for restoration. The Tax Reform Act of 1976 and the Economic Recovery Tax Act of 1981 provided tangible incentives in the form of investment tax credits for restoration and adaptive use of old buildings. A subsequent law, the Tax Reform Act of 1986 removed a portion of incentive, adversely affecting many restoration projects. Projects may find the most effective support in individual states in the office of State Historic Preservation Officer.

BIBLIOGRAPHY

General References

O. M. Bullock, Jr., *The Restoration Manual,* Silvermine Publishers, Inc., Norwalk, Conn., 1966 reprint, New York, Van Nostrand Reinhold, Co., Inc., 1983.

W. J. Murtagh, *Keeping Time, The History and Theory of Preservation in America,* Main Street Press, Pittstown, N.J., 1988.

M. F. Schmertz, et al., *New Life for Old Buildings,* New York, McGraw-Hill, Inc., 1982.

W. Seale, *Recreating the Historic House Interior,* American Assoc. for State and Local History, Nashville, Tenn., 1979.

National Park Service, *Recording Historic Buildings,* U. S. Government Printing Office, Washington, D.C. 1970.

B. Diamondstein, *Buildings Reborn, New Uses, Old Places,* New York, Harper and Row, Publishers Inc., 1978.

S. Cantacuzino, and S. Brandt, *Saving Old Buildings,* Architectural Press, London, UK 1980.

See also ADAPTIVE USE; PRESERVATION, HISTORIC

ORIN M. BULLOCK, JR., FAIA
Rock Hall, Maryland

DAVID P. FOGLE
University of Maryland
College Park, Maryland

RUGS AND CARPETS

In current usage, "rugs and carpets" refers to the entire range of textile-based floor coverings, including such diverse products as individually hand-woven specialty pieces designed by their maker, machine-woven limited edition area rugs designed by architects to reflect their individual architectural idioms, miles of mass-produced tufted synthetic greige goods to be stored and later cut and dyed to fill customers' orders, and finally, huge outdoor carpets used to cover the playing fields of many sports stadiums. However, a closer look at the uses of rugs and carpets in architecture today reveals a seeming reversion to the meanings of the roots of the two terms.

"Carpet," in medieval Latin, Middle English, and Old French, was used to refer to any thick fabric cover, including coverings for walls, floors, beds, and especially tables and chairs. The Latin and French root for the term "tapestry" was used synonymously with carpet, but generally did not refer to floor coverings. "Rug" appears to come from the same roots as the Swedish *rugg,* meaning entangled hair, and the English "rough," meaning coarse and uneven. Into the nineteenth century, "rug," in addition to referring to a floor covering, could also mean a portiere or a lap robe.

Today "carpet" and "rug" are used almost interchangeably. Although carpet can mean a smaller-than-room-size floor covering, it more often means a floor covering designed to cover the entire floor of a room, often by stitching sections together. The term "rug" rarely refers to a wall-to-wall fabric floor covering, but is more frequently used to mean a discrete piece with regular geometric dimensions and a definite unified design controlled by the dimensions of the piece. "Tapestry" refers more specifically to a type of patterned weaving, usually used as a wall hanging, in which few horizontal threads are continuous throughout the width of the piece; instead, the weft stops, returns, and starts according to the color changes in the design.

Today's methods of machine-made carpet manufacture have their origins in the methods used to make handmade rugs. The principles and components are similar to those of other textile weaving. The threads that run the length of the rug or carpet are called the warp or chain. Warp threads are stretched between two beams mounted so that there is a front half of the chain made up of alternate warp threads and a back half. The space between these two layers of threads is called the shed. A row of weft or transverse threads attached to a shuttle is run through the shed, and the loom is then adjusted so that the two planes of warp are reversed before the shuttle is returned to its starting position. The weft thus passes over and under adjacent warp threads in a pattern that reverses itself with each successive row of weft. Handmade and machine-made rugs and carpets follow this basic weaving principle and differ most in the way the pile and pattern are produced.

In handmade rugs the pile and pattern are created by pieces of dyed yarn knotted around two adjacent warp threads. Both cut ends of the pile yarn are brought forward to the face of the rug. After each row of knots, one to three rows of weft are inserted and beaten down tightly into place by a fork or comblike tool. The weft serves to anchor the knots and form the foundation of the rug. Because the form of the knot causes the cut ends to lie obliquely toward the starting end of the rug rather than stand absolutely perpendicular to the foundation, the face of the pile is made up of parts of the ends and parts of the sides of the knot yarns. This gives a handmade rug a distinctive nap.

ORIGINS

It is generally agreed that carpet weaving began as a no-madic craft in the Middle East and that the production of flat-woven carpets or *kilim* was well developed before the production of pile carpets became widely established. *Kilim* have no pile, but have elaborate geometric and representational patterns created through variations of brocading and tapestry techniques.

The oldest known fragment of a pile carpet was found in a Scythian burial mound of the fifth century BC in the Pazyryk Valley of southern Siberia near the boundaries of present-day Mongolia in northern China. The Scythians were tribes of horse-riding warriors that had extended their influence throughout the Middle East as far south as the borders of present-day Egypt during this period. It is not clear whether the Scythians were rug makers or simply collectors who acquired such treasures through their wide contacts with other peoples and tribes.

Stone paving slabs from the seventh century BC at the palace of King Assurbanipal at Nineveh were carved to represent pile rugs, including the knotted fringe of the warp and an overcast selvage on the long edges. The pattern of these rugs carved in stone bears a strong resemblance to the pattern of the later Pazyryk carpet.

Today's Oriental rugs descend most directly from the time of the Seljuk Turks. For 200 years, from 1050 AD until the empire was split apart, the Islamic Turkoman followers of Seljuk-ibn-Dakak from the Kirghy Steppes in West Turkestan controlled Persia, Mesopotamia, and Asia Minor, including Turkey and Syria. They brought with them a tradition of rug designs with a clear stylistic connection to Chinese textiles from the Han dynasty. These eleventh-century patterns lived on into the nineteenth century in Turkish and Caucasian nomadic work.

With the Mongol invasions of the thirteenth century, Persia was permanently separated from the vestiges of

the Seljuk Turk empire. By the early sixteenth century, under the Sefavid dynasty, Persian rugs produced for the court had developed a characteristic style. It was generally more detailed and curvilinear than the older Turkish designs and had a greater reliance on floral motifs. Persian court designs of this period, which typify Persian carpets to the present day, reflect contemporaneous Chinese influence, including such Ming dynasty motifs as scrolling leaves, peony blossoms, and imaginary birds. Turkish rug designs, on the other hand, rely heavily on rectilinear abstract geometric patterns arranged with rhythmic repeats.

Turkish rugs were generally all wool, including the warp, the weft, and the individual dyed yarns knotted around the warp to create the pile and the design. Persian court designs began to use silk extensively during this period. The greater tensile strength of silk allows finer warp threads, and thus more of them can be used per inch. More warp threads per inch accommodate more knots. The more knots per inch in a rug, the denser the pile, and the more luxurious and longer lasting the rug. But most importantly, the more knots per inch, the more detail there can be in the design. Silk was also sometimes used for the weft and pile as well.

The Persian quest for greater detail could also explain the predominance of the Persian knot in Persian court rug design of this period. The use of the Persian knot, also known as the asymmetrical knot, separates each warp thread by only one strand of pile yarn, whereas with the Turkish, or symmetrical knot, pairs of pile yarns are separated from each other by two strands of warp.

With the Persian knot, the yarn encircles two warp threads by passing under one and around the other. The cut ends emerge on the face of the rug separately, each to one side of a warp thread. The cut ends on the face of the rug are separated from each other by a warp thread.

With the Turkish knot, the pile yarn lies across two adjacent warps, with the cut ends encircling one warp each and then emerging as a pair between the two warps to the face of the rug. The two warp threads encircled by a knot are mirror images or symmetrical with each other.

By the beginning of the reign of the Persian Sefavid Shah Abbas the Great in 1587, Persian carpets had attained international renown. Even the Turks, with a rug-making tradition and industry of their own, seem to have preferred Persian rugs to local products. In 1683, when a large number of Oriental rugs were captured from the Turks after their defeat at the Siege of Vienna, many of the pieces were of Persian origin. Persian rug-making workshops were established during this period to produce pieces primarily for export or under commission from European royalty. This organized production under the auspices of the court continued until the collapse of the Sefavid dynasty with the invasion of the Afghans in 1722.

The spread of the art of rug making to Europe started much earlier than the seventeenth century. As a result of Moslem domination and influence in Spain from the eighth through fifteenth centuries, the Crusades of the eleventh through thirteenth centuries, the explorations of Marco Polo along the Silk Road through Turkestan, Persia, and Turkey starting in the late thirteenth century, and the conquests by the Turks of the Balkans starting in the fourteenth century, the examples and influence of this art form gradually reached Europe.

Evidence of the influence of Persian rugs on European life and design can be seen in late-fourteenth-century paintings such as the polyptych *Madonna and Child Enthroned with Six Angels* by Taddeo Geddi, in which the madonna is shown seated upon a throne draped with a rug of early Persian design. Many medieval buildings, especially in Italy, had floors inlaid with tiles in patterns inspired by Persian rugs.

Venice was well known throughout the rest of Europe as a center of trade in Oriental rugs by the early sixteenth century. By the end of the century, the British had sent a spy to Persia to bring back the secrets of wool dyeing and carpet knotting for the purpose of starting a local industry.

Turkish rugs were depicted with great detail in the fifteenth and sixteenth centuries by European portraitists, showing the value placed on Oriental rugs by both the owners and the artists. Works by Hans Holbein in England, by Venetians Giovanni Bellini and Carlo Crinelli, by Italians Ghirlandaio, il Pintoricchio, and Lorenzo Lotto, and by Flemish painters Hans Menling, Jan van Eyck, and Petrus Christus show the subjects seated or standing on carpets of recognizable Turkish patterns.

The frequency with which seventeenth-century Persian rugs appeared in the contemporaneous European paintings of Velasquez, Rubens, Van Dyck, Vermeer, Terborch, de Hooch, Bol, and Metsu indicates the large number of these rugs that were imported into Europe during this period. Rugs are shown in use as floor coverings, table coverings, and wall hangings.

In the early seventeenth century, Henry IV of France had established a workshop in the Louvre to weave carpets in the manner of the Turks. From the beginning, this effort used a unique knot and centered on producing rugs designed by European artists of repute rather than copying Turkish or Persian patterns. The rugs produced were limited to use by the French court. This workshop soon expanded into the quarters of a former soap factory, and the same Savonnerie became synonymous with knotted velvet pile rugs or carpets of European design.

The Savonnerie rug works was distinguished by its technique of creating pile by first weaving the yarn into the rug as a continuous series of loops made from a single weft thread and then cutting the loops. The single weft thread is woven into the carpet around a gauge rod, which establishes a uniform height for the loops. The end of the gauge rod has a blade attached, which cuts the loops as the rod is withdrawn. The cut loops create the pile. The resulting knot resembles the Turkish knot.

Savonnerie rugs and carpets were also the first to incorporate artistic devices such as shading into the design of the piece to create an illusion of depth in the finished composition. The flowers and animals were no longer the abstractions seen in Turkish or Persian rugs. Designs approached the representational realism of painted works on canvas, sculptural bas-relief, or *trompe l'oeil* effects employed on ceilings and wall frescoes of this period. The

Eastern influence had been completely erased. Savonnerie designs also incorporated representations of baroque, rococo, Empire, and neoclassical architectural elements in the design of the pieces.

By the mid-eighteenth century in France, pile carpets were also being made at Aubusson. Aubusson had been known for centuries for tapestry weaving. In 1743, the King's Council expanded the Aubusson workshop to make pile carpets for the bourgeoisie. The designs of Aubusson were much simpler, and many were based on Oriental models. Two types of rugs were made at Aubusson: the knotted pile type woven on vertical looms, as originated at the Savonnerie, and flat-woven thick tapestry rugs worked from the reverse side and woven on horizontal looms. The latter were often produced with the same design as the rugs with pile, but having no pile, they were more sensitive to wear.

The mid-eighteenth century in England was the age of great Georgian country houses. Carpet design for these houses took inspiration from the classical motifs of the architecture. Architect Robert Adam often designed the carpets for specific rooms he had designed, often with the carpet mirroring the design of the vaulted ceiling of the room. The furniture maker Thomas Chippendale also designed carpets to achieve a unity of design with his furniture.

By the end of the eighteenth century, the groundwork had been laid for the industrialization of carpet production. European handmade carpets lost their role in mainstream interior design to machine-made carpets over the next century.

MACHINE WEAVING

Most of the European rug weaving centers were also textile weaving centers. The textile industry was becoming mechanized during the eighteenth century, so that the carpet industry, which followed closely behind advances in the textile industry, was already almost fully industrialized by the time power carpet looms came into use in the mid-nineteenth century. Important inventions that led to the mechanization of the textile industry included the invention of the flying shuttle in 1733, the spinning jenny in 1764, the textile power loom in 1785, and most importantly for rug making, the Jacquard attachment in 1800.

Jacquard Attachment. The French Jacquard attachment is a mechanical means of recording the pattern and controlling its production in the carpet. Where hand weavers refer to a cartoon drawn on gridded paper to direct the placement of colored yarns, the Jacquard mechanism relies on a continuous loop of a series of cards punched with holes to control needles, which raise the correct colored thread to create the desired pattern. The principle is similar to that of a player piano, except that it can take over 4000 different cards to complete a 36-in. repeat in the pattern of a carpet.

Brussels Weave. The Brussels weave was developed as a result of the invention of the Jacquard attachment. The weave differs dramatically from that of over 2000 years of handmade carpet methods in that the pattern and pile are created by warp threads rather than by knots running with the weft. The carpet pattern is usually limited to five or six colors. Warp threads in all five of the colors, along with a cotton chain, are mounted at each of the warp positions, called reeds. To create each row of looped pile, the Jacquard needles lift one colored thread at each reed, forming a shed through which a wire is passed from the side across the width of the piece. At the same time, a shuttle carrying a linen, jute, or cotton weft is passed through the shed created between the two levels of cotton chain, anchoring the row of loops. Two shots of weft are used for each row of pile loops. The size of the wire determines the length of the pile, and the carpet density is determined by the number of wires or rows per inch and the pitch or number of loops of yarn across the width of the loom.

The Wilton Weave. The Wilton weave is similar to the Brussels weave except that the loops are cut by a blade at the end of the wire as it is withdrawn from each row of pile. The Brussels and Wilton weaves produce carpets that are very durable because the foundation includes five layers of pile thread below the surface in addition to the chain and weft.

E. B. Bigelow perfected the Brussels power loom in Lowell, Mass., in 1848, and both the United States and the United Kingdom quickly put it to work. Brussels carpets were the most popular type of pile carpet throughout the rest of the nineteenth century. But the Axminster carpet rapidly gained popularity after an Axminster power loom was introduced in the 1870s.

The Axminster Weave. The Axminster weave was the most popular method of carpet manufacture from the early 1900s through 1950. Like the Wilton carpet, the Axminster carpet has plush pile rather than the loop pile of the Brussels carpet. The Axminster carpet is actually tufted, as it is woven rather than made of pile from cut warp or weft loops. The Axminster loom includes a tufting mechanism that is as wide as the carpet pattern and includes as many parallel spools of this width as there are rows in the design before a repeat. Each spool is wound with as many parallel rolls of tufting yarn as there are reeds, or tufts, in the width of the design. Each roll is the color for its spot in the design. Each of the parallel spools represents a row of tufts in the pattern. The spools feed a row of tubes, with each tube producing a tuft in the width of the pattern by inserting a loop of colored yarn between the upper rows of the warp. The loop is anchored by a double weft shot through the base of the tuft so that the tuft encircles the weft. This differs from handknotted carpets, where the tuft or knot encircles the warp. A pair of broad knives then cut the tufts from the tufting mechanism. The tufting mechanism is generally the size of one repeat of the pattern. This method of producing the pattern and pile is more suited for producing a uniform repeating carpet pattern than for producing a pattern with a border and center medallion, as is typical of Oriental rugs.

The Axminster process spawned a wide range of variations of differing quality according to the layers of stuffer warp and weft and the number of tufts per inch, but because of the intricacy of the setup process, the Axminster was the most expensive of the popular machine-made carpets of the second half of the nineteenth century. The Axminster loom was later improved with the addition of a gripper mechanism that allowed preweaving preparation to be simplified and carpet production to be more economical without sacrificing the intricacy and range of colors possible in the pattern.

The Velvet and Tapestry Weave. In the nineteenth century, the Velvet weave and its loop pile counterpart, the Tapestry weave, were flexible in the designs they could accommodate because the yarn was preprinted with the pattern to be woven. The preparation of the pile yarn for use in a tapestry or velvet carpet required that it be wound onto a drum the width of the pattern to be produced and large enough in circumference to hold the full length of a single warp for the length of the piece. The yarn on the drum was then printed with a version of the desired pattern, distorted to correct for the depth of the pile in the woven carpet. The yarn was then woven into the carpet as part of the warp. The pile yarn was looped over wires and anchored into the carpet with the weft as in the Brussels weave.

The patterns for velvet or tapestry carpets could not feature strongly contrasting adjacent colors or clearly defined elements because the colors tended to bleed into one another as they were printed on a single continuous pile yarn. Although the loom and weaving method are still used today, for solid or tweed carpets with variegated pile yarns formed by twisting two colors of yarn together, the method of producing a pattern by preprinting the yarn has been abandoned.

Chenille Axminster. The most flexible of the machine-weaving methods is the chenille Axminster. It is not as limited as the Brussels or Wilton weaves in the number of colors that can be used, as limited as the Axminster in the size of the pattern before it must repeat, or as limited as the Velvet or Tapestry weaves in the contrast of the colors. It is also the only machine-woven carpet in which the pattern and pile are created by the weft.

There are two fabrics that must be made in order to weave a Chenille carpet. The first is the Chenille fur blanket, and the second is the actual carpet. As with most carpets since the Sefavid dynasty, a chenille carpet is designed on gridded paper. For a Chenille carpet, the paper carpet design is cut into a continuous strip that simulates the color changes in the weft yarn necessary to produce the desired design. The weaver uses this paper strip to guide the feeding of yarn of the needed colors into the loom to make the Chenille fur blanket. The colored yarns are the weft of this fabric, and groups of fine cotton thread set at 0.5–1-in. intervals, according to the length of pile desired in the finished carpet, are the warp. Once this fur blanket is woven, it is cut into a continuous strip so that the weft threads are cut halfway between the groups of cotton warp threads on each side of the blade. This results in a continuous strip of individual parallel lengths of fur held together in the center by a narrow woven strip of cotton thread. This strip of fur is steam set into a vee, with the cotton thread at the vortex. The crimped chenille fur is woven into the carpet through the shed between the "catcher" warp and the rest of the fabric being woven. Four shots of filling weft are woven into the fabric between each row of chenille fur to create the foundation of the carpet.

The Chenille process of carpet making requires hand labor to comb and straighten each row of chenille fur as it is woven into the carpet foundation. For this reason, it is an expensive process. It is used for custom-made carpets because it can be used to produce carpets up to 30 ft in width and allows great flexibility in pattern, color, and shape.

The Ingrain Carpet. The least expensive and most practical carpet of the nineteenth century was a flat-weave carpet known as an Ingrain, a Kidderminster, or a Scotch carpet. In its simplest form, it was woven in two colors with two layers or plies of warp and was called a two-ply ingrain. These carpets had no pile and were reversible. The weave was similar to a textile tapestry weave except that in an ingrain carpet, when a color was discontinued in the pattern, the yarn, although remaining continuous, was shifted to the other ply rather than returned in the opposite direction, as it would be in the tapestry weave. Thus, the two sides of a two-ply ingrain had reverse color schemes. One side, for example, could have a green ground with blue flowers, whereas the other side would have a blue ground with green flowers.

More complex designs were also produced in the two-ply ingrain by introducing color changes in the warp as well as the weft or by using four colors. A thicker carpet, the three-ply ingrain, used three to six colors and three plies of warp, resulting in a totally internal stuffer ply, with many possibilities for complex designs resulting. The use of two Jacquard attachments even made it possible to have three-ply ingrains with different patterns on each side.

Ingrain carpets had been made on hand looms since the mid-eighteenth century, and the invention of the Jacquard attachment in 1800 allowed intricately patterned hand-loomed ingrain carpets to be mass produced. But Bigelow's steam-powered ingrain loom, patented in 1842, before he perfected the Brussels power loom, allowed the daily production of a carpet mill to increase fourfold. The economy of production and the ease of maintenance of this nonpile, tightly woven carpet made the ingrain carpet the most popular fabric floor covering throughout the nineteenth century, an era before efficient carpet sweepers or vacuum cleaners.

THE INDUSTRIAL AGE

Even with the nineteenth-century onslaught of industrialization, important architects and designers still designed rugs to be produced by hand. A principal advantage of the hand loom over the power loom during the nineteenth century was the large size possible. The mech-

anized and power looms of the nineteenth century generally could make carpets up to only 3 ft wide. Machine-made room-size carpets were made by seaming together the necessary strips of carpet.

In 1817, architect John Nash commissioned Robert Jones to design three huge carpets for the renovation of the Brighton Pavilion for King George IV. The largest of these was 61 × 40 ft. The carpet for the Banqueting Room was round and was designed in a Chinese motif of dragons and serpents, reflecting both the domed ceiling and the chinoiserie of the rest of the decor.

In the UK the Great Exhibition of 1851 was the beginning of an examination of national architectural and decorative style as the British started to react to the impact of industrialization. An important concern was the fact that other European countries made much greater use of artists and trained designers in the manufacture of all types of machine-made goods. A criticism particular to the design of carpets was the incoherent complexity and the appearance of a third dimension in carpet designs. Objection was raised to treading on apparently three-dimensional, realistic, flamboyant woven renditions of roses, ferns, cornucopias, fruit, and the inevitable acanthus leaves. In reaction to the self-conscious virtuosity of the early industrial age, artists and designers looked to handmade Oriental rugs from Persia and Turkey.

MODERN ORIENTAL RUGS

At the Paris Exhibition of 1871 and the South Kensington International Exhibition of the same year, carpets manufactured in the UK and France were displayed that were clearly inspired by known Persian and Turkish examples. The abstracted natural motifs, subtle geometric order, and intricate frame made by the sophisticated design of the border of Oriental rugs set the standard for contemporary machine and handmade rug and carpet design. Handmade Oriental rugs were also entering a transitional period. Oriental rugs and carpets made after 1870 are inheritors of a proud tradition, but are a different product from their predecessors. Rugs made prior to 1870 are considered antique, and those from 1870 to the present are considered modern Oriental rugs.

William Morris was one of the leaders of the arts and crafts movement in the UK and a strong proponent of the excellence of Persian and Turkish rug design. He used his careful study of Persian rugs to design pieces for both machine and hand manufacture. His desire was to establish a carpet design tradition in the UK that would allow works of art to be created there that were comparable with those of the East. Later architects influenced by this movement, including C. F. A. Voysey and Charles Rennie MacKintosh, also designed carpets as part of a unified design for an entire interior. The same reaction against the excesses of the machine age also led to an almost insatiable appetite in the United States and Europe for imported authentic handmade Oriental rugs.

With the growing interest in Oriental rugs in the West, Persia sent a display to the 1873 Vienna World Exhibition, which increased the demand for Oriental rugs even more. It was also about this time that what would become the Victoria & Albert Museum began a sizable collection of Oriental rugs. Such exposure served to heighten the growing public dissatisfaction with machine-made goods. Ironically, it was the new prosperity resulting from the industrial age in Europe and the United States that greatly expanded the bourgeoisie that had the means to acquire handmade Oriental rugs.

Charles Eastlake's *Hints on Household Taste in Furniture, Upholstery and Other Details* was published during this period. In this book, Eastlake advocated the aesthetic and sanitary superiority of hand-knotted Oriental rugs. In contrast to the earlier convention of wall-to-wall machine-made carpets, Eastlake recommended that less-than-room-size Oriental rugs be laid over hardwood floors. Accommodation to the fashion of using area rugs on hardwood floors was often accomplished in more frugal households, limited to the usual pine floors, by using machine-made wall-to-wall carpets with a contrasting border seamed into the piece around the edges of the room, suggesting an Oriental rug. The reform philosophy of Eastlake and Morris and the arts and crafts or craftsman movement in general valued hand labor over machine production, and was averse to including three-dimensional realistic representations of fruit and flowers in a fabric to be walked on, and appreciated the health value of rugs that could be carried outside and beaten in this pre-vacuum-cleaner era, an appreciation that prevailed well beyond the turn of the century.

The demand for Oriental rugs generated by this change in European and U.S. tastes hit the East at a time when the hand-knotting tradition was at a low point. Because of political and military upheavals, few districts or regions of the East were advancing the design tradition of hand-knotted rugs. The works being produced were primarily coarser copies of old patterns, and there was little design vitality being introduced. To Western eyes, they were beautiful nonetheless.

With the demand for Oriental rugs increasing dramatically in the West and the art form in decline in the East, conditions were ripe for cost-cutting measures. Traditional color schemes were changed to meet the whims of Western fashion, synthetic chemical dyes replaced traditional vegetable and other natural dyes, and longer pile was used to create the appearance of greater luxury and to try to hide the fact that fewer knots per inch were being used. Such methods resulted in rugs with less durability, substantial loss of detail and clarity in delicate patterns, and simplified designs. With these changes in traditional techniques, 1870 is considered the beginning of modern Oriental rug production. Although some dealers call pre-World War II twentieth-century pieces antique, only rugs manufactured before 1870 should be considered antique.

Characteristics of an Oriental Rug

The Type of Knot. The type of knot, and the number of warps it encircles, can be the Turkish knot, the Persian knot encircling the left warp or the right warp or the Turkish or Persian knot tied around four warps as a cost cutting measure, called a jufti, making a weaker fabric.

The Knot Count. The knot count per square inch can range from 10 to 1000 knots; 60–80 knots/in.^{2} is considered standard today. By comparison, machine-made Axminster carpets, which most closely approximate the handmade Oriental rug, usually have a maximum knot count of 50 tufts/in.^{2} A good rug maker can turn out 6000 to 10,000 knots per day.

The Number of Weft Lines. The number of weft lines that separate each row of knots anchoring them into the rug's foundation is usually one to three shots or rows. If three shots are used and the first and third are pulled tight, the warp will be layered, giving the back of the carpet a ridged appearance and giving more body to the piece.

The Composition of Warp, Weft, and Pile Yarns. The composition of warp, weft, and pile yarns was most commonly silk and wool in antique rugs; the less expensive but less durable cotton and jute have become common in the warp and weft of modern rugs.

The Ply of Yarn. The ply of yarn is the direction of twist of the plies together, the direction of spin of the fibers into the thread of a ply, and the number of individual strands plied together to make the yarn of the warp, weft, and pile with more plies, or strands twisted together to make the yarn, the yarn is thicker, fewer knots need to be tied to incorporate a given amount of material into the piece, and so a less detailed design results. In modern Oriental rugs, the wool is usually machine spun.

Dimension, Finish, and Fringe. The dimensions and finish of the selvage and fringes at the end of the warps have become much more standardized as carpet weavers have been organized into large factories rather than individual workshops; machine-made copies of Oriental rugs often have a premade fringe sewn onto two opposite ends of the rug.

Colors. The use of colors, with the improvement of synthetic chemical dyes since their first use in Oriental rugs in the late nineteenth century, is no longer the liability it once was, but rugs produced as works of art rather than mere decorative or furnishing articles have returned to the use of natural dyes. In antique rugs, there are varying qualities of natural dyes; modern rugs are often bleached to look antique and treated to increase wool luster.

Style. Style is classified by geography. There are 6 main classifications by region and more than 50 identifiable styles, named according to a city or town within a district in which the style is traditional.

The Main Classifications of Modern Oriental Carpets

Persian. Persian rugs are predominantly from modern-day Iran. They make the most extensive use of stylized plants; birds and animals are used in a free-flowing and curvilinear fashion; and the ground is usually covered almost entirely by the pattern.

Turkoman. Turkoman rugs are usually from Turkestan, Bokhara, Afghanistan, or Beluchistan. They generally have a red ground and woven, rather than knotted, fringes. The design is usually composed of geometric patterns such as squares, diamonds, octagons, stars, and crosses. Because of the isolation of these regions, the designs have been the least affected by modernized influences.

Caucasian. Caucasian rugs differ from Turkoman rugs in that red is not as dominant in the designs and the rugs do not have woven fringes. Persian-inspired curvilinear forms and patterns are included with geometric forms in the designs.

Turkish. Turkish rugs rely heavily on geometric forms, but show the influence of the importation of naturalistic Persian designs during the Ottoman dynasty.

Chinese. Chinese hand-knotted rug making has a long history, but it was never considered an art form and was thus more susceptible to foreign commercial influence. The colors in an individual piece are limited but effective. Motifs or patterns usually float in the ground as individual elements rather than being intermingled and interdependent as in most other Oriental rugs.

Indian. Indian and Pakistani rugs are produced for export. India and Pakistan are currently the largest exporters of hand-knotted rugs in the world. The quality is poor, yet improving. The cost is low because the labor is the cheapest in the world. Cotton dhurries are the traditional rug. This tapestry, plain-woven rug is made in many innovative designs.

Within these six classifications, there are finer geographic subdivisions that serve as style names. These styles are also often made outside their traditional region. For example, the Esfahán rug, the archetypal Persian rug design, named after an Iranian city that was the Sefavid capital of Persia, is characterized by deep reds, a range of blues and creams, arabesques, and elaborate borders of scrolling flowers and clouds. Today, it is also made in India, Pakistan, and Romania, areas without strong indigenous traditions, but with strong modern rug export industries. These latter rugs, often of questionable quality, are called Esfahán rugs by some rug merchants. To be more accurate, these rugs should be called Esfahán-type or Esfahán-inspired rugs.

Although technique, fibers, and dyes are all crucial in the construction of Oriental rugs, there are also some important intangible elements woven into these works of art. Today's Oriental rugs have the distillation of over 2000 years of tradition, history, religion, and mythology woven into their foundation, pile, and pattern along with the warp, chain, weft, and knots. The patterns of Oriental rugs represent order in the universe with heaven above and earth below, the four points of the compass, the dome of the sky, the door into heaven, the garden of Eden, divine light, the framework of time, the continents floating in the sea among dragons and other creatures, warring good and evil, and the transitory pleasures of this world that have to be beaten in order to attain the permanent pleasures of another world. The fascination and enchantment of Oriental rugs owes as much to the depth and lost meaning of the symbolism of the designs as it does to the skill of the rug maker.

OTHER HANDMADE RUG TRADITIONS

The influence of Morris and the arts and crafts movement and the disenchantment with mid-nineteenth-century industrialized manufacture reached Scandivania as well. Both Sweden and Finland had national handicraft societies by the last quarter of the century. In Finland, at the turn of the century, architects Herman Gesellins, Armas Lindgren, and Eliel Saarinen built Hvittrask, a log-cabin-style house incorporating traditional Finnish construction techniques. Saarinen's wife designed and wove Finnish folk art inspired rugs for Hvittrask, as well as rugs for Frank Lloyd Wright in the United States. The traditional rug in Scandinavia was the *rya* or *ryiji,* which used a knot similar to the Turkish knot. Prior to the fifteenth century, these rugs had a long shaggy pile of primarily undyed yarn. Often, these rugs had pile on both sides and were used as bedcovers, in barter, and as dowries. Special rugs were woven for weddings; the couple stood on the rug during the ceremony and then used it as a covering for the marriage bed. Until the eighteenth century, these rugs were primarily black, white, and gray. Occasionally, yellow and red were also used. Motifs included boy–girl pairs for wedding rugs, pots of flowers, double hearts, and heraldic styled animals.

U.S. Navaho rugs also became popular in turn of the century decor as a result of the arts and crafts movement. The Navaho weaving tradition began in the 1700s as a translation into wool of the older cotton weaving tradition of the Pueblo Indians. The Navahos had been sheepherders since the Spaniards had introduced sheep to North America in the seventeenth century. Before the great demand created by white traders at the turn of the century, the Navahos wove primarily flat-woven blankets and garments. As with Oriental rugs, the interference of foreigners and a sudden surge of demand almost destroyed the tradition. Several traders, however, including J. B. Moore of Crystal, N. Mex. and Lorenzo Hubball of Ganado organized the local craft, adapted and standardized designs to ensure the marketability of the product, and modified the weave to produce the tapestry floor coverings that were in demand. The 1930s and 1940s followed as a period of revival of the older, simpler color schemes using vegetable dyes and traditional patterns.

TUFTED CARPET

A number of other handmade rug types were also developed in the United States. Yarn-sewn rugs on a burlap or homespun linen base, appliquéd shirred rugs, braided rugs, rag knitted and woven rugs, and hooked rugs on a variety of bases, the most popular of which was imported Indian jute burlap, were all attempts by U.S. housewives to cover their floors with affordable, decorative, thick fabric. The most important of these was developed from the craft of candlewicking.

The Candlewicking Technique

The candlewicking technique was first used in the early 1900s for the production of bedspreads. In this technique, the backing is woven separately from the final product. The pile of the carpet or bedspread is produced by locking tufts of yarn in the fabric backing. In bedspread manufacture, the tufts are locked into the backing by shrinking the backing fabric around the tufts. With the introduction of latex, adhesive for locking the tufts into the backing, and a multineedle tufting machine in the early 1940s, the machine-made tufted carpet industry was established. After 12-ft wide broadloom tufting machines were introduced in the late 1940s and the secondary backing was added in the late 1950s, the modern tufted carpet industry was in full production. Today, more than 90% of the carpet yardage produced in the United States is tufted.

Tufted carpet is manufactured using rows of needles to insert loops of pile yarn into a primary backing as the backing is fed through the tufting machine. The tufting machine works much like a sewing machine with hundreds of needles. The rows of needles are as long as the carpet is wide. Each needle inserts a "seam" of loops from the backside of the primary backing, which are caught by a hooklike looper that moves backwards and forwards in conjunction with the up-and-down movement of the needle. If the carpet is to have looped pile, much like the nineteenth-century Brussels woven carpet, then the looper does not include a blade. If the tufted carpet is to have cut pile, the looper includes a blade, and the finished product is similar in texture to the Wilton or velvet weaves.

As with woven and hand-knotted rugs and carpets, the resistance to abrasion, crushing, and soiling of the carpet is largely determined by the density of the pile. The pile density in tufted carpets is determined by multiplying the number of needles per inch across the width of the carpet and the number of stitches per inch along the length of the carpet to arrive at the number of tufts per square inch. The number of needles per inch is often referred to as the gauge of the carpet and is recorded as a fraction, with the numerator being the number of inches and the denominator being the number of needles in the length given in the numerator. These measurements of pile density are equivalent in woven carpets to the pitch, the number of loops of yarn in 27 in. across the width of the loom and rows per inch along the length of the carpet. However, in tufted carpet, the possible pile density is limited by the strength of the primary backing.

Until the mid-1960s, jute was the most commonly used backing material for both the primary and secondary backing. It can withstand the numerous close penetrations of the tufting needles necessary to produce a dense carpet without subsequently tearing when stretched for installation. But jute can also shrink and stain the surface of the carpet after it has gotten wet, and since jute is a natural fiber, it supports the growth of mold and mildew. Another factor that has led to the use of synthetic backing fabrics is that most jute must be imported from India or Pakistan. This has frequently led to an irregularity of supply.

Many tufted carpets today use woven polypropylene as a primary backing and jute as a secondary backing. Although a polypropylene primary backing limits the density possible in a tufted carpet and printing and dyeing methods using high temperatures cannot be used on piece goods made with a polypropylene primary backing, it is desirable because it is waterproof and nonabsorbent. This reduces staining and simplifies cleaning. The secondary backing of jute absorbs adhesive better than polypropylene, thus ensuring a good seal in direct glue-down installations and helping prevent delamination of the primary and secondary backing.

The latex adhesive used in the manufacture of tufted carpets is key in determining the quality and performance of tufted carpets. The quality of the latex is key in determining both the tuft bind strength of the carpet and the delamination strength. Tuft bind strength is a measure of how well the individual tufts are held in the foundation of the carpet; the industry standard is a force of 15 lb exerted on a tuft. Delamination strength is a measure of the ability of the carpet to withstand horizontal as well as vertical force without separation of the primary and secondary backing.

The material of the primary and secondary backing, the quality of the latex adhesive, and a limitation on the density of tufts per square inch are keys to evaluating the specifications of tufted carpets. Other key components of the specifications apply to all machine-made carpets, both tufted and woven.

CARPET SPECIFICATIONS

In addition to the method of manufacture, such as Axminster, Wilton, or Velvet weaves or tufting, the components of a carpet specification include pile height and pile density, face weight, fiber type, yarn characteristics, surface texture, color and dye method, and any special treatments for stain resistance or to reduce the level of static electricity buildup. These components work together to determine performance. Issues in describing performance include abrasion resistance, resistance to crushing, resilience, texture retention, soil and stain resistance, cleanability, color retention, static control, and flame resistance. The components of a specification also work together to determine the attractiveness or aesthetic appeal of a carpet.

Face Weight. Although pile density is key in determining the durability of a carpet, its resistance to crushing and soiling, and its resilience, the pile height is the main feature that determines the softness or luxurious feel of the carpet. These two characteristics determine the face weight of the carpet. A dense carpet with a low pile height can have the same face weight as a less dense carpet of the same material with a greater pile height. Even if the same amount of material went into the manufacture of both carpets, the denser carpet would retain its appearance longer.

The face weight of the carpet is a measure of the amount of yarn used in the pile of the carpet. It is measured in ounces per square yard. Pile height and density are not the only factors that determine the face weight of a carpet. Because so much of the pile yarn in a woven carpet remains in the foundation of the carpet, the face weight of a woven and tufted carpet cannot be accurately compared. The physical properties of the fiber used in the pile yarn, such as its weight for a given volume of yarn, are also factors in the face weight of a carpet. The face weights of a variety of carpets can be accurately compared only when the carpets are made from the same fiber. Today's carpets are made primarily of nylon, wool, polypropylene, acrylic, and polyester. Although acrylic and nylon are similar in weight, a carpet must have a face weight of acrylic that is more than twice that of nylon in order to wear as well as a nylon carpet. Polyester is heavier than acrylic, but for the same face weight, which is actually less yarn, the wearability is greater. Wool, the traditional yarn for rug and carpet making since the fifth century BC, is heavier than all the synthetic carpet fibers. However, wool is less than 15% heavier than Nylon, yet a face weight at least twice as great is required for equivalent durability in a carpet. In an area of average foot traffic, a carpet with a 42-oz face weight should be the minimum specified for a wool or acrylic carpet, whereas for equivalent performance, a 28-oz carpet of nylon or polypropylene would be sufficient.

Wool. Wool is the archetypal carpet fiber. Whereas less than 1% of the carpet yardage sold in the United States is wool carpet, approximately 50% of the carpet yardage sold in Europe is wool. Wool has better soil resistance and cleanability than any of the synthetic fibers. This is partially due to its static charge, which, unlike some highly positively charged synthetics, attracts less dust. It is also partially due to the construction of wool fiber, which helps hide dirt. The surface of wool fiber resembles a series of overlapping fish scales and diffuses light because it is rough. By contrast, synthetic fibers are generally smooth. Wool also has a natural crimp or curl, and thus has better texture retention and resilience than most synthetics. The combination of the rough surface and the natural crimp gives wool a soft and fluffy feel, or hand, compared with synthetic carpet fibers.

The synthetic fibers are generally formulated and engineered to imitate or improve on wool as a carpet fiber. The most advanced nylon, so-called fourth-generation nylon, has been developed with a large filament size and light-scattering striations on the formerly shiny, smooth filament surface, allowing it to surpass the soil resistance and cleanability of wool. Despite significant drawbacks, acrylic yarns continue to be used in carpet manufacture because they accept the same wide range of dyes and colors with a similar rich appearance, and the pile has a feel or hand similar to that of wool. Polypropylene and polyester are much more durable and resistant to abrasion than wool, but are being improved so that their crush resistance and resilience will compare favorably with those of wool. All of the synthetic fibers are less expensive than wool.

Nylon. Since the 1960s, nylon has served as the bench mark for measuring the relative performance of synthetic carpet fibers. With wool essentially priced out of the U.S. market (all wool carpet fiber is imported), the other synthetic fibers compete primarily with nylon. Today, almost 90% of the carpet yardage sold in the United States is nylon. Since the 1960s, nylon has been constantly improved so that all of its properties and characteristics might surpass those of wool. Its feel or hand and its range and quality of color and colorfastness have been greatly improved over the past 20 years. Its cleanability or stain resistance and the strength of its electrostatic charge are the two characteristics that have received the most attention in recent years.

Nylon producers have introduced several innovations to increase the fiber's stain resistance and cleanability. They have introduced a dye into solution nylon, before it is extruded as a fiber, in order to deluster the fiber. Delustered nylon more closely resembles the soft color quality of wool and is no longer translucent, thus allowing it to hide dirt better. Manufacturers have molded the cross section of the fiber so that it scatters light better than the original round cross section. A trilobal cross section was used by some manufacturers, but the curved sides trapped dirt. Further innovation led to the development of a fiber with an almost triangular cross section and one with an almost square, partially hollow cross section. In order to reduce further the dust-trapping surface area, the fiber cross section has been enlarged from 15–25 den to 34 den so that fewer fibers are needed to create the same weight of material, and fewer fibers means less surface area to collect dirt. Treatment of the fibers with fluorocarbon preparations, which dramatically increases the stain resistance of the yarn, has also become more common as the technology for applying them has improved. Fluorocarbon treatments are effective only as long as they stay on the fiber, so technology for adding fluorocarbon to the nylon solution before it is extruded as fiber or including the fluorocarbon in the dyeing process has been developed to replace the less effective method of spraying the completed carpet with a stain-resisting surface treatment.

Efforts to reduce the static charge built up in nylon carpet when it is stroked by the materials commonly found in shoe soles have included antistatic sprays (which wear off), thin metal filaments spun into the yarn to act essentially as lightning rods (which can break or crush easily), and carbon filaments inserted into the fiber or yarn construction (which can cause a slight discoloration in lighter colors). Static charges are a problem for both human comfort, since they can cause unpleasant shocks, and computer reliability, since the shocks to the computer can erase a whole day's work, at best. Since the computer's threshold for feeling a static shock is significantly lower than a human's and since an increasing number of workstations in a typical office are being computerized, there is still room for improvement in static control carpet technology.

Nylon, like most synthetic fibers, can be used in carpets

either as a yarn spun from staple fibers, comparable with spun wool yarn, or as a bulked continuous filament yarn. Spun staple yarns are made up of short pieces of filament, around 6 in. long, spun together to make threads that are then spun into yarns of one to six plies. Continuous filament yarns are made up of plies of continuous filaments that can be as much as 30 mi long. Except in the most advanced bulked continuous filament nylons, staple yarns are generally bulkier than filament yarns of the same weight. Bulked continuous filament yarns are given their bulk and texture by heat setting the yarn in a twist, a crimp, or a knit and then temporarily straightening it to tuft or weave it into a carpet.

Until recently, continuous filament yarns were used in loop pile carpets, and spun staple yarns were used in cut pile carpets. Advances in nylon dyeing and bulking methods have provided sufficient color and texture uniformity to allow advanced nylon bulked continuous filament yarns to be used in cut pile applications. In lower-face-weight carpets, there are several advantages to being able to use bulked continuous filament yarns in cut pile carpet manufacture. The twist of the plies of a continuous filament yarn can be tighter and more uniform than with staple yarns, and this results in better texture retention and greater resistance to matting and crushing. The continuous filament structure also reduces the fuzzing and shedding that occur in cut pile carpets made from staple yarns, which result from loose staple filaments that miss being locked into the primary backing.

Other Important Characteristics of Carpet Yarn

The Yarn Count. The yarn count, or the number of yards of yarn to the ounce, usually given as a fraction, with the numerator indicating the number of plies and the denominator indicating the length in yards of 1 oz of the yarn; the lower the number of yarns per ounce, the heavier the yarn.

The Denier. The denier, or the weight of yarn in grams per 9000 m; the lower the denier, the finer the filament of yarn.

Plies. The number of *plies* which is a factor in the texture and finish, more than in the quality or performance, of a carpet.

The variations in pile height and density and mixtures of loop and plush are the key factors in determining the texture and style of the carpet. There are eight basic tufted carpet textures.

Level Loop Pile. Level loop pile has the best durability, resilience, and resistance to crushing; variations include alternating rows of cut and uncut loops.

Cut Pile. Cut pile is often called plush, saxony, or velvet, depending on the pile height, pile density, number of plies, and amount of crimp or twist in the pile yarn.

Level Tip Shear. Level tip shear is where the pile height is even, but some texture is created by the pattern with which the loops are cut.

Random Shear and Multilevel Loop. Random shear and multilevel loop are where the tufts are at varying heights, with either all of them uncut or the highest tufts cut with the remainder uncut. When new, these textures hide dirt and crushing well, but soon wear and crush to a relatively even height.

Frieze or Twist. Frieze or twist is where the yarns are dramatically bulked with a tight heat-set crimp to increase resilience and crush resistance. This can be difficult to vacuum because of the rough surface.

Shags. Shags have an extreme pile height (1.5–2 in. long), but usually are not adequately dense to prevent the pile from crushing easily. They are limited to light-traffic residential use.

Sculptured or Carved. Sculptured or carved carpet is tufted with even pile height and then sheared at varying heights to carve or sculpt a design into the surface.

Finally, the most obvious characteristics of a carpet's style are its color and pattern. There are a variety of methods for creating carpet colors.

Stock Dyeing. Stock dyeing is used for some staple yarns; the staple fibers are dyed prior to being spun into threads to be used as plies in yarn. It is effective in increasing the color range possible in synthetic fibers such as polypropylene that accept only a limited number of dyes; yarn colors can be created by spinning staples of several colors together.

Solution Dyeing. Solution dyeing is where dye is added to synthetic fiber solutions before the fiber is extruded; the resulting yarn is extremely colorfast.

Skein Dyeing. Skein dyeing is similar to traditional hand wool dyeing methods. Yarn, either bulked continuous filament or staple, is dyed by the skein once spun.

Package Dyeing. Package dyeing is where undyed yarn is wound onto perforated packages and stored to be dyed as needed by forcing the dye into the yarn from the center of the package without unwinding or repackaging.

Space Dyeing. Space dyeing is where three or more colors are used to create a random pattern of colors when used in the carpet.

Moresque Yarns. Moresque yarns are created when a carpet yarn is made up of plies of different colors; they produce a tweed pattern.

Piece Dyeing. Piece dyeing is where color is not applied until after the carpet has been tufted. Undyed carpet called greige goods is stored in its natural color and dyed as needed. Before tufting, undyed yarns can be treated to accept color differently and then tufted to create a pattern when the piece is dyed.

Carpet Printing. Carpet printing, because of the complexities involved in tufting multicolored patterns into carpet, is used for most patterned, tufted carpet. As the technology is improved, the results are becoming quite satisfactory.

Carpet color is beset with a variety of modern quality control problems. In direct glue-down installations covering vast surfaces, such as open-plan offices or airport walkways, keeping the color constant from side to side and along the length of a run is important. With the introduction of more effective chemical and heat cleaning methods, colorfastness has become important. With sophisticated interior color schemes, exact reproducibility of the color in each dye lot is important. The technology of carpet patterning and coloring is rapidly changing to meet these demands better.

INSTALLATION

Besides the economy and durability introduced into carpet manufacture by synthetic fibers, a key factor in the recent transition of carpet from a luxury furnishing item to a basic building material was the introduction in 1965 of the direct glue-down method of installation. In direct glue-down installation, the carpet is glued directly to the floor without a pad or cushion underneath. Because the carpet is firmly attached to the floor across its entire surface, the stretching and buckling inherent in more traditional installation methods in which the carpet is anchored at the edges of the room over a cushion or pad are no longer a potential source of uneven wear and tripping hazards. The most important advantage of the direct glue-down installation method is that it allows carpet to be used over large areas, such as whole floors of office buildings. The durability of synthetic fibers allows walls to be installed over the carpet. Carpet installed using the direct glue-down method wears faster than the same carpet installed over a pad and is difficult to remove when it must be replaced. These drawbacks are not important when compared with the speed, efficiency, and dependability of direct glue-down installation.

FUTURE

The millenia-old rug and carpet industry continues to evolve to meet modern demands. The most advanced method of carpet manufacture is even more removed from traditional weaving or stitching methods than anything introduced heretofore. It is totally dependent on advances in adhesive chemistry. In this process, called fusion bonding, two parallel vertical sheets of jute backing coated with adhesive on the sides facing each other are run past a mechanism that folds yarn back and forth against the two backing sheets, embedding the yarn in the adhesive on both sheets of the jute. The adhesive is then heat set, and the yarn is sliced up the middle, creating two pieces of cut pile carpet. This method of manufacturing cut pile carpet keeps 100% of the pile yarn on the surface of the carpet, resulting in markedly better performance than that of tufted carpets with the same face weight. The heat-set adhesive creates a solid waterproof barrier that prevents liquid spills or grit from reaching the backing, thus slow-

ing its wear. The process is still more expensive and slower than tufting, but is rapidly being improved.

Another carpet manufacturing technology that is rapidly evolving is that of carpet tile. Carpet tile is often manufactured by the needle-bonding process. Needle bonding was developed in the early 1960s to make inexpensive polypropylene matting for miniature golf courses. It is actually the modern version of ancient felting and matting techniques and comes closest to the ancient meaning of "rug"—tangled hair. Carpet tiles are valuable in highly automated offices with a need for frequent access to interstitial space below the floor or that use flat cable under the carpet for electrical and communication wiring needs.

The use of rugs and carpets in the West has come full circle since the Renaissance, when Oriental rugs were taken off the walls to replace cut reeds and grasses as indoor floor coverings. Outdoor carpet has now replaced growing grass as the playing surface in outdoor stadiums, and inexpensive polyester tufted carpets without secondary backings have gone back on the wall as glued-on wall coverings with excellent acoustic properties.

BIBLIOGRAPHY

General References

R. G. Hubel, *The Book of Carpets,* Praeger Publishers, New York, 1970.

L. Shoshkes, *Contract Carpeting,* Watson Guptill Publications, New York, 1974.

A. Landreau, *American Underfoot: A History of Floor Coverings from Colonial Times to the Present,* Smithsonian Institution Press, Washington, D.C., 1976.

I. Bennett, ed., *Rugs & Carpets of the World,* New Burlington Books, London, 1977.

N. Miller, "Third Generation," *Progressive Architecture* 3(80), 110–115 (Mar. 1980).

D. Black, ed., *The MacMillan Atlas of Rugs & Carpets,* MacMillan Publishing Co., New York, 1985.

G. Winkler and R. Moss, *Victorian Interior Decoration,* Henry Holt & Co., New York, 1986.

T. McDonald, "Challenges of Synthetic Carpets," *Architecture, The AIA Journal,* 123–125 (Feb. 1988).

LAURIE PUTSCHER
Annapolis, Maryland

SCIENCE AND TECHNOLOGY CENTERS

Attendance at the 200 institutions that are members of the Association of Science-Technology Centers (ASTC) is over 50 million visitors a year, and new science-technology centers are being formed around the world.

These institutions are similar to traditional museums in that they mount exhibits for the public, have regular visits from school groups, and conduct educational programs related to the exhibits. But they are also distinguished from traditional museums, even science museums, by several characteristics:

1. Use of interactive exhibits requiring visitor participation.
2. Emphasis on contemporary science and technology, with little chronological information or historical context.
3. Elevation of public education to their primary mission, displacing research, conservation, and collection to secondary functions.

Science and technology centers have not established a tradition of external critical reviews of exhibitions and programs, such as those for art museum exhibitions. The centers often rely on the number of visitors for the major measure of the institution's success. This has led to controversial measures, such as the use of large theaters with domes or panoramic screens, to increase attendance and provide extra revenue, even if the presentations in the theaters have minimal education intent. For the centers to define their roles in a broader context of science and technology education, they will have to go beyond popularity and determine more precisely just what it is they can achieve.

At the beginning of the 20th century, the ideas of the serious-minded practical technology museum and the popular industrial exposition were combined to create the modern science and technology museum. The Deutsches Museum in Munich and the Museum of Science and Industry in Chicago are the most famous of these original institutions. Their primary goal was public education with exhibits that could be touched or even operated. Some hands-off exhibits did remain, showing that preservation and collection were additional functions.

In the 1960s the science-technology centers took this trend one step further. The success of the Russian space program, illustrated by the launching of the first Sputnik satellite, had elevated science education in the United States to a matter of national urgency. The influence of Jean Piaget's theories of learning, stressing the role of concrete experience early in the process, had inspired a new generation of "hands-on" science curricula for the schools. Science and technology centers responded to these trends by taking as models the museums of science and industry, but elevating public education to their dominant goal, with interactivity as their dominant technique.

With little or no intention of collecting, preserving, or researching valuable objects, it became an issue as to whether these institutions qualified for accreditation in the American Association of Museums, which regarded conservation and research as key elements of any museum. This was one reason for the formation of ASTC, which required interactive exhibits but did not require conservation or research as criteria for full membership. In the science-technology centers, objects were present in order to be used, not preserved. Thus the members of ASTC became a third generation science museum, so far removed from the original function of museums, to preserve and display collections, that they often dropped the name "museum." The evolution in goals of the three generations of institutions is summarized in Table 1.

The centers normally have no tenured staff or curators, whose functions are based on the model of professors in universities. Senior staff are primarily teachers and designers, rather than research scholars. Exhibit development has always been a major activity but on-site workshops, teacher training, curriculum development, outreach programs in schools and community sites, and recently educational theater programs have become significant factors in many science centers.

So far, these institutions might seem to resemble schools more than museums. Indeed many science-technology centers were set up intentionally to be extensions of schools, such as the Palais de la Decouverte in Paris and the Fernbank Center in Atlanta. But science-technology centers do not function particularly well in illustrating elements of a typical curriculum. Major topics of established curricula, such as biology, chemistry, and geography, have proven hard to treat with interactive exhibits. Many exhibits are developed almost as pieces of art, with the interests and inspirations of the staff determining the content. Exhibits on light, color, sound, and mechanics were produced by such centers as the Exploratorium in San Francisco, and widely reproduced by new centers.

The success of the interactive style of exhibitory itself has been the unique contribution which distinguishes the science-technology centers from earlier forms of museums and from other media of education.

STYLES OF INTERACTIVE EXHIBITS

"Interactivity" as a technique in science-technology centers covers a variety of possibilities. The simplest are "push the button to start" devices, where the visitor merely sets in motion a fixed activity, such as a model

Table 1. Goals of Three Generations of Science Museums

First generation (1794–)	Technology collections and training centers	Conservation Collection Research Training
Second generation (1906–)	Science and industry museums	Public education Conservation Collection Research
Third generation (1937–)	Science-technology centers	Public education

machine or an audio-visual presentation. Sometimes there is a choice of buttons, and the visitor selects the presentation he or she would like to see. But in general the term "hands-on exhibits" refers to more complex interaction, where the visitor controls one or more variables of real physical phenomena.

Typical interactive exhibits involve manipulating real phenomena and exploring the results. The visitor adjusts the mass, length, and swing amplitude of a simple pendulum, and discovers that only the length has a big effect on the time it takes for the pendulum to swing back and forth. That principle was one of Galileo's major discoveries. Visitors can turn on and off spotlights of red, green, and blue, to figure out how these colors mix to produce new colors. Visitors operate telescopes, microscopes, and other tools of the scientist or engineer, to examine the behavior of normally inaccessible parts of the world.

The quality of the individual interactive experience appears to be the common key to the success of the exhibits described above, and hence to the success of this new style of museum. Of lesser importance are the overall thematic organizations or even the particular subjects being treated. Few visitors seem to conceive of their visit as an exposure to a general thesis or a structure of knowledge. Rather, they perceive the museum visit as a set of loosely related individual experiences: a beautiful or ugly object, a successful or frustrating manipulation.

Science-technology centers demonstrate the power of a technique, interactive exhibitory, to create and sustain a new kind of institution. But the task remains to determine just what these institutions can and should accomplish with this powerful technique.

Beyond visitor counts and elementary visitor satisfaction surveys, museums in general do not have a great deal of information on what educational functions they accomplish. Research in this field, as in most educational research, is difficult, slow, and hard to generalize to experiences with other exhibits or programs in other institutions.

In general, science-technology centers have little or no research collections, and no research staff. But research and evaluation have recently been receiving increased attention. The formation of the International Laboratory for Visitor Research, based at the University of Wisconsin, Milwaukee and its excellent bibliographies by Chandler Screven have solidified this vital work.

Science-technology centers have taken their place with

Figure 2. The Technology and Innovation Center, Hallmark Inc., Kansas City, Mo. interior, interaction area. Photograph courtesy of Nick Wheeler.

the other cultural institutions of our day. To improve the public understanding of science and technology, the centers are becoming better integrated with school and university curricula and are being supported by public and private funding as contributors to an improved "quality of life" in their communities.

Figure 3. The Technology and Innovation Center, Hallmark Inc., Kansas City, Mo. interior, color laboratory. Photograph courtesy of Nick Wheeler.

Figure 1. The Technology and Innovation Center, Hallmark Inc., Kansas City, Mo. exterior principal facade. Photograph courtesy of Nick Wheeler.

Figure 4. The New York Hall of Science, Corona, New York, exterior view.

CASE STUDIES OF SCIENCE CENTERS

Technology and Innovation Center

The Technology and Innovation Center, Hallmark Inc., Kansas City, Missouri is a 200,000 square foot building by Davis, Brody & Associates, completed in 1986. This building brings together under one roof three functional groups, previously separated, but whose work demands constant interaction in both formal and informal ways.

Figure 5. The Ontario Science Centre, Toronto, Ontario, Canada. View from valley, Exhibit Building in foreground. Photograph courtesy of Panda Associates.

Figure 6. The Cité des Sciences et de l'Industrie Parc de la Villette, Paris, France, view of Geode, museum in background. Photograph courtesy of Charlie Abad.

Advanced Technical Research, Equipment Engineering and the Creative Workshop are organized in a two-level configuration whose focus is a skylit greenhouse, where staff (scientists, engineers, technicians, artists, and craftsmen) and visiting artists and engineers can meet for short or long periods to exchange ideas and learn about each other's work.

Since free communication is vital to the technical and artistic innovations developed here, the Creative Workshop adjoins, and is treated as, an extension of the atrium space. A skylit gallery, through which an escalator moves like a kinetic sculpture, visually links the machine shops on the second floor with the hub of the action on the first floor, while providing the necessary functional separation. The scale and massing of the building and its limestone facade defer to the distinguished architecture of the existing complex (Figs. 1–3).

New York Hall of Science

The New York Hall of Science, Corona, New York was originally designed as an exhibit hall for the 1964 World's Fair in Flushing Meadows Park by Harrison & Abramovitz. The building underwent extensive renovation to make it suitable for use as a science-technology

Figure 7. The Cité des Sciences et de l'Industrie Parc de la Villette, Paris, France, main hall. Photograph courtesy of Charlie Abad.

center. Virtually all of the 35,000 square feet of public space is devoted to hands-on exhibitions (Fig. 4).

Ontario Science Center

The Ontario Science Center, Toronto, Ontario, Canada, designed by Raymond Moriyama, FRAIC, represents the first major museum of science and technology in North America which was designed for hands-on participation by the public. Moriyama took advantage of the steeply sloping site to create a tri-nuclear scheme. Public access is through the Entrance Building containing coat check, dining facility, and general orientation space. From the entrance, the public crosses an enclosed bridge to the Core Building which houses the auditorium, used for multi-screen projection as well as live shows, and staff offices. The Great Hall serves as the central distribution point, directing the public through the connecting link by moving ramps and stairs to the Exhibition Building. Provision has been made for a second Exhibition Building to be connected in the same manner to the Core Building (Fig. 5).

Cité des Sciences et de l'Industrie Parc de la Villette

The Cité des Sciences et de l'Industrie Parc de la Villette, Paris, France is a redevelopment of the old slaughter-house complex in Paris. The Museum of Science and Industry was created from the frame of an existing structure, and the Geode, the complementary structure housing the hemispherical-screen cinema. The new complex was created by the competition winner, Adrien Fainsilber, Architect and Planner.

With a footprint of over 300,000 square feet, this science-technology center is one of the largest in the world. Completed in the mid-1980s, it incorporates into a volume determined by the existing frame a variety of spaces for exhibits, both hands-on and traditional. From the main floor, the visitor experiences the main space, with a clear height to underside of roof in excess of 100 feet, traversed by bridges connecting mezzanines at the upper levels and with space vehicles and other objects suspended from the major roof trusses.

In addition to the extensive permanent and temporary exhibit spaces, there is a major auditorium, meeting

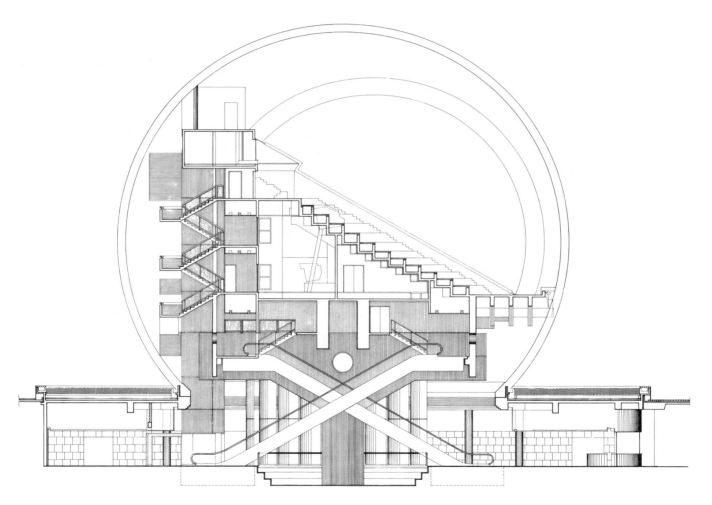

NORTH–SOUTH SECTION THROUGH GEODE

Figure 8. The Cité des Sciences et de l'Industrie Parc de la Villette, Paris, France, north-south section through Geode. Photograph courtesy of Adrien Fainsilber.

rooms, visitors' and technical information centers, library, bookstore, cafeteria, and workrooms. Because of the length of the building, two fire lanes permit fire-fighting equipment access to any interior point (Figs. 6–8).

BIBLIOGRAPHY

General References

V. J. Danilov, *Science and Technology Centers,* MIT Press, Cambridge, Mass., 1982.

Association of Science-Technology Centers, 1413 K Street, NW, 10th Fl, Washington, D.C. 20005.

International Laboratory for Visitor Studies, Dept. of Psychology, University of Wisconsin-Milwaukee, P. O. Box 413, Milwaukee, Wis. 53201.

See also AMUSEMENT PARKS; AQUARIUMS; LABORATORIES; MUSEUMS; ZOOS

ALAN J. FRIEDMAN
New York Hall of Science

ALAN SCHWARTZMAN, FAIA
Davis, Brody & Associates

SHEET METAL

Architectural sheet metal includes flexible metallic materials that are considered very thin in relation to length and width, not exceeding 3/16 in. (0.45 mm) in thickness, comprising:

1. Commercially pure metals (metallic elements with controlled amounts of impurities), best exemplified by copper.
2. Alloys (substances having metallic properties, consisting of two or more metallic elements or of metallic and nonmetallic elements that remain mixed with each other when molten and do not separate into distinct layers when solid), such as aluminum, iron, lead, stainless steel, and steel.
3. Laminates of commercially pure metals and/or alloys, such as aluminum–zinc alloy-coated steel, galvanized (zinc-coated) steel, lead-coated copper, terne (lead–tin alloy) coated stainless steel, and terne plate (lead–tin alloy-coated steel).
4. Other laminates include a base of sheet metal, often aluminum or steel, protected from the weather by a factory-applied covering. Such coverings are usually applied in a continuous process directly to one or both sides of metal sheet in coil form and include liquid coatings, film coverings, or a combination.

Historically, the use of sheet metal in architecture, other than for roofing and flashings, became fashionable through the concept of producing the appearance of other materials in classic forms, principally stone, in the exterior of buildings. For example, elements of classical architecture such as the entablature (often improperly referred to as the cornice) could be replicated faithfully and with

rather obvious savings in weight and expense by using formed sheet metal. Other ornamentations of stone and wood were executed using sheet metal. Depending upon the selection of the particular sheet metal, longer useful life and relative freedom from maintenance could provide considerable cost advantages. Its high strength and low weight made it easy to achieve the appearance of massive stone sections in which there is mostly hollow space where a supporting framework (armature) is concealed.

By early in the twentieth century, there were literally hundreds of patterns published and available to enable skilled sheet-metal mechanics to reproduce classical design elements and ornaments. The design, fabrication, and installation of sheet metal into its many other traditional forms, such as batten-seam, standing-seam and flat-seam roofing, exposed and concealed flashings, gutters and spouts, ventilators, and skylights is also well documented. Other utilitarian forms of sheet metal include heating, ventilating, air conditioning and environmental system ductwork, casings, cabinets, kitchen equipment, food service facilities, and electromagnetic and ionizing radiation shielding.

Authoritative sources of specific, detailed information concerning traditional design and use of sheet metal include metal producers, and national trade associations of producers, roofing contractors and sheet metal contractors. Product literature, specification data sheets, guide specifications and typical details are available on request from proprietary sources.

The selection of a particular sheet-metal material will depend upon installed cost as well as in-service costs which must consider the effects of exposure to the elements. Whether or not protective coatings must be relied upon to shield the base metal from such exposure and the durability of the coatings must be considered. Independent comparative test data regarding the behavior of protective coatings on sheet metal under actual or accelerated exposure to the weather, especially as it relates to the intended exposure may be crucial. Moisture, solar radiation (particularly ultraviolet), industrial or natural pollutants, marine, and other known exposure factors should be evaluated most carefully in terms of natural degradation and the effect of accidental damage to protective coatings. The ability to restore the necessary protection to the base metal during the service life therefore is an important factor in comparing relative costs.

Exposure to interior environmental factors that may be encountered or generated within the system of which sheet metal is an integral part must be evaluated. One such factor is the potential for condensation on the underside of sheet metal exposed to the exterior environment. Condensation may reduce thermal insulating values as moisture accumulates. Hidden corrosion of one or more components may degrade the performance of fasteners. For these reasons, the correct use of a vapor retarder is mandatory if the dew-point temperature can occur within the system. The vapor retarder is designed to protect against the passage of water vapor to locations within the system where the dew-point temperature may occur. The inability to altogether preclude such moisture migration is recognized by its very terminology: vapor retarder. The need to control moisture migration within a structure is found when the effect of the potential range of exterior climate is studied in relationship to the designed interior conditions. In general, the need for a positive vapor retarder is considerable when average winter month temperatures are below 40°F and interior relative humidity is 45% or greater.

The effects of electrochemical corrosion must always be considered present when dissimilar metals are in contact. A basic understanding of this subject is crucial to the success of every sheet-metal design. The galvanic series represents the order and the relative strength of the electrical potential which produces a flow of electrical current when dissimilar metals are in contact.

The galvanic series thus provides guidance for the use of the various metals which may safely be designed to come in contact. Most critical is the selection of fasteners. The closer in the galvanic series, the lower will be the rate of electrochemical corrosion between any two dissimilar metals. In simplest possible terms, the more noble metals will suffer little or not at all from contact with less noble metals. Fasteners of metals more noble in the galvanic series may be used to attach or anchor sheets of less noble metals relatively successfully but never vice versa. The smaller the relative amount of any two dissimilar metals, the more important it is that the smaller amount should be the more noble. In architectural sheet-metal design, the metals most frequently encountered are listed in Ref. 2.

Galvanic Series
(Corroded end, least noble, anodic)
Zinc—Galvanized Steel—Galvanized Wrought Iron
Aluminum—Alclad
Mild Steel—Wrought Iron—Cast Iron
50–50 Lead Tin Solder
Stainless Steel Type 304 (active)
Lead—Tin
Copper—Red Brass—Yellow Brass
Monel
Stainless Steel Type 304 (passive)
(Protected end, most noble, cathodic)

One important objective throughout the history of usage of sheet metal in architecture has been to avoid the designed use of caulks and sealants to attain weatherproof joints, if only because the sheet metal itself would invariably far outlast almost any caulk or sealant. Traditional design incorporates the use of soldering solely to provide watertight quality where necessary at joints in sheet metal, such as gutter seams. Rivets are employed at such joints to transfer stress so as to protect against fatigue failure of solder through cyclical stress.

To rely upon caulks and sealants by design necessitates the utmost care in material selection and requires careful periodic inspection and maintenance. Where access will limit inspection, joint degradation invites insidious water entry and results in hidden damage. Properly designed joints that are weatherproof without caulks and sealants are most desirable.

The development and use of predesigned, pre-engineered, prefabricated and prefinished metal-roofing systems continues to grow. Certain metal-roofing systems rely to a considerable extent upon sealants to provide weatherproof seams. Where sealing the joints practically eliminates the potential for moisture escape from within the system, unwanted buildup of condensate may occur. Conversely, the traditional design of batten and standing seam roofing permits some air flow in and out of the substrate through folded but unsealed seams.

In order to use sheet-metal materials successfully, it is important to understand a few basic structural principles in order to confront potential factors of degradation properly. In practice, the necessary thickness of sheet metal may be determined more by the ability to fabricate and install sections of sheet metal free from objectionable accidental damage rather than merely by the ability of the sections to serve their intended purpose and function as installed. For example, although continuous sections may be desirable in terms of roofing design, handling and installing very long sections in high, exposed locations may be precluded by extremely high costs to avoid the effect of wind. Where sheet metal will not be fully supported, large concentrated loading at right angles to its surface must be guarded against throughout and following installation. In other words, if permanent unsightly deformations are to be avoided, the truly successful design must contemplate every probable use, misuse and abuse. Modest increase in thickness may provide some protection against such damage.

Thanks to techniques available for fabricating large components of sheet-metal roof and wall systems on-site, transverse seams are no longer needed. Predesigned sheet-metal roof and wall systems have benefits and drawbacks. The obvious problem of heat destruction of even the most durable coatings precludes its direct application. This rules out any welding or soldering to create watertight connections between sections of precoated metal. Some base metals, such as aluminum, are not ordinarily joined in the field by either welding or soldering.

Selection of a particular type or mixture (alloy) of metal is usually influenced more by initial cost of installation than by accessibility, routine maintenance requirements, or projected service life expectancy. The cost of refinishing at some future time should be taken into account with prefinished material when such coating is to protect the base metal against the elements. Whether appearance or durability is an important or the controlling factor, refinishing costs should be accounted for in any fair cost comparison with sheet metals intended to weather.

The success of all installations of sheet metal depends greatly upon at least these listed qualifications. For example, a sheet metal roof must be:

1. Designed to accommodate thermal expansion and contraction freely without buckling or crimping. All sections of sheet metal are to be attached by means of cleats which engage folded edges and NOT by means of fasteners which would penetrate the sheet.

Figure 1. An example of a batten seam roofing, the Shrine of the Immaculate Conception, Washington, D.C. Courtesy of Stewart Bros. Photographers.

2. Designed to accommodate all loads imposed during and after construction without permanent deformation. Full support and proper anchorage must be provided by the substrate to withstand wind, ice, and snow.

3. Protected against corrosive effects of both exterior and underside exposure under foreseeable conditions. All metals in contact with each other must be the same or similar and free from potential galvanic corrosion. The substrate in contact with any part of the metal-roofing system including its fasteners must remain free from effects of condensation and/or temporary water infiltration. (Where fire-retardant treated materials form part of the substrate, make certain that no consequential, deleterious reaction can arise in the presence of moisture.) The effects of galvanic corrosion will occur when runoff from a more noble metal flows upon a less noble metal, for example, copper to aluminum.

4. Designed to remain weathertight without necessity for caulks or sealants. All seams should be capable of accommodating relative movement between sec-

Figure 2. An example of a flat-seam roofing on a shallow dome, the Shrine of the Immaculate Conception, Washington, D.C. Courtesy of Inco, Ltd.

tions of the metal as a result of thermal expansion. The construction of watertight seams involving soldering requires that the stress across the soldered joint be carried mechanically by properly installed rivets and NOT merely by the solder. (Where soldering or special shop welding is not possible, the watertight integrity cannot be achieved to the same degree.)

5. Designed to drain freely without obstructions, cascades or other unnecessary concentration of flow. Erosion of metals occurs as a result of dirt being carried by the runoff. An example of the long term effect of erosion is seen in elbows, downspouts, and gutters of copper.

Architectural sheet metals in common use include:

Aluminum. Because of its rate of thermal expansion, the design must accommodate greater movement at joints than with other metals used for roofing. Protection against atmospheric corrosion is available using electrochemical treatment or baked on coatings. Joining by means of soldering or field welding is not practicable. The use of aluminum in roofing is found primarily in proprietary rather than traditional systems.

Copper. The use of cold-rolled (cornice temper) sheet provides greater stiffness and is preferred for most applications. Copper has been used for more than two centuries in the form of batten and standing seam roofing (Fig. 1). It may be constructed readily in the form of flat-seam (all joints soldered) roofing, permitting its use on very low slopes (Fig. 2). Runoff from copper will cause some green staining which becomes more prominent on light-colored surfaces. The natural weathering process of copper results in the formation of an even, protective coating termed "patina." Despite many heroic efforts, NO artificial means yet has produced its equal either in appearance or its durability.

Lead-coated Copper. The application of a coating of lead at the rate of 7.5 lb per 100 ft^2 to each side of sheet copper gives much the same appearance as sheet lead. The structural properties of the sheet copper are practically identical as are its uses. Characteristic staining attributable to plain copper is absent.

Galvanized Steel. The protective coating of zinc on both sides of the sheet has provided excellent service. As a base metal, its use is growing in the proprietary systems. Its strength and lower rate of thermal expansion compared to aluminum are important. It can be soldered to create watertight joints.

Lead. The useful characteristics of lead, including its density, high resistance to environmental corrosion, malleability and flexibility, must all be viewed in the context of limitations imposed by its mechanical properties. Although successful roofs of sheet lead are to be found, its characteristic uses have tended more to waterproofing, flashing, soundproofing, and shielding from ionizing radiation.

Monel. The nickel–copper alloy known as monel metal offers many of the characteristics of copper. It offers greater strength than cold-rolled copper. Monel has proved inestimably durable and nonstaining. Because of its cost premium, its applications have been limited principally to monumental structures (Figs. 3 and 4).

Stainless Steel. With its resistance to atmospheric corrosion, high strength, low rate of thermal expansion and good workability, stainless steel offers highly desirable characteristics in terms of metals suitable for roofing applications. Standard mill finish offers an acceptable luster. Special matte finishes offer reduced reflectivity. Special soldering fluxes and solder are required to obtain satisfactory results. Cleaning of soldering residue is an important final step if localized corrosion is to be avoided.

Terne-coated Stainless. Type 304 stainless steel is used as the base metal which is coated with the lead–tin alloy (terne) to become TCS. Chief among its characteristics are all of those of the base metal plus the ability to create soldered joints using ordinary methods. The appearance of TCS is that of the lead–tin alloy, which weathers to a

Figure 3. The spire, an example of monel metal.

Figure 4. The spire, an example of monel metal.

medium, neutral grey, matte finish. TCS offers durability, strength, workability and uniform, neutral appearance without staining lower surfaces exposed to its runoff.

Tin. More properly called terne plate (lead–tin alloy coating on sheet steel), has been employed as standing seam roofing for over a century. Its underside should be painted prior to application and its exposed side maintained by periodic painting. (Because of the greatly increased durability offered by stainless steel as the base metal, the use of terne plate as metal roofing which requires periodic repainting may not be justified.)

BIBLIOGRAPHY

1. *SMACNA Architectural Sheet Metal Manual,* 4th ed., Sheet Metal and Air Conditioning Contractors National Association, Vienna, Va. 1987.
2. *Catalog 16,* Whitehead Metal Products Company, New York, 1950, p. 230.

General References

Copper and Common Sense, 7th ed., Revere Copper Products, Inc., Rome, N.Y., 1982.
Modern Application of Sheet Copper in Building Construction, Copper and Brass Research Association, New York, 1955.
Copper Brass Bronze Design Handbook, Sheet Copper Applications and Architectural Applications, Copper Development Association, Inc. Greenwich, Conn.
Quality Metals of Industry, Whitehead Metal Products Company, Inc., New York, 1950.
C. Hornbostel, *Materials for Architecture,* Reinhold Book Corp., New York, 1961.
W. Neubecker, *The Universal Sheet Metal Pattern Cutter,* Vol. Two, The Sheet Metal Publication Company, New York, 1923.
Handbook of Roof Construction, The Producers' Council, Washington, D.C., 1959.
Stainless Steel Data Manual, American Iron and Steel Institute, New York, 1966.
Sheet Lead The Protective Metal, Lead Industries Association, Inc., New York, 1984.
Aluminum in Modern Architecture, Reynolds Metals Company, Louisville, Ky., 1956.
Specifications Data Manual, Follansbee Steel, Follansbee, W.Va., 1988.

See also BRASS AND BRONZE; COPPER; CORROSION; ENVELOPES, BUILDING; GALVANIZED COATINGS; MOISTURE PROTECTION; ROOFING MATERIALS

ROBERT E. LINCK
Philadelphia, Pennsylvania

SIGHT-IMPAIRED, DESIGN FOR

Designing for visually impaired people may conjure up thoughts of blind people using white canes or dog guides and braille signs. It is less likely to bring to mind the problems of people with bifocals trying to read a flight schedule at ceiling height, older people going from the sunlight to a dark interior, and people who have special difficulty with glare, yet all of these require special design consideration. As a group, the visually impaired are a diverse and heterogeneous population. Some of them have minor vision deficits that can be corrected with glasses; some have no vision at all. They also vary in many characteristics such as intelligence, personality, wealth, geographic location, employment, mobility skills, orientation, and way-finding abilities, to mention a few. Because of their jobs or recreational interests, some visually impaired people travel extensively around the United States and other countries. They travel independently with the use of a cane or dog guide. Other individuals are much less independent and only travel with the assistance of a sighted guide.

Design to facilitate the independent travel of visually impaired people, which does not magnify their limitations, presents a special challenge for the designer. This may be particularly true because design professionals tend to be visually oriented, and it may be difficult for them to empathize with a user who has little or no usable vision. This section defines the visually impaired population and the orientation and mobility skills and strategies they use and describes some specific design problems and solutions.

BACKGROUND

Blindness and Visual Impairment

The word "blind" is often used to describe the entire population with vision problems. However, there are other words that are more precise, such as severe visual impairment, partially sighted, low vision, functional blindness (defined as the inability to read newspaper print with corrective lenses), and legal blindness (a classification used to determine eligibility for various benefits). Persons are considered legally blind if their central visual acuity with best correction with glasses and/or contact lenses does not exceed 20/200 in the better eye, or if their visual field is less than 20°. The classification 20/200 means that the person can see no more at 20 ft than the person with normal (20/20) vision can see at 200 ft.

Visually impaired people have a range and variety of conditions of residual vision: A person may have pieces of vision in various parts of the field of vision or the center of the visual field may be gone; they may only be able to tell if the lights are on or off (light perception) or possibly follow a line of lights in a hallway (light projection). They may also have combinations of these conditions. About 85% of the people who are legally blind have some usable vision. Therefore, the appropriate usage of the term "blind" is when referring to those persons with a complete loss of sight. All other persons with various degrees of visual loss are more appropriately referred to as "visually impaired."

There are about 11.4 million persons in the United States with some type of visual limitation (1), that is, persons who have trouble seeing even with corrective lenses. The U.S. prevalence of "severe visual impairment"—self-reported inability to see to read ordinary newsprint even with glasses—is estimated as almost 2 million Americans (2). Based on prevalence rates and 1987 population statistics, there are about 600,000 legally blind persons in the United States (3).

According to Kirchner and Peterson (4), 59% of severely visually impaired persons in the United States have one or more additional impairments. This means that it is common to have two or more types of impairment besides impaired vision, with an average of 2.49 additional impairments. The three most common combinations with visual impairment, in decreasing frequency, are hard-of-hearing, nonparalytic orthopedic impairments or deformities, and partial or complete paralysis (including cerebral palsy).

Causes of Blindness

According to the World Health Organization, there are approximately 42 million blind persons in the world. Because the major causes are infections and malnutrition, more than half the blindness in the world is preventable. In the United States the majority of causes of blindness are associated with the aging process, and approximately 78% of the severely visually impaired population is 65 years or older and about 60% of the legally blind population is 65 years or older.

The aging process is often accompanied by changes in visual acuity, accommodation, light/dark adaptation, ocular mobility, and other aspects of seeing. The leading causes of vision loss and blindness in the United States are

Macular Degeneration. This disease is associated with the aging process. Generally, with macular degeneration, vision loss is not sudden but progresses over a period of years as a result of a deterioration of the macula (the small area of the retina responsible for fine acute vision). This causes impairment of central vision, leaving side or peripheral vision intact. The person may have difficulty performing tasks such as reading signs or recognizing pictures or faces.

Cataracts. As a person ages, the lens of the eye tends to lose its transparency, producing a clouding called a cataract. Cataracts may cause no severe vision loss. However, in some people they may decrease vision substantially, necessitating removal.

Diabetic Retinopathy. Diabetes may cause damage due to hemorrhages to the small blood vessels nourishing the retina. This may leave the person totally blind, with blurred or distorted vision, irregular fields of vision, and/or visual conditions that fluctuate from day to day.

Glaucoma. With this condition, most common among persons over 40 years of age, there is an increase in pressure in the eye due to faulty draining of normal eye fluids, which can eventually damage the retina and result in vision loss.

Retinitis Pigmentosa. This syndrome is an inherited condition that results in night blindness. In addition, a person experiences a loss of the peripheral field, which leads to tunnel vision and/or total blindness.

Abilities and Disabilities of Visually Impaired Persons

The person born blind or visually impaired is considered congenitally blind or visually impaired. People who lose their vision sometime after the first few years of life are considered to be adventitiously blind or visually impaired. Although only a small percentage of the legally blind population is congenitally blind, there are many design implications for these persons.

One design implication results from the limitation in the range, variety, and accuracy of environmental concepts for many congenitally blind people. Whereas the sighted person develops and verifies many concepts informally, the visually impaired or blind person must have a structured presentation of most concepts to ensure accurate development of these fundamentals (5). Therefore, a visually impaired person may have difficulty with complex, irregular, and/or unpredictable layouts of buildings and/or cities because of a lack of experience, sufficient environmental information or cues, or for all these reasons.

Despite some popular myths to the contrary, when someone loses their vision, the other senses *do not* become more sensitive or more acute, nor do the visually impaired persons have some mysterious sixth sense to guide them. In fact, most visually impaired persons go through a special training program to teach (or retrain for the adventitiously handicapped person) them how to use their remaining senses more effectively. Through a structured program the person learns how to effectively use sounds, tactual information, kinesthetic information (ie, detecting and interpreting information from surfaces), temperature, and olfactory cues, and air currents, to mention a few. Training the use of residual vision is a major component in most rehabilitation and habilitation programs. Some sensory perceptions that may be used are

Vision. Because of the large number of persons with low vision and the diversity of visual conditions, there is a great deal of emphasis on vision training (6). A person is taught to maximize the usefulness of any remaining vision such as using light patterns in hallways as landmarks and cues.

Hearing. Hearing, like vision, provides a way of getting information from a distance (ie, beyond arms' reach). For the visually impaired person, the ability to effectively use hearing to preview the environment becomes extremely important. For example, indoors reflected sound helps a person determine if a room is large or small. Hearing also helps the visually impaired person establish and maintain orientation to the environment (7).

Touch. Touch is anything that is touched by or touches the persons body. For example, a person can gather a great deal of information about an object such as its size, weight density, texture, volume, materials, and construction. Reading a raised-line map or numbers on a door involves the sense of touch. An important capability of touch is the ability to detect temperature changes such as the cool air from an open window or the air currents that exist between buildings or from intersecting hallways. This temperature sensation is also valuable to localize the sun or feel the heat from the sun disappear as the person walks under a marquee.

Smell. Odors, while very diffuse and difficult to localize, provide information to the blind or visually impaired person. Outdoors, the person may be able to use the fragrance of a bakery or a restaurant. Indoors, a person may be able to identify the presence of someone by the fragrant aroma of a pipe or the musty smell of an attic storeroom.

Balance and Kinesthesis. Balance and kinesthesis are useful in the detection of surface inclines and declines as well as lateral tilts of various surfaces. In addition, the information from these senses also gives the person information about the body's position, movement, posture, and amount of turning (ie, 90 or 180°).

It is important for the designer to be aware of the additional sensory information that may be used by the blind or visually impaired person for the purposes of cues and landmarks to aid way-finding and safety. For blind and visually impaired people, it is important to provide "redundant cueing" where multiple forms of environmental information are provided. For instance, at an elevator both a bell and bright light may be provided to allow reinforcement of cues and to allow people with different abilities to use the information.

ORIENTATION AND MOBILITY

Definitions

The travel skills of visually impaired persons are divided into two areas: orientation and mobility. Orientation refers to the use of the remaining senses to establish one's position and relationship to other objects in the setting; mobility refers to one's ability to move from a starting point to a desired location.

Mobility Devices and Strategies

The information a blind or visually impaired person requires for safe, efficient, and effective mobility may come from a wide variety of mobility devices or aids. The mobility devices or aids currently used include sighted guides, dog guides, and canes (8). Electronic travel aids are also used, but they are generally used on a sporadic basis and usually in conjunction with another primary mobility aid (eg, sighted guide, dog guide, or cane). The choice of the device or aid used is a matter of individual preference. The cane provides a wealth of information about the environment but no protection from over-hanging obstacles, whereas the dog guide provides few environmental details but facilitates the individual staying on the path or sidewalk, traveling at a faster speed.

The majority of visually impaired persons use some type of cane (long cane, collapsible or prescription cane as it is sometimes called) in a systematic way. This type of cane is usually made of aluminum or fiberglass and is approximately ½ in. in diameter. The length of the cane is prescribed by the mobility specialist and is determined by a consideration of the individual's height and length of stride.

The cane in and of itself does a blind or visually impaired person little good; the techniques or strategies of using the cane make it a valuable mobility tool. The basic technique involves the rhythmic movement of the cane in an arc in front of the body, to ascertain the presence of objects in the path. The width of the arc is just wider than the individual's shoulders (about 24 in). In addition, when the left foot is back, the cane is put in contact with the floor surface one step ahead of the left foot. As the left foot is moved forward into this "cleared" space the cane is being moved to the space in front of the right foot. In this way the blind or visually impaired traveler is able to get information about surface texture and the presence of objects, and, most importantly, locate drop-offs. Because the cane is held at waist level, overhanging or angled objects or structures such as guy wires or tree limbs cannot be detected.

A very limited proportion of the blind and visually impaired population—about 1%—uses dog guides. The potential user group is only about 3% for several reasons: it has been found that the best candidates are either totally blind or have very limited residual vision; the person should be in good physical shape and able to walk about 3–4 miles per hour; and some people are not fond of dogs. The dog guide is trained to walk straight down a hallway or sidewalk, veering only to avoid obstacles or turning at the owner's command. Because of this training of the dog guide, the blind person makes less contact with the environment (eg, decorative trees or statues in a sidewalk area, street furniture, buildings or shorelines).

ORIENTATION AND COGNITIVE MAPPING

The design of cities and buildings can help make independent travel by blind or visually impaired people relatively easy and safe, or it can make such travel difficult, dangerous, and stressful. Poor design may even limit the extent to which people will travel independently. This section examines the skills and processes that blind and visually impaired people use in finding their way.

Orientation and Mobility

As was discussed above, independent travel by blind or visually impaired persons—or by anyone—depends on two interrelated sets of processes and skills: orientation and mobility. Orientation involves knowing where one is located with respect to the larger setting, where the goal is located, and how to get to the goal. The overall mental concept a person has of a setting is often called a "cognitive map," and it may be more or less accurate or comprehensive. Sometimes blind or visually impaired people may have an integrated maplike image of the total layout of the setting, but frequently they may conceive of the setting as a chain of instructions such as "turn left at the second corridor then go to the third door." Because using an overall image allows travelers to take shortcuts and alternative routes, mobility specialists often try to provide blind and visually impaired travelers with a comprehensive concept of a setting by using a verbal description or map of an area or through tactile maps, or both. This concept is often organized by cardinal directions (north, south, east, west), and travelers are encouraged to keep track of these directions as they move. There is evidence that these techniques do help some people, and skilled travelers may move from a chain of instructions to a more integrated mental image (9). However, other people, and especially congenitally blind people, may have considerable difficulty ever developing an overall image of a setting.

Mobility is the minute-to-minute use of environmental information that allows people to travel from place to place. As was discussed above, many visually impaired people have some amount of vision and, as a result, use visual information for travel. Depending on what specific visual abilities they have, visually impaired persons may rely on well-lit and well-differentiated environmental features such as signs with legible large type and clearly marked and prominent stair nosings or train platform

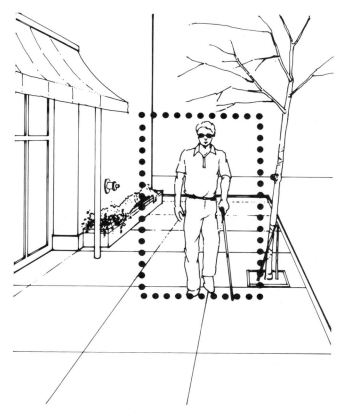

Figure 1. Many blind and visually impaired people use a long cane that sweeps an area in front of them about as wide as their shoulders. Whereas it is very useful for detecting landmarks and obstructions on the ground, it cannot detect overhanging objects.

edges. However, because most visually impaired people are older than 65, in addition to other disabilities they are often affected by a yellowing of the lens of the eye, decreased ability of the lens to focus by stretching and contracting, decreased visual acuity, and decreased ability of the pupil to accommodate to changes in light levels by dilating quickly. As a result, even older people with normal vision find some situations more difficult than do younger people: glare, differentiating blues and greens, quickly changing focus from near to far objects (or vice versa). Older people may also need much more light and large print. Because of the decreased ability to accommodate to changes in illumination levels, older people may have trouble moving from brightly lit to darker areas.

For persons who do use a mobility aid, the long cane is the most commonly used (Fig. 1). As was described above, this thin, flexible, aluminum cane becomes a primary way of gaining environmental information by sweeping a path a bit wider than the shoulders in front of the traveler (about 60 cm). Whereas the cane serves to protect the traveler by detecting obstructions and drop-offs, it can also help mobility by detecting "shorelines." A blind or visually impaired person may navigate by following a "shoreline" such as the grass at the edge of a sidewalk, the edge of carpeting, a wall, or other feature that may provide a continuous detectible edge in the direction of travel. In this case, for example, the cane makes contact with the surface on the left side, moves across in step with the stride, and touches the shoreline on the left. Although used less often, a cane user may also trail a wall by placing the hand with fingertips slightly bent in contact with the wall with the arm extended at an angle of about 45° with the wall. This may be helpful, for example, in finding a door if the traveler knows about where it is located. A cane can also be used to detect landmarks, features that are memorable because of their form, texture, resilience, sound-emitting quality, or other characteristics.

Visually impaired and blind persons rely heavily on sound cues to learn about their setting. Those with good hearing can often detect changes in room volumes or surfaces by changes in the characteristics of the echo. For example, they may know when they are moving from an entryway into a large lobby, or from a marble-clad room into one covered in soft materials. In extensive experimental testing at Georgia Tech, it was discovered that the most effective cane-detectible landmarks for concrete sidewalks were metal plates set flush with the concrete and other cues that emitted a loud noise when struck by a cane. Another effective cue was a resilient rubber mat similar to enlarged corduroy (10).

Orientation and Mobility: An Example

The relationships between orientation and mobility may be clearer in an example. For this section, assume that a hypothetical couple is moving from a bus stop to an office in a nearby office building. They are competent travelers and reasonably familiar with the route. Furthermore, assume that the man is blind and the woman is severely visually impaired. After getting off the bus, the couple attempts to orient themselves to the site and understand their relationship to the setting. If the bus reliably discharges them at the same bus stop, and the bus stop has a clear and direct relationship to their destination, they may be able to use an overall mental representation of the setting. They may know, for example, they are facing north and the building they are traveling to is one block east. However, there are those for whom such a coordinated mental map may not be their cognitive process. In any case, an overall cognitive map may be harder to develop if the route is complex or sinuous. The blind man might rely on hearing the "traffic surge" to know when to cross safely at a traffic signal—the time when the traffic moving in his direction starts. (Some blind people complain about cars turning right-on-red because they mistake it for a traffic surge.) Because he has his wife with him, the man may rely on her for crossing, particularly if the crosswalk markings have considerable visual contrast to rely on. For many blind or visually impaired long cane users, crossing large open spaces without a shoreline is extremely difficult because it requires people to rely entirely on their own kinesthetic feedback rather than environmental information. This task is even more difficult if it requires people to cross open spaces at oblique angles (11).

As they walk down the sidewalk toward their office building, the couple may rely on landmarks that they detect with their canes, cues they hear, and what the visu-

ally impaired woman may see. For example, they may hear people going into major building entries, and she may see large areas of light-colored building surfaces or glass. Street furniture such as benches or newspaper machines may serve as useful landmarks but can also turn a simple path into a complicated one if the traveler has to navigate around many obstacles. When the couple reaches their building—detected perhaps because of the color contrast and changed echo at the opening at the entry and a change in the paving—they turn into the building. If they have used the building many times, they will probably know exactly where to go, but if they are less familiar with this building, they face a difficult problem: How do they get more information about the building? Whereas a person with good eyesight may be able to see the directory or find the information desk, these may be difficult tasks for blind or visually impaired people (in fact, these are often difficult problems for people with normal eyesight, as well). Without more information, it may be difficult for travelers to plan their routes and travel strategies. Even if an information desk is found, the staff are seldom trained to give clear and useful directions to visually impaired people. In addition, if the building is unknown to them, it may be important for blind and visually impaired people to know what kind of building or area they are in: a hospital, for instance, may present the possibility that a person will wander into restricted or dangerous areas.

Building form plays a role in travel planning. As with the relationship between bus stop and building, if the building is relatively simple in form, primarily uses right angle turns, and has distinctive features, it is easier to develop an overall cognitive map and make plans about how to travel (12).

Assuming that the couple has learned what they need to know about the building (from past experience, asking directions of a passerby, or using some more "high tech" solution such as a tactual map or an information phone) and developed a strategy to find their destination, they must find the elevator or stairs. This often presents the same problems described above if no shoreline, audible sound, or clearly visual contrast is available. When the correct elevator is located—and with multiple elevators it may be difficult to find which elevator door is open—they must discover where the call button is located and where their floor button is located in the elevator car. There are many patterns for button layout: some panels are split with even and odd floors on left and right; some skip service floors; some elevators in small buildings have buttons horizontally arranged. (This elevator panel issue provides a modest example of the larger problem: the fit between the traveler's concept of the setting and its design. If the design is consistent and logical—such as by having braille and raised numbering, and even numbers on one side and odd on the other in predictably ascending order—it may be easier to act competently (13).) The travelers must also find the floor to which they are traveling. They may do this on the elevator by pushing all the buttons and counting stops, asking others on the elevator, feeling tactile numbers mounted on the jamb of the elevator, or relying on an auditory cue such as a synthesized voice that announces the floor.

When getting off the elevator, the travelers may look for a landmark or signage to reassure them that they are on the right floor and headed in the right direction. For visually impaired people, large, well-lit signs with considerable contrast between letters and background may be helpful. As the couple walks toward their office they may use one edge of the wall as a shoreline and may trail the wall when they get near their destination. Landmarks along the way such as surface changes, numbers of doors encountered, changes in room volume or surface, or for the visually impaired woman, bright lights may help them keep track of their progress and know when they have arrived. To verify the office, there may be raised letters by the door or they may ask receptionists once inside the office.

The next section discusses design strategies that work with the processes of orientation and mobility to help people travel safely and competently.

DESIGN CONSIDERATIONS

The prevalence of people with no vision or low vision requires designers to consider carefully their needs in the built environment. Their requirements for orientation information and for protection against certain types of hazard mandate a different conception of the human users of the built environment. Effective design must provide information about the environment to make it safer, and to make it understandable to those with and without vision, and at least reduce ambiguity and confusion. As people with visual impairments have less visual information available to them, thoughtful design must provide information to increase intelligibility and safety. This need not limit the designer's palette, but it may modify or add to the proposed solution. Corridors with many direction changes and obtuse angles, for example, may be more difficult for people (all people) to comprehend at first. However, with an intelligible system of landmarks, even those with no vision, or little intelligence, will find their way without too much difficulty. Similarly, people with poor vision may be more at risk from some environmental hazards—unexpected drop-offs, such as stairs or the edge of platforms at stations, for example. Even these can be made safer by drawing attention to them or reducing exposure to unprotected areas by means of adding guardrails.

Design Review Considerations

An effective design should address the following items successfully. The list is not exhaustive but is intended as an introduction to the typical problems that must be considered.

Projection Hazards. Remove objects projecting into the path of travel that someone may contact. This may be because they cannot see it, or are not paying attention, or because objects do not lie in the path swept by the long cane, such as tree branches, or fire extinguishers.

As Figure 1 shows, pathways should be trimmed to form a protective zone free from tree branches and shrubs.

Inside buildings, nothing should project into an area where people may walk. For example, one should not permit the sloping underside of a stair to be below head height (14).

Trip and Fall Hazards. Provide protection from construction site barriers, or barricades, or any chains used to prevent people from crossing a lawn, for example, or similar devices that people may fall over because they fail to see them or detect them with their canes. Tree roots causing the sidewalk to be uneven, or uneven paving stones should be corrected.

Chains that are used as barricades may not be seen, particularly at night, even by people with little visual impairment. As a general rule, chains should not be used. The crossbar of construction site barricades and other horizontal barriers may be used if they are designed to be detectable by people using canes. To this end, as indicated in Figure 2, they should not be higher than 27 in. above the ground (15).

Unprotected Drop-offs. Provide protection from steps, drop-offs, platforms, or other unprotected edges in the main travel path.

For those with little or no vision, falling into a stair or off an edge is a special danger. Two solutions can reduce the risk of a fall: detectable warning cues (16) and design strategies. Floor-surface warning cues can be used to indi-

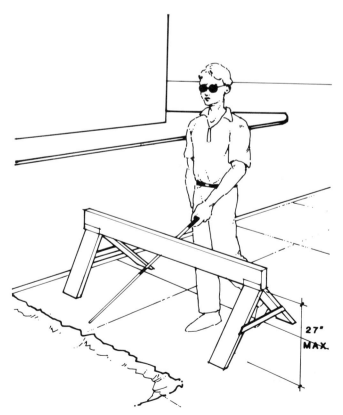

Figure 2. Hazards should be zoned out of the direction line of travel.

cate to the long-cane user that there is a stair, ramp, platform edge, or similar drop-off ahead. These cues usually take the form of a strip of flooring material that is detectably different from the rest of the floor. A cane user will then recognize this difference and act with appropriate caution. Changes of floor material are common inside and outside the building, so the change may not be adequate to convey the information. Furthermore, unless the cueing material is standardized for all the hazardous drop-offs, it may be ineffective. Two studies confirmed that materials that provide sound and resilience cues are more effective than those that rely on textural differences alone (17,18). Although these cues are prescribed in several codes and specifications, there remains some question about their efficacy (19). As it is common to find a variety of floor surface materials in buildings and on outdoor paths, some have doubted whether this sort of cueing by means of floor strips will be recognized as a warning to a cane user; it has also been suggested that it can only work if the materials used for the purpose are standardized—that the cueing material is always the same and only used where it will warn of danger. For this reason, others have suggested that the device may only work where the cane user is familiar with the particular building or environment. In terms of design, it is wise to move stairs and similar drop-offs out of the direct path of travel so that the visually impaired person is less likely to encounter a drop-off unexpectedly (Fig. 3). Obviously this countermeasure

Figure 3. Drop-offs are a serious hazard that should be clearly marked with highly visible and cane-detectible markers.

can be carried to extremes, and the drop-off becomes so concealed that people will be unable to find it when they need to. For those with some vision, additional measures should be considered, such as using contrasting colors, increased lighting, or other means to emphasize drop-offs.

Ramps and Curb Ramps. Guard against ramps of such a small pitch that blind and visually impaired people may not notice them.

Encountering a ramp obviously does not present the same degree of hazard as a drop-off, but it may still be dangerous if a long-cane user does not notice it. This may be the case with a curb ramp with a low pitch. Ramps with a gradient that is less than about 1:16 may not be detected. The cane user may unwittingly stray out into the street. For this reason, most cane users would prefer to have the curb ramps set out of the route of direct travel, or given a very distinct and detectable change of material (as discussed earlier).

Glass Doors and Screens. Protect areas of glass that people may walk into because they are difficult to see and improperly placed.

For all people, the transparency of glass is potentially hazardous in walkways. For people with visual limitations, the hazard is magnified. It is necessary to be conscious of the dangers and to devise ways to avoid the problem, such as by marking the glass or taking it out of the direct path of travel.

Environmental Information. As people move through the environment, provide enough distinctive information to enable them to locate themselves, and to plan their route to their destination.

Some types of building layout are more difficult for people, and particularly people with vision deficits, to comprehend and to establish a concept from which to act. This includes buildings with routes that have many changes of direction, particularly if the changes are not right-angled; buildings with curvilinear routes; buildings with many repetitious and undifferentiated corridors and spaces. People with little or no vision are also likely to find large open spaces such as atriums and parking lots difficult to navigate unless shorelines or other environmental or cognitive information clues are provided.

Apart from signage and other information systems, several other techniques are available to make the environment more comprehensible. People with visual limitations, and those with normal vision, depend on an understanding of the uniqueness of the place they are in, the ways in which it differs from other places, including the places they have come from and are going to. They search for landmarks, shorelines, and distinctive features that they can recognize and remember. For example, these may include a landmark such as a planter. Spaces with different acoustics may also be noticeable. The sound may be that of motor vehicles or pedestrian activity. It may result from the size of the space they are in, or the materials of the floor and walls, or by deliberately intrusive sounds from a fountain or water feature, for example. A node where a decision about change in direction is necessary may include a change in floor and wall materials that can be detected by a cane (or by a hand being trailed along a wall) as well as visually. The node may include information from air currents, odor, heat from a light, or other cues to stimulate other senses, as well. With a knowledge of the techniques that blind and visually impaired people use, one can design into the building a continuous system of information clues that assist them in navigating through the environment. One technique that seems to be effective is to provide linear guide strips on the floor, or shorelines, on both sides of the path that people who use canes can follow. Guide strips and "artificial" shorelines may be effective where no other shoreline is available, such as in large open spaces. They act as a line that can be followed, but they must be made from materials that are detectably different from the walkway area in which they are set; and they must be learned. Another solution might be to have carpeting on the desired path, with a hard surface on either side.

Maps and Information Aids. Provide sufficient information aids in the building. They should be located where visually impaired people may find them easily.

Maps are one of several tools used by blind, visually impaired (and sighted) people to develop or enhance their understanding of basic spatial relationships, to facilitate their comprehension of specific travel environments, to refresh their memory of routes and areas, and to further their skill in independent route planning (8). The orientation aids also enable these persons to travel independently in unfamiliar areas and to add to their knowledge and enjoyment of the environment.

Three basic types of orientation aids are used by blind and visually impaired people to facilitate wayfinding. These types of aids may be used separately or in combination.

Models: Three-dimensional representations of real objects or groups of objects built to scale (eg, model of a building).

Graphic aids: Tactile or visual diagrams or maps having information perceptible to touch, vision, or to both touch and vision (eg, a colored raised line on a floor-plan representation).

Verbal aids: Descriptions of the environment that may be presented by braille print, or in an auditory (voice) output, perhaps by tape recorder. These verbal descriptions may be of a large area comparable to a city map or a very specific set of directions delineating a route.

Like others, visually impaired and blind people have varying levels of skills in using these orientation aids. The previous discussion of orientation aids is based on reference 8; for more detail this reference is suggested.

Signage. Signage should be well placed and large enough to be read by people with poor vision and be comprehensible by those who read by touch. (Raised letters are readable by more people than is braille.)

Signage is the principal communication method for those with vision. Frequently the signage system is inadequate, and some people may become lost in a maze of corridors. This may arise because the basic signage does not exist, or because it is ambiguous or poorly located. For those with poor vision, the signage may be incomprehensible because of the style of lettering used, or because of the use of meaningless symbols. The signs may be too small (an additional 1 in. in height for every 25 ft is a probable minimum). The sign may even be too large, or set too high. (It should be at eye height.) It may not be decipherable by touch (lettering for signs that will be touched to be understood should have raised or indented characters, although research indicates that raised lettering is more effective). The letters should be between 5/8 and 2 in. high; and the characters should be sans serif and raised or indented to at least 1/32 in. (20).

Signage for all people should be visible, comprehensible, legible, and directed at the illiterate as well as the literate (with appropriate avoidance of meaningless or ambiguous symbols).

Audible Information Systems. Audible as well as visual information should be provided.

Without audible information those with little or no vision may be cut off from the sort of travel information that is usually provided by video monitors in large transit terminals. Departure and arrival information is usually routinely announced, but the traveler will need assistance in locating the proper gate. Audible signals at traffic lights have been used in Japan and Europe, but their success is questionable. Bells, buzzers, and bird calls have been tried, but no standard has yet been adopted for the United States. There have been complaints that the noise disturbs people at night in nearby buildings, and many claim that the sounds interfere with more important information: traffic sound.

Route Impediments. The route may contain poles, mailboxes, trash cans, drinking fountains, and other types of street and building furniture that people must avoid as they walk, and into which they may bump.

It is true that people with little or no vision use these objects as landmarks with which to navigate, but having many objects in the way adds to the difficulty of navigation and increases the probability of confusion and accidental contact with them. It is better to group these things out of the direct route, and to provide landmarks where they will be most effective as information sources.

Codes

Federal, state, and local laws mandate accessibility. The appropriate laws, building and fire codes, and specifications should be consulted. These will also give a more thorough and detailed description of the needs of those with visual impairments, and how to design for them.

CONCLUSIONS

The design of buildings and cities may be a help or hindrance in daily living for people with a wide range of visual disabilities. Appropriate design, however, is critical for the safety, mobility, and orientation of blind and visually impaired people, many of whom are older and have other disabilities. By providing necessary environmental information, the designer can produce a setting that is functional and significant without losing aesthetic appeal.

BIBLIOGRAPHY

1. National Center for Health Statistics, Prevalence of Selected Impairments: United States—1977, Vital and Health Statistics, **10**, No. 134, Hyattsville, Md., 1981.

2. Ref. 1.

3. C. Kirchner, G. Stephen, and F. Chandu, Statistics on blindness and visual impairment, in *Yearbook of the Association for Education and Rehabilitation of the Blind and Visually Impaired,* A.E.R.B.V.I., Washington, D.C. 1987.

4. C. Kirchner, and R. Peterson, Data on visual disability from NCHS, 1977, in C. Kirchner, *Data on Blindness and Visual Impairment in the U.S.* American Foundation for the Blind, Inc., New York, 1988.

5. E. Hill and B. Blasch, Concept development, in R. Welsh and B. Blasch, eds., *Foundations of Orientation and Mobility.* American Foundation for the Blind, Inc., New York, 1980.

6. R. Jose, ed., *Understanding Low Vision,* American Foundation for the Blind, Inc., New York, 1983.

7. W. Wiener, Audition in Ref. 5.

8. B. Bentzen, Mobility aids in Ref. 5.

9. J. Templer, J. D. Wineman, and C. M. Zimring, *Design Guidelines to Make Crossing Structures Accessible to the Physically Handicapped,* Office of Research and Development, Federal Highway Administration, Department of Transportation, Washington, D.C., 1982.

10. E. Pavlos, J. A. Sanford, and E. Steinfeld, *Detectible Tactile Surface Treatments,* U.S. Architectural and Transportation Compliance Board, Washington, D.C., 1985.

11. Ref. 9, p. 61.

12. Ref. 9, p. 61.

13. D. Norman, *The Psychology of Everyday Things,* Basic Books, New York, 1988.

14. American National Standards Institute, *American National Standard Specifications for Making Buildings and Facilities Accessible to and Usable by Physically Handicapped People,* ANSI 117.1, New York, 1986, pp. 25–27.

15. J. Templer, *Development of Priority Accessible Networks: An Implementation Manual,* U.S. Department of Transportation, Federal Highway Administration, Offices of Research and Development, U.S. Government Printing Office, Washington, D.C., 1980, p. 205.

16. Ref. 14, p. 30, 58.

17. Ref. 10, p. ii.

18. Ref. 9, p. 61.

19. J. A. Templer, J. Wineman, D. Hyde, J. Lehrbaum, and J. Sanford, *An Evaluation of Falls at Platform Edges, and a Discussion of Potential Solutions,* The Pedestrian Research Laboratory, Georgia Institute of Technology, Atlanta, 1988.

20. Ref. 14, p. 60.

See also Handicapped Access Laws And Codes; Physical And Mental Disability, Design For

John Templer
Craig Zimring
Georgia Institute of Technology
Atlanta, Georgia

Bruce Blasch
Veterans Administration
Medical Center
Decatur, Georgia

SILICONES

Silicones, silanes, and siloxanes have a broad range of construction applications, from additives in asphalt and concrete, to structural sealants used to adhere panels to skyscrapers, to coatings for fabric membranes in tension support structures. In fact, the durability and performance of silicones cause the list of applications to grow every year.

The first silicone building materials were construction sealants introduced in the 1960s. Silicone sealants applied at that time still show no signs of deterioration. How long today's silicone sealants will last is unknown, but they are certainly one of the most durable elastomeric materials used in construction. Many of the silicone materials covered in this article differ from the original sealants in physical form or formulation, but they share the same qualities of durability and premium performance.

The materials discussed in this article come from a basic building block of silicon, the element, a metal derived from sand. When properly reacted, molecules can be made that contain only one silicon atom with various other groups around it. These are silanes. When silanes are reacted together, they form chains or networks. These are called silicones. A siloxane is a series of alternating silicon and oxygen atoms. Siliconates and silicates are salts of the silanes or siloxanes.

SILANE AND SILICONE WATER REPELLENTS

Accelerated deterioration of concrete structures because of water and salt infiltration is a principal concern of the concrete industry. Absorbed water causes structural damage during freezing and thawing cycles. Salt corrodes the reinforcing steel of concrete structures such as bridge decks, sea walls, and parking garages. Such destruction manifests itself in the form of splitting, spalling, or scaling of the concrete surface. This damage is not limited to concrete and may also occur in masonry and stone because of their pore and capillary structures. These materials absorb water and permit deep migration of aqueous salts (1–3).

To reduce damage due to water and salt infiltration, the absorbency of the materials must be eliminated or reduced (4). However, this must not inhibit the free passage of water vapor in and out of the concrete or masonry; the material must retain the ability to breathe. Quite often, such measures must be taken without discoloring, darkening, or altering the physical appearance of the structure.

Several methods for protecting concrete and masonry from water and salt infiltration are documented in the literature (5,6). These include the use of oils, resinous acrylics, polyurethanes, hydrocarbons, silicone polymers, and silicate resins. However, many of these materials seal the surface so that the ability of the concrete to breathe is lost, or they do not effectively penetrate the surface of the concrete (7). A silicate or silicone material penetrates the substrate, and blocks liquid water, yet is permeable enough on a molecular scale to allow water vapor to pass.

The first use of silicone polymers in surface treatments was in the 1960s, and they are still widely used. Their expected lifetime is generally from 4 to 10 years, before erosion necessitates retreatment. The life expectancy depends on how long the 0.1–1-mm surface penetrated by the silicone will survive the wind and weather.

The early inorganic silicate resins are still among the most cost-effective ways of providing water repellency to stone and concrete structures, in spite of their susceptibility to erosion. One difficulty is the caustic nature of the material. Special care is required to keep it off the skin of workers and prevent damage to shrubs or glass. One popular application that avoids this problem is the treatment of new soft brick by total immersion in the silicate solution.

Difficulties with the caustic nature of inorganic silicates led to the development of less caustic or noncaustic silicones and siliconates. Many of these are solvent dispersed. This allows deeper penetration and reduces the problem of staining glass. However, this system is expensive, and working with the combustible solvents requires special care. With both the caustic and noncaustic systems, overapplication can sometimes darken the surface or leave a residue.

Alkyltrialkoxy silanes were first used to preserve concrete masonry and stone in about 1970. Silanes have several advantages. Their deep penetration prevents rapid erosion, and they act as chloride screens, preventing damage from salt and deicing chemicals. As a rule, silanes do not impart a noticeable color change to the surface of the substrate (8) or stain glass. Thus silane treatment of concrete and stone is gaining popularity.

The depth of penetration is fundamental to lasting performance. The more porous the substrate, the greater the depth of silane penetration and resin formation. Improved penetration is reportedly obtained by using a silane that has been diluted in toluene or some other aromatic solvent as opposed to an alcohol (9).

The ability to stop the capillary action of water is particularly important for masonry walls or concrete slabs that stand continuously on wet ground and do not contain a barrier below grade to prevent the upward capillary migration of water (10). This capillary rising of water in a building is often known as rising damp.

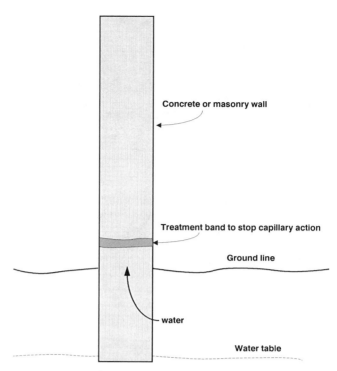

Figure 1. Treatment for rising damp.

The silanes or silicones used to treat a rising damp situation are pressure injected or gravity fed into the wall to saturate thoroughly a narrow band through the entire thickness of the wall, as shown in Figure 1. This treatment is used extensively in Europe and in such historic places as New Orleans, La., or Charleston, S.C., to preserve the old buildings and avoid the discomfort and damage caused by continual dampness.

The safety aspects of these materials are important. Workers should wear eye protection to prevent contact with silanes. Exposure to the vapors of alkyltrialkoxy silanes should be avoided. The materials are not corrosive, nor do they release acidic or basic byproducts. However, they do have a drying or defatting effect on contact with skin. The flammability, volatility, and vapor toxicity are moderate and similar to those of the corresponding alcohol.

SILANES AS ADDITIVES

Silicone polymers have silane curing chemistries and generally develop very good unprimed adhesion to metals and other mineral surfaces.

Typical commercial organofunctional silanes that have been effective in improving the adhesion of caulks and sealants are listed in Table 1.

Latex Systems

A primer that bonds two or more polymers to glass bonds the polymers to each other. Thus the silanes not only

Table 1. Typical Organofunctional Silanes for Adhesion of Caulks and Sealants

Organofunctional Group	Chemical Structure	Trade Name
Epoxy	$\overset{\displaystyle O}{\overset{\diagup\diagdown}{CH_2CHCH_2OCH_2CH_2CH_2Si(OCH_3)_3}}$	Dow Corning Z-6040
Methacrylate	$CH_2{=}\overset{CH_3}{\underset{\textstyle\vert}{C}}CO_2OCH_2CH_2CH_2Si(OCH_3)_3$	Dow Corning Z-6030
Diamino	$H_2NCH_2CH_2NHCH_2CH_2CH_2Si(OCH_3)_3$	Dow Corning Z-6020
Primary amine	$H_2NCH_2CH_2CH_2Si(OC_2H_5)_3$	UCC A-1100 (Union Carbide Corp.)

make silicones better construction materials, but also add immeasurably to the usefulness of other materials used in the construction trades, such as latexes.

Highway Construction

Functional silanes used as additives to concrete and asphalt increase tensile strength and bond strength and reduce the rate of chloride ion penetration. The result is a significant increase in highway life span, sometimes as great as 100%.

Concrete. Silane is mixed into the concrete just before it is poured (concrete ad-mix). Concrete highways with the ad-mix are considerably more durable, but for many years the cost was considered too high relative to the cost of concrete. Although the use of a silane additive can increase material costs by as much as 10%, this expense is now minor relative to the total installed cost and is more than offset by the increased durability of the concrete.

The silane additive also increases the time it takes the concrete to set. Concrete with the ad-mix typically takes 50% longer to set than untreated concrete, although it can take twice as long, depending on the concentration of the additive. Although this is not desirable in all applications, there are some benefits. Some large concrete pours experience damaging heat buildup during cure. As the reaction time is slowed, the heat generated by the reaction has time to dissipate.

Asphaltic Concrete. The stone and the asphalt liquid in some asphalts can lose their adhesion after the asphaltic concrete is in the roadway. This phenomenon is often called "stripping" and is characterized by cracks that precede the potholes and voids found in asphalt roadways. Although stripping is a function of the combination of bituminous material and the type of aggregate used to make the asphaltic concrete, it can be significantly reduced by the use of antistripping agents. Lime is a good antistripping agent, and there are also a variety of organic chemical additives sold for this purpose. When the 5- and 10-year studies are completed, this will be another large construction application for functional silanes and possibly silicones.

SILICONE SEALANTS

Silicone sealants are noted for their ability to maintain their initial physical properties after many years of exposure to constantly changing environmental conditions. It is this ability that has earned silicones the reputation of being the high-performance sealant. Their applications are as varied as sealing bath tubs, caulking windows, sealing expansion and control joints in buildings, sealing highways, and sealing and gluing glass to modern high-rise buildings.

Silicone sealants have been used in various construction applications since their introduction over 20 years ago. However, the first silicone sealants evolved acetic acid during cure, and this acidic byproduct reacted with acid sensitive surfaces such as concrete and mortar, resulting in uncertain adhesion. Since that time, however, several types of non-acid-evolving silicone sealants have been developed, and these do not react with concrete. These materials are widely used in the curtain walls in buildings, in sidewalks, and in highway joints.

Originally, silicones were regarded as too costly to use as sealants unless no other materials would work. Today, the cost gap between silicones and good organic sealants has narrowed to the point where they are competitive in most applications.

General Properties and Performance

All uncured silicone sealants contain three basic ingredients: long-chain silicone polymer, curing agents, and fillers. In the cured state, the basic polymeric structure of a silicone sealant consists of alternating silicon and oxygen atoms. This SiO linkage (similar to the structure in glass or quartz) is transparent to ultraviolet (uv) radiation; therefore, silicone sealants are virtually unaffected by weather.

Some nonsilicone sealant manufacturers incorporate 1–10% silicone additive to improve certain physical properties. They label these products "siliconized" or "silicone modified." Siliconized products may offer some improvement in physical properties over untreated organic sealants, but their weatherability and elongation are similar to those of other organic sealants.

Nearly all silicone sealants sold to the construction industry are supplied as one-part packages containing liquid silicone sealant. This liquid silicone cures to an elastomeric rubber upon exposure to atmospheric moisture. The curing process is often called room-temperature vulcanization (RTV), and the sealants are commonly referred to as RTVs. During the curing process, the silicone polymer and curing agent (cross-linker) react together to form the continuous Si–O–Si network, simultaneously releasing a byproduct. This byproduct may be acidic or neutral, depending on the particular cure system used.

For many years, the silicone market was dominated by the acid-evolving sealants, with their characteristic acetic acid or vinegar odor. Other silicons, more recently developed, release only neutral or nearly neutral byproducts such as alcohol, amides, or amines, which do not attack concrete or marble surfaces.

Modulus. Silicone sealants can differ from each other in modulus, which has an important bearing on the ability of the sealant to withstand joint movement. Modulus, as used here, is the force required to produce a 150% elongation (specific deformation) of a cured rubber tensile bar, as described in ASTM D412 (11). In addition, modulus is sometimes related to the ultimate elongation capability of the sealant at rupture for a tensile bar sample prepared according to ASTM D412 (Table 2). The last column of the table shows sealant joint movement capabilities related to job-site movement. Many of the best nonsilicone sealants currently available perform at 25% cyclic movement. Some silicones have 25% performance but some can take up to 100% movement in extension and 50% in compression. This illustrates that an entire range of silicone sealants are available to handle joint movements that are very large.

These cyclic movements are of fundamental importance when choosing a sealant for any application. There is no industry-wide agreement on the values of low-, medium-, or high-modulus silicone sealants. As a result, some producers claim a particular sealant to be low modulus, whereas other producers classify a similar sealant as medium modulus. The cyclic movement values stated on the sealant package or in the manufacturer's literature should be used to provide an appropriate match between sealant and application. The user should be aware, however, that all manufacturers do not use the same test method to obtain movement values. The test method must be considered when comparing movement values stated by a manufacturer (23).

Certain silicone sealants are characterized by very low modulus. Because they can be elongated or compressed with very little force, they place little stress on fragile surfaces like aggregate composites, weaker concrete, and lightweight exterior insulation systems. Although primers are sometimes required, they are not usually needed to obtain good adhesion to concrete, unless water immersion conditions are anticipated. These low modulus sealants are the premier sealing materials for the most difficult joints.

Some silicones, generally with neutral cure, are classi-fied as having medium modulus. Although they have less joint movement capability than the very-low-modulus silicones, they are still superior in movement capability to all known organic sealants. They have enough joint movement capability to satisfy most joint-sealing requirements. They also have greater unprimed adhesion to a wider variety of substrates. Unprimed adhesion to most substrates makes application and installation much more error free. The construction industry views these materials as general-purpose adhesives/sealants, suitable for most applications involving the sealing of dissimilar materials, like glass to aluminum, aluminum to concrete, concrete to other materials, and even concrete to concrete.

High-modulus silicones are high-strength materials. Although they can withstand less movement than other silicones, they are the equal of most premium organics in this respect. Since strength is not a factor in most sealing applications, these materials see little use as concrete joint sealants, but extensive use in structural glazing and general sealing. The nonacid, high-modulus silicones are used on all common construction surfaces. They perform as well or better than organic sealants from a joint movement point of view, and they excel over all nonsilicones in weathering ability longevity, and constant performance over a wide temperature range.

Temperature Range. Silicone sealants have other inherent characteristics that make them suitable for providing long-term service as construction industry joint sealants. Silicone sealants can be applied over a wide temperature range, from −35 to 140°F (−37 to 60°C), provided that proper surface preparation is performed. However, even though they can be applied in extreme cold, it is sometimes impractical to do so since special care has to be taken to ensure a frost-free surface. Today's silicones do not adhere to wet or frosty surfaces. This is also true for good organic joint-sealing materials.

Cured silicones maintain their rubbery properties over a wide temperature range, with less stiffening in the cold and less softening in the heat than organic sealants. The advertised working temperature range of most silicones is from −65 to 350°F. However, all silicones are slightly different, especially in their high-temperature capabilities. Some silicone sealants can take continuous service up to a high-temperature limit of 250°F; others can tolerate 425°F. Most organics have a 180°F maximum. The ability to withstand very high temperatures is not often needed in general construction sealing. When it is needed, it is advisable to consult the manufacturer's literature to ensure a proper choice.

Table 2. Elongation and Cyclic Joint Movement of Silicone Sealants

Sealant Classification	Force at 150% Elongation, psi (MPa)	Ultimate Elongation, %	Cyclic Joint Movement, %
High modulus	100 (690)	500	±25
Medium modulus	40–100 (276–690)	500–1200	±35
			±40
Low modulus	40 (276)	1200	±50
			+100 to −50

Compression Set. Compression set is a measure of how much the sealant permanently deforms when compressed under a load. If permanently deformed (or compressed), the sealant has less ability to stretch when the joint expands and may fail. When used within the manufacturer's recommendations, silicones generally recover 90–100% after compression. These values can be compared with recovery values of 80–90% for urethanes and 70–80% for polysulfides. This is an important feature of silicones and other good expansion joint sealants. It is a key feature separating good sealants from those of marginal capabilities, which may offer recoveries as low as 25–50%. Compression set resistance is the principal indicator of the ability of a sealant to take cyclic extension and compression, year after year, without rupture.

Other Properties. Many other features of silicones, such as their good weatherability, ozone resistance, and radiation resistance, could be highlighted. It is essential that a specifier look at each application and determine the needed performance. If special properties are needed in a silicone sealant, the manufacturer should be contacted. Current sealant technology permits silicone manufacturers to produce a spectrum of silicone sealants with different physical properties to meet a variety of needs.

Highway Sealants

In highway applications, concrete joints are sealed to prevent surface water, incompressibles (ie, dirt, small stones), and deicing chemicals from entering joints. Surface water in joints causes erosion of the pavement foundation, resulting in faulted pavement. Incompressibles in highway joints cause pavement joint deterioration and pavement "growth" (reduction in space provided for pavement thermal expansion). Deicing chemicals in joints corrode metal transfer load devices embedded in the pavement. Highways must be sealed and protected from these sources of damage.

The function of the sealant is to seal the joint between two concrete substrates. It does not serve as an adhesive for bonding the substrates together. The sealant's strength characteristics are less important than its ability to withstand joint movement and maintain adhesion under a variety of environmental conditions. Thus the low-modulus silicones with their large movement capability are ideal for these joints. The weather resistance of silicones is also important because sunlight hits the sealant at severe angles, and shading or other protection almost never exists on a highway. Heat stability keeps the silicone sealant from becoming soft, even in the hottest climates, so stones do not penetrate the sealant or become imbedded in it. The retention of elasticity in the cold allows for integrity of sealant and bond, even on the coldest days, when the joints are widest.

Limitations. Silicones cannot exceed their rated movement capability in highway applications. If a sealant is rated at 50% of the joint width in cyclic expansion (0.5-in. joint to 0.75 in.), then a failure can be expected if the joint moves 75% (0.5 to 0.875 in.). To avoid this, it is recom-

mended that the joint size and joint movement expectation be matched to half the movement capability of the sealant. For example, a sealant rated at ±50% should be installed in joints with expected movement of ±25%. A ±0.125-in. movement would require a 0.5-in. joint and a ±50% sealant. If two slabs move in unison in a highway application, the sealant experiences twice the anticipated movement (0.25 in), but this movement is still within the sealant's capability.

Silicones do not take abrasion well. Road traffic, scuffing, foot traffic, and rough treatment abrade a silicone. The recommended approach for using silicone in high-abrasion areas is to recess the silicone sealant below the surface, away from the source of abrasion. In a highway, the top of the sealant should be 0.25–0.5 in. below the road surface. If a road is faulted and grinding is scheduled after resealing, installation 0.75 in. below the surface is acceptable.

To minimize or eliminate the possibility of joint spalling caused by traffic or incompressibles working on the joint edge, the joint edges should be beveled and the sealant tooled to a concave or semicircular shape.

Silicones degrade in active caustics. Water-saturated concrete has active lime (a caustic) and eventually degrades a silicone. There are several possible solutions to this problem. For materials used at grade level, highway engineers should either accept the over 10-year lifetime predicted for unprimed silicones on horizontal exposed concrete in typical U.S. climates, or prime the surface of the concrete with a material that sets up a barrier coating between the silicone and the concrete. Such barrier materials are being tested by all of the major silicone producers. Accelerated tests show that they extend the useful life of silicones in wet conditions. Long-term field data are expected to prove this by the 1990s.

Only silicones with a barrier-coating primer should be used below grade on concrete, with the consent of the manufacturer. For above-grade use on concrete, no problems should be expected for at least 15 years, the age of the oldest application to date. How long a typical silicone will adhere and perform above grade on concrete has yet to be determined. The same is true for silicone applications to substrates other than concrete. The oldest installations are now only 20 years old. Most of those silicones are still performing well. No two silicone sealant formulations give identical performance in all situations. The first step toward obtaining the best sealant for an application is to identify the minimum properties needed. Next, the sealants available to satisfy those needs and those that exceed those needs must be identified. Finally, it must be decided how large an overdesign or insurance factor is needed in the sealant.

Sealant Selection

Selection of a joint sealing compound is influenced by many job-site-related requirements, such as resistance to heat, cold, mildew, and radiation; Food and Drug Administration (FDA) approval for use with food or potable water; ozone resistance; ability to withstand exposure to harsh chemicals, and fire resistance. The type of joint, working vs nonworking (less than 5% total planned movement), should also be considered. Close examination of the particular application helps determine the type of joint involved and the degree of movement expected.

Working Joints. Working joints are primarily designed to accommodate the movement associated with thermal expansion and contraction of construction materials. However, thermal expansion and contraction are not the only factors that influence joint movement. Working joints are known by several names, depending on the application. Several examples are listed below:

- Highway and building isolation joints.
- Highway contraction joints.
- Curtain-wall joints (panel to panel, panel to mullion).
- Perimeter glazing.
- Joints between dissimilar materials.

Working joints may be of several designs: butt joints, tongue-and-groove joints, lap joints, and surround joints. In a butt joint, the panels lie edge to edge, and the sealant is subjected to alternating tensile and compressive forces. In a lap joint, the panels override each other in a sliding movement, which results in shearing stresses on the sealing material. The surround joint is a combination of butt and lap joints. In this joint, the sealant may be subject simultaneously or separately to tensile, compressive, or shearing forces.

The amount of stress placed on the sealant depends on how much movement occurs, the joint configuration, and the joint size. The total movement depends on several factors working independently or collectively. However, only temperature change is widely used to predict how much joint movement will occur. A good correlation has been reported between daily temperature changes and expansion joint movement (12). Statistical analysis indicates that the daily data can be extrapolated to annual movement. This has been confirmed by actual measurements. Data for this study were obtained by measurement of movement in expansion joints in two different buildings while constantly monitoring temperature. Results of the study show that, although temperature may not be the sole cause of joint movement, calculations based only on expected temperature changes can give a good estimate of the movement that will occur. In another study, a good correlation between joint movement in highways and mid-depth concrete pavement temperature was reported (13).

The degree of joint movement for any temperature change is influenced by the construction materials. The coefficient of linear expansion is different for every material, and thus the movement is different. For example, the coefficients for precast portland cement concrete and aluminum are 10.8 cm/cm°C (6.5 × 10⁻⁶ in./in.°F) and 21.6 cm/cm°C (13 × 10⁻⁶ in./in.°F), respectively. The amount of movement for aluminum is twice the movement of concrete for a given size panel and temperature change. Knowing the degree of movement associated with construction materials is important in the sealant selection process.

The substrate temperature at the time of sealant installation determines the type of stress placed on the sealant. If the sealant is installed in a butt joint on a hot summer day, the joint between the two substrates will be at or near minimum because the substrate will be at maximum size. In this case, the sealant will undergo primarily extension during the following winter as the temperature decreases and the substrates contract. Conversely, if the sealant installation occurs during late fall or winter, the joint will be near or at the maximum opening. The sealant will undergo primarily compression during the following spring and summer months.

Temperature and field conditions can simultaneously place more than one type of stress on the sealant. Joints are at their maximum opening during winter months, when the sealants are coldest and least able to accommodate movement. At this time, highway sealants and sealants in other joints undergo extensive stresses. Under these conditions, the highway sealant also experiences shear stress caused by upward and downward deflections of two concrete slabs under traffic load. The amount of shear on the sealant can be expected (conceptually) to increase as the highway receives more use over the years. For these applications, a low-modulus silicone is often preferred because of its good movement capabilities.

Linear shear from the sealing of dissimilar materials can occur. The extent to which this is expected should be estimated. Building panel length or highway slab length also affects the degree of observed movement.

Calculations to estimate joint movement due to thermal changes are relatively simple, provided that the desired joint size, coefficient of linear expansion, and panel size are known. Using the installation temperature, the total expected movement is segmented into expansion and contraction portions, shown below.

Example of Movement Calculation

Material	Precast concrete
Coefficient of expansion	6.5×10^{-6} in./in.°F
Panel size	30 ft
Joint width	0.5 in.
Installation temperature	70°F
Expected temperature range	−30 to 130°F

Movement = (panel size)(coefficient of expansion)
              × (temperature range)

Maximum expansion:

$$= (30 \text{ ft})(12 \text{ in./ft})(6.5 \times 10^{-6} \text{ in./in.°F})(100°F)$$
$$= 0.234 \text{ in.}$$
$$= 47\%$$

Maximum compression:

$$= (30 \text{ ft})(12 \text{ in./ft})(6.5 \times 10^{-6} \text{ in./in.°F})(60°F)$$
$$= 0.140 \text{ in.}$$
$$= 28\%$$

Under these conditions, a medium-modulus silicone rated at ±50% joint movement would meet these requirements.

However, there is practically no room for error in either the panel size or the installation conditions. A low-modulus silicone rated at $+100/-50\%$ joint movement would be preferred in this case because it provides a safety factor of nearly 2 for extension and compression.

Safety factors allow for deviations between design and field movement conditions. Each sealant is rated at a particular joint movement capability based on controlled laboratory conditions. However, seldom are laboratory and field conditions the same; therefore, a margin of error must be allowed. Silicone manufacturers generally recommend a safety factor of 2 or 3 (installed sealant and one-half or one-third of its rated movement capability). This type of safety margin allows joints to be sealed that are narrower than designed. Note in the above example that the designed sealant installation temperature was 70°F (21°C). However, if the sealant were to be installed on a hot summer day at 95°F, the joints would be narrower, and the sealant would experience greater-than-planned extension during the following winter.

The *U.S. Army Manual on Sealing and Caulking* gives recommendations for a minimum safety factor (14). The manual uses the formula listed below. This formula considers the sealant's movement capacity and expected joint movement to calculate the minimum joint dimension needed.

$$\begin{array}{l} \text{Minimum} \\ \text{joint width} \end{array} = \cfrac{1}{\begin{array}{c}\text{sealant} \\ \text{movement capability} \end{array} + \begin{array}{c}\text{material and} \\ \text{construction tolerances}\end{array}} \times \begin{array}{c}\text{maximum joint} \\ \text{movement expected}\end{array}$$

Thus, if the sealant's movement capability in one direction is 25% (0.25) and the total expected movement (expansion and contraction from the example above) is 0.374 in. (approximately 0.1 cm), then the minimum joint width is 1.5 in. (3.8 cm) plus tolerances. If the sealant's movement capability is 50% (0.50), then the minimum joint size can be 0.75 in. (1.9 cm) plus tolerances. Using this rule of thumb allows for human error in installation or differences in installation temperatures.

Nonworking Joints. The same factors that influence movement in a working joint are present in a nonworking joint. However, the degree of movement is substantially less (5% or less). Thus the criteria for selecting a sealant with medium or low to medium modulus are based on something other than expected movement.

The primary function of the sealant in a nonworking joint is to act as a joint filler to seal these joints effectively for many years. Thus sealant selection should be based on factors such as adhesion (primed versus unprimed), temperature, expected cost, length of desired service, and similar considerations. In these applications, practically any sealant will perform, but attention to quality is still important.

A low-cost sealant (eg, oil-based caulk) saves money on initial installation, but the long-term performance may be inadequate. Typically, low-cost caulks become hard and

brittle and crack with the passage of time. In the brittle state, the smallest movement may cause failure of the seal. Silicone sealants and other high-performance sealants do not become hard and brittle with time and thus are capable of providing a long-term, cost-effective seal for nonworking joints.

Several publications give guidelines for proper joint sizing and proper installation techniques (15,16).

Installation

Proper installation of a sealant, whether for highways or buildings, is just as important as proper sealant selection for obtaining the maximum benefits that silicone sealants can provide. The elements of proper installation include surface preparation, joint design, and follow-up inspection.

Surface Preparation. Adequate surface preparation (cleaning) is one of the most important steps toward obtaining a successful installation. Removal of dirt and other loose foreign matter allows the sealant to be placed in intimate contact with the substrate surface, leading to the development of good adhesion. If foreign matter remains on the substrate surface, intimate contact cannot be obtained.

There are several techniques for cleaning the surface. The techniques depend on the application (buildings are different from highways, new construction is different from reseal applications). Generally, no single technique can be used for every application; field conditions dictate which technique to use.

For new concrete construction (eg, precast concrete panels, formed highway joints), cleaning the joint surface by mechanical abrasion with a wire brush followed by a high-pressure air blast is generally sufficient to remove laitance and dirt. If mold release agents are present and have penetrated into the pores of the concrete, more thorough cleaning is required. For highway joints that are sawed, residual cement dust must be removed from the joint walls. High-pressure water blasting performed immediately after sawing, followed by wire brushing after the concrete dries and high-pressure air blasting, is generally acceptable.

Some precast panels have waterproofing or a decorative coating on them. If the coating is on the walls of the joint, the sealant must bond to the coating, not the concrete. The problem then becomes the durability of the coating, its adhesion to the concrete, and the sealant's ability to bond to this particular coating. Many failure lines occur between the coating and the concrete. In such cases, the sealant may adhere well to the coating, but the coating fails and the building will leak.

Surface preparation for reseal applications where the original joint sealant is not a silicone is difficult and time consuming because removal of old sealing materials is required. On buildings, mechanical abrasion and knife cutting followed by mechanical abrasion are the two common techniques used to accomplish this. In highway joint resealing, joint widening by sawing is generally the fastest way to remove old sealing materials, particularly asphaltic types. After removal of the old sealant, the procedures described above should be used to complete the joint preparation process.

In some building resealing applications, removal of the old sealant need not be performed. A technique called a "band-aid" joint has been successfully used without removing the old sealant. This technique requires that a recommended bond breaker tape cover the old joint sealant and that new sealant be placed over the tape and overlap the joint edges by at least 0.25 in. (0.6 cm). However, the appearance of the finished joint should be considered before using this technique. If appearance is important (eg, in a building facade), this technique may be undesirable. If appearance is not important (eg, on a building roof), this procedure saves time and some labor expense. Some walls have been done this way and are quite attractive. The band-aid technique is very important when a wider joint is needed between glass or aluminum wall panels. These joints cannot be opened, thus either the band-aid joint or a lower modulus, higher movement sealant would be recommended.

If the failed sealant being replaced is silicone and the mode of failure is cohesive (not failure to adhere to substrate) because of excessive stress, repair can be easily and quickly accomplished. The old sealant should be cut out, and low-modulus high movement silicone should be installed. In this case, the joint walls have not contaminated, so no cleaning is required, and most silicone sealants adhere to themselves, unprimed. However, job-site adhesion testing should be conducted to verify the adhesion.

The best procedure for adequately cleaning the surface substrate is subject to individual preference. The one procedure that is generally not recommended for removing old sealants on concrete or porous surfaces is the use of solvents. These liquids tend to carry contaminants into the concrete pores, where they can prevent the development of good adhesion.

Joint Design. Good joint design is an important consideration for proper sealant installation. There are four elements to be considered in a joint design: joint width, joint depth, backer-rod selection, and sealant placement.

The joint width between two substrates affects the ease of sealant installation and the percentage of movement. Installing sealant into joints as small as 0.188 in. (0.50 cm) or smaller is extremely difficult, if not impossible. Therefore, the joint should be wide enough to allow for easy installation. In addition, small working joints of this type typically have a high percentage of movement. The joint must be large enough to accommodate the design movement without exceeding the sealant's capabilities. The U.S. Army formula for calculating minimum joint width was discussed in the section on working joints.

Another essential element of joint design is the use of recommended backup or backer-rod materials. There are three reasons for using backer rods. First, they act as bond breakers to prevent three-sided adhesion (the third side is the bottom or back of the joint). Only adhesion to the joint walls is desired. Three-sided adhesion places excessive stress on the sealant and drastically reduces its extension

capability. Second, they help control bead thickness. Proper backer-rod placement (depth) into the joint ensures that the correct amount of sealant is installed. Third, the backer rods serve as a tooling aid. Nonsagging sealant must be tooled into the joint to ensure intimate contact between the sealant and substrate, so that good adhesion can develop.

The type of backer used depends on the sealant and the application. Each silicone manufacturer recommends the type of backer rod to use with the seal for a particular application. Generally, open-cell polyurethane and expanded closed-cell polyethylene foams are recommended.

The last element of joint design is sealant placement. The proper amount of sealant must be placed in the joint at the recommended depth. Silicone highway sealants are installed so that the sealant's width-to-depth ratio is 2:1, but the sealant bead should never be less than 0.25 in. (0.65 cm) or greater than 0.5 in. (1.27 cm). For example, a 1-in. (2.54-cm) joint requires a sealant bead 0.5 in. (1.27 cm) thick; a 2-in. (5.108-cm) joint would also require a 0.5-in. (1.27-cm) sealant bead. This recommended placement is one factor that should be given serious thought when estimating silicone sealant cost against a lower-price and lower-performance organic sealant that usually requires a 1:1 width-to-depth sealant placement.

Follow-up Inspection. A follow-up field inspection is an equally important part of the total installation procedure. Long-term sealant performance depends on all three installation procedures: surface preparation, joint design, and follow-up inspection. The single largest cause of sealant failure for buildings and highways is improper installation. Conducting a follow-up inspection two to three weeks after installation and another one to two years later detects problem areas (if any), and corrective measures can be taken before damage is done.

Almost all initial problems are related to work quality and adhesion. If a sealant performs well after the first full-year cycle, future problems are usually related to materials or compatibility, although there are exceptions.

There are several ways to conduct a follow-up field inspection to determine the quality of the installation. One technique that measures the sealant's adhesion and elongation capability is the hand-pull test. The hand-pull test may be run on the job site after the sealant is fully cured, usually within 14–21 days.

Hand-pull Test Procedure

1. A knife cut should be made horizontally from one side of the joint to the other.
2. Two vertical cuts approximately 2 in. long should be made at the sides of the joint, meeting the horizontal cut at the top of the 2-in. cuts.
3. The 2-in. piece of sealant should be grasped firmly between the fingers just above the 1-in. mark and pulled at 90°. A ruler should be held along one side of the extended sealant.
4. If the 1-in. mark on the sealant can be matched and held at the 2-in. mark of the ruler (100% elongation)

with no failure (the sealant is not starting to pull away from the joint), the sealant will perform at 25% expansion.

5. If the 1-in. mark on the sealant can be pulled to the 3-in. mark on the ruler (200% elongation) and held there with no failure of the sealant, the sealant will perform at 50% joint expansion.

Adhesion may be adversely affected by moisture in or on the substrate during sealant application and cure, contaminated or weak surfaces, and poor application techniques.

With proper selection, silicone sealants are not only acceptable for use on concrete and other materials, but in many situations are the best available sealing materials. Nevertheless, silicone sealants require the same attention to detail by the applicator as any of the high-quality organic sealants. The cost of silicone sealants has decreased relative to the organic sealants, and they are only 10–20% more costly on a per-gallon basis and are sometimes comparable in cost on a linear foot applied basis. This cost considers only the original installation and does not include the advantages of the extended life cycle of silicones.

SILICONE SEALANTS IN STRUCTURAL GLAZING

Structural glazing is the practice of using silicone sealant as an adhesive to hold large glass windows on the sides and skylights on the roofs of buildings. The continuous bead of silicone may also serve as the seal that keeps out water and weather.

The key to adhesive reliability in structural glazing is the stability of the sealant when exposed to uv radiation. The sun shines through the glass directly on the glue line. Any deterioration of the adhesive would cause loss of adhesion. An advantage of silicone sealants for structural glazing stems from their resistance to uv radiation. Silicone sealants are elastomeric, allowing the glass to expand in the summer and contract in the winter without stressing and breaking it. Finally, silicone sealants are long lasting. The first silicone structural glazing systems were used in the 1960s, and there have been no failures of these systems to date (17).

This success is largely due to the attention to detail structural glazing systems have received (18). With structural glazing, more than any other sealing system, it is the total concept of materials plus design plus installation technique that allows the system to work.

Design Considerations

Figure 2 shows a typical structural glazing design. The formula used to calculate the amount of bonding surface (bite) required between the sealant and substrate in structural glazing is

$$\text{bite} = \frac{0.5 \times \text{smallest glass size} \times \text{wind load}}{\text{design strength of sealant}}$$

In building construction and glazing, bite by ASTM definition is the dimension by which the frame, stop, or flange of

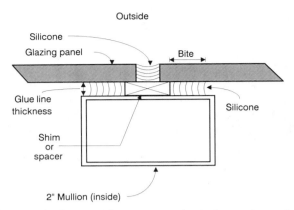

Figure 2. A glazing with no stops or physical restraints to hold the glass.

a lock-strip gasket overlaps the edge of the glass or panel. Bite in structural glazing is analogous to the lock strip. It is the dimension of the adhesive/sealant that holds the glass to the mullion.

If the glass is held on four sides with an adhesive/sealant or on two sides with an adhesive/sealant and on two sides by a conventional jamb with stops, the equation is the same. In the case of two-sided structural glazing, the theory says that the stops take care of the forces on their sides of the unit, and the sealant does its work where it is applied.

The following example shows how the bite equation should be used.

Structural Glazing Calculations

Glass dimensions: 5.5 ft (1.68 m) × 6 ft (1.83 m).

Location: Los Angeles.

Force exerted on glass by highest pulse of wind in 50 years: 50 psi (244 kg/m^2; 2.39 kPa).

Sealant design strength: 20 psi (137.8 kPa; 14.06 × 10^3 kg/m^2).

(Sealant strength is measured by forming an actual joint such as that called for in ASTM C719 (19). After proper cure, the joint is pulled in a tensometer to test its strength.)

$$\text{Bite} = \frac{0.5(1.68 \text{ m})(244 \text{ kg/m}^2)}{14 \times 10 \text{ kg/m}^2} = 0.014 \text{ m} = 14 \text{ mm}$$
$$= \frac{0.5(5.5 \text{ ft})(50 \text{ psi})}{(20 \text{ psi})} = 0.57 \text{ in.}$$

The 20-psi value is in the equation for the design strength of the adhesive/sealant unless there is specific data to indicate other values can be used. Seldom should a design value higher than 20 psi be used, as this would reduce the safety factor. Although, 20 psi is the maximum design value for the sealant in most situations, many architects call for 12 or 15 psi for the maximum dynamic stress.

Glue Line Thickness. Although the force of the wind is the primary pressure on a structural panel, the glue line

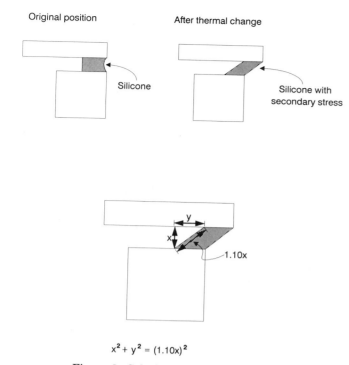

Original position   After thermal change

Silicone

Silicone with
secondary stress

$$x^2 + y^2 = (1.10x)^2$$

Figure 3. Calculation of secondary stress.

must be sufficiently thick to accommodate the movement that results from thermal expansion and contraction of the glass. Most sealants used as structural adhesives can tolerate ±25% movement, or 1.25 times their original length. This figure is used to calculate the bite necessary to withstand the wind load factor; however, the secondary stress of thermal expansion must also be considered.

Secondary stress caused by temperature change is in the shear direction. This stress can be reduced by installing an adequately thick glue line. Architects usually choose 10 or 15% movement as the maximum secondary stress contribution. Figure 3 shows a calculation of a glue line thickness allowing only 10% stretch and minimizing the secondary stress.

Y can be calculated as a simple thermal change:

Y = Shear Movement from Temperature Change
Y = thermal expansion coefficient × temperature change
    × length
X = Glue Line Thickness
    $X^2 + Y^2 = (1.10X)^2$

Adhesive/sealant manufacturers usually recommend that the glue line be kept at a 0.25-in. (6-mm) minimum, even if the final calculation indicates a smaller one. This minimum thickness is recommended because practical experience has shown that it is difficult to achieve a relatively air-free bead in a channel less than 0.25 in. wide.

The general practice since the mid-1960s, the beginning of structural glazing, has been to use 0.25–0.375 in. (6–8 mm) as the glue line, with some deep channels going to 0.5 in. (12 mm). Thus the thickness of the glue line is not governed primarily by theoretical considerations, but

by the practical need to have enough room to obtain a good installation.

Edge Clearances. Another aspect of the structural joint, the distance between the glass lites, must also be considered. The item most often taken back to the architect for reconsideration is not the bite or glue line, but the distance between the edge of the glass and the fin (or the distance between the edges of two glass lites where there is no interposing fin or mullion). Some architects, in designing for appearance, forget that this could be an expansion joint. In calculating the width of the weather seal or expansion joints, the same rules and the same formula are followed as were given earlier with the formula for minimum joint width.

Sealant Color. In the United States, most structural glazing is done with black, aluminum, or bronze sealants. Black is by far the most popular color. Only a few jobs in the United States specify clear sealant. In contrast, clear silicones are specified for most of the work in Europe and the Far East. Architects in the United States switched from clear to pigmented sealants because of the increased durability of the pigmented sealants.

Silicone sealants are the only type of sealants allowed in structural glazing because silicone polymer shows no degradation in sunlight and weather. This is also why they are gaining an increasing share of the market for expansion and control joints. However, clear silicones are almost completely transparent to sunlight, which can pass through them with little attenuation. Thus the materials under the sealant must also be stable to the uv rays of sunlight for the life of the building. If there is a coating on the metal or glass, the manufacturer should guarantee that the coating will withstand 20–30 years of direct exposure to sunlight.

Adhesion. For any joint designed for the use of sealants, adhesion is the key to success. If adhesion fails in an expansion joint, the building leaks. If adhesion fails in a structural application, panels loosen and may eventually fall.

Many architects who include structural glazing in their building designs use two procedures to minimize the possibility of adhesion problems. First, they pretest all specified materials for adhesion before construction of the building skin begins. Second, they test materials on site as they are delivered to the job.

The present field test for adhesion is the same as the hand-pull test described in the section on sealant selection, except the sealant is pulled until it breaks. With present structural sealants the sealant should break before it loses adhesion. Manufacturers generally ask that a record be kept at the site to show that adhesion tests were performed on each lot of metal or other material that arrives on the site. In industry technical committees, every major silicone supplier to the structural glazing industry has reported cases where materials delivered to some job sites were different from those pretested for the same project.

When such adhesion variation is found, work must be

stopped until cleaning procedures, primers, or sealants are changed to ensure reliable adhesion. Although no standard ASTM guideline has yet been published on adhesion testing, each manufacturer supplies detailed procedures on how these job-site lot-to-lot tests should be carried out.

Good, reliable adhesion is the key to a successful structural glazing project. Stronger sealants do not imply greater assurance of success or a greater safety factor for the job. The strongest sealant is no better than the strength of the bond. The bond is dependent on surface preparation and sealant installation techniques.

Close job inspection, compatible materials, pressure testing (or vacuum testing) of selected units, and postjob inspection increase the true safety factor and confidence that the job will not fail.

The basics of good joint design when using adhesives/sealants in structural glazing can be summed up in these points:

1. Adequate bite should be provided to hold the glass for the maximum anticipated wind load.
2. The glue line should be designed to be wide enough to produce only small stresses from lites in thermally induced shear.
3. The joint size should be large enough to accommodate all movement and provide a material tolerance in weather-sealing joints and expansion joints.
4. Adhesion and compatibility testing, including both pretesting and on-the-job testing, should be specified.
5. Print reviews should be secured from the manufacturer of the adhesive/sealant.

The last item is a good practice that more and more architects are using. A print review does not mean that the sealant manufacturer takes responsibility for the architect's design. Sealant specialists, however, see hundreds of prints each year. They become familiar with many types of oversights and faults and can often identify potential problems at an early stage. Print reviews of structural glazing projects are offered as a free service by many sealant manufacturers.

Silicone in Insulated Glass

The use of silicones in insulated glass units is growing (20–22). Silicones are used as the sealant that adheres the two glass lites of the unit together.

There are two types of insulated glass units: the single-seal type and the dual-seal type. Both can be used for any size window, and both can incorporate high-performance heat-absorbing or -reflecting glass. Both use a polysulfide or hot-metal butyl organic seal. The difference is that the dual-seal unit also uses a secondary seal of the same material or of silicone. This extra seal, although it increases the cost, improves performance dramatically and allows manufacturers to increase their warranties to 10 years, in contrast to the 5 years typical for single-seal units. Figure 4 illustrates the difference in the two types of insulated glass units.

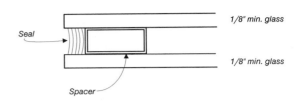

Single seal insulated glass unit

1/8" min. glass

Seal

1/8" min. glass

Spacer

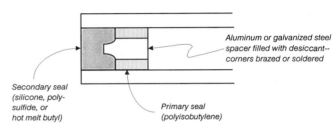

Dual seal insulated glass unit

Aluminum or galvanized steel spacer filled with desiccant--corners brazed or soldered

Secondary seal (silicone, polysulfide, or hot melt butyl)

Primary seal (polyisobutylene)

Figure 4. Single-seal and dual-seal insulated glass units.

The use of silicones in insulated glass started slowly because the polysulfide sealants give a minimum of 10 years of performance, with units typically outliving the usual 10-year warranty. Accelerated testing by various glass and sealant manufacturers indicated the probability of a longer lifetime with a silicone dual-seal unit (21), but this superiority had not yet been demonstrated in the field.

Until the advent of structural glazing, there was no pressing need to replace polysulfides with silicones. However, with the rapid growth of structural glazing and the trend toward energy conservation, there was a natural movement of insulated glass into structural glazing. Since only silicone sealants can tolerate constant exposure of the bond line to uv radiation through the glass, the use of silicone as the secondary seal of a dual-seal unit is necessary if insulated glass is to be used in structural glazing.

As manufacturers began to make the dual-seal units with silicone, they found the additional cost was only a few cents per unit, and they could sell the units at higher prices for greater profit. Many architects, who were familiar with the good durability of the standard silicone sealants, translated that into greater longevity of the insulated glass units in standard applications as well, and thus the original slow growth of silicones into the insulated glass area increased rapidly.

One issue often debated is how much silicone to use as the secondary seal when the insulated glass unit is used in structural glazing. It should be remembered that the secondary seal is a structural bond, adhering the outboard lite of the unit to the building. A difference of opinion exists as to whether the calculation for the thickness of the glue line used for structural glazing should also be used for insulated glass, or whether the controlled manufacturing environment reduces adhesion variability and makes a smaller glue line appropriate. The impact of wind loading on the individual lites in the event of a seal failure is also unclear.

Research on this debate is ongoing, and industry standards are evolving to govern the use of insulated glass in structural glazing. However, there is no question that silicone will be used as the secondary seal in a growing number of insulated glass units, particularly those going into structural glazing.

Most manufacturers use a two-part silicone for fast cure and more rapid production; others use a one-part, no-mix product. Almost all use a silicone that gives unprimed, reliable adhesion to glass and metal spacers. Adhesion is always a variable, especially with the many different finishes and cleaning techniques used with the aluminum spacers and the many coatings being applied to glass (most of which are on an inner surface, to which the sealant must adhere). ASTM and other standards exist for normal insulated glass units, and slowly such standards will be developed for insulated glass units to be used structurally.

SILICONE GASKETS

Gaskets are used in many areas of the construction industry. Gaskets include seals, spacers, and shims. They come in solid rubber, sponge rubber, webbed, chevron-shaped, and accordion-fold versions.

Silicone gaskets are used in construction projects where quality is of the highest value. These gaskets can be used almost anywhere and vary in hardness and strength. The silicone gaskets resist deterioration and are of the same general composition as the silicone sealants. They come to the job site in preformed shapes. Because they are totally formed in a factory, many varieties of strength and elasticity are available.

Silicone gaskets are made by milling a peroxide crosslinker into a long-chained polysiloxane polymer or gum and adding filters and extenders. The fillers and extenders are added to give increased hardness and strength. The homogeneous mixture is extruded through an orifice of nearly any shape and vulcanized by heat. Typically, a gasket is extruded onto a conveyor belt that takes the extrusion through an oven. Physical properties for these gaskets are determined by published ASTM test methods. The hardness of silicone gaskets is measured by a Shore A durometer and may range from 40 to 80 Shore A points. This test method is ASTM D2240 (23). For comparison, a standard pencil eraser may give a Shore A durometer reading of 30 points.

Tensile strength as measured by ASTM D412 (11) may range from 700 to 900 psi at elongations from 100 to 300%. A typical high-strength silicone sealant may exhibit properties such as a durometer reading of 30, tensile strength of 400 psi, and elongation of 500% when measured with the above ASTM tests. The most desirable properties exhibited by silicone gaskets are their excellent resistance to ozone, oxidation, heat and cold aging, uv aging, and acids. Silicone gaskets have excellent recovery characteristics at extremely hot and cold temperatures. They are not affected by thermal cycling or uv cycling.

The standard silicone gasket is not highly tear or abrasion resistant. If this property is needed, it must be specified. The standard silicone gaskets also tend to swell in hydrocarbons. If an application is exposed to hydrocarbon and swelling cannot be tolerated, a nonswelling silicone must be specified. The substitution of a trifluoropropyl group for a methyl group on the dimethylpolysiloxane polymer is one way to get a gasket or sealant that has fuel resistance, although this substitution is more expensive.

The base of the silicone gasket is clear, and most of the fillers are white. Hence, pigmenting of silicone gaskets is easy. Most gaskets are black because black pigment is the least expensive, but gaskets can be made in almost any color.

Some gasket bases incorporate blowing agents so that the finished gasket is a soft, pliable foam. Blowing agents activate during the heat cure process and increase the gasket to about two times the original size. Sponge rubber gaskets generally are not made with cavities because the blowing action closes the cavity.

Certain gasket manufacturers make gaskets with a high-strength cord, fiber, or fabric running through the extrusion to prevent stretch, hold shape, resist sag, or increase tear resistance.

Silicone gaskets' biggest competition are neoprene and ethylene–propylene terpolymer (EPDM) gaskets. These are one-third to one-half the cost of silicone gaskets, have good abrasion and tear resistance, are not as fuel sensitive, and are easier to install. However, neoprene and EPDM gaskets become brittle and deteriorate with thermal cycling and uv cycling. Because formulations rely heavily on carbon, they come in one color, black. They do not rebound as well as silicones at any temperature.

The main uses for silicone gaskets are in glazing. Dry glazing is when glass is held on a building by mechanical fasteners. The glass rests on setting blocks. Because the mechanical fasteners cannot rest directly on the glass, a gasket is installed between the glass and the fastening device. This gasket prevents air and water from leaking in around the perimeter of the window. If neoprene or EPDM gaskets are used for this purpose, they generally have to be replaced or resealed in about 10 years. A common way to fix a leaking weatherproofing gasket is to put a sealant, usually a silicone sealant, over the top of the gasket.

If a silicone gasket system is used, it can be expected that no maintenance will be required for the life of the building because silicone gaskets do not dry out, shrink, or become brittle. The use of preformed silicone gaskets in construction is relatively new, having started in the late 1970s, but long lifetimes are expected based on experience with silicone gaskets in other applications and the durability exhibited by silicone sealants.

Silicone gaskets are often used in structural glazing so that there is absolute assurance that the gasket, shim, or setting block is totally compatible with the silicone sealant for the life of the structure.

SILICONE COATINGS

Silicone sealant dispersed in a solvent becomes a coating. The durability, weatherability, and temperature stability of silicone sealants are also qualities of silicone coatings. Silicone's unique properties make it desirable for certain specific applications. Silicone is inherently a breathing system; that is, silicone allows water molecules in the vapor state to pass, but does not allow liquid water to pass (24,25). Thus the silicone coating is not a vapor barrier and cannot be used for such applications. It can be used to protect a vapor barrier from the weather. When water is trapped beneath a silicone-coated system, it can and will breathe out. This characteristic is especially desirable for roof and wall coatings.

The silicone polymer is transparent to sunlight (uv radiation). For a silicone coating to protect the surface beneath it from damage by sunlight, the coating must be pigmented and thick enough to give sufficient buildup of pigment. Existing silicone coatings require a minimum of 15 mil cured coating (26,27). When a silicone-coated roof fails, the single most common cause is improper application.

Silicone–polyurethane Roofing

Silicone–polyurethane roofing is a combination of spray-applied polyurethane foam and spray-applied silicone coating. Polyurethane foam is one of the most efficient insulating materials available for roofing. Silicone coating is the most weather resistant of the coatings available to protect the foam (28). The cured coating provides a weathertight seal that protects polyurethane foam from degradation caused by uv light, water, and other weathering agents.

Silicone-coated foam insulation started with a few test roofs in 1968, and many more tests began in the early 1970s. By the middle of the 1980s, its value was proven, and the system is now growing. The silicone–polyurethane roofing system has a number of advantages. It can be applied without seams and is lightweight and relatively strong. Its weather resistance and self-flashing capability contribute to long life. It provides high-quality insulation. Problems with the system are usually caused by improper deck preparation or improper application of the foam or coating. These problems can be avoided with proper specifications and inspection of the installation.

Like all single-ply or thin-coat systems, the silicone–polyurethane roof can be damaged by dropped objects that puncture the coating. The roof should be examined for such damage every year. Punctures, gouges, and tears can be repaired immediately by filling them with a silicone sealant. This quick, inexpensive repair can be made by regular maintenance personnel without calling in roofing experts.

Spray-applied polyurethane foam is a 1:1 mixture of an isocyanate and a polyol. Foam applied with a slight excess of isocyanate is not usually a serious problem, although cracking and a hard, glossy surface may result. The polyol component contains the fluorocarbon blowing agent. The blowing agent contributes directly to the cell structure and insulating quality of the foam. Spraying foam with excess polyol is a much more serious problem than excess isocyanate. Foam with excess polyol does not have the normal strength, density, or insulation value, and it absorbs water. This off-ratio foam must be removed and replaced. The silicone coating that is applied over the foam is a one- or two-component silicone rubber sprayed in two coats on the polyurethane foam.

Spray-applied polyurethane foam used for roofing applications must have certain physical properties in order to function properly on a roof. The foam produced must have an in-place density of at least 2.5 lb/ft³, a minimum compressive strength of 40 psi, and a 90% closed-cell content. The foam must be a minimum of 1 in. thick, and each lift of foam must be at least 0.5 in. (27). The two-component coating is mixed on site as it is dispensed. The one-component silicone coating is used as supplied without the addition of solvents, catalysts, or curing agents. It cures by reacting with water vapor in this atmosphere. The silicone coating comes in 55-gal drums and is available worldwide. The cost of the silicone–polyurethane roofing system is comparable with the costs of other roofing systems, such as single plies and polyurethane foam roofs with organic coatings.

Codes. The silicone–polyurethane roof system has been evaluated for safety by Factory Mutual and Underwriters' Laboratories (UL). When properly applied, the system passes both Factory Mutual calorimeter testing and UL 790 spread-of-flame testing (29). Factory Mutual has given the system a Class 1 rating. UL has given the system a Class A rating when used with one of many particular foams tested and not exceeding the limiting slope. To receive a Class A rating, the spread of flame may not be more than 6 ft at any given slope.

The silicone–polyurethane roof system complies with the Southern Building Code Congress International Standards. It conforms to the Building Officials and Code Administrators International Standards. The International Conference of Building Officials has accepted the system.

There are many safety precautions that should be observed in the storage and application of the polyurethane foam. All safety precautions as outlined by the Cellular Plastics Division of the Society of the Plastics Industry (SPI), the National Fire Protection Association (NFPA), the Occupational Safety and Health Act (OSHA), and the material manufacturer should be observed. A few of the precautions include the following:

1. Canister-type respirators or forced air supply masks must be worn by all personnel involved in the application of the foam.
2. Eye protection must be worn and meet the requirements of the American National Standards Institute (ANSI).
3. All skin area must be covered by protective clothing.
4. Smoking, open flames, and welding sparks are prohibited during foam application.

The silicone coating is supplied in a combustible solvent. Adequate ventilation is required during application, and sparks, flames, and smoking should be avoided.

The coating should be applied at a temperature greater than 32°F (0°C). The first coat, or base coat, dark gray, must be applied the same day the foam is installed. It can be applied within 1 or 2 h after the foam installation, but in no less than 1 h.

In theory, about 0.80 gal of coating is needed to cover 100 ft^2 of a glass-smooth surface to a 7.5 mil thickness. In practice, because of irregular foam surfaces, loss of coating due to the wind, and loss of coating in the drum, the coating must be applied at a rate of at least 1.25 gal/100 ft^2 to provide a minimum dry-film thickness of 7.5 mil (24). Depending on the surface texture, a greater rate of application may be required. Extremely rough foam surfaces should not be coated. The foam must be removed and replaced.

The base coating should be allowed to cure for approximately 2–6 h, depending on the temperature and humidity conditions (25). Two to three hours should elapse before walking on the base coat. Allowing an overnight or longer cure time is acceptable, provided the base coat is clean and completely free of all moisture before applying the finish coat.

After the base coat has cured and before the finish coat is applied, the coating should be inspected for any pinholes, cracks, or other defects. All defects, especially pinholes, must be touched up with additional base coat.

The top coat, in a contrasting color, should be applied at right angles to the base coat and should be applied within 24–72 h after the base coat. The application rate again should be a minimum of 1.25 gal/100 ft^2 (24). The finish coat should completely cover the base coat. With the two coats applied, there must be a minimum of 15 mil silicone coating. A minimum 15 mil dry-film thickness of silicone coating is required to provide long-term protection of the polyurethane foam.

If roofing granules are required or desired, they should be sprayed into a wet third coat within 5 min of its application. The granules should be applied at a rate of 50 lb/100 ft^2 (27). The granules have many interesting and pleasing colors, and the roofs have a more conventional look.

Silicone Air- and Tension-supported Roofing

Silicones have entered the roofing market in yet another way. Builders and architects have experimented with silicone-coated fiber glass fabrics since 1971 because of their light weight, high strength, and high light transmission. Early fabrics were not a commercial success, in part because of their low flexibility and poor crease resistance. The technology has advanced to the point where fabrics with excellent flexibility and crease resistance, as well as high strength and light transmission, are now commercially available.

The manufacture of these state-of-the-art silicone coated fiber glass fabrics involves a proprietary process that employs a combination of silicones to optimize the properties of the fabric. The silicones are dispersed from solvents onto rolls of woven fiber glass fabric. When the coating is properly applied, each fiber in the fabric is surrounded by a chemically bonded sheath of silicone. The fiber glass provides strength; the silicone provides a durable envelope protecting the fiber glass from abrasion and hydrolysis.

Although the need for high light transmission was the driving force behind the development of silicone-coated fiber glass fabrics, the light weight, flexibility, and strength of the fabric are often more important properties. In fact, pigments are occasionally added to the coating to reduce the light transmission as well as to provide color.

Properties. The fiber glass fabric plays an important role in determining many of the properties of the coated membrane. The properties of the fiber glass fabric itself are determined by such factors as glass composition, fiber type and diameter, strand weight, yarn construction, and weave pattern. The impact of the fiber glass on the properties of the coated fabric can be seen in Table 3, which shows selected properties of four coated fabrics. The weight of each fabric is split about equally between the fiber glass and the silicone. As the data in the table imply, stronger fabrics generally have more fiber glass, weigh more, and have lower light transmission.

The importance of properly applied silicone is shown in Table 4, which lists the properties of an uncoated fiber glass fabric and the same fabric after coating with the silicone. The table also includes a Teflon-coated (DuPont) fiber glass fabric. The higher values for the tensile, flex-fold, and tear strengths of the coated versus the uncoated fabric point out the importance of the silicone coating. Comparison of the values for the silicone-coated fiber glass and the Teflon-coated fiber glass shows the importance of surrounding each fiber with a protective coating. Although the tensile and flex-fold values of the two fabrics are similar, the tear resistance of the silicone-coated fabric is considerably higher than that of the Teflon-coated fabric. This is believed to be because the silicone is applied by a process that surrounds each individual fiber, whereas the Teflon process is not.

Aside from their strength, light weight, and high light transmission, silicone-coated fiber glass fabrics meet several other important criteria required of exterior construction materials. The weatherability of silicone-coated fabrics is excellent. Silicones have long been known for their durability in all sorts of climatic extremes, and the fiber glass, once protected from hydrolysis, can endure almost any extreme of temperature, sunlight, or moisture. A number of outdoor and machine weathering studies have confirmed the weatherability of silicone-coated fiber glass fabrics. Table 5 shows that after 13 years of exposure in the desert Southwest essentially no degradation of a silicone-coated fiber glass fabric occurred. Although this fabric was only an experimental sample based on early technology, it is indicative of the performance of newer fabrics that use silicones similar to those used initially. In Table 6, carbon arc weatherometer results further indicate the durability of fabrics produced using the newer coating technology.

The performance of silicone-coated fiber glass fabrics in

Table 3. Properties of Silicone-coated Fiber Glass Fabrics

Coated Fabric Weight, oz/yd	Translucency, % Solar Transmittance	Trapezoidal Tear Warp/Fill, lb	Breaking Strength Warp/Fill, lb/in.
12	80	12/12	130/140
16	60	35/50	175/190
32	50	100/110	500/450
36	45	100/120	750/650

Table 4. Physical Properties of Uncoated and Coated Fiber Glass Fabrics

Fabric Type	Strip Tensile, Warp × Fill	Flex Fold, Warp × Fill	Trapezoidal Tear, Warp × Fill, lb/in.
Fiber glass fabric	440 × 370	335 × 300	45 × 55
Silicone-coated fabric	750 × 650	500 × 550	100 × 120
Teflon-coated fabric	875 × 675	824 × 460	75 × 80

fire tests ranges from good to excellent. Commercially available fabrics have been rated Class B in the ASTM E108 Burning Brand test (30) and Class A in the E108 Intermittent Flame (31) and Spread-of-flame (32) tests. Their fire resistance is constantly improving.

A new method has been developed for seaming together individual pieces (gores) of the fabric. This seaming technique uses silicone adhesives to make large continuous membranes ideally suitable as lightweight roofing materials. The proprietary silicone adhesive seaming technology developed concurrently with the new fabrics produces seams having the same strength and durability as the fabric. The fabric can be joined using mechanical connections, but sewing is not used because of the brittle nature of the glass fibers. Weatherproofing is accomplished with seals, gaskets, and caulks.

Applications and Availability. The membranes created by seaming together gores of silicone-coated fiber glass fabric are ideally suitable as roofing materials for stadium covers, amphitheaters, tennis courts, and wherever large, free-span roofs are required. They have been used in both air- and tension-supported structures. They allow much more design freedom than more conventional building materials.

At this time, the principal source of silicone-coated fiber glass construction fabrics is ODC Inc., Norcross, Ga. ODC coats the fabric and provides a range of services from

engineering through erection of the structure. Sold under the Vester trademark, the fabric and services provided by ODC cover applications ranging from greenhouses to sports stadiums.

The silicone industry views this roofing concept as a huge opportunity. Not only does the system give premium performance over a longer life cycle, but it also has a lower installed cost than competing systems. Silicone-coated air- and tension-supported roofs should come into widespread use in the near future.

SILICONE FIRESTOPS AND FOAM PRODUCTS

Silicones as a class are generally fire resistant and, with special technology, can be made very fire resistant. In fact, they can be used to stop the spread of fire and the flames and toxic gases generated in fires. Silicone firestops are among the few materials approved for use in U.S. nuclear power plants.

A silicone firestop is a seal in holes or openings in a wall, such as those that carry pipes and cables from room to room. Making fire-resistant walls is relatively easy; making holes in the walls that do not let flame or intense heat pass through to the other side is more difficult. The seal must be tight enough that gases cannot pass through, strong enough that a fire hose cannot blow away the firestop, and soft enough that more wires or pipes can be put through the firestop. These requirements tend to limit the choices to fire-resistant silicone foam.

The need for such a super firestop was vividly demonstrated in the mid-1970s by the control room fire in the Tennessee Valley Authority's Brown's Ferry Nuclear Generating Station on March 22, 1975 (33–35). In that fire, a urethane foam installed previously as a penetration seal was ignited accidentally by a worker using a lighted candle to check for air movement. The fire spread quickly to cable-jacketing material and then on to other areas. Many problems were encountered in controlling the fire. A carbon dioxide fire-extinguishing system was ineffective because of gas lost through burned-out seals; thus the

Table 5. Outdoor Weathering of Silicone-coated Fiber Glass

Exposure Time, yr	Arizona		Florida	
	Light Transmission, %	Tensile Strength, pli	Light Transmission, %	Tensile Strength, pli[a]
0	86.4	120	83.4	125
5	84.4	117	81.5	116
13	83.6	119		

[a] pli = pounds per linear inch.

Table 6. Machine Weathering of Silicone-coated Fiber Glass

Exposure Time, h	Arizona		Florida	
	Light Transmission, %	Tensile Strength, pli	Light Transmission, %	Tensile Strength, pli[a]
0	45.6	795	45.6	795
1,000	46.4	810	46.1	782
7,000	45.8	824	42.8	752
11,000			43.4	760

[a] pli = pounds per linear inch.

required concentration was never reached. Losses were estimated at over $200 million because of business interruption alone.

Subsequent fires at the World Trade Center (36–38) and New York Telephone Exchange (37) also resulted in substantial loss of property and business. More recently, attention has focused on fires that resulted in loss of life. The most notable of these were the hotel fires at the MGM Grand Hotel (39,40) in Las Vegas, Nev. and at the Houston, Tex., Westchase Hilton (40,41).

These fires, along with a number of others that have occurred, are especially significant since investigations revealed that in approximately 70% of the cases death was caused by inhalation of smoke and toxic vapors, not the fire itself. In-depth studies of recent fires through autopsies (42–45) have revealed that death often occurs prior to the victim reaching fatal levels of carbon monoxide and carbon dioxide poisoning. It has become increasingly apparent that death in modern fires is being caused by combustion byproducts from organic resins, especially those types that contain nitrogen moieties and emit cyanide compounds.

The United States has the worst record in the world with regard to both property and human loss from fire (46–49). There are indications that this is primarily because of the increased use of flammable plastics throughout the construction industry. A simple glance around any building reveals the high level of "fuel loading" present in the form of furnishings and wall, floor, and ceiling coverings (40). The use of silicone firestops can reduce the risk associated with this level of flammability.

Product Types

Two types of silicone foam products are available, one based on an organotin catalyst and the other on platinum-catalyzed cure technology. Both begin as two-component liquids that cure to an elastomeric state through chemical reactions after mixing. In the platinum-catalyzed reaction, initial cross-linking occurs through an addition reaction of vinyl functional siloxane polymers with polymers that contain silicone hydrides in their structure. Simultaneously, another reaction occurs between other silicon hydrides and silanol-ended silicone polymers. This releases a small amount of hydrogen gas, which is trapped within the developing elastomer to form the foam.

The foam obtained from the tin-catalyzed reaction tends to be more open celled and somewhat lighter than that from the platinum-catalyzed reaction. Among other applications, it is used in certain medical applications as a wound dressing. However, the platinum-catalyzed product has several advantages. Of these, the most important are improved resistance to hydrolytics (water) and high-temperature reversion.

Product Characteristics

In general, a silicone RTV foam can be described as a two-component liquid system that, when mixed at a 1:1 ratio, cures and rises to form a medium-density, permanently flexible elastomeric foam. The working time, often called the "set" or "snap time," is 1–3 min. Foam rise is complete within 5 min, with slight additional cure in the next 24 h. The reaction rate is temperature dependent, increasing or decreasing as the temperature rises or falls. A fast cure version is also available that cures in 40 s at 75°F and in 7–8 s at 95°F. The foam density is 17–20 lb/ft^3 with a K-factor of 0.4–0.5 per inch and an R-factor of 2–2.5 per inch.

The liquid nature and color contrasted (black–white) appearance of the two components, coupled with the 50:50 mix ratio, make the foam simple and easy to mix. The low toxicity of the liquid components and the cured foam make handling safe and convenient. There are few special precautions required, except that the hydrogen gas released should not be allowed to accumulate.

Physical Properties

The foam is predominantly (approximately 85%) closed cell. This is an important consideration for its use in controlling the movement of fire, smoke, toxic vapors, and water during fire situations.

Its free-foam density is about 17 lb/ft^3. Its tensile strength is in the range of 33 psi. Relatively minor formulation changes can be made that allow preparation of lower-density materials, down to approximately 10 lb/ft^3. However, the physical strength decreases proportionately.

Silicones have good electrical insulation properties. An important point with respect to the use of this product in power-generating facilities is the fact that it is unnecessary to derate power cables that pass through the maximum thicknesses (12 in.) of foam used in nuclear plants. Independent tests conducted by Detroit Edison (50) and Westinghouse (51) have confirmed this.

The thermal insulation values are relatively low as compared with other products. However, the K-factor range for silicone foam of 0.4–0.5, dependent on the actual density (14–20 lb/ft^3), is often satisfactory for use in specific applications that also require high-temperature stability.

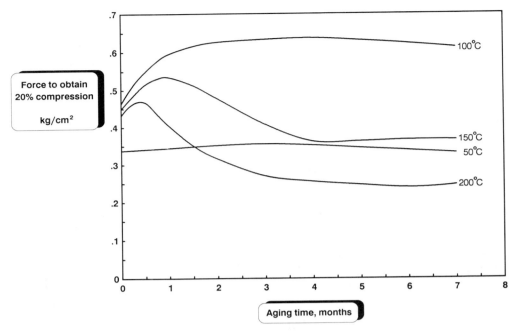

Figure 5. A series of curves illustrate the stability of the foam at various temperatures for extended periods.

Silicone foam is stable throughout the service temperature range of −55 to 200°C (−60 to 400°F). In addition, foam does not melt or show appreciable change in physical properties at slightly higher temperatures for substantial periods of time.

A series of curves shown in Figure 5 illustrates the stability of the foam at various temperatures for extended periods. Reports generated within the nuclear industry using these and other data concluded that Dow Corning 3-6548 silicone RTV foam exhibits little or no change in physical properties throughout this temperature range (up to 200°C) for a period of time considered to be the life of a nuclear power plant (more than 30 years).

Fire Tests

The most important property exhibited by silicone foam is its fire resistance. However, fire resistant does not mean noncombustible. In fact, the limited degree of combustibility exhibited by silicone foam is important for the formation of the surface char of siliceous material that acts as thermal protection for the virgin foam remaining on the nonfire side. This mechanism is similar to the ablative process used to protect aerospace reentry vehicles. During fire testing, temperatures in excess of 1500°F (800°C) are encountered. Continuous exposure to these conditions eventually causes the char to form all the way through the foam sample.

Combustion Byproducts

Several methods have been developed to study and evaluate the toxic effects of pyrolysis gases and other byproducts of various materials (45,52). Receiving particular attention recently are protocols designed by the National

Institute of Standards and Technology (NIST), the University of Pittsburgh, and the University of San Francisco. This has become a controversial subject, with questions raised regarding the most appropriate test conditions. Recent studies have centered on the NIST and Pittsburgh methods (53–55). However, the studies conducted by the University of San Francisco are thought to represent the broadest and most complete coverage of compositional types done to date (52). These studies list silicone materials among the least toxic of the over 270 materials evaluated.

The composition of smoke given off during combustion of Dow Corning 3-6548 silicone RTV foam was measured using a NIST chamber. The smoke consists of a very fine dust (amorphous silica) with smaller amounts of carbon dioxide and carbon monoxide (56). These last are typical hydrocarbon decomposition products. They are generated from the methyl groups situated along the siloxane backbone.

Foam Benefits and Applications

Fire resistance and low toxicity form the basis for the value of the platinum-catalyzed silicone RTV foam. Other attributes of interest to the construction industry include durable flexibility over a broad temperature range, the closed-cell structure, the ability of the liquid to flow and cure into different shapes and sizes, and the ease of removal or repair.

In addition to being used in over 90% of this country's nuclear power-generating plants, silicone foam has also gained wide acceptance for reducing the risk of life and property loss in nonnuclear areas. Examples include high-rise office and hotel structures, hospitals and boarding homes, and various industrial facilities like pulp and paper mills and petrochemical complexes. In addition, a number of applications are developing in the transportation industry, for example, prevention of fire spread on ships and passenger trains.

Two uses have emerged that can be classified as somewhat more specialized applications. One is the use of silicone foam to provide complete positive seals in and around computer centers, especially those areas protected by Halon-type fire extinguishing systems. Such facilities include industrial process control rooms, air traffic control centers, aviation training centers, and information handling centers. Another interesting use is in the control of sound both within (57) and between rooms. Silicone foam was specifically chosen for use in the protection of personnel and test instrumentation at a jet engine development laboratory, a severe test for any sound barrier.

New Technology

In addition to the silicone RTV foam, several other products are in the research and development stage. These include products with lower densities (10 lb/ft^3 without sacrificing physical properties), a tougher open-cell material that is also moldable, and a nonslump (with somewhat higher density) material that forms a tougher char under fire conditions.

A fire-resistant sealant is also available. This complements the silicone foam in that it is convenient to use and makes repairs fast and simple. The use of the silicone firestop sealant in small penetrations is so convenient that this is becoming the method of choice.

BIBLIOGRAPHY

1. W. A. Cordon, *Freezing and Thawing of Concrete, Mechanisms and Control,* American Concrete Institute, Detroit, Mich., 1966, p. 5.

2. J. P. Nicholson, "The Corrosion of Reinforcing Steel in Concrete: Method of Survey and Repair Strategies," National Association of Corrosion Engineers, No. 1294, p. 1.

3. *Concrete in Sea Water,* Cement and Concrete Association of Australia, Tech., Bull., The Habour Press, Sydney, Australia, 1974, p. 1.

4. *Comparison of Silicone Resins, Siliconates, Silanes, and Siloxanes as Water Repellent Treatments for Masonry,* 983-1, Prosoco, Inc., Kansas City, Mo., ConserVare No. 983-1,

5. "Concrete Sealers for Protection of Bridge Structures," National Cooperative Highway Research Program, Transportation Research Board, Washington, D.C., Rep. No. 244, 1981, p. 3.

6. Ref. 4, p. 6.

7. Ref. 5, p. 6.

8. Ref. 5, p. 10.

9. Ref. 4, p. 7.

10. *Chemical Dampcoursing—Recommended Procedures,* Prosoco, Inc., Kansas City, Mo., ConserVare No. 683-1.

11. ASTM D412–83, American Society for Testing and Materials, Philadelphia, Pa.

12. K. K. Karpati and E. V. Gibbons, Division of Building Research, National Research Council of Canada, 1979.

13. J. P. Cook, *Construction Sealants and Adhesives,* Wiley-Interscience, New York, 1970, p. 222.

14. *U.S. Army Manual on Sealing and Caulking,*

15. *Annual Book of ASTM Standards,* Vol. 4.07, ASTM, C962–81, American Society for Testing and Materials, Philadelphia, Pa., sec. 4.

16. *Sealants: The Professional's Guide,* Sealants and Water Proofer's Institute, Kansas City, Mo., Tech. Bull., 1984, p. 10.

17. *Sealant Technology in Glazing Systems,* American Society for Testing and Materials, Philadelphia, Pa., STP 638, pp. 67–99.

18. J. M. Klosowski and C. Schmidt, "The Role of Adhesive Sealants in Structural Glazing," *U.S. Glass, Metal, and Glazing,* 70–84 (July/Aug. 1984).

19. ASTM C719–79, American Society for Testing and Materials, Philadelphia, Pa.

20. "Insulated Glass," in *The Ducker Report,* Ducker Corp., Detroit, Mich., 1981, p. 8.

21. A. Sanford, "The Performance of Silicone Sealants in Insulated Glass Units," *U.S. Glass, Metal, and Glazing,* 58–64 (1983).

22. J. Spearman, "High Quality Makes I.G. Manufacturing Venture a Success," *U.S. Glass, Metal, and Glazing,* 60–63 (July/Aug. 1982).

23. ASTM D2240–86, American Society for Testing and Materials, Philadelphia, Pa.

24. *Membrane Roofing, SPEC Data,* Dow Corning Corp., Midland, Mich., Form No. 61-2711-83, 1983, p. 1.

25. *Construction Coating, Information About Building Products No. 3-5000,* Dow Corning Corp., Midland, Mich., Form No. 61-2141-82, 1982, p. 1.

26. *Dow Corning Silicone/Polyurethane Roof System, Manual of Recommended Application Techniques,* Dow Corning Corp., Midland, Mich., Form No. 61-897A-82, 1982, p. 20.

27. *Dow Corning Silicone/Polyurethane Roof System, Guide Specifications,* Dow Corning Corp., Midland, Mich., Form No. 61-376A-82, 1982, p. 1.

28. S. A. Brady, "Protecting Polyurethane Foam Roofing Insulation," *Metal Building Review* (July 1977).

29. Spread-of-flame Testing, UL 790, Underwriters' Laboratories.

30. Burning Brand Test, ASTM E108–80, American Society for Testing and Materials, Philadelphia, Pa.

31. Intermittent Flame Test, ASTM E108–80, American Society for Testing and Materials, Philadelphia, Pa.

32. Spread-of-flame Test, ASTM E108–80, American Society for Testing and Materials, Philadelphia, Pa.

33. *Fire Safety Aspects of Polymeric Materials, Buildings,* Vol. 7, National Materials Advisory Board, National Academy of Sciences, Technomics Publishing, Westport, Conn., 1979, pp. 51–56.

34. A. J. Pryor, "Brown's Ferry Nuclear Power Plant Fire," Society of Fire Protection Engineers, Boston, Mass., Technol. Rep. No. 77-2, 1977, pp. 1–14.

35. R. L. Scott, "Brown's Ferry Nuclear Power Plant Fire on March 11, 1975," *Nuclear Safety* 17(5), 592–610 (1976).

36. Ref. 49, pp. 134–136.

37. R. J. Kasper, "Minimizing Potential Damage from the Cable-tray Fires," *Plant Engineering,* 91–94 (Feb. 18, 1982).

38. "Lessons of a High-rise Fire," *Fire International* 51, 59–64 (Mar. 1976).

39. "Fire at the MGM Grand," *Fire Journal,* **76,** 19–37 (Jan. 1982).

40. "Hotel Fires—Behind the Headlines," National Fire Protection Association, Quincy, Mass., 1982

41. "Twelve Die in Fire at Westchase Hilton Hotel," *Fire Journal* **76,** 11–26, 54–56 (Jan. 1982).

42. E. G. Butcher and A. C. Parnell, *Smoke Control in Fire Safety Design,* E. and F. N. Son, Ltd., London, 1979, pp. 17–22.

43. G. F. Vickery, "Fire Safety," *Building Operating Management* **48–49,** 64–65 (Aug. 1983).

44. Ref. 49, p. 30.

45. F. B. Clarke III, "Toxicity of Combustion Products—Current Knowledge," *Fire Journal* 77, 84–97, 101–108 (Sept. 1983).

46. B. C. Levin, "Fire Deaths and Toxic Gases," *Nature* **300,** 18 (Nov. 4, 1982).

47. R. L. Rawls, "Fire Hazards of Plastics Spark Heated Debate," *Chemical and Engineering News* **61,** 9–16 (Jan. 3, 1983).

48. Ref. 49, pp. 2, 13.

49. C. J. Hilado, *Handbook of Flammability Regulations,* Technomics Publishing, Westport, Conn., 1975, p. 1.

50. V. J. Herter, R. E. Barry, and T. A. Began, "Ampacity Test of a Silicone Foam Fire Stop in a Cable Tray," in *Proceedings of the IEEE Power Engineering Society Summer Meeting,* Portland, Oreg. July 26–31, 1981, pp. 1–6.

51. C. W. Nemeth, G. B. Rackliffe, and J. R. Legro, "Ampacities for Cables in Trays with Fire Stops," in *Proceedings of the IEEE Power Engineering Society Winter Meeting,* Atlanta, Ga., Feb. 1–6, 1981, pp. 1–6.

52. H. L. Kaplan, A. F. Grand, and G. E. Harzell, *Combustion Toxicology: Principles and Test Methods,* Technomics Publishing, Lancaster, UK, 1983, pp. 108–123.

53. "Flammability—New California Toxicity Reports Disagree," *Plastics World* **41,** 4–5 (July 1983).

54. G. Forger, "Smoke Toxicity Standards," *Plastics World,* **41,** 36–38 (Aug. 1983).

55. K. P. Keller, "Battle Rages over the Toxicity of Plastics," *Building Design and Construction,* 42–44 (June 1983).

56. C. J. Hilado, C. J. Casey, D. F. Christensen, and J. Lipowitz, "Toxicity of Pyrolysis Gases from Silicone Polymers," *Journal of Combustion Technology,* 130–140 (May 5, 1978).

57. C. L. Lee and S. Spells, "Sound Absorption Property of Platinum-catalyzed Silicone RTV Foam," *Journal of Cellular Plastics* **18,** 174–177 (May/June 1982).

See also Acrylics; Adhesives; Concrete, Architectural; Envelopes, Building; Glass In Construction; Membrane Structures; Moisture Protection; Plastics; Precast Architectural Concrete; Roofing Materials; Sealants; Suspension Cable Structures

Jerome Klosowski
Dow Corning Corporation
Midland, Michigan

SITE DEVELOPMENT

Site development involves the arrangement of structures and the configuration of the landscape to develop a piece of land for some form of human activity. Site development ranges in scale from the siting of a single structure to the entire design of a city or new community. It is, however,

Figure 1. Pre-twentieth century Venice, Italy. Streets and accompanying squares and plazas acted as the rooms of the cities while buildings formed the walls.

usually considered to be the development of a specific site. Depending on scale, urban contextual issues, landscape, and other natural systems, it often requires the expertise of a range of professional input including architecture, landscape architecture, and urban design, as well as other design and professional expertise.

The article is divided into two parts, the first part includes a review of the major historical contributions in the physical evolution of cities and communities. As in all physical design processes, an understanding of past experiences provides valuable insight for the development of contemporary site designs. Although all great cities evolved over time, there were individuals such as Haussmann, Oglethorpe, Clarence Stein, and others who made major contributions to site design philosophies. The second part of the article provides approaches to site development and specific site design criteria.

HISTORY

Up to the end of the Middle Ages, western cities were functional places of residence, commerce, and security. With the arrival of the Renaissance, the renewed interest in cultural expression turned public attention to the aesthetics of the city.

In pretwentieth-century cities, streets and accompanying squares and plazas acted as the rooms of the cities while buildings formed the walls (Fig. 1). A map of early Rome shows an intricate combination of streets, plazas, and squares defined by buildings (Fig. 2). Movement throughout these spaces in cities, such as Rome and Florence, is an experience of diversity and poetics resulting

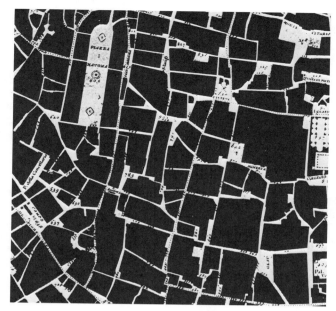

Figure 2. Rome, Italy, central area showing the intricate variety of the Renaissance city.

from the impact of the varying scale of plazas, squares, and streets; the artifacts, such as monuments and fountains; and the intricate detailing of the architecture. The city building process occurred over many centuries, and involved a sequence of different political structures and cultures that, in spite of varying needs and attitudes toward the city, were unified in their commitment to defining space.

The reconstruction of Paris, under the direction of Haussmann, took place between 1852 and 1870, and remains one of the great feats of site design. The major goal of the grand boulevard system designed by Haussmann was to glorify the city by orienting its long vistas in an axial arrangement toward major pieces of architecture and monuments. The major roads laid out by Haussmann

Figure 3. The Arc de Triomphe, Champs Elysées, Paris, France. Roads were oriented on long vistas towards major monuments.

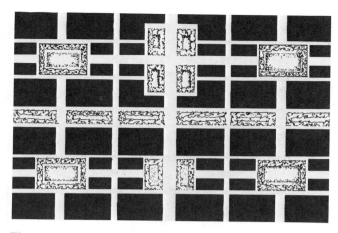

Figure 4. Savannah, Georgia, Plan of the basic interconnecting square system. Each neighborhood is defined by a common square.

clearly emphasize the important corridors over the random order of the less-important streets. The result is a visually exciting city, which remains with a clear hierarchy and ease of movement (Fig. 3).

The Grid City

Most U.S. cities were laid out in a grid pattern of rectangular blocks. One of the most successful grids is the plan for Savannah, Georgia, laid out by James Oglethorpe in the 1700s. The success of the plan in terms of creating an orderly and pleasant living environment is based on the repetition of a modular neighborhood system. The neighborhood unit was composed of a group of residential blocks centered around a square. As Savannah grew, the neighborhood unit of green squares and town houses was repeated, resulting in a series of squares interconnected with the road system (Fig. 4).

Another great U.S. city plan was prepared for Washington, D.C., by the French engineer Pierre-Charles L'Enfant. The layout is similar to Haussmann's plan for Paris in that it is a baroque plan that overlays a basic grid with a diagonal boulevard system. The diagonal road system provides unity by dominating the grid and by connecting the high points of the topography (Fig. 5). Like Paris, Washington's roads were originally designed to converge on major monuments or important public buildings.

In the 1920s, the concept of the integrated, space-defining historical city was being questioned by the emerging modern movement. The machine age, with one of its major products, the automobile, was fostering new theories in city planning and architecture. Le Corbusier, one of the most renowned architects of the twentieth century, formulated theories of city design based on the functional separation of housing, transportation, and open space. In his book *Radiant City,* Le Corbusier radically departs from the historical image of the city as an articulation of spaces formed by connected buildings. He describes a city with buildings and transportation systems floating in a field of green open space. His plan for the expansion of Paris envisioned a clean, functional separation of housing, transportation, and parks (Fig. 6).

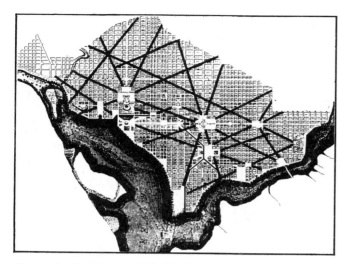

Figure 5. Washington, D.C. The baroque plan is a basic grid with a diagonal boulevard system which links important nodal points.

Suppose we are entering the city by way of the Great Park. Our fast car takes the special elevated motor track between the majestic skyscrapers; as we approach nearer, there is seen the repetition against the sky of the twenty-four skyscrapers;

to our left and right on the outskirts of each particular area are the municipal and administrative buildings, and enclosing the space are the museums and university buildings. The whole city is a park (Le Corbusier).

Frank Lloyd Wright was another modernist visionary who foresaw a utopian community generally based on an agrarian society. His concept for a low density decentralized community was in complete opposition to Le Corbusier's concepts of high density living. Wright, in an April 1935 article in *Architectural Record,* proposed his concept "Broadacre City—A New Community Plan." Wright's city was planned for 1400 families. Each family would receive a minimum 1-acre plat. The following excerpt from Wright's article basically describe his concepts.

The basis of the whole is general decentralization as an implied principle. . . . All common interests take place in a simple coordination wherein all are employed: little farms, little homes for industry, little factories, little schools, a little university going to the people mostly by way of their interest in the ground, little laboratories on their own ground for professional men. And the farm itself, notwithstanding its animals, becomes the most attractive unit of the city. The husbandry of animals at last is in decent association with them and with all else as well. True farm relief.

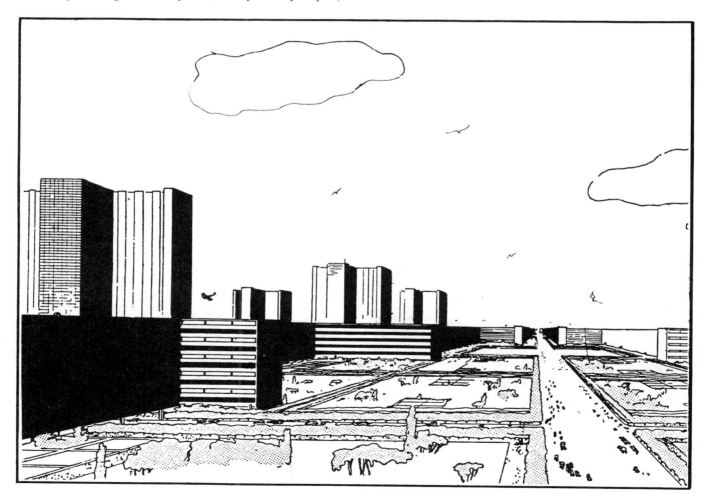

Figure 6. View of "A city for three million people," Le Corbusier. Courtesy of Orion Press, New York.

Figure 7. Local road design. This sketch demonstrates one of the most common and most successful residential arrangements. The common green unifies the residential structures while affording a vista from the roadway, site designer Raymond Unwin. Courtesy of Charles Scribner & Sons, New York.

Le Corbusier's and Wright's ideas were traditional departures from the norm and were not implemented. However, the efficient movement systems described by the modernists were built because of the increase in population and the physical spreading of the city caused by the automobile. The limited-access parkway network begun in the late 1930s and early 1940s, which later evolved into the limited-access freeway, reflects Le Corbusier's concept of providing a roadway system separated from traditional movement systems. The expressways provided a new freedom of movement, which expanded work and lifestyle opportunities for a new generation of people.

Cluster Planning

Cluster development has been a basic development pattern throughout history. Early tribal groupings were basically clusters of living units developed for social and survival needs. Essentially, a cluster is a grouping of houses usually integrated with green open space. In the United States in the 1920s during the "garden city movement," designers such as Clarence Stein were expressing their concepts in designs, such as the cluster plan for Radburn,

New Jersey. Later, the planned unit development (PUD) concept evolved principally in the 1960s, and was a more comprehensive approach to land planning than the cluster in that it provided for mixed-use development (see Fig. 1 in vol. 1, CLUSTER DEVELOPMENT). In the 1960s, the U.S. new-town planning movement resulted in significant towns including Reston, Virginia, and Columbia, Maryland. These towns incorporate various housing types, a town center, a commercial area, schools, employment centers, and even a cemetery in Columbia, Maryland. The site development of these new towns resulted from a comprehensive team effort involving both physical designers as well as social and economic specialists.

Prior to Radburn and the U.S. new-town planning, Raymond Unwin, a lesser known British urban designer, wrote one of the most significant, far-reaching books on the site design for communities, titled *Town Planning and Practice,* published in 1919. He proposed logical and accomplishable solutions to the site development of residential communities (Fig. 7). In particular, he emphasized the integration of road design within the residential community (Fig. 8).

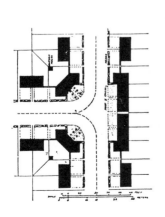
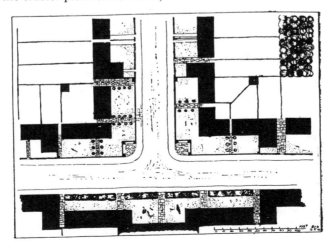
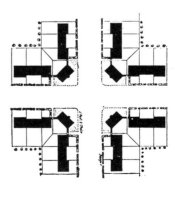

Figure 8. Raymond Unwin's sketch shows the use of architecture to reinforce the site design. The corners and the terminus of the road axis are clearly developed. Courtesy of Charles Scribner & Sons, New York.

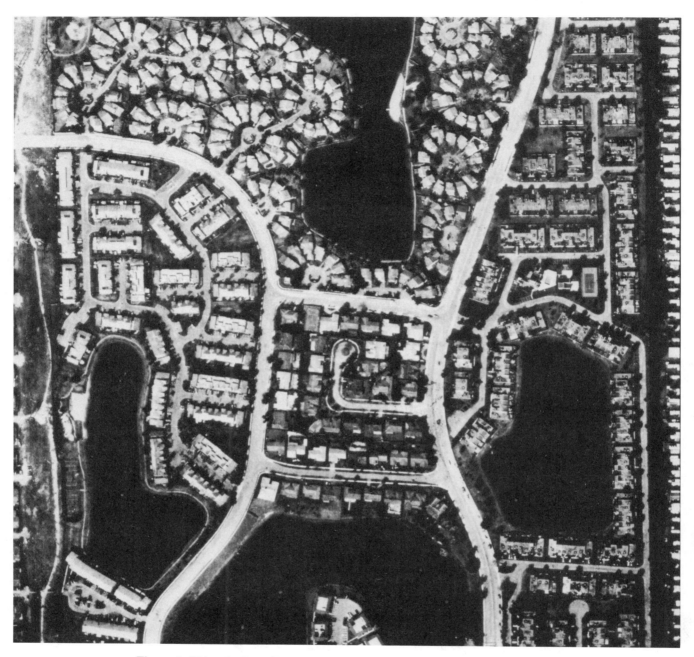

Figure 9. This suburban planning is additive or piecemeal with little overall unity.

Other major contributions from Europe were the British new towns, basically developed from the theories of Sir Ebenezer Howard. Two of several significant towns were Welwyn Garden City, developed in 1920 strongly based on Howard's concepts, and later, in 1955, Cumbernauld. These towns use the concepts of a green belt, which defines the physical limits and thereby the population limits of the town. Economic opportunities and social advantages were also basic elements of Howard's new-town philosophies.

The significant concepts of community site development that have evolved throughout history offer insight for design of contemporary communities of today. Unfortunately, the new-town concepts and other innovative approaches to comprehensive community design have lost some of their thrust in recent years. A piecemeal, unconnected pattern of development characterizes many of today's physical environments, particularly in the developing fringe areas of our cities (Fig. 9). A renewed focus in quality design by the community and those specifically charged to design our physical environment is essential for maintaining and improving our environment.

THE SITE-PLANNING PROCESS

Site planning for any significant development project should be a sequential process, beginning with broad information gathering and ending with specific, detailed design drawings. The process involves three basic stages: analysis, design, and implementation. Figure 10 indicates a planning process; however, it should be noted that the site planning process will be specific to the particular project. The following is a checklist approach to structure a project. Specifics of the site, such as physical site characteristics, urban or suburban location, and community criteria, will modify the process. The site planning process is interdisciplinary and includes both architect and landscape architect. An integrated approach to site development and architecture helps create a quality environment.

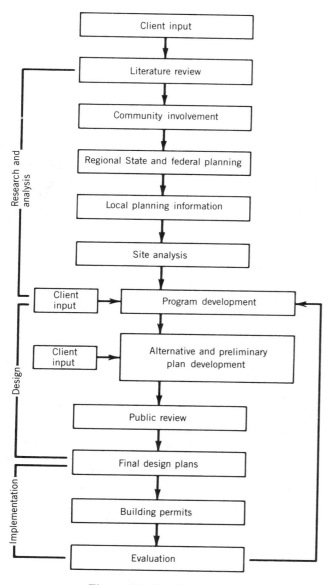

Figure 10. Planning process.

Also important, particularly in urban in-fill situations, is the involvement of the community in providing input to the design process. Although most site planning processes involve some form of public hearing, a less-structured involvement early in the design process will be useful in designing a project that responds to existing community desires and aspirations. Certain steps in the following process may be taken simultaneously, rather than on a precise step-by-step basis.

Client Contact and Input

The first step is the contact between client and site planner. Although the site planner should be involved as early as possible in the decision-making process, the client may already have some broad objectives based on financial capabilities and market feasibility. In many cases, it may be advisable for the client to retain the site planner for assistance in selecting a site that meets the client's basic aims. It is important that the site planner obtain all client data relative to the planning of the site.

Literature Review

Site planning problems vary from rural and suburban sites to intensive urban sites. It is often beneficial to review literature relevant to the nature of the particular site planning problem. There is an extensive amount of literature available for designers working within an existing urban framework, as well as suburban areas.

Community Involvement

Early in the design process it is important to contact community groups that have an interest in the proposed project. Involvement of such groups may provide valuable information relative to their conception of the existing community and their view of possible changes. It is particularly important for in-fill projects when edges of the proposed project are immediately adjacent to existing development. The compatibility of the edges of building intensity, scale, lot size, and design are typical issues that should be resolved with community participation. Also, an early cooperative effort can avoid criticism later at public-hearing stages. Citizen contact should be maintained throughout the design process.

Regional, State, and Federal Planning

In some areas of the country, regional planning agencies have been established for research and planning of intercommunity regional issues such as water management, transportation, population studies, pollution control, and other regional environmental concerns. Many communities have adopted plans that establish regional planning guidelines on land-use planning. The site planner should pinpoint regional issues pertinent to the site design.

Some projects also may be affected by state or national criteria, although this is not a common occurrence. Adopted state plans may address broad issues applicable to large sites or impose constraints on sites involving issues of statewide concern. Also, some states require environmental impact statements for large-scale projects. At the national level, the Environmental Protection Agency and the Fish and Wildlife Service, both nonpermitting agencies, have delegated their authority to various permitting agencies involved in the protection of air and water quality. Under the U.S. Clean Water Act, the U.S. Army Corps of Engineers is responsible for environmental review of proposed dredge and fill operations in navigable waters as well as wetlands. Another federal regulation that will affect many coastline projects is the Federal Flood Insurance Program, which establishes minimum elevations for potential flood areas.

Local Planning Information

At this stage the site planner becomes involved in collecting local planning information that will influence decisions made in the site planning process. Personal contact with local planning and zoning agencies is important in order to clearly comprehend local criteria. Following is a list of information to review.

Planning Documents. Many communities have adopted comprehensive plans that will indicate in general terms, and in some instances in specific terms, the particular land use and intensity of the site. Also, valuable information on the availability and phasing of public services and utilities, environmental criteria, traffic planning information, and population trends can be found in most comprehensive plans. Some communities may require that rezoning meet the criteria provided in their comprehensive plans.

In addition to the comprehensive plan, some communities adopt neighborhood or area studies that refine the comprehensive plan as it relates to subareas. Many of these studies stipulate specific zoning categories for individual parcels of land.

Urban Design Studies. Many communities have adopted urban design plans that provide guidance for the coherent development of their urban areas. These documents may range from a general conceptual nature to documents that incorporate specific zoning requirements. Some documents may include compliance with specific urban design requirements. Some provide bonuses in greater land-use intensities for incorporating urban amenities such as plazas and squares. These plans are usually developed with major input from the design professions.

Zoning. The intensity and type of land use that can occur is determined by the zoning on a tract of land. A zoning change is required if the planned project does not comply with the current zoning use.

Public Services and Utilities. Although some of this information on public services and utilities may be provided in the comprehensive plan or neighborhood study, the critical nature of the availability of these public facilities may require additional research, especially:

1. Availability of public sewer service, access to trunk lines, capacity of the trunk lines, and available increases in the flow. (If sewage lines are not immediately available, the projected phasing of these services must be determined, as well as other possible alternatives to sewage collection and treatment.)
2. Availability of potable water, with the same basic research approach as indicated for sewer service determination.
3. Local and state regulations on freshwater wells and septic tanks.
4. Access to public roads, existing and projected carrying capacity, and levels of service of the roads. (State and local road departments can provide this information.)
5. Availability and capacity of schools and other public facilities such as parks and libraries.

Site Analysis (Site Inventory)

Site analysis is one of the site planner's major responsibilities. All of the on- and off-site environmental design determinants must be evaluated and synthesized during the site analysis process.

Program Development

At the program development stage, the background research, citizen input, and the site analysis are combined with client input and synthesized into a set of site development concepts and strategies. Elements that form the basis for program development include market and financial criteria; federal, state, regional, and local planning information; development costs; and the client's basic objectives, combined with site opportunities and constraints as developed in the synthesis of environmental site determinants. Trade-offs and a balancing of the various determinants may be needed in order to develop an appropriate approach to site development. Consideration of dwelling unit type, density, marketing, time phasing, and other similar criteria, as well as graphic studies of the site, constitute the program. Graphic representations depicting design concepts should be clearly developed for presentation to the client and others who may have input to the process. If the program cannot be accomplished under the existing zoning, the decision to request a zoning change becomes a part of the program.

Alternative and Preliminary Plan Preparation

Once the program is established and accepted by the client, alternative design solutions that meet the program objectives, including basic zoning criteria, are developed. The accepted alternative is further developed into the preliminary plan. This plan should be relatively detailed, showing all spatial relationships, landscaping, and similar information.

Public Review

If a zoning change is required to implement the plan, review by the public will be required. Some communities will require substantial data, such as impact statements and other narrative and graphic exhibits, while others may only require an application for the zone change. Local requirements for changes can be complex, and it is imperative for the site planner or the client's attorney to be familiar with local criteria.

Final Design Plans

At this stage, the preliminary plan is further refined to include any modifications that may have been agreed on at a public hearing. Final design plans, including landscape plans and all required dimensioning, must be provided in the final design.

At this stage, the preliminary plans are further refined into the final site development plans. The final site development plans include fully dimensioned drawings and all landscape plans and site details. Final development plans also include those drawings such as legal plats, utilities, and street and drainage plans prepared by the engineer or surveyor. On approval, final design plans are recorded in the public records in the form of plats. In addition, homeowner association agreements, deed restrictions, and other similar legal documents must be recorded, and become binding on all owners and successive owners unless changed by legal processes. Bonding may be required for public facilities.

Building Permits

Building permits may be issued when all final documents are recorded and architectural drawings have been reviewed and approved in accordance with local building codes. Depending on the agreement between site planner and client, the planner may continue his or her services into the supervision of the site development.

Evaluation

This stage may come years later after the community has become a reality. The purpose is to review the process and the resulting program and assess it in the context of the community as it exists. This is an important aspect usually overlooked. It provides the site planner with valuable data for future planning programs.

SITE ANALYSIS PROCESS

The first step in any site analysis is the gathering of physical site data. An aerial photograph and an accurate survey showing the following information are basic to any site analysis process:

1. Scale, north arrow, benchmark, and date of survey.
2. Tract boundary lines.
3. Easements: location, width, and purpose.
4. Names and locations of existing road right-of-ways on, or adjacent to, the tract including bridges, curbs, gutters, and culverts.
5. Position of buildings and other structures such as foundations, walls, fences, steps, and paved areas.
6. Utilities on, or adjacent to, the tract, including location of gas lines, fire hydrants, electric and tele-

phone poles, and street lights; and direction, distance to, and size of nearest watermains and sewers and invert elevation of sewers.
7. Location of swamps, springs, streams, bodies of water, drainage ditches, watershed areas, floodplains, and other physical features.
8. Outline of wooded areas with names and condition of plant material.
9. Contour intervals of 2–5 ft, depending on the slope gradients, and spot elevations at breaks in grade, along all drainage channels or swales and selected points as needed.

Considerable additional information may be needed, depending on design consideration and site complexities such as soil information and studies of the geological structure of the site.

Suburban Site Analysis

As indicated in the previous site planning process, the site analysis is a major responsibility of the site planner. The physical analysis of the site is developed primarily from field inspections. Using the survey, the aerial photograph, and, where warranted, infrared aerial photographs, the site designer, working in the field and in the office, verifies the survey and notes site design determinants (Fig. 11). Site design determinants should include but not be limited to the following:

1. Areas of steep and moderate slopes.
2. Macroclimatic and microclimatic conditions, including sun angles during different seasons, prevailing breezes, wind shadows, frost pockets, and sectors where high or low points give protection from sun and wind.
3. Solar energy considerations: if solar energy appears to be feasible, a detailed climatic analysis must be undertaken considering such factors as detailed sun charts, daily averages of sunlight and cloud cover, daily rain averages, areas exposed to the sun at different seasons, solar radiation patterns, and temperature patterns.
4. Areas of potential flood zones and routes of surface water runoff.
5. Possible road access to the site, including potential conflicts with existing road systems and carrying capacities of adjacent roadways. (This information can usually be obtained from local or state road departments.)
6. Natural areas that, from an ecological and aesthetic standpoint, should be saved, all tree masses should include name and condition of tree species and understory planting.
7. Significant wildlife habitats that would be affected by site modification.
8. Soil conditions relative to supporting plant material, areas suitable for construction, erosion potential, and septic tanks, if relevant.

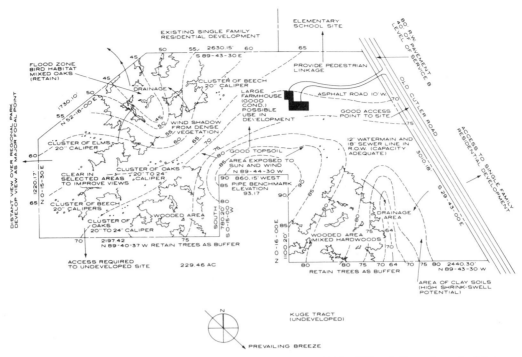

Figure 11. Topographic survey. Reprinted by permission of John Wiley & Sons, Inc., *Architectural Graphic Standards,* C. G. Ramsey and H. R. Sleeper, 8th ed., 1988.

9. Geological considerations relative to supporting structures.

10. Exceptional views, objectionable views (use on-site photographs).

11. Adjacent existing and proposed land uses with notations on compatibility and incompatibility.

12. Potential noise sources, particularly noise generated from traffic that can be mitigated by the use of plants, berming, walls, and by extending the distance between the source and the receiver.

If a site has numerous environmental design determinants, the site planner might analyze each environmental system individually in order to comprehend the environmental character of the site more clearly. This can be a complex process, and a site planner–landscape architect with expertise in environmental analysis should be retained to coordinate such an effort.

By preparing each analysis on transparencies, the site planner can use the overlay approach to site analysis, a technique popularized by Ian McHarg in his book *Design with Nature.* Values are assigned to each sheet based on impact, ranging from areas of the site where change would have minimal effect to areas where change would result in severe disruption of the site. In essence, the separate sheets become abstractions with values assigned by the site planner and associated professionals. As each sheet is superimposed, a composite develops that, when completed, constitutes the synthesis of the environmental design determinants. Lighter tones indicate areas where modification would have minimal influence, darker tones indicate areas more sensitive to change. The sketches

shown simulate the overlay process (Fig. 12). The site planner may give greater or lesser weight to certain parameters depending on the particular situation. In assigning values, the site planner should consider such factors as the value of maintaining the functioning of the individual site systems, the uniqueness of the specific site features, and the cost of modifying the site plan as an input in the site design process. Following is a list of the environmental design determinants that, depending on the particular site, may be considered and included in an overlay format:

1. *Slope.* The slope analysis is developed on the contour map; consideration should include the percentage of slope and orientation of slope relative to the infrastructure and land uses.

2. *Soil patterns.* Consideration may include the analysis of soils by erosion potential, compressibility and plasticity, capability of supporting plant growth, drainage capabilities, possible sources of pollution or toxic wastes, septic tank location (if relevant), and the proposed land uses and their infrastructure.

3. *Vegetation.* Consideration of indigenous species (values of each in terms of the environmental system), size and condition, the succession of growth toward climax conditions, uniqueness, the ability of certain species to tolerate construction activities, aesthetic values, and density of undergrowth.

4. *Wildlife.* Consideration of indigenous species, their movement patterns, the degree of changes that each species can tolerate, and feeding and breeding areas.

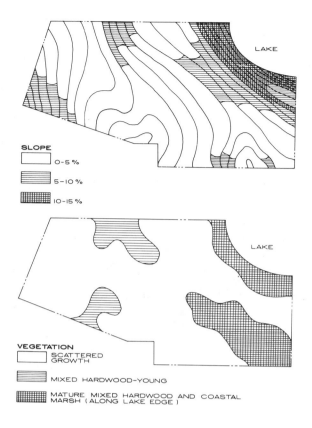

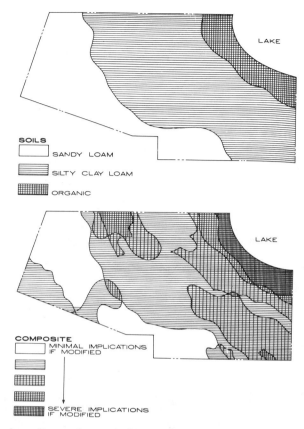

Figure 12. Environmental design determinants that may, depending on the particular site, need to be considered and included in an overlay format. Reprinted by permission of John Wiley & Sons, Inc., *Architectural Graphic Standards,* C. G. Ramsey and H. R. Sleeper, 8th ed., 1988.

5. *Geology.* Consideration of underlying rock masses, the depth of different rock layers, and the suitability of different geological formations in terms of potential infrastructure and building.

6. *Surface and subsurface water.* Consideration of natural drainage patterns, aquifer recharge areas, erosion potential, and floodplains.

7. *Climate.* Consideration of microclimatic conditions including prevailing breezes (at different times of the year), wind shadows, frost pockets, and air drainage patterns.

Computer Application

The above process is labor intensive when developed by hand on individual transparencies. However, this particular method of environmental analysis is easily adaptable to the computer aided design and drafting (CADD) system. Commercial drafting programs suitable for the overlay approach are readily available. Simplified, the method is as follows:

1. A map, such as a soil map, is positioned on the digitizer and the information is transferred to the processor through the use of the stylus. One major advantage to the use of a computer is that the scale of the map being recorded will be transferred to the selected scale by the processor. A hatched pattern is selected, with a less dense pattern for soil types that would have minimal influence and with more dense patterns for soil types that are more sensitive to change. Once this information is programmed into the computer, it is stored.

2. The same process is repeated for development of the next overlay (layer); for example, vegetation. Once again any scale map may be used. This process is repeated until all layers have been stored. At any time one or all overlays can be produced on the screen.

3. Then the individual overlays or any combination of overlays can be drawn on mylar with a plotter. If appropriate for the particular analysis, the plotter will draw in color. The resulting overlay sheets would have taken considerably longer by hand and may have been less accurate. The site can also be studied directly on the computer monitor screen. Another advantage to the use of the computer is that any part of the overlay can be enlarged for greater detail. The overlay process can be recorded by videotape or by slides from the screen for use in presentations.

Urban Site Analysis

Although much of the information presented for suburban sites may apply equally to urban sites, additional site design criteria may be necessary. The urban environment has numerous design determinants in the form of existing structures, city patterns, and microclimatic conditions.

Environmental Considerations

1. *Air movement*. Prevailing breezes characteristic of a region may be greatly modified by urban high-rise structures. Predominant air movement patterns in a city may be along roadways and between buildings. In addition, the placement, shape, and height of existing buildings can create air turbulence caused by micro air movement patterns. These patterns may influence the location of building elements such as outdoor areas and balconies. Also, a building's design and placement can mitigate or increase local wind turbulence.

2. *Sun and shadow patterns*. Existing structure, sun and shadow patterns should be studied to determine impact on the proposed building. This is particularly important for outdoor terraces and balconies where sunlight may be desirable. Sun and shadow patterns also should be considered as sources of internal heat gain or loss. Building orientation, window sizes and shading devices can modify internal heat gain or loss. Studies also should include daily and seasonal patterns, and impact on existing buildings and open spaces of shadows cast by the proposed building.

3. *Reflections*. Reflections from adjacent structures such as glass-clad buildings may be a problem. The new building should be designed to compensate for such glare, or if possible, oriented away from such glare.

Urban Contextual Analysis

1. *Building typology and hierarchy*. An analysis of the particular building type (residential, commercial, public) relative to the hierarchy of the various building types in the city is useful in deciding the general design approach of a new building. For example, public buildings may be dominant in placement and design, while residential buildings are subdominant. It is important to maintain any existing hierarchy that reinforces visual order in the city. Any predominant architectural solutions and details that may be characteristic of a building type may be useful in the new building's design to maintain a recognizable building type.

2. *Regional character*. An analysis of the city's regional architectural characteristics is appropriate in developing a design solution that responds to unique regional characteristics. Regional characteristics may be revealed through unique architectural types, vernacular building resulting from local climatic and cultural characteristics, and from historically significant architecture. Historical structures should be saved by modifying them for the proposed new use or by incorporating parts of the existing structure(s) into the proposed design.

3. *City form*. The delineation of city form created by road layout, location of major open spaces, and architecture should be analyzed. Architecture should be used to reinforce particular places within the city. For example, a building proposed for a corner site should be designed to reinforce the corner

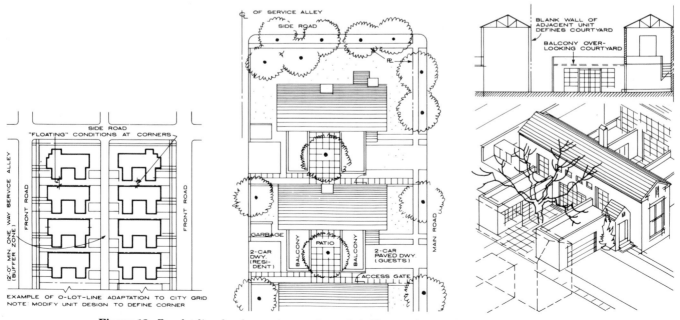

Figure 13. Zero lot-line development concepts reprinted by permission of John Wiley & Sons, Inc., *Architectural Graphic Standards*, C. G. Ramsey and H. R. Sleeper, 8th ed., 1988.

through building form, entrance and design details. A building proposed for midblock may be a visually unifying element, providing connection and continuity to adjacent buildings. Sites at the end of important vistas or adjacent to major city squares should be reserved for important public buildings.

4. *Building scale and fenestrations.* It is important to analyze the building scale and fenestration of nearby buildings. Such detailing may be reflected, although not necessarily reproduced, in the proposed building. This can provide for visual unity and continuity in the architectural character of the city. One example is the use and placement of cornice lines to define the building's lower floors in relation to adjacent buildings. Cornice lines also can define the building's relationship to pedestrians in terms of scale and use.

5. *Building transition.* Sometimes it may be appropriate to use arcades and porches to provide transition between the building's private interior and the public sidewalk. It may be especially worthy to include them if adjacent buildings provide these elements.

6. *Views.* Important city views of plazas, squares, monuments, and natural features such as waterfronts and parks should be considered. They are important as views from the proposed building (Fig. 13). It is also important to design the proposed structure to enhance and preserve such views for the public and for inhabitants of nearby buildings. Table 1 indicates the basic intensity standards for the various types of residential development.

SITE DESIGN PROCESS

The following steps illustrate a design process as indicated in Figure 14:

1. *Site Analysis.* A synthesis of the physical environmental design determinants and off-site influences.
2. *Concept Plan.* A synthesis of the site analysis, research, citizen input, and client input into design concepts. Several concept plans may be prepared.
3. *Preliminary Plan.* A further sophistication and detailing of the concept plan.

Design Scale

The site planner should be aware of four interdependent levels of design relative to the site design process.

Community. At the community, or neighborhood scale, the site planner should be aware of those elements that create design unity and give identity to the development as a whole. Major natural features, circulation systems, greenway systems, and public-use spaces such as schools, shopping, and parks act as focal points or linkages in the total design of the project.

Subcommunity. The first level down from the community scale is the subcommunity space. These are the spaces created by the grouping or clustering of housing units and associated parking, paths, and landscape into a form that responds to the environmental characteristics of the site and gives identity to the individual clusters.

Transition. Transition spaces, in the form of porches, entrance courts, patios, and yards, provide a transition from the private interior spaces of the housing unit to the public spaces. Consideration should be given to privacy for the individual unit and to environmental site characteristics such as breezes, sun angles, and landscape.

Interior. This is the smallest scale with which the site planner is involved. Emphasis should be placed on the unit's interior design for its relationship to the exterior environment and for privacy. A close working relationship between architect and landscape architect is essential.

ADVANTAGES OF PLANNED UNIT DEVELOPMENT AND CLUSTER ZONING CONCEPTS

Although the lot-by-lot type of subdivision is still the prevalent development type in many suburban areas, the amenities that can be realized by the planned unit development and cluster zoning concepts are such that these approaches should be seriously considered. In some communities the terms planned unit development (PUD) and cluster may be synonymous. Usually, however, the PUD is a more comprehensive approach than the cluster, with provisions for both single-family and multifamily development and, in some instances, commercial and industrial activities. The combination of commercial and recreational development in the town or community center can be found in some PUDs. Fee simple ownership and condominium ownership usually are permitted. Often PUDs are divided into tracts and developed over a long-term period such as 10 to 20 years. The term cluster refers to the grouping of single-family residences in clusters on lots smaller than permitted by the single-family zoning districts, and compensating for the smaller lots with common open space areas of substantial and usable configurations.

Both methods offer the designer not only the flexibility of locating structures in a manner that responds to site features, but also the opportunity for developing imaginative architectural forms. A key element of these approaches is the common green space that gives design cohesiveness to the total project.

The responsibility for the maintenance of common space and associated common facilities is a major concern that must be resolved in PUD and cluster developments. The homeowners' association is the most commonly accepted approach. The association should be established by recorded agreement before the sale of the first unit by the developer. Each homeowner is automatically a member and is assessed a proportionate share of the cost in maintaining the common facilities. The developer or his attorney should evaluate the best methods of developing a homeowners' association before the initiation of site de-

Table 1. Intensity Standards for Residential Development[a]

Dwelling Unit Type	Dwelling Units per Acre	Common Open Space as Percentage of Total Site	Parking per Unit[b]	Trees per Acre of Total Site Area[c]	Private Open Space[d]
Single family	3–5 depending on lot size	Usually not provided	2.5 +/−	15+	Depends on lot size
Duplex	5–10 depending on lot size	Usually not provided	2+ (4+ for each structure)	15+	Depends on lot size (at least 50% of lot)
Zero-lot-line[e]	4–8 units per acre	Usually not provided	2.25+	15+	At least 40% of lot
Single-family cluster[f]	4–7	25–50%	2.25+	15–20 +/− for first 3 acres, 10+ for remaining acreage	Depends on lot size (at least 40% of lot)
Atrium[g]	4–9 units per acre	Usually not provided	2.25+	15+	25% of unit square footage
Suburban town house[h]	6–9	25–40%	2.25+	15–20 +/− for first 3 acres, 10 for remaining acreage	500–700 ft² per unit
Urban town house[i]	8–16	15–25% if provided	2.0 +/− (some parking may be on street)	15–20 +/− for first 3 acres, 10 +/− for remaining acreage	400–600 ft² per unit
Walk-up apartment	10–25 (may be regulated by FAR)	25–50%	2.0 +/− (depending on number of bedrooms)	15–20 +/− for first 3 acres, 10 +/− for remaining acreage	Usually not provided except on ground floor units
Mid-rise apartment up to 6 stories	15–35 (may be regulated by FAR)	25–50%	2.0 +/− (depending on number of bedrooms)	15–20 +/− for first 3 acres, 10 +/− for remaining acreage	Usually not provided except on ground floor units
High-rise apartments	30–75 (may be 100+ in dense urban areas)	20–60% (may include roof terraces)	2.0 +/− (depending on number of bedrooms)	15–20 +/− for first 3 acres, 10 +/− for remaining acreage	Usually not provided
Planned unit development[j]	10–25 depending on type of PUD	25–60%	2.0 +/− (depending on unit type(s))	15–20 +/− for first 3 acres, 10 +/− for remaining acreage	Depends on individual unit type(s)

[a] The standards above should be used only as a basic reference to determine spatial site functions. The final determination of intensity and dwelling type of a particular site should evolve at the end of a thorough planning process. The designer also must refer to local zoning codes and ordinances for specific criteria.

[b] In determining the parking requirements per unit, the site planner should consider available public transportation and the relationship of the development's location to employment centers and supporting facilities. Overestimating parking spaces to accommodate infrequent special activities can result in excess pavement. Depending on prevailing conditions, it is better to accommodate infrequent overflow parking on grassed areas, in commercial parking areas, or in community center parking lots.

[c] A major unifying design element, trees also can act as climate modifiers. Extensive tree planting should be part of most site planning programs in appropriate climate areas unless the site already bears a substantial number of trees. The number of trees per acre should be based more on the particular locale than on a uniform standard. Trees planted along streets at 30–50 ft on center provide shading as well as visual unity for the development.

[d] Both visual and aural privacy is important in development design. Private open space for each unit may be provided by courtyards, entrance courts, porches, and rear, side, and front yards.

[e] Provides increased density over typical single-family developments by reducing individual lot sizes, and thereby reducing single-family housing costs. The zero-lot-line developments provide in-fill solutions in lower density urban areas where higher density is justified because of available urban services and higher land costs. Sketches indicate basic design considerations for zero-lot-line development.

[f] Clusters of single-family units provide maximum open space. Units may or may not be attached.

[g] A single-family unit similar to early Greek and Roman structures that incorporated interior living spaces fronting on an internal court.

[h] A single-family unit attached to other single family units with a party wall. Open space usually is a major element in suburban town house development.

[i] Early prototypes appear in many older cities. They are similar to suburban town houses, although densities are usually higher and common open space usually is provided in public open space.

[j] All housing types included in the table, plus associated retail support facilities and community amenities, may be found in a planned unit development (PUD). Emphasis is on total community design.

velopment. Many jurisdictions require a legal instrument for the association prior to final approval of the project.

The use of common open space usually allows more flexibility in effectively fitting the development to the land than does the more typical lot-by-lot approach. Following are some of the obvious advantages gained by the proper use of the planned unit development concept:

1. With smaller individual lots, excess land can be massed together to provide larger and more useful community recreational space.

2. With the use of connecting community open spaces and fewer through traffic streets, children are better protected from vehicular traffic.

3. With larger amounts of open space, the natural character of the site can be preserved.

4. With the shorter networks of streets and utilities construction costs can be reduced.

It should be emphasized that the standard subdivision approach still retains a major part of the housing market.

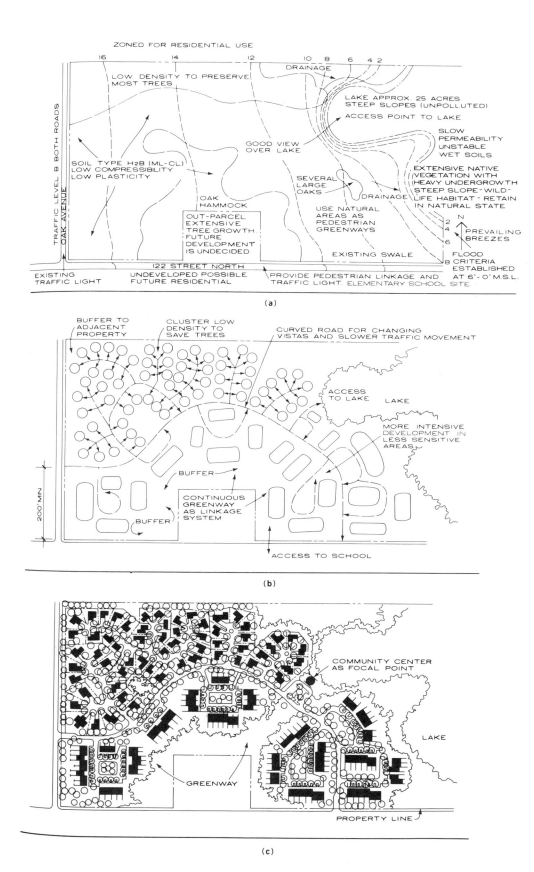

Figure 14. Design scales (**a**) site analysis; (**b**) concept planning; (**c**) preliminary plan. Reprinted by John Wiley & Sons, Inc., *Architectural Graphic Standards,* C. G. Ramsey and H. R. Sleeper, 8th ed., 1988.

Where the program suggests a more typical subdivision layout, the site planner has a responsibility to respond to the same environmental design determinants of the site as for a project being developed under more flexible zoning criteria. Creative planning can be accomplished using either approach (Fig. 15).

VEHICULAR CORRIDOR COMPONENTS

A site designer needs a basic understanding of roadway layout to design circulation systems that function on the site and are compatible with systems off the site. Basic criteria for road design is provided in Figure 16. Specific minimum standards that must be met are in effect for most municipalities.

Hierarchy of Road Systems

A site designer needs to know the hierarchy of road systems and the purposes of each system. At the upper end is the limited-access freeway, which carries up to 1000 or 2000 vehicles per lane per hour at 60 mph and up to 2000 per hour at slower speeds. Site selection is affected by accessibility to freeway systems.

Major or principal arterials and minor arterials are intercommunity connectors that can carry, respectively, 800 or more cars per lane per hour and 400–500 cars per lane per hour, depending on traffic signals, on-street parking, intersections, and other physical impediments restricting traffic flow. Site selection is affected by these streets because they usually provide the direct access to a proposed development.

Collector streets are laid out by the site planner in the development to collect traffic from the neighborhoods and local streets and direct it onto the arterials. They can carry efficiently 100–250 vehicles per lane per hour.

Traffic Generation

In projects where traffic generation is a major factor in the road system design, it may be advisable to retain the services of a transportation engineer. Technical information on traffic can be found in publications produced by the Institute of Transportation Engineers. This institute projects trip generation factors for residential development (Table 2).

Table 2. Summary of Rate Tables of the Different Types of Dwelling Units

Type	Average Weekday Vehicle Trip Ends/Unit		
	Avg.	Max.	Min.
Single-family detached unit	10.0	21.9	4.3
Apartment, general	6.1	12.3	0.5
Low-rise apartment	6.6	9.2	5.1
High-rise apartment	4.0	6.4	1.2
Condominium	5.2	11.8	0.6
Mobile home park	4.8	7.6	2.3
Retirement community	3.3	4.9	2.8
Planned unit development	7.8	14.4	5.8

Environmental Considerations for Road Design

A site's environmental characteristics affect the location and development of a road system. It is the responsibility of the site designer to develop systems that recognize the ecological constraints of the particular site. Following is a checklist of environmental considerations for road alignment:

1. Cause minimal disruption of existing topography by reducing cut and fill requirements, thus reducing erosion and sedimentation problems.
2. Cause minimal disruption of natural overland and subsurface water flows.
3. Cause minimal disruption to existing vegetation and animal life.
4. Avoid positive drainage along roadways into storm sewer systems, where such systems directly outfall into water bodies and cause pollution. Systems of swales along the roadway help to filter nutrients from the roadway surface before entering natural water bodies, thus reducing water pollution.

Other Considerations

1. Bike path grades should not exceed 5–6% for short distances (200–400 ft) or 2% for long distances. Separate bike path from roadway with swales and plantings. Where possible, bike paths can be integrated into greenway systems rather than along the roadway.
2. Tree species that tolerate smog and dust and with root systems that do not damage underground utilities or pavements should be selected. Where snow removal or icy conditions occur, trees should be placed far enough from the roadway edge to prevent damage from automobiles or chemicals applied to the roadway. Tree spacing should take into consideration species and desired effect; as a general rule shade trees should be 35–50 ft apart.
3. *Street lighting.* Design considerations for spacing between lights should relate to amount of illumination needed based on street type, pedestrian use, crime prevention, and similar criteria. Approximate spacing for vehicular street use is 100–150 ft between standards.

FINAL DEVELOPMENT PLANS

After all necessary approvals under the zoning process have been granted, final site development plans are initiated. The final presentation drawing is prepared by the site planner as part of the presentation for the zoning and public review process or as part of the final site development plans (Fig. 17). The technical site development plans, as listed below, are usually prepared by a registered surveyor or engineer. The professional preparing these plans should obtain a copy of the local subdivision code and, if available, a copy of the public works manual for specific local requirements. All drawings should show

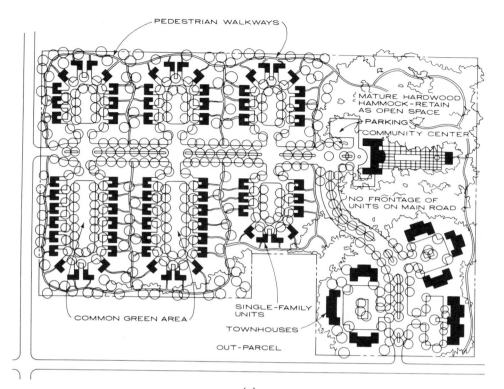

(a)

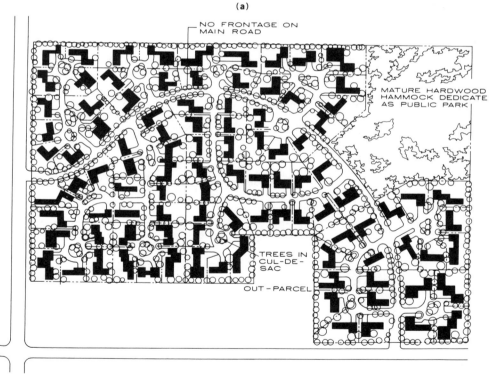

(b)

Figure 15. Comparison of conventional and planned unit development. (a) Planned unit development (two-story units); (b) conventional single-family (one-story units). Reprinted by permission of John Wiley & Sons, Inc., *Architectural Graphic Standards*, C. G. Ramsey and H. R. Sleeper, 8th ed., 1988.

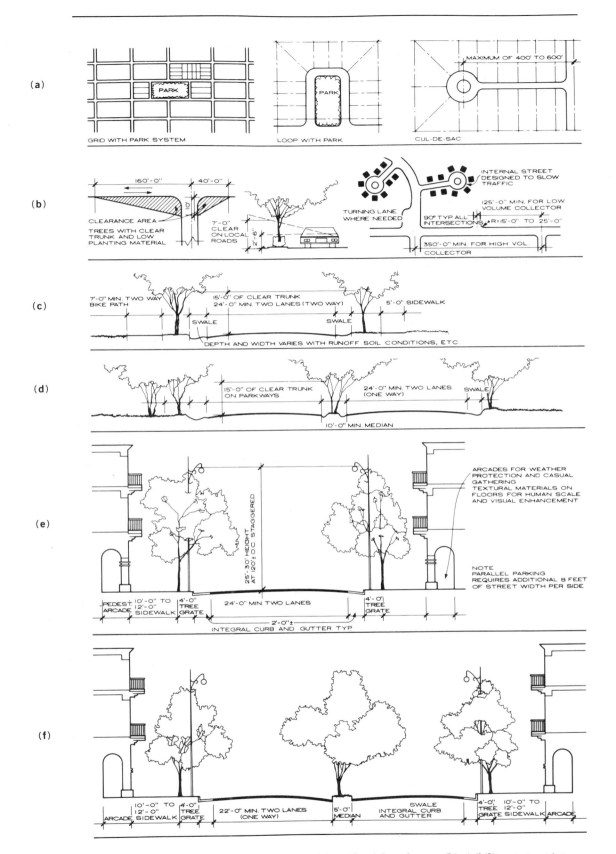

Figure 16. Vehicular corridor components **(a)** residential road types; **(b)** visibility at street intersections; **(c)** local residential street; **(d)** suburban parkway; **(e)** two-lane urban street; **(f)** four-lane urban street with landscaped median. Reprinted by permission of John Wiley & Sons, Inc., *Architectural Graphic Standards,* C. G. Ramsey and H. R. Sleeper, 8th ed., 1988.

Figure 17. An example of a final presentation drawing of a zero-lot-line as an urban infill. Note: Modify unit design to define corner. Reprinted by permission of John Wiley & Sons, Inc., *Architectural Graphic Standards,* C. G. Ramsey and H. R. Sleeper, 8th ed., 1988.

the name and location of the development, the date of preparation and any revisions, the scale, north point, datum, and approvals of local authorities. The following list of exhibits are typical requirements for most communities.

Tentative or Preliminary Plat. Platting is the process in which a piece of land, referred to as the parent tract, is subdivided into two or more parcels. A plat specifically and legally describes the layout of the development. A tentative plat is the first step in the preparation of the final drawings and indicates the layout of the development in terms of lot layout and sizes of lots, lot frontages, road right-of-ways, setbacks, sidewalks, street offsets, and other graphic information relative to the design of the project. After approval of the tentative plat, the engineer can begin the utility, street paving, and drainage plans. Even if the local regulations do not require a tentative plat, it is advised that the designer prepare a sketch of the plat and meet with local authorities to avoid problems later in the final site development plan process.

Street Paving and Drainage Plans. Street paving and drainage plans are final construction drawings prepared by an engineer indicating:

1. Streets and parking areas with starting points and radii.
2. Typical cross sections (some communities may also require road profiles).
3. Details and specifications of pavement base, surfacing and curbs.
4. Indication of methods to confine storm water runoff within the right-of-way (soil tests for percolation may be required). Also details and specifications for inlets, manholes, catch basins, and surface drainage channels.
5. Indication that roads will meet local, state, and federal flood criteria.

Utility Plans. Utility plans are final drawings prepared by an engineer that indicate the location of water supply lines, sewage disposal lines, fire hydrants, and other utility functions usually located in the road right-of-way. In addition to approval by local public works departments, some communities require review of utility plans by the public health board, fire department, and departments involved in pollution control.

Final Plat. The final plat is usually the last stage of the final site development process prior to the issuance of building permits. A subdivision plat, when accepted and recorded in the public land records, establishes a legal description of the streets, residential lots and other sites in the development. If roads and other improvements are not constructed at the time of final platting, a bond, usually in excess of the estimated cost of the improvements, will be required. Following is a typical list of information that should be shown on the final plat.

1. Right-of-way lines of streets, and easements, with accurate dimensions, bearings, and curve data.
2. Name and right-of-way width of each street or other right-of-way.
3. Location, dimensions, and purpose of any easements.
4. Identifying number for each lot or site.
5. Purpose for which sites, other than residential lots, are dedicated or reserved.
6. Minimum building setback line on all lots and other sites.
7. Location and description of monuments.
8. Reference to recorded subdivision plats of adjoining platted land by record, name, date, and number.
9. Certification by surveyor or engineer.
10. Statement by owner(s) dedicating streets, right-of-ways and any sites for public use.
11. Approval by local authorities.
12. Title, scale, north arrow, and date.

BIBLIOGRAPHY

General References

C. G. Ramsey and H. R. Sleeper, *Architectural Graphic Standards,* 8th ed., John Wiley & Sons, Inc., New York, 1988. (This publication was a major source of information.)

S. Anderson, *On Streets,* MIT Press, Cambridge, Mass., 1978.

D. Appleyard, *Livable Streets,* University of California Press, Berkeley, & Los Angeles, Calif., and London, UK, 1981.

H. F. Arnold, *Trees in Urban Design,* Van Nostrand Reinhold Co., New York, 1980.

L. Benevolo, *The History of the City,* MIT Press, Cambridge, Mass., 1981.

C. Cullen, *Townscape,* The Architectural Press, London, UK, 1961.

J. DeChiara and L. Koppelman, *Urban Planning and Design Criteria,* Van Nostrand Reinhold Co., New York, 1982.

Rational Architecture; The Reconstruction of the European City, Brussels, Editiens des Archives d'architecture Modernes, 1978.

W. R. Ewald and D. R. Mandelker, *Street Graphics,* The American Society of Landscape Architects Foundation, Washington, D.C., 1971.

D. R. Gibson, *Historic Savannah,* Dot Gibson Publications, Savannah, Ga., 1976.

G. Greenan, *The Road Corridor,* Dade County Planning Dept., Miami, Fla., 1988. (This publication was a major source of information.)

L. Halprin, *Cities,* MIT Press, Cambridge, Mass., 1973.

Le Corbusier, *The Radiant City,* N. V. Drukkerij Kochen Knuttel, The Netherlands, 1967. (First published in France in 1933.)

K. C. Lippert, ed., *C. N. Ledoux L'Architecture,* ed. remee, Princeton Architectural Press, Princeton, N.J., 1983.

K. Lynch, *Image of the City,* MIT Press, Cambridge, Mass., 1960.

K. Lynch, *Site Planning,* MIT Press, Cambridge, Mass., 1962.

H. L. Malt, *Furnishing the City,* McGraw-Hill Inc., New York, 1970.

I. McHarg, *Design with Nature,* The National History Press, Garden City, N.Y., 1969.

L. Mumford, *The City in History,* Harcourt, Brace and World, New York, 1961.

F. J. Osburn and A. Whittick, *The New Towns,* McGraw-Hill Inc., New York, 1963.

S. Rasmussen, *Town and Buildings,* MIT Press, Cambridge, Mass., 1986.

A. Rossi with texts by B. Huet and P. Lombardo, *Aldo Rossi, Three Cities,* Electa Editrice, Milano, Italy, 1984.

W. Sanders and co-workers, *Affordable Single Family Housing,* U.S. Department of Housing and Urban Development, Washington, D.C., 1984.

D. P. Spreiregan, ed., *On the Art of Designing Cities: Selected Essays of Edelbert Peets,* MIT Press, Cambridge, Mass., 1968.

S. C. Stein, *Toward New Towns for America,* MIT Press, Cambridge, Mass., 1967.

C. Tunnard and B. Pushkarev, *Man-Made America: Chaos or Control?* Yale University, New Haven, Conn., 1963.

R. Unwin, *Town Planning Practice,* Charles Scribner's Sons, New York, 1919.

The Urban Advisors to the Federal Highway Administrator, *The Freeway in the City,* U.S. Government Printing Office, Washington, D.C., 1968.

F. L. Wright, "Broadacre City: A New Community Plan," *The Architectural Record* (1935).

See also CLUSTER DEVELOPMENT AND LAND SUBDIVISION; REGULATIONS—ZONING AND BUILDING CODES; URBAN DESIGN—ARCHITECTURE AT URBAN SCALE; URBAN DESIGN—CREATION OF LIVABLE CITIES

GARY C. GREENAN
University of Miami
Coral Gables, Florida

SOVIET UNION ARCHITECTURE

The Soviet Union, known officially as the Union of Soviet Socialist Republics, is a multinational successor state of the Russian Empire that ended with the Russian Revolution of 1917. Although the Soviet Union is comprised of 15 constituent republics, here the focus is the historical development of Russian architecture, ie, the architecture of the modern Russian state.

Historically, Russian architecture may be divided into four major periods. In the first or Early period, extending from the late tenth century to the beginning of the sixteenth century, the Byzantine-inspired architectural developments embodied the diverse political and cultural milieus of the principalities of Kiev, Vladimir-Suzdal, and Novgorod-Pskov, with their varying assimilations of influences from the East and the West. The second or Muscovite period, from the sixteenth through the seventeenth centuries, was marked by the consolidation of the Muscovite state under the Moscow princes, who sought both to reassert national artistic traditions and to update them in light of current Western tendencies and techniques. The third or Imperial period, from the early eighteenth to the early twentieth centuries, was inaugurated by the reforms of Peter the Great, who broke with the traditional conservative tendencies of Russian life and in architecture caused a shift from a lingering medieval mode to one fully in the mainstream of the latest developments in western Europe. The fourth or Soviet period, dating from the Russian Revolution of 1917 to the present, has been characterized by vacillations between experimental avant-garde design and conservative tendencies in Soviet architecture.

THE EARLY PERIOD

Historically, the beginnings of Russian architecture are traceable to the Christianization of Kievan Russia late in the tenth century. Little is known of the architecture of the pre-Christian period. It was almost exclusively wooden and few material traces of it have survived save for fragments uncovered in archaeological excavations and revealed through occasional early manuscript illuminations.

With the conversion of Kievan Russia to Christianity in 988, Byzantine culture and art found fertile soil among the peoples who were later to be known as Russians and who can first be described as Eastern Slavs. The Middle

Byzantine style of architecture, epitomized by Basil I's Nea Ekklesia in Constantinople (consecrated 881), supplied the basis for developments in the leading principalities of Kiev, Vladimir-Suzdal, and Novgorod-Pskov, as an intensive building of churches set in after the acceptance of the new faith. The standard cross-in-square plan of the middle Byzantine church—the cross inscribed in a rectangular plan with semicircular apses and with one or five domes supported by pendentives resting on four piers—became the accepted type for early Russian churches. The resulting provision for designing and supporting the central dome, together with the elaborate Byzantine scheme for decorating church interiors with frescoes and mosaics to symbolize the setting of Christ's life on earth, thus determined the iconography of early Russian church architecture. In addition, certain influences that came from Serbia, Bulgaria, Georgia, and Armenia can also be discerned.

Kiev. The first church erected in the principality of Kiev was the Church of the Tithe (or the Desiatinnaia Church, 900–996; demolished). Built by Prince Vladimir, who Christianized Kievan Russia, it is known from archaeological findings to have been a domed cruciform building with nave and side aisles, six piers, three apses, and a small west porch. The Cathedral of S. Sophia (1037–1061), built by Grand Prince Yaroslav the Wise, was the largest and most splendid of the Kievan churches.

Conceived as the metropolitan see of the Kievan realm and the burial place of its grand princes, S. Sophia is the only structure of this period that still stands and retains, at least on the interior, something of its original form. It was a vast cruciform church with nave and four side aisles, five apses, and 13 domes, symbolizing Christ and the 12 apostles. Its walls, like those of all other buildings of the period, were constructed of alternating courses of roughly hewn stone and brick immersed in mortar, following the Byzantine technique of *opus mixtum*. The pyramidal massing, open galleries, massive cruciform piers, and numerous domes all marked a unique departure from Byzantine prototypes.

More typical of early Kievan churches was the smaller domed cruciform variant with nave and two side aisles and six or eight piers. Leading examples include the Cathedral of the Transfiguration in Chernigov (1017–1036), the Cathedral of the Assumption in the Monastery of the Caves (1073–1077; consecrated 1089; destroyed 1941), the church of the Monastery of St. Michael (1108–1133; extant until the 1930s), both in Kiev, and the Church of Our Saviour in Berestovo (c. 1113–1125).

The subsequent decline of Kiev's political fortunes led, by the mid-twelfth century, to a further streamlining of plan and form. The more compact variants dating from this period employed a four-pier plan with nave and two side aisles, three apses, and a narthex with a choir gallery above on the west end; stairs leading to the choir gallery were now inserted into the thickness of the west or north wall. The simplified form of a cubical mass surmounted by a central cupola over the crossing was built of even-layered brick intended for plastering instead of the earlier *opus mixtum*. Leading examples of this mid-twelfth century type are the Church of the St. Cyril Monastery near Kiev (1146–1171) and the Cathedral of the Annunciation (1186), the Cathedral of the Dormition at the Yeletski Monastery, and the Church of SS. Boris and Gleb (late twelfth century), all in Chernigov.

Vladimir-Suzdal. The northeastern principality of Vladimir-Suzdal, which began to flourish in the mid-twelfth century after Prince Andrei Bogoliubski attacked and defeated Kiev in 1169, provided a unique springboard for the fusion of Byzantine, Romanesque, and Caucasian influences. The churches built in and around Vladimir in the twelfth and early thirteenth centuries adapted the mid-twelfth century Kievan prototype, as evidenced by the Cathedral of the Transfiguration in Pereslavl-Zalessky (1152–1157). Instead of brick, however, they used white Kama limestone, which gave rise to a new system of articulation and encouraged the use of intricately carved decoration.

The articulation of wall surfaces with sharply projecting engaged columns and bands of blind arcading on ornamental colonnettes and the use of deeply splayed portals and windows are indicative of German Romanesque and Lombard influence. The character of the bas-relief ornamentation is analogous to that found on a number of Armenian and Georgian churches. In the end, however, the builders of Vladimir-Suzdal were no mere copyists, but succeeded in creating a style inimitably their own. Among the outstanding monuments of Vladimir-Suzdalian architecture are the Cathedral of the Assumption (1158–1189), which was to serve as a model for its namesake in the Moscow Kremlin; the Church of the Intercession of the Virgin at Bogoliubovo (1166), the jewel of early Russian architecture; and the Church of S. Dmitri in Vladimir (1194–1197).

Damaged by fire in 1185, the Cathedral of the Dormition was radically altered in 1185–1189, when the building was enlarged on all four sides and converted from a three-aisled to a five-aisled church. The white stone facades employed a frieze of colonnettes and arches half way up the wall and sculptured stone representing scenes with lions and female masks and figures. This practice, alien to the Byzantine tradition of Kiev, is typical of Romanesque art and had been introduced into Vladimir by stonemasons from the West, possibly emigrants from Galicia-Volynia.

Carved stone bas-reliefs were even more widely employed on the facades of the consummately crafted Church of the Intercession, beautifully sited in the surrounding landscape above the confluence of the Nerl and Kliazma rivers. In this diminutive four-piered, three-apsed structure with a single dome, the more inert Middle Byzantine cube acquired both height and grace by establishing an exquisite proportional relationship between its various architectural and decorative elements. The sharply projecting engaged columns, placed against the pilasters and leading directly into the semicircular moldings of the arched gables, and the corbel table of blind arcading set on a row of ornamental colonnettes accentuate the soaring movement of every line in the building. The bas-relief figures of King David, the lions, and the female masks decorating the upper bays of each facade serve to heighten the evocative expressive power of the building as a whole.

The Church of S. Dmitri in Vladimir (1194–1197), marked the apogee of the Vladimir-Suzdalian style. Although broader and more massive than the Intercession, it too was a four-piered church with a single dome, and with an entrance on each side on axis in the Armenian manner. Setting S. Dmitri apart from the other Vladimir-Suzdalian churches is the profusion of flatly carved bas-reliefs over the upper walls, depicting King David offering praise to his Creator amid a tapestry of animals and birds symbolizing the natural universe.

Novgorod. As the civilization of the Kievan epoch was swept away by the Mongol invasion in the mid-thirteenth century, Novgorod, with its extensive foreign trade through the Hanseatic League, emerged as the center of a unique and quite original popular Russian culture and architecture. As in Kiev, in Novgorod the development of church architecture began with the Cathedral of S. Sophia (1045–1052), which replaced a wooden 13-dome church of the same name. Although following its Kievan namesake in plan, it employed only three apses and five cupolas; similarly, its walls were more austere and its windows, small and narrow. The resulting vigor and verticality of its solid masses marked a notable departure from the Byzantine pattern.

At the beginning of the twelfth century a new tendency was inaugurated in Novgorod architecture with the construction of the Cathedral of the Nativity of the Virgin at the St. Anthony Monastery (1117) and the Cathedral of St. George at the Yuriev Monastery (1119), the latter built by Master Peter. Each employed a six-pier plan with a nave, two side aisles, and an attached stair tower. Remarkable for their size and austere monumentality, these cathedrals were cubic in form and modest in decoration. Employing a masonry technique similar to that used in Scandinavian architecture, the walls were built of roughly hewn stone set in the facades with a pink mortar; the arches, vaults, and drums were built of almost square bricks. Facades were then plastered over with pink mortar, which was applied so thinly that it could not conceal the irregularities of the masonry. The resulting rough, uneven wall surfaces yielded a "hand-crafted," picturesque effect. The severe climate and heavy snowfalls also necessitated various modifications of earlier Kievo-Byzantine forms. In time, windows were narrowed and deeply splayed, roofs became steeper, and the traditional Byzantine helmet domes gradually assumed their innately Russian bulbous form.

The regional style of Novgorod began to emerge after a city revolt deposed the princes in 1136, inaugurating the Republic of the *Veche,* or popular assembly. Thereafter, boyars, rich merchants, and craft guilds replaced the princes as the leading patrons of Novgorod building. The domed cruciform church became smaller and acquired a more simplified and intimate character. Typifying this new type of architecture were the Church of St. George in Staraya Ladoga (c. 1165) and the Church of SS. Peter and Paul on Sinichy Hill in Novgorod (1185–1192). Even the princely Church of the Saviour at Nereditsa near Novgorod (1198) followed this popular tradition. Virtually de-

molished in World War II and again rebuilt, this church epitomizes the marked austerity and compactness of late twelfth-century Novgorod architecture.

The Mongol invasion of 1238 initially led to a decline in building activity. However, the ensuing economic prosperity in the fourteenth century, stemming from the flourishing Baltic trade through the Hanseatic League, of which Novgorod was the westernmost outpost, gave rise to the Golden Age of Novgorod architecture. The period from the end of the thirteenth and throughout the fourteenth and fifteenth centuries was marked by the progressive condensing of plan and streamlining of form. The use of four piers instead of six yielded a square plan with one apse and one dome as the predominant Novgorod type. The very small Church of St. Nicholas on the Lipna (1292) embodied this emerging tendency, while at the same time signaling the turn toward a more dynamic form with the introduction of the trefoil-gabled roofline.

By the mid-thirteenth century, the size of the churches had increased, owing to improved economic conditions. The proportional relationships between the streamlined cubical body of the church and the attenuated cylindrical forms of full-height apse and tall, gracefully articulated drum served to accentuate the increasing sense of height of these merchants' cathedrals. The first full-fledged manifestation of this tendency is to be found in the Church of St. Theodore Stratilates (1360–1361). The decoration of the apse by a double blind arcade, the upper one containing two arches for each one in the lower, may be due to German influence, which was particularly strong in the fourteenth century. The Cathedral of the Transfiguration (1374) shows a greater verticality and more refined proportions. Its division of walls follows the developed late Novgorod scheme whereby four pilasters divide the wall into three panels, topped by a trefoil arch in the center and a halved trefoil for the right sides. The lavish decorative scheme, consisting of ornamental brickwork, niche groupings crowned by elaborate hood moldings, and inlaid stone devotional crosses, enlivens the appearance of the facades. This series of substantial Golden Age structures also includes the Church of SS. Peter and Paul in Kozhevkiki (1406); severely damaged in World War II and restored in the 1960s, it is even more majestic in its proportions and decorative detail.

Pskov. The Novgorod tradition was augmented in Pskov, whose opportunities were constricted both by its lesser wealth and by the pressures of its enemies, the Lithuanians to the west. The churches of Pskov were relatively tiny and squat and usually had three low apses. The cross-in-square church with two free-standing piers was, as a rule, enveloped by a deep western porch, side chapels, colonnades and storerooms. A bell gable, such as the striking exemplar at the Church of the Epiphany (1496), or a bell wall, like that of the Church of St. Nicholas on the Dry Spot (1371) was usually placed beside or above the western entrance. These distinctive church porches and bell walls marked Pskov's contribution to Russian architecture.

Because these churches were too small to contain interior columns, the Pskov builders developed the structural device of recessive rows of corbeled arches for the support of central cupola drums and domes, as in the Church of St. Nicholas by the Stone Wall (c. fifteenth century). This feature, which became a favorite Russian structural and decorative element, caused the master builders of Pskov to be repeatedly summoned to Moscow by the tsars.

THE MUSCOVITE PERIOD

The political and artistic life of Russia had experienced a decline during the century and a half of Mongol domination following the invasions of 1237–1241. Architecture fell into a state of decay everywhere but in Novgorod because of the destruction of major Russian cities during the invasion and the ensuing utter disorganization of the Vladimir-Suzdalian building crafts by the recurring Mongol conscription of skilled craftsmen.

And yet, difficulties experienced by the Golden Horde some 50 years after the Mongol invasions opened the way for the swift political rise of the grand princes of Moscow and of the Muscovite principality in the fourteenth century. Moscow, which had been founded as a Suzdalian outpost in 1147 and had remained of very minor importance, emerged in this period as the political and religious capital of the fledgling Muscovite state and its center of trade. The rise of Muscovite Russia's fortunes led to the resumption of building activity on a large scale. The Moscow Kremlin was fortified in this period with walls and towers built of limestone and embellished with several churches built in the Vladimir-Suzdalian style. These fortifications were soon imitated elsewhere in the Muscovite state.

Consolidation. The early Muscovite style of architecture grew out of an amalgam of diverse influences from other regions and traditions—most notably, those of pre-Mongol Vladimir-Suzdal and of contemporary Pskov—into a unified expression with its own composite forms and motifs. This transitional style was defined by a series of limestone churches, including the Cathedral of the Dormition in Zvenigorod (1399), the Trinity Cathedral of the Trinity-Sergius Monastery in Zagorsk (1422–1423), and the Cathedral of Our Saviour at the Andronikov Monastery in Moscow (c. 1427). Although varying in size, these churches were of a single type, recalling the earlier scheme of Vladimir-Suzdalian churches—the cubical mass springing from a four-pier plan with three apses and three entrances on axis, the triple division of the walls with a decorative frieze at mid-height, and a single dome. The decorative scheme, however, consisting of carved ornament and the prominent use of the ogee arch, presupposes some familiarity with oriental motifs as well as with Gothic architecture, which may have come to Muscovy by way of Serbia. The system of corbeling the arches above the interior crossing at the base of the drum, first encountered in the Church of St. Paraskeva in Chernigov (c. 1200), recalls the structural technique developed in Pskov.

The Ascendancy of Moscow. With the decline of Byzantine influence after the fall of Constantinople in 1453, primacy in the world of Orthodoxy shifted to Muscovite Russia. Ivan III, who succeeded in consolidating the Mus-

covite state, used his marriage to Princess Zoë Paleologus, a niece of the last Byzantine emperor and a ward of the Pope, to legitimize his claims to the succession, which later culminated in the doctrine of "Moscow, the Third Rome." Aspiring to rival the older centers of Muscovite culture and to transform his court into something more fashionable in the western style, Ivan launched a major building program.

Architects and artisans were imported from Italy to rebuild the Moscow Kremlin and its two most important churches. The resulting forms, techniques, and sensibilities of Italian Renaissance architecture transported to Russian soil took hold with varying accommodations to local architectural traditions. Marco Ruffo and the Milanese Pietro Solari, who was both an architect and an engineer, rebuilt and extended the fortifications of the Kremlin, superimposing the latest forms and building techniques of Italian Renaissance castles on a picturesque triangulated site; they also built the Faceted Palace (1487–1491) in a Renaissance style using diamond-shaped limestone blocks in the manner of the Palazzo Bevilaqua in Bologna or the Palazzo dei Diamanti in Ferrara. The Bolognese architect and fortifications expert Ridolfo Fioravanti, who had been a member of the famed Sforza circle in Milan, along with Filarete (Antonio Averlino) and Leonardo da Vinci, built the Cathedral of the Dormition (1474–1479) to replace the earlier edifice that had collapsed in the earthquake of 1474. In designing the Kremlin Dormition on the foundations of the earlier building, Fioravanti was obliged to follow the model of its twelfth-century namesake in Vladimir in affirmation of Moscow's dynastic and spiritual links to the earlier Russian principality. While introducing new brick building methods to avert a repetition of the calamity of 1474, Fioravanti's Dormition also imposed a new intellectual logic stemming from the Renaissance sense of geometrical order. This design innovation was applied to regularize the external articulation of the Vladimir prototype by dividing the walls into bays of equal width. Correspondingly, it also established what for Russian design constituted an unprecedented spaciousness within by eliminating internal galleries, replacing the traditional cruciform piers with thinner round columns, and dividing the internal space into a series of bays of equal size. In the Cathedral of the Archangel Michael (1505–1509), designed by the Venetian architect Alevisio Novi (di Montagna), the Vladimir prototype likewise determined the essential mass and plan. In contrast to the Dormition, however, it was the exterior envelope that was subjected to the most telling manifestations of Renaissance taste. These included the use of an ornate classical order—the first use of the Orders in Russian architecture—to articulate the facade in the classical manner of a two-story Renaissance palace, the crowning of each facade bay with Venetian scallop-shell gables, and the treatment of the entrance as a two-story loggia.

A third church, the Annunciation Cathedral (1484–1489), originally three-domed but subjected to extensive alterations and additions, was designed by Pskov architects in the manner of the transitional Muscovite style. The use of the ogee-arched Kokoshnik motif foreshadowed a growing tendency in which Russian ecclesiastical architecture began supplanting the Byzantine heritage with features increasingly asserting national traditions and sensibilities.

The Sixteenth Century. The boldest departure from the Middle Byzantine cross-in-square formula, whose variations on a theme had until now pretty much determined the formal contours of Russian church design, occurred in the first half of the sixteenth century with the rise of the so-called "tent" churches. Constituting the most original and impressive achievement of early Russian architecture, these striking churches were shaped by the distribution of subsidiary towers around a central tower in both plan and pyramidal silhouette, with each tower capped by a steep cone-shaped roof. The full-fledged tent-church phenomenon was initiated by the Church of the Ascension at Kolomenskoe (1530–1532), a cruciform central plan surmounted by a tall octagonal tower with a spire, built by Vasili III in honor of the long-awaited birth of his son and heir, the future Ivan IV. Next in the series was the Church of St. John the Baptist at Diakovo (1553–1554). Built by Ivan IV as a votive church for the birth of his second son, the church at Diakovo is a more complex centralized plan consisting of a central octagon flanked by four smaller octagonal chapels, with each of the five octagonal towers topped by helmet-shaped domes. The series culminates with the Cathedral of St. Basil the Blessed in Moscow (1555–1560), built by Ivan IV as a national votive monument to his victory over the Tatar khanates of Kazan and Astrakhan. St. Basil's unites eight subsidiary tower-shaped octagonal chapels around the dominant central octagonal tower, in plan and form reminiscent of the Ascension at Kolomenskoe. Echoing the traditional attenuated profiles of Russian wooden fortification towers while at the same time evincing a formal affinity to Italian Renaissance centrally planned church schemes, these unique tent churches proved the quintessential embodiment of the growing political and dynastic ambitions of the Muscovite tsars and the rising national consciousness of the Muscovite state.

Sixteenth-century architecture also included monumental five-domed cathedrals, such as those of Rostov, the Novodevichi Monastery in Moscow (1524), Vologda (1568–1570), and the Trinity-Sergius Monastery (1559–1585). Small single-domed churches with several rows of *kokoshnik* gables were also built, inaugurated by the Cathedral of the Donskoi Monastery in Moscow (1593). The phenomenon of urban parish churches also took hold in the sixteenth century with the construction of small churches with unpretentious facades and intimate interiors. In the monasteries, a special place was occupied by the refectories, which often were richly decorated.

The most common form of construction in the sixteenth century, however, was the fortification of Russian towns. Following the model of the Moscow Kremlin, earlier fortifications systems were radically altered (Ladoga, Orekhov, etc). Towns were also fortified with massive masonry walls and towers, with many of them owing their architectural image to these enclosing fortifications (Nizhni Novgorod, Kolomna, Serpukhov, Smolensk, etc). Similarly, a number of monasteries were turned into auxiliary fortifications and enclosed by massive masonry walls with rec-

tangular and round towers (the Simonov Monastery in Moscow, the Trinity-Sergius Monastery in Zagorsk, etc).

The Seventeenth Century. The seventeenth century was a closing phase in the history of early Russian architecture. The underpinnings of a new secular culture, which was to assume definitive form after the reforms of Peter the Great in the early eighteenth century, began to take hold with the enhanced economic status of merchants and craftsmen, who increasingly became leading patrons of architecture. Despite efforts by the Patriarch Nikon to reverse the secularization of architecture by mandating a return to the former severity of church building and corresponding use of the canonical three- or five-dome scheme, the tendency toward the secularization of architectural impulses and form nonetheless prevailed.

The characteristics of seventeenth-century architecture emerged between 1625 and 1650, with the severity of earlier forms giving way to a more ornate, picturesque expression. The tent roofs and spires, which had evolved as functional forms of expression in the preceding century, were reduced to the status of exterior ornamental motifs set over gable roofs and roof vaulting as well as over belfries and stair pavilions. At the same time, chapels of various shapes and sizes were added to the north and south sides of the main body of the church; small porches, covered galleries, and covered staircases rounded out these additions, the varied roof forms of which made the church silhouette seem even more irregular and picturesque. Similarly, the formerly large expanses of mainly unbroken masonry wall surfaces were replaced by rich and elaborately molded decorative paneling, embellished with ornamental motifs of white stone and colored tiles set within the wall.

Examples of these architectural tendencies in Moscow were the churches of the Trinity in Nikitniki (1628–1653), the Nativity of the Virgin in Puntinki (1649–1652), St. Nicholas on the Bersenevka (1656), and the Trinity in Ostankino (1678–1683), all of which offered a richly varied array of decorative motifs. A great deal of building was carried out in the Kremlin, where spires were added to most of the towers. At the same time, old palaces were enlarged and new ones built, including the Terem Palace (1635–1636) and the Patriarchal Palace and Church of the Twelve Apostles (1643–1655).

Several other cities also experienced significant building campaigns in the seventeenth century. The massive Kremlin in Rostov, built as a residence by the Metropolitan Jonas Sysoevich, is one of the most interesting and well-preserved architectural ensembles of the period, although its structures followed Nikon's dictates in re-asserting certain conservative tendencies in earlier Russian architecture. In Yaroslavl, wealthy local merchants built a series of less conservative churches, often surpassing those of Moscow in size. Although adhering to Nikon's injunction against the use of more than three or five domes, these churches embellished the emerging decorative program for seventeenth-century church design through the use of five-dome clusters as well as pyramidal tent roofs over side chapels and the extensive application of colored and glazed tiles as well as lavish interior fresco cycles (the churches of St. Elias the Prophet, 1647–1650;

St. John Chrysostom in Korovniki, 1649–1654; St. John the Baptist in Tolchkovo, 1671–1688; and others). The building of monasteries was also given a new impetus in this period. The walls and towers as well as refectories of such monasteries as those of SS. Boris and Gleb near Rostov, of the Saviour and St. Euthemius in Suzdal, and of St. Cyril on the White Lake are among the masterpieces of early Russian architecture.

The Moscow Baroque. Developments in the last quarter of the seventeenth century were affected by the first inroads of baroque art, which was brought to Russia from Poland by way of White Russia and the Ukraine. While the ensuing Moscow Baroque episode paved the way for transforming what was still essentially a medieval tradition into the Western-oriented and academically-derived art that followed in the wake of the reforms of Peter the Great, its highly decorative appropriation of baroque motifs, though more disciplined, still had something in common with the propensity for ornateness prevalent in earlier seventeenth century Russian architecture. Moscow Baroque architecture developed under the direct patronage of a few highly influential noble families—most notably, the Naryshkins and the Golitsyns—who had avidly cultivated Western customs and tastes.

As before, emphasis continued to be placed on achieving an expressive exterior silhouette, with the most distinctive variations involving the design of vertical structures either as a series of superimposed and pyramidally massed stories of different shapes, or in the form of towers. The forms were ornamented with richly carved portals, window frames, columns, pilasters, rosettes, conches, and purely decorative motifs executed in white stone and thus contrasting sharply with the pinkish-red background of the brick walls. All these decorative elements were combined in a distinctive, disciplined manner and placed with due regard for the contribution of each to the whole. The churches of the Moscow Baroque were also distinguished by interiors that were more spacious and filled with a greater amount of light. Classic examples of this style are the Church of the Intercession at Fili (1690–1693); the churches of the Saviour at Ubory (1694–1697) and the Trinity at Troitset-Lykovo (1698–1703), designed by Yakov Bukhvostov; and the singular Church of the Virgin of the Sign at Dubrovitsy (1690–1704).

THE IMPERIAL PERIOD

The founding of St. Petersburg in 1703 marked the beginning of a new era in Russian culture and architecture. The reforms of Peter the Great sought to overturn the old medieval order of Muscovite Russia by cultivating a new social order capable of assimilating Western ideas and bringing Russian culture into the mainstream of European developments. Secular impulses, which had surfaced in the last part of the seventeenth century, now became the preeminent underpinnings of the new culture.

The reforms in Russian architecture, reflected in the successive currents of the Baroque, Neoclassical, and Russian Empire styles, brought Russian architecture to an unprecedented level of maturity and achievement. These reforms were, in turn, facilitated by the remarkable architectural continuity obtained through the successive reigns of key sovereigns who were remarkably enlightened in matters of architectural style and taste, as well as by the succession of gifted foreign and foreign-trained Russian architects who implemented the reforms.

The Petrine Period. The newly created imperial capital of St. Petersburg (renamed Petrograd in 1914 and Leningrad in 1924) and its environs offered a fresh field for the realization of ambitious new architectural and planning projects in which western European influences gained decisive ascendancy. To be sure, the first 35 years of the new capital's existence were ones of experiment and a tentative search by the foreign architects imported by Peter the Great for the ultimate direction the city would take. Placing the greatest stamp on early St. Petersburg architecture was the sensible late Baroque northern European idiom introduced by the Swiss-Italian architect Domenico Trezzini. As Peter's chief architect, he not only developed prototypical house designs for the various classes of citizens ordered to settle in the capital, but also designed the capital's more important early buildings, including the first Summer Palace (1710–1714), the Fortress and the Cathedral of SS. Peter and Paul (1712–1733), and the Twelve Colleges (Ministries) on Vasily Island (1722–1733). Other important architects adding to Peter's program of westernizing Russian architecture included the Germans, Georg Johann Mattarnovi, who designed the Kunstkamera (1718–1725) and Gottfried Schädel, who designed the two residences for Prince Alexander Menshikov of Vasily Island (with Giovanni Maria Fontana, 1711–1716) and at Oranienbaum (now Lomonosov, 1713–1725). French input in this initial period was limited to the short-lived contributions of the architect Jean-Baptiste-Alexandre Le Blond, who published a plan for St. Petersburg (1716); designed the initial palace (1716–1717) and several pavilions at Peterhof (now Petrodvorets), Peter's country estate on the Gulf of Finland; and redesigned the Summer Garden before Le Blond's premature death in 1719.

In Moscow, where the buildings were more richly decorated, following the ancient capital's established propensity for a more ornately articulated architectural form, there persisted the old type of church surmounted by a bell tower, ranging from the Church of the Archangel Gabriel, popularly known as the Menshikov Tower, (1701–1707); the original spire burned in 1723) to the Church of St. John the Warrior (1709–1717), the central-plan domed church with two chapels and bell tower thought to have been designed by Ivan Zarudnyi.

Elizabethan Rococo. By the mid-eighteenth century, St. Petersburg and its environs had achieved greater architectural unity and cohesiveness at the hands of the Italian-born Bartolomeo Francesco Rastrelli, who not only designed all the larger government buildings and imperial palaces, but also supervised all other architectural activity in Russia for the Empress Elizabeth. Called on to deal with palaces of immense frontage, Rastrelli proved a consummate master of highly integrated and remarkably plastic large-scale architectural forms. His buildings were endowed with an urbanity and grace that made them the equals of the best contemporary European work. Among his masterpieces are the enlarged palaces at Peterhof (1747–1752), and Tsarskoe Selo (1749–1752), as well as the Summer Palace in St. Petersburg (1741–1744; demol.), the Vorontsov Palace (1749–1757), the Stroganov Palace (1750–1754), and the Winter Palace (1754–1762). His Cathedral of St. Andrew in Kiev (1747–1767) and of the Smolny Convent in St. Petersburg (1748–1757) represent an innate blending of the traditional Russian centrally planned five-dome church with an articulate flair for expressive Rococo composition.

In Moscow, the Rastrellian model was echoed in the Church of St. Clement (1754–1774), whose design is ascribed to Pietro Antonio Trezzini (no relation to Domenico). The Apraksin Mansion (ca 1766), designed by an unknown architect but evincing a plasticity and inventiveness of form and detail not unlike those of Rastrelli, exemplifies the domestic architecture of the Rococo period in Moscow, of which few traces have survived.

Catherinian Neoclassicism. The turn to Neoclassicism came with the reign of Catherine II and continued into the reign of Alexander I, culminating in the Russianized Empire Style. In this remarkable period, Russian architecture succeeded in shedding its last vestiges of provincialism and entering fully into the mainstream of European architecture (Figs. 1–3). In St. Petersburg, Neoclassicism first became perceptible in the building for the Academy of Fine Arts (1765–1772) by the French architect J.-B.-M. Vallin de la Mothe, with Alexander F. Kokorinov, and the Marble Palace (1768–1785) by the Italian Antonio Rinaldi. It then emerged vividly in the work of the Scotsman Charles Cameron, the Italian Giacomo Quarenghi, and French-trained Ivan E. Starov, all of whose work epitomized Catherine's enthusiasm for the severity of Neoclassical architecture. Cameron's Agate Pavilion (1780–1785) and Cameron Gallery (1783–1786), which were built on a site adjoining the southwest wing of Elizabeth's palace at Tsarskoe Selo (now Pushkin), represented the most classical environment achieved in Russia up to that time, inspired by the style of Robert Adam. Cameron's palace for the Grand Duke Paul at Pavlovsk (1780–1796) represented an even more lively manipulation of geometrical form and Neoclassical detail. Quarenghi, building in the style of Palladio, produced a succession of notable urban ensembles, including the State Bank (1783–1790), the Academy of Sciences (1783–1789), and the Hermitage Theater (1783–1787), which was connected to the Hermitage proper by a bridge over the intervening canal. His design for the Palace of the Dowager Empress Marie (later the Smolny Institute) provided a monumental paradigm for an urban palace that subsequently was adapted by other Russian architects. Starov's geometrically articulated church and belfry at Nikolskoe (1773–1776) was as severely neoclassical in the new Parisian sense as anything of the same date in the West. As severe but more monumental was his Tauride Palace (1783–1789) in St. Petersburg, whose magnificent colonnaded gallery came to be widely admired and copied.

In Moscow, a more intimate version of the Neoclassical style in the latter part of the eighteenth century was created by or under the influence of Vasili I. Bazhenov and Matvei F. Kazakov, who developed an idiom of remark-

Figure 1. Catherine the Great Palace, Leningrad. Courtesy of Nancy Block. See also color plates.

able purity and serenity. Bazhenov built little but exerted considerable influence. His bold project to rebuild the Moscow Kremlin as a gigantic triangular neoclassical palace complex encompassing the most important earlier palaces and churches was among the most monumental conceptions of eighteenth-century European architecture. His spirit if not his hand may be discerned in the Pashkov Palace (1784–1786, later the Rumiantsev Museum and now the old building of the Lenin Library). His Yushkov Mansion (1793; home in the 1920s of the famous Soviet art

Figure 2. Leningrad Winter Palace, Hermitage. Courtesy of Nancy Block.

Figure 3. Catherine the Great Palace, Hermitage. Courtesy of Nancy Block.

school, the VKHUTEMAS), articulated the essential elements of Moscow's variant of the Neoclassical style.

Kazakov succeeded in adapting his intimate brand of neoclassicism to a variety of monumental structures, ranging from the Senate Building in the Kremlin (1771–1785; later the Court of Justice and now the principal seat of the Supreme Soviet) to the Church of the Metropolitan Philip (1777–1788) and the Golitsyn Hospital (1796–1801, now part of the First City Hospital), as well as the numerous mansions he designed throughout Moscow. Both these mansions and the country houses for the Sheremetevs, the Golitsyns, and the Yusupovs at Kuskovo, Ostankino, and Arkhangelskoe, respectively, are less severe in their designs; the latter, produced by the owners' serf architects, conveys a greater sense of domesticity than the imperial palaces in and around St. Petersburg.

During the rebuilding of Moscow after the Napoleonic occupation, neoclassicism continued to dominate in the works of transplanted foreigners such as the French Osip I. Bove (Beauvais) and the Italian Domenico I. Gilardi, as well as of Gilardi's Russian pupil, Afanasi G. Grigoriev and others, whose work differed from that of St. Petersburg architects in its less severe manner and greater lyricism.

The Alexandrian Empire Style. A Russian version of the Empire style in its original French conception, the Alexandrian Empire Style expanded the Neoclassical aesthetic to focus on the design of monumental buildings to create an architectural organization of urban squares and ensembles. Inaugurating the style was Andrei N. Voronikhin's Cathedral of the Virgin of Kazan (1801–1811), a neoclassical reinterpretation of St. Peter's Basilica and Square in Rome, Thomas de Thomon's Exchange (1804–1810), a striking neoclassical ensemble created at the cape of Vasily Island, and Andreian D. Zakharov's transformation of the earlier Admiralty in 1806–1823 into a monumental, multipavilioned neoclassical complex.

The zenith of the Alexandrian Empire Style was reached at St. Petersburg with the work of Karl I. (Carlo) Rossi. His work, inspired by ancient and modern Rome, helped fulfill Alexander's ambition to endow St. Petersburg with a series of unrivaled public buildings and urban ensembles. Rossi's genius in urban design was amply demonstrated in his General Staff Building (1819–1829), whose vast, sweeping curved facade served to complete the Winter Palace Square, and the Alexander (now Pushkin) Theater complex (1827–1832), which deftly joined two new squares with an intervening street to create an integral monumental urban ensemble.

By the mid-nineteenth century, however, the severity of Russian Neoclassicism and the Empire Style yielded to the more ponderous idiom manifested in Auguste Ricard Montferrand's Cathedral of St. Isaac (1818–1858) in St. Petersburg, and especially in the ostentatious palaces built by A. I. Stakenschneider, which combined elements of the Neoclassic, Baroque, and Renaissance styles.

The differences between the architecture of St. Petersburg and Moscow and that of the provinces diminished as a result of the standardized designs produced by leading architects. Over 150 administrative buildings were erected according to designs produced by Zakharov; facades of houses built throughout Russia were based on designs by Vasili P. Stasov and others.

The Neo-Russian Styles and the Arts and Crafts Movement. During the last half of the nineteenth century the most progressive developments in Russian architecture were closely related to the antithetical concepts of nationalism and internationalism in Russian culture. These tendencies grew out of the controversy between the Slavophiles and the Westernizers, which had appeared in the 1840s under the reign of Nicholas I. The political and philosophical underpinnings of both programs were bolstered by the emerging scholarly investigations of the Russian artistic past.

The first attempts to discover the characteristics of a Russian national style, prompted by Nicholas I's policy of Official Nationalism, found its expression in the work of Konstantin A. Ton, who assumed the task of creating a new national style based on an insipid collage of motifs derived loosely from medieval Russian and Byzantine architecture. Ton's colossal Cathedral of Christ the Redeemer (1839–1883; demolished 1930s), built in the center of Moscow to commemorate Russia's victories over Napoleon (1812–1814), epitomized his officially sanctioned Russo-Byzantine style, as did his Grand Kremlin Palace (1839–1848), erected in the Moscow Kremlin.

The Slavophil-induced search for an authentic Russian architecture in the last quarter of the nineteenth century led to the rise of the Neo-Russian style, which sought to revive salient aspects of Muscovite architecture from the sixteenth and seventeenth centuries. Three buildings constructed around Red Square in Moscow were leading examples of the style. Vladimir O. Shervud's Historical Museum (1875–1883), standing at the north end of the square, was inspired by St. Basil's Cathedral (Figs. 4 and 5), standing at the opposite end, which Shervud regarded as a prototype for Russian architecture. Leading secular variations on a theme appeared in Aleksandr N. Pomerantsev's Retail Rows (1889–1893; now GUM, the state department store) (Fig. 6), standing along the east side of Red Square and notable for the first major use of steel, glass, and reinforced concrete in its interior galleries, and the Moscow Duma or City Hall (1890–1912; now the Central Lenin Museum) by Dmitri N. Chichagov, partially filling the angle between the Retail Rows and the Historical Museum. In religious architecture the Church of the Ascension, or of the Saviour on the Blood (1883–1907) (Fig. 7), constructed in St. Petersburg on the spot where Alexander II had been assassinated in 1881, marked architect Alfred A. Parland's attempt to synthesize the forms of St. Basil's Cathedral and the surface treatment of seventeenth-century Muscovite and Yaroslavl churches. In domestic architecture the Igumnov Mansion (1889–1893; now the French Embassy) by Niko-

Figure 5. Church of the Intercession of the Virgin known popularly as St. Basil's Cathedral, Red Square, Moscow (1555–1560), by Barma and Posknik. Courtesy of Nancy Block.

lai I. Pozdeev echoed the traditional forms memorialized by both his native Yaroslavl churches and the well-known model of the long-demolished wooden palace of Kolomenskoe.

More interesting and potentially more influential were the attempts by the art colonies at Abramtsevo and Talashkino to revive the native traditions of the peasant arts and crafts and to rework them in the spirit of a new age. This Russian equivalent of the Arts and Crafts Movement had been inspired by the aspirations of the "Itinerants," a group of artists who had seceded from the Academy of Fine Arts in 1863, two years after the emancipation of the serfs, for the sake of "bringing art to the people." Embracing the populist ideal that art should be an active force in the cause of social reform, these artists maintained that native traditions, not the classical themes imposed by the Academy, should dictate the essential content and character of Russian art. Their depiction of the pathos of peasant life was an unprecedented theme for Russian art, as was their concerted drive to seek a new national culture and art based on the long-neglected traditions of the Russian folk arts.

Figure 4. Church of the Intercession of the Virgin known popularly as St. Basil's Cathedral, Red Square, Moscow (1555–1560), by Barma and Posknik. Courtesy of Nancy Block.

Figure 6. GUM, the state department store, Red Square, Moscow (1889–1893), Aleksandr N. Pomerantsev. Courtesy of Nancy Block.

Figure 7. Church of the Resurrection of the Saviour on the Blood, St. Petersburg (1883–1907) Alfred A. Parland. Courtesy of Nancy Block. See also color plates.

In the late 1870s the railroad magnate Savva Mamontov transformed his country estate at Abramtsevo, north of Moscow, into a center for the study of Russian folk art and a retreat for a group of artists and architects who sought to incorporate native folk traditions and motifs into their work. Here, Ivan P. Ropet (pseudonym of Ivan N. Petrov) and Victor A. Hartman launched the tendency in architecture with their personalized interpretations of native log cabin forms, embellished with finely hewn adaptations of native folk embroidery motifs. In addition to designing the Workshop at Abramtsevo (1872), Hartman also designed the building for Mamontov's printing establishment in Moscow (1872) and numerous pavilions. Ropet advanced his version of the style, which became widely known as the Ropet style, in his "Teremok" Bath House at Abramtsevo (1873), as well as the Russian pavilions that he designed for the international expositions at Philadelphia (1876), Paris (1889), and Chicago (1893). The artist Victor Vasnetsov designed the chapel at Abramtsevo (1880–1882), modeled on the austere medieval church forms of Pskov; he later designed the Tretiakov Gallery in Moscow (1900–1905) on the basis of his study of medieval Russian manuscript illuminations.

The art colony at Talashkino, founded in 1887 by Princess Maria K. Tenisheva, likewise aspired to revive native Russian handicrafts and cottage industries. The artists gathered at Talashkino, the most notable of which were Nikolai K. Roerich and Sergei V. Maliutin as well as Princess Tenisheva herself, augmented their study of ancient Russian art with an investigation of native folklore themes; the exuberant interpretations of these themes endowed the work of these artists with striking overtones of

a Neoprimitivist art. Epitomizing this tendency is Maliutin's "Teremok" Cottage at Talashkino (1887) (Fig. 8) and his Pertsov Apartment House in Moscow (1905–1910).

The Modern Style, Russia's Art Nouveau. At the turn of the century Russian architecture was swept up by an enthusiasm for the *Stile moderne,* the term by which the Russian variant of the Art Nouveau was known. The Russian tendency, strongly influenced by the German, Viennese, and Scottish movements, was stimulated by the rapid growth of Russian industrialism in the 1890s and the corresponding rise of an entrepreneurial class anxious to assert its new-found prominence in a new style unhampered by inherited traditions and taste. Like its West European counterparts, the Russian modern style encompassed the stylization of motifs from nature and the conspicuous exploitation of the latest building materials and techniques. Exponents of the style shared in their vigorous pursuit of new architectural forms enlivened by a sculptural treatment of structural elements and bold use of murals, Fedor O. Shekhtel, the best-known architect working in this style, produced a number of outstanding buildings in Moscow, including the magnificent Riabushinsky House (1900–1902) and Derozhinsky House (1901–1902), as well as the Riabushinsky Bank (1902), the "Russian Morning" Printing House (1907), and the Moscow Merchants Society Building (1909).

An interesting phenomenon in Russian architecture at the turn of the century was the melding of the Neo-Russian and the modern styles, involving the stylized reworking of elements from traditional Russian architecture. Here, too, Shekhtel proved a leading exponent of this tendency, as exemplified by his imaginative wooden Russian pavilions for the Glasgow international exposition of 1901, and his striking Yaroslavl Railway Station in Moscow (1902–1904). Another innovative architect who worked in this style was Aleksei V. Shchusev. Emulating the austere medieval forms of Novgorod and Pskov, he built numerous churches in the style, including the one at the Cloister of Mary and Martha in Moscow (1908–1912).

Figure 8. Teremok cottage at Talashkino, outside Smolensk (1887) Sergei Y. Maliutin. Courtesy of Anatole Senkevitch. See also color plates.

The Neoclassical Revival. Dissatisfaction with the decorative excesses of the Neo-Russian and the moderne styles led Russian architects to the rediscovery of Russia's rich classical legacy. This tendency crystallized in St. Petersburg, the center of the classical tradition imported from the West, where interest in Russian Neoclassical architecture was aroused by the celebration in 1903 of the 200th anniversary of the founding of the imperial capital by Peter the Great. It was affirmed by the Historical Exhibition of Architecture and Industrial Arts held in 1911 in the St. Petersburg Academy of Fine Arts, itself an early Neoclassical building. The impact of this neoclassical legacy on Russian architecture was also affirmed by the Contemporary Petrograd Movement. Analogous to the City Beautiful Movement in American architecture and planning at the turn of the century, the Contemporary Petrograd Movement sought to supplant the earlier tendencies described above with an avid predilection for the neoclassical legacy of Old Petersburg; that legacy was advanced by the movement's proponents as the preeminent rational model for the continued planning and development of the imperial capital as well as other Russian cities. The leading exponents of the resulting Neoclassical Revival were Ivan A. Formin and Vladimir A. Shchuko in St. Petersburg and Ivan V. Zholtovsky and Aleksandr I. Tamanov (Tamanian); all were graduates of the architecture faculty at the Academy of Fine Arts in St. Petersburg.

The Russian pavilions that Shchuko designed for the 1911 exhibitions in Rome and in Turin heralded the advent of the Neoclassical Revival in Russian architecture, as did his two apartment buildings of 1911 on Stone Island in St. Petersburg. Fomin, who had helped organize the 1911 exhibition and compiled its catalogue, produced several articulate designs in the revived Neoclassical style, including the sumptuous Polovtsev Mansion on Stone Island (1911–1913) and the Abamelek-Lazarev Mansion on the Moika Canal (1912–1914) in Petrograd. His project for New Petersburg, a vast residential and retail development in the Goloday Island section of the city (1911–1912) that he designed in collaboration with Fedor I. Lidval, proved the quintessential embodiment of the New Petrograd Movement: The vast complex of radial avenues converging on a semicircular square enclosed by a monumental row of multistory buildings sought to emulate the large-scale Neoclassical planning schemes in nineteenth-century St. Petersburg; only two buildings of this grandiose ensemble were completed before the suspension of the development by World War I. One of the more innovative examples of the Neoclassical Revival in St. Petersburg was the Mertens Trade Building (1910–1912) by Mikhail S. Lialevich, with its glass-curtain wall suspended within the broad three-bay Corinthian arcade.

The first major building in Moscow to inaugurate the return to classical tradition was Roman I. Klein's Museum of Fine Arts in Moscow (1898–1912), the bold massing scheme of which was articulated by an innovative combination of the Ionic Order from the Erechtheum and the frieze from the Parthenon; in 1912, Klein also designed the Borodino Bridge in Moscow, rendering it as a "propylaeum" and adapting the Doric Order of the Propylaeum at the Athenian Acropolis. Zholtovsky followed his diminutive neoclassical building for the Moscow Equestrian Society of 1903–1906 with a Neo-Renaissance replication of Palladio's Palazzo Thiene for his design of the Tarasov Mansion (1909–1912; now the Italian Embassy). Tamanian's crisply articulated Shcherbatov Houses of 1912–1913, rendered as a large-scale urban Neoclassical villa U-shaped around a central courtyard, was widely admired for giving clear and certain definition to Novinsky Boulevard.

THE SOVIET PERIOD

The Twenties and Soviet Modernism

When the Bolshevik Revolution broke out in 1917, few progressive artists failed to embrace its ideals. They did so largely on the basis of what was perceived to be the Revolution's profoundly regenerative capacity to rid society of the debilitating exploitation of man by man, and to generate the socioeconomic wherewithal for building a new egalitarian society. The decadent bourgeois society, which had stifled the avant-garde's ambitions and ideals, had been shattered. A new world and a new art were to be created out of the debris. Sustained by their vision of an egalitarian society, Soviet avant-garde artists advocated a modern, socially useful art that had to express the forms and functions of the new socialist age. This was to be achieved by embodying the material needs and ideals of socialism in the process of shaping and enhancing everyday life through art.

The elaboration of these aims and ideals in Soviet architecture centered around two avant-garde tendencies: those of the Rationalist Movement and the Constructivist Movement. Rarely has the history of architecture witnessed such an opportunity for two singularly progressive tendencies, working alongside one another—*albeit,* frequently at cross-purposes, to correlate so profoundly the creative potentials and complexities of architectural form and content. Where the Rationalists succeeded in establishing a persuasive basis for articulating the expressive potentials of modern architectural form, the Constructivists succeeded in crystallizing its specific content.

The Rationalist Movement derived its primary theoretical impetus and name from the innate theory of a rational architecture advanced by Nikolai A. Ladovsky, in collaboration with Vladimir F. Krinsky and Nikolai V. Dokuchaev. A rational architecture, to Ladovsky and his colleagues, was one that helped the observer become oriented to the built environment by facilitating his perception of the spatial and expressive character of architectural form. To accomplish this objective, the architect-designer had to convey the necessary perceptual clues to the observer by using lucid geometrical principles to articulate the essential aspects of architectural form and space, as well as by communicating the form's expressive character through the visual manipulation of design motifs rooted in psychological bases of perception. The theoretical and pedagogical programs developed by Ladovsky and his colleagues, aiming at the formulation of a new language of vision, were closely related to the Suprematism of Kasimir Malevich and the "Prouns" of El Lissitzky, whose architectonic spatial compositions represented the ultimate refinement in the formulations of modern spatial form.

In 1923 Ladovsky and his colleagues, joined by El Lissitzky, formed the Association of New Architects (ASNOVA) for the purpose of countering the growing opposition of the Constructivists, who accused the Rationalists of an excessive preoccupation with abstract form. In 1928 Ladovsky and his closest followers seceded from ASNOVA to found the Association of Architects-Urbanists (ARU) to extend the Rationalist doctrine to the broader—and, in Ladovsky's view, ultimate—realm of urban form.

Principles of a Rationalist architecture had initially been formulated in the numerous experimental design studies that Ladovsky, Krinsky, and their associates had conducted in 1919–1921 within the Commission of Painterly-Sculptural-Architectural Synthesis (Zhivskulptarkh) and the Institute of Artistic Culture (Inkhuk) in Moscow. Rationalist principles of design were also elaborated on in the countless design exercises executed by students of Ladovsky, Krinsky, and Dokuchaev at the Architecture Faculty of the Moscow Vkhutemas (the Russian acronym for the Higher Artistic and Technical Studios); the most progressive Soviet art school in the 1920s, the Vkhutemas offered instruction in architecture as well as in the visual and applied arts. Rationalist principles likewise were applied in the numerous buildings designed by Konstantin S. Melnikov, including his Soviet Pavilion for the 1925 Paris Exposition of Decorative Arts and Industries, his own house (1927–1929) and several workers' clubs, as well as in Nikolai Ladovsky's Red Gates (now Lermontov) Metro Entrance in Moscow of 1935.

The Constructivist movement assumed tangible form somewhat later than that of the Soviet Rationalists. The origins of the Constructivist idea in Soviet art and architecture are traceable to Vladimir Tatlin's belief that material dictates technique and that technique, in turn, determines form. This notion, first demonstrated in his counter-reliefs and complex counter-reliefs of 1914–1917, obtained its ultimate realization in his famous Monument to the Third International, which he executed as a model in 1919–1920. Tatlin's steel-and-glass tower was conceived to symbolize a new type of monumental construction aimed at achieving an innate synthesis of artistic and utilitarian forms.

The crystallization of Constructivist principles in Soviet art occurred in 1921 with the formation within Moscow's Inkhuk of the First Working Group of Constructivists, which advanced the concept of an industrially rooted and product-oriented art. The focus of such a production art was to be the design and construction, in collaboration with industry, of useful objects and utensils required for everyday life. This objective bears a striking resemblance to the ideals espoused by William Morris in England and by Hermann Muthesius within the German Werkbund. The major differences stemmed from the Constructivists' belief that the social as well as functional purpose of this production art was further mandated and vitalized by the innate socialist underpinnings of the new society being built in the wake of the Russian Revolution.

Moisei Ginzburg's 1924 book entitled, *Style and Epoch,* emerged as a veritable manifesto of the early Constructiv-

ist movement in Soviet architecture. According to Ginzburg, the Russian Revolution had supplied the vital wherewithal not only for transforming society in the egalitarian image of socialist principles, but also for creating a new constructive phase of architectural development that would fulfill the aims and ideals of the proletariat in the new socialist phase of the industrial age. The new style of architecture emerging out of this constructive phase would facilitate the "mechanization of life," by which Ginzburg had in mind the universal civilizing force of the machine. By acting to mechanize the productive forces of society, the machine had enhanced the status of the proletariat and supplied a powerful technical and organizational base for modern architecture.

The most vivid manifestations of Ginzburg's concept of mechanized life occurred in the early designs of Alexander Vesnin who, with Ginzburg, was the founder of the Constructivist movement in Soviet architecture. Vesnin's brilliant design for the stage set for Alexander Tairov's adaptation of G. K. Chesterton's novel, *The Man Who Was Thursday,* is a brilliant manifestation of the industrialized urban imagery embraced by Ginzburg and the Constructivists. Its industrialized syntax was applied to an architectural design in the 1924 competition project for the *Leningrad Pravda* building, which Alexander Vesnin designed in collaboration with his brothers Victor and Leonid. The Vesnins' project for the Palace of Labor in Moscow (1923) (Fig. 9), although awarded only third prize in the competition, pointed the way to the emerging Constructivist ideal of utilizing both social and technical content as a prime determinant of the new building prototypes required by the new socialist society.

The pursuit of that ideal assumed a more pragmatic approach in the mid-1920s, mediating the earlier Constructivist concerns with symbolic expression. The increasing level of building activity sparked by the New Economic Policy induced Constructivist architects to streamline their design methodology to achieve a greater economy of means and ends. The pursuit of this program led the Constructivists to form the Association of Modern Architects (OSA) in 1925 under the leadership of Moisei Ginzburg and Alexander Vesnin. In the following year, the OSA began to promulgate the functional method of design in its journal, *Modern Architecture,* edited by Ginzburg and Vesnin. That method was aimed at formulating the social and technical aspects of the program to develop new building forms and types suitable for an emerging Socialist society. The buildings designed by Ginzburg and the Vesnin brothers epitomize the successful implementation of the functional method. Particularly noteworthy in that regard is Ginzburg's Narkomfin Apartment House in Moscow (1928–1930), designed with Ivan F. Milinis, and the Vesnin brothers' Palace of Culture for the Likhachev Auto Factory (1931–1937) in Moscow.

Architects who embraced modernism without formally joining either movement included Ilia G. Golosov, who designed the Zuev Workers' Club of 1929 in Moscow, and his brother Panteleimon, who designed the Pravda Building (1930–1934) in Moscow. Grigori B. Barkhin likewise expanded on the modernist idiom in a number of his designs, including the Izvestiia Building in Moscow (1925–1927).

Figure 9. Project for the Palace of Labor in Moscow (1922–1923), Alexander A., Leonid, A., and Victor A. Vesnin.

The period of the First Five-Year Plan (1928–1932) coincided with the heyday of the modern Soviet architectural tendencies, which were dominated by the Constructivists. In addition, two tendencies also vied with one another in urban planning, which likewise had risen to the fore in this period. The first was the Urbanists, who proposed the re-distribution of the urban population into satellite socialist settlements of about 50,000 inhabitants each, living in collective housing combines. The leading exponents of this concept were L. Sabsovich and the Vesnin brothers, who produced a model plan for the settlement of Kuznetsk. The second tendency, comprising the Disurbanists, advocated the dissolution of Soviet cities and merging the city and countryside through an extensive network of linear settlements. The major advocates of Disurbanism were M. Okhitovich and Moisei Ginzburg, who in 1929 produced a highly innovative design with Mikhail Barshch for the Green City settlement outside Moscow.

The older generation of architects–academicians, who had become established prior to the Revolution, worked side by side with the proponents of Modern architecture. At first their work reflected a continuation of pre-revolutionary tendencies. By the last half of the 1920s, however, it began generally to reflect the growing ascendancy of Modernism. Ivan V. Zholtovsky and Aleksei V. Shchusev were appointed directors of the architecture section within the People's Commissariat of Enlightenment. Sim-

ilarly, the Petrograd Architectural Office was headed by Vladimir A. Shchuko and Vladimir G. Gelfreikh. Zholtovsky was commissioned to prepare the master plan and design several of the pavilions for the First All-Russian Exhibition of Agricultural and Cottage Industries in Moscow (1923). Shchusev, who had been awarded the commission to prepare plans for New Moscow (1918–1923) as the new Soviet capital, was chief architect of the Agricultural exhibition. He was also chosen to design the Lenin Mausoleum on Red Square, producing two temporary wooden versions in 1924 before erecting the present austere granite monument in 1929. The most telling indication of Shchusev's embracing of the modern idiom was his Commissariat of Agriculture Building in Moscow (1928–1933). Ivan A. Fomin began the development of his Red Doric style—which he defined as a fusion of the Doric Order and Constructivist principles—with his 1922 project for the Palace of Labor competition, and continued it in his Polytechnic Institute in Ivanovo-Voznesensk (1927–1932) and his Dynamo Building of 1929 in Moscow. Shchuko, along with Gelfreikh, produced a strikingly modern design for the Gorky Theater in Rostov-on-the-Don (1930–1935). However, their earlier, more conservative design for the Lenin Library in Moscow (1928–1941) won out over submissions by the Vesnin brothers, anticipating the repudiation of modernism in 1932.

The Stalinist Period and Socialist Realism

Just as the competition for the Palace of Labor in 1923 had signaled the trend toward Modern architecture, so the competition for the Palace of Soviets in Moscow (1931–1934) marked its virtual demise. The first round of the competition was open to architects from all countries. Many Modern architects, including Le Corbusier and Walter Gropius, took part in the belief that the new socialist society held out the best hope for sustaining the development of a genuinely new architecture.

The results, announced in April 1932, proclaimed the inadequacy of all 250 submissions. While assigning the first three prizes to those of Boris M. Iofan, Ivan V. Zholtovsky, and Hector O. Hamilton from the United States, the jury directed that all further efforts "be directed toward the utilization of newer and better applications of classical architecture." These results, which came as a great surprise to both the Soviet and the West European exponents of the Modern Movement, set the tone for the complete transformation of Soviet architectural theory and practice under the Stalinist regime. In the second phase of the competition, which concluded in February 1933, Iofan's classical design was selected as the sole winning entry. At the same time, in continuing to develop his final design, Iofan was joined by Shchuko and Gelfreikh at the request of the jury. Thereafter, the palace became increasingly more rhetorical and colossal in scale, culminating in a giant statue of Lenin.

Dictating the new tendency in Soviet architecture was the doctrine of Socialist Realism, which sought to advance socialist content and nationalist form. The Stalinist regime had repudiated the stark, abstract forms of Soviet modernism for being incomprehensible, and thus alienating, to the masses. The architecture of Socialist Realism was conceived to inspire pride in the accomplishments and projected grandeur of the Soviet regime, to express the qualities unique to the Soviet experience, and to utilize a mode of expression that would be suitably appreciated and understood by the populace. Doing so involved the use of a familiar, rhetorical, and monumental style that could be executed on a scale calculated both to awe and to inspire the New Soviet Man. To a people grown intimately accustomed to the rich classical legacy of eighteenth- and nineteenth-century Russian architecture, the adaptation of the classical tradition acted to provide Soviet architecture with its requisite broad base of popular support.

Ivan Zholtovsky's Apartment House on Mokhovaya Street (1932–1934; now the Intourist Building on Marx Avenue) adapted the colossal Corinthian Order of Palladio's Loggia del Capitaniato in Vincenza and became the object of both controversy and acclaim. The Red Army Theater in Moscow (1924–1940) by Karo S. Alabian and Vladimir N. Simbirtsev aimed at integrating the expressive power of architecture with the Classical tradition to convey socialist symbolism: the floor plan of the building is a five-pointed star, the emblem of the Red Army, while the whole is encased in a colossal Corinthian colonnade. Nearby, Shchusev's "Moscow" Hotel (1936) applied overlays of simplified classical articulation to a colossal architectural form. A more monumental classical treatment was employed in the Building for the Ukrainian Council of Ministers in Kiev (1934–1938) by Ivan Fomin and Pavel Abrosimov and in Noa Trotsky's House of the Soviets in Leningrad (1941).

With the growth of nationalist sentiment in the late 1930s came a perceptible shift toward the expression of national forms in Soviet architecture. Extensive use was made of national motifs in some of the Moscow subway stations. This tendency culminated in the designs of the various pavilions at the All-Union Agricultural Exhibition in Moscow (1939–1940), with those of the Uzbek, Georgian, Armenian, and Ukrainian republics being the most distinctive. The originality of form and richness of ornament reflected the architectural traditions as well as the folk arts of the various republics.

With the outbreak of World War II, all building activity came to a halt in the threatened areas. Beginning in 1943, the first plans for the reconstruction of cities destroyed in the war proposed restoring their original aspects and integrating new buildings in terms of scale and appearance with the existing urban fabric, particularly in the more historic towns. Post-war Soviet architecture set out to reflect, in its expressive content, the country's victory over Nazi Germany. This tendency culminated in the design of the complex of eight skyscrapers, popularly referred to as "wedding cakes," of which seven were built in the years 1948–1953. The buildings included the new Moscow State University, the Ministry of Foreign Affairs Building, two hotels, several apartment houses, and an office building.

This unique urban complex of tall buildings, conceived in conjunction with the 800th anniversary of the founding of Moscow in 1147, sought to evoke the traditional pyramidal silhouette of Moscow's Kremlin and surrounding monasteries, with its crisp vertical accents, to achieve a cosmic transposition of the city's traditional skyline. Consisting of central structures rising 20–32 stories with

flanking 6–18-story wings, these pyramidally massed tower ensembles were strategically located in various locations around the city's radial plan so that their height and pyramidal bulk would encircle and bring into more expressive relief the newly-designed Palace of Soviets, and thus affect the Moscow skyline for many miles. The Palace of Soviets, crowned by a giant statue of Lenin, would tower over the resulting vast urban complex, while the seven tall building tower ensembles would form its subsidiary vertical elements. This urban design concept was developed in response to the requirement outlined in the official program, which stated that "the proportions and silhouettes of these [tall] buildings must . . . be integrated with . . . the silhouette of the future Palace of Soviets . . . [and] with the historically evolved architecture [of Moscow]." At the same time, each of the buildings was, in turn, conceived to be the focal point in the composition of its immediate neighborhood, both reflecting the architectural features of the surrounding historical fabric and setting the matrix for the contemporary building ensembles to be constructed around it.

The Post-Stalinist Thaw

The end of the Stalinist regime in 1953 ushered in a limited thaw in Soviet architectural life. Late in 1954, Party Secretary Nikita S. Khrushchev criticized the decorative excesses and high building costs of the seven tower ensembles, as well as of the other buildings inspired by them throughout the country. The ensuing 20th Party Congress in 1955 proclaimed these architectural practices to be a distortion of the country's architectural heritage and accorded national priority to the comprehensive industrialization of the Soviet building enterprise. The accommodation of mass-production techniques was to replace traditional concerns with architectural style. As a result, standardization in housing, based on utilizing prefabricated large-scale concrete panel construction and other methods, dominated the scene for the next two decades.

At the same time, these Khrushchevian initiatives also served effectively to propel Soviet architecture to re-enter the mainstream of Late Modern architecture. The second competition for the Palace of Soviets (1957–1959) affirmed the rejection of traditional styles in favor of a revived modern expression. Although that project, as the one before it, never came to fruition, the Palace of Congresses in the Moscow Kremlin (1961) by Mikhail V. Posokhin and others upheld the mandate for a return to modernism. Indeed, the work of Posokhin, who became the chief architect of Moscow, reflects most tellingly the changes that had taken place. Having designed one of the Stalinist "wedding cakes," the apartment house complex on Uprising Square (1950–1954), he then proceeded to create, in collaboration with Mdoyants and Svirsky, the leading trend-setter of Khrushchevian Neo-Modernism— the multiblock Kalinin Avenue complex (1962–1968). This monumental complex, which established a major new shopping artery for Moscow, consisted of four V-shaped apartment–office towers fronted by lower buildings on one side of the avenue and five compound rectangular towers, also flanked by lower buildings, on the other. Terminating the avenue complex at the Moscow River is the distinctively angular 32-story building for the

Council for Mutual Economic Assistance, or CMEA (1963–1970).

The ensuing stagnation of the Brezhnev era, which was consumed by an institutionalized quest for a contemporary monumentality, was marked by the erection of hulking towers, public buildings, and monuments to the Second World War. To escape the stifling bureaucratic impediments to individual creativity, a small group of young architects, mostly graduates of the Moscow Architectural Institute, created the movement of "paper architecture" and began winning competitions held by Japanese architecture publications. Echoing the sensibilities of Western Post-Modernism, this movement has sought to advance a pluralist, "post-totalitarian" program in which traditional concern for form and space has yielded to a more literary and visionary expression aimed at stimulating individual creativity and the human imagination. Rejecting the dogmatic legacy of their own constructivist and rationalist tendencies of the 1920s, the proponents of paper architecture have created playful, rhetorical designs that emphasize the subjective and emotional qualities of the environment more than functional or stylistic aspects. This movement has not only succeeded in shaking up the country's architectural bureaucracy, but also anticipated the urgent new demands advanced in the Gorbachev era by the Soviet architectural profession for its own reinvigoration.

The Gorbachev policy of "glasnost" and "perestroika" has encouraged intense discussions within the field. In 1986, the discussions and debates at the Eighth Congress of Soviet Architects led to a proposal for restructuring the entire profession. That fall, the Central Committee of the Communist Party and the Council of Ministers of the USSR issued a resolution outlining the scope of the endeavor. It sanctioned the creation of a new network of independent design studios and co-ops ("Arkhproekt") as privately based architectural practices similar to Western architectural firms. Operating under the aegis of the Union of Architects of the USSR, these independent co-ops have been conceived to compete for commissions with, and ultimately to supplant, the state system of architectural offices; there are already well over a hundred independent architectural design co-ops in the country, and their clients include factories, unions, and foreign companies. The resolution also called for enhancing the level of "individual experience" and social responsibility in Soviet architecture by raising the architects' aesthetic and social consciousness. To do so, Soviet architects have begun networking with counterparts in the other arts, including music, theater, literature, and film, as well as establishing contacts with environmental advocacy groups, in the pursuit of a Soviet architecture capable of creating a more profound aesthetic content and a more responsive humanistic environment. At the same time, the Soviet government's housing policy has begun changing, as low-rises, co-ops, and individual houses are gaining official acceptance as alternatives to the prevalent housing monoliths. Although these and other related changes are still in process of implementation, they nonetheless point to a profound and unprecedented rehabilitation of Soviet architecture.

BIBLIOGRAPHY

General References

"Aspects of Spatial Form and Perceptual Psychology in the Doctrine of the Rationalist Movement in Soviet Architecture in the 1920s," *VIA* 6, 78–115 (1983).

W. C. Brumfield, *Gold in Azure: One Thousand Years of Russian Architecture*, David R. Godine, Inc., Boston, Mass., 1983.

"Charles Cameron's Work in Eighteenth-Century Russia," *Architectural Association Quarterly*, **11** (2) 4–8 (1979).

C. Cooke, ed., *Russian Avant-garde Art and Architecture*, AD Profile 47, London, 1983.

C. Cooke, ed., *Chernikhov: Fantasy and Construction*, AD Profile 55, London, 1984.

C. Cooke and A. Kudriavtsev, *Uses of Tradition in Russian and Soviet Architecture*, AD Profile 68, London, 1987.

Iu. A. Egorov, *The Architectural Planning of St. Petersburg*, trans. E. Dluhosch, Ohio University Press, Athens, Ohio, 1969.

H. Faensen and V. Ivanov, *Early Russian Architecture*, G. P. Putnam's Sons, New York, 1975.

M. Ia. Ginzburg, *Style and Epoch*, trans. A. Senkevitch, Jr., MIT Press, Cambridge, Mass., 1983.

G. H. Hamilton, *The Art and Architecture of Russia*, 3rd ed., Penguin Books, New York, 1983.

M. A. Il'in, *Moscow: Monuments of Architecture of the 14th–17th Centuries,* trans. I. Ivianskaya, Iskusstvo, Moscow, 1973.

M. A. Il'in, *Moscow: Monuments of Architecture, 18th-First Third of the 19th Century,* trans. I. Ivianskaya, Iskusstvo, Moscow, 1975.

M. K. Karger, *Novgorod the Great*, trans. K. M. Cook, Progress, Moscow, 1973.

S. O. Khan-Magomedov, *Alexandr Vesnin and Russian Constructivism*, Rizzoli International Publications Inc., New York, 1986.

S. O. Khan-Magomedov, *Pioneers of Soviet Architecture*, Rizzoli International Publications Inc., New York, 1987.

E. I. Kirichenko, *Moscow: Architectural Monuments of the 1830s–1910s*, trans. B. Meyerovich, Iskusstvo, Moscow, 1977.

A. Kopp, *Town and Revolution: Soviet Architecture and City Planning, 1917–1935*, trans. T. E. Burton, George Braziller Inc., New York, 1970.

Ivan Leonidov, Catalogue 8, Institute for Architecture and Urban Studies, Rizzoli International Publications Inc., New York, 1981.

L. M. Lissitzky, *Russia: An Architecture for World Revolution*, rev. ed., trans. E. Dluhosch, MIT Press, Cambridge, Mass., 1984.

N. A. Miliutin, *Sotsgorod: The Problem of Building Socialist Cities*, trans. A. R. Sprague, MIT Press, Cambridge, Mass., 1974.

R. Milner-Gulland and J. Bowlt, *An Introduction to Russian Art and Architecture*, Cambridge University Press, New York, N.Y. 1980.

O. Powstenko, *The Cathedral of St. Sophia in Kiev*, Ukrainian Academy of Arts and Sciences in the U.S., New York, N.Y., 1954.

I. Rae, *Charles Cameron: Architect to the Court of Russia*, Elek Books, London, 1971.

"Russian Architecture, 1880–1910," *Apollo*, 98, 436–443 (Dec. 1973).

A. Senkevitch, Jr., *Soviet Architecture, 1917–1956: A Biblio-*

graphical Guide to Source Material, University Press of Virginia, Charlottesville, Va., 1974.

"Fedor Osipovich Shekhtel: An Architect and His Clients in Turn-of-the-Century Moscow," *Architectural Association Files*, 5, 3–31 (Jan. 1984).

O. A. Shvidkovsky, ed., *Building in the USSR, 1917–1932*, Praeger Publishers, New York, 1971.

"The Social Character of Stalinist Architecture," *Architectural Association Quarterly*, **11** (2) 49–55 (1979).

"The Soviet Approach to Architecture," *American Quarterly on the Soviet Union*, 2, 76–80, (July–Oct. 1939).

S. F. Starr, *Melnikov: Solo Architecture in a Mass Society*, Princeton University Press, Princeton, N.J., 1978.

"Theoretical Attitudes to Architecture in Russia, 1830–1910s," *Architectural Association Quarterly*, **11** (2) 9–23 (1979).

W. Thompson, *Novgorod the Great*, Praeger Publishers, New York, 1967.

N. N. Voronin, *Vladimir, Bogoliubovo, Suzdal, Yuriev-Polskoi*, Progress, Moscow, 1971.

A. Voyce, *The Moscow Kremlin*, University of California Press, Berkeley, Calif., 1954.

A. Voyce, *The Art and Architecture of Medieval Russia*, University of Oklahoma Press, Norman, Okla., 1967.

See also CHURCH ARCHITECTURE

ANATOLE SENKEVITCH, JR.
The University of Michigan
Ann Arbor, Michigan

STAIR DESIGN

Stairs, ladders, and ramps seem to be almost as old as building, yet even the earliest known varieties are still constructed today. As new variations have developed, these have usually expanded the vocabulary without displacing earlier models. The evolution of the stair catalyzed man's exploration and exploitation of architectural space. Spatial potentials demanded the invention of the stair; and the stair made possible quite new configurations and dispositions. Stairs serve many roles besides their prosthetic function. These roles may modify or even dominate completely the mundane purposes of safe, comfortable and convenient ascent and descent. For the stair has always been used to represent man's spiritual aspirations and cosmography; to demonstrate secular power and authority, prestige and status; for aesthetic, poetic, architectural, and spatial manipulation; to make adjoining floors seem close, and the ascent a gentle transition; or to accentuate the separateness of spaces, with the staircase acting as a bridge. Stairs convey meaning and have personalities. These innermost, almost archetypal, responses to stairs seem to carry with them cultural memories embedded in the psyche, part myth, part religious mystery, part dream, part fairy tale. Jacob dreams of a ladder; Sigmund Freud dreams of stairs, or sees dreams of stair climbing as sexual manifestations or representations, sexual fantasies transmuted into metaphorical icons; Gaston Bachelard reminds us that poetic daydreams reflect the complex of memory and imagination (1,2).

Figure 1. The Pyramid of the Magician, Uxmal.

STAIRS OF THE GODS

Siegfried Giedion equates the rise of the first high civilizations with the rise of the vertical as the preferred direction (3). Heaven is up, hell is below; we climb the ladder of success, take the stairway to the stars; our spirits are up, we are in the depths of despair. And, since so many of this world's gods have chosen to live and instruct from the mountain tops of Olympus, Sinai, Ida, Fuji, and the Himalayas, it is not surprising that man should have built ziggurat mountains to lure the gods into man's settlements or to bring man closer to the gods (Fig. 1). The builders of these homes for the gods were careful to ensure that these places are approached with suitable humility. For example, three flights of stairs led to the portico of the lowest tier of the ziggurat of Urnammu at Ur. They formed an approach and an entrance as demandingly obvious and unambiguous as the great ramps of the temples of Mentuhotep and Queen Hatshepsut at Deir-el-Bahari. The supplicant is at once dwarfed by the scale of the approach, mercilessly exposed, and in essence reminded of his insignificance in the cosmos and in the realms of the Gods, the king, and the powerful. Elevating temples, public, and religious buildings, symbolically and actually, above the earth plane and man, was customary. Even the meanest temple in the classical world is raised upon a crepidoma; and the number and size of these steps has a symbolic and ritualistic significance. Vitruvius writes that:

> The steps in front (of temples) must be arranged so that there shall always be an odd number of them; for thus the right foot with which one mounts the first step will also be the first to reach the level of the temple itself (4).

Rothery suggests that this has to do with the ritual of approaching the altar with right hand uplifted in submission and supplication (5). The steps leading to the choir in some medieval churches are also symbolically significant. They represent the mountain from which Christ delivered his sermon, or perhaps Calvary or the hill of Golgotha; and the frequent use of fifteen steps to the choir represents the fifteen virtues. The three steps to the altar symbolize virtuous faith, love, and hope (6). Pilgrimage steps were constructed so that the pilgrim will strive, step by step, to attain a worthy goal and shed worldly concerns.

The Scala Sancti (or Scala Pilati as it was sometimes called) which leads to the Sancta Sanctorum, the Palatine chapel of the popes in Rome, is the best known of these. Medieval tradition has it that these were the steps Jesus climbed several times on the day he was sentenced to death in Jerusalem. Pilgrims climb the 28 steps on their knees offering a prayer on each.

During the Renaissance and Baroque, under the philosophical influence of the renewed interest in the ideas of the classical world, a church that did not sit atop its own stepped podium, looked mean, visually uncomfortable, and somehow lacking in dignity—at least to the architects. A podium serves several purposes. It lifts the building up from its surroundings. This makes it seem more important, and separates it from its more mundane neighbors. The building is placed on a pedestal and given a base. Once again for the faithful, climbing the steps is an act that they must submit to before entering the house of God (or the palace of those temporal rulers in whom we trust). The steps insist that one participates in the ritual of approach. Secular demonstrations of the monumental stair are every bit as common as those erected for spiritual edifices. For wherever autocratic power is exerted over large building complexes, there flourishes the monumental stair as an immediate exhibition of the puissance of the king, his empire, and the state, and latterly the corporation and institution.

Stairs have also been fashionable and used as demonstrations of the status of the owner. As a status symbol, the turret of the medieval fortress, the towers of the homes of powerful families, and the bell towers of the church became a favored architectural device for palaces, patrician houses and other types of buildings. They symbolized in the city landscape the family's power and position. The great Baroque stairs of the seventeenth and eighteenth centuries were made the focus of the palace and their symbolic, ceremonial, and architectural possibilities of stairs were exploited with such consummate skill.

Scale, Scala, and Proportion

It did not take long for the designers of buildings to realize that stairs can also convey an idea of relative physical size. Stairs are one of the few devices in architecture that can indicate to the observers just how big a building, or part of a building, is compared to other parts or to its surroundings. Even the word used for this purpose—scale—shares the same etymological roots as the Latin word for stairs (scala). Stairs can perform this scaler function uniquely well because the dimensions of risers and treads for humankind must conform to the comfortable limits imposed by our gait. One cannot comfortably use risers that are greater than about eight and a half inches, nor a tread that is much less than about nine inches. Treads may be quite large, but risers cannot be. Steps cannot vary much in size. Therefore one can often deduce building size from steps; and one can manipulate scale by constructing superhuman scaled stairs adjoining those for human gait as in the Parthenon.

The Diagonal Accent

Buildings are composed predominantly from horizontal and vertical planes, and either may be exaggerated by the

Figure 2. Pompidou Center, Paris, France.

designer. The diagonal line or plane is comparatively unusual in the major massing of building components except as a roof cap; and architects have always sought to understand and to tame the vigorous, unruly heresy that the diagonal demonstrates within comfortable orthogonal schema. The nature of the diagonal is a forceful dynamic movement that may threaten the tranquility of the usual order and orientation. It has shock value; it surprises us and rivets our attention and is often used deliberately for this reason (Fig. 2). The stair is by nature diagonal and this only strengthens the connotations of movement implicit in the sequence of risers and treads. The Medieval world enjoyed and exploited the diagonal of stairs. It was a natural element to balance asymmetrical arrangements. The early Renaissance architects, on the other hand, tended to put stairs into their own compartments to prevent them from violating the even balance of horizontal and vertical of the rest of their compositions.

Stair Shape and Architectural Intent

Considering the stair's major influences on architecture chronologically, the earliest stairs were straight flight; helical stairs had their heyday in the middle ages; and the great formal compositions were typical of the doglegs of the Renaissance, flowered in the Baroque palaces, and have taken many forms since. The straight flight stair is the archetypal stair, and has been found in excavations of buildings in Egypt and Mesopotamia dating from earliest times, and, of course, remains in common use today. It is the simplest stair in layout, and the builder does not require a sophisticated structural knowledge. It is relatively easy to accommodate within a building. In its basic form, in the traditional Mediterranean house for example, the straight flight stair is usually tucked away out of sight and is little more than a sloping passage with walls on both sides. It is not exploited as a device to connect the two floors visually. The stair user experiences the stair passage with a tunnel-like view of the space to which the stair leads. Traditionally, these stairs frequently lacked handrails, were precipitous and ill-lit even in patrician houses. In the course of time the stair as an architectural space was gradually embellished. The corridor box of the flight was articulated and expanded spatially with painted scenes and decorative motifs. Later arches, columns, vaults, and molding, were used to break the passage up into a series of spaces to be experienced sequentially. The stair, by nature, is a sequential experience. Additional emphasis on the space was achieved by pushing out the walls and the ceiling to make much grander, more monumental spaces. Added monumentality was created by enlarging the tread, decreasing the riser, providing an excessively generous width of staircase, and increasing the size and importance of the apparent or real handrail. An even more dramatic emphasis on the sense of scale was created using false perspective as in Bernini's Scala Regia (1663–1666) seen in Figure 3.

The helical stair is also an ancient device, and was certainly known in biblical times. From the old testament *Kings,* 6:8, we learn that in Solomon's temple (970 B.C.) "they went up with winding stairs into the middle chamber." However, it was in buildings of all kinds constructed after the dissolution of the Roman empire that the helical stair became common. The helical stair is an appealing design because it occupies less floor space than other layouts. However, its design and construction requires the technical skills of a craftsman. So it is not surprising that

the epoch of the helical stair in the great castles, churches, monasteries, and palaces of Europe coincides with the development of the craft guilds in the middle ages. Within the medieval fortress, besides providing access, the helical stair was useful for defense. If an enemy succeeded in storming the walls of a castle, to take the fortress was another matter. The internal communication system was devised to give the defenders every advantage. Routes through these castles are devious, and comprehensible only to those familiar with them. Stairs rise one floor, and then continue upward in a different location. They are narrow and precipitous, and they can be blocked with little trouble. A few armed men at the landing can keep at bay a strong force of attackers, compelled to ascend in single file. If the enemy were to capture the stair, they would be menaced by overlooking shot-holes.

Architecturally, helical stairs soon began to receive special attention. They were transformed from dismal holes into sculptural objects, new spatial experiences, and symbols of pride and prestige. These stairs have more light, and can be seen as expressive elements. To achieve this, the stair was revealed by removing much of the surrounding walls. The walls of exterior stairs, also, were often replaced by the flimsiest of structural cages. The Campanile at Pisa Cathedral (ca 1174), which is in essence a fifty-two feet diameter free standing helical stair, is one of the earliest examples. The Frances I stair at Blois (1515–1525) is one of the best known. Dissolving the walls was simply a first stage in the deliberate attempt to explore the spatial possibilities of the helical stair. There followed experiments with the newel, to open up the eye of the stair and ultimately to strive for a magical stair devoid of walls or apparent support. By dissolving the solid newel into a hollow shaft or frame, light can be introduced from the top down the middle of the stair, a practical discovery for internal stairs particularly. Spatially, the well was a revolutionary discovery connecting the horizontal floors in quite a new way, making stair use a dramatic architectural experience with its increased sense of verticality experienced as a continuous spiraling journey. Stairs became as grand as their owners wished and could afford, and the grand helical stair is one of the major architectural achievements of the Renaissance.

It was quite late in the Renaissance, at the beginning of the sixteenth century, that the stairwell for helical stairs was fully developed. This was much earlier than the stairwell for straight flight or composite stairs. The most influential helical stair, a ramp with a substantial well, was built by Bramante for Pope Julius in the tower next to the Belvedere. This was soon followed by Vignola's magnificent helical stair at the Farnese Palace at Caprarola (1547–1549). Here the stairwell is opened up to almost ten feet (Fig. 4). Palladio appreciated the new device and says "I have made a staircase void in the middle, in the Monastery de la Carita in Venice, which succeeds admirably." However, opening the well presents problems as well as benefits; the greater the well, the greater the unused space. And the concept of the great stair hall of the Baroque was still in the future. The helical stair and well is like a vertical tunnel of space, with limited possibilities for spatial flow sideways. A spiraling stair forms an apparently continuous wall and strong enclosure. Even

Figure 3. The Scala Regia at the Vatican, Falda's view.

Figure 4. The Farnese Palace stair, Caprarola, Italy.

Figure 6. The Stuttgart Art Museum by James Stirling, Germany.

Frank Lloyd Wright's Guggenheim Museum with its nearly sixty foot wide well and sky lit atrium is constrained by these visual, spatial limitations. For these reasons, the Baroque designers abandoned the continuous helical stair in favor of designs that were less demanding and limiting spatially. The double helix, of obscure origins is a special variant of the circular helical stair developed and was particularly popular in France and Germany. Two stairs of equal diameter, spiral upward about a common center, but start a hundred and eighty degrees apart. Mielke says they are an old Islamic device, noting that there is such a stair in the minaret of the Suq al-ghash of Baghdad (902–908) (7). By far the most famous of these double helix stairs is at the Chambord Palace (1519–1547). It is the hub around which this Renaissance ideal castle revolves (Fig. 5). There is a persistent theory that Leonardo da Vinci designed the Chambord stair. It is certainly possible that he influenced the design, for Francis I's first architect was Italian, Domenico da Cortone. And, there is an extant sketch of such a stair by Leonardo, and also a design of his for a group of four independent straight flight stairs climbing around a fixed core. Furthermore, Leonardo was patronized by Francis I and lived near Amboise from 1516, dying there in 1519 the year that work on Chambord began. A renewed interest in the

architectonic possibilities of the grand stair in compositions has lead James Stirling, for example, to use a great helical stair set in a circular unroofed walled courtyard as the focal event of his Stuttgart Art Museum (Fig. 6). In its relationship to the plan form, it is loosely (and consciously) modelled on K. F. Schinkel's Berlin Museum (1824–1828).

Much of the Baroque fascination for, and evolvement of, the grand staircase can be traced directly to the spatial revelations of the helical stair. The helical stair was to the Medieval and Renaissance buildings what the grand stair was to the Baroque. Chronologically, we can trace an architectonic mutation from elemental straight flight or helical stairs, through dogleg, open well and square newel stairs, through garden and grand approach stairs, to the great Imperial stairs of Europe. Probably the composite stair type with the longest continuous history is the dogleg. There is a wooden staircase of this type leading from the peristyle court to the upper chambers of the Maison de la Colline at Delos (2nd century B.C.). Many of the buildings of the Roman Empire also used these double returning flights, separated by a central wall. In post-Roman Europe, the dogleg stair was seldom used. The straight flight and the helical were the stairs of choice until the advent of the Renaissance. In fact, one of the earliest uses of the dogleg in a major Renaissance building was in Brunelleschi's Foundling Hospital in Florence (1421–1445). The dogleg stair was interesting to Renaissance designers as an ordering device for the plan because it enables the exit and entry point to be located almost directly above each other. This permits floor plans to be regularized with rooms over rooms, and the whole plan to be repeated if necessary. This was particularly useful for the ideal system of repetitive structures and spaces that was to be part of Renaissance and Baroque planning.

By the sixteenth century, for the great buildings of Europe, the spatial economy and architectonic simplicity of the dogleg stair was no longer adequate. Changing theories of space, and the ceremonial use of space, led to a desire to treat the stair with as much architectural respect as any other room in the building. The general form of the Escorial *Imperial stair* presaged the advent of the great Baroque stairs, but it has little of the scenographic pres-

Figure 5. The double helix at Chambord Palace, France.

ence or spatial exuberance of those of the palaces of Bruhl, Wurzburg, Pommersfelden, or Bruchsal. The relocation of the principal rooms of noble houses and palaces from their traditional place on the ground floor to the *piano nobile* made the access stair of the Renaissance and Baroque of far greater functional importance than it had been, when the stair only served suites of rooms of lesser significance. So it is not surprising that the staircase grew in size and magnificence. The risers decreased in height and the treads increased in depth, to respond to the increased functional demands of ceremony, and traffic volume. It was the internal grand stair of the Renaissance and Baroque that the symbolic, ceremonial, and architectural possibilities of stairs came to be exploited with such consummate skill. The dividing and enclosing walls so typical of these early Italian Renaissance stairs fitted well with the extant conception of harmony derived from the theory that architectural spaces should be complete in themselves. The stairs could be used to give a controlled perspective view as well as a rich continuous experience. They could be considered as part of the sequence of the processional way and the reception spaces.

During the Baroque, by contrast, with the connection to the *piano nobile* now so important, the status of the building and its owner was expressed as much by the stair as by the facade, the portico and the reception rooms. The amount of space used to house the stair grew to stupendous dimensions. By no means the largest is Neumann's grand stair at the Wurzburg Palace which occupies about one hundred and two feet by sixty four feet. Luigi Vanvitelli's stair for the Royal Palace at Caserta occupies some 13,855 square feet, being a hundred and sixty three feet by eighty five feet. The oval staircase hall at the Episcopal Palace at Bruchsal is, significantly, the largest room in the palace. It was not, of course, sheer size that was the goal. The stair had to express the taste and elegance of the aristocracy. It had also to be an elaborate backdrop, rather like a stage set, for ceremonial occasions—with treads generous enough and risers shallow enough for ladies of fashion to negotiate not only with safety, but with poise and dignity; and stage design undoubtedly influenced these extraordinary Baroque stair fantasies.

Above all, these grand internal stairs, 'Staircases of Honor' as Guadet calls them, were designed to make the transition from the ground to the *piano nobile* and the upper floors as imperceptible a spatial barrier as possible. The stairs and the stair halls are used to distract the stair user from the act of climbing, and to integrate the vertically adjacent spaces. It was in Germany and Austria that the grandest and richest of the great Baroque stairs emerged; at the Town Palace of Prince Eugene by Fisher von Erlach; at Pommersfelden, Schlos Mirabell (Fig. 7), the palaces of Daun-Kinsky and the Belvedere by Lucas von Hildebrandt; and at the episcopal palaces at Bruchsal, Bruhl, and Wurzburg by Balthazar Neumann. These stairs cannot be considered simply as sumptuous means to pass from the ground to the reception rooms; they became an end in themselves, resplendent art objects, the jewel in the crown of the palace. They exemplified perfectly the extant theory that allowed each building element to display its own expression even if this tended to isolate it

Figure 7. Hildebrandt's stair in the Mirabell Palace, Salzburg, Austria.

from its surroundings. Surrounding walls were dissolved by means of large windows, recesses, mirrors, sculpture, and illusionary devices with dome-like ceilings transformed into artificial skies. On these stairs, the formalities of reception and departure were played out within the diplomatic protocol of the court. Visiting dignitaries were often received on the stair, and where they were received was a measure of their rank and social position; and the gentle riser-tread geometry mandated a stately, comfortable and ceremonial gait for the procession of ascent or descent. On the lower floor of the Wurzburg Palace (Fig. 8) the staircase walls have been dissolved so that the stair floats within arcades on three sides; its long impressive flight at the bottom appears to rise from within the arcade adjoining the portico. The view is at first constricted and then widens out as one ascends. After an intermediate resting place, the flight continues to the intermediate level landing. From there two flights return on either side to the great open space of the *piano nobile*, which is flooded with light from large windows. Hovering over the whole space is a great vaulted ceiling and Tiepolo's fresco. Here one is presented with its illusory world and sky above and beyond reality, where Apollo reigns over the kingdom of the arts. The stair emerges on the upper level,

Figure 8. Imperial stair in the Wuzburg Palace, Germany.

surrounded on all sides by an ambulatory, which visually expands the volume. The space of the stair is like an inverted pyramid, with the ceiling to carry the vertical space through to the infinity of the painted sky above. Neumann had proposed a frothy Rococo decorative treatment for the balustrades, akin to Hildebrandt's Mirabell, but this was abandoned for a more sedate and simpler version.

STAIR DESIGN FOR ACCIDENT AND INJURY REDUCTION

For one who is fascinated by the stair as a delightful element of architectural theater, it is disturbing to have to confront the other face of stairs that witnesses millions of injurious, crippling, and often fatal accidents on stairs every year. Steps and stairs turn out to be the most dangerous element in the home in the United States and the United Kingdom, and the second most dangerous element in Japan. Because stairs have been shown to be dangerous, does not mean that they are inevitably and incurably dangerous. It does mean that this epidemic of falls needs to be treated; aspects of the disease are known and can be addressed, and if this knowledge is used stairs can be

made to be much safer than they are now. Many stair accidents are preventable. Stairway falls may result from: the way the stair is designed; the way the stair is built; the way the stair is maintained; the way that people use stairs; and each of these must be considered if we are to reduce accidents and injuries.

THE WAY THE STAIR IS DESIGNED

Inappropriate Use. There are some locations where stairs should be avoided. The elderly, for example, have more stair accidents and are more easily injured than other people; and, for them, remedial surgery after injury is riskier, and healing takes longer. Therefore, as a general rule, stairs in homes for the elderly and other facilities for this age group are likely to be the locus of accidents. There is a correlation between alcohol consumption and stair falls so stairs that lead to bars and places that serve liquor are likely to have a higher rate of accidents. Stairs are sometimes located where they will be significantly more dangerous. For example, a restaurant should not be connected to its kitchen by a stair (nor a self-service counter with the seating area); the steps may become slippery from food slopped over it; and the trays, that are carried, may prevent an adequate view of the stair. Similarly, the parts department of a factory or a workshop should not be accessible only by means of stairs. People who carry things while they use stairs are more likely to fall (8).

Hidden Steps. Steps are sometimes located where they may not be noticed. A quite common and particularly hazardous example is where a single step occurs within a walkway, a passage, or in the form of a platform in a store. The danger is that the step(s) may not be clearly seen because the light is poor, or even if there is plenty of light, the step may visually merge with the walkway. The latter condition is an especial danger to people with impaired vision.

Dangerous Views. As a generality, it seems that anything that induces the stair user to focus attention onto the stair rather than the surroundings increases safety. Where this is not possible, then the views should be wide open at all points on the stair, not suddenly revealed at certain places and certainly not only at the top or bottom three steps by the landings, where most accidents occur.

Illumination. Poorly illuminated stairs are dangerous; many reports and studies have confirmed this. Yet one study found that about 95% of the residential stairways in a survey had light levels below the 20 footcandles recommended by the Illuminating Engineering Society for Stairways in 1972 (9). However the researchers did not report the percentage of the stairs that met the building code requirements. If they had, they might well have found that most of the stairs complied with the extant codes. After all most of the codes require a minimum lighting level of only one footcandle, one fifth to one twentieth of that recommended by the IES today (10). Why this disparity exists is puzzling. Adequate illumination, either natural or artificial must be provided. The IES recommendations (five to twenty footcandles for most applications) seem to be much more realistic for stair safety than those minima permitted by most building codes. The illumination should be reasonably constant over the whole stair. Window and artificial light sources should not be placed where the stair user must include them, and the steps, in the same direct field of vision; and shadows on the steps should be avoided. Illumination is also related to the surface, ie, the treads. In terms of reflectance, the IES recommends 21% to 31% for floors. If the stair is located where there is any risk that someone might stumble into it unexpectedly, then permanent supplementary artificial illumination should be provided. Finally, the switches that control the stair lights should be placed sufficiently far from the stair so that there is no risk of a person falling while they reach for the switch; and in the same vein three-way switches should be used at the top and bottom of the stairs.

Riser/Tread Geometry. To a large extent the dimensions of risers and treads actually control our gait, comfort, and the probability of accidents. Gait is affected by the height of the riser, the depth of the tread, and the combination of the two. Ever since Vitruvius, the quest for the perfect relationship of riser to going, and stair pitch, has been a kind of designer's philosopher's stone. Almost every architect of note for the last two thousand years has held decided and often differing views on the proper geometry of stairs for comfort and safety. But it was in France in the late seventeenth century that the first known attempt was made to devise a formula that linked stair geometry to man's gait. Francois Blondel, who became director of the Royal Academy of Architecture in 1672, was the author of, *inter alia,* the influential *Cours d'architecture* (11). Blondel noted that "the length of a comfortable pace of a man who walks on the level is . . . twenty four inches. And the [maximum comfortable] height of one climbing a vertical step is only twelve inches." The drawback to the Blondel rule that was perceived by the critics was that where the risers are higher or lower than usual, the rule produces extremely narrow or extremely wide treads. Since the first world war, researchers have used various techniques to try to relate riser and tread geometry to human gait by studying energy expenditure, analyzing gait, and anthropometrics.

Human Energy Expenditure and Riser/Tread Combinations. Energy expenditure as a measure of rhythm, comfort, and fatigue seems to offer one of the most productive approaches to the development of stair geometry criteria. Researchers sought to compare the energy demands on the human metabolism of different riser/tread combinations to see whether some were less demanding than others. They concluded that stairs with low risers demand lower rates of energy expenditure than those with high risers; however, one can choose a riser/tread combination from a range of alternatives that all have about the same energy demands; in this range, high risers are paired with small treads, and low risers with large treads. Therefore,

it is possible to use relatively high risers when this is necessary without incurring a greatly increased rate of energy expenditure, provided that the treads are small but not too small. Combinations which demand relatively low rates of energy expenditure recommend themselves for use in public places and where the aged and the frail are potential users. The findings indicate that there is a relationship between the human pace, and the riser/tread ratio, but the relationship is more flexible than Blondel envisaged. Blondel's formula is too restrictive, too narrowly idealistic, and insufficiently responsive to human adaptability.

Gait, Missteps, and Stair Geometry. Another approach to stair geometry is to examine its effect on gait. This has been studied through gait analysis of the locomotor processes exercised during stair use (12). The study concluded that stair gait is influenced by stair riser/tread geometry and speed of climb. The influence of gait is less noticeable in ascent, where much less of the shoe needs to be placed on the step; nevertheless, risers from 6.3–8.9 in. cause fewer missteps. Small risers create flights with more risers, and therefore more opportunities to trip. The steeper the stair, the greater the number of missteps in descent; and at steep angles, where the treads are small, the performance is poorest. The larger *goings* (the tread depth less the nosing overhang) 11.5–14.2 in. generate the fewest missteps; and generally stairs with goings less than about 9 in. perform very poorly. Stairs with risers from 4.6–7.2 in. and goings greater than 9 in. seem to have the safest potential in descent, particularly if the angle is low, and the pedestrian is descending at a moderate pace. As descent has been shown to be the movement direction that is most hazardous, the requirements for safe movement in descent should be of first importance. A reasonable compromise to suit ascent and descent movement, on the basis of these findings, would be a stair with risers that, to suit ascent, are not less than 6.3 in.; and to suit descent, are not more than 7.2 in., and goings that are greater than 9 in.

Anthropometry and Going Dimensions. The evidence that small goings induce missteps suggests that one should consider them in relation to human dimensions. Tread dimensions, for example, are not always large enough to accommodate the length of the shod foot, thereby forcing stair users into curiously contorted gaits. When the treads are narrow, in descent, people tend to twist their feet sideways relative to the line of travel in order to gain greater area of support for their feet and to ensure a more secure base. The more the tread of the steps is narrowed, the more the feet are twisted sideways. This demonstrates a natural effort to provide the leading foot with an adequate area to resist forward momentum and slippage in descent. It also suggests that, in descent, treads that are perceived as being narrower than the shoe length, engender a gait that is increasingly distorted as the treads are narrowed. Recommended minimum tread dimensions that were adequate for people of Blondel's time in the seventeenth century or even at the beginning of this century, may no longer be adequate, for average foot length like stature has generally increased. A 95th percentile man's foot in shoes is 12.6 in. in length. However, one must also allow a tolerance between heel and riser in descent of ¼ in. as a minimum, and assume that 1¾ in. of shoe projection beyond the nosing is about the limit for stability (to ensure that the metatarsal heads, the big bones of the foot, will be on the tread). This suggests that a going of about 11 in. is a reasonable minimum to accommodate 95% of the population.

Step Geometry, Conclusions. There is a useful range of riser/tread ratios with risers from 4.6–7.2 in. coupled with goings from 11–14 in. or more; at these levels, the rate of energy expenditure remains fairly low, and the number of missteps will be predictably small. From all the investigations, the range of dimensions shown in Table 1 fulfills the criteria of comfort and safety best within the range of the laboratory observations.

Riser and Going for Helical Stairs. For helical stairs, obviously the going varies in proportion to the distance from the center of the radius. It is important that, at the predicted walking line, the going should be adequate. The walking line is the imaginary line along which the feet travel while using the helical stair. People do not walk with their bodies touching the handrail, or adjoining wall; they leave a space. It is not clear from any studies how large this space is for people using helical stairs, but in common European usage 10.63 in. (270 mm) is judged to be the distance between the walking line and the inside of a handrail or the newel. To adhere to the same standards recommended for straight flight stairs, 11 in. minimum going at the walking line, the helical stair will need a minimum diameter of about 6 ft 9 in. (13).

The Tread Edge. Misreading the stair will set up a cognitive misinformation cycle that may translate into faulty foot placement and an accident. Precise information is needed as to the exact location of the front edge of the tread of each step. One of the commonest design failures is where, when one looks down, the treads seem to merge together. The risers cannot be seen and the stair looks more like a ramp. This is because there is no visual contrast between adjoining treads. All the treads may be black, white, or virtually any other unbroken, even color, and in certain lights, the nosing edges visually merge with the treads. The ability to detect the edge of the tread may also be defeated by inappropriate stair carpet pat-terns, or slip resistance treatments. Some stair carpets have strong decorative and repetitive patterns that dominate the visual field to the exclusion of everything including the tread edge. Misreading the location of the tread edge in ascent may cause a trip, or understepping where the foot slips off the upper tread; in descent, it may also cause a trip, catching the heel on the nosing edge, or overstepping, perhaps with the foot slipping off the step. All of these events are extremely dangerous and the cause of some of the most serious accidents.

Projecting Nosings. The idea of projecting the front edge of the tread beyond the face of the riser below, developed long ago. It appears to offer a partial solution to the problem of narrow treads, without increasing the overall depth of the tread. It provides, in ascent, extra space for the toe; and, in descent it is claimed that extra space for the heel to tuck in under the nosing projection is provided. Many of the extant construction codes in fact require nosing overhangs of half an inch or more, particularly if the going is less than ten inches. However two studies suggest that nosings greater than about three quarters of an inch may be hazardous (for reasons that are unclear). Abrupt nosing overhang projections, formed by projecting the tread beyond the riser, seem to present great difficulties for people with prosthetic feet or legs; the shod foot tends to catch on the nosing in ascent. These designs are generally prohibited in codes for accessibility. So the abrupt nosing may soon be a thing of the past. Where the nosing overhang is formed by simply sloping the riser back from the nosing edge, this seems to cause no such difficulties, and these are generally permitted. Fixing carpeting around steps that have abrupt nosing overhangs is difficult. As a result carpets are often left to bulge out around the projection without adequate fixing. The looseness of the carpet and the lack of definition of the edge of the nosing then becomes a new hazard.

Tread Materials. The appropriate choice of a material for stair treads is likely to be influenced by structural considerations, the type and volume of traffic, appearance, resistance to wear, chemicals and the climate, ease of maintenance and cleaning, cost, slip resistance, and how comfortable it is to walk on. The surface of treads should have an even and smooth surface with an adequate and uniform coefficient of friction. This principle is quite often violated by the presence of uneven joints, in brick stairs for example; by projecting nosing strips that have been added for the purpose of increasing frictional resistance; and by the use of very rough shag carpeting. If any of these materials may catch the toe or the heel of the shoe, then an accident may result. A second principle requires the tread surface to be stable. It must not be loose or move to any extent under the load of the forces applied to it by the feet. Stairs are not the places for throw rugs or temporary coverings, and carpets must be firmly fitted.

RAMPS

Gradient and Slip Resistance. Ramps have just as long a history as stairs but they have never been as prevalent as

Table 1. Range of Riser and Going Dimensions for Comfort and Safety

Rise (in.)	Going						
7.2	11						
7	11						
6.5	11	11.5	12	12.5			
6	11	11.5	12	12.5	13	13.5	14
5.5	11	11.5	12	12.5	13		
5	11	11.5	12				
4.6	11						

a building element. The reason for this is not difficult to find; for an equal rise and width, they occupy about five times as much floor space as stairs. Apart from space considerations, ramps offer clear advantages over stairs. They are less physically demanding on users, and they are also inherently safer than stairs. A fall on a ramp is less likely to cause severe injuries than a fall on a stair. A fall on a ramp is probably not much worse than a fall on the level. Ramps are also more effective than stairs for facilitating the movement of crowds of people; ramps slow the flow of mass pedestrian movement less than stairs. This makes them particularly suitable, and safer than stairs, for access and egress ways for theatres, stadia, and places where there are crowds moving, and where people may be easily distracted from the act of seeing and using stairs. Finally, ramps offer much less of a barrier than steps and stairs for wheeled vehicles such as wheelchairs, stretchers, and shopping carts. Ramps, however, are not for everyone; some people who use crutches, and others who have a certain kind of balance problem, if given the choice, will avoid ramps and use stairs.

Ramp Safety. The design of a safe ramp is less complex than it is for stairs. The main concerns are for a safe layout and gradient, a slip resistant floor surface, and hand and guardrails. A safe layout for ramps is one that follows the same principles necessary for a safe stair layout. People using a ramp should not be made to exit into congested or hazardous areas. Curb ramps, particularly, should not direct wheel chair users towards the center of a street intersection; the curb ramp should direct the user into the crosswalk. Landings and spaces where people could be crushed during emergency evacuations are potentially dangerous and must be avoided. A minimum of sixty six inches is needed at the top and bottom of ramps as a space for wheelchairs to slow down, stop and change direction.

Ramp Gradient. It might be presumed that no lower limit to ramp gradient needs to be considered, after all the less steep the ramp is, the less hazardous it is likely to be; and of course this is essentially correct. There is at least one exception to this. Severely visually disabled people who use a long cane for guidance may not be able to detect the place where a level sidewalk changes into a curb ramp, if the slope of the curb ramp is less than about 1:16. For these people the presence of this detectable level change is important as one of the clues that a road lies ahead, and without which some less skilled travellers might inadvertently stray into the street (14). Based on tests of people using short ramps, it can be concluded that ramps steeper than 1:8 are probably too dangerous, and that ramps that are 1:3.27 or steeper cannot be utilized without gait distortion (15). Obviously this does not mean that, at slopes steeper than 1:8, people will certainly fall; and that, at slopes that are less steep than 1:8, people will not fall. It does mean that the probability of a fall increases as the slope increases; and that at slopes steeper than 1:8, even the ramp users find the slope difficult to use. Ramps as steep as 1:8 are only acceptable for ascending or descending heights of no more than three inches.

For a height greater than three inches, 1:10 is preferred; and for heights greater than six inches 1:12 is preferred. Ramps will be used by some people with handicaps. For them questions of maximum gradient are linked to physical strength and stamina. A ramp that is too long, with no landing or resting place, may be daunting or even unsafe; manual wheelchairs may get out of control. Table 2 shows recommendations made for ramps that could be ascended by at least 80% of those who use manual wheelchairs.

These findings differ from the value of 1:12 that is the maximum gradient permitted in most codes and standards directed at handicapped accessibility. The reason for this is that the 1:12 requirement does not take into account the bodily strength and effort that long ramps demand.

Even with a gradient that is not too demanding, landings are necessary as resting places. Landings should be spaced increasingly close together as the total distance travelled up the ramp increases. Table 3 shows the maximum distance to the first and subsequent landings for various ramp gradients. Most codes and standards limit the distance between landings to thirty feet. Table 3 generally suggests substantially longer distances between landings, unless the ramp is very long.

Coefficient of Friction and Slip Resistance. Ramp gradient is only one part of the equation for safety, and in some respects may not be the most significant term. A ramp that is relatively steep, ie 1:10, may be much safer than one that is less steep but slippery. A ramp is dangerous to use if the frictional force between the shoe and the ramp surface is too small to prevent a slip. So, for a safe ramp, one must consider not only the ramp's gradient, but the frictional force between shoe and ramp floor surface. One can design a ramp that has a relatively safe gradient, and has a surface that provides adequate frictional resistance to a standardized test shoe. One cannot, however, control the shoes that the ramp users will wear, and one cannot totally control the presence of substances that might act to lubricate the surface between shoe and floor. Society makes an attempt to control slip resistance in building and fire codes by calling for a non-slip or nonskid surface (a virtual impossibility), and by limiting gradients; and, as will be discussed, there are some standards for slip resistance. But there are no comparable standards for con-

Table 2. Acceptable and Maximum Gradients for Ramps of Various Lengths[a]

Ramp Gradient Allowable Slope	Maximum Rise in Single Run[b]	Total Length Minus Landings[b]
1:8.00–1:10	3 in.(76 mm)	24–30 in. (610–762 mm)
1:10.1–1:11	9 (2.74 m)	91–99 (28–30 m)
1:11.1–1:13	14 (4.27 m)	155–182 (47–55 m)
1:13.1–1:15	16 (4.88 m)	210–240 (64–73 m)
1:15.1–1:16	20 (6.10 m)	302–320 (92–98 m)

[a] Building, fire, and handicapped codes may require different gradients.
[b] Feet unless otherwise noted.

Table 3. Optimum Distance Between Landings[a]

No. of Landing	Gradient					
	1:15.9	1:14.3	1:13.7	1:12.7	1:11.6	1:10.0
1st	95(5.9)[b]	85(6.0)	80(5.8)	75(5.9)	65(5.6)	45(4.5)
2nd	170(10.7)	155(10.9)	145(10.6)	130(10.3)	120(10.3)	90(9.0)
3rd	215(13.5)	200(14.0)	190(13.9)	175(13.8)	165(14.2)	
4th	245(15.4)	230(16.1)	220(16.1)			
5th	275(17.3)					
6th	305(19.2)					

[a] in feet.

[b] Figures in parenthesis indicate the total height, in feet, ascended.

trolling the slipperiness of shoes. Shoes are still sold that have soles that are as smooth as glass, and many types of shoe sole material remain relatively slippery permanently.

The whole subject of acceptable slip resistance levels has little consensus. The problem is that the Coefficient of Friction (COF) is dependent not only on the characteristics of the floor surface. The minimum value of COF needed for safe locomotion is also affected by waste deposits and precipitation on the surface; temperature and humidity; the composition of the materials of the shoes; any coating on the floor material; and on human factors. The minimum value of COF needed for safe locomotion is influenced by the fit of the shoes; individual gait and speed; age, physical condition, and walking skill level; direction of movement, type of task being performed, ie, pushing something; and behavioral responses (16). Not all of these can be accurately assessed, and certainly not their cumulative and interactive affects. The first part of the international controversy revolves around whether static or dynamic COF's are the most meaningful; and there is equipment available for measuring either or both. In the United States, a preference for static values has been shown recently. The question that arises is whether one can control slip resistance by specifying minimum values of COF. It is not unusual to find that a static COF of 0.5 is recommended as a minimum COF. Is this the correct value? A tabular summary of key quantitative findings by various writers going back to 1943 noted that "The minimum required COF for normal pace walking . . . ranges between 0.2 and 0.4 depending on the author's research methodology . . . ," and depending, one might add, on whether the author has included a safety factor (17). What can one conclude from all this? ASTM and the Underwriters Laboratory (for polish coated floor surfaces) and others have recommended 0.5 as a minimum acceptable value (18). Others have recommended values from 0.2 to 0.7, but there is no international nor national consensus. A COF of 0.5 includes, by all accounts, a safety factor and therefore has some merit as a cautious recommendation (particularly as a precaution against slippery shoes). If, however, a floor surface does not meet this standard, it does not follow that it is dangerous. 0.4 or even 0.3 may be the minimum for safety. A COF of 0.5 is no guarantee of safety; it may not provide adequate protection for people running, nor for people turning left or right, nor for people walking on ramps, nor for wet surfaces, nor for people using very slippery shoes.

When the contact area between shoe and surface is lubricated by water, oil, dust, or any similar substance, the COF may be substantially reduced. "Nearly all combinations of dry and clean shoes and surfaces have COF values greater than 0.5 while only selected combinations of wet shoes and surfaces result in a COF value greater than 0.4 (19)." Floor surfaces exposed to the weather or any other potential lubricating factor should be finished with materials that, when wet, will still have an adequate COF; and when floors are being washed, people should not walk on them unless the wet COF is adequate. In industrial or commercial environments, where admission of people is controlled, a possible alternative would be to supply or specify the shoes to be worn.

A flooring material that provides an adequate frictional resistance when used for level walkways may be quite inadequate on a ramp (20). Floor surfaces on a slope will require a higher COF to cancel out the effects of the slope. If a ramp has a gentle slope, say 1:12, then a person's speed on the ramp will probably be much the same as on the level sidewalk. If, for example, a coefficient of friction of 0.5 is required to prevent someone from slipping on the level sidewalk, then the material of the ramp will need to have a coefficient of 0.61 if it is to be as effective as the level walkway in preventing slips. So there is clearly an argument for choosing a ramp material that compensates for the slope. It is not easy to find materials that will give an adequate slip resistance for the steeper gradients. This is part of the reason why steep ramps have a poor safety record; and particularly ramps out in the open that are not protected from precipitation and other lubricating materials.

STEPS

Slip Resistance and Steps. The surface of stair treads, and of course landings, must have an adequate and uniform resistance to slip forces. Mishaps can occur at any stage in the gait cycle. However accidents caused by slips usually occur as the weight is being transferred from, or onto, a foot at the beginning, or end, of the swing phase. As heel-strike represents such a small contact area, the potential for slippage is much greater than at toe-off where much of the sole of the shoe remains in contact with the horizontal surface. If the frictional force between foot and step is insufficient to effectuate the weight transfers at first contact, and later the toe-off, then the foot will slip

Figure 9. Abrasive tread.

and the body will be thrown off-balance. However, normal gait on stairs is unlikely to result in slips because the peak horizontal force generated between the foot and the tread is much less than the equivalent forces generated during walking on the level. Nevertheless special attention must be paid to slip resistance at the step nosings, and particularly the nosing at the landing at the top of a flight. The mechanics of slip mishaps point up the necessity for a large enough tread, and adequately abrasive surface, particularly at the front of the tread; and, out-of-doors, the necessity for a wash or slope to throw water off the tread during rain and to prevent ice formation. The risks of slipping on stairs have been so overplayed in safety literature that there have been several misguided and potentially hazardous responses from the building industry. One response has been to make treads with aggressively abrasive surfaces; some like cheese graters Fig. 9. This is quite unnecessary and is quite likely to cause accidents when the stair user trips on this very rough surface. If anyone is unfortunate enough to fall on to such a surface, the resulting abrasions are likely to be extensive.

Garden Steps. Garden stairs may be no more than rough cut steps on a mountain trail or a stair as monumental, fantastic, and elaborate as any interior stair. The question that is raised here is what are the characteristics of a safe garden stair? It is tempting to suggest that all steps and stairs should follow the same standards of design, in principle that is so. Perhaps a more realistic answer, however, is to say that where a stair appears to be part of a carefully constructed exterior pedestrian walkway system, then the usual standards are expected by the user and should apply. But if the steps and stairs are obviously part of an informal rough mountain trail, then the users' expectations are attuned to these different circumstances and they can react appropriately. It is the perception of the stair user that must be considered. If the stair looks like a conventional stair, then the user expects it to be so, and to be just as safe. If the stair looks obviously rough, uneven, and organic, then the user proceeds with the same caution with which he climbs a trail.

HANDRAILS, GUARDRAILS, AND BALUSTRADES

As one might suspect, from the literature on stair accidents there is a consensus that handrails help to reduce the incidence and severity of stair accidents. Studies suggest that injury severity is reduced if a handrail is at hand for the victim to use; and if there is no handrail available, the injury is likely to be more severe. However the effectiveness of a handrail is governed by its location, its height above the stair, the distance between the handrail and the adjoining wall, its shape and size, and the materials from which it is made.

Handrail Location. Where stair handrails are inconveniently located and force the stair user to take a significantly longer route, on a wide monumental stair for example, handrail use decreases. There is no evidence that users select routes to be closer to handrails. Most of the model building codes quite rightly require the handrail to be continuous the entire length of the flight, and several require the rail to extend the equivalent of one tread or more beyond the last riser. This is to enable people to have a rail at hand as they negotiate the first and last step. This railing projection must be treated carefully so that it does not project into a walkway and become a hazard for people with limited vision.

Many model building codes use a 22 in. module to prescribe the relationship between stair width and the location of handrails. Some permit a single rail on one side for stairs up to 44 in. and two rails for stairs up to 88 in. From anthropometric studies a stair that is 35 in. wide between the walls and with a rail on one side has the maximum feasible width, if the rail must fall within the reach of adult users. A 47 in. wide stair with handrails on both sides is the maximum width for both rails to be always available to adult users.

Handrail Height. For many years, 30–34 in. has been considered to be the ideal height for handrails to be set above the stair nosing regardless of the pitch, and most model codes require conformity within this range. Recently, some Canadian researchers have questioned these standards. On the basis of their laboratory studies they concluded that the optimum range of handrail heights for young subjects lies between 36 and 38 in.; for elderly subjects, between 36 and 40 in. They also asked the subjects to indicate a preferred handrail height, and found that the mean was approximately 36 in. For children's handrails, on the basis of anthropometric data researchers have suggested that, to allow for children from ages 4 to 15, the rail should be 21.8–28.7 in. for places (21), such as kindergarten and other schools where the handrail can be located to suit the needs of the specific age group, or 24 in. where children of all ages may be present (22).

Handrail-to-Wall Clearance. For the handrail to be usable, there must be sufficient space for someone to be able to grab the rail in an emergency as well as for normal use. The codes generally set this distance at 1½ in. Obviously, the space between the handrail and wall must be, as a minimum, large enough for the hand to enter and grasp the rail. The bare hand thickness at the third metacarpal is 1.42 in. for the 95th percentile of the population. Gloves may increase this value by 0.2 in. to a total of 1.62 in.; and flexion of the hand will cause an unknown increase in this thickness. This recommendation does not take into account the situation where the wall has a rough, abrasive surface and when the rail has to be grabbed in an emergency. The worst case example of this is where the rail is to be grabbed horizontally from the side and the extended fingers strike the wall. In this event, there must be sufficient clearance for the length of fingers extended fully (4.9 in. for the 95th percentile male) plus some clearance, say ¼ in. For a 1½ in. diameter handrail, the wall clearance should be no less than 3.65 in. (4.9 in. + .125 in. − 1.5 in.). In actuality the action of the handrail in the crotch of the thumb decreases the effective finger length, however this additional tolerance probably counterbalances the stretch of the tissues as the hand is thrust against the rail.

Handrail Shape and Size. Handrails must be able to transmit forces and moments to and from the human hand effectively. Increasing the congruence between the rail and the hand will increase the contact forces and, perhaps, the effective normal force by increasing the number of finger segments in contact with the handrail. Furthermore, by increasing the contact area, the forces can be spread over a larger area thereby reducing the stresses and strains on the tissues of the hand. Those who have examined the question of handrail shape have agreed that a 1½ in. circular shape permits a power grip and will maximize tangential forces over a wide range of hand sizes and shapes. Rectangular rails and molded decorative rails usually limit use to the less effective pinch grip.

Handrail Materials. Many factors enter into the choice of appropriate materials for handrails: friction, tactility, resilience, surface and structural integrity, and appearance. Each of these can influence comfort and safety, and comfort probably also influences safety; a rail that is uncomfortable to use because of its shape or tactile qualities may discourage or even prevent handrail use.

The selection of materials with an appropriate coefficient of friction for the ambient environmental circumstances is not merely a question of comfort but is imperative for safety and for injury reduction. A handrail that will become too slippery may actually cause falls if the user is leaning on it, or pulling up using it. A handrail that is too abrasive may discourage people from using it and may cause abrasions, avulsions, and lacerations, when some part of the hand or body is forcibly moved over the surface. On the one hand, to avoid trauma, materials should be selected to minimize the frictional forces; on the other hand the materials must be chosen that will not tend to slip out of the hand. The padded automobile steering wheel may well be a useful model for the stair handrail. The material can be relatively smooth with a low coefficient of friction, but the coefficient of friction and the grip can be increased when necessary by simply holding the rail tighter and compressing the padding into greater congruence with the hand.

When one considers handrails as a tactile material, one should consider the problem of materials that are good absorbers and conductors of heat—particularly the metals. Handrails exposed to the sun and the cold may become too hot or cold to touch, or they may cause trauma to those people who use them and who suffer from diminished tactile sense (a not uncommon aspect of aging, and diabetes).

The surface of the handrail is rendered less useful by awkward fixing brackets that interfere with continuous hand movement along the rail; and some brackets are fixed using bolts that protrude from the handrail in a way that can injure the hand, or any other part of the body that impacts it. Finally, the material of the handrail must retain its original integrity and must be maintained to prevent deterioration. Most materials deteriorate with age, particularly when used externally. Wood tends to become brittle and to splinter, ferrous metals tend to become rusted and pitted; and both of these conditions will prevent or discourage handrail use.

The literature on stair safety seldom discusses handrail visibility; and yet the need for visibility seems obvious. Consider, for example, a white painted handrail fixed to a white wall; or a dark wooden handrail to be viewed against a background of similar hue. It may be quite difficult to perceive the handrail with precision during a fall; and this is likely to be a major problem for those with visual impairments. It seems to make good sense that the handrail, as the first line of defense should be highly visible and stand out against the background.

Balustrades. Although a comparatively small number of injuries are caused by people striking the balustrading during a fall, these can be reduced by avoiding sharp projections or edges; or better still, by providing an energy absorbing material. An additional risk of injury may result from a design that can trap a hand, arm, or some other body part during a fall; a design with some sort of wedge shaped crevice, for example. A special concern of this sort has been recognized for a long time, the risk of a baby's head becoming caught; or a baby falling through balusters that are too widely spaced. One standard requires that any railing system shall be arranged so that a sphere 5 in. in diameter, representing a baby's head, cannot be passed through the system (23). This is posited on the grounds that, by the age of two years in normal child development, children can negotiate stairs unaided. Anthropometric data shows that the 50th percentile 2 year old has a hip depth of 4 in., and can still fall through a 5 in. space leaving the child caught by the head. For one year old children who may not be able to use stairs, crawling to a guardrail or a stair is quite a likely eventuality. This suggests that a spacing that is no greater than 3½ in. should be chosen (24).

Guardrails. Stair handrails, and guardrails are needed for very different purposes. A guardrail is one of several ways of preventing people from falling over the edge of a landing, platform, balcony, stair, ramp etc. A stair or ramp handrail serves to help people keep their balance;

provides guidance for people with impaired vision; reassures some people who use stairs; helps people pull themselves up in ascent; aborts or limits falls after one has lost one's balance. But a handrail is usually too low to prevent people from falling over an edge.

From these definitions, a handrail can only serve as a guardrail if it can prevent people from falling off an edge. This is usually impossible because of the low minimum handrail heights permitted by the model building codes. So stairs, ramps, and escalators with handrails but no edge protection have a limited ability to act as guardrails. Other means must be provided to obviate this risk. One of many solutions is to provide an additional rail, at guardrail height, above the handrail. The choice of an effective height for a guardrail at an edge has been studied using anthropomorphic dummies to simulate various postures of humans leaning against or walking into a guardrail at a brisk speed (25).

It was concluded that the guardrail should be set approximately equal to the height of the centroid of the 95th percentile composite male population in the United States (42 in.) with the subject in a straight posture on a level surface. As the width of the guardrail is increased, the risk of overbalancing apparently decreases, so a relaxation of the 42 in. rule has been suggested where the width of the horizontal guardrail is greater than 6 in., and the adjoining interior floor surface is level. Under these circumstances, the minimum height of the guardrail should not be less than 48 in. minus B, where B is the minimum width of the top surface of the guardrail. Thus, if the width of the top surface of the guardrail is 10 in., then the height may be 38 in. (48 in. less 10 in.). However in no case should the rail be less than 30 in.

STAIR CAPACITY

A stair which is inadequate for the volume of traffic is at best irritating, is certainly uncomfortable, and may be downright dangerous. People seem to understand subconsciously how much space is needed for safe ambulation at various speeds. One begins to feel uneasy as crowds throng and start to press around us. Their proximity, their penetration of our personal space, and certainly unsought physical contact may be offensive to us. And as congestion increases, what was merely distasteful and uncomfortable, may become quite suddenly threatening. Body contact pressures build up; and the crowd coalesces into a unified conflux with individual responses impossible. People are swept along involuntarily, and even lifted off their feet; injury and death may be inevitable.

For people ascending or descending a stair in single file, 38 in. between walls for comfort is needed; and 29 in. as a minimum for a public place. Handrails occupy at least 3 in. on each side, however, no further lateral tolerance is necessary as the arm swing and lateral displacement occurs mostly above the handrail. Comparable figures for residential interiors, assuming no heavy clothing, would be 37 in. and 27.5 in. However, the effective width is mediated by the presence of adjoining walls and handrails;

people tend to maintain a distance of about six inches between themselves and a wall, and three and a half inches between themselves and the centerline of a graspable handrail (26). For people to be able to walk side-by-side, some codes require a minimum of 44 in. Unless the stair is to serve a very select population, this seems to be too little. Therefore a stair which will allow people to walk side by side in heavy clothing between walls should be at least 56 in. wide; 69 in. between walls is more comfortable.

In any pedestrian movement system, the component parts are interlocked and dependent on each other; the walkway capacity is controlled by the stair that terminates it; the stair's capacity is affected by its location. Pedestrian flow is primarily related to the speed and spatial demands of the pedestrians, and, from these, the capacity of the route can be gauged. Other factors act to modify, or are modified by, the flow of the pedestrians directional conflicts, overtaking movements, reverse flow, and bulk arrivals or platoons—but the effect of these can also be taken into account. Stairway movement, flow and capacity is markedly different from that on level and inclined walkways. In the first place, for a normal, free, unobstructed speed, much less room is necessary on stairs—11 square feet per pedestrian for ascent and 15 square feet for descent, compared to about 35 square feet on walkways (27). Because the horizontal component of pedestrian speed is much less on stairs, even in descent, than on level walkways, free flow is reached in ascent at a speed of about 100 feet per minute, and 120 feet per minute in descent (and this would be a shuffling speed on a level walkway); compared to around 300 feet per minute for walking on the level in free flow. Because of the reduced speed, both the theoretical and observed maximum capacity of stairs is less than for walkways of similar dimensions. Theoretically this means that a stair in a corridor should be about a third wider than the corridor. But if the corridor and stair are sized to allow a flow of about 15 pedestrians per minute per foot width, there is no need to increase the stair width unless to allow for extreme, unpredictable events. This would be a sensible precaution where capacities are unpredictable and where the stair might become a bottleneck.

Reverse flow appears to affect stairways much more than walkways, probably because of the limitations on agility imposed by stairs. If a stair is only wide enough for two people side by side, at even moderate rates of flow, the capacity may be halved by a reverse flow of only a very small number of people, depending on the length of the stair (28). With light reverse flow (one to three people), flow drops to 11.2 pedestrians per minute per foot. With heavy reverse flow (more than three people), queues will still form at a flow rate of 7.6 pedestrians per minute per foot. The level-of-service concept was developed by traffic engineers to indicate the levels of performance that could be expected to result from flow design choices. Table 4 summarizes pedestrian flow characteristics on stairs into six levels-of-service. The use of levels higher than E is not recommended. However, to avoid queues forming, level E should be avoided also, and level D used with discretion.

Table 4. Level-of Service for Stairs

Average Area per Person[a]	Characteristics
Less than 4	• Flow: up to 20 people per minute per foot width; flow attains a maximum, but is erratic with frequent stoppages and verges on complete breakdown, • Average speed: shuffling, 0–70 (horizontal) ft/min
F	• Choice of speed: none • Passing: impossible • Queuing at stair entrance: yes
4–7	• Flow: 13–17 p/min/ft, intermittent stoppages • Average speed: 70–90 ft/min
E	• Choice of speed: none • Passing: impossible • Queuing at stair entrance: yes
7–10	• Flow: 10–13 p/min/ft • Average speed: 90–95 ft/min
D	• Choice of speed: restricted • Passing: impossible • Queuing at stair entrance: some at higher flow level
10–15	• Flow: 7–10 p/min/ft • Average speed: 95–100 ft/min
C	• Choice of speed: restricted • Passing: impossible • Queuing at stair entrance: none
15–20	• Flow: 5–7 p/min/ft • Average speed: 100 ft/min
B	• Choice of speed: freely selected • Passing: restricted • Queuing at stair entrance: none
More than 20	• Flow: 5 or less p/min/ft • Average speed: 100 ft/min
A	• Choice of speed: freely selected • Passing: at will • Queuing at stair entrance: none

[a] Square feet.

THE WAY THE STAIR IS BUILT

Some of the greatest gains in accident reduction can be reaped simply by insisting that stairs are constructed according to the original design, and that a reasonable level of precision is present in the finished product. Frequently this is not the case. Handrails are not fixed firmly in place and pull loose from the wall. Stair carpets break loose from too few fastenings. Risers, treads, and nosing overhangs are built with little dimensional uniformity. Where risers and treads are constructed with heights or depths that vary from step to step, several studies have identified this as a cause of accidents. The problem, it seems, is that stairs, if they are wooden (or the original formwork, if they are made of concrete), are often constructed without sufficient precision. A second problem is that the top or bottom riser is sometimes substantially different from the rest, because the carpenter has not taken into account the thickness of the two floor finishes to be constructed later; or because carpet or some other material is placed over the original floor material during alterations. Dimensional

inconsistency of the nosing overhang has also been found to be a cause of accidents. Most building codes wisely insist that the differences in dimension between the largest and smallest in a flight, and between those in adjoining steps should not exceed three sixteenths of an inch. This is by no means too exacting a standard for contemporary building practices.

THE WAY THE STAIR IS MAINTAINED

Many stair accidents result from poorly maintained stairs. Levels of deterioration and damage that might be acceptable for level walkway surfaces cannot be tolerated on stairs; the risk of a serious injury is too great. Obviously the greatest danger comes from any structural weakness that may cause any part of the stair to break during use. Nearly as bad is the condition where the treads on the surface material are chipped, torn, splintered, loose, or excessively worn. Of almost as much concern are handrails and balusters that are broken, missing, or loose. Finally, there is the hazard caused by objects or deposits allowed to accumulate on the stairs, ie, toys, things stored on the stair, water, ice, snow, sand, dirt, grease, and industrial process powders etc. Stairs should never be used as a location for storing objects. Stairs must be kept clean and free from precipitation, dust, dirt, and anything that might act to trigger slips and trips. The surface finish of treads and carpets especially must not be allowed to deteriorate noticeably. Handrails and balustrades must be kept in good repair, firmly fixed, and structurally sound. Artificial illumination sources must be kept in good operating condition.

THE WAY PEOPLE USE STAIRS

There is not a great deal that one can point to as dangerous behavior on stairs, but there is some. In one study it was found, for example that there were more accidents than expected from those who wore shoes with flat soles with no heels. Why this should be is not clear. One might have expected high heel shoes or boots to be dangerous, but no evidence of this was found. The only other clothing factor that was significant was the length of clothing below the waist. It was found that there were more incidents than expected from those whose clothing only reached above the knee. But then it was found that this was the same as saying that children have more accidents. It was also found that there were more incidents from those who were accompanied by one or more persons. But, again, this probably mostly reflected children accompanied by adults. In the same study it was found that people tended to change their attention just before a misstep; some were watching other people just before the incident; and some had suddenly changed direction on the stair. All of these acts represent inattention or distraction and this is hazardous. Finally, as mentioned earlier, it was found, as others have, that it is dangerous to carry things on stairs. There were more incidents than expected by those carrying objects, regardless of how they were carried.

REDUCING INJURIES FROM STAIR FALLS

In the foregoing, it has been suggested that stair accidents can be reduced by intelligent design, construction, maintenance, and use. This is not enough. This is rather like designing, building, and using cars in such a way that they are inherently safer and less likely to be involved in accidents; but not worry about what happens to the passengers if there is an accident. Injuries are caused by the force of the impact of the body, or a part of the body striking the steps, handrail, balustrade, or walls of the stair, or anything projecting into the stair. In terms of a conceptual model for injury reduction, anything that at any place can decrease the force of an impact will reduce the magnitude of any injury. One must remove or modify anything that might stab, cut, lacerate, or bruise the victim. Stab wounds are those that would be caused if the victim fell against or grabbed some fairly sharp projecting feature. This type of design may be an integral part of some elaborate wrought iron balustrades, but it may simply be the sharp corner of a stringer. Most cuts will come from bumping up against edges and corners such as one sometimes finds on nosings, or metal nosing inserts. Balustrades and handrails frequently are made from rectangular or square bars or wood sections, and stringers are formed from timber or plates. Frequently these sections are left with corners that become sharp edges if struck forcibly by some part of the body. Lacerations will be caused by falling against any rough surface on the side walls, or the treads or balustrade. Commonly one finds walls, adjoining the stair finished with rough concrete, plaster, brick, or even wood. Some treads are given a surface akin to a cheese grater under the misguided belief that this will reduce slips. Balustrades may be constructed with ornamentation that will cause severe lacerations if one happens to fall against them. Finally the stair, or more usually the balustrading, may have construction bolts and protruding nuts that no one would make contact with in normal stair use, but during a fall these may become part of the hostile environment. Bruises, fractures, and concussions will result from striking against nosing edges, the rods and bars that are typical of many balustrades, square or rectangular handrails, and any other projections. In effect the force of the fall is absorbed by 'a blunt instrument', as shown in Figure 10. All of these hostile elements can and should be modified or eliminated from stairs, or at least from the areas where falls may occur. The stair should be free from projecting elements, sharp edges and corners, any rough surfaces, bars, rods, and plate of small section. Instead, like the interior of the car, smooth flat surfaces should be used, or gentle curves.

These design tactics will lessen the incidence and severity of many types of wound, but severe traumatic injury may still occur even if the body strikes a relatively smooth flat surface with sufficient force. Therefore another strategy (used in the design of automobile interiors) is directed at absorbing the energy of the impact by the use of padding. Just as a stunt man can fall several floors onto a pile of mattress-like devices without getting hurt, so the same principles can be used within a car or for a stair. Most injuries from stair falls are caused by collision

Figure 10. The sharp stair.

with the steps and landings, so the greatest rewards in injury reduction will be derived from softening these—rounding the nosings and reducing the hardness of the surfaces. These measures must be taken with due discretion. The rounding of the nosing must not substantially reduce the size of the tread; and the walking surfaces must not be made so soft that this interferes with a normal gait. There is unfortunately little research available that can help us to set out the limits of acceptable and effective softness. However the future probably lies with materials or underlayment similar to those used for tumbling, acrobatics, and judo in gymnasiums. These materials are relatively firm to walk upon and, because of their thickness, composition, and resilience, can readily absorb falls from heights. For the time being, one can at least make use of the ubiquitous carpets and underlayment available, so long as these materials have no adverse effect on gait. Conceptually the Soft Stair can be realized, and practically stairs can be designed so that accidents will be infrequent, and injuries minimized.

BIBLIOGRAPHY

1. S. Freud, "The Dream-Work: Representation by symbols in Dreams," *The Complete Psychological Works,* Vol. V, Hogarth Press, London, UK, 1948, p. 355.

2. G. Bachelard, *The Poetics of Space,* Beacon Press, Boston, Mass., 1969, p. 57.

3. S. Giedion, *The Eternal Present,* Pantheon Books, New York, 1964.

4. Vitruvius, *The Ten Books on Architecture,* M. H. Morgan, translator, Harvard University Press, Cambridge, Mass., 1926, p. 88.

5. G. C. Rothery, *Staircases and Garden Steps,* Stokes and Co., New York, undated, p. 16.

6. F. Mielke, *Die Geschichte der Deutschen Treppen,* Wilhelm Ernst, Berlin, Germany, 1966, p. 150.

7. *Ibid.* p. 42.

8. J. Templer, G. M. Mullet, J. Archea, S. T. Margulis, *An Analysis of the Behavior of Stair Users,* U. S. Department of Commerce, National Bureau of Standards, NBSIR 78–1554, Washington, D.C., 1978, p. 9.

9. J. Kaufman, J. Christensen, eds., *IES Lighting Handbook,* the Illuminating Engineering Society of North America, New York, 1972, p. 9–99.

10. J. Kaufman, H. Haynes, eds., *IES Lighting Handbook,* the Illuminating Engineering Society of North America, New York, 1981, p. A–5.

11. F. Blondel, *Cours d'Architecture Enseigne dans l'Academie Royale d'Architecture,* Lambert Roulland, Paris, France, 1675–1683.

12. J. Templer, *Stair Shape and Human Movement,* diss., Columbia University, New York, 1974, p. 140.

13. G. M. B. Webber, "Specifying the Geometry of Helical and Spiral Stairs," *IBCO: The Journal of the Institution of Building Control Officers,* X(1), 14–18 (1983).

14. J. Templer, *Provisions for Elderly and Handicapped Pedestrians,* Vol. 3, The Development and Evaluation of Countermeasures, Offices of Research and Development, Federal Highway Administration, Department of Transportation, Washington D.C., 1980.

15. J. A. Templer, J. Wineman, C. Zimring. *Design Guidelines to Make Crossing Structures Accessible to the Physically Handicapped,* Offices of Research and Development, Federal Highway Administration, Department of Transportation, Washington D.C., 1982.

16. M. J. Pfauth, J. M. Miller, "Work Surface Friction Coefficients: a Survey of Relevant Factors and Measurement Methodology," *Journal of Safety Research* 8(2) (1976).

17. J. M. Miller, "Slippery Work Surfaces: Towards a Performance Definition and Quantitative Coefficient of Friction Criteria," *Journal of Safety Research* 14, 145–158 (1983).

18. *ASTM Standard Consumer Safety Specification for Slip-resistant Bathing Facilities* (F 462–79 (Reapproved 1985) requires a static coefficient of friction of no less than 0.04 but this is for a bathing facility tested using a soap solution.

19. Ref. 17, p. 150.

20. F. C. Harper, W. J. Warlow, B. C. Clarke, *The Forces Applied to the Foot in Walking* HMSO, National Building Studies Research Paper No. 32, 1967.

21. K. Lunau, *Industrial Design: Development of a Safe Handrail for Stairs,* West Park Research, Toronto, for the National Research Council of Canada, contract no. 0SZ85–00148 (1986).

22. J. Pauls, *Are Functional Handrails within our Grasp?,* National Research Council, Ottawa, Canada, 1986, p. 6.

23. Teledyne Brown Engineering, *A Design Guide for Home Safety,* U. S. Department of Housing and Urban Development, Washington D.C., 1972, p. 2–13.

24. J. Archea, B. Collins, F. Stahl, *Guidelines for Stair Safety,* NBS Building Science Series 120, National Bureau of Standards, Washington D.C., 1979, p. 65.

25. S. G. Fattal, L. E. Cattaneo, G. E. Turner, S. N. Robinson. *A Model Performance Standard for Guardrails.* NBSIR 76–1131 Center for Building Technology, Institute for Applied Technology, National Bureau of Standards, Washington D.C., 1976.

26. J. Pauls, *Effective-width Model for Crowd Evacuation Flow on Stairs,* National Research Council, Ottawa, Canada, paper to the 6th International Fire Protection Seminar, Karlsruhe, Germany, Sept. 1982.

27. J. J. Fruin, *Pedestrian Planning and Design,* Metropolitan Association of Urban Designers and Environmental Planners, New York, 1971, p. 58.

28. B. S. Pushkarev and J. M. Zupan. *Urban Space for Pedestrians,* MIT Press, Cambridge, Mass., 1975.

General References

Unless otherwise referenced, the material in this article is based on the manuscript of J. Templer, *Views of the Staircase,* 1989.

See also STAIRS AND RAMPS—SAFETY DESIGN ASPECTS

JOHN TEMPLER
Georgia Institute of Technology
Atlanta, Georgia

STEEL, WEATHERING

Architects and design engineers have indicated a desire for a structural material for building exteriors that is relatively inexpensive and requires little or no expenditure of funds for maintenance. Such a product is required for commercial, monumental, and industrial buildings. One of the most significant developments in the construction industry in the last 25 years has been the use of corrosion-resistant, high-strength low-alloy steels in the unpainted condition. Characteristically, these steels contain small amounts of alloying elements that result in atmospheric corrosion resistance superior to unpainted carbon steel. When exposed to moderate industrial and urban environments, these steels develop a tightly adherent protective oxide film that substantially seals the surface against further attack. As a result of this behavior no protective finishes are necessary.

Weathering steels for use in the unpainted condition have been available now for some 55 years. They were introduced first in 1933 for coal-carrying hopper cars. Later the use was extended to building applications where they were covered by ASTM Specification A242 from 1941 through some 17 revisions. Recognizing the need for a steel composition capable for use in bridge construction, the steel industry developed A588 steel, which was adopted by introducing certain changes in the A242 specification. The 1942 revision of A242–41 recognized the enhanced atmospheric corrosion resistance such steel compositions possessed together with their higher yield strengths. The historical development and evolution of the current A242 and A588 ASTM specifications involve improved weldability and an increase in section thickness available with A588 steel while continuing to retain the high yield strength and enhanced atmospheric corrosion resistance.

Thus the current A588–88 specification covers high-strength low-alloy structural steel shapes, plates and bars for welded and bolted connections. The steel is intended primarily for use in welded bridges and buildings where savings in weight and increased corrosion resistance in the unpainted condition are desired. The A588 steel as described in the current edition of the *ASTM Book of Specifications* comes in five grades.

During this half century of high-strength low-alloy steel usage, considerable experience has been accumulated in a variety of applications. The earliest railroad hopper cars were still in service after 25 years though experiencing considerable denting because relatively thin plates were used. The oldest monumental buildings have now reached the age of 25 years and continue in excellent condition with little or no maintenance requirements. However, not all buildings have come through unscathed without some basic problem troubling their continued service life. The reasons for their difficulty lie in the oldest of adages; namely, the directions were not carefully followed, nor did the design personnel seek out the necessary information from the originators or sources of the weathering steel compositions.

OBJECTIVES

One of the objectives herein is to offer a brief historical overview of the evolution of the high-strength low-alloy steels beginning with the influence of copper. This is followed by the results of adding other alloying elements that have led to the currently available compositions. This will be followed by a description of the data from exposure tests performed in various environments. This resulted in recommendations for the kind of locations where satisfactory performance could be expected, and instances where difficulties might be encountered. Finally, some of the results of current experience will be described so that the information can be put to more effective use.

HISTORICAL BACKGROUND

As is well known, the current grades of the various A588 bridge steels contain copper, chromium, silicon, and nickel for enhanced corrosion resistance in the atmosphere, and manganese, vanadium, and carbon for their strengthening effects. The A242 architectural grades contain, in addition, phosphorous but do not contain vanadium. Lower amounts of carbon and larger amounts of chromium and nickel are used. The designation high-strength low-alloy (HSLA) steel is very broad and has never been precisely defined. Even the origin of the term is unclear. Traditionally, low-carbon mild steel has been used for structural applications. For example, ASTM A36 steel can contain up to 0.29% carbon and up to 1.20% manganese, and have a minimum yield strength of 36 ksi (250 MPa). The evolution of the HSLA steels arises from this carbon steel base. The term HSLA, however, is generally limited to low alloy steels produced as hot-rolled plates, shapes and bars, and as hot-rolled or cold-rolled sheet and strip.

It was noted in the early 1800s, and reported in 1827, that copper when present in foundry products resisted corrosion somewhat in sulfuric acid. Burgess and Aston in 1913 at the University of Wisconsin, studied the effects of different element additions and verified the benefits conferred by copper to plain carbon steel (1).

Buck reported on his work in the same publication as did Burgess, wherein he exposed corrugated steel sheets containing varying amounts of copper from 0.06% to 0.34% (2). The large 24 by 96 in. sheets (61 by 244 cm) of 16-gauge and 24-gauge steel were exposed at an angle of 18° serving as a roof for a shedlike structure. Exposure

tests were at a site near Atlantic City, New Jersey, and by coke-oven furnaces near Connellsville, Pennsylvania. Buck found the panels with 0.15 to 0.34% copper resisted the effects of the coke-oven atmosphere from one and a half to two times as well as the copper-free steel sheets.

In 1916, Buck and Handy reported the results of a large number of experiments in which both the copper and sulfur levels in the steel were varied (3). Test exposures were at the coke-oven site and in the less severe industrial city of McKeesport, Pennsylvania. They found among their test sheets that sulfur in the presence of less than 0.25% copper resulted in early failure. The minimum level of copper to protect against sulfur was established at 0.20% as still found in various ASTM specifications today.

In 1919, Buck reported on experiments with 12 different levels of copper ranging from 0.012 to 0.25% (4). The specimens were exposed at the coke oven site in the Gary, Indiana mill. Working with two sulfur levels, he decisively demonstrated the beneficial effect of copper in controlling the adverse effects of sulfur in steel. Buck further demonstrated the beneficial effects achieved by only 0.02 to 0.03% copper.

The foregoing discussion indicates the origin of statements appearing in the literature and specifications covering the weathering steels. In 1953, Larrabee reported on a number of experimental findings concerning the results obtained using 4 by 6 in. (10 by 15 cm) test panels exposed on test racks inclined 30° to the horizontal and facing south (5). He showed that on the basis of repeated tests at different periods that copper-bearing steel (0.20%) could exhibit levels of superiority over copper-free steels (less than 0.02%) from one and a half to four times.

It should be evident from this historical review that the experimental findings have established that when small, unpainted test panels of copper-free and copper-bearing carbon steel are exposed under the same conditions on a test rack next to one another, the aforementioned difference ratios will be achieved. The performance of any other configuration of specimens would have to be established by similar exposure tests.

USS COR-TEN STEEL

This proprietary high-strength low-alloy steel grade was the first composition to be commercially marketed back in 1933. The name was derived from properties conferred upon the steel after being alloyed with copper, silicon, chromium, nickel, and phosphorus. The "COR" was derived from the increased corrosion resistance while the "TEN" came from the increased tensile strength. In 1962, Larrabee and Coburn's paper showed the results of exposing 270 different compositions of steel in three environments to assess individually and together the contribution of the above alloying elements (6). The sulfur content of the master batch of steel was fixed at 0.02%. The significance of 0.012 and 0.04% copper is dramatic in their demonstration of the importance of minute changes in low levels of copper. This is evident in the abbreviated tabulation shown in Table 1, Material Numbers 1, 2, 3, 4, and 5. Also evident is the influence of each of the foregoing elements with the two levels of copper.

Table 1. Average Reduction in Thickness After 15.5 Years, mils[a]

| | Wt, % | | | | | Location | |
Material No.	Cu	Ni	Cr	Si	P	Kearney, New Jersey (Industrial)	Kure Beach, North Carolina 250-m (800 ft) Lot (Moderate Marine)
1	0.012					28.8	52.0
2	0.04					8.8	14.3
3	0.24					6.1	11.2
4	0.008	1				6.1	9.6
5	0.2	1				4.4	8.0
6	0.01		0.61			41.7	15.8
7	0.22		0.63			4.6	9.0
8	0.01			0.22		14.7	21.5
9	0.22			0.20		6.0	9.9
10	0.02				0.06	7.8	14.1
11	0.21				0.06	4.9	9.1
12		1	1.2	0.05	0.12	2.6	3.9
13	0.21		1.2	0.62	0.11	1.9	3.3
14	0.2	1		0.16	0.11	3.3	5.7
15	0.18	1	1.3		0.09	1.9	3.8
16	0.22	1	1.3	0.46		1.9	3.7
17	0.21	1	1.2	0.48	0.06	1.9	3.3
18	0.21	1	1.2	0.18	0.10	1.9	3.8

[a] 1 mil = 25.4 μm, 1 mil = 0.001 inches; to convert mil to μm, multiply by 25.4.

It is evident from this comprehensive study that from the standpoint of reduction in corrosion rate a number of compositions are capable of achieving the desired result. However, from the standpoint of the metallurgist and production personnel, certain preferred compositions are necessary to achieve workability, mechanical properties and cost of alloying elements.

SPECIFICATIONS FOR THE BUILDING AND BRIDGE STEELS

The most popular of the high-strength low-alloy steels are those in the sheet and plate categories. The ASTM specification covering the early architectural applications was A242. Its current scope covers "high-strength low-alloy structural steel shapes, plates, and bars of welded, riveted, or bolted construction intended primarily for use as structural members where savings in weight or added durability are important." The chemical requirements are shown in Table 2.

The specification further states that additional alloy-ing elements include chromium, nickel, silicon, vanadium, titanium, and zirconium. The tensile requirements exceed those of A36 steel up to four inches in thickness.

The scope in Specification A606-85 high-strength low-alloy steel covers hot- and cold-rolled sheet and strip in cut lengths or coils intended for use in structural and miscellaneous purposes where savings in weight or added durability are important. These steels have enhanced atmospheric corrosion resistance and are supplied in two types. The degree of corrosion resistance is based on data acceptable to the consumer. The maximum limits of carbon, manganese, and sulfur are shown in Table 3.

The specification further states that the manufacturer shall use such alloying elements combined with those in Table 3 to satisfy the mechanical properties, such as the tensile requirements, and when requested supply acceptable data of corrosion resistance to the purchaser.

The last specification, A588–88a, has the same scope as A242 but includes the added phase ". . . intended for use in welded bridges and buildings where savings in weight or added durability are important." Listed in this specification are five grades: A, B, C, D, and K, each of which is supplied by a different producer. An illustration of the compositions available in the sheet and plate grades examples have been taken from the brochure of United States Steel and shown in Table 4.

Table 2. Chemical Requirements (Heat Analysis)

Element	Composition, Type 1
Carbon, max	0.15
Manganese, max	1.00
Phosphorus, max	0.15
Sulfur, max	0.05
Copper, max	0.20

Table 3. Chemical Requirements (Heat Analysis)

Element	Composition max, %
Carbon	0.22
Manganese	1.25
Sulfur	0.05

Table 4. Chemical Compositions, wt%, Ladle Analysis

Element	USS COR-TEN A (A242 Type)	USS COR-TEN B (A588 Type)
Carbon	0.12 max	0.19 max
Manganese	0.20/0.50	0.80/1.25
Phosphorus	0.07/0.15	0.04 max
Sulfur	0.05 max	0.05 max
Silicon	0.25/0.75	0.30/0.65
Copper	0.25/0.55	0.25/0.40
Chromium	0.30/1.25	0.40/0.65
Nickel	0.65 max	0.40 max
Vanadium		0.02/0.10

PROPERTIES AND BEHAVIOR OF THE WEATHERING STEELS

The weathering steels have been licensed by United States Steel (USX) in Canada, Europe, and Japan. Exposure tests of the type described earlier have been conducted in each of these countries as well as in some South American countries. In every instance the HSLA steel composition proved superior to the copper-bearing steel though not necessarily to the same degree as found in the United States. Experience from Buck's early work up to the present has shown that the protective oxide film results as a consequence of the nightly condensation of dew that contains varying amounts of sulfuric acid. This acid is produced as a result of the sulfur oxide exhaust gases emanating from power stations burning fossil/fuels such as sulfur-bearing coal and oil.

Much of our knowledge has been based originally on the performance on test racks of small test panels exposed at an angle of 30° facing south. The test racks were placed either in a grassy plot or over sand or soil. It was evident early that the skyward face of a test panel exhibited a relatively smooth though slightly pitted surface after the initial two years exposure in a moderate industrial environment. In contrast, the groundward faces in all environments exhibited a coarse, granular appearance with much of the early corrosion product still loosely attached to the panel. While the top face was rapidly dried by the combined effects of wind and sun, the bottom face tended to retain some dampness. The quantitative behavior of such test panels are made up of the combined losses in weight from both faces.

Larrabee established these relationships in 1941 for specimens exposed at Kearney, New Jersey, which at the time had a severe industrial environment, and in 1943 at what alternated between a semirural to a semiindustrial environment depending upon industrial activity in the nearby mill town of Vandergrift, Pennsylvania. Larrabee exposed panels for four years at South Bend, Pennsylvania, beginning in 1939, and for 3-½ years at Kearney, New Jersey, and reported the results in 1943 (7). Averaging the losses for each test site, the results are shown in Table 5.

It is clear from the foregoing that, on average, when loss in weight data were being presented in terms of reduction in thickness, the groundward face or bottom of the test panel was contributing approximately 63% of the loss while the skyward surface or top of the panel was contributing 37%. These data together with the description of the nature and texture of the oxide film tell in significant detail what the boldly exposed faces are likely to experience and what the sheltered faces are likely to exhibit. It is significant that these respective ratios were consistent for each of the three steel compositions in two environments.

However, since structures are erected in a vertical rather than on an inclined plane, it is important to refer to studies in which panel tests were performed in both planes at the same time. Such data are available for panels exposed for one and two year intervals. The results are shown in Table 6.

It is evident from these data that the combined corrosion rate for a vertical panel is about 20 to 25% greater than for an inclined plane. The reason is that often the rain is vertical in character and, therefore, does not wash the test panel just as the groundward face of an inclined test panel is never washed. Hence, the corrosion rate is likely to be higher, and particularly so close to the shoreline where the panel is likely to receive seawater mist.

Table 6. Effect of Position on Corrosion Rates

Location	Environment	Ratio of Losses Vertical/Inclined
Kearney, N.J.	Industrial	1.25
Vandergrift, Penn.	Industrial	1.26
South Bend, Penn.	Semirural	1.20
Kure Beach, N.C.	Marine	
800 ft from ocean	Moderate	1.25
80 ft from ocean	Severe	1.40

Table 5. Establishment of Weight Loss Ratio Between Skyward and Groundward Faces of Test Panels in Different Environments[a]

	COR-TEN Steel		Copper-Bearing Steel		Carbon Steel		Average Loss	
	Top	Bottom	Top	Bottom	Top	Bottom	Top	Bottom
South Bend, Penn.	34.3	65.7	39	61	36.4	63.6	36.6	63.4
Kearney, N.J.	37	63	36.6	63.4	39	61	37.5	62.5
							37.1[b]	62.9[b]

[a] Weight loss, percent
[b] Average.

Table 7. Failure Time for Copper-bearing Steel Sheet by Position

Sheet Face	Months to Severe Rusting	Performance Ratio
Bottom of trough	25	1
Sides of trough	25	1
Vertical surface facing north	130	5.2
Inclined surface facing south	170	6.8

As more and more interest was being shown in the possibilities of the unpainted weathering steels in the middle 1930s, Pilling and Wesley exposed a sheet of copper-bearing steel on a 30° inclined test rack (8). The lower edge was shaped to form a trough that would catch rainwater. The upper edge was folded back in a vertical plane facing the north. A small horizontal ledge was fixed over the vertical portion to shelter it somewhat from rain. The failure time of the various faces is shown in Table 7.

It is quite evident that the washing and drying action of the rain, wind, and sun play a role in the performance of the various surfaces. Based on the data in Table 7, it can be seen that the HSLA steels would perform better but would experience similar results in the trough beneath water as well as on the sides of the trough where dampness constantly wicks upwards.

With the foregoing experimental field data in hand, corrosion engineers of the major suppliers of the weathering steels began to develop their recommendations for the effective use of these steels in the many conceivable types of structures that would be designed by architects and design engineers. The controlling parameters that the corrosion engineers found to characterize the weathering steels and, therefore, control the manner in which they would perform are

1. For optimum performance in the unpainted condition the structure should be boldly exposed to the weather as much as possible.

2. The development of the protective oxide film is best achieved under conditions of normal exposure wherein the surfaces are wet at night by dew formation and dry during the daylight hours owing to wind and/or sun.

3. Because this wet-dry cycle cannot occur when the steel is buried in the soil, or immersed in water, the protective oxide will not form, and the performance will resemble that of mild carbon steel exposed to the same conditions. An example of a soil effect is that of Figure 1 which shows the bottom of a full-scale weathering steel column on a concrete pad. Note how moisture has wicked upward from the soil below and stimulated the formation of lamellar sheets of rust. To avoid this condition and obtain long term protection it is necessary to apply a water-resistant coating of the coal-tar epoxy type to the buried portion of the column and extending up a short distance above grade.

The aforementioned "rules-of-the-road" are a result of studying the performance of small test panels exposed in both the vertical and inclined condition combined with

Figure 1. Lamellar corrosion due to soil moisture wicking up against unpainted steel column.

results exhibited by the sheet of copper-bearing steel rolled into a trough to retain water. The same kind of information was obtained from the over 1,000,000 railroad hopper cars and numerous coal-carrying barges that have been built as well as the numerous light standards and transmission towers of varying size that have been installed over the past half-century.

To "fine-tune" the numerous observations made and arrange them in a fashion the design engineer and architect can find their way through this extensive experience, it will be useful to organize these findings in terms of the aforementioned controlling parameters. The first is the effect of weather and the environment. Historically, when this was a coal-burning economy and smoke stacks were relatively short, such as 100 to 200 ft (30 to 60 m), the weathering steels developed their tightly adherent oxide film most rapidly. Thus, the aggressive industrial atmosphere turned out to be the best place to use the unpainted weathering steel. In distant rural areas, far from powerhouse exhaust stacks, the weathering steels continued to develop their protective oxide coating and outperformed the uncoated carbon steels despite the latter corroding at a much lower rate. In marine environments, likewise, where there was an industrial component to the environment, the weathering steel outperformed the carbon steel. Again, this information came from test-panel exposure sites in the eastern and western coastal areas; namely, Kure Beach, North Carolina, and Point Reyes, California.

While the west coast and the east coast tests and structures in these areas continue to perform satisfactorily, the Gulf Coast has some unique problems. Test on the intercoastal waterway in Freeport, Texas, did not reveal what has been seen on actual structures in more exposed locations close to the Gulf of Mexico. However, bridges very close to the onshore breezes of the Gulf of Mexico, particularly the below deck structure and the side facing the southerly breeze, accumulated deposits of sea salts that resulted in a granular texture leaving a suggestion that corrosion was continuing at a very slow rate and that the formation of the protective oxide coating was, likewise, proceeding at a slow rate. A rather pock marked appearance characterizes such a sandblasted girder.

This experience demonstrated the need to calibrate the specific environment of interest prior to commitment to erect a structure. This finding poses another requirement implied by the results of regional studies, and that is the general performance of metal structures in the vicinity where one wishes to erect a structure. The behavior of steel fences, cars, trucks, small boats, mail boxes, gutters, house properties, utility poles, etc, provide useful clues as to the aggressiveness of the local environment. Combining these observations with questions addressed to people living and working in the vicinity as to their maintenance problems, paint requirements and paint life, one can obtain a reasonable assessment of the local environment. Then, if at least 18 to 24 months is available a test rack can be installed and test panels exposed through a couple of seasons.

NOTABLE STRUCTURES IN WEATHERING STEEL

John Deere Building

The first major step toward obtaining public acceptance of the appearance of rusted steel was made in 1958 by Eero Saarinen who used unpainted USS COR-TEN high-strength low-alloy steel in his unique design for the John Deere and Company's Administration Building in Moline, Illinois. A general view of the eight-story administration building designed by Saarinen for the John Deere and Company is shown in Figure 2. The first floor is an exhibition hall connected to an upper story of the administration building through a glass-enclosed flying bridge framed in low-alloy A steel. To preserve an outdoor view and avoid the use of drapes and window blinds, sunshading louvers of low-alloy A steel were incorporated into the exterior framing of the administration building. All other exterior metal elements such as columns, posts, beams, and girders were also made of low-alloy A steel.

Chicago Civic Center

Low-alloy A steel has been used to sheath the entire Chicago Civic Center (Fig. 3). This 31-story building stands 647 feet and 11 inches above its plaza. The amount of steel exposed to the weather approximates 275,000 square feet. This includes column covers, spandrel panels, louvers,

Figure 2. John Deere headquarters building utilizing high-strength low-alloy USS COR-TEN A steel throughout.

Figure 3. Chicago Civic Center utilizing USS COR-TEN A steel.

and window frames. On the granite plaza, three flagpoles were erected from low-alloy B steel. Also, a 50-foot tall sculpture was erected in low-alloy B steel from a design created by Pablo Picasso.

Fresno Convention Center

An interesting application for low-alloy A sheet steel in an unusual environment is the Fresno Convention Center situated in the heart of the agricultural though arid San Joaquin Valley in California. It consists of three large assembly-hall-type buildings. Two of the structures utilized low-alloy A steel in a mansard-style roofing application; the third employs the industrial-building-type wall panels as vertical siding.

Ford Foundation Building

The headquarters building for the Ford Foundation was erected in midtown Manhattan, New York City. The building contains 11 floors with its offices arranged on two sides in an L-shape from the second to the ninth floors. Offices on the tenth and eleventh floors ring the building. Within the interior courtyard, a "temperate zone" group of plants, shrubs, and trees has been installed.

The entire inner court is framed in low-alloy A steel girders and glass. The exterior likewise is framed in large horizontal low-alloy A steel girders that join the concrete columns of the building, which are clad with a mahogany-tinted South Dakota granite. The interior court remained open to the atmosphere for 20 months to permit weathering the low-alloy A steel columns and spandrels. During this period the formation of the oxide film proceeded at a rapid rate stimulated by the urban atmosphere that characterizes the midtown area. After the interior court was closed, the low-alloy A steel interior walls were brushed (with bristle brushes) to remove the final traces of construction debris and loose oxide.

Although the outside low-alloy A steel members will continue to weather and assume a somewhat darker tone, it is expected that the interior members will retain their

Figure 4. USX Tower, Pittsburgh, Pennsylvania, employing USS COR-TEN A steel in the spandrels and COR-TEN B steel in the saltwater-filled columns.

present appearance because of the prevailing relative humidity of about 50%, the recirculating air, and the lack of moisture condensation necessary for the further weathering of the steel.

The USX Tower, Pittsburgh, Pennsylvania

The USX Tower in the words of its management "has been conceived and designed as a corporate facility. It is as much a facility as any mill or mine . . ." That statement emphasizes the fact that "the building was *not* designed as a corporate monument with a prestige budget."

This remarkable 64-story triangular building, whose design was selected on the basis of wind-load studies, is 841 feet above its triangular plaza of 41,000 square feet, and houses the second largest office structure in the world, Figure 4.

The low-alloy A steel was selected for the exterior spandrel, mullions and window framing; the low-alloy B steel was selected for the salt-filled supporting columns. To increase the amount of interior working space, the 18 supporting columns were placed on the outside of the building. These H-shaped box columns were fabricated of welded low-alloy B steel plates. The box sections are divided into 200-ft-tall zones. The entire column system is a

self-contained fire-protection unit holding 500,000 gallons of water and 740 tons of potassium carbonate. This salt will perform the double function of acting as an antifreeze component and a corrosion inhibitor.

Each column will be divided by diaphragms into four zones, each approximately 200 ft high located at the 16th, 34th, 50th, and 64th floors. These levels were selected to maintain the hydrostatic pressure within reasonable limits. For each 200-ft section there is a piping system consisting of a lower loop and an upper loop that connects all 18 columns together and to an expansion tank. Should a fire occur, the available water with its latent heat of evaporation will dissipate the heat without overheating the steel columns. This system thus saves conventional fireproofing and column covers permitting the full architectural expression of bare steel.

Finally, the stability of the exterior columns required that they be attached to the floor system at only every third floor. These are termed primary floors. The two floors between are referred to as secondary floors. The beams extending from the core perimeter wall to the outside wall are 13 ft on center. The construction of the secondary floors, relative to the primary floors can be compared to construction of a series of three-story buildings within a three-story framework. The outside ends of the beams are supported by two-story columns which, in turn, rest on a box spandrel girder at the primary floor. The box spandrels that surround the primary floors also stabilize the exterior columns.

It is of further interest that the family of steels has played a large part in the design of the steel building. These begin with the structural grade carbon steel having a yield point of 36.0 ksi and range to the heat-treated constructional alloy steel having a yield strength of 100 ksi. The major portion of the structural frame; however, is comprised of the A36 carbon steel and the low-alloy B steel with a yield point of 50 ksi. To further enhance the corrosion resistance of the unpainted exterior low-alloy A steel the interior face, where the protective oxide film cannot form, is galvanized.

GUIDELINES FOR EFFECTIVE USE

The results of long-term corrosion tests and observations of low-alloy A and B steel structures have provided valuable guidelines for the effective use of these steels. Some of the more important of these are described below.

Cleaning of Exposed Surfaces

To obtain optimum and uniform appearance, regardless of environmental exposure conditions, all low-alloy A and B steel components for exterior architectural applications should be freed of mill scale. Acid pickling or blast cleaning are satisfactory methods of removing mill scale. Blast cleaning should be done in accordance with provisions of the Steel Structures Painting Council Surface Preparation Specifications, Near-White Metal Blast Cleaning SSPC-SP 10 (1985).

Foreign matter such as grease, oil, chalk, crayon, concrete, mortar, and plaster on weathering steel should be removed because their presence will interfere with the normal development of a uniform oxide film. Welding flux, slag, and spatter should also be removed from all exposed surfaces.

Joining

Welding. Low-alloy A and B steels can be welded, with the use of good shop practice, by the shielded metal-arc, submerged-arc, gas metal-arc, and electrical resistance processes. For bare-steel appplications, when the welded area is required to match or approach the color of low-alloy A and B steels after atmospheric exposure, or have atmospheric-corrosion resistance similar to that of the base metal, single-pass welds may be made by using the mild-steel welding materials provided that the procedure used ensures suitable composition enrichment of the weld metal. In built-up or multiple-pass welds where such a color match is desired, ASTM A316 E8016-Cl or E8016-C2 electrodes or wires and wire-flux combinations providing 2-1/2 or 3-1/2 % nickel weld-metal or a suitable Cr–Si–Cu–Ni composition electrode should be used. The above procedures for multiple-pass welds may also be used for single-pass welds. Further, in multiple-pass butt welds where surface color match is important, consideration should be given to the use of the mild-steel welding materials for most of the joint and to the use of the alloy-steel welding materials for the completion of the joint. For more detailed welding instructions, the supplier of the steel should be consulted.

Bolting. Low-alloy A steel bolts and nuts are satisfactory for bearing-type connections. Field observations of unpainted COR-TEN steel bolted joints indicate that joints must be stiff and tight. To provide this stiffness and tightness, the following guidelines are suggested:

1. The pitch on a line of fasteners adjacent to a free edge of plates or shapes in contact with one another should not exceed 14 times the thickness of the thinnest part, and, in any event, not exceed seven inches.
2. The distance from the center of any bolt to the nearest free edge of plates or shapes in contact with one another should not exceed eight times the thickness of the thinnest part, and, in any event, should not exceed five inches. (Edges of elements sandwiched between splice plates need not meet this requirement.)
3. Preferable fasteners are ASTM A325 Type 3 bolts installed to the "Specifications for Structural Joints Using ASTM A325 or A490 Bolts" approved by the Research Council on Riveted and Bolted Structural Joints.

Compatibility with Other Materials

In the formation of the protective oxide film about two mils (0.002 in.) of metal is lost. About one-half is consumed in the formation of loosely attached, inert iron oxide particles. Normally, these dust away in the wind. However, during periods of drainage by rain water and nightly dew, these particles can contact adjacent materials of construction such as concrete walls, sidewalks, and window panes. Drainage of such material continues for the better part of two to three years with substantial diminution thereafter. Permanent provisions should be made through design, detailing, and the selection of materials and colors to accommodate this run-off drainage or divert it from sensitive surfaces.

Adjacent building components subject to minimal staining that are readily cleaned include semigloss and glossy porcelain enamels, stainless steels, anodized aluminum, extruded neoprene, ceramic tile and glazed brick, and glass (which will require special maintenance). Materials that are difficult or impossible to clean include concrete and stucco, unpainted galvanized steel, unglazed brick, porous stone, and wood. Brown or colorless anodized aluminum often can be used in contact with the weathering steels, and as a gutter for the drainage diversion of building drippage.

Badly stained and neglected glass can be cleaned using stainless-steel wool wetted with a stream of water while rubbing in a vertical plane only. Likewise, a proprietary abrasive such as Zud is capable of removing such stains by rubbing in a vertical plane. Acid solutions should never be used as the drainage may become lodged in a crevice and continue to attack the steel. Reflective-type coated glass should never be installed with the coated surface to the exterior because abrasive cleaning could damage the coating.

Sidewalk staining has been overcome in various imaginative fashions. For example, the plaza of the Deere Administration Building is composed of a gray-brown traprock which exhibited a not-too-intense brown band about 10 to 15 ft wide, situated immediately below the exterior sunshade and louvre elements. The stain was easily removed by the application of a proprietary acid cleaner contained in the wash water. The cleaner is commonly used for removing stains from bricks and is available at building supply dealers.

The 85,000 square-foot Rockville granite plaza of the Chicago Civic Center exhibits a considerable amount of pedestrian dirt intermixed with a hardly noticeable brownish stain immediately beneath the curtain wall and extending a distance of about 10 to 15 ft beyond the building line. Maintenance personnel periodically use an acid-based cleaner to wash the entire plaza. This cleaning procedure is effective in restoring the granite plaza to its original appearance.

The Fresno Convention Center has experienced a small amount of sidewalk and column stain; however, it was planned to attach a gutter to retain the drippage from those structural elements that overhang the sidewalks and the brick columns.

Vertical and horizontal structural weathering steel members in small buildings represent another source of stain as in their use in a car showroom employing large plate-glass windows. To dispose of drainage product that would normally stain the sidewalk, a narrow plot of soil extending out a distance of about 18 in. was used for the planting of flowers. In fact drippage from vertical and horizontal columns and girders can be handled in several other ways. For example, in the rear or at the sides of a one- or two-story building, or if parking is permitted in the front of such a building, an asphalt- or black-topped walk or drive can be used in place of concrete, in which case the brown stains are effectively masked by the black surface. Drippage in the front of a building from a horizontal girder can also be effectively handled with a 24-in. wide bush planter located immediately below the girder. Another effective means of handling the drainage of small vertical columns as well as any other free-standing vertical members is to surround the structural member with large egg-shaped or small rounded river bed stones. These multicolored stones, whose colors are predominantly reddish brown, are most effective in masking drainage stains.

A technique to prevent staining of walls is to arrange for the horizontal COR-TEN steel fascia elements to extend beyond the curtain wall a distance of a few inches. This permits taking advantage of the fact that hanging water droplets will fall in a vertical plane and not contact the adjacent wall. Figure 5 illustrates the stain-free appearance of a white, glazed brick wall which is topped by a COR-TEN A steel fascia girder that extends a distance of about four inches. After five years exposure, the entire height of wall continues to be free of brown drippage stains; only the white gravel on the foundation shelf immediately below the fascia and hidden from view is discolored.

Limitations

The test of time has proven the usefulness of the unpainted weathering steels in such applications as buildings, bridges, rail hopper cars, transmission towers, highway appurtenances, and the like. However, the indiscriminate use of these steels through lack of attention to their characteristic inability to remain wet for extended periods such as a bridge in a rain forest or when exposed to

Figure 5. Staining of glazed brick wall avoided by extending horizontal girders several inches beyond plane of wall.

the constant on-shore sea breeze off the Gulf of Mexico, or crevices that retain water for long periods, or loosely bolted joints that catch and retain nightly dew condensate, or when contacted by damp vegetation overgrowth, all contribute the one hazard to the successful use of these unique steel compositions.

The most effective means for avoiding such problems is to design around this characteristic. By visiting the sites of the aforementioned buildings together with a careful reading of the brochures supplied by the producers of the weathering steels, architects and design engineers can see at first hand the value of adhering to the information derived through experience and tests.

BIBLIOGRAPHY

1. C. F. Burgess and Aston, Jr., "Influence of Various Elements on the Corrodibility of Iron," *The Journal of Industrial and Engineering Chemistry* **5,** 458 (1913).

2. D. M. Buck, "Copper in Steel—The Influence on Corrosion," *The Journal of Industrial and Engineering Chemistry* **5,** 447 (1913).

3. D. M. Buck, and J. O. Handy, "Research on the Corrosion Resistance of Copper Steel," *The Journal of Industrial and Engineering Chemistry* **8,** 209 (1916).

4. D. M. Buck, "The Influence of Very Low Percentages of Copper in Retarding the Corrosion of Steel," *Proceedings of the American Society for Testing and Materials* **19,** 224 (1919).

5. C. P. Larrabee, "Corrosion Resistance of High-Strength Low-Alloy Steels as Influenced by Composition and Environment," *Corrosion* **9,** 259 (1953).

6. C. P. Larrabee and S. K. Coburn, "The Atmospheric Corrosion of Steels as Influenced by Changes in Chemical Composition," *First International Congress on Metallic Corrosion,* London, Butterworth, 1962.

7. C. P. Larrabee, "The Effect of Specimen Position on Atmospheric Corrosion Testing of Steel," *Transactions of the Electrochemical Society,* 297 (1945).

8. N. P. Pilling and W. A. Wesley, "Atmospheric Durability of Steels Containing Nickel and Copper," *Proceedings of the American Society for Testing and Materials* **40,** 643 (1940).

See also CORROSION; STAINLESS STEEL; STEEL IN CONSTRUCTION; STRUCTURAL STEEL

SEYMOUR K. COBURN
Corrosion Consultants, Inc.
Pittsburgh, Pennsylvania

In retrospect a debt of gratitude is owed to such pioneers as D. M. Buck of the original United States Steel Corporation for his work with copper-bearing steel in the first decade of the 20th century. Building upon this was the work by George Schramm and C. P. Larrabee that led to the development of the high-strength low-alloy steels by mid-century. Finally, these steels reached the public over the past quarter century through the commercial efforts of S. C. Lore, and the creativity of some of the great architects practicing during this past quarter century.

STYRENE RESINS

The use of styrene plastics in the building and construction industry dates back to the introduction of extruded foams and expandable foam beads in the late 1940s and early 1950s (1). Although styrene monomer and polystyrene were commercially introduced in 1937, the initial cost of manufacture of the early products was too high to warrant economically viable construction systems. With the rapid expansion of styrene monomer production during World War II, to supply the demands of the GR-S synthetic rubber program, came the economies of scale and improved manufacturing efficiency. This dramatically increased the availability of styrene monomer, while significantly reducing costs, and made the use of styrene resins economically feasible for construction uses. From this inception period, the uses of styrene resins in the building and construction industry have increased to the current consumption levels of hundreds of millions of pounds of fabricated products.

Insulation systems utilizing extruded polystyrene and molded bead foams consume more than 300 million pounds of polystyrene and represent the largest construction usage of styrene resins (2). The use of acrylonitrile–butadiene–styrene (ABS) copolymers in plastic piping systems for the residential construction market is the second largest area of use, consuming more than 160 million pounds for extruded pipe and injection molded fittings. An additional 40 million pounds of ABS and styrene copolymer impact modifiers (toughening agents) are consumed in polyvinyl chloride (PVC) formulations. The third and most recent use of styrene-based resins is that of acrylonitrile–saturated elastomer–styrene (AES) and acrylonitrile–styrene–acrylate (ASA) copolymers in residential exterior siding and windows. Styrene resins are also consumed in a host of decorative applications such as tub and shower surrounds, bathroom and kitchen fixtures, and light diffusers and decorative tile.

THE CHEMISTRY AND MANUFACTURE OF STYRENE RESINS

Polystyrene prepared by the homopolymerization of styrene monomer (Eq. 1) is a clear, hard, polymeric material of high molecular weight. Typical commercial materials incorporate in excess of 1000 monomer units ($n = >1000$) in the polymer chain (3,4):

$$\underset{\mathrm{C_6H_5}}{CH{=}CH_2} \rightarrow \underset{\mathrm{C_6H_5}}{H(CH{-}CH_2)_nH} \qquad (1)$$

Polystyrene exhibits excellent resistance to moisture, good dielectric properties, and maintains its rigidity up to its glass-transition temperature of 98°C. The last property is key to its use in insulation systems as opposed to PVC, which has a performance temperature threshold of 65–70°C. The physical properties of polystyrene are shown in Table 1 (5–9).

Table 1. Physical Properties of Polystyrene

Property	Value	Ref.
Specific gravity (g/cm³)	1.05	3
Tensile yield, MPa	42.0	3
Modulus, MPa	3170	3
Elongation, %	1.8	4
Notched Izod impact, J/M	21	4
Vicat softening point, °C	96	4
Coefficient of linear thermal expansion, per °C	$6–8 \times 10^{-5}$	5
Dielectric constant	2.54–2.55	6
Heat capacity, kJ/(kg·K)		
at 0°C	1.185	7
at 50°C	1.256	7
at 100°	1.838	7
Heat of combustion, kJ/mol	-4.33×10^3	8
Heat of fusion, kJ/mol	8.37 ± 0.08	9
Refractive index, n_D	1.59–1.60	6
Thermal conductivity, W/(m·K)		
at 0°C	0.105	6
at 100°C	0.128	6

Two chemical processes are used in the manufacture of polystyrene for use in the construction industry; both involve free-radical polymerization. Mass or bulk polymerization is the predominant process used to make resin for extruded foam and molded applications. In this continuous process, the styrene monomer is polymerized in either a continuous stirred-tank reactor or a series of linear plug-flow reactors to 60–80% conversion. The residual styrene monomer is then stripped in a devolatilizer to be recycled and the polymer extruded and chopped into pellets (10). Most resin used for expandable bead foam is manufactured in a batch suspension process (11–13). In this process, styrene monomer is polymerized by suspending it in water along with two or more initiators in a jacketed reactor. The temperature is programmed from 80°C to 120°C for 16–24 hours. The blowing agent may be imbibed into the expandable beads and the product centrifuged and dried. The resultant beads are then used to make beadboard. Foamed polystyrene beads have also been admixed with concrete to produce lightweight masonry structures (14).

Acrylonitrile–butadiene–styrene resins are comprised of a rigid, brittle, styrene–acrylonitrile matrix that is toughened by small 0.1–1 μ polybutadiene rubber particles. Typically, the matrix composition is 20–30% acrylonitrile and 70–80% styrene. Rubber is generally 15–25% by weight of the total composition. Copolymerization of acrylonitrile with the styrene increases both the functional heat-distortion temperature (HDT) and resistance to chemicals relative to polystyrene or high impact polystyrene that also contains rubber. Additionally, ABS has higher tensile strength and toughness than styrene homopolymers, making it an excellent material for piping systems and other applications requiring high strength and durability. The polybutadiene rubber phase imparts excellent low temperature toughness that eliminates breakage during installation and handling in cold weather. ABS resins offer excellent ease of fabrication and have a low tendency to orient or develop mechanical anisotropy on molding. This provides fittings and parts with uniform toughness (15,16). ABS may also be readily painted, vacuum metallized, or electroplated for a variety of uses such as in plumbing fixtures (17–20). Electroplating significantly strengthens the ABS part (18).

The physical properties of ABS polymers are specifically tailored for a given application by varying the monomer compositions, rubber concentration, rubber particle size, molecular weight, and molecular-weight distribution. In addition, various additives and stabilizers may be incorporated to further improve performance. This variation of performance has made ABS one of the most versatile of the engineering thermoplastics. Table 2 compares the physical properties of several types of ABS products used in manufacturing building products. ABS is produced and sold in the United States under the trade names CYCOLAC (Borg Warner Corporation), MAGNUM (The Dow Chemical Company), and LUSTRAN (Monsanto).

Commercial manufacture of ABS resins is carried out via emulsion and mass (bulk) polymerization as well as combinations of the two processes. In the predominate process, emulsion polymerization, the cross-linked polybutadiene rubber particles are initially formed as a polybutadiene latex in an aqueous batch process. A shell of styrene–acrylonitrile (SAN) is then chemically grafted to the rubber particle by feeding the monomers to the latex reactor under heat and pressure. The resultant product containing 30–70% rubber may be mixed with a SAN latex or coagulated and later compounded with a SAN polymer. The latex is coagulated by addition of acid or inorganic salts, and is washed and dried to obtain a powder. Colorants and additives are then added to the ABS in an extruder or Banbury mixer prior to pelletizing (21,22).

The mass process for ABS entails the dissolving of polybutadiene rubber or styrene–butadiene block copolymer in the styrene and acrylonitrile monomer mixture. This rubber solution is then passed through a series of agitated linear plug-flow reactors where the rubber particle size is controlled by agitation speed (23). The polymer solution is then devolatilized, extruded, and pelletized as in the polystyrene process. As shown in Figures 1 and 2, the rubber particles formed in mass polymerization are larger and highly occluded with SAN when compared to the solid polybutadiene particles formed in the emulsion process. In general, mass-produced ABS has better processibility, color and thermal stability, and toughness per unit rubber. Emulsion products have higher gloss, tensile strength, and higher toughness.

In general, ABS resins cannot be used in exterior applications unless painted or coated to provide protection from oxidative degradation of the polybutadiene rubber. Therefore, weatherable styrene resins have been developed using saturated rubbers, such as ethylene–propylene elastomers (EPDM) and butyl acrylate. Acrylonitrile–EPDM–styrene (AES) polymers are manufactured by a mass or suspension process in which styrene and acrylonitrile are grafted onto the EPDM rubber chains (24–26). Butyl acrylate systems are manufactured by an emulsion process where a butyl acrylate rubber particle is initially prepared and then grafted with a SAN shell analogous to the emulsion ABS process previously described (27).

Acrylonitrile–EPDM–styrene resins have excellent toughness at high and low temperatures and good retention of properties over long periods of outdoor exposure. The higher heat-distortion temperatures of these systems relative to PVC have enabled fabricators to manufacture dark-colored residential siding without the oil canning or chalking experienced in earlier vinyl systems (Figs. 3 and 4). Acrylonitrile–styrene–acrylate (ASA) polymers, while having lower toughness and much reduced low temperature toughness, are also used in exterior systems. The comparative physical properties of these weatherable resins are shown in Table 3.

AES resins are sold under the trade name ROVEL (The Dow Chemical Company). ASA resins are produced and sold under the trade names GELOY (General Electric) and CENTREX (Monsanto).

Table 2. Physical Properties of ABS Resins

Property	High Impact Extrusion[a]	Extrusion Blending[b]	Molded Fittings[c]	Plating Grade[d]
Specific gravity (g/cm^3)	1.02	1.05	1.05	1.05
Tensile yield, MPa	36	29	38	41
Ultimate tensile, MPa	34	29	33	33
Modulus, MPa	1.7	2.0	2.0	2.4
Elongation, %	35	50	40	56
Notched Izod impact				
at 23°C, J/m	427	134	223	214
at −40°C, J/m	107	70	90	85
Falling dart impact				
at 23°C, J (73.4°F)	>36	34	35	36
at −20°C, J (−4°F)	>36	19	27	17
Melt flow rate, g/10 min (230°C/3.8 Kg)	0.6	4.2	2.6	5.5
Heat-deflection temperature at 1820 kPa, annealed, °C	100	96	96	102
Coefficient of thermal expansion (cm/cm/°C)	0.0009	0.0006	0.0006	0.0007

[a] CYCOLAC LDG 4113N (Borg Warner Corporation)
[b] MAGNUM PG 912 (The Dow Chemical Company)
[c] MAGNUM FG 960 (The Dow Chemical Company)
[d] ABS XU-74036 (The Dow Chemical Company)

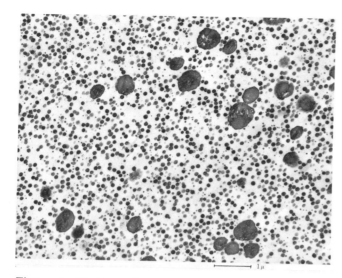

Figure 1. Electron micrographs (28,200× magnification) of emulsion process ABS with small dense rubber particles.

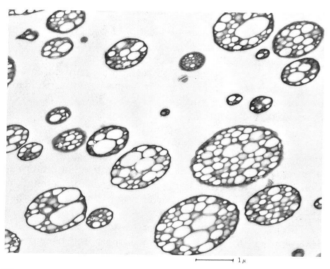

Figure 2. Electron micrographs (28,200× magnification) of mass process ABS with larger occluded rubber particles.

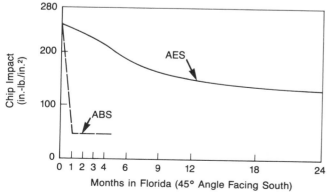

Figure 3. Comparison of chip impact retention of ABS and AES plastics in Florida under 45° south outdoor exposure conditions.

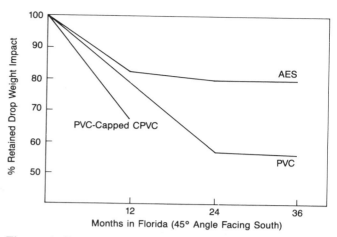

Figure 4. Comparison of impact retention of AES, PVC, and PVC-capped CPVC siding in Florida under 45° south outdoor exposure conditions.

ABS USE IN PLASTIC PIPING SYSTEMS

Pipe Fabrication and Specifications

Acrylonitrile–butadiene–styrene copolymers have been used successfully in piping systems since the early 1960s. This family of resins is known for good chemical resistance and excellent toughness over a wide temperature range. ABS is also less expensive, lighter, and easier to assemble during installation than copper, cast-iron, steel, or clay pipe. The largest use of ABS piping systems is in drain, waste, and vent (DWV) applications in residential and commercial plumbing systems. The specific resins used for pipe and fittings are classified under ASTM D-1788 and D-3965 to meet the requirements of the finished articles as specified by the respective ASTM standards. ABS pipe applications are identified by the following American Society for Testing and Materials (ASTM) standards:

ASTM D-2661—ABS Plastic Drain, Waste, and Vent
    Pipe and Fittings
ASTM D-2680—ABS Composite Sewer Pipe

Table 3. Physical Properties of Weatherable Styrene Resins

Property	AES[a]	ASA[b]	ASTM Method
Specific gravity (g/cm³)	1.02	1.02	D-792
Tensile yield, MPa	33.1	30.0	D-638
Tensile modulus, GPa	1.86	1.52	D-638
Yield elongation, %	39	35	D-638
Notched Izod impact			D-256
at 23°C, J/m	769	368	
at −40°C, J/m	91	21	
Instrumented dart impact			D-3763
at 23°C, J	38.6	28.4	
at −29°C, J	46.6	19.3	
Heat-deflection temperature			D-648
at 264 psi, annealed, °C	99	100	

[a] ROVEL 401 (The Dow Chemical Company)
[b] GELOY 1120 (General Electric)

ASTM D-2750—ABS Plastics Utilities Conduit and Fittings

ASTM D-2751—ABS Sewer Pipe and Fittings

ASTM F-628—ABS Plastic Drain, Waste, and Vent Pipe Having a Foam Core

ASTM D-1527—ABS Schedule 40 and Schedule 80 Plastic Pipe

ASTM D-2282—ABS Plastic Pressure Pipe in Standard Dimension Ratio (SDR) Sizes

ASTM D-2468—ABS Plastic Pipe Fittings Schedule 40

ASTM D-2469—ABS Plastic Pipe Fittings Schedule 80

ASTM D-2235—Solvent Cement For ABS Plastic Pipe and Fittings

ASTM F-409—Thermoplastic Accessible and Replaceable Plastic Tube and Tubular Fittings

ASTM F-480—Thermoplastic Water-Well Casing Pipe and Couplings Made in Standard Dimension Ratios (SDR)

ASTM F-481—Installation of Thermoplastic Pipe and Corrugated Tubing in Septic-Tank Leach Fields

Initially, ABS pipe and fittings were solid wall constructions. The pipe was manufactured by feeding the ABS pellets through a single- or twin-screw extruder into a pipe die of the desired diameter to shape the product. The pipe was then pulled through a vacuum tank containing a sizing sleeve and placed into a water bath for cooling by a haul-off system. The pipe was then cut to the desired length by a rotary cut-off saw. Due to escalating hydrocarbon raw material costs and price pressure from PVC systems, the solid wall segment has been declining in importance since the late 1970s in favor of lower density foam-core pipe.

Co-extrusion technology allowed the manufacture of foam-core pipe surrounded by two concentric solid skin layers of solid ABS (28,29). In this process two extruders feeding a single coextrusion pipe die are used. The foam-core layer is achieved by incorporating a chemical blowing agent such as azodicarbonamide with the ABS in the core extruder. When the polymer melt reaches the appropriate temperature, the blowing agent decomposes to release nitrogen and carbon dioxide in the melt. The fine cell foam core is simultaneously coated with the solid skin layers from the other extruder in which no blowing agent is used. The net effect of this process is a reduction in the amount of resin needed to produce a given length of pipe. Unit weight reductions of up to 30% can be achieved by this process, whereas the structural integrity of the pipe is actually increased by the foam core's added rigidity. By 1987, most ABS pipe manufacturers had converted to this process to gain the more competitive reduced cost of manufacture. The pipe fittings for both types of pipe are manufactured by standard injection-molding procedures. Here the low tendency for ABS to orient and not display anisotropy is important to ensure uniform directional toughness and integrity.

It is common practice in the industry to blend a high impact extrusion resin with a special reduced viscosity blending grade such as those described in Table 2. This practice helps increase the extrusion rates from the extruders and reduces surging of the pipeline, producing a more uniform and reliable product. All DWV pipe made from ABS is colored black as specified by the ASTM standards. Other uses of ABS pipe may be colored at the discretion of the manufacturer or as prescribed by a particular code body. Pipe manufactured to ASTM standards is marked with the standard specifications for the respective products.

Acrylonitrile–butadiene–styrene pipe and fittings are available in the sizes appropriate for the specific end use applications. For DWV uses, sizes include 1.25, 1.5, 2, 3, 4, and 6-in. diameter products. The geometries of the various fittings are described in ASTM Standard D-3311. For sewer pipe and fittings, available sizes include 3, 4, 6, 8, 10, 12, and 15-in. diameters. These sewer products are also available with belled-end pipe and fittings for joining with elastomeric gaskets or with uniform-diameter ends for solvent cement welded joints. ABS utilities conduit and fittings are supplied in 1, 1.5, 2, 3, 3.5, 4, 5, and 6-in. diameter sizes. Pipe for pressure uses is produced in 1/8 to 12-in. diameter sizes.

Physical and Chemical Performance Characteristics

Regardless of the pipe application, ABS has distinct advantages over traditional materials such as cast iron, steel, copper, or clay. It is lightweight and has excellent corrosion resistance, chemical resistance, joint integrity, and toughness, enabling it to withstand heavy earth loads as well as abuse in shipping and handling. It is easily fabricated and installed and should damage occur, it is readily repaired. Compared to other plastic piping systems, its advantages include reduced weight, higher toughness with excellent impact resistance at low temperature, good rigidity at elevated temperature, and fabrication of high integrity joints with a one-step cement as opposed to two-step cement or ultrasonic welders in other systems.

The physical strength properties for ABS resin material required for DWV pipe (its largest end usage) and fittings are shown in Table 4 as specified by ASTM standards D-2661 and F-628 for the solid wall and foam-core types, respectively (30). Resin requirements for the other type of ABS pipe products may be found in the ASTM standards for products such as those listed previously.

The chemical resistance properties of ABS resins and, hence, the pipe and fittings produced from them, are a function of the specific chemical, its concentration, the exposure temperature, the length of contact, and the service exposure conditions that may lead to stress concentrations in the pipe fitting. In general, ABS pipe used in plumbing applications experiences exposure to dilute concentrations of common household chemicals in water. ABS pipe used in sewer-type applications accessible to automobiles or machinery may experience exposures to petroleum products that most likely have been washed down with water, making the exposure less severe. In any case, ABS piping withstands these types of chemical exposures without deleterious effects. A list of ABS exposure resistance to some common materials and chemicals is shown in Table 5 (31). Additional chemical exposure data can be found in Ref. 31.

Table 4. Minimum Requirements for ABS Resin Compounds

Property	ASTM Method	DWV Pipe	DWV Fittings
Notched Izod impact (at 23°C, J/m)	D-256	320	210
Heat-deflection temperature under 1.82 MPa Load, °C	D-648	82	82
Tensile stress at yield min., MPa	D-638	31	33
Specific gravity (g/cm³)			
Minimum	D-792	1.0	1.0
Maximum		1.2	1.2

Agency Code Approvals

Acrylonitrile–butadiene–styrene pipe and fittings are manufactured to meet ASTM standards for the intended use application. These detailed specifications for each product are the criteria for ensuring that the products are satisfactory for a specific end use. Manufacturers that meet these criteria can gain approval of third-party certifying organizations and can apply the certification logos of these organizations on the products signifying such approval for the end use application. In many municipalities, such third-party certifications are necessary to meet local building codes. One such organization is The Na-

Table 5. Chemical Resistance of ABS Plastic Pipe

Chemical	Concentration	Performance Rating[a]		
		23°C	48.9°C	71.1°C
Acetic acid	5%	R	R	
Acetone	100%	N	N	N
Alcohol, ethyl		R to N	N	N
Alcohol, isopropyl		R		
Alcohol, methyl		R to N	N	N
Ammonia, aqueous		R		R
Bleach liquor, 12.5% active chlorine		R		N
Calcium salts (aqueous)		R		R
Calcium chloride		R	R	
Caustic soda (dry and solution)		R		R
Copper salts, aqueous		R		R
Copper sulphate, aqueous	All	R	R	
Diethylene glycol		R	R	
Esters		N		N
Fatty Acids		R		R
Ferric chloride	All	R	R	
Heptane		R		
Hydrochloric acid	20%	C	C	
Kerosene		R		
Ketones		N		N
Magnesium salts		R		R
Milk		R	R	R
Mineral oil		R		
Oils and fats		R		N
Oleic acid		R	C	R
Oxalic acid		R		R
Perchloroethylene		N		
Petroleum		R		N
Potassium salts		R		R
Sewage, residential		R		
Soap solutions		R		N
Sodium carbonate	25%	R	R	
Sodium chromate		R	R	
Sodium hydrogen sulfite		R	R	
Sodium hypochlorite		R to N	R	N
Sodium phosphate, saturated		R	R	
Sulfite liquor		R		C
Sulfuric acid	15%	R	R	
Sulfuric acid	50%	R	C	C
Tanning liquor		R		R
Triethylene glycol		R		
Trisodium phosphate		R		
Turpentine		N		N
Urine		R		R
Vinegar		R		N

[a] Ratings: R = generally resistant; C = less resistant than R but still suitable under some conditions; N = not resistant; blank = not tested

tional Sanitation Foundation (NSF). Its logo for DWV pipe is, for example, NSF-DWV. The International Association of Plumbing and Mechanical Officials (IAPMO) is another such organization that certifies products with a logo bearing the letters UPC within a shield. In Canada, the Canadian Standards Association (CSA) approves and monitors all ABS pipe.

Acrylonitrile–butadiene–styrene pipe installations in nonfire-resistive construction are recognized in three model codes: (1) the Uniform Plumbing Code of the International Conference of Building Officials (ICBO); (2) the Standard Plumbing Code of the Southern Building Code Congress International (SBCCI); and (3) the Basic/National Plumbing Code of the Building Officials and Code Administrators International (BOCAI). In addition, ABS has state or local approval for installation in all 50 United States and the 10 Canadian provinces.

Although plumbing codes govern the types of piping systems installed in construction, such systems in fire-resistive construction are subject to building codes that define the requirements for fire performance of construction to maintain structural integrity of buildings when penetrations occur. ABS piping can be installed with accepted fire-stopping materials, techniques, and devices where penetration of fire-rated structures are necessary. The satisfactory performance of these installations depends on strict adherence to the installation requirements for them. Typical generic fire-stopping materials used are gypsum-based cement, fiberglass thermal insulation, mineral wool, and metal. Also available are proprietary fire-stopping materials and devices that have been tested for a given type of installation and rated for a specific fire-endurance period. In all cases, generic and proprietary materials and devices that are acceptable for fire stopping have been tested nationally by recognized laboratories using ASTM E-119 or ASTM E-814 test standards. A compilation of such tested materials and devices is available in a design and installation data manual issued by the Plastics Pipe and Fittings Association (32).

Uses of ABS Piping in Construction

Acrylonitrile–butadiene–styrene piping systems are used primarily in nonpressure applications in both nonfire-resistive and fire-resistive structures. Drain, waste, and vent plumbing systems are installed in conventional residential homes, mobile and modular homes, and recreational vehicles as well as in multistory apartment buildings and commercial buildings such as hotels and motels.

The toughness of ABS and its resistance to chemicals and heat have made it suitable for drainage of industrial and commercial buildings. Waste collection and disposal through ABS sewer systems (residential as well as municipal) has been done successfully for more than 25 years. With the improving technology of fire-stopping materials and devices and the acceptance by the model building codes, the use of ABS in fire-resistive construction will continue to expand.

Acrylonitrile–butadiene–styrene systems are suitable for pressure piping applications in schedule 40 and schedule 80. Industrial uses in pneumatic systems have been

successfully installed. Potable water distribution systems require that all plastic piping systems be certified by an accredited laboratory for that use. Such potable systems are marked with the certifying laboratory's seal of approval.

The excellent electrical insulating properties of ABS make it acceptable for handling communication and electrical wire and cable for underground installation as well as for use in construction. Optical fiber communication and business computer linkage constructed of ABS conduit have performed well.

STYRENE COPOLYMERS FOR EXTERIOR SIDING AND ACCESSORIES

Weatherable Styrenic Construction Uses

Since the introduction of PVC exterior house siding in the early 1970s, the use of plastics in building and construction has experienced substantial growth and consumer acceptance due to its low maintenance costs, durability, and economical installation. Due to the low heat-distortion temperature of PVC, these systems have been limited to white and light pastel colors. Attempts to manufacture dark colors such as brown or red have met with difficulty due to heat sag or "oil canning" or with whitening or chalking of the surface after outdoor exposure. Although it has sufficient temperature resistance, ABS is not an acceptable material for siding due to the vulnerability of the butadiene rubber to oxidative and uv degradation. Exterior exposure of ABS results in a rapid decline in toughness and surface yellowing. Lamination of the surface with weather-resistant films provides only marginal improvement.

To meet this need, saturated elastomer reinforced SAN copolymers were developed. These systems contain either grafted EPDM rubber (AES) or butyl acrylate rubber (ASA). Figure 3 compares the toughness retention during outdoor exposure of AES and ABS. Figure 4 shows the excellent retention of impact resistance of AES polymer as compared to PVC and PVC co-extruded over a CPVC substrate. Based on extensive test-home programs and more than six years of successful performance, the first commercially viable dark-colored AES house siding was intro-

Figure 5. Typical single family residence protected with dark red ROVEL siding.

Figure 6. Millwork lineal with extruded AES profile as weather protection.

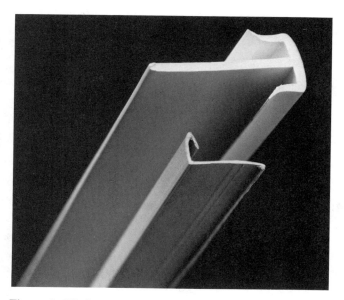

Figure 8. Window weather strip using dark colored AES to provide stable colors and heat resistance.

duced to the building industry in 1987. This introduction has met with good acceptance due to consumer demand for dark colors to harmonize with earth-tone windows and roofing (Fig. 5). The principal uses of weatherable styrenics in building and construction are in siding, frames for dark-colored windows, door components, and trim accessories. In each case, weatherable styrenics are selected because they retain their color, maintain a useful balance of physical properties, are resistant to high surface temperature, and provide low maintenance at a relatively low initial cost.

Windows constructed of weatherable styrenics fall into two categories: low maintenance millwork windows and all-plastic windows. In dark-colored millwork windows, cladding is made by extruding a profile in the shape of the wood frame, which may incorporate an integral co-extruded gasket or seal. This construction, known as dual

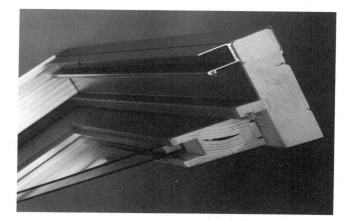

Figure 7. Millwork window construction with AES capping on the lineal and as a jambliner. Overlapping corners allow for expansion and contraction.

durometer extrusion, snaps or is glued in place to protect the wood. In addition to the sash and frame, weatherable styrenics are used for colored jambs in double-hung windows as well as hardware components where they provide corrosion resistance particularly in salt-air environments. Figures 6 and 7 show a cross section of a wooden window profile capped with a dark-colored weatherable styrenic.

Solid plastic windows use weatherable styrenics modified with inorganic fillers to reduce the coefficient of expansion and increase stiffness. The material is extruded into profiles for the sash, as well as the more complex profiles for the frame that are designed to accept metal stiffeners to achieve additional structural integrity. Dual durometer extrusion techniques are used to make glazing beads where the rigid styrenic supports and a flexible lip seals the glass. Figure 8 shows a weatherable styrenic weather strip used in window assemblies.

A major material of construction for dark-colored doors continues to be the structural aluminum frame; however, weatherable styrenics are being used for dent- and scratch-resistant panels. These panels, which are styrenic sheet over a rigid structural foam board or particleboard, have proved to be superior over traditional aluminum kick panels. Figure 9 shows a storm-door panel with a particleboard-backed AES sheet. Door sweeps incorporating flexible plastic fins by dual durometer extrusion are commercially available with a weatherable styrenic "U" channel and flexible PVC seal fin.

Fabrication Methods

Processing of AES–ASA resins can be divided into profile extrusion, sheet extrusion, co-extrusion, and injection molding. Profiles are used to extrude specific geometric cross sections to be used as component parts in the fabrication of windows and doors, or for decorative coverings such as siding and mobile-home skirting.

Figure 9. Storm door composite panel constructed by lamination of an AES skin over a particle board substrate.

Sheet extrusions and co-extrusions typically require further processing such as thermoforming to produce component parts. Frequently, AES–ASA materials are used as cap stocks over less expensive PVC or ABS substrates in co-extrusions. This is particularly typical for residential house siding where a modified PVC substrate is used under an AES cap layer. AES co-extruded over ABS sheet is widely used for in ground steps in swimming pools and for spa and hot tub shells. In these cases, AES offers superior resistance to chlorinated water in addition to toughness and weatherability. Other typical uses include louvers, shutters, and garage doors. When co-extrusion techniques are used, it is important that the thickness of the AES layer be a minimum of 15 mils after thermoforming to protect the nonweatherable substrate layer.

Extrusion of AES and ASA polymers can be done on typical thermoplastic extrusion equipment. It is recommended that these products be dried in a forced-air desiccant hopper dryer for a minimum of 4 h at 85°C. Best results are achieved with single-screw, one-stage, nonvented extruders having a minimum length/diameter ratio of 24:1. High shear, high mixing screws work best to provide the shear necessary for producing a uniformly fluxed melt to the die. Mixing pins placed in the metering flights, or a mixing head, provide additional means of dispersing pigment and homogenizing the melt. Typical screw recommendations are shown in Table 6 for a 2.5-in. extruder. Typical processing conditions for the various fabrication methods are shown in Table 7.

Blends of weatherable styrenics with PVC for ignition resistance and scratch resistance are also used commercially. For these blends, it is recommended that a PVC-type screw be used that is cored to accept oil cooling with the appropriate screw tip. Both the screw and the barrel of

Table 6. Typical Dimensions for a 2.5-in. Single-stage Screw

Feed zone	5 flights at 0.300″
Transition zone	6 flights at constant taper
Metering zone	13 flights at 0.100″
Mixing pins	2–4 rows
Compression ratio	3:1
Length/diameter	24:1

Table 7. Typical Processing Conditions for AES/ASA Polymers

Injection Molding Conditions

Cylinder temperatures, °F (°C)	
Nozzle	490 (254)
Front	510 (266)
Middle	480 (249)
Rear	450 (232)
Mold temperature, °F (°C)	160 (71)
Injection pressure, psi (MPa)	
Primary	1200–1500 (8.3–10.3)
Secondary	800–1000 (5.5–6.9)
Back pressure, psi (MPa)	50–150 (0.3–1.0)
Injection speed	slow to moderate (25–40 gms/sec)
Cycle times, s	
Primary injection	8
Secondary injection	12
Clamp	40
Melt temperature, °F (°C)	480–530

Sheet Extrusion Conditions

Barrel temperatures, °F (°C)	380 (193) Rear
	420 (216) Front
Stock temperature, °F (°C)	450 (232)
Die temperature, °F (°C)	420 (216)
Roll temperatures, °F (°C)	
(Up stack	
configuration) Top	200–230 (93–110)
Middle	200–230 (93–110)
Bottom	180 (82)

Profile Extrusion Conditions

Barrel temperature, °F (°C)	
Zone 1 hopper	375 (191)
Zone 2	385 (196)
Zone 3	395 (202)
Zone 4	400 (204)
Zone 5 adapter	430 (221)
Die temperature, °F (°C)	420 (216)
Stock temperature, °F (°C)	435–460 (224–238)

the extruder should be nitrided to prevent corrosive attack from liberated HCl and to reduce wear.

Injection molding is used to produce a variety of component parts, including crankcase covers for casement windows, patio door handles, and fittings for gutter systems. AES polymers show a linear decrease in melt viscosity (Figs. 10 and 11) with increasing temperature. This is different from similar impact ABS grades that stiffen at higher temperatures. As a result, molds fill more easily than might be predicted from melt-flow-rate measurements. Typical molding conditions are shown in Table 7.

PHYSICAL PROPERTIES OF AES AND ASA POLYMERS

AES/ASA polymers exhibit an outstanding blend of physical properties and color retention required for outdoor applications. Differences in typical physical properties between AES and ASA polymers are given in Table 8.

Table 8. Physical Properties of Weatherable Styrenics

Property	Units	Test Method	AES	ASA
Tensile yield	psi	ASTM D638	5400	4600
	(MPa)		(37)	(32)
Tensile rupture	psi		4700	3300
	(MPa)		(32)	(23)
Tensile modulus	psi		300,000	250,000
	(MPa)		(2068)	(1724)
Yield elongation	%		2.9	3.1
Ultimate elongation	%		32	23
Flexural strength	psi	ASTM D790	7700	8000
	(MPa)		(53)	(55)
Flexural modulus	psi		280,000	264,000
	(MPa)		(1930)	(1820)
Izod impact strength	ft lbs/in. (J/m)	ASTM D256		
73°F			13.9 (750)	7.6 (410)
0°F			2.6 (140)	1.4 (75)
−40°F			1.1 (60)	0.7 (38)
Deflection temperatures	°F (°C)	ASTM D648		
Unannealed, 264 psi	(1.8 MPa)		198 (92)	190 (88)
Annealed, 264 psi	(1.8 MPa)		209 (98)	210 (99)
Hardness	Rockwell "R"	ASTM D785	100	85
Melt-flow rate	gms/10 min	ASTM D1238 230°C/3.8 Kg	1.0	0.9
Specific gravity		ASTM D792	1.02	1.06
Coefficient of Thermal Expansion	10^{-5} in/in/°F (10^{-5} cm/cm/°C)	ASTM D696	4.4 (7.9)	5.9 (10.6)
Flammability		UL-94	HB	HB

TESTING PROCEDURES AND CODES

Since weatherable styrenics must perform reliably for years in actual use, the testing of these materials to assure performance is quite critical. This includes color retention as well as toughness retention. Due to the relatively new commercial status of weatherable styrenics, there are few ASTM standards written specifically for styrenics, however, PVC procedures are followed as guidelines pending issuance of formal standards. The most important of these are:

ASTM D-4226—Test method for impact resistance of rigid PVC building products

ASTM D-3679—Specifications for rigid PVC siding

ASTM D-4099—Specification for PVC prime windows

ASTM D-3678—Specifications for rigid PVC interior profile extrusions

ASTM D-737—Practice for installation of storm windows, replacement windows, multiglazing, storm doors, and replacement doors in residential buildings

ASTM D-1042—Test method for linear-dimensional change of plastics

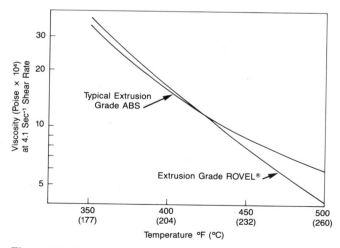

Figure 10. Viscosity versus temperature comparison of ABS and AES resins under extrusion.

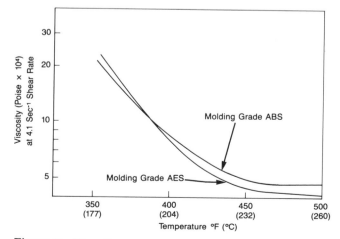

Figure 11. Viscosity versus temperature comparison of ABS and AES resins under injection molding conditions.

Table 9. Hunter Color Values AES vs PVC after Florida Exposure of 12 Months (45° South)

	White AES	White PVC	Brown AES	Brown PVC
Hunter color-meter reading un-aged sample	$L = 93.46$ $a = -.41$ $b = 4.56$	$L = 87.1$ $a = -5.9$ $b = 7.4$	$L = 24.69$ $a = 6.49$ $b = 7.05$	$L = 39.5$ $a = 1.4$ $b = 7.4$
Change in reading after 12-month Florida aging	$\Delta L = -.86$ $\Delta a = .48$ $\Delta b = -.12$	$\Delta L = 1.6$ $\Delta a = 0.3$ $\Delta b = -0.8$	$\Delta L = .65$ $\Delta a = -.66$ $\Delta b = .23$	$\Delta L = 1.8$ $\Delta a = -0.4$ $\Delta b = 0.1$
Total color difference after aging	$\Delta E = .99$	$\Delta E = 1.8$	$\Delta E = .95$	$\Delta E = 1.8$

ASTM D-1435—Recommended practice for outdoor weathering of plastics

ASTM D-2244—Instrumental evaluation of color differences of opaque materials

Laboratory weathering instruments such as the Xenon Arc or QUV weatherometer are often used to accelerate outdoor exposure studies of test specimens. Care must be taken to relate these to actual outdoor exposure data. Typically, the Xenon Arc provides the most suitable results. Certain test methods will produce degradative differences in samples, however, show very little correlation to outdoor exposure data.

Color retention of AES–ASA polymers have also been studied to determine the extent of color shift due to outdoor exposure.

A common means used to measure color shift is colorimetric data, which is determined by instrumented devices such as a MacBeth or Hunter Colorimeter. These devices are capable of mathematically measuring color shift from red to green (a value), yellow to blue (b value), and light to dark (L value). The total color change is measured as $\Delta E = (\Delta L^2 + \Delta a^2 + \Delta b^2)^{1/2}$ when comparing a standard (control) sample to any other sample. Hunter color-meter readings comparing white and brown AES to PVC after exposure in Florida (45° South) for 12 months are given in Table 9. Color retention of ivory AES vs ASA or Xenon exposure is given in Table 10.

Table 10. Color Retention of Ivory AES vs ASA Xenon Exposure

Exposure Period	Hunter Color Values	AES	ASA
Initial	L	87.67	88.80
	a	-1.22	-1.75
	b	15.16	16.71
1000 h	ΔL	3.40	0.05
	Δa	-0.58	-0.20
	Δb	-0.67	0.65
	ΔE	3.52	0.68
2000 h	ΔL	3.51	-1.31
	Δa	-0.29	-0.13
	Δb	-2.65	1.43
	ΔE	4.41	1.94
3000 h	ΔL	3.25	-1.23
	Δa	-0.18	0.00
	Δb	-3.31	0.96
	ΔE	4.64	1.56

STYRENE PLASTIC FOAM

Since the commercial inception of foamed polystyrene in 1940, this application has grown to consume hundreds of millions of pounds in a variety of uses in the construction industry. Used primarily in insulation and roofing, the board is either extruded directly from polystyrene polymer or molded from expandable polystyrene beads.

In 1984, the total usage of foamed styrene plastics was estimated to be 2.01×10^9 board feet and projected to grow at 6% annually (33,34). Roofing represents the largest single usage (750 MM board feet), followed by residential housing (500 MM board feet), commercial construction (300 MM board feet), and an additional 410 MM board feet consumed in miscellaneous other applications. Extruded polystyrene board provides high insulating value, excellent compressive strength, and good handling properties.

Nomenclature

The nomenclature of plastics foam is not centered around uses, but rather is defined by material type such as the American Society for Testing and Materials (ASTM) for Polystyrene Foam Thermal Insulation ASTM C578-83 (35). A foamed plastic is defined as a plastic the apparent density of which has been decreased by the presence of numerous cells distributed throughout its mass (36). These cells are small pockets of gas suspended in the polymer matrix. If the cell structure readily allows gas movement from one cell to another, the foam is termed "open cell." If gas movement is restricted, the foam is described as "closed cell." This molecular architecture is controlled by the material, type of blowing agent, and the method of manufacture.

Foam Manufacture

The original process of manufacture as used by the Dow Chemical Company when it introduced STYROFOAM in 1940 was the extrusion process. This is still the largest and most important process used today. A schematic of the extrusion process in shown in Figure 12. In this process a mixture of polystyrene, blowing agent, and various additives are fused into a molten mass in a plasticating extruder. The molten mass is then forced under pressure through an extrusion die onto a conveying system. After exiting the die the blowing agent expands, producing the cellular structure while the polymer melt is simulta-

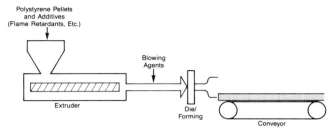

Figure 12. Manufacturing process for extruded polystyrene foam board.

neously cooled, fixing the final board dimensions and the foam morphology. The resultant foam is of the closed-cell type. This cell structure is critical for obtaining good insulating properties and mechanical properties. The cellular structure of an extruded foam is shown in Figure 13. Typical physical properties of polystyrene foamed plastics are shown in Table 11.

In contrast to extrusion, expanded bead foam is a two-step process. Rather than starting with polymer, pre-

formed beads containing the blowing agent are utilized. In the first step (pre-expansion) the beads are partially expanded by exposing them to heat in the form of steam or hot air. After pre-expansion, a mold is filled with the pre-expanded beads and additional heat applied to form the desired product. The process schematic is shown in Figure 14. The secondary expansion of the beads actually causes them to fuse together to form a continuous polystyrene matrix. A photomicrograph of the bead network is shown in Figure 15. While the final properties of bead board are inferior to extruded foam as seen in Table 11, the ability to form a variety of shapes by using molds of differing configuration is a decided advantage of the bead process over extrusion.

Application

There is a wide variety of uses of polystyrene foams in the construction industry. Thermal retrofitting of old structures (Fig. 16), siding (Fig. 17), sheathing, and foundation insulation are among the uses of extruded foam in the residential market. Commercial applications include interior and cavity wall insulation, foundation insulation, and membrane roofing systems. Due to the moisture resistance of extruded foam, it is the only recommended material suitable for use above waterproofing membranes (37). Generally, a moisture content of 4%–6% reduces insulation capability by about 20%. Figures 18, 19, and 20 indicate the effect that a certain percentage of water has on the insulating value of a plastic foam. Since water can enter the foam by a variety of mechanisms, it is important to consider the impact of moisture vapor, direct absorption, and structural damage caused by freeze–thaw cycles (38–40). These expanded plastics are also used as core materials in panel construction because of their excellent structural properties (41,42). Lamination of weatherable plastic systems to the foam core are currently being utilized in garage and external doors in the residential market.

Molded-bead polystyrene foam is also used in residential and commercial applications for siding and foundation insulation. Molded-foam plastics have also found utility in low temperature applications and sandwich panel construction. Specialized products utilizing bead plastics are manufactured by laminating a wide variety of facing

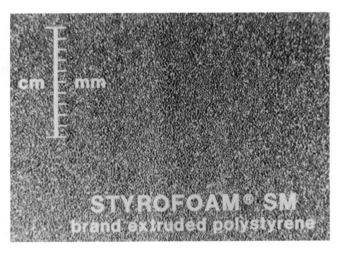

Figure 13. Photomicrograph showing the cellular structure of 1.9 lb/ft³ (30.4 Kg/m³) extruded polystyrene foam.

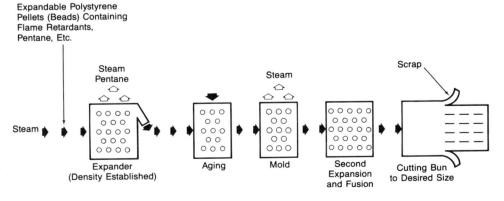

Figure 14. Manufacturing process for molded bead polystyrene foam.

Table 11. Typical Product Properties—Summary of Literature Values of Various Foamed Plastics for 1-in. (2.54-cm) Thick Product

	k Factor (BTU/h·ft²·°F/in.) (75°F Mean Test Temperature) (λ in w/mk) ASTM Test Density lbs/ft³ (kg/m³)	R-Value (h·°F·ft²/BTU) (75°F Mean Test Temperature per Inch of Thickness) (m²k/w) C177–76 or C518–76	Vertical Compression Strength (10% or Yield, Whichever Occurs First) (psi) (PePa) C177–76 or C518–76
Molded-bead polystyrene	1.0 (16.0)	.26 (0.037)	3.8 (0.68)
	1.25 (20.0)	.25 (0.036)	3.9 (0.69)
	1.5 (24.0)	.24 (0.035)	4.2 (0.73)
	2.0 (32.0)	.23 (0.033)	4.3 (0.77)
Polyisocyanurate–polyurethane	2.0 (32.0)	.14[a] (0.020)	7.2[a] (1.3)
Extruded polystyrene	1.9 (30.4)	0.20[c] (0.029)	5.0[c] (0.9)
	1.4 (22.4)	0.20[d] (0.029)	5.0[d] (0.9)
Phenolic	2.7 (43.2)	0.12[a] (0.017)	8.3[a] (1.5)

[a] Aged at 180 d at 75°F before testing.
[b] This measurement of wvt is not only of foam core, but on product with facers.
[c] Value of material aged 5 yr at 75°F.
[d] Aging criteria not available from manufacturing.
[e] This value in perms.

materials such as foil, paper, and fibrous board to serve as chemical and thermal separators.

While cellular plastic foams are generally poor materials for reducing sound transmission, they can be effective in absorbing certain frequencies. The sound absorption of several foamed plastics has been reported in the literature (43–46).

Safety

Products of combustion of various plastic foams have been identified (47). The primary products of combustion are carbon dioxide and carbon monoxide similar to those of organic materials. Considerable investigation into the behavior of foamed plastics in real fire situations has been done. Small-scale tests do not accurately reflect the behavior of polystyrene foam in real fire situations (48). Building codes often require that foamed plastics meet specific test parameters developed by Factory Mutual or Underwriters Laboratories, Incorporated, or that they be installed according to specific criteria.

Certain additives may limit the use of specific foams where food or human contact are anticipated. Manufacturers should be contacted for specific recommendations on the use of their products.

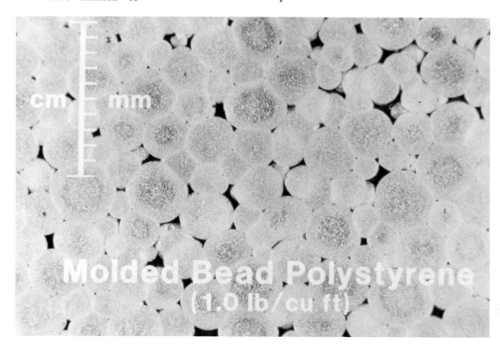

Figure 15. Photomicrograph showing cellular structure of 1.0 lb/ft³ (16.0 Kg/m³) molded bead polystyrene foam.

Flexural Strength (Extrusion) (psi) (kPa) D1621–73	Tensile Strength (Vertical) (psi) (kPa) C203–82	Shear Strength (Extrusion) (psi) (kPa) D1623–78	Water Vapor Transmission (Perm-in) (ng/Pa S M) C273–61	Water Absorption (% by Volume) E 96–80	Coefficient of Thermal Expansion (in./in.·°F) (cm/cm·K) C272–76	Max Service Temperature (°F) (Long Term) (°C) D696–74
10–14	25–30	16–20	18–22	1.2–3.0	<2.5	3.5×10^{-5} 167
(69–96)	(172–207)	(110–138)	(124–152)	(1.8–4.4)		(1.9×10^{-5}) (75)
13–18	32–38	17–21	23–25	1.1–2.8	<2.5	3.5×10^{-5} 167
(90–124)	(221–262)	(117–145)	(159–172)	(1.6–4.1)		(1.9×10^{-5}) (75)
15–21	40–50	18–22	26–32	0.9–2.5	<2.0	3.5×10^{-5} 167
(103–145)	(276–295)	(124–152)	(179–221)	(1.3–3.6)		(1.9×10^{-5}) (75)
25–33	55–75	23–27	33–37	0.6–1.5	<1.0	3.5×10^{-5} 167
(172–227)	(379–517)	(159–186)	(227–255)	(0.9–2.2)		(1.9×10^{-5}) (75)
25	50–55	50	25–30	<0.03[b]	<0.3	1.3×10^{-5} 250
(172)	(295–379)	(295)	(172–207)	(0.04)		(7.2×10^{-6}) (121.1)
40	80–90	65	35–40	0.4–0.7	<0.1	3.5×10^{-5} 165
(276)	(552–621)	(448)	(241–276)	(0.6–1.0)		(1.9×10^{-5}) (73.9)
15–20	50–70	25	N/A	N/A	<0.1	3.5×10^{-5} 165
(103–138)	(345–483)	(172)				(1.9×10^{-5}) (73.9)
30	50	40	40	1.4[e]	1.8	1.3×10^{-5} 250
(207)	(345)	(276)	(275.8)	(2.0)		(7.2×10^{-6}) (121.1)

Figure 16. Housing unit retrofitted with polystyrene foam insulation to improve energy efficiency and reduce heating costs. Here, three inches of foam create an envelope as part of the INSUL/CRETE exterior wall insulation and finishing system. Photograph courtesy of Newport News Redevelopment and Housing Authority.

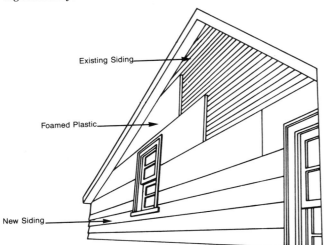

Figure 17. Foam insulation beneath new siding in a residential retrofit application.

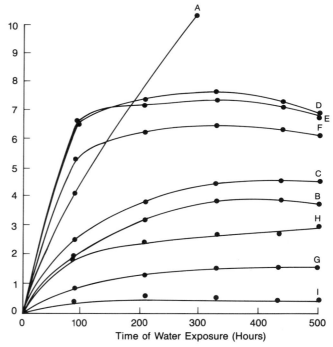

Figure 18. (A) 1.0 in (2.54 cm) thick fiberboard, 10.6 lb/ft³ (169.8 Kg/m³); (B) 1.0 in (2.54 cm) thick molded bead polystyrene, 1.6 lb/ft³ (26.2 Kg/m³), 31% void; (C) 2.1 in (5.33 cm) thick molded bead polystyrene, 1.7 lb/ft³ (26.8 Kg/m³), 27% void; (D) 1.4 in (3.56 cm) thick molded bead polystyrene, 1.3 lb/ft³ (21.3 Kg/m³), 27% void; (E) 2.0 in (5.08 cm) thick molded bead polystyrene, 1.2 lb/ft³ (19.7 Kg/m³), 37% void; (F) 2.0 in (5.08 cm) thick molded bead polystyrene, 1.0 lb/ft³ (16.5 Kg/m³), 27% void; (G) 2.0 in (5.08 cm) thick cellular glass, 8.4 lb/ft³ (133.9 Kg/m³); (H) 2.0 in (5.08 cm) thick polyurethane, 3.1 lb/ft³ (50.1 Kg/m³), aluminum skins; 1.0 in (2.54 cm) thick polyisocyanurate, 2.6 lb/ft³ (41.3 Kg/m³) aluminum skins, glass reinforced; (I) 2.0 in (5.08 cm) thick German molded bead polystyrene, 2.2 lb/ft³ (35.6 Kg/m³), 10% void, 1.4 in (3.56 cm) thick extruded polystyrene skinboard, 2.3 lb/ft³ (36.5 Kg/m³), 1.5 in (3.81 cm) thick extruded polystyrene skinboard, 2.3 lb/ft³ (46.5 Kg/m³). Percent volume of water absorbed per unit volume of foam over 504 hours (21 days). Courtesy of ASTM STP 660.

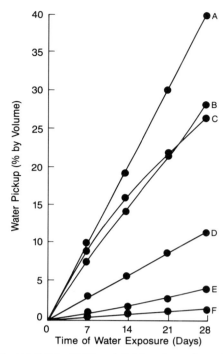

Figure 19. (A) 2.2 in (5.59 cm) thick polyurethane laminated with paper, 2.3 lb/ft³ (37.6 Kg/m³); (B) 2.0 in (5.08 cm) thick polyurethane without skins, 2.1 lb/ft³ (33.0 Kg/m³); (C) 2.0 in (5.08 cm) thick molded bead polystyrene, 1.6 lb/ft³ (25.3 Kg/m³); (D) 2.0 in (5.08 cm) thick cut cell molded bead polystyrene, 3.5 lb/ft³ (55.4 Kg/m³); (E) 2.0 in (5.08 cm) thick molded bead polystyrene, 2.1 lb/ft³ (33.6 Kg/m³); (F) 2.0 in (5.08 cm) thick extruded polystyrene skinboard, 2.2 lb/ft³ (35.2 Kg/m³). Water pick up (percent by volume) versus time (days). Courtesy of ASTM STP 660.

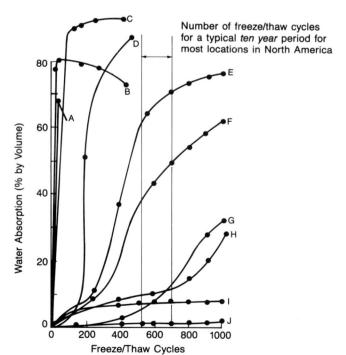

Figure 20. (A) 1.5 in (3.81 cm) thick cellular glass, 9 lb/ft³ (144.2 Kg/m³); (B) 1.0 in (2.54 cm) thick fiberglass roof insulation, 13.8

BIBLIOGRAPHY

1. R. N. Kennedy in R. J. Bender, ed., *Handbook of Foamed Plastics,* Lake Publishing Co., Libertyville, Ill., 1965.
2. V. Wigotsky, ed., in *Plastics Engineering,* October 1984, p. 23.
3. R. F. Boyer, H. Keskkula, A. E. Platt in N. M. Bikales, ed., *Encyclopedia of Polymer Science and Technology,* Vol. 13, John Wiley & Sons, Inc., New York, 1970, pp. 128–447.
4. A. E. Platt, T. C. Wallace, *Kirk-Othmer: Encyclopedia of Chemical Technology,* Vol. 21, 3rd ed., John Wiley & Sons, Inc., New York, 1983, pp. 801–847.
5. R. H. Boundy, R. F. Boyer, and S. Stoesser, *Styrene, Its Polymers, Copolymers and Derivatives,* American Chemical Society 115, Reinhold Publishing Corp., New York, 1952.
6. A. H. Scott and J. R. Kinard, Jr., *J. Res. Nat. Bur. Stand.* **71**(2), 119 (1967).
7. K. Uebereiter and E. Otto-Laupenmuhlen, *Naturforsch.* **8,** 664 (1953).
8. D. E. Roberts et al., *J. Polym. Sci.* **2,** 420 (1947); R. M. Joshi and B. J. Zwolinski, *Macromolecules* 1(1), 25 (1968).
9. R. Dedeurwaerder and J. F. M. Oth, *J. Chem. Phys.* **56,** 940 (1959).
10. G. Molau and H. Keskkula, *J. Polym. Sci. Part A* **4,** 1595 (1966).
11. M. Munzer and E. Trommsdorf in C. E. Schildknecht and I. Skeist, eds., *Polymerization Processes,* John Wiley and Sons, Inc., New York, 1977, pp. 106–142.
12. R. B. Bishop, *Practical Polymerization for Polystyrene,* Cahners Books, Boston, Mass., 1971.
13. L. F. Albright, *Processes for Major Addition-type Plastics and Their Monomers,* McGraw-Hill Inc., New York, 1974.
14. L. C. Rubens, *J. Cell. Plast.* **9,** 232 (1973).
15. H. Keskkula, G. M. Simpson, and F. L. Dicken, *Soc. Plast. Eng. Annu. Tech. Conf.* **12,** XV-2 (1966).
16. *Br. Plast.* **38,** 708 (1965).
17. G. M. Kraynak, *Soc. Plast. Eng. Annu. Tech. Conf.* **13,** 896 (1967).
18. *Vacuum Metallizing Cycolac,* Technical Report P 135, Borg Warner Corporation Chicago, Ill., 1980.
19. E. N. Hendreth, *Modern Plastics Encyclopedia,* Vol. 43, McGraw-Hill Inc., New York, 1966, p. 991.
20. K. Stoeckhert, *Kunststoffe,* **55,** 857 (1965).
21. C. H. Basdekis, *ABS Plastics,* Reinhold Publishing Corp., New York, 1964.

lb/ft³ (221.4 Kg/m³); (C) 1.0 in (2.54 cm) thick fiberboard, 10.2 lb/ft³ (163.2 Kg/m³); (D) 1.0 in (2.54 cm) thick polyisocyanurate, glass reinforced with aluminum facings, 2.6 lb/ft³ (41.6 Kg/m³); (E) 1.0 in (2.54 cm) thick molded beam polystyrene, 1.0 lb/ft³ (16.0 Kg/m³); (F) 2.0 in (5.08 cm) thick molded bead polystyrene, 1.7 lb/ft³ (27.2 Kg/m³); (G) 2.0 in (5.08 cm) thick German molded bead polystyrene, 2.2 lb/ft³ (35.2 Kg/m³); (H) 1.4 in (3.56 cm) thick polyurethane with asphalt felt facing, all sides sealed in asphalt, 2.4 lb/ft³ (38.4 Kg/m³); (I) 1.0 in (2.54 cm) thick polyurethane without skins; (J) 1.0 in (2.54 cm) and 2.0 in (5.08 cm) thick extruded polystyrene skinboard, 2.1 to 2.5 lb/ft³ (33.6 to 40.0 Kg/m³). Water absorption of various insulations after freeze-thaw exposure following ASTM Method C 666–73. Courtesy of ASTM STP 660.

22. U.S. Pat. 4,419,496 (1963), D. E. Henton and T. M. O'Brien, (to Dow Chemical).

23. G. E. Molau and H. Keskkula, *J. Appl. Polym. Sci.* **7**, pp. 35, 1968.

24. E. Zahn, *Appl. Polym. Symp.* **11**, 209 (1969).

25. U.S. Pat. 3,489,821 (Jan. 13, 1970), H. S. Witt and C. S. Paddock (to Uniroyal, Inc.)

26. U.S. Pat. 4,202,498 (1980), W. J. Peascoe (to Uniroyal, Inc.).

27. U.S. Pat. 3,944,631 (Mar. 16, 1976), A. Yu and R. E. Gallagher (to Stauffer Chemical).

28. U.S. Pat. 4,249,875 (Feb. 10, 1981), E. Hart and R. Rutledge (to Cosden Technology, Inc.).

29. F. R. Bush and G. C. Rollefson, *paper presented at the 38th Society of Plastics Engineers-ANTEC,* New York, 1980.

30. *ASTM 1986 Annual Book of ASTM Standards,* Vol. 08.04 Plastic Pipe and Building Products, Philadelphia, Pa., 1986.

31. *Thermoplastic Piping of The Transport of Chemicals,* Technical Report PPI-TR19, Plastics Pipe Institute, Division of the Society of the Plastics Industry, Inc. New York, October 1984.

32. Data manual, Plastic Pipe and Fittings Association, Glen Ellyn, Ill., 1986.

33. *Insulated Sheathing,* Quantum Enterprises, Inc., Lencroft, N.J., December 1984.

34. *Study to Industry Roofing Usage Factors in 26 Dow Sales Regions,* Ducker Research Company, Inc., Birmingham, Mich., August, 1984.

35. ASTM C578-83, American Society for Testing and Materials, Philadelphia, Pa., 1983.

36. ASTM D 833-83, American Society for Testing and Materials, Philadelphia, Pa., 1983.

37. F. J. Dechow and K. A. Epstein, ASTM STP 660, *Thermal Transmission Measurement of Insulation,* American Society for Testing and Materials, Philadelphia, Pa., 1978.

38. *Thermal and Moisture Protection,* Sweets Catalog File 7, Sweets Division, McGraw-Hill Information System Co., New York, 1984.

39. S.-H. Thorsen, *Determination of the Expansion Coefficient, Water Absorption, Moisture Diffusivity, as Well as Thermal Conductivity at Different Moisture Contents for Polystyrene and Urethane Cellular Plastics,* Institute for Building Technology, Chalmers University of Technology, Goteborg, Sweden, August 1973.

40. C. W. Kaplar, *Moisture and Freeze/Thaw Effects on Rigid Thermal Insulations,* Technical Report 249, CRREL, Hanover, N.H., April 1974.

41. S. C. A. Praskevopoulos, *J. Cell. Plast.* **i** (1), 132 (1965).

42. *Forming Thin Shells,* Bulletin, The Dow Chemical Company, Midland, Mich., 1962.

43. A. F. Randolph, ed., *Plastics Engineering Handbook,* 3rd ed., Reinhold Publishing Corp., New York, 1960.

44. A. Cooper, *Plast. Inst. Trans.* **26**, 299 (1958).

45. *Ibid.,* **29** (321), 62 (1964).

46. G. L. Ball II, M. Schwartz, and J. S. Long, *Off. Dig. Fed. Soc. Paint Technol.* **32**, 817 (1960).

47. C. Hilado, H. Cumming, and C. Casey, *J. Cell. Plast.* **15** (4), 205 (1979).

48. FTC Consent Agreement, File #7323040, The Dow Chemical Company, Midland, Mich., 1974.

See also ACRYLICS; EPOXY RESINS; FLUOROPOLYMERS; FOAMED PLASTICS; PHENOLIC RESINS; PLASTICS; PLASTICS, ABS; POLYAMIDES; POLYCARBONATES; POLYESTERS; SILICONES

THOMAS C. KLINGLER
BRYCE KOSLAN
WAYNE E. PETERSON, JR.
KARL ZUPIC
JAMES ZISKA
The Dow Chemical Company
Midland, Michigan

INDEX

Bold faced type identifies exact titles of articles and therefore they are major references. *Italicized numbers* are illustrations. Italicized titles are publications. Quotation marks are used to identify articles, speeches, and titles of exhibitions. Non-English terms, names, and locations may be spelled differently by authors or may vary from country to country. The index uses a single spelling. Dates of buildings given are approximate, and there may be variations among dates given by authors. The index lists a single time span. The index is not exhaustive, and the reader is urged to consult the major references for detailed information and additional reading.